THE PARAGON HOUSE
SPELLING DICTIONARY

THE PARAGON HOUSE

Spelling Dictionary

PARAGON HOUSE
NEW YORK

PARAGON HOUSE
New York

First U.S. edition, 1993

Published in the United States by

Paragon House
90 Fifth Avenue
New York, N.Y. 10011
Reprinted by arrangement with Penguin Books Limited
Copyright © 1990 by Market House Books Ltd.

All rights reserved. No part of this book may be
reproduced, in any form, without written permission
from the publishers, unless by a reviewer who wishes
to quote brief passages.

Manufactured in the United States of America

Library of Congress Cataloging-in-Publication Data

The Paragon house spelling dictionary / [prepared by Market House Books]. — 1st U.S. ed.
    p.   cm.
    Revised ed. of: The Penguin spelling dictionary.
    ISBN 1-55778-597-X

    1. English language—Orthography and spelling—Dictionaries.
2. Spellers. I. Market House Books Ltd. II. Penguin spelling dictionary.
PE1146.P26   1993
423'.1—dc20   92-32326
                                                                     CIP

TABLE OF CONTENTS

Preface vii

The Rules of Spelling ix

The Spelling Dictionary 1

First names 521

Biographical names 539

PREFACE

English is a difficult language to spell correctly – and not only for the foreigner. Native speakers, too, find it hard. The problem is that modern English is such a rich and resourceful language, derived from so many sources, that its spelling does not obey simple rules. Although much of the language *is* regular, in the sense that it does obey rules, there are very large numbers of exceptions to the common patterns. While the only safe way to be sure of a spelling is to look it up in this dictionary, the basic rules are given on the following pages.

The Paragon House Spelling Dictionary is divided into three sections: the main spelling list; a list of first names; and a list of biographical names.

SPELLING LIST

This, the largest section, contains normal vocabulary words, place names, some trademarks, and biblical and mythological names not included in the names lists (see below). Unhyphenated two-word compounds (e.g. phrasal verbs and nouns) are usually not listed, as each element will have its own entry. Exceptions include compounds with irregular inflections (see below) and some eponymous terms (terms derived from the name of a person), in which both elements are included as an aid to the sense.

Centred dots within a word indicate the points at which it can be hyphenated. These divisions are phonetic, rather than etymological, and correspond to syllabification breaks; note, however, that when syllabification breaks are not acceptable hyphenation points are not shown. Monosyllabic words should never be hyphenated, nor – if possible – should people's names.

Inflections (changes in the form of a word to indicate changes in grammatical function) are included if they are irregular. In general, regular inflections are not included. For rules on the formation of regular and irregular inflections, see under **The Rules of Spelling** on the following pages.

US spellings and British variant spellings are included after the preferred spelling of the word; they also have their own entries, with an appropriate gloss, if they are widely separated alphabetically from the preferred spelling.

Short glosses are provided for unfamiliar words and to avoid confusion between similarly spelt or pronounced words. Most of the proper names in this section are also glossed.

A few common misspellings are included in the list. These words are bracketed and the correct spelling indicated.

FIRST NAMES

This section comprises a comprehensive list of English first names, together with their spelling variants. It does not include the more obscure biblical and mythological names (many of which are listed in the main section of the dictionary) or the names of monarchs and other rulers that are unfamiliar or foreign (many of these are listed under the biographical names).

BIOGRAPHICAL NAMES

This section includes the names of people from all countries, past and present, who have achieved fame in some sphere of human activity. Monarchs are generally not included if their names appear in the first names list. Biographical names are listed in alphabetical order of the surname, followed by first names and any titles; the less familiar names of a subject are bracketed. Variant spellings and pseudonyms are also listed, and similar names are glossed to avoid confusion.

THE RULES OF SPELLING

Nouns

REGULAR INFLECTIONS

Regular plurals are formed by adding -*s*; for nouns ending in -*s*, -*x*, -*z*, -*ch*, or -*sh*, add -*es*.

IRREGULAR INFLECTIONS

1

Nouns of Latin origin ending in -*a*, especially in scientific or technical usage, usually have the plural ending -*ae* (e.g. **alga/algae; nebula/nebulae**).

Such nouns ending in -*ma* usually have the plural ending -*mata* (e.g. **stoma/stomata**).

2

Nouns ending in -*f* either form regular plurals (e.g. **chief/chiefs**) or have the plural ending -*ves* (e.g. **calf/calves**).

Most nouns ending in -*fe* from regular plurals (e.g. **safe/safes**) but a few have the plural ending -*ves* (e.g. **wife/wives**).

3

Nouns ending in -*i* usually form regular plurals but a few have the plural ending -*ies* (e.g. **chilli/chillies**).

4

Nouns ending in -*is* either form regular plurals (e.g. **iris/irises**) or having the plural ending -*es* (e.g. **basis/bases**). Some scientific and technical nouns have the plural ending -*ides* (e.g. **apsis/apsides**).

5

Most nouns ending in -*o* either form regular plurals (e.g. **albino/abinos**) or have the plural ending (-*oes* (e.g. **tomato/tomatoes**). Nouns of Italian origin have the plural form -*i*, either as the only plural or as an alternative (e.g. **graffito/graffiti, virtuoso/virtuosos** *or* **virtuosi**).

6

Some nouns of Greek origin ending in -*on* have the plural ending -*a* (e.g. **criterion/criteria**).

7

Nouns of Latin origin ending in -*um*, especially in scientific or technical usage, have the plural ending -*a* (e.g. **bacterium/bacteria; stratum/strata**).

8

Many nouns of Latin origin ending in -*us*, especially in scientific or technical usage, have the preferred or alternative plural ending -*i* (e.g. **fungus/fungi; stylus/styli** *or* **styluses**). A few such nouns have the plural ending -*era* or -*ora* (e.g. **genus/genera; corpus/corpora**).

9

Most nouns ending in -*x* form regular plurals (e.g. **tax/taxes**) but a few, usually in scientific or technical usage, have the plural ending -*ces* (e.g. **appendix/appendices**).

Such nouns ending in -*ex* have the plural ending -*ices* (e.g. **index/indices**).

Such nouns ending in -*nx* have the plural ending -*nges* (e.g. **meninx/meninges**).

10

Nouns ending in -*y* preceded by a vowel form regular plurals (e.g. **donkey/donkeys**). Nouns ending in -*y* preceded by a consonant or -*qu-* have the plural ending -*ies* (e.g. **family/families; colloquy/colloquies**). Note that proper names ending in -*y* form regular plurals, irrespective of the preceding letter (e.g. **Sally/Sallys**).

11

In phrasal nouns and most other hyphenated nouns, the final element is pluralized (e.g. **lay-by/lay-bys**), but in some hyphenated and multiword nouns the noun element may be pluralized irrespective of its position (e.g. **looker-on/lookers-on; court martial/court martials** *or* **courts martial**).

Note, however, that this does not apply to nouns ending in -*ful* (e.g. **spoonful/spoonfuls**; *not* **spoonsful**).

12

Some nouns, especially animals, have the same singular and plural forms (e.g. **sheep/sheep; fish/fish** *or* **fishes**).

13

Abbreviations and numberals usually have the plural ending -*s* (e.g. **MPs; 1920s**).

SUFFIXES

Many nouns are formed by adding suffixes to the corresponding verb or adjective. A few general rules apply.

1 -*ation*

For words ending in -*l* preceded by a single vowel, the -*l* is doubled (e.g. **cancel/cancellation**).

2 -er and -or

Either of these suffixes may be added to form nouns meaning the 'doer' of the corresponding verb, but the -*er* forms greatly outnumber the -*or* forms. For some verbs, both forms exist; in these cases the following rules may apply:

(a) the -*or* form is used for objects and the -*er* form for people (e.g. **resister**, person who resists; **resistor**, electrical component).

(b) the *or* form is preferred in legal or scientific contexts (e.g. **bailer**, one who bails; **bailor**, transferer of goods by bailment).

3 -ment

(a) For words ending in -*dge*, the preferred form is to drop the -*e* (e.g. **judge/judgment**).

(b) For words ending in -*ll*, the terminal -*l* is dropped (e.g. **install/instalment**).

(c) For words of more than one syllable ending in -*y* preceded by a consonant, the -*y* is changed to -*i* (e.g. **merry/merriment**).

4 -ness

For words of more than one syllable preceded by a consonant, the -*y* is changed to -*i* (e.g. **happy/happiness**).

Adjectives

REGULAR INFLECTIONS

Regular comparatives and superlatives, for adjectives of one or two syllables, are formed by adding -*er* and -*est*, respectively.

For adjectives ending in -*e*, the -*e* is dropped before adding -*er* or -*est* (e.g. **nice/nicer, nicest; free/freer, freest**).

Adjectives of three or more syllables are preceded by *more* and *most* to form the comparative and superlative respectively.

IRREGULAR INFLECTIONS

1

For adjectives ending in -*y* preceded by a consonant, the comparative and superlative are formed by dropping the -*y* and adding -*ier* and -*iest* respectively (e.g. **tidy/tidier, tidiest**).

2

For monosyllabic adjectives ending in a consonant preceded by a single vowel, the comparative and superlative are formed by doubling the terminal consonant before adding -*er* and -*est* respectively (e.g. **hot/hotter, hottest**).

SUFFIXES
-*able* and -*ible*

The great majority of these adjectives have the ending -*able*; they are derived from native English verbs and nouns. Certain verbs and nouns of Latin origin, however, take the suffix -*ible*; some common examples are **accessible, comprehensible, convertible, divisible, eligible, perceptible, permissible, tangible**. Some can end in either -*able* or -*ible* (e.g. **collectable/collectible, discussible/discussable**).

For adjectives ending in -*able*, the following rules generally apply, although there are exceptions:

(a) For verbs and nouns ending in -*e*, the -*e* is dropped before adding -*able* unless it is preceded by -*c*- or -*g*- (e.g. **noticeable, changeable**) or when its retention aids pronunciation (e.g. **blameable, saleable**).

(b) For words ending in -*y* preceded by a consonant, the -*y* is changed to -*i* before adding -*able* (e.g. **justifiable**).

(c) For verbs ending in -*l* preceded by a single vowel, the -*l* is doubled before adding -*able* (e.g. **distil/distillable**).

Verbs

REGULAR INFLECTIONS

1
The third person singular is formed by adding -*s* or, for verbs ending in -*s*, -*x*, -*z*, -*ch*, or -*sh*, by adding -*es*.

2
The present participle is formed by adding -*ing*.

3
The past tense and past participle are formed by adding -*ed*.

4
For verbs ending in -*e* preceded by a consonant, the -*e* is dropped before adding -*ing* or -*ed* (compare **Irregular inflections** 3 and 4).

IRREGULAR INFLECTIONS

1
For verbs ending in -*y* preceded by a consonant, the past tense and past participle are formed by dropping the -*y* and adding -*ied* (e.g. **marry/married**).

2
In monosyllabic verbs ending in a consonant preceded by a single

vowel, the terminal consonant is doubled when inflecting (e.g. **pat/ patting, patted**).
With some exceptions, this rule also applies to verbs of more than one syllable, notably when:
(a) the terminal consonant is -*l* (e.g. **marvel/marvelling, marvelled**); note that in American English the -*l* is not doubled.
(b) the stress is on the last syllable (e.g. **refer/referring, referred**).

3

For verbs ending in -*e* preceded by a vowel, the -*e* is dropped before adding -*ed* but retained before -*ing* (e.g. **hoe/hoeing, hoed**).

4 For a few verbs ending in -*e* preceded by a consonant, the -*e* is dropped before adding -*ed* but retained before -*ing*, usually to avoid confusion with very similar words (e.g. **singe/singeing, singed**).

5

For verbs ending in -*ac*- or -*ic*, the present participle is formed by adding -*king* and the past tense and participle by adding -*ked* (e.g. **traffic/trafficking, trafficked**).

SUFFIXES

1 -*ize* and -*ise*

Most of these verbs have the preferred ending -*ize*, with -*ise* as an acceptable variant in British English (but not in American English); the same applies to the derived nouns (e.g. **specialize/specialization**). Exceptions include **advertise, compromise, improvise, supervise**; for these verbs -*ise* is the only acceptable ending in British and American English.

2 -*yse* and -*yze*

-*yse* is the only acceptable form in British English; -*yze* is the US spelling (e.g. **catalyse/US catalyze; paralyse/US paralyze**).

Adverbs

Many adverbs are formed by adding -*ly* to the corresponding adjectives or noun. Note:

1

For adjectives or nouns ending in -*e*, the -*e* is usually, but not always, retained (e.g. **pale/palely; rude/rudely**). Exceptions include **true/truly, whole/wholly**.

2
For adjectives or nouns ending in *-l*, the *-l* is retained (e.g. **eventual/eventually**).

3
For adjectives ending in *-ll*, the penultimate *-l* is dropped before adding *-ly* (e.g. **full/fully**).

4
For adjectives or nouns ending in *-y*, the adverb is formed by dropping the *-y* and adding *-ily* (e.g. **merry/merrily**).

Common spelling problems

1 *-cede* or *-ceed*

There is no general rule here: the usual ending is *-cede* (e.g. **concede**, **precede**); the only verbs ending in *-ceed* are **exceed**, **proceed**, and **succeed**. Note particularly the spelling of **supersede**.

2 *-ei-* or *-ie-*

The rule 'i before e except after c' works fairly well when the sound is pronounced 'ee' (e.g. **niece**, **siege**; but **receipt**, **receive**). Exceptions include **seize**, **weir**, **weird**.
When the sound is pronounced 'ai' (as in paid), the spelling is *-ei-* (e.g. **deign**, **neighbour**, **weigh**).

3 *Difficult words*

A few words cause many people problems because they follow no rules:

acco**mm**odate	exa**gg**erate	phenomenon
anomalous	forty	pursue
business	gauge	surprise
comme**m**orate	harass	threshold
desi**cc**ate	ino**c**ulate	with**h**old
ecstasy	necessary	
emba**rr**ass	parallel	

xiv

A

aa rock
Aachen West German city
Aal·borg (or Ål·) Danish port
aalii shrub
aard·vark
aard·wolf (plural ·wolves)
Aar·gau Swiss canton
Aar·hus (or År·) Danish port
aba·ca fibre
aback
ab·ac·ti·nal zoology term
aba·cus (plural ·ci or ·cuses)
Aba·dan Iranian port
Abad·don the devil
abaft nautical term
aba·lo·ne mollusc
ab·am·pere electrical unit
aban·don
aban·doned
aban·doned·ly
aban·donee legal term
aban·don·ment
abase
abase·ment
abash
abash·ed·ly
abat·able
abate
abate·ment
aba·tis (or ab·at·tis) fortifications term
aba·tor legal term
ab·at·toir
ab·ax·ial away from the axis; compare adaxial
ab·ba·cy (plural ·cies)
Abbasid dynasty of caliphs
ab·ba·tial
abbé French abbott
ab·bess
Abbe·vill·ian archaeological period
ab·bey
ab·bot
ab·bre·vi·ate
ab·bre·via·tion

ab·bre·via·tor
(abcess) incorrect spelling of abscess
ab·cou·lomb electrical unit
ab·di·cable
ab·di·cate
ab·di·ca·tion
ab·dica·tive
ab·di·ca·tor
ab·do·men
ab·domi·nal
ab·domi·nal·ly
ab·du·cens nerve
ab·du·cent anatomy term
ab·duct
ab·duc·tion
abeam nautical term
abece·dar·ian learner
abed
abele poplar
Abelian maths term
abel·mosk plant
Ab·eo·ku·ta Nigerian town
Ab·er·dare Welsh town
Ab·er·deen
Ab·er·do·nian
ab·er·nethy biscuit
ab·er·rance (or ·ran·cy)
ab·er·rant
ab·er·ra·tion
Ab·er·yst·wyth
abet (abet·ting, abet·ted)
abet·ment
abet·ter (or esp. in legal contexts ·tor)
abey·ance
abey·ant
ab·far·ad electrical unit
ab·hen·ry (plural ·ries) electrical unit
ab·hor (·hor·ring, ·horred)
ab·hor·rence
ab·hor·rent
ab·hor·rer
abid·ance
abide (abid·ing, abode or abid·ed)
abid·er

abid·ing
abid·ing·ly
Abid·jan Ivory Coast port
abi·et·ic acid
abi·gail maid
Abi·lene Texan city
abil·ity (plural ·ities)
Ab·ing·don
ab ini·tio Latin from the start
abio·gen·esis biological theory
abio·genet·ic
abiog·enist
abio·sis absence of life
abiot·ic
ab·ir·ri·tant relieving irritation
ab·ir·ri·tate
ab·ject
ab·jec·tion
ab·ju·ra·tion
ab·jure renounce; compare adjure
ab·jur·er
Ab·khaz (plural ·khaz) Soviet people
Ab·kha·zia Soviet republic
ab·late
ab·la·tion
ab·la·tive grammar term
ab·la·tor heat shield
ab·laut linguistics term
ablaze
able
able-bodied
abloom
ab·lu·tion
ab·lu·tion·ary
ably
ab·ne·gate
ab·ne·ga·tion
ab·ne·ga·tor
ab·nor·mal
ab·nor·mal·ity (plural ·ities)
ab·nor·mal·ly
aboard
abode

abohm

ab·ohm electrical unit
aboi·deau (*plural* ·deaus *or* ·deaux) Canadian dyke
abol·ish
abol·ish·er
abol·ish·ment
abo·li·tion
abo·li·tion·ary
abo·li·tion·ism
abo·li·tion·ist
abo·ma·sum ruminant's stomach
abomi·nable
abomi·nably
abomi·nate
abomi·na·tion
abomi·na·tor
ab·oral zoology term
Abo·rigi·nal
abo·rigi·nal
Abo·rigi·ne native Australian
abo·rigi·ne an original inhabitant
abort
abor·ti·cide
abor·ti·fa·cient inducing abortion
abor·tion
abor·tion·al
abor·tion·ist
abor·tive
Abou·kir battle site
abou·lia variant spelling of abulia
abound
about
about-turn (*or esp. US* about-face)
above
ab·ra·ca·dab·ra
abra·dant
abrade
abrad·er
abran·chi·ate (*or* ·chial) zoology term
abra·sion
abra·sive
abrax·as magic charm
ab·re·act psychology term
ab·re·ac·tion
ab·re·ac·tive
abreast
abridg·able (*or* abridge·)
abridge
abridg·er
abridg·ment (*or* abridge·)
abroad
ab·ro·gate
ab·ro·ga·tion
ab·ro·ga·tor
ab·rupt
ab·rup·tion breaking off
ab·rupt·ness
Abruz·zi Italian region
ab·scess
ab·scise to separate
ab·scis·sa (*plural* ·sas *or* ·sae) maths term
ab·scis·sion shedding of plant parts
ab·scond
ab·scond·er
ab·seil mountaineering term
ab·sence
ab·sent
ab·sen·tee
ab·sen·tee·ism
ab·sent·er
ab·sen·te reo *Latin* the defendant being absent
absent-minded
absent-minded·ness
ab·sinthe (*or* ·sinth)
ab·sit omen *Latin* may the foreboding not be realized
ab·so·lute
ab·so·lute·ly
ab·so·lu·tion
ab·so·lut·ism
ab·solu·tory
ab·solv·able
ab·solve
ab·solv·er
ab·sorb take into or permeate; *compare* adsorb
ab·sorb·abil·ity
ab·sorb·able
ab·sorb·ance physics term
ab·sorb·ed·ly
ab·sor·be·fa·cient inducing absorption
ab·sorb·en·cy
ab·sorb·ent
ab·sorb·er
ab·sorb·ing
ab·sorb·ing·ly
ab·sorp·tance physics term
ab·sorp·tion
ab·sorp·tive
ab·sorp·tiv·ity physics term
ab·squatu·late decamp
ab·stain
ab·stain·er
ab·ste·mi·ous
ab·sten·tion
ab·sten·tious
ab·ster·gent cleansing
ab·sti·nence
ab·sti·nent
ab·stract
ab·stract·ed·ly
ab·stract·ed·ness
ab·strac·tion
ab·strac·tion·ism theory of abstract art
ab·strac·tive
ab·stric·tion biology term
ab·struse
ab·struse·ness
ab·surd
ab·surd·ity (*or* ·ness; *plural* ·ities *or* ·nesses)
Abu Dha·bi sheikdom
abu·lia (*or* abou·) loss of willpower
abu·lic
abun·dance
abun·dant
abuse
abus·er
Abu Sim·bel Egyptian temple
abu·sive
abu·sive·ness
abut (abut·ting, abut·ted)
abu·ti·lon shrub
abut·ment (*or* abut·tal)
abut·tals legal term
abut·ter owner of adjoining property
abuzz
ab·volt electrical unit
ab·watt electrical unit
Aby·dos ancient Egyptian town
abysm *Archaic* abyss
abys·mal immeasurable; very bad
abys·mal·ly
abyss
abys·sal of ocean depths
Ab·ys·sinia *former name of Ethiopia*

Ab·ys·sin·ian
aca·cia
aca·deme
aca·demia
aca·dem·ic
aca·dem·ical·ly
aca·dem·icals academic dress
acad·emi·cian
aca·demi·cism (or acad·emism) conventionalism
acad·emy (plural ·emies)
Aca·dia Canadian region; compare Arcadia
Aca·dian of Acadia; compare Accadian
aca·jou mahogany
ac·an·tha·ceous botany term
acan·thine
acan·tho·cepha·lan wormlike animal
acan·thoid spiny
ac·an·thop·ter·yg·ian fish
acan·thous thornlike
acan·thus (plural ·thuses or ·thi) plant; architectural ornament
a cap·pel·la musical term
Aca·pul·co Mexican port
aca·ria·sis tick or mite infestation
aca·rid (or acari·dan) tick or mite
aca·roid
aca·rol·ogy
acar·pel·lous lacking carpels
acar·pous producing no fruit
aca·rus mite
acata·lec·tic verse form
acau·dal (or ·date) having no tail
acau·les·cent having no stem
Ac·cad variant spelling of Akkad
Ac·cad·ian variant spelling of Akkadian; compare Acadian
ac·cede
ac·ced·ence
ac·ced·er
ac·cel·era·ble

ac·cel·er·an·do (plural ·dos) musical term
ac·cel·er·ant
ac·cel·er·ate
ac·cel·era·tion
ac·cel·era·tive (or ·tory)
ac·cel·era·tor
ac·cel·er·om·eter
ac·cent
ac·cen·tor bird
ac·cen·tual rhythmical
ac·cen·tu·ate
ac·cen·tua·tion
ac·cept
ac·cept·abil·ity (or ·able·ness)
ac·cept·able
ac·cept·ably
ac·cept·ance
ac·cept·ant
ac·cep·ta·tion
ac·cept·ed·ly
ac·cep·ter (or esp. in legal contexts, chemistry, and electronics ·tor)
ac·cess
ac·ces·sa·ry (plural ·ries) variant spelling of accessory
ac·ces·sibil·ity
ac·ces·sible
ac·ces·sibly
ac·ces·sion
ac·ces·sion·al
ac·ces·so·rial
ac·ces·so·ri·ly
ac·ces·so·ri·ness
ac·ces·so·ry (or in legal contexts ·sa·ry; plural ·ries)
ac·ciac·ca·tu·ra (plural ·ras or ·re) musical term
ac·ci·dence linguistics term
ac·ci·dent
ac·ci·den·tal
ac·ci·den·tal·ly
ac·ci·die apathy
ac·cipi·ter hawk
ac·cipi·tral (or ·trine)
ac·claim
ac·cla·ma·tion
ac·clama·tory
ac·cli·ma·tiz·able (or ·ma·tis·able, ·mat·able)

ac·cli·ma·ti·za·tion (or ·ma·ti·sa·tion, ·ma·tion)
ac·cli·ma·tize (or ·ma·tise, ·mate)
ac·cli·ma·tiz·er (or ·tis·er)
ac·clivi·tous (or ·cli·vous)
ac·cliv·ity (plural ·ities) upward slope
ac·co·lade
ac·com·mo·date
ac·com·mo·dat·ing
ac·com·mo·dat·ing·ly
ac·com·mo·da·tion
ac·com·mo·da·tive
(accomodate) incorrect spelling of accommodate
ac·com·pa·ni·er
ac·com·pa·ni·ment
ac·com·pa·nist (or esp. US ·pa·ny·ist)
ac·com·pa·ny (·nies, ·ny·ing, ·nied)
ac·com·plice
ac·com·plish
ac·com·plish·able
ac·com·plish·er
ac·com·plish·ment
ac·cord
ac·cord·able
ac·cord·ance
ac·cord·ant
ac·cord·er
ac·cord·ing
ac·cord·ing·ly
ac·cor·di·on
ac·cor·di·on·ist
ac·cost
ac·cost·able
ac·count
ac·count·abil·ity
ac·count·able
ac·count·ably
ac·count·an·cy
ac·count·ant
ac·count·ing
ac·cou·ple·ment supporting beam
ac·cou·tre (US ·ter)
ac·cou·tre·ment (US ·ter·)
Ac·cra Ghanaian capital
ac·cred·it
ac·credi·ta·tion
ac·cres·cent botany term
ac·crete

accretion

ac·cre·tion
ac·cre·tive (or
　ac·cre·tion·ary)
Ac·cring·ton
ac·cru·al (or ·ment)
ac·crue (·cru·ing, ·crued)
ac·cul·tur·ate
ac·cul·tura·tion
ac·cum·ben·cy
ac·cum·bent botany term
ac·cu·mu·lable
ac·cu·mu·late
ac·cu·mu·la·tion
ac·cu·mu·la·tive
ac·cu·mu·la·tor
ac·cu·ra·cy (plural ·cies)
ac·cu·rate
ac·cu·rate·ly
ac·curs·ed
ac·cus·al
ac·cu·sa·tion
ac·cu·sa·ti·val
ac·cu·sa·tive grammar term
ac·cu·sa·to·rial (or ·tory)
ac·cuse
ac·cused
ac·cus·er
ac·cus·ing·ly
ac·cus·tom
ac·cus·tomed
Ac·cu·tron (Trademark)
　watch
ace
acedia apathy
acel·lu·lar
acen·tric
acepha·lous headless
ac·er·ate variant of acerose
ac·er·bate embitter
acer·bic
acer·bity (plural ·bities)
ac·er·ose (or ·ous, ·ate)
　needle-shaped
acer·vate growing in
　clusters
aces·cence (or ·cen·cy)
aces·cent turning sour
ac·etabu·lum (plural ·la)
　cavity in hipbone
ac·etal chemical compound
ac·et·al·de·hyde
ac·et·am·ide (or ·id)
ac·et·ani·lide (or ·lid)
ac·etate
acetic acid

aceti·fi·ca·tion
aceti·fi·er
aceti·fy (·fies, ·fy·ing,
　·fied) convert into vinegar
ac·etom·eter
ac·etone
ac·etous (or ·etose)
　resembling vinegar
acetum vinegar
ac·etyl
acety·late
acety·la·tion
acetyl·cho·line biochemical
　compound
acety·lene
acety·len·ic
acety·lide
ac·etyl·sali·cyl·ic acid
　chemical name for aspirin
acey-deucy backgammon
Achaea (or Achaia) region
　of Greece
Achae·an (or Achaian)
Achaemenid member of
　Persian dynasty
Acha·tes loyal friend
ache
ach·ing·ly
achene (or akene) botany
　term
achenial (or akenial)
Acher·nar star
Ach·er·on mythological
　river
Acheu·lian (or ·lean)
　archaeological period
achiev·able
achieve
achieve·ment
achiev·er
Ach·il·lean
Achilles
ach·la·myd·eous lacking
　petals and sepals
achlor·hy·dria lacking
　stomach acid
achon·drite meteorite
achon·drit·ic
achon·dro·pla·sia skeletal
　disorder
achon·dro·plas·tic
ach·ro·mat type of lens
ach·ro·mat·ic
ach·ro·mati·cal·ly
achro·ma·tin part of cell
　nucleus

achro·ma·tism (or ·tic·ity)
achro·ma·ti·za·tion (or
　·sa·tion)
achro·ma·tize (or ·tise)
　remove colour from
achro·ma·tous
a·chro·mic (or
　achro·mous) colourless
ach-y-fi Welsh expression of
　disgust
acicu·la (plural ·lae)
　needle-shaped structure
acicu·lar
acicu·late (or ·lat·ed)
acicu·lum (plural ·lums or
　·la) zoology term
acid
acid-fast
acid-forming
acid·ic
acidi·fi·able
acidi·fi·ca·tion
acidi·fi·er
acidi·fy (·fies, ·fy·ing,
　·fied)
aci·dim·eter
acidi·met·ric (or ·ri·cal)
aci·di·met·ri·cal·ly
aci·dim·etry
acid·ity (plural ·ities)
acid·ness
aci·dom·eter hydrometer
　for acids
aci·do·phil (or ·phile)
　biology term
aci·do·phil·ic (or
　·dophi·lous)
aci·dophi·lus bacterium
aci·do·sis medical condition
aci·dot·ic
acidu·late make acid
acidu·la·tion
acidu·lous (or ·lent)
aci·er·ate change into steel
aci·era·tion
aci·naci·form botany term
acin·ic (or aci·nous,
　aci·nose)
acini·form
aci·nus (plural ·ni) biology
　term
Acis mythological character
ack-ack anti-aircraft fire
ackee (or akee) fruit
ac·knowl·edge

ac·knowl·edge·able
ac·knowl·edg·er
ac·knowl·edg·ment (or ·edge·)
aclin·ic line magnetic equator
acme peak
acne skin disease
ac·no·dal
ac·node maths term
Acol bridge term
aco·lyte
aco·nite (or ·ni·tum)
aco·nit·ic
acorn
acoty·ledon botany term
acoty·ledon·ous
acou·chi (or ·chy) rodent
acous·tic (or ·ti·cal)
acous·ti·cal·ly
acous·ti·cian
acous·tics
ac·quaint
ac·quaint·ance
ac·quaint·ance·ship
ac·quaint·ed
ac·qui·esce
ac·qui·es·cence
ac·qui·es·cent
ac·quir·able
ac·quire
ac·quire·ment
ac·quir·er
ac·qui·si·tion
ac·quisi·tive
ac·quisi·tive·ness
ac·quit (·quit·ting, ·quit·ted)
ac·quit·tal
ac·quit·tance
ac·quit·ter
acre
acre·age
acred having acres of land
acre-foot (plural -feet)
acre-inch
ac·rid
ac·ri·dine chemical compound
acrid·ity (or ·ness)
ac·ri·fla·vine antiseptic
Ac·ri·lan (Trademark)
ac·ri·mo·ni·ous
ac·ri·mo·ny (plural ·nies)
ac·ro·bat

ac·ro·bat·ic
ac·ro·bati·cal·ly
ac·ro·bat·ics
ac·ro·car·pous botany term
ac·ro·dont zoology term
ac·ro·drome botany term
ac·ro·gen botany term
ac·ro·gen·ic (or acrog·enous)
acro·lein chemical compound
ac·ro·lith type of sculpture
ac·ro·me·gal·ic
ac·ro·mega·ly hormonal disease
acro·mi·on (plural ·mia) part of shoulder blade
acrony·chal (or ·cal) occurring at sunset
ac·ro·nym
ac·ro·nym·ic (or acrony·mous)
acrop·etal botany term
ac·ro·pho·bia fear of heights
ac·ro·pho·bic
Acropo·lis
ac·ro·spire botany term
across
acros·tic
acros·ti·cal·ly
acro·ter architectural term
acryl·ic
ac·ry·lo·ni·trile
ac·ry·lyl
act
act·abil·ity
act·able
ac·tin protein
ac·ti·nal zoology term
act·ing
ac·tinia (plural ·tiniae or ·tinias) sea anemone
ac·tin·ic type of radiation
ac·tini·cal·ly
ac·ti·nide (or ·non)
ac·tini·form (or ac·ti·noid) star-shaped
ac·tin·ism
ac·tin·ium radioactive element
ac·ti·noid variant of actiniform
ac·tino·lite mineral
ac·ti·no·mere biology term

ac·ti·nom·eter radiation measurer
ac·ti·no·met·ric (or ·ri·cal)
ac·ti·nom·etry
ac·ti·no·mor·phic (or ·phous) botany term
ac·ti·no·my·cete bacterium
ac·ti·no·my·cin antibiotic
ac·ti·no·my·co·sis bacterial infection
ac·ti·no·my·cot·ic
ac·ti·non variant of actinide
ac·tino·pod protozoan
ac·ti·no·thera·py radiotherapy
ac·ti·no·ura·nium isotope of uranium
ac·ti·no·zo·an marine organism
ac·tion
ac·tion·able
ac·tion·ably
action-packed
Ac·ti·um ancient Greek town
ac·ti·vate
ac·ti·va·tion
ac·ti·va·tor
ac·tive
ac·tive·ly
ac·tive·ness
ac·tiv·ism
ac·tiv·ist
ac·tiv·ity (plural ·ities)
ac·to·myo·sin protein
Ac·ton London district
ac·tor
ac·tress
ac·tual
ac·tu·al·ity (plural ·ities)
ac·tu·ali·za·tion (or ·sa·tion)
ac·tu·al·ize (or ·ise)
ac·tu·al·ly
ac·tu·ari·al
ac·tu·ary (plural ·aries)
ac·tu·ate
ac·tua·tion
ac·tua·tor
acu·ity
acu·leate (or ·leat·ed) pointed
acu·leus (plural ·lei) prickle
acu·men

acuminate

acu·mi·nate pointed
acu·mi·na·tion
acu·mi·nous
acu·punc·ture
acut·ance photography term
acute
acute·ly
acute·ness
acy·clic chemistry term
acyl
ad *Slang* advertisement
adac·ty·lous without fingers or toes
ad·age
ada·gio (*plural* ·gios) musical term
ada·mant
ada·man·tine very hard
Ada·ma·wa language group
Ad·am·ite nudist
Ad·ams US mountain
ad·ams·ite tear gas
Ada·na Turkish city
adapt
adapt·abil·ity (*or* ·able·ness)
adapt·able
adapt·ably
ad·ap·ta·tion
adapt·er one who adapts; *compare* adaptor
adap·tive
adapt·or electrical device; *compare* adapter
ad·ax·ial towards the axis; *compare* abaxial
add
ad·dax antelope
ad·dend number added to
ad·den·dum (*plural* ·da)
ad·der snake
add·er calculator
ad·dict
ad·dic·tion
ad·dic·tive
Ad·dis Aba·ba Ethiopian capital
ad·di·tion
ad·di·tion·al
ad·di·tion·al·ly
ad·di·tive
ad·dle
ad·dress
ad·dressee
ad·dress·er (*or* ·dres·sor)

Ad·dres·so·graph (*Trademark*)
ad·duce
ad·duce·able (*or* ·duc·ible)
ad·du·cent
ad·duct pull towards
ad·duc·tion
ad·duc·tor muscle
Ad·elaide Australian city
ademp·tion legal term
Aden capital of South Yemen
ad·enec·to·my (*plural* ·mies) removal of gland
ad·enine biochemical compound
ad·eni·tis inflammation of a gland
ad·eno·car·ci·no·ma (*plural* ·mas *or* ·ma·ta) tumour
ad·eno·hy·phophy·sis part of pituitary gland
ad·enoid resembling a gland
ad·enoi·dal affected by enlarged adenoids
ad·enoid·ec·to·my (*plural* ·mies)
ad·enoids tonsil tissue
ad·eno·ma (*plural* ·mas *or* ·ma·ta) glandular tumour
adeno·sine biochemical compound
ad·eno·vi·rus
adept
ad·equa·cy
ad·equate
à deux *French* of or for two persons
ad·here
ad·her·ence
ad·her·ent (*noun, adj*)
ad·he·sion
ad·he·sive
ad·he·sive·ness
ad hoc *Latin* for a particular purpose
ad ho·mi·nem *Latin* to the man
adia·bat·ic physics term
adi·aph·or·ism theological term
adi·apho·rist
adi·apho·ris·tic
adi·apho·rous medical term

adieu (*plural* adieus *or* adieux) goodbye
ad in·fi·ni·tum *Latin* without end
ad in·ter·im *Latin* for the meantime
adi·os *Spanish* goodbye
adi·po·cere waxy substance
adi·poc·er·ous
adi·pose fatty
adi·pos·ity
Adi·ron·dacks US mountains
adit mine shaft
Adi·va·si Indian people
ad·ja·cen·cy
ad·ja·cent
ad·jec·ti·val
ad·jec·tive
ad·join
ad·join·ing
ad·joint maths term
ad·journ
ad·journ·ment
ad·judge
ad·ju·di·cate
ad·ju·di·ca·tion
ad·ju·di·ca·tive
ad·ju·di·ca·tor
ad·junct
ad·junc·tive
ad·ju·ra·tion
ad·jura·tory
ad·jure appeal to solemnly; *compare* abjure
ad·jur·er (*or* ·ju·ror)
ad·just
ad·just·able
ad·just·ment
ad·ju·tan·cy
ad·ju·tant
ad·ju·vant helping; auxiliary
ad lib spontaneously; freely
ad-lib (-libbing, -libbed) improvise
ad-libber
ad·man (*plural* ·men)
ad·mass people susceptible to advertising
ad·meas·ure
ad·meas·ure·ment
Admetus mythological king
ad·min *short for* administration
ad·mini·cle legal term

ad·min·is·ter
ad·min·is·trable
ad·min·is·trate
ad·min·is·tra·tion
ad·min·is·tra·tive
ad·min·is·tra·tor (*fem*
 ·trix *in legal contexts*)
ad·mi·rable
ad·mi·rably
ad·mi·ral
ad·mi·ral·ty (*plural* ·ties)
ad·mi·ra·tion
ad·mire
ad·mirer
ad·mir·ing·ly
ad·mis·sibil·ity (*or*
 ·sible·ness)
ad·mis·sible
ad·mis·sion
ad·mis·sive
ad·mit (·mit·ting,
 ·mit·ted)
ad·mit·tance
ad·mit·ted·ly
ad·mix
ad·mix·ture
ad·mon·ish
ad·mon·ish·er (*or*
 ·moni·tor)
ad·mo·ni·tion
ad·moni·tory
ad·nate botany term
ad nau·seam *Latin* to a
 disgusting extent
ad·nomi·nal word
 modifying a noun
ad·noun adjective used as
 noun
ado
ado·be building term
ado·les·cence
ado·les·cent
Adon·ic type of verse line
Adonis mythological
 character
adopt
adopt·able
adopt·ed
adop·tee
adopt·er
adop·tion
adop·tion·ism (*or* ·tian·)
adop·tion·ist (*or* ·tian·)
adop·tive
ador·able

ador·ably
ado·ra·tion
adore
ador·er
adorn
adorn·ment
ad rem *Latin* to the point
ad·re·nal gland
adrena·line hormone
ad·ren·er·gic biology term
adre·no·cor·ti·co·troph·ic
 (*US* ·trop·ic) stimulating
 adrenal cortex
Adri·at·ic
adrift
adroit
adroit·ness
ad·sci·ti·tious additional
ad·sorb accumulate on a
 surface; *compare* absorb
ad·sorb·abil·ity
ad·sorb·able
ad·sorb·ate
ad·sor·bent
ad·sorp·tion
adu·laria mineral
adu·late
adu·la·tion
adu·la·tor
adu·la·tory
adult
adul·ter·ant
adul·ter·ate
adul·tera·tion
adul·ter·ator
adul·ter·er (*fem* ·ess)
adul·ter·ine fake
adul·ter·ous
adul·tery (*plural* ·teries)
adult·hood
ad·um·bral shadowy
ad·um·brate
ad·um·bra·tion
ad·um·bra·tive
Adu·wa Ethiopian town
ad va·lo·rem *Latin*
 according to value
ad·vance
ad·vanced
ad·vance·ment
ad·vanc·er
ad·vanc·ing·ly
ad·van·tage
ad·van·ta·geous
ad·van·ta·geous·ness

ad·vec·tion
Ad·vent coming of Christ
ad·vent arrival
Ad·ven·tist
ad·ven·ti·tia anatomy term
ad·ven·ti·tious happening
 by chance; growing in
 abnormal position
ad·ven·tive
ad·ven·ture
ad·ven·tur·er (*fem* ·ess)
ad·ven·tur·ism
ad·ven·tur·ist
ad·ven·tur·ous
ad·verb
ad·ver·bial
ad·ver·sary (*plural*
 ·saries)
ad·ver·sa·tive linguistics
 term
ad·verse
ad·ver·sity (*plural* ·sities)
ad·vert refer to; *Slang*
 advertisement
ad·vert·ence (*or* ·en·cy)
ad·vert·ent·ly
ad·ver·tise
ad·ver·tise·ment
ad·ver·tis·er
ad·ver·tis·ing
(advertize) *incorrect spelling
 of* advertise
ad·vice
ad·vis·abil·ity
ad·vis·able
ad·vise
ad·vised
ad·vis·ed·ly
ad·vise·ment *US* careful
 consideration
ad·vis·er (*or* ·vi·sor)
ad·vi·so·ry
ad·vo·caat
ad·vo·ca·cy (*plural* ·cies)
ad·vo·cate
ad·vo·ca·tion
ad·vo·ca·tory
Ady·gei (*plural* ·gei *or*
 ·geis) Soviet people
ady·na·mia weakness
ady·nam·ic
adze (*US* adz) tool
Adzhar
Adzha·ria Soviet republic
ad·zuki (*or* ·su·ki) bean

aecio·spore
aecium (*or* **aecid·ium**; *plural* **aecia** *or* ·**ia**) fungal structure
aedes mosquito
aedile (*US also* **edile**) Roman magistrate
Aeëtes mythological king
Aegean
Aegi·na Greek island
Aegir Norse god
aegis (*US also* **egis**)
aegro·tat university degree
Aegyptus mythological king
Aeneas mythological prince
Aene·id epic poem
Aeo·lian
aeo·lian harp
Aeol·ic ancient Greek dialect
aeoli·pile model steam turbine
Aeo·lis Greek god
aeon (*US* **eon**)
aeo·nian (*or* **eo·**) everlasting
aepy·or·nis extinct bird
aer·ate
aera·tion
aera·tor
aer·en·chy·ma plant tissue
aer·ial relating to air; radio or TV device; *compare* **ariel**
aeri·al·ist trapeze artist
aerie *variant spelling of* **eyrie**
aeri·fi·ca·tion
aeri·form gaseous
aeri·fy (·**fies**, ·**fy·ing**, ·**fied**)
aero·bal·lis·tics
aero·bat·ics
aer·obe (*or* **aero·bium**; *plural* ·**obes** *or* ·**bia**)
aero·bic requiring oxygen
aero·bics exercises
aero·bio·sis
aero·bio·tic
aero·bium *variant of* **aerobe**
aero·do·net·ics study of gliding flight
aero·drome
aero·dy·nam·ic
aero·dy·nami·cal·ly
aero·dy·nam·ics
aero·dyne heavier-than-air machine
aero·em·bo·lism nitrogen in the blood
aero-engine
aero·foil
aero·gel solid foam
aero·gram (*or* ·**gramme**)
aer·og·ra·phy
aero·lite meteorite
aero·lo·gic (*or* ·**logi·cal**)
aer·olo·gist
aer·ol·ogy study of the atmosphere
aero·mechan·ic
aero·mechani·cal
aero·mechan·ics
aer·om·eter
aero·met·ric
aer·om·etry branch of physics
aero·naut
aero·nau·ti·cal (*or* **aero·nau·tic**)
aero·naut·ics
aero·neu·ro·sis
aero·pause region of upper atmosphere
aero·pha·gia swallowing of air
aero·pho·bia
aero·pho·bic afraid of draughts
aero·plane
aero·sol
aero·space
aero·sphere earth's atmosphere
aero·stat lighter-than-air craft
aero·stat·ic (*or* ·**stati·cal**)
aero·stat·ics
aero·sta·tion
aero·ther·mo·dy·nam·ic
aero·ther·mo·dy·nam·ics
aeru·go verdigris
aeru·gin·ous
aery *variant spelling of* **eyrie**; *poetic* airy; insubstantial
Aes·cu·la·pian
Aesculapius Roman god
Aesir Norse gods
aes·the·sia (*US* **es·**) normal sensitivity
aes·thete (*US also* **es·**)
aes·thet·ic (*or* ·**theti·cal**; *US also* **es·**)
aes·theti·cal·ly (*US also* **es·**)
aes·the·ti·cian (*US also* **es·**)
aes·theti·cism (*US also* **es·**)
aes·thet·ics (*US also* **es·**)
aes·ti·val (*US* **es·**) occurring in the summer
aes·ti·vate (*US* **es·**)
aes·ti·va·tion (*US* **es·**) biology term
aes·ti·va·tor (*US* **es·**)
aether *former spelling of* **ether** (anaesthetic); *variant spelling of* **ether** (hypothetical medium)
aethe·real *rare spelling of* **ethereal**
aethe·real·ity *rare spelling of* **ethereality**
aetio·logi·cal (*US* **etio·**)
aeti·olo·gist (*US* **eti·**)
aeti·ol·ogy (*US* **eti·**) study of causes
Aeto·lia Greek region
afar
afebrile without fever
af·fabil·ity
af·fable
af·fably
af·fair
af·faire *French* love affair
af·fect have an effect on; *compare* **effect** (*verb*)
af·fec·ta·tion
af·fect·ed
af·fect·ed·ly
af·fect·ed·ness
af·fect·ing
af·fect·ing·ly
af·fec·tion
af·fec·tion·al
af·fec·tion·ate
af·fec·tive arousing emotions
af·fec·tiv·ity (*or* ·**tive·ness**)
af·fen·pin·scher dog
af·fer·ent conducting inwards; *compare* **efferent**
af·fet·tuo·so musical term
af·fi·ance betroth

agglutinable

af·fi·ant *US* person who makes an affidavit
af·fi·da·vit
af·fili·ate
af·filia·tion
af·fine maths term
af·fined closely related
af·fini·tive
af·fin·ity (*plural* ·ities)
af·firm
af·firm·able
af·fir·ma·tion
af·firma·tive
af·firm·er (*or* ·ant)
af·fix
af·fix·ture
af·fla·tus creative power
af·flict
af·flic·tion
af·flic·tive
af·flu·ence
af·flu·ent
af·flux flowing towards
af·ford
af·for·est
af·for·esta·tion
af·fran·chise release from obligation
af·fran·chise·ment
af·fray
af·freight·ment
af·fri·cate
af·frica·tive phonetics term
af·fright
af·front
af·fu·sion baptism
Af·ghan hound
Af·ghan (*or* ·ghani) people
af·ghan shawl
af·ghani Afghan currency
Af·ghani·stan
afi·cio·na·do (*plural* ·dos) supporter
afield
afire
aflame
af·la·tox·in
afloat
aflut·ter
afoot
afore
afore·men·tioned
afore·said
afore·thought

a for·tio·ri *Latin* for a stronger reason
afoul
afraid
af·reet Arabian demon
afresh
Af·ri·ca
Af·ri·can
Af·ri·can·ism
Af·ri·kaans language of Afrikaners
Af·ri·kan·der (*or* ·can·) cattle
Af·ri·ka·ner White South African
Af·ri·ka·ner·dom
Afro (*plural* Afros) hairstyle
Afro-American
Afro-Asian
Afro-Asiatic
af·ror·mo·sia wood
aft
af·ter
after·birth
after·body (*plural* ·bodies) discarded part of rocket
after·brain
after·burner
after·burning
after·care
after·damp gas in mines
after·deck
after·effect
after·glow
after·heat
after·image
after·life
after·math
after·noon
after·pains
after·piece brief additional comic play
af·ters *Slang* dessert
after·sensation
after·shaft type of feather
after·shave
after·shock
after·taste
after·thought
after·wards (*or esp. US* ·ward)
after·word postscript
after·world

aga (*or* agha) Turkish title
Aga·dir Moroccan port
again
against
agal·loch tree
aga·ma lizard
Agamemnon mythological king
agam·ete biology term
agam·ic biology term
agami·cal·ly
aga·mo·gen·esis biology term
aga·mo·genet·ic
aga·mo·geneti·cal·ly
aga·pan·thus lily
Agape Christian love
agape gaping
agar seaweed product
aga·ric mushroom
agari·ca·ceous
Agar·ta·la Indian city
ag·ate
agate·ware
aga·ve plant
age (age·ing *or esp. US* ag·ing, aged)
aged (*adj, noun*)
agee *Scot* awry
age·ing (*or esp. US* ag·ing)
age·less
agen·cy (*plural* ·cies)
agen·da (*or* ·dum; *plural* ·das *or* ·dums)
agen·esis imperfect development
agenet·ic
agent
agen·tial
agen·tive (*or* ·tial) linguistics term
agent pro·vo·ca·teur (*plural* agents pro·vo·ca·teurs)
ag·era·tum plant
ag·ger Roman earthwork
ag·gior·na·men·to (*plural* ·ti) updating Catholic church
ag·glom·er·ate
ag·glom·era·tion
ag·glom·era·tive
ag·glu·ti·nabil·ity
ag·glu·ti·nable

agglutinant

ag·glu·ti·nant
ag·glu·ti·nate
ag·glu·ti·na·tion
ag·glu·ti·na·tive
ag·glu·ti·nin antibody
ag·glu·tino·gen
ag·grada·tion
ag·grade geology term
ag·gran·dize (or ·dise)
ag·gran·dize·ment (or ·dise·ment)
ag·gran·diz·er (or ·dis·er)
ag·gra·vate
ag·gra·va·tion
ag·gre·gate
ag·gre·ga·tion
ag·gress
ag·gres·sion
ag·gres·sive
ag·gres·sor
ag·grieve
ag·griev·ed·ly
ag·gro *Slang* aggression
aghast
ag·ile
agil·ity
Ag·in·court
ag·ing variant spelling (*esp. US*) *of* ageing
agio·tage business of currency exchange
agist legal term
agi·tate
agi·ta·tion
agi·ta·to musical term
agi·ta·tor
agit·prop communist propaganda
Aglaia Greek goddess
agleam
ag·let (*or* aiglet) shoelace tag
agley *Scot* awry
aglit·ter
aglow
agma phonetic symbol
ag·mi·nate gathered together
ag·nate having common male ancestor
ag·no·men (*plural* ·nomi·na) ancient Roman's fourth name
ag·nomi·nal
ag·nos·tic

ag·nos·ti·cism
Ag·nus Dei liturgical chant
ago
agog
à gogo *French* as much as one likes
agon (*plural* ago·nes) ancient Greek festival
agon·ic forming no angle
ago·nist
ago·nis·tic
ago·nize (*or* ·nise)
ago·niz·ing·ly (*or* ·nis·)
ago·ny (*plural* ·nies)
ago·ra (*plural* ·rae *or* ·ras) Greek marketplace
ago·ra (*plural* ·rot) Israeli coin
ago·ra·pho·bia
ago·ra·pho·bic
agou·ti (*plural* ·tis *or* ·ties) rodent
Agra Indian city
agraffe fastening
agran·ulo·cy·tosis blood disorder
ag·ra·pha sayings of Christ
agraphia inability to write
agrar·ian
agrari·an·ism
agree (agree·ing, agreed)
agree·able
agree·able·ness
agree·ably
agreed
agree·ment
agres·tal growing as a weed
agres·tic rural
ag·ri·busi·ness
ag·ri·cul·tur·al
ag·ri·cul·ture
ag·ri·cul·tur·ist (*or* ·tur·al·ist)
ag·ri·mo·ny (*plural* ·nies) plant
ag·ro·bio·logi·cal
ag·ro·bi·olo·gist
ag·ro·bi·ol·ogy
ag·ro·logi·cal
agrol·ogy study of soils
ag·ro·nom·ic (*or* ·nomi·cal)
ag·ro·nom·ics land economics
agrono·mist

agrono·my science of cultivation
ag·ros·tol·ogy study of grasses
aground
ag·ryp·not·ic of insomnia
Aguas·ca·lien·tes Mexican state
ague malaria
ague·weed
Agul·has South African headland
ah
aha
ahead
ahem
Ah·meda·bad (*or* ·mada·) Indian city
Ah·med·na·gar (*or* ·mad·) Indian city
ahoy
Ah·waz (*or* ·vaz) Iranian town
ai (*plural* ais) animal
aid help
aide assistant
aide-de-camp (*plural* aides-)
aide-mémoire (*plural* aides-)
aid·er
aigrette (*or* aigret) feather on hat
aiguille mountain peak
aiguil·lette military ornament
aikido self-defence
ail
ailan·thus (*plural* ·thuses) tree
ailer·on
ail·ing
ail·ment
ailu·ro·phile cat lover
ailu·ro·philia
ailu·ro·phobe fearer of cats
ailu·ro·phobia
aim
aim·less
aim·less·ness
ain *Scot* own
ain't *Nonstandard* am not
Ainu (*plural* Ainus *or* Ainu) Japanese people
aïoli garlic mayonnaise
Aïr Saharan region

Alcestis

air
air·borne
air·brick
air·brush
air·burst
air·bus
air-conditioned
air-conditioner
air-conditioning
air-cool
air·craft (*plural* ·craft)
air·craft·man (*or* ·crafts·; *plural* ·men)
air·craft·woman (*or* ·crafts·; *plural* ·women)
air·crew
Air·drie Scottish town
air·drop (·drop·ping, ·dropped) delivery by parachute
air-dry (-dries, -dry·ing, -dried)
Aire·dale Yorkshire district; terrier
air·field
air·flow
air·foil
air·frame part of aircraft
air·glow
air·head military term
airi·ly
airi·ness
air·ing
air-intake
air·less
air·less·ness
air·lift
air·line
air·lin·er
air·lock
air·man (*plural* ·men)
air·plane *US* aeroplane
air·port
air·screw propeller
air·ship
air·sick
air·sick·ness
air·space
air·speed
air·stream
air·strip
air·tight
air·waves
air·way

air·woman (*plural* ·women)
air·worthi·ness
air·worthy
airy (airi·er, airi·est)
airy-fairy
aisle
Aisne French river
ait *Dialect* islet
aitch letter H
aitch·bone cut of beef
Aix-en-Provence French city
Ajac·cio Corsican port
ajar
Ajax mythological character
Aj·mer Indian city
Ake·la cub-scout leader
akha·ra Indian gymnasium
akim·bo
akin
Ak·kad (*or* Ac·cad) Babylonian city
Ak·ka·dian (*or* Ac·ca·)
Ak·tyu·binsk Soviet city
à la *French* in the style of
ala (*plural* alae) winglike structure
Ala·bama
Ala·bam·ian
ala·bas·ter
à la carte
alack
alacka·day
alac·ri·tous
alac·rity
Aladdin
Ala·go·as Brazilian state
Alai Soviet mountain range
ala·meda *US* tree-lined promenade
Ala·mo
à la mode fashionable
ala·mode silk
ala·nine amino acid
alan·nah Irish term of endearment
alap Indian music
alar of wings
alarm
alarmed
alarm·ing
alarm·ing·ly
alarm·ism
alarm·ist

alar·um *Archaic* alarm
alary of wings
alas
Alas·ka
Alas·kan
alate winged
al·ba·core fish
Alba Lon·ga ancient city
Al·ba·nia
Al·ba·nian
Al·ba·ny *US* city; Canadian river; Australian port
al·ba·ta alloy
al·ba·tross
al·be·do (*plural* ·dos) physics term
al·be·it
Al·bert *former name of* Mobutu
Al·ber·ta Canadian province
al·bert·ite variety of bitumen
al·bes·cence
al·bes·cent becoming white
Al·bi·gen·ses medieval heretics
Al·bi·gen·sian
al·bin·ic (*or* ·bin·is·tic)
al·bi·nism
al·bi·no (*plural* ·nos)
Al·bi·on *Archaic* Britain
al·bite mineral
al·bit·ic
Ål·borg variant spelling of Aalborg
al·bum
al·bu·men white of egg; *compare* albumin
al·bu·menize (*or* ·menise)
al·bu·min a protein; *compare* albumen
al·bu·mi·nate
al·bu·mi·noid
al·bu·mi·nous
al·bu·mi·nu·ria urine containing albumin
Al·bu·quer·que *US* city
al·bur·num sapwood
Al·bu·ry Australian city
Al·ca·ic verse form
al·caide Spanish commander
al·cal·de Spanish mayor
Al·ca·traz *US* island
al·ca·zar Moorish palace
Alcestis mythological queen

alchemic

al·chem·ic (or ·chemi·cal, ·chem·is·tic)
al·che·mist
al·che·mize (or ·mise)
al·che·my (plural ·mies)
al·che·rin·ga Aboriginal golden age
al·ci·dine ornithology term
al·co·hol
al·co·hol·ic
al·co·hol·ic·ity
al·co·hol·ism
al·co·holi·za·tion (or ·sa·tion)
al·co·hol·ize (or ·ise)
al·co·hol·om·eter
Al·co·ran Koran
al·cove
Alcyone (or Halcyone) mythological character
Al·dab·ra Indian Ocean islands
Al·deba·ran star
al·de·hyde
al den·te Italian cooked until still firm
al·der
al·der·man (plural ·men)
al·der·man·ic
Al·der·mas·ton
Al·der·ney Channel Island
Al·der·shot
al·dol chemical compound
al·dose sugar
al·dos·terone hormone
ald·ox·ime chemical compound
al·drin insecticide
ale
alea·to·ry dependent on chance
ale·cost plant
alee nautical term
al·egar malt vinegar
ale·house
Ale·man·ni Germanic people
Al·eman·nic
alem·bic
alem·bi·cat·ed excessively refined
aleph Hebrew letter
aleph-null (or -zero) maths term
Alep·po Syrian city

alert
alert·ness
Ales·san·dria Italian town
alethic logic term
aleu·rone (or ·ron) plant protein
al·evin young fish
ale·wife fish
al·ex·an·ders plant
Al·ex·an·dria Egyptian port
Al·ex·an·drian
Al·ex·an·drine type of verse
al·ex·an·drite gemstone
alexia word blindness
alex·in immunology term
al·fal·fa
al·fila·ria (or ·fil·eria) plant
al·fres·co
al·gae (sing. alga)
al·gal
al·gar·ro·ba (or ·ga·ro·ba) tree
al·ge·bra
al·ge·bra·ic (or ·brai·cal)
al·ge·brai·cal·ly
al·ge·bra·ist
Al·ge·ci·ras Spanish port
Al·ge·ria
Al·ge·rian (or ·rine)
al·gerine fabric
al·gi·cide
al·gid chilly
Al·giers Algerian capital
al·gin biochemical compound
al·gi·nate
al·gin·ic acid
al·goid resembling algae
Al·gol star; computer language
al·go·lag·nia sexual perversion
al·go·lag·nic
al·go·lag·nist
al·golo·gist
al·gol·ogy study of algae
al·gom·eter
al·gom·etry
Al·gon·quian (or ·kian)
Al·gon·quin (or ·kin; plural ·quins, ·quin or ·kins, ·kin) American Indian

al·go·pho·bia fear of pain
al·gor chill
al·go·rism counting system
al·go·ris·mic
al·go·rithm maths term
al·go·rith·mic
al·go·rith·mi·cal·ly
Al·ham·bra Spanish citadel
Al·ham·bresque
Al Hasa Saudi Arabian province
Al Hu·fuf (or Ho·fuf) Saudi Arabian town
ali·as (plural ·ases)
Ali Baba
ali·bi (plural ·bis)
Ali·can·te Spanish town
ali·cy·clic chemistry term
ali·dade (or ·dad) surveying instrument
al·ien
al·ien·abil·ity
al·ien·able
al·ien·age
al·ien·ate
al·iena·tion
al·iena·tor
al·ienee legal term
al·ien·ism
al·ien·ist US psychiatrist
al·ien·or legal term
ali·form wing-shaped
Ali·garh Indian city
alight (alight·ing, alight·ed or alit)
align
align·ment
alike
ali·ment
ali·men·ta·ry
ali·men·ta·tion
ali·men·ta·tive
ali·mo·ny
aline rare spelling of align
ali·ped having winglike limbs
ali·phat·ic chemistry term
ali·quant maths term
ali·quot maths term
aliun·de from another source
alive
aliza·rin dye
al·ka·hest (or ·ca·) alchemical solvent

al·ka·li (*plural* ·lis *or* ·lies)
al·kal·ic
al·ka·li·fy (·fies, ·fy·ing, ·fied)
al·ka·lim·eter
al·ka·li·met·ric
al·ka·lim·etry
al·ka·line
al·ka·lin·ity
al·ka·liz·able (*or* ·lis·able)
al·ka·lize (*or* ·lise)
al·ka·loid plant compound
al·ka·lo·sis medical condition
al·kane chemistry term
al·ka·net plant
al·kene chemistry term
al·kyd
al·kyl
al·kyla·tion chemistry term
al·kyne chemistry term
all
Allah
Al·laha·bad Indian city
al·lan·ite mineral
al·lan·to·ic
al·lan·toid
al·lan·toi·dal
al·lan·to·is (*plural* ·ides) embryology term
al·lar·gan·do musical term
al·lay
(alledge) *incorrect spelling of* allege
al·le·ga·tion
al·lege
al·leged
al·leg·ed·ly
al·le·giance
al·le·gori·cal (*or* ·gor·ic)
al·le·gori·cal·ly
al·le·go·rist
al·le·gori·za·tion (*or* ·sa·tion)
al·le·go·rize (*or* ·rise)
al·le·go·ry (*plural* ·ries)
al·le·gret·to (*plural* ·tos) musical term
al·le·gro (*plural* ·gros)
al·lele (*or* al·le·lo·morph) genetics term
al·lel·ic
al·lel·ism
al·le·luia (*or* hal·le·lu·jah; note Handel's Hallelujah Chorus)
alle·mande musical term
Al·len Irish bog
Al·len·town US city
Al·lep·pey Indian port
al·ler·gen allergy-causing substance
al·ler·gen·ic
al·ler·gic
al·ler·gist allergy specialist
al·ler·gy (*plural* ·gies)
al·le·thrin insecticide
al·le·vi·ate
al·le·via·tion
al·le·via·tive
al·le·via·tor
al·ley narrow lane; *compare* ally
alley·way
All·hal·lows
All·hal·low·tide
all·heal plant
al·lia·ceous of allium
al·li·ance
al·lied
Al·lier French river
Al·lies in World War II
al·lies *plural of* ally
al·li·ga·tor
all-important
all-inclusive
al·lit·er·ate
al·lit·era·tion
al·lit·era·tive
al·lium onion genus
Al·loa Scottish town
al·lo·cate
al·lo·ca·tion
al·loch·tho·nous geology term
al·lo·cu·tion formal speech
al·lo·dial
al·lo·dium (*or* al·lod; *plural* ·dia *or* ·lods) legal term
al·loga·mous
al·loga·my biology term
al·lo·graph signature written for another
al·lo·graph·ic
al·lom·er·ism chemistry term
al·lom·er·ous
al·lo·met·ric
al·lom·etry biology term
al·lo·morph
al·lo·mor·phic
al·lo·mor·phism chemistry term
al·lo·nym assumed name
al·lo·path (*or* ·lopa·thist) medical practitioner
al·lo·path·ic
al·lo·pathi·cal·ly
al·lopa·thy
al·lo·pat·ric biology term
al·lo·pat·ri·cal·ly
al·lo·phane mineral
al·lo·phone linguistics term
al·lo·phon·ic
al·lo·plasm biology term
al·lo·plas·mic
al·lo·pu·ri·nol anti-gout drug
al·lot (·lot·ting, ·lot·ted)
al·lot·ment
al·lo·trope chemistry term
al·lo·trop·ic
al·lo·tropi·cal·ly
al·lot·ro·py (*or* ·pism)
al·lot·tee
al·low
al·low·able
al·low·ance
Al·lo·way Scottish village
al·low·ed·ly
al·loy
all-round
all·rounder
all·seed plant
all·spice
all-star (*adj*)
all-time (*adj*)
al·lude refer; *compare* elude; illude
al·lure
al·lure·ment
al·lur·er
al·lur·ing
al·lu·sion reference; *compare* illusion
al·lu·sive
al·lu·sive·ness
al·lu·vial
al·lu·vion overflow
al·lu·vium (*plural* ·viums *or* ·via) soil; *compare* eluvium

ally

ally (*verb* **allies, ally·ing, allied**; *noun, plural* **allies**) friend; *compare* **alley**
al·lyl
Alma-Ata Soviet city
Al·ma·da Portuguese city
Al·ma·gest astronomy treatise
alma ma·ter *Latin* one's school or university
al·ma·nac
al·ma·nack almanac; *Archaic except in proper names, as* **Whitaker's Almanack**
al·man·dine gemstone
Al Marj Libyan town
al·me·mar platform in synagogue
Al·mería Spanish port
al·mighti·ly
al·mighti·ness
Al·mighty God
al·mighty
Al·mo·hades Muslim group
al·mond
al·mon·er
al·mon·ry
Al·mo·ra·vides Muslim group
al·most
alms
alms·house
al·mu·can·tar astronomy term
al·muce monk's cape
Al·ni·co (*Trademark*)
aloe (*plural* **aloes**) plant
aloes purgative drug
alo·etic
aloft
alo·ha Hawaiian greeting
alo·in chemical compound
alone
along
along·shore
along·side
aloof
aloof·ness
alo·pecia
aloud
alow nautical term
alp
al·paca

alpen·glow
alpen·horn *variant of* **alphorn**
alpen·stock
Alpes-de-Haute-Pro·vence French department
Alpes Ma·ri·times French department
al·pes·trine
al·pha
al·pha·bet
al·pha·beti·cal (*or* ·**bet·ic**)
al·pha·beti·cal·ly
al·pha·beti·za·tion (*or* ·**sa·tion**)
al·pha·bet·ize (*or* ·**ise**)
al·pha·bet·iz·er (*or* ·**is·er**)
Al·pha Cen·tau·ri constellation
al·pha·nu·mer·ic (*or* **al·pha·mer·ic**)
al·pha·nu·meri·cal·ly (*or* **al·pha·meri·cal·ly**)
alp·horn (*or* **alpen·horn**)
al·pho·sis absence of skin pigmentation
Al·pine of the Alps
al·pine of mountains
al·pin·ism
al·pin·ist
Alps
al·ready
al·right *variant spelling of* **all right**, *regarded by some as nonstandard*
Al·sace French region
Alsace-Lorraine French region
Al·sa·tia ancient name of Alsace
Al·sa·tian
al·sike plant
also
also-ran
alt high in pitch
Al·tai Asian mountains
Al·ta·ic language group
Al·tair star
al·tar table in church; *compare* **alter**
altar·piece
alt·azi·muth astronomical instrument
al·ter to change; *compare* **altar**

al·ter·abil·ity
al·ter·able
al·tera·tion
al·tera·tive therapeutic drug
al·ter·cate
al·ter·ca·tion
al·ter ego
al·ter·nant
al·ter·nate
al·ter·nate·ly
al·ter·na·tion
al·ter·na·tive
al·ter·na·tive·ly
al·ter·na·tor
al·thaea (*US* ·**thea**) plant
Al·thing Icelandic parliament
alt·horn brass instrument
al·though
al·time·ter
al·ti·met·ri·cal
al·tim·etry
Al·ti·pla·no Andean plateau
al·tis·si·mo musical term
al·ti·tude
al·ti·tu·di·nal
alto (*plural* **altos**)
alto·cu·mu·lus (*plural* ·**li**) cloud
al·to·geth·er entirely; *note* **all together** all at the same time
Al·to·na German port
al·to re·lie·vo (*or* **ri·**; *plural* ·**vos**) sculpture term
al·to·stra·tus (*plural* ·**ti**) cloud
al·tri·cial ornithology term
Al·trin·cham English town
al·tru·ism
al·tru·ist
al·tru·is·tic
al·tru·is·ti·cal·ly
alu·del chemical vessel
alu·la (*plural* ·**lae**) tuft of feathers
alum
alu·mi·na aluminium oxide
alu·mi·nate
alu·mi·nif·er·ous
alu·min·ium (*US* ·**min·um**)
alu·mi·nize (*or* ·**nise**)
alu·mi·nos·ity

alu·mi·no·ther·my chemical process
alu·mi·nous resembling aluminium
alu·mi·num US spelling of aluminium
alum·nus (fem ·na; plural ·ni, fem ·nae) US former student
alum·root
Alun·dum (Trademark)
alu·nite mineral
al·veo·lar
al·veo·late
al·veo·la·tion
al·veo·lus (plural ·li) anatomy term
al·vine anatomy term
al·ways
alys·sum plant
Alzheimer's dis·ease
am
ama·da·vat variant of avadavat
ama·dou fungal substance
Ama·ga·sa·ki Japanese city
amah Eastern nurse
amal·gam
amal·gam·ate
amal·gama·tion
(amalgum) incorrect spelling of amalgam
amo·ni·ta fungus
amanu·en·sis (plural ·ses)
ama·ranth plant
ama·ran·tha·ceous
ama·ran·thine
ama·relle cherry
Ama·rll·lo US city
ama·ryl·li·da·ceous
Ama·ryl·lis Poetic shepherdess
ama·ryl·lis plant
amass
amass·er
ama·teur
ama·teur·ish
ama·teur·ish·ness
ama·teur·ism
Amati violin
ama·tol explosive substance
ama·tory (or ·to·rial)
amau·ro·sis blindness
amau·rot·ic

amaut Eskimo woman's hood
amaze
amaze·ment
amaz·ing
amaz·ing·ly
Ama·zon South American river; female warrior
ama·zon aggressive female
Ama·zo·nas Brazilian state
Ama·zo·nian
ama·zon·ite gemstone
Am·ba·la Indian city
am·ba·ry (or ·ri; plural ·ries or ·ris) plant; fibre
am·bas·sa·dor ·
am·bas·sa·dor·ial
am·bas·sa·dor·ship
am·bas·sa·dress
am·ber
amber·gris substance from sperm whale
amber·jack fish
am·ber·oid (or am·broid) synthetic amber
am·bi·dex·ter·ity (or ·dex·trous·ness)
am·bi·dex·trous
am·bi·ence (or ·ance)
am·bi·ent
am·bi·gu·ity (plural ·ities)
am·bigu·ous
am·bigu·ous·ness
am·bit
am·bi·tion
am·bi·tious
am·biva·lence (or ·len·cy)
am·biva·lent
am·bi·ver·sion
am·bi·vert psychology term
am·ble
am·bler
am·blygo·nite mineral
am·blyo·pia impaired vision
am·bly·op·ic
ambo (plural ambos) pulpit
am·bo·cep·tor immune substance
Am·boi·na Indonesian island
am·boy·na (or ·boi·) wood
am·bro·sia
am·bro·sial (or ·sian)

am·bro·type photography term
am·bry (or aum·; plural ·bries) cupboard
ambs·ace lowest throw at dice
am·bu·lac·ral
am·bu·lac·rum (plural ·ra) band on starfish
am·bu·lance
am·bu·lant
am·bu·late
am·bu·la·tion
am·bu·la·tory (plural ·tories)
am·bus·cade ambush
am·bush
ameba US spelling of amoeba
ame·lio·rant
ame·lio·rate
ame·lio·ra·tion
ame·lio·ra·tive
ame·lio·ra·tor
amen
ame·nabil·ity (or ·nable·ness)
ame·nable
ame·nably
amend change; compare emend
amend·able
amenda·tory US corrective
amend·er
amend·ment
amends
amen·ity (plural ·ities)
amen·or·rhoea (US ·rhea)
Amen-Ra Egyptian god
ament mentally deficient person
am·ent (or am·en·tum; plural ·ents or ·ta) catkin
amen·tia mental deficiency
Ameri·ca
Ameri·can
Ameri·ca·na
Ameri·can·ism
Ameri·cani·za·tion (or ·sa·tion)
Ameri·can·ize (or ·ise)
Ameri·can·iz·er (or ·is·er)
am·eri·cium radioactive element

Amerindian 16

Am·er·in·dian North American Indian
Am·er·in·dic
am·ethyst
am·ethys·tine
am·etro·pia eye disorder
Am·ha·ra Ethiopian province
Am·har·ic Ethiopian language
ami·abil·ity (*or* ·**able·ness**)
ami·able
ami·ably
ami·an·thine (*or* ·**thoid**, ·**thoid·al**)
ami·an·thus variety of asbestos
ami·cabil·ity (*or* ·**cable·ness**)
ami·cable
ami·cably
am·ice part of priest's vestment
ami·cus cu·riae *Latin* friend of the court
amid
am·ide chemical compound
amid·ic
Ami·dol (*Trademark*) photographic developer
amid·ships
amidst
Ami·ens French city
ami·go (*plural* ·**gos**)
amine organic base; *compare* **ammine**
ami·no acid
ami·no·ben·zo·ic acid
ami·no·phenol
ami·no·py·rine
amir Afghan ruler
amiss
ami·to·sis form of cell division
ami·tot·ic
ami·toti·cal·ly
am·ity (*plural* ·**ities**)
Am·man Jordanian capital
am·meter
am·mine ammonia compound; *compare* **amine**
ammo *short for* **ammunition**
am·mo·coete zoology term
am·mo·nal explosive compound
am·mo·nate
am·mo·nia
am·mo·ni·ac gum resin
am·mo·nia·cal
am·mo·ni·ate
am·mo·nia·tion
am·mon·ic
am·moni·cal
am·moni·fi·ca·tion
am·moni·fy (·**fies**, ·**fy·ing**, ·**fied**)
am·mo·nite fossil
am·mo·nit·ic
am·mo·nium
am·mu·ni·tion
am·ne·sia
am·ne·si·ac (*or* **am·ne·sic**)
am·nes·ty (*noun, plural* ·**ties**; *verb* ·**ties**, ·**ty·ing**, ·**tied**)
am·nio·cen·tesis
am·ni·on (*plural* ·**ni·ons** *or* ·**nia**) fetal membrane
am·ni·ot·ic
amoe·ba (*US* **ame·**; *plural* ·**bae** *or* ·**bas**)
am·oebaean (*or* ·**oebean**; *US* **am·ebean**) verse form
am·oebia·sis (*US* **am·ebia·**; *plural* ·**ses**) parasitic infection
amoe·bic (*US* **ame·**)
amoe·bo·cyte (*US* **ame·**)
amoe·boid (*US* **ame·**)
amok (*or* **amuck**)
among (*or* **amongst**)
amon·til·la·do (*plural* ·**dos**) sherry
amor·al morally neutral; *compare* **immoral**
amo·ral·ity
amor·al·ly
amo·ret·to (*or* ·**ri·no**; *plural* ·**ret·ti** *or* ·**ri·ni**) cupid
amo·rist
amo·ro·so musical term
amo·rous
amo·rous·ness
amor pa·triae *Latin* love of one's country
amor·phism
amor·phous
amor·tiz·able (*or* ·**tis·able**)
amor·ti·za·tion (*or* ·**sa·tion**)
amor·tize (*or* ·**tise**)
amor·tize·ment (*or* ·**tise·ment**)
amount
amour love affair
amour-propre self-respect
Amoy Chinese port
amp
am·pe·lop·sis vine
am·per·age
am·pere
ampere-hour
ampere-turn
am·per·sand the character &
am·pheta·mine
am·phi·ar·thro·sis (*plural* ·**ses**) anatomy term
am·phi·as·ter biology term
am·phib·ian
am·phi·bi·ot·ic zoology term
am·phibi·ous
am·phi·blas·tu·la sponge larva
am·phi·bole mineral
am·phi·bol·ic (*or* ·**phibo·lous**)
am·phibo·lite rock
am·phibo·logi·cal
am·phi·bol·ogy (*or* **am·phibo·ly**; *plural* ·**ogies** *or* ·**lies**) ambiguity
am·phi·brach metrical foot
am·phi·brach·ic
am·phi·chro·ic (*or* **am·phi·chro·mat·ic**) producing two colours
am·phi·coe·lous zoology term
am·phic·ty·on ancient Greek religious councillor
am·phic·ty·on·ic
am·phic·tyo·ny (*plural* ·**nies**)
am·phi·dip·loid biology term
am·phi·gor·ic
am·phi·go·ry (*or* ·**gou·ri**; *plural* ·**ries** *or* ·**ris**) nonsense writing
am·phima·cer metrical foot

anagram

am·phi·mix·is (*plural* ·mixes) sexual reproduction
am·phi·ox·us (*plural* ·oxi *or* ·ox·uses) aquatic organism
am·phi·pod aquatic organism
am·phip·ro·sty·lar
am·phip·ro·style architectural term
am·phis·bae·na (*plural* ·nae *or* ·nas) worm lizard
am·phis·bae·nic
am·phi·sty·lar architectural term
am·phi·thea·tre (*US* ·ter)
am·phi·thecium (*plural* ·thecia) botany term
am·phit·ri·cha bacteria
am·phit·ri·chous
Amphitrite Greek goddess
am·phit·ro·pous botany term
Amphitryon mythological character
am·pho·ra (*plural* ·rae *or* ·ras)
am·pho·ter·ic chemistry term
am·ple
am·plexi·caul botany term
am·pli·fi·able
am·pli·fi·ca·tion
am·pli·fi·er
am·pli·fy (·fies, ·fy·ing, ·fied)
am·pli·tude
am·ply
am·poule (*or esp. US* ·pule) container for injectable liquids
am·pul·la (*plural* ·lae) flask
am·pul·la·ceous (*or* ·ceal)
am·pul·lar (*or* ·lary)
am·pu·tate
am·pu·ta·tion
am·pu·tee
Am·ra·va·ti Indian town
am·ri·ta (*or* ·ree·) Hindu concept
Am·rit·sar Indian city
Am·ster·dam

amuck *variant spelling of* amok
amu·let
Amur Asian river
amuse
amuse·ment
amus·ing
amus·ing·ly
amyg·da·la (*plural* ·lae) anatomy term
amyg·da·late of almonds
amyg·dale geology term
amyg·da·lin almond extract
amyg·da·line relating to tonsils or almonds
amyg·da·loid rock
amyg·da·loi·dal
amyl
amy·la·ceous starchy
am·yl·ase enzyme
am·yl·ene chemical compound
amy·loid starchlike protein
amy·loly·sis biology term
amy·lo·pec·tin component of starch
amy·lop·sin enzyme
am·yl·ose component of starch
amy·lum starch
Amy·tal (*Trademark*) drug
an
ana·bae·na plant
ana·ban·tid fish
Ana·bap·tist Protestant sect
ana·bas fish
anaba·sis (*plural* ·ses) military expedition
ana·bat·ic
ana·bio·sis resuscitation
ana·bleps (*plural* ·bleps) fish
ana·bol·ic
anabo·lism
anabo·lite
anabo·lit·ic
ana·branch
ana·car·dia·ceous botany term
anacho·rism geographical misplacement
ana·chron·ic out of date order
anach·ro·nism

anach·ro·nis·tic
anach·ro·nis·ti·cal·ly
ana·cli·nal geology term
ana·cli·sis
ana·clit·ic psychology term
ana·co·lu·thia lack of grammatical sequence
ana·co·lu·thic
ana·co·lu·thon (*plural* ·tha)
ana·con·da
ana·cous·tic soundless
ana·cru·sis (*plural* ·ses) linguistics term
ana·crus·tic
ana·dem garland
ana·di·plo·sis rhetorical term
anad·ro·mous migrating up river; *compare* catadromous
anaemia (*US* anemia)
anaemic (*US* anemic)
an·aer·obe (*or* ·aero·bium; *plural* ·aer·obes *or* ·aero·bia)
an·aero·bic not requiring oxygen
an·aero·bi·cal·ly
an·aes·the·sia (*US* ·es·)
an·aes·thet·ic (*US* ·es·)
an·aes·thet·ics (*US* an·es·the·si·ology)
anaes·the·tist (*US* an·es·the·si·olo·gist) doctor specializing in anaesthetics; *compare* anesthetist
anaes·the·ti·za·tion (*or* ·sa·tion; *US* anes·the·ti·za·tion)
anaes·the·tize (*or* ·tise; *US* anes·the·tize)
ana·glyph stereoscopic picture
ana·glyph·ic (*or* ·glyphi·cal, ·glyp·tic, ·glyp·ti·cal)
Ana·glyp·ta (*Trademark*) wallpaper
ana·go·ge (*or* ·gy) allegorical interpretation
ana·gog·ic (*or* ·gogi·cal)
ana·gogi·cal·ly
ana·gram

anagrammatic

ana·gram·mat·ic (*or* ·mati·cal)
ana·gram·mati·cal·ly
ana·gram·ma·tism
ana·gram·ma·tist
ana·gram·ma·tize (*or* ·tise)
Ana·heim Californian city
anal
(analagous) *incorrect spelling of* analogous
anal·cite (*or* ·cine) mineral
ana·lec·tic
ana·lects (*or* ·lec·ta)
ana·lem·ma (*plural* ·mas *or* ·ma·ta) type of sundial
ana·lem·mat·ic
ana·lep·tic restorative drug
an·al·gesia (*or* ·gia)
an·alge·sic
ana·log *US variant spelling of* analogue
ana·logi·cal (*or* ·log·ic)
analo·gist
analo·gize (*or* ·gise) draw comparisons
analo·gous
ana·logue (*US also* analog; *in the UK the US spelling is often used in computer science and in electronics*)
anal·ogy (*plural* ·ogies)
an·al·pha·bet·ic
an·al·pha·beti·cal·ly
ana·lys·able
analy·sand person undergoing psychoanalysis
ana·ly·sa·tion
ana·lyse (*US* ·lyze)
ana·lys·er (*US* ·lyz·)
analy·sis (*plural* ·ses)
ana·lyst analyser; *compare* annalist
ana·lyt·ic (*or* ·lyti·cal)
ana·lyti·cal·ly
Anam·bra Nigerian state
an·am·ne·sis (*plural* ·ses) recollection
an·am·nes·tic
an·am·nes·ti·cal·ly
ana·mor·phic
ana·mor·phism geology term

ana·mor·pho·scope optical device
ana·mor·pho·sis (*plural* ·ses) distorted image
an·an·drous botany term
Ananias biblical character
an·an·thous flowerless
ana·pest (*or* ·paest) metrical foot
ana·pes·tic (*or* ·paes·)
ana·phase biology term
anapho·ra rhetorical device
anapho·ral (*or* ana·phor·ic)
ana·phori·cal·ly
an·aph·ro·disia
an·aph·ro·dis·iac
ana·phy·lac·tic
ana·phy·lac·ti·cal·ly
ana·phy·lax·is type of allergy
ana·pla·sia biology term
ana·plas·tic
ana·plas·ty plastic surgery
an·ap·tyc·tic
an·ap·tyx·is (*plural* ·tyxes) linguistics term
an·ar·chic (*or* ·chi·cal)
an·ar·chi·cal·ly
an·ar·chism
an·ar·chist
an·ar·chis·tic
an·ar·chy
an·ar·thria loss of speech
an·ar·throus
ana·sar·ca medical term
ana·sar·cous
an·as·tig·mat type of lens
an·as·tig·mat·ic
anas·to·mose
anas·to·mo·sis (*plural* ·ses)
anas·to·mot·ic
anas·tro·phe rhetorical device
ana·tase mineral
anath·ema (*plural* ·emas)
anath·ema·ti·za·tion (*or* ·sa·tion)
anath·ema·tize (*or* ·tise)
Ana·to·lia part of Turkey
Ana·to·lian
ana·tomi·cal
ana·tomi·cal·ly
anato·mist

18

anato·mi·za·tion (*or* ·sa·tion)
anato·mize (*or* ·mise)
anato·miz·er (*or* ·mis·er)
anato·my (*plural* ·mies)
anat·ro·pous botany term
an·bury (*plural* ·buries) animal tumour
an·ces·tor
an·ces·tral
an·ces·tral·ly
an·ces·tress
an·ces·try (*plural* ·tries)
Anchises mythological prince
an·chor
An·chor·age Alaskan city
an·chor·age
an·cho·rite (*fem* ·ress) recluse; *compare* ankerite
an·cho·veta fish
an·cho·vy (*plural* ·vies *or* ·vy)
an·chu·sa plant
an·cien ré·gime (*plural* an·ciens ré·gimes) *French* pre-Revolutionary France
an·cient
an·cient·ness
an·cil·lary (*plural* ·laries)
an·cipi·tal (*or* ·tous) biology term
an·con (*or* ·cone; *plural* ·cones) architectural term
An·co·na Italian port
an·co·nal (*or* ·neal)
an·cy·los·to·mia·sis (*or* an·ky·, an·chy·) hookworm disease
and
An·da·lu·sia Spanish region
an·da·lu·site mineral
an·dan·te musical term
an·dan·ti·no (*plural* ·nos) musical term
An·dean
An·der·lecht Belgian town
An·der·son Canadian river
An·des
an·desine mineral
an·desite rock
An·dhra Pra·desh Indian state
and·iron
An·di·zhan Soviet city

anguine

An·dor·ra
An·dor·ra La Vel·la capital of Andorra
An·dor·ran
And·over
an·dra·dite gemstone
Androcles legendary character
an·dro·clin·ium botany term
an·droe·cial
an·droe·cium (*plural* ·cia) stamens of flower
an·dro·gen hormone
an·dro·gen·ic
an·drog·enous producing only male offspring; *compare* androgynous
an·dro·gyne
an·drogy·nous having male and female characteristics; *compare* androgenous
an·droid
Andromache mythological character
An·drom·eda constellation
An·dros Greek island
an·dro·sphinx (*plural* ·sphinxes *or* ·sphinges)
an·dros·ter·one hormone
Andvari mythological character
ane *Scot* one
an·ec·dot·age
an·ec·do·tal
an·ec·dote
an·ec·dot·ic
an·ec·dot·ist
an·echo·ic
anemia *US spelling of* anaemia
anemic *US spelling of* anaemic
anemo·chore botany term
anemo·graph
anemo·graph·ic
anemo·graphi·cal·ly
an·emog·ra·phy recording wind measurements
an·emol·ogy
an·emom·eter
an·emo·met·ric
an·emo·met·ri·cal
an·emom·etry
anemo·ne

an·emophi·lous wind-pollinated
an·emophi·ly
anemo·scope
anent *Scot* concerning
aner·gic lacking energy
an·er·gy
an·er·oid
an·es·the·sia *US spelling of* anaesthesia
an·es·thesi·olo·gist *US* anaesthetist
an·es·thesi·ology *US* anaesthetics
an·es·the·tist *US* person qualified to administer anaesthetics, not necessarily a doctor; *compare* anaesthetist
an·es·trus *US spelling of* anoestrus
an·ethole organic compound
an·eu·ploid biology term
aneu·rin vitamin
aneu·rysm (*or* ·rism) blood-vessel defect
aneu·rys·mal (*or* ·ris·mal, ·rys·mat·ic, ·ris·mat·ic)
anew
an·frac·tu·os·ity (*plural* ·ities)
an·frac·tu·ous convoluted
An·garsk Soviet city
an·ga·ry legal term
an·gel
An·ge·leno (*plural* ·nos) inhabitant of Los Angeles
angel·fish (*plural* ·fish *or* ·fishes)
an·gel·ic
an·gel·ica
an·geli·cal
an·gel·ol·ogy
An·ge·lus Roman Catholic prayers
an·ger
An·gers French town
An·ge·vin inhabitant of Anjou
an·gi·na
an·gi·nal
an·gi·na pec·to·ris
an·gi·nose (*or* ·nous)
an·gi·ol·ogy branch of medicine

an·gio·ma (*plural* ·mas *or* ·ma·ta) tumour
an·gi·oma·tous
an·gio·sperm botany term
an·gio·sper·mous
Ang·kor Cambodian region
An·gle ancient German invader
an·gle
an·gler
An·gle·sey
an·gle·site mineral
angle·worm
An·glian of Angles or East Anglia
An·gli·can of Church of England
An·gli·can·ism
An·gli·cism English idiom
An·gli·cist
an·gli·ci·za·tion (*or* ·sa·tion)
an·gli·cize (*or* ·cise)
an·gli·fy (·fies, ·fy·ing, ·fied)
an·gling
Anglo-American
Anglo-Catholic
Anglo-Catholicism
Anglo-Irish
An·glo·ma·nia
An·glo·phile (*or* ·phil)
An·glo·philia
An·glo·phili·ac (*or* ·phil·ic)
An·glo·phobe
An·glo·pho·bia
An·glo·phone native English speaker
Anglo-Saxon
An·go·la
An·go·lan
an·go·ra
An·gos·tu·ra bitter-tasting bark
An·gos·tu·ra Bit·ters (*Trademark*)
an·gri·ly
an·gry (·gri·er, ·gri·est)
angst anxiety
ang·strom unit of length
An·guil·la West Indian island
an·guil·li·form eel-shaped
an·guine snakelike

anguish

an·guish
an·gu·lar
an·gu·lar·ity (*plural* ·ities)
an·gu·late
an·gu·la·tion
An·gus former Scottish county
ang·wan·ti·bo (*plural* ·bos) animal
An·halt German region
an·he·dral
an·hin·ga bird
An·hwei Chinese province
an·hy·dride
an·hy·drite
an·hy·drous
ani (*plural* anis) bird
Ani·ak·chak Alaskan volcano
an·icon·ic
anil shrub
an·ile like an old woman
ani·line organic compound
anil·ity
ani·ma
ani·mad·ver·sion
ani·mad·vert
ani·mal
ani·mal·cu·lar
ani·mal·cule (*or* ·cu·lum; *plural* ·cules *or* ·cu·la) microscopic animal
ani·mal·ism
ani·mal·ist
ani·mal·ity
ani·mali·za·tion (*or* ·sa·tion)
ani·mal·ize (*or* ·ise)
ani·mate
ani·ma·tion
ani·ma·tism
ani·ma·to music term
ani·ma·tor (*or* ·mat·er)
ani·mé resin
ani·mism
ani·mist
ani·mis·tic
ani·mos·ity (*plural* ·ities)
ani·mus
an·ion chemistry term
ani·on·ic
an·ise plant
ani·seed
an·isei·ko·nia visual defect
an·isei·kon·ic

ani·sette liqueur
ani·so·dac·tyl zoology term
ani·so·dac·ty·lous
ani·soga·mous
ani·soga·my type of sexual reproduction
ani·sole chemical compound
an·isom·er·ous botany term
an·iso·met·ric
an·iso·metro·pia visual disorder
an·iso·trop·ic
an·isot·ro·py
An·jou French province
An·ka·ra Turkish city
an·ker·ite mineral; *compare* anchorite
ankh Egyptian cross
An·king Chinese city
an·kle
ankle·bone
an·klet
an·ky·lo·saur dinosaur
an·ky·lose (*or* ·chy·)
an·ky·lo·sis (*or* ·chy·) immobility of joint
an·ky·lot·ic (*or* ·chy·)
an·lace medieval dagger
an·la·ge (*plural* ·gen *or* ·ges) biology term
An·na·ba Algerian port
an·na·berg·ite mineral
an·nal
an·nal·ist compiler of annals; *compare* analyst
an·nal·is·tic
an·nals
An·nam (*or* Anam) part of Vietnam
An·napo·lis US city
An·na·pur·na (*or* Ana·) Nepalese mountains
an·nates pope's revenue
an·nat·to (*or* anat·; *plural* ·tos) tree
an·neal
an·neal·er
Anne·cy French lake
an·nelid worm
an·neli·dan
an·nex take over or add on; *compare* annexe
an·nexa·tion
an·nexa·tion·al
an·nexa·tion·ism

20

an·nexa·tion·ist
an·nexe addition to building; *compare* annex
an·ni·hil·able
an·ni·hi·late
an·ni·hi·la·tion
an·ni·hi·la·tive
an·ni·hi·la·tor
an·ni·ver·sa·ry (*plural* ·saries)
anno Domi·ni Latin year of our Lord
an·no·tate
an·no·ta·tion
an·no·ta·tive
an·no·ta·tor
an·nounce
an·nounce·ment
an·nounc·er
an·noy
an·noy·ance
an·nual
an·nual·ly
an·nui·tant
an·nu·ity (*plural* ·ities)
an·nul (·nul·ling, ·nulled)
an·nu·lar
an·nu·late ringed
an·nu·la·tion
an·nu·let architectural moulding
an·nul·lable
an·nul·ment
an·nu·lose segmented
an·nu·lus (*plural* ·li *or* ·luses)
an·nun·ci·ate announce; *compare* enunciate
An·nun·cia·tion Christian feast
an·nun·cia·tion announcement
an·nun·cia·tive (*or* ·tory)
an·nun·cia·tor
anoa cattle
an·ode
an·od·ic
ano·dize (*or* ·dise)
ano·dyne painkiller
an·oes·trus (*US* ·es·)
anoint
anoint·er
anoint·ment
anole lizard
anoma·lis·tic

anoma·lis·ti·cal·ly
anoma·lous
anoma·ly (*plural* ·lies)
anom·ic
an·omie (*or* ·omy) lack of social standards
anon *Archaic* soon
ano·nym pseudonym
ano·nym·ity
anony·mous
anophe·les (*plural* ·les) mosquito
ano·rak
ano·rexia ner·vo·sa
ano·rex·ic
an·or·thite mineral
an·or·thit·ic
an·or·tho·site rock
an·os·mat·ic (*or* an·os·mic)
an·os·mia inability to smell
an·oth·er
an·ox·aemia (*US* ·emia) oxygen deficiency in blood
an·ox·aemic (*US* ·emic)
an·oxia lack of oxygen
an·ox·ic
an·sate having a handle
An·schluss union of Austria with Germany
an·ser·ine (*or* ·ous) of geese
An·shan Chinese city
an·swer
an·swer·abil·ity (*or* ·able·ness)
an·swer·able
ant
anta architectural term
An·ta·buse (*Trademark*)
ant·acid
an·tago·nism
an·tago·nist
an·tago·nis·tic
an·tago·nis·ti·cal·ly
an·tago·niz·able (*or* ·nis·able)
an·tago·ni·za·tion (*or* ·sa·tion)
an·tago·nize (*or* ·nise)
ant·al·ka·li (*plural* ·lis *or* ·lies)
ant·al·ka·line
An·ta·na·na·ri·vo Madagascan capital

Ant·arc·tic
Ant·arc·ti·ca
An·tar·es star
ante stake in poker; advance payment; *compare* anti
ant·eater
ante·bel·lum
ante·cede
ante·ced·ence
ante·ced·ent
an·te·ced·ents
ante·choir part of church
ante·date
ante·di·lu·vian
ante·fix (*plural* ·fixes *or* ·fixa) roof ornament
ante·fix·al
ante·lope
ante·me·rid·ian (*adj*)
ante me·ridi·em *Latin* before noon
ante-mortem (*adj*) before death
ante·na·tal
an·ten·na (*plural* ·nae) insect feelers
an·ten·na (*plural* ·nas) aerial
an·ten·nule
ante·pen·dium (*plural* ·dia) altar covering
ante·penult
ante·penul·ti·mate
ante·ri·or
ante·room
ante·type earlier form
ante·ver·sion
ante·vert tilt forwards
ant·he·li·on (*plural* ·lia) meteorology term
ant·he·lix (*or* anti·; *plural* ·heli·ces *or* ·he·lixes) ear cartilage
an·thel·min·tic (*or* ·thic) vermifuge
an·them
an·themi·on (*plural* ·mia) Greek design
an·ther
an·ther·idial
an·ther·id·ium (*plural* ·ia) botany term
an·thero·zo·id botany term
an·thesis flowering
an·tho·cya·nin (*or* ·cy·an) pigment

an·tho·dium (*plural* ·dia) botany term
an·tho·logi·cal
an·tholo·gist
an·tholo·gize (*or* ·gise)
an·thol·ogy (*plural* ·ogies)
an·tho·phore botany term
an·tho·taxy botany term
an·tho·zo·an marine organism
an·thra·cene chemical compound
an·thra·cite coal
an·thra·cit·ic
an·thrac·nose fungal disease
an·thra·coid
an·thra·qui·none chemical compound
an·thrax (*plural* ·thra·ces)
an·thro·po·cen·tric
an·thro·po·cen·trism
an·thro·po·gen·esis (*or* ·geny) study of man's origin
an·thro·po·genet·ic (*or* ·gen·ic)
an·thro·poid
an·thro·poi·dal
an·thro·po·logi·cal
an·thro·polo·gist
an·thro·pol·ogy
an·thro·po·met·ric (*or* ·ri·cal)
an·thro·po·met·ri·cal·ly
an·thro·pome·trist
an·thro·pom·etry
an·thro·po·mor·phic
an·thro·po·mor·phism
an·thro·po·mor·phist
an·thro·po·mor·phize (*or* ·phise)
an·thro·po·mor·pho·sis
an·thro·po·mor·phous
an·thro·po·path·ic
an·thro·popa·thy (*or* ·thism) attribution of human passions to a deity
an·thro·popha·gi (*sing.* ·gus) cannibals
an·thro·po·phag·ic
an·thro·popha·gite
an·thro·popha·gy cannibalism
an·thro·po·soph·ic
an·thro·poso·phy

anthurium

an·thu·ri·um plant
anti *Slang* opposed to; *compare* ante
anti-aircraft
an·ti·ar tree
anti·bary·on physics term
An·tibes French port
anti·bi·o·sis
anti·bi·ot·ic
anti·body (*plural* ·bodies)
an·tic
anti·cata·lyst
anti·cath·ode
anti·chlor
anti·chlo·ris·tic
anti·cho·lin·er·gic physiology term
anti·cho·lin·es·ter·ase enzyme
Anti·christ
an·tici·pant
an·tici·pate
an·tici·pa·tion
an·tici·pa·tive
an·tici·pa·tor
an·tici·pa·to·ri·ly
an·tici·pa·tory
anti·clas·tic maths term
anti·cleri·cal
anti·cli·mac·tic
anti·cli·mac·ti·cal·ly
anti·cli·max
anti·cli·nal
anti·cline geology term
anti·cli·no·rium (*plural* ·ria) geology term
anti·clock·wise
anti·co·agu·lant
anti·con·vul·sant
An·ti·cos·ti Canadian island
anti·cy·clone
anti·cy·clon·ic
anti·de·pres·sant
anti·dote
anti·drom·ic biology term
An·tie·tam US battle site
anti·febrile
anti·fer·ro·mag·ne·tism
anti·foul·ing protective paint
anti·freeze
anti·gen
anti·gen·ic
anti·geni·cal·ly

Antigone mythological character
An·ti·gua West Indian island
anti·ha·la·tion photography term
anti·he·ro (*plural* ·roes)
anti·his·ta·mine
anti·icer
anti·imperi·al·ism
anti·imperi·al·ist
anti·knock petrol additive
anti·lep·ton physics term
An·til·les West Indian islands
anti·log
anti·loga·rithm
anti·loga·rith·mic
an·tilo·gism philosophy term
an·til·ogy (*plural* ·ogies) contradiction in terms
anti·ma·cas·sar
anti·mag·net·ic
anti·ma·lar·ial
anti·masque grotesque dance
anti·mat·ter
anti·mere biology term
anti·mer·ic
an·tim·er·ism
anti·mis·sile
anti·mo·nar·chic
anti·mo·nar·chist
anti·mo·nial
anti·mo·nic
anti·mo·nous
anti·mo·ny chemical element; *compare* antinomy
anti·mo·nyl
anti·na·tion·al·ist
anti·na·tion·al·is·tic
anti·neu·tri·no (*plural* ·nos)
anti·neu·tron
anti·nod·al
anti·node physics term
anti·nom·ic
anti·nomi·cal·ly
an·tino·my (*plural* ·mies) paradox; *compare* antimony
anti·nu·cleon
An·ti·och Turkish city

anti·oxi·dant
anti·par·al·lel
anti·par·ticle
anti·pas·to (*plural* ·ti) Italian hors d'oeuvres
anti·pa·thet·ic (*or* ·ical)
anti·pa·theti·cal·ly
an·tipa·thy (*plural* ·thies)
anti·peri·od·ic
anti·peri·stal·sis physiology term
anti·per·son·nel
anti·per·spi·rant
anti·phlo·gis·tic
anti·phon
an·tipho·nal
an·tipho·nal·ly
an·tipho·nary (*plural* ·naries) collection of biblical passages
an·tipho·ny (*plural* ·nies) type of choral singing
an·tiph·ra·sis rhetorical device
an·tipo·dal
anti·pode
an·tipo·dean
An·tipo·des Australia and New Zealand
an·tipo·des points diametrically opposite on Earth
anti·pope
anti·prag·mat·ic
anti·prag·ma·tism
anti·pro·ton
anti·psy·chia·try
anti·py·resis
anti·py·ret·ic
anti·py·rine
anti·quar·ian
anti·quary (*plural* ·quaries)
anti·quate
anti·quat·ed
anti·qua·ted·ness
an·tique
an·tiq·uity (*plural* ·uities)
anti·ra·chit·ic preventing rickets
anti·racism
anti·racist
anti·repub·li·can
anti·revo·lu·tion·ary
an·tir·rhi·num

anti·scor·bu·tic preventing scurvy
anti-Semite
anti-Semitic
anti-Semitism
anti·sep·sis
anti·sep·tic
anti·sep·ti·cal·ly
anti·serum (*plural* ·serums *or* ·sera)
anti·slav·ery
anti·so·cial
anti·spas·mod·ic
anti·stat·ic
an·tis·tro·phe
anti·stroph·ic
anti·sub·ma·rine
anti·tank
an·tith·esis (*plural* ·ses)
anti·theti·cal (*or* ·thet·ic)
anti·theti·cal·ly
anti·tox·ic
anti·tox·in
anti·trades winds
an·tit·ra·gus (*plural* ·gi) part of ear
anti·tus·sive alleviating coughing
anti·type
anti·ven·in
anti·vivi·sec·tion
anti·vivi·sec·tion·ist
anti·world world composed of antimatter
ant·ler
ant·lered
Ant·lia constellation
ant·like
ant·li·on insect
An·to·fa·gas·ta Chilean port
an·to·no·ma·sia figure of speech
an·to·no·mas·tic
an·to·no·mas·ti·cal·ly
an·to·nym
an·tony·mous
an·tre cavern
An·trim
an·trorse directed upwards
an·trum (*plural* ·tra) anatomy term
An·tung Chinese port
Ant·werp
Anubis Egyptian god

anu·ran tailless amphibian
anu·resis inability to urinate
anu·ria inability to form urine
anu·rous tailless
anus
an·vil
anxi·ety (*plural* ·eties)
anx·ious
anx·ious·ness
any
An·yang Chinese town
any·body
any·how
any·one
any·thing
any·way
any·where
any·wise
An·zac Australian and New Zealand Army Corps
An·zio Italian port
aorist linguistics term
aoris·tic
aoris·ti·cal·ly
aor·ta (*plural* ·tas *or* ·tae)
aor·tic (*or* ·tal)
aou·dad sheep
apace
Apache (*plural* Apaches *or* Apache) American Indian
apache gangster
apa·go·ge logic term
apa·gog·ic (*or* ·gogi·cal)
apa·gogi·cal·ly
ap·an·age *variant spelling of* appanage
Apar·ri Philippine port
apart
apart·heid
apart·ment
apa·tet·ic of animal coloration
apa·thet·ic
apa·theti·cal·ly
apa·thy
apa·tite mineral
ape
apeak
Apel·doorn Dutch town
ape·like
ape·man (*plural* ·men)
Ap·en·nines

aper·çu *French* outline or insight
aperi·ent
aperi·od·ic at irregular intervals
aperi·odi·cal·ly
aperio·dic·ity
apé·ri·tif drink before meal; *compare* aperitive
ape·ri·tive laxative; *compare* apéritif
ap·er·ture
ap·ery (*plural* ·eries) imitative behaviour
apet·al·ous petal-less
apet·aly
apex (*plural* apexes *or* api·ces)
aphaer·esis (*or* apher·; *plural* ·ses) linguistics term
apha·gia inability to swallow
apha·nite rock
apha·sia language disorder
apha·sic
ap·he·lian
ap·he·li·on (*plural* ·lia) point in planet's orbit
ap·he·lio·trop·ic botany term
apher·esis *variant spelling of* aphaeresis
aph·esis linguistics term
aphet·ic
apheti·cal·ly
aphid
aphidi·ous
aphis (*plural* aphi·des)
apho·nia (*or* ·ny) loss of voice
aphon·ic
apho·rism
apho·rist
apho·ris·tic
apho·rize (*or* ·rise)
apho·tic without light
aph·ro·di·sia
aph·ro·disi·ac
Aphrodite Greek goddess
aph·tha (*plural* ·thae) ulcer
aphyl·lous leafless
aphyl·ly
apian of bees
api·ar·ian of beekeeping

apiarist

apia·rist
api·ary (*plural* ·aries)
    beehive; *compare* aviary
api·cal
api·cal·ly
api·ces *plural of* apex
apicu·late
api·cul·tur·al
api·cul·ture
api·cul·tur·ist
apiece
à pied *French* on foot
Api·ezon (*Trademark*)
Apis sacred bull
ap·ish
ap·ish·ness
apiv·or·ous bee-eating
apla·cen·tal
ap·la·nat·ic physics term
ap·la·nati·cal·ly
aplano·sphere
aplano·spore
apla·sia congenital absence of organ
aplas·tic
aplen·ty
ap·lite (*or* hap·) rock
ap·lit·ic (*or* hap·)
aplomb
ap·noea (*US* ·nea) inability to breath
Apo Philippine mountain
apoca·lypse
apoca·lyp·tic
apoca·lyp·ti·cal·ly
apo·carp
apo·car·pous botany term
apo·chro·mat
apo·chro·mat·ic physics term
apo·chro·ma·tism
apoco·pate
apoco·pa·tion
apoco·pe linguistics term
apo·crine physiology term
Apoc·ry·pha Old Testament appendix
apoc·ry·phal of doubtful authenticity
apoc·ry·phal·ly
apocy·na·ceous botany term
apo·cyn·thi·on astronomy term
apo·dal without feet

apo·dic·tic (*or* ·deic·) unquestionably true
apo·dic·ti·cal·ly (*or* ·deic·)
apodo·sis (*plural* ·ses) grammar term
apo·en·zyme
apo·gam·ic
apoga·mous
apoga·my type of plant reproduction
apo·gee
apo·geo·trop·ic botany term
apo·geot·ro·pism
apo·liti·cal
apo·liti·cal·ly
Apol·li·naris mineral water
Apollo Greek god
Apol·lo spacecraft
Ap·ol·lo·nian
Apollyon the Devil
apolo·get·ic
apolo·geti·cal·ly
apolo·get·ics branch of theology
apo·lo·gia
apolo·gist
apolo·gize (*or* ·gise)
apolo·giz·er (*or* ·gis·er)
apo·logue moral fable
apol·ogy (*plural* ·ogies)
apo·lune astronomy term
apo·mict
apo·mic·tic
apo·mixis (*plural* ·mixes) asexual reproduction
apo·mor·phine alkaloid
apo·neu·ro·sis (*plural* ·ses) anatomy term
apo·neu·rot·ic
apopha·sis rhetorical device
apo·phthegm (*or* apo·thegm) cryptic remark; *compare* apothem
apophy·ge architectural term
apophyl·lite mineral
apophy·sate
apophy·sial
apophy·sis (*plural* ·ses) outgrowth
apo·plec·tic
apo·plexy
aport nautical term
apo·semat·ic zoology term

apo·sio·pe·sis (*plural* ·ses) rhetorical device
apo·sio·pet·ic
apo·spory botany term
apos·ta·sy (*plural* ·sies)
apos·tate
apos·ta·tize (*or* ·tise)
a pos·terio·ri *Latin* from effect to cause; *compare* a priori
apos·til marginal note
apos·tle
apos·to·late
ap·os·tol·ic
apos·tro·phe
apos·troph·ic
apos·tro·phize (*or* ·phise)
apoth·ecary (*plural* ·ecaries)
apo·the·cial
apo·the·cium (*plural* ·cia)
apo·thegm variant spelling *of* apophthegm
apo·them geometry term; *compare* apophthegm
apoth·eo·sis (*plural* ·ses)
apoth·eo·size (*or* ·sise) glorify
apo·tro·pa·ic preventing evil
ap·pal (*US* ·pall; ·pal·ling, ·palled)
Ap·pa·la·chia US region
Appa·la·chian
ap·pal·ling
ap·pal·ling·ly
Ap·pa·loo·sa horse
ap·pa·nage (*or* apa·nage) perquisite
ap·pa·rat·us (*plural* ·rat·us *or* ·rat·uses)
ap·par·el (·el·ling, ·elled; *US* ·el·ing, ·eled)
ap·par·ent
ap·par·ent·ness
ap·pa·ri·tion
ap·pari·tor ecclesiastical court officer
ap·pas·sio·na·to musical term
ap·peal
ap·peal·able
ap·peal·er
ap·peal·ing·ly
ap·pear
ap·pear·ance

ap·peas·able
ap·pease
ap·peas·er
ap·pease·ment
ap·pel fencing term
ap·pel·lant
ap·pel·late
ap·pel·la·tion
ap·pel·la·tive
ap·pel·lee
ap·pend
ap·pend·age
ap·pen·dant
ap·pen·di·cec·to·my (or esp. US ap·pen·dec·to·my; plural ·mies)
ap·pen·di·ci·tis
ap·pen·di·cle small appendage
ap·pen·dicu·lar
ap·pen·dix (plural ·dixes or ·di·ces)
Ap·pen·zell Swiss canton
ap·per·cc·ive
ap·per·cep·tion psychology term
ap·per·cep·tive
ap·per·tain
ap·pes·tat hunger control centre in brain
ap·pe·tence (or ·ten·cy; plural ·tences or ·ten·cies)
ap·pe·tite
ap·pe·tiz·er (or ·tis·er)
ap·pe·tiz·ing (or ·tis·ing)
ap·plaud
ap·plaud·er
ap·plaud·ing·ly
ap·plause
ap·ple
apple·cart
apple·jack
apple·snits Canadian apple dish
ap·pli·ance
ap·plic·abil·ity
ap·pli·cable
ap·pli·cably
ap·pli·cant
ap·pli·ca·tion
ap·plica·tive
ap·pli·ca·tor
ap·pli·ca·tory

ap·plied
ap·pli·er
ap·pli·qué (·qué·ing, ·quéd)
ap·ply (·plies, ·ply·ing, ·plied)
ap·pog·gia·tu·ra (plural ·ras or ·re) musical term
ap·point
ap·poin·tee
ap·point·er
ap·point·ment
ap·poin·tor legal term
Ap·po·mat·tox US battle site
ap·por·tion
ap·por·tion·able
ap·por·tion·er
ap·por·tion·ment
ap·pose
ap·po·site apt; compare opposite
ap·po·si·tion
ap·posi·tive linguistics term
ap·prais·able
ap·prais·al (or ·praise·ment)
ap·praise assess; compare apprise
ap·prais·er
ap·prais·ing·ly
ap·prais·ive
ap·pre·ci·able
ap·pre·ci·ate
ap·pre·cia·tion
ap·pre·cia·tive (or ·tory)
ap·pre·cia·tive·ness
ap·pre·hend
ap·pre·hen·sibil·ity
ap·pre·hen·sible
ap·pre·hen·sion
ap·pre·hen·sive
ap·pre·hen·sive·ness
ap·pren·tice
ap·pren·tice·ship
ap·pressed pressed closely against
ap·prise (or ·prize) inform; compare appraise
ap·proach
ap·proach·abil·ity (or ·able·ness)
ap·proach·able
ap·pro·bate Scottish legal term; US approve

ap·pro·ba·tion
ap·pro·ba·tive (or ·tory)
ap·pro·pri·able
ap·pro·pri·ate
ap·pro·pri·ate·ness
ap·pro·pria·tion
ap·pro·pria·tor
ap·prov·al
ap·prove
ap·proved
ap·proxi·mal situated side by side
ap·proxi·mate
ap·proxi·mate·ly
ap·proxi·ma·tion
ap·proxi·ma·tive
ap·pulse astronomy term
ap·pul·sive
ap·pur·te·nance
ap·pur·te·nant
apraxia disorder of nervous system
aprax·ic (or aprac·tic)
après-ski
apri·cot
April
a prio·ri Latin from cause to effect; compare a posteriori
apri·or·ism
apri·or·ity
apron
ap·ro·pos
apse recess in church
ap·si·dal
ap·sis (plural ·si·des) point in planet's orbit
apt
ap·ter·al architectural term
ap·ter·ous wingless
ap·ter·yg·ial lacking fins or wings
ap·ter·yx kiwi
ap·ti·tude
apt·ness
Apu·lia Italian region
Apu·ri·mac Peruvian river
apy·re·tic
Aqa·ba (or Aka·ba) Jordanian port
aqua (plural aquae or aquas)
aqua·cul·ture cultivation of marine organisms; compare aquiculture
aqua·lung

aquamarine

aqua·marine
aqua·naut
aqua·pho·bia
aqua·plane
aqua re·gia strong acid
aqua·relle
aqua·rel·list water-colour painter
aqua·rist aquarium curator
aquar·ium (*plural* aquar·iums *or* aquaria)
Aquar·ius
aquat·ic
aquat·ics
aqua·tint
aqua·vit aromatic spirit
aqua vi·tae *Archaic* brandy
aque·duct
aque·ous
aqui·cul·tur·al
aqui·cul·ture hydroponics; *compare* aquaculture
aqui·cul·tur·ist
aqui·fer water-containing rock
Aqui·la constellation
aqui·legia
aqui·line
Aqui·taine French region
Ara constellation
Arab
ara·besque
Ara·bia
Ara·bian
Ara·bic language
arabi·nose sugar
Ar·ab·ist
ar·able
Ara·by *Archaic* Arabia
Ara·ca·jú Brazilian port
Arachne mythological character
arach·nid spider
arach·ni·dan
arach·noid membrane covering brain
Arad Romanian city
Ara·gon Spanish region
Ara·go·nese
arago·nite mineral
Ara·guaia Brazilian river
Arak Iranian town
arak *variant spelling of* arrack
Aral·dite (*Trademark*)

ara·lia·ceous botany term
Ara·ma·ic language
Aran Irish islands; type of sweater; *compare* Arran
ara·neid spider
Arapa·ho (*plural* ·hos *or* ·ho) American Indian
ara·pai·ma fish
Ara·rat Turkish mountain
ara·ro·ba tree; medicinal substance
Aras Asian river
Arau·ca·nia Chilean region
Arau·ca·nian
arau·ca·ria tree
Ara·wak·an American Indian language
ar·ba·lest crossbow
ar·bi·ter
ar·bi·trable
ar·bi·trage financial term
ar·bi·tral
ar·bit·ra·ment
ar·bi·trari·ly
ar·bi·trari·ness
ar·bi·trary
ar·bi·trate
ar·bi·tra·tion
ar·bi·tra·tor
ar·bi·tress
ar·bor rotating shaft; *US spelling of* arbour
ar·bora·ceous
ar·bor·eal
ar·bo·reous
ar·bo·res·cence
ar·bo·res·cent
ar·bo·retum (*plural* ·ta *or* ·tums)
ar·bori·cul·ture
ar·bor·ist
ar·bori·za·tion (*or* ·sa·tion)
ar·bor vi·tae tree
ar·bour (*US* ·bor) tree-lined shelter; *compare* arbor
Ar·broath Scottish port
ar·bu·tus (*plural* ·tuses) shrub
arc part of curve; *compare* ark
ar·cade
Ar·ca·dia department of Greece; *compare* Acadia

Ar·ca·dian
Ar·ca·dy (*or* ·dia) rustic paradise
ar·ca·na tarot cards
ar·cane
ar·ca·num (*plural* ·na)
ar·ca·ture small arcade
arch
Ar·chaean (*or esp. US* ·chean) geology term
ar·chaeo·logi·cal (*US also* ·cheo·)
ar·chaeo·logi·cal·ly (*US also* ·cheo·)
ar·chae·olo·gist (*US also* ·che·)
ar·chae·ol·ogy (*US also* ·che·)
ar·chaeo·mag·net·ism (*US also* ·cheo·)
ar·chae·op·ter·yx
ar·chae·or·nis extinct bird
Ar·chaeo·zo·ic (*US also* ·cheo·)
ar·cha·ic
ar·chai·cal·ly
ar·cha·ism
ar·cha·ist
ar·cha·is·tic
ar·cha·is·ti·cal·ly
ar·cha·ize (*or* ·ise)
ar·cha·iz·er (*or* ·is·er)
Arch·an·gel Soviet port
arch·angel
arch·angelic
arch·bishop
arch·bishop·ric
arch·deacon
arch·deacon·ry (*plural* ·ries)
arch·dioc·esan
arch·dio·cese
arch·ducal
arch·duchess
arch·duchy (*plural* ·duchies)
arch·duke
arched
ar·che·go·nium (*plural* ·nia) botany term
arch·en·emy (*plural* ·emies)
ar·chen·ter·ic
ar·chen·ter·on embryology term

ar·che·ol·ogy US variant spelling of archaeology
arch·er
archer·fish (plural ·fish or ·fishes)
ar·chery
ar·che·spore (or ·spo·rium; plural ·spores or ·spo·ria) spore-making cell
ar·che·spo·rial
ar·che·typ·al (or ·typi·cal)
ar·che·typ·al·ly (or ·typi·cal·ly)
ar·che·type
arch·fiend
archi·carp fungal structure
archi·di·aco·nal
archi·di·aco·nate
archi·epis·co·pal
archi·epis·co·pate (or ·co·pa·cy)
ar·chil variant spelling of orchil
archi·mage great magician
archi·man·drite head of Orthodox monastery
Archi·medean
archi·pelag·ic (or ·pe·lagian)
archi·pela·go (plural ·gos or ·goes)
archi·tect
archi·tec·ton·ic
archi·tec·toni·cal·ly
archi·tec·ton·ics
archi·tec·tur·al
archi·tec·tur·al·ly
archi·tec·ture
archi·trave moulding
ar·chiv·al
ar·chive
archi·vist
archi·volt moulding around arch
arch·ness
ar·cho·plasm (or archi·) type of protoplasm
ar·cho·plas·mic
arch·priest
arch·way
arco·graph geometric instrument
Arc·tic North Pole region
arc·tic very cold

Arc·to·gaea (US ·gea) zoogeographical area
Arc·to·gaean (US ·gean)
Arc·tu·rian
Arc·tu·rus star
ar·cu·ate arc-shaped
ar·cua·tion
ar·deb unit of measure
Ar·dèche French department
Arden (Forest of)
ar·den·cy
Ar·dennes W European hills
ar·dent
ar·dour (US ·dor)
ar·du·ous
ar·du·ous·ness
are
area
areal
area·way passageway
ar·eca palm tree
arena
ar·ena·ceous geology term
ar·enico·lous living in sandy places
ar·enite sandstone
ar·enit·ic
aren't are not
ar·eog·ra·phy description of Mars
areo·la (plural ·lae or ·las)
areo·lar (or ·late)
areo·la·tion
Arequi·pa Peruvian city
Ares Greek god
arête mountain ridge
ar·ethu·sa plant
Arez·zo Italian city
ar·ga·li (or ar·gal; plural ·ga·li or ·gals) wild sheep
ar·gent silver
Ar·gen·teuil Parisian suburb
ar·gen·tic
ar·gen·tif·er·ous
Ar·gen·ti·na
Ar·gen·tine of Argentina
ar·gen·tine of silver
Ar·gen·tin·ean
ar·gen·tite mineral
ar·gen·tous

ar·gil potter's clay
ar·gil·la·ceous
ar·gil·lif·er·ous
ar·gil·lite rock
ar·gil·lit·ic
ar·gi·nine amino acid
Argo Jason's ship; constellation
ar·gol deposit in wine vats
Ar·go·lis region of ancient Greece
ar·gon chemical element
Ar·go·naut
Ar·gonne French region
ar·go·non gas
Ar·gos ancient Greek city
ar·go·sy (plural ·sies) large merchant ship
ar·got
ar·got·ic
ar·gu·able
ar·gu·ably
ar·gue (·gu·ing, ·gued)
ar·gu·er
ar·gu·fy (·fies, ·fy·ing, ·fied)
ar·gu·ment
ar·gu·men·ta·tion
ar·gu·men·ta·tive
ar·gu·men·ta·tive·ness
ar·gu·men·tum (plural ·ta) Latin argument
Argus mythological giant
argy-bargy (plural -bargies)
ar·gyle fabric
Ar·gyll (or ·gyll·shire) former Scottish county
År·hus variant spelling of Aarhus
aria
Arian follower of Arianism; compare Aryan
Ari·an·ism heretical doctrine
arid
arid·ity (or ar·id·ness)
Ariège French department
Ari·el satellite of Uranus
ari·el gazelle; compare aerial
Aries constellation; sign of the zodiac
ari·et·ta (plural ·et·tas, ·et·te or ·ettes) short aria
aright

aril

aril botany term
ar·il·late
ar·il·lode
Ari·ma·thea Palestinian town
ario·so musical term
arise (**aris·ing, arose, aris·en**)
aris·ta (*plural* **·tae**) bristle
Ar·is·tar·chus moon crater
aris·tate
ar·is·toc·ra·cy (*plural* **·cies**)
aris·to·crat
aris·to·crat·ic
aris·to·crati·cal·ly
Ar·is·to·telian
arith·me·tic (*noun*)
arith·met·ic (*or* **·meti·cal;** *adj*)
arith·meti·cal·ly
arith·meti·cian
Ari·zo·na
ark Noah's boat; *compare* **arc**
Ar·kan·sas
ar·kose sandstone
Ar·ling·ton US county
arm
ar·ma·da
ar·ma·dil·lo (*plural* **·los**)
Ar·ma·ged·don
Ar·magh
Ar·ma·gnac French brandy
ar·ma·ment
ar·ma·men·tar·ium (*plural* **·tar·iums** *or* **·taria**) doctor's equipment
ar·ma·ture moving electrical part
arm·band
arm·chair
Arm·co (*Trademark*) safety barrier
armed
Ar·me·nia
Ar·me·nian
Ar·men·tières French town
ar·met medieval helmet
arm·ful
arm·hole
ar·mi·ger heraldic term
ar·mil·lary of bracelets
arm·ing
Ar·mini·an
Ar·mini·an·ism Protestant doctrine
ar·mipo·tence
ar·mipo·tent strong in battle
ar·mi·stice
arm·less
arm·let
ar·moire cabinet
ar·mo·ri·al
ar·mour (*US* **·mor**)
ar·moured (*US* **·mored**)
ar·mour·er (*US* **·mor·**)
ar·moury (*US* **·mory;** *plural* **·mouries,** *US* **·mories**)
arm·pit
arm·rest
arms
ar·mure fabric
army (*plural* **armies**)
Arn·hem Dutch city
ar·ni·ca plant
Arno Italian river
ar·oid botany term
aro·ma
aro·mat·ic
aro·mati·cal·ly
aro·ma·tic·ity
aro·ma·ti·za·tion (*or* **·sa·tion**)
aro·ma·tize (*or* **·tise**)
arose
around
arous·al
arouse
arous·er
ar·peg·gio (*plural* **·gios**)
ar·que·bus (*or* **har·**) early musket
ar·rack (*or* **arak**) alcoholic spirit
ar·raign
ar·raign·er
ar·raign·ment legal term
Ar·ran Scottish island; *compare* **Aran**
ar·range
ar·range·able
ar·range·ment
ar·rang·er
ar·rant
Ar·ras French town
ar·ras hanging tapestry; *compare* **arris**

ar·ray
ar·ray·al
ar·rears
ar·rest
ar·rest·able
ar·rest·er
ar·rest·ing
ar·rest·ing·ly
ar·rhyth·mia abnormal heartbeat
arrière-pensée (*plural* **arrière-pensées**) French mental reservation
Ar Ri·mal Arabian desert
ar·ris (*plural* **·ris** *or* **·rises**) sharp edge; *compare* **arras**
ar·ri·val
ar·rive
ar·riv·er
ar·ri·viste ambitious person
ar·ro·ba unit of weight
ar·ro·gance
ar·ro·gant
ar·ro·gate claim without justification
ar·ro·ga·tion
ar·roga·tive
ar·ro·ga·tor
ar·ron·disse·ment French district
ar·row
arrow·head
arrow·root
arrow·wood
arrow·worm
arro·yo *US* gully
ars antiqua 13th-century music style; *compare* **ars nova**
arse
ar·senal
ar·senate
ar·senic
ar·seni·cal
ar·senide
ar·seni·ous (*or* **·sen·ous**)
ar·senite
ar·seno·py·rite mineral
ar·sine chemical compound
ar·sis (*plural* **·ses**) prosody term
ars nova 14th-century music style; *compare* **ars antiqua**
ar·son

ars·phena·mine drug
arsy-versy *Slang* backwards
art
Art Deco 1920-40 art style; *compare* Art Nouveau
ar·te·fact (*or* ·ti·)
ar·tel Soviet cooperative union
Artemis Greek goddess
ar·te·mi·sia plant
ar·te·rial
ar·te·ri·ali·za·tion (*or* ·sa·tion)
ar·te·ri·al·ize (*or* ·ise)
ar·te·ri·ole subdivision of artery
ar·te·rio·sclero·sis
ar·te·rio·sclerot·ic
ar·te·rio·venous
ar·te·ri·tis
ar·tery (*plural* ·teries)
ar·te·sian
art·ful
art·ful·ly
art·ful·ness
ar·thral·gia joint pain
ar·thral·gic
ar·thrit·ic
ar·thri·tis
arthro·mere zoology term
arthro·mer·ic
arthro·pod
ar·thropo·dous (*or* ·dal)
arthro·spore
ar·thro·spor·ic (*or* ·ous)
Ar·thu·rian
ar·ti·choke
ar·ti·cle
ar·ticu·lar
ar·ticu·late
ar·ticu·late·ness (*or* ·la·cy)
ar·ticu·la·tion
ar·ticu·la·tor
ar·ticu·la·tory
ar·ti·fact *variant spelling of* artefact
ar·ti·fice
ar·tifi·cer
ar·ti·fi·cial
ar·ti·fi·ci·al·ity
ar·til·lery
ar·tillery·man (*plural* ·men)
arti·ness
ar·tio·dac·tyl zoology term
ar·tio·dac·ty·lous
ar·ti·san
art·ist person skilled in art, etc.
ar·tiste entertainer
ar·tis·tic
ar·tis·ti·cal·ly
art·ist·ry
art·less
art·less·ness
Art Nouveau 1890-1910 art style; *compare* Art Deco
Ar·tois former French province
art·work
arty (arti·er, arti·est)
Aru·ba West Indian island
arum
Aru·na·chal Pra·desh Indian state
Ar·un·del
arun·di·na·ceous resembling a reed
Aru·wi·mi Zaïrian river
Aryan (*or* Arian) non-Jewish Caucasian; *compare* Arian
Ary·an·ize (*or* ·ise)
aryl chemistry term
ary·te·noid (*or* ·tae·) anatomy term
ary·te·noid·al
as
asa·foeti·da (*or esp. US* ·feti·) resin
Asan·te·he·ne Ghanaian ruler
asa·ra·bac·ca plant
asa·rum dried ginger root
as·bes·tos (*US also* ·tus)
as·bes·to·sis
as·ca·ria·sis
as·ca·rid parasitic worm
as·cend
as·cend·ancy (*or* ·ency, ·ance, ·ence)
as·cend·ant (*or* ·ent)
as·cend·er
As·cen·sion Christian feast; S Atlantic island
as·cen·sion
as·cen·sion·al
As·cen·sion·tide

as·cent upward movement; *compare* assent
as·cer·tain
as·cer·tain·able
as·cer·tain·ment
as·cesis (*plural* ·ceses) self-discipline
as·cet·ic
as·ceti·cal·ly
as·ceti·cism
asci *plural of* ascus
Ascii computer language
as·cid·ian marine animal
as·cid·ium (*plural* ·cidia) botany term
as·ci·tes medical term
as·cit·ic
as·cle·pia·da·ceous botany term
Asclepius Greek god
as·co·carp part of a fungus
as·co·go·nium (*plural* ·nia) fungal reproductive body
as·co·my·cete fungus
as·co·my·cetous
ascor·bic acid
as·co·spore
As·cot Berkshire town; racecourse
as·cot cravat
as·crib·able
as·cribe
as·crip·tion (*or* ad·scrip·)
as·cus (*plural* asci) fungal part
as·dic echo sounder
ase·ity philosophy term
asep·al·ous
asep·sis
asep·tic
asexu·al
asexu·al·ity
asexu·al·ly
As·gard home of Norse gods
ash
ashamed
asham·ed·ly
Ashan·ti Ghanaian region
ash·en
Ashes cricket trophy
ashet *Dialect* dish
Ash·ke·na·zi (*plural* ·zim) Jew of E European descent

ash·key

ash·key
Ash·kha·bad Soviet city
ash·lar (*or* ·ler)
ash·lar·ing building material
ashore
(ashphalt) *incorrect spelling of* asphalt
ash·plant
ash·ram Hindu religious retreat
Ashtoreth biblical character
ash·tray
ashy (ashi·er, ashi·est)
Asia
Asian
Asi·at·ic
aside
asi·nine
asi·nin·ity
Asir Saudi Arabian region
ask
askance (*or* askant)
ask·er
askew
aslant
asleep
As·ma·ra Ethiopian city
Asmodeus Jewish demon
As·nières Parisian suburb
aso·cial
aso·cial·ly
asp
as·para·gine amino acid
as·para·gus
as·par·tic acid
as·pect
as·pec·tual linguistics term
as·pen
as·per Turkish coin
as·per·gil·lo·sis (*plural* ·ses)
as·per·gil·lus (*plural* ·li) fungus
as·per·ity (*plural* ·ities)
as·perse
as·pers·er
as·per·sion
as·per·sive
as·per·so·rium (*plural* ·ria) basin for holy water
as·phalt
as·phal·tic
as·phal·tite
as·phal·tum

as·pho·del plant
as·phyxia
as·phyx·ial
as·phyxi·ant
as·phyxi·ate
as·phyxia·tion
as·phyxia·tor
as·pic
as·pi·dis·tra
as·pir·ant
as·pi·rate
as·pi·ra·tion
as·pi·ra·tor
as·pira·tory
as·pire
as·pir·er
as·pi·rin (*plural* ·rin *or* ·rins)
as·pir·ing
(asprin) *incorrect spelling of* aspirin
asquint
ass
as·sai musical term; palm tree
as·sail
assail·able
as·sail·ant
as·sail·er
assail·ment
As·sam Indian state
As·sa·mese (*plural* ·mese)
as·sas·sin
as·sas·si·nate
as·sas·si·na·tion
as·sault
as·sault·er
as·say test; *compare* essay
as·say·able
as·say·er
as·se·gai (*or* ·sa·; *plural* ·gais) spear
as·sem·blage
as·sem·ble
as·sem·bler
as·sem·bly (*plural* ·blies)
as·sembly·man (*plural* ·men)
as·sent consent; *compare* ascent
as·sen·ta·tion servile agreement
as·sen·tient approving
as·sen·tor
as·sert

as·sert·er (*or* ·ser·tor)
as·sert·ible
as·ser·tion
as·ser·tive
as·ser·tive·ness
as·sess
as·sess·able
as·sess·ment
as·ses·sor
as·ses·so·rial
as·set
asset-stripper
asset-stripping
as·sev·er·ate declare emphatically
as·sev·era·tion
as·sibi·late phonetics term
as·sibi·la·tion
as·si·du·ity (*plural* ·ities)
as·sidu·ous
as·sidu·ous·ness
as·sign
as·sign·abil·ity
as·sign·able
as·sig·nat former French currency
as·sig·na·tion
as·signee legal term
as·sign·er
as·sign·ment
as·sign·or legal term
as·simi·lable
as·simi·late
as·simi·la·tion
as·simi·la·tive (*or* ·tory)
As·sini·boine Canadian river
as·sist
as·sis·tance
as·sis·tant
as·sist·er
as·size
as·sizes
as·so·ci·able
as·so·ci·ate
as·so·cia·tion
as·so·cia·tion·ism psychology term
as·so·cia·tive
as·so·nance grammar term
as·so·nant
as·so·nan·tal
as·sort
as·sorta·tive (*or* ·sort·ive)
as·sort·ed

as·sort·er
as·sort·ment
as·suage
as·suage·ment
as·suag·er
as·sua·sive
as·sum·able
as·sume
as·sumed
as·sum·er
as·sum·ing
As·sump·tion Christian feast
as·sump·tion
as·sump·tive
Assur Assyrian god
as·sur·able
as·sur·ance *note* life assurance; *compare* insurance
as·sure
as·sured
as·sur·ed·ly
as·sur·ed·ness
as·sur·er
as·sur·gent curving upwards
(assymetric) *incorrect spelling of* asymmetric
(assymptote) *incorrect spelling of* asymptote
As·syria
As·syr·ian
As·syri·olo·gist
As·syri·ol·ogy
Astarte Phoenician goddess
astat·ic unstable
astati·cal·ly
astati·cism
as·ta·tine chemical element
as·ter
as·te·ri·at·ed crystallography term
as·ter·isk
as·ter·ism
astern
aster·nal anatomy term
as·ter·oid
as·teroi·dal
as·the·nia (*or* ·ny)
as·then·ic weak
as·the·no·pia eyestrain
as·the·nop·ic
as·theno·sphere layer of atmosphere

asth·ma
asth·mat·ic
asthmati·cal·ly
Asti Italian town
as·tig·mat·ic
as·tig·mati·cal·ly
astig·ma·tism (*or* astig·mia)
astil·be plant
astir
Asti Spumante wine
As·to·lat Arthurian town
astoma·tous biology term
aston·ish
aston·ish·ing
aston·ish·ing·ly
aston·ish·ment
As·to·ria US port
astound
astound·ed
astound·ing
astound·ing·ly
astrad·dle
as·tra·gal architectural moulding
astraga·lus anklebone
As·tra·khan Soviet city
as·tra·khan fur
as·tral
as·tra·pho·bia (*or* ·tro·) fear of thunderstorms
as·tra·pho·bic (*or* ·tro·)
astray
astride
as·trin·gen·cy (*or* ·gence)
as·trin·gent
as·tro·bi·ol·ogy
as·tro·bota·ny
as·tro·com·pass
as·tro·cyte cytology term
as·tro·dome
as·tro·dy·nam·ics
as·tro·geol·ogy
as·troid maths term
as·tro·labe astronomers' instrument
as·trolo·ger (*or* ·gist)
as·tro·logi·cal
as·tro·logi·cal·ly
as·trol·ogy
as·tro·met·ric (*or* ·ri·cal)
as·trom·etry branch of astronomy
as·tro·naut
as·tro·nau·tic (*or* ·ti·cal)

as·tro·nau·ti·cal·ly
as·tro·nau·tics
as·tro·navi·ga·tion
as·tro·navi·ga·tor
as·trono·mer
as·tro·nomi·cal (*or* ·nom·ic)
as·tro·nomi·cal·ly
as·trono·my
as·tro·photo·graph·ic
as·tro·pho·tog·ra·phy
as·tro·physi·cal
as·tro·physi·cist
as·tro·phys·ics
as·tro·sphere cytology term
As·tu·ri·as former Spanish kingdom
as·tute
as·tute·ness
Astyanax mythological character
asty·lar architectural term
Asun·ción Paraguayan capital
asun·der
As·wan Egyptian city
aswarm
asyl·lab·ic
asy·lum
asym·met·ric (*or* ·ri·cal)
asym·met·ri·cal·ly
asym·me·try
asymp·to·mat·ic
asymp·to·mati·cal·ly
as·ymp·tote geometry term
as·ymp·tot·ic (*or* ·toti·cal)
as·ymp·toti·cal·ly
asyn·chro·nism
asyn·chro·nous
as·yn·det·ic
as·yn·deti·cal·ly
asyn·de·ton (*plural* ·deta) grammar term
Asyut (*or* As·siut) Egyptian city
at
atac·tic chemistry term
Atalanta mythological character; *compare* Atlanta
ata·man (*plural* ·mans) Cossack leader
ata·rac·tic (*or* ·rax·ic)
ata·raxia (*or* ·raxy) peace of mind
ata·vism

atavist

ata·vist
ata·vis·tic (*or* ·vic)
ata·vis·ti·cal·ly
ataxia (*or* ataxy) lack of muscular coordination
atax·ic (*or* atac·tic)
At·ba·ra Sudanese town
Ate Greek goddess
ate
at·elec·ta·sis lung collapse
at·el·ier *French* workshop
Atha·bas·ka Canadian lake
athe·ism
athe·ist
athe·is·tic (*or* ·ti·cal)
athe·is·ti·cal·ly
ath·el·ing Anglo-Saxon prince
ath·emat·ic musical term
Athena Greek goddess
Ath·enaeum
ath·enaeum (*US also* ath·eneum) institution of learning
Athe·nian
Ath·ens
ather·man·cy
ather·ma·nous opaque to radiant heat
ath·ero·ma (*plural* ·mas *or* ·ma·ta)
ath·er·oma·tous
ath·ero·scle·ro·sis (*plural* ·ses)
ath·ero·scle·rot·ic
athirst
ath·lete
ath·let·ic
ath·leti·cal·ly
ath·leti·cism
ath·let·ics
atho·dyd ramjet
at-home social gathering
athwart
athwart·ships
atilt
At·lan·ta US city; *compare* Atalanta
At·lan·tean
at·lan·tes architectural term
At·lan·tic
At·lan·tis legendary continent
At·las mountain range
at·las

Atli legendary king
at·man Hindu self
at·moly·sis (*plural* ·ses)
at·mom·eter
at·mom·etry
at·mos·phere
at·mos·pher·ic (*or* ·pheri·cal)
at·mos·pheri·cal·ly
at·mos·pher·ics
at·oll
atom
atom·ic
atomi·cal·ly
ato·mic·ity
at·om·ism
at·om·ist
at·om·is·tic (*or* ·ti·cal)
at·om·is·ti·cal·ly
at·omi·za·tion (*or* ·sa·tion)
at·om·ize (*or* ·ise)
at·om·iz·er (*or* ·is·er)
aton·able (*or* atone·)
aton·al musical term
aton·al·ism
ato·nal·ity
ato·nal·ly
atone
atone·able *variant spelling of* atonable
atone·ment
aton·er
aton·ic
ato·nic·ity
ato·ny
atop
atrial
atrio·ven·tricu·lar
atrip nautical term
atrium (*plural* atria)
atro·cious
atro·cious·ness
atroc·ity (*plural* ·ities)
atroph·ic
at·ro·phy (*noun, plural* ·phies; *verb* ·phies, ·phy·ing, ·phied)
at·ro·pine (*or* ·pin) alkaloid
atta·boy
at·tach
at·tach·able
at·ta·ché diplomat
at·tach·er

32

at·tach·ment
at·tack
at·tack·er
at·tain
at·tain·abil·ity (*or* ·able·ness)
at·tain·able
at·tain·der legal term
at·tain·ment
at·taint
at·tar (*or* ot·) essential oil
(attachment) incorrect spelling *of* attachment
at·tempt
at·tempt·able
at·tempt·er
at·tend
at·tend·ance
at·tend·ant
at·tend·er
at·ten·tion
at·ten·tive
at·ten·tive·ness
at·tenu·ant
at·tenu·ate
at·tenua·tion
at·tenua·tor physics term
at·test
at·test·able
at·test·ant (*or* ·test·er)
at·tes·ta·tion
at·test·or (*or* ·test·ta·tor) legal term
At·tic of Attica
at·tic
At·ti·ca Greek region
at·ti·cism clear expression
at·tire
at·ti·tude
at·ti·tu·di·nal
at·ti·tu·di·nize (*or* ·nise)
at·ti·tu·di·niz·er (*or* ·nis·er)
at·torn
at·tor·ney
at·torn·ment
at·tract
at·tract·able
at·tract·ant
at·trac·tion
at·trac·tive
at·trac·tive·ness
at·trac·tor (*or* ·tract·er)
at·trib·ut·able
at·trib·ute

at·trib·ut·er (or ·trib·u·tor)
at·tri·bu·tion
at·tri·bu·tive
at·tri·tion
at·tri·tion·al
at·tri·tive
Attu island off Alaska
at·tune
atypi·cal
atypi·cal·ly
aubade ode
Aube French river
auberge French inn
auber·gine
Auber·vil·liers Parisian suburb
aubrie·tia (or aubre·) plant
au·burn
Aubus·son French town
Auck·land New Zealand city; S Pacific islands
au cou·rant French up-to-date
auc·tion
auc·tion·eer
auc·to·rial of an author
auda·cious
auda·cious·ness
audac·ity (plural ·ities)
Aude French department
audibil·ity (or audible·ness)
audible
audi·ence
audile psychology term
audio
audio·gen·ic
audio·logi·cal
audi·olo·gist
audi·ol·ogy
audi·om·eter
audio·met·ric
audio·met·ri·cal·ly
audi·om·etrist
audi·om·etry
audio·phile hi-fi enthusiast
audio·typ·ing
audio·typist
audio·visual
audi·phone hearing aid
audit
audi·tion
audi·tor

audi·to·rium (plural ·riums or ·ria)
audi·tory
au fait French well-informed
au fond French fundamentally
auf Wie·der·seh·en German goodbye
Augean mythological stables; very dirty
augend number added
auger boring tool; compare augur
aught (or ought) Archaic anything; zero; compare ought
augite mineral
au·git·ic
aug·ment
aug·ment·able
aug·men·ta·tion
aug·menta·tive
aug·men·tor (or ·ment·er)
Augs·burg West German city
augur predict; compare auger
augur·al
augu·ry (plural ·ries)
August month
august imposing
Au·gus·ta Sicilian port
Augus·tan of Emperor Augustus; literary period
Augus·tin·ian of St Augustine
auk
auk·let
au lait French with milk
auld lang syne Scot old times; compare langsyne
aulic of a royal court
Aulis ancient Greek town
aum·bry variant spelling of ambry
au na·tu·rel French nude or raw
aunt
auntie (or aunty; plural aunties)
au pair
aura (plural auras or aurae)
aural of the ear; compare oral
aural·ly

Australoid

aure·ate gilded
aure·ole (or aureo·la) halo
Aureo·my·cin (Trademark) antibiotic
aure·us (plural aurei) Roman coin
au re·voir
auric chemistry term
auri·cle anatomical part
auricu·la (plural ·lae or ·las) primrose
auricu·lar
auricu·late (or ·lat·ed) having ears
aurif·er·ous
Auri·ga constellation
Aurig·na·cian Palaeolithic culture
aurist ear specialist
aurochs extinct cattle
Aurora Roman goddess
auro·ra (plural ·ras or ·rae)
auro·ra aus·tra·lis
auro·ra bo·real·is
auro·ral
aur·ous
aurum gold
Ausch·witz
aus·cul·tate
aus·cul·ta·tion
aus·cul·ta·tor
aus·form·ing steel heat treatment
aus·pex (plural ·pices) Roman soothsayer
aus·pice (plural ·pices) omen; guidance
aus·pi·cious
aus·pi·cious·ness
aus·ten·ite metallurgy term
aus·ten·it·ic
aus·tere
aus·tere·ness
aus·ter·ity (plural ·ities)
Aus·ter·litz battle site
aus·tral of the south
Aus·tral·asia
Aus·tral·asian
Aus·tralia
Aus·tral·ian
Aus·tral·ia·na
Aus·trali·an·ism
Aus·trali·an·ize (or ·ise)
Aus·tra·loid

australopithecine 34

aus·tra·lo·pithe·cine fossil man
Aus·tra·lo·pithe·cus genus of fossil men
Aus·tral·orp domestic fowl
Aus·tria
Aus·trian
Austro-Asiatic
Aus·tro·nesia S Pacific islands
Aus·tro·nesian
auta·coid body secretion
autar·chic (*or* ·chi·cal)
autar·chy (*plural* ·chies) unrestricted rule; *compare* autarky
autar·kic (*or* ·ki·cal, ·chic, ·chi·cal)
autar·ky (*or* ·chy; *plural* ·kies *or* ·chies) economic self-sufficiency; *compare* autarchy
aut·eco·logi·cal
aut·ecol·ogy
auteur film director
authen·tic
authen·ti·cal·ly
authen·ti·cate
authen·ti·ca·tion
au·then·ti·ca·tor
au·then·tic·ity
author
author·ess
autho·rial
authori·tar·ian
authori·tari·an·ism
authori·ta·tive
authori·ta·tive·ness
author·ity (*plural* ·ities)
authori·za·tion (*or* ·sa·tion)
author·ize (*or* ·ise)
author·iz·er (*or* ·is·er)
author·ship
autism
autis·tic
auto (*plural* **autos**) *Slang* motor car
auto·anti·body (*plural* ·bodies)
auto·bahn
auto·bi·og·ra·pher
auto·bio·graphi·cal
auto·bi·og·ra·phy (*plural* ·phies)
auto·cade *US* motorcade
auto·ca·taly·sis (*plural* ·ses) chemistry term
auto·chang·er record-changing device
autoch·thon (*plural* ·thons *or* ·tho·nes) earliest known inhabitant
autoch·thon·ism (*or* ·tho·ny)
autoch·tho·nous (*or* ·tho·nal)
auto·clave
auto·cor·re·la·tion
autoc·ra·cy (*plural* ·cies)
auto·crat
auto·crat·ic
auto·crati·cal·ly
auto·cross
auto·cue
auto-da-fé (*plural* **autos-da-fé**) ceremony of Spanish Inquisition
auto·di·dact self-taught person
autoe·cious botany term
autoe·cism
autoga·mous (*or* auto·gam·ic)
autoga·my biology term
auto·gen·esis (*or* autog·eny)
auto·genet·ic
autog·enous
auto·gi·ro (*or* ·gy·; *plural* ·ros)
auto·graft
auto·graph
auto·graph·ic
auto·graphi·cal·ly
autog·ra·phy
auto·hyp·no·sis
auto·hyp·not·ic
auto·hyp·noti·cal·ly
autoi·cous botany term
auto·im·mune
auto·im·mun·ity
auto·ioni·za·tion (*or* ·sa·tion)
auto·ki·net·ic
Autoly·cus moon crater
Autolycus mythological character
auto·lyse (*US* ·lyze)
auto·ly·sin
autoly·sis self-destruction of cells
auto·lyt·ic
auto·mat
automa·ta *plural of* **automaton**
auto·mate
auto·mat·ic
auto·mati·cal·ly
auto·ma·tion
automa·tism
automa·tist
automa·tize (*or* ·tise)
automa·ton (*plural* ·tons *or* ·ta)
automa·tous
auto·mo·bile
auto·mo·bil·ist
auto·mo·tive
auto·nom·ic
auto·nomi·cal·ly
autono·mist
autono·mous
autono·my (*plural* ·mies)
auto·phyte botany term
auto·phyt·ic
auto·phyti·cal·ly
auto·pi·lot
auto·pis·ta Spanish motorway
auto·plas·tic
auto·plas·ty transplantation from own body
autop·sy (*plural* ·sies)
auto·put Yugoslav motorway
auto·radio·graph
auto·radio·graph·ic
auto·ra·di·og·ra·phy
auto·ro·ta·tion
auto·so·mal
auto·some type of chromosome
auto·sta·bil·ity
auto·stra·da Italian motorway
auto·sug·ges·tion
auto·sug·ges·tive
auto·tim·er
auto·tom·ic
autoto·mize (*or* ·mise)
autoto·my (*plural* ·mies) shedding of body part
auto·tox·ic
auto·tox·in
auto·trans·form·er
auto·troph·ic biology term

auto·type
auto·typ·ic
auto·typy
autoxi·da·tion chemistry term
autumn
autum·nal
autun·ite mineral
Auvergne French region
auxa·nom·eter
aux·esis biology term
aux·ilia·ry (*plural* ·ries)
aux·in hormone
auxo·chrome chemistry term
ava·da·vat (*or* ama·) bird
avail
avail·abil·ity
avail·able
avail·ably
ava·lanche
Ava·lon Arthurian paradise
avant-garde
Avar former European people
ava·rice
ava·ri·cious
avast nautical interjection
ava·tar manifestation of Hindu deity
ave *Latin* welcome; farewell
Ave·bury Wiltshire village; Neolithic stone circle
Ave·lla·ne·da Argentine city
avenge
aveng·er
av·ens (*plural* ·ens) plant
Av·en·tine Roman hill
aven·tu·rine (*or* aven·tu·rin, avan·tu·rine) dark glass
av·enue
aver (aver·ring, averred)
av·er·age
aver·ment
averse
aver·sion
aver·sive
avert
avert·ible (*or* ·able)
Aves·ta Zoroastrian scriptures
Aves·tan

Avey·ron French department
avian of birds
aviary (*plural* aviaries) place for keeping birds; *compare* apiary
avi·ate
avia·tion
avia·tor
avia·trix (*or* ·tress)
avi·cul·ture bird-rearing
avi·cul·tur·ist
avid
avi·din a protein
avid·ity
avid·ness
Avie·more Scottish resort
avi·fau·na
avi·fau·nal
Avi·gnon French city
avi·on·ic
avi·on·ics
aviru·lent
avita·mino·sis (*plural* ·ses)
avi·zan·dum Scottish legal term
avo·ca·do (*plural* ·dos)
avo·cet (*or* ·set) bird
avoid
avoid·able
avoid·ance
avoid·er
av·oir·du·pois system of weights
Avon English county and river
avow
avow·able
avow·al
avowed
avow·er
avul·sion
avun·cu·lar
avun·cu·late
await
awake (awak·ing, awoke *or* awaked, awok·en *or* awaked)
awak·en
award
award·able
awardee
award·er
aware

aware·ness
awash
away
awe
aweath·er nautical term
aweigh
awe-inspiring
awe·some
awe·some·ness
awe-stricken (*or* awe-struck)
aw·ful
aw·ful·ly
aw·ful·ness
awhile
awk·ward
awk·ward·ness
awl
awl·wort plant
awn plant bristle
awn·ing
awoke
awry
axe (*US* ax)
axel ice-skating jump; *compare* axil; axle
axen·ic uncontaminated
ax·ial
axil angle between leaf and stem; *compare* axel; axle
ax·ile attached to an axis
ax·il·la (*plural* ·lae) armpit
ax·il·lary (*plural* ·laries) of armpit; feather
axio·logi·cal
axi·olo·gist
axi·ol·ogy study of values
axi·om
axio·mat·ic (*or* ·mati·cal)
axio·mati·cal·ly
Axis Nazi alliance
axis (*plural* axes)
axle mechanical part; *compare* axel; axil
axle·tree carriage axle
Ax·min·ster Devon town; carpet
axo·lotl salamander
axon part of nerve cell
ax·seed plant
ay (*or* aye) *Archaic* always; *compare* aye
ayah maid
aya·huas·ca plant
ayatollah

Ay·cliffe English town
aye (*or* **ay**) *Archaic or dialect* yes; *compare* **ay**
aye-aye animal
Ayles·bury
Ay·ma·ra (*plural* **·ras** *or* **·ra**) South American Indian
Ayr Scottish port
Ayr·shire cattle
Ayur·veda Hindu medical treatise
Ayut·tha·ya Thai city
azalea
azan Islamic call to prayer

aza·thio·prine drug
Az·bine Saharan region
azeda·rach medicinal bark
azeo·trope chemistry term
azeo·trop·ic
Azer·bai·jan region of Iran; Soviet republic
Azer·bai·ja·ni (*plural* **·ni** *or* **·nis**)
az·ide
azi·muth astronomy term
azi·muth·al
az·ine
azo·ben·zene
azo·ic without life

az·ole chemical compound
Azores Atlantic islands
az·ote *Obsolete* nitrogen
azo·tae·mia (*US* **·te·**) uraemia
azo·tae·mic (*US* **·te·**)
az·oth mercury
azot·ic of nitrogen
azo·to·bac·ter bacterium
Az·tec
az·ure
az·ur·ite mineral
azy·gous

B

Ba soul in Egyptian mythology
baa (**baa·ing, baaed**)
Baal Semitic god
Baal·bek Lebanese town
baba cake
ba·bas·su palm tree
bab·bitt line with alloy
Bab·bitt met·al
bab·ble
bab·bler
babe
Ba·bel biblical tower
ba·biche rawhide thongs
babi·ru·sa wild pig
ba·boon
(**babtize**) *incorrect spelling of* **baptize**
ba·bul acacia tree
baby (*noun, plural* **babies**; *verb* **babies, ba·by·ing, ba·bied**)
ba·by·hood
ba·by·ish
Baby·lon city
Baby·lo·nia kingdom
Baby·lo·nian
baby's-breath (*or* **babies'-**) plant
baby-sit (**-sitting, -sat**)
baby-sitter
baby-snatch·er
bac·ca·lau·re·ate
bac·ca·rat

bac·cate berry-like
Bac·chae priestesses of Bacchus
bac·cha·nal
bac·cha·na·lia
bac·cha·na·lian
bac·chant (*fem* **·chan·te**; *plural* **·chants** *or* **·chan·tes**, *fem* **·chan·tes**) drunken reveller
Bac·chic
bac·chius (*plural* **·chii**) metrical foot
Bacchus god of wine
bac·cif·er·ous
bac·ci·form
bac·civ·or·ous
bac·cy *Slang* tobacco
bach·elor
bachelor's-buttons plant
ba·cil·lary (*or* **·lar**)
ba·cil·li·form
ba·cil·lus (*plural* **·li**) rod-shaped bacterium
baci·tra·cin antibiotic
back
back·ache
back·bencher
back·bend
back·bite (**·bit·ing, bit, bit·ten** *or* **bit**)
back·board
back·bone

back·breaker
back·breaking
back·chat
back·cloth (*or* **·drop**)
back·comb
back·cross genetics term
back·date
back·door
back·er
back·fill archaeology term
back·fire
back·gam·mon
back·ground
back·hand
back·hand·ed
back·handed·ly
back·handed·ness
back·hand·er
back·ing
back·lash
back·less
back·list
back·log
back·most
back-pedal (**-pedalling, -pedalled**; *US* **-pedaling, -pedaled**)
back·saw
Backs Cambridge college grounds
back·scratch·er
back·side
back·sight
back-slapping

back·slide (·slid·ing, ·slid, ·slid or ·slid·den)
back·slid·er
back·space
back·spin
back·stage
back·stairs
back·stay nautical term
back·stitch
back·stop
back·street
back·stroke
back·swept
back·track
back·up (*noun*)
back·veld South African rural area
back·ward (*adj*)
back·warda·tion stock exchange term
back·ward·ness
back·wards (*US* ·ward; *adv*)
back·wash
back·water
back·woods·man (*plural* ·men)
Ba·co·lod Philippine town
ba·con
ba·con·er pig
bac·te·rae·mia (*US* ·re·) bacteria in the blood
bac·te·ria *plural of* bacterium
bac·te·rial
bac·te·ri·cid·al
bac·te·ri·cide
bac·te·rin vaccine
bac·te·rio·logi·cal
bac·te·ri·olo·gist
bac·te·ri·ol·ogy
bac·te·ri·oly·sis disintegration of bacteria
bac·te·rio·lyt·ic
bac·te·rio·phage virus that destroys bacteria
bac·te·rio·phag·ic
bac·te·ri·opha·gous
bac·te·rio·sta·sis
bac·te·rio·stat·ic
bac·te·rio·stati·cal·ly
bac·te·rium (*plural* ·ria)
bac·ter·oid
Bac·tria ancient Asian country

Bac·trian
ba·cu·li·form rod-shaped
bacu·lum (*plural* ·la *or* ·lums)
bad (worse, worst)
Ba·da·joz Spanish city
Ba·da·lo·na Spanish port
bad·der·locks seaweed
bad·dy (*or* ·die; *plural* ·dies)
bade
Ba·den former German state; Swiss spa
Baden-Baden West German spa
Baden-Wurttem·berg West German state
badge
badg·er
badi·nage
bad·lands
bad·ly
bad·man (*plural* ·men)
bad·min·ton
bad·mouth
bad·ness
Bae·de·ker travel guidebook
bael tree
Baf·fin Canadian island and bay
baf·fle
baf·fle·ment
baf·fler
bag (bag·ging, bagged)
Ba·gan·da (*plural* ·da *or* ·das) African people
ba·gasse sugar-cane pulp
baga·telle
ba·gel (*or* bei·) bread roll
bag·gage
bag·gi·ly
bag·gi·ness
bag·ging
bag·gy (·gier, ·gi·est)
bagh Indian garden
Bagh·dad (*or* Bag·dad)
bag·man (*plural* ·men)
bag·pipe
ba·guette (*or* ·guet)
bag·wig 18th-century wig
bag·worm
Ba·hai
Ba·ha·ism religion
Ba·ha·ist

Ba·ha·mas
Ba·ha·mian
Ba·hia Brazilian town
Ba·hía Blan·ca Argentine port
Bah·rain (*or* ·rein)
Bah·rai·ni (*or* ·rei·)
baht Thai currency
ba·hu·vri·hi linguistics term
Bai·kal Soviet lake
bail (*noun*) security for prisoner; part of wicket; *compare* bale
bail (*or* bale; *verb*) remove water from boat
bail·able
bailee legal term
bail·er (*or* bal·) one who bails water
bai·ley castle wall
Bailey bridge
bailie *Scot* magistrate
bail·iff
baili·wick legal term
bail·ment legal term
bail·or legal term
bails·man (*plural* ·men) one who stands bail
bain·ite component of steel
bain-marie (*plural* bains-marie) cooking utensil
Bai·ram Muslim festival
bairn
bait enticement; to torment; *compare* bate
baize
bake
bake·house
Ba·ke·lite (*Trademark*)
bak·er
bak·ery (*plural* ·eries)
Bake·well English town; tart
bak·la·va cake
bak·sheesh
Baku Soviet port
Bala Welsh lake
Balaam biblical character
Bala·cla·va helmet
Bala·kla·va (*or* ·cla·) Soviet port
bala·lai·ka
bal·ance
bal·ance·able
bal·anc·er

balas

bal·as gemstone
bala·ta tree
Ba·la·ton Hungarian lake
Bal·boa Panamanian port
bal·boa Panamanian currency
bal·brig·gan fabric
bal·co·nied
bal·co·ny (*plural* ·nies)
bald
bal·da·chin brocade
Balder Norse god
bal·der·dash
bald·headed
bald·ing
bald·money plant
bald·ness
bald·pate
bal·dric sash for sword
bale (*noun*) block of hay; *compare* bail
bale (*verb*) make bales; jump from aircraft; *variant spelling of* bail
Bal·ear·ic Is·lands
ba·leen whalebone
bale·ful
bale·ful·ly
bale·ful·ness
bal·er agricultural machine; *variant spelling of* bailer
Bali Indonesian island
bali·bun·tal straw hat
Ba·lik·pa·pan Indonesian city
Ba·li·nese (*plural* ·nese)
balk (*or* baulk) stop short; avoid; timber beam; *compare* baulk
Bal·kan
Bal·kani·za·tion (*or* ·sa·tion)
balk·er (*or* baulk·)
balky (*or* baulky; balki·er *or* baulki·er, balki·est *or* baulki·est)
ball
bal·lad
bal·lade verse form
bal·lad·eer
bal·lad·ry
Bal·la·rat Australian town
bal·last
bal·le·ri·na
bal·let

bal·let·ic
bal·leto·mane
bal·leto·ma·nia
ball·flower architectural ornament
bal·lis·ta (*plural* ·tae) ancient catapult
bal·lis·tic
bal·lis·ti·cal·ly
bal·lis·tics
bal·locks *variant spelling of* bollocks
bal·lo·net gas compartment in balloon
bal·loon
bal·loon·ist
bal·lot (·lot·ing, ·lot·ed)
bal·lotte·ment medical term
ball·park
ball·point
ball·room
bal·ly slang term
bal·ly·hoo
balm
bal·ma·caan overcoat
balmi·ly
balmi·ness
Bal·mor·al Scottish castle; flat cap
balmy (balmi·er, balmi·est) soft and soothing; *variant spelling* (*esp. US*) *of* barmy
bal·ne·al
bal·neo·logi·cal
bal·ne·olo·gist
bal·ne·ol·ogy study of therapeutic baths
ba·lo·ney (*or* bo·)
bal·sa wood
bal·sam
bal·sam·ic
bal·sam·if·er·ous
bal·sa·mi·na·ceous
Balt person from Baltic States
Bal·tic
Bal·ti·more
Ba·lu·chi (*or* ·lo·; *plural* ·chis *or* ·chi) Muslim people
Ba·lu·chi·stan region of Asia
bal·us·ter
bal·us·trade

38

Ba·ma·ko capital of Mali
Bam·ba·ra (*plural* ·ra *or* ·ras) African people
Bam·berg West German town
bam·bi·no (*plural* ·nos *or* ·ni)
bam·boo (*plural* ·boos)
bam·boo·zle
bam·boo·zle·ment
bam·boo·zler
ban (ban·ning, banned)
ba·nal
ba·nal·ity
ba·na·na
Ban·at plain in E Europe
ba·nau·sic utilitarian
Ban·bury
banc legal term
band
band·age
ban·dan·na (*or* ban·dana)
band·box
ban·deau (*plural* ·deaux) headband
ban·de·ril·la bullfighter's dart
ban·de·ril·lero (*plural* ·leros) bullfighter's assistant
ban·de·role (*or* ·de·rol, ·ne·rol) flag
ban·di·coot
ban·dit (*plural* ·dits *or* ·dit·ti)
ban·dit·ry
Band·jar·ma·sin (*or* Ban·jer·ma·sin) Indonesian port
band·master
ban·do·leer (*or* ·lier) shoulder belt
ban·do·line hairdressing substance
ban·dora (*or* pan·) musical instrument
bands·man (*plural* ·men)
band·spreading radio tuning control
band·stand
Ban·dung Indonesian city
band·wagon
band·width
ban·dy (*adj* ·di·er, ·di·est; *verb* ·dies, ·dy·ing, ·died)

barograph

bandy-bandy (*plural* -bandies) snake
bane
bane·berry (*plural* ·berries)
bane·ful
Banff former Scottish county; Canadian town
bang
Ban·ga·lore Indian city
bang·er
Bang·ka Indonesian island
Bang·kok
Bang·la·desh
Bang·la·deshi
ban·gle
Bangor Welsh or Northern Irish town
Ban·gui capital of Central African Republic
ban·ish
ban·ish·ment
ban·is·ter
ban·jo (*plural* ·jos *or* ·joes)
ban·jo·ist
Ban·jul Gambian capital
bank
bank·able
bank·book
bank·er
bank·et gold-bearing rock
bank·ing
bank·roll
bank·rupt
bank·rupt·cy (*plural* ·cies)
bank·sia shrub
banned
ban·ner
ban·ner·ette
ban·ning
(bannister) *incorect spelling of* banister
ban·nock Scottish cake
Ban·nock·burn Scottish battle site
banns (*or* bans) of marriage
ban·quet feast
ban·quette seat
ban·shee
bant *Dialect* string
ban·tam
bantam·weight
ban·ter

ban·ter·er
Ban·toid language
Ban·tu (*plural* ·tu *or* ·tus)
Ban·tu·stan South African homeland
ban·yan (*or* ·ian) tree
ban·zai Japanese salutation
bao·bab tree
bap
bap·tism
bap·tis·mal
Bap·tist member of Christian sect
bap·tist·ry (*or* ·tis·tery; *plural* ·ries *or* ·teries)
bap·tize (*or* ·tise)
bar (bar·ring, barred)
Barabbas biblical character
bara·thea fabric
barb
Bar·ba·dian
Bar·ba·dos
bar·bar·ian
bar·bar·ian·ism
bar·bar·ic
bar·bari·cal·ly
bar·bar·ism
bar·bar·ity (*plural* ·ities)
bar·ba·rize (*or* ·rise)
bar·ba·rous
bar·ba·rous·ness
Bar·ba·ry N African region
bar·bate
bar·becue (·becu·ing, ·becued)
bar·bel fish; bristle
bar·bell weight
bar·bel·late covered with bristles
bar·ber
bar·ber·ry (*plural* ·ries)
barber·shop
bar·bet bird
bar·bette gun platform
Bar·bi·can area of London
bar·bi·can fortified place
bar·bi·cel
bar·bi·tone (*US* ·tal)
bar·bi·tu·rate
Bar·bu·da West Indian island
bar·bule
bar·ca·role (*or* ·rolle)
Bar·ce·lo·na

bar·chan (*or* ·khan, ·chane, ·kan) sand dune
bard
bard·ic
bar·dola·try
bare uncovered; naked; expose; *compare* bear
bare·back (*or* ·backed)
bare·faced
bare·fac·ed·ness
bare·foot (*or* ·footed)
bare·handed
bare·headed
Ba·reil·ly Indian city
bare·ly
bare·ness
Bar·ents Arctic sea
bar·gain
barge
bar·gee
barge·pole
Bari Italian port
bar·ic of atmospheric pressure
ba·ril·la plant extract
bari·tone
bar·ium
bark dog's cry; outer layer of tree; *compare* barque
bark·er
Bark·ing London borough
bar·ley
barley·corn
barm *Dialect* yeast
bar·maid
bar·man (*plural* ·men)
Bar·mecide (*or* ·mecid·al) illusory
bar mitz·vah
bar·my (*or esp. US* balmy; ·mi·er, ·mi·est) *Slang* crazy; *compare* balmy
barn
bar·na·cle
Bar·na·ul Soviet city
barn-brack *Dialect* fruit muffin
Bar·net London borough
bar·ney *Slang* argument
barn·storm
barn·yard
Ba·ro·da Indian state
baro·gram
baro·graph

barographic

baro·graphic
ba·rom·eter
baro·met·ric
baro·met·ri·cal·ly
bar·on
bar·on·age
bar·on·ess
bar·on·et
bar·on·et·age
bar·on·et·cy (*plural* ·cies)
ba·rong Philippine knife
ba·ro·nial
baro·ny (*plural* ·nies)
ba·roque
baro·recep·tor
baro·scope
baro·stat
Ba·rot·se (*plural* ·se *or* ·ses) African people
Ba·rot·se·land Zambian region
ba·rouche horse-drawn carriage
barque (*US also* bark) boat; *compare* bark
bar·quen·tine (*or* ·quan·)
Bar·qui·si·me·to Venezuelan city
bar·rack (*verb*)
bar·racks
bar·ra·cou·ta fish
bar·ra·cu·da (*plural* ·da *or* ·das) fish
bar·rage
bar·ra·mun·da (*or* ·di; *plural* ·das, ·da; *or* ·dis, ·dies, di) fish
bar·ran·ca *US* ravine
Bar·ran·quil·la Colombian port
bar·ra·tor
bar·ra·trous (*or* bar·retrous)
bar·ra·try (*or* bar·retry) legal term
bar·ré music term
barred
bar·rel (·rel·ling, ·relled; *US* ·rel·ing, ·reled)
bar·ren
bar·ren·ness
bar·rens *US* barren land
barren·wort plant
bar·ret cap
bar·rette hair clasp

bar·ri·cade
bar·ri·cad·er
bar·ri·er
bar·ring
bar·ris·ter
bar·room
bar·row
Bar·ry Welsh port
Bar·sac wine
bar·tender
bar·ter
bar·ter·er
bar·ti·zan small turret
Bart·lett pear
bary·cen·tre centre of mass
bar·ye unit
bary·on physics term
bary·sphere
ba·ry·tes mineral
bary·ton bass viol
ba·sal
bas·alt
basalt·ware
bas·cule bridge
base
base·ball
base·board
base·born
Ba·sel (*or* Basle) Swiss city
base·less
base·line
base·man (*plural* ·men) baseball fielder
base·ment
base·ness
Ba·sen·ji dog
ba·ses *plural of* base *or* basis
bash
Ba·shan biblical region
bash·ful
bash·ful·ly
bash·ful·ness
bashi·ba·zouk Turkish soldier
Bash·kir (*plural* ·kir *or* ·kirs) Mongoloid people
ba·sic
ba·si·cal·ly
ba·sic·ity chemistry term
ba·sid·ial
ba·sidio·my·cete fungus
ba·sidio·my·cet·ous
ba·sidio·spore
ba·sidio·spor·ous

40

ba·sid·ium (*plural* ·ia) fungal structure
basi·fixed botany term
basi·fy (·fies, ·fy·ing, ·fied) make basic
bas·il herb
basi·lar anatomy term
basi·lary
Ba·sil·don Essex town
Ba·sil·ian Eastern monk
ba·sil·ic vein
ba·sili·ca Roman building
ba·sil·i·can (*or* ·sil·ic)
Ba·si·li·ca·ta Italian region
basi·lisk lizard
ba·sin
basi·net medieval helmet; *compare* bassinet
ba·sin·ful
Ba·sing·stoke Hampshire town
ba·sion anatomy term
ba·sip·etal botany term
ba·sis (*plural* ·ses)
bask
Baskerville style of type
bas·ket
basket·ball
bas·ket·ry
basket-star starfish
basket·work
Basle *variant spelling of* Basel
ba·so·phil (*or* ·phile, ·phil·ic) stained by basic dyes
Ba·so·tho (*plural* ·tho *or* ·thos) African people
Basque Pyrenean people and language
Bas·ra (*or* Bas·rah, Bus·ra, Bus·rah) Iraqi port
bas-relief (*or* bas·relief)
Bas-Rhin French department
bass voice; singer
bass (*plural* bass *or* basses) fish
Bas·sein Burmese city
Bas·sen·thwaite
bas·set
Basse-Terre West Indian island
bas·si·net cradle; *compare* basinet

bass·ist double bass player
bas·so (*plural* ·sos *or* ·si) bass singer
bas·soon
bas·soon·ist
bass·wood
bast plant tissue
bas·tard
bas·tardi·za·tion (*or* ·sa·tion)
bas·tard·ize (*or* ·ise)
bas·tard·ry *Austral* malicious behaviour
bas·tardy illegitimacy
baste
Bas·tille fortress
bas·ti·na·do (*noun, plural* ·does; *verb* ·does, ·do·ing, ·doed) torture
bast·ing
bas·ti·on
bast·naes·ite (*or* ·nas·ite) mineral
Ba·su·to·land *former name of* Lesotho
bat (bat·ting, bat·ted)
Ba·tan·gas Philippine port
batch
(**batchelor**) *incorrect spelling of* bachelor
bate restrain; *Slang* rage; *compare* bait
ba·teau boat
bat·ed
bat·fish (*plural* ·fish *or* ·fishes)
Bath English city; order of knighthood
bath container; wash in bath
bathe swim; wash wound, etc.
bath·er
ba·thet·ic
bath·house
bath·ing
batho·lith (*or* ·lite) granite mass
batho·lith·ic (*or* ·lit·ic)
ba·thom·eter
batho·met·ric
batho·met·ri·cal·ly
ba·thom·etry
ba·thos
bath·robe
bath·room
bath·tub

Bath·urst Australian city; *former name of* Banjul
bathy·al of ocean depths
bathy·met·ric
bathy·met·ri·cal·ly
ba·thym·etry
bathy·scaph (*or* ·scaphe, ·scape)
bathy·sphere
ba·tik (*or* bat·tik) fabric-printing process
ba·tiste fabric
Bat·ley Yorkshire town
bat·man (*plural* ·men)
ba·ton
Bat·on Rouge US city
ba·tra·chi·an amphibian
bats·man (*plural* ·men)
bats·man·ship
batt quilt wadding
bat·tal·ion
bat·ted
bat·ten
Bat·ten·burg cake
bat·ter
bat·ter·er
bat·tery (*plural* ·teries)
bat·ting
bat·tle
battle-axe
bat·tle·dore racket game
battle·field
bat·tle·ment
battle·piece
bat·tler
battle-scarred
battle·ship
bat·tue hunting term
bat·ty (·ti·er, ·ti·est)
Ba·tum (*or* Ba·tu·mi) Soviet city
bat·wing
bat·woman (*plural* ·women)
bau·ble
Bau·chi Nigerian state
baud unit of speed; *compare* bawd
Bau·haus school of arts
bau·hinia plant
baulk billiards term (*US* balk); *variant spelling of* balk
Bau·tzen East German city
baux·ite

Ba·varia
Ba·var·ian
baw·bee former Scottish coin
bawd brothel keeper; *compare* baud
bawdi·ly
bawdi·ness
bawd·ry
bawdy (bawdi·er, bawdi·est)
bawdy·house
bawl
bawl·er
bay
ba·ya·dere Hindu dancing girl
Ba·ya·mon Puerto Rican city
bay·berry (*plural* ·berries)
Ba·yeux French town
bayo·net (·net·ing, ·net·ed *or* ·net·ting, ·net·ted)
bayou marshy stream
bay·wood
ba·zaar (*or* ·zar)
ba·zoo *US* mouth
ba·zoo·ka
bdel·lium tree
be
beach shore; *compare* beech
beach·comber
beach·head
Beach-la-Mar Pacific language
bea·con
Bea·cons·field English town
bead
beadl·ly
beadi·ness
bead·ing
bea·dle
beady (beadi·er, beadi·est)
bea·gle
beak
beaked
beak·er
beaky
beam
beam-ends
beamy
bean

beanbag

bean·bag
bean·ery (*plural* ·eries)
  US cheap restaurant
bean·feast
beanie *US* close-fitting hat
beano (*plural* beanos)
  Slang party
bean·pole
beanstalk
bear (bear·ing, bore,
  borne) support; convey;
  endure; *compare* bare
bear (bear·ing, bore,
  born) give birth to
bear (*plural* bears *or*
  bear) animal
bear·able
bear·ably
bear·berry (*plural*
  ·berries)
beard
beard·ed
beard·less
bear·er
bear·ish
Bé·ar·naise sauce
bear's-breech (*or*
  -breeches) plant
bear's-foot plant
bear·skin
beast
beast·ings *US spelling of*
  beestings
beast·li·ness
beast·ly (·lier, ·liest)
beat (beat·ing, beat,
  beat·en *or* beat)
beat·able
beat·er
bea·tif·ic
bea·tifi·cal·ly
be·ati·fi·ca·tion
be·ati·fy (·fies, ·fy·ing,
  ·fied)
be·ati·tude
beat·nik
beau (*plural* beaus *or*
  beaux)
Beau·fort meteorological
  scale
beau·jo·lais (*or* Beau·)
  wine
beau monde fashionable
  society
Beau·mont Texan city
Beaune French city; wine

beaut *Slang* good
beau·te·ous
beau·ti·cian
beau·ti·fi·ca·tion
beau·ti·ful
beau·ti·ful·ly
beau·ti·fy (·fies, ·fy·ing,
  ·fied)
beau·ty (*plural* ·ties)
Beau·vais French town
beaux-arts fine art
bea·ver
Beaver·board
  (*Trademark*)
be·bee·rine alkaloid
Beb·ing·ton English town
be·bop jazz
be·calmed
be·came
be·cause
bec·ca·fi·co (*plural* ·cos)
  bird
bé·cha·mel sauce
bêche-de-mer marine
  organism
Bechua·na·land *former*
  name of Botswana
beck
beck·et nautical term
beck·on
beck·on·er
be·cloud
be·come (·com·ing,
  ·came, ·come)
be·com·ing·ly
bed (bed·ding, bed·ded)
be·daub
be·daz·zle
be·daz·zle·ment
bed·bug
bed·dable
bed·ded
bed·der
bed·ding
be·deck
be·dev·il (·il·ling, ·illed;
  US ·il·ing, ·iled)
be·dev·il·ment
be·dew
bed·fellow
Bed·ford
Bed·ford·shire
be·dim (·dim·ming,
  ·dimmed)
bed·lam

Bed·ling·ton terrier
Bedou·in (*or* Bedu·in;
  plural ·ins *or* ·in)
bed·pan
bed·plate
bed·post
be·drag·gle
bed·rail
bed·rid·den
bed·rock
bed·roll
bed·room
bed·side
bed·sitter (*or* ·sit)
bed·sore
bed·spread
bed·stead
bed·straw plant
bed·time
bed·warmer
bee
bee·bread
beech tree; *compare* beach
beech·nut
bee-eater
beef (*plural* beeves) cattle
beef (*plural* beefs) cut of
  meat; complaint
beef·bur·ger
beef·cake
beef·eater
beefi·ness
beef·steak
beef·wood
beefy (beefi·er, beefi·est)
bee·hive
bee·keeper
bee·line
Beelzebub the Devil
been
beep
beep·er
beer
beeri·ness
Beer·she·ba Israeli town
beery (beeri·er, beeri·est)
beest·ings (*or* biest·ings;
  US also beast·ings)
  cow's first milk
bees·wax
bees·wing crust in port
beet
beet·fly (*plural* ·flies)
bee·tle
beet·root

Belshazzar

bee·zer *Slang* fellow
be·fall (·fal·ling, ·fell, ·fall·en)
be·fit (·fit·ting, ·fit·ted)
be·fit·ting·ly
be·fog (·fog·ging, ·fogged)
be·fool
be·fore
before·hand
be·foul
be·foul·er
be·foul·ment
be·friend
be·fud·dle
beg (beg·ging, begged)
be·gan
be·get (·get·ting, ·got *or* ·gat, ·got·ten *or* ·got)
be·get·ter
beg·gar
beg·gar·li·ness
beg·gar·ly
beggar·weed
beg·gary
begged
beg·ging
be·gin (gin·ning, ·gan, ·gun)
be·gin·ner
be·gird surround
be·gone
be·gonia
be·gor·ra Irish exclamation
be·got
be·got·ten
be·grime
be·grudge
be·grudg·ing·ly
be·guile (·guil·ing, ·guiled)
be·guile·ment
be·guil·er
be·guil·ing·ly
be·guine dance
be·gum (*or* ·gam) Muslim woman ruler
be·gun
be·half
be·have
be·hav·iour (*US* ·ior)
be·hav·iour·al (*US* ·ior·)
be·hav·iour·ism (*US* ·ior·)
be·hav·iour·ist (*US* ·ior·)
be·hav·iour·is·tic (*US* ·ior·)

be·head
be·held
be·he·moth biblical monster
be·hest
be·hind
behind·hand
be·hold (·hold·ing, ·held)
be·hold·en
be·hold·er
be·hove (*US* ·hoove)
beige
bei·gel variant spelling of bagel
Bei·jin Chinese name for Peking
be·ing
Bei·ra Mozambique port
Bei·rut (*or* Bey·routh) Lebanese capital
be·jew·el (·el·ling, ·elled; *US* ·el·ing, ·eled)
bel unit of power
be·la·bour (*US* ·bor)
be·lah tree
be·lat·ed
be·lat·ed·ness
be·lay (·lay·ing, ·layed) make secure
belch
belch·er
be·lea·guer
Be·lém Brazilian port
be·lem·nite fossil
Bel·fast
Bel·fort French department
bel·fry (*plural* ·fries)
Bel·gae Celtic people
Bel·gian
Bel·gium
Bel·grade Yugoslav capital
Bel·gra·via London district
Belial demon
be·lie (·ly·ing, ·lied)
be·lief
be·li·er
be·liev·able
be·lieve
be·liev·er
Belisha traffic beacon
be·lit·tle
be·lit·tle·ment
be·lit·tler
be·lit·tling·ly
Be·lize Central American state

bell
bel·la·don·na
bel·lar·mine jar
Bel·la·trix star
bell·bird
bell·boy
belle beautiful woman
belle epoque *French* period before World War I
Bel·leek porcelain
Bellerophon mythological hero
belles-lettres *French* literary works
bel·let·rist
bel·let·ris·tic
bell·hop
bel·li·cose
bel·li·cos·ity
bel·lig·er·ence
bel·lig·er·en·cy
bel·lig·er·ent
Bellona Roman goddess
bel·low
bel·low·er
bel·lows
bell·pull
bell·push
bell·ringer
bell·ringing
bell·wether flock leader
bell·wort plant
bel·ly (*noun, plural* ·lies; *verb* ·lies, ·ly·ing, ·lied)
belly·band part of harness
belly·button
belly-flop (-flopping, -flopped)
bel·ly·ful
Bel·mo·pan Belize capital
Belo Ho·ri·zon·te Brazilian city
be·long
be·long·ings
Be·lo·rus·sia (*or* Bye·) Soviet republic
Be·lo·rus·sian (*or* Bye·)
be·lov·ed
Be·lo·vo (*or* Bye·) Soviet city
be·low
Bel Pa·ese cheese
Bel·sen concentration camp
Belshazzar biblical character

belt

belt
Bel·tane Celtic festival
belt·way *US* ring road
be·lu·ga sturgeon
bel·vedere building with view
bema Athenian speaker's platform
Bem·ba (*plural* ·ba *or* ·bas) African people
be·mire
be·moan
be·muse
be·mused
ben *Scot* mountain peak
Bena·dryl (*Trademark*)
Be·na·res Indian city
bench
bench·er a judge
bend (bend·ing, bent)
Ben·del Nigerian state
bend·er
Ben·di·go Australian city
bends decompression sickness
bendy (bendi·er, bendi·est)
be·neath
Ben·edi·ci·te canticle
ben·edi·ci·te blessing
Ben·edic·tine order of monks; liqueur
ben·edic·tion
ben·edic·tory
Ben·edic·tus canticle
ben·efac·tion
ben·efac·tor
ben·efac·tress
be·nef·ic *rare variant of* beneficient
ben·efice
be·nefi·cence
be·nefi·cent
ben·efi·cial
ben·efi·cial·ly
bene·fi·ciary (*plural* ·ciaries)
ben·efit
Bene·lux
Be·ne·ven·to Italian city
be·nevo·lence
be·nevo·lent
Ben·gal
Ben·ga·lese
Ben·ga·li

ben·ga·line fabric
Ben·gha·zi (*or* ·ga·si) Libyan port
be·night·ed
be·nign
be·nig·nan·cy
be·nig·nant
be·nig·nity (*plural* ·nities)
Be·nin African republic
beni·son
ben·ne plant
Ben Ne·vis
ben·ny *Slang* amphetamine tablet
Be·no·ni South African city
bent
ben·thic
ben·thos (*or* ·thon) biology term
ben·ton·ite clay
bent·wood
Be·nue Nigerian state
be·numb
ben·zal·de·hyde
Ben·ze·drine (*Trademark*)
ben·zene chemical compound; *compare* benzine
ben·zi·dine
ben·zine (*or* ·zin) petrol; *compare* benzene
ben·zo·ate
ben·zo·caine anaesthetic
Ben·zo·drine (*Trademark*)
ben·zo·fu·ran
ben·zo·ic
ben·zo·in gum resin
ben·zol (*or* ·zole)
ben·zo·phe·none
ben·zo·qui·none
ben·zo·yl
ben·zyl
Beo·wulf epic poem
be·queath
be·queath·er
be·quest
Be·rar Indian region
be·rate
Ber·ber Caucasoid Muslim
Ber·bera Somalian port
ber·beri·da·ceous botany term
ber·ber·ine alkaloid

ber·ber·is shrub
ber·ceuse lullaby
Berch·tes·ga·den West German town
be·reave
be·reave·ment
be·reft
be·ret
Be·rez·ni·ki Soviet city
berg iceberg; mountain; *compare* burg; burgh
Ber·ga·mo Italian city
ber·ga·mot tree; oil
Ber·gen Norwegian port
berg·schrund crevasse in glacier
beri·beri disease
Bering Arctic sea and strait
berk *variant spelling of* burk
Berkeley Californian city
ber·kelium radioactive element
Berk·shire
Ber·lin
berm narrow ledge
Ber·mu·da
Bern (*or* Berne) Swiss capital
Ber·nese
ber·ry (*noun, plural* ·ries; *verb* ·ries, ·ry·ing, ·ried)
ber·sa·gliere Italian soldier
ber·seem plant
ber·serk
berth
Ber·wick former Scottish county
Berwick-upon-Tweed English town
ber·yl mineral
ber·yl·ine
be·ryl·lium chemical element
Bes Egyptian god
Be·san·çon French city
be·seech (·seech·ing, ·sought)
be·set (·set·ting, ·set)
be·side
be·sides
be·siege
be·sieg·er
be·smear
be·smirch

be·som
be·sot·ted
be·span·gle
be·spat·ter
be·speak (·speak·ing, ·spoke, spo·ken or ·spoke)
be·spec·ta·cled
be·spoke
be·spread
be·sprent sprinkled over
be·sprin·kle
Bes·sa·ra·bia Soviet region
best
bes·tial
bes·ti·al·ity (*plural* ·ities)
bes·ti·al·ize (*or* ·ise)
bes·tial·ly
bes·ti·ary (*plural* ·aries)
be·stir (·stir·ring, ·stirred)
be·stow
be·stow·al (*or* ·ment)
be·stow·er
be·strew (·strew·ing, ·strewed, ·strewn *or* ·strewed)
be·stride (·strid·ing, ·strode *or* ·strid, ·strid·den *or* ·strid)
bet (bet·ting, bet *or* bet·ted)
beta
be·ta·ine alkaloid
be·take (·tak·ing, ·took, ·tak·en)
be·ta·tron particle accelerator
be·tel plant
Be·tel·geuse (*or* ·geux) star
bête noire (*plural* bêtes noires) pet hate
beth Hebrew letter
Betha·ny biblical village
Beth·el biblical town
Beth·le·hem
be·tide
bê·tise folly
be·to·ken
beto·ny (*plural* ·nies) plant
be·took
be·tray
be·tray·al
be·tray·er

be·troth
be·troth·al
be·trothed
bet·ta fish
bet·ter improved
bett·er one who bets
bet·ter·ment
betu·la·ceous botany term
be·tween
be·tween·times
be·twixt
Beu·lah biblical place
beva·tron synchrotron
bev·el (·el·ling, ·elled; *US* ·el·ing, ·eled)
bev·er·age
Bev·er·ly Hills Californian city
bev·vy (*plural* ·vies) *Dialect* alcoholic drink
bevy (*plural* bevies) flock
be·wail
be·wail·er
be·ware
be·wil·der
be·wil·der·ing·ly
be·wil·der·ment
be·witch
be·witch·ing·ly
bey Turkish title
Bey·og·lu district of Istanbul
be·yond
bez·ant gold coin
bez·el face of tool or gem
be·zique card game
be·zoar hairball
Bha·gal·pur Indian city
Bha·ga·vad-Gita Hindu text
bhang narcotic
Bha·rat *Hindi* India
Bha·ra·ti·ya Indian
Bhat·pa·ra Indian city
bha·van house
Bhav·na·gar Indian port
bhin·di vegetable
Bho·pal Indian port
Bhu·ba·nes·war Indian city
Bhu·tan Asian kingdom
Bhu·tan·ese
Bi·afra Nigerian region
Bia·ly·stok Polish city
bi·an·nual twice a year; *compare* biennial

bi·an·nual·ly
bi·an·nu·late zoology term
Biar·ritz French town
bias (·as·ing, ·ased *or* ·as·sing, ·assed)
bi·ath·lon sport
bi·auricu·late (*or* ·lar)
bi·ax·ial
bib (bib·bing, bibbed)
bib·ber
bib·cock tap with nozzle
bi·belot trinket
Bi·ble
bib·li·cal
Bib·li·cist
bib·lio·graph·er (*or* ·graph)
bib·lio·graph·ic (*or* ·graphi·cal)
bib·li·og·ra·phy (*plural* ·phies)
bib·li·ola·try
bib·lio·man·cy
bib·lio·ma·nia
bib·lio·ma·ni·ac
bib·lio·phile (*or* ·phil)
bib·li·ophi·lis·tic
bib·li·oph·ism
bib·lio·pole (*or* ·li·opo·list) dealer in rare books
bib·lio·the·ca (*plural* ·cas *or* ·cae) library
bibu·lous
bi·cam·er·al
bi·cap·su·lar
bicarb
bi·car·bo·nate
bice blue colour
bi·cen·tenary (*plural* ·tenaries)
bi·cepha·lous two-headed
bi·ceps (*plural* ·ceps *or* ·cepses)
bi·chlo·ride
bi·cip·i·tal of the biceps
bick·er
bick·er·er
bi·col·lat·er·al
bi·col·our (*or* ·oured; *US* ·or *or* ·ored)
bi·con·cave
bi·con·cav·ity
bi·con·vex

bicorn 46

bi·corn (*or* ·cor·nate, ·cor·nu·ate)
bi·cus·pid
bi·cus·pi·date
bi·cy·cle
bi·cy·clic (*or* ·cli·cal)
bi·cy·clist (*or* ·cler)
bid (bid·ding; bad, bade, *or* bid; bid·den *or* bid)
bi·dar·ka (*or* ·kee) Eskimo canoe
bid·dable
bid·der
bid·dy (*plural* ·dies)
bide (bid·ing, bid·ed *or* bode, bid·ed)
bi·den·tate
bi·det
Bie·der·mei·er furniture and art style
(biege) *incorrect spelling of* beige
Biel Swiss town
bield *Dialect* refuge
Bie·lefeld West German city
Bielskó-Biala Polish town
bi·en·nial every two years; *compare* biannual
bi·en·nial·ly
bier coffin support; *compare* byre
bier·kel·ler
bi·fa·cial
bi·fari·ous botany term
biff
bif·fin apple
bi·fid divided into two lobes
bi·fid·ity
bi·fi·lar having two parallel threads
bi·flag·el·late biology term
bi·fo·cal
bi·fo·cals
bi·fo·li·ate having two leaves
bi·fo·lio·late having two leaflets
bi·fo·rate having two openings
bi·form
Bif·rost Norse mythological rainbow
bi·fur·cate forked
bi·fur·ca·tion
big (big·ger, big·gest)

biga·mist
biga·mous
biga·my (*plural* ·mies)
big·ar·reau cherry
bi·gen·er hybrid organism
bi·gener·ic
big·eye fish
big·ger
big·gest
big·gin close-fitting cap
big·gish
big·head
big·headed
big·headed·ness
big·horn (*plural* ·horns *or* ·horn)
bight bay; bend in rope; *compare* bite; byte
big·mouth
big·no·nia shrub
big·no·nia·ceous
big·ot
big·ot·ed
big·ot·ry (*plural* ·ries)
bi·gua·nide biochemical compound
big·wig
Bi·har Indian state
Bi·ha·ri
Bi·ja·pur Indian city
bi·jec·tion maths term
bi·jec·tive
bi·jou (*plural* ·joux)
bi·jou·terie jewellery
bi·ju·gate (*or* ·gous) botany term
Bi·ka·ner Indian city
bike
bi·ki·ni
bi·la·bial
bi·la·bi·ate
bil·an·der cargo ship
bi·lat·er·al
bi·lat·er·al·ly
Bil·bao Spanish port
bil·berry (*plural* ·berries)
bil·boes ankle shackles
bile
bile·stone
bilge
bil·har·zia parasite
bil·har·zia·sis
bili·ary
bi·lin·ear
bi·lin·gual

bi·lin·gual·ism
bili·ous
bil·ious·ness
bili·ru·bin bile pigment
bili·ver·din bile pigment
bilk thwart
bilk·er
bill
bil·la·bong
bill·board
bil·let
billet-doux (*plural* billets-doux) love letter
bill·fish (*plural* ·fish *or* ·fishes)
bill·fold
bill·hook
bil·liard
bill·ing
Bil·lings·gate
bil·lion (*plural* ·lions *or* ·lion)
bil·lion·aire
bil·lionth
bil·lon alloy
bil·low
bil·lowi·ness
bil·lowy
bill·poster
bil·ly (*plural* ·lies)
bil·ly·can
bill·yo slang term
bi·lo·bate (*or* ·lobed)
bi·locu·lar (*or* ·late)
Bim native of Barbados
bima·nous two-handed
bim·bo (*plural* ·bos *or* ·boes)
bi·mes·trial lasting two months
bi·me·tal·lic
bi·met·al·lism economic doctrine
bi·mo·lec·u·lar
bi·month·ly (*plural* ·lies)
bi·morph electronics term
bin (bin·ning, binned)
bi·nal twofold
bi·na·ry (*plural* ·ries)
bi·nate occurring in pairs
bin·aural
bind (bind·ing, bound)
bind·er
bind·ery (*plural* ·eries)
bindi-eye plant

birthwort

bind·weed
bine *botany term*
binge
bin·gey *Austral* stomach
bin·gle *Austral* minor crash
bin·go
bin·na·cle
binned
bin·ning
bin·ocu·lar (*adj*)
bin·ocu·lars
bi·no·mial
bi·nomi·nal biology term
bint *Slang* girl
bin·tu·rong animal
bi·nu·cle·ar
bi·nu·cle·ate
bio·assay
bio·as·tro·nau·tics
bio·cata·lyst
bio·cata·lyt·ic
bi·oc·el·late biology term
bio·cenol·ogy branch of ecology
bio·chemi·cal
bio·chemi·cal·ly
bio·chem·ist
bio·chem·is·try
bio·cid·al
bio·cide
bio·cli·ma·tol·ogy
bio·cy·cle ecological region
bio·degrad·able
bio·deg·ra·da·tion
bio·dy·nam·ic (*or* ·nami·cal)
bio·dy·nam·ics
bio·en·er·get·ics
bio·en·gi·neer
bio·en·gi·neer·ing
bio·feed·back
bio·fla·vo·noid vitamin
bio·gen hypothetical protein
bio·gen·esis
bio·genet·ic (*or* bio·geneti·cal, biog·enous)
bio·geneti·cal·ly
bio·geo·graphi·cal
bio·geog·ra·phy
bi·og·ra·pher
bio·graphi·cal
bi·og·ra·phy (*plural* ·phies)
bio·herm organic rock

bio·logi·cal (*or* ·log·ic)
bio·logi·cal·ly
bi·olo·gist
bi·ol·ogy
bio·lu·mi·nes·cence
bio·lu·mi·nes·cent
bi·oly·sis
bio·lyt·ic
bio·mass ecology term
bi·ome ecology term
bio·met·ric
bio·met·ri·cal·ly
bi·om·etry (*or* bio·met·rics)
bi·on·ic
bi·on·ics
bio·nom·ic
bio·nomi·cal·ly
bio·nom·ics ecology
bi·ono·mist
bio·physi·cal
bio·physi·cist
bio·phys·ics
bio·plasm
bio·plas·mic
bio·poi·esis biology term
bi·op·sy (*plural* ·sies)
bi·op·tic
bio·rhythm
bio·scope
bi·os·co·py (*plural* ·pies)
bio·sphere ecology term
bio·stat·ic
bio·stati·cal·ly
bio·stat·ics
bio·strome fossil-rich rock
bio·syn·the·sis
bio·syn·thet·ic
bio·syn·theti·cal·ly
bio·ta biology term
bio·tech·no·logi·cal
bio·tech·nolo·gist
bio·tech·nol·ogy
bi·ot·ic
bio·tin vitamin
bio·tite mineral
bio·tit·ic
bio·tope ecological area
bio·type biology term
bio·typ·ic
bi·pa·ri·etal
bip·ar·ous
bi·par·ti·san (*or* ·zan)
bi·par·ti·san·ship (*or* ·zan·)

bi·par·tite
bi·par·ti·tion
bi·ped
bi·ped·al
bi·pet·al·ous
bi·phen·yl
bi·pin·nate *botany term*
bi·plane
bi·pod
bi·po·lar
bi·pro·pel·lant
bi·quad·rate maths term
bi·quad·rat·ic
bi·quar·ter·ly
bi·ra·cial
bi·ra·dial
bi·ra·mous divided into two parts
birch
bird
bird·bath
bird-brained
bird·cage
bird·house
birdie
bird·like
bird·lime
bird·man (*plural* ·men)
bird·seed
bird's-eye (*adj*)
bird's-foot (*or* bird-; *plural* -foots) plant
bird-watcher
bird-watching
bi·refrin·gence
bi·refrin·gent
bi·reme ship
bi·ret·ta (*or* ber·ret·ta) clerical cap
bi·ria·ni Indian food
Bir·ken·head
Bir·ming·ham
Biro (*Trademark*; *plural* Biros)
Bi·ro·bi·dzhan Soviet city
birr make whirring sound; *compare* bur; burr
birth
birth·day
birth·mark
birth·place
birth·right
birth·root plant
birth·stone
birth·wort plant

Biscay

Bis·cay (Bay of)
bis·cuit
bise wind
bi·sect
bi·sec·tion
bi·sec·tor
bi·sec·trix (*plural* ·tri·ces) maths term
bi·ser·rate botany term
bi·sex·ual
bi·sexu·al·ism (*or* ·ity)
bish *Slang* mistake
bish·op
bishop·bird
bish·op·ric
Bis·kra Algerian town
Bis·marck US city
bis·muth
bis·muth·al
bis·mu·thic
bis·muth·in·ite mineral
bis·muth·ous
bi·son (*plural* ·son)
bisque colour; soup; sports term
Bis·sau (*or* ·sao) capital of Guinea-Bissau
bis·sex·tile of a leap year
bis·ter US *spelling of* bistre
bis·tort plant
bis·tou·ry (*plural* ·ries) surgical knife
bis·tre (*US* ·ter) drawing pigment
bis·tro (*plural* ·tros) restaurant
bi·sul·cate cleft
bi·sul·phate (*US* ·fate)
bi·sul·phide (*US* ·fide)
bi·sul·phite (*US* ·fite)
bi·sym·met·ric (*or* ·ri·cal)
bi·sym·met·ri·cal·ly
bi·sym·met·ry
bit
bi·tar·trate
bitch
bitchi·ly
bitchy (bitchi·er, bitchi·est)
bite (bit·ing, bit, bit·ten) grip with teeth; *compare* bight; byte
Bi·thynia ancient Asian country
bit·ing·ly

bit·ing·ness
bit·ser *Austral* mongrel dog
bit·stock
bitt mooring post
bit·ten
bit·ter
Bit·ter Lakes
bit·ter·ling fish
bit·tern bird
bit·ter·ness
bitter·nut
bit·ters drink
bitter·sweet
bitter·weed
bitter·wood
bit·ty (·ti·er, ·ti·est)
bi·tu·men
bi·tu·mi·ni·za·tion (*or* ·sa·tion)
bi·tu·mi·nize (*or* ·nise)
bi·tu·mi·nous
bi·va·len·cy
bi·va·lent
bi·valve
bi·val·vu·lar
bivou·ac (·ack·ing, ·acked)
biv·vy (*plural* ·vies) *Slang* tent
bi·week·ly (*plural* ·lies)
bi·year·ly
Biysk (*or* Biisk, Bisk) Soviet town
bi·zarre
Bi·zer·te (*or* ·ta) Tunisian port
blab (blab·bing, blabbed)
blab·ber
blabber·mouth
black
black·ball
black·berry (*plural* ·berries)
black·bird
black·board
black·buck antelope
Black·burn
black·butt tree
black·cap bird
black·cock male grouse
black·cur·rant
black·damp
black·en
black·fish (*plural* ·fish *or* ·fishes)

black·fly (*plural* ·flies)
Black·foot (*plural* ·feet *or* ·foot) American Indian
black·guard
black·guard·ism
black·guard·ly
black·head
black·heart plant disease
black-hearted
black·ing
black·ish
black·jack
black·leg (·leg·ging, ·legged)
black·list
black·mail
black·mail·er
black-market (*verb*)
black·ness
black·out
black·poll bird
Black·pool
Black·shirt fascist
black·smith
black·snake
black·tail deer
black·thorn
black·top US paving material
Black·wood bridge term
black·wood Australian tree
blad·der
blad·der·ket·mia plant
bladder·nose seal
bladder·nut
bladder·wort
bladder·wrack
blade
blah silly talk
blain blister
blam·able (*or* blame·)
blame
blame·ful
blame·ful·ness
blame·less
blame·less·ness
blame·worthi·ness
blame·worthy
blanch make white; *compare* blench
blanc·mange
bland
blan·dish
blan·dish·ment
bland·ness

blank
blan·ket
blank·ly
Blan·tyre-Limbe Malawian city
blare
blar·ney
bla·sé indifferent
blas·pheme
blas·phem·er
blas·phe·mous
blas·phe·my (*plural* ·**mies**)
blast
blasted
blas·te·ma (*plural* ·**mas** *or* ·**ma·ta**) biology term
blas·tem·ic
blast·ing
blas·to·coel (*or* ·**coele**) embryology term
blas·to·cyst
blas·to·derm (*or* ·**disc**) embryology term
blas·to·derm·ic
blast·off
blas·to·gen·esis
blas·to·gen·ic (*or* ·**genet·ic**)
blas·to·mere embryology term
blas·to·mer·ic
blas·to·pore embryology term
blas·to·por·ic (*or* ·**al**)
blas·to·sphere
blas·tu·la (*plural* ·**las** *or* ·**lae**) embryology term
blas·tu·lar
blat *US* bleat
bla·tan·cy
bla·tant
blath·er (*or* **bleth**·)
blather·skite talkative person
blau·bok (*plural* ·**bok** *or* ·**boks**) antelope
Blay·don English town
blaze
blaz·er
bla·zon
bla·zon·ry (*plural* ·**ries**)
bleach
bleach·able
bleach·er

bleak
bleak·ness
blear
bleari·ness
bleary (**bleari·er**, **bleari·est**)
bleat
bleat·er
bleat·ing·ly
bleb blister
bleed (**bleed·ing**, **bled**)
bleed·er
bleep
blem·ish
blem·ish·er
blench shy away; *compare* blanch
blench·er
blench·ing·ly
blend combine
blende type of ore
blend·er
Blen·heim West German village
blen·ni·oid fish
blen·ny (*plural* ·**nies**)
blepha·ri·tic
blepha·ri·tis inflammation of eyelids
bles·bok (*or* ·**buck**; *plural* ·**boks**, ·**bok** *or* ·**bucks**, ·**buck**) antelope
bless (**bless·ing**, **blessed** *or* **blest**)
bless·ed (*adj*)
bless·ed·ness
blest
blet fruit decay
blew
blew·its edible fungus; *compare* bluet
Bli·da Algerian city
blight
blight·er
Blighty *Slang* England
bli·mey
blimp
blimp·ish
blind
blind·age military screen
blind·er
blind·fish (*plural* ·**fish** *or* ·**fishes**)
blind·fold
blind·ing

blind·ly
blind·ness
blind·storey (*or* ·**story**)
blind·worm
blini (*or* **blin·is**) pancake
blink
blink·er
blink·ers
blink·ing
blintz (*or* **blintze**) filled pancake
blip (**blip·ping**, **blipped**)
bliss
bliss·ful
bliss·ful·ly
bliss·ful·ness
blis·ter
blis·ter·ing·ly
blithe
blithe·ness
blith·er·ing
blithe·some
blitz
blitz·krieg
bliz·zard
bloat
bloated
bloat·er
blob (**blob·bing**, **blobbed**)
bloc group of nations
block
block·ade
block·ad·er
block·age
block·board
block·bust·er
block·bust·ing
block·er
block·head
block·house
Bloem·fon·tein South African city
bloke
blond (*fem* **blonde**)
blond·ness (*fem* **blonde·ness**)
blood
blood·curdling
blood·ed
blood·fin
blood·hound
bloodi·ly
bloodi·ness
blood·less
blood-letting

bloodroot

blood·root
blood·shed
blood·shot
blood·stain
blood·stained
blood·stock
blood·stone
blood·sucker
blood·thirsti·ly
blood·thirsti·ness
blood·thirsty (·thirsti·er,
 ·thirsti·est)
blood·worm
bloody (adj bloodi·er,
 bloodi·est; verb
 blood·ies, bloody·ing,
 blood·ied)
bloody-minded
bloom
bloom·er
bloom·ers
bloom·ery (plural ·eries)
 ironworks
bloom·ing
Blooms·bury
bloop·er US blunder
blos·som
blot (blot·ting, blot·ted)
blotch
blotchi·ly
blotchi·ness
blotchy (blotchi·er,
 blotchi·est)
blot·ter
blot·to Slang drunkenly
 unconscious
blouse
blou·son
blow (blow·ing, blew,
 blown)
blow-dry (-dries, -dry·ing,
 -dried)
blow·er
blow·fish (plural ·fish or
 ·fishes)
blow·fly (plural ·flies)
blow·hard boastful person
blow·hole
blow·lamp
blown
blow·out (noun)
blow·pipe
blow·torch
blow·wave

blowy (blowi·er,
 blowi·est)
blowzi·ly (or blowsi·)
blowzi·ness (or
 blowsi·ness)
blowzy (or blowsy;
 blowzi·er, blowzi·ier or
 blowsi·er, blowsi·est)
blub (blub·bing, blubbed)
blub·ber
blub·bery
bludge Austral scrounge
bludg·eon
bludg·eon·er
blue (adj blu·er, blu·est;
 verb blue·ing or
 blu·ing, blued)
Blue·beard
blue·bell
blue·berry (plural
 ·berries)
blue·bill
blue·bird
blue-blooded
blue·bonnet Scottish hat
blue·book government
 publication
blue·bottle
blue·fish (plural ·fish or
 ·fishes)
blue·gill fish
blue·grass
blue·ing (or blu·ing)
blue·jacket
blue·ness
blue·nose US puritanical
 person
blue·print
blues
blue·stocking
blue·stone
bluet plant; compare blewits
blue·throat bird
blue·tit
blue·tongue lizard
blu·ey Austral blanket
bluff
bluff·er
bluff·ness
blu·ing variant spelling of
 blueing
blu·ish (or blue·ish)
blun·der
blun·der·buss
blun·der·er

50

blun·der·ing·ly
blunge ceramics term
blung·er
blunt
blunt·ness
blur (blur·ring, blurred)
blurb
blur·red·ly
blur·red·ness
blur·ry
blurt
blush
blush·er
blush·ing·ly
blus·ter
blus·ter·er
blus·ter·ing·ly (or ·ous·ly)
blus·tery (or ·ter·ous)
Blyth English port
B'nai B'rith Jewish society
boa
boar male pig; compare
 boor; bore
board
board·er
board·ing
board·room
board·walk US wooden
 promenade
boar·fish (plural ·fish or
 ·fishes)
boar·hound
boar·ish coarse; sensual;
 compare boorish
boar·ish·ness
boast
boast·er
boast·ful
boast·ful·ly
boast·ful·ness
boast·ing·ly
boat
boat·el waterside hotel
boat·er
boat·hook
boat·house
boat·ing
boat·load
boat·man (plural ·men)
boat·swain (or bo·sun)
bob (bob·bing, bobbed)
bob·bery (plural ·beries)
 pack of dogs
bob·bin
bob·bi·net fabric

bona fides

bob·ble
bob·by (*plural* ·bies)
bob·cat
bob·float fishing float
bob·let bobsleigh
bobo·link bird
bo·bo·tie curried dish
bob·owler *Dialect* moth
bob·sleigh (*or esp. US* ·sled)
bob·stay
bob·tail
bob·white bird
bo·cage wooded country
boc·cia bowls game
Boche *Slang* German
Bo·chum West German city
bock beer
bod *Slang* person
bode
bo·dega wine shop
bodge
bodg·er
bodgie *Austral* unruly man
Bo·dhi·satt·va Buddhist divine
bod·ice
bodi·less
bodi·ly
bod·kin
Bod·lei·an Oxford library
Bod·min
Bo·do·ni style of type
body (*noun, plural* bodies; *verb* bodies, body·ing, bod·ied)
body-centred
body-check
body-guard
body-snatcher
body-work
boehm·ite mineral
Boeo·tia region of ancient Greece
Boeo·tian
Boer Dutch South African
boeuf Bour·gui·gnon beef casserole
bof·fin
bog (bog·ging, bogged)
bo·gan *Canadian* side stream
bo·gey golf term; *compare* bogie

bo·gey (*or* **bogy**; *plural* ·geys *or* bogies) evil spirit; *compare* bogie
bogey·man (*plural* ·men)
bog·gart *Dialect* poltergeist
bog·gi·ness
bog·gle
bog·gy (·gi·er, ·gi·est)
bo·gie wheeled undercarriage; *compare* bogey
bo·gle *Dialect* bogey
Bog·nor Re·gis
bo·gong moth
Bo·gor Indonesian city
Bo·go·tá Colombian capital
bo·gus
bog·wood
bogy variant spelling of bogey
bo·hea China tea
Bo·he·mia
Bo·he·mian
Bo·hol Philippine island
boil
boil·able
boil·er
boiler·maker
boiler·plate
boiler·suit
boil·ing·ly
Bois de Bou·logne Parisian park
Boi·se US city
bois·ter·ous
bois·ter·ous·ness
bok·ma·kie·rie bird
bola weapon
Bo·land South African region
bold
bold·face (*adj*)
bold·ness
bole tree trunk; *compare* bowl
bo·lec·tion architectural term
bo·lero (*plural* ·ros)
bo·letus (*plural* ·letuses *or* ·leti) fungus
bo·lide meteor
boli·var (*plural* ·vars *or* ·vares) Venezuelan currency
Bo·livia

Bo·liv·ian
boll
bol·lard
bol·locks (*or* bal·locks)
boll·worm
bolo (*plural* bolos) knife
Bo·lo·gna Italian city
Bo·lo·gnese
bo·lom·eter
bo·lo·met·ric
bo·lo·met·ri·cal·ly
bo·lo·ney variant spelling of baloney
Bol·she·vik (*plural* ·viks *or* ·vi·ki)
Bol·she·vism
Bol·she·vist
Bol·shie (*or* ·shy)
bol·son US desert valley
bol·ster
bol·ster·er
bol·ster·ing·ly
bolt
bolt·er
Bol·ton
bol·to·nia plant
bolt·rope rope on a sail
bo·lus (*plural* ·luses) chewed food
Bol·za·no Italian city
bomb
bom·ba·ca·ceous botany term
bom·bard
bom·bar·dier
bom·bard·ment
bom·bar·don musical instrument
bom·bast
bom·bas·tic
bom·bas·ti·cal·ly
Bom·bay
bom·ba·zine
bom·be dessert
bom·bé furniture style
bomb·er
bom·bora submerged reef
bomb·shell
bomb·sight bomb-aiming device
bomb site bomb-destroyed area
bom·by·cid moth
bona fide genuine
bona fides good faith

Bonaire

Bon·aire West Indian island
bo·nan·za
Bo·na·part·ism
bona va·can·tia unclaimed goods
bon·bon
bonce Slang head
bond
bond·age
bond·ed
bond·holder
bond·maid
bond·servant
bonds·man (plural ·men)
bone
bone·black
bone·fish (plural ·fish or ·fishes)
bone·head
bone·less
bon·er Slang blunder
bone·set plant
bone·set·ter
bone·shaker
bone·yard
bon·fire
bong
bon·go (plural ·gos or ·goes) drum
bon·go (plural ·go or ·gos) antelope
bon·ho·mie
boni·ness
bon·ism
bo·ni·to (plural ·tos or ·toes) fish
bonk·ers
bon mot (plural bons mots) fitting remark
Bonn West German capital
bon·net
bon·ny (·ni·er, ·ni·est)
bon·sai (plural ·sai)
bon·sela African gift
bon·spiel curling match
bon·te·bok (plural ·boks or ·bok) antelope
bo·nus
bony (boni·er, boni·est)
bonze Buddhist priest
boo (boo·ing, booed)
boob
boo·bi·al·la shrub
boo·book owl
boo·by (plural ·bies)

booby-trap (verb; -trap·ping, -trapped)
boo·dle
booed
boo·gie
boogie-woogie
boo·hoo (·hoo·ing, ·hooed)
boo·ing
book
book·binder
book·bindery (plural ·binderies)
book·bind·ing
book·case
bookie
book·ing
book·ish
book·ish·ness
book-keeper
book-keeping
book-learning
book·let
book·louse insect
book·maker
book·making
book·mark (or ·marker)
book·plate
book·rack
book·sell·er
book·shelf (plural ·shelves)
book·shop
book·stall
book·stand
book·worm
Bool·ean type of algebra
boom
boom·er
boom·er·ang
boom·slang snake
boon
boon·docks US wild country
boon·dog·gle US do futile work
boor unpleasant person; compare boar; bore
boor·ish ill-mannered; insensitive; compare boarish
boor·ish·ness
boost
boost·er
boot

boot·black
boot·ed
bootee
Boö·tes constellation
booth
boot·lace
Boo·tle
boot·leg (·leg·ging, ·legged)
boot·leg·ger
boot·less
boot·lick
boot·lick·er
boot·loader
boot·strap
boo·ty (plural ·ties)
booze
booz·er
boozi·ness
boozy (boozi·er, boozi·est)
bop (bop·ping, bopped)
bora north wind
Bora Bora Pacific island
bo·ra·cic
bo·ra·cite mineral
bor·age plant
bo·ragi·na·ceous
bo·rak Austral nonsense
bo·rane chemical compound
bo·rate
bo·rax (plural ·raxes or ·ra·ces)
bo·ra·zon chemical compound
bor·bo·ryg·mus (plural ·mi) stomach rumbling
Bor·deaux French port; wine
Bor·delaise sauce
bor·del·lo (plural ·los)
bor·der
bor·dereau (plural ·dereaux) insurance invoice
bor·der·er
border·land
border·line
Bor·ders Scottish region
bor·dure heraldry term
bore dull person; drill hole; compare boar; bore
bo·real of the north
Boreas Greek god
bore·dom

boree tree
bor·er
bo·ric
bo·ride chemical compound
bor·ing
born given birth to
borne carried
Bor·neo Malaysian island
bor·neol chemical compound
born·ite mineral
Bor·nu Nigerian state
Bo·ro·di·no battle site
bo·ron chemical element
bo·ro·nia shrub
bo·ro·sili·cate
bor·ough
bor·row
bor·row·er
bor·stal
bort (*or* **boart, bortz**) inferior diamond
bor·zoi (*plural* ·**zois**)
bos·cage (*or* ·**kage**) thicket
bosch·vark wild pig
bosh
bosk small wood
bos·ket (*or* ·**quet**) thicket
Bos·kop prehistoric African race
bosky (**boski·er, boski·est**)
Bos·nla Yugoslav region
Bos·nian
bos·om
bos·omy
bos·on physics term
Bos·po·rus (*or* **Bos·pho·rus**) Turkish strait
boss
bos·sa nova dance
bossi·ly
bossi·ness
bossy (**bossi·er, bossi·est**)
Bos·ton
bo·sun *variant spelling of* **boatswain**
Bos·worth battle site
bot (*or* **bott**) botfly larva
bo·tani·cal (*or* ·**tan·ic**)
bota·nist
bota·nize (*or* ·**nise**)
bota·ny (*plural* ·**nies**)

bo·tar·go (*plural* ·**goes**) fish roe
botch
botch·er
botchi·ly
botchiness
botchy (**botchi·er, botchi·est**)
bot·fly (*plural* ·**flies**)
both
both·er
both·era·tion
both·er·some
bothy (*plural* **bothies**) *Scot* small shelter
bot·ryoi·dal (*or* ·**ry·ose**)
bots horse disease
Bot·swa·na
bot·tle
bottle·brush shrub
bottle·neck
bottle·nose dolphin
bot·tom
bot·tom·less
bottom·most
bot·tom·ry (*plural* ·**ries**) legal term
Bot·trop West German city
botu·lin toxin
botu·li·nus (*plural* ·**nuses**) bacterium
botu·lism
Boua·ke Ivory Coast town
bou·chée vol-au-vent
Bouches-du-Rhone French department
bou·clé knobbly yarn
bou·clée support for billiard cue
bou·doir
bouf·fant
Bou·gain·ville Pacific island
bou·gain·vil·lea (*or* ·**laea**) plant
bough
bought
bought·en *Dialect* bought
bou·gie catheter
bouil·la·baisse fish soup
bouil·lon broth
boul·der
boule gem; *compare* **boulle**
boule·vard

bovver

boule·var·di·er fashionable man
boule·verse·ment *French* upheaval
boulle (*or* **boule, buhl**) marquetry; *compare* **boule**
Bou·logne
bounce
bounc·er
bounci·ly
bounci·ness
bounc·ing
bouncy (**bounci·er, bounci·est**)
bound
bounda·ry (*plural* ·**ries**)
bound·en
bound·er
bound·less
bound·less·ness
bounds
boun·te·ous
boun·te·ous·ness
boun·ti·ful
boun·ti·ful·ness
boun·ty (*plural* ·**ties**)
bou·quet
bou·quet gar·ni (*plural* **bou·quets gar·nis**)
bour·bon US whiskey
bour·don organ stop
bourg French market town
bour·geois (*fem* ·**geoise**)
bour·geoi·sie
bourn stream
bourne (*or* **bourn**) destination; boundary
Bourne·mouth
bour·rée dance
Bourse French stock exchange
bouse (*or* **bowse**) nautical term
bou·stro·phedon alternately ordered word lines
bout
bou·tique
bou·ton·ni·ere buttonhole flower
bou·zouki
bo·vid
bo·vine
Bov·ril (*Trademark*)
bov·ver *Slang* rowdiness

bow

bow
bowd·ler·ism
bowd·leri·za·tion (or ·sa·tion)
bowd·ler·ize (or ·ise)
bow·el
bow·er
bower·bird
Bow·ery New York street and area
bow·fin fish
bow·head whale
bow·ing
bow·knot
bowl basin; wooden ball; compare bole
bow-legged
bowl·er
bowl·ful
bow·line
bowl·ing
bowls
bow·man (plural ·men)
bow·saw
bowse variant spelling of bouse
bow·ser fuel tanker
bow·shot
bow·sprit
bow·string
bow-wow
bow·yer maker of archery bows
box
box·berry (plural ·berries)
box·board
box·car US closed railway van
box·er
box·ing
box·room
box·wood
boy
boy·ar
boy·cott
boy·friend
boy·hood
boy·ish
boy·ish·ness
boy·la Aboriginal witch doctor
Boyne Irish river
boysen·berry (plural ·berries)

bra
Bra·bant Belgian province
brace
brace·let
brac·er
bra·chial of the arm
bra·chi·ate
bra·chia·tion
bra·chio·pod marine invertebrate
bra·chio·saur·us
bra·chium (plural ·chia) armlike part
brachy·cephal·ic (or ·cepha·lous) broad-headed
brachy·cepha·ly (or ·lism)
brachy·dac·tylia (or ·tyl·ism)
brachy·dac·tyl·ic
bra·chylo·gous
bra·chyl·ogy (plural ·ogies) concise style
bra·chyp·ter·ous short-winged
brachy·ur·an crustacean
brac·ing
brac·ing·ly
brack·en
brack·et
brack·ish
brack·ish·ness
Brack·nell Berkshire town
bract
bract·eal
brac·te·ate
brac·teo·late
brac·te·ole
brad small nail
brad·awl
Brad·ford
Bradshaw railway timetable
brady·car·dia abnormally slow heartbeat
brady·car·di·ac
brady·kin·in blood protein
brae Scot hill
brag (brag·ging, bragged)
Bra·ga Portuguese city
brag·ga·do·cio (plural ·cios) boasting
brag·gart
brag·ger
brag·ging·ly
Brah·ma Hindu god

Brah·man (or ·min; plural ·mans, ·min, or ·mins) Hindu caste
Brah·ma·na Hindu treatise
Brah·ma·ni (plural ·nis) woman Brahman
Brah·man·ic (or ·min·ic)
Brah·man·ism (or ·min·ism)
Brah·ma·pu·tra Asian river
Brah·min variant spelling of Brahman
Bra·hui Pakistani language
braid
braid·ed
braid·er
braid·ing
brail nautical term
Braille writing for blind
brain
brain·child (plural ·children)
braini·ness
brain·less
brain·less·ness
brain·pan
brain·sick
brain·stem
brain·storm
brain·storm·er
brain·storm·ing
brain·wash
brain·wash·er
brain·wash·ing
brainy (braini·er, braini·est)
braise cook; compare braze
brake
brakes·man (plural ·men)
bram·ble
bram·bling bird
Bram·ley apple
bran
branch
bran·chia (plural ·chiae) animal's gill
bran·chial
bran·chi·ate
branch·ing
bran·chio·pod crustacean
brand
Bran·den·burg East German city
bran·dish
bran·dish·er

54

brand·ling earthworm
brand-new
bran·dy (*plural* **·dies**)
bran·le dance
brash
brashi·ness state of being brashy
brash·ly
brash·ness
brashy (**brashi·er, brashi·est**) fragmented
Bra·sília Brazilian capital
Bra·şou Romanian city
brass
bras·sard (*or* **·sart**) armband
brass·bound
bras·se·rie
bras·si·ca vegetable
bras·si·ca·ceous
brassie (*or* **brassy**; *plural* **brassies**) golf club
bras·siere
brassi·ly
brassi·ness
brassy (**brassi·er, brassi·est**)
brat
Bra·ti·sla·va Czech city
brat·tice mining term
brat·tish·ing architectural term
brat·wurst sausage
braun·ite mineral
bra·va·do (*plural* **·does** *or* **·dos**)
brave
brave·ness
brav·ery (*plural* **·eries**)
bra·vo (*plural* **·voes** *or* **·vos**)
bra·vu·ra
braw *Scot* excellent
brawl
brawl·er
brawn
brawni·ly
brawni·ness
brawny (**brawni·er, brawni·est**)
braxy sheep disease
bray
bray·er
braze solder metal; *compare* **braise**

bra·zen
bra·zen·ness
braz·er one who brazes
bra·zi·er brass worker; charcoal-burning pot
Bra·zil
bra·zil·ein (*or* **·sil·ein**) red dye
Bra·zil·ian
brazi·lin (*or* **brasi·lin**) yellow dye
Braz·za·ville Congolese capital
breach break; gap; *compare* **breech**
bread
bread·board
bread·crumb
bread·fruit (*plural* **·fruits** *or* **·fruit**)
bread·line
bread·nut
bread·root plant
breadth
bread·winner
break (**break·ing, broke, brok·en**)
break·able
break·age
break·away
break·down
break·er
break·fast
break·front
break-in (*noun*)
break·neck
break-out (*noun*)
break·point
break·through (*noun*)
break-up (*noun*)
break·water
bream (*plural* **bream**)
breast
breast·bone
breast-feed (**-feed·ing, -fed**)
breast·pin
breast·plate
breast·stroke
breast·work fortification
breath
breatha·lyse
Breatha·lyz·er (*or* **·lys·er**) (*Trademark*)
breathe

breath·er
breathi·ly
breathi·ness
breath·ing
breath·less
breath·less·ness
breath·taking
breathy (**breathi·er, breathi·est**)
brec·cia rock
brec·ci·at·ed
Brec·on (*or* **Breck·nock**) Welsh town
Brec·on·shire (*or* **Breck·nock·shire**) former Welsh county
bred
Bre·da Dutch city
bree *Scot* thin soup
breech part of gun; buttocks (*note* **breech birth**); *compare* **breach**
breech·block
breech·clout loincloth
breeches
breech·ing harness strap
breech·loader
breech-loading
breed (**breed·ing, bred**)
breed·er
breeze
breezi·ly
breezi·ness
breezy (**breezi·er, breezi·est**)
breg·ma (*plural* **·ma·ta**) part of skull
Bre·men West German city
Brem·er·ha·ven West German port
brems·strah·lung physics term
Bren gun
Bren·ner Pass
Brent London borough
brent (*plural* **brents** *or* **brent**) goose
br'er *US dialect* brother
Bre·scia Italian city
Brest French port
breth·ren
Bret·on of Brittany
breve accent; musical note
bre·vet (**·vet·ting, ·vet·ted** *or* **·vet·ing, ·vet·ed**) military term

brevetcy

brev·et·cy
brevia·ry (*plural* ·ries)
bre·vier size of type
brevi·ros·trate ornithology term
brev·ity (*plural* ·ities)
brew
brew·age
brew·er
brew·ery (*plural* ·eries)
brew·ing
brew·is *Dialect* gravy-soaked bread
bri·ar (*or* ·er) tobacco pipe; *variant spelling of* brier
Briareus Greek giant
briar·root (*or* brier·)
brib·able (*or* bribe·able)
bribe
brib·er
brib·ery (*plural* ·eries)
bric-a-brac
brick
brick·bat
brickie *Slang* bricklayer
brick·layer
brick·laying
brick·le *Dialect* brittle
brick·work
brick·yard
bri·cole billiards term
brid·al
bride
bride·groom
brides·maid
bride·well jail
bridge
bridge·able
bridge·board
bridge·head
Bridge·port US port
bridge·work
bridg·ing
Bridg·wa·ter Somerset town
bri·die *Scot* meat pie
bri·dle
bri·dler
bri·doon horse's bit
Brie cheese
brief
brief·case
brief·ing
brief·ly
bri·er (*or* ·ar) thorny shrub; *compare* briar

bri·ery (*or* ·ary)
brig
bri·gade
briga·dier
briga·low tree
brig·and
brig·an·dine armour
brig·an·tine ship
bright
bright·en
bright·en·er
bright·ness
Bright·on
brights *US* headlights
bright·work metal car trimmings
brill (*plural* brill *or* brills)
bril·liance (*or* ·lian·cy)
bril·liant
bril·lian·tine
brim (brim·ming, brimmed)
brim·ful (*or* ·full)
brim·mer
brim·stone
brin·dle
brin·dled
brine
bring (bring·ing, brought)
brini·ness
brink
brink·man·ship
brin·ny (*plural* ·nies) *Austral* a stone
briny (brini·er, brini·est)
bri·oche
brio·lette jewel
bri·quette
bri·sance power of explosion
Bris·bane
brise-soleil window protection
brisk
bris·ket
bris·ling fish
bris·tle
bristle-grass
bristle·tail insect
bris·tly
Bris·tol
bris·tols *Slang* breasts
Brit *Slang* Briton
brit young herring
Brit·ain

Bri·tan·nia
Bri·tan·nic
Briti·cism
Brit·ish
Brit·ish·er
Brit·ish·ism
Brit·on
Brit·ta·ny
brit·tle
brit·tle·ness
brittle-star starfish
Brno Czech city
broach raise topic; tap container; *compare* brooch
broach·er
broad
broad·bill bird
broad·brim hat
broad·cast (cast·ing, ·cast *or* ·cast·ed)
broad·cast·er
broad·cloth
broad·en
broad·leaf (*plural* ·leaves) tobacco plant
broad-leaved denoting nonconiferous trees
broad·loom
broad·ly
broad-minded
broad-minded·ness
Broad·moor
Broads East Anglian lakes
broad·sheet
broad·side
broad·sword
broad·tail Persian lamb
Broad·way
Brob·ding·nag
bro·cade
broca·telle brocade
broc·co·li
broch Scottish tower
bro·ché woven with raised design
bro·chette skewer
bro·chure
brock badger
brock·et deer
brod·dle *Dialect* poke
bro·de·rie an·glaise
Broeder·bond South African society
bro·gan boot
brogue

broil
broil·er
broke
bro·ken
broken-down
broken-hearted
bro·ker
bro·ker·age
brol·ga bird
brol·ly (*plural* ·lies)
bro·mal sedative
bro·mate
brome grass
bro·melia·ceous
bro·meli·ad botany term
brom·eo·sin dye
bro·mic
bro·mide
bro·mid·ic dull
bro·min·ate chemistry term
bro·mina·tion
bro·mine chemical element
bro·mism (*or* bro·min·ism) bromine poisoning
bro·mo·form chemical compound
Broms·grove English town
bron·chi *plural of* bronchus
bron·chia bronchial tubes
bron·chial
bron·chi·ec·ta·sis bronchial disease
bron·chio·lar
bron·chi·ole
bron·chit·ic
bron·chi·tis
bron·cho·pneu·mo·nia
bron·cho·scope
bron·cho·scop·ic
bron·chos·co·pist
bron·chos·co·py
bron·chus (*plural* ·chi)
bron·co (*or* ·cho; *plural* ·cos *or* ·chos) wild pony
bronco-buster
bron·to·sau·rus (*or* ·to·saur)
Bronx New York borough
bronze
bronzy
brooch piece of jewellery; *compare* broach
brood
brood·er

broodi·ness
broody (broodi·er, broodi·est)
brook
brook·able
brook·ite mineral
brook·let
brook·lime trailing plant
Brook·lyn New York borough
brook·weed
broom
broom·corn sorghum
broom·rape plant
broom·stick
brose *Scot* porridge
broth
broth·el
broth·er
brother·hood
brother-in-law (*plural* brothers-)
broth·er·li·ness
broth·er·ly
brough·am carriage
brought
brou·ha·ha
brow
brow·band part of bridle
brow·beat (·beat·ing, ·beat, ·beat·en)
brown
browned-off
Brownie junior Guide
brownie chocolate cake
brown·ing
brown·ish
brown·out *US* power reduction
browse
brows·er
bru·cel·lo·sis
bruc·ine alkaloid
Bruges Belgian city
bru·in
bruise
bruised
bruis·er
bruis·ing
bruit *Archaic* report
bru·mal wintry
brume mist
Brum·ma·gem *Slang* Birmingham

Brum·mie *Slang* Birmingham native
brum·ous
brunch
Bru·nei Malaysian state
bru·nette
Brunhild (*or* Brünnhilde) legendary queen
Bruns·wick West German city
brunt
brush
brush·er
brush·off (*noun*)
brush-up (*noun*)
brush·wood
brush·work
brusque
brusque·ness
Brus·sels
brut denoting dry champagne
bru·tal
bru·tal·ity (*plural* ·ities)
bru·tali·za·tion (*or* ·sa·tion)
bru·tal·ize (*or* ·ise)
bru·tal·ly
brute
bru·ti·fy (·fies, ·fy·ing, ·fied) brutalize
brut·ish
brut·ish·ness
Bry·ansk Soviet city
bryo·logi·cal
bry·olo·gist
bry·ol·ogy study of mosses
bryo·ny (*or* brio·; *plural* ·nies)
bryo·phyte botany term
bryo·phyt·ic
bryo·zoan invertebrate animal
Bry·thon·ic language group
bu·bal (*or* bu·ba·lis) antelope
bu·ba·line
bub·ble
bub·bler
bub·bly (·bli·er, ·bli·est)
bubo (*plural* buboes) swelling
bu·bon·ic
bu·bono·cele medical term

Bucaramanga

Bu·ca·ra·man·ga Colombian city
buc·cal of the cheek
buc·ca·neer
buc·ci·na·tor muscle
bu·cen·taur Venetian barge
Bu·cha·rest Romanian capital
Buch·en·wald concentration camp
bu·chu shrub
buck
bucka·roo US cowboy
buck·bean
buck·board carriage
buck·et
buck·et·ful (*plural* ·fuls)
buck·eye tree
buck·horn
buck·hound
Buck·ing·ham
Buck·ing·ham·shire
buck·jump·er *Austral* untamed horse
buck·le
buckler-fern
buck·ling bloater
bucko *Irish* young fellow
buck·ram (ram·ing, ·ramed)
buck·saw
buck·shee
buck·shot
buck·skin
buck·thorn
buck·tooth (*plural* ·teeth)
buck·wheat
bu·col·ic
bu·coli·cal·ly
bud (bud·ding, bud·ded)
Bu·da·pest Hungarian capital
Bud·dhism
Bud·dhist
bud·ding
bud·dle trough
bud·dleia
bud·dy (*plural* ·dies)
budge
budg·eri·gar
budg·et
budgie
Bue·na·ven·tu·ra Colombian port
Bue·nos Aires
buff
Buf·fa·lo port in New York State
buf·fa·lo (*plural* ·loes, ·los, *or* ·lo)
buff·er
buf·fet restaurant; sideboard
buf·fet (·fet·ing, ·fet·ed) to batter; a blow
buf·fet·er
buffle·head duck
buf·foon
buf·foon·ery
bug (bug·ging, bugged)
buga·boo source of fear
Bu·gan·da Ugandan state
bug·bane plant
bug·bear
bugged
bug·ger
bug·gery
bug·ging
bug·gy (*noun, plural* ·gies; *adj* ·gi·er, ·gi·est)
bu·gle
bu·gler
bugle·weed
bu·gloss
buhl *variant spelling of* boulle
buhr·stone (*or* bur· *or* burr·)
build (build·ing, built)
build·er
build·ing
build-up (*noun*)
built
built-in
built-up
(buisness) *incorrect spelling of* business
Bu·jum·bu·ra capital of Burundi
Bu·kha·ra (*or* Bo·) Soviet city
Bu·ko·vi·na (*or* ·co·) E European region
Bu·la·wa·yo Zimbabwean city
bul·ba·ceous
bulb·ar
bulb·if·er·ous
bul·bil (*or* ·bel) small bulb
bulb·ous
bul·bul bird
Bul·garia
Bul·gar·ian
bulge
bulgi·ness
bulg·ing·ly
bulgy
bu·limia insatiable hunger
bulk
bulk·head
bulki·ly
bulki·ness
bulky (bulki·er, bulki·est)
bull
bul·la (*plural* ·lae) seal on papal bull; blister
bul·lace damson
bul·late blistered
bull·bat bird
bull·dog
bull·doze
bull·doz·er
bul·let
bul·letin
bullet·proof
bull·fight
bull·fighter
bull·fighting
bull·finch
bull·frog
bull·head fish
bul·lion
bull·ish
bull-necked
bull·ock
bull·pen
bull·ring
bull's-eye
bull·shit
bull·whip
bul·ly (*noun, plural* ·lies; *verb* ·lies, ·ly·ing, ·lied)
bully·rag (·rag·ging, ·ragged)
bul·rush
bul·wark
bum (bum·ming, bummed)
bum·bailiff
bum·ble
bumble·bee
bum·bler
bum·boat
bum·ma·lo (*plural* ·lo) Bombay duck
bum·mer
bump

bump·er
bumph (*or* **bumf**) *Slang* documents
bumpi·ly
bumpi·ness
bump·kin
bump·tious
bump·tious·ness
bumpy (**bumpi·er, bumpi·est**)
bun
Buna (*Trademark*) rubber
bunch
bunchi·ness
bunchy (**bunchi·er, bunchi·est**)
bun·combe *US variant spelling of* **bunkum**
Bund (*plural* **Bunds** *or* **Bün·de**) federation
bund embankment
Bun·da·berg Australian city
Bun·del·khand Indian region
Bun·des·rat West German federal council
Bun·des·tag West German legislative assembly
bundh Indian strike
bun·dle
bun·dler
bun·du *S African* wild region
bung
bun·ga·low
bung·hole
bun·gle
bun·gler
bun·gling
bun·ion
bunk
bun·ker
bun·kum (*US also* **·combe**)
bun·ny (*plural* **·nies**)
bun·raku Japanese puppet theatre
Bun·sen burn·er
bunt
bunt·al straw
bunt·ing
bunt·line
bunya-bunya tree
bun·yip Australian monster
buoy

buoy·age
buoy·an·cy
buoy·ant
bu·pres·tid beetle
bur (**bur·ring, burred**) seed vessel; *compare* **birr; burr**
bu·ran blizzard
Bu·ray·dah (*or* **·rai·da**) Saudi Arabian town
Bur·ber·ry (*Trademark*; *plural* **·ries**)
bur·ble
bur·bler
bur·bot (*plural* **·bots** *or* **·bot**) fish
bur·den
bur·den·some
bur·dock
bu·reau (*plural* **·reaus** *or* **·reaux**)
bu·reau·cra·cy (*plural* **·cies**)
bu·reau·crat
bu·reau·crat·ic
bu·reau·crati·cal·ly
bu·reau·crat·ism
bu·reau·cra·tize (*or* **·tise**)
bu·rette (*or esp. US* **·ret**)
burg fortified town; *compare* **berg; burgh**
Bur·gas Bulgarian port
bur·gee ship's flag
Bur·gen·land Austrian province
bur·geon (*or* **bour·geon**)
burg·er hamburger
bur·gess citizen of borough
burgh Scottish town; *compare* **berg; burg**
burgh·al
burgh·er citizen
bur·glar
bur·glar·ize *US* burgle
bur·gla·ry (*plural* **·ries**)
bur·gle
bur·go·mas·ter
bur·go·net helmet
bur·grave German governor
Bur·gun·dian
Bur·gun·dy
bur·ial
buri·er
bu·rin chisel
burk (*or* **berk**) *Slang* fool

bur·ka Muslim garment
burke suffocate
Bur·kina Faso African country
burl small lump
bur·lap fabric
burl·er
bur·lesque (*or* **·lesk; ·lesqu·ing, ·lesqued** *or* **·lesk·ing, ·lesked**)
bur·les·quer (*or* **·lesk·er**)
bur·ley tobacco
bur·li·ness
Bur·ling·ton Canadian and US cities
bur·ly (**·li·er, ·li·est**)
Bur·ma
Bur·mese
burn (**burn·ing, burnt** *or* **burned**)
burn·er
bur·net plant
burn·ing
burn·ing·ly
bur·nish
burn·ish·able
burn·ish·er
Burn·ley Lancashire town
bur·noose (*or* **bur·nous** *or* **bur·nouse**) Arab hood
burn·sides *US* side-whiskers
burnt
bu·roo *Dialect* dole
burp
burr rough edge; small drill; dialect characteristic; *compare* **birr; bur**
bur·ra·wang plant
burred
bur·ring
bur·ro (*plural* **·ros**) donkey
bur·row
bur·row·er
bur·ry (**·ri·er, ·ri·est**) prickly
Bur·sa Turkish city
bur·sa (*plural* **·sae** *or* **·sas**) medical term; *compare* **bursar**
bur·sal
bur·sar financial official; *compare* **bursa**
bur·sar·ial
bur·sa·ry (*plural* **·ries**)
burse *Scot* student allowance

burseraceous

bur·ser·aceous botany term
bur·si·form
bur·si·tis
burst (burst·ing, burst)
burst·er
bur·ton hoisting tackle
Burton-upon-Trent
Bu·run·di African republic
bur·weed
Bury town in Greater Manchester
bury (buries, bury·ing, bur·ied)
Bur·yat Mongoloid people
Bury St Ed·munds
bus (noun, plural buses or busses; verb bus·ing or bus·sing, bused or bussed)
bus·bar electrical conductor
bus·by (plural ·bies)
bu·sera Ugandan drink
bush
bush·baby (plural ·babies)
bush·buck (or bosch·bok; plural ·bucks, ·buck or ·boks, ·bok) antelope
bush·el (·el·ing, ·elled; US ·el·ing, ·eled) unit; US mend garment
bush·el·ler (US ·el·er)
bush·hammer
Bu·shi·do samurai code
bushi·ness
bush·ing
Bu·shire Iranian port
Bush·man (plural ·man or ·men) S African people
bush·man (plural ·men) bush dweller
bush·master snake
bush·pig
bush·ranger
bush·tit bird
Bush·veld
bush·whack
bush·whacker
bushy (bushi·er, bushi·est)
busi·ly
busi·ness trade, etc.; compare busyness
business·like
business·man (plural ·men)
business·woman (plural ·women)
bus·ing (or bus·sing)
busk
busk·er
bus·kin boot
bust
bus·tard
bust·er
bus·tle
bus·tler
busty (busti·er, busti·est)
bu·suu·ti garment
busy (adj busi·er, busi·est; verb busies, busy·ing bus·ied)
busy·body (plural ·bodies)
busy Liz·zie plant
busy·ness state of being busy; compare business
but
bu·ta·di·ene
bu·tane
bu·ta·nol
bu·ta·none
butch
butch·er
butcher·bird
butcher's-broom shrub
butch·ery (plural ·eries)
bu·tene
but·ler
but·lery (plural ·leries)
butt
butte steep-sided hill
but·ter food
butt·er one that butts
but·ter·bur plant
butter·cup
butter·fat
butter·fingered
butter·fingers
butter·fish (plural ·fish or ·fishes)
butter·fly (plural ·flies)
but·ter·ine artificial butter
But·ter·mere lake
butter·milk
butter·nut
butter·scotch
butter·wort plant
but·tery (plural ·teries)
but·tock
but·ton
button·hole
button·hook
button·mould (US ·mold)
but·ton·wood
but·tress
but·ty (plural ·ties) Dialect sandwich
bu·tyl
bu·tyra·ceous
bu·tyr·al·de·hyde
bu·tyr·ate
bu·tyr·ic acid
bu·tyr·in
bux·om
bux·om·ness
Bux·ton Derbyshire town
buy (buys, buy·ing, bought)
buy·er
buzz
buz·zard
buzz·er
bwa·na
by
by-bidder
by-blow
Byd·goszcz Polish city
bye sports term; something incidental
by-election (or bye-election)
Bye·lo·rus·sia variant spelling of Belorussia
Bye·lo·rus·sian variant spelling of Belorussian
Bye·lo·vo variant spelling of Belovo
by·gone
by·law (or bye-law)
by-line
by·pass (·pass·ing, ·passed or ·past)
by·path
by-product
byre cowshed; compare bier
byr·nie armour
by·road
By·ron·ic
bys·si·no·sis lung disease
bys·sus (plural ·suses or ·si) zoology term
by·stander
by·street
byte computer term; compare bight; bite

By·tom Polish city
by·way
by·word
Byz·an·tine
By·zan·tium

C

cab
ca·bal (·**bal·ling**, ·**balled**) secret group
ca·bal·le·ro (*plural* ·**ros**)
ca·ba·na tent
Ca·ba·na·tuan Philippine city
caba·ret
cab·bage
cabbage·town city slum
cab·ba·la (*or* **ca·ba·la, kab·ba·la, ka·ba·la**) Jewish teaching
cab·ba·lism (*or* **caba·, kab·ba·, kaba·**)
cab·ba·list (*or* **caba·, kab·ba·, kaba·**)
cab·ba·lis·tic (*or* **caba·, kab·ba·, kaba·**)
cab·by (*or* **cab·bie**; *plural* ·**bies**)
ca·ber
cab·ezon (*or* ·**ezone**) fish
Ca·bi·mas Venezuelan town
cab·in
Cabi·net government
cabi·net furniture
cabinet-maker
cabinet·work
ca·ble
ca·ble·gram
cable-laid
ca·blet small cable
cable·way
cab·man (*plural* ·**men**)
cabo·chon polished gem
ca·boo·dle
ca·boose
Ca·bo·ra Bas·sa African dam
cabo·tage coastal navigation
ca·bret·ta leather
ca·bril·la fish
cab·ri·ole furniture leg
cab·rio·let horse-drawn carriage
ca·cao cocoa tree

cac·cia·to·re (*or* ·**ra**) cookery term
cacha·lot whale
cache
ca·chec·tic weakened
cache·pot flowerpot container
ca·chet
ca·chexia (*or* ·**chexy**) weakness
cach·in·nate laugh loudly
cach·in·na·tion
ca·chou lozenge; *variant of* catechu; *compare* cashew
ca·chu·cha dance
ca·cique American Indian chief
cack-handed
cack·le
cack·ler
caco·demon
caco·dyl chemical compound
caco·epy bad pronunciation
caco·ethes uncontrollable urge
caco·eth·ic
caco·gen·ics
caco·graph·ic
ca·cog·ra·phy bad handwriting
ca·col·ogy bad speech
caco·mis·tle (*or* ·**mix·le**) animal
caco·phon·ic
ca·copho·nous
ca·copho·ny (*plural* ·**nies**)
cac·ta·ceous
cac·tus (*plural* ·**tuses** *or* ·**ti**)
ca·cu·mi·nal phonetics term
cad
ca·das·ter (*or* ·**tre**) property register
ca·dav·er
ca·dav·er·ic
ca·dav·er·ine chemical compound

ca·dav·er·ous
ca·dav·er·ous·ness
cad·die (*or* ·**dy**; *noun, plural* ·**dies**; *verb* ·**dies,** ·**dy·ing**, ·**died**) golf term; *compare* caddy
cad·dis fly
cad·dis (*or* ·**dice**) textile
cad·dish
Cad·do·an language group
cad·dy (*plural* ·**dies**) tea container; *compare* caddie
cade tree
ca·delle beetle
ca·dence
ca·den·cy (*plural* ·**cies**) heraldic term
ca·dent
ca·den·za
ca·det
cadge
cadg·er
cadi Muslim judge
Cadillac (*Trademark*)
Cá·diz Spanish port
cad·mium
ca·dre trained personnel
ca·du·ceus (*plural* ·**cei**) medical emblem
ca·du·city senility
ca·du·cous biology term
cae·cal (*US* **ce·**)
cae·cil·ian amphibian
cae·cum (*US* **ce·**; *plural* ·**ca**) part of intestine
Cae·llan Roman hill
Cae·lum constellation
Caen French city
cae·no·gen·esis (*or* **cai·, kai·**; *US* **ce·** *or* **ke·**) biology term
cae·no·genet·ic (*or* **cai·, kai·**; *US* **ce·** *or* **ke·**)
caeo·ma botany term
Caer·leon Welsh town
Caer·nar·von
Caer·nar·von·shire
Caer·phil·ly

caesalpiniaceous

caes·al·pinia·ceous botany term
Caesa·rea Israeli port
Cae·sar·ean (*or* ·ian) of Caesar
Cae·sar·ean sec·tion (*or* cae·; *US* ce·sar·ean sec·tion)
Cae·sar·ism autocratic government
cae·sium (*US* ce·)
caes·pi·tose (*US* ces·) growing in tufts
cae·su·ra (*plural* ·ras *or* ·rae)
café
caf·eteria
caf·feine (*or* ·fein)
caf·tan *variant spelling of* kaftan
cage
cage·ling
cag·ey (*or* cagy; cagi·er, cagi·est)
cagi·ly
cagi·ness
Ca·glia·ri Sardinian port
cag·mag *Dialect* chat
ca·goule
ca·hier *French* notebook
ca·hoots
Caiaphas biblical character
Cai·cos West Indian islands
Cain biblical character
Cai·no·zo·ic *variant spelling of* Cenozoic
caïque boat
cairn
cairn·gorm quartz
Cairngorm Scottish mountains
Cai·ro
cais·son watertight structure
Caith·ness
cai·tiff cowardly person
ca·jole
ca·jol·ery (*plural* ·eries)
Ca·jun Acadian descendant
caju·put (*or* caj·eput) shrub
cake
cake·walk
Cala·bar Nigerian port
cala·bash tree
Ca·lab·ria Italian region

ca·la·dium plant
Cal·ais
cala·lu Caribbean leaves
cala·man·co fabric
cala·man·der wood
cala·mine lotion
cala·mint plant
cala·mite plant
ca·lami·tous
ca·lam·ity (*plural* ·ities)
cala·mon·din fruit
cala·mus (*plural* ·mi) plant; cane
cal·an·dria heat-exchanger vessel
ca·lash (*or* ·leche) carriage
cala·thus (*plural* ·thi) Greek symbol
ca·lav·er·ite mineral
cal·ca·neal (*or* ·nean)
cal·ca·neus (*or* ·neum; *plural* ·nei) heel bone
cal·car (*plural* ·caria) spur
cal·car·eous containing lime
cal·ca·rif·er·ous
cal·cei·form (*or* ·ceo·late) botany term
cal·ceo·lar·ia plant
cal·ces (*plural of* calx)
cal·cic containing calcium
cal·ci·cole lime-loving plant
cal·cico·lous
cal·cif·er·ol vitamin
cal·cif·er·ous
cal·cif·ic
cal·ci·fi·ca·tion
cal·ci·fu·gal
cal·ci·fuge acid-loving plant
cal·cifu·gous
cal·ci·fy (·fies, ·fy·ing, ·fied)
cal·ci·mine (*or* kal·so·mine) wash for walls
cal·ci·na·tion
cal·cine chemistry term
cal·cite mineral
cal·cit·ic
cal·ci·ton·in hormone
cal·cium
calc·sinter rock
cal·cu·la·bil·ity (*plural* ·ities)
cal·cu·lable

cal·cu·late
cal·cu·la·tion
cal·cu·la·tive
cal·cu·la·tor
cal·cu·lous
cal·cu·lus (*plural* ·luses) maths term
cal·cu·lus (*plural* ·li) stone in body
Cal·cut·ta
cal·dar·ium Roman bathroom
cal·de·ra volcanic crater
cal·dron *variant spelling of* cauldron
Cal·edo·nia
Cal·edo·nian
cal·efa·cient
cal·efac·tion
cal·efac·tory (*plural* ·tories)
cal·en·dar dates; *compare* colander
cal·en·der smoothing machine; *compare* colander
cal·ends (*or* kal·ends)
ca·len·du·la plant
cal·en·ture fever
calf (*plural* calves)
calf·skin
Cal·ga·ry Canadian city
Cali Colombian city
cali·brate
cali·bra·tion
cali·bra·tor (*or* ·brat·er)
cali·bre (*US* ·ber)
cali·bred (*US* ·bered)
cali·ces *plural of* calix
ca·li·che geology term
cali·co (*plural* ·coes *or* ·cos)
Cali·cut Indian port
Cali·for·nia
cali·for·nium radioactive element
cali·pash (*or* cal·li·pash) turtle meat
cali·pee turtle meat
cali·per *US spelling of* calliper
ca·liph (*or* ca·lif, ka·lif, kha·lif)
ca·li·phate (*or* ca·li·fate, ka·li·fate)
cali·sa·ya cinchona bark

cal·is·then·ic *variant spelling of* callisthenic
ca·lix (*plural* cali·ces) chalice; *compare* calyx
calk *variant spelling of* caulk
calk (*or* cal·kin) spike on shoe
call
cal·la plant
call·able
cal·lais ornamental stone
cal·lant (*or* ·lan) youth
Ca·llao Peruvian port
call·boy
call·er one who calls
cal·ler *Scot* fresh food
cal·lig·ra·pher (*or* ·phist)
cal·li·graph·ic
cal·li·graphi·cal·ly
cal·lig·ra·phy
call·ing
cal·lio·pe *US* steam organ
cal·li·pash *variant spelling of* calipash
cal·li·per (*US* cali·per)
cal·li·pyg·ian (*or* ·py·gous) having shapely buttocks
cal·lis·then·ic (*or* cal·is·)
cal·lis·then·ics (*or* cal·is·)
Cal·lis·to satellite of Jupiter
cal·los·ity (*plural* ·ities)
cal·lous (*adj*)
cal·lous·ness
cal·low
cal·low·ness
cal·lus (*noun; plural* ·luses)
calm
cal·ma·tive
calm·ness
calo·mel purgative
Cal·or (*Trademark*)
ca·lor·ic
calo·ric·ity (*plural* ·ities)
Calo·rie kilocalorie
calo·rie
calo·rif·ic
calo·rifi·cal·ly
calo·rim·eter
calo·ri·met·ric (*or* ·ri·cal)
calo·ri·met·ri·cal·ly
calo·rim·etry
ca·lotte priest's skullcap

calo·yer Greek Orthodox monk
cal·pac (*or* cal·pack, kal·pak) brimless hat
calque (calqu·ing, calqued) linguistics term
cal·trop (*or* ·trap, ·throp) plant
calu·met peace pipe
ca·lum·ni·ate
ca·lum·nia·tion
ca·lum·ni·ous (*or* ·nia·tory)
cal·um·ny (*plural* ·nies)
calu·tron physics term
Cal·va·dos French department; brandy
cal·varia top of skull
Cal·va·ry Crucifixion site
cal·va·ry (*plural* ·ries) suffering
calve (*verb*)
calves *plural of* calf
Cal·vin·ism
Cal·vin·ist
Cal·vin·is·tic
cal·vi·ti·es baldness
calx (*plural* calxes *or* cal·ces) oxide
caly·cate having a calyx
caly·cine (*or* ca·lyci·nal) of a calyx
caly·cle (*or* ca·lycu·lus; *plural* ·cles *or* ·li) biology term
Calypso mythological character
ca·lyp·so (*plural* ·sos) song
ca·lyp·tra botany term
ca·lyp·trate
ca·lyp·tro·gen
ca·lyx (*plural* ca·lyxes *or* caly·ces) sepals of plant; *compare* calix
Cam river
cam machinery
Ca·ma·güey Cuban city
ca·mail armour
ca·ma·ra·derie
cama·ril·la Spanish cabal
cam·ass (*or* ·as) plant
cam·ber
Cam·ber·well
cam·bial of cambium

cam·bist foreign-exchange dealer
cam·bist·ry (*plural* ·ries)
cam·bium (*plural* ·biums *or* ·bia) plant tissue
Cam·bo·dia
Cam·bo·dian
cam·bo·gia gum resin
cam·boose lumberjack's cabin
Cam·brai French town
Cam·bria *Latin* Wales
Cam·brian geological period
cam·bric fabric
Cam·bridge
Cam·bridge·shire
Cam·den London borough
came
cam·el
cam·el·eer
ca·mel·lia
ca·melo·pard giraffe
Ca·melo·par·dus (*or* ·da·lis) constellation
Cam·elot
Cam·em·bert cheese
cameo (*noun, plural* cameos; *verb* cameos, cameo·ing, cam·eoed)
cam·era
cam·er·al
cam·era lu·ci·da
camera·man (*plural* ·men)
cam·era ob·scu·ra
camera-ready
cam·er·len·go (*or* ·lin·go; *plural* ·gos) papal treasurer
Cam·eroon
cami·knick·ers
cami·on lorry
ca·mise smock
cami·sole
cam·let cloth
camo·mile (*or* chamo·)
ca·moo·di snake
Ca·mor·ra secret society
camou·flage
camp
Cam·pa·gna Italian plain
cam·paign
cam·paign·er
Cam·pa·nia Italian region

campanile

cam·pa·ni·le bell tower
cam·pa·nolo·gist
cam·pa·nol·ogy
cam·panu·la flower
cam·panu·la·ceous
cam·panu·late bell-shaped
Cam·peche Mexican state
camp·er
cam·pes·tral of fields
cam·phene
cam·phire henna
cam·phor
cam·pho·rate
cam·phor·ic
Cam·pi·nas Brazilian city
camp·ing
cam·pi·on
cam·po Brazilian savanna
campo·ree Scout meeting
Cam·pos Brazilian city
cam·pus (*plural* **·puses**)
cam·shaft
cam·wood
can (**can·ning, canned**)
Cana biblical town
Ca·naan biblical region
Ca·naan·ite
Cana·da
Ca·na·dian
Ca·na·di·an·ism
ca·nai·gre plant
ca·naille *French* mob
ca·nal (**·nal·ling, ·nalled**;
  US **·nal·ing, ·naled**)
cana·licu·lar
cana·licu·lus (*plural* **·li**)
  small channel
cana·li·za·tion (*or*
  ·sa·tion)
cana·lize (*or* **·lise**)
cana·pé
ca·nard rumour
ca·nary (*plural* **·naries**)
Ca·nary Is·lands (*or*
  Ca·naries)
ca·nas·ta card game
can·as·ter tobacco
Ca·nav·er·al US cape
Can·ber·ra
can·can
can·cel (**·cel·ling, ·celled**;
  US **·cel·ing, ·celed**)
can·cel·late (*or* **·lous,
  ·lat·ed**) medical term
can·cel·la·tion

can·cel·ler (*US* **·cel·er**)
Can·cer sign of zodiac
can·cer disease
can·cer·ous
can·croid
can·de·la unit
can·de·la·brum (*or* **·bra**;
  plural **·bra, ·brums,** *or*
  ·bras)
can·did
can·di·da·cy (*or* **·da·ture**)
can·di·date
can·did·ness
can·died
Can·di·ot Cretan
can·dle
candle·berry (*plural*
  ·berries)
candle·fish (*plural* **·fish** *or*
  ·fishes)
candle·light
Candle·mas
candle·nut
candle·pins bowling game
candle·power
can·dler
candle·stick
candle·wick
candle·wood
can·dour (*US* **·dor**)
can·dy (*noun, plural*
  ·dies; *verb* **·dies,
  ·dy·ing, ·died**)
candy·floss
candy-striped
candy·tuft
cane
cane·brake US thicket
ca·nel·la spice
can·er
ca·nes·cent hoary
can·field card game
cangue wooden collar
Ca·nicu·la the star Sirius
ca·nicu·lar of Sirius
ca·nine
can·ing
can·is·ter
can·ker
can·ker·ous
canker·worm
can·na plant
can·na·bic
can·na·bin
can·na·bis

Can·nae battle site
canned
can·nel coal
can·nel·lo·ni (*or* **·ne·lo·ni**)
can·ne·lure groove
can·ner
can·nery (*plural* **·neries**)
Cannes French town
can·ni·bal
can·ni·bal·ism
can·ni·bal·is·tic
can·ni·bali·za·tion (*or*
  ·sa·tion)
can·ni·bal·ize (*or* **·ise**)
can·ni·kin (*or* **cana·kin,
  cani·kin**) small can
can·ni·ly
can·ni·ness
can·ning
Can·nock Staffordshire
  town
can·non (*plural* **·nons** *or*
  ·non) artillery; *compare*
  canon
can·non·ade
cannon·ball
can·non·eer
can·non·ry (*plural* **·ries**)
  artillery; *compare* **canonry**
can·not
can·nu·la (*or* **canu·la**;
  plural **·las** *or* **·lae**)
  surgical tube
can·nu·late (*or* **canu·late**)
can·ny (**·ni·er, ·ni·est**)
ca·noe (**·noes, ·noe·ing,
  ·noed**)
ca·noe·ist
can·on priest; decree;
  compare **cannon**
can·on·ess
ca·noni·cal
ca·noni·cate office of canon
can·on·ic·ity
can·on·ist
can·oni·za·tion (*or*
  ·sa·tion)
can·on·ize (*or* **·ise**)
can·on·ry (*plural* **·ries**)
  office of canon; *compare*
  cannonry
ca·noo·dle
Ca·no·pus Egyptian port
cano·py (*noun, plural*
  ·pies; *verb* **·pies,
  ·py·ing, ·pied**)

Ca·nos·sa Italian castle
cans *Slang* headphones
cant platitudes; slope
can't cannot
can·ta·bi·le musical term
Can·ta·brian Spanish mountains
Can·ta·brig·ian of Cambridge
Can·tal French department; cheese
can·ta·la plant
can·ta·loupe (*or* ·loup)
can·tan·ker·ous
can·ta·ta
can·ta·trice singer
can·teen
can·ter
Can·ter·bury
can·thari·des (*sing.* ·tha·ris) medicine
can·thus (*plural* ·thi) corner of eye
cant·ic
can·ti·cle
can·ti·lena musical term
can·ti·lever
can·til·late
can·til·la·tion
can·ti·na Spanish bar
cant·ing
can·tle saddle part
can·to (*plural* ·tos)
Can·ton Chinese port
can·ton division of Switzerland
can·ton·al
Can·ton·ese (*plural* ·ese)
can·ton·ment
can·tor religious singer
can·tor·is musical term
can·trip magic spell
can·tus (*plural* ·tus) medieval church singing
canty *Dialect* lively
can·vas cloth
canvas·back (*plural* ·backs *or* ·back) duck
can·vass solicit
can·vass·er
can·yon
can·zo·na musical term
can·zo·ne (*plural* ·ni) song
can·zo·net song
caou·tchouc rubber

cap (cap·ping, capped)
ca·pa·bil·ity (*plural* ·ities)
ca·pable
ca·pably
ca·pa·cious
ca·paci·tance physics term
ca·paci·tate
ca·paci·ta·tion
ca·paci·tive
ca·paci·tor
ca·pac·ity (*plural* ·ities)
cap-a-pie from head to foot
ca·pari·son
cape
cap·elin (*or* cap·lin) fish
Ca·pel·la star
ca·per
cap·er·cail·lie (*or* ·cail·zie)
Ca·per·na·um Israeli town
Cape Roca Portuguese cape
cape·skin
Capet French dynasty
Ca·petian
Cape Verde island country
ca·pi·as legal term
cap·il·la·ceous hairy
cap·il·lar·ity surface tension
ca·pil·lary (*plural* ·laries)
capi·tal
capi·tal·ism
capi·tal·ist
capi·tal·is·tic
capi·tali·za·tion (*or* ·sa·tion)
capi·tal·ize (*or* ·ise)
capi·tal·ly
capi·tate headlike
capi·ta·tion
capi·ta·tive
Capi·tol US Congress building
Capi·to·line Roman hill
ca·pitu·lar
ca·pitu·lary (*plural* ·laries)
ca·pitu·late
ca·pitu·la·tion
ca·pitu·la·tor
ca·pitu·lum (*plural* ·la) biology term
capo (*plural* capos) guitar attachment
ca·pon
ca·pon·ize (*or* ·ise)

capo·ral tobacco; *compare* corporal
ca·pote cloak
Cap·pa·do·cia ancient Asian region
cap·pa·ri·da·ceous botany term
capped
cap·per
cap·pie *Scot* ice-cream cone
cap·ping
cap·puc·ci·no (*plural* ·nos)
cap·reo·late botany term
Ca·pri
ca·pric·cio (*plural* ·cios *or* ·ci) musical work
ca·pric·cio·so musical term
ca·price
ca·pri·cious
ca·pri·cious·ness
Cap·ri·corn sign of zodiac
Cap·ri·cor·nus (*plural* ·ni) constellation
cap·ri·fi·ca·tion
cap·ri·fig wild fig
cap·ri·fo·lia·ceous botany term
cap·rine of goats
cap·ri·ole
cap·sai·cin alkaloid
cap·si·cum
cap·sid plant bug
cap·size
cap·stan
cap·stone (*or* cope·)
cap·su·lar
cap·su·late (*or* ·lat·ed)
cap·su·la·tion
cap·sule
cap·sul·ize (*or* ·ise)
cap·tain
cap·tain·cy (*or* ·tain·ship; *plural* ·cies *or* ·ships)
cap·tion
cap·tious
cap·ti·vate
cap·ti·va·tion
cap·ti·va·tor
cap·tive
cap·tiv·ity (*plural* ·ities)
cap·tor
cap·ture
Capua Italian town
ca·puche friar's hood

Capuchin

Capu·chin friar
capu·chin monkey
ca·put (*plural* **capi·ta**) head; *compare* **kaput**
capy·ba·ra rodent
car
cara·bao water buffalo
cara·bid beetle
cara·bi·neer (*or* **·nier**) *variants of* **carbineer**
ca·ra·bi·nie·re (*plural* **·ri**) Italian policeman
cara·cal lynx
ca·ra·ca·ra bird
Ca·ra·cas Venezuelan capital
cara·cole (*or* **·col**) dressage term
cara·cul fur; *variant spelling of* **karakul**
ca·rafe
cara·geen *variant spelling of* **carrageen**
ca·ram·ba (*or* **·bo·la**) tree; fruit
cara·mel
cara·mel·ize (*or* **·ise**)
ca·ran·gid (*or* **·goid**) fish
cara·pace
car·at weight; *compare* **caret**
cara·van (**·van·ning**, **·vanned**)
cara·van·se·rai (*or* **·sa·ry**; *plural* **·rais** *or* **·ries**)
cara·vel (*or* **car·vel**) ship
cara·way
car·ba·mate
car·bami·dine
car·ban·ion chemistry term
car·ba·zole
car·bene chemistry term
car·bide
car·bine rifle
car·bi·neer (*or* **cara·bi·neer**, **cara·bi·nier**) soldier
car·bo·hy·drate
car·bo·lat·ed
car·bol·ic
car·bo·lize (*or* **·lise**)
car·bon
car·bo·na·ceous
car·bo·nade beef stew
car·bo·na·do (*noun*, *plural* **·does** *or* **·dos**; *verb*

·do·ing, **·doed**) grilled meat; industrial diamond
Car·bo·na·ri political society
car·bon·ate
car·bona·tion
car·bon·ic
car·bon·if·er·ous
car·boni·za·tion (*or* **·sa·tion**)
car·bon·ize (*or* **·ise**)
car·bon·ous
car·bon·yl
Car·bo·run·dum (*Trademark*)
car·box·yl
car·box·yl·ase enzyme
car·box·yl·ate
car·box·yl·ic
car·boy large bottle
car·bun·cle
car·bun·cu·lar
car·bu·ra·tion
car·bu·ret (**·ret·ting**, **·ret·ted**; *US* **·ret·ing**, **·ret·ed**)
car·bu·ret·tor (*or* **·ter**; *US* **·retor**)
car·bu·ri·za·tion (*or* **·sa·tion**)
car·bu·rize (*or* **·rise**)
car·byla·mine
car·cass (*or* **·case**)
Car·chem·ish ancient Syrian city
car·cino·gen
car·cino·gen·ic
car·ci·no·ma (*plural* **·mas** *or* **·ma·ta**)
car·ci·no·ma·toid (*or* **·tous**)
car·ci·no·ma·to·sis
card
car·da·mom (*or* **·mum**, **·mon**) spice
card·board
card-carrying
car·di·ac
car·di·al·gia heart pain
car·di·al·gic
Car·diff
Car·di·gan Welsh bay
car·di·gan
car·di·nal
car·di·nal·ate (*or* **·ship**)

car·di·nal·ly
card·ing
car·dio·gram record
car·dio·graph instrument
car·di·og·ra·pher
car·dio·graph·ic (*or* **·graphi·cal**)
car·di·og·ra·phy
car·di·oid
car·dio·logi·cal
car·di·olo·gist
car·di·ol·ogy
car·dio·mega·ly heart enlargement
car·dio·vas·cu·lar
car·di·tis
car·doon plant
card·sharp (*or* **·sharper**)
car·dua·ceous botany term
care
ca·reen nautical term
ca·reer
ca·reer·ist
care·free
care·ful
care·ful·ly
care·ful·ness
care·less
care·less·ness
ca·ress
ca·ress·er
ca·ress·ing·ly
car·et printing symbol; *compare* **carat**
care·taker
care·worn
car·fare *US* bus fare
car·fax crossroads
car·go (*plural* **·goes** *or* **·gos**)
car·hop
Caria ancient Asian region
Car·ib (*plural* **·ibs** *or* **·ib**) American Indian
Car·ib·bean
Car·ib·bees West Indian islands
cari·bou (*plural* **·bous** *or* **·bou**)
cari·ca·ture
cari·ca·tur·ist
cari·es (*plural* **cari·es**) tooth decay
ca·ril·lon (**·lon·ning**, **·lonned**)

ca·ril·lon·neur
Ca·ri·na constellation
ca·ri·na (*plural* ·nae *or* ·nas) keel-shaped part
cari·nate (*or* ·nat·ed)
Ca·rin·thia Austrian province
cario·ca dance
cario·gen·ic producing tooth decay
cari·ole (*or* car·ri·ole) cart
cari·os·ity (*or* cari·ous·ness)
cari·ous
car·line plant
car·ling (*or* ·line) ship's beam
Car·lisle Cumbrian city
Car·low Irish county
Carl·ton English town
car·ma·gnole French costume
car·man (*plural* ·men)
Car·mar·then
Car·mar·then·shire former Welsh county
Car·mel Israeli mountain
Car·mel·ite friar or nun
car·mina·tive
car·mine
car·nage
car·nal
car·nal·ist
car·nal·ity
car·nall·ite mineral
car·nal·ly
car·nas·sial tooth
Car·nat·ic Indian region
car·na·tion
car·nau·ba wax
car·nel·ian *variant spelling of* cornelian
car·net travel document; customs licence
car·ni·fi·ca·tion
car·ni·fy (·fies, ·fy·ing, ·fied) medical term
Car·nio·la Yugoslav region
car·ni·val
car·ni·vore
car·nivo·rous
car·no·tite
car·ny (*or* ·ney; ·nies, ·ny·ing, ·nied *or* ·neys, ·ney·ing, ·neyed) coax

car·ob
ca·roche carriage
car·ol (·ol·ling, ·olled; *US* ·ol·ing, ·oled)
car·ol·er
Caro·li·na
Caro·line (*or* Caro·lean) of King Charles
Caro·lin·gian Frankish dynasty
Caro·lin·ian of Carolina
caro·lus (*plural* ·luses *or* ·li) coin
car·om billiards term
caro·tene (*or* ·tin) orange pigment
ca·rot·enoid
ca·rot·id artery
ca·rot·id·al
ca·rous·al drinking party; *compare* carousel
ca·rouse
carou·sel *US* merry-go-round; *compare* carousal
ca·rous·er
carp
car·pal of the wrist; *compare* carpel
Car·pa·thian Moun·tains
car·pel flower part; *compare* carpal
car·pel·lary
car·pel·late
Car·pen·ta·ria Australian gulf
car·pen·ter
car·pen·try
car·pet
carpet·bag
carpet·bag·ger
car·phol·ogy medical term; *compare* carpology
car·po·go·nial
car·po·go·nium (*plural* ·nia) botany term
car·po·logi·cal
car·polo·gist
car·pol·ogy branch of botany; *compare* carphology
car·po·meta·car·pus bird bone
car·popha·gous feeding on fruit
car·po·phore botany term
car·port

car·po·spore
car·pus (*plural* ·pi) wrist
car·rack galleon
car·ra·geen (*or* ·gheen, cara·geen) seaweed
Car·ra·ra Italian town
car·re·four crossroads
car·rel (*or* ·rell) library cubicle
car·riage
carriage·way
car·rick
car·ri·er
car·ri·on
car·ron·ade cannon
car·rot
car·roty
car·ry (·ries, ·ry·ing, ·ried)
carry·all
carry·cot
carse *Scot* low-lying land
car·sey *variant spelling of* carzey
car·sick
car·sick·ness
cart
cart·age
Car·ta·gena Colombian port
carte blanche (*plural* cartes blanches)
car·tel
car·tel·ize
car·teli·za·tion
Car·tesian of Descartes
cart·ful
Car·thage
Car·tha·gin·ian
cart·horse
Car·thu·sian monk
car·ti·lage
car·ti·lagi·nous
cart·load
car·to·gram map
car·tog·ra·pher
car·to·graph·ic
car·to·graphi·cal
car·tog·ra·phy
carto·man·cy fortune-telling
car·ton
car·toon
car·toon·ist
car·touche (*or* ·touch)

cartridge

car·tridge
car·tu·lary (*or* **char·**; *plural* **·laries**) legal records
cart·wheel
car·un·cle fleshy outgrowth
car·un·cu·lar (*or* **·lous**)
car·un·cu·late (*or* **·lat·ed**)
carve
car·vel *variant of* **caravel**
carvel-built
carv·er
carv·ery (*plural* **·eries**)
carv·ing
cary·at·id (*plural* **·ids** *or* **·ati·des**)
cary·ati·dal (*or* **·dean, cary·at·ic, cary·atid·ic**)
caryo·phyl·la·ceous botany term
cary·op·sis (*plural* **·ses** *or* **·si·des**) botany term
car·zey (*or* **·sey**) *Slang* lavatory
ca·sa·ba (*or* **cas·sa·ba**) melon
Casa·blan·ca
cas·bah *variant spelling of* **kasbah**
cas·cade
cas·ca·ra
cas·ca·ril·la shrub
case
ca·sease enzyme
ca·seate medical term
ca·sea·tion
case-bound
ca·sefy (**·sefies, ·sefy·ing, ·sefied**) become cheesy
case-harden
ca·sein protein
ca·seino·gen protein
case·mate part of ship
case·ment
ca·seose biochemical compound
ca·seous cheeselike
ca·sern (*or* **·serne**) soldier's billet
Ca·ser·ta Italian town
case·work
cash
cash·able
cash-and-carry
cash-book

cash·ew nut; *compare* **cachou**
cash·ier
cash·mere
cas·ing
ca·si·no (*plural* **·nos**) gaming house; *compare* **cassino**
cask
cas·ket
Cas·lon style of type
Cas·pian Sea
casque helmet
casqued
cas·sa·reep cassava juice
cas·sa·ta ice cream
cas·sa·tion legal term
cas·sa·va plant
Cas·se·grain·ian telescope
cas·se·role
cas·sette
cas·sia plant
cas·si·mere (*or* **casi·mere**) cloth
cas·si·no (*or* **ca·si·no**) card game; *compare* **casino**
Cas·sio·peia constellation
cas·sis liqueur
cas·sit·er·ite mineral
cas·sock priest's garment; *compare* **hassock**
cas·socked
cas·sou·let French stew
cas·so·wary (*plural* **·waries**) bird
cast (**·ing, cast**)
cas·ta·net
cast·away
caste Hindu class
cas·tel·lan keeper of castle
cas·tel·lat·ed
cas·tel·la·tion
cast·er one who casts; *compare* **castor**
cas·ter (*or* **·tor**) sugar dispenser; wheel on furniture; *compare* **castor**
cas·ti·gate
cas·ti·ga·tion
cas·ti·ga·tor
Cas·tile (*or* **Cas·til·la**)
Cas·til·ian
cast·ing
cas·tle
cas·tled

68

cast-off (*adj*)
cast·off (*noun*)
Cas·tor star; mythological character
cas·tor plant oil; beaver secretion; *compare* **caster**
cas·trate
cas·tra·tion
cas·tra·to (*plural* **·ti** *or* **·tos**)
cas·tra·tor
cas·ual
casu·al·ly
casu·al·ty (*plural* **·ties**)
casua·ri·na tree
casu·ist
casu·is·tic (*or* **·ti·cal**)
casu·is·ti·cal·ly
casu·ist·ry (*plural* **·ries**)
ca·sus bel·li *Latin* occasion of war
cat
ca·taba·sis (*plural* **·ses**) descent
cata·bat·ic
cata·bol·ic (*or* **kata·**)
cata·boli·cal·ly (*or* **kata·**)
ca·tabo·lism (*or* **ka·**)
ca·tabo·lite
cata·caus·tic physics term
cata·chre·sis incorrect use of words
cata·chres·tic (*or* **·ti·cal**)
cata·cla·sis (*plural* **·ses**) geology term
cata·clas·tic
cata·cli·nal geology term
cata·clysm
cata·clys·mic (*or* **·mal**)
cata·comb
ca·tad·ro·mous migrating down river; *compare* **anadromous**
cata·falque
Cata·lan language or inhabitant of Catalonia
cata·lase enzyme
cata·lec·tic prosody term
cata·lep·sy medical term
cata·lep·tic
cata·logue (*US* **·log**)
cata·logu·er (*or* **·logu·ist**; *US* **·log·**)
Cata·lo·nia Spanish region
ca·tal·pa tree

cata·lyse (*US* ·lyze)
cata·lys·er (*US* ·lyz·)
ca·taly·sis (*plural* ·ses)
cata·lyst
cata·lyt·ic
cata·ma·ran
cata·menia menstruation
cata·menial
cata·mite homosexual boy
cata·mount (*or* ·mount·ain) animal
Ca·ta·nia Sicilian port
cata·pho·resis chemistry term
cata·phyll leaf
cata·pla·sia pathology term
cata·plasm poultice
cata·plas·tic
cata·plexy paralysis
cata·pult
cata·ract
ca·tarrh
ca·tarrh·al (*or* ·ous)
cat·arrh·ine zoology term
ca·tas·tro·phe
cata·stroph·ic
cata·strophi·cal·ly
ca·tas·tro·phism geological theory
ca·tas·tro·phist
cata·to·nia schizophrenia
cata·ton·ic
Ca·taw·ba (*plural* ·bas *or* ·ba) American Indian people
cat·bird
cat·boat
cat·call
catch (catch·ing, caught)
catch·er
catch·fly (*plural* ·flies) plant
catchi·ness
catch·ing
catch·ment
catch·penny (*plural* ·pennies)
catch·pole sheriff's officer
catch·up *US variant of* ketchup
catch·weight
catch·word
catchy (catchi·er, catchi·est)

cate·cheti·cal (*or* cat·echet·ic) teaching method
cat·echeti·cal·ly
cat·echin chemical compound
cat·echism
cat·echis·mal
cat·echist (*or* cate·chiz·er, cate·chis·er)
cat·echis·tic (*or* ·ti·cal)
cat·echi·za·tion (*or* ·sa·tion)
cat·echize (*or* ·ise)
cat·echol chemical compound
cat·echola·mine
cat·echu (*or* ca·chou, cutch) resin
cat·echu·men convert
cat·ego·rial
cat·egori·cal (*or* ·egor·ic)
cat·egori·cal·ly
cat·ego·ri·za·tion (*or* ·sa·tion)
cat·ego·rize (*or* ·rise)
cat·ego·ry (*plural* ·ries)
ca·tena (*plural* ·tenae) biblical comments
cat·enane chemistry term
cat·enar·ian
ca·tena·ry (*plural* ·ries) geometric curve
cat·enate biology term
cat·ena·tion
cat·enoid geometric surface
ca·tenu·late botany term
ca·ter
cat·er·an brigand
ca·ter·er
ca·ter·ing
cat·er·pil·lar
cat cr waul
cat·fall nautical term
cat·fish (*plural* ·fish *or* ·fishes)
cat·gut
Cath·ar (*plural* ·ars *or* ·ari) heretical Christian
Cath·ar·ism
ca·thar·sis
ca·thar·tic purgative
ca·thar·ti·cal·ly
Ca·thay *Archaic* China
cat·head nautical term

ca·thec·tic psychology term
ca·thedra (*plural* ·thedrae) bishop's throne
ca·thedral
ca·thep·sin enzyme
Cathe·rine wheel firework
cath·eter
cath·eteri·za·tion (*or* ·sa·tion)
cath·eter·ize (*or* ·ise)
ca·thex·is (*plural* ·thexes) psychiatry term
ca·thod·al
cath·ode
ca·thod·ic (*or* ·thodi·cal)
Catholic religion
catho·lic universal
Ca·tholi·cism
catho·lic·ity
ca·tholi·ci·za·tion (*or* ·sa·tion)
ca·tholi·cize (*or* ·cise)
ca·tholi·con universal remedy
cati·on positive ion
cati·on·ic
cat·kin
cat·like
cat·ling surgical knife
cat·mint (*or esp. US* ·nip)
cat·nap (*verb* ·nap·ping, ·napped)
cat-o'-nine-tails (*plural* -tails)
ca·top·tric (*or* ·tri·cal)
ca·top·trics branch of optics
cat's-ear plant
cat's-eye
cat's-foot (*plural* -feet) plant
cat's-paw
cat·sup *US variant of* ketchup
cat·ta·lo (*or* cata·lo; *plural* ·loes *or* ·los) cattle
cat·tery (*plural* ·teries)
cat·ti·ly
cat·ti·ness
cat·tish
cat·tle
cattle·man (*plural* ·men)
catt·leya orchid
cat·ty (·ti·er, ·ti·est)
cat·walk

Caucasia

Cau·ca·sia
Cau·ca·sian
Cau·ca·soid
Cau·ca·sus mountain range
cau·cus (*plural* ·cuses)
cau·dad towards the tail
cau·dal of the tail
cau·dal·ly
cau·date (*or* ·dat·ed)
cau·da·tion
cau·dex (*plural* ·di·ces *or* ·dexes) stem
cau·dil·lo (*plural* ·los) Spanish leader
cau·dle spiced wine
caught
caul
caul·dron (*or* cal·dron)
cau·les·cent
cau·li·cle plant stalk
cau·li·flow·er
cau·line
caulk (*or* calk) fill cracks
caulk·er (*or* calk·er)
caus·abil·ity
caus·able
caus·al
cau·sal·gia pathology term
cau·sal·ity (*plural* ·ities)
cau·sal·ly
cau·sa·tion
causa·tive
cause cé·lè·bre (*plural* causes cé·lè·bres)
caus·er
cau·serie informal talk
cause·way
caus·tic
caus·ti·cal·ly
caus·tic·ness (*or* ·tic·ity)
cau·ter·ant caustic
cau·teri·za·tion (*or* ·sa·tion)
cau·ter·ize (*or* ·ise)
cau·tery (*plural* ·teries)
cau·tion
cau·tion·ary
cau·tious
cau·tious·ness
cav·al·cade
cava·lier
cava·lier·ism
ca·val·la (*or* ·ly; *plural* ·la, ·las, *or* ·lies) fish
cav·al·ry (*plural* ·ries)

cav·al·ry·man (*plural* ·men)
Cav·an Irish county
cava·ti·na (*plural* ·ne) musical work
cave
ca·veat warning
ca·veat emp·tor *Latin* let the buyer beware
ca·vea·tor legal term
cave·fish (*plural* ·fish *or* ·fishes)
cave·man (*plural* ·men)
cav·en·dish tobacco
cav·er
cav·ern
cav·ern·ous
cav·es·son horse's noseband
ca·vet·to (*plural* ·ti) architectural moulding
cavi·ar (*or* ·are)
cavi·corn hollow-horned
ca·vie *Scot* hen coop
cav·il (·il·ling, ·illed; *US* ·il·ing, ·iled)
cav·il·ler
cav·ing
cavi·ta·tion
Ca·vi·te Philippine port
cav·ity (*plural* ·ities)
cavo-relievo (*or* -rilievo; *plural* cavo-relievos *or* cavi-rilievi) architectural term
ca·vort
cavy (*plural* cavies) rodent
caw
Cawn·pore Indian city
Cax·ton style of type
cay low island or bank
cay·enne
cay·man (*or* cai·man; *plural* ·mans) crocodile
Cay·man Is·lands
cay·use *US* small pony
cea·no·thus shrub
Cea·ra Brazilian state
cease
cease·fire
cease·less
ce·cal *US spelling of* caecal
ce·ci·ty blindness
Cecrops mythological character

ce·cum *US spelling of* caecum
ce·dar tree; *compare* ceder
cede
ced·er one who cedes; *compare* cedar
cedi Ghanaian currency
ce·dil·la
cei·ba tree
cei·lidh Gaelic party
ceil·ing
ceil·om·eter
cela·don porcelain
cel·an·dine
Ce·la·ya Mexican city
Cel·ebes Indonesian island
cel·ebrant
cel·ebrate
cel·ebra·tion
cel·ebra·tive
cel·ebra·tor
cel·ebra·tory
ce·leb·rity (*plural* ·rities)
ce·leri·ac vegetable
ce·ler·ity speed
cel·ery
ce·les·ta (*or* ·leste) musical instrument
ce·les·tial
ce·les·tial·ly
cel·es·tite (*or* ·tine) mineral
ce·li·ac *US spelling of* coeliac
celi·ba·cy (*plural* ·cies)
celi·bate
cell
cel·la (*plural* ·lae) room in temple
cel·lar
cel·lar·age
cel·lar·er monastic official
cel·lar·et bottle stand
Cel·le West German city
cel·list
cel·lo (*plural* ·los)
cel·lo·bi·ose (*or* cel·lose) biochemical compound
cel·lo·phane
cel·lu·lar
cel·lu·lase enzyme
cel·lule
cel·lu·li·tis

70

Cel·lu·loid (*Trademark*)
cel·lu·lose
cel·lu·lo·sic
ce·lom *US spelling of* coelom
ce·lo·mate *US spelling of* coelomate
Celsius temperature scale
celt axe
Celt (*or* Kelt) people
Celt·ic (*or* Kelt·ic)
Celti·cist (*or* Celt·ist, Kelti·cist, Kelt·ist)
cem·ba·lo (*plural* ·los) harpsichord
ce·ment
ce·men·ta·tion
ce·ment·er
ce·ment·ite chemical compound
ce·men·tum tooth substance
cem·etery (*plural* ·eteries)
cena·cle (*or* coena·cle) supper room
ce·nes·the·sia variant spelling of coenesthesia
ce·no·bite variant spelling of coenobite
ce·no·gen·esis *US spelling of* caenogenesis
ce·no·genet·ic *US spelling of* caenogenetic
ce·no·spe·cies (*plural* ·spe·cies) biology term
ceno·taph
ceno·taph·ic
ce·no·te well
Ce·no·zo·ic (*or* Cai·) geological era
cense burn incense
cen·ser incense container
cen·sor suppressor; to ban; *compare* sensor
cen·sor·able
cen·so·rial
cen·so·ri·ous
cen·so·ri·ous·ness
cen·sor·ship
cen·sual of a census; *compare* sensual
cen·sur·able
cen·sure
cen·sus (*plural* ·suses)
cent
cen·tal unit

cen·taur
Cen·tau·rus constellation
cen·tau·ry (*plural* ·ries) plant
cen·te·nar·ian
cen·te·nary (*plural* ·naries)
cen·ten·nial
cen·ter *US spelling of* centre
cen·tesi·mal hundredth
cen·tesi·mo (*plural* ·mos) monetary unit
cen·ti·are (*or* cen·tare) unit
cen·ti·grade
cen·ti·gram (*or* ·gramme)
cen·ti·li·tre (*US* ·ter)
cen·til·lion (*plural* ·lions *or* ·lion) 10^{600}
cen·time
cen·ti·me·tre (*US* ·ter)
cen·ti·pede
centi·poise unit
cent·ner
cen·to (*plural* ·tos) type of poem
cen·tral
cen·tral·ism
cen·tral·ity (*plural* ·ities)
cen·trali·za·tion (*or* ·sa·tion)
cen·tral·ize (*or* ·ise)
cen·tral·ly
cen·tre (*US* ·ter)
centre·board (*US* center·) keel
centre·fire (*US* center·)
centre·fold (*US* center·)
centre·piece (*US* center·)
cen·tric (*or* ·tri·cal)
cen·tric·ity
cen·trifu·gal
cen·trifu·gal·ly
cen·trifu·ga·tion
cen·tri·fuge
cen·tring (*US* ·tering)
cen·tri·ole biology term
cen·trip·etal
cen·trip·etal·ly
cen·trist moderate
cen·tro·bar·ic
cen·tro·cli·nal geology term
cen·troid
cen·tro·mere chromosome part

cen·tro·mer·ic
cen·tro·some cell part
cen·tro·som·ic
cen·tro·sphere
cen·trum (*plural* ·trums *or* ·tra) part of vertebra
cen·tum linguistics term
cen·tu·pli·cate
cen·tu·rial
cen·tu·ri·on
cen·tu·ry (*plural* ·ries)
cep fungus
cepha·lad towards the head
cepha·lal·gia headache
ce·phal·ic
cepha·lin (*or* kepha·) biochemical compound
cepha·li·za·tion (*or* ·sa·tion)
cepha·lo·chor·date zoology term
cepha·lom·eter
cepha·lo·met·ric
cepha·lom·etry
Cepha·lo·nia Greek island
cepha·lo·pod mollusc
cepha·lopo·dan
cepha·lo·pod·ic (*or* ·lopo·dous)
cepha·lo·tho·rac·ic
cepha·lo·tho·rax (*plural* ·raxes *or* ·races)
Ce·pheus constellation
ce·ra·ceous waxy
Ce·ram Indonesian island
ce·ram·ic
ce·ram·ics
cera·mist (*or* ce·rami·cist)
ce·rar·gy·rite mineral
ce·ras·tes (*plural* ·tes) snake
ce·rate ointment
ce·rat·ed ornithology term
ce·rato·dus (*plural* ·duses) extinct fish
Cerberus mythological dog
cer·cal zoology term
cer·caria (*plural* ·cariae) larva
cer·car·ial (*or* ·ian)
cer·cis plant
cer·co·pi·thecoid monkey
cer·cus (*plural* ·ci) zoology term

cere

cere swelling on bird's beak; compare **sere**
ce·real crop; compare **serial**
cer·ebel·lar
cer·ebel·lum (plural ·**lums** or ·**la**)
cer·ebral
cer·ebral·ly
cer·ebrate
cer·ebra·tion
cer·ebric
cer·ebroid
cer·ebro·side biochemical compound
cer·ebro·spi·nal
cer·ebro·vas·cu·lar
cer·ebrum (plural ·**ebrums** or ·**ebra**)
cere·cloth waxed cloth
cere·ment burial clothes
cer·emo·nial
cer·emo·ni·al·ism
cer·emo·ni·al·ist
cer·emo·nial·ly
cer·emo·ni·ous
cer·emo·ny (plural ·**nies**)
Ce·res asteroid
Ceres Roman goddess
cer·esin wax
ce·reus cactus
ce·ria chemical compound
ce·ric
ce·rise
ce·rium chemical element
cer·met metal–ceramic material
cer·nu·ous drooping
cero (plural **cero** or **ceros**) fish
ce·ro·graph·ic (or ·**graphi·cal**)
ce·rog·ra·phist
ce·rog·ra·phy engraving on wax
ce·ro·plas·tic
ce·ro·plas·tics
ce·ro·type printing process
ce·rous
cert Slang certainty
cer·tain
cer·tain·ly
cer·tain·ty (plural ·**ties**)
cer·ti·fi·able
cer·ti·fi·ably
cer·tifi·cate
cer·ti·fi·ca·tion
cer·tifi·ca·tory

cer·ti·fy (·**fies**, ·**fy·ing**, ·**fied**)
cer·tio·ra·ri legal term
cer·ti·tude
ce·ru·lean deep blue
ce·ru·men earwax
ce·ru·mi·nous
ce·ruse white lead
ce·rus·site (or ·**ru·site**) mineral
cer·ve·lat sausage
cer·vi·cal
cer·vi·ci·tis
cer·vid zoology term
cer·vine of deer
cer·vix (plural ·**vixes** or ·**vi·ces**)
ce·sar·ean sec·tion US spelling of **Caesarean section**
ce·sium US spelling of **caesium**
ces·pi·tose US spelling of **caespitose**
cess
ces·sa·tion
ces·ser legal term
ces·sion act of ceding; compare **session**
ces·sion·ary (plural ·**aries**) legal term
cess·pool (or ·**pit**)
ces·tode tapeworm
ces·toid ribbon-shaped
ce·ta·cean whale
ce·ta·ceous
ce·tane chemical compound
cete group of badgers
ce·teris pa·ri·bus Latin other things being equal
ce·to·logi·cal
ce·tolo·gist
ce·tol·ogy study of whales
Ce·tus constellation
Ce·vennes mountain range
Cey·lon
Cey·lon·ese
chaba·zite mineral
chab·lis wine
cha·cha (or **cha-cha-cha**)
chac·ma baboon
cha·conne musical term
Chad African republic; lake
Chad·ean
Chad·ic language group
chae·ta (plural ·**tae**) bristle on worm

72

chae·tog·nath wormlike animal
chae·to·pod worm
chafe
chaf·er beetle
chaff
chaff·er (noun)
chaf·fer (verb) haggle
chaf·finch
chaffy
chaf·ing
Cha·gas' dis·ease
cha·grin
chain
chain·man (plural ·**men**)
chain·plate
chain-react
chain-smoke
chain-stitch
chain-store
chair
chair·borne
chair·man (plural ·**men**)
chair·man·ship
chair·person
chair·woman (plural ·**women**)
chaise carriage
chaise longue (plural **chaise longues** or **chaises longues**)
cha·la·za (plural ·**zas** or ·**zae**) biology term
cha·la·zal
chal·can·lite mineral
chal·cedon·ic
chal·cedo·ny (plural ·**nies**)
chal·cid insect
Chal·cidi·ce Greek peninsula
Chal·cis Greek city
chal·co·cite mineral
chal·cog·ra·pher (or ·**phist**)
chal·co·graph·ic (or ·**graphi·cal**)
chal·cog·ra·phy engraving
chal·co·lith·ic archaeology term
chal·co·py·rite mineral
Chal·dea (or ·**daea**) Babylonian region
Chal·dean (or ·**daean**)
Chal·dee language
chal·dron unit
cha·let

chal·ice goblet; *compare* challis
chali·co·there extinct mammal
chalk
chalk·board *US* blackboard
chalki·ness
chalk·pit
chalky (chalki·er, chalki·est)
chal·lah (*or* hal·lah; *plural* ·lahs *or* ·loth) Jewish bread
chal·lenge
chal·lenge·able
chal·leng·er
chal·lis (*or* ·lie) fabric; *compare* chalice
chal·one internal secretion
cha·lyb·eate containing iron
cha·made military signal
cham·ber
cham·ber·lain
chamber·maid
cham·bray cloth
cha·me·le·on
cha·meleon·ic
cham·fer
cham·fer·er
cham·ois (*plural* ·ois)
Cha·mo·nix French town
champ
cham·pac (*or* ·pak) tree
Cham·pagne French region
cham·pagne wine
cham·paign open country
cham·pers *Slang* champagne
cham·per·tous
cham·per·ty (*plural* ·ties) legal term
cham·pi·gnon mushroom
cham·pi·on
cham·pion·ship
champ·le·vé enamelling process
Champs Ely·sées
chance
chan·cel
chan·cel·lery (*or* ·lo·ry; *plural* ·leries *or* ·lo·ries)
chan·cel·lor

chan·cel·lor·ship
chan·cery (*plural* ·ceries)
chanci·ly
chan·cre pathology term
chan·croid ulcer
chan·croi·dal
chan·crous
chancy (chanci·er, chanci·est)
chan·de·lier
chan·delle aeronautics term
Chan·der·na·gore Indian port
Chan·di·garh Indian city
chan·dler
chan·dlery (*plural* ·dleries)
Chang·chia·kow (*or* ·k'ou) Chinese city
Chang·chow (*or* Ch'ang·chou) Chinese city
Chang·chun (*or* Ch'ang Ch'un) Chinese city
change
change·abil·ity (*or* ·able·ness)
change·able
change·ably
change·ful
change·less
change·less·ness
change·ling
change·over
chang·er
change-ringing
Chang·sha (*or* Ch'ang·sha) Chinese port
Chang·teh (*or* Ch'ang-te) Chinese port
chan·nel (·nel·ling, ·nelled; *US* ·nel·ing, ·neled)
chan·nel·ize (*or* ·ise)
chan·nel·ler (*US* ·nel·er)
chan·son *French* song
chant
chant·er
chan·te·relle mushroom
chan·teuse
chan·tey *US spelling of* shanty
chan·ti·cleer (*or* ·cler) cock

Chan·til·ly French town
chan·try (*plural* ·tries)
chan·ty variant spelling of shanty
Chao·an Chinese city
cha·os
cha·ot·ic
cha·oti·cal·ly
chap (chap·ping, chapped)
chapa·rejos cowboy's overalls
chap·ar·ral wooded area
cha·pat·ti (*or* ·pa·ti; *plural* ·ti *or* ·tis) bread
chap·book
chape scabbard mounting
cha·peau (*plural* ·peaux *or* ·peaus) hat
chap·el
chap·er·on (*or* ·one)
chap·er·on·age
chap·fallen (*or* chop·) dejected
chapi·ter architectural term
chap·lain
chap·lain·cy (*plural* ·cies)
chap·let strung beads
chap·let·ed
chap·pal sandal
chapped
chap·pie *Slang* fellow
chap·ping
chaps *short for* chaparejos
chap·stick *US* lip salve
chap·ter
chap·ter·house
char (char·ring, charred)
char (*or* charr; *plural* char, chars *or* charr, charrs) fish
chara·banc
chara·cin (*or* ·cid) fish
char·ac·ter
char·ac·ter·ful
char·ac·ter·is·tic
char·ac·ter·is·ti·cal·ly
char·ac·teri·za·tion (*or* ·sa·tion)
char·ac·ter·ize (*or* ·ise)
char·ac·ter·less
cha·rade
char·as hashish

charcoal 74

char·coal
chard
Cha·rente French river
Charent-Maritime French department
charge
charge·abil·ity
charge·able
char·gé d'af·faires (plural char·gés d'af·faires)
charg·er
Cha·ri African river
chari·ly
chari·ness
Char·ing Cross
Chari-Nile language group
chari·ot
chari·ot·eer
cha·ris·ma (or char·ism)
char·is·mat·ic
char·is·mati·cal·ly
chari·table
chari·table·ness
chari·tably
char·ity (plural ·ities)
cha·ri·va·ri (or shiva·ree) mock serenade
char·kha (or ·ka) spinning wheel
char·lady (plural ·ladies)
char·la·tan
char·la·tan·ism (or ·ry)
char·la·tan·is·tic
Charles·ton US city
charles·ton dance
char·lie Slang fool
char·lock plant
Char·lotte US city
char·lotte pudding
Charlotte Ama·lie capital of Virgin Islands
charm
charm·er
Char·meuse (Trademark) fabric
Char·mi·nar Indian monument
charm·ing
char·nel sepulchral
Char·ol·lais cattle
Charon mythological character
char·poy (or ·pai) bedstead
char·qui dried meat
char·quid

chart
chart·able
char·ter
char·tered
Char·ter·house Carthusian monastery
Chart·ism reform movement
Chart·ist
chart·ist share analyst
Char·tres French city
char·treuse liqueur
char·woman plural ·women
chary (chari·er, chari·est)
Cha·ryb·dis mythological monster
chase
chas·er
chasm
chas·mal (or ·mic)
chas·sé ballet step
chas·seur French huntsman
chas·sis (plural ·sis)
chaste
chas·ten
chas·ten·er
chas·tis·able
chas·tise
chas·tise·ment
chas·tity
chasu·ble
chat (chat·ting, chat·ted)
cha·teau (or châ·; plural ·teaux or ·teaus)
chat·elain (fem ·elaine) castle keeper
Chat·ham Kent town; Pacific islands
cha·toy·an·cy
cha·toy·ant changing in lustre
Chat·ta·noo·ga US city
chat·tel
chat·ter
chatter·box
chat·ter·er
chat·ti·ly
chat·ty (·ti·er, ·ti·est)
Chau·cerian
chaud·froid sauce
chauf·fer (or chau·fer) heater
chauf·feur (fem ·feuse)
chaul·moo·gra tree
chausses medieval garment

chau·vin·ism
chau·vin·ist
chau·vin·is·tic
chau·vin·is·ti·cal·ly
chaw Dialect chew tobacco
cha·yo·te plant
cheap inexpensive; compare cheep
cheap·en
cheap·ness
cheap·skate
cheat
cheat·er
Che·bo·ksa·ry Soviet port
Che·chen (plural ·chens or ·chen) Soviet people
Checheno-Ingush Soviet republic
check pause; pattern; etc.; US spelling of cheque
check·able
check·book US spelling of chequebook
check·er one who checks; US spelling of chequer
check·ered US spelling of chequered
checker·berry (plural ·berries)
checker·bloom plant
checker·board US draughtboard
check·ers US draughts
check-in (noun)
check·mate
check·out (noun)
check·point
check·up (noun)
checky heraldic term
Ched·dar
chedd·ite explosive
cheek
cheek·bone
cheeki·ly
cheeki·ness
cheek·piece
cheeky (cheeki·er, cheeki·est)
cheep chirp; compare cheap
cheep·er
cheer
cheer·ful
cheer·ful·ly
cheer·ful·ness
cheeri·ly

cheeri·ness
cheerio
cheer·leader
cheer·less
cheer·less·ness
cheers
cheery (cheeri·er, cheeri·est)
cheese
cheese·board
cheese·burg·er
cheese·cake
cheese·cloth
cheese·mon·ger
cheese·paring
cheesi·ness
cheesy (cheesi·er, cheesi·est)
chee·tah (*or* che·tah)
chef
chef-d'oeuvre (*plural* chefs-d'oeuvre) *French* masterpiece
Che·kiang Chinese province
che·la (*plural* ·lae) claws
che·la (*plural* ·las) Hindu disciple
che·la·ship
che·late chemistry term
che·la·tion
che·lic·era (*plural* ·erae) spider's claw
che·lic·er·al
che·lic·cr·ate
che·lif·er·ous
che·li·form
Chelms·ford
che·loid *variant spelling of* keloid
che·lo·nian tortoise or turtle
chelp *Dialect* chatter
Chel·sea
Chel·ten·ham
Chel·ya·binsk Soviet city
chemi·cal
chemi·cal·ly
chemi·lu·mi·nes·cence
chemi·lu·mi·nes·cent
che·min de fer gambling game
che·mise
chemi·sette underbodice
chemi·sorb (*or* chemo·)
chemi·sorp·tion
chem·ist

chem·is·try (*plural* ·tries)
chemo·pro·phy·lac·tic
chemo·pro·phy·lax·is
chemo·recep·tor (*or* chemo·cep·tor)
chem·os·mo·sis
chem·os·mot·ic
chemo·sphere layer of atmosphere
chemo·spher·ic
che·mo·stat
chemo·syn·thesis
chemo·syn·thet·ic
chemo·syn·theti·cal·ly
chemo·tac·tic
chemo·tac·ti·cal·ly
chemo·tax·is biology term
chemo·thera·pist
chemo·thera·py
chemo·trop·ic
chemo·tropi·cal·ly
che·mot·ro·pism botany term
chem·pa·duk tree
chem·ur·gic (*or* ·gi·cal)
chem·ur·gy branch of chemistry
Che·nab Himalayan river
Cheng·chow (*or* Cheng-chou) Chinese city
Cheng·teh Chinese city
Cheng·tu (*or* Ch'eng-tu) Chinese city
che·nille
che·no·pod plant
che·no·po·dia·ceous
cheong·sam Chinese dress
cheque (*US* check)
cheque·book (*US* check·)
cheq·uer (*US* check·) pattern of squares; *compare* checker
chequer·board (*US* checker·)
cheq·uered (*US* check·ered)
Cheq·uers premier's country house
cheq·uers *US* draughts game
Cher French river
Cher·bourg French port
Che·rem·kho·vo Soviet city
cher·ish
cher·ish·able

cher·ish·er
Cher·nov·tsy Soviet city
cher·no·zem (*or* tscher·no·sem) black soil
Chero·kee (*plural* ·kees *or* ·kee)
che·root
cher·ry (*plural* ·ries)
cher·so·nese peninsula
chert quartz
Chert·sey Surrey town
cherty
cher·ub (*plural* ·ubs *or* cheru·bim)
che·ru·bic
che·ru·bi·cal
cher·vil
cher·vo·nets Soviet coin
Chesa·peake US bay
Chesh·ire
chess
chess·board
ches·sel cheese mould
chess·man (*plural* ·men)
chest
chest·ed
Ches·ter
Ches·ter·field Derbyshire town
ches·ter·field sofa
chesti·ly
chesti·ness
chest·nut
chesty (chesti·cr, chesti·est)
cheval-de-frise barrier of spikes
cheva·lier
che·vet part of church
Che·vi·ot hills; sheep
che·vi·ot fabric
chev·rette goat skin
chev·ron
chev·ro·tain animal
chew
chew·able
chew·er
chewy (chewi·er, chewi·est)
Chey·enne American Indian; US city
chez *French* at the home of
chi Greek letter
chi·ack *Austral* to tease

chianti 76

chi·an·ti
Chi·apas Mexican state
chia·ro·scur·ism
chia·ro·scu·rist
chia·ro·scu·ro (*plural*
 ·ros) art term
chi·as·ma (*or* chi·asm;
 plural ·mas, ·ma·ta, *or*
 ·asms) biology term
chi·as·mal
chi·as·mic
chi·as·mus (*plural* ·mi)
 rhetoric term
chi·as·tic
chi·as·to·lite mineral
Chi·ba Japanese city
chi·bouk (*or* ·bouque)
 Turkish pipe
chic
Chi·ca·go
chi·ca·lo·te poppy
chi·cane
chi·can·er
chi·can·ery (*plural* ·eries)
Chich·es·ter
chi·chi
Chi·chi·haerh (*or* Ch'i-
 ch'i-haerh) Chinese city
chick
chicka·bid·dy
chicka·dee bird
chicka·ree squirrel
Chicka·saw (*plural* ·saws
 or ·saw) American Indian
chick·en
chicken-hearted (*or*
 -livered)
chicken·pox
chick·pea
chick·weed
Chi·cla·yo Peruvian city
chic·le gum
chi·co shrub
chico·ry (*or* chic·co·ry;
 plural ·ries)
chide (chid·ing; chid·ed
 or chid; chid·ed, chid,
 or chid·den)
chid·er
chief
chief·ly
chief·tain
chiff·chaff bird
chif·fon

chif·fo·nier (*or* ·fon·nier)
 furniture
chig·etai wild ass
chig·ger larva
chi·gnon
chigoe flea
Chi·hua·hua Mexican state;
 dog
chil·blain
child (*plural* chil·dren)
child·bed
child·birth
child·hood
child·ish
child·ish·ness
child·less
child·less·ness
child·like
chil·dren *plural of* child
Chile
Chil·ean
chili·ad group of one
 thousand
chili·ad·al (*or* ·ad·ic)
chili·asm theology term
chili·ast
chili·as·tic
chill
chil·li (*plural* ·lies)
chil·li con car·ne
chil·li·ness
Chil·lon Swiss castle
chil·lum clay pipe
chil·ly (·li·er, ·li·est)
chi·lo·pod invertebrate
Chil·tern Hills; Hundreds
Chi·lung (*or* Chi-lung)
 Taiwanese port
chi·maera fish; *compare*
 chimera
Chim·bo·te Peruvian port
chime
chi·mera (*or* ·maera)
 monster; biology term;
 compare chimaera
chi·mere (*or* chim·er,
 chim·ar) bishop's gown
chi·meri·cal (*or* ·mer·ic)
 fanciful
Chim·kent Soviet city
chim·ney
chimney·piece
chimney·pot
chimp
chim·pan·zee

chin
Chi·na country
chi·na porcelain
china·berry (*plural*
 ·berries)
China·graph
 (*Trademark*)
China·man (*plural* ·men)
China·town
china·ware
chinch *US* bedbug
chin·che·rin·chee plant
chin·chil·la
Chin-Chou (*or*
 Chin·chow) Chinese city
Chin·dit
Chin·dwin Burmese river
chine
chi·né mottled
Chi·nee *Slang* Chinaman
Chi·nese (*plural* ·nese)
Ching (*or* Ch'ing) Chinese
 dynasty
chink
Chin·kiang (*or* Cheng-
 chiang) Chinese port
chin·less
chino (*plural* chinos) cloth
chi·noi·serie
Chi·nook (*plural* ·nook *or*
 ·nooks) American Indian
chi·nook wind
Chi·nook·an
chin·qua·pin (*or* ·ca·pin,
 ·ka·pin) tree
chintz
chintzy (chintzi·er,
 chintzi·est)
chin·wag (·wag·ging,
 ·wagged)
chi·ono·doxa plant
Chios Greek island
chip (chip·ping, chipped)
chip·board
chip·munk
chipo·la·ta
chip·per
chip·ping
chip·py (*noun, plural*
 ·pies; *adj* ·pi·er, ·pi·est)
chir·al chemistry term
chi·ral·ity
chirm chirp
chi·rog·ra·pher

chi·ro·graph·ic (or
  ·graphi·cal)
chi·rog·ra·phy calligraphy
chi·ro·man·cy palmistry
Chiron centaur
chi·ropo·dist
chi·ropo·dy
chi·ro·prac·tic
chi·ro·prac·tor
chi·rop·ter bat
chi·rop·ter·an
chirp
chirp·er
chirpi·ly
chirpi·ness
chirpy (chirpi·er,
  chirpi·est)
chirr (or chirre, churr)
  make shrill sound
chir·rup
chir·rup·er
chir·rupy
chis·el (·el·ling, ·elled;
  US ·el·ing, ·eled)
chis·el·ler (US ·el·er)
chi-square statistics term
chit
Chi·ta Soviet city
chi·tal deer
chi·tar·ro·ne (plural ·ni)
  lute
chit·chat (·chat·ting,
  ·chat·ted)
chi·tin biochemical
  compound
chi·tin·oid
chi·tin·ous
chi·ton Greek tunic
Chit·ta·gong Bangladeshi
  port
chit·ter US twitter
chit·ter·lings (or chit·lins,
  chit·lings) pig intestines
chiv Slang knife
chiv·al·ric
chiv·al·rous
chiv·al·ry (plural ·ries)
chive (or chives)
chivy (or chiv·vy; chivies,
  chivy·ing, chiv·ied or
  chiv·vies, ·vy·ing, ·vied)
chlamy·date zoology term
chla·myd·eous botany term
chla·mydo·spore
chlor·acne skin disease

chlo·ral chemical compound
chlo·ram·bu·cil drug
chlo·ra·mine chemical
  compound
chlo·ram·pheni·col
  antibiotic
chlo·rate
chlor·dane (or ·dan)
  insecticide
chlo·rel·la alga
chlo·ren·chy·ma plant
  tissue
chlo·ric
chlo·ride
chlo·rid·ic
chlo·rin·ate
chlo·rina·tion
chlo·rina·tor
chlo·rine (or ·rin)
chlo·rite mineral
chlo·rit·ic
chlo·ro·ben·zene
chlo·ro·form
chlo·ro·hy·drin
Chlo·ro·my·ce·tin
  (Trademark)
chlo·ro·phyll (or ·phyl)
chlo·ro·phyl·loid
chlo·ro·phyl·lous
chlo·ro·pic·rin (or
  chlor·pic·rin) pesticide
chlo·ro·plast
chlo·ro·plast·ic
chlo·ro·prene chemical
  compound
chlo·ro·quine drug
chlo·ro·sis disease
chlo·ro·thia·zide
chlo·rot·ic
chlo·rous of chlorine
chlor·proma·zine drug
chlor·pro·pa·mide drug
cho·ano·cyte zoology term
choc-ice
chock
chock-a-block
chock·er Slang fed up
chock-full
choco·late
choco·laty
Choc·taw (plural ·taws or
  ·taw) American Indian
Chog·yal Indian ruler
choice
choice·ly

choice·ness
choir choral group; compare
  quire
choir·boy
choir·master
Choi·seul Pacific island
choke
choke·able
choke·berry (plural
  ·berries)
choke·bore shotgun
choke·cherry (plural
  ·cherries)
chok·er
choky (or ·ey)
cho·lecal·cif·er·ol vitamin
chol·an·gi·og·raphy bile-
  duct examination
chol·ecys·tec·to·my
  (plural ·mies) removal of
  gall bladder
chol·ecys·tog·raphy gall-
  bladder examination
chol·er anger
chol·era
chol·er·ic
chol·eroid
cho·les·ter·ol (or ·ter·in)
cho·li bodice
cho·line biochemical
  compound
cho·lin·er·gic biology term
cho·lin·es·ter·ase enzyme
choll·la cactus
Cho·lon Vietnamese city
chomp
chon Korean coin
chon·dri·fi·ca·tion
chon·dri·fy (·fies, ·fy·ing,
  ·fied) change into
  cartilage
chon·drio·so·mal
chon·drio·some biology
  term
chon·drite meteorite
chon·drit·ic
chon·dro·ma (plural ·mas
  or ·ma·ta) tumour
chon·dro·ma·tous
chon·drule meteorology
  term
Chong·jin (or Chung·)
  Korean port
Chon·ju Korean city
choose (choos·ing, chose,
  cho·sen)

chooser 78

choos·er
choosi·ly
choosi·ness
choosy (choosi·er, choosi·est)
chop (chop·ping, chopped)
cho·pine shoe
chop·logic
chop·per
chop·pi·ly
chop·pi·ness
chop·py (·pi·er, ·pi·est)
chop·stick
cho·ra·gus Greek chorus leader
cho·ral (*adj*)
cho·rale (*noun*)
cho·ral·ly
chord maths and music senses; *compare* cord
chord·al
chor·date animal with notochord; *compare* cordate
chord·ing musical term
chordo·phone musical instrument
chore
cho·rea neurological disorder
cho·real (*or* cho·re·ic)
cho·reo·dra·ma
cho·reo·graph
cho·reog·ra·pher (*or* ·reg·ra·pher)
cho·reo·graph·ic (*or* ·regraph·ic)
cho·reo·graphi·cal·ly (*or* ·regraphi·)
cho·reog·ra·phy (*or* ·reg·ra·phy)
cho·ri·amb (*or* ·am·bus; *plural* ·ambs *or* ·am·bi) prosody term
cho·ri·am·bic
cho·ric of a chorus
cho·ri·on embryonic membrane
cho·ri·on·ic (*or* cho·rial)
chor·is·ter
Chor·ley Lancashire town
cho·rog·ra·pher
cho·ro·graph·ic (*or* ·graphi·cal)
cho·ro·graphi·cal·ly

cho·rog·ra·phy mapping regions
cho·roid membrane of eyeball
cho·rol·ogy geography term
chor·tle
cho·rus (*plural* ·ruses)
Chor·zow Polish city
chose
cho·sen
Cho·ta Nag·pur Indian plateau
Chou Chinese dynasty
chou (*plural* choux) cabbage; *compare* choux
chough bird
choux pastry; *plural of* chou
chow
chow-chow
chow·der soup
chow mein Chinese food
chre·ma·tis·tic of money-making
chres·ard biology term
chrism (*or* chris·om) anointing oil; *compare* chrisom
chris·mal
chris·ma·tory (*plural* ·tories) receptacle for consecrated oil
chris·om baptismal robe; *compare* chrism
Christ
Chris·ta·del·phian
Christ·church New Zealand city; Dorset town
chris·ten
Chris·ten·dom
chris·ten·er
chris·ten·ing
Chris·tian
Chris·tia·nia *former name for* Oslo
Chris·ti·an·ity
Chris·tiani·za·tion (*or* ·sa·tion)
Chris·tian·ize (*or* ·ise)
Chris·tian·iz·er (*or* ·is·er)
Chris·tian·ly
Christ·like
Christ·mas
Christ·mas·sy
Christmas·tide
Chris·to·logi·cal
Chris·tol·ogist

Chris·tol·ogy
Christ's-thorn plant
chro·ma physics term
chro·mate
chro·mat·ic
chro·mati·cal·ly
chro·mati·cism
chro·ma·tic·ity physics term
chro·mat·ic·ness physics term
chro·mat·ics (*or* chro·ma·tol·ogy) science of colour
chro·ma·tid chromosome part
chro·ma·tin substance of chromosomes
chro·ma·tin·ic
chro·ma·tist (*or* chro·ma·tolo·gist)
chro·ma·to·gram
chro·ma·tog·ra·pher
chro·ma·to·graph·ic
chro·ma·to·graphi·cal·ly
chro·ma·tog·ra·phy chemical analysis
chro·ma·tol·ogy *variant of* chromatics
chro·ma·toly·sis cytology term
chro·ma·to·phore zoology term
chro·ma·to·phor·ic
chro·ma·toph·or·ous
chrome
chro·mic
chro·mi·nance physics term
chro·mite mineral
chro·mium
chro·mo·gen
chro·mo·gen·ic colour-producing
chro·mo·litho·graph
chro·mo·li·thog·ra·pher
chro·mo·litho·graph·ic
chro·mo·li·thog·ra·phy
chro·mo·mere cytology term
chro·mo·nema (*plural* ·nema·ta) biology term
chro·mo·nemal (*or* ·nemat·ic, ·nemic)
chro·mo·phore chemistry term
chro·mo·phor·ic (*or* ·ous)

chro·mo·plast part of cell
chro·mo·pro·tein
chro·mo·so·mal
chro·mo·some
chro·mo·sphere layer of sun
chro·mo·spher·ic
chro·mous
chro·myl
chro·naxie (or ·naxy) physiology term
chron·ic
chroni·cal·ly
chro·nic·ity
chroni·cle
chroni·cler
Chroni·cles Old Testament book
chrono·bi·ol·ogy
chrono·gram
chrono·gram·mat·ic (or ·mati·cal)
chrono·graph time recorder
chro·nog·ra·pher
chrono·graph·ic
chrono·logi·cal
chrono·logi·cal·ly
chro·nolo·gist
chro·nol·ogy (plural ·ogies)
chro·nom·eter timepiece
chrono·met·ric (or ·ri·cal)
chrono·metri·cal·ly
chro·nom·etry
chro·non unit
chrono·scope
chrono·scop·ic
chrysa·lis (plural ·lises, ·lids, or chry·sali·des)
chry·san·themum
chrysa·ro·bin drug
chrys·el·ephan·tine statuary term
chryso·ber·yl
chryso·lite gemstone
chryso·lit·ic
chryso·prase gemstone
chryso·tile mineral
chtho·nian (or ·nic) of the underworld
chub (plural chub or chubs)
Chubb (Trademark) lock
chub·bi·ness
chub·by (·bi·er, ·bi·est)

chuck
chuck·le
chuck·ler
chuck·wal·la lizard
chuck-will's-widow bird
chud·dar Indian shawl
chu·fa sedge
chuff
chuffed
chuf·fy Scot chubby
chug (chug·ging, chugged)
chu·kar partridge
Chuk·chi Soviet peninsula
chuk·ker (or ·ka) polo term
chum (chum·ming, chummed)
chum·mi·ly
chum·mi·ness
chum·my (·mi·er, ·mi·est)
chump
chump·ing Dialect collecting wood
chun·der
chun·der·ous Austral nauseating
Chung·king (or Ch'ung-ch'ing) Chinese port
chunk
chunki·ly
chunki·ness
chunky (chunki·er, chunki·est)
Chun·nel Channel tunnel
chun·ter
church
church·goer
church·going
Church·ill Canadian river
church·man (plural ·men)
church·warden
church·woman (plural ·women)
church·yard
chu·ri·dars Indian trousers
chu·rin·ga Aboriginal amulet
churl
churl·ish
churn
churr variant spelling of chirr
chute
chut·ney (or ·nee)

chut·tie Austral chewing gum
Chu·vash (plural ·vash or ·vashes) Soviet people
chy·la·ceous (or chy·lous)
chyle intestinal fluid
chyme digested food
chy·mo·sin rennin
chy·mo·tryp·sin enzyme
chy·mo·tryp·sino·gen enzyme precursor
chy·mous
ciao Italian greeting
ci·bo·rium (plural ·ria) communion vessel
ci·ca·da (or ci·ca·la; plural ·das, ·dae or ·las, ·le)
cica·tri·cial
cica·tric·le biology term
ci·cat·ri·cose
cica·trix (plural ·tri·ces) scar
cica·tri·zant (or ·sant)
cica·tri·za·tion (or ·sa·tion)
cica·trize (or ·trise) heal
cica·triz·er (or ·tris·er)
cic·ely plant
cic·ero (plural ·eros) unit
cic·ero·ne (plural ·nes or ·ni) tourist guide
Cic·ero·nian eloquent
cich·lid fish
cich·loid
ci·der
ci·gar
ciga·rette
ciga·ril·lo (plural ·los) cigar
cig·gy (plural ·gles) Slang cigarette
cilia plural of cilium
cili·ary
cili·ate
cili·at·ed
cili·ation
cil·ice haircloth
cilio·late
cil·ium (plural cilia) minute hair
cim·ba·lom dulcimer
Cim·bri Germanic people
Cim·brian
Cim·bric

cimex

ci·mex (*plural* **cimi·ces**) bedbug
Cim·me·rian very dark
cinch
cin·cho·na tree bark
cin·choni·dine alkaloid
cin·cho·nine alkaloid
cin·chon·ism poisoning
cin·cho·ni·za·tion (*or* ·sa·tion)
cin·cho·nize (*or* ·nise)
Cin·cin·nati
cinc·ture surround
cin·der
cin·dery
cine film
cin·easte film enthusiast
cin·ema
Cin·ema·scope (*Trademark*)
cin·ema·theque small cinema
cin·emat·ic
cin·emati·cal·ly
cin·emato·graph
cin·ema·tog·ra·pher
cin·emato·graph·ic
cin·ema·tog·ra·phy
cin·eol (*or* ·eole) eucalyptol
Cin·era·ma (*Trademark*)
cin·eraria plant
cin·erar·ium (*plural* ·eraria) place for cremation ashes
cin·erary (*adj*)
cin·era·tor cremation furnace
ci·ner·eous (*or* **cin·eri·tious**) greyish
cin·erin chemical compound
cin·gu·late (*or* ·lat·ed)
cin·gu·lum (*plural* ·la) anatomical part
cin·na·bar mineral
cin·na·mon
cin·na·mon·ic (*or* **ci·nam·ic**)
cin·quain poem
cinque five
cinque·foil plant
Cinque Ports
Cin·za·no (*Trademark*)
ci·pher (*or* **cy·pher**) secret writing; *compare* **sypher**

cipo·lin marble
cir·ca
cir·ca·dian daily
Cir·cas·sia Soviet region
Cir·cas·sian
Circe mythological character
cir·ci·nate botany term
Cir·ci·nus constellation
cir·cle
cir·cler
cir·clet
cir·cuit
cir·cuit·al of a circuit
cir·cui·tous indirect
cir·cui·tous·ly
cir·cuit·ry circuit system
cir·cu·ity (*plural* ·ities)
cir·cu·lar
cir·cu·lar·ity (*or* ·ness)
cir·cu·lari·za·tion (*or* ·sa·tion)
cir·cu·lar·ize (*or* ·ise)
cir·cu·lar·iz·er (*or* ·is·er)
cir·cu·late
cir·cu·la·tion
cir·cu·la·tive
cir·cu·la·tor
cir·cu·la·tory
cir·cum·am·bi·ence (*or* ·en·cy)
cir·cum·am·bi·ent
cir·cum·am·bu·late
cir·cum·am·bu·la·tion
cir·cum·am·bu·la·tor
cir·cum·am·bu·la·tory
cir·cum·ben·di·bus circumlocution
cir·cum·cise
cir·cum·ci·sion
cir·cum·fer·ence
cir·cum·fer·en·tial
cir·cum·flex
cir·cum·flex·ion
cir·cum·flu·ous surrounded by water
cir·cum·fuse
cir·cum·fu·sion
cir·cum·lo·cu·tion
cir·cum·locu·tory
cir·cum·lu·nar
cir·cum·navi·gable
cir·cum·navi·gate
cir·cum·navi·ga·tion
cir·cum·navi·ga·tor

80

cir·cum·nu·tate botany term
cir·cum·nu·ta·tion
cir·cum·po·lar
cir·cum·scis·sile botany term
cir·cum·scribe
cir·cum·scrip·tion
cir·cum·spect
cir·cum·spec·tion
cir·cum·spec·tive
cir·cum·stance
cir·cum·stan·tial
cir·cum·stan·ti·ality (*plural* ·alities)
cir·cum·stan·tial·ly
cir·cum·stan·ti·ate
cir·cum·stan·tia·tion
cir·cum·val·late surround with fortification
cir·cum·val·la·tion
cir·cum·vent
cir·cum·vent·er (*or* **ven·tor**)
cir·cum·ven·tion
cir·cum·vo·lu·tion
cir·cum·vo·lu·tory
cir·cus (*plural* ·cuses)
ciré waxed
Ci·ren·ces·ter
cirque mountain feature
cir·rate (*or* **cir·rose**, **cir·rous**) biology term
cir·rhosed
cir·rho·sis
cir·rhot·ic
cir·ri·pede (*or* ·ped) marine animal
cir·ro·cu·mu·lus (*plural* ·li)
cir·rose (*or* ·rous)
cir·ro·stra·tus (*plural* ·ti)
cir·rus (*plural* ·ri) cloud; tentacle; *compare* **schirrhus**
cir·soid medical term
cis·al·pine
cis·co (*plural* ·coes *or* ·cos) fish
cis·lu·nar between earth and moon
cis·mon·tane
cis·soid curve
cist box; *compare* **cyst**
cis·ta·ceous botany term
Cis·ter·cian monk

cis·tern
cis·ter·na (*plural* ·nae)
　anatomy term
cis·tron genetics term
cit·able (*or* cite·able)
cita·del
ci·ta·tion
cite
citha·ra (*or* kitha·ra)
　musical instrument
citi·fy (*or* city·fy; ·fies,
　·fy·ing, ·fied)
citi·zen
citi·zen·ry (*plural* ·ries)
citi·zen·ship
Ci·tlal·té·petl Mexican
　volcano
cit·ral plant oil
cit·rate
cit·re·ous greenish-yellow
cit·ric
cit·ri·cul·ture
cit·rin vitamin
cit·rine gemstone
cit·ron fruit
cit·ron·el·la grass
cit·ron·el·lal plant oil
cit·rul·line amino acid
cit·rus (*plural* ·ruses)
cit·tern musical instrument
City London's commercial
　area
city (*plural* cities)
civ·et
civ·ic
civi·cal·ly
civ·ics
civ·il
ci·vil·ian
ci·vil·ity (*plural* ·ities)
civi·li·za·tion (*or* ·sa·tion)
civi·lize (*or* ·lise)
civi·liz·er (*or* ·lis·er)
civ·il·ly
civ·vy (*plural* ·vies) *Slang*
　civilian
clack
Clack·man·nan former
　Scottish county
Clac·ton Essex town
Clac·to·nian Palaeolithic
　culture
clad (clad·ding, clad)
clade
cla·dis·tic

cla·dis·tics
cla·doc·er·an animal
clad·ode (*or* clado·phyll)
　plant stem
claim
claim·able
claim·ant
claim·er
clair·audi·ence psychology
　term
clair-obscure art term
clair·voy·ance
clair·voy·ant
clam (clam·ming,
　clammed)
cla·mant noisy
clama·to·rial ornithology
　term
clam·bake
clam·ber
clam·mi·ly
clam·mi·ness
clam·my (·mi·er, ·mi·est)
clam·or·ous
clam·our (*US* ·or)
clamp
clamp·er shoe spike
clan
clan·des·tine
clang
clang·er that which clangs;
　mistake
clang·or (*or* ·our) loud
　noise
clang·or·ous (*or* ·our·ous)
clank
clan·nish
clans·man (*plural* ·men)
clans·woman (*plural*
　·women)
clap (clap·ping, clapped)
clap·board
Clap·ham
clap·per
clapper·board
clap·trap
claque hired applauders
clara·bel·la (*or* clari·)
　organ stop
clar·ence carriage
Clar·en·don village near
　Salisbury
clar·en·don typeface
clar·et
clari·fi·ca·tion

clari·fier
clari·fy (·fies, ·fy·ing,
　·fied)
clari·net
clari·net·ist (*or* ·net·tist)
cla·rino musical term
clari·on
clario·net *Obsolete* clarinet
clar·ity
clarkia plant
cla·ro cigar
clarts *Dialect* lumps of mud
clary (*plural* claries) plant
clash
clash·er
clasp
clasp·er
class
class-conscious
class-conscious·ness
clas·sic
clas·si·cal
clas·si·cal·ism
clas·si·cal·ity
clas·si·cal·ly
clas·si·cism (*or*
　clas·si·cal·ism)
clas·si·cist (*or*
　clas·si·cal·ist)
clas·si·cis·tic
clas·sics
clas·si·fi·able
clas·si·fi·ca·tion
clas·si·fi·ca·tion·al
clas·si·fi·ca·tory
clas·si·fi·er
clas·si·fy (·fies, ·fy·ing,
　·fied)
classi·ly
classi·ness
clas·sis (*plural* ·ses)
　church elders
class·less
class·less·ness
class·mate
class·room
classy (classi·er,
　classi·est)
clas·tic geology term
clath·rate netlike
clat·ter
clat·tery
clau·di·ca·tion lameness
claus·al
clause

claustral 82

claus·tral *variant spelling of* cloistral
claus·tro·phobe
claus·tro·pho·bia
claus·tro·pho·bic
claus·tro·pho·bi·cal·ly
cla·vate (*or* clavi·form) club-shaped
clav·er *Scot* gossip
clavi·chord
clavi·chord·ist
clavi·cle
clavi·corn beetle
cla·vicu·lar
cla·vier musical instrument
Cla·vi·us moon crater
claw
claw·er
clay
clay·bank *US* brown colour
clay·ey
clay·like
clay·more sword
clay·pan clay layer
clay·stone
clay·to·nia plant
clean
clean·able
clean-cut
clean·er
clean-limbed
clean·li·ness
clean·ly (·li·er, ·li·est)
clean·ness
cleans·able
cleanse
cleans·er
clean-shaven
clear
clear·ance
clear·cole wall whiting
clear-cut
clear-eyed
clear-headed
clear-headed·ness
clear·ing
clear·ness
clear-sighted
clear·way
clear·wing moth
cleat
cleav·able
cleav·age

cleave (cleav·ing; cleaved *or* clove; cleft, cleaved, *or* clo·ven)
cleav·er
cleav·ers goosegrass
cleck *Dialect* gossip
cleek golf club
Clee·thorpes English resort
clef
cleft
cleg horsefly
cleis·toga·mous (*or* ·to·gam·ic)
cleis·toga·my botany term
clem (clem·ming, clemmed) *Dialect* be hungry
clema·tis
clem·en·cy (*plural* ·cies)
clem·ent
clem·en·tine
clench
cleo·me plant
clep·to·ma·nia *variant spelling of* kleptomania
clere·storied (*or* clear·storied)
clere·story (*or* clear·; *plural* ·stories) church windows
cler·gy (*plural* ·gies)
clergy·man (*plural* ·men)
cler·ic
cleri·cal
cleri·cal·ism
cleri·cal·ly
cleri·hew verse
clerk
clerk·dom
clerk·ly
clerk·ship
Clermont-Ferrand French city
cle·ru·chy Athenian colony
cleve·ite mineral
Cleve·land
clev·er
clev·er·ly
clev·er·ness
clev·is coupling device
clew yarn; *compare* clue
cli·ché
cli·ché'd (*or* ·chéd)
Cli·chy Parisian suburb
click

click·er
cli·ent
cli·en·tal of a client
cli·en·tele customers
cliff
cliff·hanger
cliff·hanging
cli·mac·ter·ic critical period
cli·mac·teri·cal
cli·mac·tic (*or* ·ti·cal) of a climax
cli·mate
cli·mat·ic (*or* ·mati·cal *or* ·mat·al)
cli·ma·to·log·ic (*or* ·logi·cal)
cli·ma·tolo·gist
cli·ma·tol·ogy
cli·max
climb
climb·er
clime climate
clin·al of a cline
cli·nan·drium (*plural* ·dria) botany term
clinch
clinch·er
cline ecology term
cling (cling·ing, clung)
cling·er
cling·fish (*plural* ·fish *or* ·fishes)
clingi·ness (*or* cling·ing·ness)
cling·stone peach
clingy
clin·ic
clini·cal
cli·ni·cian
clink
clink·er
clinker-built (*or* clincher-)
clink·stone
cli·nom·eter surveying instrument
cli·no·met·ric (*or* ·ri·cal)
cli·nom·etry
cli·no·stat botany term
clin·quant tinsel
clin·to·nia plant
clip (clip·ping, clipped)
clip·board
clip-clop
clip·per

clip·pers
clip·pie *Slang* bus conductress
clip·ping
clique
cli·quey (*or* ·quy)
cli·quish
clish·ma·clav·er *Scot* gossip
cli·tel·lum (*plural* ·la) part of worm
clit·ic unstressed
clito·ral
clito·ris
cloa·ca (*plural* ·cae) zoology term
cloa·cal
cloak
cloak·room
clob·ber
cloche
clock
clock·maker
clock·wise
clock·work
clod
clod·dish
clod·dy
clod·hop·per
clod·hop·ping
clog (clog·ging, clogged)
clog·gi·ness
clog·gy (·gi·er, ·gi·est)
cloi·son·né enamel work
clois·ter
clois·tered
clois·tral (*or* claus·tral)
clomp
clon·al
clone (*or* clon)
clon·ic medical term
clo·nic·ity
clonk
clo·nus convulsion
clop (clop·ping, clopped)
close
close-down (*noun*)
close-fisted
close-grained
close-hauled sailing term
close-knit
close·ly
close·ness
clos·er
close-stool
clos·et

close-up (*noun*)
clos·ing
clos·trid·ial (*or* ·ian)
clos·trid·ium (*plural* ·iums *or* ·ia) bacterium
clo·sure
clot (clot·ting, clot·ted)
cloth
cloth·bound
clothe (cloth·ing, clothed *or* clad)
clothes
clothes·horse
clothes·line
clothes-press
clo·thi·er
cloth·ing
clo·ture *US* closure
cloud
cloud·berry (*plural* ·berries)
cloud·burst
cloud-cuckoo-land
cloudi·ly
cloudi·ness
cloud·less
cloud·let
cloud·scape
cloudy (cloudi·er, cloudi·est)
clough *Dialect* gorge
clout
clove
clo·ven
clo·ver
clover·leaf (*plural* ·leaves)
clown
clown·ery
clown·ish
cloy
cloy·ed·ness
cloy·ing·ly
cloy·ing·ness
club (club·bing, clubbed)
club·bable (*or* ·able)
club·by (·bi·er, ·bi·est)
club-footed
club·haul nautical term
club·house
club·land
club·man (*plural* ·men)
cluck
clucky *Austral* pregnant

clue (clu·ing, clued) evidence; *compare* clew
clue·less
Cluj Romanian city
clum·ber spaniel
clump
clump·ish (*or* clump·like)
clumpy
clum·si·ly
clum·si·ness
clum·sy (·si·er, ·si·est)
clung
Clu·ni·ac of Cluny
clunk
Clu·ny French town
clu·peid fish
clu·peoid
clus·ter
clus·tery
clutch
clut·ter
Clw·yd Welsh county
Clyde Scottish river
Clyde·bank Scottish town
Clydes·dale horse
clype *Scot* tell tales
clyp·eal (*or* clype·ate)
clyp·eus (*plural* clypei) part of insect's head
clys·ter enema
cni·dar·ian zoology term
cnido·blast zoology term
Cni·dus ancient Greek city
Cnos·sus *variant spelling of* Knossos
co·ac·er·vate chemistry term
co·ac·er·va·tion
coach
coach·er
coach·ing
coach·man (*plural* ·men)
coach·work
co·ac·tion
co·ac·tive
co·ac·tiv·ity
co·ad·ju·tant
co·ad·ju·tor bishop's assistant
co·adu·nate biology term
co·adu·na·tion
co·adu·na·tive
co·agu·lable
co·agu·lant (*or* co·agu·la·tor)

coagulase 84

co·agu·lase enzyme
co·agu·late
co·agu·la·tion
co·agu·la·tive
co·agu·lum (*plural* ·la) coagulated mass
Coa·hui·la Mexican state
coal
coal·er coal transporter
coa·lesce
coa·les·cence
coa·les·cent
coal·face
coal·field
coal·fish (*plural* ·fish *or* ·fishes)
coa·li·tion
coa·li·tion·al
coa·li·tion·ist (*or* ·er)
coal·man (*plural* ·men)
Coal·port china
coaly
coam·ing nautical term
co·ap·ta·tion joining two surfaces
co·arc·tate zoology term
co·arc·ta·tion
coarse rough; *compare* corse; course
coarse·ly
coars·en
coarse·ness
coast
coast·al
coast·er
coast·guard
coast·line
coat
coat·ed
coatee small coat
coa·ti (*or* coati-mundi) animal
coat·ing
coat·less
coat-tail
co·author
coax
coax·er
co·ax·ial (*or* ·ax·al)
cob
co·balt
co·bal·tic
co·bal·tite (*or* ·tine) mineral
co·bal·tous

cob·ber *Austral* friend
cob·ble
cob·bler
cobble·stone
co·bel·lig·er·ent
co·bia fish
co·ble *Scot* fishing boat
Co·blenz variant spelling of Koblenz
cob·nut
Cobol computer language
co·bra
Co·burg West German city
co·burg loaf
cob·web
cob·webbed
cob·web·by
coca shrub
Coca-Cola (*Trademark*)
co·caine (*or* ·cain)
co·cain·ism
co·caini·za·tion (*or* ·sa·tion)
co·cain·ize (*or* ·ise)
coc·cal
coc·ci *plural of* coccus
coc·cid insect
coc·cidi·oi·do·my·co·sis fungal disease
coc·cidio·sis (*plural* ·ses) animal disease
coc·cif·er·ous
coc·coid
coc·co·lith geology term
coc·cous (*adj*)
coc·cus (*plural* ·ci) bacterium
coc·cyg·eal
coc·cyx (*plural* ·cy·ges)
Co·cha·bam·ba Bolivian city
Co·chin Indian region and port
cochi·neal
coch·lea (*plural* ·leae) ear part
coch·lear
coch·leate shell-shaped
cock
cock·ade
cock-a-doodle-doo
cock-a-hoop
Cock·aigne imaginary land
cock-a-leekie soup

cocka·lo·rum self-important person
cocka·tiel (*or* ·teel) parrot
cocka·too (*plural* ·toos) parrot
cocka·trice monster
cock·chafer beetle
cock·crow
cock·er
cock·er·el
cock·eye
cock·eyed
cock·fight
cock·horse
cocki·ly
cocki·ness
cock·le
cockle·bur weed
cockle·shell
cock·loft garret
cock·ney
cock·ney·fi·ca·tion (*or* ·ni·)
cock·ney·fy (*or* ·ni·; ·fies, ·fy·ing, ·fied)
cock·ney·ism
cock·pit
cock·roach
cocks·comb (*or* cox·comb)
cocks·foot (*plural* ·foots) grass
cock·shy throw
cock·spur grass
cock·sure
cock·swain variant spelling of coxswain
cock·tail
cock·up
cocky (cocki·er, cocki·est)
coco (*plural* cocos) short *for* coconut
co·coa
coco de mer tree
coco·nut
co·coon
co·co·pan mining wagon
co·cotte
co·co·yam vegetable
cod (*noun, plural* cod *or* cods; *verb* cod·ding, cod·ded)
coda
cod·dle

cod·dler
code
co·dec·li·na·tion
co·deine
cod·er
co·dex (*plural* co·di·ces)
cod·fish (*plural* ·fish *or* ·fishes)
codg·er
codi·cil
codi·cil·la·ry
co·di·col·ogy
codi·fi·ca·tion
codi·fi·er
codi·fy (·fies, ·fy·ing, ·fied)
cod·ling (*or* ·lin) apple
co·do·main maths term
co·don genetics term
cod·piece
co·driver
cods·wallop
co·ed
co·edit
co·edi·tion
co·edi·tor
co·edu·ca·tion
co·edu·ca·tion·al
co·edu·ca·tion·al·ly
co·ef·fi·cient
coe·la·canth primitive fish
coe·len·ter·ate animal
coe·len·ter·ic
coe·len·ter·on (*plural* ·tera) zoology term
coe·li·ac (*US* ce·) of the abdomen
coe·lom (*US* ce·) body cavity
coe·lo·mate (*US* ce·)
coe·lo·stat astronomical instrument
coe·nes·the·sia (*or* ·sis, ce·)
coe·nes·thet·ic (*or* ce·)
coe·no·bite (*or* ce·) member of religious order
coe·no·cyte botany term
coe·no·cyt·ic
coe·no·sarc zoology term
coe·nu·rus larva
co·en·zyme
co·equal
co·equali·ty
co·equal·ly

co·erce
co·er·cible
co·er·cion
co·er·cion·ary
co·er·cion·ist
co·er·cive
co·er·cive·ness
co·er·civ·ity physics term
co·es·sen·tial
co·es·sen·tial·ity (*or* ·ness)
co·eter·nity
co·eval contemporary
co·eval·ity
co·eval·ly
co·ex·ist
co·ex·ist·ence
co·ex·ist·ent
co·ex·tend
co·ex·ten·sion
co·ex·ten·sive
coff *Scot* buy
cof·fee
coffee·pot
cof·fer
coffer·dam underwater chamber
cof·fin
cof·fle chained slaves
cog (cog·ging, cogged)
co·gen·cy
co·gent
cogi·tate
cogi·ta·tion
cogi·ta·tive
cogi·ta·tor
Cog·nac French town; brandy
cog·nate
cog·na·tion relatedness
cog·ni·tion perception
cog·ni·tive
cog·ni·zable (*or* ·sable)
cog·ni·zance (*or* ·sance)
cog·ni·zant (*or* ·sant)
cog·nize (*or* ·nise) perceive
cog·no·men Roman family name
co·gno·scen·ti (*or* cono·scen·ti; *sing.* ·te)
co·gon grass
cog·wheel
co·hab·it
co·hab·it·ant (*or* ·it·er)
co·habi·ta·tion

co·heir
co·here
co·her·ence (*or* ·en·cy)
co·her·ent
co·her·er
co·he·sion
co·he·sive
coho (*plural* coho *or* cohos) fish
co·ho·bate redistil
co·hort
co·hosh plant
co·hune palm tree
coif cap
coif·feur (*fem* ·feuse) hairdresser
coif·fure hair style
coign (*or* coigne) *variant spellings of* quoin; *compare* coin
coil
coil·er
Co·im·ba·tore Indian city
Coim·bra Portuguese city
coin currency; *compare* quoin
coin·age
co·in·cide
co·in·ci·dence
co·in·ci·dent
co·in·ci·dent·al
co·in·ci·dent·al·ly
coin·er
coin-op
co·in·sur·ance
co·in·sure
Coin·treau (*Trademark*)
coir coconut fibre
coit *Austral* buttocks
coi·tal
coi·tus (*or* ·tion)
Coke (*Trademark*) Coca-Cola
coke
coku·lo·ris film term
col
cola (*or* kola) tree; nut
col·an·der sieve; *compare* calendar; calender
co·lati·tude
col·can·non cabbage dish
Col·ches·ter
col·chi·cine alkaloid
col·chi·cum plant

Colchis

Col·chis ancient Asian country
col·co·thar rouge
cold
cold-blooded
cold-blooded·ness
cold-drawn metallurgy term
cold-hearted
cold·ish
cold·ness
cold-weld
cole cabbage
co·lec·to·my (*plural* ·mies)
cole·man·ite mineral
col·eop·ter·an (*plural* ·ter·ans *or* ·tera) beetle
col·eop·ter·ist
col·eop·ter·ous
col·eop·tile botany term
col·eo·rhi·za (*plural* ·zae) botany term
cole·slaw
co·leus (*plural* ·uses) plant
col·ey fish; *compare* coly
col·ic
col·icky
colic·root
colic·weed
Co·li·ma Mexican state and city
coli·seum (*or* col·os·seum)
co·li·tic
co·li·tis (*or* colo·ni·tis)
col·labo·rate
col·labo·ra·tion
col·labo·ra·tive
col·labo·ra·tor
col·lage
col·la·gen protein
col·la·gen·ic (*or* ·gen·ous)
col·lag·ist
col·lap·sar black hole
col·lapse
col·laps·ibil·ity
col·laps·ible (*or* ·able)
col·lar
collar·bone
col·lard cabbage
col·lar·ette
col·late
col·lat·er·al
col·lat·er·al·ly

col·la·tion
col·la·tive
col·la·tor
col·league
col·lect
col·lect·able (*or* ·ible)
col·lec·ta·nea miscellany
col·lec·tion
col·lec·tive
col·lec·tiv·ism
col·lec·tiv·ist
col·lec·tiv·is·tic
col·lec·tiv·ity (*plural* ·ities)
col·lec·tivi·za·tion (*or* ·sa·tion)
col·lec·ti·vize (*or* ·vise)
col·lec·tor
col·lec·to·rate
col·leen *Irish* girl
col·lege
col·le·gial
col·legian
col·legi·ate
col·legium (*plural* ·legiums *or* ·legia)
col·lem·bo·lan insect
col·len·chy·ma plant tissue
Colles' frac·ture
col·let jewellery setting
col·lide
col·lie
col·li·er
col·liery (*plural* ·lieries)
col·li·gate join
col·li·ga·tion
col·li·ga·tive
col·li·mate
col·li·ma·tion
col·li·ma·tor optical device
col·lin·ear
col·lin·ear·ity
col·lin·sia plant
col·li·sion
col·lo·cate
col·lo·ca·tion
col·lo·cu·tor
col·lo·di·on (*or* ·dium) liquid
col·logue (·lo·guing, ·logued) conspire
col·loid
col·loi·dal
col·loi·dal·ity
col·lop *Dialect* meat slice

col·lo·quial
col·lo·qui·al·ism
col·lo·qui·al·ly
col·lo·quium (*plural* ·quiums *or* ·quia)
col·lo·quy (*plural* ·quies)
(collossus) *incorrect spelling of* colossus
col·lo·type printing process
col·lo·typ·ic
col·lude
col·lu·sion
col·lu·sive
col·lu·vial
col·lu·vium (*plural* ·via *or* ·viums) rock fragments
col·ly *Dialect* soot
col·lyr·ium (*plural* ·lyria *or* ·lyr·iums) eye lotion
col·ly·wob·bles
colo·bus monkey
colo·cynth plant
co·loga·rithm
co·logne perfume
Co·logne West German city
Co·lom·bia South American republic; *compare* Columbia
Co·lom·bian
Co·lom·bo Sri Lankan capital
co·lon
Co·lón Panamanian port
colo·nel
colo·nel·cy (*or* colo·nel·ship)
co·lo·nial
co·lo·ni·al·ism
co·lo·ni·al·ist
co·lo·ni·al·ly
co·lon·ic
colo·nist
colo·ni·tis *variant of* colitis
colo·niz·able (*or* ·nis·able)
colo·ni·za·tion (*or* ·sa·tion)
colo·nize (*or* ·nise)
colo·niz·er (*or* ·nis·er)
col·on·nade
col·on·nad·ed
Col·on·say Hebridean island
colo·ny (*plural* ·nies)
colo·phon emblem

co·lopho·ny rosin
col·or US spelling of colour
Colo·ra·do
col·or·ant
col·ora·tion
colo·ra·tu·ra (or col·ora·ture) musical term
col·or·if·ic
col·or·im·eter
col·ori·met·ric (or ·ri·cal)
col·or·im·etry
co·los·sal
co·los·sal·ly
Col·os·seum Roman amphitheatre
col·os·seum variant spelling of coliseum
co·los·sus (plural ·si or ·suses)
co·los·to·my (plural ·mies) artificial colon opening
co·los·tral
co·los·trum first breast milk
co·loto·my (plural ·mies)
col·our (US col·or)
col·our·able (US ·or·)
col·our·ant (US ·or·)
(colouration) incorrect spelling of coloration
colour-blind (US color-)
col·oured (US ·ored)
colour·fast (US color·)
col·our·ful (US ·or·)
col·our·ful·ly (US ·or·)
col·our·ing (US ·or·)
col·our·ist (US ·or·)
col·our·is·tic (US ·or·)
col·our·ize (·ise; US col·or·ize)
col·our·less (US ·or·)
colour·man (US color·; plural ·men) paint dealer
col·oury (or ·ory)
col·pi·tis medical term
col·por·teur book pedlar
Colt (Trademark) revolver
colt
col·ter US spelling of coulter
colt·ish
colts·foot (plural ·foots) plant
colu·brid snake
colu·brine of snakes

co·lu·go lemur
Co·lum·ba constellation
col·um·bar·ium (plural ·ia) dovecote
Co·lum·bia US river and city; compare Colombia
Co·lum·bian
co·lum·bic
Col·um·bine pantomime character
col·um·bine plant
co·lum·bite mineral
co·lum·bium chemical element
Co·lum·bus US city
colu·mel·la (plural ·lae) biology term
colu·mel·lar
col·umn
co·lum·nar
col·umned (or ·um·nat·ed)
co·lum·nia·tion
col·umn·ist
co·lure circle on sphere
Col·wyn Bay
coly (plural colies) bird; compare coley
col·za rape plant
coma (plural comas) unconsciousness
coma (plural comae) cloud round comet
com·al
Co·man·che (plural ·ches or ·che)
Co·man·chean
co·mate hairy
co·ma·tose
co·matu·lid (or ·matu·la; plural ·lids or ·lae) marine animal
comb
com·bat
com·bat·able
com·bat·ant
com·bat·er
com·bat·ive
combe variant spelling of coomb
comb·er
com·bin·able
com·bi·na·tion
com·bi·na·tive (or ·to·rial, ·tory)
com·bine

commandment
com·bin·er
comb·ing
com·bo (plural ·bos) jazz band
com·bust
com·bus·tibil·ity (or ·tible·ness)
com·bus·tible
com·bus·tion
com·bus·tor engine part
come (com·ing, came)
come·back
Com·econ Communist economic association
co·median
co·medic
co·medi·enne
com·edo (plural ·edos or ·edo·nes) blackhead
come·down
com·edy (plural ·edies)
come·ly (·li·er, ·li·est)
come-on (noun)
com·er
co·mes·tible
com·et
come·up·pance
com·fit sweet
com·fort
com·fort·able
com·fort·ably
com·fort·er
com·fort·ing
com·fort·less
com·frey plant
com·fy (·fi·er, ·fi·est)
com·ic
comi·cal
comi·cal·ly
Com·in·form Communist Information Bureau
com·ing
Com·in·tern international Communist organization
co·mi·tia Roman assembly
com·ity (plural ·ities) courtesy
com·ma
com·mand
com·man·dant
com·man·deer
com·mand·er
com·mand·er·ship
com·mand·ing
com·mand·ment

commando 88

com·man·do (*plural* ·dos *or* ·does)
com·mea·sure
com·media dell'arte Italian comic theatre
comme il faut *French* as it should be
com·memo·rate
com·memo·ra·tion
com·memo·ra·tive (*or* ·tory)
com·memo·ra·tor
com·mence
com·mence·ment
com·mend
com·mend·able
com·mend·ably
com·men·dam Church office
com·men·da·tion
com·menda·tory
com·men·sal biology term
com·men·sal·ism (*or* ·sal·ity)
com·men·su·rable
com·men·su·rate
com·men·su·ra·tion
com·ment
com·men·tar·ial
com·men·tary (*plural* ·taries)
com·men·tate
com·men·ta·tor
com·ment·er
com·merce
com·mer·cial
com·mer·cial·ism
com·mer·cial·ist
com·mer·cial·is·tic
com·mer·ci·al·ity
com·mer·ciali·za·tion (*or* ·sa·tion)
com·mer·cial·ize (*or* ·ise)
com·mer·cial·ly
com·mère female compere
com·mi·na·tion threatening vengeance
com·mina·tory
com·min·gle
com·mi·nute reduce to fragments
com·mi·nu·tion
com·mis agent
com·mis·er·ate
com·mis·era·tion

com·mis·era·tive
com·mis·era·tor
com·mis·sar
com·mis·sar·ial
com·mis·sari·at
com·mis·sary (*plural* ·saries)
com·mis·sion
com·mis·sion·aire
com·mis·sion·al (*or* ·ary)
com·mis·sion·er
com·mis·su·ral
com·mis·sure anatomy term
com·mit (·mit·ting, ·mit·ted)
com·mit·ment
com·mit·tal
com·mit·tee
committee·man (*plural* ·men)
com·mit·ter
(committment) *incorrect spelling of* commitment
com·mode
com·mo·di·ous
com·mod·ity (*plural* ·ities)
com·mo·dore
com·mon
com·mon·able legal term
com·mon·age legal term
com·mon·al·ity commonness
com·mon·al·ty (*or* ·ity) ordinary people
com·mon·er
com·mon·ly
com·mon·ness
common·place
Com·mons (House of)
common·weal *Archaic* common goods; commonwealth
Common·wealth of Nations; republican England
common·wealth independent community
com·mo·tion
com·mo·tion·al
com·mu·nal
com·mu·nal·ism
com·mu·nal·ist
com·mu·nal·is·tic
com·mu·nal·ity

commu·nali·za·tion (*or* ·sa·tion)
com·mu·nal·ize (*or* ·ise)
Com·mu·nade supporter of Paris Commune
com·mu·nard member of a commune
Com·mune Paris Revolutionary government
com·mune
com·mu·ni·cabil·ity (*or* ·cable·ness)
com·mu·ni·cable
com·mu·ni·cant
com·mu·ni·cate
com·mu·ni·ca·tion
com·mu·ni·ca·tive
com·mu·ni·ca·tor
com·mu·ni·ca·tory
Com·mun·ion Eucharist
com·mun·ion
com·mun·ion·al
com·mun·ion·ist
com·mu·ni·qué
com·mun·ism
Com·mun·ist political party
com·mun·ist supporter of communism
com·mu·nis·tic
com·mu·ni·tar·ian
com·mu·nity (*plural* ·nities)
com·mu·ni·za·tion (*or* ·sa·tion)
com·mu·nize (*or* ·nise) nationalize
com·mut·able exchangeable
com·mu·tate
com·mu·ta·tion
com·mu·ta·tive involving substitution
com·mu·ta·tor electrical device
com·mute
com·mut·er
Como Italian city and lake
Como·ros island country
co·mose hairy
comp *Slang* compositor
com·pact
com·pact·er
com·pact·ness
com·pan·der sound transmission
com·pan·ion

comradeship

com·pan·ion·able
com·pan·ion·ably
com·pan·ion·able
com·pan·ion·ate
com·pan·ion·ship
com·pan·ion·way stairway on ship
com·pa·ny (*plural* ·nies)
com·pa·rabil·ity
com·pa·rable
com·pa·rably
com·para·tive
com·para·tive·ly
com·para·tor
com·pare
com·par·er
com·pari·son
com·part·ment
com·part·men·tal
com·part·men·tali·za·tion (*or* ·sa·tion)
com·part·men·tal·ize (*or* ·ise)
com·part·men·ted
com·pass
com·pass·able
com·pas·sion
com·pas·sion·ate
com·pat·ibil·ity
com·pat·ible
com·pat·ibly
com·pat·ri·ot
com·pat·ri·ot·ic
com·pat·ri·ot·ism
com·peer equal status
com·pel (·pel·ling, ·pelled)
com·pel·ler
com·pen·di·ous
com·pen·dium (*plural* ·diums *or* ·dia)
com·pen·sate
com·pen·sa·tion
com·pen·sa·tive
com·pen·sa·tor
com·pen·sa·tory
com·pere
com·pete
com·pe·tence
com·pe·ten·cy (*plural* ·cies) legal term
com·pe·tent
com·pe·ti·tion
com·peti·tive
com·peti·tor

com·pi·la·tion
com·pile
com·pil·er
com·pla·cen·cy (*or* com·pla·cence; *plural* ·cencies *or* ·cences) self-satisfaction; *compare* complaisance
com·pla·cent
com·plain
com·plain·ant
com·plain·er
com·plaint
com·plai·sance willingness to comply; *compare* complacency
com·plai·sant
com·ple·ment complete; that which completes; *compare* compliment
com·ple·men·tary (*or* ·tal)
com·ple·men·tiz·er grammar term
com·plete
com·plete·ness
com·plet·er
com·ple·tion
com·ple·tive
com·plex
com·plex·ion
com·plex·ity (*plural* ·ities)
com·pli·ance (*or* ·an·cy)
com·pli·ant (*or* ·able)
com·pli·cate
com·pli·cat·ed
com·pli·ca·tion
com·plic·ity (*plural* ·ities)
com·pli·er
com·pli·ment praise; *compare* complement
com·pli·men·tary
com·pline (*or* ·plin) canonical hour
com·ply (·plies, ·ply·ing, ·plied)
com·po (*plural* ·pos) mixture; *Austral* compensation
com·po·nent
com·po·nen·tial
com·po·ny (*or* ·ne) heraldic term
com·port
com·port·ment
com·pose

com·pos·er
com·po·site
com·po·si·tion
com·po·si·tion·al
com·posi·tor
com·pos men·tis *Latin* sane
com·post
com·po·sure
com·pote
com·pound
com·pound·er
com·pra·dor foreign agent
com·pre·hend
com·pre·hen·sibil·ity (*or* ·sible·ness)
com·pre·hen·sible (*or* ·hend·ible)
com·pre·hen·sibly
com·pre·hen·sion
com·pre·hen·sive
com·press
com·press·ibil·ity (*or* ·ible·ness)
com·press·ible
com·pres·sion
com·pres·sion·al
com·pres·sive
com·pres·sor
com·pris·able
com·pris·al
com·prise
com·pro·mise
com·pro·mis·er
Comp·tom·eter (*Trademark*)
comp·trol·ler
com·pul·sion
com·pul·sive
com·pul·so·ry
com·pul·so·ri·ly
com·punc·tion
com·punc·tious
com·put·abil·ity
com·put·able
com·pu·ta·tion
com·pu·ta·tion·al
com·pute
com·put·er
com·put·eri·za·tion (*or* ·sa·tion)
com·put·er·ize (*or* ·ise)
com·rade
com·rade·ship

comsat

com·sat *short for* communications satellite
com·stock·ery *US* excessive censorship
Comus Roman god
con (con·ning, conned)
con amo·re musical term
co·na·tion psychology term
cona·tive linguistics term
co·na·tus (*plural* ·tus) striving
con brio musical term
con·cat·enate
con·cat·ena·tion series of events
con·cave
con·cav·ity (*plural* ·ities)
concavo-concave
concavo-convex
con·ceal
con·ceal·ment
con·cede
con·ced·er
con·ceit
con·ceit·ed
con·ceiv·able
con·ceiv·ably
con·ceive
con·cel·ebrate
con·cel·ebra·tion (concensus) *incorrect spelling of* consensus
con·cen·trate
con·cen·tra·tion
con·cen·tra·tive
con·cen·tra·tor
con·cen·tre to concentrate
con·cen·tric (*or* ·tri·cal)
con·cen·tri·cal·ly
con·cen·tric·ity
Con·cep·ción Chilean city
con·cept
con·cep·ta·cle botany term
con·cep·tion
con·cep·tion·al
con·cep·tive
con·cep·tual
con·cep·tu·al·ism
con·cep·tu·al·ist
con·cep·tu·al·is·tic
con·cep·tu·ali·za·tion (*or* ·sa·tion)
con·cep·tu·al·ize (*or* ·ise)
con·cern
con·cerned

con·cern·ed·ly
con·cern·ing
con·cert
con·cer·tan·te musical work
con·cert·ed
con·cert·go·er
con·cer·ti·na (·nas, ·na·ing, ·naed)
con·cer·ti·no (*plural* ·ni) musical work
con·cer·tize
con·cer·to (*plural* ·tos *or* ·ti)
con·cer·to gros·so (*plural* ·ti gros·si)
con·ces·sible
con·ces·sion
con·ces·sion·aire (*or* ·er, ·ary; *plural* ·aires, ·ers, *or* ·aries)
con·ces·sion·ary
con·ces·sive
conch (*plural* conchs *or* conches) mollusc
con·cha (*plural* ·chae) shell-shaped part
con·chal
con·chif·er·ous
con·chio·lin protein
con·choid geometric curve
con·choi·dal geology term
con·cho·logi·cal
con·cholo·gist
con·chol·ogy study of shells
con·chy (*plural* ·chies) *Slang* conscientious objector
con·ci·erge
con·cili·ar of ecclesiastical councils
con·cili·ate
con·cili·ation
con·cilia·tive
con·cili·ator
con·cilia·tory (*or* ·tive)
con·cin·nity (*plural* ·nities) harmonious arrangement
con·cin·nous
con·cise
con·ci·sion
con·clave
con·clav·ist
con·clude
con·clu·sion
con·clu·sive

con·coct
con·coct·er (*or* ·coc·tor)
con·coc·tion
con·coc·tive
con·comi·tance
con·comi·tant
Con·cord US and Australian cities; *compare* Concorde
con·cord agreement
con·cord·ance
con·cord·ant
con·cor·dat treaty
Con·corde airliner; *compare* Concord
con·course
con·cres·cence biology term
con·crete
con·cre·tion
con·cre·tion·ary
con·cre·tive
con·creti·za·tion (*or* ·sa·tion)
con·cre·tize (*or* ·tise)
con·cu·bi·nage
con·cu·bine
con·cu·pis·cence
con·cu·pis·cent
con·cur (·cur·ring, ·curred)
con·cur·rence
con·cur·rent
con·cuss
con·cus·sion
con·cus·sive
con·demn
con·demn·able
con·dem·na·tion
con·dem·na·tory
con·demn·er
con·den·sabil·ity (*or* ·sibil·ity)
con·den·sable (*or* ·sible)
con·den·sate
con·den·sa·tion
con·dense
con·dens·er
con·de·scend
con·de·scend·ence legal term
con·de·scend·ing
con·de·scen·sion
con·dign well-deserved
con·di·ment

con·di·tion
con·di·tion·al
con·di·tion·al·ity
con·di·tion·al·ly
con·di·tioned
con·di·tion·er
con·di·tion·ing
con·do·la·tory
con·dole
con·do·lence (*or* ·dole·ment)
con·dol·er
con·dom
con·do·min·ium (*plural* ·iums)
con·do·na·tion
con·done
con·don·er
con·dor vulture
con·dot·tiere (*plural* ·tieri) mercenary
con·duce
con·duc·er
con·duc·ible
con·du·cive
con·duct
con·duct·ance physics term
con·duct·ible
con·duc·tion
con·duc·tive
con·duc·tiv·ity (*plural* ·ities)
con·duc·tor (*fem* ·tress)
con·duit
con·du·pli·cate botany term
con·du·pli·ca·tion
con·dy·lar
con·dyle bone projection
con·dy·loid
con·dy·lo·ma (*plural* ·mas *or* ·ma·ta) tumour
con·dy·loma·tous
cone
cone·flower
co·ney *variant spelling of* cony
Co·ney Is·land US resort
con·fab *Slang* chat
con·fabu·late
con·fabu·la·tion
con·fabu·la·tor
con·fabu·la·tory
con·fect combine ingredients
con·fec·tion

con·fec·tion·ary (*plural* ·aries) place where confections are made
con·fec·tion·er
con·fec·tion·ery (*plural* ·eries) sweets
Con·fed·era·cy seceding US states
con·fed·era·cy (*plural* ·cies)
Con·fed·er·ate
con·fed·er·ate
Con·fed·era·tion original US states
con·fed·era·tion
con·fed·era·tion·ism
con·fed·era·tion·ist
con·fer (·fer·ring, ·ferred)
con·feree (*or* ·fer·ree)
con·fer·ence
con·fer·en·tial
con·fer·ment (*or* ·fer·ral)
con·fer·rable
con·fer·rer
con·fer·va (*plural* ·vae *or* ·vas) alga
con·fer·val
con·fer·void
con·fess
confessant
con·fess·ed·ly
con·fes·sion
con·fes·sion·al
con·fes·sion·ary
con·fes·sor
con·fet·ti
con·fi·dant (*fem* ·dante) person in whom one confides
con·fide
con·fi·dence
con·fi·dent self-assured
con·fi·den·tial
con·fi·den·ti·al·ity (*or* ·tial·ness)
con·fi·den·tial·ly
con·fid·er
con·fid·ing
con·figu·ra·tion
con·figu·ra·tion·al (*or* ·ra·tive)
con·figu·ra·tion·ism Gestalt psychology
con·figu·ra·tion·ist
con·fin·able (*or* ·fine·able)

confutation

con·fine
con·fine·ment
con·firm
con·firm·and candidate for confirmation
con·fir·ma·tion
con·firma·tory (*or* ·tive)
con·fis·cable
con·fis·cate
con·fis·ca·tor
con·fis·ca·tory
Con·fit·eor prayer
con·fi·ture confection
con·fla·gra·tion
con·fla·gra·tive
con·flate combine
con·fla·tion
con·flict
con·flic·tion
con·flic·tive (*or* ·tory)
con·flu·ence (*or* con·flux)
con·flu·ent
con·fo·cal
con·form
con·form·abil·ity (*or* ·able·ness)
con·form·able
con·form·ably
con·for·mal maths term
con·for·ma·tion
con·form·er
con·form·ist
con·form·ity (*or* ·ance; *plural* ·ities *or* ·ances)
con·found
con·found·er
con·fra·ter·nal
con·fra·ter·nity (*plural* ·nities)
con·frère fellow member
con·front
con·fron·ta·tion (*or* con·front·ment)
con·front·er
Con·fu·cian
Con·fu·cian·ism
Con·fu·cian·ist
con fuo·co musical term
con·fus·able
con·fuse
con·fus·ed·ly
con·fus·ing
con·fus·ing·ly
con·fu·sion
con·fu·ta·tion

confutative

con·fu·ta·tive
con·fute
con·fut·er
con·ga (·ga·ing, ·gaed) dance; *compare* conger
con·gé dismissal
con·geal
con·geal·ment
con·ge·la·tion
con·ge·ner member of group
con·ge·ner·ic
con·gen·ial
con·ge·ni·al·ity (*or* con·gen·ial·ness)
con·gen·ial·ly
con·geni·tal present from birth
con·geni·tal·ly
con·ger eel; *compare* conga
con·ge·ries collection
con·gest
con·gest·ible
con·ges·tion
con·ges·tive
con·gi·us (*plural* ·gii) unit
con·glo·bate form into ball
con·glo·ba·tion
con·glom·er·ate
con·glom·er·at·ic (*or* ·it·ic)
con·glom·era·tion
con·glu·ti·nant
con·glu·ti·nate heal together
con·glu·ti·na·tive
Con·go African republic
con·go eel
Con·go·lese
con·gou (*or* ·go) China tea
con·grats
con·gratu·late
con·gratu·la·tion
con·gratu·la·tor
con·gratu·la·tory
con·gre·gant
con·gre·gate
con·gre·ga·tion
Con·gre·ga·tion·al evangelical church
con·gre·ga·tion·al
Con·gre·ga·tion·al·ism
Con·gre·ga·tion·al·ist
con·gre·ga·tive

con·gre·ga·tor (*or* ·gre·gant)
Con·gress US legislature
con·gress
Con·gres·sion·al
con·gres·sion·al
Con·gres·sion·al·ist
con·gres·sion·al·ist
Congress·man (*plural* ·men)
Congress·woman (*plural* ·women)
con·gru·ence (*or* ·en·cy; *plural* ·ences *or* ·cies)
con·gru·ent
con·gru·ity (*plural* ·ities)
con·gru·ous
con·ic (*or* coni·cal)
con·ics
co·nid·ial (*or* ·ian)
co·nidio·phore
co·nid·ium (*plural* ·nidia) fungal spore
co·ni·fer
co·nif·er·ous
co·ni·ine (*or* co·nin, co·nine) alkaloid
Con·is·ton lake
co·nium hemlock
con·jec·tur·al
con·jec·ture
con·jec·tur·er
con·join
con·join·ed·ly
con·join·er
con·joint
con·ju·gable
con·ju·gal
con·ju·gal·ly
con·ju·gal·ity
con·ju·gant
con·ju·gate
con·ju·ga·tion
con·ju·ga·tion·al
con·ju·ga·tive
con·ju·ga·tor
con·junct
con·junc·tion
con·junc·tion·al
con·junc·ti·va (*plural* ·vas *or* ·vae) eyeball membrane
con·junc·ti·val
con·junc·tive
con·junc·ti·vi·tis

con·junc·tur·al
con·junc·ture
con·jura·tion
con·jure
con·jur·er (*or* ·or)
conk
conk·er
con moto musical term
Con·nacht Northern Irish province
con·nate
con·natu·ral
Con·naught *former name of* Connacht
con·nect
con·nect·ible (*or* ·able)
Con·necti·cut
con·nec·tion (*or* ·nex·ion)
con·nec·tion·al (*or* ·nex·ion·al)
con·nec·tive
con·nec·tor (*or* ·er)
conned
Con·ne·ma·ra
con·ning
con·nip·tion US rage
con·niv·ance (*or* ·ence)
con·nive
con·niv·ent
con·niv·er
con·nois·seur
con·no·ta·tion
con·no·ta·tive (*or* con·no·tive)
con·note
con·nu·bial
con·nu·bi·al·ity
con·nu·bi·al·ly
co·no·dont fossil tooth
co·noid geometry term
co·noi·dal
con·quer
con·quer·or
con·quest
con·quis·ta·dor (*plural* ·dors *or* ·do·res)
con·san·guin·eous (*or* ·guine)
con·san·guin·ity
con·science
conscience-stricken
con·sci·en·tious
con·sci·en·tious·ness
con·scion·able
con·scious

con·scious·ness
con·script
con·scrip·tion
con·scrip·tion·al
con·scrip·tion·ist
con·se·crate
con·se·cra·tion
con·se·cra·tor
con·se·cra·tory (*or* ·tive)
con·se·cu·tion sequence of events
con·secu·tive
con·sen·sual
con·sen·sus
con·sent
con·sent·er
con·sen·tience
con·sen·tient in agreement
con·se·quence
con·se·quent
con·se·quen·tial
con·se·quen·tial·ly
con·se·quen·ti·al·ity (*or* ·tial·ness)
con·se·quent·ly
con·serv·able
con·serv·an·cy (*plural* ·cies)
con·ser·va·tion
con·ser·va·tion·al
con·ser·va·tion·ist
con·serva·tism
Con·serva·tive political party
con·serva·tive opposed to change
con·serva·toire musical institution
con·ser·va·tor custodian
con·serva·tory (*plural* ·tories)
con·serve
con·serv·er
Con·sett Durham town
con·sid·er
con·sid·er·able
con·sid·er·ably
con·sid·er·ate
con·sid·era·tion
con·sid·er·er
con·sign
con·sign·able
con·signa·tion
con·signee
con·sign·ment

con·sign·or (*or* ·er)
con·sist
con·sist·en·cy (*or* ·ence; *plural* ·cies *or* ·ences)
con·sist·ent
con·sis·to·rial (*or* ·rian)
con·sis·tory (*plural* ·tories) diocesan court
con·so·ci·ate
con·so·cia·tion
con·so·cies (*plural* ·cies) ecology term
con·sol·able
con·so·la·tion
con·sola·tory
con·sole
con·sol·er
con·soli·date
con·soli·da·tion
con·soli·da·tor
con·sols government securities
con·so·lute chemistry term
con·som·mé
con·so·nance (*or* ·nan·cy; *plural* ·nances *or* ·cies) agreement
con·so·nant
con·so·nan·tal
con·sort
con·sort·er
con·sor·tial
con·sor·tium (*plural* ·tia)
con·spe·cif·ic
con·spec·tus overall view
con·spicu·ous
con·spicu·ous·ness
con·spira·cy (*plural* ·cies)
con·spira·tor
con·spira·to·rial (*or* con·spira·tory)
con·spira·to·rial·ly
con·spira·tress
con·spire
con·sta·ble
con·stabu·lary (*plural* ·laries)
Con·stance European lake
Con·stance (*or* Kon·stanz) West German city
con·stan·cy
con·stant
Con·stan·ţa Romanian port
con·stant·an alloy

Con·stan·tine Algerian city
Con·stan·ti·no·ple
con·sta·ta·tion establishing truth
con·stel·late form clusters
con·stel·la·tion
con·stel·la·tory
con·ster·nate
con·ster·na·tion
con·sti·pate
con·sti·pat·ed
con·sti·pa·tion
con·stitu·en·cy (*plural* ·cies)
con·stitu·ent
con·sti·tute
con·sti·tut·er (*or* ·tu·tor)
con·sti·tu·tion
con·sti·tu·tion·al
con·sti·tu·tion·al·ism
con·sti·tu·tion·al·ist
con·sti·tu·tion·al·ity
con·sti·tu·tion·al·ly
con·sti·tu·tive
con·strain
con·strain·er
con·straint
con·strict
con·stric·tion
con·stric·tive
con·stric·tor
con·struct
con·struct·ible
con·struc·tion
con·struc·tion·al
con·struc·tive
con·struc·tiv·ism art movement
con·struc·tiv·ist
con·struc·tor (*or* ·ter)
con·strue (·stru·ing, ·strued)
con·stru·er
con·sub·stan·tia·tion Christian doctrine
con·suetude custom
con·suetu·di·nary
con·sul
con·su·lar
con·su·late
con·sult
con·sul·tan·cy (*plural* ·cies)
con·sult·ant
con·sul·ta·tion

consultative

con·sul·ta·tive (*or* ta·tory, con·sul·tive)
con·sult·er (*or* ·sul·tor)
con·sum·able
con·sume
con·sum·er
con·sum·er·ism
con·sum·mate
con·sum·ma·tion
con·sum·ma·tive (*or* ·tory)
con·sum·ma·tor
con·sump·tion
con·sump·tive
con·tact
con·tac·tor
con·tac·tual
con·ta·gion
con·ta·gious
con·ta·gious·ness
con·ta·gium (*plural* ·gia) transmission of disease
con·tain
con·tain·er
con·tain·eri·za·tion (*or* ·sa·tion)
con·tain·er·ize (*or* ·ise)
con·tain·ment
con·tami·nant
con·tami·nate
con·tami·na·tion
con·tami·na·tor
con·tan·go (*noun, plural* ·gos; *verb* ·goes, ·go·ing, ·goed) stock-exchange term
conte *French* short story
con·té crayon
con·temn scorn
con·temn·er (*or* ·tem·nor)
con·tem·nible
con·tem·plate
con·tem·pla·tion
con·tem·pla·tive
con·tem·pla·tor
con·tem·po·ra·neity
con·tem·po·ra·neous
con·tem·po·rari·ly
con·tem·po·rary (*plural* ·raries)
con·tem·po·rize (*or* ·rise) synchronize
con·tempt
con·tempt·ibil·ity (*or* ·ible·ness)

con·tempt·ible
con·temp·tu·ous
con·tend
con·tend·er
con·tent
con·tent·ed
con·ten·tion
con·ten·tion·al
con·ten·tious
con·tent·ment
con·ter·mi·nous
con·test
con·test·able
con·test·ant
con·tes·ta·tion
con·test·er
con·text
con·tex·tual
con·tex·tu·al·ize (*or* ·ise)
con·tex·tual·ly
con·tex·tur·al
con·tex·ture weaving
con·ti·gu·ity
con·tigu·ous
con·ti·nence (*or* con·ti·nen·cy)
Con·ti·nent mainland Europe
con·ti·nent large landmass
Con·ti·nen·tal
con·ti·nen·tal
Con·ti·nen·tal·ism
Con·ti·nen·ta·list
con·ti·nen·tal·ity
con·tin·gence
con·tin·gen·cy (*plural* ·cies)
con·tin·gent
con·tinu·able
con·tin·ual
con·tinu·al·ity (*or* ·al·ness)
con·tin·ual·ly
con·tinu·ance
con·tinu·ant
con·tinu·ation
con·tinu·ative linguistics term
con·tinu·ator
con·tinue
con·tinu·er
con·tinu·ing·ly
con·ti·nu·ity (*plural* ·ities)
con·tinuo (*plural* ·tinuos) musical term

94

con·tinu·ous
con·tin·uum (*plural* ·tinua *or* ·tin·uums)
con·to (*plural* ·tos) Portuguese currency
con·tort
con·tor·tion
con·tor·tion·al
con·tor·tion·ist
con·tor·tion·is·tic
con·tour
contra·band
contra·band·ist
contra·bass musical instrument
contra·bass·ist
contra·bas·soon
contra·bas·soon·ist
contra·cep·tion
contra·cep·tive
con·tract
con·tract·able able to enter contract
con·tract·ibil·ity (*or* ·ible·ness)
con·tract·ible able to be shortened
con·trac·tile
con·trac·til·ity
con·trac·tion
con·trac·tion·al
con·trac·tive
con·trac·tor
con·trac·tual
con·trac·tual·ly
con·trac·ture muscle disorder
contra·dict
contra·dict·able
contra·dict·er (*or* ·dic·tor)
contra·dic·tion
contra·dic·tive (*or* ·tious)
contra·dic·tory
contra·dis·tinc·tion
contra·dis·tinc·tive
contra·dis·tin·guish
con·trail aircraft vapour trail
contra·in·di·cant
contra·in·di·cate
contra·in·di·ca·tion
con·tral·to (*plural* ·tos *or* ·ti)
contra·po·si·tion
con·trap·tion

contra·pun·tal
contra·pun·tal·ly
contra·pun·tist (*or* ·tal·ist)
contra·ri·ety (*plural* ·eties)
con·tra·ri·ly
con·tra·ri·ness
con·tra·ri·wise
con·tra·ry (*plural* ·ries)
con·trast
con·tras·tive
con·trasty
contra·val·la·tion fortifications
contra·vene
contra·ven·er
contra·ven·tion
contra·yer·va plant root
con·tre·danse dance
con·tre·temps (*plural* ·temps)
con·trib·ute
con·tri·bu·tion
con·tribu·tive
con·tribu·tor
con·tribu·to·rial
con·tribu·tory
con·trite
con·tri·tion
con·triv·ance
con·trive
con·trol (·trol·ling, ·trolled)
con·trol·lable
con·trol·lably
con·trol·ler
con·tro·ver·sial
contro·ver·sial·ism
contro·ver·sial·ist
con·tro·ver·sial·ly
con·tro·ver·sy (*plural* ·sies)
con·tro·vert deny
contro·vert·er
contro·vert·ible
con·tu·ma·cious obstinate
con·tu·ma·cy (*plural* ·cies)
con·tu·meli·ous insolent
con·tu·mely (*plural* ·melies)
con·tuse bruise
con·tu·sion
con·tu·sioned
con·tu·sive

co·nun·drum
con·ur·ba·tion
con·ure parrot
con·va·lesce
con·va·les·cence
con·va·les·cent
con·vec·tion
con·vec·tion·al
con·vec·tive
con·vec·tor
con·ven·able
con·ve·nance French propriety
con·vene
con·ven·er
con·veni·ence
con·veni·ent
con·vent
con·ven·ti·cle secret assembly
con·ven·tion
con·ven·tion·al
con·ven·tion·al·ism
con·ven·tion·al·ist
con·ven·tion·al·ity (*plural* ·ities)
con·ven·tion·ali·za·tion (*or* ·sa·tion)
con·ven·tion·al·ize (*or* ·ise)
con·ven·tion·al·ly
con·ven·tual of a convent
con·verge
con·ver·gence
con·ver·gen·cy
con·ver·gent
con·vers·able
con·ver·sance (*or* ·san·cy)
con·ver·sant
con·ver·sa·tion
con·ver·sa·tion·al
con·ver·sa·tion·al·ist (*or* ·tion·ist)
con·ver·sa·tion·al·ly
con·ver·sa·zio·ne (*plural* ·zio·ni *or* ·zio·nes) *Italian* artistic discussion
con·verse
con·vers·er
con·ver·sion
con·ver·sion·al (*or* ·ary)
con·vert
con·vert·er (*or* ·ver·tor)
con·vert·ibil·ity (*or* ·ible·ness)

con·vert·ible
con·verti·plane (*or* ·verta·, ·verto·)
con·vex
con·vex·ity (*plural* ·ities)
convexo-concave
convexo-convex
con·vey
con·vey·able
con·vey·ance
con·vey·anc·er
con·vey·anc·ing
con·vey·or (*or* ·er)
con·vict
con·vict·able (*or* ·ible)
con·vic·tion
con·vic·tive convincing
con·vince
con·vinc·er
con·vinc·ible
con·vinc·ing
con·viv·ial
con·vivi·al·ity
con·viv·ial·ly
con·vo·ca·tion legislative assembly
con·vo·ca·tion·al
con·voca·tive
con·vo·ca·tor
con·voke summon
con·vok·er
con·vo·lute
con·vo·lut·ed
con·vo·lu·tion
con·volve coil
con·vol·vu·la·ceous
con·vol·vu·lus (*plural* ·luses *or* ·li) plant
con·voy
con·vul·sant
con·vulse
con·vul·sion
con·vul·sive
cony (*or* co·ney; *plural* conies *or* ·neys)
coo (coo·ing, cooed)
Cooch Be·har Indian city
cooee (*or* coo·ey)
cook
cook·able
cook·book
cook·er
cook·ery
cook·house
cookie

cooking

cook·ing
cook·out *US* barbecue
cool
coo·la·bah (*or* ·li·) tree
cool·ant
cool·er
coolie (*or* cooly; *plural* coolies)
cool·ly (*adv*)
cool·ness
coomb (*or* combe, coombe) valley
coon
coon·can card game
coon·skin
coon·tie plant
coop
co-op
coop·er barrel-maker
coop·er·age
co·oper·ate (*or* co-operate)
co·opera·tion (*or* co-operation)
co·opera·tive (*or* co-operative)
co·opera·tor (*or* co-operator)
coop·ery
co-opt (*or* co-opt)
co·opta·tion (*or* co-optation)
co·opta·tive (*or* co-optative)
co·option (*or* co-option)
co·or·di·nal (*or* co-ordinal) biology term
co·or·di·nate (*or* co-ordinate)
co·or·di·na·tion (*or* co-ordina·tion)
co·or·di·na·tor (*or* co-ordina·tor)
Coorg former Indian province
coot
cootch hiding place
cootie *US* louse
cop (cop·ping, copped)
co·pai·ba (*or* ·va) resin
co·pal resin
co·palm resin
co·par·cenary (*or* ·ceny) joint ownership
co·par·cener
co·part·ner

cope
Co·pen·ha·gen
co·pepod plankton constituent
co·per horse dealer
Co·per·ni·can
cope·stone
copi·er
co·pilot
cop·ing
co·pi·ous
co·pla·nar
co·pla·nar·ity
co·poly·mer chemistry term
co·poly·meri·za·tion (*or* ·sa·tion)
co·poly·mer·ize (*or* ·ise)
cop·per
cop·per·as chemical compound
copper·head snake
copper·plate
copper·smith
cop·pery
cop·pice *variant of* copse
cop·ra coconut kernel
cop·ro·la·lia obscene language
cop·ro·lite fossilized faeces
cop·ro·lit·ic
cop·ropha·gous
cop·ropha·gy
cop·ro·philia abnormal interest in faeces
co·prophi·lous growing on dung
copse (*or* cop·pice)
Copt
cop·ter *short for* helicopter
Cop·tic language; Church
copu·la (*plural* ·las *or* ·lae) linking verb; *compare* cupola
copu·lar
copu·late
copu·la·tion
copu·la·tive
copy (*noun, plural* copies; *verb* copies, copy·ing, copied)
copy·book
copy-edit
copy-editor
copy·hold
copy·holder

copy·ist
copy·read *US* subedit
copy·right
copy·writer
copy·writing
coq au vin chicken dish
coque·li·cot corn poppy
co·quet (·quet·ting, ·quet·ted) to flirt
co·quet·ry (*plural* ·ries)
co·quette
co·quet·tish
co·quille seafood
co·qui·na limestone
co·qui·to (*plural* ·tos) tree
cora·cii·form ornithology term
cora·cle
cora·coid zoology term
cor·al animal; jewellery; *compare* corral
cor·al·line (*or* ·loid)
cor·al·lite fossil coral
coral·root
cor an·glais (*plural* cors an·glais) musical instrument
cor·ban biblical gift
cor·beil (*or* ·beille) architectural ornament
cor·bel (·bel·ling, ·belled) bracket on building
cor·bicu·la (*plural* ·lae) pollen basket
cor bli·mey
cord string; anatomical senses; *compare* chord
cord·age
cor·date heart-shaped; *compare* chordate
cord·ed
Cor·delier Franciscan friar
Cor·deliers French political club
cor·dial
cor·di·al·ity (*plural* ·ities)
cor·di·al·ly
cor·di·er·ite mineral
cor·di·form heart-shaped
cor·dil·lera mountain range
Cor·dil·leras American mountain range
cord·ite explosive
cord·less
Cór·do·ba Argentinian and Spanish cities

cor·do·ba Nicaraguan currency
cor·don
cor·don bleu
cor·do·van leather
cords corduroy trousers
cor·du·roy
cord·wood
core
co·reli·gion·ist
co·reop·sis plant
corer
co·respon·den·cy
co·respond·ent adulterer; *compare* **correspondent**
corf (*plural* **corves**) wagon
Cor·fam (*Trademark*)
Cor·fu
cor·gi (*plural* **·gis**)
co·ria·ceous of leather
co·ri·an·der
Cor·inth Greek port; region of ancient Greece
Co·rin·thian
Co·rin·thians New Testament book
co·rium (*plural* **·ria**) layer beneath skin
Cork
cork
cork·age
cork·board
corked
cork·er
cork·ing
cork·screw
cork·wood
corky
corm
cor·mel new corm
cor·mo·phyte botany term
cor·mo·phyt·ic
cor·mo·rant
cor·mous
corn
cor·na·ceous botany term
corn·cob
corn·cockle plant
corn·crake bird
corn·crib *US* maize store
cor·nea (*plural* **·neas** or **·neae**) eye layer
cor·neal
corned
cor·nel plant

cor·nel·ian of cornel
cor·nel·ian (*or* **car·**) gemstone
cor·neous horny
cor·ner
corner·stone
cor·net
cor·net·ist (*or* **·net·tist**)
cor·nett (*or* **·net**) old woodwind instrument
corn·field
corn·flakes
corn·flour cooking ingredient
corn·flower plant
corn·husk
cor·nice architectural embellishment
cor·niche coastal road
cor·nicu·late horned
Cor·nish
corn·stalk *Austral* native Australian
corn·starch *US* cornflour
cor·nu (*plural* **·nua**) anatomical part
cor·nual
cor·nu·co·pia
cor·nute (*or* **·nut·ed**) hornlike
Corn·wall
corny (**corni·er, corni·est**)
co·rol·la flower petals
cor·ol·la·ceous
cor·ol·lary (*plural* **·laries**)
co·ro·na (*plural* **·nas** or **·nae**)
Co·ro·na Aus·tra·lis constellation
Co·ro·na Bo·real·is constellation
co·ro·nach *Scot* dirge
co·ro·na·graph (*or* **·no·**) optical instrument
coro·nal
coro·nary (*plural* **·naries**) artery; thrombosis
coro·na·tion
coro·ner
coro·ner·ship
coro·net
coro·net·ed
cor·po·ra *plural of* **corpus**
cor·po·ral NCO; of the body; *compare* **corporeal**; **caporal**

cor·po·ra·le altar cloth
cor·po·ral·ity
cor·po·ral·ship
cor·po·rate
cor·po·ra·tion
cor·po·ra·tive
cor·po·ra·tor member of corporation
cor·po·real physical; *compare* **corporal**
cor·po·real·ly
cor·po·real·ity (*or* **·ness**)
cor·po·reity bodily nature
cor·po·sant atmospheric phenomenon
corps (*plural* **corps**) group of people
corpse dead body
cor·pu·lence (*or* **·len·cy**)
cor·pu·lent
cor·pus (*plural* **·po·ra**)
Cor·pus Chris·ti Christian festival
cor·pus·cle
cor·pus·cu·lar
cor·pus de·lic·ti legal term
cor·pus lu·teum (*plural* **cor·po·ra lu·tea**) tissue in ovary
cor·pus stria·tum (*plural* **cor·po·ra stria·ta**) brain part
cor·pus vile (*plural* **cor·po·ra vilia**) *Latin* worthless body
cor·rade geology term
cor·ral (**·ral·ling, ·ralled**) animal enclosure; *compare* **coral**
cor·ra·sion geology term; *compare* **corrosion**
cor·ra·sive
cor·rect
cor·rect·able (*or* **·ible**)
cor·rec·tion
cor·recti·tude
cor·rec·tive
cor·rect·ness
cor·rec·tor
Cor·regi·dor Philippine island
cor·re·late
cor·re·la·tion
cor·rela·tive mutually related

correlativeness

cor·rela·tive·ness (*or* ·tiv·ity)
cor·re·spond
cor·re·spond·ence
cor·re·spond·ent one who corresponds; *compare* co-respondent
Cor·rèze French region
cor·ri·da *Spanish* bullfight
cor·ri·dor
cor·rie hollow in hill
Cor·rie·dale sheep
Cor·ri·en·tes Argentine port
cor·ri·gen·dum (*plural* ·da)
cor·ri·gibil·ity
cor·ri·gible
cor·robo·rant
cor·robo·rate
cor·robo·ra·tion
cor·robo·ra·tive
cor·robo·ra·tor
cor·robo·ree *Austral* noisy gathering
cor·rod·ant (*or* ·ent)
cor·rode
cor·rod·er
cor·rod·ibil·ity
cor·rod·ible
cor·ro·sion wearing away; *compare* corrasion
cor·ro·sive
cor·ru·gate
cor·ru·gat·ed
cor·ru·ga·tion
cor·ru·ga·tor muscle
cor·rupt
cor·rupt·er (*or* ·rup·tor)
cor·rupt·ibil·ity (*or* ·ible·ness)
cor·rup·tible
cor·rup·tion
cor·rup·tion·ist
cor·rup·tive
cor·sac fox
cor·sage
cor·sair
corse *Archaic* corpse; *compare* coarse; course
corse·let (*or* cors·let)
cor·set
cor·setière (*masc* ·setier)
cor·set·ry
Cor·si·ca

Cor·si·can
cor·tege (*or* ·tège)
Cor·tes Spanish parliament
cor·tex (*plural* ·ti·ces)
cor·ti·cal
cor·ti·cate (*or* ·cat·ed) having rind or bark
cor·ti·ca·tion
cor·ti·co·ster·oid (*or* cor·ti·coid) hormone
cor·ti·co·ster·one
cor·ti·co·tro·phic (*US* ·pic)
cor·ti·co·tro·phin (*US* ·pin) hormone
cor·ti·sol hormone
cor·ti·sone
co·run·dum mineral
Co·run·na *variant of* La Coruña
co·rus·cate sparkle
cor·us·ca·tion
cor·vée feudal labour
corves *plural of* corf
cor·vette
cor·vine of crows
co·ryda·lis plant
cor·ymb botany term
co·rym·bose (*or* ·bous)
cory·phaeus (*plural* ·phaei) chorus leader
cory·phée ballet dancer
co·ry·za head cold
cos lettuce; *short for* cosine
co·sec *short for* cosecant
co·secant geometry term
co·sech geometry term
co·seis·mal (*or* ·mic)
Co·sen·za Italian city
cosh
cosh·er
co·sig·na·tory
co·si·ly (*US* ·zi·)
co·sine geometry term
co·si·ness
cos·met·ic
cos·meti·cal·ly
cos·me·ti·cian
cos·mic (*or* ·mi·cal)
cos·mine (*or* ·min) zoology term
cos·mo·drome zoology term
cos·mogo·nal

cos·mo·gon·ic (*or* ·goni·cal)
cos·mogo·nist
cos·mogo·ny (*plural* ·nies) origin of universe
cos·mog·ra·phy mapping of universe
cos·moid fish scale
cos·mo·logi·cal (*or* ·log·ic)
cos·molo·gist
cos·mol·ogy study of universe
cos·mo·naut
cos·mopo·lis international city
cos·mo·poli·tan
cos·mo·poli·tan·ism
cos·mopo·lite cosmopolitan plant or animal
cos·mopo·lit·ism
cos·mos
Cos·mo·tron particle accelerator
coss Indian unit
Cos·sack
cos·set
cost (cost·ing, cost)
cos·ta (*plural* ·tae) rib
Cos·ta Bra·va
cos·tal of ribs
co-star (-star·ring, -starred)
cos·tard apple
Cos·ta Rica
Cos·ta Ri·can
cos·tate
cost-effective
cos·ter·mon·ger
cost·ing
cos·tive constipated
cost·li·ness
cost·ly (·li·er, ·li·est)
cost·mary (*plural* ·maries) plant
cos·toto·my (*plural* ·mies)
cost-plus
cos·tume
cos·tumi·er (*or* ·tum·er)
cosy (*US* cozy; *noun, plural* cosies, *US* cozies; *adj* cosi·er, cosi·est, *US* coz·ier, cozi·est)
cot
co·tan·gent geometry term

cote shelter for doves
Côte d'Azur
Côte-d'Or French department
co·ten·an·cy
co·ten·ant
co·terie
co·ter·mi·nous
Côtes-du-Nord French department
co·tid·al
co·til·lion dance
co·tin·ga bird
co·to·neas·ter shrub
Coto·paxi volcano in Ecuador
Cots·wold sheep
Cots·wolds hills
cot·ta surplice; *compare* **cotter**
cot·tage
cot·tag·er
cot·ter securing pin; peasant farmer; *compare* **cotta**
cot·tier Irish smallholder
cot·ton
cot·ton·ade fabric
cotton·seed (*plural* ·**seeds** *or* ·**seed**)
cotton·tail US rabbit
cotton·weed
cotton·wood
cot·tony
coty·ledon seed leaf
coty·ledo·nal
coty·ledo·na·ry
coty·ledo·nous (*or* ·**noid**)
coty·loid (*or* ·**oi·dal**) cup-shaped
cou·cal bird
couch
cou·chant heraldic term
couch·er
cou·chette
couch·ing embroidery; eye surgery
cou·dé telescope
cou·gar
cough
could
couldn't
cou·lee lava
cou·lisse timber
cou·loir gully
cou·lomb unit

cou·lom·eter (*or* ·**lomb·meter**)
coul·ter (*US* **col·**) plough blade
cou·ma·ric (*or* **cu·**)
cou·ma·rin (*or* **cu·**)
cou·ma·rone
coun·cil assembly
coun·cil·lor (*US* ·**ci·lor**) council member
coun·cil·lor·ship (*US* ·**ci·lor·**)
coun·sel (·**sel·ling**, ·**selled**; *US* ·**sel·ing**, ·**seled**) advice; advise
coun·sel·lor (*US* ·**sel·or**) advisor
count
count·down
coun·te·nance
count·er
counter·act
counter·ac·tion
counter·ac·tive
counter·at·tack
counter·bal·ance
counter·blast
counter·change
counter·charge
counter·check
counter·claim
counter·claim·ant
counter·clockwise *US* anticlockwise
counter·culture
counter·es·pio·nage
counter·feit
counter·feit·er
counter·foil
counter·glow glow in sky
counter·in·sur·gen·cy
counter·in·tel·li·gence
counter·ir·ri·tant
counter·ir·ri·ta·tion
counter·mand
counter·march
counter·meas·ure
counter·mine
counter·move
counter·of·fen·sive
counter·pane
counter·part
counter·plot (·**plot·ting**, ·**plot·ted**)
counter·point

Courland

counter·poise
counter·pro·duc·tive
counter·proof printing term
counter·pro·pos·al
Counter-Reformation religious movement
counter-revolu·tion
counter-revo·lu·tion·ary
counter·scarp fortification
counter·shad·ing
counter·shaft
counter·sign
counter·sink (·**sink·ing**, ·**sank**, ·**sunk**)
counter·spy (*plural* ·**spies**)
counter·ten·or
counter·type
counter·vail
counter·weigh
counter·weight
counter·word
counter·work
coun·tess
count·less
coun·tri·fy (*or* ·**try·fy**; ·**fies**, ·**fy·ing**, ·**fied**)
coun·try (*plural* ·**tries**)
country·man (*plural* ·**men**)
country·side
country·woman (*plural* ·**women**)
coun·ty (*plural* ·**ties**)
coup
coup de grâce (*plural* **coups de grâce**)
coup d'état (*plural* **coups d'état**)
coupe dish; ice-cream
cou·pé car; carriage
cou·ple
cou·pler
cou·plet
cou·pling
cou·pon
cour·age
cou·ra·geous
cou·rante musical work
cour·gette
cou·ri·er messenger; *compare* **currier**
cour·lan bird
Cour·land (*or* **Kur·land**) Soviet region

course

course direction, etc.;
   compare coarse; corse
cours·er
cours·ing hunting
court
Cour·telle (*Trademark*)
cour·teous
cour·tesan (*or* ·tezan)
cour·tesy (*plural* ·tesies)
court·house
cour·ti·er
court·ing
court·ly (·li·er, ·li·est)
court mar·tial (*noun*,
   plural court mar·tials
   or courts mar·tial)
court-martial (*verb*
   -martial·ling,
   -martialled; *US*
   -martial·ing,
   -martialed)
court·room
court·ship
court·yard
cous·cous spicy dish;
   compare cuscus
cous·in relation; *compare*
   cozen
cou·teau knife
couth refined
couthie *Scot* friendly
cou·ture
cou·tu·ri·er (*fem* ·ère)
cou·vade primitive custom
co·va·len·cy (*US*
   ·va·lence) chemistry term
co·va·lent
co·vari·ance
cove
cov·en
cov·enant
cov·enan·tal
cov·enan·tee
Cov·enant·er Scottish
   Presbyterian
cov·enan·tee
cov·enant·er (*or*
   ·enan·tor)
Cov·en·try
cov·er
cov·er·age
cov·er·er
cov·er·ing
cov·er·less
cov·er·let
co·vers maths term

cov·ert
cov·er·ture legal term
cover-up
cov·et
cov·et·er
cov·et·ous
cov·et·ous·ness
cov·ey flock
cov·in conspiracy
cow
cow·age (*or* ·hage) plant
cow·ard
cow·ard·ice
cow·ard·li·ness
cow·ard·ly
cow·bane plant
cow·bell
cow·berry (*plural*
   ·berries)
cow·bind plant
cow·bird
cow·boy
cow·er
Cowes
cow·fish (*plural* ·fish *or*
   ·fishes)
cow·girl
cow·hand
cow·herb
cow·herd
cow·hide
cow·itch plant
cowl
cow·lick
cowl·ing
cow·man (*plural* ·men)
co-worker
cow·pat
cow·pea plant
cow·pox
cow·ry (*or* ·rie; *plural*
   ·ries) mollusc
cow·shed
cow·slip
cox
coxa (*plural* coxae) hip
   joint
cox·al
cox·al·gia
cox·al·gic
cox·comb
cox·comb·ry (*plural* ·ries)
cox·swain (*or* cock·)
coy
coy·ness

100

coy·ote (*plural* ·otes *or*
   ·ote)
co·yo·til·lo (*plural* ·los)
   shrub
coy·pu (*plural* ·pus *or*
   ·pu)
co·zen to trick; *compare*
   cousin
coz·en·age
coz·en·er
cozy *US spelling of* cosy
crab (crab·bing, crabbed)
crab-apple
crab·ber fisherman
crab·by (·bi·er, ·bi·est)
crab·stick
crab·wise
crack
crack·brain
crack·brained
cracked
crack·er
cracker·jack
crack·et *Dialect* stool
crack·ing
crack·jaw
crack·le
crack·ling
crack·nel
crack·pot
Cra·cow Polish city
cra·dle
cradle-snatch·er
cradle·song
craft skill; *compare* kraft
crafti·ly
crafti·ness
crafts·man (*plural* ·men)
crafts·man·ship
crafty (crafti·er,
   crafti·est)
crag
crag·ged *US* craggy
crag·gy (·gi·er, ·gi·est)
Cra·iova Romanian city
crake bird
cram (cram·ming,
   crammed)
cram·bo (*plural* ·boes)
   word game
cram·mer
cramoi·sy crimson
cramp
cram·pon (*or* ·poon)
cran herring measure

cran·age
cran·berry (*plural* ·berries)
crane
cranes·bill
cra·nial
cra·ni·ate having a skull
cra·nio·log·i·cal
cra·ni·ol·o·gist
cra·ni·ol·o·gy
cra·ni·om·eter
cra·nio·met·ric (*or* ·ri·cal)
cra·ni·om·etry
cra·ni·oto·my (*plural* ·mies)
cra·nium (*plural* ·niums *or* ·nia)
crank
crank·case
cranki·ly
cranki·ness
crank·pin
crank·shaft
cranky (cranki·er, cranki·est)
cran·nied
cran·ny (*plural* ·nies)
crap (crap·ping, crapped)
crape *variant spelling of* crepe
crap·pie (*plural* ·pies) fish
crap·py *Slang* worthless
craps US dice game
crap·shooter
crapu·lence
crapu·lous (*or* ·lent) drunken
cra·que·lure cracks on paintings
crash
crash·ing
crash-land
crash-landing
cra·sis (*plural* ·ses) linguistics term
crass
crass·ness (*or* cras·si·tude)
cras·su·la·ceous botany term
cratch fodder rack
crate
cra·ter
cra·ter·ous
craunch *Dialect* crunch

cra·vat
crave
cra·ven
crav·ing
craw animal stomach
craw·fish *variant spelling of* crayfish
crawl
crawl·er
Craw·ley Sussex town
cray *Austral* crayfish
cray·fish (*or* craw·; *plural* ·fish *or* ·fishes)
cray·on
cray·on·ist
craze
crazed
cra·zi·ly
cra·zi·ness
cra·zy (·zi·er, ·zi·est)
creak noise; *compare* creek
creaki·ness
creaky (creaki·er, creaki·est)
cream
cream·cups flower
cream·er
cream·ery (*plural* ·eries)
cream·laid (*or* ·woven) type of paper
creamy (creami·er, creami·est)
crease
crease·less
cre·ate
crea·tine (*or* ·tin) biochemical compound
cre·ati·nine biochemical compound
crea·tion
crea·tion·al
crea·tion·ism theological belief
crea·tive
crea·tive·ly
crea·tiv·ity
crea·tor
crea·tur·al (*or* ·ture·ly)
crea·ture
crèche
Cré·cy battlefield
cred·al *variant spelling of* creedal
cre·dence

crenellation
cre·den·dum (*plural* ·da) article of faith
cre·dent *Archaic* believing
cre·den·tial
cre·den·za sideboard
cred·ibil·ity (*or* ·ible·ness)
cred·ible
cred·ibly
cred·it
cred·it·able
cred·it·able·ness (*or* ·abil·ity)
cred·it·ably
credi·tor
cre·do (*plural* ·dos)
cre·du·lity
credu·lous
Cree American Indian
creed
creed·al (*or* cred·al)
creek inlet; *compare* creak
creel basket
creep (creep·ing, crept)
creep·er
creepie *Scot* stool
creepi·ly
creepi·ness
creeps (*noun*)
creepy (creepi·er, creepi·est)
creepy-crawly (*plural* -crawlies)
cre·mate
cre·ma·tion
cre·ma·tion·ism
cre·ma·tion·ist
cre·ma·tor
crema·to·rium (*plural* ·riums *or* ·ria)
crema·tory (*adj*)
crème *French* cream
crème cara·mel
crème de menthe liqueur
Cre·mo·na Italian city
cre·nate (*or* ·nat·ed) scalloped
cre·na·tion (*or* crena·ture)
cren·el (*or* ·nelle)
cren·el·late (US ·el·ate) supply with battlements; indent
cren·el·la·tion (US ·ela·tion)

crenulate

crenu·late (*or* ·lat·ed) notched
crenu·la·tion
creo·dont extinct mammal
Cre·ole people
cre·ole language
creo·lized (*or* ·lised)
Creon legendary king
cre·opha·gous flesh-eating
cre·opha·gy
creo·sol constituent of creosote; *compare* cresol
creo·sote
creo·sot·ic
crepe (*or* crape) fabric
crêpe pancake
crepe de Chine fabric
crêpe su·zette (*plural* crêpes su·zettes) orange pancake
crepi·tant
crepi·tate crackle
crepi·ta·tion
crepi·tus medical term
crept
cre·pus·cu·lar active at dusk
cre·scen·do (*plural* ·dos)
cres·cent
cres·cen·tic
cre·sol disinfectant; *compare* creosol
cress
cres·set
crest
crest·ed
crest·fallen
crest·ing
cre·syl·ic
Cre·ta·ceous geological period
cre·ta·ceous of chalk
Cre·tan
Crete
cre·tic metrical foot
cret·in
cret·in·ism
cret·in·oid
cret·in·ous
cre·tonne fabric
Creuse French region
cre·vasse glacier crack
crev·ice cleft
crew
Crewe Cheshire town

crew·el yarn; *compare* cruel
crew·el·ist
crewel·work
crew-neck (*or* -necked)
crib (crib·bing, cribbed)
crib·bage
cri·bel·lum spider's organ
crib·ri·form (*or* crib·rous) sievelike
crib·work timber framework
crick
crick·et
crick·et·er
cri·coid anatomy term
cried
cri·er
cri·key
crim *Austral* criminal
crime
Cri·mea
Cri·mean
crime pas·sio·nel (*plural* crimes pas·sio·nel)
crimi·nal
crimi·nal·ity (*plural* ·ities)
crimi·nal·ly
crimi·no·logi·cal (*or* ·log·ic)
crimi·nolo·gist
crimi·nol·ogy
crimp
crimp·er
crim·ple crumple
Crimp·lene (*Trademark*)
crim·son
cringe
crin·gle nautical term
cri·nite having hairs
crin·kle
crinkle-root plant
crin·kly
crinkum-crankum twisted object
cri·noid marine organism
crino·line
cri·num plant
cri·ol·lo (*plural* ·los) cocoa
cripes slang expression
crip·ple
crip·pling
cri·sis (*plural* ·ses)
crisp
cris·pate (*or* ·pat·ed) curled
cris·pa·tion

102

crisp·bread
crisp·er
crisp·ness
crispy (crispi·er, crispi·est)
cris·sal of a crissum
criss·cross
cris·sum (*plural* ·sa) ornithology term
cris·ta (*plural* ·tae) biology term
cris·tate (*or* ·tat·ed) crested
cri·teri·on (*plural* ·teria *or* ·terions)
crit·ic
criti·cal
criti·cal·ly
criti·cism
criti·cize (*or* ·cise)
criti·cizer (*or* ·ciser)
cri·tique
crit·ter *US* creature
croak
croak·er
croaki·ly
croaki·ness
croaky
Cro·at
Croa·tia Yugoslav republic
Croa·tian
cro·cein dye
cro·chet (·chet·ing, ·cheted) knitting; *compare* crotchet
cro·chet·er
cro·cido·lite asbestos
crock
crock·ery
crock·et architectural ornament
Crock·ford clergy directory
croco·dile
croco·dil·ian
cro·co·ite (*or* ·coi·site) mineral
cro·cus (*plural* ·cuses)
croft
croft·er
crois·sant
Cro-Magnon prehistoric man
crom·bec bird
crom·lech prehistoric structure

Crom·wel·lian
crone
cronk *Austral* unsound
Cronus Titan
cro·ny (*plural* ·nies)
crook
crook·ed
crook·ed·ness
croon
croon·er
crop (crop·ping, cropped)
crop-eared
crop·per
cro·quet (·quet·ing, ·queted) game
cro·quette savoury cake
cro·sier (*or* ·zier) bishop's crook
cross
cross·bar
cross·beam
cross·bill
cross·bones
cross·bow
cross·breed (·breed·ing, ·bred)
cross·check
cross-country
cross·current
cross·cut (·cut·ting, cut)
crosse lacrosse stick
cross-examina·tion
cross-examine
cross-examiner
cross-eye
cross-eyed
cross-fertili·za·tion (*or* ·sa·tion)
cross-fertilize (*or* -fertilise)
cross fire
cross-garnet hinge
cross-grained
cross·hatch
cross·head
cross-index
cross·ing
cross·jack sail
cross-legged
cross·let heraldry term
cross-link
cros·sop·te·ryg·ian primitive fish
cross-over
cross·patch

cross·piece
cross-ply (*adj*)
cross-pollinate
cross-pollina·tion
cross-purposes
cross-question
cross-question·ing
cross-refer
cross-reference
cross·road (*or* ·roads)
cross·ruff bridge term
cross-section·al
cross-slide
cross-stitch
cross·talk
cross·tree nautical term
cross·walk *US* pedestrian crossing
cross·wind
cross·wise (*or* ·ways)
cross·word
cross·wort plant
crotch
crotch·et musical note; *compare* crochet
crotch·ety *Slang* irritable
cro·ton shrub
crouch
croup disease
croup (*or* croupe) horse's hindquarters
crou·pi·er
croup·ous (*or* croupy)
crouse *Dialect* saucy
croute toast
crou·ton cookery garnish
crow (crow·ing, crowed *or* crew)
crow·bar
crow·berry (*plural* ·berries)
crow·boot Eskimo boot
crowd
crowd·ed
crow·er
crow·foot (*plural* ·foots) plant
crown
crown·piece bridle part
crown·work
crow's-foot (*plural* -feet)
crow's-nest
Croy·don
croze barrel recess

cro·zier *variant spelling of* crosier
cru vineyard
cru·ces *plural of* crux
cru·cial important
cru·cial·ly
cru·cian fish
cru·ci·ate
cru·ci·ble
cru·ci·fer plant
cru·cif·er·ous
cru·ci·fier
cru·ci·fix
cru·ci·fix·ion
cru·ci·form
cru·ci·fy (·fies, ·fy·ing, ·fied)
cruck roof timber
crud *Slang* rubbish
crude
crud·ity (*or* crude·ness; *plural* ·ities *or* ·nesses)
cru·el (·el·ler, ·el·lest) unkind; *compare* crewel
cru·el·ly
cru·el·ty (*plural* ·ties)
cru·et
cruise sea trip; *compare* cruse
cruis·er
cruiser·weight
cruise·way
crul·ler cake
crumb
crum·ble
crum·bly (·bli·er, ·bli·est)
crumby (crumbi·er, crumbi·est) full of crumbs; *compare* crummy
crum·horn musical instrument
crum·my (·mi·er, ·mi·est) *Slang* inferior; *compare* crumby
crump to thud
crum·pet
crum·ple
crum·ply
crunch
crunchi·ly
crunchi·ness
crunchy (crunchi·er, crunchi·est)
cru·node maths term
crup·per saddle strap

cru·ra *plural of* **crus**
cru·ral
crus (*plural* **cru·ra**) lower leg
cru·sade
cru·sad·er
cruse small pot; *compare* **cruise**
crush
crush·er
crust
crus·ta·cean
crus·ta·ceous
crus·tal
crust·ed
crusti·ly
crusti·ness
crusty (**crusti·er, crusti·est**)
crutch
crux (*plural* **cruxes** *or* **cru·ces**)
crux an·sa·ta ankh
cru·zei·ro (*plural* **·ros**) Brazilian currency
crwth musical instrument
cry (*noun, plural* **cries**; *verb* **cries, cry·ing, cried**)
cry·baby (*plural* **·babies**)
cryo·bi·olo·gist
cryo·bi·ol·ogy
cryo·gen freezing mixture
cryo·gen·ics
cryo·hy·drate
cryo·lite mineral
cry·om·eter
cry·om·etry
cry·on·ics
cryo·phil·ic
cryo·phyte plant growing on snow
cryo·plank·ton
cryo·scope
cryo·scop·ic
cry·os·co·py
cryo·stat
cryo·sur·gery
cryo·thera·py (*or* **cry·mo·thera·py**)
cryo·tron electronic device
crypt
cryp·taes·thesia (*US* **·tes·**) extrasensory perception
crypt·al of crypts; *compare* **cryptic**
crypt·analy·sis study of codes
crypt·ana·lyst
crypt·ana·lyt·ic
cryp·tic (*or* **·ti·cal**) obscure; *compare* **cryptal**
cryp·ti·cal·ly
cryp·to·clas·tic geology term
cryp·to·crys·tal·line
cryp·to·gam plant
cryp·to·gam·ic (*or* **·toga·mous**)
cryp·to·gen·ic of unknown origin
cryp·to·gram
cryp·to·graph
cryp·tog·ra·pher (*or* **·phist**)
cryp·to·graph·ic (*or* **·graphi·cal**)
cryp·tog·ra·phy (*or* **·tol·ogy**) study of codes
cryp·tolo·gist
cryp·to·meria tree
cryp·to·zo·ic living in dark places
cryp·to·zo·ite malarial parasite
crys·tal
crys·tal·line
crys·tal·lin·ity
crys·tal·lite
crys·tal·lit·ic
crys·tal·lize (*or* **·tal·ize, ·tal·lise, ·tal·ise**)
crys·tal·log·ra·pher
crys·tal·lo·graph·ic
crys·tal·log·ra·phy
crys·tal·loid
cte·nid·ium (*plural* **·ia**) mollusc's gill
cte·noid comblike
cte·nopho·ran
cteno·phore invertebrate
cub (**cub·bing, cubbed**)
Cuba
cub·age
Cu·ban
cub·ane chemical compound
cu·ba·ture cubic contents
cubbed
cub·bing
cubby·hole
cube
cu·beb plant
cu·bic
cu·bi·cal (*adj*) of volume
cu·bi·cle (*noun*) small room
cu·bicu·lum burial chamber
cu·bi·form
cub·ism
cub·ist
cu·bis·tic
cu·bit unit
cu·bi·tal of the forearm
cu·boid
Cu-bop jazz music
cuck·old
cuck·old·ry
cuckoo (*plural* **cuckoos**)
cuckoo·pint
cu·cu·li·form ornithology term
cu·cul·late hood-shaped
cu·cum·ber
cu·cur·bit plant
cu·cur·bi·ta·ceous
Cú·cu·ta Colombian city
cud
cud·bear lichen
cud·dle
cud·dle·some
cud·dly (**·dli·er, ·dli·est**)
cud·dy (*plural* **·dies**) cabin
cudg·el (**·el·ling, ·elled;** *US* **·el·ing, ·eled**)
cudg·el·ler (*US* **·el·er**)
cudg·erie tree
cud·weed
cue (**cu·ing, cued**) signal; billiard shaft; *compare* **queue**
Cuer·na·va·ca Mexican city
cues·ta ridge
cuff
Cuia·bá (*or* **Cu·ya·bá**) Brazilian port and river
cu·ing
cui·rass armour
cui·ras·sier
cuir-bouilli leather
cui·sine
cuisse armour
culch (*or* **cultch**) oyster bed
cul-de-sac (*plural* **culs-de-sac** *or* **cul-de-sacs**)

cu·let armour
cu·lex (*plural* ·li·ces) mosquito
Cu·lia·cán Mexican city
cu·lic·id mosquito
culi·nary
cull
cull·er
cul·let waste glass
cul·lis gutter
Cul·lod·en battlefield
cul·ly (*plural* ·lies) *Slang* pal
culm stem
cul·mif·er·ous
cul·mi·nant
cul·mi·nate
cul·mi·na·tion
cu·lottes women's trousers
cul·pa (*plural* ·pae) fault
cul·pabil·ity
cul·pable
cul·pably
cul·prit
cult
cul·tic
cul·ti·gen plant
cult·ism
cult·ist
cul·ti·vable (*or* cul·ti·vat·able)
cul·ti·var plant
cul·ti·vate
cul·ti·vat·ed
cul·ti·va·tion
cul·ti·va·tor
cul·trate (*or* ·trat·ed) knife-shaped
cul·tur·al
cul·tur·al·ly
cul·ture
cul·tured
cul·tur·ist
cul·ver *Archaic* dove
cul·ver·in cannon
cul·vert
Cu·ma·ná Venezuelan city
cum·ber
Cum·ber·land former English county
Cum·ber·nauld Scottish town
cum·ber·some
cum·brance
Cum·bria

Cum·brian
cum·in (*or* cum·min) herb
cum·mer·bund (*or* kum·)
cum·shaw tip; gift
cu·mu·late
cu·mu·la·tion
cu·mu·la·tive
cu·mul·et pigeon
cu·mu·li·form cloud-shaped
cu·mu·lo·nim·bus (*plural* ·bi *or* ·buses) cloud
cu·mu·lo·stra·tus (*plural* ·ti)
cu·mu·lous (*adj*)
cu·mu·lus (*noun*; *plural* ·li)
cu·neal
cu·neate
cu·nei·form writing
cun·jevoi plant
cun·ni·lin·gus
cun·ning
cunt
cup (cup·ping, cupped)
cup·bearer
cup·board
cup·cake
cu·pel (·pel·ling, ·pelled; *US* ·pel·ing, ·peled)
cu·pel·la·tion metallurgical process
cup·ful (*plural* ·fuls)
Cupid
cu·pid·ity
cu·po·la dome; *compare* copula
cu·po·lat·ed
cupp·a (*or* ·per) *Slang* cup of tea
cupped
cup·ping
cu·pre·ous
cu·pric
cu·prif·er·ous
cu·prite mineral
cu·pro·nick·el
cu·prous
cu·pu·late (*or* ·lar) cup-shaped
cu·pule
cur
cur·abil·ity
cur·able
Cu·ra·çao Carribean island; liqueur

curmudgeonly

cu·ra·cy (*plural* ·cies)
cu·ra·re (*or* ·ri) poison
cu·ra·rine muscle relaxant
cu·ra·ri·za·tion (*or* ·sa·tion)
cu·ra·rize (*or* ·rise)
cu·ras·sow bird
cu·rate
cu·ra·tive
cu·ra·tor museum keeper
cu·ra·to·rial
curb restrain; *US spelling of* kerb
curch woman's cap
cur·cu·lio (*plural* ·lios) weevil
cur·cu·ma plant
curd
curdi·ness
cur·dle
cur·dler
curdy
cur·able
cure
cure-all
cu·rette (*or* ·ret; ·ret·ting, ·ret·ted) surgical instrument
cu·ret·tage (*or* ·rette·ment)
cur·few
cu·ria (*plural* ·riae) papal court
Cu·ria Re·gis Norman king's court
cu·rie unit
cu·rio (*plural* ·rios) collector's item
cu·rio·sa curiosities
cu·ri·os·ity (*plural* ·ities)
cu·ri·ous
cu·ri·ous·ness
Cu·ri·ti·ba Brazilian city
cu·rium radioactive element
curl
curl·er
cur·lew
cur·li·cue (*or* ·ly·)
curli·ness
curl·ing
curl·paper
curly (curli·er, curli·est)
cur·mudg·eon
cur·mudg·eon·ly

currant

cur·rant fruit; *compare* current
cur·ra·jong *variant spelling of* kurrajong
cur·ra·wong bird
cur·ren·cy (*plural* ·cies)
cur·rent flow; up-to-date; *compare* currant
cur·ri·cle carriage
cur·ricu·lar
cur·ricu·lum (*plural* ·la *or* ·lums)
cur·ricu·lum vi·tae (*plural* ·la vi·tae)
cur·ri·er leather worker; *compare* courier
cur·ri·ery (*plural* ·eries)
cur·rish rude
cur·ry (*noun, plural* ·ries; *verb* ·ries, ·ry·ing, ·ried)
curry·comb
curse
curs·ed (*or* curst)
cur·sive printing term
cur·sor VDU device
cur·so·rial adapted for running
cur·sori·ly
cur·sory hasty
curt
cur·tail
cur·tail·ment
cur·tain
curtain-raiser
cur·ta·na sword
cur·ti·lage enclosed land
curt·ness
curt·sy (*or* ·sey; *noun, plural* ·sies *or* ·seys; *verb* ·sies, ·sy·ing, ·sied *or* ·seys, ·sey·ing, ·seyed)
cur·va·ceous
cur·va·ture
curve
cur·vet (·vet·ting *or* ·vet·ing, ·vet·ted *or* ·vet·ed) dressage term
cur·vi·lin·ear (*or* ·eal)
cur·vi·lin·ear·ity
curvy (curvi·er, curvi·est)
cus·cus marsupial; *compare* couscous
cu·sec unit
Cush biblical character

cush·ion
cush·iony
Cush·it·ic language
cushy *Slang* easy
cus·pate (*or* ·pat·ed, cusped)
cus·pid
cus·pi·date (*or* ·dat·ed, ·pidal)
cus·pi·da·tion architectural term
cus·pi·dor spittoon
cuss
cuss·ed
cuss·ed·ness
cus·tard
cus·to·dial
cus·to·dian
cus·to·dy (*plural* ·dies)
cus·tom
cus·tom·ari·ly
cus·tom·ary
custom-built
cus·tom·er
cus·tom·ize (*or* ·ise)
cus·tos (*plural* cus·to·des) Franciscan
cus·tu·mal customary
cut (cut·ting, cut)
cu·ta·neous
cut·away
cut·back
Cutch *variant spelling of* Kutch
cutch *variant of* catechou
cute
cute·ness
cu·ti·cle
cu·ticu·la (*plural* ·lae) cuticle
cu·ticu·lar (*adj*)
cutie
cu·tin plant substance
cu·tin·ize (*or* ·ise)
cu·tis (*plural* ·tes *or* ·tises) skin
cut·lass
cut·ler
cut·lery
cut·let
cut-price
cut·purse pickpocket
Cut·tack Indian city
cut·ter
cut·throat

cut·ting
cut·tle
cuttle·bone
cuttle·fish (*plural* ·fish *or* ·fishes)
cut·ty *Dialect* short
cut·water
cut·work embroidery
cut·worm caterpillar
cu·vette dish
Cux·ha·ven West German port
Cuz·co (*or* Cus·co) Peruvian city
cwm valley
Cwm·bran Welsh town
cyan blue colour
cy·ana·mide (*or* ·mid)
cya·nate
cy·an·ic
cya·ni·da·tion
cya·nide
cya·nine (*or* ·nin) dye
cya·nite mineral
cya·nit·ic
cya·no·co·bala·min vitamin
cy·ano·gen poisonous gas
cya·no·hy·drin
cya·no·sis blueness of skin
cya·not·ic
cy·ano·type blueprint
Cybele Phrygian goddess
cy·ber·nate
cy·ber·na·tion
cy·ber·net·ic
cy·ber·neti·cist
cy·ber·net·ics
cy·cad plant
cyca·da·ceous
Cyc·la·des Aegean islands
cy·cla·mate
cyc·la·men
cy·cle
cy·clic (*or* ·cli·cal)
cy·cli·cal·ly
cy·clist
cy·clo·al·kane
cy·clo·hex·ane
cy·cloid
cy·cloi·dal
cy·clom·eter
cy·clom·etry
cy·clone

cy·clon·ic (*or* **·cloni·cal,** **·clo·nal**)
cy·clo·nite explosive
Cy·clo·pean
cy·clo·pedia (*or* **·pae·dia**)
cy·clo·pedic (*or* **·pae·dic**)
cy·clo·pen·tane
cy·clo·plegia medical term
cy·clo·pro·pane
Cy·clops one-eyed giant
cy·clops crustacean
cy·clo·rama
cy·clo·ram·ic
cy·clo·sis (*plural* **·ses**) biological process
cy·clos·to·mate (*or* **·clo·stoma·tous**)
cy·clo·stome primitive vertebrate
cy·clo·style
cy·clo·thy·mia mood swings
cy·clo·thy·mic (*or* **·mi·ac**)
cy·clo·tron physics term
cyg·net young swan; *compare* **signet**
Cyg·nus constellation
cyl·in·der
cy·lin·dri·cal (*or* **·dric**)
cy·lin·dri·cal·ly
cyl·in·droid
cyma (*plural* **cymae** *or* **cymas**) architectural moulding
cy·mar woman's jacket
cy·ma·tium architectural moulding
cym·bal musical instrument; *compare* **symbol**
cym·bal·er (*or* **·eer,** **·bal·ist**)
cym·ba·lo (*plural* **·los**) dulcimer
cyme botany term
cy·mene chemical compound
cy·mif·er·ous
cy·mo·gene *US* petroleum distillate

cy·mo·graph *variant spelling of* **kymograph**
cy·moid like a cyma
cy·mo·phane mineral
cy·mose of a cyme
Cym·ric (*or* **Kym·**) Welsh language
Cym·ry (*or* **Kym·**) Welsh people
cyn·ic
cyni·cal
cyni·cal·ly
cyni·cism
cy·no·sure
cy·pher *variant spelling of* **cipher**
cy·pera·ceous botany term
cy pres legal term
cy·press tree; *compare* **Cyprus**
Cyp·rian
cy·pri·nid fish
cy·prino·dont fish
cy·pri·noid carplike
Cyp·ri·ot (*or* **·ote**)
cyp·ri·pedium orchid
Cy·prus country; *compare* **cypress**
cyp·sela (*plural* **·selae**) botany term
Cyr·enai·ca (*or* **Cir·**) Libyan region
Cy·ril·lic Slavonic alphabet
cyst lump; sac; *compare* **cist**
cys·tec·to·my (*plural* **·mies**) removal of bladder
cys·teine amino acid
cys·tein·ic
cyst·ic
cys·ti·cer·coid larva
cys·ti·cer·cus (*plural* **·ci**) larva
cys·tine amino acid
cys·ti·tis bladder inflammation
cys·to·carp botany term

cys·to·carp·ic
cys·to·cele
cys·toid
cys·to·lith bladder stone
cys·to·scope medical term
cys·to·scop·ic
cys·tos·co·py (*plural* **·pies**)
cys·toto·my (*plural* **·mies**)
cy·tas·ter cytology term
Cyth·era Greek island
cyti·dine biochemical compound
cy·to·chemi·cal
cy·to·chem·is·try
cy·to·chrome biochemical compound
cy·to·gen·esis (*or* **·tog·eny**) origin of cells
cy·to·genet·ics
cy·to·ki·nesis
cy·to·logi·cal
cy·tolo·gist
cy·tol·ogy study of cells
cy·toly·sin
cy·toly·sis
cy·ton nerve-cell body
cy·to·plasm
cy·to·plasm·ic
cy·to·plast
cy·to·sine biochemical compound
cy·to·taxo·nom·ic
cy·to·tax·ono·mist
cy·to·tax·on·omy
Cyzi·cus ancient Greek colony
czar *variant spelling of* **tsar**
czar·das dance
Czech
Czecho·slo·vak
Czecho·slo·va·kia
Czecho·slo·va·kian
Czę·sto·cho·wa Polish city

D

dab (**dab·bing, dabbed**)
dab·ber
dab·ble
dab·bler
dab·chick
da capo musical term

Dacca

Dac·ca variant of **Dhaka**
dace
da·cha (or **·tcha**) Russian country house
dachs·hund
da·coit armed robber
da·coity
Da·cron (Trademark)
dac·tyl metrical foot; finger
dac·tyl·ic
dac·tyli·cal·ly
dac·tylo·gram US fingerprint
dac·tyl·og·ra·phy
dac·ty·lol·ogy (plural **·ogies**) sign language
dad
Dada artistic movement
Da·da·ism
Da·da·ist
Da·da·is·tic
Da·da·is·ti·cal·ly
dad·dy (plural **·dies**)
dado (plural **da·does** or **da·dos**) lower part of wall
Daedalus mythological character
dae·mon (or **dai·**) spirit; demigod; compare **demon**
dae·mon·ic (or **dai·**)
daff Scot to frolic; Slang daffodil
daf·fo·dil
daffy (**daffi·er, daffi·est**) Slang daft
daft
Da·gan Babylonian god
Dag·en·ham
Da·ge·stan (or **Da·ghe·stan**) Soviet republic
dag·ga narcotic
dag·ger
dagger·board
dag·lock encrusted wool
da·go (plural **·gos** or **·goes**)
da·go·ba Buddhist shrine
da·guerreo·type
da·guerreo·typ·er (or **·ist**)
da·guerreo·typy
dah Morse code sound
dahl·ia
Dah·na Arabian desert
Da·ho·man (or **Da·ho·mean**)
Da·ho·mey former name of Benin
Dáil Ei·rann Irish parliament
dai·ly (plural **·lies**)
dai·mon variant spelling of **daemon**
dain·ti·ly
dain·ti·ness
dain·ty (noun, plural **·ties**; adj **·ti·er, ·ti·est**)
dai·qui·ri (plural **·ris**) drink
dairy (plural **dairies**)
dairy·ing
dairy·man (plural **·men**)
dais platform
dai·sy (plural **·sies**)
daisy·cutter cricket
Da·kar Senegalese capital
Da·ko·ta
Da·ko·tan
dal Indian food
Dalai Lama Tibetan leader
da·la·si Gambian currency
dale
Dales Yorkshire region
dales·man (plural **·men**)
Dal·las US city
dal·li·ance
dal·ly (**·lies, ·ly·ing, ·lied**)
Dal·ma·tia Yugoslav region
Dal·ma·tian
dal·mat·ic tunic
dal·ton unit
dal·ton·ic
dal·ton·ism colour blindness
dam (**dam·ming, dammed**) river barrier; female parent; compare **damn**
dam·age
dam·age·abil·ity
dam·age·able
dam·ag·er
dam·ages
Da·man Indian region
Da·man·hûr Egyptian city
Da·ma·ra (plural **·ras** or **·ra**) African people
Dama·scene of Damascus
dama·scene decorate metal

108

Da·mas·cus Syrian capital
dam·ask
dame
Dami·et·ta Egyptian town
dam·mar (or **da·mar, dam·mer**) resin
dammed obstructed; compare **damned**
dam·ming
damn condemn; compare **dam**
dam·nabil·ity
dam·nable
dam·nably
dam·na·tion
dam·na·tory
damned condemned; compare **dammed**
damned·est
dam·ni·fi·ca·tion
dam·ni·fy (**·fies, ·fy·ing, ·fied**) injure
Damocles mythological character
damp
damp·course
damp·en
damp·en·er
damp·er
damp·ly
damp·ness
dam·sel
damsel·fish (plural **·fish** or **·fishes**)
damsel·fly (plural **·flies**)
dam·son
dan buoy; judo grade
Danaë mythological character
dance
danc·er
danc·ing
dan·de·lion
dan·der
Dan·die Din·mont terrier
dan·di·fi·ca·tion
dan·di·fy (**·fies, ·fy·ing, ·fied**)
dan·di·prat coin
dan·dle fondle
dan·dler
dan·druff (or **·driff**)
dan·druffy (or **·driffy**)
dan·dy (plural **·dies**)
dandy·ish

dandy·ism
Dane
Dane·geld (*or* **·gelt**)
   Anglo-Saxon tax
Dane·law (*or* **·lagh**)
   England under Danish law
dane·wort shrub
dang damn
dan·ger
dan·ger·ous
dan·ger·ous·ness
dan·gle
dan·gler
danio (*plural* **danios**) fish
Dan·ish
dank
dank·ness
dan·seur (*fem* **·seuse**)
   French dancer
Dan·ube
Danu·bian
Dan·zig Gdańsk; pigeon
dap (**dap·ping, dapped**)
daphne shrub
daph·nia flea
Daph·nis mythological character
dap·per
dap·ple
dapple-grey (*US* **-gray**)
dar·af unit
dar·bies *Slang* handcuffs
Dar·dan (*or* **·da·nian**)
   Trojan
Dar·da·nelles
Dar·da·nus mythological character
Dar·dic language group
dare
dare·devil
dare·devil·ry (*or* **·try**)
dar·er
Dar es Sa·laam Tanzanian capital
Dar·fur Sudanese province
darg *Dialect* day's work
dar·ic coin
Dari·en part of Panama
dar·ing
dari·ole cookery mould
Dar·jee·ling Indian town; tea
dark
dark·en
dark·en·er

dar·kle darken
dark·ly
dark·ness
dark·room
dark·some
darky (*or* **darkie, dark·ey**; *plural* **darkies** *or* **·eys**)
Dar·ling Australian river
dar·ling
Dar·ling·ton Durham town
Darm·stadt West German city
darn
darned
dar·nel grass
darn·er
darn·ing
dart
dart·board
dart·er
Dart·ford Kent town
Dart·moor
Dart·mouth Devon port
darts
Dar·win Australian port
Dar·win·ian
Dar·win·ism
Dar·win·ist
dash
dash·board
da·sheen plant
dash·er
da·shi·ki garment
dash·ing
dash·pot vibration damper
Dasht-i-Lut (*or* **-e-**) Iranian desert
das·sie animal
das·tard
das·tard·li·ness
das·tard·ly
dasy·ure marsupial
da·ta information; *plural of* **datum**
dat·able (*or* **date·**)
dat·able·ness (*or* **date·**)
da·ta·ry (*plural* **·ries**) Catholic official
date
dat·ed
dat·ed·ness
date·less
date·line
dat·er

dat·ing
da·ti·val
da·tive
dato Philippine chief
da·to·lite mineral
da·tum (*plural* **·ta**) fact; *compare* **data**
da·tu·ra plant
daub smear
daube stew
daub·er
daub·ery (*or* **·ry**)
dauby
Dau·gav·pils Soviet city
daugh·ter
daughter-in-law (*plural* **daughters-**)
daugh·ter·li·ness
daugh·ter·ly
daunt
daunt·er
daunt·ing
daunt·less
dau·phin heir to French throne
Dau·phi·né former French province
dau·phine (*or* **·phin·ess**) wife of dauphin
dav·en·port desk
dav·it
daw jackdaw
daw·dle
daw·dler
dawn
Daw·son Canadian town
day
day·book
day·boy
day·break
day·dream
day·dream·er
day·dream·ing
day·dreamy
day·flower
day·light
day·long
day-neutral botany term
day·star sun
day·time
day-to-day
Day·ton US city
Day·to·na Beach US city
day-tripper
daze

dazzle 110

daz·zle
dea·con
dea·con·ess
dea·con·ry (*plural* ·ries)
dea·con·ship
de·ac·tiv·ate
de·ac·ti·va·tion
de·ac·ti·va·tor
dead
dead·beat
dead·en
dead·en·er
dead·eye nautical term
dead·fall trap
dead·head
dead·light nautical term
dead·line
dead·li·ness
dead·lock
dead·ly (·li·er, ·li·est)
dead·ness
dead-nettle
dead·pan
dead·wood
deaf
deaf-and-dumb
deaf·en
deaf-mute
deaf-muteness (*or* -mutism)
deaf·ness
deal (deal·ing, dealt) take action, etc.; *compare* dele
dea·late (*or* ·lat·ed) wingless
dea·la·tion
deal·er
deal·fish (*plural* ·fish *or* ·fishes)
deal·ing
dealt
de·ami·nate (*or* ·am·in·ize, ·am·in·ise) biochemistry term
de·ami·na·tion (*or* ·ami·ni·za·tion, ·ami·ni·sa·tion)
dean university official, etc.; *compare* dene
dean·ery (*plural* ·eries)
dean·ship
dear
dear·ly
dear·ness
dearth

deary (*or* dearie; *plural* dearies)
death
death·bed
death·blow
death·less
death·li·ness
death·ly
death's-head
death·trap
death·watch
Deau·ville French resort
deb *short for* debutante
de·ba·cle
de·bag (·bag·ging, ·bagged)
de·bar (·bar·ring, ·barred)
de·bark disembark
de·bar·ka·tion
de·bar·ment
de·base
de·bas·ed·ness
de·base·ment
de·bas·er
de·bat·able (*or* ·bate·able)
de·bat·ably
de·bate
de·bat·er
de·bauch
debau·chee
de·bauch·er
de·bauch·ery (*or* ·ment)
de·ben·ture bond
de·bili·tate
de·bili·ta·tion
de·bili·ta·tive
de·bil·ity (*plural* ·ities)
deb·it
debo·nair (*or* deb·on·naire)
de·bouch move into larger space
de·bouch·ment (*or* ·bou·chure)
De·bre·cen Hungarian city
dé·bride·ment surgical term
de·brief
de·bris (*or* dé·)
debt
debt·or
de·bug (·bug·ging, ·bugged)
de·bunk
de·bunk·er

de·bus (·bus·ing, ·bused *or* ·bus·sing, ·bussed) unload; alight
de·but
debu·tante
de·ca·dal
dec·ade
deca·dence (*or* ·den·cy)
deca·dent
de·caf·fein·ate
deca·gon
de·cago·nal
deca·he·dral
deca·he·dron
de·cal transferred design
de·cal·ci·fi·ca·tion
de·cal·ci·fi·er
de·cal·ci·fy (·fies, ·fy·ing, ·fied)
de·cal·co·ma·nia transferring designs
de·ca·les·cence physics term
de·ca·les·cent
Deca·logue Ten Commandments
de·camp
de·camp·ment
de·ca·nal of a dean
dec·ane chemical compound
dec·ane·dio·ic acid
de·ca·ni musical term
deca·no·ic acid
de·cant
de·cant·er
de·capi·tate
de·capi·ta·tion
de·capi·ta·tor
deca·pod crustacean
de·capo·dal (*or* ·dan, ·dous)
de·car·bon·ate
de·car·boni·za·tion (*or* ·sa·tion)
de·car·bon·ize (*or* ·ise)
de·car·bon·iz·er (*or* ·is·er)
de·car·boxy·la·tion
dec·are unit
deca·style architectural term
deca·syl·lab·ic
deca·syl·lable
de·cath·lete
de·cath·lon
de·cay

Dec·can Indian plateau
de·cease
de·ceased
de·cedent deceased
de·ceit
de·ceit·ful
de·ceit·ful·ly
de·ceiv·able
de·ceiv·able·ness (or ·abil·ity)
de·ceive
de·ceiv·er
de·cel·er·ate
de·cel·era·tion
de·cel·era·tor
de·cel·erom·eter
De·cem·ber
De·cem·brist Russian revolutionary
de·cena·ry (or de·cen·na·ry) of tithing
de·cen·cy (plural ·cies)
de·cen·nial
de·cen·nium (or de·cen·na·ry; plural ·niums, ·nia, or ·naries) decade
de·cent
de·cen·tral·ist
de·cen·trali·za·tion (or ·sa·tion)
de·cen·tral·ize (or ·ise)
de·cep·tion
de·cep·tive
de·ce·rebrate remove brain
de·ce·rebra·tion
de·cern legal term
deci·are unit
deci·bel
de·cid·able
de·cide
de·cid·ed
de·cid·ed·ly
de·cid·er
de·cidua (plural ·cid·uas or ·ciduae) anatomy term
de·cid·ual (or ·cidu·ate)
de·cidu·ous
dec·ile statistics term
de·cil·lion 10^{60}
de·cil·lionth
deci·mal
deci·mali·za·tion (or ·sa·tion)

deci·mal·ize (or ·ise)
deci·mate
deci·ma·tion
deci·ma·tor
deci·metre (US ·meter)
de·ci·pher
de·ci·pher·abil·ity
de·ci·pher·able
de·ci·pher·er
de·ci·pher·ment
de·ci·sion
de·ci·sion·al
de·ci·sive
de·ci·sive·ness
deck
deck·house
deck·le (or ·el) frame
deckle-edged
de·claim
de·claim·er
dec·la·ma·tion
de·clama·to·ri·ly
de·clama·tory
de·clar·able
de·clar·ant
dec·la·ra·tion
de·clara·tive
de·clara·tor legal term
de·clara·to·ri·ly
de·clara·tory
de·clare
de·clar·er
de·class
dé·clas·sé (fem ·sée) French having lost status
de·clas·si·fi·able
de·clas·si·fi·ca·tion
de·clas·si·fy (·fies, ·fy·ing, ·fied)
de·clen·sion
de·clen·sion·al
de·clen·sion·al·ly
de·clin·able
dec·li·nate drooping
dec·li·na·tion
de·cli·na·tory
de·cline
de·clin·er
dec·li·nom·eter
de·clivi·tous
de·cliv·ity (plural ·ities) downward slope
de·clutch
de·coct
de·coc·tion

de·code
de·cod·er
de·coke
de·col·late separate
de·col·la·tion
de·col·la·tor
dé·colle·tage low neckline
dé·colle·té
de·colo·nize (or ·nise)
de·col·or·ant
de·col·ori·za·tion (or ·sa·tion, de·col·ora·tion)
de·col·or·ize (or ·ise, de·col·our)
de·com·pos·abil·ity
de·com·pos·able
de·com·pose
de·com·pos·er
de·com·po·si·tion
de·com·pound type of leaf
de·com·press
de·com·pres·sion
de·com·pres·sive
de·com·pres·sor
de·con·gest·ant
de·con·secrate
de·con·tami·nant
de·con·tami·nate
de·con·tami·na·tion
de·con·tami·na·tive
de·con·tami·na·tor
de·con·trol (·trol·ling, ·trolled)
dé·cor (or de·)
deco·rate
deco·ra·tion
deco·ra·tive
deco·ra·tor
deco·rous
de·cor·ti·cate remove shell
de·cor·ti·ca·tion
de·cor·ti·ca·tor
de·co·rum
de·cou·page decoration
de·cou·pling electronics term
de·coy
de·coy·er
de·crease
de·creas·ing·ly
de·cree (·cree·ing, ·creed)
de·cree·able
de·cree nisi
de·cre·er

decrement 112

dec·re·ment diminution
de·crep·it
de·crepi·tate crackle on heating
de·crepi·ta·tion
de·crepi·tude
de·cres·cence
de·cres·cent decreasing
de·cre·tal papal edict
de·cre·tal·ist
de·cre·tive
dec·re·tory
de·cri·al
de·cri·er
de·cry (·cries, ·cry·ing, ·cried)
de·crypt decode
de·cum·bence (or ·ben·cy)
de·cum·bent lying flat
de·cu·ple increase tenfold
de·cu·ri·on Roman councillor
de·cur·rent botany term
de·curved bent downwards
decu·ry (plural ·ries) ten Roman soldiers
de·cus·sate intersect
de·cus·sa·tion
De·dé·ag·ach Greek port
dedi·cate
dedi·cat·ed
dedi·ca·tee
dedi·ca·tion
dedi·ca·tor
dedi·ca·tory (or ·tive)
de·dif·fer·en·tia·tion
de·duce
de·duc·ibil·ity (or ·ible·ness)
de·duc·ible
de·duct
de·duct·ibil·ity
de·duct·ible
de·duc·tion
de·duc·tive
Dee river
deed
deek *Dialect* look at
deem consider; *compare* deme
deem·ster (or demp·) Manx magistrate
deep
deep·en

deep·en·er
deep·freeze (*noun*)
deep-freeze (*verb*; -freez·ing, -froze or -freezed, -frozen or -freezed)
deep-fry (-fries, -fry·ing, -fried)
deep-laid
deep·ness
deep-rooted (or -seated)
deer (*plural* deer or deers)
deer·grass
deer·hound
deer·skin
deer·stalker
de-escalate
de-escala·tion
de·face
de·face·able
de·face·ment
de·fac·er
de fac·to
(defaecate) *incorrect spelling of* defecate
de·fal·cate legal term
de·fal·ca·tion
de·fal·ca·tor
defa·ma·tion
de·fama·to·ri·ly
de·fama·tory
de·fame
de·fam·er
de·fault
de·fault·er
de·fea·sance annulment
de·fea·sible
de·feat
de·feat·er
de·feat·ism
de·feat·ist
def·ecate
def·eca·tion
def·eca·tor
de·fect
de·fec·tion
de·fec·tive
de·fec·tor
de·fence (*US* ·fense)
de·fence·less (*US* ·fense·)
de·fence·less·ness (*US* ·fense·)
de·fend
de·fend·able

de·fend·ant
de·fend·er
de·fen·es·tra·tion throwing from window
de·fen·sibil·ity (or ·sible·ness)
de·fen·sible
de·fen·sibly
de·fen·sive
de·fer (·fer·ring, ·ferred)
def·er·ence
def·er·ent
def·er·en·tial
def·er·en·tial·ly
de·fer·ment (or ·fer·ral)
de·fer·rable (or ·fer·able)
de·fer·ral
de·ferred
de·fer·rer
de·fi·cient
defi·cit
de·fi·er
defi·lade military term
de·file
de·file·ment
de·fil·er
de·fin·able
de·fine
de·fin·er
de·fini·en·dum (*plural* ·da) thing defined
de·fini·ens (*plural* ·en·tia) definition
defi·nite
defi·nite·ly
defi·nite·ness
defi·ni·tion
defi·ni·tion·al
de·fini·tive
de·fini·tive·ly
de·fini·tude
def·la·grate burn
def·la·gra·tion
de·flate
de·fla·tion
de·fla·tion·ary
de·fla·tion·ist
de·fla·tor
de·flect
de·flec·tion (or ·flex·ion)
de·flec·tive
de·flec·tor
de·flexed
de·floc·cu·late disperse
de·floc·cu·la·tion

de·flo·ra·tion
de·flow·er
de·flow·er·er
de·fo·li·ant
de·fo·li·ate
de·fo·lia·tion
de·fo·lia·tor
de·force withhold
de·force·ment
de·for·ciant legal term
de·for·est
de·for·esta·tion
de·for·est·er
de·form
de·form·able
de·for·ma·tion
de·formed
de·form·ed·ness
de·form·er
de·form·ity (*plural* ·ities)
de·fraud
de·frau·da·tion
de·fraud·er
de·fraud·ment
de·fray
de·fray·able
de·fray·al (*or* ·ment)
de·fray·er
de·frock
de·frost
de·frost·er
deft
deft·ness
de·funct
de·func·tive
de·fuse
defy (·fies, ·fy·ing, ·fied)
dé·ga·gé *French* casual
de·gas (·gas·ses *or* ·gases, ·gas·sing, ·gassed)
de·gas·ser
de·gauss demagnetize
de·gen·era·cy (*plural* ·cies)
de·gen·er·ate
de·gen·er·ate·ness
de·gen·era·tion
de·gen·era·tive
de·glu·ti·nate extract gluten
de·glu·ti·na·tion
de·glu·ti·tion swallowing
de·gra·dable
deg·ra·da·tion
de·grade
de·grad·ed

de·grad·er
de·grad·ing
de·grease
de·gree
degree-day unit
de·gres·sion decrease
de·hisce burst open
de·his·cence
de·his·cent
de·horn
Deh·ra Dun Indian city
de·hu·mani·za·tion (*or* ·sa·tion)
de·hu·man·ize (*or* ·ise)
de·hu·midi·fi·ca·tion
de·hu·midi·fi·er
de·hu·midi·fy (·fies, ·fy·ing, ·fied)
de·hy·drate
de·hy·dra·tion
de·hy·dra·tor
de·hydro·gen·ase enzyme
de·hydro·gen·ate (*or* ·ize, ·ise) remove hydrogen
de·hydro·gena·tion
de·hydro·geni·za·tion (*or* ·sa·tion)
de·hyp·no·tize (*or* ·ise)
de-ice
de-icer
dei·ci·dal
dei·cide killing a god
deic·tic logic term
deic·ti·cal·ly
de·ific godlike
dei·fi·ca·tion
dei·fi·er
dei·form
dei·fy (·fies, ·fy·ing, ·fied)
deign
deil *Scot* devil
de·in·dus·tri·ali·za·tion (*or* ·sa·tion)
de·in·dus·tri·al·ize (*or* ·ise)
de·ism
de·ist
de·ist·ic (*or* ·is·ti·cal)
de·ity (*plural* ·ities)
deix·is linguistics term
déjà vu
de·ject
de·jec·ta body waste
de·ject·ed
de·ject·ed·ness

de·jec·tion
de jure *Latin* according to law
dek·ko (*plural* ·kos) *Slang* look
de·laine fabric
de·lami·nate divide into layers
de·lami·na·tion
(delapidate) *incorrect spelling of* dilapidate
de·late denounce
Dela·ware US state
Dela·war·ean
de·lay
de·lay·er
dele (de·leing, de·led) symbol for deletion; *compare* deal
de·lec·table
de·lec·table·ness (*or* ·tabil·ity)
de·lec·tably
de·lec·ta·tion
del·egable
del·ega·cy (*plural* ·cies) committee
del·egate
del·ega·tion
de·lete
del·eteri·ous
de·letion
Delft Dutch town; earthenware
Del·hi Indian capital
deli *short for* delicatessen
De·lian of Delos
de·lib·er·ate
de·lib·er·ate·ness
de·lib·era·tion
de·lib·era·tive
de·lib·era·tor
deli·ca·cy (*plural* ·cies)
deli·cate
deli·ca·tes·sen
de·li·cious
de·lict civil wrong
de·light
de·light·ed
de·light·er
de·light·ful
de·light·ful·ly
de·light·ful·ness
de·lim·it (*or* ·limi·tate)
de·limi·ta·tion

de·lim·i·ta·tive
de·lin·eable
de·lin·eate
de·lin·ea·tion
de·lin·ea·tive
de·lin·ea·tor tailor's pattern
de·lin·quen·cy (*plural* ·cies)
de·lin·quent
deli·quesce chemistry term
deli·ques·cence
deli·ques·cent
de·liri·ant
de·liri·ous
de·liri·ous·ness
de·lir·i·um (*plural* ·lir·iums *or* ·liria)
de·lir·i·um tre·mens
deli·tes·cence medical term
deli·tes·cent
de·liv·er
de·liv·er·able
de·liv·er·ance
de·liv·er·er
de·liv·ery (*plural* ·eries)
dell
Del·mar·va US peninsula
de·lo·cali·za·tion (*or* ·sa·tion)
de·lo·cal·ize (*or* ·ise)
De·los Greek island
de·louse
Del·phi Greek oracle
Del·phian
Del·phic
del·phin·i·um (*plural* ·phin·iums *or* ·phinia)
Del·phi·nus constellation
del·ta
del·ta·ic (*or* del·tic)
del·ti·olo·gist
del·ti·ol·ogy collecting postcards
del·toid muscle
de·lude
de·lud·er
del·uge
de·lu·sion
de·lu·sion·al
de·lu·sive
de·lu·so·ry
de luxe
delve
delv·er

de·mag·neti·za·tion (*or* ·sa·tion)
de·mag·net·ize (*or* ·ise)
de·mag·net·iz·er (*or* ·is·er)
dema·gog·ic (*or* ·gogi·cal)
dema·gogi·cal·ly
dema·gogue (*US also* ·gog)
dema·gogu·ery (*or* ·ism)
dema·gogy (*plural* ·gogies)
de·mand
de·mand·able
de·mand·ant
de·mand·er
de·mand·ing
de·man·toid gemstone
de·mar·cate
de·mar·ca·tion (*or* ·ka·tion)
de·mar·ca·tor
dé·marche French diplomatic manoeuvre
de·ma·teri·al·ize (*or* ·ise)
Dema·vend Iranian volcano
deme biology term; ancient local-government unit; *compare* deem
de·mean
de·mean·ing
de·mean·our (*US* ·or)
de·ment
de·ment·ed
de·ment·ed·ness
de·men·tia
Dem·erara Guyanese river
dem·erara sugar
de·mer·it
de·meri·to·ri·ous
de·mer·sal living in deep water
de·mesne land
Demeter Greek goddess
demi·bas·ti·on fortification
demi·can·ton
demi·god (*fem* ·god·dess)
demi·john bottle
de·mili·ta·ri·za·tion (*or* ·sa·tion)
de·mili·ta·rize (*or* ·rise)
demi·lune crescent shape
demi·mon·daine unrespectable woman
demi·monde

114

de·min·er·al·ize (*or* ·ise)
demi·relief
de·mis·able
de·mise
demi·semi·qua·ver
de·mis·sion giving up office
de·mist
de·mist·er
demi·tasse small coffee cup
demi·urge philosophy term
demi·vierge French promiscuous virgin
demi·volt (*or* ·volte)
demo (*plural* demos) *Slang* demonstration
de·mob (·mob·bing, ·mobbed)
de·mo·bi·li·za·tion (*or* ·sa·tion)
de·mo·bi·lize (*or* ·lise)
de·moc·ra·cy (*plural* ·cies)
Demo·crat political party member
demo·crat
Demo·crat·ic
demo·crat·ic
demo·crati·cal·ly
de·moc·ra·ti·za·tion (*or* ·sa·tion)
de·moc·ra·tize (*or* ·tise)
dé·mo·dé French out of fashion
de·modu·late
de·modu·la·tion electronics term
de·modu·la·tor
De·mo·gor·gon underworld god
de·mog·ra·pher (*or* ·phist)
de·mo·graph·ic (*or* ·graphi·cal)
de·mo·graphi·cal·ly
de·mog·ra·phy
demoi·selle damsel; bird
de·mol·ish
de·mol·ish·er
de·mol·ish·ment
demo·li·tion
demo·li·tion·ist
de·mon devil; *compare* daemon
de·mon·eti·za·tion (*or* ·sa·tion)
de·mon·etize (*or* ·etise)
de·mo·ni·ac (*or* ·nia·cal)

de·mo·nia·cal·ly
de·mon·ic
de·moni·cal·ly
de·mon·ism
de·mon·ist
de·mon·ize (or ·ise)
de·mon·ola·ter demon worshipper
de·mon·ola·try
de·mono·logi·cal
de·mon·olo·gist
de·mon·ol·ogy
de·mon·strabil·ity (or ·strable·ness)
de·mon·strable
de·mon·strably
dem·on·strate
dem·on·stra·tion
de·mon·stra·tion·al
de·mon·stra·tion·ist
de·mon·stra·tive
de·mon·stra·tor
de·mor·ali·za·tion (or ·sa·tion)
de·mor·al·ize (or ·ise)
de·mor·al·iz·er (or ·is·er)
de·mos nation
de·mote
de·mot·ic of the people
de·mo·tion
de·mot·ist
de·mount
de·mount·able
demp·ster variant of deemster
de·mul·cent soothing
de·mul·si·fi·ca·tion
de·mul·si·fi·er
de·mul·si·fy (·fies, ·fy·ing, ·fied)
de·mur (·mur·ring, ·murred)
de·mure
de·mure·ness
de·mur·rable
de·mur·rage
de·mur·ral
de·mur·rer objection
demy paper size
de·mys·ti·fi·ca·tion
de·mys·ti·fy (·fies, ·fy·ing, ·fied)
de·my·tholo·gize (or ·gise)
den (den·ning, denned)

de·nar·ius (plural ·narii) coin
de·nary based on ten
de·na·tion·ali·za·tion (or ·sa·tion)
de·na·tion·al·ize (or ·ise)
de·natu·rali·za·tion (or ·sa·tion)
de·natu·ral·ize (or ·ise)
de·na·tur·ant
de·na·tura·tion
de·na·ture (or ·tur·ize, ·tur·ise)
de·na·zi·fy (·fies, ·fy·ing, ·fied)
Den·bigh·shire former Welsh county
den·dri·form branching
den·drite part of nerve cell
den·drit·ic (or ·driti·cal)
den·driti·cal·ly
den·dro·chrono·logi·cal
den·dro·chro·nolo·gist
den·dro·chro·nol·ogy
study of tree rings
den·droid (or ·droi·dal) treelike
den·dro·logi·cal (or ·log·ic, ·drolo·gous)
den·drolo·gist
den·drol·ogy
dene wooded valley; compare dean
Den·eb star
de·nega·tion
den·gue viral disease
de·ni·able
de·ni·al
de·nico·tin·ize (or ·ise)
de·ni·er one who denies
den·ier unit of weight
deni·grate
deni·gra·tion
deni·gra·tor
den·im
de·ni·trate chemistry term
de·ni·tra·tion
de·ni·tri·fi·ca·tion
de·ni·tri·fy (·fies, ·fy·ing, ·fied)
deni·zen
Den·mark
denned
den·ning
de·nomi·nable

de·nomi·nate
de·nomi·na·tion
de·nomi·na·tion·al
de·nomi·na·tion·al·ism
de·nomi·na·tion·al·ist
de·nomi·na·tive naming
de·nomi·na·tor
de·not·able
de·no·ta·tion
de·no·ta·tive
de·note
de·note·ment
de·noue·nment
de·nounce
de·nounce·ment
de·nounc·er
dense
dense·ness
den·sim·eter
den·si·met·ric
den·sim·etry
den·si·tom·eter
den·si·to·met·ric
den·si·tom·etry
den·sity (plural ·sities)
dent
den·tal
den·ta·lium (plural ·liums or ·lia) mollusc
den·tate
den·ta·tion state of having teeth; compare dentition
den·tex fish
den·ti·cle small tooth
den·ticu·late
den·ticu·la·tion
den·ti·form
den·ti·frice
den·til architectural term
den·ti·la·bial
den·ti·lin·gual phonetics term
den·tin·al
den·tine (or ·tin) tooth tissue
den·tist
den·tis·try
den·ti·tion set of teeth; compare dentation
den·toid
Den·ton Lancashire town
den·ture
de·nu·cleari·za·tion (or ·sa·tion)
de·nu·clear·ize (or ·ise)

denudate 116

denu·date
denu·da·tion
de·nude
de·nud·er
de·nu·mer·able
de·nun·ci·ate
de·nun·cia·tion
de·nun·cia·tor
de·nun·cia·tory
Den·ver US city
deny (de·nies, de·ny·ing, de·nied)
deo·dand legal term
deo·dar tree
de·odor·ant
de·odori·za·tion (or ·sa·tion)
de·odor·ize (or ·ise)
de·odor·iz·er (or ·is·er)
de·on·tic logic term
de·on·to·logi·cal
de·on·tolo·gist
de·on·tol·ogy branch of ethics
de·oxi·di·za·tion (or ·sa·tion)
de·oxi·dize (or ·dise)
de·oxi·diz·er (or ·dis·er)
de·oxy·cor·ti·co·ster·one (or de·oxy·cor·tone) hormone
de·oxy·gen·ate (or ·ize, ·ise)
de·oxy·gena·tion
de·oxy·ri·bo·nu·cle·ic acid (or des·)
de·oxy·ri·bose (or des·) a sugar
de·part
de·part·ment
de·part·men·tal
de·part·men·tal·ism
de·part·men·tali·za·tion (or ·sa·tion)
de·part·ment·al·ize (or ·ise)
de·part·men·tal·ly
de·par·ture
de·pas·ture
de·pend
de·pend·abil·ity (or ·able·ness)
de·pend·able
de·pend·ably
de·pend·ant (noun)

de·pend·ence (US also ·ance)
de·pend·en·cy (US also ·an·cy; plural ·cies)
de·pend·ent (US also ·ant; adj)
de·per·son·ali·za·tion (or ·sa·tion)
de·per·son·al·ize (or ·ise)
de·pict
de·pict·er (or ·pic·tor)
de·pic·tion
de·pic·tive
de·pic·ture
depi·late
depi·la·tion
depi·la·tor
de·pila·tory (plural ·tories)
de·plane
de·plet·able
de·plete
de·ple·tion
de·ple·tive (or ·tory)
de·plor·able
de·plor·able·ness (or ·abil·ity)
de·plor·ably
de·plore
de·plor·er
de·plor·ing·ly
de·ploy
de·ploy·ment
de·plu·ma·tion
de·plume deprive of feathers
de·po·lari·za·tion (or ·sa·tion)
de·po·lar·ize (or ·ise)
de·po·lar·iz·er (or ·is·er)
de·po·liti·cize (or ·cise)
de·pone Scot testify
de·po·nent linguistics term; deposition maker
de·popu·late
de·popu·la·tion
de·port
de·port·able
de·por·ta·tion
de·por·tee
de·port·ment
de·pos·able
de·pos·al
de·pose
de·pos·er

de·pos·it
de·posi·tary (plural ·taries) person; compare depository
depo·si·tion
de·posi·tor
de·posi·tory (plural ·tories) warehouse; compare depositary
de·pot
dep·ra·va·tion corruption; compare deprivation
de·prave
de·praved
de·praved·ness
de·prav·er
de·prav·ity (plural ·ities)
dep·re·cate protest against; compare depreciate
dep·re·ca·tion
dep·re·ca·tive
dep·re·ca·tor
dep·re·ca·to·ri·ly
dep·re·ca·tory
de·pre·ciable
de·pre·ci·ate lose value; compare deprecate
de·pre·cia·tion
de·pre·cia·tor
de·pre·cia·tory (or ·tive)
dep·re·date plunder
dep·re·da·tion
de·press
de·pres·sant
de·pressed
de·press·ible
de·press·ing
de·pres·sion
de·pres·sive
de·pres·so·mo·tor physiology term
de·pres·sor
de·pres·suri·za·tion (or ·sa·tion)
de·pres·sur·ize
de·priv·able
dep·ri·va·tion (or de·priv·al) loss; compare depravation
de·prive
de·prived
de·priv·er
dep·side chemistry term
depth
depu·rate purify

depu·ra·tion
depu·ra·tive purifying
depu·ra·tor
depu·ta·tion
de·pute
depu·tize (or ·tise)
depu·ty (plural ·ties)
de·rac·in·ate uproot
de·raci·na·tion
de·rail
de·rail·leur bicycle gear
de·rail·ment
de·range
de·range·ment
de·ra·tion
Der·by
Der·by·shire
de·reg·is·ter
der·elict
der·elic·tion
de·re·strict
de·re·strict·ed
de·re·stric·tion
de·ride
de·rid·er
de ri·gueur
de·ris·ible
de·ri·sion
de·ri·sive (or ·sory)
de·ri·sive·ness
de·riv·able
deri·va·tion
deri·va·tion·al
de·riva·tive
de·rive
de·riv·er
der·ma skin
der·mal
der·ma·ti·tis
der·mato·gen plant tissue
derma·to·glyph·ics skin pattern
der·ma·toid
der·ma·to·logi·cal
der·ma·tolo·gist
der·ma·tol·ogy
der·ma·tome surgical instrument
der·ma·tom·ic
der·ma·to·phyte parasitic fungus
der·ma·to·phyt·ic
der·ma·to·phy·to·sis
der·ma·to·plas·tic

der·ma·to·plas·ty skin grafting
der·ma·to·sis (plural ·ses) skin disease
der·mic
der·mis skin layer
der·moid
dero·gate disparage
dero·gation
de·roga·tive
de·roga·to·ri·ly
de·roga·to·ri·ness
de·roga·tory
der·rick
der·rière buttocks
derring-do bold action
der·rin·ger (or der·in·ger) pistol
der·ris plant
Der·ry Londonderry
der·ry Austral grudge
derv diesel oil
der·vish
Der·went river
Derwent·water lake
de·sali·nate (or ·nize, ·nise)
de·sali·na·tion (or ·ni·za·tion, ·ni·sa·tion)
de·scale
des·cant
des·cant·er
de·scend
des·cend·able
de·scend·ant (noun)
de·scend·ent (adj)
de·scend·er
de·scend·ible (or ·able)
de·scent
de·school
de·scrib·able
de·scribe
de·scrib·er
de·scri·er
de·scrip·tion
de·scrip·tive
de·scrip·ti·vism
de·scry (·scries, ·scry·ing, ·scried)
des·ecrate
des·ecra·tion
des·ecra·tor (or ·ter)
de·seg·re·gate
de·seg·re·ga·tion
de·seg·re·ga·tion·ist

de·sen·si·ti·za·tion (or ·sa·tion)
de·sen·si·tize (or ·tise)
de·sen·si·tiz·er (or ·tis·er)
des·ert plantless region; compare dessert
de·sert abandon; merit; compare dessert
de·sert·ed
de·sert·er
des·ert·ifi·ca·tion
de·ser·tion
de·serve
de·serv·ed·ly
de·serv·ed·ness
de·serv·er
de·serv·ing
de·sexu·ali·za·tion (or ·sa·tion)
de·sexu·al·ize (or ·ise)
des·ha·bille variant spelling of dishabille
des·ic·cant
des·ic·cate
des·ic·ca·ted
des·ic·ca·tion
des·ic·ca·tive
des·ic·ca·tor
de·sid·er·ate long for
de·sid·era·tion
de·sid·era·tive
de·sid·era·tum (plural ·ta) something wanted
de·sign
de·sign·able
des·ig·nate
des·ig·na·tion
des·ig·na·tive (or ·tory)
des·ig·na·tor
de·sign·ed·ly
de·sign·er
de·sign·ing
desi·nence word ending
desi·nent (or ·nen·tial)
de·sir·abil·ity (or ·sirable·ness)
de·sir·able
de·sire
de·sir·er
de·sir·ous
de·sist
de·sist·ance (or ·ence)
desk
des·man (plural ·mans) animal

desmid

des·mid alga
des·mid·ian
des·moid tumour
Des Moines US city
deso·late
deso·lat·er (or ·or)
deso·la·tion
de·sorb chemistry term
de·sorp·tion
des·pair
des·patch variant spelling of dispatch
des·pe·ra·do (plural ·does or ·dos)
des·per·ate
des·pera·tion
des·pi·cabil·ity (or ·cable·ness)
des·pic·able
des·pic·ably
des·pise
de·spis·er
de·spite
de·spoil
de·spoil·er
de·spoil·ment
de·spo·lia·tion
de·spond
de·spond·en·cy (or ·ence)
de·spond·ent
des·pot
des·pot·ic (or ·poti·cal)
des·poti·cal·ly
des·pot·ism
des·pu·mate clarify
des·pu·ma·tion
des·qua·mate
des·qua·ma·tion
Des·sau East German city
des·sert sweet; compare desert
dessert·spoon
des·sia·tine Russian unit
(dessicate) incorrect spelling of desiccate
des·ti·na·tion
des·tine
des·tined
des·ti·ny (plural ·nies)
des·ti·tute
des·ti·tu·tion
de·stroy
de·stroy·able
de·stroy·er
de·struct

de·struc·tibil·ity
de·struct·ible
de·struc·tion
de·struc·tion·ist
de·struc·tive
de·struc·tive·ness (or ·tiv·ity)
de·struc·tor furnace
desue·tude state of disuse
des·ul·to·ri·ly
des·ul·to·ri·ness
des·ul·tory
de·tach
de·tach·abil·ity
de·tach·able
de·tached
de·tach·er
de·tach·ment
de·tail
de·tailed
de·tain
de·tain·able
de·tainee
de·tain·er
de·tain·ment
de·tect
de·tect·able (or ·ible)
de·tec·tion
de·tec·tive
de·tec·tor
de·tent locking device
dé·tente easement
de·ten·tion
de·ter (·ter·ring, ·terred)
de·terge cleanse
de·ter·gen·cy (or ·gence)
de·ter·gent
de·terio·rate
de·terio·ra·tion
de·terio·ra·tive
de·ter·ment
de·ter·mi·nable
de·ter·mi·nant
de·ter·mi·nate
de·ter·mi·na·tion
de·ter·mi·na·tive
de·ter·mine
de·ter·mined
de·ter·mined·ly
de·ter·mined·ness
de·ter·min·er
de·ter·min·ism
de·ter·min·ist
de·ter·min·is·tic
de·ter·rence

118

de·ter·rent
de·ter·sive
de·test
de·test·abil·ity (or ·able·ness)
de·test·able
de·tes·ta·tion
de·test·er
de·throne
de·throne·ment
de·thron·er
deti·nue legal term
Det·mold West German city
deto·nate
deto·na·tion
deto·na·tive
deto·na·tor
de·tour
de·toxi·cant
de·toxi·cate
de·toxi·ca·tion
de·toxi·fi·ca·tion
de·toxi·fy (·fies, ·fy·ing, ·fied)
de·tract
de·trac·tion
de·trac·tive (or ·tory)
de·trac·tor
de·train
de·train·ment
de·trib·ali·za·tion (or ·sa·tion)
de·trib·al·ize (or ·ise)
det·ri·ment
det·ri·men·tal
det·ri·men·tal·ly
de·tri·tal
de·tri·tion wearing away
de·tri·tus debris
De·troit US city
de trop French superfluous
de·trude thrust out
de·trun·cate
de·trun·ca·tion
de·tru·sion
de·tu·mes·cence
Deucalion mythological character
deuce
deu·ced
deus ex machi·na Latin providential resolver
deu·ter·ago·nist drama term

deu·tera·nope
deu·tera·no·pia green blindness
deu·ter·an·op·ic
deu·ter·ide chemistry term
deu·ter·ium hydrogen isotope
deu·tero·ca·noni·cal
deu·ter·oga·mist
deu·ter·oga·my
deu·ter·on deuterium nucleus
Deu·ter·ono·my biblical book
deu·to·plasm (or deu·tero·) egg yolk
deu·to·plas·mic (or ·tic)
Deut·sche Mark
deut·zia shrub
Deux-Sèvres French city
deva oriental god; compare diva
de·valua·tion
de·value (or ·valu·ate; ·valu·ing, ·val·ued or ·at·ing, ·ated)
De·va·na·ga·ri Indian script
dev·as·tate
dev·as·ta·tion
dev·as·ta·tive
dev·as·ta·tor
de·vel·op
de·vel·op·able
de·vel·op·er
de·vel·op·ment
de·vel·op·men·tal
de·vel·op·men·tal·ly
de·vi·ance
de·vi·ant
de·vi·ate
de·via·tion
de·via·tion·ism
de·via·tion·ist
de·via·tor
de·via·tory
de·vice contrivance; plan; compare devise
dev·il (·il·ling, ·illed; US ·il·ing, ·iled)
devil·fish (plural ·fish or ·fishes)
dev·il·ish
dev·il·ish·ness
dev·il·ment
dev·il·ry (plural ·ries)

de·vi·ous
de·vi·ous·ness
de·vis·able
de·vis·al act of devising
de·vise to plan; leave by will; a gift by will; compare device
de·vi·see inheritor
de·vis·er (or in legal contexts ·vi·sor) one who devises; compare divisor
de·vi·tali·za·tion (or ·sa·tion)
de·vi·tal·ize (or ·ise)
de·vit·ri·fi·ca·tion
de·vit·ri·fy (·fies, ·fy·ing, ·fied) chemistry term
de·vo·cal·ize (or ·ise)
de·voice phonetics term
de·void
de·voirs (plural) French compliments
de·vo·lu·tion
de·vo·lu·tion·ary
de·vo·lu·tion·ist
de·volve
de·volve·ment
Dev·on
De·vo·nian
Dev·on·shire
de·vote
de·vot·ed
de·vot·ed·ness
devo·tee
de·vote·ment
de·vo·tion
de·vo·tion·al
de·vo·tion·al·ity (or ·ness)
de·vour
de·vour·er
de·vour·ing·ly
de·vout
de·vout·ness
dew
de·wan Indian minister
dew·berry (plural ·berries)
dew·claw
dew·drop
dewi·ly
dewi·ness
dew·lap
Dews·bury Yorkshire town
dewy (dewi·er, dewi·est)

dewy-eyed
Dex·edrine (Trademark)
dex·ter
dex·ter·ity
dex·ter·ous (or dex·trous)
dex·ter·ous·ness (or dex·trous·ness)
dex·tral
dex·tral·ity
dex·tral·ly
dex·tran biochemical compound
dex·trin (or ·trine) adhesive gum
dextro·am·pheta·mine
dextro·glu·cose
dextro·gy·rate (or ·gyre)
dextro·ro·ta·tion
dextro·ro·ta·tory (or dextro·ro·ta·ry)
dex·trorse (or ·tror·sal) spiralling left to right
dex·trose form of glucose
dex·trous
dey Algerian ruler
Dhah·ran Saudi Arabian town
dhak tree
Dhaka (or Dac·ca) Bangladeshi capital
dhal vegetable
dhar·ma Hindu custom
dhar·na Indian sit-in
Dhau·la·gi·ri Nepalese mountain
dho·bi Indian washerman
dhole animal
dho·ti (or dhoo·ti, dhoo·tie, dhu·ti) loincloth
dhow boat
dia·base rock
dia·ba·sic
dia·be·tes
dia·bet·ic
dia·ble·rie devilry
dia·bol·ic
dia·boli·cal
dia·boli·cal·ly
dia·boli·cal·ness
diabo·lism
di·abo·list
di·abo·lize (or ·lise)
di·abo·lo (plural ·los) game

diacaustic

dia·caus·tic physics term
di·ac·etyl·mor·phine
dia·chron·ic linguistics term
di·acid
dia·cid·ic
di·aco·nal of a deacon
di·aco·nate
dia·crit·ic phonetic symbol
dia·criti·cal
di·ac·tin·ic physics term
di·ac·tin·ism
dia·del·phous botany term
dia·dem
di·ad·ro·mous fan-shaped
di·aer·esis variant spelling of dieresis
di·aeret·ic variant spelling of dieretic
dia·gen·esis chemistry term
dia·geo·trop·ic
dia·geot·ro·pism response to gravity
di·ag·nos·able
di·ag·nose
di·ag·no·sis (plural ·ses)
di·ag·nos·tic
di·ag·nos·ti·cal·ly
di·ag·nos·ti·cian
di·ag·nos·tics
di·ago·nal
di·ago·nal·ly
dia·gram (·gram·ming, ·grammed; US ·gram·ing, ·gramed)
dia·gram·mat·ic
dia·gram·mati·cal·ly
dia·graph drawing instrument
dia·ki·nesis biology term
dial (dial·ling, dialled; US dial·ing, dialed)
dia·lect
dia·lec·tal
dia·lec·tic
dia·lec·ti·cal
dia·lec·ti·cal·ly
dia·lec·tics branch of logic
dia·lec·to·logi·cal
dia·lec·tolo·gist
dia·lec·tol·ogy
di·al·lage mineral
dial·ler
di·alo·gism philosophy term
di·alo·gist
dia·lo·gis·tic (or ·ti·cal)

di·alo·gize (or ·gise)
dia·logue (US also ·log)
dia·logu·er
dia·lys·abil·ity
dia·lys·able
dia·ly·sa·tion
dia·lyse (US ·lyze)
dia·lys·er (US ·lyz·)
di·aly·sis (plural ·ses)
dia·lyt·ic
dia·lyti·cal·ly
dia·mag·net
dia·mag·net·ic
dia·mag·neti·cal·ly
dia·mag·net·ism
dia·man·té decorated with sequins
dia·man·tine of diamonds
di·am·eter
di·am·etral
dia·met·ric (or ·ri·cal)
dia·met·ri·cal·ly
dia·mine chemistry term
dia·mond
diamond·back terrapin
di·an·drous botany term
dia·no·et·ic of thought
dia·noia philosophy term
di·an·thus (plural ·thuses) plant
dia·pa·son organ stop
dia·pa·son·al (or ·son·ic)
dia·pause suspended growth
dia·pede·sis medical term
dia·pedet·ic
dia·per
di·apha·nous
di·apha·nous·ness (or ·nei·ty)
dia·phone linguistics term
dia·phon·ic
di·apho·ny musical term
dia·pho·resis
dia·pho·ret·ic causing perspiration
dia·pho·to·trop·ic biology term
dia·photo·trop·ism
dia·phragm
dia·phrag·mat·ic
dia·phrag·mati·cal·ly
dia·phys·ial
di·aphy·sis bone shaft
dia·pir geological fold
di·apo·phys·ial

120

dia·pophy·sis (plural ·ses) anatomy term
dia·posi·tive positive transparency
di·arch botany term
di·ar·chic (or di·ar·chi·cal, di·ar·chal, dy·)
di·ar·chy (or dy·; plural ·chies) two-state government
dia·rist
di·ar·rhoea (US ·rhea)
di·ar·rhoeal (or ·rhoe·ic; US ·rheal or ·rhe·ic)
di·ar·thro·dial
di·ar·thro·sis (plural ·ses) movable joint
dia·ry (plural ·ries)
dia·scope projector
Di·as·po·ra Jews' dispersion
dia·spore mineral
dia·stal·sis (plural ·ses) physiology term
dia·stal·tic
dia·stase enzyme
dia·sta·sic
dia·sta·sis (plural ·ses) separation
dia·stat·ic
dia·ste·ma (plural ·ma·ta) fissure
di·as·ter biology term
di·as·to·le dilation of heart
di·as·tol·ic
di·as·tral biology term
dia·stroph·ic
di·as·tro·phism movement of earth's crust
dia·style architectural term
dia·tes·sa·ron musical term
dia·ther·man·cy (plural ·cies) heat transmission
dia·ther·man·ous
dia·ther·mic
dia·ther·my (or ·mia) medical term
diath·esis (plural ·eses) susceptibility to disease
dia·thet·ic
dia·tom alga
dia·to·ma·ceous
dia·tom·ic
di·ato·mic·ity
di·ato·mite rock
dia·ton·ic musical term
dia·toni·cal·ly

dia·toni·cism
dia·tribe
dia·trop·ic
di·at·ro·pism biology term
dia·zine (*or* ·zin) chemistry term
di·azo (*plural* ·azos *or* ·azoes) chemistry term
dia·zole
di·azo·methane
dia·zo·nium
dia·zo·ti·za·tion (*or* ·sa·tion)
dia·zo·tize (*or* ·tise)
dib (dib·bing, dibbed)
di·ba·sic
di·ba·sic·ity
dib·ber
dib·ble garden tool
dib·bler
di·bran·chi·ate zoology term
di·bro·mide
di·car·box·yl·ic acid
dic·ast Athenian juror
dice
di·cen·tra plant
di·cepha·lism
di·cepha·lous two-headed
di·cer
dicey (dici·er, dici·est)
di·cha·sial
di·cha·sium (*plural* ·sia) botany term
di·chla·myd·eous botany term
di·chlo·ride
di·chloro·di·fluoro·methane
di·chloro·di·phenyl-tri·chloro·ethane DDT
di·choga·mous (*or* ·cho·gam·ic)
di·choga·my botany term
di·choto·mist
di·choto·mi·za·tion (*or* ·sa·tion)
di·choto·mize (*or* ·mise)
di·choto·mous (*or* ·cho·tom·ic)
di·choto·my (*plural* ·mies)
di·chro·ic (*or* di·chro·it·ic)
di·chro·ism crystallography term
di·chro·ite

di·chro·mate chemistry term
di·chro·mat·ic having two colours
di·chro·mati·cism crystallography term
di·chro·ma·tism
di·chro·mic involving two colours
di·chro·scope (*or* ·chroi·scope, ·chroo·scope) optical instrument
di·chro·scop·ic (*or* ·chroi·scop·ic, ·chroo·scop·ic)
dick·ens slang term
Dick·en·sian
dick·er *US* barter
dicky (*or* dick·ey; *noun, plural* dickies *or* dick·eys; *adj* dicki·er, dicki·est)
di·cli·nism
di·cli·nous botany term
di·cli·ny
di·coty·ledon botany term
di·coty·ledon·ous
di·crot·ic (*or* ·cro·tal) having a double pulse
di·cro·tism
dic·ta *plural of* dictum
Dic·ta·phone (*Trademark*)
dic·tate
dic·ta·tion
dic·ta·tion·al
dic·ta·tor
dic·ta·tor·ial
dic·ta·tor·ial·ly
dic·ta·tor·ship
dic·ta·tress (*or* ·trix)
dic·tion
dic·tion·ary (*plural* ·aries)
Dic·to·graph (*Trademark*)
dic·tum (*plural* ·tums *or* ·ta)
di·cyno·dont extinct reptile
did
Dida·che treatise
di·dac·tic
di·dac·ti·cal·ly
di·dac·ti·cism
di·dac·tics teaching
did·dle

did·geri·doo musical instrument
didi·coy (*or* did·di·coy, dida·kai; *plural* ·coys *or* ·kais) gypsy
didn't
Dido mythological character
didst
di·dym·ium chemistry term
didy·mous in pairs
di·dyna·mous botany term
die (*verb*; dy·ing, died) expire; *compare* dye
die (*noun*) tool; *Archaic* dice; *compare* dye
die·back tree disease
die-cast (-casting, -cast)
di·ecious *variant spelling* (*esp. US*) *of* dioecious
die-hard
die-hardism
diel·drin insecticide
di·elec·tric
di·elec·tri·cal·ly
Dien Bien Phu Vietnamese battle site
di·en·cephal·ic
di·en·cepha·lon brain part
Di·eppe French port
di·er·esis (*or* ·aer·; *plural* ·eses) phonetics symbol; *compare* diuresis
di·eret·ic (*or* ·aeret·) of dieresis; *compare* diuretic
die·sel
diesel-electric
diesel-hydrau·lic
di·esis (*plural* ·eses) printing term
die·stock tool
di·estrus *US spelling of* dioestrus
diet
di·etary
di·et·er
di·etet·ic (*or* ·eteti·cal)
di·eteti·cal·ly
di·etet·ics
di·ethyl·stil·boes·trol (*US* ·bes·)
di·eti·tian (*or* ·cian)
dif·fer
dif·fer·ence
dif·fer·ent
dif·fer·en·tia (*plural* ·tiae) logic term

differentiability 122

dif·fer·en·ti·abil·ity
dif·fer·en·ti·able
dif·fer·en·tial
dif·fer·en·ti·ate
dif·fer·en·tia·tion
dif·fer·en·tia·tor
dif·fi·cult
dif·fi·cul·ty (*plural* ·ties)
dif·fi·dence
dif·fi·dent
dif·fract
dif·frac·tion
dif·frac·tive
dif·frac·tom·eter
dif·fuse
dif·fuse·ness
dif·fus·er (*or* ·fu·sor)
dif·fus·ibil·ity (*or* ·ible·ness)
dif·fus·ible
dif·fu·sion
dif·fu·sive
dif·fu·siv·ity
dig (dig·ging, dug)
diga·mist
di·gam·ma obsolete Greek letter
diga·mous
diga·my (*plural* ·mies) second marriage
di·gas·tric jaw muscle
di·gen·esis zoology term
di·genet·ic
di·gest
di·gest·ant
di·gest·er
di·gest·ibil·ity (*or* ·ible·ness)
di·gest·ible
di·ges·tif *French* digestive drink
di·ges·tion
di·ges·tion·al
di·ges·tive (*or* ·tant)
dig·ger
dig·ging
dig·it
digi·tal
digi·tal·in chemical compound
digi·tal·is
digi·tal·ism
digi·tali·za·tion (*or* ·sa·tion)
digi·tal·ize (*or* ·ise)

digi·tal·ly
digi·tate (*or* ·tat·ed)
digi·ta·tion
digi·ti·form
digi·ti·grade walking on toes
dig·iti·za·tion (*or* ·sa·tion)
dig·it·ize (*or* ·ise)
digi·tox·in chemical compound
digi·tron electronics term
di·glot bilingual
di·glot·tic
dig·ni·fy (·fies, ·fy·ing, ·fied)
dig·ni·tary (*plural* ·taries)
dig·nity (*plural* ·nities)
di·graph two-letter sound
di·graph·ic
di·gress
di·gress·er
di·gres·sion
di·gres·sion·al
di·gres·sive
di·he·dral
di·he·dron
di·hy·brid
di·hy·brid·ism
Di·jon French city
dik-dik antelope
dike variant spelling of dyke
dik·tat decree
di·lapi·date
di·lapi·da·ted
di·lapi·da·tion
di·lapi·da·tor
di·lat·abil·ity (*or* ·able·ness)
di·lat·able
di·la·tan·cy physics term
di·la·tant
di·la·ta·tion
dila·ta·tion·al
di·late
di·la·tion
di·la·tive
dila·tom·eter
dila·to·met·ric
dila·to·met·ri·cal·ly
dila·tom·etry
di·la·tor (*or* ·lat·er, di·la·ta·tor)
dila·to·ri·ness
di·la·tory

dil·do (*or* ·doe; *plural* ·dos *or* ·does) artificial penis
di·lem·ma
dil·em·mat·ic (*or* dil·em·mic)
dil·et·tante (*plural* ·tan·tes *or* ·tan·ti)
dil·et·tan·tish (*or* ·teish)
dil·et·tan·tism (*or* ·teism)
dili·gence
dili·gent
dill
dil·ly *Slang* remarkable person
dilly-dally (-dallies, -dally·ing, -dallied)
dilu·ent
di·lute
di·lu·tee
di·lut·er
di·lu·tion
di·lu·vial (*or* ·vian)
di·lu·vium (*plural* ·via) geology term
dim (*adj* dim·mer, dim·mest; *verb* dim·ming, dimmed)
dime
di·men·hy·dri·nate drug
di·men·sion
di·men·sion·al
di·men·sion·al·ity
di·men·sion·less
di·mer chemistry term
di·mer·cap·rol drug
di·mer·ic
dim·er·ism
dim·er·ous divided into two
dim·eter verse line
di·methyl·sulph·ox·ide
di·met·ric crystallography term
di·midi·ate halve; divided in halves
di·midi·ation
di·min·ish
di·min·ish·able
di·min·ish·ment
di·minu·en·do (*plural* ·dos)
dimi·nu·tion
di·minu·tive
dim·is·sory permission to depart

dim·ity (*plural* ·ities) fabric
dim·ly
dimmed
dim·mer
dim·mest
dim·ming
dim·ness
di·morph
di·mor·phism
di·mor·phous (*or* ·phic) chemistry term
dim·ple
dim·ply
dim·wit
dim-witted
dim-witted·ness
din (din·ning, dinned)
di·nar currency
dine
din·er
di·ner·ic chemistry term
di·nette
ding
ding·bat *US* unnamed object
ding·bats *Austral* delirium tremens
ding-dong
dinge
din·ghy (*or* ·gy, ·gey; *plural* ·ghies, ·gies, *or* ·geys)
din·gi·ly
din·gi·ness
din·gle dell
din·go (*plural* ·goes)
din·gy (·gi·er, ·gi·est)
di·ni·tro·ben·zene
dink *Scot* ncat
Din·ka (*plural* ·kas *or* ·ka) Sudanese people
din·kum
dinky (dinki·er, dinki·est)
dinned
din·ner
din·ning
di·noc·er·as extinct mammal
di·no·flag·el·late unicellular organism
di·no·saur
di·no·saur·ian
di·no·there extinct mammal
dint

di·oc·esan
dio·cese
di·ode
di·oecious (*or esp. US* ·ecious, ·oicious) botany term
di·oestrus (*US* ·estrus) biology term
Diomedes mythological king
Dio·ny·sia ancient Greek festivals
Dio·nysi·ac
Dio·ny·sian
Dionysus Greek god
di·op·side mineral
di·op·tase mineral
di·op·tom·eter
di·op·tom·etry
di·op·tral
di·op·tre (*US* ·ter) unit
di·op·tric (*or* ·tri·cal)
di·op·tri·cal·ly
di·op·trics
dio·ra·ma display
dio·ram·ic
dio·rite rock
dio·rit·ic
di·ox·an (*or* ·ane) chemical compound
di·ox·ide
dip (dip·ping, dipped)
di·pep·tide
di·pet·al·ous having two petals
di·phase (*or* ·phas·ic) physics term
di·phenyl biphenyl
di·phenyl·amine
di·phos·gene
diph·thcria
diph·therial (*or* ·therit·ic, ·ther·ic)
diph·theroid
diph·thong
diph·thon·gal
diph·thongi·za·tion (*or* ·sa·tion)
diph·thong·ize (*or* ·ise)
di·phy·cer·cal zoology term
di·phy·let·ic descent from two ancestors
di·phyl·lous having two leaves
diphy·odont dentition

di·plegia paralysis
di·plegic
di·plex electronics term
di·plex·er
dip·lo·blas·tic zoology term
dip·lo·car·di·ac zoology term
dip·lo·coc·cal (*or* ·cic)
dip·lo·coc·cus (*plural* ·coc·ci) bacterium
dip·lo·do·cus (*plural* ·cuses) dinosaur
dip·loë bone
dip·loid biology term
dip·loi·dic
dip·loidy
di·plo·ma
di·plo·ma·cy (*plural* ·cies)
dip·lo·mat
dip·lo·mate
dip·lo·mat·ic (*or* ·mati·cal)
dip·lo·mati·cal·ly
dip·lo·mat·ics study of historical documents
di·plo·ma·tist
dip·lont biology term
di·plo·pia double vision
di·plop·ic
dip·lo·pod invertebrate
di·plo·sis biology term
dip·lo·ste·mo·nous botany term
dip·lo·tene genetics term
dip·noan lungfish
dipo·dy (*plural* ·dies) metrical unit
di·po·lar
di·pole physics term
dipped
dip·per
dip·ping
dip·py *Slang* crazy
di·pro·pel·lant
di·proto·dont marsupial
dip·so·ma·nia
dip·so·ma·ni·ac
dip·so·ma·nia·cal
dip·stick
dip·ter·al architectural term
dip·ter·an (*or* ·on) two-winged insect
dip·tero·car·pa·ceous botany term
dip·ter·ous two-winged

(diptheria)

(diptheria) *incorrect spelling of* diphtheria
(dipthong) *incorrect spelling of* diphthong
dip·tych
dire
di·rect
di·rec·tion
di·rec·tion·al
di·rec·tion·al·ity
di·rec·tion·al·ly
di·rec·tive
di·rect·ly
di·rect·ness
Di·rec·toire French Revolutionary government
di·rec·tor
di·rec·to·rate
di·rec·to·rial
di·rec·tor·ship
di·rec·tory (*plural* ·tories)
di·rec·tress
di·rect·rix (*plural* ·rixes *or* ·rices) geometry term
dire·ful
dirge
dir·ham Moroccan currency
diri·gibil·ity
di·rig·ible steerable
di·ri·ment invalidating
dirk
dirndl dress or skirt
dirt
dirti·ly
dirti·ness
dirty (*adj* dirti·er, dirti·est; *verb* dirties, dirty·ing, dirt·ied)
Dis Roman god
dis·abil·ity (*plural* ·ities)
dis·able
dis·able·ment
dis·abus·al
dis·abuse
di·sac·cha·ride (*or* ·rid)
dis·ac·cord
dis·ac·cred·it
dis·ac·cus·tom
dis·ad·vant·age
dis·ad·van·taged
dis·ad·van·ta·geous
dis·af·fect
dis·af·fect·ed·ly
dis·af·fec·tion
dis·af·fili·ate

dis·af·fili·ation
dis·af·firm
dis·af·fir·mance (*or* ·ma·tion)
dis·af·for·est legal term
dis·af·for·es·ta·tion (*or* dis·af·for·est·ment)
dis·agree (·agree·ing, ·agreed)
dis·agree·able
dis·agree·able·ness (*or* ·abil·ity)
dis·agree·ably
dis·agree·ment
dis·al·low
dis·al·low·able
dis·al·low·ance
dis·am·bigu·ate
dis·an·nul (·nul·ling, ·nulled)
dis·an·nul·ment
dis·ap·pear
dis·ap·pear·ance
dis·ap·point
dis·ap·point·ed
dis·ap·point·er
dis·ap·point·ing
dis·ap·point·ment
dis·ap·pro·ba·tion
dis·ap·prov·al
dis·ap·prove
dis·ap·prov·er
dis·arm
dis·arma·ment
dis·arm·er
dis·arm·ing
dis·ar·range
dis·ar·range·ment
dis·ar·ray
dis·ar·ticu·late
dis·ar·ticu·la·tion
dis·ar·ticu·la·tor
dis·as·sem·ble
dis·as·sem·bly
dis·as·so·ci·ate
dis·as·so·cia·tion
dis·as·ter
dis·as·trous
dis·avow
dis·avow·al
dis·avow·ed·ly
dis·avow·er
dis·band
dis·band·ment

124

dis·bar (·bar·ring, ·barred)
dis·bar·ment
dis·be·lief
dis·be·lieve
dis·be·liev·er
dis·be·liev·ing·ly
dis·branch
dis·bud (·bud·ding, ·bud·ded)
dis·bur·den
dis·bur·den·ment
dis·burs·able
dis·burse
dis·burse·ment (*or* ·burs·al)
dis·burs·er
disc (*US* disk) circular plate; record; *compare* disk
dis·calced barefooted
dis·card
dis·card·er
dis·cern
dis·cern·er
dis·cern·ible (*or* ·able)
dis·cern·ing
dis·cern·ment
dis·charge
dis·charge·able
dis·charg·er
dis·ci·ple
dis·ci·ple·ship
dis·ci·plin·able
dis·ci·pli·nal
dis·ci·pli·nant member of Catholic sect
dis·ci·pli·nar·ian
dis·ci·pli·nary
dis·ci·pline
dis·ci·plin·er
dis·cipu·lar of disciples
dis·claim
dis·claim·er
dis·cla·ma·tion
dis·cli·max ecology term
dis·close
dis·clos·er
dis·clo·sure
dis·co (*plural* ·cos)
dis·cobo·lus (*or* ·los; *plural* ·li) discus thrower
dis·cog·ra·pher
dis·cog·ra·phy (*plural* ·phies) record catalogue
dis·coid

dis·coi·dal
dis·col·ora·tion
dis·col·our (US ·or)
dis·col·our·ment (US ·or·)
dis·com·bobu·late confuse
dis·com·fit disconcert
dis·com·fit·er
dis·com·fi·ture
dis·com·fort
dis·com·mend
dis·com·mode
dis·com·mo·di·ous
dis·com·mod·ity (plural ·ities) economics term
dis·com·mon legal term
dis·com·pose
dis·com·pos·ed·ly
dis·com·pos·ing·ly
dis·com·po·sure
dis·con·cert
dis·con·cert·ed
dis·con·cert·ing·ly
dis·con·cer·tion (or ·cert·ment)
dis·con·form·ity (plural ·ities)
dis·con·nect
dis·con·nect·ed
dis·con·nect·er
dis·con·nec·tion (or ·nex·ion)
dis·con·nec·tive
dis·con·so·late
dis·con·so·la·tion (or ·late·ness)
dis·con·tent
dis·con·tent·ed
dis·con·tent·ed·ness
dis·con·tent·ment
dis·con·tinu·ance
dis·con·tinua·tion
dis·con·tinue (·tinu·ing, ·tinued)
dis·con·ti·nu·ity (plural ·ities)
dis·con·tinu·ous
dis·co·phile (or ·phil) record collector
dis·cord
dis·cord·ance (or ·an·cy)
dis·cord·ant
dis·co·theque
dis·count
dis·count·able

dis·coun·tenance
dis·count·er
dis·cour·age
dis·cour·age·ment
dis·cour·ag·er
dis·cour·ag·ing·ly
dis·course
dis·cours·er
dis·cour·teous
dis·cour·tesy (plural ·tesies)
dis·cov·er
dis·cov·er·able
dis·cov·er·er
dis·cov·ert legal term
dis·cov·er·ture
dis·cov·ery (plural ·eries)
dis·cred·it
dis·cred·it·able
dis·cred·it·ably
dis·creet tactful; compare discrete
dis·creet·ness
dis·crep·an·cy (plural ·cies)
dis·crep·ant
dis·crete distinct; separate; compare discreet
dis·crete·ness
dis·cre·tion
dis·cre·tion·ari·ly (or ·tion·al·ly)
dis·cre·tion·ary (or ·al)
dis·cri·mi·nant
dis·crimi·nate
dis·crimi·nat·ing
dis·crimi·na·tion
dis·crimi·na·tion·al
dis·crimi·na·tor
dis·crimi·na·to·ri·ly (or dis·crimi·na·tive·ly)
dis·crimi·na·tory (or ·tive)
dis·cur·sive
dis·cus (plural ·cuses or ·ci) disc
dis·cuss debate
dis·cus·sant (or ·cuss·er)
dis·cuss·ible (or ·able)
dis·cus·sion
dis·cus·sion·al
dis·dain
dis·dain·ful
dis·dain·ful·ly
dis·ease
dis·eased

dis·em·bark
dis·em·bar·ka·tion (or ·bark·ment)
dis·em·bar·rass
dis·em·bar·rass·ment
dis·em·bod·ied
dis·em·bodi·ment
dis·em·body (·bodies, ·body·ing, ·bod·ied)
dis·em·bogue (·bogu·ing, ·bogued) discharge
dis·em·bogue·ment
dis·em·bow·el (·el·ling, ·elled; US ·el·ing, ·eled)
dis·em·bow·el·ment
dis·em·broil
dis·en·able
dis·en·able·ment
dis·en·chant
dis·en·chant·er
dis·en·chant·ment
dis·en·cum·ber
dis·en·cum·ber·ment
dis·en·dow
dis·en·dow·er
dis·en·dow·ment
dis·en·fran·chise
dis·en·fran·chise·ment
dis·en·gage
dis·en·gage·ment
dis·en·tail
dis·en·tail·ment
dis·en·tan·gle
dis·en·tan·gle·ment
dis·en·thral (or ·thrall; ·thral·ling, ·thralled)
dis·en·thral·ment (or ·thrall·)
dis·en·ti·tle
dis·en·tomb
dis·en·twine
di·sepa·lous botany term
dis·equi·lib·rium
dis·es·tab·lish
dis·es·tab·lish·ment
dis·es·teem
di·seur (fem ·seuse) French monologue performer
dis·fa·vour (US ·vor)
dis·fea·ture
dis·fea·ture·ment
dis·fig·ure

disfigurement

dis·fig·ure·ment (*or* ·ura·tion)
dis·fig·ur·er
dis·fran·chise
dis·fran·chise·ment
dis·gorge
dis·gorge·ment
dis·gorg·er
dis·grace
dis·grace·ful
dis·grace·ful·ly
dis·grac·er
dis·grun·tle
dis·grun·tled
dis·grun·tle·ment
dis·guis·able
dis·guise
dis·guis·er
dis·gust
dis·gust·ed·ly
dis·gust·ing
dish
dis·ha·bille (*or* des·) half-dressed
dis·har·mo·ni·ous
dis·har·mo·ny (*plural* ·nies)
dish·cloth
dis·heart·en
dis·heart·en·ment
dished
di·shev·el (·el·ling, ·elled; *US* ·el·ing, ·eled)
di·shev·el·ment
dis·hon·est
dis·hon·es·ty (*plural* ·ties)
dis·hon·our (*US* ·or)
dis·hon·our·able (*US* ·or·)
dis·hon·our·ably (*US* ·or·)
dis·hon·our·er (*US* ·or·)
dish·washer
dish·water
dishy (dishi·er, dishi·est)
dis·il·lu·sion
dis·il·lu·sion·ment
dis·il·lu·sive
dis·in·cen·tive
dis·in·cli·na·tion
dis·in·cline
dis·in·fect
dis·in·fect·ant
dis·in·fec·tion
dis·in·fec·tor
dis·in·fest
dis·in·fes·ta·tion
dis·in·fla·tion
dis·in·genu·ous
dis·in·genu·ous·ness
dis·in·her·it
dis·in·heri·tance
dis·in·te·grable
dis·in·te·grate
dis·in·te·gra·tion
dis·in·te·gra·tive
dis·in·te·gra·tor
dis·in·ter (·ter·ring, ·terred)
dis·in·ter·est
dis·in·ter·est·ed impartial; *compare* **uninterested**
dis·in·ter·ment
dis·ject break apart
dis·join separate
dis·join·able
dis·joint dislocate
dis·joint·ed
dis·junct
dis·junc·tion (*or* ·ture)
dis·junc·tive
disk computer device; *US spelling of* disc
dis·lik·able (*or* ·like·)
dis·like
dis·limn efface
dis·lo·cate
dis·lo·ca·tion
dis·lodge
dis·lodg·ment (*or* ·lodge·)
dis·loy·al
dis·loy·al·ty (*plural* ·ties)
dis·mal
dis·mal·ly
dis·mal·ness
dis·man·tle
dis·man·tle·ment
dis·man·tler
dis·mast
dis·mast·ment
dis·may
dis·mem·ber
dis·mem·ber·er
dis·mem·ber·ment
dis·miss
dis·mis·sal
dis·miss·ible
dis·miss·ive
dis·mount
dis·mount·able
Dis·ney·land
dis·obedi·ence
dis·obedi·ent
dis·obey
dis·obey·er
dis·oblige
dis·oblig·ing
dis·op·era·tion ecology term
dis·or·der
dis·or·der·li·ness
dis·or·der·ly
dis·or·gani·za·tion (*or* ·sa·tion)
dis·or·gan·ize (*or* ·ise)
dis·or·gan·iz·er (*or* ·is·er)
dis·ori·en·tate (*or* dis·ori·ent)
dis·ori·en·ta·tion
dis·own
dis·own·er
dis·own·ment
dis·par·age
dis·par·age·ment
dis·par·ag·er
dis·par·ate
dis·par·ity (*plural* ·ities)
dis·pas·sion detachment
dis·pas·sion·ate
dis·pas·sion·ate·ness
dis·patch (*or* des·)
dis·patcher (*or* des·)
dis·pel (·pel·ling, ·pelled)
dis·pel·ler
dis·pen·sabil·ity (*or* ·sable·ness)
dis·pen·sable
dis·pen·sa·ry (*plural* ·ries)
dis·pen·sa·tion
dis·pen·sa·tion·al
dis·pen·sa·tory (*plural* ·tories) drug catalogue
dis·pense
dis·pens·er
di·sper·mous botany term
dis·per·sal
dis·per·sant
dis·perse
dis·pers·er
dis·per·sion
dis·per·sive
dis·per·soid chemistry term
dis·pir·it
dis·pir·it·ed
dis·pir·it·ing
dis·place
dis·place·able

dis·place·ment
dis·plac·er
dis·play
dis·play·er
dis·please
dis·pleas·ure
dis·port
dis·pos·abil·ity (or ·able·ness)
dis·pos·able
dis·pos·al
dis·pose
dis·posed
dis·pos·er
dis·po·si·tion
dis·po·si·tion·al
dis·pos·sess
dis·pos·ses·sion
dis·pos·ses·sor
dis·pos·ses·so·ry
dis·praise
dis·prais·er
dis·proof
dis·pro·por·tion
dis·pro·por·tion·able
dis·pro·por·tion·ate
dis·pro·por·tiona·tion
dis·prov·able
dis·prov·al
dis·prove
dis·put·abil·ity (or ·able·ness)
dis·put·able
dis·put·ably
dis·pu·tant
dis·pu·ta·tion
dis·pu·ta·tious (or ·tive)
dis·pute
dis·put·er
dis·quali·fi·able
dis·quali·fi·ca·tion
dis·quali·fi·er
dis·quali·fy (·fies, ·fy·ing, ·fied)
dis·qui·et
dis·qui·et·ed·ly (or dis·qui·et·ly)
dis·qui·et·ed·ness (or dis·qui·et·ness)
dis·qui·et·ing
dis·qui·etude
dis·qui·si·tion formal discourse
dis·rate reduce to lower rank

dis·re·gard
dis·re·gard·er
dis·re·gard·ful
dis·rel·ish
dis·re·pair
dis·repu·tabil·ity (or ·table·ness)
dis·repu·table
dis·repu·tably
dis·re·pute
dis·re·spect
dis·re·spect·abil·ity
dis·re·spect·able
dis·re·spect·ful
dis·re·spect·ful·ly
dis·robe
dis·robe·ment
dis·rob·er
dis·rupt
dis·rupt·er (or ·rup·tor)
dis·rup·tion
dis·rup·tive
dis·sat·is·fac·tion
dis·sat·is·fac·tory
dis·sat·is·fy (·fies, ·fy·ing, ·fied)
dis·sect
dis·sec·tible
dis·sec·tion
dis·sec·tor
dis·seise (or ·seize) legal term
dis·sei·sin (or ·zin)
dis·sei·sor (or ·zor)
dis·sem·blance
dis·sem·ble
dis·sem·bler
dis·semi·nate
dis·semi·na·tion
dis·semi·na·tive
dis·semi·na·tor
dis·semi·nule botany term
dis·sen·sion
dis·sent
dis·sent·er
dis·sen·tience (or ·tien·cy)
dis·sen·tient dissenting
dis·sen·tious argumentative
dis·sepi·ment dividing membrane
dis·sepi·men·tal
dis·ser·tate
dis·ser·ta·tion
dis·ser·ta·tion·al

dis·ser·ta·tion·ist
dis·ser·vice
dis·ser·vice·able
dis·sev·er break off
dis·sev·er·ance (or ·er·ment, ·era·tion)
dis·si·dence
dis·si·dent
dis·simi·lar
dis·simi·lar·ity (plural ·ities)
dis·simi·late phonetics term; compare dissimulate
dis·simi·la·tion
dis·simi·la·tive
dis·simi·la·tory
dis·si·mili·tude
dis·simu·late pretend; compare dissimilate
dis·simu·la·tion
dis·simu·la·tive
dis·simu·la·tor
dis·si·pate
dis·si·pat·ed
dis·si·pat·er (or ·pa·tor)
dis·si·pa·tion
dis·si·pa·tive
dis·so·ci·abil·ity (or ·able·ness)
dis·so·ci·able
dis·so·ci·ate
dis·so·cia·tion
dis·so·cia·tive
dis·sol·ubil·ity (or ·uble·ness)
dis·sol·uble
dis·so·lute
dis·so·lute·ness
dis·so·lu·tion
dis·so·lu·tive
dis·solv·abil·ity (or ·able·ness)
dis·solv·able
dis·solve
dis·sol·vent
dis·solv·er
dis·so·nance (or ·nan·cy)
dis·so·nant
dis·suad·able
dis·suade
dis·suad·er
dis·sua·sion
dis·sua·sive
dis·sua·sive·ness
dis·syl·lab·ic (or di·syl·)

dissyllable

dis·syl·la·ble (*or* di·syl·)
dis·sym·met·ric (*or* ·ri·cal)
dis·sym·me·try (*plural*
 ·tries)
dis·taff
dis·tal anatomy term
dis·tal·ly
dis·tance
dis·tant
dis·taste
dis·taste·ful
dis·taste·ful·ly
dis·tem·per
dis·tend
dis·tend·er
dis·ten·si·bil·ity
dis·ten·sible
dis·ten·sion (*or* ·tion)
dis·tich poem
dis·ti·chal
dis·ti·chous in two rows
dis·til (*US* dis·till;
 ·til·ling, ·tilled)
dis·till·able
dis·til·late
dis·til·la·tion (*or*
 dis·till·ment)
dis·til·la·tory
dis·till·er
dis·till·ery (*plural* ·eries)
dis·tinct
dis·tinc·tion
dis·tinc·tive
dis·tinc·tive·ness
dis·tinct·ness
dis·tin·gué (*fem* ·guée)
 French distinguished
dis·tin·guish
dis·tin·guish·able
dis·tin·guish·ably
dis·tin·guished
dis·tin·guish·er
dis·tort
dis·tort·ed
dis·tort·er
dis·tor·tion
dis·tor·tion·al
dis·tor·tive
dis·tract
dis·tract·ed
dis·tract·er
dis·tract·ibil·ity
dis·tract·ible
dis·trac·ting
dis·trac·tion

dis·trac·tive
dis·train
dis·train·able
dis·trainee legal term
dis·train·ment
dis·trai·nor (*or* ·train·er)
dis·traint legal term
dis·trait absent-minded
dis·traught
dis·tress
dis·tressed
dis·tress·ful
dis·tress·ful·ly
dis·tress·ing
dis·trib·ut·able
dis·tribu·tary (*plural*
 ·taries) stream
dis·trib·ute
dis·tribu·tee legal term
dis·tri·bu·tion
dis·tri·bu·tion·al
dis·tribu·tive
dis·tribu·tor (*or* ·tribut·er)
dis·trict
dis·trin·gas legal term
dis·trust
dis·trust·er
dis·trust·ful
dis·trust·ful·ly
dis·turb
dis·turb·ance
dis·turbed
dis·turb·er
di·sul·fi·ram drug
di·sul·phate (*US* ·fate)
di·sul·phide (*US* ·fide)
di·sul·phu·ric (*US* ·fu·)
dis·un·ion
dis·unite
dis·unity (*plural* ·unities)
dis·use
dis·used
dis·util·ity
dit Morse code sound
dita shrub
ditch
ditch·er
di·theism
di·theist
di·theis·tic
dith·er
dith·er·er
di·thio·nite chemical
 compound

128

dithy·ramb ancient Greek
 hymn
dithy·ram·bic
dithy·ram·bi·cal·ly
dit·tan·der plant
dit·ta·ny (*plural* ·nies)
 plant
dit·to (*noun, plural* ·tos;
 verb ·tos, ·to·ing, ·toed)
dit·to·graph·ic
dit·tog·ra·phy (*plural*
 ·phies) repetition
dit·ty (*plural* ·ties)
di·uresis increased
 urination; *compare* dieresis
di·uret·ic increasing
 urination; *compare* dieretic
di·ureti·cal·ly
di·ur·nal of the day
di·ur·nal·ly
div *Slang* stupid person
diva (*plural* divas *or* dive)
 prima donna; *compare*
 deva
di·va·lency
di·va·lent
di·van
di·vari·cate branching
di·vari·ca·tion
di·vari·ca·tor zoology term
dive (div·ing, dived (*US*
 dove))
dive-bomb
div·er
di·verge
di·ver·gence (*or* ·gen·cy;
 plural ·gences *or* ·cies)
di·ver·gent
di·vers *Archaic* several
di·verse varied
di·ver·si·fi·abil·ity
di·ver·si·fi·able
di·ver·si·fi·ca·tion
di·ver·si·fi·er
di·ver·si·form
di·ver·si·fy (·fies, ·fy·ing,
 ·fied)
di·ver·sion
di·ver·sion·al (*or* ·ary)
di·ver·sity
di·vert
di·vert·ed·ly
di·vert·er
di·vert·ible
di·ver·ticu·lar

di·ver·ticu·li·tis
di·ver·ticu·lo·sis
di·ver·ticu·lum (*plural* ·la) anatomical pouch
di·ver·ti·men·to (*plural* ·ti) musical work
di·vert·ing·ly
di·ver·tisse·ment brief entertainment
di·ver·tive
Dives biblical character
di·vest
di·vest·ible
di·vesti·ture (*or* ·ves·ture, ·vest·ment)
di·vid·able
di·vide
divi·dend
di·vid·er
di·vid·ers measuring compass
divi-divi (*plural* -divis *or* -divi) tree
di·vin·able
divi·na·tion
di·vina·tory
di·vine
di·vin·er
div·ing
di·vin·ing
di·vin·ity (*plural* ·ities)
divi·ni·za·tion (*or* ·sa·tion)
divi·nize (*or* ·nise) deify
di·vis·ibil·ity
di·vi·sible
di·vi·sion
di·vi·sion·al (*or* ·ary)
di·vi·sion·ism
di·vi·sion·ist
di·vi·sive
di·vi·sor maths term; *compare* deviser
di·vorce
di·vor·cé (*fem* ·cée) divorced person
di·vorce·able
di·vorce·ment
di·vorc·er
di·vor·cive
div·ot turf
di·vulge
di·vul·gence (*or* ·vulge·ment)
di·vulg·er
di·vul·sion tearing apart

di·vul·sive
div·vy (*plural* ·vies) *Slang* dividend
Dixie southern states of USA
dixie metal pot
Dixie·land jazz
Di·yar·ba·kir (*or* ·bekir) Turkish city
diz·zi·ly
diz·zi·ness
diz·zy (*adj* ·zi·er, ·zi·est; *verb* ·zies, ·zy·ing, ·zied)
Dja·ja variant spelling of Jaya
Dja·ja·pu·ra variant spelling of Jajapura
Dja·kar·ta (*or* Ja·) variant spelling of Jakarta
Djam·bi (*or* Jam·) variant spelling of Jambi
Djer·ba Tunisian island
Dji·bou·ti (*or* Ji·) African republic
djin·ni (*or* ·ny) variant spellings of jinni
Djok·ja·kar·ta variant spelling of Jogjakarta
Dne·pro·dzer·zhinsk Soviet city
Dne·pro·petrovsk Soviet city
Dnie·per (*or* Dnepr) Soviet river
Dnie·ster (*or* Dnestr) Soviet river
do (*verb* does, do·ing, did, done; *noun*, *plural* dos *or* do's)
doab land between rivers
do·able
dob·bin
dob·by (*plural* ·bies) loom attachment
Do·ber·man pin·scher dog
do·bla coin
Do·bro (*Trademark*; *plural* ·bros) guitar
Do·bru·ja E European region
dobson·fly (*plural* ·flies)
doc *Slang* doctor
do·cent US lecturer
do·cent·ship
Do·cetism heresy

doc·ile
do·cil·ity
dock
dock·age dock charge
dock·er
dock·et
dock·land
dock·yard
doc·tor
doc·tor·al (*or* ·to·rial)
doc·tor·ate
doc·tri·naire
doc·tri·nair·ism (*or* ·nar·ism)
doc·tri·nal
doc·tri·nal·ity
doc·tri·nar·ian
doc·trine
doc·trin·ism
docu·ment
docu·men·ta·ri·ly
docu·men·tary (*plural* ·taries)
docu·men·ta·tion
dod·der totter, tremble (*verb*); plant (*noun*)
dod·der·er
dod·der·ing
dod·dery
dod·dle
do·deca·gon 12-sided figure
do·de·cago·nal
do·deca·he·dral
do·deca·he·dron 12-faced solid
Do·deca·nese Aegean islands
do·deca·phon·ic musical term
do·deca·phon·ism
do·deca·phon·ist
do·deca·phony
dodge
Dodg·em (*Trademark*)
dodg·er
dodgy (dodgi·er, dodgi·est)
dodo (*plural* dodos *or* dodoes)
dodo·ism
Do·do·ma Tanzanian town
Do·do·na Greek town
doe (*plural* does *or* doe)
doek African headscarf
doer

does

does (*present tense of* do; *plural of* doe)
doe·skin
doff
doff·er
dog (dog·ging, dogged)
dog·bane plant
dog·berry (*plural* ·berries) shrub
dog·berry·ism officialdom
dog·cart
doge Venetian magistrate
dog-ear
dog-eared
dog·fight
dog·fish (*plural* ·fish *or* ·fishes)
dog·ged (*adj*)
dog·ged·ness
Dog·ger North Sea sandbank
dog·ger fishing vessel
dog·ger·el (*or* dog·rel)
dog·gery (*plural* ·geries) surly behaviour
dog·gish
dog·go *Slang* in hiding
dog·gone US slang term
dog·gy (*adj*; ·gi·er, ·gi·est)
dog·gy (*or* ·gie; *noun*; *plural* ·gies)
dog·house
do·gie *US* motherless calf
dog·leg (·leg·ging, ·legged) bend sharply
dog·leg·ged (*adj*)
dog·ma (*plural* ·mas *or* ·ma·ta)
dog·man (*plural* ·men) *Austral* crane-driver's assistant
dog·mat·ic (*or* ·mati·cal)
dog·mati·cal·ly
dog·mat·ics
dog·ma·tism
dog·ma·tist
dog·ma·ti·za·tion (*or* ·sa·tion)
dog·ma·tize (*or* ·tise)
dog·ma·tiz·er (*or* ·tis·er)
do-gooder
dogs·body (*plural* ·bodies)
dog's-tail grass
dog-tired

dog·tooth (*plural* ·teeth)
dog·trot
dog·vane wind vane
dog·watch nautical term
dog·wood
doh musical note
Doha capital of Qatar
doi·ly (*or* doy·ley, doy·ly; *plural* ·lies *or* ·leys)
do·ing
doit coin
do-it-yourself
dol unit of pain
do·lab·ri·form (*or* ·rate) hatchet-shaped
Dol·by (*Trademark*) recording system
dol·ce musical term
dol·ce vita *Italian* luxurious life
dol·drums
dole
dole·ful
dole·ful·ly
dole·ful·ness
dol·er·ite rock
dol·er·it·ic
doli·cho·cephal·ic (*or* cepha·lous) long-headed
doli·cho·cepha·lism (*or* ·ly)
do·li·na (*or* ·ne) ground depression
doll
dol·lar
dollar·bird
dollar·fish (*plural* ·fish *or* ·fishes)
doll·ish
dol·lop
dol·ly (*noun, plural* ·lies; *verb* ·ly·ing, ·lied)
dol·man (*plural* ·mans) robe
dol·mas (*or* ·ma) stuffed vine leaves
dol·men tomb
do·lo·mite mineral
Do·lo·mites mountain range
dolo·mit·ic
dol·or·im·etry pain measurement
do·lo·ro·so musical term
dol·or·ous
dol·our (*US* ·or) grief

130

dol·phin
dol·phin·ar·ium
dolt
dolt·ish
dom monk's title
do·main
dome
dome·like
domes·day *variant spelling of* doomsday
Domes·day Book (*or* Dooms·)
do·mes·tic
do·mes·ti·cable
do·mes·ti·cal·ly
do·mes·ti·cate
do·mes·ti·ca·tion
do·mes·ti·ca·tive
do·mes·ti·ca·tor
do·mes·ti·city (*plural* ·cities)
domi·cal (*or* do·mic) of a dome
domi·cile
domi·cili·ary
domi·cili·ate
domi·nance
domi·nant
domi·nate
domi·na·tion
domi·na·tive
domi·na·tor
do·mi·nee Afrikaner clergyman
domi·neer
Domi·ni·ca West Indian country
do·mini·cal relating to the Lord
Do·mini·can Republic; friar
domi·nie *Scot* schoolmaster
do·min·ion
do·min·ium (*or* ·ion) legal term
domi·no (*plural* ·noes)
Don Spanish title; Soviet river
don (don·ning, donned)
Doña Spanish woman's title
Donar Germanic god
do·nate
do·na·tion
dona·tive gift
do·na·tor

Don·bass (*or* **·bas**) Soviet industrial region
Don·cas·ter
done
do·nee receiver of gift
Don·egal Irish county
Do·nets Soviet river
Do·netsk Soviet city
dong
don·jon castle keep
Don Juan legendary seducer
don·key
Don·na Italian woman's title
donned
don·nert *Scot* stunned
don·ning
don·nish
donny·brook rowdy brawl
do·nor
do·nor·ship
don't do not
do·nut *variant spelling (esp. US) of* **doughnut**
doo·dah
doo·dle
doodle·bug
doo·dler
doom
dooms·day (*or* **domes·**)
door
door·bell
do-or-die
door·frame
door·jamb
door·keeper
door·man (*plural* **·men**)
door·mat
door·nail
door·post
door·sill
door·step
door·stop
door·way
door·yard *US* outside yard
do·pant chemistry term
dope
dopey (*or* **dopy**; **dopi·er**, **dopi·est**)
dopi·ness
Dop·pel·gäng·er ghost
Dop·per Afrikaner churchgoer
dor beetle

Do·ra·do constellation
Dor·ches·ter
Dor·dogne French region and river
Dor·drecht Dutch port
Do·rian ancient Greek
Dor·ic architectural term
Do·ris region of ancient Greece
Dor·king
dorm *Slang* dormitory
dor·man·cy
dor·mant
dor·mer
dor·mie (*or* **·my**) golf term
dor·mi·tory (*plural* **·tories**)
Dor·mo·bile (*Trademark*)
dor·mouse (*plural* **·mice**)
dor·nick (*or* **·neck**) cloth
do·roni·cum plant
dorp South African village
dor·sad towards the back
dor·sal of the back
dor·sal·ly
Dor·set
dor·si·grade walking on backs of toes
dor·si·ven·tral having upper and lower surfaces
dor·si·ven·tral·ity
dor·so·ven·tral from back to belly
dor·so·ven·tral·ly
dor·sum (*plural* **·sa**) the back
Dort·mund West German city
dorty *Scot* sullen
dory (*plural* **dories**) fish; boat
dos·age
dose
dos·er
do-si-do dance figure
do·sim·eter (*or* **dose·meter**)
do·si·met·ric
do·si·metri·cian (*or* **do·sim·etrist**)
do·sim·etry
doss
dos·sal (*or* **·sel**) church hanging
dos·ser *Slang* tramp; dosshouse

doss·house
dos·si·er
dot (**dot·ting**, **dot·ted**)
dot·age
do·tard
do·ta·tion endowment
dote
dot·er
dotted
dot·ted
dot·ter
dot·ter·el (*or* **·trel**)
dot·ti·ly
dot·ti·ness
dot·ting
dot·tle (*or* **·tel**) tobacco in pipe
dot·ty (**·ti·er**, **·ti·est**)
Douai French city
Doua·la (*or* **Dua·la**) Cameroon port
Dou·ay bible
dou·ble
double-acting
double-barrelled (*US* **-barreled**)
double-bass (*adj*)
double-blind
double-breasted
double-check
double-cross
double-dealing
double-decker
double-dotted musical term
double-edged
dou·ble en·ten·dre
double-faced
double-glazing
double-header
double-hung
double-jointed
double-park
double-quick
dou·bler
double-reed
dou·bles tennis
double-space
double-stop (**-stopping**, **-stopped**)
dou·blet
double-think
dou·ble·ton bridge term
double-tongue (**-tonguing**, **-tongued**) musical term

doubletree 132

double·tree horizontal bar on vehicle
dou·bloon (*or* **do·blon**) coin
dou·blure lining inside book
dou·bly
Doubs French river
doubt
doubt·able
doubt·er
doubt·ful
doubt·ful·ly
doubt·ful·ness
doubt·less
douc monkey
douce *Scot* sedate
dou·ceur bribe
douche
dough
dough·boy *Slang* dumpling
dough·nut (*or esp. US* **do·nut**)
doughti·ly
dough·ty (·**ti·er**, ·**ti·est**) hardy
doughy (**doughi·er**, **doughi·est**)
Doug·las Manx town
Dou·kho·bors Russian sect
doum (*or* **doom**) palm tree
dour sullen; *compare* **dower**
dou·rine horse disease
dour·ness
Dou·ro Spanish–Portuguese river
dou·rou·cou·li monkey
douse (*or* **dowse**) drench; *compare* **dowse**
dous·er (*or* **dows·**)
dove bird; *US past tense of* **dive**
dove·cote (*or* ·**cot**)
dove·kie (*or* ·**key**) bird
Do·ver
dove·tail
dov·ish
dow·able legal term
dowa·ger
dow·di·ly
dow·di·ness
dow·dy (*noun, plural* ·**dies**; *adj* ·**di·er**, ·**di·est**)
dow·el
dow·er widow's inheritance; *compare* **dour**

(**dowery**) *incorrect spelling of* **dowry**
dow·itch·er bird
Dow-Jones av·er·age *US* stock exchange index
down
down·beat
down-bow
down·cast
down·com·er (*or* ·**come**) plumbing term
down·fall
down·fallen
down·grade
down·haul nautical term
down·hearted
down·hearted·ness
down·hill
downi·ness
Down·ing Street
down-market
Down·pat·rick Irish town
down·pipe
down·pour
down·range
down·right
Downs Sussex hills
downs chalk uplands
down·side
down·spout *US* drainpipe
Down's syn·drome
down·stage
down·stairs
down·state *US* S part of state
down·stream
down·swing
down·throw
down-to-earth
down·town
down·trod·den (*or* ·**trod**)
down·turn
down·ward (*adj*)
down·wards (*adv*)
down·wash
down·wind
downy (**downi·er**, **downi·est**)
dow·ry (*plural* ·**ries**)
dowse to divine water; *variant spelling of* **douse**
dows·er
dows·ing
dox·as·tic logic term
doxo·logi·cal

dox·ol·ogy (*plural* ·**ogies**)
doxy (*plural* **doxies**)
doy·en (*fem* ·**enne**)
doze
doz·en
doz·enth
doz·er
dozy (**dozi·er**, **dozi·est**)
drab (**drab·ber**, **drab·best**)
drab·bet fabric
drab·ble make wet
drab·ly
drab·ness
dra·cae·na plant
drachm fluid dram
drach·ma (*plural* ·**mas** *or* ·**mae**) Greek currency
Dra·co constellation
dra·cone container towed by ship
Dra·co·nian (*or* ·**con·ic**) harsh
Dra·co·ni·an·ism
dra·con·ic dragon-like
dra·coni·cal·ly
draff husks
draffy
draft sketch; military selection; money order; *US spelling of* **draught**
draftee
draft·er
drafts·man (*plural* ·**men**) document drafter; *compare* **draughtsman**
drag (**drag·ging**, **dragged**)
dra·gée sweet
drag·gle trail
drag·hound
drag·line
drag·net
dra·go·man (*plural* ·**mans** *or* ·**men**) interpreter
drag·on
drag·on·ess
drag·on·et fish
dragon·fly (*plural* ·**flies**)
dragon·head (*or* **dragon's-head**) plant
drag·on·ish
drag·on·nade persecution by dragoons
dragon·root
dra·goon
dra·goon·age

drag·rope
drail weighted hook
drain
drain·able
drain·age
drain·er
drain·pipe
drake
Dra·kens·berg African mountain
dram 1/16 ounce; tot; *compare* **drachm**
dra·ma
Dra·ma·mine (*Trademark*)
dra·mat·ic
dra·mati·cal·ly
dra·mat·ics
dra·ma·tis per·so·nae characters in a play
drama·tist
drama·tiz·able (*or* ·tis·able)
drama·ti·za·tion (*or* ·sa·tion)
drama·tize (*or* ·tise)
drama·tiz·er (*or* ·tis·er)
drama·turge (*or* ·tur·gist) dramatist
drama·tur·gic (*or* ·gi·cal)
drama·tur·gy
Drambuie (*Trademark*)
drank
drap·able (*or* **drape·able**)
drape
drap·er
dra·per·ied
dra·pery (*plural* ·peries)
drapes *US* curtains
dras·tic
dras·ti·cal·ly
drat
drat·ted
draught (*US* **draft**) air current; drink; load pulling; *compare* **draft**
draught·board (*or* draughts·)
draught·er (*US* **draft·**)
draughti·ness (*US* **drafti·**)
draughts game
draughts·man (*US* **drafts·**; *plural* ·men) plan drafter; *compare* **draftsman**

draughts·man·ship (*US* **drafts·**)
draughty (*US* **drafty**; **draughti·er, draughti·est**; *US* **drafti·er, drafti·est**)
Dra·va European river
Dra·vid·ian language group
draw (**draw·ing, drew, drawn**)
draw·able
draw·back
draw·bar
draw·bridge
drawee
draw·er
drawer·ful
drawers undergarment
draw·ing
draw·knife (*or* ·shave; *plural* ·knives *or* ·shaves) woodcutting tool
drawl
drawl·er
drawly
drawn
draw·plate extrusion plate
draw·string
draw·tube
dray cart; *compare* **drey**
dray·horse
dread
dread·ful
dread·fully
dread·ful·ness
dread·nought (*or* ·naught) battleship
dream (**dream·ing, dreamt** *or* **dreamed**)
dream·er
dreami·ly
dreami·ness
dream·ing·ly
dream·less
dream·like
dreamy (**dreami·er, dreami·est**)
dreari·ly
dreari·ness
dreary (**dreari·er, dreari·est**)
dredge
dredg·er
dree *Scot* endure
dreg

dreg·gy (·gi·er, ·gi·est)
drench
drench·er
Dren·the Dutch region
Dres·den East German city
dress
dres·sage
dressed
dress·er
dressi·ly
dressi·ness
dress·ing
dress·maker
dress·making
dressy (**dressi·er, dressi·est**)
drew
drey squirrel's nest; *compare* **dray**
drib·ble
drib·bler
drib·let (*or* ·blet) small amount
dried
dri·er (*adj*)
dri·est
drift
drift·age
drift·er
drift·wood
drifty
drill
drill·able
drill·er
drill·ing
drill·master
drill·stock tool part
dri·ly
drink (**drink·ing, drank, drunk**)
drink·able
drink·er
drip (**drip·ping, dripped**)
drip-dry (-dries, -dry·ing, -dried)
drip·ping
drip·py (·pi·er, ·pi·est)
drip·stone
driv·able (*or* **drive·**)
drive (**driv·ing, drove, driv·en**)
drive-in
driv·el (·el·ling, ·elled; *US* ·el·ing, ·eled)
driv·el·ler (*US* ·el·er)

driven

driv·en
driv·er
driv·er·less
drive·way
driv·ing
driz·zle
driz·zly
drogue
droit right
droll
droll·ery (*plural* ·eries)
droll·ness
Drôme French department
drom·edary (*plural* ·edaries) camel
drom·ond sailing vessel
drone
dron·go (*plural* ·gos) bird
dron·ish
drool
droop sag; *compare* drupe
droopi·ly
droopi·ness
droopy (droopi·er, droopi·est)
drop (drop·ping, dropped)
drop·let
drop·light
drop·out
drop·per
drop·pings
drop·si·cal
drop·sied
drop·sonde meteorological device
drop·sy fluid in body
drop·wort plant
drosh·ky (*or* dros·ky; *plural* ·kies) carriage
dro·sophi·la (*plural* ·las *or* ·lae) fruit fly
dross
drossi·ness
drossy (drossi·er, drossi·est)
drought (*or* drouth)
droughty
drove
drov·er
drown
drown·er
drowse
drowsi·ly
drowsi·ness

drowsy (drowsi·er, drowsi·est)
drub (drub·bing, drubbed) beat
drub·ber
drudge
drudg·er
drudg·ery (*plural* ·eries)
druf·fen *Dialect* drunk
drug (drug·ging, drugged)
drug·get fabric
drug·gist
drug·store
dru·id (*fem* ·id·ess)
dru·id·ic (*or* ·idi·cal)
dru·id·ism
drum (drum·ming, drummed)
drum·beat
drum·fire
drum·fish (*plural* ·fish *or* ·fishes)
drum·head
drum·lin landform
drum·mer
drum·stick
drunk
drunk·ard
drunk·en
drunk·en·ness
dru·pa·ceous
drupe fruit; *compare* droop
drupe·let (*or* dru·pel) small fruit
Dru·ry Lane
Druse (*or* Druze) religious sect
druse crystals lining cavity
dry (*adj* dri·er, dri·est; *verb* dries, dry·ing, dried)
dry·able
dry·ad (*plural* ·ads *or* ·ades) wood nymph
dry·ad·ic
dry-clean
dry-cleaner
dry-cleaning
dry·er (*noun*)
dry·ness
dryo·pith·ecine extinct ape
dry-salt preserve by salting
dry-stone wall
dual two; *compare* duel

134

Du·ala (*plural* ·ala *or* ·alas) African people
dual·ism
dual·ist
dual·is·tic
dual·is·ti·cal·ly
dual·ity (*plural* ·ities)
dual-purpose
dub (dub·bing, dubbed)
Du·bai sheikdom
dub·bin (*or* dub·bing) leather grease
du·bi·ety (*or* du·bi·os·ity; *plural* ·ties)
du·bi·ous
du·bi·ous·ness
du·bi·table
du·bi·ta·tion doubt
Dub·lin
Du·bon·net (*Trademark*)
Du·brov·nik Yugoslav port
du·cal
duc·at coin
duce *Italian* leader
duch·ess
duchy (*plural* duchies)
duck
duck·board
duck·er
duck·ling
ducks trousers
duck·weed
ducky (*or* duckie; *plural* duckies)
duct
duc·tile
duc·til·ity (*or* ·tile·ness)
dud
dude
du·deen clay pipe
dudg·eon anger
Dud·ley English town
due
duel (duel·ling, duelled; *US* duel·ing, dueled) fight; *compare* dual
duel·ler (*or* ·list; *US* ·er *or* ·ist)
du·el·lo (*plural* ·los) duelling
du·en·na chaperon
duet (*or* du·ette)
duet·tist
duff
duf·fel (*or* ·fle)

duf·fer
dug
du·gong animal
dug·out
dui·ker (*plural* ·kers *or* ·ker) antelope
Duis·burg West German city
duke
duke·dom
dul·cet
dul·ci·ana organ stop
dul·ci·fy (·fies, ·fying, ·fied) sweeten
dul·ci·mer musical instrument
du·lia veneration for saints
dull
dull·ard
dull·ness (*or* dul·ness)
dulls·ville boredom
dul·ly in a dull way
du·lo·sis zoology term
dulse seaweed
Du·luth US port
duly appropriately
dumb
Dum·bar·ton Scottish town
dumb·bell
dumb-cane plant
dumb·found (*or* dum·)
dumb·found·er (*or* dum·)
dumb·ness
dumb·struck (*or* ·stricken)
dumb·waiter stand for dishes
dum·dum bullet
Dum·fries
dum·my (*noun, plural* ·mies; *verb* ·mies, ·my·ing, ·mied)
du·mor·ti·crite mineral
dump
dump·er
dumpi·ness
dump·ling
dumpy (dumpi·er, dumpi·est)
Dum·yat Egyptian town
dun (*verb* dun·ning, dunned; *adj* dun·ner, dun·nest)
Dun·bar Scottish port
dunce

Dun·dalk Irish town
Dun·dee
dunder·head
dune
Dun·edin New Zealand port
Dun·ferm·line
dung
dun·ga·ree fabric
dun·ga·rees overalls
Dun·ge·ness Kent headland
dun·geon
dung·hill
dungy
dun·ite rock
dunk
dunk·er
Dun·kirk French port
Dun Laoghaire Irish port
dun·lin bird
dun·nage cargo-packing material
dun·na·kin *Dialect* lavatory
dunned
dun·ner
dun·nest
dun·ning
dun·nite explosive
dun·nock bird
dun·ny *Scot* cellar
Du·noon Scottish town
Dun·si·nane Scottish hill
Dun·sta·ble
dunt *Dialect* a blow
duo (*plural* duos *or* dui)
duo·deci·mal of 12
duo·deci·mo (*plural* ·mos) book size
duo·denal
duo·dena·ry
duo·deni·tis
duo·denum (*plural* ·dena *or* ·denums)
duo·logue
duo·mo (*plural* ·mos) cathedral
duo·tone printing process
dup *Dialect* open
dup·abil·ity
dup·able
dupe
dup·er
dup·ery
du·ple musical term
du·plet chemistry term
du·plex

du·plex·ity
du·pli·cabil·ity
du·pli·cable
du·pli·cate
du·pli·ca·tion
du·pli·ca·tive
du·pli·ca·tor
du·plic·ity (*plural* ·ities)
du·pon·dius coin
du·rabil·ity (*or* ·rable·ness)
du·rable
Du·ralu·min (*Trademark*) aluminium alloy
dura ma·ter membrane round brain
du·ra·men wood
du·rance imprisonment
Du·ran·go Mexican state
du·ra·tion
du·ra·tion·al
du·ra·tive linguistics term
Dur·ban South African port
dur·bar African court
du·ress
Du·rex (*Trademark*) condom
Dur·ham
du·rian (*or* ·ri·on) fruit
dur·ing
dur·mast tree
duro (*plural* duros) coin
Du·roc US pig
dur·ra (*or* dou·ra, dou·rah) grass
durst *past tense of* dare
du·rum wheat
Du·shan·be Soviet city
dusk
duski·ness
dusky (duski·er, duski·est)
Düs·sel·dorf West German city
dust
dust·bin
dust·cart
dust·er
dusti·ly
dusti·ness
dust·man (*plural* ·men)
dust·pan
dust·sheet
dust-up *Slang* fight
dusty (dusti·er, dusti·est)

Dutch
Dutch·man (*plural* ·men)
du·teous *Archaic* dutiful
du·ti·abil·ity
du·ti·able
du·ti·ful
du·ti·ful·ly
du·ti·ful·ness
duty (*plural* duties)
duty-free
du·vet
du·vetyn (*or* ·vetine, ·vetyne) fabric
dux *Scot* best pupil
dvan·dva compound word
dwale deadly nightshade
dwarf (*plural* dwarfs *or* dwarves)
dwarf·ish
dwarf·ish·ness
dwarf·ism
dwell (dwell·ing, dwelt *or* dwelled)
dwell·er
dwell·ing
dwin·dle
dy·able (*or* dye·able)
dyad maths term
dy·ad·ic twofold
Dyak (*plural* Dyaks *or* Dyak) Malaysian people
dy·ar·chic (*or* ·chi·cal, ·chal) *variant spelling of* diarchic
dy·ar·chy (*plural* ·chies) *variant spelling of* diarchy
dyb·buk (*plural* ·buks *or* ·buk·kim) Hebrew spirit
dye (dye·ing, dyed) colour; *compare* die
dye·ing colouring; *compare* dying
dye·line blueprint
dy·er
dyer's-greenweed
dyer's-weed
dye·stuff

dye·wood
Dyf·ed Welsh county
dy·ing expiring; *compare* dyeing
dyke (*or* dike)
dy·nam·eter
dy·nam·ic
dy·nami·cal·ly
dy·nam·ics
dy·na·mism philosophical theory
dy·na·mist
dy·na·mis·tic
dy·na·mite
dy·na·mit·er (*or* ·mit·ist)
dy·na·mit·ic
dy·na·mo (*plural* ·mos)
dy·na·mo·elec·tric (*or* ·tri·cal)
dy·na·mom·eter
dy·na·mo·met·ric (*or* ·ri·cal)
dy·na·mom·etry
dy·na·mo·tor
dyn·ast ruler
dy·nas·tic (*or* ·ti·cal)
dyn·as·ty (*plural* ·ties)
dy·na·tron type of oscillator
dyne unit
dy·node electrode
dys·en·ter·ic
dys·en·tery
dys·func·tion
dys·gen·ic
dys·gen·ics reducing quality of race
dys·graphia impaired writing ability
dys·lexia impaired reading ability
dys·lex·ic (*or* ·lec·tic)
dys·men·or·rhoea (*US* ·rhea)
dys·men·or·rhoeal (*US* ·rheal)

dys·pep·sia (*or* ·sy) indigestion
dys·pep·tic (*or* ·ti·cal)
dys·pha·gia difficulty in swallowing
dys·phag·ic
dys·pha·sia impaired speech
dys·pha·sic
dys·phe·mism substitution of offensive word
dys·pho·nia impaired speech
dys·phon·ic
dys·pho·ria uneasy feeling
dys·phor·ic
dys·pla·sia abnormal organ development
dys·plas·tic
dysp·noea (*US* ·nea) difficulty in breathing
dysp·noeal (*or* ·noe·ic; *US* ·neal *or* ·ne·ic)
dys·pro·sium chemical element
dys·tel·eol·ogy philosophy term
dys·thy·mia neurotic condition
dys·thy·mic
dys·to·pia worst possible place
dys·troph·ic
dys·tro·phy (*or* ·phia) wasting of tissues
dys·uria painful urination
dys·uric
dy·tis·cid beetle
Dyu·la (*plural* ·la *or* ·las) African people
Dzer·zhinsk Soviet city
Dzong·ka Asian language
Dzun·ga·ria (*or* Zun·) Chinese region

E

each
eager keen; *compare* eagre
eager·ly

eager·ness
eagle
eagle-eyed

eagle·stone
eaglet
eagle·wood

eagre (or eager) tidal bore; compare eager
eal·dor·man Anglo-Saxon official
Ealing
ear
ear·ache
ear·bash Austral talk
ear·drop
ear·drum
eared
ear·flap
ear·ful
ear·ing nautical term
earl
ear·lap
earl·dom
ear·li·ness
ear·ly (·li·er, ·li·est)
Ear·ly Bird satellite
ear·mark
ear·muff
earn
earn·er
ear·nest
ear·nest·ness
earn·ings
ear·phone
ear·piece
ear·plug
ear·ring
ear·shot
ear·splitting
earth
earth·born
earth·bound
earth·en
earthen·ware
earthi·ly
earthi·ness
earth·light variant of earthshine
earth·li·ness
earth·ling
earth·ly (·li·er, ·li·est)
earth·nut
earth·quake
earth·rise
earth·shaking
earth·shine (or ·light) earth's reflected light
earth·star fungus
earth·wards (or esp. US ·ward)
earth·work

earth·worm
earthy (earthi·er, earthi·est)
ear·wax
ear·wig
ease
ease·ful
ease·ful·ness
easel
ease·ment
eas·er
easi·ly
easi·ness
east
East An·glia
East An·glian
East Ber·lin
East Ber·lin·er
east·bound
East·bourne
East·er
Easter-ledges plant
east·er·ly (plural ·lies)
east·ern
east·ern·er
east·ern·most
East·er·tide
East Ger·man
East Ger·ma·ny
East In·dian
East In·dies
east·ing nautical term
East Kil·bride Scottish town
East·leigh Hampshire town
east-northeast
east-southeast
east·ward (adj)
east·ward·ly
east·wards (adv)
easy (easi·er, easi·est)
easy-going
eat (eat·ing, ate, eat·en)
eat·able
eat·age Dialect grazing rights
eat·en
eat·er
eau de Co·logne
eau de Ja·velle bleaching solution
eau de nil greenish colour
eau de vie brandy
eaves

eaves·drop (·drop·ping, ·dropped)
eaves·drop·per
ebb
Ebbw Vale
ebon ebony
eb·on·ite rubber
eb·on·ize (or ·ise)
eb·ony (plural ·onies)
Ebora·cum Latin York
ebrac·te·ate
ebul·lience (or ·lien·cy)
ebul·lient
ebul·li·os·co·py chemistry term
ebul·li·tion boiling
ebur·na·tion bone condition
ecad ecology term
écar·té card game
Ec·bata·na Iranian city
ec·bol·ic medi term
ec·cen·tric
ec·cen·tri·cal·ly
ec·cen·tri·city (plural ·cities)
ec·chy·mo·sis (plural ·ses) skin condition
Ec·cles English town; cake
ec·cle·sia (plural ·siae) church congregation
ec·cle·si·arch sacristan
Ec·cle·si·as·tes Old Testament book
ec·cle·si·as·tic
ec·cle·si·as·ti·cal
ec·cle·si·as·ti·cal.ly
ec·cle·si·as·ti·cism
Ec·cle·si·as·ti·cus book of Apocrypha
ec·cle·si·ola·ter
ec·cle·si·ola·try ecclesiastical obsession
ec·cle·sio·logi·cal (or ·log·ic)
ec·cle·si·olo·gist
ec·cle·si·ol·ogy study of Church
ec·crine
ec·crin·ol·ogy study of glands
ec·dys·ial
ec·dysi·ast striptease artist
ec·dy·sis (plural ·ses) moulting
ec·dy·sone hormone

ecesis 138

ecesis ecology term
ec·hard biology term
eche·lon
ech·eve·ria plant
echid·na (*plural* ·nas *or* ·nae) spiny anteater
echi·nate (*or* ·nat·ed) having bristles
echi·no·coc·cus tapeworm
echi·no·derm marine animal
echi·no·der·mal (*or* ·ma·tous)
echi·noid marine animal
echi·nus (*plural* ·ni) sea urchin
echo (*noun, plural* echoes; *verb* echoes, echo·ing, ech·oed)
echo·ic
echo·ism linguistics term
echo·la·lia psychiatric term
echo·la·lic
echo·location
echo·prac·tic
echo·praxia (*or* ·prax·is) psychiatric term
echo·virus
éclair
ec·lamp·sia pregnancy condition
ec·lamp·tic
éclat acclaim
ec·lec·tic selecting the best
ec·lec·ti·cism
eclipse
eclips·er
eclip·sis linguistics term
eclip·tic astronomy term
eclip·ti·cal·ly
ec·lo·gite rock
ec·logue poem
eclo·sion emergence of insect
eco·cide environmental destruction
eco·logi·cal (*or* ·log·ic)
eco·logi·cal·ly
ecolo·gist
ecol·ogy
econo·met·ric (*or* ·ri·cal)
econo·me·tri·cian (*or* ·met·rist)
econo·met·rics economics
eco·nom·ic

eco·nomi·cal
eco·nomi·cal·ly
eco·nom·ics
econo·mist
econo·mi·za·tion (*or* ·sa·tion)
econo·mize (*or* ·mise)
econo·miz·er (*or* ·mis·er)
econo·my (*plural* ·mies)
écor·ché anatomical figure
eco·spe·cies
eco·spe·cif·ic
eco·sphere
écoss·aise dance
eco·sys·tem
eco·ton·al
eco·tone ecology term
eco·type
eco·typ·ic
eco·typi·cal·ly
écra·seur surgical device
ecru yellowish colour
ec·sta·sy (*plural* ·sies)
ec·stat·ic
ec·stati·cal·ly
ec·stat·ics
ec·thy·ma skin condition
ec·to·blast biology term
ec·to·blas·tic
ec·to·derm (*or* exo·derm) embryo part
ec·to·der·mal (*or* ·mic)
ec·to·en·zyme
ec·to·gen·esis
ec·tog·enous (*or* ·to·gen·ic) biology term
ec·to·mere embryology term
ec·to·mer·ic
ec·to·morph
ec·to·mor·phic thin
ec·to·morphy
ec·to·para·site
ec·to·para·sit·ic
ec·to·phyte parasitic plant
ec·to·pia congenital displacement
ec·top·ic in abnormal position; *compare* entopic
ec·to·plasm
ecto·plas·mic
ec·to·proct animal
ec·to·sarc amoeba ectoplasm
ecto·sar·cous

ec·ty·pal
ec·type copy
Ecua·dor
Ecua·do·rian (*or* ·ran)
ecu·men·ic
ecu·meni·cal (*or* oecu·)
ecu·meni·cal·ism (*or* ·cism) Christian unity
ecu·meni·cal·ly
écu·rie motor-racing team
ec·ze·ma
ec·zema·tous
eda·cious greedy
eda·cious·ness
edac·ity
Edam
edaph·ic of soil
edaphi·cal·ly
Edda Norse poems
eddo plant
eddy (*noun, plural* eddies; *verb* eddies, eddy·ing, eddied)
Ed·dy·stone rocks; lighthouse
Ede Dutch city
edel·weiss
ede·ma US spelling of oedema
edema·tous US spelling of oedematous
Eden biblical garden
eden·tate zoology term
eden·tu·lous (*or* ·late) toothless
edge
Edge·hill English battle site
edg·er
edge·ways
edgi·ly
edgi·ness
edg·ing
edgy (edgi·er, edgi·est)
edh runic character
ed·ibil·ity (*or* ·ible·ness)
ed·ible
edict
edic·tal
edi·fi·ca·tion
edifi·ca·tory
edi·fice
edi·fi·cial
edi·fi·er
edi·fy (·fies, ·fy·ing, ·fied)
edi·fy·ing·ly

edile *US variant spelling of* oedile
Ed·in·burgh
edit
edi·tion
edi·tio prin·ceps (*plural* edi·tio·nes prin·ci·pes) *Latin* first edition
edi·tor
edi·to·rial
edi·to·ri·al·ist
edi·to·ri·ali·za·tion (*or* ·sa·tion)
edi·to·ri·al·ize (*or* ·ise)
edi·to·ri·al·iz·er (*or* ·is·er)
edi·to·ri·al·ly
edi·tor·ship
Ed·mon·ton Canadian city
Edom biblical people
edu·cabil·ity (*or* educat·abil·ity)
edu·cable (*or* ·cat·able)
edu·cate
edu·cat·ed
edu·ca·tion
edu·ca·tion·al
edu·ca·tion·al·ist (*or* ·tion·ist)
edu·ca·tion·al·ly
edu·ca·tive
edu·ca·tor
edu·ca·tory
educe logic term
educ·ible
educt chemistry term
educ·tion
educ·tive
edul·co·rate wash
edul·co·ra·tion
Ed·ward·ian
eel
eel·grass
eel-like
eel·pout fish
eel·worm
e'er ever; *compare* ere
eerie (eeri·er, eeri·est) weird; *compare* eyrie
eeri·ly
eeri·ness
eff
ef·fable expressible
ef·face
ef·face·able
ef·face·ment

ef·fac·er
ef·fect (*noun*) result; (*verb*) cause; *compare* affect
ef·fect·er
ef·fect·ible
ef·fec·tive
ef·fec·tive·ly
ef·fec·tive·ness
ef·fec·tor physiology term
ef·fects
ef·fec·tual
ef·fec·tu·al·ity (*or* ·al·ness)
ef·fec·tu·al·ly
ef·fec·tu·ate bring about
ef·fec·tu·ation
ef·femi·na·cy (*or* ·nate·ness)
ef·femi·nate
ef·fen·di (*plural* ·dis) Turkish title
ef·fer·ence
ef·fer·ent conducting outwards; *compare* afferent
ef·fer·vesce
ef·fer·ves·cence
ef·fer·ves·cent
ef·fer·ves·cible
ef·fer·ves·cing·ly
ef·fete weak
ef·fi·ca·cious
ef·fi·ca·cy (*or* ·cious·ness)
ef·fi·cien·cy (*plural* ·cies)
ef·fi·cient
ef·fig·ial
ef·fi·gy (*plural* ·gies)
ef·flo·resce
ef·flo·res·cence
ef·flo·res·cent
ef·flu·ence (*or* ef·flux)
ef·flu·ent
ef·flu·vial
ef·flu·vium (*plural* ·via *or* ·viums) bad smell
ef·flux *variant of* effluence
ef·fort
ef·fort·ful
ef·fort·less
ef·fort·less·ness
ef·fron·tery (*plural* ·teries)
ef·ful·gence
ef·ful·gent radiant
ef·fuse spread out

ef·fu·si·om·eter physics apparatus
ef·fu·sion
ef·fu·sive
ef·fu·sive·ness
Efik (*plural* Efik *or* Efiks) African people
eft newt
egad
egali·tar·ian
egali·tari·an·ism
Egeria female adviser
egest excrete
eges·ta
eges·tion
eges·tive
egg
egg-beater
eg·ger (*or* ·gar) moth
egg·head
egg·nog (*or* egg-noggin)
egg·plant *US* aubergine
egg·shell
eggy
Eg·ham Surrey town
egis *US variant spelling of* aegis
eg·lan·tine plant
Eg·mont extinct volcano
ego (*plural* egos)
ego·cen·tric
ego·cen·tric·ity
ego·cen·trism
ego·ism self-interest; *compare* egotism
ego·ist
ego·is·tic (*or* ·ti·cal)
ego·ma·nia
ego·ma·ni·ac
ego·ma·nia·cal
ego·tism self-centredness; *compare* egoism
ego·tist
ego·tis·tic (*or* ·ti·cal)
ego·tis·ti·cal·ly
egre·gious bad
egre·gious·ness
egress
egres·sion
egret bird
Egypt
Egyp·tian
Egyp·to·logi·cal
Egyp·tolo·gist
Egyp·tol·ogy

eh

eh
eider
eider·down
eidet·ic psychology term
eideti·cal·ly
eido·lon (*plural* ·la *or*
  ·lons) apparition
Eiffel Tower
eigen·func·tion physics
  term
Eiger Swiss mountain
eight
eight·een
eight·een·mo (*plural*
  ·mos)
eight·eenth
eight·fold
eighth
eighti·eth
eight·some
eighti·vo (*plural* ·vos)
eighty (*plural* eighties)
Eilat Israeli port
Eind·ho·ven Dutch city
ein·korn wheat
Ein·stein·ian
ein·stein·ium radioactive
  element
Eire
eireni·con (*or* ireni·)
  philosophy term
eise·gesis (*plural* ·geses)
  text interpretation
Eisen·ach East German city
eistedd·fod (*plural* ·fods
  or ·fodau)
eistedd·fod·ic
ei·ther
ejacu·late
ejacu·la·tion
ejacu·la·tive
ejacu·la·tor
ejacu·la·tory
eject
ejec·ta volcanic material
ejec·tion
ejec·tive phonetics term
ejec·tor
eke
ekis·ti·cal (*or* ·tic)
ekis·tics human settlements
elabo·rate
elabo·rate·ness
elabo·ra·tion
elabo·ra·tive

elabo·ra·tor
el·aeop·tene *variant spelling
  of* eleoptene
El Ala·mein Egyptian
  battle site
Elam ancient kingdom
Elam·ite (*or* ·it·ic)
élan style
eland antelope
élan vital philosophy term
ela·pid snake
elapse
elas·mo·branch fish
elas·mo·saur reptile
elas·tance physics term
elas·tic
elas·ti·cal·ly
elas·ti·cate
elas·ti·ca·tion
elas·tici·ty
elas·ti·cize (*or* ·cise)
elas·tin protein
elas·to·mer rubbery
  material
elas·to·mer·ic
Elas·to·plast
  (*Trademark*)
elate
elat·ed
elat·ed·ness
ela·ter biology term
elat·er·id beetle
elat·er·in purgative
elat·er·ite bitumen
ela·terium purgative
ela·tion
ela·tive linguistics term
Elba Italian island
Elbe European river
el·bow
elbow·room
El·brus Soviet mountain
el·der
elder·berry (*plural*
  ·berries)
el·der·li·ness
el·der·ly
el·der·ship
eld·est
El Do·ra·do legendary city
el·dritch (*or* ·drich)
  unearthly
Ele·at·ic
Ele·ati·cism philosophy
  term

140

ele·cam·pane plant
elect
elect·able
elec·tion
elec·tion·eer
elec·tion·eer·er
elec·tion·eer·ing
elec·tive
elec·tiv·ity (*or* ·tive·ness)
elec·tor
elec·tor·al
elec·tor·ate
elec·tor·ship
Electra mythological
  character
elec·tret physics term
elec·tric
elec·tri·cal
elec·tri·cal·ly
elec·tri·cian
elec·tric·ity
elec·tri·fi·able
elec·tri·fi·ca·tion
elec·tri·fi·er
elec·tri·fy (·fies, ·fy·ing,
  ·fied)
elec·tro (*plural* ·tros)
elec·tro·acous·tic (*or*
  ·ti·cal)
elec·tro·acous·tics
elec·tro·analy·sis
elec·tro·ana·lytic (*or*
  ·lyti·cal)
elec·tro·car·dio·gram
elec·tro·car·dio·graph
elec·tro·car·dio·graph·ic
  (*or* ·graphi·cal)
elec·tro·car·di·og·ra·phy
elec·tro·chemi·cal
elec·tro·chem·ist
elec·tro·chem·is·try
elec·tro·con·vul·sive
elec·tro·cor·ti·co·gram
  record of brainwaves
elec·tro·cute
elec·tro·cu·tion
elec·trode
elec·tro·de·pos·it
elec·tro·depo·si·tion
  chemistry term
elec·tro·di·aly·sis
elec·tro·dy·nam·ic (*or*
  ·nami·cal)
elec·tro·dy·nam·ics
elec·tro·dy·na·mom·eter

elec·tro·en·cepha·lo·gram
elec·tro·en·cepha·lo·graph
elec·tro·en·cepha·lo-graph·ic
elec·tro·en·cepha·lo-graphi·cal·ly
elec·tro·en·cepha·log·ra-phy
elec·tro·form form by electrolysis
elec·tro·graph printing term
elec·tro·graph·ic
elec·tro·graphi·cal·ly
elec·trog·ra·phy
elec·tro·jet physics term
elec·tro·ki·net·ic
elec·tro·ki·net·ics
elec·tro·lu·mi·nes·cence
elec·tro·lu·mi·nes·cent
elec·tro·ly·sa·tion (US ·za·tion)
elec·tro·lyse (US ·lyze)
elec·tro·lys·er (US ·lyz·er)
elec·troly·sis
elec·tro·lyte
elec·tro·lyt·ic (or ·lyti·cal)
elec·tro·mag·net
elec·tro·mag·net·ic
elec·tro·mag·neti·cal·ly
elec·tro·mag·ne·tism
elec·tro·me·chani·cal
elec·tro·mer·ism chemistry term
elec·tro·met·al·lur·gi·cal
elec·tro·me·tal·lur·gist
elec·tro·met·al·lur·gy
elec·trom·eter
elec·tro·met·ric (or ·ri·cal)
elec·trom·etry
elec·tro·mo·tive current-producing
elec·tron
elec·tro·nega·tive
elec·tro·nega·tiv·ity
elec·tron·ic
elec·troni·cal·ly
elec·tron·ics
elec·tron·volt unit
elec·tro·phil·ic chemistry term
elec·tro·phone musical term

elec·tro·phon·ic
elec·tro·pho·resis physics term
elec·tro·pho·ret·ic
elec·tropho·rus physics apparatus
elec·tro·physio·logi·cal
elec·tro·physi·olo·gist
elec·tro·physi·ol·ogy
elec·tro·plate
elec·tro·plat·er
elec·tro·po·si·tive
elec·tro·scope
elec·tro·scop·ic
elec·tro·stat·ic
elec·tro·stati·cal·ly
elec·tro·stat·ics
elec·tro·stric·tion physics term
elec·tro·sur·gery
elec·tro·sur·gi·cal
elec·tro·thera·peu·tic (or ·ti·cal)
elec·tro·thera·peu·tics
elec·tro·thera·pist
elec·tro·thera·py
elec·tro·ther·mal
elec·tro·ton·ic
elec·troto·nus physiology term
elec·tro·type printing term
elec·tro·typ·er
elec·tro·va·len·cy (or ·lence) chemistry term
elec·tro·va·lent
elec·trum alloy
elec·tu·ary (plural ·aries) medical term
el·eemosy·nary dependent on charity
el·egance (or el·egan·cy; plural ·egances or ·cies)
el·egant
el·egi·ac
el·egist
el·egize (or ·egise)
el·egy (plural ·egies)
el·ement
el·ement·al
el·emen·ta·ri·ness
el·emen·ta·ry
el·emi (plural ·emis) resin
elen·chus (plural ·chi) logic term

elenc·tic
el·eop·tene (or ·aeop·) chemistry term
el·ephant (plural ·ephants or ·ephant)
el·ephan·ti·as·ic
el·ephan·tia·sis disease
el·ephan·tine
el·ephan·toid
elephant's-ear plant
elephant's-foot (or elephant-) plant
Eleu·sin·ian
Eleu·sis Greek town
el·evate
el·evat·ed
el·eva·tion
el·eva·tor
elev·en
eleven-plus
elev·en·ses
elev·enth
el·evon aircraft control surface
elf (plural elves)
El Fai·yum (or Al Fai·yum) Egyptian city
elfin
elf·ish (or elv·)
elf·lock
Elgin Scottish town; marbles
El Giza Egyptian city
Elia Greek department
elic·it evoke; compare illicit
elic·it·able
elici·ta·tion
elici·tor
elide linguistics term
elid·ible
eli·gibil·ity
eli·gible
eli·gibly
elimi·nable
elimi·nant
elimi·nate
elimi·na·tion
elimi·na·tive (or ·tory)
elimi·na·tor
Elis ancient Olympic Games site
eli·sion linguistics term
elite (or élite)
elit·ism
elit·ist

elixir

elix·ir
Eliza·bethan
elk
elk·hound
ell unit of length
Elles·mere Canadian Island
el·lipse flattened circle
el·lip·sis (*plural* ·ses) missing words
el·lip·soid
el·lip·soi·dal
el·lip·tic
el·lip·ti·cal
el·lip·ti·cal·ly
el·lip·ti·cal·ness
el·lip·ti·city
elm
El Man·su·ra (*or* Al Man·su·rah) Egyptian city
El Min·ya Egyptian port
El Mis·ti Peruvian volcano
El Obeid Sudanese city
elo·cu·tion
elo·cu·tion·ary
elo·cu·tion·ist
elon·gate
elon·ga·tion
elon·ga·tive
elope
elope·ment
elop·er
elo·quence
elo·quent
elo·quent·ness
El Paso Texan city
El Sal·va·dor
else·where
El·si·nore
elu·ant *variant spelling of* eluent
elu·ci·date
elu·ci·da·tion
elu·ci·da·tive (*or* ·da·tory)
elu·ci·da·tor
elude escape from; *compare* allude; illude
elud·er
elu·ate chemistry term
elu·ent (*or* ·ant)
elu·sion
elu·sive evasive; *compare* illusive
elu·sive·ness
elute chemistry term

elu·tri·ant
elu·tri·ate
elu·tria·tion
elu·tria·tor
elu·vial
elu·via·tion
elu·vium (*plural* ·via) rock particles; *compare* alluvium
el·ver eel
elves *plural of* elf
elv·ish *variant spelling of* elfish
Ely
Ély·sée Parisian palace
Ely·sian
Ely·sium mythological heaven
ely·troid (*or* ·trous)
ely·tron (*or* ·trum; *plural* ·tra) beetle's wing
em printer's measure; *compare* en
ema·ci·ate
ema·ci·a·ted
ema·ci·a·tion
ema·nate
ema·na·tion
ema·na·tion·al
ema·na·tive
ema·na·tor
ema·na·tory
eman·ci·pate
eman·ci·pa·tion
eman·ci·pa·tion·ist
eman·ci·pa·tive
eman·ci·pa·tor
eman·ci·pa·tory
emar·gi·nate (*or* ·nat·ed) notched
emar·gi·na·tion
emas·cu·late
emas·cu·la·tion
emas·cu·la·tive (*or* ·tory)
emas·cu·la·tor
em·balm
em·balm·er
em·balm·ment
em·bank
em·bank·ment
(**embarass**) *incorrect spelling of* embarrass
em·bar·go (*noun, plural* ·goes; *verb* ·goes, ·go·ing, ·goed)
em·bark

em·bar·ka·tion
em·bark·ment
em·bar·rass
em·bar·rass·ing
em·bar·rass·ment
em·bas·sy (*plural* ·sies)
em·bat·tle
em·bay
em·bay·ment bay-shaped
em·bed (·bed·ding, ·bed·ded)
em·bed·ment
em·bel·lish
em·bel·lish·er
em·bel·lish·ment
em·ber
em·bez·zle
em·bez·zle·ment
em·bez·zler
em·bit·ter
em·bit·ter·er
em·bit·ter·ment
em·bla·zon
em·bla·zon·ment
em·bla·zon·ry
em·blem
em·blem·at·ic (*or* ·ati·cal)
em·blem·ati·cal·ly
em·blema·tize (*or* ·tise, ·blem·ize, ·blem·ise)
em·ble·ments legal term
em·bodi·ment (*or* im·)
em·body (·bod·ies, ·body·ing, ·bod·ied)
em·bold·en
em·bo·lec·to·my (*plural* ·mies)
em·bol·ic
em·bo·lism
em·bo·lis·mic
em·bo·lus (*plural* ·li) material blocking blood vessel
em·bo·ly (*plural* ·lies) embryology term
em·bon·point French plumpness
em·boss
em·boss·er
em·boss·ment
em·bou·chure (*plural* ·chures)
em·bow architecture term
em·bow·el
em·bow·er

em·bow·ment
em·brace
em·brace·able
em·brace·ment
em·brac·er
em·brac·ery *Obsolete* jury bribing
em·branch·ment
em·bra·sure fortification
em·bra·sured
em·brec·to·my (*plural* ·mies)
em·bro·cate
em·bro·ca·tion
em·broi·der
em·broi·der·er
em·broi·dery (*plural* ·deries)
em·broil
em·broil·er
em·broil·ment
em·bry·ec·to·my (*plural* ·mies)
em·brue *variant spelling of* imbrue
em·bryo (*plural* ·bryos)
em·bryo·gen·ic
em·bry·og·eny development of embryo
em·bry·oid
em·bryo·logi·cal (*or* ·log·ic)
em·bry·olo·gist
em·bry·ol·ogy
em·bry·on·ic (*or* ·bryo·nal)
em·bry·oni·cal·ly
em·bus (·bus·ing, ·bused *or* ·bus·sing, ·bussed)
emend improve text; *compare* amend
emend·able
emen·da·tion
emen·da·tor
emen·da·tory
em·er·ald
emerge
emer·gence
emer·gen·cy (*plural* ·cies)
emer·gent
emeri·tus
emersed botany term
emer·sion emerging; *compare* immersion
em·ery mineral

em·esis vomiting
emet·ic
emeti·cal·ly
em·etine (*or* ·etin) alkaloid
emi·grant
emi·grate leave country; *compare* immigrate
emi·gra·tion
emi·gra·tion·al
emi·gra·tive
émi·gré *French* emigrant
Emilia-Romagna Italian region
Emi·nence (*or* ·nen·cy; *plural* ·nences *or* ·nen·cies) cardinal's title
emi·nence (*or* ·nen·cy; *plural* ·nences *or* ·nen·cies) superiority
émi·nence grise (*plural* emi·nences grises) *French* powerful person
emi·nent distinguished; *compare* immanent; imminent
emir (*or* emeer) Islamic ruler
emir·ate (*or* emeer·)
em·is·sary (*plural* ·saries)
emis·sion
emis·sive
emis·siv·ity physics term
emit (emit·ting, emit·ted)
emit·ter
Em·men Dutch city
em·mena·gog·ic
em·mena·gogue medical term
Em·men·thal (*or* ·tal, ·thal·er, ·tal·er) cheese
em·mer wheat
em·met *Dialect* ant
em·me·tro·pia perfect vision
em·me·trop·ic
Emmy television award
emol·lience
emol·lient soothing
emolu·ment salary
emote
emot·er
emo·tion
emo·tion·al
emo·tion·al·ism
emo·tion·al·ist
emo·tion·al·is·tic

empress
emo·tion·al·ity
emo·tion·ali·za·tion (*or* ·sa·tion)
emo·tion·al·ize (*or* ·ise)
emo·tion·al·ly
emo·tive
emo·tive·ness (*or* ·tiv·ity)
emo·ti·vism
em·pale *less common spelling of* impale
em·pan·el (*US* im·; ·el·ling, ·elled, *US* ·el·ing, ·eled)
em·pan·el·ment (*US* im·)
em·path·ic (*or* ·pa·thet·ic)
em·pathi·cal·ly (*or* ·pa·theti·cal·ly)
em·pa·thize (*or* ·thise)
em·pa·thy
em·pen·nage aircraft tail
em·per·or
em·per·or·ship
em·pery power
em·pha·sis (*plural* ·ses)
em·pha·size (*or* ·sise)
em·phat·ic
em·phati·cal·ly
em·phati·cal·ness
em·phy·sema lung condition
em·phy·sema·tous
em·pire
em·pir·ic
em·piri·cal
em·piri·cal·ly
em·piri·cal·ness
em·piri·cism
em·piri·cist
em·place
em·place·ment
em·plane
em·ploy
em·ploy·abil·ity
em·ploy·able
em·ployee
em·ploy·er
em·ploy·ment
em·poi·son
em·po·rium (*plural* ·riums *or* ·ria)
em·pov·er·ish *less common spelling of* impoverish
em·pow·er
em·pow·er·ment
em·press

empt

empt *Dialect* empty
emp·ti·able
emp·ti·ly
emp·ti·ness
emp·ty (*adj* ·ti·er, ·ti·est; *verb* ·ties, ·ty·ing, ·tied)
empty-handed
empty-headed
em·py·ema pus accumulation
em·py·emic
em·py·real
em·py·rean heavens
em·py·reu·ma burning smell
emu
emu·late
emu·la·tion
emu·la·tive
emu·la·tor
emu·lous competitive
emu·lous·ness
emul·si·fi·able (*or* emul·sible)
emul·si·fi·ca·tion
emul·si·fi·er
emul·si·fy (·fies, ·fy·ing, ·fied)
emul·sion
emul·sive
emul·soid chemistry term
emunc·tory (*plural* ·tories) excretory organ
en half an em; *compare* em
en·able
en·abler
en·act
en·ac·tion
en·ac·tive
en·act·ment
en·ac·tor
en·ac·tory
enam·el (·el·ling, ·elled; *US* ·el·ing, ·eled)
enam·el·ler (*US* ·el·er)
enam·el·list (*US* ·el·ist)
enam·el·work
en·am·our (*US* ·or)
en·am·oured (*US* ·ored)
en·antio·morph crystal form
en·antio·mor·phic
en·antio·morph·ism
en·ar·thro·dial

en·ar·thro·sis (*plural* ·ses) ball-and-socket joint
enate of the mother
enat·ic
en bloc *French* in a block
en·cae·nia festival
en·cage
en·camp
en·camp·ment
en·cap·su·late
en·cap·su·la·tion
en·case (*or* in·)
en·case·ment (*or* in·)
en·cash
en·cash·able
en·cash·ment
en·caus·tic ceramics term
en·caus·ti·cal·ly
en·ceinte pregnant
Enceladus mythological giant
en·cephal·ic of the brain
en·cepha·lin (*or* ·kepha·) brain chemical
en·cepha·li·tic
en·cepha·li·tis
en·cepha·lo·gram
en·cepha·lo·graph
en·cepha·lo·graphi·cal
en·cepha·log·ra·phy
en·cepha·lo·ma (*plural* ·mas *or* ·ma·ta) tumour
en·cepha·lo·my·eli·tic
en·cepha·lo·my·eli·tis
en·cepha·lon (*plural* ·la) brain
en·cepha·lous
en·chain
en·chain·ment
en·chant
en·chant·er
en·chant·ing
en·chant·ment
en·chant·ress
en·chase engrave
en·chi·la·da Mexican food
en·chon·dro·ma (*plural* ·mas *or* ·ma·ta) tumour
en·chon·droma·tous
en·cho·rial (*or* ·ric) of a particular country
en·ci·pher
en·ci·pher·er
en·ci·pher·ment
en·cir·cle

144

en·cir·cle·ment
en·clasp
en·clave
en·clit·ic linguistics term
en·cliti·cal·ly
en·clos·able (*or* in·)
en·close
en·clos·er
en·clo·sure
en·code
en·code·ment
en·cod·er
en·co·mi·ast writer of eulogies
en·co·mi·as·tic (*or* ·ti·cal)
en·co·mi·as·ti·cal·ly
en·co·mium (*plural* ·miums *or* ·mia)
en·com·pass
en·com·pass·ment
en·core
en·coun·ter
en·coun·ter·er
en·cour·age
en·cour·age·ment
en·cour·ag·er
en·cour·ag·ing·ly
en·cri·nite fossil
en·croach
en·croach·er
en·croach·ing·ly
en·croach·ment
en·crust (*or* in·)
en·crust·ant (*or* in·)
en·crus·ta·tion (*or* in·)
en·cul·tu·ra·tion
en·cul·tu·ra·tive
en·cum·ber (*or* in·)
en·cum·ber·ing·ly (*or* in·)
en·cum·brance (*or* in·)
en·cum·branc·er legal term
en·cyc·lic
en·cyc·li·cal letter from pope
en·cy·clo·pedia (*or* ·pae·dia)
en·cy·clo·pedic (*or* ·pae·dic)
en·cy·clo·pedi·cal·ly (*or* ·pae·di·)
en·cy·clo·pedism (*or* ·pae·dism)
en·cy·clo·pedist (*or* ·pae·dist)
en·cyst biology term

en·cyst·ment (or ·ta·tion)
end
en·dam·age
en·dam·age·ment
en·da·moeba (US ·meba; plural ·moebae or ·moebas, US ·mebas)
en·dan·ger
en·dan·ger·ment
end·arch botany term
end-blown music term
end·brain
en·dear
en·dear·ing
en·dear·ing·ly
en·dear·ment
en·deav·our (US ·or)
en·deav·our·er (US ·or·)
en·dem·ic (noun) localized disease; compare epidemic
en·dem·ic (or ·demi·al, ·demi·cal; adj)
en·demi·cal·ly
en·de·mism (or ·mic·ity)
end·er
en·der·mic absorbed through skin
end·game
end·ing
en·dive
end·less
end·less·ness
end·long
end·most
endo·blast embryology term
endo·blas·tic
endo·car·dial (or ·di·ac)
endo·car·di·tic
endo·car·di·tis
endo·car·dium (plural ·dia) heart membrane
endo·carp part of fruit
endo·car·pal (or ·pic)
endo·cen·tric linguistics term
endo·cra·nium (plural ·nia) anatomy term
endo·crin·al
endo·crine ductless; compare exocrine
endo·crin·ic
endo·crino·log·ic (or ·ic·al)
endo·cri·nolo·gist

endo·cri·nol·ogy study of hormones
en·doc·ri·nous
endo·derm (or ento·) part of embryo
endo·der·mal (or ento·)
endo·der·mic (or ento·)
endo·derm·is botany term
endo·don·tia
endo·don·tic
endo·don·tics dentistry term
endo·don·tist
endo·don·tol·ogy
endo·en·zyme
endo·er·gic energy-absorbing; compare exoergic
en·doga·mous (or endo·gam·ic)
en·doga·my
en·dog·enous developing in an organism
en·dog·eny
endo·lymph fluid in ear
endo·lym·phat·ic
endo·metrial
endo·metrio·sis
endo·metrium (plural ·metria) womb lining
endo·morph
endo·mor·phic heavily built
endo·mor·phism geology term
endo·mor·phy
endo·neu·rium anatomy term
endo·para·site
endo·para·sit·ic
endo·pep·ti·dase enzyme
endo·phyte (or ento·) parasitic plant
endo·phyt·ic (or ento·)
endo·plasm biology term
endo·plas·mic
en·dor·phin brain chemical
en·dors·able (or in·)
en·dorse (or in·)
en·dor·see (or in·)
en·dorse·ment (or in·)
en·dors·er (or ·dor·sor, in·)
endo·scope medical instrument
endo·scop·ic
en·dos·co·pist

en·dos·co·py
endo·skel·etal
endo·skel·eton
en·dos·mo·sis biology term
en·dos·mot·ic
en·dos·moti·cal·ly
endo·some cell nucleus part
endo·sperm seed tissue
endo·sper·mic
endo·spore
en·dos·por·ous
en·dos·teal
en·dos·teum (plural ·tea) anatomy term
en·dos·to·sis (plural ·ses) physiology term
endo·thecial
endo·thecium (plural ·thecia) botany term
endo·thelial
endo·theli·oid
endo·thelio·ma (plural ·mata) tumour
endo·thelium (plural ·thelia) anatomy term
endo·ther·mic (or ·mal) heat-absorbing; compare exothermic
endo·ther·mi·cal·ly
endo·ther·mism
endo·tox·ic
endo·tox·in
en·dow
en·dow·er
en·dow·ment
end·paper part of book
end·plate
end·play bridge term
en·due (or in·; ·dues, ·du·ing, ·dued) endow
en·dur·abil·ity (or ·dur·able·ness)
en·dur·able
en·dur·ance
en·dure
en·dur·ing
en·dur·ing·ly
end·ways
Endymion mythological character
en·ema (plural ·emas or ·ema·ta)
en·emy (plural ·emies)
en·er·get·ic
en·er·geti·cal·ly

energeticist

en·er·geti·cist
en·er·get·ics
en·er·gid biology term
en·er·gize (or ·gise)
en·er·giz·er (or ·gis·er)
en·er·gu·men possessed person
en·er·gy (plural ·gies)
en·er·vate weaken; compare innervate; innovate
en·er·va·tion
en·er·va·tive
en·er·va·tor
en·face
en face French facing forwards
en·face·ment
en fa·mille French informally
en·fant ter·ri·ble (plural en·fants ter·ri·bles) French indiscreet person
en·fee·ble
en·fee·ble·ment
en·fee·bler
en·feoff legal term
en·feoff·ment
En·field London borough; rifle
en·fi·lade military term
en·fleu·rage French perfume-making
en·fold (or in·)
en·fold·er (or in·)
en·fold·ment (or in·)
en·force
en·force·abil·ity
en·force·able
en·forc·ed·ly
en·force·ment
en·forc·er
en·fran·chise
en·fran·chise·ment
en·fran·chis·er
En·ga·dine Swiss region
en·gage
en·gagé French committed
en·gaged
en·gage·ment
en·gag·er
en·gag·ing
en·gag·ing·ly
en·gag·ing·ness
en garde French on guard
en·gen·der

en·gen·der·er
en·gen·der·ment
en·gine
en·gi·neer
en·gi·neer·ing
en·gine·ry (plural ·ries)
en·gla·cial
Eng·land
Eng·lish
Eng·lish·ism
English·man (plural ·men)
English·woman (plural ·women)
en·glut devour
en·gorge
en·gorge·ment
en·graft (or in·)
en·graf·ta·tion (or en·graft·ment, in·)
en·grail indent coin
en·grail·ment
en·grain variant spelling of ingrain
en·grained variant spelling of ingrained
en·gram psychology term
en·gram·mic (or ·gram·at·ic)
en·grave
en·grav·er
en·grav·ing
en·gross
en·gross·ed·ly
en·gross·er
en·gross·ing·ly
en·gross·ment
en·gulf (or in·)
en·gulf·ment
en·hance
en·hance·ment
en·hanc·er
en·hanc·ive
en·har·mon·ic
en·har·moni·cal·ly
enig·ma
en·ig·mat·ic (or ·mati·cal)
en·ig·mati·cal·ly
Eni·we·tok Pacific atoll
en·jamb·ment (or ·jambe·) poetry term
en·join
en·join·er
en·join·ment
en·joy

146

en·joy·able
en·joy·ably
en·joy·er
en·joy·ment
en·kepha·lin variant spelling of encephalin
en·kin·dle
en·kin·dler
en·lace
en·lace·ment
en·large
en·large·able
en·large·ment
en·larg·er
en·light·en
en·light·en·er
en·light·en·ing·ly
En·light·en·ment 18th-century movement
en·light·en·ment
en·list
en·list·er
en·list·ment
en·liv·en
en·liv·en·er
en·liv·en·ing·ly
en·liv·en·ment
en masse French in a mass
en·mesh (or in·, im·)
en·mity (plural ·mities)
en·nage printing term
en·nead group of nine
en·nead·ic
en·nea·gon
en·nea·he·dral
en·nea·he·dron (plural ·drons or ·dra)
En·nis Irish town
En·nis·kil·len (or In·nis·kil·ling) Northern Irish town
en·no·ble
en·no·ble·ment
en·no·bler
en·no·bling·ly
en·nui apathy
enol chemistry term
enol·ogy US spelling of aenology
enor·mity (plural ·mities)
enor·mous
eno·sis union of Greece and Cyprus
enough
enounce enunciate

en pas·sant *French* in passing
en·phy·tot·ic *botany term*
en·plane
en·quire (*or esp. US* in·) ask; *compare* inquire
en·quir·er (*or esp. US* in·)
en·quiry (*or esp. US* in·; *plural* ·quiries)
en·rage
en·rag·ed·ly
en·rage·ment
en rap·port *French* in sympathy
en·rap·ture
en·rich
en·rich·er
en·rich·ment
en·robe
en·rob·er
en·rol (*US* ·roll; ·rol·ling, ·rolled)
en·rol·lee
en·rol·ler
en·rol·ment (*US* ·roll·)
en·root
en route *French* on the way
ens *metaphysics term*
en·san·guine stain with blood
En·schede Dutch city
en·sconce
en·sem·ble
en·shrine (*or* in·)
en·shrine·ment
en·shroud
en·si·form sword-shaped
en·sign
en·sign·ship (*or* ·cy; *plural* ·ships *or* ·cies)
en·si·labil·ity
en·si·lage
en·sile store in silo
en·slave
en·slave·ment
en·slav·er
en·snare (*or* in·)
en·snare·ment
en·snar·er
en·soul (*or* in·)
en·sphere (*or* in·)
en·sta·tite mineral
en·sue (·su·ing, ·sued)
en·su·ing·ly

en suite forming a unit
en·sure make sure; *compare* insure
en·sur·er
en·swathe
en·tab·la·ture
en·ta·ble·ment platform
en·tail
en·tail·er
en·tail·ment
en·ta·moeba (*or* en·da·; *US* ·meba; *plural* ·moebae *or* ·moebas, *US* ·mebas) amoeba
en·tan·gle
en·tan·gle·ment
en·tan·gler
en·ta·sia
en·ta·sis (*plural* ·ses) *architectural term*
En·teb·be Ugandan town
en·tel·echy (*plural* ·echies) *philosophy term*
en·tel·lus monkey
en·tente cor·diale *French* friendly relations
en·ter
en·ter·able
en·ter·al·ly
en·ter·er
en·ter·ic (*or* ·al) intestinal
en·teri·tis
en·tero·gas·trone hormone
en·tero·ki·nase enzyme
en·ter·on (*plural* ·tera) digestive tract
en·ter·os·to·my (*plural* ·mies)
en·ter·ot·omy (*plural* ·omies)
en·tero·vi·rus (*plural* ·ruses)
en·ter·prise
en·ter·pris·er
en·ter·pris·ing
en·ter·tain
en·ter·tain·er
en·ter·tain·ing
en·ter·tain·ing·ly
en·ter·tain·ment
en·thal·py *physics term*
en·thet·ic *medical term*
en·thral (*US* ·thrall; ·thral·ling, ·thralled)
en·thrall·er

en·thral·ling·ly
en·thral·ment (*US* ·thrall·)
en·throne
en·throne·ment
en·thuse
en·thu·si·asm
en·thu·si·ast
en·thu·si·as·tic
en·thu·si·as·ti·cal·ly
en·thy·memat·ic (*or* ·ical)
en·thy·meme *logic term*
en·tice
en·tice·ment
en·tic·er
en·tic·ing·ly
en·tic·ing·ness
en·tire
en·tire·ly
en·tire·ness
en·tirety (*plural* ·tireties)
en·ti·tle
en·ti·tle·ment
en·tity (*plural* ·tities)
ento·blast *embryology term*
ento·blas·tic
ento·derm *variant of* endoderm
ento·der·mal (*or* ·mic)
en·tomb
en·tomb·ment
en·tom·ic of insects
ento·mo·logi·cal (*or* ·log·ic)
ento·molo·gist
ento·mo·lo·gize (*or* ·gise)
ento·mol·ogy study of insects; *compare* etymology
ento·mopha·gous
ento·mophi·lous insect-pollinated
ento·mophi·ly
ento·mos·tra·can crustacean
ento·mos·tra·cous
ento·phyte *variant of* endophyte
ento·phyt·ic *variant of* endophytic
en·top·ic in normal position; *compare* ectopic
en·tou·rage
ento·zo·ic living inside an animal

entozoon

en·to·zo·on (*or* ·an; *plural* ·zoa)
en·tr'acte *French* interval between acts
en·trails
en·train board a train
en·train·ment
en·tram·mel (·mel·ling, ·melled; *US* ·mel·ing, ·meled) obstruct
en·trance
en·trance·ment
en·tranc·ing·ly
en·trant
en·trap (·trap·ping, ·trapped)
en·trap·ment
en·trap·per
en·treat
en·treat·ing·ly
en·treat·ment
en·treaty (*plural* ·treaties)
en·tre·chat ballet movement
en·tre·côte
en·trée
en·tre·mets (*plural* ·mets) dessert
en·trench
en·trench·er
en·trench·ment
en·tre nous *French* between ourselves
en·tre·pôt trading centre
en·tre·pre·neur
en·tre·pre·neur·ial
en·tre·pre·neur·ship
en·tre·sol *French* between floors
en·tro·py (*plural* ·pies) physics term
en·trust
en·trust·ment
en·try (*plural* ·tries)
en·twine
en·twine·ment
enu·cleate remove nucleus
enu·clea·tion
enu·clea·tor
Enu·gu Nigerian city
enu·mer·able countable; *compare* innumerable
enu·mer·ate
enu·mera·tion
enu·mera·tive
enu·mera·tor
enun·ci·abil·ity
enun·ci·able
enun·ci·ate articulate; *compare* annunciate
enun·cia·tion
enun·cia·tive (*or* ·tory)
enun·cia·tor
en·ure *variant spelling of* inure
enu·resis bedwetting
enu·ret·ic
en·vel·op (*verb*)
en·velope (*noun*)
en·vel·op·ment
en·ven·om
en·ven·omed
en·vi·able
en·vi·able·ness
en·vi·ably
en·vi·er
en·vi·ous
en·vi·ous·ness
en·vi·ron (*verb*) encircle
en·vi·ron·ment
en·vi·ron·men·tal
en·vi·ron·men·tal·ism
en·vi·ron·men·tal·ist
en·vi·ron·men·tal·ly
en·vi·rons (*noun*) vicinity
en·vis·age
en·vis·age·ment
en·vi·sion
en·voy
en·vy (*noun, plural* ·vies; *verb* ·vies, ·vy·ing, ·vied)
en·vy·ing·ly
en·wind (·wind·ing, ·wound)
en·womb
en·wrap (*or* ·in; ·wrap·ping, ·wrapped)
en·wreath
en·zo·ot·ic veterinary term
en·zo·oti·cal·ly
en·zy·mat·ic (*or* ·zy·mic)
en·zyme catalyst
en·zy·mo·logi·cal
en·zy·molo·gist
en·zy·mol·ogy
en·zy·moly·sis (*or* ·mo·sis)
en·zy·mo·lyt·ic
eobi·ont biology term
Eocene geological period
Eogene geological period
eohip·pus fossil horse
eolith stone tool
Eolith·ic Stone Age period
eon *US spelling of* aeon
eonism psychiatry term
Eos Greek goddess
eosin (*or* eosine) dye
eosin·ic
eosino·phil blood cell
eosino·phil·ic (*or* eosi·nophi·lous)
Eozo·ic geological period
epact astronomy term
ep·arch Eastern bishop
ep·ar·chial
ep·ar·chy (*or* ·chate; *plural* ·chies *or* ·chates)
ep·aulet (*or* ·aulette)
épée sword
épée·ist
epei·ric (*or* epei·ro·gen·ic, epei·ro·genet·ic) of continental drift
ep·ei·rog·eny (*or* epi·rog·eny, ep·ei·ro·gen·esis)
ep·en·cephal·ic
ep·en·cepha·lon (*plural* ·la) part of brain
epen·thesis (*plural* ·theses) linguistics term
ep·en·thet·ic
epergne table ornament
ep·ex·egesis (*plural* ·egeses) linguistics term
ep·ex·eget·ic (*or* ·egeti·cal)
ep·ex·egeti·cal·ly
ephah Hebrew unit
ephebe Greek youth
ephed·rine (*or* ·rin) alkaloid
ephem·era (*plural* ·eras *or* ·erae) short-lived insect; *compare* emphemeron
ephem·er·al
ephem·er·al·ity (*or* ·al·ness)
ephem·er·id mayfly
ephem·er·is (*plural* eph·emer·ides) astronomical table

ephem·er·on (*plural* **·era** *or* **·er·ons**) transitory thing; *compare* **ephemera**
Ephesian
Eph·esus ancient Greek city
ephod vestment
eph·or Greek magistrate
epi·blast embryology term
epi·blas·tic
epi·bol·ic
epibo·ly (*plural* **·lies**) embryology term
epic
epi·ca·lyx (*plural* **·lyxes** *or* **·ly·ces**) botany term
epi·can·thus (*plural* **·thi**) anatomy term
epi·car·di·ac (*or* **·dial**)
epi·car·dium (*plural* **·dia**) anatomy term
epi·carp (*or* **exo·**) botany term
epi·cene
epi·cen·ism
epi·cen·tral
epi·cen·tre (*US* **·ter**)
epi·clesis theology term
epi·con·ti·nen·tal
epi·cot·yl botany term
epi·cri·sis medical term
epi·crit·ic anatomy term
epi·cure
Epi·cu·rean of Epicurus
epi·cu·rean devoted to pleasure
Epi·cu·rean·ism
epi·cur·ism (*or* **·cu·rean·ism**)
epi·cy·cle
epi·cy·clic (*or* **·cli·cal**)
epi·cy·cloid geometric curve
epi·cy·cloid·al
Epi·daur·us Greek port
epi·deic·tic (*or* **·dic·tic**) rhetorical term
epi·dem·ic widespread disease; *compare* **endemic**
epi·demi·cal
epi·demio·logi·cal
epi·demi·olo·gist
epi·demi·ol·ogy
epi·der·mal (*or* **·mic**, **·moid**)
epi·der·mis
epi·dia·scope projector

epi·didy·mal
epi·di·dy·mis (*plural* **·dymi·des**) anatomy term
epi·dote mineral
epi·dot·ic
epi·dur·al anaesthetic
epi·fo·cal geology term
epi·gas·tric (*or* **·trial**)
epi·gas·trium (*plural* **·tria**) abdominal part
epi·geal (*or* **·gean**, **·geous**) botany term
epi·gene formed at earth's surface
epi·gen·esis biology theory
epi·gen·esist (*or* **epig·enist**)
epi·genet·ic
epi·geneti·cal·ly
epig·enous
epi·glot·tal (*or* **·tic**)
epi·glot·tis (*plural* **·tises** *or* **·ti·des**) anatomy term
epi·gone (*or* **·gon**) imitator
epi·gram saying
epi·gram·mat·ic
epi·gram·mati·cal·ly
epi·gram·ma·tism
epi·gram·ma·tist
epi·gram·ma·tize (*or* **·tise**)
epi·graph inscription
epig·ra·pher
epi·graph·ic (*or* **·graphi·cal**)
epi·graphi·cal·ly
epig·ra·phist
epig·ra·phy
epigy·nous botany term
epigy·ny
epi·lep·sy
epi·lep·tic
epi·lep·ti·cal·ly
epi·lep·toid (*or* **·lep·ti·form**)
epi·lim·ni·on lake water
epilo·gist
epi·logue
epi·mere embryology term
epi·mor·phic
epi·mor·pho·sis zoology term
epi·my·sium (*plural* **·sia**) anatomy term
epi·nas·tic

epi·nas·ty (*plural* **·ties**) botany term
epi·neph·rine *US* adrenaline
epi·neu·rial
epi·neu·rium anatomy term
epi·phan·ic
Epipha·ny Christian festival
epipha·ny (*plural* **·nies**) manifestation
epi·phenom·enal
epi·phenom·enal·ism philosophy term
epi·phenom·enal·ist
epi·phenom·enon (*plural* **·ena**)
epi·phragm shell
epi·phys·eal (*or* **·ial**)
epiphy·sis (*plural* **·ses**) anatomy term
epi·phyte botany term
epi·phyt·ic (*or* **·phyti·cal**)
epi·phyti·cal·ly
epi·phy·tot·ic
epi·ro·gen·ic (*or* **·genet·ic**) variants of **epeirogenic**
epi·rog·eny variant spelling of **epeirogeny**
Epi·rus Greek region
epis·co·pa·cy (*plural* **·cies**) church government
epis·co·pal
epis·co·pa·lian
epis·co·pa·lian·ism
epis·co·pal·ism
epis·co·pal·ly
epis·co·pate
epi·scope projector
epi·semat·ic zoology term
epi·si·oto·my (*plural* **·mies**) medical term
epi·sode
epi·sod·ic (*or* **·sodi·cal**)
epi·sodi·cal·ly
epi·some
epi·spas·tic producing a blister
epi·sta·sis medical term
epi·stat·ic
epi·stax·is nosebleed
ep·is·tem·ic relating to knowledge
epis·temo·logi·cal
epis·temolo·gist
epis·temol·ogy

episternum

epi·ster·num (*plural* ·na) breastbone part
epis·tle
epis·tler (*or* ·to·ler, ·to·list)
epis·to·lary (*or* epi·stol·ic, epis·to·la·tory)
epis·to·ler
epis·tro·phe rhetorical term
epi·style architectural term
epi·taph inscription
epi·taph·ic
epi·taph·ist
epita·sis drama term
epi·tax·ial
epi·taxy (*or* ·tax·is) crystal growth
epi·tha·lam·ic
epi·tha·la·mium (*or* ·mi·on; *plural* ·mia) nuptial ode
epi·thelial (*or* ·theli·oid)
epi·thelio·ma (*plural* ·mas *or* ·ma·ta) tumour
epi·theli·oma·tous
epi·thelium (*plural* ·thelia) tissue
epi·thet
epi·thet·ic (*or* theti·cal)
epito·me typical example
epi·tom·ic (*or* ·tomi·cal)
epito·mist
epito·mi·za·tion (*or* ·sa·tion)
epito·mize (*or* ·mise)
epito·miz·er (*or* ·mis·er)
epi·zo·ic zoology term
epi·zo·ism
epi·zo·ite
epi·zo·on (*plural* ·zoa) animal parasite
epi·zo·ot·ic veterinary term
epi·zo·oti·cal·ly
ep·och
ep·och·al
epoch-making
ep·ode prosody term
epo·nym something named after a person
epony·mous (*or* epo·nym·ic)
epony·my
épo·pée (*or* epo·poeia) poem
epos body of poetry
epox·ide

epoxy
Ep·ping
Ep·si·lon astronomy term
ep·si·lon Greek letter
Ep·som
epyl·li·on (*plural* ·lia) poem
eq·uabil·ity (*or* ·uable·ness)
eq·uable
eq·uably
equal (equal·ling, equalled; *US* equal·ing, equaled)
equal-area cartography term
equali·tar·ian
equali·tari·an·ism
equali·ty (*plural* ·ties)
equali·za·tion (*or* ·sa·tion)
equal·ize (*or* ·ise)
equal·iz·er (*or* ·is·er)
equal·ly
equa·nim·ity
equani·mous
equat·abil·ity
equat·able
equate
equa·tion
equa·tion·al
equa·tor
equa·to·rial
Equa·to·rial Guinea African republic
eq·uer·ry (*plural* ·ries)
eques·trian
eques·tri·an·ism
eques·tri·enne
equi·an·gu·lar
equi·dis·tance
equi·dis·tant
equi·lat·eral
equili·brant
equili·brate
equi·li·bra·tion
equi·li·bra·tor
equili·brist
equili·bris·tic
equi·lib·rium (*plural* ·riums *or* ·ria)
equi·mo·lecu·lar
equine
equin·ity
equi·noc·tial
equi·nox

equip (equip·ping, equipped)
equi·page carriage
equi·par·ti·tion physics term
equip·ment
equi·poise equilibrium
equi·pol·lence (*or* ·len·cy)
equi·pol·lent equal in effect
equi·pon·der·ance (*or* ·ancy)
equi·pon·der·ant
equi·pon·der·ate counterbalance
equi·po·tent
equi·po·ten·tial physics term
equi·po·ten·ti·al·ity
equip·per
equi·setum (*plural* ·setums *or* ·seta) plant
equi·table
equi·table·ness
equi·tably
equi·tant botany term
equi·ta·tion horsemanship
equi·tes Roman cavalry
equi·ty (*plural* ·ties)
equiva·lence
equi·va·len·cy (*or* ·va·lence) chemistry term
equiva·lent
equivo·cal
equivo·cal·ity (*or* ·ca·cy)
equivo·cal·ly
equivo·cate
equivo·cat·ing·ly
equivo·ca·tion
equivo·ca·tory
equi·voque (*or* ·voke) pun
Equul·eus constellation
era
era·di·ate radiate
era·dia·tion
eradi·cable
eradi·cant
eradi·cate
eradi·ca·tion
eradi·ca·tive
eradi·ca·tor
eras·able
erase
eras·er
era·sion

Eras·ti·an·ism state supremacy over church
eras·ure
Er·bil (*or* **Ir·bil, Ar·bil**) Iraqi city
er·bium chemical element
ere *Poetic* before; *compare* **e'er**
Erebus Greek god
Erech·theum (*or* **·thei·on**) Athenian temple
erect
erect·able
erect·er (*or* **erec·tor**)
erec·tile
erec·til·ity
erec·tion
erect·ness
erec·tor (*or* **·ter**)
er·emite hermit
er·emit·ic (*or* **·emiti·cal**)
er·emit·ism
erep·sin enzyme
er·ethism medical term
er·ethis·mic (*or* **·ethis·tic, ·ethit·ic**)
Er·furt East German city
erg unit
er·ga·toc·ra·cy (*plural* **·cies**) government by workers
ergo *Latin* therefore
er·go·graph muscle-measuring instrument
er·gom·eter dynamometer
er·go·nom·ic
er·go·nom·ics
er·gono·mist
er·gos·terol biochemical compound
er·got crop disease
er·got·ism human disease
eri·ca shrub
eri·ca·ceous
Erida·nus constellation
Erie Canadian lake
erig·er·on plant
Erin *Archaic* Ireland
eri·na·ceous of hedgehogs
Eris Greek goddess
er·is·tic logic term
er·is·ti·cal
Eri·trea Ethiopian province
Eri·trean
erk *Slang* aircraftsman

Er·lang unit
erl·king malevolent spirit
er·mine (*plural* **·mines** *or* **·mine**)
erne eagle
Er·nie computer lottery
erode
erod·ent
ero·genei·ty
erog·enous (*or* **ero·gen·ic**)
Eros
erose uneven
ero·sion
ero·sion·al
ero·sive
ero·sive·ness
ero·tema (*or* **·teme, ·tesis**) rhetorical question
ero·temat·ic (*or* **·tet·ic**)
erot·ic (*or* **eroti·cal**)
eroti·ca
eroti·cal·ly
eroti·cism (*or* **ero·tism**)
ero·to·gen·ic *variant of* erogenous
erot·ol·ogy
ero·to·ma·nia
ero·to·ma·ni·ac
err
er·ran·cy (*plural* **·cies**)
er·rand
er·rant
er·rant·ry (*plural* **·tries**)
er·ra·ta *plural of* erratum
er·rat·ic
er·rati·cal·ly
er·rati·cism
er·ra·tum (*plural* **·ta**) printing error
er·rhine causing nasal secretion
Er Rif Moroccan region
er·ro·neous
er·ro·neous·ness
er·ror
er·satz artificial
Erse Gaelic
erst·while
eru·bes·cence redness
eru·bes·cent
eruct (*or* **eruc·tate**) belch
eruc·ta·tion
eruc·ta·tive
eru·dite

escapement

eru·di·tion (*or* **eru·dite·ness**)
erum·pent bursting out
erupt break out; *compare* irrupt
erupt·ible
erup·tion
erup·tion·al
erup·tive
erup·tiv·ity (*or* **·tive·ness**)
Ery·man·thus Greek mountain
eryn·go (*or* **erin·**; *plural* **·goes** *or* **·gos**) plant
ery·sip·elas skin disease
ery·si·pela·tous
ery·sip·eloid
ery·thema skin redness
ery·themat·ic (*or* **·thema·tous, ·themic**)
eryth·rism abnormal redness
ery·thris·mal
eryth·rite mineral
eryth·ri·tol (*or* **·rite**) drug
eryth·ro·blast marrow cell
eryth·ro·blas·tic
eryth·ro·blas·to·sis blood disease
eryth·ro·cyte blood cell
eryth·ro·cyt·ic
eryth·ro·cy·tom·eter
eryth·ro·cy·tom·etry
eryth·ro·my·cin antibiotic
eryth·ro·poi·esis red blood cell formation
eryth·ro·poi·et·ic
Er·zu·rum Turkish city
Es·bjerg Danish port
es·ca·drille aircraft squadron; *compare* espadrille
es·ca·lade scaling walls
es·ca·lad·er
es·ca·late
es·ca·la·tion
es·ca·la·tor
es·cal·lo·nia shrub
es·cal·lope scallop
es·ca·lope veal slice
es·cap·able
es·ca·pade
es·cape
es·capee
es·cape·ment

escaper

es·cap·er
es·cap·ism
es·cap·ist
es·ca·polo·gist
es·ca·pol·ogy
es·carp fortification
es·carp·ment steep slope
escha·lot shallot
es·char scab
es·cha·rot·ic
es·cha·to·logi·cal
es·cha·tolo·gist
es·cha·tol·ogy theology
es·cheat legal term
es·chew avoid
es·chew·al
es·chew·er
es·co·lar (*plural* ·lars *or* ·lar) fish
Es·co·rial Spanish village
es·cort
es·cri·toire
es·crow legal term
es·cu·do (*plural* ·dos) Portuguese currency
es·cu·lent edible
es·cutch·eon heraldry term
es·cutch·eoned
Es·dra·elon Israeli plain
es·em·plas·tic unifying
es·er·ine alkaloid
Es·fa·han *variant spelling of* Isfahan
Esher
es·ker (*or* ·kar) glacial deposit
Eskil·stu·na Swedish city
Es·ki·mo (*plural* ·mos *or* ·mo)
Es·ki·moan
Es·ki·moid
Es·ki·sehir Turkish city
esopha·gus *US spelling of* oesophagus
eso·ter·ic abstruse; *compare* exoteric
eso·teri·cal·ly
eso·teri·cism
es·pa·drille canvas shoe; *compare* escadrille
es·pal·ier wall-trained tree
es·par·to (*plural* ·tos) grass
es·pe·cial
es·pe·cial·ly
Es·pe·ran·to artificial language
es·pial
espi·er
es·pio·nage
Es·pí·ri·to San·to Brazilian state
Es·pí·ri·tu San·to Pacific island
es·pla·nade
es·pous·al
es·pouse
es·pous·er
es·pres·so (*plural* ·sos) coffee
es·prit liveliness
es·prit de corps group pride
espy (espies, espy·ing, espied)
es·quire
es·say composition; attempt; *compare* assay
es·say·ist
Es·sen West German city
es·sence
Es·sene Jewish sect
es·sen·tial
es·sen·tial·ism philosophical doctrine
es·sen·tial·ist
es·sen·tial·ity (*or* ·ness)
es·sen·tial·ly
Es·sequi·bo South American river
Es·sex
Es·sonne French department
es·tab·lish
es·tab·lish·er
es·tab·lish·ment
es·tab·lish·men·tar·ian
es·tab·lish·men·tar·ian·ism
es·ta·mi·net French café
es·tan·cia ranch
es·tate
es·teem
es·ter chemistry term
es·ter·ase enzyme
es·teri·fi·ca·tion
es·teri·fy (·fies, ·fy·ing, ·fied)
es·ti·mable
es·ti·mable·ness
es·ti·mate
es·ti·ma·tion
es·ti·ma·tive
es·ti·ma·tor
estipu·late (*or* ex·stipu·) botany term
es·thete *US variant spelling of* aesthete
es·thetic *US variant spelling of* aesthetic
es·ti·val *US spelling of* aestival
es·ti·vate *US spelling of* aestivate
Es·to·nia Soviet republic
Es·to·nian
es·top (·top·ping, ·topped) legal term
es·top·page
es·top·pel
es·to·vers legal term
es·trade dais
es·tra·di·ol *US spelling of* oestradiol
es·tra·gon tarragon
es·trange
es·tranged
es·trange·ment
es·trang·er
es·tray
es·treat legal term
Es·tre·ma·du·ra Spanish region
es·tri·ol *US spelling of* oestriol
es·tro·gen *US spelling of* oestrogen
es·trone *US spelling of* oestrone
es·trous *US spelling of* oestrous
es·trus *US spelling of* oestrus
es·tu·ar·ial
es·tua·rine
es·tu·ary (*plural* ·aries)
esu·ri·ence (*or* ·en·cy)
esu·ri·ent greedy
eta Greek letter
etae·rio (*plural* ·rios) botany term
éta·gère *French* ornament stand
eta·lon physics device
eta·mine (*or* ·min) fabric
et cet·era and so on

et·cet·eras (*plural noun*)
extra things
etch
etch·ant etching acid
etch·er
etch·ing
eter·nal
eter·nal·ity (*or* ·ness)
eter·nali·za·tion (*or*
eter·ni·, ·sa·tion)
eter·nal·ize (*or* eter·nize,
·ise)
eter·nal·ly
eter·nity (*plural* ·nities)
ete·sian meteorology term
ethane
ethane·di·ol
etha·nol
eth·ene *variant of* ethylene
ether anaesthetic
ether (*or* aether)
hypothetical medium
ethe·real
ethe·real·ity (*or* ·ness)
ethe·reali·za·tion (*or*
·sa·tion)
ethe·real·ize (*or* ·ise)
ethe·real·ly
ether·ic
etheri·fi·ca·tion
etheri·fy (·fies, ·fy·ing,
·fied)
etheri·za·tion (*or* ·sa·tion)
ether·ize (*or* ·ise)
ether·iz·er (*or* ·is·er)
eth·ic
ethi·cal
ethi·cal·ly
ethi·cal·ness (*or* ·cali·ty)
ethi·cist
ethi·cize (*or* ·cise)
eth·ics
Ethio·pia
Ethio·pian
Ethio·pic
eth·moid facial bone
eth·moi·dal
eth·narch Roman ruler
eth·nar·chy (*plural* ·chies)
eth·nic (*or* ·ni·cal)
eth·ni·cal·ly
eth·no·bota·ny botanical folklore
eth·no·cen·tric
eth·no·cen·tri·cal·ly

eth·no·cen·tric·ity
eth·no·cen·trism belief in
group's superiority
eth·no·gen·ic
eth·nog·enist
eth·nog·eny origin of races
eth·nog·ra·pher
eth·no·graph·ic (*or*
·graphi·cal)
eth·no·graphi·cal·ly
eth·nog·ra·phy
anthropology term
eth·no·log·ic (*or* ·logi·cal)
eth·nolo·gist
eth·nol·ogy study of races;
compare ethology
etho·log·ic (*or* ·logi·cal)
etho·logi·cal·ly
etholo·gist
ethol·ogy study of animal
behaviour; *compare*
ethnology
etho·none chemical
compound
ethos
eth·ox·ide
eth·oxy·ethane
ethyl
eth·yl·ate
eth·yla·tion
eth·yl·ene (*or* eth·ene)
eth·yl·enic
ethyl·ic
ethyne chemical compound
etio·late
etio·la·tion
eti·ol·ogy *US spelling of*
aetiology
eti·quette
Etna
Eton
Eto·nian
Etru·ria ancient Italian
country
Etrus·can (*or* Etru·rian)
étude musical composition
étui needle case
ety·mo·logi·cal (*or* ·log·ic)
ety·molo·gist
ety·mol·ogy (*plural*
·ogies) study of words;
compare entomology
ety·mon (*plural* ·mons *or*
·ma) original word form
Etzel legendary king

eubac·te·ria (*sing.* ·rium)
Euboea Greek island
Euboean
eucaine anaesthetic
euca·lyp·tol (*or* ·tole)
essential oil
euca·lyp·tus (*or* ·lypt;
plural ·tuses, ·ti *or*
·lypts)
eucha·ris plant
Eucha·rist sacrament
Eucha·ris·tic (*or* ·ti·cal)
Eucha·ris·ti·cal·ly
euchlo·rine (*or* ·rin)
explosive gas
euchre US card game
euchro·mat·ic
euchro·ma·tin chromosome
part
Euclid·ean (*or* ·ian)
eudemon benevolent spirit
eudemo·nia (*or*
eudaemo·) happiness
eudemon·ic (*or*
eudaemon·)
eudemon·ics (*or*
eudaemon·)
eudemon·ism (*or*
eudaemon·)
eudemon·is·ti·cal·ly (*or*
eudaemon·)
eudi·om·eter chemistry
term
eudio·met·ric (*or* ·ri·cal)
eudio·met·ri·cal·ly
eudi·om·etry
eugen·ic (*or* eugeni·cal)
eugeni·cal·ly
eugeni·cist
eugen·ics
eugenol essential oil
euglena protozoan
euhe·mer·ism study of
myths
euhe·mer·ist
euhe·mer·is·tic
euhe·mer·is·ti·cal·ly
euhe·mer·ize (*or* ·ise)
eula·chon (*or* ·chan;
plural ·chons, ·chon *or*
·chans, ·chan) fish
eulo·gia holy bread
eulo·gist (*or* ·giz·er,
·gis·er)
eulo·gis·tic (*or* ·ti·cal)
eulo·gis·ti·cal·ly

eulogize

eulo·gize (or ·gise)
eulogy (plural eulogies)
Eumeni·des Greek Furies
eunuch
euony·mus (or evony·) tree
eupa·to·rium plant
eupat·rid Greek landowner
eupep·sia (or ·sy) good digestion
eupep·tic
euphau·si·id crustacean
euphemism inoffensive word; compare euphuism
euphemist
euphemis·tic (or ·ti·cal)
euphemis·ti·cal·ly
euphemize (or euphemise)
euphemiz·er (or euphemis·er)
euphon·ic (or euphoni·cal)
euphoni·cal·ly
eupho·ni·ous
eupho·ni·ous·ly
eupho·ni·ous·ness
eupho·nium musical instrument
eupho·nize (or ·nise)
eupho·ny (plural ·nies) pleasing sound
euphor·bia plant
euphor·bia·ceous
eupho·ria elation
eupho·ri·ant
euphor·ic
euphori·cal·ly
eupho·tic ecology term
euphra·sy (plural ·sies) plant
Euphra·tes Asian river
euphroe (or uphroe) nautical term
Euphrosyne Greek goddess
euphuism prose style; compare euphemism
euphu·ist
euphu·is·tic (or ·ti·cal)
euphu·is·ti·cal·ly
euplas·tic healing quickly
euploid biology term
eup·noea (US ·nea) normal breathing
eup·noe·ic (US ·ne·)

Eura·sia
Eura·sian
Eur·at·om European Atomic Energy Commission
Eure French department
Eure-et-Loir French department
eureka
eurhyth·mic (or ·mi·cal)
eurhyth·mics
eurhyth·my
euri·pus (plural ·pi) channel
Euroc·ly·don biblical wind
Euro·com·mun·ism
Euro·crat EEC administrator
Euro·dol·lar
Euro·mar·ket (or ·mart)
Eu·ro·pa satellite of Jupiter
Europa mythological character
Europe
Euro·pean
Euro·pean·ism
Euro·peani·za·tion (or ·sa·tion)
Euro·pean·ize (or ·ise)
euro·pium chemical element
Euro·poort Dutch port
Euro·vis·ion broadcasting network
Eurus mythological wind
Eurydice dryad
euryp·ter·id extinct animal
eury·ther·mal (or ·mic, ·mous) ecology term
eury·trop·ic ecology term
euspo·ran·gi·ate botany term
Eusta·chian tube anatomy term
eusta·sy
eustat·ic geology term
eustati·cal·ly
eutec·tic (or ·toid) physics term
Euterpe Greek Muse
eutha·na·sia
euthen·ics environmental study
euthen·ist
euthe·rian zoology term
eutroph·ic ecology term
eutrophi·ca·tion

154

eux·enite mineral
evacu·ant
evacu·ate
evacu·ation
evacu·ative
evacu·ator
evac·uee
evad·able (or ·ible)
evade
evad·er
evad·ing·ly
evagi·nate turn inside out
evagi·na·tion
evalu·ate
evalu·ation
evalu·ative
evalu·ator
eva·nesce fade gradually
eva·nes·cence
eva·nes·cent
evan·gel gospel
evan·geli·cal
evan·geli·cal·ism
evan·geli·cal·ly
evan·gelism
evan·gelist
evan·gelis·tic
evan·gelis·ti·cal·ly
evan·geli·za·tion (or ·sa·tion)
evan·gelize (or ·gelise)
evan·geliz·er (or ·gelis·er)
Ev·ans·ville US city
evapo·rabil·ity
evapo·rable
evapo·rate
evapo·ra·tion
evapo·ra·tive
evapo·ra·tor
evapo·rim·eter (or ·rom·)
evapo·rite rock
evapo·tran·spi·ra·tion
eva·sion
eva·sive
eva·sive·ness
eve
evec·tion astronomy term
evec·tion·al
even
even-handed
even-handed·ness
eve·ning
even·ness
evens betting term
even·song

event
even-tempered
event·ful
event·ful·ly
event·ful·ness
even·tide
even·tual
even·tu·al·ity (*plural* ·ities)
even·tu·al·ly
even·tu·ate result in
even·tua·tion
ever
Ev·er·est
Ever·glades Florida region
ever·green
ever·lasting
ever·lasting·ness
ever·more
ever·sible
ever·sion
evert turn inside out
evert·or muscle
every
every·body
every·day
Every·man medieval play
every·one
every·thing
every·where
Eve·sham
evict
evic·tion
evic·tor
evi·dence
evi·dent
evi·den·tial
evi·den·tial·ly
evi·dent·ly
evil
evil·doer
evil·doing
evil·ly
evil-minded
evil-minded·ness
evil·ness
evince
evin·cible
evin·cive
evis·cer·ate disembowel
evis·cera·tion
evis·cera·tor
evo·cable
evo·ca·tion
evoca·tive

evoca·tive·ness
evo·ca·tor biology term
evoke
evok·er
evo·lute geometry term
evo·lu·tion
evo·lu·tion·ary (*or* ·al)
evo·lu·tion·ism
evo·lu·tion·ist
evo·lu·tion·is·tic
evolv·able
evolve
evolve·ment
evolv·er
evony·mus *variant spelling of* euonymus
ev·zone Greek soldier
ewe
ewe-neck
ewer
ex
ex·ac·er·bate aggravate
ex·ac·er·bat·ing·ly
ex·ac·er·ba·tion
ex·act
ex·act·able
ex·act·ing
ex·act·ing·ness
ex·ac·tion
ex·acti·tude
ex·act·ly
ex·act·ness
ex·ac·tor (*or* ·ter)
ex·ag·ger·ate
ex·ag·ger·at·ed
ex·ag·ger·at·ed·ly
ex·ag·ger·at·ing·ly
ex·ag·gera·tion
ex·ag·gera·tive (*or* ·tory)
ex·ag·gera·tor
ex·alt
ex·al·ta·tion
ex·alt·ed
ex·alt·ed·ly
ex·alt·ed·ness
ex·alt·er
exam
exa·men examination of conscience
ex·am·in·able
ex·ami·na·tion
ex·ami·na·tion·al
ex·am·ine
ex·ami·nee
ex·am·in·er

excerption

ex·am·ple
ex·ani·mate
ex·ani·ma·tion
ex·an·thema (*or* ·them; *plural* ·thema·ta, ·themas, *or* ·thems) rash
ex·an·thema·tous (*or* ·themat·ic)
exa·rate entomology term
ex·arch Eastern bishop; botany term
ex·arch·al
ex·arch·ate (*or* ·ar·chy; *plural* ·ates *or* ·chies)
ex·as·per·ate
ex·as·per·at·ed·ly
ex·as·per·at·er
ex·as·per·at·ing·ly
ex·as·pera·tion
Ex·cali·bur magic sword
ex ca·thedra *Latin* with authority
ex·cau·date tailless
ex·ca·vate
ex·ca·va·tion
ex·ca·va·tor
ex·ceed
ex·ceed·able
ex·ceed·er
ex·ceed·ing·ly
ex·cel (·cel·ling, ·celled)
ex·cel·lence
Ex·cel·len·cy (*or* ·lence; *plural* ·cies *or* ·lences) title
ex·cel·lent
ex·cel·si·or
ex·cept
ex·cept·able
ex·cept·ing
ex·cep·tion
ex·cep·tion·able objectionable
ex·cep·tion·able·ness
ex·cep·tion·al very good
ex·cep·tion·al·ity
excep·tion·al·ly
ex·cep·tion·al·ness
ex·cep·tive
ex·cerpt book extract; *compare* exert; exsert
ex·cerpt·er (*or* ·cerp·tor)
ex·cerpt·ible
ex·cerp·tion

excess

ex·cess
ex·ces·sive
ex·ces·sive·ly
ex·ces·sive·ness
ex·change
ex·change·abil·ity
ex·change·able
ex·chang·er
Ex·cheq·uer Treasury
ex·cipi·ent medical term
ex·cis·able
ex·cise
ex·cise·man (plural ·men)
ex·ci·sion
ex·cit·abil·ity (or ·able·ness)
ex·cit·able
ex·cit·ant
ex·ci·ta·tion
ex·cita·tive (or ·tory)
ex·cite
ex·cit·ed
ex·cit·ed·ly
ex·cit·ed·ness
ex·cite·ment
ex·cit·er oscillator
ex·cit·ing
ex·cit·ing·ly
ex·ci·ton chemistry term
ex·ci·tor nerve
ex·claim
ex·claim·er
ex·cla·ma·tion
ex·cla·ma·tion·al
ex·clama·to·ri·ly
ex·clama·tory
ex·claus·tra·tion release of nun or monk
ex·clave
ex·clo·sure
ex·clud·abil·ity
ex·clud·able (or ·ible)
ex·clude
ex·clud·er
ex·clu·sion
ex·clu·sion·ary
ex·clu·sion·ist
ex·clu·sive
ex·clu·sive·ness (or ·sivi·ty)
ex·cogi·tate devise
ex·cog·ita·tion
ex·cogi·ta·tive
ex·cogi·ta·tor
ex·com·muni·cable
ex·com·muni·cate
ex·com·mu·ni·ca·tion
ex·com·mu·ni·ca·tive (or ·tory)
ex·com·mu·ni·ca·tor
ex·co·ri·ate
ex·co·ria·tion
ex·cre·ment
ex·cre·men·tal (or ·ti·tious)
ex·cres·cence
ex·cres·cen·cy (plural ·cies)
ex·cres·cent
ex·cre·ta
ex·cre·tal
ex·crete
ex·cret·er
ex·cre·tion
ex·cre·tive
ex·cre·tory
ex·cru·ci·ate
ex·cru·ci·at·ing
ex·cru·ci·at·ing·ly
ex·cru·cia·tion
ex·cul·pable
ex·cul·pate vindicate
ex·cul·pa·tion
ex·cul·pa·tory
ex·cur·rent flowing outwards
ex·cur·sion
ex·cur·sion·ist
ex·cur·sive
ex·cur·sive·ness
ex·cur·sus (plural ·suses or ·sus) digression
ex·cus·able
ex·cus·able·ness
ex·cus·ably
ex·cusa·tory
ex·cuse
ex-directory (adj)
ex·eat leave of absence
ex·ecrable
ex·ecrable·ness
ex·ecrate loathe
ex·ecra·tion
ex·ecra·tive (or ·tory)
ex·ecut·able
ex·ecu·tant
ex·ecute
ex·ecut·er one who executes something; compare executor
ex·ecu·tion
ex·ecu·tion·er
ex·ecu·tive
ex·ecu·tor trustee of will; compare executer
ex·ecu·to·rial
ex·ecu·tor·ship
ex·ecu·tory legal term
ex·ecu·trix (plural ·tri·ces or ·trixes) female executor
ex·edra continuous bench
ex·egesis (plural ·egeses) Bible interpretation
ex·egete (or ·egetist)
ex·eget·ic (or ·egeti·cal)
ex·egeti·cal·ly
ex·eget·ics
ex·em·plar
ex·em·pla·ri·ly
ex·em·pla·ri·ness
ex·em·pla·ry
ex·em·pli·fi·able
ex·em·pli·fi·ca·tion
ex·em·pli·fi·ca·tive
ex·em·pli·fi·er
ex·em·pli·fy (·fies, ·fy·ing, ·fied)
ex·em·pli gra·tia Latin for the sake of example
ex·em·plum (plural ·pla) example
ex·empt
ex·empt·ible
ex·emp·tion
ex·en·ter·ate remove surgically
ex·en·tera·tion
ex·equa·tur official authorization
ex·equies funeral rites
ex·er·cis·able
ex·er·cise train; use; compare exorcise
ex·er·cis·er
ex·ergual
ex·ergue date on coin
ex·ert make effort; compare excerpt; exsert
ex·er·tion
ex·er·tive
Ex·eter
ex·eunt Latin they leave
ex·fo·li·ate
ex·fo·lia·tion

ex·fo·lia·tive
ex gra·tia *Latin* gratuitous
ex·hal·able
ex·hal·ant
ex·ha·la·tion
ex·hale
ex·haust
ex·haust·er
ex·haust·ibil·ity
ex·haust·ible
ex·haus·tion
ex·haus·tive
ex·haust·ive·ness
ex·hib·it
ex·hi·bi·tion
ex·hi·bi·tion·er scholarship student
ex·hi·bi·tion·ism
ex·hi·bi·tion·ist
ex·hi·bi·tion·is·tic
ex·hibi·tive illustrative
ex·hibi·tor (*or* ·hib·it·er)
ex·hibi·tory
ex·hil·ar·ant
ex·hila·rate
ex·hil·arat·ing·ly
ex·hila·ra·tion
ex·hila·ra·tive (*or* ·tory)
ex·hila·ra·tor
ex·hort
ex·hor·ta·tion
ex·hor·ta·tive (*or* ·tory)
ex·hort·er
ex·hu·ma·tion
ex·hume
ex·hum·er
exi·gen·cy (*or* exi·gence; *plural* ·cies *or* ·gences)
exi·gent urgent
exi·gible required
exi·gu·ity (*or* ex·igu·ous·ness)
ex·igu·ous meagre
ex·ile
ex·il·ic (*or* ·ian)
ex·ist
ex·ist·ence
ex·ist·ent
ex·is·ten·tial
ex·is·ten·tial·ism
ex·is·ten·tial·ist
ex·is·ten·tial·ly
exit
exi·tance physics term

ex li·bris *Latin* from the library of
Ex·moor
exo·bi·olo·gist
exo·bi·ol·ogy astrobiology
exo·cen·tric linguistics term
exo·crine having a duct; *compare* endocrine
exo·derm *variant of* ectoderm
exo·don·tics dentistry
exo·don·tist
Exo·dus Old Testament book
exo·dus
exo·en·zyme
exo·er·gic energy-emitting; *compare* endoergic
ex of·fi·cio *Latin* by right of office
ex·oga·mous (*or* exo·gam·ic)
ex·oga·my marrying into another tribe
ex·og·enous
ex·on·er·ate
ex·on·era·tion
ex·on·era·tive
ex·on·era·tor
exo·nym foreigner's version of placename
exo·pep·ti·dase enzyme
ex·oph·thal·mic
ex·oph·thal·mos (*or* ·mus, ·mia) protrusion of eyeball
exo·rabil·ity
exo·rable moved by pleading
ex·or·bi·tance
ex·or·bi·tant
ex·or·cise (*or* ·cize) expel evil spirit; *compare* exercise
ex·or·cis·er (*or* ·ciz·er)
ex·or·cism
ex·or·cist
ex·or·dial
ex·or·dium (*plural* ·diums *or* ·dia) beginning of speech
exo·skel·etal
exo·skel·eton
ex·os·mo·sis biology term
ex·os·mot·ic (*or* ex·os·mic)

exo·sphere atmospheric layer
exo·spore botany term
exo·spor·ous
ex·os·to·sis (*plural* ·ses) outgrowth from bone
exo·ter·ic comprehensible; *compare* esoteric
exo·teri·cal·ly
exo·teri·cism
exo·ther·mic (*or* ·mal) heat-emitting; *compare* endothermic
exo·ther·mi·cal·ly (*or* ·ther·mal·ly)
ex·ot·ic
ex·oti·ca
ex·oti·cal·ly
ex·oti·cism
ex·ot·ic·ness
exo·tox·ic
exo·tox·in
ex·pand
ex·pand·able (*or* ·ible)
ex·pand·er
ex·panse
ex·pan·sibil·ity
ex·pan·sible
ex·pan·sile
ex·pan·sion
ex·pan·sion·ary
ex·pan·sion·ism
ex·pan·sion·ist
ex·pan·sion·is·tic
ex·pan·sive
ex·pan·sive·ness
ex par·te legal term
ex·pa·ti·ate enlarge upon; *compare* expiate
ex·pa·tia·tion
ex·pa·tia·tor
ex·pat·ri·ate
ex·pat·ria·tion
ex·pect
ex·pect·able
ex·pec·tan·cy (*or* ·tance; *plural* ·cies *or* ·tances)
ex·pec·tant
ex·pec·ta·tion
ex·pec·ta·tive
ex·pec·to·rant
ex·pec·to·rate
ex·pec·to·ra·tion spitting
ex·pec·to·ra·tor

expediency

ex·pedi·en·cy (*or* ·ence; *plural* ·cies *or* ·ences)
ex·pedi·ent
ex·pedi·en·tial
ex·pedite
ex·pedit·er (*or* ·pedi·tor)
ex·pedi·tion
ex·pedi·tion·ary
ex·pedi·tious
ex·pedi·tious·ness
ex·pel (·pel·ling, ·pelled)
ex·pel·lable
ex·pel·lant (*or* ·lent)
ex·pel·lee
ex·pel·ler
ex·pend
ex·pend·abil·ity
ex·pend·able
ex·pend·er
ex·pendi·ture
ex·pense
ex·pen·sive
ex·pen·sive·ness
ex·peri·ence
ex·peri·en·tial
ex·peri·ment
ex·peri·men·tal
ex·peri·men·tal·ism
ex·peri·men·tal·ist
ex·peri·men·tal·ly
ex·peri·men·ta·tion
ex·peri·ment·er
ex·pert
ex·per·tise
ex·pert·ness
ex·pi·able
ex·pi·ate atone; *compare* expatiate
ex·pia·tion
ex·pia·tor
ex·pia·tory
ex·pi·ra·tion
ex·pira·tory of exhalation
ex·pire
ex·pir·er
ex·pi·ry (*plural* ·ries)
ex·plain
ex·plain·able
ex·plain·er
ex·pla·na·tion
ex·plana·to·ri·ly
ex·plana·tory (*or* ·tive)
ex·plant biology term
ex·plan·ta·tion
ex·pletive swear word

ex·pli·cable
ex·pli·cate explain
ex·pli·ca·tion
ex·pli·ca·tive (*or* ·tory)
ex·pli·ca·tor
ex·plic·it
ex·plic·it·ness
ex·plode
ex·plod·er
ex·ploit
ex·ploit·able (*or* ·ploita·tive)
ex·ploi·ta·tion
ex·plo·ra·tion
ex·plora·tory (*or* ·tive)
ex·plore
ex·plor·er
ex·plo·sion
ex·plo·sive
ex·plo·sive·ness
ex·po·nent
ex·po·nen·tial maths term
ex·po·nen·tial·ly
ex·pon·ible needing explanation
ex·port
ex·port·abil·ity
ex·port·able
ex·por·ta·tion
ex·port·er
ex·pos·able
ex·pos·al
ex·pose
ex·po·sé exposure of scandal
ex·posed
ex·pos·ed·ness
ex·pos·er
ex·po·si·tion
ex·po·si·tion·al
ex·posi·tor expounder
ex·posi·to·ri·ly (*or* ·tive·ly)
ex·posi·tory (*or* ·tive)
ex post fac·to *Latin* retrospective
ex·pos·tu·late dissuade
ex·pos·tu·lat·ing·ly
ex·pos·tu·la·tion
ex·pos·tu·la·tor
ex·pos·tu·la·tory (*or* ·tive)
ex·po·sure
ex·pound
ex·pound·er
ex·press

158

ex·press·age conveyance by express
ex·press·er
ex·press·ible
ex·pres·sion
ex·pres·sion·al
ex·pres·sion·ism
ex·pres·sion·ist
ex·pres·sion·is·tic
ex·pres·sion·less
ex·pres·sive
ex·pres·sive·ness
ex·pres·siv·ity
(**expresso**) *incorrect spelling of* espresso
ex·press·way US motorway
ex·pro·pri·able
ex·pro·pri·ate
ex·pro·pria·tion
ex·pro·pria·tor
ex·pul·sion
ex·pul·sive
ex·punc·tion
ex·punge
ex·pung·er
ex·pur·gate
ex·pur·ga·tion
ex·pur·ga·tor
ex·pur·ga·tory (*or* ·to·rial)
ex·quis·ite
ex·quis·ite·ness
ex·san·gui·nate drain blood from
ex·san·guin·ation
ex·san·guine (*or* ·gui·nous)
ex·san·guin·ity
ex·scind (*or* ·sect) cut off
ex·sect cut out
ex·sec·tion
ex·sert protrude; *compare* excerpt; exert
ex·ser·tile
ex·ser·tion
ex·sic·cate dry
ex·sic·ca·tion
ex·sic·ca·tive
ex·sic·ca·tor
ex·stipu·late (*or* es·tipu·late) botany term
(**extasy**) *incorrect spelling of* ecstasy
ex·stro·phy medical term
ex·tant surviving

ex·tem·po·ra·neous (*or*
 ·po·rary)
ex·tem·po·ra·neous·ness
ex·tem·po·rari·ly
ex·tem·po·rari·ness
ex·tem·po·re impromptu
ex·tem·po·ri·za·tion (*or*
 ·sa·tion)
ex·tem·po·rize (*or* ·rise)
ex·tem·po·riz·er (*or*
 ·ris·er)
ex·tend
ex·tend·ed·ness
ex·tend·er
ex·tend·ibil·ity (*or*
 ·abil·ity)
ex·tend·ible (*or* ·able)
ex·ten·sibil·ity (*or*
 ·sible·ness)
ex·ten·sible (*or* ·sile)
ex·ten·sion
ex·ten·sion·al
ex·ten·sion·al·ity (*or* ·ism)
ex·ten·sity psychology term
ex·ten·sive
ex·ten·sive·ness
ex·ten·som·eter (*or* ·sim·)
 physics term
ex·ten·sor muscle
ex·tent
ex·tenu·ate
ex·tenu·at·ing·ly
ex·tenu·ation
ex·tenu·ator
ex·tenu·atory
ex·te·ri·or
ex·te·ri·ori·za·tion (*or*
 ·sa·tion)
ex·te·ri·or·ize (*or* ·ise)
 medical term
ex·ter·mi·nable
ex·ter·mi·nate
ex·ter·mi·na·tion
ex·ter·mi·na·tive (*or*
 ·tory)
ex·ter·mi·na·tor
ex·tern (*or* ·terne) US
 nonresident hospital
 doctor
ex·ter·nal
ex·ter·nal·ism
ex·ter·nal·ist
ex·ter·nal·ity (*plural*
 ·ities)
ex·ter·nali·za·tion (*or*
 ·sa·tion)
ex·ter·nal·ize (*or* ·ise)
ex·ter·nal·ly
ex·tero·cep·tive
ex·tero·cep·tor biology
 term
ex·ter·ri·to·rial
ex·ter·ri·to·ri·al·ity
ex·tinct
ex·tinc·tion
ex·tinc·tive
ex·tine (*or* ·ine) botany
 term
ex·tin·guish
ex·tin·guish·able
ex·tin·guish·ant
ex·tin·guish·er
ex·tin·guish·ment
ex·tir·pate destroy
ex·tir·pa·tion
ex·tir·pa·tive
ex·tir·pa·tor
ex·tol (*US* ·toll; ·tol·ling,
 ·tolled)
ex·tol·ler
ex·tol·ling·ly
ex·tol·ment
ex·tort
ex·tort·er
ex·tor·tion
ex·tor·tion·able
ex·tor·tion·ary
ex·tor·tion·ate
ex·tor·tion·ist (*or* ·er)
ex·tor·tive
ex·tra
extra·ca·noni·cal outside
 scripture
extra·cel·lu·lar
ex·tract
ex·tract·abil·ity (*or*
 ·ibil·ity)
ex·tract·able (*or* ·ible)
ex·trac·tion
ex·trac·tive
ex·trac·tor
extra·cur·ricu·lar
extra·dit·able
extra·dite
extra·di·tion
extra·dos (*plural* ·dos *or*
 ·doses) architecture term
extra·ga·lac·tic
extra·ju·di·cial
extra·mari·tal
extra·mun·dane outside
 the world
extra·mu·ral
extra·neous
extra·neous·ness
extra·nu·clear
extraor·di·nari·ly
extraor·di·nari·ness
ex·traor·di·nary
ex·trapo·late
ex·trapo·la·tion
ex·trapo·la·tive (*or* ·tory)
ex·trapo·la·tor
extra·po·si·tion
extra·sen·so·ry
extra·ter·res·trial
extra·ter·ri·to·rial (*or*
 ex·ter·)
extra·ter·ri·to·ri·al·ity
extra·uter·ine
ex·trava·gance
ex·trava·gant
ex·trava·gan·za
ex·trava·gate *Archaic* roam
ex·trava·ga·tion
ex·trava·sate exude
ex·trava·sa·tion
extra·vas·cu·lar
extra·vehicu·lar outside a
 spacecraft
extra·vert *variant spelling of*
 extrovert
ex·treme
ex·treme·ly
ex·treme·ness
ex·trem·ism
ex·trem·ist
ex·trem·ity (*plural* ·ities)
ex·tri·cable
ex·tri·cate
ex·tri·ca·tion
ex·trin·sic not contained
 within; *compare* intrinsic
ex·trin·si·cal·ly
(extrordinary) *incorrect
 spelling of* extraordinary
ex·trorse (*or* ·tror·sal)
 turned outwards
extro·ver·sion (*or* extra·)
extro·ver·sive (*or* extra·)
extro·vert (*or* extra·)
extro·vert·ed (*or* extra·)
ex·trude
ex·tru·sion
ex·tru·sive

exuberance

exu·ber·ance (*or* ·ancy)
exu·ber·ant
exu·ber·ate
exu·da·tion
exu·da·tive
ex·ude
ex·ult
ex·ult·ant
ex·ul·ta·tion
ex·ult·ing·ly
ex·ur·bia *US* outside suburbs
exu·viae shed skin
exu·vial
exu·vi·ate
exu·via·tion
ex-works excluding delivery cost
eyas nestling hawk
eye (eye·ing *or* ey·ing, eyed)
eye·ball
eye·bath
eye·bolt
eye·bright plant
eye·brow
eye-catcher
eye-catching
eye·cup
eyed
eye·dropper
eye·ful
eye·glass
eye·glasses *US* spectacles
eye·hole
eye·ing (*or* ey·ing)
eye·lash
eye·less
eye·let
eye·let·eer
eye·lid
eye·liner
eye-opener
eye·piece
eye·shade
eye·shot
eye·sight
eye·sore
eye·spot
eye·stalk
eye·strain
eye·tooth (*plural* ·teeth)
eye·wash
eye·witness
eyra animal
Eyre Canadian lake; Australian peninsula
ey·rie (*or* aerie, aery; *plural* ey·ries *or* aeries) eagle's nest; *compare* eerie
ey·rir (*plural* aurar) Icelandic coin

F

fa (*or* fah) musical note
fab
fa·ba·ceous botany term
Fa·bian
Fa·bi·an·ism
fa·ble
fa·bled
fa·bler
fab·ric
fab·ri·cate
fab·ri·ca·tion
fab·ri·ca·tive
fab·ri·ca·tor
Fab·ri·koid (*Trademark*) waterproof fabric
fabu·list teller of fables
fabu·lous
fabu·lous·ness
fa·çade (*or* ·cade)
face
face·able
face·bar wrestling hold
face-centred (*US* -centered) crystallography term
face-harden metallurgy term
face·less
face·less·ness
face-lift
face-off ice hockey term
face·plate lathe part
fac·er
face-saving
fac·et (*verb* ·et·ing, ·et·ed *or* ·et·ting, ·et·ted)
fa·cetiae witty sayings
fa·cetious
fa·cetious·ness
fa·cia *variant spelling of* fascia
fa·cial
fa·cial·ly
fa·cies (*plural* ·cies) appearance; *compare* fasces; fascia
fac·ile
fac·ile·ly
fac·ile·ness
fa·cili·tate
fa·cili·ta·tion
fa·cili·ta·tive
fa·cili·ta·tor
fa·cil·ity (*plural* ·ities)
fac·ing
fac·simi·le (·le·ing, ·led)
fact
fact·ful
fac·tice rubbery material
fac·tion
fac·tion·al
fac·tion·al·ism
fac·tion·al·ist
fac·tious factional; *compare* factitious
fac·tious·ness
fac·ti·tious contrived; *compare* factious; fictitious
fac·ti·tious·ness
fac·ti·tive linguistics term
fac·tor
fac·tor·abil·ity
fac·tor·able
fac·tor·age commission paid to factor
fac·torial
fac·to·ri·al·ly
fac·tor·ing business term
fac·tori·za·tion (*or* ·sa·tion)
fac·tor·ize (*or* ·ise)
fac·tor·ship
fac·to·ry (*plural* ·ries)
fac·to·tum

fac·tual
fac·tu·al·ism
fac·tu·al·ist
fac·tu·al·is·tic
fac·tu·al·ly
fac·tu·al·ness (*or* ·ity)
facu·la (*plural* ·lae) sun spot
facu·lar
fac·ul·ta·tive optional
fac·ul·ty (*plural* ·ties)
fad
fad·able
fad·di·ness
fad·dish
fad·dism
fad·dist
fad·dy (·di·er, ·di·est)
fade
fad·ed
fad·ed·ness
fade-in
fade·less
fade-out
fad·er
fadge *Dialect* agree
fad·ing
fae·cal (*US* fe·)
fae·ces (*US* fe·)
Fa·en·za Italian city
fae·rie (*or* ·ry; *plural* ·ries) *Archaic* fairyland
Fae·roes (*or* Fa·roes) North Atlantic islands
Faero·ese (*or* Faro·; *plural* ·ese)
faff *Slang* fuss
fag (fag·ging, fagged)
fa·ga·ceous botany term
fagged
fag·ging
fag·got (*or esp. US* fag·ot)
fag·got·ing (*or esp. US* fag·ot·) needlework term
fah *variant spelling of* fa
fahl·band rock
Fahr·en·heit temperature scale
faï·ence (*or* fai·) pottery
fail
fail·ing
faille fabric
fail-safe
fail·ure

fain
fai·ne·ance (*or* ·an·cy)
fai·né·ant (*or* ·ne·) idle
faint pale; collapse; *compare* feint
faint·er
faint·ing
faint·ing·ly
faint·ish
faint·ly
faint·ness
faints *variant spelling of* feints
fair just; not dark; event; *compare* fare
Fair·banks Alaskan city
fair·ground
fair·ing
fair·ish
fair·lead (*or* ·leader) nautical term
fair·ly
fair-minded
fair-minded·ness
fair·ness
fair-spoken
fair·way
fair-weather (*adj*)
fairy (*plural* fairies)
fairy·land
fairy-like
fait ac·com·pli (*plural* faits accomplis) *French* something done
faith
faith·ful
faith·ful·ly
faith·ful·ness
faith·less
faith·less·ness
Faiza·bad Afghan city; *variant spelling of* Fyzabad
fake
fak·er one who fakes
fa·kir (*or* ·qir, ·keer) holy man
fa-la refrain
Fa·lange Spanish Fascist movement
Fa·lang·ism
Fa·lan·gist
fal·ba·la gathered frill
fal·cate (*or* ·ci·form) sickle-shaped
fal·chion sword

fal·con
fal·con·er
fal·con·et small falcon
fal·coni·form
fal·con·ry
fal·deral (*or* fal·derol, fol·derol) trifle
fald·stool bishop's seat
Fa·lerii ancient Italian city
Fa·lis·can language
Fal·kirk Scottish town
Falk·land Is·lands
fall (fall·ing, fell, fall·en)
fal·la·cious
fal·la·cious·ness
fal·la·cy (*plural* ·cies)
fal·lal ornament
fal·lal·ery
fall·en
fall·er
fall·fish (*plural* ·fish, ·fishes)
fal·libil·ity (*or* ·lible·ness)
fal·lible
fal·li·bly
Fal·lo·pian tube anatomy term
fall-out
fal·low
fal·low·ness
Fal·mouth Cornish port
false
false-card bridge term
false·hood
false·ly
false·ness
fal·set·to (*plural* ·tos)
false·work framework
fal·sies false breasts
fal·si·fi·able
fal·si·fi·ca·tion
fal·si·fi·er
fal·si·fy (·fies, ·fy·ing, ·fied)
fal·sity (*plural* ·sities)
falt·boat collapsible boat
fal·ter
fal·ter·er
fal·ter·ing·ly
Fa·lun Swedish city
Fa·ma·gu·sta Cypriot port
fame
fa·mil·ial
fa·mili·ar
fa·mili·ar·ity (*plural* ·ities)

familiarization

fa·mil·iari·za·tion (or
  ·sa·tion)
fa·mil·iar·ize (or ·ise)
fa·mil·iar·iz·er (or ·is·er)
fa·mili·ar·ness
Fami·list member of sect
fa·mille Chinese porcelain
fami·ly (plural ·lies)
fam·ine
fam·ish
fam·ish·ment
fa·mous
fa·mous·ness
famu·lus (plural ·li)
  sorcerer's attendant
fan (fan·ning, fanned)
Fana·ga·lo (or ·ka·lo)
  African language
fa·nat·ic
fa·nati·cal
fa·nati·cal·ly
fa·nati·cism
fa·nati·cize (or ·cise)
fan·cied
fan·ci·er
fan·ci·ful
fan·ci·ful·ly
fan·ci·ful·ness
fan·ci·ly
fan·ci·ness
fan·cy (adj ·ci·er, ·ci·est;
  noun, plural ·cies; verb
  ·cies, ·cy·ing, ·cied)
fancy-free
fancy·work
fan·dan·gle ornament
fan·dan·go (plural ·gos)
  dance
fan·fare
fang
fanged
fan·go mud from thermal
  springs
fan·ion surveyor's flag
fan·jet jet engine
fan·kle Scot entangle
fan·light
fanned
fan·ner
fan·ning
fan·ny (plural ·nies) Slang
  female genitals
fan·on vestment
fan·tail
fan-tailed

fan-tan game
fan·ta·sia
fan·ta·size (or ·sise)
fan·tast visionary
fan·tas·tic (or ·ti·cal)
fan·ta·sy (or phan·; noun,
  plural ·sies; verb ·sies,
  ·sy·ing, ·sied)
Fan·ti (plural ·tis or ·ti)
  Ghanaian people
fan·toc·ci·ni marionettes
far (far·ther or fur·ther,
  far·thest or fur·thest)
far·ad unit
fara·day unit
fa·rad·ic physics term
fara·dism medical use of
  electricity
fara·di·za·tion (or
  ·sa·tion)
fara·dize (or ·dise)
fara·diz·er (or ·dis·er)
far·an·dole dance
far·away
farce
far·ceur (fem ·ceuse) farce
  writer
far·ci stuffed
far·ci·cal
far·ci·cal·ity (or ·ness)
far·ci·cal·ly
far·cy (plural ·cies) animal
  disease
far·del bundle
fare payment; food; to
  manage; compare fair
Fare·ham Hampshire town
far·er
fare·well
far-fetched
far-flung
fa·ri·na flour
fari·na·ceous containing
  starch
fari·nose flourlike
farl (or farle) cake
farm
farm·able
farm·er
farm·house
farm·ing
farm·land
farm·stead
farm·yard

162

Farn·bor·ough Hampshire
  town
far·nesol chemical
  compound
far·ness
Farn·ham Surrey town
faro card game
Fa·roes variant spelling of
  Faeroes
Faro·ese variant spelling of
  Faeroese
far-off
fa·rouche sullen
far·ragi·nous
far·ra·go (plural ·goes)
  hotchpotch
far-reaching
far·ri·er
far·ri·ery (plural ·eries)
far·row
far-seeing
far-sighted
far-sighted·ly
far-sighted·ness
fart
far·ther (or fur·) more
  distant; compare further
farther·most
far·thest (or fur·)
far·thing
far·thin·gale hoop under
  skirt
fart·lek sports term
fas·ces (plural noun; sing.
  ·cies) Roman insignia;
  compare facies
fas·cia (or fa·cia; plural
  ·ciae) flat surface; fibrous
  tissue; compare facies
fas·cial (or fa·cial)
fas·ci·ate (or ·at·ed)
fas·cia·tion botany term
fas·ci·cle bundle
fas·ci·cled
fas·cicu·lar (or ·late)
fas·cicu·la·tion
fas·ci·cule instalment
fas·ci·cu·lus (plural ·li)
fas·ci·nate
fas·ci·nat·ed·ly
fas·ci·nat·ing
fas·ci·na·tion
fas·ci·na·tive
fas·cine bundle of sticks
fas·cism

fas·cist
fa·scis·tic
fa·scis·ti·cal·ly
fash *Scot* worry
fash·ion
fash·ion·able
fash·ion·ably
fash·ion·able·ness
fash·ion·er
Fa·sho·da Sudanese town
fast
fast·back car
fast-breeder nuclear reactor
fas·ten
fas·ten·er
fas·ten·ing
fast·er
fas·tidi·ous
fas·tidi·ous·ness
fas·tigi·ate (*or* ·at·ed) biology term
fast·ness
fat (fat·ter, fat·test)
fa·tal
fa·tal·ism
fa·tal·ist
fa·tal·is·tic
fa·tal·is·ti·cal·ly
fa·tal·ity (*plural* ·ities)
fa·tal·ly
fat·back pork fat
fate
fat·ed
fate·ful
fate·ful·ly
fate·ful·ness
Fates Greek goddesses
fat·head
fa·ther
father·hood
father-in-law (*plural* fathers-)
father·land
fa·ther·less
father-like
fa·ther·li·ness
fa·ther·ly
fath·om
fath·om·able
fath·om·er
Fa·thom·eter (*Trademark*)
fath·om·less
fa·tid·ic (*or* ·tidi·cal) prophetic

fati·gabil·ity (·gable·ness)
fa·tig·able
fa·tigue (·tigu·ing, ·tigued)
fat·ling fattened young animal
fat·ness
Fat·shan Chinese city
fat·so (*plural* ·sos *or* ·soes)
fat-soluble
fat·ted
fat·ten
fat·ten·able
fat·ten·er
fat·ti·ly
fat·ti·ness
fat·tish
fat·ty (*adj* ·ti·er, ·ti·est; *noun, plural* ·ties)
fa·tui·tous fatuous; *compare* fortuitous
fa·tu·ity (*plural* ·ities)
fatu·ous
fatu·ous·ness
fau·bourg French suburb
fau·cal (*or* ·cial)
fau·ces (*plural* ·ces) anatomy term
fau·cet *US* tap
faugh exclamation
fault
fault-finder
fault-finding
faulti·ly
faulti·ness
fault·less
fault·less·ness
faulty (faulti·er, faulti·est)
faun Roman deity; *compare* fawn
fau·na (*plural* ·nas *or* ·nae) animals
fau·nal
Faust (*or* Faustus) legendary magician
Faust·ian
faute de mieux *French* lacking better
fau·teuil armchair
Fauv·ism art movement
Fauv·ist
faux pas (*plural* faux pas)

fa·veo·late honeycombed
fa·vo·nian of the west wind
fa·vour (*US* ·vor)
fa·vour·able (*US* ·vor)
fa·vour·ably (*US* ·vor·)
fa·vour·able·ness (*US* ·vor·)
fa·vour·er (*US* ·vor·)
fa·vour·ing·ly (*US* ·vor·)
fa·vour·ite (*US* ·vor·)
fa·vour·it·ism (*US* ·vor·)
Fav·rile glass
fa·vus skin disease
fawn animal; colour; cringe; *compare* faun
fawn·er
fawn·ing·ly
fax facsimile transmission
fay fairy; *compare* fey
fay·al·ite mineral
faze *US* disconcert
fe·al·ty (*plural* ·ties) feudal loyalty
fear
fear·er
fear·ful
fear·ful·ly
fear·ful·ness
fear·less
fear·less·ness
fear·nought (*or* ·naught) fabric
fear·some
fear·some·ly
fear·some·ness
fea·sibil·ity (*or* ·sible·ness)
fea·sible
fea·sibly
feast
feast·er
feat exploit; *compare* feet
feath·er
feather·bed (·bedding, ·bedded)
feather·bedding overmanning
feather·brain
feather·brained
feather·edge
feath·er·ing
feather·stitch
feather-veined
feather·weight
feath·ery

feature

fea·ture
feature-length (*adj*)
fea·ture·less
fea·ture·less·ness
feaze nautical term
fe·bric·ity
feb·ri·fa·cient
fe·brif·ic (*or* ·brif·er·ous)
fe·brifu·gal
feb·ri·fuge fever-reducing drug
fe·brile feverish
fe·bril·ity
Feb·ru·ary (*plural* ·aries)
fe·cal *US spelling of* faecal
fe·ces *US spelling of* faeces
fe·cit *Latin* made it
feck·less
feck·less·ness
fecu·la (*plural* ·lae) starch
fecu·lence
fecu·lent filthy
fe·cund fertile
fe·cun·date
fe·cun·da·tion
fe·cun·da·tor
fe·cun·da·tory
fe·cun·dity
fed
fe·da·yee (*plural* ·yeen) Arab commando
fed·er·al
fed·er·al·ly
fed·er·al·ism
fed·er·al·ist
fed·er·al·is·tic
fed·er·ali·za·tion (*or* ·sa·tion)
fed·er·al·ize (*or* ·ise)
fed·er·ate
fed·era·tion
fed·era·tive
fe·do·ra hat
fee (fee·ing, feed)
fee·ble
feeble-minded
feeble-minded·ly
feeble-minded·ness
fee·ble·ness
feed (feed·ing, fed)
feed·able
feed·back
feed·bag
feed·er
feed·lot

feel (feel·ing, felt)
feel·er
feel·ing
feet *plural of* foot; *compare* feat
feeze *Dialect* beat
feign
feign·er
feign·ing·ly
feint mock action; printing term; *compare* faint
feints (*or* faints) whisky residue
feld·spar (*or* fel·spar) mineral
feld·spath·ic (*or* fel·)
feld·spath·ose (*or* fel·)
fe·li·cif·ic making happy
fe·lici·tate
fe·lici·ta·tion
fe·lici·ta·tor
fe·lici·tous apt
fe·lici·tous·ness
fe·lic·ity (*plural* ·ities)
fe·lid animal
fe·line
fe·lin·ity (*or* ·line·ness)
fell
fell·able
fel·lah (*plural* ·lahs, ·la·hin, *or* ·la·heen) Arab peasant
fel·la·tio oral sex
fell·er
fell·monger animal skin dealer
fel·loe (*or* ·ly; *plural* ·loes *or* ·lies) wheel segment
fel·low
fel·low·ship
felo de se (*plural* fe·lo·nes de se *or* fe·los de se) suicide
fel·on
fe·lo·ni·ous
fe·lo·ni·ous·ness
fel·on·ry (*plural* ·ries)
felo·ny (*plural* ·nies)
fel·site (*or* ·stone) rock
fel·sit·ic
felt
felt·ing
fe·luc·ca boat
fel·wort plant
fe·male

fe·male·ness
feme woman (*in legal contexts*)
femi·nine
femi·nine·ly
femi·nin·ity
femi·nism
femi·nist
femi·ni·za·tion (*or* ·sa·tion)
femi·nize (*or* ·nise)
femme de cham·bre (*plural* femmes de cham·bre) chambermaid
femme fa·tale (*plural* femmes fa·tales) seductive woman
femo·ral of the thigh
fe·mur (*plural* ·murs *or* femo·ra) thigh bone
fen
fence
fenc·er
fenc·ing
fend
fend·er
fend·ered
fen·es·tel·la (*plural* ·lae) wall niche
fe·nes·tra (*plural* ·trae) biology term
fe·nes·tral
fe·nes·trat·ed (*or* ·trate) having windows
fen·es·tra·tion
Fe·nian Irish revolutionary
fen·nec fox
fen·nel
fennel-flower
fen·ny marshy
Fenrir (*or* Fenris, Fenriswolf) mythological wolf
Fens
fenu·greek plant
feoff *variant spelling of* fief
fe·ral (*or* ·rine) wild
fer·bam fungicide
fer-de-lance snake
fer·etory (*plural* ·etories) shrine
Fer·ga·na Asian region
fe·ria (*plural* ·rias *or* ·riae) weekday
fe·rial
fe·rine *variant of* feral

fer·ity wildness
Fer·man·agh Northern Irish county
fer·ma·ta (*plural* **·tas** *or* **·te**) musical term
fer·ment undergo fermentation; *compare* **foment**
fer·ment·abil·ity
fer·ment·able
fer·men·ta·tion
fer·menta·tive
fer·menta·tive·ness
fer·ment·er
fer·mi unit
fer·mi·on particle
fer·mium radioactive element
fern
fern·ery (*plural* **·eries**)
ferny
fe·ro·cious
fe·roc·ity (*or* **·ro·cious·ness**)
Fer·ra·ra Italian city
fer·rate chemistry term
fer·reous containing iron
fer·ret
fer·ret·ing silk tape
fer·ret·er
fer·rety
fer·ri·age
fer·ric chemistry term
fer·ri·cy·an·ic acid
fer·ri·cya·nide
fer·rif·er·ous producing iron
fer·ri·mag·net·ic
fer·ri·mag·net·ism
Fer·ris wheel fairground wheel
fer·rite ceramic
fer·ri·tin protein
fer·ro·cene chemical compound
fer·ro·chro·mium (*or* **fer·ro·chrome**)
fer·ro·con·crete
fer·ro·cy·an·ic acid
fer·ro·cya·nide
fer·ro·elec·tric
fer·ro·elec·tri·cal·ly
fer·ro·elec·tric·ity
fer·ro·mag·ne·sian
fer·ro·mag·net·ic
fer·ro·mag·net·ism
fer·ro·man·ga·nese
fer·ro·sili·con
fer·ro·type photography term
fer·rous
fer·ru·gi·nous containing iron
fer·rule (*or* **fer·ule**) metal cap; *compare* **ferule**
fer·ry (*noun, plural* **·ries**; *verb* **·ries, ·ry·ing, ·ried**)
fer·tile
fer·til·ity (*or* **·tile·ness**)
fer·ti·liz·able (*or* **·lis·able**)
fer·ti·li·za·tion (*or* **·sa·tion**)
fer·ti·lize (*or* **·lise**)
fer·ti·liz·er (*or* **·lis·er**)
feru·la (*plural* **·las** *or* **·lae**) plant
feru·la·ceous
fer·ule flat cane; *compare* **ferrule**
fer·ven·cy
fer·vent (*or* **·vid**)
fer·vent·ly (*or* **·vid·ly**)
fer·vid *variant of* **fervent**
fer·vour (*US* **·vor**)
fes·cue grass
fesse (*or* **fess**) heraldry term
fes·tal festive
fes·ter
fes·ti·na·tion quickening of gait
fes·ti·val
fes·tive
fes·tive·ly
fes·tive·ness
fes·tiv·ity (*plural* **·ities**)
fes·toon
fes·toon·ery
fest·schrift (*plural* **·schrift·en** *or* **·schrifts**) commemorative writings
feta cheese
fe·tal (*or* **foe·**)
fe·ta·tion (*or* **foe·**) pregnancy
fetch
fetch·er
fetch·ing
fête (*or* **fete**)

fiacre

fe·tial (*plural* **fe·tia·les**) Roman herald
fet·ich *variant spelling of* **fetish**
fe·ti·cid·al (*or* **foe·**)
fe·ti·cide (*or* **foe·**) destruction of fetus
fet·id (*or* **foet·**) foul-smelling
fe·tipa·rous (*or* **foe·**) of marsupial birth
fet·ish (*or* **·ich**)
fet·ish·ism (*or* **·ich·**)
fet·ish·ist (*or* **·ich·**)
fet·lock (*or* **fetter·**) part of horse's leg
fe·tor (*or* **foe·**) stench
fet·ter
fet·ter·er
fet·ter·less
fet·tle
fet·tling refractory material
fet·tu·ci·ne (*or* **·tuc·ci·, tu·ci·ni**) pasta
fe·tus (*or* **foe·**; *plural* **·tuses**)
feud
feu·dal
feu·dal·ism
feu·dal·ist
feu·dal·is·tic
feu·dal·ity (*plural* **·ities**)
feu·dali·za·tion (*or* **·sa·tion**)
feu·dal·ize (*or* **·ise**)
feu·da·tory
feud·ist
feuil·le·ton review section of paper
feuil·le·ton·ism
feuil·le·ton·ist
feuil·le·ton·is·tic
fe·ver
fe·vered
fe·ver·few plant
fe·ver·ish (*or* **·ous**)
fe·ver·ish·ness
fever·wort plant
few
few·ness
fey whimsical; *compare* **fay**
fez (*plural* **fez·zes**)
Fez·zan Libyan region
fezzed
fia·cre carriage

fiancé

fi·an·cé (*fem* ·cée)
Fi·an·na Fail Irish political party
fi·as·co (*plural* ·cos *or* ·coes)
Fiat (*Trademark*)
fiat decree
fib (fibbed, fib·bing)
fib·ber
fi·bre (*US* ·ber)
fibre·board (*US* fiber·)
fi·bred (*US* ·bered)
fibre·fill (*US* fiber·)
fibre·glass (*US* fiber·)
fibre-optic (*adj*; *US* fiber-)
fibre optics (*noun*; *US* fiber optics)
fibre·scope (*US* fiber·)
fi·bri·form
fi·bril (*or* ·bril·la; *plural* ·brils *or* ·bril·lae) small fibre
fi·bri·lar (*or* ·bril·lar, ·bril·lose)
fi·bril·la·tion muscle twitching
fi·bril·li·form
fi·brin blood-clotting protein
fi·brino·gen
fi·brino·gen·ic (*or* ·ous)
fi·brino·geni·cal·ly
fi·bri·noly·sin enzyme
fi·bri·noly·sis
fi·bri·no·lyt·ic
fi·brin·ous
fi·bro·blast tissue cell
fi·bro·blas·tic
fi·bro·cement
fi·broid
fi·bro·in protein
fi·bro·ma (*plural* ·ma·ta *or* ·mas) tumour
fi·broma·tous
fi·bro·sis
fi·bro·si·tis
fi·brot·ic
fi·brous
fi·brous·ness
fi·bro·vas·cu·lar botany term
fibu·la (*plural* ·lae *or* ·las) leg bone
fibu·lar
fiche *short for* microfiche

fichu scarf
fick·le
fick·le·ness
fic·tile moulded from clay
fic·tion
fic·tion·al
fic·tion·ali·za·tion (*or* ·sa·tion)
fic·tion·al·ize (*or* ·ise)
fic·tion·al·ly
fic·tion·ist (*or* fic·tion·eer)
fic·ti·tious not genuine; compare factitious
fic·ti·tious·ness
fic·tive of fiction
fid nautical term
fid·dle
fiddle-de-dee
fiddle-faddle
fiddle·head (*or* ·neck) nautical term
fid·dler
fiddle·stick violin bow
fiddle·sticks nonsense
fiddle·wood
fid·dling
fid·dly (·dli·er, ·dli·est)
fid·ei·com·mis·sary (*plural* ·saries) legal term
fid·ei·com·mis·sum (*plural* ·sa)
fi·deism
fi·deist
fi·deis·tic
fi·del·ity (*plural* ·ities)
fidg·et
fidg·et·ing·ly
fidg·ety
fi·du·cial
fi·du·ci·ary trustee
fie exclamation
fief (*or* feoff) property granted to vassal
field
field·er
field·fare bird
field-holler Negro singing style
field·mouse
field·piece gun
fields·man (*plural* ·men)
field·stone
field·work

fiend
fiend·ish
fiend·ish·ness
fierce
fierce·ly
fierce·ness
fi·eri fa·ci·as legal term
fiery
Fie·so·le Italian town
fi·es·ta
Fife Scottish region
fife
fif·er
fif·teen
fif·teenth
fifth
fif·ti·eth
fif·ty (*plural* ·ties)
fifty-fifty
fig
fight (fight·ing, fought)
fight·er
fighter-bomber
fight·ing
fig·ment
figu·ral
figu·rant (*fem* ·rante) dancer
fig·ur·ate musical term
fig·ura·tion
fig·ura·tive
fig·ura·tive·ly
fig·ura·tive·ness
fig·ure
fig·ured
figure-ground psychology term
figure·head
fig·ur·er
figu·rine statuette
fig·wort
Fiji
Fi·jian
fil *variant of* fils
fila·gree *variant spelling of* filigree
fila·ment
fila·men·tary (*or* ·tous)
fi·lar of thread
fi·laria (*plural* ·lariae) worm
fi·lar·ial (*or* ·ian)
fila·ria·sis
fila·ture silk spinning
fil·bert nut

filch
filch·er
file
file·card
file·fish (*plural* ·fish *or* ·fishes)
fil·er
fi·let lace; meat fillet
fi·let mi·gnon (*plural* fi·lets mi·gnons) beef cut
fil·ial
fil·ial·ly
fil·ial·ness
fili·ate legal term
fili·ation lineage
fili·beg (*or* fil·li·, phili·) kilt
fili·bus·ter
fili·bus·ter·er
fili·bus·ter·ism
fili·cid·al
fili·cide killing son or daughter
fili·form threadlike
fili·gree (*or* fila·, filla·; ·gree·ing, ·greed)
fil·ings
Fili·pi·no (*plural* ·nos) inhabitant of Philippines
fill
filla·gree *variant spelling of* filigree
filled
fill·er
fil·let
fill·ing
fil·lip
fil·lis·ter (*or* fil·is·ter, fil·les·ter) wood plane
fil·ly (*plural* ·lies)
film
film·ic
film·ly
filmi·ness
fil·mog·ra·phy (*plural* ·phies)
film·set (·setting, ·set)
film·setter
film·setting
filmy (filmi·er, filmi·est)
filo thin pastry
filo·plume feather
fi·lose threadlike
filo·selle thread

fils (*or* fil; *plural* fils) Middle Eastern coin
fil·ter separating device; *compare* philtre
fil·ter·abil·ity (*or* ·able·ness)
fil·ter·able (*or* fil·trable)
filter-tipped
filth
filthi·ly
filthi·ness
filthy (filthi·er, filthi·est)
fil·trat·able *variant of* filterable
fil·trate
fil·tra·tion
fi·lum (*plural* ·la) anatomy term
fim·ble plant
fim·bria (*plural* ·briae) anatomy term
fim·brial
fim·bri·ate (*or* ·bri·at·ed, ·bril·late) fringed
fim·bria·tion
fin (fin·ning, finned)
fin·able (*or* fine·)
fi·na·gle use trickery
fi·na·gler
fi·nal
fi·na·le
fi·nal·ism philosophical doctrine
fi·nal·ist
fi·nal·ity (*plural* ·ities)
fi·na·li·za·tion (*or* ·sa·tion)
fi·nal·ize (*or* ·ise)
fi·nal·ly
fi·nals
fi·nance
fi·nan·cial
fi·nan·cial·ly
fi·nan·ci·er
fin·back whale
finch
find (find·ing, found)
find·able
find·er
fin de siè·cle *French* end of 19th century
find·ing
fine
fine·able *variant spelling of* finable

Finnish

fine-cut
fine-draw (-drawing, -drew, -drawn)
Fine Gael Irish political party
fine-grain
fine-grained
fine·ly
fine·ness
fin·ery (*plural* ·eries)
fine·spun
fi·nesse
fine-tooth (*or* -toothed) comb
fin·foot (*plural* ·foots) bird
Fin·gal's Cave
fin·ger
finger·board
fin·gered
fin·ger·er
fin·ger·ing
fin·ger·ling young fish
finger·mark
finger·nail
finger·print
finger·stall
finger·tip
Fin·go (*plural* ·go *or* ·gos) African people
fi·nial
fi·ni·aled
fin·icky (*or* ·ick·ing)
fin·ing clarifying liquid
fin·is the end
fin·ish
fin·ish·er
Fin·is·tère French department
Fin·is·terre Spanish headland
fi·nite
fi·nite·ly
fi·nite·ness
fink *Slang* blackleg
Fin·land
Finn
fin·nan had·dock (*or* Fin·nan had·die)
finned
fin·ner whale
Finn·ic language group
fin·ning
Finn·ish

Finnmark

Finn·mark Norwegian county
Finno-Ugric (*or* **-Ugrian**) language group
fin·ny (**·ni·er**, **·ni·est**)
fino sherry
fi·nochio (*or* **·noc·chio**) fennel
Fin·ster·aar·horn Swiss mountain
fiord *variant spelling of* **fjord**
fio·rin grass
fip·ple mouthpiece
fir
fire
fire·able
fire-and-brimstone
fire·arm
fire·back
fire·ball
fire·bird
fire·boat
fire·bomb
fire·box
fire·brand
fire·brat insect
fire·break
fire·brick
fire·bug arsonist
fire·cracker
fire·crest bird
fire·damp
fire·dog
fire·drake dragon
fire·eater
fire·eating
fire-extinguish·er
fire·fly (*plural* **·flies**) beetle
fire·guard
fire·man (*plural* **·men**)
fire·pan
fire·place
fire·proof
fir·er
fire·side
fire·stone
fire·thorn
fire·trap
fire·warden
fire·water whisky
fire·weed
fire·wood
fire·work
fir·ing

fir·kin barrel
firm
fir·ma·ment
fir·ma·men·tal
fir·mer chisel
firm·ness
firm·ware computer term
first
first-born
first-class (*adj*)
first-foot (*or* **·footer**)
first-footing
first-hand
first·ling first offspring
first-nighter
first-rate
firth (*or* **frith**)
fis·cal
fish (*plural* **fish** *or* **fishes**)
fish·able
fish·bolt
fish·bowl
fish·er
fisher·man (*plural* **·men**)
fish·ery (*plural* **·eries**)
fish-eye camera lens
fish·finger
fish·gig pole for impaling fish
fish-hook
fishi·ly
fishi·ness
fish·ing
fish·monger
fish·net
fish·plate metal joint
fish·tail dance step
fish·wife (*plural* **·wives**)
fishy (**fishi·er**, **fishi·est**)
fis·sile physics term
fis·sil·ity
fis·sion
fis·sion·abil·ity
fis·sion·able
fis·si·pal·mate ornithology term
fis·sipa·rous reproducing by fission
fis·si·ped (*or* **·sip·edal**) zoology term
fis·si·ros·tral ornithology term
fis·sure
fist
fist·ic of boxing

fisti·cuffs
fist·mele archery term
fis·tu·la (*plural* **·las** *or* **·lae**) medical term
fis·tu·lous (*or* **·lar**, **·late**)
fit (*verb* **fit·ting**, **fit·ted**; *adj* **fit·ter**, **fit·test**)
fitch (*or* **fitch·et**) polecat
fit·ful
fit·ful·ly
fit·ful·ness
fit·ment
fit·ness
fit·table
fit·ted
fit·ter
fit·ting
fit·ting·ly
fit·ting·ness
five
five-finger plant
five·fold
five·penny
five·pins
fiv·er
fives ball game
five-star (*adj*)
fix
fix·able
fix·ate
fixa·tion
fixa·tive
fixed
fix·ed·ly
fix·ed·ness
fix·er
fix·ity (*plural* **·ities**) stability
fix·ture
fiz·gig
fizz
fizz·er
fizzi·ness
fiz·zle
fizzy (**fizzi·er**, **fizzi·est**)
fjeld (*or* **field**) rocky plateau
fjord (*or* **fiord**)
flab
flab·ber·gast
flab·bi·ly
flab·bi·ness
flab·by (**·bi·er**, **·bi·est**)
fla·bel·late (*or* **·bel·li·form**) fan-shaped

fla·bel·lum (*plural* ·la)
flac·cid
flac·cid·ity (*or* ·ness)
flac·on bottle
flag (flag·ging, flagged)
flag·el·lant (*or* ·la·tor)
flag·el·lant·ism
fla·gel·lar
flag·el·late
flag·el·lat·ed
flag·el·la·tion
fla·gel·li·form
fla·gel·lum (*plural* ·la *or* ·lums) whiplike part
flageo·let musical instrument
flagged
flag·ger
flag·ging
flag·gy (·gi·er, ·gi·est) limp
fla·gi·tious wicked
flag·man (*plural* ·men)
flag·on
flag·pole
fla·gran·cy (*or* ·grance)
fla·grant
fla·gran·te de·lic·to red-handed
flag·ship
flag·staff (*plural* ·staffs *or* ·staves)
flag·stone
flag-waver
flag-waving
flail
flair talent; *compare* flare
flak (*or* flack)
flake
flak·er
flaki·ly
flaki·ness
flaky (flaki·er, flaki·est)
flam (flam·ming, flammed) *Dialect* deceive
flam·bé (*or* ·bée) cookery term
flam·beau (*plural* ·beaux *or* ·beaus) torch
Flam·bor·ough Head English promontory
flam·boy·ance (*or* ·an·cy)
flam·boy·ant
flame
flame·like

fla·men (*plural* ·mens *or* fla·mi·nes) Roman priest
fla·men·co (*plural* ·cos)
flame-of-the-forest tree
flame·out
flame·proof
flam·er
flame-thrower
flam·ing
fla·min·go (*plural* ·gos *or* ·goes)
flam·mabil·ity
flam·mable
flamy (flami·er, flami·est)
flan
Flan·ders
flâne·rie idleness
flâ·neur
flange
flang·er
flank
flank·er
flan·nel (·nel·ling, ·nelled; *US* ·nel·ing, ·neled)
flan·nel·ette
flan·nel·ly
flap (flap·ping, flapped)
flap·doodle *Slang* nonsense
flap·jack
flap·per
flare flame; widen; *compare* flair
flare-up (*noun*)
flash
flash·back
flash·board
flash·bulb
flash·cube
flash·er
flashi·ly
flashi·ness
flash ing
flash·light
flash·over electric discharge
flashy (flashi·er, flashi·est)
flask
flask·et basket
flat (flat·ter, flat·test)
flat·boat
flat·fish (*plural* ·fish *or* ·fishes)
flat·foot
flat-footed

flat-footed·ly
flat-footed·ness
flat·head (*plural* ·head *or* ·heads) fish
flat·iron
flat·let
flat·mate
flat·ness
flat·ten
flat·ten·er
flat·ter
flat·ter·able
flat·ter·er
flat·ter·ing
flat·ter·ing·ly
flat·tery (*plural* ·teries)
flat·ting metallurgy term
flat·tish
flat·top *US* aircraft carrier
flatu·lence (*or* ·len·cy)
flatu·lent
fla·tus (*plural* ·tuses)
flat·ways
flat·worm
flaunch (*or* flaunch·ing) slope round chimney
flaunt
flaunt·er
flaunt·ing·ly
flaunty (flaunti·er, flaunti·est)
flau·tist (*US* flut·ist)
fla·ves·cent turning yellow
fla·vin (*or* ·vine) pigment
fla·vone plant pigment
fla·vo·pro·tein enzyme
fla·vo·pur·pu·rin dye
fla·vor·ous
fla·vour (*US* ·vor)
fla·vour·er (*US* ·vor·)
fla·vour·ful (*US* ·vor·)
fla·vour·ing (*US* ·vor·)
fla·vour·less (*US* ·vor·)
fla·vour·some (*US* ·vor·)
flaw
flaw·less
flaw·less·ness
flawy squally
flax
flax·en (*or* flaxy)
flax·seed
flay
flay·er
flea
flea·bag

fleabane

flea·bane plant
flea·bite
flea-bitten
fleam lancet
flea·pit
flea·wort plant
flèche spire
flé·chette missile
fleck
flec·tion *variant spelling (esp. US) of* flexion
fled
fledge
fledg·ling (*or* fledge·)
fledgy (fledgi·er, fledgi·est) feathered
flee (flee·ing, fled)
fleece
fleeci·ly
fleeci·ness
fleecy (fleeci·er, fleeci·est)
fle·er one who flees
fleer sneer
fleet
fleet·ing
fleet·ness
Fleet·wood Lancashire port
Flem·ing native of Flanders
Flem·ish
flense (*or* flench, flinch) strip blubber from whale
flens·er (*or* flench·, flinch·)
flesh
flesh·er *Scot* butcher
fleshi·ness
flesh·ings tights
flesh·li·ness
flesh·ly (·li·er, ·li·est)
flesh·pots
fleshy (fleshi·er, fleshi·est)
fletch
fletch·er arrow maker
Fletch·er·ism chewing food thoroughly
fletch·ings arrow feathers
fleur-de-lis (*or* -lys; *plural* fleurs-de-lis *or* -lys)
fleu·rette (*or* ·ret) ornament
fleur·on ornament
fleu·ry *variant of* flory

flew
flews bloodhound's lip
flex
flexi·bil·ity (*or* ·ible·ness)
flex·ible
flex·ibly
flex·ile
flex·ion (*or esp. US* flection)
flex·ion·al
flexi·time
flex·or muscle
flexu·ous (*or* ·ose) having many bends
flex·ur·al
flex·ure
fley *Dialect* be afraid
flib·ber·ti·gib·bet
flick
flick·er
flick·er·ing·ly
flick·ery
fli·er (*or* fly·)
flies
flight
flighti·ly
flighti·ness
flight·less
flighty (flighti·er, flighti·est)
flim·flam (·flam·ming, ·flammed)
flim·si·ly
flim·si·ness
flim·sy (·si·er, ·si·est)
flinch
flinch·er
flinch·ing·ly
fling (fling·ing, flung)
fling·er
Flint Welsh town
flint quartz
flinti·ly
flinti·ness
flint·lock firearm
Flint·shire former Welsh county
flinty (flinti·er, flinti·est)
flip (flip·ping, flipped)
flip-flop (-flopping, -flopped)
flip·pan·cy
flip·pant
flip·per
flip·ping

flirt
flir·ta·tion
flir·ta·tious
flir·ta·tious·ness
flirt·er
flirt·ing·ly
flit (flit·ting, flit·ted)
flitch pork
flite (*or* flyte) *Scot* scold
flit·ter
flitter·mouse (*plural* ·mice) *Dialect* bat
fliv·ver old car
float
float·abil·ity
float·able
float·age *variant spelling of* flotage
floata·tion *variant spelling of* flotation
float·er
float·ing
floaty (floati·er, floati·est) light
floc *variant of* floccule
floc·cose tufted
floc·cu·lant anticoagulant; *compare* flocculent
floc·cu·late aggregate
floc·cu·la·tion
floc·cule (*or* floc·cu·lus, flock, floc) mass of particles
floc·cu·lence (*or* ·len·cy)
floc·cu·lent fleecy; *compare* flocculant
floc·cu·lus (*plural* ·li) marking on sun
floc·cus (*plural* ·ci) down
flock
flocky
Flod·den battlefield
floe ice; *compare* flow
flog (flog·ging, flogged)
flog·ger
flog·ging
flong printing term
flood
flood·able
flood·er
flood·gate
flood·light (·light·ing, ·lit)
floor
floor·age
floor·board

floor·ing
floo·zy (*or* ·zie, ·sy;
  plural ·zies *or* ·sies)
flop (flop·ping, flopped)
flop·pi·ly
flop·pi·ness
flop·py (·pi·er, ·pi·est)
Flora Roman goddess
flo·ra (*plural* ·ras *or* ·rae)
  plant life
flo·ral
flo·ral·ly
Flor·ence Italian city
Flor·en·tine
flo·res·cence flowering;
  compare fluorescence
flo·ret
Flo·ria·nópo·lis Brazilian
  port
flo·ri·at·ed (*or* ·reated)
  architectural term
flo·ri·bun·da rose
flo·ri·cul·tur·al
flo·ri·cul·ture
flo·ri·cul·tur·ist
flor·id
Flori·da
flo·rid·ity (*or* ·ness)
flo·ri·gen hormone
flo·ri·legium (*plural*
  ·legia) book about
  flowers
flor·in
flo·rist
flo·ris·tic
flo·ris·ti·cal·ly
flo·ris·tics branch of botany
flo·ru·it *Latin* flourished
flo·ry (*or* fleu·) heraldic
  term
flos fer·ri mineral
floss
flossy (flossi·er,
  flossi·est)
flo·tage (*or* float·age)
flo·ta·tion (*or* floata·tion)
flo·til·la
flot·sam
flounce
flounc·ing
floun·der (*plural* ·der *or*
  ·ders) fish; to struggle;
  compare founder
flour
flour·ish

flour·ish·er
floury
flout
flout·er
flout·ing·ly
flow liquid movement;
  compare floe
flow·age
flow·er
flow·er·age
flower·bed
flow·ered
flow·er·er
flow·er·et
flow·eri·ness
flow·er·ing
flow·er·less
flower-like
flower-of-an-hour plant
flower·pot
flow·ery
flown
flu illness; *compare* flue
fluc·tu·ant
fluc·tu·ate
fluc·tua·tion
flue pipe; *compare* flu
flued
flu·en·cy
flu·ent
fluff
fluffi·ly
fluffi·ness
fluffy (fluffi·er, fluffi·est)
flu·gel·horn musical
  instrument
flu·id
flu·id·al
fluid·extract
  pharmaceutical term
flu·id·ic
flu·id·ics
flu·id·ity (*or* ·ness)
flu·idi·za·tion (*or* ·sa·tion)
flu·id·ize (*or* ·ise)
flu·id·iz·er (*or* ·is·er)
flu·id·ly (*or* flu·id·al·ly)
fluke
fluki·ness
fluky (*or* fluk·ey; fluki·er,
  fluki·est)
flume ravine
flum·mery (*plural*
  ·meries)
flum·mox

flung
flunk *Slang* fail
flunky (*or* flunk·ey;
  plural flunkies *or* ·eys)
  servant
flu·or *variant of* fluorspar
fluo·rene chemical
  compound; *compare*
  fluorine
fluo·resce
fluo·res·cein (*or* ·ceine)
  chemical compound
fluo·res·cence radiation
  emission; *compare*
  florescence
fluo·res·cent
flu·or·ic of fluorine
fluori·date
fluori·da·tion
fluo·ride
fluo·rim·eter *variant of*
  fluorometer
fluori·nate treat with
  fluorine
fluori·na·tion
fluo·rine (*or* ·rin) chemical
  element; *compare* fluorene
fluo·ro·car·bon
fluo·rom·eter (*or* ·rim·)
fluo·ro·met·ric (*or* ·ri·)
fluo·rom·etry (*or* ·rim·)
fluoro·scope X-ray
  instrument
fluoro·scop·ic
fluoro·scopi·cal·ly
fluor·os·co·py
fluo·ro·sis
flu·or·spar (*or* flu·or)
  mineral
flur·ry (*noun, plural* ·ries;
  verb ·ries, ·ry·ing,
  ·ried)
flush
flush·er
Flush·ing Dutch port
flus·ter
flute
flut·ed
flut·er
flut·ing
flut·ist *US* flautist
flut·ter
flut·ter·er
flut·ter·ing·ly
flut·tery
fluty (fluti·er, fluti·est)

fluvial

flu·vial (*or* **·via·tile**) of a river
flu·vio·ma·rine of sea and river
flux
flux·ion change
flux·ion·al (*or* **·ary**)
flux·meter
fly (*noun, plural* **flies**; *verb* **flies, fly·ing, flew, flown**)
fly·able
fly·away
fly·back physics term
fly·blow (**·blow·ing, ·blew, ·blown**)
fly·boat
fly·book angler's fly case
fly·by (*plural* **·bys**)
fly-by-night
fly·catcher
fly·er *variant spelling of* **flier**
fly-fish
fly-fisher
fly-fishing
fly·ing
fly·leaf (*plural* **·leaves**)
fly·over
fly·paper
fly·past
Flysch Alpine rock
fly·speck
flyte *variant spelling of* **flite**
fly·trap
fly·weight
fly·wheel
foal
foam
foam·flower
foami·ly
foami·ness
foam·like
foamy (**foami·er, foami·est**)
fob (**fob·bing; fobbed**)
fo·cal
fo·cali·za·tion (*or* **·sa·tion**)
fo·cal·ize (*or* **·ise**) focus
fo·cal·ly
fo'c's'le (*or* **fo'c'sle**) *variant spellings of* **forecastle**
fo·cus (*noun, plural* **·cuses** *or* **·ci**; *verb* **·cuses, ·cus·ing, ·cused**)

fo·cus·able
fo·cus·er
fod·der
foe
foehn *variant spelling of* **föhn**
foe·man
foe·tal *variant spelling of* **fetal**
foe·ta·tion *variant spelling of* **fetation**
foe·ti·cide *variant spelling of* **feticide**
foet·id *variant spelling of* **fetid**
foe·tipa·rous *variant spelling of* **fetiparous**
foe·tor *variant spelling of* **fetor**
foe·tus *variant spelling of* **fetus**
fog (**fog·ging, fogged**)
fog·bound
fog·bow light in fog
fog·dog white spot in fog
fogged
Fog·gia Italian city
fog·gi·ly
fog·gi·ness
fog·ging
fog·gy (**·gi·er, ·gi·est**)
fog·horn
fogy (*or* **fo·gey**; *plural* **fogies** *or* **·geys**)
fo·gy·ish (*or* **·gey·**)
föhn (*or* **foehn**) wind
foi·ble
foil
foil·able
foils·man (*plural* **·men**)
Fo·ism Chinese Buddhism
foi·son plentiful supply
Fo·ist
foist
fola·cin folic acid
fold
fold·able
fold·away
fold·boat
fold·ed
fold·er
fol·derol *variant spelling of* **falderal**
fold·ing
fold-out printing term
fo·lia·ceous

fo·li·age
fo·li·ar of leaves
fo·li·ate
fo·li·at·ed
fo·lia·tion
fo·lic acid vitamin
fo·lio (*noun, plural* **·lios**; *verb* **·lios, ·lio·ing, ·lioed**)
fo·lio·late botany term
fo·li·ose leafy
fo·lium (*plural* **·lia**) geometrical curve
folk
Folke·stone
folk·ish
folk·lore
folk·lor·ic
folk·lor·ist
folk·lor·is·tic
folk·moot medieval assembly
folk-rock
folk·si·ness
folk·sy (**·si·er, ·si·est**)
folk·ways sociology term
fol·li·cle
fol·licu·lar
fol·licu·late (*or* **·lat·ed**)
fol·licu·lin hormone
fol·low
fol·low·able
fol·low·er
fol·low·ing
follow-on (*noun*)
follow-through (*noun*)
follow-up (*noun*)
fol·ly (*plural* **·lies**)
Fol·som man early man
Fo·mal·haut star
fo·ment instigate; *compare* **ferment**
fo·men·ta·tion
fo·ment·er
fond
fon·dant
fon·dle
fon·dler
fon·dling·ly
fond·ness
fon·due cookery term
font baptismal bowl; *variant spelling* (*esp. US*) *of* **fount**
Fon·taine·bleau French town

font·al
fon·ta·nelle (*or* **·nel**) anatomy term
Foo·chow (*or* **Fu-chou**) Chinese port
food
food·stuff
fool
fool·ery (*plural* **·eries**)
fool·har·di·ness
fool·hardy (**·hardi·er, hardi·est**)
fool·ish
fool·ish·ness
fool·proof
fools·cap
fool's-parsley
foot (*plural* **feet**)
foot·age
foot-and-mouth disease
foot·ball
foot·ball·er
foot·board
foot·boy
foot·bridge
foot-candle unit
foot·er
foot·fall
foot·gear
foot·hill
foot·hold
footie variant spelling of footy
foot·ing
foot-lambert unit
foot·le potter
foot·lights
foot·ling trivial
foot·loose
foot·man (*plural* **·men**)
foot·mark
foot·note
foot·pace platform before altar
foot·pad highwayman
foot·path
foot·plate
foot-pound unit
foot-poundal unit
foot·print
foot·rest
foot·rope
foots dregs
foot·sie

foot·slog (**·slog·ging, ·slogged**)
foot·sore
foot·stalk
foot·stall base of column
foot·step
foot·stool
foot-ton unit
foot·wall geology term
foot·way
foot·wear
foot·work
foot·worn
footy (*or* **footie**) *Slang* football
foo yong (*or* **foo yoong, foo yung, fu yung**) Chinese omelette
foo·zle bungle golf shot
foo·zler
fop
fop·pery (*plural* **·peries**)
fop·pish
fop·pish·ness
for
for·age
for·ag·er
fo·ra·men (*plural* **·rami·na** *or* **·ra·mens**) hole in bone
fo·rami·nal
fora·mini·fer protozoan
fo·rami·nif·er·al (*or* **·ous**)
for·as·much as
for·ay
for·ay·er
for·bade (*or* **·bad**)
for·bear (**·bear·ing, ·bore, ·borne**) to refrain; variant spelling of forebear
for·bear·ance
for·bear·er
for·bear·ing·ly
for·bid (**·bid·ding, ·bade** *or* **·bad, ·bid·den** *or* **·bid**)
for·bid·dance
for·bid·den
for·bid·der
for·bid·ding·ly
for·bore
for·borne
for·by *Scot* besides
force
force·able

forced
forc·ed·ly
forc·ed·ness
force-feed (**-feeding, -fed**)
force·ful
force·ful·ly
force·ful·ness
force ma·jeure
force·meat
for·ceps (*plural* **·ceps** *or* **·ci·pes**)
forc·er
for·cible
for·cible·ness (*or* **·cibil·ity**)
for·cibly
forc·ing·ly
ford
ford·able
fore
fore-and-aft (*adj*)
fore-and-after vessel
fore·arm
fore·bear (*or* **for·**) ancestor; *compare* forbear
fore·bode
fore·bod·er
fore·bod·ing
fore·brain
fore·cast (**·cast·ing, ·cast** *or* **·cast·ed**)
fore·cast·er
fore·cas·tle (*or* **fo'c's'le, fo'c'slc**)
fore·clos·able
fore·close
fore·clo·sure
fore·course boat's sail
fore·court
fore·deck
fore·doom
fore·father
fore·finger
fore·foot (*plural* **·feet**)
fore·front
fore·gather variant spelling of forgather
fore·go (**·goes, ·go·ing, ·went, ·gone**) precede; variant spelling of forgo
fore·go·er
fore·going
fore·gone
fore·gone·ness

foreground

fore·ground
fore·gut
fore·hand
fore·handed
fore·head
fore·hock bacon
for·eign
for·eign·er
for·eign·ism
for·eign·ness
fore·judge prejudge; *variant spelling of* forjudge
fore·judg·ment (*or* ·judg·)
fore·know (·know·ing, ·knew, ·known)
fore·know·able
fore·know·ing·ly
fore·knowl·edge
fore·land
fore·leg
fore·limb
fore·lock
fore·man (*plural* ·men)
fore·man·ship
fore·mast
fore·most
fore·name
fore·named
fore·noon
fo·ren·sic of the law; *compare* forensics
fo·ren·si·cal·ity
fo·ren·si·cal·ly
fo·ren·sics debating; *compare* forensic
fore·or·dain
fore·or·dain·ment (*or* ·di·na·tion)
fore·part
fore·paw
fore·peak nautical term
fore·play
fore·quar·ter
fore·reach nautical term
fore·run (·run·ning, ·ran, ·run)
fore·run·ner
fore·sail
fore·see (·see·ing, ·saw, ·seen)
fore·see·able
fore·seen
fore·seer
fore·shad·ow
fore·shad·ow·er

fore·shank
fore·sheet nautical term
fore·shock *US* minor earthquake
fore·shore
fore·short·en
fore·side
fore·sight
fore·sighted
fore·sighted·ness
fore·skin
for·est
for·est·al (*or* fo·res·tial)
fore·stall
fore·stall·er
fore·stal·ment
for·esta·tion
fore·stay nautical term
forestay·sail
for·est·ed
for·est·er
forest-like
for·est·ry
fore·taste
fore·tell (·tell·ing, ·told)
fore·tell·er
fore·thought
fore·thought·ful
fore·time the past
fore·to·ken foreshadow
fore·told
fore·tooth (*plural* ·teeth)
fore·top platform on foremast
fore·topgal·lant nautical term
fore·topmast
fore·topsail
fore·tri·an·gle nautical term
for·ever
for·ever·more
fore·warn
fore·warn·er
fore·warn·ing·ly
fore·went
fore·wind
fore·wing
fore·word
fore·yard nautical term
for·feit
for·feit·able
for·feit·er
for·fei·ture
for·fend *US* protect; *Archaic* prevent

for·fi·cate forked
for·gath·er (*or* fore·) assemble
for·gave
forge
forge·able
forg·er
for·gery (*plural* ·geries)
for·get (·get·ting, ·got, ·got·ten)
for·get·ful
for·get·ful·ly
for·get·ful·ness
forget-me-not
for·get·table
for·get·ter
forg·ing
for·giv·able
for·giv·ably
for·give (·giv·ing, ·gave, ·giv·en)
for·give·ness
for·giv·er
for·giv·ing·ly
for·giv·ing·ness
for·go (*or* fore·; ·goes, ·go·ing, ·went, ·gone) give up; *compare* forego
for·go·er (*or* fore·)
for·got
for·got·ten
for·judge (*or* fore·) legal term; *compare* forejudge
for·judg·ment (*or* fore·)
fork
forked
fork·ed·ly
fork·ed·ness
fork·ful
fork-lift truck
For·lì Italian city
for·lorn
form shape, etc.; *US spelling of* forme
form·able
for·mal
for·mal·de·hyde
for·ma·lin (*or* for·mol)
for·mal·ism
for·mal·ist
for·mal·is·tic
for·mal·ity (*plural* ·ities)
for·mali·za·tion (*or* ·sa·tion)
for·mal·ize (*or* ·ise)

for·mal·iz·er (*or* ·is·er)
for·mal·ly in a formal way; compare formerly
for·mal·ness
for·mant acoustics term
for·mat (·mat·ting, ·mat·ted)
for·mate chemistry term
for·ma·tion
for·ma·tion·al
forma·tive
forma·tive·ly
forma·tive·ness
forme (*US* form) printing term; compare form
for·mer
for·mer·ly in the past; compare formally
for·mic of ants; acid
For·mi·ca (*Trademark*)
for·mi·cary (*or* ·car·ium; *plural* ·caries *or* ·caria) ant hill
for·mi·ca·tion skin sensation
for·mi·dabil·ity (*or* ·dable·ness)
for·mi·dable
for·mi·dably
form·less
form·less·ness
for·mol variant of formalin
For·mo·sa former name of Taiwan
for·mu·la (*plural* ·las *or* ·lae)
for·mu·laic
for·mu·lari·za·tion (*or* ·sa·tion)
for·mu·lar·ize (*or* ·ise)
for·mu·lar·iz·er (*or* ·is·er)
for·mu·lary (*plural* ·laries)
for·mu·late
for·mu·la·tion
for·mu·la·tor
for·mu·lism
for·mu·list
for·mu·lis·tic
form·work concrete mould
for·myl chemistry term
For·nax constellation
for·nenst *Scot* situated against
for·ni·cal of a fornix
for·ni·cate

for·ni·ca·tion
for·ni·ca·tor
for·nix (*plural* ·ni·ces) body structure
for·sake (·sak·ing, ·sook, ·sak·en)
for·sak·en
for·sak·en·ness
for·sak·er
for·sook
for·sooth
for·ster·ite mineral
for·swear (·swear·ing, ·swore, ·sworn)
for·swear·er
for·sworn
for·sythia
fort
For·ta·leza Brazilian port
for·ta·lice small fort
Fort-de-France Martinican capital
forte strength
for·te musical term
forte-piano musical term
forte·piano piano
Forth Scottish river
forth forward; compare fourth
forth·com·ing
forth·com·ing·ness
forth·right
forth·right·ness
forth·with
for·ti·eth
for·ti·fi·able
for·ti·fi·ca·tion
for·ti·fi·er
for·ti·fy (·fies, ·fy·ing, ·fied)
for·tis (*plural* ·tes) phonetics term
for·tis·si·mo (*plural* ·mos *or* ·mi)
for·ti·tude
for·ti·tu·di·nous
Fort Knox
fort·night
fort·night·ly
Fortran computer language
for·tress
for·tui·tism philosophy term
for·tui·tist
for·tui·tous unplanned; compare fatuitous

foundry

for·tui·tous·ness
for·tu·ity (*plural* ·ities)
Fortuna Roman goddess
for·tu·nate
for·tu·nate·ly
for·tu·nate·ness
for·tune
fortune-hunter
fortune-teller
fortune-telling
for·ty (*plural* ·ties)
forty-niner prospector
fo·rum (*plural* ·rums *or* ·ra)
for·ward (*adj*)
for·ward·er (*noun*)
for·ward·ness
for·wards (*adv*)
for·went
for·zan·do musical term
fos·sa (*plural* ·sae) anatomical depression
fosse (*or* foss) ditch
fos·sette bone depression
fos·sil
fos·sil·if·er·ous
fos·sil·iz·able (*or* ·is·able)
fos·sili·za·tion (*or* ·sa·tion)
fos·sil·ize (*or* ·ise)
fos·so·rial used for burrowing
fos·ter
fos·ter·age
fos·ter·er
fos·ter·ing·ly
fos·ter·ling foster child
fou·droy·ant sudden
fou·et·té ballet step
fought
foul bad; compare fowl
fou·lard fabric
foul·ly
foul-mouthed
Foul·ness Essex island
foul·ness
found
foun·da·tion
foun·da·tion·al
foun·da·tion·ary
found·er one who founds; to sink; compare flounder
found·ing
found·ling
found·ry (*plural* ·ries)

fount

fount fountain; source
fount (*or esp. US* **font**) printing term
foun·tain
fountain·head
four
four-ball golfing term
four-chette anatomy term
four-colour (*US* -**color**) photography term
four-dimension·al
Four·drini·er paper-making machine
four·fold
four-handed
Fou·ri·er·ism social system
Fou·ri·er·ist (*or* ·**ite**)
Fou·ri·er·is·tic
four-in-hand carriage
four-leaf (*or* -**leaved**) clover
four·pence
four·penny
four-poster
four·ra·gère ornamental cord
four·score
four·some
four·square
four-stroke en·gine
four·teen
four·teenth
fourth 4th; *compare* **forth**
four-way (*adj*)
four-wheel drive
fo·vea (*plural* ·**veae**) anatomy term
fo·veal
fo·veate (*or* ·**veat·ed**)
fo·veo·la (*plural* ·**lae**) small fovea
fo·veo·lar
fo·veo·late (*or* ·**lat·ed**)
Fowey Cornish village
fowl chicken; *compare* **foul**
fowl·er bird hunter
Fow·liang (*or* **Fou-liang**) Chinese city
fowl·ing
fox (*plural* **foxes** *or* **fox**)
fox·fire glow
fox·glove
fox·hole
fox·hound
fox-hunter
fox-hunting
foxi·ly
foxi·ness
fox·ing part of shoe
fox·like
fox·tail grass
fox·trot (·**trot·ting**, ·**trot·ted**)
foxy (**foxi·er**, **foxi·est**)
foy·er
Fra monk's title
fra·cas (*plural* ·**cas**; *US* ·**cases**) uproar
frac·tion
frac·tion·al (*or* ·**ary**)
frac·tion·al·ly
frac·tion·ate
frac·tiona·tion
frac·tiona·tor
frac·tioni·za·tion (*or* ·**sa·tion**)
frac·tion·ize (*or* ·**ise**)
frac·tious
frac·to·cu·mu·lus (*plural* ·**li**)
frac·to·stra·tus (*plural* ·**ti**)
frac·tura·ble
frac·tur·al
frac·ture
frae *Scot* from
frae·num (*or* **fre**··; *plural* ·**na**) fold
frag (**frag·ging**, **fragged**) US military slang term
frag·ile
frag·ile·ly
fra·gil·ity (*or* ·**gile·ness**)
frag·ment
frag·men·tal
frag·men·tal·ly
frag·men·tari·ly
frag·men·tari·ness
frag·men·tary
frag·men·ta·tion
fra·grance (*or* ·**gran·cy**; *plural* ·**grances** *or* ·**gran·cies**)
fra·grant
frail
frail·ly
frail·ness
frail·ty (*plural* ·**ties**)
fraise tool; neck ruff; rampart
Frak·tur typeface

fram·able (*or* **frame·**)
fram·boe·sia (*US* ·**be·**) disease
fram·boise liqueur
frame
frame·less
fram·er
frame-up
frame·work
fram·ing
franc
France
Franche-Comté French region
fran·chise
fran·chise·ment
Fran·cis·can
fran·cium chemical element
fran·co·lin partridge
Fran·co·nian language group
Fran·co·phile (*or* ·**phil**)
Fran·co·phobe
Fran·co·pho·bia
Fran·co·phone native French speaker
frang·er *Austral* condom
fran·gibil·ity (*or* ·**gible·ness**)
fran·gible breakable
fran·gi·pane almond pastry
fran·gi·pani (*plural* ·**panis** *or* ·**pani**) shrub
Frang·lais French with English words
frank
frank·able
frank·al·moign legal term
Frankenstein
frank·er
Frank·furt
frank·fur·ter
frank·in·cense
Frank·ish
Frank·lin Canadian district
frank·lin medieval landowner
frank·lin·ite mineral
frank·ness
frank·pledge medieval tithing system
fran·tic
fran·ti·cal·ly (*or* **fran·tic·ly**)

frap (frap·ping, frapped) nautical term
frap·pé *French* chilled
frass insect excrement
fratchy quarrelsome
fra·ter friar
fra·ter·nal
fra·ter·nal·ly
fra·ter·nal·ism
fra·ter·nity (*plural* ·nities)
frat·er·ni·za·tion (*or* ·sa·tion)
frat·er·nize (*or* ·nise)
frat·er·niz·er (*or* ·nis·er)
frat·ri·cid·al
frat·ri·cide
Frau (*plural* Frau·en *or* Fraus) *German* woman; Mrs
fraud
fraudu·lence (*or* ·len·cy)
fraudu·lent
fraught
Fräu·lein (*plural* ·lein *or* ·leins) *German* young woman; Miss
fraxi·nel·la plant
fray
fra·zil ice spikes
fraz·zle
freak
freaki·ly
freaki·ness
freak·ish
freak·ish·ness
freaky (freaki·er, freaki·est)
freck·le
freck·led (*or* ·ly)
Fred·er·iks·berg Danish city
free (*adj* fre·er, fre·est; *verb* free·ing, freed)
free·bie *Slang* free gift
free·board
free·boot
free·booter
free·born
freed·man (*plural* ·men)
free·dom
freed·woman (*plural* ·women)
free-floater uncommitted person
free-floating
free-for-all
free-handed
free-hearted
free·hold
free·holder
free·lance
free·lancer
free-liver
free-living
free·load *US* be a sponger
free·ly
free·man (*plural* ·men)
free·martin female twin calf
Free·mason member of secret order
free·mason stonemason
Free·masonic
free·masonic
Free·masonry
free·masonry
free-range
free·sheet free newspaper
free·sia
free-spoken
free·standing
free·stone
free·style
free-swimmer
free-swimming
free·thinker
free·thinking
Free·town capital of Sierra Leone
free-trader
free·way
free·wheel
free·wheeling
freez·able
freeze (freez·ing, froze, fro·zen)
freeze-dry (·dries, -drying, -dried)
freez·er
freeze-up
freez·ing
Frei·burg West German city
freight
freight·age
freight·er
freight·liner
Fre·man·tle Australian port
fremi·tus (*plural* ·tus) medical term
Fre·mont *US* city
French
Frenchi·fy (·fies, ·fy·ing, ·fied)
French·man (*plural* ·men)
French·woman (*plural* ·women)
fre·net·ic
fre·neti·cal·ly
frenu·lum (*plural* ·la) zoology term
fre·num *variant spelling of* fraenum
fren·zied
fren·zy (*noun, plural* ·zies; *verb* ·zies, ·zy·ing, ·zied)
Fre·on (*Trademark*)
fre·quen·cy (*plural* ·cies) physics and statistics term
fre·quen·cy (*or* fre·quence) frequent occurrence
fre·quent
fre·quent·able
fre·quen·ta·tion
fre·quen·ta·tive linguistics term
fre·quent·er
fre·quent·ly
fres·co (*plural* ·coes *or* ·cos)
fresh
fresh·en
fresh·en·er
fresh·er (*or* ·man; *plural* ·ers *or* ·men)
fresh·et river overflowing
fresh·man *variant of* fresher
fresh·ness
fresh·water (*adj*)
fres·nel unit
Fres·no *US* city
fret (fret·ting, fret·ted)
fret·ful
fret·ful·ly
fret·ful·ness
fret·less
fret·ted
fret·work
Freud·ian
Freudi·an·ism
Frey Norse god
Freya Norse goddess
fri·abil·ity (*or* ·able·ness)
fri·able
fri·ar

friarbird

friar·bird
fri·ary (*plural* ·aries)
frib·ble fritter away
frib·bler
Fri·bourg Swiss town
fric·an·deau (*or* ·do; *plural* ·deaus, deaux, *or* ·does) cookery term
fric·as·see (·see·ing, ·seed) cookery term
frica·tive phonetics term
fric·tion
fric·tion·al
Fri·day
fridge
fried
friend
friend·less
friend·less·ness
friend·li·ly
friend·li·ness
friend·ly (·li·er, ·li·est)
friend·ship
fri·er *variant spelling of* fryer
fries
Frie·sian cattle; *variant spelling of* Frisian
Fries·land Dutch province
frieze decorative strip
frig (frig·ging, frigged)
frig·ate
frig·ging
fright
fright·en
fright·en·able
fright·en·er
fright·en·ing
fright·en·ing·ly
fright·ful
fright·ful·ly
frig·id
Frig·id·aire (*Trademark*)
fri·gid·ity (*or* frig·id·ness)
fri·jol (*plural* ·joles) French bean
frill
frilled
frilli·ness
frilly (frilli·er, frilli·est)
fringe
frin·gil·line (*or* ·lid) ornithology term
fringy
frip·pery (*plural* ·peries)
frip·pet frivolous woman

Fris·bee (*Trademark*)
Fris·co *Slang* San Francisco
fri·sé fabric
fri·sette (*or* ·zette) fringe
fri·seur *French* hairdresser
Fri·sian (*or* Frie·) language; of Friesland
Fri·sian Is·lands
frisk
frisk·er
frisk·et printing term
friski·ly
friski·ness
frisky (friski·er, friski·est)
fris·son shiver
frit (*or* fritt; frit·ting, frit·ted) glassy material
frith *variant of* firth
fri·til·lary (*plural* ·laries) butterfly; plant
fritt *variant spelling of* frit
frit·ter
frit·ter·er
Friu·li European region
Friu·lian
Friuli-Venezia Giu·lia Italian region
friv·ol (·ol·ling, ·olled)
fri·vol·ity (*plural* ·ities)
friv·ol·ler
frivo·lous
frivo·lous·ness
fri·zette *variant spelling of* frisette
frizz
frizz·er
friz·zi·ness (*or* ·zli·ness)
friz·zle
friz·zler
friz·zy (*or* ·zly; ·zi·er, ·zi·est *or* ·zli·er, ·zli·est)
fro from; *compare* froe
frock
frock·ing coarse material
froe (*or* frow) tool; *compare* fro
frog (frog·ging, frogged)
frog-bit plant
frog·fish (*plural* ·fish *or* ·fishes)
frogged
frog·ging
frog·gy

frog·hopper insect
frog·man (*plural* ·men)
frog-march
frog·mouth bird
frog·spawn
frol·ic (·ick·ing, ·icked)
frol·ick·er
frol·ic·some (*or* frol·icky)
from
fro·men·ty *variant of* frumenty
frond
Fronde French rebellion
frond·ed
fron·des·cence botany term
fron·des·cent (*or* fron·dose, fron·dous)
Fron·deur French rebel
frons (*plural* fron·tes) entomology term
front
front·age
front·al
fron·tal·ity
fron·tal·ly
front·bencher
fron·tier
fron·tiers·man (*plural* ·men)
fron·tis·piece
front·let forehead decoration
fron·to·gen·esis meteorology term
fron·toly·sis meteorology term
front-runner
front·wards (*or esp. US* ·ward)
frost
frost·bite
frost·bitten
frost·ed
frosti·ly
frosti·ness
frost·ing
frost·work
frosty (frosti·er, frosti·est)
froth
frothi·ly
frothi·ness
frothy (frothi·er, frothi·est)
frott·age rubbing

178

frou·frou swishing sound
frow variant spelling of **froe**
fro·ward obstinate
frown
frown·er
frown·ing·ly
frowst
frows·ty stale
frowzi·ness (or **frowsi·**)
frowzy (or **frowsy**; **frowzi·er, frowzi·est** or **frowsi·er, frows·iest**) shabby
froze
fro·zen
fro·zen·ness
fruc·tif·er·ous fruit-bearing
fruc·ti·fi·ca·tion
fruc·ti·fi·er
fruc·ti·fy (·**fies,** ·**fy·ing,** ·**fied**)
fruc·tose sugar
fruc·tu·ous
fru·gal
fru·gal·ly
fru·gal·ity (or ·**ness**)
fru·giv·or·ous fruit-eating
fruit
fruit·age
frui·tar·ian
fruit·cake
fruit·er fruit grower
fruit·er·er fruit seller
fruit·ful
fruit·ful·ly
fruit·ful·ness
fruiti·ness
frui·tion
fruit·less
fruit·less·ness
fruity (fruiti·er, fruiti·est)
fru·men·ta·ceous resembling wheat
fru·men·ty (or **fro·, fur·**) porridge
frump
frump·ish (or **frumpy**)
frump·ish·ness (or **frumpi·ness**)
Frun·ze Soviet city
frus·trate
frus·trat·er
frus·tra·tion
frus·tule botany term

frus·tum (plural ·**tums** or ·**ta**) geometric solid
fru·tes·cence
fru·tes·cent (or ·**ti·cose**) shrublike
fry (noun, plural **fries**; verb **fries, fry·ing, fried**)
fry·er (or **fri·**)
fry·ing
Fu-chou variant spelling of **Foochow**
fuch·sia shrub
fuch·sin (or ·**sine**) dye
fuck
fuck·er
fuck·ing
fu·coid
fu·coid·al (or **fu·cous**)
fu·cus (plural ·**ci** or ·**cuses**) seaweed
fud·dle
fuddy-duddy (plural **-duddies**)
fudge
Fueh·rer variant spelling of **Führer**
fuel (fuel·ling, fuelled; US **fuel·ing, fueled)**
fuel·ler (US **fuel·er**)
fug
fu·ga·cious fleeting
fu·gac·ity
fu·gal of a fugue
fu·gal·ly
fu·ga·to musical term
fu·gi·tive
fu·gi·tive·ly
fugle·man (plural ·**men**) one used as example
fugue
fu·gulst
Füh·rer (or **Fueh·**) German leader
Fuji (or **Fujiyama, Fujisan**) Japanese mountain
Fu·kien Chinese province
Fu·kuo·ka Japanese city
Fu·ku·shi·ma Japanese city
Fula (or **Fu·lah**; plural **Fula** or **Fulas** or **Fu·lah, Fu·lahs**) African people
Fu·la·ni language
ful·crum (plural ·**crums** or ·**cra**)

ful·fil (US ·**fill**; ·**fil·ling,** ·**filled**)
ful·fil·ler
ful·fil·ment (US ·**fill·**)
ful·gent (or ·**gid**) resplendent
ful·gu·rant
ful·gu·rate flash like lightning
ful·gu·rat·ing painful
ful·gu·ra·tion surgical procedure
ful·gu·rite mineral
ful·gu·rous
Ful·ham
fu·ligi·nous smoky
full
full·back
full-blooded
full-blown
full-bodied
full·er
full-faced
full-frontal (adj)
full-length
full-mouthed
full·ness
full-rigged
full-sailed
full-scale
full-time (adj)
full-timer
ful·ly
fully-fledged
ful·mar bird
ful·mi·nant sudden
ful·mi·nate
ful·mi·na·tion
ful·mi·na·tor
ful·mi·na·tory
ful·mln·ic acid
ful·some
ful·some·ly
ful·some·ness
ful·vous tawny
fu·mar·ic acid
fu·ma·role volcano vent
fu·ma·rol·ic
fu·ma·to·rium (or ·**tory**; plural ·**riums,** ·**ria,** or ·**tories**) fumigation chamber
fu·ma·tory of fumigation; compare **fumitory**
fum·ble

fumbler

fum·bler
fum·bling·ly
fum·bling·ness
fume
fume·less
fum·er
fu·mi·gant
fu·mi·gate
fu·mi·ga·tion
fu·mi·ga·tor
fum·ing
fu·mi·tory (*plural* ·tories) plant; *compare* fumatory
fumy (fumi·er, fumi·est)
fun (fun·ning, funned)
fu·nam·bu·lism
fu·nam·bu·list tightrope walker
Fun·chal capital of Madeira
func·tion
func·tion·al
func·tion·al·ism
func·tion·al·ist
func·tion·al·ly
func·tion·ary (*plural* ·aries)
fund
fun·da·ment
fun·da·men·tal
fun·da·men·tal·ism
fun·da·men·tal·ist
fun·da·men·tal·is·tic
fun·da·men·tal·ity (*or* ·ness)
fun·da·men·tal·ly
fund·ed
fun·di mechanic
fun·dic
fun·dus (*plural* ·di) anatomy term
Fun·dy Canadian bay
fu·ner·al
fu·ner·ary
fu·nereal
fun·fair
fun·gal
fun·gi *plural of* fungus
fun·gibil·ity
fun·gible legal term
fun·gic
fun·gi·cid·al
fun·gi·cide
fun·gi·form
fun·gi·stat
fun·gi·stat·ic
fun·goid
fun·gous (*adj*)
fun·gus (*noun*; *plural* ·gi *or* ·guses)
fu·ni·cle botany term
fu·nicu·lar
fu·nicu·late
fu·nicu·lus (*plural* ·li) anatomy term
funk
funk·er
funky (funki·er, funki·est)
fun·nel (·nel·ling, ·nelled; US ·nel·ing, ·neled)
fun·ni·ly
fun·ni·ness
fun·ny (·ni·er, ·ni·est)
fur (fur·ring, furred)
fur·al·de·hyde
fu·ran (*or* fur·fu·ran) chemical compound
fur·below ornamental trim
fur·bish
fur·bish·er
fur·cate fork
fur·cat·ed
fur·ca·tion
fur·cu·la (*or* ·lum; *plural* ·lae *or* ·la) forklike organ
fur·fur (*plural* ·fures) scaling of skin
fur·fu·ra·ceous of bran
fur·fur·al·de·hyde
fur·fu·ran *variant of* furan
fu·rio·so musical term
fu·ri·ous
fu·ri·ous·ness
furl
furl·able
furl·er
fur·long unit
fur·lough US leave
fur·men·ty *variant of* frumenty
fur·nace
Fur·ness Cumbrian peninsula
fur·nish
fur·nish·er
fur·nish·ings
fur·ni·ture
fu·ro·re (*or esp. US* fu·ror)
fur·phy (*plural* ·phies) Austral rumour
furred
fur·ri·er fur dealer; more furry
fur·ri·ery (*plural* ·eries)
fur·ri·ly
fur·ri·ness
fur·ring
fur·row
fur·row·er
fur·rowy
fur·ry (·ri·er, ·ri·est)
fur·ther additional; *variant of* farther
fur·ther·ance
fur·ther·er
further·more
further·most
fur·thest
fur·tive
fur·tive·ly
fur·tive·ness
fu·run·cle boil
fu·run·cu·lar (*or* ·lous)
fu·run·cu·lo·sis skin condition
fury (*plural* furies)
furze gorse
furzy
fu·sain charcoal
fus·cous brownish
fuse
fu·see (*or* ·zee) clock part; match
fu·sel oil
fu·selage
(fushia) *incorrect spelling of* fuchsia
Fu·shun Chinese city
fu·sibil·ity (*or* fusible·ness)
fu·sible
fu·sibly
fu·si·form spindle-shaped
fu·sil musket
fu·sile (*or* ·sil) easily melted
fu·si·lier
fu·sil·lade rapid gunfire
fu·sion
fu·sion·ism
fu·sion·ist
fuss
fuss·er

fussi·ly
fussi·ness
fuss·pot
fussy (fussi·er, fussi·est)
fus·ta·nel·la (or ·nelle) Greek skirt
fus·tian fabric
fus·tic tree
fus·ti·ly
fus·ti·ness
fus·ty (·ti·er, ·ti·est)
fu·thark (or ·tharc, ·thork, ·thorc) phonetic alphabet
fu·tile
fu·tile·ly
fu·tili·tar·ian
fu·tili·tari·an·ism
fu·til·ity (plural ·ities)
fut·tock part of boat
fu·ture
fu·tur·ism
fu·tur·ist
fu·tur·is·tic
fu·tur·is·ti·cal·ly
fu·tur·ity (plural ·ities)
fu·tur·olo·gist
fu·tur·ol·ogy

fu yung variant of foo yong
fu·zee variant spelling of fusee
fuzz
fuzzi·ly
fuzzi·ness
fuzzy (fuzzi·er, fuzzi·est)
fyke US fishing net
Fylde region of Lancashire
fyrd Anglo-Saxon militia
Fyza·bad (or Faiza·) Indian city; compare Faizabad

G

Ga (or Gã; plural Ga, Gas or Gã, Gãs) African people
gab (gab·bing, gabbed)
gab·ar·dine variant spelling of gaberdine
gab·ber
gab·ble
gab·bler
gab·bro (plural ·bros) rock
gab·bro·ic (or ·it·ic)
gab·by (·bi·er, ·bi·est) talkative
ga·belle French salt tax
gab·cr·dine fabric
gab·er·dine (or ·ar·) cloak
Ga·bès Tunisian port
gab·fest US gathering
ga·bi·on stone-filled cylinder
ga·bi·on·ade (or ·on·nade)
ga·ble
ga·bled
ga·blet small gable
Ga·bon
Gabo·nese
Gabo·ro·ne Botswanan capital
gaby (plural gabies) simpleton
gad (gad·ding, gad·ded)
gad·about
gad·der
gad·fly (plural ·flies)
gadg·et

gadg·eteer lover of gadgetry
gadg·et·ry
gadg·ety
Gad·hel·ic Gaelic language
ga·did fish
ga·doid
gado·lin·ic
gado·lin·ite mineral
gado·lin·ium chemical element
ga·droon (or go·) decorative moulding
ga·drooned (or go·)
gad·wall (plural ·walls or ·wall) duck
Gael Gaelic speaker
Gael·ic
gaff angling pole; nautical boom; Slang home
gaffe blunder
gaf·fer
gaff-rigged
gaff-sail
gaff-topsail
gag (gag·ging, gagged)
gaga Slang senile
Ga·gau·zi Russian language
gage pledge; greengage; US spelling of gauge
gagged
gag·ger
gag·ging
gag·gle
gahn·ite mineral
gai·ety (plural ·eties)

gail·lar·dia plant
gai·ly
gain
gain·able
gain·er
gain·ful
gain·ful·ly
gain·ful·ness
gain·li·ness
gain·ly
gain·say (·say·ing, ·said)
gain·say·er
gait walk
gait·er
gal Slang girl; unit
gala
ga·lac·ta·gogue inducing milk secretion
ga·lac·tic
gal·ac·tom·eter
gal·ac·tom·etry
ga·lac·to·poi·esis milk production
ga·lac·to·poi·etic
ga·lac·tose sugar
ga·la·go (plural ·gos) bushbaby
ga·lah bird
Galahad
ga·lan·gal plant
gal·an·tine glazed pressed meat
Ga·lá·pa·gos Is·lands
Gala·shiels Scottish town
Ga·la·ta Turkish port

Galatea

Galatea mythological character
gala·tea fabric
Ga·laţi Romanian port
Ga·la·tia ancient Asian region
Ga·la·tians New Testament book
Gal·axy solar system
gal·axy (*plural* **·axies**) any star system; distinguished gathering
gal·ba·num gum resin
gale
ga·lea (*plural* **·leae**) helmet-shaped structure
ga·leate (*or* **·leat·ed**)
ga·lei·form
ga·lena (*or* **·lenite**) mineral
Ga·len·ic of Galen's medical system
ga·leni·cal pharmacology term
Ga·len·ism
Ga·len·ist
ga·lère *French* undesirable people
Ga·li·bi (*plural* **·bi** *or* **·bis**) American Indian
Ga·li·cia European region
Ga·li·cian
Gali·lean of Galilee; of Galileo
Gali·lee Israeli region
gali·lee church porch
gal·in·gale (*or* **ga·lan·gal**) plant
gali·ot (*or* **gal·li·ot**) small galley
gali·pot (*or* **gal·li·pot**) pine resin
gall
Gal·la (*plural* **·las** *or* **·la**) African people
gal·lant
gal·lant·ness
gal·lant·ry (*plural* **·ries**)
gall blad·der
Gal·le Sri Lankan port
gal·leass (*or* **·li·ass**) warship
gal·leon
gal·ler·ied
gal·lery (*plural* **·leries**)
gal·ley
gall·fly (*plural* **·flies**)

gal·li·am·bic verse metre
gal·liard dance
Gal·lic of France or Gaul
gal·lic chemistry term; of galls
Gal·li·can
Gal·li·can·ism French Catholic movement
Gal·lice *Latin* in French
Gal·li·cism
Gal·li·ci·za·tion (*or* **·sa·tion**)
Gal·li·cize (*or* **·cise**)
Gal·li·ciz·er (*or* **·cis·er**)
gal·li·gas·kins men's breeches
gal·li·mau·fry (*plural* **·fries**) *US* hotchpotch
gal·li·na·cean
gal·li·na·ceous ornithology term
gall·ing
gal·li·nule bird
gal·li·ot variant spelling of galiot
Gal·lipo·li Turkish port
gal·li·pot earthenware pot; variant spelling of galipot
gal·lium chemical element
gal·li·vant (*or* **gali·vant, gala·vant**)
gal·li·wasp lizard
gall·nut (*or* **gall-apple**)
gal·lo·glass (*or* **·low·**) Irish military retainer
gal·lon
gal·lon·age
gal·loon decorative cord
gal·lop horse's gait; compare galop
gal·lop·er
gal·lous chemistry term
Gal·lo·way Scottish area
gal·lows (*plural* **·lowses** *or* **·lows**)
gall·stone
gal·luses *Dialect* braces
ga·loot *US* clumsy person
gal·op dance; compare gallop
ga·lore
ga·loshes (*or* **go·**)
ga·lumph
gal·van·ic (*or* **·vani·cal**)
gal·vani·cal·ly
gal·va·nism

gal·va·ni·za·tion (*or* **·sa·tion**)
gal·va·nize (*or* **·nise**)
gal·va·niz·er (*or* **·nis·er**)
gal·va·nom·eter
gal·va·no·met·ric (*or* **·ri·cal**)
gal·va·nom·etry
gal·va·no·scope
gal·va·no·scop·ic
gal·va·nos·co·py
gal·va·no·trop·ic
gal·va·not·ro·pism botany term
gal·vo (*plural* **·vos**) short for galvanometer
Gal·way Irish county
Gal·we·gian
gal·yak (*or* **·yac**) fur
gam school of whales
gam·ba·do (*plural* **·dos** *or* **·does**) leather stirrup
gam·beson medieval garment
Gam·bia
Gam·bian
gam·bier (*or* **·bir**) astringent
Gam·bier Is·lands
gam·bit
gam·ble bet; compare gambol
gam·bler
gam·bling
gam·boge gum resin
gam·bo·gian
gam·bol (**·bol·ling, ·bolled;** *US* **·bol·ing, ·boled**) frolic; compare gamble
gam·brel horse's hock; type of roof
game
game·cock
game·keeper
game·keeping
gam·elan oriental orchestra
game·ly
game·ness
games·man (*plural* **·men**)
games·man·ship
game·some merry
game·ster
ga·met·al (*or* **·ic**)
gam·etan·gial

gam·etan·gium (*plural* ·gia)
gam·ete reproductive cell
ga·meto·cyte
gam·eto·gen·esis (*or* ·etog·eny)
gam·eto·gen·ic (*or* ·etog·enous)
ga·meto·phore plant part
ga·meto·phor·ic
ga·meto·phyte plant producing gametes
gam·eto·phyt·ic
gam·ey *variant spelling of* gamy
gam·ic biology term
gam·in street urchin
gam·ine boyish girl
gami·ness
gam·ing
gam·ma Greek letter
gam·ma·di·on (*plural* ·dia) swastika
gam·mer *Dialect* old woman
gam·mon
gam·mon·er *Slang* deceiver
gam·my (·mi·er, ·mi·est) *Slang* lame
gamo·gen·esis biology term
gamo·genet·ic (*or* ·geneti·cal)
gamo·pet·al·ous botany term
gamo·phyl·lous
gamo·sep·al·ous
gamp umbrella
gam·ut
gamy (*or* gam·ey; gami·er, gami·est)
gan (gan·ning, ganned) *Dialect* to go
Gan·da (*plural* ·das *or* ·da) African people
gan·der
Gan·dhian
Gan·dhi·ism (*or* ·dhism)
ga·nef *US* opportunist
gang
gang·bang
ganged
gang·er labourers' foreman
Gan·ges Indian river
gang·land
gan·glial (*or* gan·gli·ar)
gan·gling (*or* ·gly)

gan·gli·on (*plural* ·glia *or* ·gli·ons) nerve tissue; cyst
gan·gli·on·ic (*or* ·at·ed)
gang·plank (*or* ·way)
gan·grene
gan·gre·nous
gang·ster
Gang·tok Indian city
gangue (*or* gang) worthless ore
gang·way
gan·is·ter (*or* gan·nis·) rock
gan·ja cannabis
gan·net
gan·oid zoology term
gan·sey *Dialect* pullover
gant·let rail track; *variant spelling of* gauntlet
gant·line nautical term
gan·try (*or* gaun·; *plural* ·tries)
Gany·mede satellite of Jupiter
Ganymede mythological character
gaol *variant spelling of* jail
gaol·er *variant spelling of* jailer
gap (gap·ping, gapped)
gape
gap·er
gapes fowl disease
gape·worm
gap·ing·ly
gapped
gap·ping grammar term
gar (*plural* gar *or* gars) fish
gar·age
Gara·mond typeface
garb
gar·bage
gar·ble
gar·bler
garb·less
gar·board nautical term
gar·çon French waiter
Gard French department
Gar·da Italian lake
gar·den
gar·den·er
gar·denia
gar·den·ing

gar·fish (*plural* ·fish *or* ·fishes)
gar·ga·ney duck
gar·gan·tuan
gar·get cattle disease
gar·gety
gar·gle
gar·gler
gar·goyle
gar·goyled
gar·ial *variant of* gavial
gari·bal·di blouse; biscuit
gar·ish
gar·ish·ness
gar·land
gar·lic
gar·licky
gar·ment
gar·ner
gar·net
gar·ni·er·ite mineral
gar·nish
gar·nishee (·nishee·ing, ·nisheed) legal term
gar·nish·er
gar·nish·ment legal notice
gar·ni·ture decoration
Ga·ronne French river
ga·rotte *variant spelling of* garrotte
gar·pike fish
gar·ret
gar·ri·son
gar·rotte (*or* gar·rote, ga·rotte) execution
gar·rott·er (*or* gar·rot·er, ga·rott·er)
gar·ru·lous
gar·ru·lous·ness (*or* gar·ru·lity)
gar·rya shrub
gar·ter
garth cloistered courtyard
Gary US port
gas (*noun*, *plural* gases *or* gas·ses; *verb* gases *or* gas·ses, gas·sing, gassed)
gas·bag
Gas·con of Gascony
gas·con·ade boastful talk
Gas·cony
gas·eous
gas·eous·ness
gases (*or* gas·ses)

gash

gash
gas·holder
gasi·fi·able
gasi·fi·ca·tion
gasi·fi·er
gasi·form
gasi·fy (·fies, ·fy·ing, ·fied)
gas·ket
gas·kin part of horse's thigh
gas·light
gas·man (plural ·men)
gas·olier (or ·elier) fitting for gaslights
gaso·line (or ·lene) US petrol
gaso·lin·ic
gas·om·eter
gaso·met·ric (or ·ri·cal)
gas·ometry
gasp
Gas·pé Canadian peninsula
gasp·er
gasp·ing·ly
gassed
gas·ser
gas·si·ness
gas·sing
gas·sy (·si·er, ·si·est)
(gasteropod) incorrect spelling of gastropod
gas·tight
gas·tight·ness
gas·tral·gia stomach pain
gas·tral·gic
gas·trec·to·my (plural ·mies)
gas·tric
gas·trin hormone
gas·trit·ic
gas·tri·tis
gas·tro·en·ter·ic
gas·tro·en·terit·ic
gas·tro·en·teri·tis
gas·tro·en·te·rolo·gist
gas·tro·en·ter·ol·ogy (or gas·trol·ogy)
gas·tro·en·ter·os·to·my (plural ·mies) operation
gas·tro·in·tes·ti·nal
gas·tro·lith stomach stone
gas·trol·ogy variant of gastroenterology

gas·tro·nome (or ·trono·mer, ·trono·mist)
gas·tro·nom·ic (or ·nomi·cal)
gas·tro·nomi·cal·ly
gas·trono·mist
gas·trono·my cooking
gas·tro·pod mollusc
gas·tropo·dan
gas·tropo·dous
gas·tro·scope medical instrument
gas·tro·scop·ic
gas·tros·co·pist
gas·tros·co·py
gas·tros·to·my (plural ·mies) artificial stomach opening
gas·tro·to·my (plural ·mies) stomach operation
gas·tro·trich aquatic animal
gastro·vas·cu·lar
gas·tru·la (plural ·las or ·lae) embryology term
gas·tru·lar
gas·tru·la·tion
gas·works
gate
gâ·teau (or ga·; plural ·teaux)
gate-crash
gate-crasher
gated
gate·fold folded oversize page
gate·house
gate·keeper
gate-leg (or -legged) table
gate·post
Gates·head
gate·way
Gath biblical city
gath·er
gath·er·able
gath·er·er
gath·er·ing
Gatling gun
gauche
gauche·ly
gauche·ness
gau·cherie
gau·cho (plural ·chos) cowboy

gaud trinket
gaud·ery (plural ·eries)
gaudi·ly
gaudi·ness
gaudy (gaudi·er, gaudi·est)
gauf·fer variant spelling of goffer
gauge (US also gage) measure; compare gage
gauge·able (US also gage·)
gauge·ably (US also gage·)
gaug·er (US also gag·)
Gau·ha·ti Indian city
Gaul Roman province
Gau·lei·ter German governor
Gaul·ish
Gaull·ism policies of de Gaulle
Gaull·ist
gaul·theria shrub
gaunt
gaunt·let (or gant·)
gaunt·ness
gaun·try variant spelling of gantry
gaur cattle
gauss (plural gauss) unit
gauss·meter
gauze
gauzi·ly
gauzi·ness
gauzy (gauzi·er, gauzi·est)
ga·vage forced feeding
gave
gav·el hammer
gav·el·kind land tenure
ga·vial (or ghar·ial, gar·ial) crocodile
Gäv·le Swedish port
ga·votte (or ·vot)
gawk
gawki·ly (or gawk·ish·)
gawki·ness (or gawk·ish·)
gawky (or gawk·ish; gawki·er, gawki·est)
gawp
gay
Gay Gor·dons dance
Gaza Israeli-occupied city

Gaz·an·ku·lu South African homeland
gaze
ga·zebo (*plural* ·**zebos** *or* ·**zeboes**)
gaze·hound
ga·zelle (*plural* ·**zelles** *or* ·**zelle**)
gaz·er
ga·zette
gaz·et·teer
Ga·zi·an·tep Turkish city
gaz·pa·cho soup
ga·zump
ga·zump·er
Gdańsk Polish port
Gdy·nia Polish port
gean cherry
ge·anti·cli·nal
ge·anti·cline geology term
gear
gear·box
gear·ing
gear·shift *US* gear lever
gear·wheel
gecko (*plural* **geckos** *or* **geckoes**)
ge·dact (*or* ·**deckt**) organ pipe
gee (**gee·ing, geed**)
gee-gee
geek sideshow performer
Gee·long Australian port
gee·pound unit
geese
geest German heathland
gee·zer *Slang* old man; *compare* **geyser**
ge·gen·schein glow in sky
Ge·hen·na place of torment
geh·len·ite mineral
Geiger count·er
gei·sha (*plural* ·**sha** *or* ·**shas**)
gel (**gel·ling, gelled**) jellylike substance; form gel; *variant spelling of* **jell**
ge·la·da baboon
ge·län·de·sprung ski jump
gela·tin (*or* ·**tine**)
ge·lati·ni·za·tion (*or* ·**sa·tion**)
ge·lati·nize (*or* ·**nise**)
ge·lati·niz·er (*or* ·**nis·er**)
ge·lati·noid

ge·lati·nous
ge·la·tion freezing
geld (**geld·ing, geld·ed** *or* **gelt**)
Gel·der·land (*or* **Guel·**) Dutch province
gel·id very cold
ge·lid·ity (*or* ·**ness**)
gel·ig·nite
gelled
gel·ling
gel·se·mium (*plural* ·**miums** *or* ·**mia**) shrub
Gel·sen·kir·chen West German city
gelt *Slang* money
gem (**gem·ming, gemmed**)
gemi·nate in pairs
gemi·na·tion
Gemi·ni constellation; sign of zodiac
gem·ma (*plural* ·**mae**) plant structure
gem·ma·ceous
gem·mate
gem·ma·tion
gemmed
gem·ming
gem·mipa·rous reproducing by gemmae
gem·mu·la·tion
gem·mule reproductive body
gemo·logi·cal (*or* **gem·mo·**)
gem·olo·gist (*or* **gem·molo·**)
gem·ol·ogy (*or* **gem·mol·**) study of gems
ge·mot Anglo-Saxon assembly
gems·bok (*or* ·**buck**; *plural* ·**bok**, ·**boks** *or* ·**buck**, ·**bucks**) antelope
gem·stone
ge·müt·lich German cosy
gen *Slang* information
ge·nappe worsted
gen·darme
gen·dar·me·rie (*or* ·**ry**)
gen·der
gene
ge·nea·logi·cal (*or* ·**log·ic**)
ge·nealo·gist

genital

ge·neal·ogy (*plural* ·**ogies**)
gen·era *plural of* **genus**
gen·er·able able to be generated
gen·er·al
gen·er·al·is·si·mo (*plural* ·**mos**)
gen·er·al·ist
gen·er·al·ity (*plural* ·**ities**)
gen·er·ali·za·tion (*or* ·**sa·tion**)
gen·er·al·ize (*or* ·**ise**)
gen·er·al·iz·er (*or* ·**is·er**)
gen·er·al·ly
gen·er·al·ness
gen·er·al·ship
gen·er·ate
gen·era·tion
gen·era·tive
gen·era·tor
gen·era·trix (*plural* ·**tri·ces**) geometry term
ge·ner·ic (*or* ·**neri·cal**)
ge·neri·cal·ly
gen·er·os·ity (*plural* ·**ities**)
gen·er·ous
gen·er·ous·ness
Gen·esis Old Testament book
gen·esis (*plural* ·**eses**) beginning
gen·et (*or* **ge·nette**) catlike animal; *variant spelling of* **jennet**
ge·net·ic (*or* ·**neti·cal**)
ge·neti·cal·ly
ge·neti·cist
ge·net·ics
Ge·neva
Ge·nevan (*or* **Gen·evese**; *plural* ·**evans** *or* ·**evese**)
gen·ial cheerful
ge·nial of the chin
ge·ni·al·ity (*or* **gen·ial·ness**)
ge·ni·al·ly
gen·ic of a gene
ge·nicu·late bending sharply
ge·nicu·la·tion
ge·nie (*plural* **ge·nies** *or* **ge·nii**)
geni·pap (*or* **gen·ip**) fruit
geni·tal

genitalic

geni·tal·ic
geni·tals (or ·ta·lia)
geni·ti·val
geni·tive grammar term
geni·tor biological father
genito·uri·nary
ge·ni·us (plural
 ge·ni·uses)
ge·ni·zah synagogue
 storeroom
Genoa Italian city
genoa yacht sail
geno·cid·al
geno·cide
Geno·ese (or ·vese;
 plural ·ese or ·vese)
ge·nome (or ·nom)
 genetics term
geno·type genetics term
geno·typ·ic (or ·typi·cal)
geno·ty·pic·ity
gen·re
gens (plural gen·tes)
 Roman aristocratic family
gent
gen·teel
gen·teel·ly
gen·teel·ness
gen·tian plant
gen·tia·na·ceous
gen·tian·el·la plant
Gen·tile not Jewish
gen·tile grammar term
gen·til·ity (plural ·ities)
gen·tle
gentle·folk
gentle·man (plural ·men)
gen·tleman-at-arms
 (plural ·tlemen-)
gentle·man·li·ness
gentle·man·ly
gen·tle·ness
gentle·woman (plural
 ·women)
gen·tly
gen·tri·fi·ca·tion
gen·tri·fy (·fies, ·fy·ing,
 ·fied)
gen·try
genu (plural genua) knee
genu·flect
genu·flec·tion (or
 ·flex·ion)
genu·flec·tor
genu·ine

genu·ine·ly
genu·ine·ness
ge·nus (plural gen·era or
 ge·nuses)
geo·cen·tric
geo·cen·tri·cal·ly
geo·chemi·cal
geo·chem·ist
geo·chem·is·try
geo·chrono·logi·cal
geo·chro·nol·ogy
ge·ode rock cavity
geo·des·ic
ge·od·esist
geod·esy (or geo·det·ics)
 measurement of earth
geo·det·ic
ge·od·ic
geo·dy·nam·ic
geo·dy·nami·cist
geo·dy·nam·ics
ge·og·nos·tic
ge·og·no·sy study of earth's
 structure
ge·og·ra·pher
geo·graphi·cal (or
 ·graph·ic)
geo·graphi·cal·ly
ge·og·ra·phy (plural
 ·phies)
ge·oid shape of earth
geo·logi·cal (or ·log·ic)
geo·logi·cal·ly
ge·olo·gist (or ·ger)
ge·olo·gize (or ·gise)
ge·ol·ogy
geo·mag·net·ic
geo·mag·ne·tism
geo·man·cer
geo·man·cy prophecy
geo·man·tic
geo·mechan·ics
ge·om·eter (or
 ge·om·etri·cian)
geo·met·ric (or ·ri·cal)
geo·met·ri·cal·ly
ge·om·etrid moth
ge·om·etrize (or ·etrise)
ge·om·etry
geo·mor·phic of earth's
 surface
geo·mor·pho·logi·cal (or
 ·log·ic)
geo·mor·pho·logi·cal·ly

geo·mor·pholo·gy (or
 ·phog·eny)
ge·opha·gist
ge·opha·gous
ge·opha·gy (or
 geo·pha·gia,
 ge·opha·gism) eating soil
geo·physi·cal
geo·physi·cist
geo·phys·ics
geo·phyte botany term
geo·phyt·ic
geo·po·liti·cal
geo·poli·ti·cian
geo·poli·tics
geo·pon·ic
geo·pon·ics agricultural
 science
Geor·dic Tynesider
geor·gette fabric
Geor·gia US state; Soviet
 republic
Geor·gian
geor·gic poem
geo·sci·ence
geo·stat·ic
geo·stat·ics geology term
geo·strat·egy
geo·stroph·ic meteorology
 term
geo·syn·chro·nous
geo·syn·cli·nal
geo·syn·cline geology term
geo·tac·tic
geo·tac·ti·cal·ly
geo·tax·is biology term
geo·tec·ton·ic of earth's
 crust
geo·ther·mal (or ·mic)
geo·trop·ic
geo·tropi·cal·ly
ge·ot·ro·pism botany term
ge·rah Hebrew weight
ge·ra·nia·ceous botany
 term
ge·ra·nial chemistry term
ge·ra·ni·ol chemical
 compound
ge·ra·nium
gera·to·log·ic
gera·tol·ogy study of
 elderly
ger·bil (or ·bille, jer·bil)
ger·ent manager
ger·enuk antelope

ger·fal·con *variant spelling of* **gyrfalcon**
geri·at·ric
geria·tri·cian (*or* **geri·at·rist**)
geri·at·rics
germ
ger·man of close relationship; *compare* **germen**
Ger·man
ger·man·der plant
ger·mane relevant
ger·mane·ly
ger·mane·ness
Ger·man·ic of Germany
ger·man·ic chemistry term
Ger·man·ism
ger·man·ite mineral
ger·ma·nium chemical element
Ger·mani·za·tion (*or* **·sa·tion**)
Ger·man·ize (*or* **·ise**)
Ger·man·iz·er (*or* **·is·er**)
Ger·mano·phile (*or* **·phil**)
Ger·mano·philia
Ger·mano·phobe
Ger·mano·pho·bia
ger·man·ous chemistry term
Ger·ma·ny
ger·men (*plural* **·mens** *or* **·mi·na**) biology term; *compare* **german**
ger·mi·cid·al
ger·mi·cide
ger·mi·nable (*or* **·na·tive**)
ger·mi·nal embryonic
ger·mi·nal·ly
ger·mi·nant
ger·mi·nate
ger·mi·na·tion
ger·mi·na·tor
Ger·mis·ton South African city
ger·on·toc·ra·cy (*plural* **·cies**) government by old men
ge·ron·to·crat·ic
ger·on·to·logi·cal
ger·on·tolo·gist
ger·on·tol·ogy study of ageing
ger·ry·man·der
ger·und grammar term

ge·run·dial
ge·run·di·val
ge·run·dive grammar term
ges·so (*plural* **·soes**) white plaster
ge·stalt (*plural* **·stalts** *or* **·stal·ten**) overall structure
Ge·sta·po
ges·tate
ges·ta·tion
ges·ta·tion·al (*or* **·tive**)
ges·ta·to·ry
ges·ticu·late
ges·ticu·la·tion
ges·ticu·la·tive
ges·ticu·la·tor
ges·tur·al
ges·ture
ges·tur·er
get (**get·ting, got**)
get·able (*or* **get·table**)
get-at-able
get·away (*noun*)
Geth·sema·ne
get-out (*noun*)
get·ter
get-together
Get·tys·burg US town
get-up (*noun*)
geum plant
gew·gaw showy trinket
gey·ser hot spring; water heater; *compare* **geezer**
gey·ser·ite mineral
Ge·zi·ra Sudanese region
Gha·na
Gha·na·ian (*or* **Gha·nian**)
ghar·ial *variant of* **gavial**
ghar·ry (*or* **·rl**; *plural* **·ries**) Indian vehicle
ghast·li·ness
ghast·ly (**·li·er, ·li·est**)
ghat steps to river
Ghats Indian mountains
gha·zi Muslim fighter
ghee butter
Ghent Belgian port
gher·kin pickled cucumber; *compare* **jerkin**
ghet·to (*plural* **·tos** *or* **·toes**)
Ghib·el·line political faction
Ghib·el·lin·ism

ghib·li (*or* **gib·**) hot wind
ghil·lie laced shoe; *variant spelling of* **gillie**
ghost
ghost·like
ghost·li·ness
ghost·ly (**·li·er, ·li·est**)
ghost·write (**·writ·ing, ·wrote, ·writ·ten**)
ghost·writ·er
ghoul
ghoul·ish
gi·ant
gi·ant·ess
gi·ant·ism *variant of* **gigantism**
giaour non-Muslim
gib (**gib·bing, gibbed**)
gib·ber
gib·ber·el·lin plant hormone
gib·ber·ish
gib·bet
gib·bing
gib·bon
gib·bous (*or* **·bose**)
gib·bous·ness
gibbs·ite mineral
gibe (*or* **jibe**) taunt; *compare* **gybe**
Gib·eon Palestinian town
gib·er (*or* **jib·**)
gib·ing·ly (*or* **jib·**)
gib·lets
gib·li *variant spelling of* **ghibli**
Gi·bral·tar
Gi·bral·tar·ian
Gib·son Australian desert; US cocktail
gid sheep disease
gid·di·ly
gid·di·ness
gid·dy (*adj* **·di·er, ·di·est**; *verb* **·dies, ·dy·ing, ·died**)
giddy-up
gidgee (*or* **gidjee**) tree
gie *Scot* give
gift
gift·ed
gift·ed·ness
gift·wrap (**·wrap·ing, ·wrapped**)
gig (**gig·ging, gigged**)

gigahertz

gi·ga·hertz (*plural* ·hertz) physics term
gi·gan·tesque
gi·gan·tic
gi·gan·ti·cal·ly
gi·gan·tic·ness
gi·gan·tism (*or* gi·ant·ism)
gi·gan·toma·chy battle of giants
gig·gle
gig·gler
gig·gly
gigo·lo (*plural* ·los)
gi·got leg of mutton
gigue music
Gi·jón Spanish port
gil·bert unit
Gil·ber·tian of W. S. Gilbert
Gil·bert Is·lands *former name of* Kiribati
gild (gild·ing, gild·ed *or* gilt) cover with gold; *compare* guild
gild·er one who gilds; *variant spelling of* guilder
gild·ing
Gil·ead mountain region; biblical character
gi·let bodice
gil·gai *Austral* water hole
Gilgamesh legendary king
gill
gilled
gil·lie (*or* ghil·lie, gil·ly; *plural* ·lies) huntsman's attendant; *compare* ghillie
Gil·ling·ham towns in Kent and Dorset
gil·lion one thousand million
gill-less
gil·ly·flower (*or* ·li·)
Gil·son·ite (*Trademark*) asphalt
gilt covered in gold; gilding substance; pig; *compare* guilt
gilt-edged
gilt·head fish
gim·bals suspension device
gim·crack
gim·let
gim·mal mechanical joint
gim·me *Slang* give me
gim·mick

gim·mick·ry
gim·micky
gimp (*or* guimpe) fabric trimming
gin (gin·ning, ginned)
gin·ger
ginger·bread
gin·ger·li·ness
gin·ger·ly
gin·gery
ging·ham
gin·gi·li (*or* ·gel·li, ·gel·ly) sesame oil
gin·gi·va (*plural* ·vae) gum
gin·gi·val
gin·gi·vi·tis
gin·gly·mus (*plural* ·mi) anatomy term
gink *Slang* man or boy
gink·go (*or* ging·ko; *plural* ·goes *or* ·koes) tree
gin·nel *Dialect* passageway
gin·seng
gip·py (*plural* ·pies) *Slang* an Egyptian; gipsy
gip·sy (*or* gyp·; *plural* ·sies)
gipsy·wort
gi·raffe (*plural* ·raffes *or* ·raffe)
gir·an·dole (*or* gi·ran·do·la) candle-holder
gira·sol (*or* giro·sol, gira·sole) opal
gird (gird·ing, gird·ed *or* girt)
gird·er
gir·dle
gir·dler
girl
girl·friend
girl·hood
girlie
girl·ish
girl·ish·ness
giro (*plural* ·ros) credit transfer; *compare* gyro
gi·ron (*or* gy·) heraldic term
Gi·ronde French river
Gi·ron·dism
Gi·ron·dist French revolutionary

gi·ron·ny (*or* gy·) heraldic term
girt
girth
gi·sarme battle-axe
Gis·borne New Zealand port
gist
git
git·tern ancient guitar
giu·sto musical term
giv·able (*or* give·able)
give (giv·ing, gave, giv·en)
give·away (*noun*)
giv·en
giv·er
giz·zard
gla·bel·la (*plural* ·lae) anatomy term
gla·bel·lar
gla·brous (*or* ·brate) smooth-skinned
gla·brous·ness
gla·cé (·cé·ing, ·céed)
gla·cial
gla·ci·al·ist
gla·ci·al·ly
gla·ci·ate
gla·cia·tion
glaci·er
glacio·logi·cal (*or* ·log·ic)
glaci·olo·gist (*or* gla·ci·al·ist)
glaci·ol·ogy
glac·is (*plural* ·ises *or* ·is) slope
glad (glad·der, glad·dest)
glad·den
glad·den·er
glade
gladi·ate sword-shaped
gladia·tor
gladia·to·rial
gladio·lus (*plural* ·li *or* ·luses)
glad·ly
glad·ness
glad·some
Glago·lit·ic Slavic alphabet
glair bookbinding glaze
glairi·ness
glairy (*or* glair·eous)
Gla·mor·gan

188

glam·ori·za·tion (*or*
  ·sa·tion)
glam·or·ize (*or* ·ise; *US*
  also ·our·)
glam·or·iz·er (*or* ·is·er)
glam·or·ous (*or* ·our·)
glam·or·ous·ness (*or*
  ·our·)
glam·our (*US also*
  glam·or)
glance
glanc·ing·ly
gland
glan·dered
glan·der·ous
glan·ders disease
glan·du·lar (*or* ·lous)
glan·dule small gland
glans (*plural* glan·des)
  anatomy term
glare
glar·ing
glar·ing·ly
glar·ing·ness
glary
Glas·gow
glass
glass-blower
glass-blowing
glasses
glass·house
glassi·ly
glass·ine book covering
glassi·ness
glass·like
glass-maker
glass-making
glass·man (*plural* ·men)
glass·ware
glass·work
glass-worker
glass·works
glass·wort plant
glassy (glassi·er,
  glassi·est)
Glas·ton·bury
Glas·we·gian of Glasgow
Glauce mythological
  character
glau·co·ma eye disease
glau·co·ma·tous
glau·co·nite mineral
glau·co·nit·ic
glau·cous waxy
glaze

glaz·er
gla·zi·er
gla·zi·ery
glaz·ing
gleam
gleam·ing·ly
glean
glean·able
glean·er
glean·ings
glebe clergyman's benefice
glee
glee·ful
glee·ful·ly
glee·ful·ness
gleet medical term
gleety
glen
Glen·coe Scottish massacre
Glen·dale US city
glen·gar·ry (*plural* ·ries)
  Scottish cap
gle·noid anatomy term
Glen·roth·es Scottish town
gley soil
glia·din (*or* ·dine) protein
glib (glib·ber, glib·best)
glib·ness
glide
glid·er
glid·ing
glid·ing·ly
glim *Slang* lamp
glim·mer
glim·mer·ing
glimpse
glimps·er
glint
glio·ma (*plural* ·ma·ta *or*
  ·mas) tumour
glio·ma·tous
glis·sade ballet step
glis·sad·er
glis·san·do (*plural* ·di)
  musical term
glis·ten
glis·ten·ing·ly
glis·ter glitter
glit·ter
glit·ter·ing
glit·tery
Gli·wi·ce Polish city
gloam·ing dusk
gloat
gloat·er

gloat·ing·ly
glob
glob·al
glob·al·ly
glo·bate (*or* ·bat·ed)
globe
globe·flower
globe-trotter
globe-trotting
glo·big·eri·na (*plural* ·nas
  or ·nae) tiny animal
glo·bin protein
glo·boid
glo·bose (*or* ·bous)
  spherical
glo·bosi·ty (*or* ·bose·ness)
globu·lar (*or* ·lous)
glob·ule
globu·lif·er·ous
globu·lin protein
glo·chidi·ate
glo·chid·ium (*plural*
  ·chidia) biology term
glock·en·spiel
glogg alcoholic drink
glom·er·ate
glom·era·tion cluster
glo·meru·lar
glo·meru·late
glom·er·ule
glo·meru·lus (*plural* ·li)
  anatomy term
gloom
gloom·ful
gloomi·ly
gloomi·ness
gloomy (gloomi·er,
  gloomi·est)
Glo·ria hymn
glo·ria fabric
glo·ri·fi·able
glo·ri·fi·ca·tion
glo·ri·fi·er
glo·ri·fy (·fies, ·fy·ing,
  ·fied)
glo·ri·ous
glo·ri·ous·ness
glo·ry (*noun, plural* ·ries;
  verb ·ries, ·ry·ing,
  ·ried)
glory-of-the-snow plant
gloss
glos·sa (*plural* ·sae *or*
  ·sas) tongue
glos·sal

glossarial

glos·sar·ial
glos·sa·rist
glos·sa·ry (*plural* ·ries)
glos·sa·tor gloss writer
glos·sec·to·my (*plural* ·mies) removal of tongue
gloss·eme linguistics term
gloss·er
glossi·ly
glossi·ness
glos·sit·ic
glos·si·tis inflammation of tongue
glos·sog·ra·pher
glos·sog·ra·phy
glos·so·la·lia gift of tongues
glossy (*adj* glossi·er, glossi·est; *noun, plural* glossies)
glot·tal
glot·tic
glot·tide·an
glot·tis (*plural* ·tises *or* ·ti·des)
glot·to·chro·nol·ogy branch of linguistics
Glouces·ter
Glouces·ter·shire
glove
glov·er
glow
glow·er
glow·er·ing·ly
glow-worm
glox·inia plant
glu·ca·gon hormone
glu·ci·num (*or* ·cin·ium) beryllium
glu·co·cor·ti·cord biochemistry term
glu·co·gen·esis biochemistry term
glu·co·genet·ic
glu·co·neo·gen·esis
glu·co·pro·tein *variant of* glycoprotein
glu·cose
glu·cos·ic
glu·co·sid·al (*or* ·ic)
glu·co·side
glu·co·su·ria *variant of* glycosuria
glue (glu·ing, glued)
glu·er
gluey (glui·er, glui·est)

glum (glum·mer, glum·mest)
glu·ma·ceous
glume botany term
glum·ness
glu·on hypothetical physics particle
glut (glut·ting, glut·ted)
glu·ta·mate
glu·ta·mine amino acid
glu·ta·thi·one biochemical compound
glu·teal (*or* ·taeal)
glu·telin protein
glu·ten protein
glu·tenous of gluten; *compare* glutinous
glu·teus (*or* ·taeus; *plural* ·tei *or* ·taei) buttock muscle
glu·ti·nous sticky; *compare* glutenous
glu·ti·nous·ness (*or* ·nos·ity)
glut·ton
glut·ton·ous
glut·tony (*plural* ·tonies)
gly·cer·ic of glycerol
glyc·er·ide chemical compound
glyc·er·in (*or* ·ine)
glyc·er·ol syrupy liquid
glyc·er·yl chemistry term
gly·cine amino acid
gly·co·gen biochemical compound
gly·co·gen·esis
gly·co·genet·ic
gly·co·gen·ic
gly·col antifreeze
gly·col·ic (*or* ·col·lic)
gly·coly·sis breakdown of glucose
gly·co·pro·tein (*or* glu·co·)
gly·co·side biochemical compound
gly·co·sid·ic
gly·co·su·ria (*or* glu·) sugar in urine
gly·co·su·ric (*or* glu·)
glyph groove on frieze
glyph·ic
glypho·graph
gly·phog·ra·pher

190

glypho·graph·ic (*or* ·graphi·cal)
gly·phog·ra·phy printing process
glyp·tic
glyp·tics engraving gems
glyp·to·dont extinct mammal
glyp·tog·ra·pher
glyp·to·graph·ic (*or* ·graphi·cal)
glyp·tog·ra·phy engraving gems
gnarl
gnarled (*or* gnarly)
gnash
gnash·ing·ly
gnat
gnat·catcher bird
gnath·ic (*or* ·al) of the jaw
gna·thi·on anatomy term
gna·thite zoology term
gna·thon·ic deceitfully flattering
gnaw (gnaw·ing, gnawed, gnawed *or* gnawn)
gnaw·able
gnaw·er
gneiss rock
gneiss·ic (*or* ·oid, ·ose)
gnoc·chi dumplings
gnome
gno·mic (*or* ·mi·cal) of aphorisms
gno·mi·cal·ly
gnom·ish
gno·mon part of sundial
gno·mon·ic
gno·moni·cal·ly
gno·sis (*plural* ·ses) spiritual knowledge
gnos·tic (*or* ·ti·cal)
Gnos·ti·cism
Gnos·ti·cize (*or* ·cise)
gno·to·bi·oti·cal·ly
gno·to·bi·ot·ics biology term
gnu (*plural* gnus *or* gnu)
go (*verb* goes, go·ing, went, gone; *noun, plural* goes)
Goa Indian district
goa gazelle
goad
go-ahead (*noun, adj*)

goal
goalie
goal-keeper
goal-keeping
goal-less
goal-mouth
go·an·na lizard
goat
goatee beard
goat-eed
goat-herd
goat-ish
goats-beard (or goat's-) plant
goat-skin
goat's-rue plant
goat-sucker bird
gob (gob·bing, gobbed)
gob·bet
gob·ble
gob·ble·de·gook (or ·dy·)
gob·bler
Go·belin tapestry
go-between
Gobi desert; compare goby
Go·bian
go·bi·oid zoology term
gob·let
gob·lin
gobo (plural gobos or goboes) microphone shield
gob·stopper
gobu·lar·ity (or ·ness)
goby (plural goby or gobies) fish; compare Gobi
god
god·child (plural ·children)
god·damn
god·daughter
god·dess
go·detia plant
god·father
god·fearing
god·forsaken
god·head
god·hood
god·less
god·less·ness
god·like
god·li·ness
god·ly (·li·er, ·li·est)
god·mother

go·down warehouse
god·parent
go·droon variant spelling of gadroon
god·send
god·son
God·speed
Godt·haab capital of Greenland
god·wit bird
goer
goe·thite (or gö·) mineral
gof·fer (or gauf·) to crimp; compare gopher
Gog biblical character
go-getter
gog·gle
goggle-box
goggle-eyed
gog·gles
Goiâ·nia Brazilian city
Goi·ás Brazilian state
Goi·del Gaelic-speaking Celt
Goi·del·ic (or Goi·dhel·ic, Ga·dhel·ic)
go·ing
goi·tre (US ·ter) thyroid swelling
goi·trous
go-kart
Gol·con·da ruined Indian town
gold
gold-beater
gold-beating
gold·crest bird
gold-dig·ger
gold-digging
gold·en
golden·eye (plural ·eyes or ·eye) duck
golden·rod plant
golden·seal plant
gold·eye (plural ·eyes or ·eye) fish
gold·finch
gold·fish (plural ·fish or ·fishes)
goldi·locks plant
gold-miner
gold-mining
gold-of-pleasure plant
gold-plate (verb)
gold·smith

gold·thread plant
go·lem resurrected being
golf
golf·er
gol·iard medieval scholar
gol·iard·ery
Goliath
gol·li·wog (or ·wogg)
gol·lop to eat greedily
gol·lop·er
gol·ly (plural ·lies)
go·loshes variant spelling of galoshes
gom·broon pottery
Go·mel Soviet city
Go·mor·rah
gom·pho·sis (plural ·ses) anatomy term
go·mu·ti palm tree
gon·ad sex organ
gon·ad·al (or go·na·dial, go·nad·ic)
gon·ado·troph·ic (US ·trop·ic)
gon·ado·tro·phin (US ·tro·pin) hormone
Gond tribal Indian
Gon·dar Ethiopian city
Gon·di Gond language
gon·do·la
gon·do·lier
Gond·wa·na·land ancient continent
gone
gon·er Slang one beyond help; compare gonna
gon·fa·lon (or ·non) banner
gon·fa·lon·ier magistrate
gong
Gon·go·la Nigerian state
Gon·go·rism literary style
go·nia·tite fossil
go·nid·ial (or ·nid·ic)
go·nid·ium (plural ·ia) botany term
go·ni·om·eter angle measurer
go·nio·met·ric (or ·ri·cal)
go·ni·om·etry
go·ni·on (plural ·nia) anatomy term
gonk toy
gon·na Slang going to; compare goner

gonococcal

gono·coc·cal (*or* ·cic)
gono·coc·coid
gono·coc·cus (*plural* ·coc·ci) bacterium
gono·cyte
gono·phore biology term
gono·phor·ic (*or* go·nopho·rous)
gono·pore zoology term
gon·or·rhoea (*US* ·rhea)
gon·or·rhoeal (*or* ·rhoe·ic; *US* ·rheal *or* ·rhe·ic)
goo
goo·ber peanut
good (bet·ter, best)
good·bye
good-for-nothing
good-humoured
good-humoured·ly
good·ish
good·li·ness
good-looking
good·ly (·li·er, ·li·est)
good·man (*plural* ·men) *Archaic* husband
good-natured
good-natured·ly
good·ness
good-night
goods
good-sized
good·wife (*plural* ·wives)
Good·win Sands
goody (*plural* goodies)
goody-goody (*plural* -goodies)
goo·ey (gooi·er, gooi·est)
goof
goofi·ly
goofi·ness
goofy (goofi·er, goofi·est)
goog·ly (*plural* ·lies) cricket term
goo·gol large number
goo·gol·plex large number
Goole Humberside port
goon
goop *US* rude person
goos·an·der duck
goose (*plural* geese)
goose·berry (*plural* ·berries)
goose·foot (*plural* ·foots) plant

goose·gog *Dialect* gooseberry
goose·grass
goose·neck nautical term
goose-step (-stepping, -stepped)
goosi·ness
goosy (*or* goos·ey; goosi·er, goosi·est)
go·pak dance
go·pher animal; *compare* goffer
Go·rakh·pur Indian city
go·ral antelope
Gor·bals Glaswegian suburb
gor·cock male grouse
gore
go·reng pi·sang Malaysian dish
gorge
gorge·able
gor·geous
gor·geous·ness
gorg·er
gor·ger·in architectural term
Gor·gon mythological monster
gor·go·nian coral
Gor·gon·zo·la cheese
go·ril·la ape; *compare* guerrilla
go·ril·lian (*or* ·line)
go·ril·loid
gori·ly
gori·ness
Gor·ki (*or* ·ky) Soviet city
Gor·lov·ka Soviet city
gor·mand·ize (*or* ·ise) eat greedily; *compare* gourmandise
gor·mand·iz·er (*or* is·er)
gorm·less
Gorno-Altai Soviet region
Gorno-Badakh·shan Soviet region
gorse
Gor·sedd bardic institution
gory (gori·er, gori·est)
gosh
gos·hawk
Go·shen biblical region
gos·ling
go-slow

192

Gos·pel New Testament book
gos·pel truth; doctrine
gos·pel·ler (*US* ·pel·er)
Gos·plan Soviet commission
gos·po·din (*plural* ·po·da) Russian title of address
Gos·port
gos·sa·mer
gos·sip
gos·sip·er
gos·sip·ing·ly
gossip-monger
gos·sipy
gos·soon *Irish* servant
gos·ter *Dialect* laugh
got
Gö·teborg (*or* Goth·en·burg) Swedish port
Goth Germanic people
Goth·ic
Gothi·cal·ly
Gothi·cism
Got·land Swedish island
got·ten
Göt·tin·gen West German city
gouache art term
Gou·da cheese
gouge
goug·er
gou·lash
gou·ra·mi (*plural* ·mi *or* ·mis) fish
gourd
gour·mand (*or* gor·) greedy person; *compare* gourmet
gour·man·dise love of food; *compare* gormandize
gour·mand·ism
gour·met epicure; *compare* gourmand
gout
gouti·ness
gout·weed
gouty
gov·ern
gov·ern·abil·ity (*or* ·able·ness)
gov·ern·able
gov·ern·ance
gov·er·ness
gov·ern·ment

gov·ern·men·tal
gov·er·nor
gov·er·nor·ship
gow·an *Scot* daisy
Gower Welsh peninsula
gown
grab (grab·bing, grabbed)
grab·ber
grab·ble grope
grab·bler
gra·ben trough of land
grace
grace-and-favour
grace·ful
grace·ful·ly
grace·ful·ness
grace·less
Graces Greek goddesses
grac·ile slender
gra·cil·ity (*or* grac·ile·ness)
gra·cious
gra·cious·ness
grack·le bird
grad *Slang* graduate
grad·abil·ity (*or* ·able·ness)
grad·able
gra·date to cause to change
gra·da·tion
gra·da·tion·al
grade
grad·er
gra·di·ent
gra·din (*or* ·dine) step or ledge
grad·ual
gradu·al·ism
gradu·al·ist
gradu·al·is·tic
gradu·al·ly
gradu·al·ness
gradu·and person about to graduate
gradu·ate
gradua·tion
gradua·tor
gra·dus (*plural* ·dus·es) book of musical exercises
Grae·cism (*or esp. US* Gre·)
Grae·cize (*or esp. US* Gre·)
Graeco-Roman (*or esp. US* Greco·)

graf·fi·ti (*sing.* ·to)
graft
graft·er
graft·ing
Grail legendary bowl
grain
grain·er
graini·ness
grain·ing
grainy (graini·er, graini·est)
gral·la·to·rial ornithology term
gram plant
gram (*or* gramme) unit
gra·ma pasture grass
grama·rye magic
gra·mer·cy *Archaic* thanks
grami·ci·din antibiotic
gra·min·eous (*or* ·mina·ceous) of grasses
grami·nivo·rous grass-eating
gram·mar
gram·mar·ian
gram·mati·cal
gram·mati·cal·ly
gram·ma·tolo·gist
gram·ma·tol·ogy study of writing systems
gramme variant spelling of gram
gram-molecu·lar (*or* -molar)
Gram-negative bacteriology term
gramo·phone
Gram·pian Scottish mountains and region
Gram-positive bacteriology term
gram·pus (*plural* ·puses) dolphin
Gra·na·da Spanish city
grana·dil·la fruit
grana·ry (*plural* ·ries)
grand
grand·aunt variant of great-aunt
grand·child (*plural* ·children)
Grand Cou·lee US dam
grand·dad
grand·daughter
gran·dee
gran·deur

grand·father
gran·dilo·quence
gran·dilo·quent
gran·di·ose
gran·di·ose·ly
gran·di·os·ity
grandio·so musical term
grand·ma (*or* ·mama)
grand mal epilepsy
grand·master
grand·mother
grand·nephew variant of great-nephew
grand·niece variant of great-niece
grand·pa (*or* ·papa)
grand·parent
grand·son
grand·stand
grange
grang·er·ism
grang·eri·za·tion (*or* ·sa·tion)
grang·er·ize (*or* ·ise) illustrate with borrowed pictures
grang·er·iz·er (*or* ·is·er)
gran·ite
granite·ware
gra·nit·ic (*or* gran·it·oid)
gran·it·ite type of granite
grani·vore
gra·nivo·rous grain-eating
gran·ny (*or* ·nie; *plural* ·nies)
grano·dio·rite rock
grano·lith paving material
grano·lith·ic
grano·phyre rock
grano·phyr·ic
grant
Gran·ta River Cam
grant·able
grantee legal term
grant·er
grant-in-aid (*plural* grants-)
gran·tor
gran tur·is·mo touring car
granu·lar
granu·lar·ity
granu·late
granu·la·tion
granu·la·tive
granu·la·tor (*or* ·lat·er)

granule

gran·ule
granu·lite rock
granu·lit·ic
granu·lo·cyte
granu·lo·cyt·ic
granu·lo·ma (*plural* ·mas or ·ma·ta) tumour
granu·loma·tous
grape
grape·fruit (*plural* ·fruit or ·fruits)
grapes veterinary term
grape·shot
grape·vine
grap·ey (*or* grapy)
graph
graph·eme linguistics term
gra·phemi·cal·ly
graph·ic (*or* graphi·cal)
graphi·cal·ly
graphi·cal·ness (*or* graph·ic·ness)
graph·ics
graph·ite
gra·phit·ic
graphi·ti·za·tion (*or* ·sa·tion)
graphi·tize (*or* ·tise) convert into graphite
grapho·log·ic (*or* ·logi·cal)
graph·olo·gist
graph·ol·ogy study of handwriting
grapho·mo·tor
grap·nel
grap·pa grape spirit
grap·ple
grap·pler
grap·pling
grap·to·lite fossil
grapy *variant spelling of* grapey
Gras·mere Cumbrian village
grasp
grasp·able
grasp·er
grasp·ing
grass
grass·finch
grass·hook sickle
grass·hopper
grassi·ness
grass·land
grass·quit bird

grassy (grassi·er, grassi·est)
grate
grate·ful
grate·ful·ly
grate·ful·ness
grat·er
grati·cule grid
grati·fi·ca·tion
grati·fi·er
grati·fy (·fies, ·fy·ing, ·fied)
grati·fy·ing·ly
gra·tin cookery term
grat·ing
grat·ing·ly
gra·tis free
grati·tude
gra·tui·tous
gra·tu·ity (*plural* ·ities)
Grau·bün·den Swiss canton
grau·pel hail
grav unit
gra·va·men (*plural* ·vami·na) legal term
grave burial place; accent; serious; engrave
gra·ve musical term
grav·el (·el·ling, ·elled; *US* ·el·ing, ·eled)
grav·el·ish
grav·el·ly
grav·en
grave·ly
grave·ness
grav·er engraving tool
Graves wine
Graves·end
grave·stone
Gra·vett·ian Palaeolithic culture
grave·yard
grav·id pregnant
gra·vid·ity (*or* ·ness)
gra·vim·eter
gravi·met·ric (*or* ·ri·cal)
gra·vim·etry
gravi·tate
gravi·tat·er
gravi·ta·tion
gravi·ta·tion·al
gravi·ta·tion·al·ly
gravi·ta·tive
gravi·ton physics term
grav·ity (*plural* ·ities)

gra·vure printing method
gra·vy (*plural* ·vies)
gray *US spelling of* grey; unit
gray·back *US spelling of* greyback
gray·beard *US spelling of* greybeard
gray·ling (*plural* ·ling *or* ·lings) fish
gray·wacke *US spelling of* greywacke
graze
graz·er animal
gra·zi·er farmer
graz·ing
grease
grease·paint
greas·er
grease·wood (*or* ·bush)
greasi·ly
greasi·ness
greasy (greasi·er, greasi·est)
great
great-aunt (*or* grand·)
great·coat
great·est
great·ly
great-nephew (*or* grand·)
great·ness
great-niece (*or* grand·)
Greats course at Oxford University
great-uncle (*or* grand·)
greave armour
greaves tallow residue
grebe
Gre·cian
Gre·cism *variant spelling* (*esp. US*) *of* Graecism
Gre·cize *variant spelling* (*esp. US*) *of* Graecize
Greco-Roman *variant spelling* (*esp. US*) *of* Graeco-Roman
Greece
greed
greedi·ly
greedi·ness
greedy (greedi·er, greedi·est)
Greek
green
green·back *US* currency note

groaner

green·bottle fly
green·brier
green·ery (*plural* ·eries)
green·finch
green·fly (*plural* ·flies)
green·gage
green·grocer
green·grocery (*plural* ·groceries)
green·head male mallard
green·heart tree
green·horn
green·house
green·ing cooking apple
green·ish
Green·land
Green·land·er
green·let bird
green·ling fish
green·ness
Green·ock Scottish port
green·ock·ite mineral
green·room
green·sand
Greens·boro US city
green·shank bird
green·stick fracture
green·stone
green·stuff
green·sward turf
Green·wich
green·wood
greet
greet·er
greet·ing
grega·rine zoology term
gre·gari·ous
gre·gari·ous·ness
Gre·go·rian
greige undyed
grei·sen rock
gre·mi·al bishop's cloth
grem·lin
Gre·na·da West Indian state
gre·nade
grena·dier
grena·dine fabric; syrup
Grena·dines West Indian islands
Grendel legendary monster
Gre·no·ble French city
gres·so·rial (*or* ·ri·ous) ornithology term
Gret·na Green

grew
grey (*US* gray) colour; *compare* gray
grey·back (*US* gray·) animal
grey·beard (*US* gray·)
grey·hen female black grouse
grey·hound
grey·ish (*US* gray·)
grey·lag goose
grey·ness (*US* gray·)
grey-state undyed
grey·wacke (*US* gray·) rock
grib·ble wood-boring animal
grid
grid·dle
griddle·cake
gride grate
grid·iron
grief
griev·ance
grieve
griev·er
griev·ing
griev·ous
griev·ous·ness
griffe architectural ornament
grif·fin (*or* grif·fon, gryph·on) winged monster
grif·fon dog; vulture; *variant spelling of* griffin
grig
gri·gri (*or* gris-gris, gree·gree; *plural* ·gris *or* ·grees) talisman
grill cooking senses; *compare* grille
gril·lage building term
grille (*or* grill) metal screen; *compare* grill
grilled
grill·er
grill·room
grilse (*plural* grilses *or* grilse) salmon
grim (grim·mer, grim·mest)
gri·mace
gri·mac·er
gri·mac·ing·ly
Gri·mal·di moon crater
gri·mal·kin old cat
grime

grim·ness
Grims·by
grimy (grim·ier, grim·iest)
grin (grin·ning, grinned)
grind (grind·ing, ground)
grin·de·lia plant
Grin·del·wald Swiss valley
grind·er
grind·ery (*plural* ·eries)
grind·stone
grin·go (*plural* ·gos)
grin·ner
grip (grip·ping, gripped)
gripe
grip·er complainer; *compare* gripper
grip·ing·ly
grippe influenza
grip·per one that grips; *compare* griper
grip·ping
grip·ping·ly
gri·saille painting term
gris·eous greyish
gri·sette French girl
gris·kin pork cut
gris·li·ness
gris·ly (·li·er, ·li·est) gruesome; *compare* gristly; grizzly
gri·son animal
grist
gris·tle
gris·tli·ness
gris·tly having gristle; *compare* grisly; grizzly
grist·mill
grit (grit·ting, grit·ted)
grith place of safety
grits coarsely ground grain
grit·ti·ly
grit·ti·ness
grit·ty (·ti·er, ·ti·est)
griv·et monkey
griz·zle become grey; *Slang* whine
griz·zled
griz·zler
griz·zly (*adj* ·zli·er, ·zli·est; *noun, plural* ·zlies) grey-haired; bear; *compare* grisly; gristly
groan
groan·er

groaningly

groan·ing·ly
groat old coin
groats crushed grain
gro·cer
gro·cery (*plural* ·ceries)
grock·le *Dialect* tourist
Grod·no Soviet city
grog
grog·gi·ly
grog·gi·ness
grog·gy (·gi·er, ·gi·est)
grog·ram fabric
groin abdominal region; vault; *compare* groyne
Gro·li·er bookbinding style
grom·met (*or* grum·)
grom·well plant
Gro·ning·en Dutch province
groom
groom·er
groom·ing
grooms·man (*plural* ·men)
groove
groovy (groovi·er, groovi·est)
grope
grop·er
grop·ing·ly
gros·beak bird
gro·schen (*plural* ·schen) Austrian coin
gros·grain fabric
gross
gross·ness
gros·su·lar·ite gemstone
grot grotto
gro·tesque
gro·tesque·ly
gro·tesque·ness
gro·tes·query (*or* ·querie; *plural* ·queries)
grot·to (*plural* ·toes *or* ·tos)
grouch
grouchi·ly
grouchi·ness
grouchy (grouch·ier, grouch·iest)
ground
ground·age anchorage fee
ground·ing
ground·less
ground·ling

ground·mass
ground·nut
ground·sel
ground·sheet
ground·sill joist
grounds·man (*plural* ·men)
ground·speed
ground·work
group
group·er (*plural* ·er *or* ·ers) fish
groupie
group·ing
grouse (*plural* grouse *or* grouses)
grous·er complainer
grout
grout·er
grouts coffee grounds
grouty (grouti·er, grouti·est) *Dialect* muddy
grove
grov·el (·el·ling, ·elled; *US* ·el·ing, ·eled)
grov·el·ler (*US* ·el·er)
grov·el·ling·ly (*US* ·el·ing·ly)
grow (grow·ing, grew, grown)
grow·able
grow·er
growl
growl·er
grown
grown-up
growth
groyne jetty; *compare* groin
Groz·ny Soviet city
grub (grub·bing, grubbed)
grub·ber
grub·bi·ly
grub·bi·ness
grub·by (grub·bi·er, grub·bi·est)
grudge
grudg·er
grudg·ing
grudg·ing·ly
gru·el
gru·el·ling (*US* ·el·ing)
grue·some (*or* grew·)
gruff

196

gruff·ish
gruff·ness
gru·gru palm tree
grum·ble
grum·bler
grum·bling·ly
grum·bly
grum·met variant spelling of grommet
gru·mous (*or* ·mose) botany term
grump
grumpi·ly (*or* grump·ish·ly)
grumpi·ness (*or* grump·ish·ness)
grumpy (*or* grump·ish; grumpi·er, grumpi·est)
Grun·dy narrow-minded critical person
grun·ion fish
grunt
grunt·er
grunt·ing·ly
grun·tled contented
Grus constellation
Gru·yère cheese
gryph·on variant spelling of griffin
grys·bok antelope
gua·ca·mo·le (*or* ·cha·) avocado dish
gua·co (*plural* ·cos) plant
Gua·dal·ca·nal Pacific island
Gua·dal·qui·vir Spanish river
Gua·de·loupe
(guage) incorrect spelling of gauge
guaia·col medicinal liquid
guaia·cum (*or* guaio·) tree or resin
Guam Pacific island
guan bird
Gua·na·ba·ra former Brazilian state
gua·na·co (*plural* ·cos) animal
Gua·na·jua·to Mexican state
gua·nase enzyme
guani·dine (*or* ·din) biochemical compound
gua·nine biochemical compound

gua·no (*plural* **·nos**) bird excrement
gua·no·sine biochemical compound
Guan·ta·na·mo Cuban city
Gua·ra·ni (*plural* **·ni** *or* **·nis**) Paraguayan people
gua·ra·ni (*plural* **·ni** *or* **·nis**) currency
guar·an·tee (**·tee·ing**, **·teed**)
guar·an·tor
guar·an·ty (*plural* **·ties**) legal term
guard
guard·able
guar·dant (*or* **gar·**) heraldic term
guard·ed
guard·ed·ly
guard·ed·ness
guard·er
guard·house
guard·ian
guardi·an·ship
guard·rail
guard·room
Guards regiment
guards·man (*plural* **·men**)
Gua·te·ma·la
gua·va fruit
Gua·ya·quil Ecuadorian port
gua·yu·le shrub
gub·bins
gu·ber·na·to·rial of a governor
guck slimy substance
gudg·eon fish
guelder-rose
Guelph (*or* **Guelf**) political faction
Guelph·ic (*or* **Guelf·**)
Guelph·ism (*or* **Guelf**)
gue·non monkey
guer·don reward
Guer·ni·ca Spanish town
Guern·sey Channel island
guern·sey sweater
Guer·rero Mexican state
guer·ril·la (*or* **gue·ril·la**) fighter; *compare* **gorilla**
guer·ril·la·ism (*or* **gue·**)
guess
guess·able

guess·er
guess·ti·mate
guess·work
guest
guest·house
guff *Slang* ridiculous talk
guf·faw
Gui·ana South American region
Guia·nese (*or* **Gui·an·an**)
guid·able
guid·ance
guide
guide·line
guide·post
guid·er
guid·ing
guid·ing·ly
gui·don flag
Gui·enne (*or* **Guy·enne**) former French province
guild (*or* **gild**) organization; *compare* **gild**
guil·der (*or* **gild·er**, **gul·den**; *plural* **·ders**, **·der** *or* **·dens**, **·den**) currency; *compare* **gilder**
Guild·ford
guild·hall (*or* **gild·**)
guilds·man (*or* **gilds·**; *plural* **·men**)
guile
guile·ful
guile·ful·ly
guile·ful·ness
guile·less
guil·lemot
guil·loche architectural border
guil·lo·tine
guil·lo·tin·er
guilt guiltiness; remorse; *compare* **gilt**
guilti·ly
guilti·ness
guilt·less
guilty (**guilti·er**, **guilti·est**)
guimpe blouse; variant spelling of **gimp**
Guinea African republic
guinea coin
Guinea-Bissau African republic
Guin·ean
guinea pig

gun

Guinevere legendary queen
gui·pure lace
guise
gui·tar
guitar·fish (*plural* **·fish** *or* **·fishes**)
gui·tar·ist
Gu·ja·rat (*or* **·je·**) Indian state
Gu·ja·ra·ti (*or* **·je·**)
Guj·ran·wa·la Pakistani city
Gu·lag Soviet administrative department
gu·lar of the throat
gulch *US* ravine
gul·den variant of **guilder**
gules heraldic term
gulf
gulf·weed
gull
Gul·lah (*plural* **·lahs** *or* **·lah**) Negro people
gul·let
gul·li·bil·ity (*or* **·la·**)
gul·lible (*or* **·lable**)
gul·li·bly (*or* **·la·**)
gull-wing
gul·ly (*noun*, *plural* **·lies**; *verb* **·lies**, **·ly·ing**, **·lied**)
gulp
gulp·er
gulp·ing·ly
gum (**gum·ming**, **gummed**)
Gum·bo French patois
gum·bo (*or* **gom·**; *plural* **·bos**) thick stew
gum·boil
gum·boot
gum·bo·til clay
gum·drop
gum·ma (*plural* **·mas** *or* **·ma·ta**) tumour
gum·ma·tous
gum·mi·ly
gum·mi·ness
gum·mite mineral
gum·mo·sis plant disease
gum·my (**·mi·er**, **·mi·est**)
gump·tion
gum·shield
gum·shoe
gum·tree
gun (**gun·ning**, **gunned**)

gunboat

gun·boat
gun·cotton
gun·fight
gun·fighter
gun·fire
gun·flint
gunge
gun·gy
gunk *Slang* slimy substance
gun·lock
gun·man (*plural* ·men)
gun·metal
gunned
gun·nel fish; variant spelling of gunwale
gun·ner
gun·nery
gun·ning
gun·ny (*plural* ·nies) US fabric
gun·paper
gun·play
gun·point
gun·powder
gun·runner
gun·running
gun·shot
gun-shy
gun·slinger
gun·smith
gun·smithing
gun·stock
Gun·tur Indian city
gun·wale (*or* gun·nel) nautical term
gun·yah *Austral* bush hut
Guo·min·dang variant spelling of Kuomintang
gup·py (*plural* ·pies) fish
Gur language
gurd·wa·ra Sikh place of worship
gur·gi·ta·tion surging movement
gur·gle
gur·gling·ly
gur·jun tree
Gur·kha (*plural* ·khas *or* ·kha)
Gur·kha·li language
Gur·mu·khi Punjabi script
gur·nard (*or* gur·net; *plural* ·nard, ·nards *or* ·net, ·nets) fish
guru (*plural* gurus)

gush
gush·er
gush·ing·ly
gushy
gus·set
gust
gus·ta·tion tasting
gus·ta·tory (*or* ·tive)
gusti·ly
gusti·ness
gus·to
gusty (gusti·er, gusti·est)
gut (gut·ting, gut·ted)
gut·bucket jazz
gut·less
gutsy (gutsi·er, gutsi·est)
gut·ta (*plural* ·tae) drop
gutta-percha
gut·tate (*or* ·tat·ed) biology term
gut·ted
gut·ter
gut·ter·ing
gutter·snipe
gut·ting
gut·tur·al
gut·tur·ali·za·tion (*or* ·sa·tion)
gut·tur·al·ize (*or* ·ise)
gut·tur·al·ly
gut·tur·al·ness (*or* ·ity, ·ism)
gut·ty (*plural* ·ties) Irish urchin
guv *Slang* governor
guy
Guy·ana South American republic
Guya·nese (*or* Guy·an·an)
Guy·enne variant spelling of Guienne
guy·ot submerged mountain
guz·zle
guz·zler
Gwa·li·or Indian city
Gwe·lo Zimbabwean town
Gwent Welsh county
Gwyn·edd Welsh county
gwyni·ad fish
gybe (*or* jibe) nautical term; *compare* gibe
gym
gym·kha·na

198

gym·na·si·arch Greek magistrate
gym·na·si·ast
gym·na·sium (*plural* ·siums *or* ·sia)
gym·nast
gym·nas·tic
gym·nas·ti·cal·ly
gym·nas·tics
gym·noso·phist Indian ascetic
gym·no·sperm conifer
gym·no·sper·mous
gym·slip
gy·nae·ceum (*plural* ·cea) women's apartments; *compare* gynoecium
gy·nae·cium variant spelling of gynoecium
gy·nae·coc·ra·cy (*US* ·ne·; *plural* ·cies) government by women
gy·nae·co·crat·ic (*US* ·ne·)
gy·nae·coid (*US* ·ne·)
gy·nae·co·logi·cal (*or* ·log·ic; *US* ·ne·)
gy·nae·co·logi·cal·ly (*US* ·ne·)
gy·nae·colo·gist (*US* ·ne·)
gy·nae·col·ogy (*US* ·ne·)
gy·nae·co·mas·tia (*US* ·ne·) male breast development
gy·nan·dro·morph biology term
gy·nan·dro·mor·phic (*or* ·phous)
gy·nan·dro·morph·ism (*or* ·mor·phy)
gy·nan·drous botany term
gy·nan·dry (*or* ·drism)
gy·narch·ic
gyn·ar·chy (*plural* ·chies) gynaecocracy
gy·noe·cium (*or* ·nae·; *US* ·ne·; *plural* ·cia) part of flower; *compare* gynaeceum
gy·no·phore botany term
gy·no·phor·ic
gyp *Slang* pain
gyp·se·ous
gyp·sif·er·ous
gyp·sophi·la plant
gyp·sum

gyp·sy *variant spelling of* gipsy
gy·ral rotating
gy·rate
gy·ra·tion
gy·ra·tor
gy·ra·tory
gyre circular movement
gyr·fal·con (*or* **ger·**)

gyro (*plural* **gyros**) gyrocompass; gyroscope; *compare* giro
gy·ro·com·pass
gy·ro·mag·net·ic
gy·ro·plane
gy·ro·scope (*or* **·stat**)
gy·ro·scop·ic
gy·ro·scop·ics

gy·rose botany term
gy·ro·sta·bi·liz·er (*or* **·lis·er**)
gy·ro·stat·ic of rotating bodies
gy·ro·stat·ics
gy·rus (*plural* **gyri**) anatomy term
gyve *Archaic* fetter

H

ha (*or* **hah**) exclamation
haaf fishing ground
Haar·lem Dutch city; *compare* Harlem
haar fog
Habakkuk prophet
Ha·ba·na *Spanish* Havana
ha·ba·nera dance
ha·beas cor·pus
hab·er·dash·er
hab·er·dash·ery
hab·er·geon (*or* **hau·ber·geon**) coat of mail
hab·ile skilful
ha·bili·ment dress
ha·bili·tate
ha·bili·ta·tion
ha·bili·ta·tor
hab·it
hab·it·abil·ity (*or* **·able·ness**)
hab·it·able
hab·it·ably
hab·it·ant
habi·tat
habi·ta·tion
habi·ta·tion·al
hab·it·ed
ha·bitu·al
ha·bitu·al·ly
ha·bitu·al·ness
ha·bitu·ate
ha·bitu·a·tion
habi·tude
habi·tu·di·nal
ha·bitué
habi·tus (*plural* **·tus**) physical state
Habsburg (*or* **Hapsburg**) royal dynasty

habu snake
háček phonetic symbol
ha·chure shading
haci·en·da
hack
hacka·more *US* rope halter
hack·berry (*plural* **·berries**)
hack·but (*or* **hag·**) gun
hack·but·eer (*or* **hag·**)
hack·er
hack·ing
hack·le
hack·ler
hack·les
Hack·ney London borough
hack·ney carriage; make banal
hack·neyed
hack·ney·ism
hack·saw
had
ha·dal of ocean depths
hada·way *Dialect* hurry
had·dock
hade geology term
Ha·de·an
Ha·des underworld
Ha·dhra·maut Arabian plateau
Had·ith Mohammedan tradition
hadj *variant spelling of* hajj
hadj·i *variant spelling of* hajji
hadn't
had·ron elementary particle
had·ron·ic
had·ro·saur (*or* **·saur·us**)
hadst *Archaic* had
hae *Scot* have

haematogenic

haec·ce·ity (*plural* **·ities**) philosophy term
Haeck·elian of Haeckel
haem (*US* **heme**) organic pigment
haema·chrome *variant spelling of* haemochrome
haema·cy·tom·eter (*US* **hema·**)
hae·mag·glu·tin·ate (*US* **he·**)
hae·mag·glu·ti·nin (*US* **he·**) antibody
haema·gogue (*US* **hema·gogue** *or* **·gog**)
hae·mal (*US* **he·**)
haema·tein (*US* **hema·**) biological stain
haema·tem·esis (*US* **hema·**)
hae·mat·ic (*US* **he·**)
haema·tin (*US* **hema·**) dark pigment
haema·tin·ic (*US* **hema·**) medicinal drug
haema·tite (*US* **hema·**) mineral
haema·tit·ic (*US* **hema·**)
hae·mato·blast (*US* **he·**)
hae·mato·blas·tic (*US* **he·**)
haema·to·cele (*US* **hema·**)
haema·to·crit (*US* **hema·**) medical term
haema·to·cry·al (*US* **hema·**) zoology term
haema·to·gen·esis (*US* **hema·**)
haema·to·gen·ic (*US* **hema·**)

haematogenous

haema·tog·enous (*US* **hema·**)
haema·toid (*or* **hae·moid**; *US* **hema·** *or* **he·**)
haema·to·log·ic (*or* **·logi·cal**; *US* **hema·**)
haema·tolo·gist (*US* **hema·**)
haema·tol·ogy (*US* **hema·**)
haema·toly·sis *variant of* haemolysis
haema·to·ma (*US* **hema·**; *plural* **·mas** *or* **·mata**) blood tumour
haema·to·poi·esis (*or* **haemo·poi·esis**; *US* **hema·** *or* **hemo·**)
haema·to·poi·et·ic (*or* **haemo·poi·et·ic**; *US* **hema·** *or* **hemo·**)
haema·to·sis (*US* **hema·**)
haema·to·ther·mal (*US* **hema·**) warm-blooded
haema·toxy·lin (*US* **hema·**) dye
haema·toxy·lon tree
haema·to·zo·on (*US* **hema·**; *plural* **·zoa**)
haema·tu·ria (*US* **hema·**)
haema·tu·ric
hae·mic (*US* **he·**)
hae·min (*US* **he·**)
haemo·chrome (*or* **haema·**; *US* **hemo·** *or* **hema·**)
haemo·coel (*US* **hemo·**) zoology term
haemo·cya·nin (*US* **hemo·**)
haemo·cyte (*US* **hemo·**)
haemo·cy·tom·eter (*US* **hemo·**)
haemo·di·aly·sis (*US* **hemo·**)
haemo·flag·el·late (*US* **hemo·**) protozoan
haemo·glo·bin (*US* **hemo·**)
haemo·glo·bi·nu·ria (*US* **hemo·**)
hae·moid *variant of* haematoid
haemo·ly·sin (*US* **hemo·**)

hae·moly·sis (*or* **haema·toly·sis**; *US* **he·** *or* **hema·**; *plural* **·ses**)
haemo·lyt·ic (*US* **hemo·**)
haemo·phile (*US* **hemo·**)
haemo·philia (*US* **hemo·**)
haemo·phili·ac (*US* **hemo·**)
haemo·phil·ic (*US* **hemo·**)
haemo·poi·esis *variant of* haematopoiesis
haemo·poi·et·ic *variant of* haematopoietic
haem·op·ty·sis (*US* **hem·**) coughing blood
haem·or·rhage (*US* **hem·**)
haem·or·rhag·ic (*US* **hem·**)
haem·or·rhoid (*US* **hem·**)
haem·or·rhoi·dal (*US* **hem·**)
haem·or·rhoid·ec·to·my (*US* **hem·**; *plural* **·mies**)
haemo·sta·sis (*or* **·sia**; *US* **hemo·**)
haemo·stat (*US* **hemo·**)
haemo·stat·ic (*US* **hemo·**)
hae·re·mai Maori welcome
hae·res *variant spelling of* heres
Ha·erh·pin *variant spelling of* Harbin
ha·fiz Islamic title
haf·nium chemical element
haft
Haf·ta·rah (*or* **Haph·ta·rah**; *plural* **·ta·roth** *or* **·ta·rahs**) biblical reading
haft·er
hag
Hagar biblical character
hag·but *variant spelling of* hackbut
Ha·gen West German city
Hagen legendary character
hag·fish (*plural* **·fish** *or* **·fishes**)
Hag·ga·dah (*or* **·da**; *plural* **·dahs**, **·das**, *or* **·doth**) Jewish literature
hag·gad·ic (*or* **·gadi·cal**)
hag·ga·dist
hag·ga·dist·ic

200

Haggai biblical prophet
hag·gard
hag·gard·ness
hag·gis
hag·gish
hag·gish·ness
hag·gle
hag·gler
hagi·archy (*plural* **·archies**) government by saints
hagi·oc·ra·cy (*plural* **·cies**)
Hagi·og·ra·pha Old Testament section
hagi·og·ra·pher (*or* **·phist**)
hagi·o·graph·ic (*or* **·graphi·cal**)
hagi·og·ra·phy (*plural* **·phies**)
hagi·ola·ter
hagi·ola·trous
hagi·ola·try veneration of saints
hagi·o·log·ic (*or* **·logi·cal**)
hagi·olo·gist
hagi·ol·ogy (*plural* **·ogies**) writings about saints
hagi·o·scope architectural term
hagi·o·scop·ic
hag·like
Hague
hah *variant spelling of* ha
ha·ha (*or* **haw-haw**) sunken fence
Hai·da (*plural* **·da** *or* **·das**) American Indian
Hai·dan
Hai·duk (*or* **Hey·duck**, **Hei·duc**) brigand
Hai·fa Israeli port
haik (*or* **haick**) Arabian garment
hai·ku (*or* **hok·ku**; *plural* **·ku**) Japanese verse
hail frozen rain; greet; *compare* hale
hail·er
hail·stone
hail·storm
Hai·nan (*or* **Hai·nan Tao**) Chinese island
Hai·naut (*or* **·nault**) Belgian province
Hai·phong Vietnamese port

hair
hair·ball
hair·brush
hair·cloth
hair·cut
hair·do (*plural* ·dos)
hair·dresser
hair·dressing
hair·grip
hair·if plant
hairi·ness
hair·less
hair·like
hair·line
hair·net
hair·piece
hair·pin
hair-raising
hair's-breadth
hair·splitter
hair·splitting
hair·spring
hair·streak butterfly
hair·style
hair·stylist
hair·tail fish
hair·weaving
hair·worm
hairy (hairi·er, hairi·est)
Hai·ti
Hai·tian
hajj (*or* hadj; *plural* hajjes *or* hadjes) Muslim pilgrimage
haj·ji (*or* hadji, haji)
hake (*plural* hake *or* hakes)
ha·kea shrub
ha·kim (*or* ·keem) Muslim judge or physician
Ha·ko·da·te Japanese port
Ha·la·fian Neolithic culture
Ha·la·kah (*or* ·cha) Jewish literature
Ha·lak·ic (*or* ·lach·ic)
hal·al (*or* hall·al) Muslim custom
ha·la·tion photography term
ha·la·vah *variant of* halvah
hal·berd (*or* ·bert)
hal·ber·dier
hal·cy·on
Halcyone *variant of* Alcyone

hale healthy; to haul; *compare* hail
Ha·lea·ka·la Hawaiian volcano
hale·ness
ha·ler (*plural* ·lers *or* ·leru) Czech coin
Hales·ow·en English town
half (*plural* halves)
half·back
half·baked
half·beak fish
half-caste
half-day
half-hearted
half-hearted·ly
half-hearted·ness
half-life
half-light
half-mast
half-naked
half-open
half·penny (*plural* ·pennies *or* ·pence)
half·penny·worth
half-price
half-shut
half-time
half·tone
half·way
half·wit
half·witted
half·witted·ly
half·witted·ness
hali·but (*plural* ·but *or* ·buts)
Ha·liç Turkish Golden Horn
Hali·car·nas·si·an
Hali·car·nas·sus ancient Greek city
hal·ide (*or* ·id) chemical compound
hali·dom *Archaic* holy thing
Hali·fax Canadian port; British town
hal·ite mineral
hali·to·sis
hall
hal·lah *variant spelling of* challah
hall·al *variant spelling of* halal
Hal·lel Jewish chant
hal·le·lu·jah *variant of* alleluia

hal·liard *variant spelling of* halyard
hall·mark
hal·lo *variant spelling of* halioo *or* hello
hal·loo (*or* ·lo; *noun, plural* ·loos *or* ·los; *verb* ·loos, ·loo·ing, ·looed; *or* ·los, ·loing, ·loed) shout; *compare* hello
hal·low
hal·lowed
hal·lowed·ness
Hal·low·e'en (*or* Hal·low·een)
hal·low·er
Hal·low·mas (*or* ·mass)
Hall·statt archaeology term
Hall·stat·tian
hal·lu·ci·nate
hal·lu·ci·na·tion
hal·lu·ci·na·tion·al (*or* ·na·tive)
hal·lu·ci·na·tor
hal·lu·ci·na·tory
hal·lu·cino·gen drug
hal·lu·ci·no·gen·ic
hal·lu·ci·no·sis mental disorder
hal·lux (*plural* ·luces) first digit on foot
hall·way
halm *variant spelling of* haulm
hal·ma
Hal·ma·he·ra Indonesian island
halo (*noun, plural* haloes *or* halos; *verb* haloes *or* halos, halo·ing, haloed)
ha·lo·bi·ont salt-water organism
halo·gen
halo·gen·ate
halo·gen·a·tion
halo·gen·oid
ha·log·enous
hal·oid
halo-like
halo·phyte plant
halo·phyt·ic
halo·phyt·ism
halo·thane
halt

Haltemprice

Hal·tem·price Hull suburb
hal·ter
hal·tere zoology term
halter-like
halt·ing
halt·ing·ness
hal·vah (*or* **hal·va, ha·la·vah**) sweetmeat
halve
hal·yard (*or* **hal·liard**)
ham (**ham·ming, hammed**)
Hama Syrian city
Hama·dān (*or* **Ham·edān**) Iranian city
hama·dry·ad nymph
hama·dry·as baboon
ha·mal (*or* **ham·mal, ha·maul**) Oriental servant
Ha·ma·ma·tsu Japanese city
hama·meli·da·ceous botany term
ha·mate hook-shaped
Ham·ble·to·nian horse
Ham·burg
ham·burg·er
hame harness attachment
Ham·elin (*or* **Ha·meln**) West German town
Ham·ers·ley Australian mountain range
Ham·il·ton Canadian port
Ham·il·to·ni·an maths term
Ham·ite African people
Ham·it·ic
ham·let
ham·mer
ham·mer·er
hammer·head animal
hammer·headed
ham·mer·less
hammer-like
Ham·mer·smith
hammer·toe
ham·mock
hammock-like
Ham·mond US city
ham·my (**ham·mi·er, ham·mi·est**)
ham·per
ham·pered·ness
ham·per·er
Hamp·shire
Hamp·stead

Hamp·ton US city
ham·shack·le fetter a horse
ham·ster
ham·string (**·string·ing, ·strung**)
hamu·lar
hamu·lus (*plural* **·li**) hooklike projection
ham·za (*or* **·zah**) Arabic phonetic sign
Han Chinese dynasty; river
hana·per wickerwork basket
hance (*or* **haunch**) architectural term
hand
hand·bag
hand·ball
hand·baller
hand·barrow
hand·bell
hand·bill
hand·book
hand·brake
hand·breadth
hand·cart
hand·clasp
hand·craft
hand·cuff
hand·fast *Archaic* agreement
hand·fasting
hand·feed (**·feed·ing, ·fed**)
hand·ful
hand·grip
hand·gun
hand·hold
handi·cap (**·cap·ping, ·capped**)
handi·cap·per
handi·craft
handi·crafts·man (*plural* **·men**)
handi·ly
handi·ness
handi·work
hand·ker·chief
han·dle
han·dle·able
handle·bar
han·dled
han·dle·less
han·dler
hand·less
hand·like
han·dling
hand·made

hand·maiden (*or* **·maid**)
hand-me-down
hand-out (*noun*)
hand·rail
hand·saw
hand·sel (*or* **han·**) *Dialect* new year gift
hand·set
hand·shake
hand·some good-looking; *compare* **hansom**
hand·some·ly
hand·some·ness
hand·spike lever
hand·spring
hand·stand
hand·stroke bell-ringing term
hand·writing
hand·written
handy (**handi·er, handi·est**)
handy·man (*plural* **·men**)
hang (**hang·ing, hung** *or* **hanged**)
hang·ar aircraft shed; *compare* **hanger**
hang·bird
Hang·chow (*or* **Hang·chou**) Chinese port
hang·dog
hanged killed; *compare* **hung**
hang·er support; one that hangs; *compare* **hangar**
hanger-on (*plural* **hangers-on**)
hang·man (*plural* **·men**)
hang·nail
hang·over
hang-up (*noun*)
hank
hank·er
(**hankerchief**) incorrect spelling *of* **handkerchief**
hank·er·er
Han·kow (*or* **Han-k'ou**) former Chinese city
hanky (*or* **hankie**; *plural* **hankies**)
hanky-panky
Ha·noi Vietnamese capital
Hano·ver
Hano·verian
Han·sard parliamentary report

Hanse (*or* Han·sa)
   medieval guild
Han·seat·ic
han·sel *variant spelling of*
   handsel
han·som cab; *compare*
   handsome
Ha·nuk·kah Jewish festival
Hanu·man monkey god
hanu·man monkey
Han·yang former Chinese
   city
hap (hap·ping, happed)
   Archaic happen; luck
ha·pax le·go·menon
   (*plural* ha·pax
   le·go·mena) nonce word
ha'·penny (*plural*
   ·pennies)
hap·haz·ard
hap·haz·ard·ness
Haph·ta·rah *variant spelling*
   of Haftarah
hap·less
hap·less·ness
hap·lite *variant spelling of*
   aplite
hap·lit·ic *variant spelling of*
   aplitic
hap·log·ra·phy (*plural*
   ·phies) omission of letter
   in writing
hap·loid biology term
hap·loidy
hap·lo·log·ic
hap·lol·ogy (*plural* ·ogies)
   omission of syllable in
   speech
hap·lo·sis biology term
hap·ly
ha'·p'orth
hap·pen
hap·pen·ing
hap·pen·stance
hap·pi·ly
hap·pi·ness
hap·py (·pi·er, ·pi·est)
happy-go-lucky
Hapsburg *variant spelling of*
   Habsburg
hap·ten (*or* ·tene) medical
   term
hap·ter·on botany term
hap·tic of touch
hap·to·trop·ism botany
   term

ha·ra·ki·ri (*or* ha·ri·ka·ri)
   Japanese suicide
ha·ram·bee African chant
ha·rangue
ha·rangu·er
Ha·rap·pa Pakistani city
Ha·rap·pan
Ha·rar (*or* Har·rar)
   Ethiopian city
Ha·rare Zimbabwean
   capital
har·ass
har·ass·er
har·ass·ing·ly
har·ass·ment
Har·bin (*or* Ha·erh·pin)
   Chinese city
har·bin·ger
har·bour (*US* ·bor)
har·bour·age (*US* ·bor·)
har·bour·er (*US* ·bor·)
har·bour·less (*US* ·bor·)
hard
hard·back
hard·bake almond toffee
hard·board
hard·en
hard·ened
hard·en·er
hard·en·ing
hard·hack plant
hard·headed
hard·headed·ly
hard·headed·ness
hard·heads plant
hard·hearted
hard·hearted·ly
hard·hearted·ness
har·di·hood
har·di·ly
har·di·ness
hard·ly
hard·ness
hard·pan clay layer
hards (*or* hurds) coarse
   fibres
hard·ship
hard·tack
hard·top
hard·ware
hard·wood
har·dy (·di·er, ·di·est)
hare
hare·bell
hare·brained

hare·like
hare·lip
hare·lipped
har·em (*or* ·eem)
Har·gei·sa Somalian city
hari·cot
(haridan) *incorrect spelling*
   of harridan
Ha·ri·jan Indian
   untouchable
ha·ri·ka·ri *variant spelling of*
   harakiri
Ha·rin·gey London
   borough
hark
hark·en *US variant spelling*
   of hearken
harl *variant spelling of* herl
Har·lem New York district;
   compare Haarlem
har·lequin
har·lequin·ade
Har·ley Street
har·lot
har·lot·ry
Har·low Essex town
harm
har·mat·tan Saharan wind
harm·er
harm·ful
harm·ful·ly
harm·ful·ness
harm·less
harm·less·ness
har·mon·ic
har·moni·ca
har·moni·cal·ly
har·mon·ics
har·mo·ni·ous
har·mo·nist
har·mo·nis·tic
har·mo·nis·ti·cal·ly
har·mo·nium
har·mo·niz·able
har·mo·ni·za·tion
har·mo·nize (*or* ·nise)
har·mo·niz·er
har·mo·ny (*plural* ·nies)
har·mo·tome
har·ness
har·ness·er
har·ness·less
harness-like
Har·ney *US* mountain
harp

harper

harp·er
harp·ings (*or* ·ins) nautical term
har·poon
har·poon·er
har·poon-like
harp·si·chord
harp·si·chord·ist
har·py (*plural* ·pies)
har·que·bus *variant spelling of* arquebus
Har·rar Ethiopian city (harrass) *incorrect spelling of* harass
har·ri·dan
har·ri·er
Har·ris Scottish island
Har·ris·burg US city
Har·ro·gate Yorkshire town
Har·ro·vian
Har·row London borough
har·row tool
har·row·er
har·row·ing
har·row·ment
har·rumph
har·ry (·ries, ·ry·ing, ·ried)
harsh
harsh·ly
harsh·ness
hars·let *variant spelling of* haslet
hart (*plural* hart *or* harts)
har·tal
har·te·beest (*or* hart·beest) antelope
Hart·ford US port
Har·tle·pool
harts·horn
harum-scarum
ha·rus·pex (*plural* ha·rus·pi·ces) Roman priest
ha·rus·pi·cal
ha·rus·pi·cy
Har·vard
har·vest
har·vest·er
har·vest·ing
har·vest·less
harvest·man (*plural* ·men)
Har·wich Essex port
Har·ya·na Indian state

Harz German mountain range
has
Ha·sa Saudi Arabian province
has-been
hash
Hash·e·mite descendant of Mohammed
hash·ish
Ha·sid·ic (*or* Has·sid·ic)
Hasi·dim (*or* Has·si·dim) Jewish sect
Has·id·ism (*or* Has·sid·ism)
hask *Dialect* cough
has·let (*or* hars·) meat loaf
hasn't
hasp
has·sle
has·sock kneeling cushion; *compare* cassock
hast
has·tate botany term
haste
haste·ful
haste·ful·ly
has·ten
has·ten·er
hasti·ly
hasti·ness
Hast·ings
has·ty (·ti·er, ·ti·est)
hat (hat·ting, hat·ted)
hat·able *variant spelling of* hateable
hat·band
hat·box
hatch
hatch·able
hatch·back
hatch·el (·el·ling, ·elled; *US* ·el·ing, ·eled) comb flax
hatch·el·ler (*US* ·el·er)
hatch·er
hatch·ery (*plural* ·eries)
hatch·et
hatchet-like
hatch·ing
hatch·ment heraldic term
hatch·way
hate
hate·able (*or* hat·)
hate·ful

hate·ful·ly
hate·ful·ness
hater
Hat·field Hertfordshire town
hath
Hath·or Egyptian goddess
Ha·thor·ic
hat·less
hat·like
hat·pin
ha·tred
hat·ter
Hat·ter·as US cape
hau·ber·geon *variant spelling of* habergeon
hau·berk coat of mail
haugh *Dialect* flat valley base
haugh·ti·ly
haugh·ti·ness
haugh·ty (·ti·er, ·ti·est)
haul
haul·age
haul·er (*or* ·ier)
haulm (*or* halm) plant stem
haunch
haunched
haunt
haunt·ed
haunt·er
haunt·ing
Hau·ra·ki New Zealand gulf
Hau·sa (*plural* ·sas *or* ·sa) African people
haus·frau
haus·tel·late
haus·tel·lum (*plural* ·la) entomology term
haus·to·ri·al
haus·to·rium (*plural* ·ria) plant organ
haut·boy strawberry
haute cou·ture
haute cui·sine
hau·teur
Ha·vana Cuban capital
Hav·ant Hampshire town
have (has, hav·ing, had)
have·lock protective cap cover
ha·ven
ha·ven·less
have-not (*noun*)

haven't
ha·ver dither
Ha·ver·ing London borough
hav·er·sack
Ha·ver·sian anatomy term
hav·er·sine maths term
hav·il·dar Indian NCO
hav·ing
hav·oc (·ock·ing, ·ocked)
hav·ock·er
haw
Ha·waii
Ha·wai·ian
Hawes English lake
haw·finch
Haw·ick Scottish town
hawk
hawk·bit plant
hawk·er
hawk·ing
hawk·ish
hawk·like
hawks·bill turtle
hawk·weed
Ha·worth Yorkshire village
hawse nautical term
hawse·hole
hawse·pipe
haws·er
haw·thorn
hay
hay·box
hay·cock pile of hay
hay·fork
hay·maker
hay·making
hay·mow
hay·rack
hay·rick
hay·seed
hay·stack
hay·ward Obsolete parish officer
hay·wire
haz·ard
haz·ard·able
haz·ard-free
haz·ard·ous
haz·ard·ous·ness
haze
ha·zel
hazel·hen
hazel·nut
haz·er nautical term

ha·zi·ly
ha·zi·ness
hazy (ha·zi·er, ha·zi·est)
he
head
head·ache
head·achy
head·band
head·board
head·cheese US brawn
head·dress
head·ed
head·er
head·fast mooring rope
head·first
head·gear
head-hunt
head-hunter
head-hunting
headi·ly
headi·ness
head·ing
head·less
head·light (or ·lamp)
head·like
head·line
head·lin·er
head·lock
head·long
head·man (plural ·men)
head·master (fem ·mistress)
head·master·ship (fem ·mistress·)
head·most
head-on
head·phones
head·piece
head·pin
head·quarters
head·race
head·rail billiards term
head·reach nautical term
head·rest
head·room
head·sail
head·scarf (plural ·scarves)
head·set
head·ship
head·shrinker
heads·man (plural ·men) executioner
head·spring
head·square

head·stall
head·stand
head·stock part of machine tool
head·stone
head·stream
head·strong
head·strong·ness
head·wards (or esp. US ·ward)
head·waters
head·way
head·wind
head·word
head·work
head·worker
heady (head·ier, head·iest)
heal cure; compare heel
heal·able
heal·er
heal·ing·ly
health
health·ful
health·ful·ly
health·ful·ness
healthi·ly
healthi·ness
healthy (health·ier, health·iest)
heap
heap·er
heap·ing
hear (hear·ing, heard)
hear·able
hear·er
hark·en (US also hark·)
hark·en·er
hear·say
hearse
hcart
heart·ache
heart·beat
heart·break
heart·breaker
heart·breaking
heart·breaking·ly
heart·broken
heart·broken·ly
heart·broken·ness
heart·burn
heart·en
heart·en·ing·ly
heart·felt
hearth

hearthstone

hearth·stone
hearti·ly
hearti·ness
heart·land
heart·less
heart·less·ness
heart-rending
hearts·ease wild pansy
heart·sick
heart·sickness
heart·some
heart·some·ly
heart·some·ness
heart·strings
heart·wood
heart·worm
hearty (heart·ier, hearti·est)
heat
heat·ed
heat·ed·ly
heat·ed·ness
heat·er
heath
heath·berry (plural ·berries)
hea·then (plural ·thens or ·then)
hea·then·dom
hea·then·ish
hea·then·ish·ness
hea·then·ism
hea·then·ize
hea·then·ness
heath·er
heath·ered
heath·ery
heath·fowl
heath·like
heathy
heat·ing
heat·less
heat·stroke
heaume medieval helmet
heave (heav·ing, heaved or hove)
heav·en
heav·en·li·ness
heav·en·ly
heav·en·ward (adj)
heav·en·wards (adv)
heav·er
heaves horse disease
heavi·ly
heavi·ness

heavy (adj heavi·er, heavi·est; noun, plural heavies)
heavy-handed
heavy-handed·ly
heavy-handed·ness
heavy·weight
heb·do·mad Obsolete seven
heb·doma·dal (or ·da·ry) weekly
heb·doma·dal·ly
Hebe Greek goddess
he·be·phre·nia schizophrenia
he·be·phren·ic
heb·etate blunt
heb·eta·tion
he·bet·ic of puberty
heb·e·tude lethargy
heb·etu·di·nous
He·bra·ic (or ·brai·cal)
He·bra·i·cal·ly
He·bra·ism
He·bra·ist
He·bra·is·tic
He·bra·is·ti·cal·ly
He·bra·i·za·tion
He·bra·ize
He·bra·iz·er
He·brew
Heb·ri·dean
Heb·ri·des
Heb·ron Jordanian city
Heca·te (or Heka·te) Greek goddess
heca·tomb sacrifice
heck
heck·el·phone oboe
heck·le
heck·ler
hec·tare
hec·tic
hec·ti·cal·ly
hec·to·coty·lus zoology term
hec·to·gram
hec·to·graph copying process
hec·to·graph·ic
hec·to·graphi·cal·ly
hec·tog·ra·phy
hec·tor
Hec·u·ba mythological character
he'd

hed·dle part of loom
hedge
hedge·hog
hedge·hop (·hop·ping, ·hopped)
hedge·hop·per
hedg·er
hedge·row
hedgy
He·djaz Saudi Arabian region
he·don·ic
he·don·ics branch of psychology
he·don·ism
he·don·ist
heebie-jeebies
heed
heed·er
heed·ful
heed·ful·ly
heed·ful·ness
heed·less
heed·less·ly
heed·less·ness
hee-haw
heel part of foot; compare heal
heel·ball
heeled
heel·er
heel·less
heel·piece
heel·post
heel·tap
Heer·len Dutch city
heft
heft·er
hefti·ly
hefti·ness
hefty (hefti·er, hefti·est)
He·geli·an
He·geli·an·ism school of philosophy
heg·emon·ic
he·gemo·ny
Hegi·ra (or Heji·ra) flight of Mohammed
he·gu·men (or ·menos) Eastern Church leader
heh exclamation
Hei·del·berg West German city
Hei·duc variant spelling of Haiduk

heif·er
heigh-ho
height tallness; *compare* hight
height·en
height·en·er
Hei·lung·kiang Chinese province
Heim·dall (*or* Heim·dal, Heim·dallr) Norse god
hei·nous
hei·nous·ness
heir
heir·dom
heir·ess
heir·less
heir·loom
heir·ship
heist
heist·er
hei·ti·ki Maori ornament
He·jaz (*or* Hi·jaz) Saudi Arabian province
Heji·ra *variant spelling of* Hegira
Heka·te *variant spelling of* Hecate
Hek·la Icelandic volcano
Hel (*or* Hela) Norse goddess
held
Hel·ena US city
Hel·go·land *variant spelling of* Heligoland
he·li·a·cal astronomy term; *compare* helical
he·li·an·thus (*plural* ·thuses) sunflower
heli·cal spiral; *compare* heliacal
heli·cal·ly
hell·ces *plural of* helix
heli·chrysum plant
heli·cline spiral ramp
heli·co·graph
heli·coid
heli·coi·dal·ly
heli·con tuba
Heli·con Greek mountain
heli·cop·ter
Heli·go·land (*or* Hel·go·) North Sea island
helio·cen·tric
helio·cen·tri·cal·ly
helio·cen·tric·i·ty (*or* helio·cen·tri·cism)

Helio·chrome (*Trademark*)
helio·chro·mic
helio·graph
he·li·og·ra·pher
helio·graph·ic
heliog·ra·phy
helio·gra·vure printing term
he·li·ola·ter
he·li·ola·trous
he·li·ola·try sun worship
he·lio·lith·ic
he·li·om·eter telescope
helio·met·ric
helio·met·ri·cal·ly
he·li·om·etry
He·li·opo·lis ancient Egyptian city
Helios sun god
helio·stat
helio·stat·ic
helio·tac·tic
helio·tax·is biology term
helio·thera·py
helio·trope plant
helio·trop·ic growing towards sunlight
helio·trop·i·cal·ly
he·li·ot·ro·pin chemical compound
he·li·ot·ro·pism
helio·type printing process
helio·typ·ic
helio·zo·an biology term
heli·port
he·lium chemical element
he·lix (*plural* heli·ces *or* he·lixes)
hell
he'll he will; he shall
Hel·ladic archaeology term
Hel·las ancient Greece
hell·bender
hell·bent
hell·box
hell·cat
hell·diver bird
Hel·le mythological character
hel·le·bore plant
hel·le·bor·ine orchid
Hel·len legendary king
Hel·lene (*or* Hel·le·nian) Greek

Hel·len·ic
Hel·leni·cal·ly
Hel·len·ism
Hel·len·ist
Hel·len·is·tic
Hel·len·is·ti·cal·ly
Hel·leni·za·tion (*or* ·sa·tion)
Hel·len·ize (*or* ·ise)
Hel·len·iz·er (*or* ·is·er)
hel·ler (*plural* ·ler) German coin
hell·ery wild behaviour
Hel·les Turkish cape
Hel·les·pont Dardanelles
hell·fire
hell·gram·mite insect larva
hell·hole
hell·hound
hel·lion
hell·ish
hell·ish·ness
hel·lo (*or* hal·lo, hul·lo; *plural* ·los)
helm
Hel·mand Asian river
hel·met
hel·met·ed
helmet-like
hel·minth parasitic worm
hel·min·thia·sis
hel·min·thic
hel·min·thoid
hel·min·tho·logi·cal
hel·min·tholo·gist
hel·min·thol·ogy
helm·less
helms·man (*plural* ·men)
Helot ancient Greek class
helot serf
hel·ot·ism
hel·ot·ry
help
help·able
help·er
help·ful
help·ful·ly
help·ful·ness
help·ing
help·less
help·less·ness
help·mate
help·meet *Archaic* helpmate
Hel·sin·ki
helter-skelter

helve

helve tool handle
Hel·vel·lyn English mountain
Hel·ve·tia Switzerland
Hel·ve·tian
Hel·vet·ic
Hel·vetii Celtic tribe
hem (**hem·ming, hemmed**)
hema· (*or* **hemato·**) *US spelling of words beginning with* **haemo·** *or* **haemato·**
he·mal *US spelling of* **haemal**
he-man (*plural* **-men**)
heme *US spelling of* **haem**
Hem·el Hemp·stead
hem·ely·tron (*or* **hemi·**; *plural* **·tra**) zoology term
hem·era·lo·pia day blindness
hem·era·lop·ic
hemi·al·gia pain on one side
hemi·an·ops·ia sight defect
he·mic *US spelling of* **haemic**
hemi·cel·lu·lose
hemi·chor·date zoology term
hemi·cy·cle
hemi·cy·clic
hemi·demi·semi·qua·ver
hemi·ely·tron *variant spelling of* **hemelytron**
hemi·he·dral crystallography term
hemi·hy·drate
hemi·hy·drat·ed
hemi·mor·phic crystallography term
hemi·mor·phism (*or* **·phy**)
hemi·mor·phite mineral
he·min *US spelling of* **haemin**
hemio·la musical term
hemi·ol·ic
hemi·para·site
hemi·plegia
hemi·ple·gic
hemi·pode (*or* **·pod**) bird
he·mip·ter·an (*or* **·on**) insect
he·mip·ter·ous
hemi·sphere
hemi·spher·ic (*or* **·spheri·cal**)
hemi·spher·oid
hemi·spher·oi·dal
hemi·stich half line of verse
hemi·ter·pene chemistry term
hemi·trope chemistry term
hemi·trop·ic
hemi·tro·pism (*or* **he·mit·ro·py**)
hem·line
hem·lock
hem·mer
hemo· *US spelling of words beginning with* **haemo·**
hemp
hemp·en
hem·stitch
hem·stitch·er
hen
hen·bane plant
hen·bit plant
hence
hence·forth
hence·forward
hench·man (*plural* **·men**)
hen·coop
hen·deca·gon
hen·de·cago·nal
hen·deca·he·dron
hen·deca·syl·lab·ic
hen·deca·syl·la·ble
hen·dia·dys rhetorical device
hen·equen (*or* **hen·equin, heni·quen**) fibre
henge archaeology term
Heng-yang Chinese city
hen·house
Hen·ley Oxfordshire town
hen·na
hen·nery (*plural* **·neries**) poultry house
heno·theism worship of one deity
heno·theist
heno·theis·tic
hen·peck
hen·pecked
hen·ry (*plural* **·ry, ·ries,** *or* **·rys**) unit
hent *Archaic* seize
hep
hepa·rin biochemical substance
he·pat·ic of liver
he·pati·ca plant
hepa·ti·tis

hep·cat
Hephaestus (*or* **Hephaistos**) Greek god
hep·tad
hep·ta·deca·no·ic acid
hep·ta·gon
hep·tago·nal
hep·ta·he·dral
hep·ta·he·dron
hep·tam·er·ous
hep·tam·eter type of verse line
hep·ta·met·ri·cal
hep·tane chemical compound
hep·tan·gu·lar
hep·tarch
hep·tar·chic
hep·tar·chy (*plural* **·chies**)
hep·ta·stich
Hep·ta·teuch Old Testament books
hep·tava·lent
hep·tose
her
Hera (*or* **Here**) Greek goddess
Hera·clea ancient Greek colony
Hera·clean
Heracles (*or* **Herakles**) *variants of* **Hercules**
Hera·cli·dan
Hera·clid (*or* **·klid**) descendant of Hercules
her·ald
he·ral·dic
he·ral·di·cal·ly
her·ald·ist
her·ald·ry
He·rat Afghan city
herb
her·ba·ceous
herb·age
herb·al
herb·al·ist
her·bar·ial
her·bar·ium (*plural* **·iums** *or* **·ia**)
her·bi·cid·al
herbi·cide
her·bi·vore
her·bivo·rous
her·bivo·rous·ness
herb·like

herby (herbi·er, herbi·est)
Her·cego·vi·na (or **·zego·**) Yugoslav region
Her·cu·la·neum ancient Italian city
her·cu·lean
Her·cu·les constellation
Hercules (or **Heracles, Herakles**) mythological hero
Her·cyn·ian geology term
herd
herd·er
her·dic US small carriage
herds·man (plural **·men**)
Herd·wick sheep
here
here·abouts
here·after
here·at
here·by
he·redes plural of heres
he·redi·tabil·ity
he·redi·table
he·redi·tably
her·edita·ment legal term
he·redi·tari·an·ism psychology term
he·redi·tari·ly
he·redi·tari·ness
he·redi·tary
he·redi·tist
he·red·ity (plural **·ities**)
Her·eford
here·in
here·in·after
here·in·before
here·into
here·of
here·on
He·rero (plural **·rero** or **·reros**) African people
he·res (or **hae·**; plural **·redes**) heir
he·resi·arch heretical leader
her·esy (plural **·esies**)
her·etic
he·reti·cal
he·reti·cal·ly
here·to
here·to·fore
here·under
here·unto
here·upon
here·with
heri·ot medieval death duty
her·it·abil·ity
her·it·able
her·it·ably
her·it·age
heri·tor (fem **·tress**)
herl (or **harl**) angling term
herm
her·maph·ro·dite
her·maph·ro·dit·ic
her·maph·ro·diti·cal·ly
her·maph·ro·dit·ism
Hermaphroditus mythological character
her·meneu·tic
her·meneu·ti·cal·ly
her·meneu·tics
her·meneu·tist
Hermes Greek god
Her·mes asteroid
her·met·ic air-tight; compare hermitic
her·meti·cal·ly
her·mit
her·mit·age
Her·mit·ian maths term
her·mit·ic hermit-like; compare hermetic
her·miti·cal·ly
her·mit-like
Her·mon mountain
Her·mou·po·lis Greek port
hern Dialect heron
her·nia
her·nial
her·ni·at·ed
her·ni·or·rha·phy (plural **·phies**) hernia surgery
Hero mythological character
hero (plural **heroes**)
Herodias mother of Salome
he·ro·ic
he·roi·cal·ly
he·ro·ics
hero·in drug
hero·ine heroic female
hero·ism
her·on
her·on·ry (plural **·ries**)
her·pes
her·pes sim·plex
her·pes zos·ter
her·pet·ic
her·pe·to·log·ic (or **·logi·cal**)
her·pe·to·logi·cal·ly
her·pe·tolo·gist
her·pe·tol·ogy study of reptiles
Herr (plural **Her·ren**) German title of address
her·ring (plural **·rings** or **·ring**)
herring·bone
hers of her
her·self
Herst·mon·ceux (or **Hurst·**)
Hert·ford
Hert·ford·shire
hertz (plural **hertz**) unit
Hertz·ian physics term
Hertzsprung-Russell diagram
Her·zego·vi·na variant spelling of Hercegovina
he's he is; he has
Hesi·od·ic of Hesiod
Hesione mythological princess
hesi·tan·cy
hesi·tant
hesi·tant·ly
hesi·tate
hesi·tat·er
hesi·tat·ing·ly
hesi·ta·tion
hesi·ta·tive
Hes·per·ia western land
Hes·pe·rian
Hesperides mythological characters
Hes·per·id·ian (or **·ean**)
hes·peri·din biochemical compound
hes·per·id·ium botany term
Hes·per·us evening star
Hesse West German state
Hes·sian of Hesse
hes·sian fibre
hes·site mineral
hes·so·nite gemstone
hest behest
Hestia Greek goddess
Hesy·chast Greek Orthodox mystic
Hesy·chast·ic
het Archaic heated

hetaera

he·tae·ra (*or* ·tai·; *plural* ·tae·rae *or* ·tai·rai) Greek prostitute
he·tae·ric (*or* ·tai·)
he·tae·rism (*or* ·tai·)
he·tae·rist (*or* ·tai·)
he·tae·ris·tic (*or* ·tai·)
hetero·cer·cal zoology term
hetero·chro·mat·ic
hetero·chro·ma·tin
hetero·chro·ma·tism
hetero·chro·mo·some
hetero·chro·mous
hetero·clite grammar term
hetero·clit·ic
hetero·cy·clic
hetero·dac·tyl ornithology term
hetero·dont zoology term
hetero·dox
hetero·doxy
hetero·dyne electronics term
het·er·oecious botany term
het·er·oecism
hetero·gam·ete
heteroga·mous
het·er·oga·my botany term
hetero·geneity
hetero·geneous of different parts; *compare* heterogenous
hetero·gen·esis
hetero·genet·ic
hetero·genetical·ly
hetero·gen·ous of different origin; *compare* heterogeneous
heter·ogeny
het·er·ogo·nous
heter·ogo·ny biology term
hetero·graft
hetero·graph·ic
het·er·og·ra·phy grammar term
het·er·ogy·nous
hetero·leci·thal
het·er·olo·gous
het·er·ol·ogy
het·er·oly·sis
hetero·lyt·ic
het·er·om·er·ous
hetero·mor·phic
hetero·mor·phism
het·er·ono·mous

het·er·ono·my
hetero·nym grammar term
het·er·ony·mous
Hetero·ousian Christian sect
het·er·opho·ny musical term
hetero·phyl·lous
hetero·phyl·ly
hetero·phyte
hetero·plas·tic
hetero·plas·ty (*plural* ·ties) surgical transplant
hetero·po·lar
hetero·po·larity
het·er·op·ter·ous zoology term
hetero·scedas·tic·ity statistics term
hetero·sex·ism
hetero·sex·ist
hetero·sex·ual
hetero·sexu·al·ity
hetero·sex·ual·ly
hetero·sis
het·er·os·po·rous
het·er·os·po·ry
hetero·sty·lous
hetero·sty·ly botany term
hetero·tac·tic
hetero·tax·is
hetero·thal·lic botany term
hetero·to·pia (*or* het·er·oto·py) displacement of body part
hetero·top·ic
hetero·troph·ic biology term
hetero·typ·ic (*or* ·typi·cal) biology term
hetero·zy·go·sis
hetero·zy·gote
hetero·zy·gous genetics term
heth (*or* cheth) Hebrew letter
het·man (*plural* ·men) Cossack leader
heu·land·ite mineral
heu·ris·tic
heu·ris·ti·cal·ly
hew (hew·ing, hewed, hewed *or* hewn) cut; *compare* hue
hew·er
hex *US* bewitch

210

hexa·chloro·cyclo·hex·ane
hexa·chloro·ethane
hexa·chloro·phene
hexa·chord musical term
hexa·co·sa·no·ic acid
hex·ad six
hexa·decane
hexa·deci·mal
hex·adic
hexa·em·er·ic
hexa·em·er·on (*or* ·hem·er·on) the Creation
hexa·gon
hex·ago·nal
hex·ag·o·nal·ly
hexa·gram
hexa·gram·moid
hexa·he·dral
hexa·he·dron
hexa·hy·drate
hexa·hy·drat·ed
hex·am·er·ism
hex·am·er·ous (*or* ·eral)
hex·am·eter
hexa·methylene·tetramine
hexa·met·ric
hex·ane
hex·an·gu·lar
hexa·no·ic acid
hexa·pla Old Testament edition
hexa·plar (*or* ·plar·ic)
hexa·pod insect
hexa·pod·ic
hex·apo·dy (*plural* ·dies) verse form
hexa·stich (*or* hex·as·ti·chon) six-line poem
hexa·stich·ic
hexa·style architecture term
Hexa·teuch Old Testament books
Hexa·teu·chal
hexa·va·lent
hex·one chemical compound
hexo·san biochemical compound
hex·ose sugar
hex·yl
hexyl·resor·cin·ol
hey exclamation
hey·day

Hey·duck *variant spelling of* Haiduk
Hey·sham Lancashire port
Hey·wood English town
Hezekiah biblical character
hi
Hia·leah US city
hia·tal
hia·tus (*plural* **·tuses** *or* **·tus**)
hi·ba·chi brazier
hi·ber·nacu·lum (*or* **·nac·le**; *plural* **·ula** *or* **·les**)
hi·ber·nal
hi·ber·nate
hi·ber·na·tion
hi·ber·na·tor
Hi·ber·nia Ireland
Hi·ber·nian
Hi·ber·ni·an·ism
Hi·ber·ni·cism
hi·bis·cus
hic·cup (**·cup·ing**, **·cuped** *or* **·cup·ping**, **·cupped**)
hick
hick·ey US gadget
hicko·ry (*plural* **·ries**)
hid
hid·able
hi·dal·go (*plural* **·gos**) Spanish nobleman
Hi·dal·go Mexican state
hid·den
hid·den·ite gemstone
hid·den·ness
hide (**hid·ing**, **hid**, **hid·den** *or* **hid**)
hide-and-seek
hide·away
hide·bound
hide·less
hid·eous
hid·eous·ly
hid·eous·ness (*or* **hid·eos·ity**)
hid·er
hid·ing
hi·dro·sis sweating
hi·drot·ic
hie (**hie·ing** *or* **hy·ing**, **hied**) hurry
hie·land *Scot* easily tricked
hi·emal of winter

hi·era·co·sphinx (*plural* **·sphinxes** *or* **·sphin·ges**)
hi·er·arch
hi·er·ar·chal
hi·er·ar·chi·cal
hi·er·ar·chi·cal·ly
hi·er·arch·ism
hi·er·ar·chy (*plural* **·chies**)
hi·er·at·ic of priests
hi·er·ati·cal·ly
hi·er·oc·ra·cy (*plural* **·cies**)
hi·ero·crat·ic
hi·ero·dule Greek slave
hi·ero·du·lic
hi·ero·glyph
hi·ero·glyph·ic
hi·ero·glyphi·cal·ly
hi·ero·glyph·ics
hi·ero·glyph·ist
hi·ero·gram sacred symbol
hi·ero·log·ic
hi·er·olo·gist
hi·er·ol·ogy (*plural* **·ogies**) sacred literature
hi·ero·phant ancient Greek priest
hi·ero·phant·ic
hi·ero·phan·ti·cal·ly
hi·fa·lu·tin *variant spelling of* highfalutin
hi-fi
hig·gle
hig·gledy-pig·gle·dy
high
high·ball
high·bind·er US gangster
high·born
high·boy US tallboy
high·brow
high·chair
high·fa·lu·tin (*or* **hi·**)
high-flier (*or* **-flyer**)
high-flown
high-handed
high-handed·ly
high-handed·ness
high·jack *less common spelling of* hijack
high·jack·er *less common spelling of* hijacker
High·land of Scottish Highlands
high·land

high·land·er
High·lander
High·lands
high·life
high·light
high·ly
highly-strung
high-minded
high-minded·ness
high·ness high condition
High·ness title for royalty
high-rise
high·road
high-spirit·ed
high-spirit·ed·ness
hight *Archaic* named; *compare* height
high·tail
high-tech (*or* **hi-**)
High·veld South African region
high·way
highway·man (*plural* **·men**)
High Wy·combe
hi·jack (*or* **high·**)
hi·jack·er (*or* **high·**)
Hi·jaz *variant spelling of* Hejaz
hike
hik·er
hi·lar anatomy term
hi·lari·ous
hi·lari·ous·ness
hi·lar·ity
hill
Hil·la Iraqi town
hill·bil·ly (*plural* **·lies**)
hill·er
hill·fort
Hil·ling·don London borough
hill·ock
hill·ocked (*or* **·ocky**)
hill·side
hilly (**hilli·er**, **hilli·est**)
hilt
hi·lum (*plural* **·la**) botany term
hi·lus (*plural* **·li**) anatomy term
Hil·ver·sum Dutch city
him
Hi·ma·chal Pra·desh Indian state

Himalayan

Hima·la·yan
Hima·la·yas
hi·mati·on (*plural* ·matia) Greek cloak
Hi·meji Japanese city
Hims *variant of* Homs
him·self
Him·yar·ite Arabian people
Him·yar·it·ic language group
hin Hebrew unit
Hi·na·ya·na Buddhism
Hi·na·ya·nist
Hi·na·ya·nis·tic
Hinck·ley English town
hind (*adj* hind·er, hind·most *or* hinder·most; *noun*, *plural* hinds *or* hind)
hind·brain
hin·der obstruct
hind·er at the rear
hin·der·er
hin·der·ing·ly
hind·gut
Hin·di language; *compare* Hindu
hind·most (*or* hinder·most)
Hin·doo *former spelling of* Hindu
Hin·doo·ism *former spelling of* Hinduism
hind·quarter
hin·drance
hind·sight
Hin·du (*plural* ·dus) people; *compare* Hindi
Hin·du·ism
Hin·du Kush Asian mountains
Hin·du·stan
Hin·du·sta·ni
hinge
hinge·like
hing·er
hin·ny (*noun, plural* ·nies; *verb* ·nies, ·ny·ing, ·nied)
hint
hint·er
hinter·land
hip
hip·bone
hip·less
hip·like

hip·parch ancient Greek cavalry commander
Hip·par·chus moon crater
hip·pe·as·trum plant
hipped
hip·pie (*or* ·py; *plural* ·pies)
hip·po (*plural* ·pos)
hippo·campal
hippo·campus (*plural* ·campi)
hip·po·cras wine
Hip·po·crat·ic of Hippocrates
Hip·po·crene ancient Greek spring
Hip·po·crenian
hippo·drome
hip·po·griff mythological monster
Hippolyta (*or* Hippolyte) Amazonian queen
Hippolytus son of Theseus
Hip·pomenes mythological character
hippo·pota·mus (*plural* ·muses *or* ·mi)
Hip·po Re·gius ancient African city
hip·py *variant spelling of* hippie
hip·sters trousers
hir·able (*or* hire·)
hi·ra·ga·na Japanese writing
Hi·ram biblical character
hir·cine lascivious
hire
hire·ling
hir·er
Hi·ro·shi·ma
hir·sute
hir·sute·ness
hiru·din anticoagulant
hi·run·dine of swallows
his
His·pania Iberia
His·pan·ic
His·pani·cism
His·pani·cist
His·pani·ci·za·tion (*or* ·sa·tion)
His·pani·cize (*or* ·cise)
His·panio·la West Indian island
his·pid bristly
his·pid·ity

hiss
hiss·er
hist
his·tami·nase enzyme
his·ta·mine
his·ta·min·ic
his·ti·dine amino acid
his·tio·cyte
his·tio·cyt·ic
his·to·chemi·cal
his·to·chem·is·try
his·to·gen plant tissue
his·to·gen·esis (*or* his·tog·eny)
his·to·genet·ic (*or* ·gen·ic)
his·to·geneti·cal·ly (*or* ·geni·cal·ly
his·to·gram
his·toid
his·to·logi·cal (his·to·log·ic)
his·to·logi·cal·ly
his·tolo·gist
his·tol·ogy study of tissues
his·toly·sis
his·to·lyt·ic
his·to·lyti·cal·ly
his·tone protein
his·to·patho·logi·cal
his·to·pa·thol·ogy
his·to·plas·mo·sis
his·to·rian
his·to·ri·at·ed decorated
his·tor·ic
his·tori·cal
his·tori·cal·ly
his·tor·i·cal·ness
his·tori·cism
his·tori·cist
his·to·ric·ity
his·to·ri·og·ra·pher
his·to·rio·graph·ic
his·to·ri·og·ra·phy
his·to·ry (*plural* ·ries)
his·tri·on·ic (*or* ·oni·cal)
his·tri·oni·cal·ly
histrionics
hit (hit·ting, hit)
hitch
hitch·er
hitch·hike
hitch·hik·er
hi-tech *variant spelling of* high-tech
hith·er

hither·most
hither·to
Hit·ler·ism
hit·ter
Hit·tite
hive
hive·like
hives nettle rash
ho exclamation; compare hoe
ho·act·zin variant spelling of hoatzin
hoar
hoard store; compare horde
hoard·er
hoard·ing
hoar·frost
hoar·hound variant spelling of horehound
hoari·ly
hoari·ness
hoarse grating; compare horse
hoarse·ly
hoars·en
hoarse·ness
hoary (hoari·er, hoari·est)
hoatch·ing Scot infested
ho·at·zin (or ·act·) bird
hoax
hoax·er
hob (hob·bing, hobbed)
Ho·bart Tasmanian capital
Hobbes·ian
Hob·bism political philosophy
Hob·bist
hob·ble
hobble·dehoy
hob·bler
hob·by (plural ·bies)
hobby·horse
hob·byist
hob·goblin
hob·like
hob·nail
hob·nailed
hob·nob (·nob·bing, ·nobbed)
hobo (plural hobos or hoboes) vagrant
hobo·ism
Ho·bo·ken Belgian city
hobson-jobson folk etymology

Hoch·hei·mer wine
hock
hock·er
hock·ey
Hock·tide former festival
ho·cus (·cus·ing, cused, or ·cus·sing, ·cussed)
hocus-pocus (-pocusing, -pocused or -pocussing, -pocussed)
hod
hod·den coarse cloth
hod·din
Ho·dei·da Yemeni port
hodge·podge US hotchpotch
hod·man (plural ·men)
ho·dom·eter variant of odometer
hodo·scope
hoe (hoe·ing, hoed) gardening tool; compare ho
hoe·down dance
Hoek van Hol·land Hook of Holland
hoe·like
hoer
Ho·fei Chinese city
hog (hog·ging, hogged)
ho·gan American Indian dwelling
Ho·garth·ian
hog·back narrow ridge
hog·fish plural ·fish or ·fishes
hogged
hog·ger
hog·ging
hog·gish
hog·gish·ly
hog·gish·ness
hog·like
Hog·ma·nay
hog·nose snake
hog·nut
hogs·head
hog·tie (·ty·ing, ·tied) US tie limbs
hog·wash
hog·weed
hoick
hoi·den variant spelling of hoyden
hoi pol·loi
hoist

hoist·er
hoity-toity
hoke overact
hokey cokey song and dance
ho·key-pokey hocus-pocus
Hok·kai·do Japanese island
hok·ku variant spelling of haiku
ho·kum
Hol·arc·tic zoogeographical term
hold (hold·ing, held)
hold·able
hold·all
hold·er
hold·er·ship
hold·fast
hold·ing
hole
holey
holi·day
holi·ly
Ho·li·ness pope's title
ho·li·ness
ho·lism
ho·lis·tic
ho·lis·ti·cal·ly
hol·la variant of hollo
hol·land cloth
Hol·land
hol·lan·daise sauce
Hol·land·er
Hol·lands Dutch gin
hol·ler Slang shout
hol·lo (or ·la; plural ·los or ·las) shout
hol·low
hol·low·ly
hol·low·ness
hol·ly (plural ·lies)
hol·ly·hock
Hol·ly·wood
holm Dialect river island
hol·mic
hol·mium chemical element
holo·blas·tic
holo·blas·ti·cal·ly
holo·caust
hol·o·caus·tal (or ·caus·tic)
Holo·cene geological period
holo·crine physiology term
holo·en·zyme

hologram 214

holo·gram handwritten document
holo·graph three-dimensional image
holo·graph·ic
hol·o·graphi·cal·ly
ho·log·ra·phy
holo·he·dral
holo·he·drism
holo·mor·phic
holo·phras·tic
holo·phyte
holo·phyt·ic
holo·plank·ton
holo·thu·rian zoology term
holo·type
holo·typ·ic
holo·zo·ic
hol·pen *Archaic* helped
Hol·stein West German region; cattle
hol·ster
hol·stered
holt *Archaic* woodland
holus-bolus *Slang* all at once
holy (*adj* ho·li·er, ho·li·est; *noun, plural* holies)
Holy·head
ho·ly·stone
holy·tide
hom (*or* homa) sacred plant
hom·age
hom·bre *US* man
hom·burg hat
home
home·bred
home·coming
home·land
home·less
home·less·ness
home·like
home·li·ness
home·ly (·li·er, ·li·est) unpretentious; *US* ugly; *compare* homy
home·mak·ing
homeo·mor·phic (*or* homoeo·)
homeo·mor·phism (*or* homoeo·)
homeo·path·ic (*or* homoeo·)

homeo·pathi·cal·ly (*or* homoeo·)
homeopa·thist (*or* homoepa·)
homeopa·thy (*or* homoeopa·)
homeo·sta·sis (*or* homoeo·)
homeo·stat·ic (*or* homoeo·)
homeo·typ·ic (*or* ·typi·cal, homoeo·) biology term
hom·er
Ho·merian
Ho·mer·ic
Ho·meri·cal·ly
home·sick
home·sick·ness
home·spun
home·stead
home·stead·er
home·ward (*adj*)
home·wards (*adv*)
home·work
homey variant spelling of homy
homey·ness variant spelling of hominess
homi·ci·dal
homi·ci·dal·ly
homi·cide
homi·let·ic (*or* homi·leti·cal)
homi·leti·cal·ly
homi·let·ics art of preaching sermons
homi·list
homi·ly (*plural* ·lies)
homi·ness (*or* homey·ness)
hom·ing
homi·nid
homi·noid
homi·ny *US* ground maize
homo (*plural* homos) *Slang* homosexual
homo·cen·tric
homo·cen·tri·cal·ly
homo·cer·cal zoology term
homo·chro·mat·ic
homo·chro·ma·tism
homo·chro·mous
homo·cy·clic
homo·dont
homoeo· variant spelling of words beginning homeo·

homo·erotic
homo·eroti·cism
homo·ero·tism
ho·moga·mous
ho·moga·my botany term
ho·mog·enate
homo·genei·ty
homo·geneous uniform; *compare* homogenous
homo·geneous·ness
ho·mog·eni·za·tion (*or* ·sa·tion)
ho·mog·enize (*or* ·enise)
ho·mog·eniz·er (*or* ·enis·er)
ho·mog·enous similar through common ancestry; *compare* homogeneous
ho·mog·eny
ho·mogo·nous
ho·mog·ony botany term
homo·graft
homo·graph
homo·graph·ic
ho·moio·ther·mic warm-blooded
ho·moio·ther·my
Ho·moi·ou·sian
Ho·moi·ou·si·an·ism Christian sect
homo·log *US variant spelling of* homologue
ho·molo·gate ratify
ho·molo·ga·tion
homo·logi·cal homologous
homo·logi·cal·ly
ho·molo·gize (*or* ·gise)
ho·molo·giz·er (*or* ·gis·er)
ho·molo·gous
homo·lo·graph·ic
homo·logue (*US also* ·log)
ho·mol·ogy (*plural* ·ogies)
ho·mol·o·sine cartography term
ho·moly·sis
ho·mo·lyt·ic
homo·mor·phic (*or* ·phous)
homo·mor·phism
homo·nym
homo·nym·ic
homo·nym·ity
Homo·ou·sian

Homo·ou·si·an·ism
   Christian sect
homo·phile
homo·phone
homo·phon·ic
homo·phoni·cal·ly
ho·mopho·nous
ho·mopho·ny linguistics
   term
homo·phyl·lic
ho·mophy·ly biology term
homo·plas·tic
homo·plas·ti·cal·ly
homo·plas·ty
homo·po·lar chemistry term
homo·po·lar·ity
ho·mop·ter·ous entomology
   term
ho·mor·gan·ic linguistics
   term
Homo sa·pi·ens
homo·scedas·tic·ity
   statistics term
homo·sex·ual
homo·sex·ual·ity
homo·sex·ual·ly
ho·mos·po·rous botany
   term
ho·mos·po·ry
homo·taxi·al·ly
homo·tax·ic
homo·tax·is
homo·thal·lic
homo·thal·lism botany
   term
homo·zy·go·sis
homo·zy·gote
homo·zy·got·ic
homo·zy·gous genetics
   term
Homs (*or* Hims, Humms)
   Syrian city
ho·mun·cu·lar
ho·mun·cu·lus (*plural* ·li)
   miniature man
homy (*or* homey;
   homi·er, homi·est)
   cosy; *compare* homely
ho·nan fabric
Honda (*Trademark*)
Hon·do *variant of* Honshu
Hon·du·ran
Hon·du·ras
hone
hon·est

hon·est·ly
hon·est·ness
hon·es·ty (*plural* ·ties)
hone·wort plant
hon·ey
honey·bee
honey·bunch
honey·comb
honey·dew
hon·ey·dewed
honey-eater bird
hon·eyed (*or* ·ied)
hon·eyed·ly (*or* ·ied·)
honey-like
honey·moon
honey·moon·er
honey·sucker bird
honey·suckle
hong Chinese factory
Hong Kong
Ho·nia·ra capital of
   Solomon Islands
hon·ied *variant spelling of*
   honeyed
Honi·ton lace
honk
honk·er
honky (*plural* honkies)
   US slang white man
honky-tonk
Hono·lu·lu
hon·or *US spelling of* honour
hono·rar·ium (*plural*
   ·rar·iums *or* ·raria)
hon·or·ary
hon·or·if·ic
hon·or·ifi·cal·ly
hon·our (*US* ·or)
Hon·our·able title of
   respect
hon·our·able (*US* ·or·)
hon·our·able·ness (*US*
   ·or·)
hon·our·ably (*US* ·or·)
hon·our·er (*US* ·or·)
hon·our·less (*US* ·or·)
Hon·shu (*or* Hon·do)
hooch
hood
hood·ed
hoodie crow
hood·less
hood·like
hood·lum
hood·lum·ism

hoo·doo (*plural* ·doos)
hoo·doo·ism
hood·wink
hood·wink·er
hoo·ey
hoof (*plural* hoofs *or*
   hooves)
hoof·bound veterinary term
hoofed
hoof·er
hoof·less
hoof·like
Hoogh·ly Indian river
hoo-ha
hook
hook·ah oriental pipe
hooked
hook·ed·ness
hook·er
hook·less
hook·like
hook·nose
hook·nosed
hook·worm
hooky (*or* hookey)
hoo·li·gan
hoo·li·gan·ism
hoop
hooped
hoop·er
hoop·la
hoop·like
hoo·poe bird
hoo·rah (*or* ·ray) *variants*
   of hurrah
hoose·gow *US* jail
hoot
hoot·en·an·ny (*or*
   hoot·nan·ny; *plural*
   ·nies) *US* folksinging
hoot·er
Hoo·ver (*Trademark*)
hoo·ver (*verb*)
hooves
hop (hop·ping, hopped)
hope
hope·ful
hope·ful·ly
hope·ful·ness
Ho·peh Chinese province
hope·less
hope·less·ly
hope·less·ness
hop·er
hop·head *Slang* drug addict

Hopi

Hopi (*plural* **Hopis** *or* **Hopi**) American Indian
hop·lite Greek soldier
hop·lit·ic
hop·lol·ogist
hop·lol·ogy study of weapons
hop·per
hop·ping
hop·ple hobble
hop·pler
Hop·pus foot unit
hop·sack
hop·scotch
hora dance
Horae Roman goddesses
ho·ral hourly
ho·ra·ry *Archaic* hourly
Ho·ra·tian of the poet Horace
Horatius legendary Roman hero
horde mob; *compare* **hoard**
hor·dein protein
Ho·reb biblical mountain
hore·hound (*or* **hoar·**) plant
ho·ri·zon
ho·ri·zon·less
hori·zon·tal
hori·zon·tal·ly
hori·zon·tal·ness
hor·me psychology term
hor·mic
hor·mo·nal
hor·mone
Hor·muz (*or* **Or·muz**) Iranian island
horn
horn·beam
horn·bill
horn·blende mineral
horn·blen·dic
horn·book
horned
horn·ed·ness
hor·net
horn·fels rock
horni·ly
horni·ness
horn·less
horn·like
horn·pipe
horn-rimmed
horn·stone
horns·wog·gle *Slang* cheat
horn·tail insect
horn·wort plant
horny (**horni·er**, **horni·est**)
horo·loge timepiece
horo·log·ic
ho·rol·o·gist (*or* **ho·rolo·ger**)
horo·lo·gium (*plural* **·gia**) clock tower
ho·rol·ogy
horo·scope
horo·scop·ic
ho·ros·co·py (*plural* **·pies**)
hor·ren·dous
hor·ri·ble
hor·ri·ble·ness
hor·ri·bly
hor·rid
hor·rid·ness
hor·rif·ic
hor·rifi·cal·ly
hor·ri·fi·ca·tion
hor·ri·fy (**·fies**, **·fy·ing**, **·fied**)
hor·ri·fy·ing·ly
hor·ripi·la·tion gooseflesh
hor·ror
horror-stricken (*or* **-struck**)
hors de com·bat *French* injured
hors d'oeu·vre (*plural* **hors d'oeu·vre** *or* **hors d'oeu·vres**)
horse animal; *compare* **hoarse**
horse·back
horse·box
horse·flesh
horse·fly (*plural* **·flies**)
horse·hair
horse·hide
horse·leech
horse·less
horse·like
horse·man (*plural* **·men**)
horse·man·ship
horse·mint
horse·play
horse·power (*plural* **horse·power**) unit
horse·radish
horse·shoe (**·shoe·ing**, **·shoed**)
horse·tail plant
horse·weed
horse·whip (**·whip·ping**, **·whipped**)
horse·whip·per
horse·woman (*plural* **·women**)
horsi·ly
horsi·ness
horst ridge
horsy (*or* **horsey**; **horsi·er**, **horsi·est**)
hor·ta·to·ri·ly
hor·ta·tory (*or* **·tive**) urging
hor·ti·cul·tur·al
hor·ti·cul·tur·al·ly
hor·ti·cul·ture
hor·ti·cul·tur·ist
hor·tus sic·cus collection of dried plants
Horus Egyptian god
ho·san·na
hose
Hosea biblical character
ho·sier
ho·siery
hos·pice
hos·pi·table
hos·pi·table·ness
hos·pi·tably
hos·pi·tal
hos·pi·tal·ity
hos·pi·tali·za·tion (*or* **·sa·tion**)
hos·pi·tal·ize (*or* **·ise**)
Hos·pi·tal·ler religious knight
hos·pi·tal·ler (*US* **·tal·er**) hospital worker
hos·pit·ium (*plural* **·ia**) travellers' refuge
hos·po·dar Ottoman ruler
host
hos·ta plant
hos·tage
hos·tel
hos·tel·ler (*US* **·tel·er**)
hos·tel·ling (*US* **·tel·ing**)
hos·tel·ry (*plural* **·ries**)
host·ess
hos·tile
hos·tile·ly

hos·til·ity (*plural* ·ities)
host·ler *variant of* ostler
hot (*adj* hot·ter, hot·test; *verb* hot·ting, hot·ted)
hot·bed
hot-blooded
hot-blooded·ness
hotch·pot legal term
hotch·potch (*US* hodge·podge)
ho·tel
ho·tel·ier
hot·foot
hot·head
hot-headed
hot-headed·ly
hot-headed·ness
hot·house
Ho·tien (*or* Ho-t'ien, Kho·tan) Chinese oasis
hot·ly
hot·ness
hot·plate
hot·pot
hot·spur impetuous person
Hot·ten·tot (*plural* ·tot *or* ·tots)
hot·tish
Hou·dan fowl
hough hock
Houghton-le-Spring Tyneside town
hou·mous (*or* ·mus) *variant of* hummus
hound
hound·er
Houns·low
hour
hour·glass
hou·ri (*plural* ·ris) Muslim nymph
hour·ly
house
house·boat
house·bound
house·boy
house·break·er
house·break·ing
house·carl medieval servant
house·coat
house·fath·er
house·fly (*plural* ·flies)
house·hold
house·holder
house·holder·ship

house·keeper
house·keeping
hou·sel *Archaic* Eucharist
house·leek
house·less
house·line nautical term
house·maid
house·man (*plural* ·men)
house·master
house·mistress
house·moth·er
house-proud
house·room
house·top
house·wife (*plural* ·wives)
house·wife·li·ness
house·wife·ly
house·wif·ery
house·work
house·worker
housey-housey
hous·ing
Hou·ston Texan port
hous·to·nia plant
hout·ing fish
hove
Hove Sussex town
hov·el (·el·ling, ·elled; *US* ·el·ing, ·eled)
hov·er
hover·craft
hov·er·er
hov·er·ing·ly
hover·port
hover·train
how
how·be·it
how·dah seat on elephant
how·dy *US* hello
howe'er
how·ever
howf *Scot* public house
how·itz·er
howl
How·land Pacific island
howl·er
how·let owl
howl·ing
How·rah Indian city
how·so·ever
how·tow·die Scottish chicken dish
hoy
hoya plant
hoy·den (*or* hoi·)

hoy·den·ish (*or* hoi·)
hoy·den·ish·ness (*or* hoi·)
Hoy·lake English town
Hsi *variant spelling of* Si
Hsian *variant spelling of* Sian
Hsiang *variant spelling of* Siang
Hsin-hai-lien *variant spelling of* Sinhailien
Hsi·ning *variant spelling of* Sining
Hsü-chou *variant spelling of* Süchow
Huai-nan Chinese city
Huang Hai *variant spelling of* Hwang Hai
Huang Ho *variant spelling of* Hwang Ho
hub
hubble-bubble
hub·bub
hub·by (*plural* ·bies)
hub·cap
Hub·li Indian city
hu·bris (*or* hy·bris)
hu·bris·tic
hucka·back fabric
huck·le
huckle·berry (*plural* ·berries)
huck·le·bone *Archaic* anklebone
huck·ster
huck·ster·ism
Hud·ders·field
hud·dle
hud·dler
hu·di·bras·tic mock-heroic
Hud·son Canadian bay; *US* river
hue colour; *compare* hew
hued
huff
huffi·ly
huffi·ness
huff·ish
huffy (huffi·er, huffi·est)
hug (hug·ging, hugged)
huge
huge·ly
huge·ness
hug·gable
hug·ger
hug·ger·mug·ger

Huguenot

Hu·guenot
Hu·guenot·ic
Hu·guenot·ism
huh *exclamation*
Hu·he·hot (*or* Hu-ho-hao-t'e) Chinese town
hula (*or* hula-hula) Hawaiian dance
hulk
hulk·ing
hull
Hull English port; Canadian city
hul·la·ba·loo (*or* ·bal·loo; *plural* ·loos)
hull·er
hull-less
hul·lo *variant spelling of* hello
hum (hum·ming, hummed)
hu·man
hu·mane
hu·mane·ly
hu·mane·ness
hu·man·ism
hu·man·ist
hu·man·ist·ic
hu·mani·tar·ian
hu·mani·tari·an·ism
hu·mani·tari·an·ist
hu·man·ity (*plural* ·ities)
hu·mani·za·tion (*or* ·sa·tion)
hu·man·ize (*or* ·ise)
hu·man·iz·er (*or* ·is·er)
human·kind
hu·man-like
hu·man·ly
hu·man·ness
hu·man·oid
Hum·ber
Humber·side
hum·ble
hum·ble·bee
hum·ble·ness
hum·bler
hum·bling·ly
hum·bly
Hum·boldt cur·rent
hum·bug (·bug·ging, ·bugged)
hum·bug·ger
hum·bug·gery
hum·ding·er

hum·drum
hum·drum·ness
hu·mec·tant
hu·mer·al
hu·mer·us (*plural* ·meri) arm bone; *compare* humorous
hu·mic
hu·mid
hu·midi·fi·ca·tion
hu·midi·fi·er
hu·midi·fy (·fies, ·fy·ing, ·fied)
hu·midi·stat
hu·mid·ity
hu·mid·ness
hu·mi·dor tobacco container
hu·mili·ate
hu·mili·at·ing·ly
hu·milia·tion
hu·mil·ia·tive
hu·mili·a·tor
hu·mil·ia·tory
hu·mil·ity (*plural* ·ities)
hummed
hum·mel *Scot* hornless
hum·mer
hum·ming
humming·bird
hum·mock
hum·mocky
hum·mus (*or* hou·mus, ·mous) Middle Eastern food
hu·mor *US spelling of* humour
hu·mor·al of body fluids
hu·mor·esque
hu·mor·ist
hu·mor·is·tic
hu·mor·ous funny; *compare* humerus
hu·mor·ous·ness
hu·mour (*US* ·mor)
hu·mour·ful (*US* ·mor·)
hu·mour·less (*US* ·mor·)
hu·mour·less·ness (*US* ·mor·)
hu·mour·some (*US* ·mor·)
hump
hump·back
hump·backed
humph
humpi·ness

hump·like
hump·ty (*plural* ·ties) padded seat
humpy (humpi·er, humpi·est)
Hums *variant of* Homs
hu·mus
Hun
Hu·nan Chinese province
hunch
hunch·back
hunch·backed
hun·dred (*plural* ·dreds *or* ·dred)
hun·dredth
hundred·weight (*plural* ·weights *or* ·weight)
hung suspended; *compare* hanged
Hun·gar·ian
Hun·ga·ry
hun·ger
Hung·nam North Korean port
hun·gri·ly
hun·gri·ness
hun·gry (·gri·er, ·gri·est)
hunk
hunk·ers *Dialect* haunches
hunky-dory
Hun-like
Hun·nish
Hun·nish·ly
Hun·nish·ness
hunt
hunt·ed
hunt·er
hunt·ing
Hun·ting·don Cambridgeshire town
Hun·ting·don·shire former English county
hunts·man (*plural* ·men)
Hunts·ville US city
Huon Tasmanian river
Hu·peh (*or* ·pei) Chinese province
hup·pah Jewish wedding ceremony
hur·dle
hur·dler
hurds *variant of* hards
hurdy-gurdy (*plural* -gurdies)
hurl

hurl·er
hur·ley hurling stick
hurl·ing
hurly-burly (*plural* -burlies)
Hu·ron (*plural* ·rons or ·ron) American Indian
Hu·ron (Lake)
hur·rah (*or* hoo·ray, hoo·rah)
hur·ri·cane
hur·ried
hur·ried·ly
hur·ried·ness
hur·ry (*verb* ·ries, ·ry·ing, ·ried; *noun, plural* ·ries)
hur·ry·ing·ly
hurst *Archaic* wood
Hurst·mon·ceux *variant spelling of* Herstmonceux
hurt (hurt·ing, hurt)
hur·ter
hurt·ful
hurt·ful·ly
hurt·ful·ness
hurt·le
hus·band
hus·band·er
hus·band·less
husband·man (*plural* ·men)
hus·band·ry
hush
husha·by
husk
husk·er
huski·ly
huski·ness
husk·like
husky (*adj* huski·er, huski·est; *noun, plural* huskies)
huss dogfish
hus·sar
Huss·ism (*or* Huss·it·ism)
Huss·ite heretical Christian
hus·sy (*plural* ·sies)
hus·tings
hus·tle
hus·tler
hut
hutch
hut·like
hut·ment

Hu·tu (*plural* ·tu *or* ·tus) African people
huz·zah *Archaic* hurrah
hwan *variant of* won
Hwang Hai (*or* Huang Hai) Chinese sea
Hwang Ho (*or* Huang Ho) Chinese river
hwyl poetic fervour
hya·cinth
hya·cin·thine
Hyacinthus mythological character
Hya·des (*or* Hy·ads) star cluster
hy·aena *variant spelling of* hyena
hya·lin biochemical substance
hya·line translucent
hya·lite variety of opal
hya·loid transparent
hya·lu·ron·ic acid
hya·lu·roni·dase enzyme
hy·brid
hy·brid·ism
hy·brid·ity
hy·brid·iz·able (*or* ·is·able)
hy·bridi·za·tion (*or* ·sa·tion)
hy·brid·ize (*or* ·ise)
hy·brid·iz·er (*or* ·is·er)
hy·bris *variant spelling of* hubris
hy·dan·to·in crystalline substance
hy·da·thode botany term
hy·da·tid tapeworm cyst
Hyde English town
Hy·dera·bad
hyd·no·car·pate
hyd·no·car·pic acid
hy·dra (*plural* ·dras *or* ·drae) marine animal
Hy·dra mythological character
hy·drac·id acid without oxygen
hy·dran·gea
hy·drant
hy·dranth zoology term
hy·drar·gy·ric
hy·drar·gy·rum mercury
hy·dras·tine biochemical compound

hy·dras·ti·nine biochemical compound
hy·dras·tis plant
hy·drate
hy·drat·ed
hy·dra·tion
hy·dra·tor
hy·drau·lic
hy·drau·li·cal·ly
hy·drau·lics
hy·dra·zine
hy·dra·zo·ic acid
hy·dria ancient Greek jar
hy·dric
hy·dride
hy·dri·od·ic
hy·dro (*plural* ·dros)
hydro·bro·mic
hydro·car·bon
hydro·cele pathology term
hydro·cel·lu·lose
hydro·cephal·ic
hydro·cepha·lus (*or* ·cephaly)
hydro·chlo·ric
hydro·chlo·ride
hy·dro·cor·al (*or* ·cor·al·line) zoology term
hydro·cor·ti·sone
hydro·cy·an·ic
hydro·dy·nam·ic
hydro·dy·nami·cal·ly
hydro·dy·nam·ics
hydro·elec·tric
hydro·elec·tric·ity
hydro·flu·or·ic
hydro·foil
hydro·gen
hydro·gen·ate
hydro·gena·tion
hydro·gena·tor
hydro·geni·za·tion (*or* ·sa·tion)
hydro·gen·ize (*or* ·ise)
hydro·gen·oly·sis
hy·drog·enous
hydro·graph
hy·drog·ra·pher
hydro·graph·ic (*or* ·graphi·cal)
hydro·graphi·cal·ly
hy·drog·ra·phy mapping oceans and rivers
hy·droid

hydrokinetic

hydro·ki·net·ic (*or* ·neti·cal)
hydro·ki·net·ics
hydro·log·ic (*or* ·logi·cal)
hydro·logi·cal·ly
hy·drolo·gist
hy·drol·ogy
hydro·lys·able (*US* ·lyz·)
hy·droly·sate
hydro·ly·sa·tion (*US* ·za·tion)
hydro·lyse (*US* ·lyze)
hydro·lys·er (*US* ·lyz·er)
hy·droly·sis
hydro·lyte
hydro·lyt·ic
hydro·mag·net·ics
hydro·manc·er
hydro·man·cy divination by water
hydro·man·tic
hydro·mechani·cal
hydro·mechan·ics
hydro·medu·sa (*plural* ·sas *or* ·sae) zoology term
hydro·medu·san
hydro·mel mead
hydro·met·al·lur·gi·cal
hydro·met·al·lur·gy
hydro·meteor
hydro·meteoro·logi·cal
hydro·meteor·ol·ogy
hy·drom·eter
hydro·met·ric (*or* ·met·ri·cal)
hy·drom·etry
hydro·path·ic (*or* ·pathi·cal)
hy·dropa·thist (*or* hydro·path)
hy·dropa·thy water cure
hydro·phane variety of opal
hydro·phil·ic
hy·drophi·lous botany term
hy·drophi·ly
hydro·pho·bia
hydro·pho·bic
hydro·phone underwater microphone
hydro·phyte
hydro·plane
hydro·poni·cal·ly
hydro·pon·ics
hydro·pow·er
hydro·scope
hydro·ski hydrofoil on seaplane
hydro·sphere
hydro·stat
hydro·stat·ic
hydro·stat·ics
hydro·sul·phide (*US* ·fide)
hydro·thera·peu·tic
hydro·thera·pist
hydro·thera·py
hydro·trop·ic growing towards water
hy·drous
hy·drox·ide
hy·droxy chemistry term
hy·droxyl
hydro·zoan zoology term
Hy·drus constellation
hy·ena (*or* ·aena)
hy·eto·graph rainfall chart
hy·eto·graph·ic (*or* ·graphi·cal)
hy·eto·graphi·cal·ly
hy·etog·ra·phy
Hygeia Greek goddess
hy·giene
hy·gien·ic
hy·gieni·cal·ly
hy·gien·ics
hy·gien·ist
hygro·graph
hy·grom·eter humidity measurer
hygro·met·ric
hygro·met·ri·cal·ly
hy·grom·etry
hygro·phi·lous botany term
hygro·scope
hygro·scop·ic
hygro·scopi·cal·ly
Hyk·sos (*plural* ·sos) Asian nomad
hyla tree frog
hy·lo·zo·ism philosophical doctrine
hy·lo·zo·ist
Hymen god of marriage
hy·men anatomical membrane
hy·men·al of the hymen
hy·meneal of marriage
hy·menium (*plural* ·menia) fungal tissue

220

hy·menop·ter·an (*plural* ·ter·ans *or* ·tera) insect
hymn
hym·nal
hym·nic
hym·nist (*or* hym·no·dist)
hym·no·dy
hym·nolo·gist
hym·nol·ogy
hy·oid bone
hy·os·cine
hy·os·cya·mine
hype
hyper·ac·id (*adj*)
hyper·acid·ity
hyper·ac·tive
hyper·ac·tiv·ity
hyper·aemia (*US* ·emia) pathology term
hyper·aemic (*US* ·emic)
hyper·aes·the·sia (*US* ·es·) increased sensitivity
hyper·aes·thet·ic (*US* ·es·)
hyper·bar·ic of high pressure
hyper·ba·ton reversed word order
hyper·bo·la (*plural* ·las *or* ·lae) geometrical curve
hyper·bo·le exaggeration
hyper·bol·ic (*or* ·boli·cal)
hyper·bo·lize (*or* ·lise) exaggerate
hyper·bo·loid
Hyper·bo·rean mythological character
hyper·bo·rean of extreme north
hyper·charge
hyper·criti·cal
hyper·criti·cal·ly
hyper·criti·cism
hyper·du·lia veneration for Virgin Mary
hyper·du·lic (*or* hyper·du·li·cal)
hyper·gly·cae·mia (*US* ·cemia) excess blood sugar
hyper·gly·cae·mic (*US* ·cemic)
hyper·gol·ic spontaneously flammable
hyper·icum plant
hyper·in·fla·tion

hyper·in·su·lin·ism
Hyperion Greek god
hyper·ki·nesia (*or* ·nesis)
hyper·ki·net·ic
hyper·mar·ket
hyper·meter verse line
hyper·met·ric (*or* ·metri·cal)
hyper·metro·pia (*US* hyper·opia) long-sightedness
hyper·metrop·ic
hy·perm·ne·sia psychology term
hyper·on elementary particle
hyper·opia *US* hypermetropia
hyper·plasia enlargement of body part
hyper·plas·tic
hy·perp·noea (*US* ·nea) increased breathing rate
hyper·py·rexia high fever
hyper·sen·si·tive
hyper·sen·si·tiv·ity
hyper·sen·si·tize (*or* ·tise) photography term
hyper·son·ic
hyper·space
hyper·spa·tial
hyper·ten·sion
hyper·ten·sive
hyper·ther·mia (*or* ·ther·my)
hyper·thy·roid
hyper·thy·roid·ism
hyper·ton·ic
hyper·troph·ic
hyper·tro·phy (*noun, plural* ·phies; *verb* ·phies, ·phy·ing, ·phied)
hyper·ven·ti·la·tion
hyper·vita·mi·no·sis
hy·pha (*plural* ·phae) part of fungus
hy·phen
hy·phen·ate
hy·phena·tion
hyp·na·gog·ic psychology term
hyp·noid
hyp·nol·ogy study of sleep

hyp·no·pae·dia
hyp·no·sis (*plural* ·ses)
hyp·no·thera·py
hyp·not·ic
hyp·noti·cal·ly
hyp·no·tism
hyp·no·tist
hyp·no·tize (*or* ·tise)
hypo (*plural* hypos) photographic fixer; syringe
hypo·acid·ity
hypo·caust Roman heating system
hypo·cen·tre (*US* ·ter)
hypo·chlor·ite
hypo·chlor·ous
hypo·chon·dria
hypo·chon·dri·ac
hypo·chon·dria·cal·ly
hypo·chon·drium (*plural* ·dria) anatomy term
hy·poco·rism pet name
hy·poc·ri·sy (*plural* ·sies)
hypo·crite
hypo·criti·cal
hypo·criti·cal·ly
hypo·cy·cloid geometric curve
hypo·cy·cloi·dal
hypo·der·mic
hypo·der·mis biology term
Hy·po·do·rian musical term
hypo·gas·tric
hypo·gas·trium (*plural* ·tria) anatomy term
hypo·geal (*or* ·geous) botany term
hypo·gene geology term
hy·pog·enous botany term
hypo·gen·ic
hypo·geum (*plural* ·gea) burial vault
hypo·glos·sal anatomy term
hypo·gly·cae·mia (*US* ·cemia) low blood sugar
hypo·gly·caem·ic (*US* ·cemic)
hy·poid
hypo·lim·nion bottom layer in lake
hypo·ma·nia

hypo·man·ic
hypo·nas·tic
hypo·nas·ty botany term
hypo·phys·eal
hy·pophy·sis (*plural* ·ses) pituitary gland
hypo·plasia (*or* ·plas·ty)
hypo·sen·si·tize (*or* ·tise)
hypo·stat·ic
hypos·ta·sis (*plural* ·ses)
hy·pos·ta·tize (*or* ·tise)
hypo·style architectural term
hypo·ten·sion
hypo·ten·sive
hy·pot·enuse
hypo·thala·mus (*plural* ·mi)
hy·poth·ecate legal term
hy·poth·eca·tion
hy·poth·eca·tor
hypo·ther·mia
hy·poth·esis (*plural* ·eses)
hy·poth·esize (*or* ·esise)
hypo·theti·cal
hypo·theti·cal·ly
hypo·thy·roid
hypo·thy·roid·ism
hypo·ton·ic
hy·poxia oxygen deficiency
hy·pox·ic
hyp·so·met·ric (*or* ·ri·cal)
hyp·som·etry altitude measurement
hy·rax animal
hy·son Chinese tea
hys·sop herb
hys·ter·ec·to·my (*plural* ·mies)
hys·te·re·sis physics term
hys·te·ria
hys·ter·ic
hys·teri·cal
hys·teri·cal·ly
hys·ter·ics
hys·tero·gen·ic
hys·ter·oid (*or* ·teroi·dal)
hys·ter·oto·my (*plural* ·mies) incision into uterus
hys·tri·co·morph rodent

I

iamb (*or* **iam·bus**; *plural*
iambs, iam·bi, *or*
iam·buses) metrical foot
iam·bic
iam·bi·cal·ly
Iap·etus satellite of Saturn
iat·ric (*or* **·ri·càl**) of
medicine
iat·ro·gen·ic
iat·ro·genic·ity
Iba·dan Nigerian city
Iba·gué Colombian city
I-beam girder
Iberia
Iberian
ibex (*plural* **ibexes,**
ibi·ces, *or* **ibex**) goat
Ibibio (*plural* **Ibibio** *or*
Ibibios) Nigerian people
ibis (*plural* **ibises** *or* **ibis**)
bird
Ibi·za (*or* **Ivi·za**) Spanish
island
Ibo (*or* **Igbo**; *plural* **Ibos,**
Ibo *or* **Igbos, Igbo**)
African people
Icaria Greek island
Icar·ian
Icarus mythological
character
ice
ice·berg
ice·blink
ice·bound
ice·box
ice·breaker
ice·cap
ice cream
ice·fall
Ice·land
Ice·land·er
Ice·land·ic
Iceni ancient British tribe
Ichang (*or* **I-ch'ang**)
Chinese port
I Ching Chinese book of
divination
Ichi·no·mi·ya Japanese
town

ich·neu·mon mongoose;
insect
ich·nite (*or* **·no·lite**) fossil
footprint
ich·no·graph·ic (*or*
·graphi·cal)
ich·no·graphi·cal·ly
ich·nog·ra·phy ground-plan
drawing
ich·no·logi·cal
ich·nol·ogy study of fossil
footprints
ichor
ichor·ous
ich·thy·ic of fishes
ich·thy·oid (*or* **·oid·al**)
ich·thyo·log·ic (*or*
·logi·cal)
ich·thyo·logi·cal·ly
ich·thy·olo·gist
ich·thy·ol·ogy
ich·thy·opha·gous
ich·thy·opha·gy
ich·thy·or·nis extinct bird
ich·thyo·saur (*or* **·saur·us;**
plural **·saurs,**
·saur·uses, *or* **·sau·ri**)
ich·thyo·sis skin disease
ich·thy·ot·ic
ici·cle
ici·cled
ici·ly
ici·ness
ic·ing
icon (*or* **ikon**)
icon·ic (*or* **iconi·cal**)
icono·clasm
icono·clast
icono·clas·tic
icono·clas·ti·cal·ly
ico·nog·ra·pher
icono·graph·ic (*or*
·graphi·cal)
ico·nog·ra·phy (*plural*
·phies)
ico·nola·ter
ico·nola·trous
ico·nola·try
icono·logi·cal
ico·nolo·gist

ico·nol·ogy
icono·mat·ic representing
sounds with pictures
icono·mati·cism
icono·scope
ico·sa·he·dral
ico·sa·he·dron (*plural*
·drons *or* **·dra**)
ic·ter·ic
ic·ter·us jaundice
ic·tus (*plural* **·tuses** *or*
·tus) poetry term
icy (**ici·er, ici·est**)
I'd I had; I would
id
Ida Cretan mountain
Ida·ho
ide fish
idea
ideal
ideal·ism
ideal·ist
ideal·is·tic
ideal·is·ti·cal·ly
ideal·ity (*plural* **·ities**)
ideali·za·tion (*or* **·sa·tion**)
ideal·ize (*or* **·ise**)
ideal·iz·er (*or* **·is·er**)
ideal·ly
ideate imagine
idea·tion
idea·tion·al
idea·tive
idea·tum (*plural* **·ta**)
philosophy term
idée fixe (*plural* **idées**
fixes)
idem·po·tent maths term
iden·tic diplomacy term
iden·ti·cal
iden·ti·cal·ly
iden·ti·cal·ness
iden·ti·fi·able
iden·ti·fi·able·ness
iden·ti·fi·ca·tion
iden·ti·fi·er
iden·ti·fy (**·fies, ·fy·ing,**
·fied)
Iden·ti·kit (*Trademark*)
iden·tity (*plural* **·tities**)

ideo·gram (*or* ·graph) symbol
id·eog·ra·phy
ideo·logi·cal (*or* ·log·ic)
ideo·logi·cal·ly
ideolo·gist (*or* ideo·logue)
ideol·ogy (*plural* ·ogies)
ideo·mo·tor physiology term
ides day in Roman calendar
idio·blast plant cell
idio·blas·tic
idio·cy (*plural* ·cies)
idio·graph·ic
idio·lect individual's language
idio·lect·al (*or* ·ic)
idi·om
idio·mat·ic (*or* ·mati·cal)
idio·mati·cal·ly
idio·mor·phic mineralogy term
idio·mor·phi·cal·ly
idio·mor·phism
idio·path·ic
idi·opa·thy (*plural* ·thies) disease of unknown cause
idio·phone musical instrument
idio·phon·ic
idio·syn·cra·sy (*plural* ·sies)
idio·syn·crat·ic
idio·syn·crati·cal·ly
idi·ot
idi·ot·ic
idi·oti·cal·ly
idle lazy; *compare* idol
idle·ness
idler
idly
idol image; *compare* idle
idola·ter (*fem* ·tress)
idola·trize (*or* ·trise)
idola·triz·er (*or* ·tris·er)
idola·trous
idola·try
idoli·za·tion (*or* ·sa·tion)
idol·ize (*or* ·ise)
idol·iz·er (*or* ·is·er)
idyll (*or* idyl)
idyl·lic
idyl·li·cal·ly
idyl·list
if

Ife Nigerian town
Igbo *variant spelling of* Ibo
ig·loo (*or* iglu; *plural* ·loos *or* iglus)
ig·ne·ous geology term
ig·nes·cent giving off sparks
ig·nit·abil·ity (*or* ·ibil·ity)
ig·nit·able (*or* ·ible)
ig·nite
ig·nit·er
ig·ni·tion
ig·ni·tron physics term
ig·no·bil·ity (*or* ·ble·ness)
ig·no·ble
ig·no·bly
ig·no·mini·ous
ig·no·miny (*plural* ·minies)
ig·nor·able
ig·no·ra·mus (*plural* ·muses)
ig·no·rance
ig·no·rant
ig·no·ra·tio elen·chi logic term
ig·nore
ig·nor·er
Igraine (*or* Ygerne) King Arthur's mother
Igua·çú (*or* Iguas·sú) South American river
igua·na lizard
igua·nian
iguano·don dinosaur
ih·ram Muslim pilgrim's robes
IJs·sel·meer (*or* Ys·) Dutch lake
ikeba·na Japanese flower arranging
ikon *variant spelling of* icon
il·eac (*or* ·eal) of ileum; *compare* iliac
Île-de-France
il·ei·tis intestinal disorder
il·eos·to·my (*plural* ·mies) abdominal operation
Ilesha Nigerian town
il·eum small intestine; *compare* ilium
il·eus intestinal obstruction
ilex tree
ili·ac of ilium; *compare* ileac
Ili·ad
Ili·ad·ic

Il·ium Troy
il·ium (*plural* ·ia) hip bone; *compare* ileum
ilk
Il·kes·ton Derbyshire town
I'll I will; I shall
ill
ill-advised
ill-assorted
il·la·tive linguistics term
Il·la·war·ra Australian district
ill-bred
ill-breed·ing
ill-considered
Ille-et-Vilaine French department
il·legal
il·legal·ity (*plural* ·ities)
il·legali·za·tion (*or* ·sa·tion)
il·legal·ize (*or* ·ise)
il·legal·ly
il·leg·ibil·ity (*or* ·ible·ness)
il·leg·ible
il·leg·ibly
il·legiti·ma·cy (*or* ·mate·ness)
il·legiti·mate
il·legiti·mate·ly
ill-fated
ill-favoured (*US* -favored)
ill-gotten
il·lib·er·al
il·lib·er·al·ity (*or* ·ness, ·ism)
il·lic·it illegal; *compare* elicit
il·lim·it·abil·ity (*or* ·able·ness)
il·lim·it·able
Il·li·nois
Il·li·nois·an (*or* ·noian, ·nois·ian)
il·liq·uid
il·lit·era·cy (*plural* ·cies)
il·lit·er·ate
ill-mannered
ill-natured
ill·ness
il·locu·tion philosophy term
il·lo·cu·tion·ary
il·logi·cal
il·logi·cal·ity (*or* ·ness)

illogically

il·log·i·cal·ly
ill-omened
ill-starred
ill-timed
ill-treat
ill-treatment
il·lude deceive; *compare* allude; elude
il·lume
il·lu·mi·nance
il·lu·mi·nant
il·lu·mi·nate
il·lu·mi·na·ti (*sing.* ·to) enlightened people
il·lu·mi·na·tion
il·lu·mi·na·tive
il·lu·mi·na·tor
il·lu·mine
il·lu·mi·nism belief in enlightenment
il·lu·mi·nist
ill-use (*verb*)
ill-use (*or* -usage)
il·lu·sion delusion; *compare* allusion
il·lu·sion·ary (*or* ·al)
il·lu·sion·ism
il·lu·sion·ist
il·lu·sion·is·tic
il·lu·sive illusory; *compare* elusive
il·lu·so·ri·ly
il·lu·so·ri·ness
il·lu·so·ry
il·lus·trat·able
il·lus·trate
il·lus·tra·tion
il·lus·tra·tion·al
il·lus·tra·tive
il·lus·tra·tor
il·lus·tri·ous
il·lu·vi·a·tion
Il·lyria Adriatic region
Il·lyr·ian
il·men·ite mineral
Iloi·lo Philippine port
Ilor·in Nigerian city
I'm
(imaculate) *incorrect spelling of* immaculate
im·age
im·age·ry (*plural* ·ries)
im·ag·i·nable
im·ag·i·nably

im·ag·i·nal of an image or imago
im·ag·i·nari·ly
im·ag·i·nary
im·ag·i·na·tion
im·ag·i·na·tive
im·ag·ine
im·ag·in·er
im·ag·ism poetic movement
im·ag·ist
im·ag·is·tic
im·ag·is·ti·cal·ly
ima·go (*plural* ·gos, ·goes, *or* ·gi·nes) adult insect; psychiatry term
imam (*or* imaum) Islamic priest
imam·ate
ima·ret Turkish hospice
im·bal·ance
im·becile
im·becil·ity (*plural* ·ities)
im·bed *less common spelling of* embed
im·bibe
im·bib·er
im·bi·bi·tion
im·bri·cate (*or* ·cat·ed)
im·bri·ca·tion
im·bro·glio (*plural* ·glios)
im·brue (*or* em·; ·bru·ing, ·brued) to stain; *compare* imbue
im·bue (·bu·ing, ·bued) instil; *compare* imbrue
im·id·az·ole
im·ide chemistry term
im·id·ic
(imigrate) *incorrect spelling of* immigrate
imine chemistry term
imi·ta·bil·ity (*or* ·table·ness)
imi·table
imi·tate
imi·ta·tion
imi·ta·tion·al
imi·ta·tive
imi·ta·tor
im·macu·la·cy (*or* ·late·ness)
im·macu·late
im·ma·nence (*or* ·nen·cy)
im·ma·nent existing within; *compare* eminent; imminent

im·ma·nent·ism religious belief
im·ma·terial
im·ma·teri·al·ism
im·ma·teri·al·ist
im·ma·terial·ity (*or* ·teri·al·ness)
im·ma·teri·al·ize (*or* ·ise)
im·ma·ture
im·ma·tu·rity (*or* ·ture·ness)
im·meas·ur·abil·ity (*or* ·able·ness)
im·meas·ur·able
im·meas·ur·ably
im·media·cy (*or* im·medi·ate·ness)
im·medi·ate
im·medi·ate·ly
im·medi·cable
im·memo·ri·able
im·memo·rial
im·memo·ri·al·ly
im·mense
im·mense·ly
im·men·si·ty (*plural* ·ties)
im·men·su·rable
im·merse
im·mers·ible
im·mer·sion immersing; *compare* emersion
im·mer·sion·ism Christian doctrine
im·mer·sion·ist
im·methodi·cal
im·methodi·cal·ly
im·mi·grant
im·mi·grate enter country; *compare* emigrate
im·mi·gra·tion
im·mi·gra·tory
im·mi·gra·tor
im·mi·nence
im·mi·nent impending; *compare* eminent; immanent
Im·ming·ham Humberside port
im·mis·cibil·ity
im·mis·cible
im·mis·cibly
im·mo·bile
im·mo·bil·ism political policy
im·mo·bil·ity

im·mo·bi·li·za·tion (*or* ·sa·tion)
im·mo·bi·lize (*or* ·lise)
im·mo·bi·liz·er (*or* ·lis·er)
im·mo·der·ate
im·mo·der·ate·ly
im·mod·era·tion (*or* ·er·ate·ness)
im·mod·est
im·mod·es·ty
im·mo·late sacrifice
im·mo·la·tion
im·mo·la·tor
im·mor·al morally bad; *compare* amoral
im·mor·al·ist
im·mo·ral·ity (*plural* ·ities)
im·mor·al·ly
im·mor·tal
im·mor·tal·ity
im·mor·tali·za·tion (*or* ·sa·tion)
im·mor·tal·ize (*or* ·ise)
im·mor·tal·iz·er (*or* ·is·er)
im·mor·tal·ly
im·mor·telle everlasting flower
im·mo·tile
im·mo·til·ity
im·mov·abil·ity (*or* ·mov·able·ness)
im·mov·able (*or in legal contexts* ·move·)
lm·mov·ably
im·mune
im·mu·nity (*plural* ·nities)
im·mu·ni·za·tion (*or* ·sa·tion)
im·mu·nize (*or* ·nise)
im·mu·niz·er (*or* ·nis·er)
im·mu·no·as·say
im·mu·no·chem·is·try
im·mu·no·genet·ic (*or* ·geneti·cal)
im·mu·no·genet·ics
im·mu·no·gen·ic
im·mu·no·geni·cal·ly
im·mu·no·globu·lin
im·mu·no·log·ic (*or* ·logi·cal)
im·mu·no·logi·cal·ly
im·mu·nolo·gist
im·mu·nol·ogy
im·mu·no·reac·tion

im·mu·no·sup·pres·sion
im·mu·no·sup·pres·sive
im·mu·no·thera·py
im·mure
im·mu·tabil·ity (*or* ·table·ness)
im·mu·table
im·mu·tably
Imo Nigerian state
imp
im·pact
im·pact·ed
im·pac·tion
im·pair
im·pair·er
im·pair·ment
im·pa·la (*plural* ·las *or* ·la) antelope
im·pale
im·pale·ment
im·pal·er
im·pal·pa·bil·ity
im·pal·pable
im·pal·pably
im·pa·na·tion Christian ritual
im·pan·el US spelling of empanel
im·pari·pin·nate botany term
im·pari·syl·la·bic
im·par·ity (*plural* ·ities) disparity
im·part
im·par·ta·tion (*or* ·part·ment)
im·part·er
im·par·tial
im·par·ti·al·ity (*or* ·ness)
im·par·tial·ly
im·part·ibil·ity
im·part·ible legal term
im·pass·abil·ity (*or* ·able·ness)
im·pass·able
im·pass·ably
im·passe
im·pas·sion
im·pas·sioned
im·pas·sioned·ly
im·pas·sive
im·pas·sive·ness (*or* ·siv·ity)
im·pas·ta·tion
im·paste paint thickly

imperforate

im·pas·to paint applied thickly
im·pa·tience
im·pa·ti·ens (*plural* ·ens) plant
im·pa·tient
im·peach
im·peach·abil·ity
im·peach·able
im·peach·er
im·peach·ment
im·pearl
im·pec·cabil·ity
im·pec·cable
im·pec·cably
im·pec·cant sinless
im·pecu·ni·ous
im·pecu·ni·ous·ness (*or* ·os·ity)
im·ped·ance physics term
im·pede
im·ped·er
im·pedi·ment
im·pedi·men·ta impeding objects
im·pedi·men·tal (*or* ·tary)
im·ped·ing·ly
im·pel (·pel·ling, ·pelled)
im·pel·ient
im·pel·ler
im·pend
im·pend·ence (*or* ·en·cy)
im·pend·ing
im·pen·etrabil·ity
im·pen·etrable
im·pen·etrably
im·peni·tence (*or* ·ten·cy, ·tent·ness)
im·peni·tent
im·pera·tive
im·pera·tor
im·per·cep·tibil·ity (*or* ·tible·ness)
im·per·cep·tible
im·per·cep·tibly
im·per·cep·tion
im·per·cep·tive
im·per·cep·tiv·ity (*or* ·tive·ness)
im·per·cipi·ent
im·per·cipi·ence
im·per·fect
im·per·fec·tion
im·per·fec·tive
im·per·fo·rate

imperforation

im·per·fo·ra·tion
im·perial
im·peri·al·ism
im·peri·al·ist
im·peri·al·is·tic
im·peri·al·is·ti·cal·ly
im·peri·al·ly
im·per·il (·il·ling, ·illed; US also ·il·ing, ·iled)
im·peri·ous
im·per·ish·abil·ity (or ·able·ness)
im·per·ish·able
im·perium (plural ·peria) ancient Roman supreme power
im·per·ma·nence (or ·nen·cy)
im·per·ma·nent
im·per·meabil·ity (or ·meable·ness)
im·per·meable
im·per·mis·sibil·ity
im·per·mis·sible
im·per·son·al
im·per·son·al·ity
im·per·son·ali·za·tion (or ·sa·tion)
im·per·son·al·ize (or ·ise)
im·per·son·al·ly
im·per·son·ate
im·per·sona·tion
im·per·sona·tor
im·per·ti·nence (or ·nen·cy)
im·per·ti·nent
im·per·turb·abil·ity (or ·able·ness)
im·per·turb·able
im·per·turb·ably
im·per·tur·ba·tion
im·per·vi·ous
im·petigi·nous
im·peti·go skin disease
im·petrate obtain by prayer
im·petra·tion
im·petra·tive
im·petra·tor
im·petu·os·ity (or ·ous·ness)
im·petu·ous
im·petus (plural ·petuses)
Im·phal Indian city

impi (plural impi or impies) Bantu warrior group
im·pi·ety (plural ·eties)
im·pinge
im·pinge·ment
im·ping·er
im·pi·ous
imp·ish
im·plac·abil·ity (or ·able·ness)
im·plac·able
im·plac·ably
im·plant
im·plan·ta·tion
im·plant·er
im·plau·sibil·ity (or ·sible·ness)
im·plau·sible
im·plau·sibly
im·plead prosecute
im·plead·able
im·plead·er
im·ple·ment tool; to carry out
im·ple·men·tal
im·ple·men·ta·tion
im·ple·ment·er (or ·or)
im·pli·cate
im·pli·ca·tion
im·plica·tive
im·plic·it
im·plic·it·ness (or ·plic·ity)
(impliment) incorrect spelling of implement
im·plode
im·plo·ra·tion
im·plo·ra·tory
im·plore
im·plor·er
im·plor·ing·ly
im·plo·sion
im·plo·sive phonetics term
im·ply (·plies, ·ply·ing, ·plied)
im·poli·cy (plural ·cies)
im·po·lite
im·po·lite·ness
im·poli·tic
im·poli·tic·ly
im·pon·dera·bilia
im·pon·der·abil·ity (or ·able·ness)
im·pon·der·able

226

im·pon·der·ably
im·po·nent
im·port
im·port·able
im·por·tance
im·por·tant
im·por·ta·tion
im·port·er
im·por·tu·nate
im·por·tune
im·por·tun·er
im·por·tu·nity (plural ·nities)
im·pos·able
im·pose
im·pos·er
im·pos·ing
im·pos·ing·ly
im·po·si·tion
im·pos·sibil·ity (plural ·ities)
im·pos·sible
im·pos·sibly
im·post customs duty
im·pos·tor (or ·post·er)
im·pos·trous (or ·tur·ous)
im·pos·ture
im·po·tence (or ·ten·cy, ·tent·ness)
im·po·tent
im·pound
im·pound·age (or ·ment)
im·pound·er
im·pov·er·ish
im·pov·er·ish·er
im·pov·er·ish·ment
im·prac·ti·cabil·ity (or ·cable·ness)
im·prac·ti·cable not feasible
im·prac·ti·cably
im·prac·ti·cal not practical
im·prac·ti·cal·ity (or ·ness)
im·prac·ti·cal·ly
im·pre·cate
im·pre·ca·tion
im·pre·ca·tory
im·pre·cise
im·pre·ci·sion (or ·cise·ness)
im·preg·nabil·ity (or ·nable·ness)
im·preg·nable (or im·preg·na·table)

im·preg·nate
im·preg·na·tion
im·preg·na·tor
im·pre·sa (or im·prese) emblem
im·pre·sa·rio (plural ·rios)
im·pre·scrip·tibil·ity
im·pre·scrip·tible legal term
im·press
im·press·er
im·press·ible
im·pres·sion
im·pres·sion·abil·ity (or ·able·ness)
im·pres·sion·able
im·pres·sion·al
im·pres·sion·al·ly
im·pres·sion·ism
im·pres·sion·ist
im·pres·sion·is·tic
im·pres·sive
im·pres·sive·ness
im·press·ment conscription
im·prest
im·pri·ma·tur sanction
im·print
im·print·er
im·print·ing
im·pris·on
im·pris·on·er
im·pris·on·ment
im·prob·abil·ity (or ·able·ness)
im·prob·able
im·pro·bity (plural ·bities)
im·promp·tu
im·prop·er
im·pro·pri·ate transfer to laity
im·pro·pria·tion
im·pro·pria·tor
im·pro·pri·ety (plural ·eties)
im·prov·abil·ity (or ·able·ness)
im·prov·able
im·prove
im·prove·ment
im·prov·er
im·provi·dence
im·provi·dent
im·prov·ing·ly
im·provi·sa·tion
im·provi·sa·tion·al

im·pro·vise
im·pro·vis·er
im·pru·dence
im·pru·dent unwise; compare **impudent**
im·pu·dence (or ·den·cy)
im·pu·dent impertinent; compare **imprudent**
im·pugn
im·pug·na·tion (or ·pugn·ment)
im·pugn·er
im·pu·is·sance
im·pu·is·sant
im·pulse
im·pul·sion
im·pul·sive
im·pul·sive·ness
im·pu·nity (plural ·nities)
im·pure
im·pu·rity (plural ·rities)
im·put·abil·ity (or ·able·ness)
im·put·able
im·pu·ta·tion
im·pu·ta·tive
im·pute
im·put·er
in
in·abil·ity (plural ·ities)
in ab·sen·tia Latin in the absence of
in·ac·ces·sibil·ity (or ·sible·ness)
in·ac·ces·sible
in·ac·ces·sibly
in·ac·cu·ra·cy (plural ·cies)
in·ac·cu·rate
in·ac·tion
in·ac·ti·vate
in·ac·ti·va·tion
in·ac·tive
in·ac·tiv·ity (or ·tive·ness)
in·ad·equa·cy (plural ·cies)
in·ad·equate
in·ad·mis·sibil·ity
in·ad·mis·si·ble
in·ad·mis·sibly
in·ad·vert·ence (or ·en·cy)
in·ad·vert·ent
in·ad·vis·abil·ity (or ·able·ness)
in·ad·vis·able

in·ad·vis·ably
in·al·ien·abil·ity (or ·able·ness)
in·al·ien·able
in·al·ien·ably
in·al·ter·abil·ity (or ·able·ness)
in·al·ter·able
in·al·ter·ably
in·amo·ra·ta (masc ·to; plural ·tas or ·tos) lover
in·ane
in·ani·mate
ina·ni·tion
in·ani·mate·ness (or ·ma·tion)
in·an·ity (plural ·ities)
in·ap·pli·cabil·ity (or ·cable·ness)
in·ap·pli·cable
in·ap·po·site
in·ap·pre·ciable
in·ap·pre·cia·tive
in·ap·pre·hen·sive
in·ap·proach·abil·ity
in·ap·proach·able
in·ap·pro·pri·ate
in·ap·pro·pri·ate·ness
in·apt inappropriate; compare **inept**
in·ap·ti·tude (or ·apt·ness)
in·arch botany term
in·ar·ticu·late
in·ar·tis·tic
in·ar·tis·ti·cal·ly
in·as·much
in·at·ten·tion (or ·tive·ness)
in·at·ten·tive
In·audibil·ity (or ·audlble·ness)
in·audible
in·audibly
in·augu·ral
in·augu·rate
in·augu·ra·tion
in·augu·ra·tor
in·augu·ra·tory
in·aus·pi·cious
in·board
in·born
in·bound
in·bred
in·breed (·breed·ing, ·bred)

Inca

Inca (*plural* Inca *or* Incas)
In·caic
in·cal·cu·labil·ity (*or* ·lable·ness)
in·cal·cu·lable
in·cal·cu·lably
in·ca·les·cence
in·ca·les·cent *chemistry term*
in cam·era *Latin* in private
In·can
in·can·desce
in·can·des·cence (*or* ·cen·cy)
in·can·des·cent
in·can·ta·tion
in·can·ta·tion·al (*or* ·ta·tory)
in·ca·pabil·ity (*plural* ·ities)
in·ca·pable
in·ca·pably
in·ca·paci·tate
in·ca·paci·ta·tion
in·ca·pac·ity (*plural* ·ities)
in·cap·su·late *less common spelling of* encapsulate
in·car·cer·ate
in·car·cera·tion
in·car·cera·tor
in·car·di·nate
in·car·di·na·tion
in·car·nate
in·car·na·tion
in·cau·tious
in·cau·tious·ness (*or* ·cau·tion)
in·cen·dia·rism
in·cen·di·ary (*plural* ·aries)
in·cense
in·cen·so·ry (*plural* ·ries) incense-burner
in·cen·tive
in·cept
in·cep·tion
in·cep·tive
in·cept·or
in·cer·ti·tude
in·ces·san·cy (*or* ·sant·ness)
in·ces·sant
in·cest
in·ces·tu·ous

inch
inch·meal inch by inch
in·cho·ate
in·choa·tion
in·choa·tive
In·chon (*or* ·cheon) South Korean port
inch·worm
in·ci·dence
in·ci·dent
in·ci·den·tal
in·ci·den·tal·ly
in·cin·er·ate
in·cin·era·tion
in·cin·era·tor
in·cipi·ence (*or* ·en·cy)
in·cipi·ent
in·ci·pit *Latin* here begins
in·cise
in·ci·sion
in·ci·sive
in·ci·sor
in·ci·sur·al
in·ci·sure
in·ci·ta·tion
in·cite
in·cite·ment
in·cit·er
in·cit·ing·ly
in·ci·vil·ity (*plural* ·ities)
in·clem·en·cy (*or* ·ent·ness)
in·clem·ent
in·clin·able
in·cli·na·tion
in·cli·na·tion·al
in·cline
in·clin·er
in·cli·nom·eter
in·close *less common spelling of* enclose
in·clos·ure *less common spelling of* enclosure
in·clud·able (*or* ·ible)
in·clude
in·clu·sion
in·clu·sive
in·co·er·cible
in·cog·ni·to (*fem* ·ta; *plural* ·tos *or* ·tas)
in·cog·ni·zance
in·cog·ni·zant
in·co·her·ence (*or* ·en·cy, ·ent·ness)
in·co·her·ent

in·com·bus·tibil·ity (*or* ·tible·ness)
in·com·bus·tible
in·com·bus·tibly
in·come
in·com·ing
in·com·men·su·rabil·ity (*or* ·rable·ness)
in·com·men·su·rable
in·com·men·su·rably
in·com·men·su·rate
in·com·mode
in·com·mo·di·ous
in·com·mod·ity (*plural* ·ities)
in·com·mu·ni·cabil·ity (*or* ·cable·ness)
in·com·mu·ni·cable
in·com·mu·ni·cably
in·com·mu·ni·ca·do
in·com·mu·ni·ca·tive
in·com·mut·abil·ity (*or* ·able·ness)
in·com·mut·able
in·com·mut·ably
in·com·pa·rabil·ity (*or* ·rable·ness)
in·com·pa·rable
in·com·pa·rably
in·com·pat·ibil·ity (*or* ·ible·ness)
in·com·pat·ible
in·com·pat·ibly
in·com·pe·tence (*or* ·ten·cy)
in·com·pe·tent
in·com·plete
in·com·plete·ness (*or* ·ple·tion)
in·com·pli·ance (*or* ·an·cy)
in·com·pli·ant
in·com·pre·hen·sibil·ity (*or* ·sible·ness)
in·com·pre·hen·sible
in·com·pre·hen·sibly
in·com·pre·hen·sion
in·com·pre·hen·sive
in·com·press·ibil·ity (*or* ·ible·ness)
in·com·press·ible
in·com·press·ibly
in·com·put·abil·ity
in·com·put·able
in·con·ceiv·abil·ity (*or* ·able·ness)

in·con·ceiv·able
in·con·ceiv·ably
in·con·clu·sive
in·con·den·sabil·ity (*or* ·sibil·)
in·con·den·sable (*or* ·sible)
in·con·form·ity
in·con·gru·ity (*plural* ·ities)
in·con·gru·ous (*or* ·ent)
in·con·gru·ous·ness (*or* ·gru·ence)
in·con·sequence (*or* ·sequent·ness)
in·con·sequen·tial (*or* ·sequent)
in·con·sequen·ti·al·ity (*or* ·tial·ness)
in·con·sequen·tial·ly
in·con·sid·er·able
in·con·sid·er·ate
in·con·sid·era·tion
in·con·sist·en·cy (*plural* ·cies)
in·con·sist·ent
in·con·sol·abil·ity (*or* ·able·ness)
in·con·sol·able
in·con·sol·ably
in·con·so·nance
in·con·so·nant
in·con·spicu·ous
in·con·stan·cy (*plural* ·cies)
in·con·stant
in·con·sum·able
in·con·sum·ably
in·con·test·abil·ity (*or* ·able·ness)
in·con·test·able
in·con·test·ably
in·con·ti·nence (*or* ·nen·cy)
in·con·ti·nent
in·con·tro·vert·ibil·ity (*or* ·ible·ness)
in·con·tro·vert·ible
in·con·tro·vert·ibly
in·con·ven·ience
in·con·ven·ient
in·con·vert·ibil·ity (*or* ·ible·ness)
in·con·vert·ible
in·con·vert·ibly

in·con·vin·cibil·ity (*or* ·cible·ness)
in·con·vin·cible
in·co·ordi·nate
in·co·ordi·na·tion
in·cor·po·rable
in·cor·po·rate
in·cor·po·rat·ed
in·cor·po·ra·tion
in·cor·po·ra·tive
in·cor·po·ra·tor
in·cor·po·real
in·cor·po·real·ly
in·cor·po·reity (*or* ·real·ity)
in·cor·rect
in·cor·rect·ness
in·cor·ri·gibil·ity (*or* ·gible·ness)
in·cor·ri·gible
in·cor·ri·gibly
in·cor·rupt
in·cor·rupt·ibil·ity (*or* ·ible·ness)
in·cor·rupt·ible
in·cor·rupt·ibly
in·cras·sate (*or* ·sat·ed) thickened
in·cras·sa·tion
in·creas·able
in·crease
in·creas·ing·ly
in·creas·er
in·cred·ibil·ity (*or* ·ible·ness)
in·cred·ible
in·cred·ibly
in·cre·du·lity
in·credu·lous
in·cre·ment
in·cre·men·tal
in·cres·cent
in·cre·tion secretion into bloodstream
in·cre·tion·ary (*or* ·tory)
in·crimi·nate
in·crimi·na·tion
in·crimi·na·tor
in·crimi·na·tory
in·cross inbreed
in·crust *variant spelling of* encrust
in·cu·bate
in·cu·ba·tion
in·cu·ba·tion·al

in·cu·ba·tive (*or* ·tory)
in·cu·ba·tor
in·cu·bus (*plural* ·bi *or* ·buses) male demon
in·cu·date (*or* ·dal) of incus
in·cul·cate
in·cul·ca·tion
in·cul·ca·tor
in·cul·pabil·ity (*or* ·pable·ness)
in·cul·pable
in·cul·pate
in·cul·pa·tion
in·cul·pa·tive (*or* in·cul·pa·to·ry)
in·cum·ben·cy (*plural* ·cies)
in·cum·bent
in·cu·nabu·la (*sing.* ·lum) early books
in·cu·nabu·lar
in·cur (·cur·ring, ·curred)
in·cur·abil·ity (*or* ·able·ness)
in·cur·able not curable; *compare* incurrable
in·cu·ri·os·ity (*or* ·ous·ness)
in·cu·ri·ous
in·cur·rable liable to incur; *compare* incurable
in·cur·rence
in·cur·rent
in·cur·sion
in·cur·sive
in·cur·vate
in·cur·va·tion
in·cur·va·ture
in·curve
in·cus (*plural* ·cu·des) ear bone
in·cuse design on coin
Ind India
in·da·mine chemical compound
in·debt·ed
in·debt·ed·ness
in·de·cen·cy (*plural* ·cies)
in·de·cent
in·de·cidu·ous
in·de·ci·pher·abil·ity (*or* ·able·ness)
in·de·ci·pher·able
in·de·ci·sion
in·de·ci·sive

indeclinable

in·de·clin·able
in·deco·rous
in·de·co·rum
in·deed
in·de·fati·gabil·ity (*or* ·gable·ness)
in·de·fati·gable
in·de·fati·gably
in·de·fea·sibil·ity (*or* ·sible·ness)
in·de·fea·sible
in·de·fea·sibly
in·de·fen·sibil·ity (*or* ·sible·ness)
in·de·fen·sible
in·de·fin·able
in·de·fin·ably
in·defi·nite
in·de·his·cence
in·de·his·cent botany term
in·del·ibil·ity (*or* ·ible·ness)
in·del·ible
in·del·ibly
in·deli·ca·cy (*plural* ·cies)
in·deli·cate
in·dem·ni·fi·ca·tion
in·dem·ni·fi·er
in·dem·ni·fy (·fies, ·fy·ing, ·fied)
in·dem·nity (*plural* ·nities)
in·de·mon·strable
in·dene chemical compound
in·dent
in·den·ta·tion
in·dent·er (*or* den·tor)
in·den·tion indentation
in·den·ture
in·den·ture·ship
in·de·pend·ence
in·de·pend·en·cy (*plural* ·cies)
in·de·pend·ent
in·de·scrib·abil·ity (*or* ·able·ness)
in·de·scrib·able
in·de·scrib·ably
in·de·struct·ibil·ity (*or* ·ible·ness)
in·de·struct·ible
in·de·struct·ibly
in·de·ter·mi·nable
in·de·ter·mi·na·cy (*or* ·na·tion, ·nate·ness)
in·de·ter·mi·nate
in·de·ter·min·ism
philosophy term
in·de·ter·min·ist
in·de·ter·min·is·tic
in·dex (*plural* ·dexes *or esp. in mathematical contexts* ·di·ces)
in·dex·er
in·dexi·cal
index-linked
In·dia
In·dian
In·di·ana US state
In·di·an·apo·lis US city
In·dic language group
in·di·can chemical compound
in·di·cant
in·di·cat·able
in·di·cate
in·di·ca·tion
in·dica·tive
in·di·ca·tor
in·dica·tory
in·di·ces *plural of* index
in·di·cia (*sing.* ·cium) distinguishing markings
in·di·cial
in·dict accuse; *compare* indite
in·dict·able
in·dictee
in·dict·er (*or* ·dic·tor)
in·dict·ment
In·dies
in·dif·fer·ence
in·dif·fer·ent
in·dif·fer·ent·ism
indifference to religion
in·dif·fer·ent·ist
in·di·gence
in·di·gene (*or* ·gen) a native
in·dig·enous
in·dig·enous·ness (*or* in·di·gen·ity)
in·di·gent
in·di·gest·ibil·ity (*or* ·ible·ness)
in·di·gest·ible
in·di·ges·tion
in·di·ges·tive
in·dign undeserving
in·dig·nant

230

in·dig·na·tion
in·dig·nity (*plural* ·nities)
in·di·go (*plural* ·gos *or* ·goes)
in·di·goid
in·di·got·ic
in·di·rect
in·di·rec·tion
in·di·rect·ness
in·dis·cern·ible
in·dis·cern·ibly
in·dis·ci·pline
in·dis·creet tactless
in·dis·crete undivided
in·dis·cre·tion
in·dis·cre·tion·ary
in·dis·crimi·nate
in·dis·crimi·na·tion
in·dis·crimi·na·tive
in·dis·pen·sabil·ity (*or* ·sable·ness)
in·dis·pen·sable
in·dis·pen·sably
in·dis·pose
in·dis·posed
in·dis·po·si·tion
in·dis·put·abil·ity (*or* ·able·ness)
in·dis·put·able
in·dis·put·ably
in·dis·sol·ubil·ity (*or* ·uble·ness)
in·dis·sol·uble
in·dis·sol·ubly
in·dis·tinct
in·dis·tinc·tive
in·dis·tin·guish·abil·ity (*or* ·able·ness)
in·dis·tin·guish·able
in·dis·tin·guish·ably
in·dite *Archaic* write; *compare* indict
in·dium chemical element
in·di·vid·ual
in·di·vidu·al·ism
in·di·vidu·al·ist
in·di·vidu·al·is·tic
in·di·vidu·al·is·ti·cal·ly
in·di·vidu·al·ity (*plural* ·ities)
in·di·vidu·ali·za·tion (*or* ·sa·tion)
in·di·vidu·al·ize (*or* ·ise)
in·di·vidu·al·iz·er (*or* ·is·er)

in·di·vid·ual·ly
in·di·vidu·ate
in·di·vidu·ation
in·di·vid·ua·tor
in·di·vis·ibil·ity (or ·ible·ness)
in·di·vis·ible
in·di·vis·ibly
Indo·china (or Indo-China)
Indo·chinese (or Indo-Chinese)
in·do·cile
in·do·cil·ity
in·doc·tri·nate
in·doc·tri·na·tion
in·doc·tri·na·tor
Indo-European
in·dole (or ·dol) chemical compound
in·dole·acetic acid
in·dole·bu·tyr·ic acid
in·do·lence
in·do·lent
In·dolo·gist
In·dol·ogy
in·do·metha·cin
in·domi·tabil·ity (or ·table·ness)
in·domi·table
in·domi·tably
In·do·nesia
In·do·nesian
in·door (adj)
in·doors (adv)
Indo-Pacific
in·do·phenol
In·dore Indian city
in·dorse variant spelling of endorse
In·dox·yl chemical compound
in·draught (US ·draft)
in·drawn
Indre French department
Indre-et-Loire French department
in·dris (or ·dri) animal
in·du·bi·tabil·ity (or ·table·ness)
in·du·bi·table
in·du·bi·tably
in·duce
in·duce·ment
in·duc·er

in·duc·ible
in·duct
in·duct·ance electrical property
in·duc·tee US military conscript
(inducter) incorrect spelling of inductor
in·duc·tile not pliant
in·duc·til·ity
in·duc·tion
in·duc·tion·al
in·duc·tive
in·duc·tor
in·dulge
in·dul·gence
in·dul·gent
in·dulg·er
in·dulg·ing·ly
in·du·line (or ·lin) dye
in·dult Catholic dispensation
in·du·pli·cate (or ·cat·ed)
in·du·pli·ca·tion
in·du·rate
in·du·ra·tion
in·du·ra·tive
In·dus Asian river
in·du·sial
in·du·sium (plural ·sia) membrane
in·dus·trial
in·dus·tri·al·ism
in·dus·tri·al·ist
in·dus·tri·ali·za·tion (or ·sa·tion)
in·dus·tri·al·ize (or ·ise)
in·dus·tri·al·ly
in·dus·tri·ous
in·dus·try (plural ·tries)
in·dwell (·dwell·ing, ·dwelt)
in·earth bury
in·ebri·ant
in·ebri·ate
in·ebri·at·ed
in·ebria·tion
in·ebri·ety
in·ed·ibil·ity
in·ed·ible
in·ed·it·ed
in·edu·cabil·ity
in·edu·cable
in·ef·fabil·ity (or ·fable·ness)
in·ef·fable

in·ef·fably
in·ef·face·abil·ity
in·ef·face·able
in·ef·fec·tive
in·ef·fec·tual
in·ef·fec·tu·al·ity (or ·ness)
in·ef·fec·tual·ly
in·ef·fi·ca·cious
in·ef·fi·ca·cy (or ·ca·cious·ness)
in·ef·fi·cien·cy
in·ef·fi·cient
in·elas·tic
in·elas·tic·al·ly
in·elas·tic·ity
in·el·egance (or ·egan·cy)
in·el·egant
in·eli·gibil·ity (or ·gible·ness)
in·eli·gible
in·elo·quence
in·elo·quent
in·eluc·tabil·ity
in·eluc·table
in·eluc·tably
in·ept incompetent; compare inapt
in·epti·tude
in·equal·ity (plural ·ities)
in·equi·table
in·equi·tably
in·equi·ty (plural ·ties)
in·eradi·cable
in·eradi·cably
in·ert
in·er·tia
in·er·tial
in·es·cap·able
in·es·cap·ably
in·es·cutch·eon heraldic term
in esse Latin actually existing
in·es·sen·tial
in·es·sen·ti·al·ity
in·es·sive linguistics term
in·es·ti·mabil·ity (or ·mable·ness)
in·es·ti·mable
in·es·ti·mably
in·evi·tabil·ity (or ·table·ness)
in·evi·table
in·evi·tably

inexact

in·ex·act
in·ex·acti·tude
in·ex·cus·abil·ity (or
  ·able·ness)
in·ex·cus·able
in·ex·cus·ably
in·ex·haust·ibil·ity (or
  ·ible·ness)
in·ex·haust·ible
in·ex·haust·ibly
in·ex·ist·ence (or ·en·cy)
in·ex·ist·ent
in·exo·rabil·ity (or
  ·rable·ness)
in·exo·rable
in·exo·rably
in·ex·pe·di·ence (or
  ·en·cy)
in·ex·pe·di·ent
in·ex·pen·sive
in·ex·pe·ri·ence
in·ex·pe·ri·enced
in·ex·pert
in·ex·pi·able
in·ex·pi·ably
in·ex·pli·cabil·ity (or
  ·cable·ness)
in·ex·pli·cable
in·ex·pli·cably
in·ex·plic·it
in·ex·press·ibil·ity (or
  ·ible·ness)
in·ex·press·ible
in·ex·press·ibly
in·ex·pres·sive
in·ex·ten·sibil·ity
in·ex·ten·sible
in·ex·tin·guish·able
in·ex·tir·pable
in ex·tre·mis *Latin* in
  extremity
in·ex·tri·cabil·ity (or
  ·cable·ness)
in·ex·tri·cable
in·ex·tri·cably
in·fal·libil·ity (or
  ·lible·ness)
in·fal·lible
in·fal·libly
in·fam·ize (or ·ise) make
  infamous
in·fa·mous
in·fa·my (*plural* ·mies)
in·fan·cy (*plural* ·cies)
in·fant

in·fan·ta Spanish princess
in·fan·te Spanish prince
in·fan·ti·cid·al
in·fan·ti·cide
in·fan·tile
in·fan·ti·lism
in·fan·til·ity
in·fan·try (*plural* ·tries)
in·fantry·man (*plural*
  ·men)
in·farct dead tissue
in·farct·ed
in·farc·tion
in·fare *Dialect* wedding
  reception
in·fatu·ate
in·fatu·at·ed
in·fatu·at·ed·ly
in·fat·ua·tion
in·fect
in·fec·tion
in·fec·tious
in·fec·tious·ness
in·fec·tive
in·fec·tive·ness (or
  ·tiv·ity)
in·fec·tor (or ·fect·er)
in·fe·cund
in·fe·cun·dity
in·fe·lici·tous
in·fe·lic·ity (*plural* ·ities)
in·fer (·fer·ring, ·ferred)
in·fer·able (or ·ible,
  ·rable, ·rible)
in·fer·ence
in·fer·en·tial
in·fe·ri·or
in·fe·ri·or·ity
in·fer·nal
in·fer·nal·ity
in·fer·nal·ly
in·fer·no (*plural* ·nos)
in·ferred
in·fer·rer
in·fer·ring
in·fer·tile
in·fer·til·ity
in·fest
in·fes·ta·tion
in·fest·er
in·fi·del
in·fi·del·ity (*plural* ·ities)
in·field
in·fielder
in·fighter

in·fighting
in·fil·trate
in·fil·tra·tion
in·fil·tra·tive
in·fil·tra·tor
in·fi·nite
in·fi·nite·ly
in·fini·tesi·mal
in·fini·tesi·mal·ly
in·fini·ti·val
in·fini·tive
in·fini·tude
in·fin·ity (*plural* ·ities)
in·firm
in·fir·ma·ry (*plural* ·ries)
in·fir·mity (*plural* ·mities)
in·fix
in·fix·ion
in·flame
in·flam·er
in·flam·ing·ly
in·flam·mabil·ity (or
  ·mable·ness)
in·flam·mable
in·flam·ma·tion
in·flam·ma·to·ri·ly
in·flam·ma·tory
in·flat·able
in·flate
in·flat·ed·ly
in·flat·er (or ·fla·tor)
in·fla·tion
in·fla·tion·ary
in·fla·tion·ism
in·fla·tion·ist
in·flect
in·flect·ed·ness
in·flec·tion (or ·flex·ion)
in·flec·tion·al (or
  ·flex·ion·)
in·flec·tive
in·flec·tor
in·flexed botany term
in·flex·ibil·ity (or
  ·ible·ness)
in·flex·ible
in·flex·ibly
in·flex·ion variant spelling of
  inflection
in·flict
in·flict·er (or ·flic·tor)
in·flic·tion
in·flic·tive
in·flo·res·cence
in·flo·res·cent

in·flow
in·flu·ence
in·flu·ence·able
in·flu·enc·er
in·flu·ent flowing in
in·flu·en·tial
in·flu·en·tial·ly
in·flu·en·za
in·flu·en·zal
in·flux
info *Slang* information
in·fold *variant spelling of* enfold
(inforce) *incorrect spelling of* enforce
in·form
in·for·mal
in·for·mal·ity (*plural* ·ities)
in·for·mal·ly
in·form·ant
in·for·ma·tion
in·for·ma·tion·al
in·forma·tive (*or* ·tory)
in·forma·tive·ly
in·form·ed·ly
in·form·er
in·form·ing·ly
infra·cos·tal anatomy term
in·fract violate
in·frac·tion
in·frac·tor
in·fra dig
infra·lap·sar·ian theology term
infra·lap·sari·an·ism
in·fran·gibil·ity (*or* ·gible·ness)
in·fran·gible
infra·red
infra·son·ic
infra·soni·cal·ly
infra·sound
infra·struc·ture
in·fre·quen·cy (*or* ·quence)
in·fre·quent
in·fringe
in·fringe·ment
in·fring·er
in·fu·lae (*sing.* ·la) ribbons on bishop's mitre
in·fun·dibu·lar (*or* ·late)
in·fun·dibu·li·form

in·fun·dibu·lum (*plural* ·la) anatomical part
in·furi·ate
in·furi·at·ing·ly
in·furia·tion
in·fus·cate (*or* ·cat·ed) tinged with brown
in·fuse
in·fus·er
in·fu·sibil·ity (*or* ·sible·ness)
in·fu·sible
in·fu·sion
in·fu·sion·ism theology term
in·fu·sion·ist
in·fu·sive
in·fu·so·rial
in·gath·er
in·gen·ious skilful; *compare* ingenuous
in·gé·nue naive girl
in·genu·ity (*plural* ·ities)
in·genu·ous naive; *compare* ingenious
in·gest
in·ges·ta (*plural*) food
in·gest·ible
in·ges·tion
in·ges·tive
in·gle
ingle·nook
in·glo·ri·ous
in·go·ing
in·got
in·graft *variant spelling of* engraft
in·grain (*or* en·)
in·grained (*or* en·)
in·grain·ed·ly (*or* en·)
in·grain·ed·ness (*or* en·)
in·grate
in·gra·ti·ate
in·gra·ti·at·ing (*or* in·gra·tia·tory)
in·gra·tia·tion
in·grati·tude
in·gra·ves·cence
in·gra·ves·cent becoming worse
in·gre·di·ent
in·gress
in·gres·sion
in·gres·sive
in·group

in·grow·ing
in·grown
in·growth
in·gui·nal of the groin
in·gur·gi·tate to gorge
in·gur·gi·ta·tion
In·gush (*plural* ·gushes *or* ·gush) Soviet people
in·hab·it
in·hab·it·abil·ity
in·hab·it·able
in·hab·it·an·cy (*or* ·ance)
in·hab·it·ant
in·habi·ta·tion
in·hal·ant
in·ha·la·tion
in·ha·la·tor device aiding breathing
in·hale
in·hal·er
in·har·mon·ic
in·har·mo·ni·ous
in·har·mo·ny
in·haul (*or* ·haul·er) nautical term
in·here
in·her·ence (*or* ·en·cy)
in·her·ent
in·her·it
in·her·it·abil·ity (*or* ·able·ness)
in·her·it·able
in·her·it·ance
in·heri·tor (*fem* ·tress *or* ·trix; *plural* ·tors, ·tresses, *or* ·tri·ces)
in·he·sion inherence
in·hib·it
in·hib·it·able
in·hib·it·er (*or* ·hibi·tor)
in·hi·bi·tion
in·hibi·tive (*or* ·tory)
in·hibi·tor
in·hos·pi·table
in·hos·pi·tably
in·hos·pi·tal·ity
in·house
in·hu·man
in·hu·mane
in·hu·man·ity (*plural* ·ities)
in·hu·ma·tion
in·hume inter
in·hum·er
in·imi·cal

inimically

in·imi·cal·ly
in·imi·cal·ness (or ·ity)
in·imi·tabil·ity (or
 ·table·ness)
in·imi·table
in·imi·tably
ini·on anatomy term
in·iqui·tous
in·iquity (plural ·iquities)
ini·tial (·tial·ling, ·tialled;
 US ·tial·ing, ·tialed)
ini·tial·er (or ·tial·ler)
ini·tiali·za·tion (or
 ·sa·tion)
ini·tial·ize (or ·ise)
 computer term
ini·tial·ly
ini·ti·ate
ini·tia·tion
ini·tia·tive
ini·tia·tor
ini·tia·tory
ini·tia·tress (or ·trix)
in·ject
in·ject·able
in·jec·tion
in·jec·tive
in·jec·tor
in·ju·di·cious
In·jun US American Indian
in·junc·tion
in·junc·tive
in·jur·able
in·jure
in·jur·er
in·ju·ri·ous
in·ju·ry (plural ·ries)
in·jus·tice
ink
ink·berry (plural ·berries)
ink·blot
ink-cap fungus
In·ker·man Crimean battle
ink·horn
inki·ness
in·kle linen tape
ink·ling
ink·stand
ink·well
inky (inki·er, inki·est)
in·laid
in·land
in·land·er
in-law
in·lay (·lay·ing, ·laid)

in·lay·er
in·let (·let·ting, ·let)
in·li·er geology term
in loco pa·ren·tis
in·mate
in me·mo·ri·am
in·mi·grant immigrant
in·most
inn
in·nards
in·nate
in·ner
inner·most
in·ner·vate supply with
 nerves; compare enervate;
 innovate
in·ner·va·tion
in·nerve stimulate
in·ning baseball term
in·nings (plural ·nings)
inn·keeper
in·no·cence
in·no·cent
(innoculate) incorrect
 spelling of inoculate
in·nocu·ous
in·nomi·nate
in nomi·ne musical term
in·no·vate introduce new
 ideas; compare enervate;
 innervate
in·no·va·tion
in·no·va·tion·al
in·no·va·tion·ist
in·no·va·tive (or ·tory)
in·no·va·tor
in·nox·ious harmless
Inns·bruck Austrian city
in·nu·en·do (plural ·dos
 or ·does)
In·nu·it (or Inu·it; plural
 ·it or ·its) Eskimo
in·nu·mer·abil·ity (or
 ·able·ness)
in·nu·mer·able (or ·ous)
in·nu·mer·ably
in·nu·mer·ate
in·nu·tri·tion
in·nu·tri·tious
in·ob·serv·ance
in·ob·serv·ant
in·ocu·labil·ity
in·ocu·lable
in·ocu·late
in·ocu·la·tion

234

in·ocu·la·tive
in·ocu·la·tor
in·ocu·lum (or ·lant;
 plural ·la or ·lants)
in·odor·ous
in·of·fen·sive
in·of·fi·cious contrary to
 moral duty
in·op·er·abil·ity (or
 ·able·ness)
in·op·er·able
in·op·era·tive
in·op·por·tune
in·op·por·tune·ness (or
 ·tun·ity)
in·or·di·na·cy (or
 ·nate·ness)
in·or·di·nate
in·or·gan·ic
in·or·gani·cal·ly
in·os·cu·late
in·os·cu·la·tion
ino·si·tol chemical
 compound
ino·trop·ic physiology term
in·pa·tient
in per·pe·tuum
in pos·se Latin possible
in·put (·put·ting, ·put)
in·qi·lab Indian revolution
in·quest
in·qui·et
in·qui·etude
in·qui·line biology term
in·qui·lin·ism (or ·ity)
in·qui·li·nous
in·quire formally
 investigate; US spelling of
 enquire
in·quir·er
in·quiry (plural ·quiries)
 formal investigation; US
 spelling of enquiry
in·qui·si·tion
in·qui·si·tion·al
in·qui·si·tion·ist
in·quisi·tive
in·quisi·tive·ness
in·quisi·tor
in·quisi·to·rial
in·quisi·to·rial·ly
in re legal term
in rem legal term
in·road
in·rush

in·sali·vate
in·sali·va·tion
in·sa·lu·bri·ous
in·sa·lu·bri·ty
in·sane
in·sani·tari·ness (or ·ta·tion)
in·sani·tary
in·san·ity (plural ·ities)
in·sa·tiabil·ity (or ·tiable·ness, ·ti·ate·ness)
in·sa·tiable (or ·ti·ate)
in·sa·tiably (or ·ti·ate·ly)
in·scape person's nature
in·scrib·able
in·scribe
in·scrib·er
in·scrip·tion
in·scrip·tion·al
in·scrip·tive
in·scru·tabil·ity (or ·table·ness)
in·scru·table
in·sect
in·sec·tar·ium (or ·tary; plural ·tar·iums, ·tar·ia, or ·taries)
in·sec·tean (or ·tan, ·tile)
in·sec·ti·cid·al
in·sec·ti·cide
in·sec·ti·vore
in·sec·tivo·rous
in·secure
in·secu·rity (plural ·rities)
in·sel·berg rocky hill
in·scmi·nate
in·semi·na·tion
in·semi·na·tor
in·sen·sate
in·sen·sibil·ity (or ·sible·ness)
in·sen·sible
in·sen·sibly
in·sen·si·tive
in·sen·si·tiv·ity
in·sen·ti·ence (or ·en·cy)
in·sen·ti·ent
in·sepa·rabil·ity (or ·rable·ness)
in·sepa·rable
in·sepa·rably
in·sert
in·sert·able
in·sert·er
in·ser·tion
in·ser·tion·al
in·ses·so·rial ornithology term
in·set (·set·ting, ·set)
in·set·ter
in·shore
in·side
in·sid·er
in·sidi·ous
in·sight
in·sight·ful
in·sig·nia (plural ·nias or ·nia)
in·sig·nifi·cance (or ·can·cy)
in·sig·nifi·cant
in·sin·cere
in·sin·cere·ly
in·sin·cer·ity (plural ·ities)
in·sinu·ate
in·sin·ua·tion
in·sinua·tive (or ·tory)
in·sinua·tor
in·sip·id
in·si·pid·ity (or ·ness)
in·sist
in·sist·ence (or ·en·cy)
in·sist·ent
in·sist·er
in situ
in·so·bri·ety
in so far (US in·so·far)
in·so·late expose to sun; compare insulate
in·so·la·tion
in·sole
in·so·lence
in·so·lent
in·sol·ubil·ity (or ·uble·ness)
in·sol·uble
in·sol·ubly
in·solv·abil·ity
in·solv·able
in·sol·ven·cy
in·sol·vent
in·som·nia
in·som·ni·ac
in·som·ni·ous
in·so·much
in·sou·ci·ance
in·sou·ci·ant

instinct

in·span (·span·ning, ·spanned) harness
in·spect
in·spect·able
in·spec·tion
in·spec·tion·al
in·spec·tive
in·spec·tor
in·spec·to·ral (or ·rial)
in·spec·tor·ate
in·spec·tor·ship
in·spir·able
in·spi·ra·tion
in·spi·ra·tion·al
in·spira·tive
in·spira·tory
in·spire
in·spir·er
in·spir·ing
in·spir·it
in·spir·it·er
in·spir·it·ing·ly
in·spir·it·ment
in·stabil·ity (plural ·ities)
in·stall (or ·stal; ·stall·ing, ·stalled or ·stal·ling, ·stalled)
in·stal·la·tion
in·stall·er
in·stal·ment (US ·stall·)
in·stance
in·stant
in·stan·ta·neous
in·stan·ta·neous·ness (or ·neity)
in·stan·ter without delay
in·stan·ti·ate represent by example
in·stant·ly
in·star zoology term
in·state
in·state·ment
in·stead
in·step
in·sti·gate
in·sti·ga·tion
in·sti·ga·tive
in·sti·ga·tor
in·stil (or ·still; ·stil·ling, ·stilled or ·still·ing, ·stilled)
in·stil·la·tion
in·still·er
in·stil·ment (or ·still·)
in·stinct

instinctive

in·stinc·tive (*or* ·tual)
in·sti·tute
in·sti·tu·tion
in·sti·tu·tion·al
in·sti·tu·tion·al·ism
in·sti·tu·tion·al·ist
in·sti·tu·tion·ali·za·tion (*or* ·sa·tion)
in·sti·tu·tion·al·ize (*or* ·ise)
in·sti·tu·tion·ary
in·sti·tu·tive
in·sti·tu·tor (*or* ·tut·er)
in·struct
in·struct·ible
in·struc·tion
in·struc·tion·al
in·struc·tive
in·struc·tor
in·struc·tor·ship
in·struc·tress
in·stru·ment
in·stru·men·tal
in·stru·men·tal·ism philosophy term
in·stru·men·tal·ist
in·stru·men·tal·ity
in·stru·men·tal·ly
in·stru·men·ta·tion
in·sub·or·di·nate
in·sub·or·di·na·tion
in·sub·stan·tial
in·sub·stan·ti·al·ity
in·sub·stan·tial·ly
in·suf·fer·able
in·suf·fer·ably
in·suf·fi·cien·cy (*or* ·cience)
in·suf·fi·cient
in·suf·flate
in·suf·fla·tion
in·suf·fla·tor
in·su·la (*plural* ·lae) anatomy term
in·sul·ant
in·su·lar
in·su·lar·ity (*or* ·ism)
in·su·late isolate; *compare* insolate
in·su·la·tion
in·su·la·tor
in·su·lin hormone; *compare* inulin
in·sult
in·sult·er

in·su·per·abil·ity (*or* ·able·ness)
in·su·per·able
in·su·per·ably
in·sup·port·able
in·sup·port·ably
in·sup·press·ible
in·sur·abil·ity
in·sur·able
in·sur·ance financial protection; *insurance against death is* life assurance
in·sure protect against loss; *compare* ensure
in·sured
in·sur·er
in·sur·gence
in·sur·gen·cy (*plural* ·cies)
in·sur·gent
in·sur·mount·abil·ity (*or* ·able·ness)
in·sur·mount·able
in·sur·mount·ably
in·sur·rec·tion
in·sur·rec·tion·al
in·sur·rec·tion·ary
in·sur·rec·tion·ism
in·sur·rec·tion·ist
in·sus·cep·tibil·ity
in·sus·cep·tible
in·swing cricket term
in·swinger
in·tact
in·tag·li·at·ed
in·tag·lio (*plural* ·lios *or* ·li) engraving
in·take
in·tan·gibil·ity (*or* ·gible·ness)
in·tan·gible
in·tan·gibly
in·tar·sia mosaic of wood
in·te·ger
in·te·gral
in·te·gral·ly
in·te·grand maths term
in·te·grant part of whole
in·te·grate
in·te·gra·tion
in·te·gra·tion·ist
in·te·gra·tive
in·te·gra·tor
in·teg·rity

in·tegu·ment
in·tegu·men·tary (*or* ·men·tal)
in·tel·lect
in·tel·lec·tion thought
in·tel·lec·tive
in·tel·lec·tual
in·tel·lec·tu·al·ism
in·tel·lec·tu·al·ist
in·tel·lec·tu·al·is·tic
in·tel·lec·tu·al·is·ti·cal·ly
in·tel·lec·tu·al·ity (*or* ·ness)
in·tel·lec·tu·ali·za·tion (*or* ·sa·tion)
in·tel·lec·tu·al·ize (*or* ·ise)
in·tel·lec·tu·al·iz·er (*or* ·is·er)
in·tel·lec·tu·al·ly
in·tel·li·gence
in·tel·li·gent
in·tel·li·gent·sia
in·tel·li·gibil·ity (*or* ·gible·ness)
in·tel·li·gi·ble
in·tel·li·gibly
In·tel·sat communications satellite
in·tem·per·ance
in·tem·per·ate
in·tend
in·tend·ance French public department
in·tend·an·cy
in·tend·ant provincial official
in·tend·ed
in·tend·er
in·tend·ment legal term
in·ten·er·ate make tender
in·tense
in·ten·si·fi·ca·tion
in·ten·si·fi·er
in·ten·si·fy (·fies, ·fy·ing, ·fied)
in·ten·sion logic term; *compare* intention
in·ten·sion·al
in·ten·sity (*plural* ·sities)
in·ten·sive
in·tent
in·ten·tion purpose; *compare* intension
in·ten·tion·al
in·ten·tion·al·ity

236

in·ten·tion·al·ly
in·tent·ly
in·ter (·ter·ring, ·terred)
inter·act
inter·ac·tion
inter·ac·tion·al
inter·ac·tive
in·ter·ac·tiv·i·ty
in·ter alia *Latin* among other things
in·ter ali·os *Latin* among other people
inter·atom·ic
inter·bed·ded
inter·brain
inter·breed (·breed·ing, ·bred)
inter·ca·lari·ly
inter·ca·lary
inter·ca·late
inter·ca·la·tion
inter·ca·la·tive
inter·cede
inter·ced·er
inter·cel·lu·lar
inter·cept
inter·cep·tion
inter·cep·tive
inter·cep·tor (*or* ·cept·er)
inter·ces·sion
inter·ces·sion·al (*or* inter·ces·sory)
inter·ces·sor
inter·ces·so·ri·al
inter·change
inter·change·abil·i·ty (*or* ·able·ness)
inter·change·able
inter·change·ably
inter·city
inter·clavi·cle
inter·cla·vicu·lar
inter·col·legi·ate
inter·co·lum·nar
inter·co·lum·nia·tion
inter·com
inter·com·mu·ni·cabil·i·ty
inter·com·mu·ni·cable
inter·com·mu·ni·cate
inter·com·mu·ni·ca·tion
inter·com·mu·ni·ca·tive
inter·com·mu·ni·ca·tor
inter·com·mun·ion
inter·con·nect
inter·con·nec·tion

inter·con·ti·nen·tal
inter·cos·tal anatomy term
inter·course
inter·crop (·crop·ping, ·cropped)
inter·cross crossbreed
inter·cur·rence
inter·cur·rent
inter·denomi·na·tion·al
inter·denomi·na·tion·al·ism
inter·den·tal
inter·de·part·men·tal
inter·de·pend·ence (*or* ·en·cy)
inter·de·pend·ent
inter·dict
inter·dic·tion
inter·dic·tive (*or* ·tory)
inter·dic·tor
inter·dis·ci·pli·nary
in·ter·est
in·ter·est·ed
in·ter·est·ed·ly
in·ter·est·ing
inter·face
inter·fa·cial
inter·fa·cial·ly
inter·fac·ing
inter·fere
inter·fer·ence
inter·feren·tial
inter·fer·er
inter·fer·ing
inter·fer·om·eter physics instrument
inter·fero·met·ric
inter·fero·met·ri·cal·ly
inter·fer·om·etry
inter·fer·on biochemical substance
Inter·fer·tile
inter·fer·til·i·ty
inter·file
inter·flu·ent flowing together
inter·fluve land between rivers
inter·flu·vial
inter·fuse
inter·fu·sion
inter·ga·lac·tic
inter·gla·cial
inter·gov·ern·men·tal
inter·gra·da·tion

inter·gra·da·tion·al
inter·grade
inter·gra·di·ent
inter·group
in·ter·im
in·te·ri·or
inter·ject
inter·jec·tion
inter·jec·tion·al (*or* ·tion·ary, ·tur·al)
inter·jec·tor
inter·jec·tory
inter·lace
inter·lace·ment
In·ter·la·ken Swiss town
inter·lami·nar
inter·lami·nate
inter·lami·na·tion
inter·lard
inter·lay (·lay·ing, ·laid)
inter·leaf (*noun*; *plural* ·leaves)
inter·leave (*verb*)
inter·line
inter·lin·ear (*or* ·eal)
inter·lin·eate
inter·line·ation
inter·lin·er
Inter·lin·gua language
inter·lin·ing
inter·link
inter·lock
inter·lock·er
inter·lo·cu·tion
inter·locu·tor
inter·locu·to·ri·ly
inter·locu·tory
inter·locu·tress (*or* ·trice, ·trix)
inter·lope
inter·lop·er
inter·lude
inter·lu·nar
inter·lu·na·tion period of moon's invisibility
inter·mar·riage
inter·mar·ry (·ries, ·ry·ing, ·ried)
inter·media·cy
inter·medi·ary (*plural* ·aries)
inter·medi·ate
inter·media·tor
in·ter·ment burial; *compare* internment

intermezzo

inter·mez·zo (*plural* ·zos *or* ·zi)
inter·mi·gra·tion
in·ter·mi·nable
in·ter·mi·nable·ness (*or* ·nabil·ity)
in·ter·mi·nably
inter·min·gle
inter·mis·sion
inter·mis·sive
inter·mit (·mit·ting, ·mit·ted)
inter·mit·tence (*or* ·ten·cy)
inter·mit·tent sporadic; *compare* intromittent
inter·mit·tor
inter·mix
inter·mix·able
inter·mix·ture
inter·mo·lecu·lar
in·tern
in·ter·nal
in·ter·nal·ity (*or* ·ness)
in·ter·nali·za·tion (*or* ·sa·tion)
in·ter·nal·ize (*or* ·ise)
in·ter·nal·ly
inter·na·tion·al
inter·na·tion·al·ism
inter·na·tion·al·ist
inter·na·tion·al·ity
inter·na·tion·ali·za·tion (*or* ·sa·tion)
inter·na·tion·al·ize (*or* ·ise)
inter·na·tion·al·ly
inter·necine
in·ternee
inter·neu·rone (*or* ·ron)
in·tern·ist
in·tern·ment confinement; *compare* interment
inter·nod·al
inter·node part of plant stem
in·tern·ship
inter·nun·cial
inter·nun·cio (*plural* ·cios) papal ambassador
intero·cep·tive
intero·cep·tor physiology term
inter·os·cu·late biology term
inter·os·cu·la·tion

inter·page
inter·pel·lant
inter·pel·late question in parliament; *compare* interpolate
in·ter·pel·la·tion
in·ter·pel·la·tor
inter·pen·etrable
inter·pen·etrant
inter·pen·etrate
inter·pen·etra·tion
inter·pen·etra·tive
inter·per·son·al
inter·phase
inter·phone
inter·plan·etary
inter·play
inter·plead (·plead·ing, ·plead·ed, ·plead *or* ·pled) legal term
inter·plead·er
Inter·pol
in·ter·po·late insert; *compare* interpellate
in·ter·po·lat·er (*or* ·la·tor)
in·ter·po·la·tion
in·ter·po·la·tive
inter·pos·able
inter·pos·al
inter·pose
inter·pos·er
inter·po·si·tion
in·ter·pret
in·ter·pret·abil·ity (*or* ·able·ness)
in·ter·pret·able
in·ter·pre·ta·tion
in·ter·pre·ta·tion·al
in·ter·pre·ta·tive
in·ter·pret·er
in·ter·pre·tive
inter·ra·cial
inter·ra·cial·ly
inter·ra·di·al
inter·reg·nal
inter·reg·num (*plural* ·nums *or* ·na)
inter·re·late
inter·re·la·tion
inter·re·la·tion·ship
inter·rex (*plural* ·re·ges)
interim ruler
in·ter·ro·bang (*or* ·tera·bang) punctuation mark

in·ter·ro·gate
in·ter·ro·gat·ing·ly
in·ter·ro·ga·tion
in·ter·ro·ga·tion·al
in·ter·rogative
in·ter·ro·ga·tor
in·ter·roga·to·ri·ly
in·ter·roga·tory (*plural* ·tories)
in·ter·rupt
in·ter·rupt·er (*or* ·rup·tor)
in·ter·rupt·ible
in·ter·rup·tion
in·ter·rup·tive
inter·scho·las·tic
inter·sect
inter·sec·tion
inter·sec·tion·al
inter·sex
inter·sex·ual
inter·sexu·al·ity (*or* ·ism)
inter·sex·ual·ly
inter·space
inter·spa·tial
inter·sperse
inter·sper·sion (*or* ·sal)
inter·sta·dial interglacial
inter·state
inter·stel·lar
in·ter·stice
in·ter·sti·tial
inter·strati·fi·ca·tion
inter·strati·fy (·fies, ·fy·ing, ·fied) geology term
inter·tex·ture
inter·tid·al
inter·trib·al
inter·tri·go (*plural* ·gos) chafed skin
inter·tropi·cal
inter·twine
in·ter·val
inter·vene
inter·ven·er (*or* ·ve·nor)
inter·ven·tion
inter·ven·tion·al
inter·ven·tion·ism
inter·ven·tion·ist
inter·view
inter·viewee
inter·view·er
in·ter vivos legal term
inter·vo·cal·ic between vowels

inter·vo·cali·cal·ly
inter·weave (·weav·ing, ·wove or ·weaved, ·woven or ·weaved)
inter·weav·er
inter·wind (·wind·ing, ·wound)
inter·woven
in·tes·ta·cy
in·tes·tate
in·tes·ti·nal
in·tes·tine
in·ti·ma (*plural* ·mae) anatomy term
in·ti·ma·cy (*plural* ·cies)
in·ti·mal
in·ti·mate
in·ti·ma·tion
in·timi·date
in·timi·da·tion
in·timi·da·tor
in·tinc·tion part of Communion
in·tine botany term
into
in·tol·er·abil·ity (*or* ·able·ness)
in·tol·er·able
in·tol·er·ably
in·tol·er·ance
in·tol·er·ant
in·to·nate
in·to·na·tion
in·to·na·tion·al
in·tone
in·ton·er
in·tor·sion botany term
in toto *Latin* entirely
in·toxi·cable
in·toxi·cant
in·toxi·cate
in·toxi·cat·ing·ly
in·toxi·ca·tion
in·toxi·ca·tive
in·toxi·ca·tor
intra-atomic
intra·car·di·ac
intra·cel·lu·lar
intra·cos·tal anatomy term
intra·cra·nial
in·trac·tabil·ity (*or* ·table·ness)
in·trac·table
in·trac·tably
intra·cu·ta·neous

intra·der·mal (*or* ·mic)
in·tra·dos (*plural* ·dos *or* ·doses) inner curve of arch
intra·mo·lecu·lar
intra·mu·ral
intra·mus·cu·lar
in·tran·si·gence (*or* ·gen·cy)
in·tran·si·gent
in·tran·si·gent·ist
in·tran·si·tive
intra·nu·clear
intra·state
intra·tel·lu·ric
intra·uter·ine
in·trava·sa·tion
intra·venous
(intravert) *incorrect spelling of* introvert
in·treat *Archaic* entreat
in·trench *less common spelling of* entrench
in·trep·id
in·tre·pid·ity (*or* ·trep·id·ness)
in·tri·ca·cy (*plural* ·cies)
in·tri·cate
in·tri·cate·ness
in·trigue (·trigu·ing, ·trigued)
in·tri·guer
intrigu·ing
in·trin·sic (*or* ·si·cal)
in·trin·si·cal·ly
in·tro (*plural* ·tros)
intro·duce
intro·duc·er
intro·duc·ible
intro·duc·tion
intro·duc·to·ri·ly
intro·duc·tory
in·tro·gres·sion
in·troit prayer
in·troi·tal
intro·ject
intro·jec·tion psychology term
intro·jec·tive
intro·mis·sion insertion
intro·mit·tent insertable; *compare* intermittent
in·trorse turned inwards
intro·spect
intro·spec·tion

intro·spec·tion·al
intro·spec·tion·ist
intro·spec·tive
intro·ver·sion
intro·ver·sive (*or* ·tive)
intro·vert
in·trude
in·trud·er
in·trud·ing·ly
in·tru·sion
in·tru·sion·al
in·tru·sive
in·trust *less common spelling of* entrust
in·tu·bate
in·tu·ba·tion
in·tu·it
in·tu·it·able
in·tui·tion
in·tui·tion·al
in·tui·tion·ism (*or* ·tion·al·ism)
in·tui·tion·ist (*or* tion·al·ist)
in·tui·tive
in·tui·tiv·ism
in·tui·tiv·ist
in·tu·mesce
in·tu·mes·cence (*or* ·cen·cy)
in·tu·mes·cent
in·tus·sus·cept
in·tus·sus·cep·tion medical and biology term
in·tus·sus·cep·tive
in·twine *less common spelling of* entwine
inu·lin plant compound; *compare* insulin
in·unc·tion
in·un·dant (*or* ·da·tory)
in·un·date
in·un·da·tion
in·un·da·tor
in·ure (*or* en·)
in·ur·ed·ness (*or* en·)
in·urn
in ut·ero *Latin* in the womb
in·utile
in·util·ity
in va·cuo *Latin* in a vacuum
in·vad·able
in·vade
in·vad·er
in·vagi·nable

invaginate

in·vagi·nate
in·vagi·na·tion
in·va·lid disabled person
in·val·id not valid
in·vali·date
in·vali·da·tion
in·vali·da·tor
in·va·lid·ism being an invalid
in·va·lid·ity (or ·val·id·ness) being not valid
in·valu·able
in·valu·ably
In·var (Trademark)
in·vari·abil·ity (or ·able·ness)
in·vari·able
in·vari·ably
in·vari·ance (or ·an·cy)
in·vari·ant
in·va·sion
in·va·sive
in·vec·tive
in·veigh rail against
in·veigh·er
in·vei·gle cajole
in·vei·gle·ment
in·vei·gler
in·vent
in·vent·ible (or ·able)
in·ven·tion
in·ven·tion·al
in·ven·tive
in·ven·tive·ness
in·ven·tor
in·ven·to·ri·able
in·ven·to·ri·al
in·ven·tory (noun, plural ·tories; verb ·tories, ·tory·ing, ·toried)
in·ve·rac·ity (plural ·ities)
In·ver·car·gill New Zealand city
In·ver·ness
in·verse
in·ver·sion
in·ver·sive
in·vert
in·vert·ase enzyme
in·ver·te·bra·cy (or ·tebrate·ness)
in·ver·te·bral
in·ver·tebrate
in·vert·er (or ·ver·tor)

in·vert·ibil·ity
in·vert·ible
in·vest
in·vest·able (or ·ible)
in·ves·ti·gable
in·ves·ti·gate
in·ves·ti·ga·tion
in·ves·ti·ga·tion·al
in·ves·ti·gative (or ·ga·tory)
in·ves·ti·ga·tor
in·ves·ti·tive
in·ves·ti·ture
in·vest·ment
in·ves·tor
in·vet·era·cy (or ·er·ate·ness)
in·vet·er·ate
in·vi·abil·ity (or ·able·ness)
in·vi·able
in·vidi·ous
in·vigi·late
in·vigi·la·tion
in·vigi·la·tor
in·vig·or·ate
in·vig·or·at·ing·ly
in·vig·ora·tion
in·vig·ora·tive
in·vig·ora·tor
in·vin·cibil·ity (or ·cible·ness)
in·vin·cible
in·vin·cibly
in·vio·labil·ity (or ·lable·ness)
in·vio·lable
in·vio·lably
in·vio·la·cy (or ·late·ness)
in·vio·late
in·vis·ibil·ity (or ·ible·ness)
in·vis·ible
in·vis·ibly
in·vi·ta·tion
in·vi·ta·tory
in·vite
in·vit·er
in·vit·ing
in vi·tro outside the body
in vivo within the body
in·vo·cable
in·vo·ca·tion
in·vo·ca·tion·al
in·voca·tory

in·voice
in·voke
in·vok·er
in·volu·cel (or ·cel·lum; plural ·cels or ·cel·la) botany term
in·volu·cel·ate (or ·at·ed)
in·vo·lu·cral
in·vo·lu·crate
in·vo·lu·cre (or ·crum; plural ·cres or ·cra) botany term
in·vol·un·tari·ly
in·vol·un·tari·ness
in·vol·un·tary
in·vo·lute (or lut·ed)
in·vo·lu·tion
in·vo·lu·tion·al
in·volve
in·volved
in·volve·ment
in·volv·er
in·vul·ner·abil·ity (or ·able·ness)
in·vul·ner·able
in·vul·ner·ably
in·vul·tua·tion making images for witchcraft
in·ward (adj)
in·ward·ly
in·wards (adv)
in·weave (·weav·ing, ·wove or ·weaved, ·wo·ven or ·weaved)
in·wrought
Io satellite of Jupiter
iodate chemistry term
ioda·tion
iod·ic chemistry term
iodide
iodine
iodism iodine poisoning
iodi·za·tion (or ·sa·tion)
iodize (or iodise)
iodiz·er (or iodis·)
iodo·form antiseptic
iodo·met·ric (or ·ri·cal)
iodo·met·ri·cal·ly
iodom·etry chemistry term
iodop·sin retinal pigment
iodous chemistry term
ion
Io·na Scottish island
Ionia Aegean region
Ionian

Ion·ic architecture term
ion·ic of ions
ioni·za·tion (*or* **·sa·tion**)
ion·ize (*or* **·ise**)
ionone plant extract
iono·pause
iono·sphere
iono·spher·ic
ion·to·pho·resis
  biochemical technique
iota
iota·cism
IOU (*plural* **IOUs**)
Iowa
ip·ecac (*or* **·ecacu·an·ha**)
  purgative
Ipoh Malaysian city
ipo·moea plant
ipso facto
Ips·wich
ira·cund easily angered
Irá·kli·on Cretan port
Iran
Ira·nian
Iraq
Ira·qi
iras·cibil·ity (*or*
  ·cible·ness)
iras·cible
iras·cibly
irate
Ir·bid Jordanian town
ire
Ire·land
iren·ic (*or* **ireni·cal**)
  conciliatory
ireni·cal·ly
iren·ics branch of theology
iri·da·ceous botany term
iri·dec·to·my (*plural*
  ·mies) eye surgery
iri·des·cence
iri·des·cent
Irid·ic
irid·ium chemical element
iri·doto·my (*plural* **·mies**)
  eye surgery
iris (*plural* **irises**) flowers
iris (*plural* **iri·des** *or*
  irises) part of eye
Irish
Irish·ism
Irish·man (*plural* **·men**)
Irish·woman (*plural*
  ·women)

irit·ic
iri·tis eye disease
irk
irk·some
Ir·ku·tsk Soviet city
iron
iron·bark tree
iron·bound unyielding
iron·clad
iron·er
iron·ic (*or* **ironi·cal**)
ironi·cal·ly
iron·ing
iro·nist
iro·nize indulge in irony
iron·monger
iron·mongery
Ironsides Cromwell's
  cavalry
iron·stone
iron·ware
iron·wood
iron·work
iro·ny (*plural* **·nies**)
  sarcasm
irony containing iron
Iro·quoi·an
Iro·quois (*plural* **·quois**)
  American Indian
ir·ra·di·ance
ir·ra·di·ant
ir·ra·di·ate
ir·ra·dia·tion
ir·ra·dia·tive
ir·ra·dia·tor
Ir·ra·tion·al
ir·ra·tion·al·ity (*or* **·ism**)
ir·ra·tion·al·ly
Ir·ra·wad·dy Burmese river
ir·re·claim·abil·ity (*or*
  ·able·ness)
ir·re·claim·able
ir·re·claim·ably
ir·rec·on·cil·abil·ity (*or*
  ·able·ness)
ir·rec·on·cil·able
ir·rec·on·cil·ably
ir·re·cov·er·able
ir·re·cov·er·ably
ir·re·cu·sable unable to be
  rejected
ir·re·deem·abil·ity (*or*
  ·able·ness)
ir·re·deem·able
ir·re·deem·ably

irreproachably

ir·re·den·tism
ir·re·den·tist territorial
  claimant
ir·re·duc·ibil·ity (*or*
  ·ible·ness)
ir·re·duc·ible
ir·re·duc·ibly
ir·ref·ra·gabil·ity (*or*
  ·gable·ness)
ir·ref·ra·gable indisputable
ir·ref·ra·gably
ir·re·fran·gibil·ity (*or*
  ·gible·ness)
ir·re·fran·gible inviolable
ir·refu·tabil·ity (*or*
  ·table·ness)
ir·refu·table
ir·refu·tably
ir·regu·lar
ir·regu·lar·ity (*plural*
  ·ities)
ir·rela·tive unrelated
ir·rel·evance (*or* **·evan·cy**;
  plural **·evances** *or*
  ·cies)
ir·rel·evant
ir·re·liev·able
ir·re·li·gion
ir·re·li·gion·ist
ir·re·li·gious
ir·re·medi·able
ir·re·medi·ably
ir·re·mis·sibil·ity (*or*
  ·sible·ness)
ir·re·mis·sible
ir·re·mis·sibly
ir·re·mov·abil·ity (*or*
  ·able·ness)
ir·re·mov·able
ir·re·mov·ably
ir·repa·rabil·ity (*or*
  ·rable·ness)
ir·repa·rable
ir·repa·rably
ir·re·place·able
ir·re·plevi·able (*or* **·sable**)
  legal term
ir·re·press·ibil·ity (*or*
  ·ible·ness)
ir·re·press·ible
ir·re·press·ibly
ir·re·proach·abil·ity (*or*
  ·able·ness)
ir·re·proach·able
ir·re·proach·ably

irresistibility

ir·re·sist·ibil·ity (or ·ible·ness)
ir·re·sist·ible
ir·re·sist·ibly
ir·reso·lubil·ity
ir·reso·luble
ir·reso·lute
ir·reso·lu·tion
ir·re·solv·abil·ity (or ·able·ness)
ir·re·solv·able
ir·re·spec·tive
ir·re·spir·able
ir·re·spon·sibil·ity (or ·sible·ness)
ir·re·spon·sible
ir·re·spon·sibly
ir·re·spon·sive
ir·re·ten·tive
ir·re·triev·abil·ity (or ·able·ness)
ir·re·triev·able
ir·re·triev·ably
ir·rev·er·ence
ir·rev·er·ent (or ·eren·tial)
ir·re·vers·ibil·ity (or ·ible·ness)
ir·re·vers·ible
ir·re·vers·ibly
ir·revo·cabil·ity (or ·cable·ness)
ir·revo·cable
ir·revo·cably
(irridescent) *incorrect spelling of* **iridescent**
ir·ri·gable
ir·ri·gate
ir·ri·ga·tion
ir·ri·ga·tion·al
ir·ri·ga·tive
ir·ri·ga·tor
ir·ri·tabil·ity
ir·ri·table
ir·ri·tably
ir·ri·tant
ir·ri·tate
ir·ri·ta·tion
ir·ri·ta·tive
ir·ri·ta·tor
ir·rupt enter or increase suddenly; *compare* **erupt**
ir·rup·tion
ir·rup·tive
Ir·tysh (*or* **Ir·tish**) Asian river

Ir·vine Scottish town
is
isa·go·ge
isa·gog·ic
isa·gog·ics introductory studies
is·al·lo·bar line on map
Isar European river
isa·tin (*or* ·tine)
isa·tin·ic
Iscariot biblical character
is·chae·mia (*US* ·che·) inadequate blood supply
is·chaem·ic (*US* ·chem·)
Is·chia Mediterranean island
is·chial
is·chium (*plural* ·chia) hip bone
is·en·trop·ic physics term
Isère French river
Is·fa·han (*or* **Es·**) Iranian city
Ishmael biblical character
isin·glass
Isis Thames at Oxford; Egyptian goddess
Is·ken·de·run Turkish port
Is·lam
Is·lama·bad Pakistani capital
Is·lam·ic
Is·lam·ize
is·land
is·land·er
Is·lay Scottish island
isle
Isle of Wight
is·let
Is·ling·ton
ism
Is·mai·li Muslim sect
Is·mai·lia Egyptian city
isn't
iso·ag·glu·ti·na·tion
iso·ag·glu·ti·na·tive
iso·ag·glu·ti·nin
iso·anti·gen
iso·bar
iso·bar·ic
iso·bar·ism
iso·bath line on map
iso·bath·ic
iso·cheim (*or* ·chime) line on map

iso·chei·mal (*or* ·menal, ·chi·mal)
iso·chor (*or* ·chore) line on graph
iso·chor·ic
iso·chro·mat·ic
isoch·ro·nal (*or* ·nous)
isoch·ro·nize (*or* ·nise)
isoch·ro·ous of uniform colour
iso·cli·nal (*or* ·clin·ic)
iso·cline geology term
isoc·ra·cy (*plural* ·cies) political equality
iso·crat·ic
iso·cya·nide
iso·dia·met·ric
iso·dia·phere physics term
iso·di·mor·phism chemistry term
iso·di·mor·phous (*or* ·phic)
iso·dy·nam·ic
iso·elec·tric
iso·elec·tron·ic
iso·gam·ete biology term
iso·ga·met·ic
isoga·mous
isoga·my
isog·enous genetically uniform
isog·eny
iso·geo·therm
iso·geo·ther·mal (*or* ·mic)
iso·gloss linguistics term
iso·glos·sal
iso·glot·tic
iso·gon maths term
iso·gon·ic (*or* isogo·nal)
iso·hel line on map
iso·hy·et line on map
iso·labil·ity
iso·lable
iso·late
iso·la·tion
iso·la·tion·ism
iso·la·tion·ist
iso·la·tive
iso·la·tor
iso·leci·thal biology term
iso·leu·cine amino acid
iso·lex linguistics term
iso·line isopleth
isolo·gous chemistry term
iso·logue

iso·mag·net·ic
iso·mer
iso·mer·ic
isom·er·ism
isom·eri·za·tion (or ·sa·tion)
isom·er·ize (or ·ise)
isom·er·ous
iso·met·ric
iso·met·ri·cal
iso·met·rics exercises
iso·metro·pia physiology term
isom·etry maths term
iso·morph
iso·mor·phic (or ·phous)
iso·mor·phism
iso·nia·zid medicinal drug
isono·my equality before the law
iso·octane chemical compound
iso·phone linguistics term
iso·pi·es·tic having equal atmospheric pressure
iso·pi·es·ti·cal·ly
iso·pleth line on map
iso·pod crustacean
isopo·dan (or ·dous)
iso·prene chemical compound
iso·pro·pyl
iso·rhyth·mic musical term
isos·celes geometry term
iso·seis·mal
is·os·mot·ic
iso·spon·dy·lous zoology term
isos·ta·sy (plural ·sies) geological theory
iso·stat·ic
iso·ster·ic chemistry term
iso·tac·tic

isoth·er·al
iso·there line on map
iso·therm
iso·ther·mal
iso·tone chemistry term
iso·ton·ic
iso·to·nic·ity
iso·tope
iso·top·ic
iso·topi·cal·ly
isoto·py
iso·tron physics apparatus
iso·trop·ic
iso·tropi·cal·ly
isot·ro·pous
isot·ro·py
Is·ra·el
Is·rae·li (plural ·lis or ·li)
Is·rael·ite
Is·ra·fil Islamic archangel
is·su·able
is·su·ance
is·su·ant
is·sue (·su·ing, ·sued)
is·su·er
Is·sus battle
Is·tan·bul
isth·mi·an
isth·moid
isth·mus (plural ·muses or ·mi)
is·tle (or ix·) fibre
Is·tria Adriatic peninsula
Is·trian
it
Ita·colu·mite sandstone
Ital·ian
Ital·ian·ate
Ital·ian·esque
Ital·ian·ism
Ital·ian·ize
Ital·ic language

ital·ic type or print
Itali·cism
itali·ci·za·tion (or ·sa·tion)
itali·cize (or ·cise)
Ita·ly
itch
itchi·ness
itch·ing
itchy (itchi·er, itchi·est)
item
itemi·za·tion (or ·sa·tion)
item·ize (or ·ise)
it·er·ant
it·er·ate
it·era·tion (or ·er·ance)
it·era·tive
Itha·ca Greek island
Itha·can
ithy·phal·lic poetry term
itin·er·an·cy (or ·era·cy; plural ·cies)
itin·er·ant
itin·er·ary (plural ·aries)
itin·er·ate travel about
itin·era·tion
it'll it will; it shall
its of it
it's it is
it·self
Iva·no·vo Soviet city
I've I have
ivied
ivo·ry (plural ·ries)
ivy (plural ivies)
Iwo Jima Pacific island
ixia plant
ix·tle variant spelling of istle
izard chamois
Izhevsk Soviet city
Iz·mir Turkish port
Iz·mit Turkish town

J

jab (jab·bing, jabbed)
Jab·al·pur (or Jub·bul·pore) Indian city
jabbed
jab·ber
jab·ber·er

jab·ber·wocky nonsense verse
jab·bing
jabi·ru bird
jabo·ran·di shrub
ja·bot frill
jaca·mar bird

ja·ça·na bird
jaca·ran·da tree
ja·cinth gemstone
jack
jack·al
jacka·napes
jack·ass

jackboot

jack·boot
jack·daw
jack·eroo (*or* **jacka·roo**; *plural* **·roos**) *Austral* trainee sheep-station manager
jack·et
jack·et·ed
jack·fish (*plural* **·fish** *or* **·fishes**)
jack·fruit
jack·hammer
jack·knife (*plural* **·knives**)
jack·pot
jacks game
jack·shaft
jack·smelt (*plural* **·smelts** *or* **·smelt**) fish
jack·snipe (*plural* **·snipe** *or* **·snipes**) bird
Jack·son US city
Jack·son·ville US port
jack·stay nautical term
jack·straws game
Jaco·bean of James I
Ja·co·bian maths term
Jaco·bin French radical
Jaco·bin·ic (*or* **·bini·cal**)
Jaco·bin·ism
Jaco·bite of James II
Jaco·bit·ic
Jaco·bit·ism
ja·co·bus (*plural* **·buses**) coin
jaco·net fabric
Jac·quard fabric; loom
jac·ti·ta·tion boasting
Ja·cuzzi (*Trademark*)
jade
jad·ed
jade·ite mineral
jae·ger marksman; bird
Jael biblical character
Jaf·fa Israeli port
Jaff·na Sri Lankan port
jag (**jag·ging, jagged**)
jag·ged
jag·ged·ly
jag·ged·ness
jag·gery (*or* **·gary, ·ghery**) date sugar
jag·ging
jag·gy (**·gi·er, ·gi·est**)
jagu·ar

ja·gua·ron·di (*or* **·run·**; *plural* **·dis**) feline
jai alai Spanish game
jail (*or* **gaol**)
jail·bird (*or* **gaol·**)
jail·break (*or* **gaol·**)
jail·er (*or* **·or, gaol·er**)
jail·house
Jain (*or* **Jai·na**) Hindu
Jain·ism
Jain·ist
Jai·pur Indian city
Ja·ja·pu·ra (*or* **Dja·**) Indonesian port
Ja·kar·ta (*or* **Dja·**) Indonesian capital
jal·ap (*or* **·op**) purgative
ja·lap·ic
Ja·lis·co Mexican state
ja·lopy (*or* **·lop·py**; *plural* **·lopies** *or* **·lop·pies**)
jalou·sie shutter
jam (**jam·ming, jammed**) crowd; preserve; *compare* jamb
Ja·mai·ca
Ja·mai·can
jamb (*or* **jambe**) part of frame; *compare* jam
jam·ba·laya Creole dish
jam·bart (*or* **jam·beau, jam·ber**; *plural* **·barts, ·beaux,** *or* **·bers**) armour
Jam·bi (*or* **Djam·**) Indonesian port
jam·bo·ree
jammed
jam·mer
jam·ming
Jam·mu Indian city
jam·my (**·mi·er, ·mi·est**)
Jam·na·gar Indian city
jam·pan sedan chair
Jam·shed·pur Indian city
Jamshid (*or* **Jamshyd**) mythological king
Ja·na·ta Indian political party
jan·gle
jan·gler
Ja·nicu·lum Roman hill
jan·is·sary (*or* **jani·zary**; *plural* **·saries** *or* **·zaries**) Turkish guard
jani·tor (*fem* **·tress**)

jani·to·ri·al
Jan·sen·ism Catholic doctrine
Jan·sen·ist
Jan·sen·is·tic (*or* **·ti·cal**)
Janu·ary (*plural* **·aries**)
Janus Roman god
Ja·pan
ja·pan (**·pan·ning, ·panned**) lacquer
Japa·nese
jape
jap·er
jap·ery
Japheth biblical character
jap·ing·ly
ja·poni·ca shrub
Ja·pu·rá South American river
jar (**jar·ring, jarred**)
jar·di·nière plant holder
jar·ful
jar·gon language
jar·gon (*or* **·goon**) gemstone
jar·goni·za·tion (*or* **·sa·tion**)
jar·gon·ize (*or* **·ise**)
jarl Scandinavian chieftain
jaro·site mineral
jarp (*or* **jaup**) *Dialect* to smash
jar·rah tree
jarred
jar·ring
jar·ring·ly
Jar·row English port
jar·vey (*or* **·vie**) coachman
jas·mine
jas·pé variegated
jas·per
Jat (*plural* **Jat** *or* **Jats**) Indo-European people
jato (*plural* **·tos**) jet-assisted takeoff
jaun·dice
jaunt
jaun·ti·ly
jaun·ty (**·ti·er, ·ti·est**)
Java
Java·nese (*or* **Ja·van**)
jave·lin
jaw
Ja·wan Indian soldier
jaw·bone

jaw·breaker
jay
Jaya (or Dja·ja) Indonesian mountain
jay·walk
jay·walk·er
jay·walk·ing
jazz
jazzi·ly
jazzi·ness
jazzy (jazzi·er, jazzi·est)
jeal·ous
jeal·ous·ly
jeal·ousy (plural ·ousies)
jeans
jeb·el (or djeb·) Arab hill
Jeb·el Musa Moroccan mountain
Jed·da variant spelling of Jidda
jeep
jeer
jeer·er
jeer·ing·ly
je·had variant spelling of jihad
Je·hol Chinese region
Je·ho·vah
Je·ho·vian (or ·vic)
je·ju·nal
je·june naive
je·june·ly
je·june·ness (or je·jun·ity)
je·ju·num small intestine
Jekyll and Hyde
jell (or gel; jel·ling, jelled or gel·ling, gelled) congeal; compare gel
jel·laba (or ·lab·ah) cloak
jel·lied
jel·li·fi·ca·tion
jel·li·fy (·fies, ·fy·ing, ·fied)
jello US jelly
jel·ly (noun, plural ·lies; verb ·lies, ·ly·ing, ·lied)
jelly·bean
jelly·fish (plural ·fish or ·fishes)
jem·my (noun, plural ·mies; verb ·mies, ·my·ing, ·mied)
jen·net (or gen·et, gen·net) female donkey; compare genet

jen·ny (plural ·nies) machine; female animal
jeop·ard·ize (or ·ise)
jeop·ardy
je·quir·ity (or ·quer·; plural ·ties) plant
jer·bil variant spelling of gerbil
jer·boa
jer·emi·ad lamentation
Je·rez Spanish town
Jeri·cho
je·rid javelin
jerk
jerk·er
jerki·ly
jer·kin jacket; compare gherkin
jerky (jerki·er, jerki·est)
jero·bo·am wine bottle
Jer·ry (plural ·ries) Slang German
jer·ry (plural ·ries) Slang chamber pot
jerry-build (-building, -built)
Jer·sey island; cattle
jer·sey garment
Je·ru·sa·lem
jess falconry term
jes·sa·mine Archaic jasmine
jest
jes·ter
Jesu
Jesu·it
Jesu·it·ic (or ·iti·cal)
Jesu·it·ism (or ·it·ry)
Jesus
jet (jet·ting, jet·ted)
jeté ballet step
jet·liner
jet·port
jet-propelled
jet·sam (or ·som)
jet·setter
jet·ti·ness
jet·ti·son
jet·ton gambling token
jet·ty (plural ·ties)
Jew
jew·el (·ell·ing, ·elled; US ·el·ing, ·eled)
jewel·fish (plural ·fish or ·fishes)
jew·el·ler (US ·el·er)

jew·el·lery (US ·el·ry)
Jew·ess
jew·fish (plural ·fish or ·fishes)
Jew·ish
Jew·ish·ness
Jew·ry (plural ·ries)
jew's-ear fungus
jew's-harp
Jezebel biblical character
jezebel shameless woman
Jhan·si Indian city
jib (jib·bing, jibbed)
jib·ber
jib·bons Dialect spring onions
jibe variant spelling of gibe or gybe
jib-headed
Ji·bou·ti variant spelling of Djibouti
Jid·da (or ·dah, Jed·) Saudi Arabian port
jif·fy (or jiff; plural jif·fies or jiffs)
jig (jig·ging, jigged)
jig·ger
jig·gered
jigger·mast
jiggery-pokery
jig·ging
jig·gle
jig·gly
jig·saw
ji·had (or jc·) Islamic holy war
jil·lion large number
jil·lionth
jilt
jilt·er
jin·gle
jin·gler
jin·gly (·gli·er, ·gli·est)
jin·go (plural ·goes)
jin·go·ism
jin·go·ist
jin·go·is·tic
jin·go·is·ti·cal·ly
Jin·ja Ugandan town
jink
jinks high spirits; compare jinx
jin·ni (or ·nee, djin·ni, djin·ny; plural jinn or djinn) Muslim spirit

jinx

jinx bad luck; *compare* **jinks**
ji·pi·ja·pa plant
jit·ter
jit·ter·bug (**·bug·ging,** **·bugged**)
jit·tery
jive
Joab biblical character
Job biblical character
job (**job·bing, jobbed**)
job·ber
job·bery corruption
job·bing
Job·cen·tre
job·less
job·less·ness
Jocasta mother of Oedipus
Jock *Slang* Scot
jock·ey
jock·strap
jo·cose
jo·cose·ly
jo·cose·ness (*or* **jo·cos·ity**)
jocu·lar
jocu·lar·ity
joc·und
jo·cun·dity (*or* **joc·und·ness**)
Jodh·pur Indian city
jodh·purs riding trousers
Jodo Buddhist sect
joey *Austral* young kangaroo
jog (**jog·ging, jogged**)
jog·ger
jog·gle
jog·gler
Jog·ja·kar·ta variant spelling of **Yokyakarta**
jog-trot (**-trot·ting, -trot·ted**)
jo·han·nes (*or* **·an·**; *plural* **·nes**) Portuguese coin
Jo·han·nes·burg
John Dory fish
john·ny (*plural* **·nies**) *Slang* man; condom
John o'Groats
John·so·nian of Samuel Johnson
Jo·hore Malaysian state
joie de vivre
join
join·der legal term
join·er
join·ery
joint
joint·ed
joint·er
joint·ly
joint·ress legal term
join·ture legal term
joint·worm
joist
jo·joba tree; oil
joke
jok·er
jok·ey (*or* **joky; joki·er, joki·est**)
jok·ing·ly
jol·li·fi·ca·tion
jol·li·fy (**·fies, ·fy·ing, ·fied**)
jol·lity (*plural* **·lities**)
jol·ly (*adj* **·li·er, ·li·est;** *verb* **·lies, ·ly·ing, ·lied**)
Jolo Philippine island
jolt
jolt·er
jolt·ing·ly
jolty
Jön·kö·ping Swedish city
jon·nock *Dialect* genuine
jon·quil
Jop·pa biblical Jaffa
Jor·dan
Jor·da·nian
jo·rum drinking bowl
Jos Nigerian city
josh *US* tease
joss Chinese deity
jos·tle
jos·tler
jot (**jot·ting, jot·ted**)
jot·ter
joual Canadian French dialect
joule unit of energy
jounce jolt
jour·nal
jour·nal·ese
jour·nal·ism
jour·nal·ist
jour·nal·is·tic
jour·nal·is·ti·cal·ly
jour·nali·za·tion (*or* **·sa·tion**)
jour·nal·ize (*or* **·ise**) record in journal
jour·nal·iz·er (*or* **·is·er**)
jour·ney
jour·ney·er
journey·man (*plural* **·men**) craftsman
journo (*plural* **journos**) *Austral* journalist
joust
joust·er
Jove Roman god
jo·vial
jo·vi·al·ity (*or* **·ness**)
jo·vi·al·ly
Jo·vian
jowl
joy
joy·ful
joy·ful·ly
joy·ful·ness
joy·less
joy·less·ness
joy·ous
joy·ous·ness
joy·pop (**·pop·ping, ·popped**) *Slang* take drugs
joy-ride (**-riding, -rode, -ridden**)
joy·rider
Juan de Fuca US–Canadian strait
juba Negro dance
Ju·bal biblical character
Jub·bul·pore variant spelling of **Jabalpur**
jube church gallery
ju·bi·lance (*or* **·lan·cy**)
ju·bi·lant
ju·bi·late
ju·bi·la·tion
ju·bi·lee
Ju·daea (*or* **·dea**)
Ju·daean (*or* **·dean**)
Ju·da·ic (*or* **·dai·cal**)
Ju·dai·ca Jewish literature
Ju·da·ism
Ju·da·ist
Ju·da·is·tic
Ju·dai·za·tion (*or* **·sa·tion**)
Ju·da·ize (*or* **·ise**)
Ju·da·iz·er (*or* **·is·er**)
Judas traitor
ju·das peephole
jud·der
judge

judge·able
judg·er
judge·ship
judg·ing·ly
judg·ment (*or* judge·)
judg·men·tal (*or* judge·)
ju·di·cable
ju·di·ca·tive
ju·di·ca·tor judge
ju·di·ca·to·rial
ju·di·ca·tory
ju·di·ca·ture
ju·di·cial
ju·di·cial·ly
ju·di·ci·ary (*plural* ·aries)
ju·di·cious
ju·di·cious·ly
ju·di·cious·ness
judo
ju·do·gi judo costume
ju·do·ist
ju·do·ka judo expert
Judy (*or* judy; *plural* Judies *or* judies) *Slang* girl
jug (jug·ging, jugged)
ju·gal cheekbone
ju·gate botany term
jug·ful (*plural* ·fuls)
jugged
Jug·ger·naut Hindu idol
jug·ger·naut vehicle; destructive force
jug·ging
jug·gins silly fellow
jug·gle
jug·gler
jug·glery
jug·gling
ju·glan·da·ceous botany term
Ju·go·sla·via *variant spelling of* Yugoslavia
jugu·lar
ju·gum biology term
juice
juici·ly
juici·ness
juicy (juici·er, juici·est)
ju·jit·su (*or* ju·jut·su, jiu·)
juju African fetish
ju·ju·ism
ju·ju·ist
ju·jube plant; sweet
juke·box

ju·lep drink
Jul·ian of Julius Caesar
ju·li·enne cookery term
Jul·lun·dur Indian city
July (*plural* Julies)
jum·ble
jum·bler
jum·bly (·bli·er, ·bli·est)
jum·bo (*plural* ·bos)
jum·buck *Austral* sheep
Jum·na Indian river
jump
jump·able
jump·er
jumpi·ly
jumpi·ness
jump-off (*noun*)
jump-start
jumpy (jumpi·er, jumpi·est)
jun·ca·ceous botany term
jun·co (*plural* ·cos) bird
junc·tion
junc·tion·al
junc·ture
Jun·diaí Brazilian city
June
Ju·neau Alaskan capital
Jung·frau Swiss mountain
Jung·ian psychiatry term
jun·gle
jun·gly (·gli·er, ·gli·est)
jun·ior
ju·ni·per
junk
Jun·ker Prussian landowner
jun·ket
jun·ket·er (*or* ·ket·ter, ·ke·teer)
junkie (*or* junky; *plural* junkies)
junk·yard
Juno Roman goddess; asteroid
Ju·no·esque
jun·ta
Ju·pi·ter planet
Jupiter Roman god
ju·pon garment
Jura European mountains; Scottish island
jura *plural of* jus
ju·ral of the law
Ju·ras·sic geological period
ju·rat legal term

ju·ra·tory
ju·rel fish
ju·ridi·cal (*or* ·rid·ic)
ju·ris·con·sult legal advisor
ju·ris·dic·tion
ju·ris·dic·tion·al
ju·ris·dic·tion·al·ly
ju·ris·dic·tive
ju·ris·pru·dence
ju·ris·pru·dent
ju·ris·pru·den·tial
ju·ris·pru·den·tial·ly
ju·rist
ju·ris·tic (*or* ·ti·cal)
ju·ror
Ju·ruá South American river
jury (*plural* juries)
jury·man (*plural* ·men)
jury-rigged nautical term
jury·woman (*plural* ·women)
jus (*plural* jura) legal right
jus ci·vi·le civil law
jus di·vi·num divine law
jus na·tu·ra·le natural law
jus·sive grammar term
jus soli legal term
just
jus·tice
jus·tice·ship
jus·ti·ci·abil·ity
jus·ti·ci·able subject to jurisdiction
jus·ti·ci·ar medieval legal officer
jus·ti·ci·ar·ship
jus·ti·ci·ary (*plural* ·aries)
jus·ti·fi·abil·ity (*or* ·able·ness)
jus·ti·fi·able
jus·ti·fi·ably
jus·ti·fi·ca·tion
jus·ti·fi·ca·tory (*or* ·tive)
jus·ti·fi·er
jus·ti·fy (·fies, ·fy·ing, ·fied)
jus·ti·fy·ing·ly
jus·tle jostle
just·ly
just·ness
jut (jut·ting, jut·ted)
Jute Germanic tribe
jute fibre
Jut·ish
Jut·land Danish peninsula

Jutlander

Jut·land·er
jut·ted
jut·ting
ju·venes·cence youth
ju·venes·cent
ju·venile
ju·venilia
ju·venil·ity (*plural* ·ities)
jux·ta·pose
jux·ta·po·si·tion
jux·ta·po·si·tion·al

K

kab·ba·la (*or* ka·ba·la) *variant spellings of* cabbala
ka·ba·ra·go·ya lizard
Ka·bardino-Balkar Soviet republic
ka·bu·ki Japanese drama
Ka·bul Afghan capital
Ka·byle (*plural* ·byles *or* ·byle) Berber people
ka·chang pu·teh Malaysian dish
ka·chi·na American Indian spirit
Kad·dish (*plural* kad·di·shim) Jewish prayer
Ka·di·yev·ka Soviet city
Ka·du·na Nigerian state
Kaf·fir (*plural* ·firs *or* ·fir) S African people
kaf·fir sorghum
Kaf·ir (*plural* ·irs *or* ·ir) Afghan people
kaf·tan (*or* caf·)
Ka·gera African river
Ka·go·shi·ma Japanese port
kai·ak *variant spelling of* kayak
Kai·feng Chinese city
kail *variant spelling of* kale
kai·nite mineral
kai·no·gen·esis *variant spelling of* caenogenesis
Kai·ser
kai·ser·dom (*or* ·ism)
Kai·sers·lau·tern West German city
kaka parrot
ka·ka·po (*plural* ·pos) parrot
ka·kemo·no (*plural* ·nos) Japanese wall hanging
kaki (*plural* kakis) fruit
kala-azar disease
Ka·la·ha·ri African desert
Kala·ma·zoo US city

Ka·lat (*or* Khe·) Pakistani region
kale (*or* kail) cabbage
ka·lei·do·scope
ka·lei·do·scop·ic
ka·lei·do·scopi·cal·ly
kal·ends *variant spelling of* calends
kale·yard (*or* kail·) Scot vegetable garden
Kal·goor·lie Australian city
Kali Hindu goddess
kali plant
kal·ian hookah
ka·lif (*or* kha·) *variant spellings of* caliph
Ka·li·nin Soviet city
Ka·li·nin·grad Soviet port
kal·mia shrub
Kal·muck (*or* ·myk; *plural* ·mucks, ·muck *or* ·myks, ·myk) Mongoloid people
ka·long fruit bat
kal·so·mine *variant spelling of* calcimine
Ka·lu·ga Soviet city
Kama Soviet river; Hindu god
kama·cite alloy
Kama·ku·ra Japanese city
ka·ma·la tree
Ka·ma·su·tra Hindu text
Kam·chat·ka Soviet peninsula
kame mound
Kamensk-Uralski Soviet city
Ka·met Indian mountain
kami (*plural* kami) Japanese spirit
ka·mi·ka·ze
Kam·pa·la Ugandan capital
kam·pong Malaysian village
Kampuchea
Kampuchean

kana Japanese writing
kana·my·cin antibiotic
Ka·nan·ga Zaïrian city
Ka·na·ra (*or* Ca·) Indian region
Ka·na·rese (*or* Ca·; *plural* ·rese)
Kana·za·wa Japanese port
Kan·chi·pu·ram Indian city
Kan·da·har Afghan city
Kan·dy Sri Lankan city
kan·ga (*or* khan·) African garment
kan·ga·roo (*plural* ·roos)
Kang·chen·jun·ga (*or* Kan·chen·) Himalayan mountain
Ka·Ngwa·ne South African homeland
Kan·na·da Indian language
Kano Nigerian state
Kan·pur Indian city
Kan·sas
Kan·su Chinese province
kan·tar unit of weight
Kant·ian
Kant·ian·ism (*or* Kant·ism) philosophy
Kao·hsiung (*or* Kao-hsiung) Chinese port
kao·li·ang sorghum
kao·lin (*or* ·line)
kao·lin·ic
kao·lin·ite mineral
kaon physics particle
ka·pell·meis·ter (*plural* ·ter)
ka·pok
kap·pa Greek letter
ka·put *Slang* not functioning; *compare* caput
kara·bi·ner mountaineering clip
Karachai-Cherkess Soviet region
Ka·ra·chi Pakistani city

Ka·ra·gan·da Soviet city
Kara·ite Jewish sect
Kara-Kalpak Soviet republic
Ka·ra·ko·ram mountain range
Ka·ra·ko·rum Mongolian city
kara·kul (*or* **cara·**) sheep; *compare* **caracul**
ka·ra·te
Kar·ba·la (*or* **Ker·be·**) Iraqi town
Ka·relia Soviet republic
Ka·relian
Ka·ren (*plural* **·rens** *or* **·ren**) Thai language and people
Ka·ri·ba African lake and dam
Karl-Marx-Stadt East German city
Karls·ruhe West German city
kar·ma destiny
kar·mic
Kar·na·taka Indian state
Ka·roo (*or* **Kar·roo**) South African plateau
ka·roo (*or* **kar·roo**; *plural* **·roos**) plateau
ka·ross African garment
kar·ri tree
karst limestone scenery
karst·ic
karyo·gam·ic
kary·oga·my biology term
karyo·ki·nesis
karyo·ki·net·ic
karyo·lymph
kary·oly·sis
karyo·lyt·ic
karyo·plasm
karyo·plas·mic (*or* **·mat·ic**)
karyo·some
karyo·type
karyo·typ·ic (*or* **·typi·cal**)
Ka·sai African river
kas·bah (*or* **cas·**)
ka·sher *variant spelling of* **kosher**
Kash·gar Chinese city
Kash·mir
Kash·miri (*plural* **·miris** *or* **·miri**)
Kash·mir·ian
Kas·sa·la Sudanese city
Kas·sel West German city
kat (*or* **khat**) narcotic
kata·bat·ic meteorology term
ka·ta·ka·na Japanese writing
Ka·tan·ga Zaïrian province
Kat·an·gese
Ka·thia·war Indian peninsula
Kat·mai Alaskan volcano
Kat·man·du (*or* **Kath·**) Nepalese capital
Ka·to·wi·ce Polish city
Kat·si·na Nigerian city
Kat·te·gat Scandinavian strait
ka·ty·did insect
Ka·uai Hawaiian island
Kau·nas Soviet city
kau·ri (*or* **·ry**; *plural* **·ris** *or* **·ries**) tree
kava drink
Ka·wa·sa·ki Japanese port
kay·ak (*or* **kai·**) canoe
Kay·seri Turkish city
ka·za·chok dance
Ka·zakh (*or* **·zak**; *plural* **·zakhs** *or* **·zaks**) Soviet people
Ka·zan Soviet city
Kaz·bek Soviet volcano
ka·zoo (*plural* **·zoos**) musical instrument
ke·bab
keck retch
Ked·ah Malaysian state
ked·dah *variant spelling of* **kheda**
kedge nautical term
ked·geree
Ke·di·ri Indonesian city
keek *Scot* peep
keel
keel·haul
keel·son (*or* **kel·**)
keen
keen·ness
keep (**keep·ing, kept**)
keep·er
keep·net
keep·sake
kees·hond (*plural* **·honds** *or* **·honden**) dog
Kee·wa·tin Canadian district
keg
Keigh·ley Yorkshire town
keis·ter (*or* **kees·**) *US* buttocks
keit·loa rhinoceros
Ke·lan·tan Malaysian state
ke·loid (*or* **che·**) scar tissue
ke·loi·dal (*or* **che·**)
kelp seaweed
kel·pie (*or* **·py**; *plural* **·pies**) sheepdog
kel·son *variant spelling of* **keelson**
Kelt *variant spelling of* **Celt**
kelt salmon
kel·ter (*or esp. US* **kil·**)
Kelt·ic *variant spelling of* **Celtic**
kel·vin unit
Ke·mero·vo Soviet city
kempt tidy
ken (**ken·ning, kenned** *or* **kent**)
ke·naf fibre
Ken·dal Cumbrian town
ken·do Japanese sport
Ken·il·worth Warwickshire town
kenned (*or* **kent**)
ken·nel (**·nel·ling, ·nelled;** *US* **·nel·ing, ·neled**)
ke·no (*or* **kee·no, ki·no, qui·no**) US game
ke·no·sis theology term
ke·not·ic
Ken·sing·ton
ken·speckle *Scot* easily recognized
Kent
ken·te fabric
Kent·ish
kent·ledge ship's ballast
Ken·tuck·ian
Ken·tucky
Ken·ya
Ken·yan
Keos Greek island
kep *Dialect* to catch
kepi (*plural* **kepis**) military cap
kept

Kerala

Ker·a·la Indian state
kera·tin protein
ke·rat·ini·za·tion (*or* **·sa·tion**)
ke·rat·in·ize (*or* **·ise**)
kera·ti·tis eye disease
kera·tog·enous
kera·toid horny
kera·to·plas·tic
kera·to·plas·ty (*plural* **·ties**) eye surgery
kera·tose zoology term
kera·to·sis skin condition
kerb (*US* **curb**) pavement edge; *compare* **curb**
Ker·be·la variant spelling of **Karbala**
kerb·ing (*US* **curb·**)
kerb·stone (*US* **curb·**)
Kerch Soviet port
ker·chief
ker·chiefed
kerf saw cut
ker·fuf·fle
Ker·gue·len Is·lands
Ker·man Iranian city
Ker·man·shah Iranian city
ker·mes insect; dye
ker·mis Dutch carnival
kern (*or* **kerne**) printing term
ker·nel
ker·nite mineral
kero·sene (*or* **·sine**)
Ker·ry Irish county
Ker·ry (*plural* **·ries**) cattle
ker·sey woollen cloth
ker·sey·mere woollen cloth
Kes·te·ven Lincolnshire region
kes·trel
Kes·wick
ketch sailing vessel
ketch·up (*US also* **catch·up, cat·sup**)
ke·tene toxic gas
keto chemistry term
ke·tone
ke·ton·ic
ke·to·nu·ria
ke·tose sugar
ke·to·sis medical term
ke·tox·ime
Ket·ter·ing Northamptonshire town
ket·tle
kettle·drum
kettle·drummer
kettle·ful
kev·el nautical term
Kew
kex plant
key
key·board
key·hole
Keynes·ian·ism economic theory
key·note
key·stone
key·stroke
key·way
Kha·ba·rovsk Soviet port
khad·dar (*or* **kha·di**) Indian cloth
Kha·kass Soviet region
kha·ki (*plural* **·kis**)
Khal·kha Mongolian language
kham·sin (*or* **kam·seen, ·sin**) wind
khan
khan·ate
khan·ga variant spelling of **kanga**
kha·rif Indian crop
Khar·kov Soviet city
Khar·toum (*or* **·tum**)
khat variant spelling of **kat**
kha·yal Indian music
kheda (*or* **khed·ah, ked·dah**) elephant enclosure
khe·dive viceroy of Egypt
Kher·son Soviet port
Khmer Cambodian people
Khmer·ian
Khoi·khoi language group
Khoi·san language
Kho·tan variant of **Hotien**
Khul·na Bangladeshi city
khus·khus grass
Khy·ber Pass
ki·aat tree
ki·ang wild ass
Kiang·si Chinese province
Kiang·su Chinese province
Kiao·chow Chinese territory
kib·ble
kib·butz (*plural* **·but·zim**)
kib·butz·nik
kibe chilblain
kib·itz *US* interfere
kib·lah (*or* **·la**) direction of Mecca
ki·bosh
kick
kick·able
kick·back
kick·er
kick·off
kick·shaw trinket
kick·sorter physics apparatus
kick·stand
kick-start
kid (**kid·ding, kid·ded**)
kid·der
Kid·der·min·ster
kid·ding
kid·dle device for catching fish
Kid·dush Jewish blessing
kid·dy (*or* **·die**; *plural* **·dies**)
kid·nap (**·nap·ping, ·napped;** *US* **·nap·ing, ·naped**)
kid·nap·per (*US* **·nap·er**)
kid·ney
kid·skin
Kiel West German port
Kiel·ce Polish city
kier bleaching vat
kie·sel·guhr soft rock
kie·ser·ite mineral
Kiev
kif (*or* **kaif, keef, kef, kief**) marijuana
ki·koi cloth
kiku·mon Japanese emblem
Ki·ku·yu (*plural* **·yus** *or* **·yu**) African people
Kil·dare
Kili·man·ja·ro
Kil·ken·ny
kill
Kil·lar·ney
kill·deer (*plural* **·deer** *or* **·deers**) bird
kill·er
kil·lick (*or* **·lock**) anchor
Kil·lie·cran·kie Scottish battle site
kil·li·fish (*plural* **·fish** *or* **·fishes**)

kill·ing
kill·ing·ly
kill-joy
Kil·mar·nock
kiln
kilo (*plural* kilos)
kilo·calo·rie
kilo·cycle
kilo·gram (*or* ·gramme)
kilo·hertz
kilo·metre (*US* ·meter)
kilo·met·ric (*or* ·ri·cal)
kilo·ton
kilo·volt
kilo·watt
kilowatt-hour
kilt
kilt·ed
kil·ter *variant spelling (esp. US) of* kelter
Kim·ber·ley South African city
kim·ber·lite rock
ki·mo·no (*plural* ·nos)
ki·mo·noed
kin
Kina·ba·lu Malaysian mountain
kin·aes·the·sia (*or* ·sis; *US* ·es·) physiology term
kin·aes·thet·ic (*US* ·es·)
ki·nase biochemical agent
Kin·car·dine (*or* Kin·car·dine·shire) former Scottish county
kin·cob fabric
kind
kin·der·gar·ten
kin·der·gar·ten·er
kind-hearted
kind-hearted·ly
kind-hearted·ness
kin·dle
kin·dler
kind·less *Archaic* heartless
kind·li·ness
kin·dling
kind·ly (·li·er, ·li·est)
kind·ness
kin·dred
kin·dred·ness (*or* kin·dred·ship)
kine cattle
kin·emat·ic
kin·emati·cal·ly

kin·emat·ics branch of physics
ki·nesics study of body language
ki·net·ic
ki·neti·cal·ly
ki·net·ics branch of mechanics
ki·neto·nu·cle·us
ki·neto·plast
king
king·bird
king·bolt
king·cup
king·dom
king·fish (*plural* ·fish *or* ·fishes)
king·fisher
king·let
king·li·ness
king·ly
king·maker
king-of-arms (*plural* kings-)
king·pin
king·ship
king-size (*or* -sized)
King's Lynn
King·ston Jamaican capital; Canadian port
Kingston upon Thames
Kings·town West Indian port
King·wa·na African language
king·wood
ki·nin protein
kink
kin·ka·jou animal
kinki·ly
kinki·ness
kinky (kinki·er, kinki·est)
kin·ni·kin·nick (*or* ·ki·nic) mixture for smoking
kino resin
Kin·ross former Scottish county
kins·folk
Kin·sha·sa Zaïrian capital
kin·ship
kins·man (*plural* ·men)
kins·woman (*plural* ·women)
ki·osk
kip (kip·ping, kipped)

kip·per
Kir·ghiz (*or* ·giz; *plural* ·ghiz *or* ·giz) Soviet people
Kir·ghi·zia (*or* ·gi·)
Ki·ri·ba·ti island republic
kiri·gami paper cutting
Ki·rin Chinese province
kirk
Kirk·by Merseyside town
Kirk·cal·dy Scottish port
Kirk·cud·bright Scottish county
kirk·man (*plural* ·men) *Scot* church member
Kirk·patrick Antarctic mountain
Kir·kuk Iraqi city
Kirk·wall Scottish town
Kir·man Persian carpet
Ki·rov Soviet city
Ki·ro·va·bad Soviet city
Ki·ro·vo·grad Soviet city
Kirsch (*or* Kirsch·was·ser) cherry brandy
Ki·run·di African language
Kis·an·ga·ni Zaïrian city
kish graphite
Ki·shi·nev Soviet city
kis·met
kiss
kiss·able
kis·sel Russian dessert
kiss·er
kiss·ing
kist *Dialect* large coffer
kit (kit·ting, kit·ted)
Ki·ta·kyu·shu Japanese port
kit·bag
kitch·en
Kitch·ener Canadian town
kitch·en·ette (*or* ·et)
kitchen·ware
kite
kith
kitsch
kit·ten
kit·ten·ish
kit·ten·ish·ness
kit·ti·wake
kit·tle *Scot* capricious
kit·ty (*plural* ·ties)
Kit·we Zambian city

kiva

ki·va underground room
Ki·wa·nis US organization
kiwi (*plural* **kiwis**)
Klai·pe·da Soviet port
klang·far·be musical term
Klans·man (*plural* **·men**) Ku Klux Klan member
klax·on
Kleen·ex (*Trademark*; *plural* **·ex** *or* **·exes**)
klepht Greek brigand
kleph·tic
klep·to·ma·nia (*or* **clep·**)
klep·to·ma·ni·ac (*or* **clep·**)
klip·spring·er antelope
Klon·dike Canadian region
kloof mountain pass
klys·tron electronics apparatus
knack
knack·er
knack·ery
knack·wurst (*or* **knock·**) sausage
knag knot in wood
knap (**knap·ping, knapped**) *Dialect* hill crest; to hit
knap·per
knap·sack
knap·weed
knar *variant spelling of* **knur**
knave
knav·ery (*plural* **·eries**)
knav·ish
knav·ish·ness
knaw·el plant
knead
knead·er
knee (**knee·ing, kneed**)
knee·cap (**·cap·ping, ·capped**)
knee-deep
knee·hole
kneel (**kneel·ing, knelt** *or* **kneeled**)
kneel·er
knee·pad
knee·pan kneecap
knees-up
knell
knelt
Knes·set Israeli parliament
knew

Knickerbocker *US* New Yorker
knick·er·bock·ers
knick·ers
knick·knack (*or* **nick·nack**)
knick·point
knife (*plural* **knives**)
knif·er
knife·rest
knight
knight-errant (*plural* **knights-**)
knight-errantry
knight·head nautical term
knight·hood
knight·li·ness
knight·ly
knish dumpling
knit (**knit·ting, knit·ted** *or* **knit**)
knit·table
knit·ter
knit·ting
knit·wear
knob (**knob·bing, knobbed**) projection; *compare* **nob**
knob·bly (**·bli·er, ·bli·est**)
knob·by (**·bi·er, ·bi·est**)
knob·ker·rie stick
knock
knock·down (*adj*)
knock·er
knock-kneed
knock-on
knock·out
knoll
Knos·sos (*or* **Cnos·sus**) Cretan city
knot (**knot·ting, knot·ted**)
knot·grass
knot·hole
knot·ted
knot·ter
knot·ti·ly
knot·ti·ness
knot·ting
knot·ty (**·ti·er, ·ti·est**)
knot·weed
knout whip
know (**know·ing, knew, known**)
know·able
know-all

252

know·er
know-how
know·ing
know·ing·ly
know·ing·ness
knowl·edge
knowl·edge·able (*or* **·edg·able**)
knowl·edge·ably
known
Knox·ville US city
knuck·le
knuckle·bone
knuckle-duster
knuckle·head
knuck·ly
knur (*or* **knurr, knar**) knot in wood
knurl (*or* **nurl**) ridge
knurled
KO (*verb* **KO's, KO'ing, KO'ed**; *noun*, *plural* **KO's**)
koa tree
koa·la
koan Buddhist riddle
kob antelope
Kobe Japanese port
Ko·blenz (*or* **Co·**) West German city
kob·old mythological spirit
Ko·chi Japanese port
Kodak (*Trademark*)
Ko·di·ak bear; Alaskan island
Ko·dok Sudanese town
kof·ta Indian food
koft·gar Indian goldsmith
Ko·hi·ma Indian city
Kohi·noor (*or* **·nor, ·nur**) diamond
kohl cosmetic
kohl·ra·bi (*plural* **·bies**) cabbage
Ko·hou·tek comet
koi·ne common language
Ko·kand Soviet city
ko·kanee salmon
Koko Nor (*or* **Kuka Nor**) Chinese lake
kola *variant spelling of* **cola**
Kol·ha·pur Indian city
ko·lin·sky (*plural* **·skies**) mink

kol·khoz (*or* **·khos, ·koz**) collective farm
Kol Ni·dre Jewish prayer
kolo (*plural* **kolos**) dance
Ko·lom·na Soviet city
Ko·ly·ma Soviet river
Ko·ma·ti African river
ko·mat·ik Eskimo sledge
Komi (*plural* **·mi** *or* **·mis**) Finnish people
Kom·mu·narsk Soviet city
Ko·mo·do Indonesian island
Kom·so·mol Soviet association
Kom·so·molsk Soviet city
Kon·go (*plural* **·gos** *or* **·go**) African people
kon·go·ni animal
ko·ni·ol·ogy (*or* **co·**)
Kon·stanz variant spelling of **Constance**
Kon·ya (*or* **Konia**) Turkish city
koo·doo variant spelling of **kudu**
kook *US* eccentric person
kooka·bur·ra
kooky (*or* **kookie; kooki·er, kooki·est**) *US* crazy
Koo·te·nay (*or* **·nai**) *US* river
kop hill
ko·peck (*or* **·pek, co·peck**) Soviet coin
Ko·peisk (*or* **·peysk**) Soviet city
kop·je (*or* **·pie**) hill
Ko·ran
Ko·ran·ic
Kor·do·fan Sudanese province
Ko·rea
Ko·rean
kor·ma food
ko·ru·na Czech coin
Kos Greek island
kos (*plural* **kos**) Indian unit of distance
Kos·ci·us·ko Australian mountain
ko·sher (*or* **ka·**)
Koši·ce Czech city
Kosovo-Metohi·ja Yugoslav region
Ko·stro·ma Soviet city

Kota (*or* **Ko·tah**) Indian city
koto (*plural* **kotos**) musical instrument
kou·li·bia·ca (*or* **cou·**) food
kou·mis (*or* **·miss**) variant spellings of **kumiss**
Kov·rov Soviet city
kow·hai tree
Kow·loon part of Hong Kong
kow·tow
kow·tow·er
Ko·zhi·kode Indian port
Kra Thai isthmus
kraal (*or* **craal**) African village
kraft wrapping paper; compare **craft**
krait snake
Kra·ka·toa (*or* **·tau**) Indonesian island
kra·ken sea monster
Kra·ma·torsk Soviet city
kra·meria shrub
Kras·no·dar Soviet city
Kras·no·yarsk Soviet city
Kre·feld West German city
Kre·men·chug Soviet city
Krem·lin
krieg·spiel war game
krill (*plural* **krill**)
krim·mer (*or* **crim·**) lambswool
Krio African language
kris knife
Krish·na
Krish·naism
Kriss Krin·gle *US* Santa Claus
Kris·tian·sand Norwegian port
Kris·tian·stad Swedish town
kro·mes·ky savoury dish
kró·na (*plural* **·nur**) Icelandic or Swedish coin
kro·ne (*plural* **·ner**) Danish or Norwegian coin
Kron·stadt Soviet port
kroon (*plural* **kroons** *or* **krooni**) former Estonian coin
Kru·gers·dorp South African city

kryp·ton
Kua·la Lum·pur
Ku·ching Malaysian port
ku·dos prestige
kudu (*or* **koo·doo**) antelope
kud·zu plant
Ku·fic (*or* **Cu·**) Arabic script
Kui·by·shev (*or* **Kuy·**) Soviet port
Ku Klux Klan
Ku Klux·er (*or* **Ku Klux Klan·ner**)
kuk·ri (*plural* **·ris**) Gurkha knife
kula Pacific island ceremony
ku·lak wealthy Russian peasant
Ku·ma·mo·to Japanese city
Ku·masi Ghanaian city
kum·ba·loi worry beads
ku·miss (*or* **kou·miss, kou·mis, kou·myss**) drink
küm·mel German liqueur
kum·quat (*or* **cum·**) fruit
kung fu
Kun·gur Chinese mountain
Kun·lun (*or* **Kuen·, Kwen·**) Chinese mountains
Kun·ming (*or* **K'un·ming**) Chinese city
kunz·ite gemstone
Kuo·min·tang (*or* **Guo·min·dang**) political party
Ku·ra Asian river
Kurd Turkic people
Kurd·ish
Kur·di·stan (*or* **Kur·destan, Kor·destan**)
Kure Japanese port
Kur·gan Soviet city
Ku·ril Is·lands
kur·ra·jong (*or* **cur·**) tree
kur·saal building at health resort
Kursk Soviet city
kur·to·sis statistics term
Kus·ko·kwim Alaskan river
Ku·tai·si Soviet city
Kutch (*or* **Cutch**) former Indian state

Kuwait

Ku·wait
Ku·wai·ti
Kuz·netsk Ba·sin Soviet region
kvass (*or* **kvas, quass**) drink
Kwa language group
kwa·cha Zambian currency
Kwa·ja·lein Pacific atoll
Kwa·ki·utl (*plural* **·utl** *or* **·utls**) American Indian
Kwang·chow·an Chinese region
Kwang·ju Korean city
Kwangsi-Chuang Chinese region
Kwang·tung Chinese province
kwan·za Angolan currency
kwashi·or·kor protein deficiency
Kwa·zu·lu South African homeland
Kwei·chow (*or* **Kuei·chou**) Chinese province
Kwei·lin (*or* **Kuei-lin**) Chinese city
Kwei·yang (*or* **Kuei-yang**) Chinese city
kwe·la African music
ky·ani·za·tion (*or* **·sa·tion**)
ky·an·ize (*or* **·ise**) treat timber
kyat Burmese currency
kyle *Scot* narrow strait
ky·lix (*or* **cy·lix;** *plural* **·li·kes**) drinking vessel
ky·loe cattle
ky·mo·graph (*or* **cy·**) medical instrument
ky·mo·graph·ic (*or* **cy·**)
Kyo·to (*or* **Kio·**) Japanese city
ky·pho·sis (*plural* **·ses**) spinal curvature
ky·phot·ic
Kyrie elei·son
kyu judo grade
Kyu·shu (*or* **Kiu·**) Japanese island

L

laa·ger (*or* **la·**) African camp; *compare* **lager**
lab
laba·rum (*plural* **·ra**) Christian banner
lab·da·num (*or* **la·**) plant resin
la·bel (**·bel·ling, ·belled;** *US* **·bel·ing, ·beled**)
la·bel·ler (*US* **·bel·er**)
la·bel·loid
la·bel·lum (*plural* **·la**) biology term
la·bia *plural of* **labium**
la·bial
la·bi·al·ism
la·bi·al·ity
la·bi·ali·za·tion (*or* **·sa·tion**)
la·bi·al·ize (*or* **·ise**)
la·bial·ly
la·bi·ate plant
la·bile
la·bil·ity
la·bio·den·tal
la·bio·na·sal
la·bio·velar
la·bium (*plural* **·bia**)
lab·lab bean
la·bora·tory (*plural* **·tories**)
La·bor Australian political party
la·bor *US spelling of* **labour**
la·bo·ri·ous
la·bo·ri·ous·ly
la·bo·ri·ous·ness
La·bour British political party
la·bour (*US* **·bor**)
la·boured (*US* **·bored**)
la·boured·ly (*US* **·bored·**)
la·bour·er (*US* **·bor·**)
la·bour·ism (*US* **·bor·**)
la·bour·ist (*US* **·bor·**)
La·bour·ite Labour Party supporter
Lab·ra·dor Canadian peninsula; dog
lab·ra·dor·ite mineral
la·bret lip ornament
lab·roid (*or* **·rid**) fish
la·brum (*plural* **·bra**) lip
La·buan Malaysian island
la·bur·num
Laby·rinth mythological maze
laby·rinth
laby·rin·thi·cal·ly
laby·rin·thine (*or* **·thian, ·thic**)
lac resin; *variant spelling of* **lakh**
iac·co·lith (*or* **·lite**) geology term
lac·co·lith·ic (*or* **·lit·ic**)
lace
Lac·edae·mon Sparta
Lac·edae·mo·nian
lac·er
lac·er·abil·ity
lac·er·able
lac·er·ant distressing
lac·er·ate
lac·era·tion
lac·era·tive
La·cer·ta constellation
lac·er·til·ian lizard
lace-up (*adj, noun*)
lace·wing insect
(lacey) *incorrect spelling of* **lacy**
lach·es (*sing.*) legal term
lach·ry·mal *variant spelling of lacrimal*
lach·ry·ma·tory (*plural* **·tories**) vessel; *variant spelling of* **lacrimatory**
lach·ry·mose
lach·ry·mose·ly
lach·ry·mos·ity
laci·ly
laci·ness
lac·ing

la·cini·ate (or ·cinia·ted) jagged
la·cinia·tion
lack
lacka·dai·si·cal
lacka·dai·si·cal·ly
lacka·dai·si·cal·ness
lack·ey
lack·lustre (US ·luster)
La·co·nia ancient Greek country
La·co·nian
la·con·ic (or ·coni·cal) of few words
la·coni·cal·ly
La Co·ru·ña (or Co·run·na) Spanish port
lac·quer
lac·quer·er
lac·ri·mal (or lach·ry·, lac·ry·)
lac·ri·ma·tion
lac·ri·ma·tor (or lach·ry·, lac·ry·) substance causing tear flow
lac·ri·ma·tory (or lach·ry·, lac·ry·; adj) of tears; compare lachrymatory
la·crosse
lac·tal·bu·min
lac·tam chemical group
lac·ta·ry of milk
lac·tase enzyme
lac·tate
lac·ta·tion
lac·ta·tion·al
lac·ta·tion·al·ly
lac·teal
lac·teal·ly
lac·tes·cence
lac·tes·cent
lac·tic
lac·tif·er·ous
lac·to·ba·cil·lus (plural ·li)
lac·to·gen·ic
lac·tom·eter
lac·tone chemical compound
lac·ton·ic
lac·to·pro·tein
lac·to·scope
lac·tose milk sugar
la·cu·na (plural ·nae or ·nas)

la·cu·nar (plural ·nars or ·nar·ia) ceiling panel; of lacunae
la·cu·nose (or ·nal, ·nary)
lacu·nos·ity
la·cus·trine
lacy (laci·er, laci·est)
lad
lad·der
lad·die
lade (lad·ing, lad·ed, lad·en or lad·ed) load cargo; compare laid
lad·er
la-di-da (or lah-di-dah)
la·dies plural of lady
la·dies' man
lad·ing cargo
La·di·no language
la·di·no (plural ·nos) clover
la·dle
ladle·ful
la·dler
lady (plural la·dies)
lady·bird
la·dy·fy (or ·di·; ·fy·ing, ·fied)
lady-in-waiting (plural ladies-)
lady-killer
lady·like
lady·love
la·dy·ship
lady's maid (plural la·dies' maids)
La·dy·smith South African city
lady's-slipper orchid
lady's-smock plant
Laertes mythological character
lae·vo·ro·ta·tion (US le·)
lae·vo·ro·ta·tory (or ·ro·ta·ry; US le·)
laevu·lin (US levu·)
laevu·lose (US levu·) a sugar
lag (lag·ging, lagged)
lag·an (or li·gan) wreckage
la·gena bottle
la·ger beer; compare laager
lag·gard
lag·gard·ly
lag·gard·ness

lagged
lag·ging
la·gniappe (or ·gnappe) US small gift
lago·morph type of mammal
lago·mor·phic (or ·phous)
la·goon
La·gos Nigerian port
lah musical note
lah-di-dah variant spelling of la-di-da
Lahn·da language
La·hore Pakistani city
Lah·ti Finnish town
laic (or lai·cal) secular
lai·cal·ly
lai·cism
lai·ci·za·tion (or ·sa·tion)
lai·cize (or ·cise)
laid past tense and past participle of lay; compare lade; lain
laik Dialect to play
lain past participle of lie; compare laid
lair
laird
lairy (lairi·er, lairi·est) Austral gaudy
lais·sez faire (or lais·ser faire)
laissez-faireism (or laisser-)
lais·sez pas·ser
la·ity
lake
Lake·land the Lake District
lak·er lake cargo boat
lakh (or lac) 100 000 Indian rupees
Lak·shad·weep Indian islands
laky (laki·er, laki·est) reddish
Lala Indian form of address
la·lang grass
Lal·lans (or ·lan) Scottish dialect
lal·la·tion speech defect
lal·ly·gag (·gag·ging, ·gagged) US loiter
lam (lam·ming, lammed)
lama Tibetan priest; compare llama

Lamaism

La·ma·ism form of Buddhism
La·ma·ist
La·ma·is·tic
La·marck·ian
La·marck·ism theory of evolution
la·ma·sery (*plural* **·series**)
lamb
lam·baste (*or* **·bast**) *Slang* beat severely
lamb·da Greek letter
lamb·da·cism phonetics term
lamb·doid (*or* **·doi·dal**)
lam·ben·cy
lam·bent
lam·bert unit of illumination
Lam·beth
lamb·kin
lam·bre·quin ornamental hanging
lamb·skin
lamé fabric
lame
la·mel·la (*plural* **·lae** *or* **·las**) thin layer
la·mel·lar (*or* **lam·el·late, la·mel·lose**)
lam·el·lat·ed
lam·el·la·tion
la·mel·li·branch mollusc
la·mel·li·bran·chi·ate
la·mel·li·corn beetle
la·mel·li·form
la·mel·li·ros·tral (*or* **·trate**) zoology term
lam·el·los·ity
lame·ly
lame·ness
la·ment
lam·en·table
lam·en·table·ness
lam·en·tably
la·men·ta·tion
La·men·ta·tions biblical book
la·ment·ed
la·ment·er
la·mia (*plural* **·mias** *or* **·miae**) mythological monster
lami·na (*plural* **·nae** *or* **·nas**) thin plate
lami·nable

lami·nar (*or* **·nose**)
lami·naria seaweed
lami·nate
lami·na·ted
lami·na·tion
lami·na·tor
lami·ni·tis horse disease
Lam·mas religious feast
lam·mer·gei·er (*or* **·gey·er**) vulture
lamp
lam·pas animal disease; fabric
lamp·black
Lam·pedu·sa Mediterranean island
lam·pern lamprey
lam·pion oil lamp
lamp·lighter
lam·poon
lam·poon·er (*or* **·ist**)
lam·poon·ery
lamp·post
lam·prey
lam·pro·phyre rock
La·nai Hawaiian island
la·nai veranda
Lan·ark Scottish town
la·nate (*or* **·nose**) woolly
Lan·ca·shire
Lan·cas·ter
Lan·cas·trian
lance
lance·let tiny animal
lan·ceo·late tapering
lanc·er
lan·cers dance
lan·cet surgical knife
lan·cet·ed architectural term
lance·wood
Lan·chow (*or* **Lan·chou**) Chinese city
lan·cin·ate
lan·ci·na·tion
Land (*plural* **Län·der**) German state
land
land·am·mann Swiss official
lan·dau
lan·dau·let (*or* **·lette**)
land·ed
Landes French region
Lan·des·haupt·mann Austrian governor

land·fall
land·form
land·grave German ruler
land·gra·vine landgrave's wife
land·ing
land·lady (*plural* **·ladies**)
land·locked
land·lop·er *Scot* vagrant
land·lord
land·lub·ber
land·mark
land·mass
land·owner
land·owner·ship
land·owning
land·race pig breed
land·scape
land·scap·ist
Land's End
land·shark land profiteer
land·side part of plough
lands·knecht a mercenary
land·slide
lands·man (*plural* **·men**)
Land·tag German assembly
land·ward
lane
lang *Scot* long
lang·lauf cross-country skiing
lang·läuf·er
lan·gouste spiny lobster
lang·syne *Scot* long ago; *compare* **auld lang syne**
lan·guage
langue linguistics term
langue de chat biscuit
Langue·doc French region
langue d'oc language
lan·guid
lan·guid·ness
lan·guish
lan·guish·er
lan·guish·ment
lan·guor weariness; *compare* **langur**
lan·guor·ous
lan·guor·ous·ness
lan·gur monkey; *compare* **languor**
lan·iard variant spelling of **lanyard**
la·ni·ary (*plural* **·aries**) tooth

la·nif·er·ous (*or* ·nig·)
   wool-bearing
lank
lanki·ly
lanki·ness
lank·ly
lank·ness
lanky (lanki·er, lanki·est)
lan·ner falcon
lan·ner·et male lanner
lano·lat·ed
lano·lin (*or* ·line)
Lan·sing US city
lans·que·net gambling game
lan·ta·na shrub
lan·tern
lan·tha·nide (*or* ·non) chemistry term
lan·tha·num chemical element
la·nu·go (*plural* ·gos) fine hair
lan·yard (*or* ·iard)
Lao (*plural* Lao *or* Laos) Asian people
Laoag Philippine city
Laocoon mythological priest
La·odi·cea ancient Greek city
La·odi·cean
la·odi·cean indifferent
Laoigh·is Irish county
Laos
Lao·tian
lap (lap·ping, lapped)
lapa·rot·omy (*plural* ·omies) abdominal surgery
La Paz Bolivian capital
lap·board
lap-chart
la·pel
la·pelled
lapi·dar·ian
lapi·dary (*plural* ·daries)
lapi·date to stone
lapi·da·tion
la·pidi·fy (·fy·ing, ·fied) change into stone
la·pil·lus (*plural* ·li) piece of lava
lap·is lazu·li
Lap·land

Lap·land·er
Lapp
lapped
lap·per
lap·pet
lap·pet·ed
lap·ping
Lapp·ish
laps·able (*or* ·ible)
lapse
laps·er
lap·strake nautical term
lap·sus (*plural* ·sus) error
lap·wing
lar·board
lar·cenist (*or* ·cener)
lar·cenous
lar·ceny (*plural* ·cenies)
larch
lard
lar·der
lar·don (*or* ·doon) strip of fat
lardy
lares Roman gods
large
large·ly
large-minded
larg·en
large·ness
large-scale
lar·gess (*or* ·gesse)
lar·ghet·to (*plural* ·tos) music term
larg·ish
lar·go (*plural* ·gos)
lari·at lasso
lar·ine of gulls
Lá·ri·sa (*or* La·ris·sa) Greek city
lark
lark·er
lark·ish·ness
lark·some
lark·spur
lar·nax terracotta coffin
La Ro·chelle French port
lar·ri·gan leather boot
lar·ri·kin *Austral* hooligan
lar·rup *Dialect* to beat
lar·va (*plural* ·vae) preadult animal; *compare* lava
lar·val
lar·vi·cid·al

lar·vi·cide
lar·yn·geal (*or* la·ryn·gal)
la·ryn·ges *plural of* larynx
lar·yn·git·ic
lar·yn·gi·tis
la·ryn·go·logi·cal (*or* ·log·ic)
lar·yn·golo·gist
lar·yn·gol·ogy
la·ryn·go·scope
la·ryn·go·scop·ic
la·ryn·gos·co·pist
la·ryn·gos·co·py
lar·yn·got·omy (*plural* ·omies)
lar·ynx (*plural* la·ryn·ges *or* lar·ynxes)
la·sa·gne (*or* ·gna)
La Salle Canadian city
las·car (*or* lash·kar) East Indian sailor
Las·caux French cave
las·civi·ous
las·civi·ous·ly
las·civi·ous·ness
lase act as laser
la·ser
lash
lash·er
lash·ing
Lashio Burmese town
lash·kar *variant spelling of* las·car
lash-up (*noun*)
las·ket nautical term
Las Pal·mas
La Spe·zia Italian port
lass
Las·sa fe·ver
las·sic
las·si·tude
las·so (*noun, plural* ·sos *or* ·soes; *verb* ·sos *or* ·soes, ·so·ing, ·soed)
las·so·er
last
last·er
last·ing
last·ing·ly
last·ly
Las Ve·gas
lat (*plural* lats, latu, *or* lati) Latvian currency
Lata·kia Syrian port
latch

latchet

latch·et *Archaic* shoelace
latch·key
late
late·comer
la·teen *nautical term*
lateen-rigged
(lateish) *incorrect spelling of* latish
late·ly
la·ten·cy
late·ness
la·tent
lat·er
lat·er·al
lat·er·al·ly
Lat·er·an *Roman palace*
lat·er·ite *clay*
lat·er·it·ic
lat·ero·ver·sion
lat·est
la·tex (*plural* ·texes *or* lati·ces)
lath (*plural* laths) *wood strip*
lathe *machine*
lath·er
lath·ery
la·thi *Indian stick*
lati·cif·er·ous *botany term*
lati·meria *fish*
Lat·in
Lat·in·ate
Lat·in·ism
Lat·in·ist
La·tin·ity
Lat·ini·za·tion (*or* ·sa·tion)
Lat·in·ize (*or* ·ise)
Lat·in·iz·er (*or* ·is·er)
La·ti·no (*plural* ·nos) *US Latin American*
lat·ish
lati·tude
lati·tu·di·nal
lati·tu·di·nal·ly
lati·tu·di·nar·ian
lati·tu·di·nari·an·ism
La·tium *Italian region*
la·tria *Catholic worship*
la·trine
lat·ten *sheet metal*
lat·ter
latter-day
lat·ter·ly
latter·most

lat·tice
lat·ticed
Lat·via
Lat·vian
laud
laud·abil·ity (*or* ·able·ness)
laud·able
laud·ably
lau·da·num
lau·da·tion *praise*
lauda·tory (*or* ·tive)
laud·er
laugh
laugh·able
laugh·able·ness
laugh·ably
laugh·er
laugh·ing·ly
laugh·ter
launch
launch·er
laun·der
laun·der·er
Laun·der·ette (*Trademark*)
laun·dress
Laun·dro·mat (*Trademark*)
laun·dry (*plural* ·dries)
laundry·man (*plural* ·men)
laundry·woman (*plural* ·women)
lau·ra·ceous *botany term*
Laura·sia *ancient continent*
lau·reate
lau·reate·ship
lau·rea·tion
lau·rel (·rel·ling, ·relled; *US* ·rel·ing, ·reled)
Lau·ren·tian *of St Lawrence river; compare* Lawrentian
lau·rus·ti·nus *shrub*
Lau·sanne
lav *short for* lavatory
lava *molten rock; compare* larva
lava·bo (*plural* ·boes *or* ·bos)
lav·age *medical procedure*
La·val *Canadian city*
la·va·tion *washing*
la·va·tion·al

258

lava·tory (*plural* ·tories)
lav·en·der
la·ver *seaweed; font*
lav·er·ock *Dialect* skylark
lav·ish
lav·ish·er
lav·ish·ly
lav·ish·ness
law
law-abiding
law·breaker
law·breaking
law·ful
law·ful·ly
law·ful·ness
law·giver
law·giving
law·less
law·less·ly
law·less·ness
law·man (*plural* ·men)
lawn
lawny
law·ren·cium *chemical element*
Law·ren·tian *of D. H. Lawrence; compare* Laurentian
law·suit
law·yer
lax
laxa·tion *defecation*
laxa·tive
lax·ity (*or* lax·ness)
lax·ly
lay (lay·ing, laid)
lay·about
lay-by
(layed) *incorrect spelling of* laid
lay·er
lay·er·ing
lay·ette
lay·ing
lay·man (*plural* ·men)
lay·shaft
lay·woman (*plural* ·women)
laz·ar *leper*
laza·ret·to (*or* ·ret, ·rette; *plural* ·tos, ·rets, ·rettes) *ship's locker; leper hospital*
laze
la·zi·ly

la·zi·ness
lazu·lite mineral
lazu·rite lapis lazuli
lazy (la·zi·er, la·zi·est)
lazy·bones
L-dopa
lea meadow; unit of length; *compare* lee; ley
leach percolate; *compare* leech
leach·er
lead (lead·ing, led) guide
lead (lead·ing, lead·ed) metal
lead·en
lead·en·ly
lead·en·ness
lead·er
lead·er·ship
lead-in (*noun*)
lead·ing
leads·man (*plural* ·men)
lead·wort shrub
leady
leaf (*plural* leaves)
leaf·age
leaf-climber
leaf-cutter ant
leaf-hopper insect
leafi·ness
leaf·let
leaf·stalk
leafy (leafi·er, leafi·est)
league (leagu·ing, leagued)
leak hole; escape; *compare* leek
leak·age
leak·er
leaki·ness
leaky (leaki·er, leaki·est)
leal *Scot* loyal
Leam·ing·ton
lean (lean·ing, leant *or* leaned)
Leander mythological character
lean·ness
leant
lean-to (*plural* -tos)
leap (leap·ing, leapt *or* leaped)
leap·er
leap·frog (·frog·ging, ·frogged)

leapt
learn (learning, learnt *or* learned)
learn·able
learn·ed wise
learn·ed·ly
learn·ed·ness
learn·er
learn·ing
learnt
leary *variant spelling of* leery
leas·able
lease
lease·back property transaction
lease·hold
lease·holder
leas·er
leash
least
least·ways
leat trench
leath·er
leather·back turtle
Leath·er·ette (*Trademark*)
Leath·er·head Surrey town
leather·head bird
leath·eri·ness
leather·jacket fish; insect
leath·ern
leather·neck *Slang* US marine
leather·wood
leath·ery
leave (leav·ing, left)
leaved with leaves
leav·en
leav·en·ing
leav·er
leaves *plural of* leaf *or* leave; *present tense of* leave
leave-taking
leav·ing
Leba·nese
Leba·non
leb·en curdled milk
Le·bens·raum *German* territory
leb·ku·chen (*plural* ·chen) biscuit
Lech European river
lech lust
lech·er
lech·er·ous

lech·ery (*plural* ·eries)
leci·thin biochemical compound
le·cithi·nase enzyme
lec·tern
lec·tion variant reading
lec·tion·ary (*plural* ·aries) book of church readings
lec·tor lecturer
lec·tor·ate (*or* ·ship)
lec·ture
lec·tur·er
lec·ture·ship
lecy·thus (*plural* ·thi) Greek vase
led
Leda mythological character
le·der·ho·sen leather shorts
ledge
ledged
ledg·er
ledg·er line (*or* leg·) musical term
ledgy
lee sheltered side; *compare* lea; ley
lee·board
leech bloodsucker; *compare* leach
leech (*or* leach) nautical term; *compare* leach
Leeds
leek vegetable; *compare* leak
leer
leer·ing·ly
leery (*or* leary; leeri·er, leeri·est *or* leari·er, leari·est)
lees sediment
leet manorial court
lee·ward
Lee·ward Is·lands
lee·way
left
left-hand (*adj*)
left-handed
left-handed·ly
left-handed·ness
left-hander
left·ism
left·ist
left·over
left·wards
left-winger
lefty (*plural* lefties)

leg

leg (leg·ging, legged)
lega·cy (*plural* ·cies)
le·gal
le·gal·ese legal jargon
le·gal·ism
le·gal·ist
le·gal·is·tic
le·gal·is·ti·cal·ly
le·gal·ity (*plural* ·ities)
le·gali·za·tion (*or* ·sa·tion)
le·gal·ize (*or* ·ise)
le·gal·ly
leg·ate envoy
lega·tee recipient of legacy
leg·ate·ship
lega·tine
le·ga·tion
le·ga·tion·ary
le·ga·to (*plural* ·tos) music term
lega·tor bequeather
lega·to·rial
leg·end
leg·end·ary (*adj*)
leg·end·ry (*noun*)
leg·er·demain
leg·er·demain·ist
leg·er line *variant spelling of* ledger line
legged *past tense of* leg
leg·ged having legs
leg·gi·ness
leg·ginged
leg·gings
leg·gy (·gi·er, ·gi·est)
Leg·horn Livorno; domestic fowl
leg·horn straw hat
leg·ibil·ity (*or* ·ible·ness)
leg·ible
leg·ibly
le·gion
le·gion·ary (*plural* ·aries)
le·gion·naire
leg·is·late
leg·is·la·tion
leg·is·la·tive
leg·is·la·tor
leg·is·la·to·rial
leg·is·la·tress
leg·is·la·ture
le·gist legal expert
le·git *Slang* legitimate
le·giti·ma·cy (*or* ·mate·ness)

le·giti·mate
le·giti·mate·ly
le·giti·ma·tion
le·giti·ma·ti·za·tion (*or* ·sa·tion) legitimization
le·giti·ma·tize (*or* ·tise) legitimize
le·giti·mism
le·giti·mist supporter of legitimate ruler
le·giti·mis·tic
le·giti·mi·za·tion (*or* ·sa·tion)
le·giti·mize (*or* ·mise)
leg·less
leg·man (*plural* ·men) US newspaper reporter
leg·room
leg·ume pod
le·gu·min protein
le·gu·mi·nous botany term
leg·work
Le Ha·vre French port
lei Hawaiian garland
Leices·ter
Leices·ter·shire
Lei·den (*or* Ley·) Dutch city
Leigh English town
Lein·ster Irish province
Leip·zig East German city
leish·ma·nia protozoan
leish·mania·sis (*or* ·ma·nio·sis) infection
leis·ter fishing spear
lei·sure
lei·sured
lei·sure·li·ness
lei·sure·ly
Leith Scottish port
leit·mo·tiv (*or* ·tif)
Lei·trim Irish county
lek Albanian currency
Le Mans French city
lem·ma (*plural* ·mas *or* ·ma·ta) logic term
lem·ming
lem·nis·cate maths term
lem·nis·cus (*plural* ·nis·ci) anatomy term
Lem·nos (*or* Lím·) Greek island
lem·on
lem·on·ade
lem·ony

260

lem·pi·ra Honduran currency
le·mur
lemu·roid (*or* ·rine)
Lena Soviet river
lend (lend·ing, lent)
lend·er
lend-lease
length
length·en
length·en·er
lengthi·ly
lengthi·ness
length·ways (*or* ·wise)
lengthy (lengthi·er, lengthi·est)
le·ni·en·cy (*or* ·ni·ence)
le·ni·ent
le·ni·ent·ly
Le·ni·na·bad Soviet town
Le·ni·na·kan Armenian city
Le·nin·grad
Len·in·ism political theory
Len·in·ist (*or* ·ite)
le·nis (*plural* le·nes) linguistics term
leni·tive soothing pain
len·ity (*plural* ·ities)
leno (*plural* lenos) fabric weave
lens
Lent
lent
len·ta·men·te musical term
Len·ten of Lent
len·tic ecology term
len·ti·cel botany term
len·ti·cel·late
len·ticu·lar (*or* ·ti·form)
len·ti·form
len·tigi·nous (*or* ·nose)
len·ti·go (*plural* ·tigi·nes) freckle
len·til
len·tis·si·mo music term
len·to (*plural* ·tos) music term
Leo constellation
León cities in Spain, Mexico, and Nicaragua
Leo·nid (*plural* Leo·nids *or* Le·oni·des) meteor shower
leo·nine
leop·ard

leop·ard·ess
leopard's-bane plant
leo·tard
lep·er
le·pido·lite mineral
lepi·dop·ter·an (*plural* ·ter·ans *or* ·tera)
lepi·dop·ter·ist
lepi·dop·ter·ous
lepi·do·si·ren fish
lepi·dote biology term
lepo·rid hare
lepo·rine of hares
lep·re·chaun
lep·ro·sar·ium (*plural* ·ia) leper hospital
lep·rose
lep·ro·sy
lep·rous
lep·rous·ness
lep·to·cepha·lus (*plural* ·li) eel larva
lep·ton (*plural* ·ta) Greek currency
lep·ton (*plural* ·tons) physics particle
lep·to·phyl·lous botany term
lep·tor·rhine zoology term
lep·to·some slender person
lep·to·so·mic (*or* ·mat·ic)
lep·to·spi·ro·sis disease
lep·to·tene biology term
le·quear ceiling panel
Ler·wick Scottish town
Les·bian of Lesbos
les·bian female homosexual
les·bi·an·ism
Les·bos Greek island
Les Cayes Haitian port
lese-majesty (*or* lèse-majesté)
le·sion
Le·so·tho African kingdom
less
les·see one to whom lease is granted
les·see·ship
less·en
less·er less great; *compare* lessor
les·son
les·sor one who grants lease; *compare* lesser
lest

let (let·ting, let)
le·thal
le·thal·ity
le·thal·ly
le·thar·gic (*or* ·gi·cal)
le·thar·gi·cal·ly
leth·ar·gy (*plural* ·gies)
Leth·bridge Canadian city
Le·the mythological river
Leto mother of Apollo
let's
Lett a Latvian
let·ter
let·tered
let·ter·er
letter·head
let·ter·ing
letter·press
let·ter·set
let·ting
Let·tish Latvian
let·tuce
leu·cine (*or* ·cin) amino acid
leu·cite mineral
leu·cit·ic
leu·co·crat·ic geology term
leu·co·cyte (*US* ·ko·)
leu·co·cyt·ic (*US* ·ko·)
leu·co·cy·to·sis (*US* ·ko·)
leu·co·cy·tot·ic (*US* ·ko·)
leu·co·der·ma (*US* ·ko·) unpigmented skin
leu·co·der·mal (*or* ·mic; *US* ·ko·)
leu·co·ma corneal scar
leu·co·maine biochemical compound
leu·co·penia (*US* ·ko·)
leu·co·penic (*US* ·ko·)
leu·co·plast (*or* ·plas·tid) structure in plant cell
leu·co·poi·esis (*US* ·ko·)
leu·co·poi·et·ic (*US* ·ko·)
leu·cor·rhoea (*US* ·kor·rhea) vaginal discharge
leu·cor·rhoeal (*US* ·kor·rheal)
leu·cot·omy brain surgery
leu·kae·mia (*US* ·ke·mia)
leuko *US spelling of some words beginning with* leuco·
lev (*plural* leva) Bulgarian currency

Le·val·loi·sian (*or* ·lois) Palaeolithic culture
Le·vant Middle Eastern region
le·vant leather
le·vant·er wind
Le·van·tine of Levant
le·van·tine silk cloth
le·va·tor
levee
lev·el (·el·ling, ·elled; *US* ·el·ing, ·eled)
level-headed
level-headed·ly
level-headed·ness
Lev·el·ler radical Parliamentarian
lev·el·ler (*US* ·el·er)
lev·el·ly
Le·ven Scottish loch
lev·er
lev·er·age
lev·er·et young hare
Le·ver·ku·sen West German town
levi·able
le·via·than biblical monster
levi·er
levi·gate grind into powder
levi·ga·tion
levi·ga·tor
levi·rate marrying brother's widow
Le·vis (*Trademark*) jeans
levi·tate
levi·ta·tion
levi·ta·tor
Le·vite priest
Le·viti·cal (*or* Le·vit·ic)
Le·viti·cus biblical book
lev·ity (*plural* ·ities)
le·vo·ro·ta·tion *US spelling of* laevorotation
le·vo·ro·ta·tory *US spelling of* laevorotatory
levu·lin *US spelling of* laevulin
levu·lose *US spelling of* laevulose
levy (*verb* levies, levy·ing, levied; *noun, plural* levies)
lewd
lewd·ly
lewd·ness

Lewes

Lew·es Sussex town
Lew·is Scottish island
lew·is (*or* **lew·is·son**) lifting device
Lewi·sham
lew·is·ite war gas
lex (*plural* **leges**) body of laws
lex·eme linguistics term
lexi·cal
lexi·cal·ity
lexi·cal·ly
lexi·cog·ra·pher
lexi·co·graph·ic (*or* **·graphi·cal**)
lexi·co·graphi·cal·ly
lexi·cog·ra·phy
lexi·co·logi·cal
lexi·co·logi·cal·ly
lexi·colo·gist
lexi·col·ogy
lexi·con
lexi·co·sta·tis·tics
lexi·gra·phy
Lex·ing·ton US city
lex·is vocabulary
lex loci law of the place
ley prehistoric track; *compare* **lea; lee**
Ley·den *variant spelling of* **Leiden**
Ley·te Philippine island
Lha·sa Tibetan capital
li unit of length
lia·bil·ity (*plural* **·ities**)
lia·ble
li·aise
liai·son
lia·na (*or* **li·ane**) plant
lia·noid
Liao·ning Chinese province
Liao·tung (*or* **·dong**) Chinese peninsula
Liao·yang Chinese city
liar
Li·ard Canadian river
li·ard coin
Lias rock series
lias blue limestone
Li·as·sic
lib *Slang* liberation
li·ba·tion
li·ba·tion·al (*or* **·ary**)
li·bec·cio (*or* **·chio**) Corsican wind

li·bel (**·bel·ling**, **·belled**; *US* **·bel·ing**, **·beled**)
li·bel·lant (*US* **·bel·ant**)
li·bel·lee (*US* **·bel·ee**)
li·bel·ler (*or* **li·bel·ist**; *US* **·bel·er** *or* **·bel·ist**)
li·bel·lous (*US* **·bel·ous**)
Lib·er·al political party
lib·er·al progressive; abundant
lib·er·al·ism
lib·er·al·ist
lib·er·al·is·tic
lib·er·al·ity (*plural* **·ities**)
lib·er·ali·za·tion (*or* **·sa·tion**)
lib·er·al·ize (*or* **·ise**)
lib·er·al·iz·er (*or* **·is·er**)
lib·er·al·ly
lib·er·al·ness
lib·er·ate
lib·era·tion
lib·era·tor (*fem* **·tress**)
Li·beria
Li·berian
lib·er·tar·ian freethinker; *compare* **libertine**
lib·er·tari·an·ism
li·ber·ti·cid·al
li·ber·ti·cide destruction of freedom
lib·er·tine dissolute person; *compare* **libertarian**
lib·er·tin·ism (*or* **·age**)
lib·er·ty (*plural* **·ties**)
li·bidi·nal
li·bidi·nous
li·bi·do (*plural* **·dos**)
Li·bra constellation; sign of zodiac
Lib·ran
li·brar·ian
li·brar·ian·ship
li·brary (*plural* **·braries**)
li·brate waver
li·bra·tion
li·bra·tion·al
li·bra·tory
li·bret·tist
li·bret·to (*plural* **·tos** *or* **·ti**)
Li·breville Gabonese capital
li·bri·form botany term
Lib·rium (*Trademark*)

Libya
Liby·an
lice
li·cence (*US* **·cense**) a permit
li·cens·able
li·cense to grant licence; *US spelling of* **licence**
li·cen·see
li·cens·er (*or* **·cen·sor**)
li·cen·ti·ate licence holder; *compare* **licentious**
li·cen·ti·ate·ship
li·cen·tia·tion
li·cen·tious promiscuous; *compare* **licentiate**
li·cen·tious·ness
li·chee (*or* **·chi**) *variant spelling of* **litchi**
li·chen
li·chen·in chemical compound
li·chen·oid
li·chen·ol·ogy
li·chen·ous (*or* **·ose**)
Lich·field Staffordshire city
lich gate (*or* **lych gate**)
lic·it lawful
lick
lick·er
lick·er·ish *Archaic* lustful; *compare* **liquorice**
lickety-split *US* very quickly
lick·ing
lick·spit·tle
lico·rice *US spelling of* **liquorice**
lic·tor Roman official
lid
lid·ded
lid·less
lido (*plural* **lidos**)
lie (**ly·ing, lied**) tell untruth; *compare* **lye**
lie (**ly·ing, lay, lain**) recline; *compare* **lye**
Lieb·frau·milch (*or* **·frau·en·milch**) wine
Liech·ten·stein
lied (*plural* **lied·er**) song
lief *Archaic* willingly
Li·ège Belgian city
liege owed allegiance
liege·man (*plural* **·men**)

lien legal term
lien·al
li·en·ter·ic
li·en·tery medical term
li·erne architectural term
Li·etu·va Lithuania
lieu
lieu·ten·an·cy
lieu·ten·ant
life (*plural* lives)
life·blood
life·boat
life·guard
life·less
life·less·ly
life·less·ness
life·like
life·line
life·long for life; *compare* livelong
lif·er
life-saver
life-saving
life-size (*or* -sized)
life·time
Lif·fey Irish river
lift
lift·able
lift·boy
lift·er
lift·off
liga·ment
liga·men·tous (*or* ·tal, ·ta·ry)
li·gan *variant spelling of* lagan
lig·and chemistry term
li·gate constrict with ligature
li·ga·tion
liga·tive
liga·ture
li·ger animal
light (light·ing, light·ed *or* lit)
light·en
light·en·er
light·en·ing making lighter; *compare* lightning
light·er
light·er·age
lighter·man (*plural* ·men)
light-fast
light-fingered
light-footed
light-headed

light-headed·ly
light-headed·ness
light-hearted
light-hearted·ly
light-hearted·ness
light·house
light·ing
light·ish
light·ly
light·ness
light·ning light flash; *compare* lightening
light·ship
light·some
light·weight
lign·al·oes tree
lig·ne·ous
lig·ni·fi·ca·tion
lig·ni·form
lig·ni·fy (·fies, ·fy·ing, ·fied) make woody
lig·nin plant tissue
lig·nite brown coal
lig·nit·ic
lig·no·caine anaesthetic
lig·no·cel·lu·lose
lig·num vi·tae wood
lig·ro·in chemical compound
ligu·la (*plural* ·lae *or* ·las) part of insect's lip
ligu·lar
ligu·late
lig·ule plant part
ligu·loid
lig·ure biblical gem
Li·gu·ria Italian region
Li·gu·ri·an
lik·able (*or* like·)
lik·able·ness (*or* like·)
Li·ka·si Zaïrian city
like
like·li·hood (*or* ·ness)
like·ly (·li·er, ·li·est)
like-minded
like-minded·ly
like-minded·ness
lik·en
like·ness
like·wise
lik·ing
li·lac
lilia·ceous
lil·ied
Lilith biblical demon
Lille French city

limitless

Lil·li·pu·tian tiny person
lilly-pilly tree
Lilo (*Trademark*; *plural* Lilos)
Li·long·we Malawian capital
lilt
lilting
lily (*plural* lilies)
lily-livered
Lima Peruvian capital
lima bean
lima·cine of slugs
li·ma·çon maths term
Li·mas·sol Cypriot port
limb
lim·bate botany term
lim·ber
lim·bic anatomy term
limb·less
lim·bo (*plural* ·bos)
Lim·burg (*or* ·bourg) Belgian or Dutch province
Lim·burg·er cheese
lim·bus (*plural* ·bi) anatomy term
lime
lime·ade
lime·kiln
lime·light
li·men (*plural* ·mens *or* limi·na) psychology term
Lim·er·ick Irish port and county
lim·er·ick comic verse
li·mes (*plural* limi·tes) boundary of Roman empire
lime·stone
lime·water
lim·ey *US* Briton; *compare* limy
li·micu·line ornithology term
li·mico·lous living in mud
limi·nal psychology term
limi·ness
lim·it
lim·it·able
limi·tar·ian
limi·tary
limi·ta·tion
lim·it·ed
lim·it·er
lim·it·less

limitlessly

lim·it·less·ly
lim·it·less·ness
limi·trophe near a frontier
limn to draw
lim·ner
lim·net·ic ecology term
lim·no·logi·cal (*or* **·log·ic**)
lim·nolo·gist
lim·nol·ogy study of lakes
Lím·nos *variant spelling of* **Lemnos**
Li·moges French city
limo·nene chemical compound
li·mo·nite mineral
Li·mou·sin French region
lim·ou·sine car
limp
limp·er
lim·pet
lim·pid
lim·pid·ity (*or* **·ness**)
limp·ing·ly
limp·kin bird
limp·ness
Lim·po·po African river
limu·lus (*plural* **·li**) crab
limy (**limi·er**, **limi·est**) of lime; *compare* **limey**
lin·able (*or* **line·**)
lin·age (*or* **line·**) number of lines; *compare* **lineage**
lin·alo·ol (*or* **·alol**)
linch·pin pin for wheel; *compare* **lynch**
Lin·coln
Lin·coln·shire
lin·crus·ta embossed wallpaper
linc·tus (*plural* **·tuses**)
lin·dane pesticide
lin·den
Lin·dis·farne
line (**lin·ing**, **lined**)
lin·eage descent from ancestor; *variant spelling of* **linage**
lin·eal
lin·eal·ly directly; *compare* **linearly**
linea·ment facial feature; *compare* **liniment**
linea·men·tal
lin·ear
lin·ear·ity

lin·ear·ly in a line; *compare* **lineally**
lin·eate (*or* **·eat·ed**)
lin·ea·tion
line·caster
line·engrav·er
line·engrav·ing
line·man (*plural* **·men**) US footballer; rail worker; *compare* **linesman**
lin·en fabric; *compare* **linin**
lineo·late (*or* **·lat·ed**)
line·out
lin·er
lines·man (*plural* **·men**) sporting official; rail worker; *compare* **lineman**
line·up (*noun*)
ling heather
ling (*plural* **ling** *or* **lings**) fish
ling·cod (*plural* **·cod** *or* **·cods**) fish
lin·ger
lin·ger·er
lin·gerie
lin·ger·ing·ly
lin·go (*plural* **·goes**)
lin·gua (*plural* **·guae**) the tongue
lin·gua fran·ca (*plural* **lin·gua fran·cas** *or* **lin·guae fran·cae**) common language
lin·gual
lin·gual·ly
lin·gui·form
lin·gui·ni pasta
lin·guist
lin·guis·tic
lin·guis·ti·cal·ly
lin·guis·tics
lin·gu·late (*or* **·lat·ed**)
lin·hay *Dialect* farm building
lini·ment topical medicine; *compare* **lineament**
li·nin biology term; *compare* **linen**
lin·ing
link
link·able
link·age
link·boy torch carrier
link·man (*plural* **·men**) broadcaster
Lin·kö·ping Swedish city

264

link·up (*noun*)
link·work
Lin·lith·gow Scottish town
linn *Scot* waterfall
Lin·nean (*or* **·naean**) of Linnaeus; *note* **Linnean Society**
lin·net
Lin·nhe Scottish loch
lino (*plural* **linos**)
li·no·cut
li·no·leate
li·no·leum
Li·no·type (*Trademark*)
Li·no·typ·er (*or* **·ist**)
lin·sang animal
lin·seed
linsey-woolsey fabric
lin·stock
lint
lin·tel
lin·telled (*US* **·teled**)
lint·er
lint·white *Scot* linnet
linty
Linz Austrian port
lion
li·on·ess
lion·fish (*plural* **·fish** *or* **·fishes**)
lion-hearted
li·oni·za·tion (*or* **·sa·tion**)
li·on·ize·r (*or* **·ise**)
li·on·iz·er (*or* **·is·er**)
lip (**lip·ping**, **lipped**)
li·pase enzyme
Li·petsk Soviet city
li·pid
lip·oid fatty
lip·oi·dal
li·poly·sis
lipo·lyt·ic
li·po·ma (*plural* **·mas** *or* **·mata**) tumour
li·poma·tous
lipo·phil·ic (*or* **lipo·trop·ic**) chemistry term
lipo·pro·tein
Lip·pe German river
Lip·pi·zan·er horse
lip·py (**·pi·er**, **·pi·est**) *US* insolent
lip-read (**-reading**, **-read**)
lip-reader

lip·stick
li·quate separate by melting
li·qua·tion
liq·ue·fa·cient
liq·ue·fac·tion (*or* ·ui·)
liq·ue·fac·tive (*or* ·ui·)
liq·ue·fi·able (*or* ·ui·)
liq·ue·fi·er (*or* ·ui·)
liq·ue·fy (*or* ·ui·; ·fies, ·fy·ing, ·fied)
li·quesce
li·ques·cence (*or* ·cen·cy)
li·ques·cent
li·queur
liq·uid
liq·uid·am·bar balsam
liq·ui·date
liq·ui·da·tion
liq·ui·da·tor
li·quid·ity
liq·uid·ize (*or* ·ise)
liq·uid·iz·er (*or* ·is·er)
liq·ui·fy variant spelling of liquefy
liq·uor
liquo·rice (*US* lico·) confectionery; *compare* lickerish
lira (*plural* lire *or* liras)
lirio·den·dron (*plural* ·drons *or* ·dra) tree
liri·pipe (*or* ·poop) tip of graduate's hood
Lis·bon
lisle
lisp
lis pen·dens legal term
lisp·er
lis·som (*or* ·some)
lis·som·ness (*or* ·some·)
list
list·able
list·ed
lis·tel architectural term
lis·ten
lis·ten·er
lis·ter plough
lis·teri·osis food poisoning
list·ing
list·less
list·less·ness
lit
lita·ny (*plural* ·nies)

li·tchi (*or* ·chee, ·chi, ly·chee; *plural* ·tchis, ·chees, ·chis, *or* ·chees)
li·ter *US spelling of* litre
lit·era·cy
lit·er·al of words or letters; *compare* littoral
lit·er·al·ism
lit·er·al·ist
lit·er·al·is·tic
lit·er·al·is·ti·cal·ly
lit·er·al·ly
lit·er·al·ness (*or* ·ity)
lit·er·ari·ly
lit·er·ari·ness
lit·er·ary
lit·er·ate
lit·era·ti scholarly people
lit·era·tim letter for letter
lit·era·tion
lit·era·tor *variant of* littérateur
lit·era·ture
lith·arge lead compound
lithe
lithe·ly
lithe·ness
lithe·some
lithia lithium compound
li·thia·sis medical term
lith·ic of stone
lith·ium
li·tho (*plural* ·thos) lithograph
litho·graph
li·thog·ra·pher
litho·graph·ic (*or* ·graphi·cal)
litho·graphi·cal·ly
li·thog·ra·phy
lith·oid (*or* li·thoi·dal)
litho·log·ic (*or* ·logi·cal)
litho·logi·cal·ly
li·thol·o·gist
li·thol·ogy study of rocks
litho·marge kaolin
litho·meteor
litho·phyte
litho·phyt·ic
litho·pone pigment
litho·sol soil
litho·sphere
litho·tom·ic (*or* ·tomi·cal)
li·thoto·mist

li·thoto·my (*plural* ·mies) removal of bladder stone
li·thot·rity (*plural* ·rities) crushing of bladder stone
Lithua·nia
Lithua·nian
liti·gable
liti·gant
liti·gate
liti·ga·tion
liti·ga·tor
li·ti·gious
lit·mus
li·to·tes (*plural* ·tes) understatement
li·tre (*US* ·ter)
lit·ter
lit·té·ra·teur (*or* lit·era·tor) professional writer
litter·bug
lit·tle
lit·to·ral of the shore; *compare* literal
li·tur·gi·cal (*or* ·gic)
li·tur·gi·cal·ly
li·tur·gics study of liturgies
lit·ur·gism
lit·ur·gist
lit·ur·gis·tic
lit·ur·gy (*plural* ·gies)
liv·abil·ity (*or* live·)
liv·able (*or* live·)
liv·able·ness (*or* live·)
live
live·able *variant spelling of* livable
live·li·hood
live·li·ness
live·long very long; entire; *compare* lifelong
live·ly (·li·er, ·li·est)
liv·en
liv·en·er
liv·er
liv·er·ied
liv·er·ish
liv·er·ish·ness
Liv·er·pool
Liv·er·pud·lian
liver·wort plant
liver·wurst sausage
liv·ery (*plural* ·eries)
liv·ery·man (*plural* ·men)
live·stock

livetrap

live·trap (·trap·ping, ·trapped)
live·ware computer workers
liv·id
liv·id·ly
liv·id·ness (or li·vid·ity)
liv·ing
Li·vo·nia former Russian province; US city
Li·vo·nian
Li·vor·no Italian port
lix·ivi·ate chemistry term
lix·ivia·tion
lix·iv·ium (plural ·iums or ·ivia) alkaline solution
liz·ard
Lju·blja·na Yugoslav city
lla·ma animal; compare lama
Llan·daff Cardiff suburb
Llan·dud·no Welsh town
Llan·elli (or ·elly) Welsh town
lla·no (plural ·nos) grassland
Lla·no Es·ta·ca·do Texan region
Lloyd's underwriters
lo exclamation
loach
load burden, etc.; compare lode
load·ed
load·er
load·ing
load·star variant spelling of lodestar
load·stone variant spelling of lodestone
loaf (plural loaves)
loaf·er
loam
loami·ness
loamy (loami·er, loami·est)
loan
loan·able
loan·er
loath (or loth) reluctant
loathe to hate
loath·er
loath·ing
loath·ly
loath·some
loath·some·ness
loaves plural of loaf

lob (lob·bing, lobbed)
lo·bar
lo·bate (or ·bat·ed)
lobbed
lob·bing
lob·by (noun, plural ·bies; verb ·bies, ·by·ing, ·bied)
lob·by·er
lob·by·ism
lob·by·ist
lobe
lo·bec·to·my (plural ·mies)
lo·belia
lo·beline alkaloid
Lo·bi·to Angolan port
lob·lol·ly (plural ·lies) tree
lo·boto·my (plural ·mies)
lob·scouse sailor's stew
lob·ster (plural ·sters or ·ster)
lobu·lar (or ·late, ·lat·ed, ·lose)
lobu·la·tion
lob·ule
lo·cal
lo·cale (noun)
lo·cal·ism
lo·cal·ist
lo·cal·is·tic
lo·cal·ity (plural ·ities)
lo·cal·iz·able (or ·is·able)
lo·cali·za·tion (or ·sa·tion)
lo·cal·ize (or ·ise)
lo·cal·iz·er (or ·is·er)
lo·cal·ly
lo·cat·able
lo·cate
lo·cat·er
lo·ca·tion
loca·tive
loch
lochia vaginal discharge
loch·ial
loci plural of locus
lock
lock·able
lock·age canal locks
lock·er
lock·et
lock·jaw
lock·nut
lock·out (noun)
lock·smith

lock·smithery (or ·smithing)
lock·up (noun)
loco (plural locos) Slang locomotive; US insane
lo·co·ism cattle disease
lo·co·man (plural ·men) engine driver
lo·co·mo·tion
lo·co·mo·tive
lo·co·mo·tor of locomotion
lo·co·weed
locu·lar (or ·late) biology term
locu·la·tion
loc·ule (or locu·lus; plural ·ules or ·li) biology term
lo·cum short for locum tenens
lo·cum te·nens (plural lo·cum te·nen·tes) professional stand-in
lo·cus (plural loci)
lo·cust
lo·cu·tion
Łód Israeli town
lode ore deposit; compare load
lo·den wool
lode·star (or load·)
lode·stone (or load·)
lodge
lodge·able
lodg·er
lodg·ing
lodg·ings
lodg·ment (or lodge·)
lodi·cule botany term
Łódź Polish city
lo·ess soil
lo·ess·ial (or ·al)
Lo·fo·ten Is·lands
loft
loft·er golf club
lofti·ly
lofti·ness
lofty (lofti·er, lofti·est)
log (log·ging, logged)
Lo·gan Canadian mountain
logan·berry (plural ·berries)
lo·ga·nia·ceous botany term
loga·oedic verse form

loga·rithm
loga·rith·mic (*or* **·mi·cal**)
loga·rith·mi·cal·ly
log·book
loge theatre box
logged
log·ger
log·ger·head
log·gia (*plural* **·gias** *or* **·gie**) roofed gallery; *compare* **logia**
log·ging
logia *plural of* **logion**; *compare* **loggia**
log·ic
logi·cal
logi·cal·ity (*or* **·ness**)
logi·cal·ly
lo·gi·cian
logi·cism
logi·on (*plural* **logia**) saying of Christ
lo·gis·tic
lo·gis·ti·cal
lo·gis·ti·cal·ly
log·is·ti·cian
lo·gis·tics
log·log maths term
logo (*plural* **logos**)
logo·gram (*or* **·graph**)
logo·gram·mat·ic (*or* **·graph·ic**, **·graphi·cal**)
logo·gram·mati·cal·ly (*or* **·graphi·cal·ly**)
lo·gog·ra·pher
lo·gog·ra·phy
logo·griph word puzzle
logo·griph·ic
lo·goma·chist
lo·goma·chy (*plural* **·chies**) word argument
logo·paedic (*US* **·pedic**)
logo·paedics (*US* **·pedics**) speech therapy
log·or·rhoea (*US* **·rhea**) talkativeness
Log·os second person of Trinity
log·os reason
logo·type printing term
lo·go·typy
log·wood
logy (**logi·er**, **logi·est**) *US* dull or listless

Lohengrin legendary character
loin
loin·cloth
Loire French river
Loire-Atlantique French department
Loi·ret French department
Loir-et-Cher French department
loi·ter
loi·ter·er
loi·ter·ing·ly
Loki Norse god
loll
Lol·lard
Lol·lardy (*or* **·lard·ry**, **·lard·ism**)
loll·er
loll·ing·ly
lol·li·pop
lol·lop
lol·ly (*plural* **·lies**)
Lom·bard
Lom·bar·dic
Lom·bardy
Lom·bok Indonesian island
Lomé capital of Togo
lo·ment (*or* **·men·tum**; *plural* **·ments** *or* **·men·ta**) plant pod
lo·men·ta·ceous
Lo·mond Scottish lake
Lon·don
Lon·don·der·ry
Lon·don·er
Lon·dri·na Brazilian city
lone
lone·li·ness
lone·ly (**·li·er**, **·li·est**)
lone·ness
lon·er
lone·some
lone·some·ly
lone·some·ness
long
lon·gan fruit
lon·ga·nim·ity patience
lon·gani·mous
long·boat
long·bow
long·cloth
long-distance (*adj*)
long-drawn-out
lon·geron part of aircraft

looniness

lon·gev·ity
lon·gevous
Long·ford Irish county
long-haired
long·hand
long-headed shrewd
long·horn cattle
lon·gi·corn beetle
long·ing
long·ing·ly
long·ish
lon·gi·tude
lon·gi·tu·di·nal
lon·gi·tu·di·nal·ly
long johns underpants
long-lived
long-range (*adj*)
long·ship
long·shore
long·shore·man (*plural* **·men**)
long-sighted
long-sighted·ly
long-sighted·ness
long·spur bird
long-standing
long-suffer·ance
long-suffer·ing
long-term
long·time (*adj*)
Lon·gueuil Canadian city
lon·gueur *French* boredom
long·ways (*US* **·wise**)
long-winded
long-winded·ly
long-winded·ness
Long·year·byen Norwegian village
lo·nic·era honeysuckle
loo (*plural* **loos**)
loo·by (*plural* **·bies**) fool
loo·fah (*US also* **·fa**, **luf·fa**)
look
look·alike
look·er
looker-on (*plural* **lookers-**)
look-in (*noun*)
look·out
loom
loom-state undyed
loon
looni·ness

loony

loony (*or* looney; *adj* looni·er, looni·est; *noun, plural* loonies)
loop
loop·er caterpillar
loop·hole
loopi·ness
loopy (loopi·er, loopi·est)
loose
loose·box
loose-jointed
loose-leaf (*adj*)
loose·ly
loos·en
loos·en·er
loose·ness
loose·strife plant
loose-tongued
loos·ish
loot
loot·er
lop (lop·ping, lopped)
lope
lop-eared
lop·er
lo·pho·branch fish
lopho·bran·chi·ate
lo·pho·phor·ate
lo·pho·phore zoology term
lop·ing
lopped
lop·per
lop·ping
lop·sided
lop·sided·ly
lop·sided·ness
lo·qua·cious
lo·quac·ity (*or* lo·qua·cious·ness)
lo·quat fruit
lo·qui·tur *Latin* he or she speaks
lor exclamation
lo·ran navigation system
Lord God
lord nobleman
lord·li·ness
lord·ling
lord·ly (·li·er, ·li·est)
lor·do·sis spinal curvature
lor·dot·ic
lord·ship
lordy exclamation
lore knowledge; zoology term; *compare* **law**

Lo·relei siren
lor·gnette
lor·gnon
lo·ri·ca (*plural* ·cae) shell
lori·cate (*or* ·cat·ed)
lori·keet parrot
lori·mer (*or* ·ner) metalworker
lo·ris (*plural* ·ris) animal
lorn forsaken
Lor·raine
lor·ry (*plural* ·ries) vehicle
lory (*plural* lories) parrot
los·able
Los An·ge·les
lose (los·ing, lost)
lo·sel *Dialect* worthless person
los·er
los·ing
loss
los·sy dissipating energy
lost
lot (lot·ting, lot·ted)
lota (*or* lo·tah) water container
Lot-et-Garonne French department
loth *variant spelling of* loath
Lo·thario (*plural* ·tharios) libertine
Lo·thian Scottish region
lo·tic ecology term
lo·tion
lot·ted
lot·tery (*plural* ·teries)
lot·ting
lot·to
lo·tus (*or* lo·tos)
lotus-eater
louche shifty
loud
loud·en
loud-hailer
loud·ish
loud·ly
loud·mouth
loud·ness
loud·speaker
lough
Lough·bor·ough Leicestershire town
lou·is (*or* lou·is d'or; *plural* lou·is *or* lou·is d'or) coin

268

Lou·is·burg (*or* ·bourg) Canadian fortress
Loui·si·ana
Lou·is·ville US port
lounge
loung·er
loupe magnifying glass
lour (*or* low·er) look menacing
Lourdes French town
lour·ing·ly (*or* low·er·)
louse (*plural* lice)
louse·wort
lousi·ly
lousi·ness
lousy (lousi·er, lousi·est)
lout
Louth Irish county
lout·ish
lout·ish·ly
lout·ish·ness
Lou·vain Belgian town
lou·var fish
Lou·vre French museum
lou·vre (*US* ·ver) slat
lou·vred (*US* ·vered)
lov·abil·ity (*or* love·)
lov·able (*or* love·)
lov·ably (*or* love·)
lov·age plant
lov·at fabric
love
love·bird
love·less
love·li·ness
love·lock
love·lorn
love·ly (*adj* ·li·er, ·li·est; *noun, plural* ·lies)
love·making
lov·er
love·sick
love·sick·ness
lov·ey
lovey-dovey
lov·ing
lov·ing·ly
lov·ing·ness
low
low·an bird
low·born (*or* ·bred)
low·boy US table with drawers
low·bred
low·brow

low·brow·ism
low-down (*noun*)
low-down (*adj*)
low·er less high; *variant spelling of* lour
low·er·able
low·er·ing·ly *variant spelling of* louringly
lower·most
low·est
Lowes·toft
low-key (*or* -keyed)
Low·land of Lowlands
low·land flat ground
Low·land·er
low·land·er
Low·lands Scottish region
low·li·ness
low·ly (·li·er, ·li·est)
low-minded
low·ness
low-pitched
low-rise (*adj*)
low-spirit·ed
lox smoked salmon
loxo·drom·ic (*or* ·dromi·cal)
loxo·dromi·cal·ly
loxo·drom·ics (*or* lox·od·ro·my) navigation technique
loy·al
loy·al·ism
Loy·al·ist Northern Irish Protestant
loy·al·ist
loy·al·ly
loy·al·ty (*plural* ·ties)
Lo·yang Chinese city
loz·enge
loz·engy heraldic term
Lo·zère French department
Lozi Zambian language
Lu·an·da Angolan capital
Luba (*plural* Luba) African people
lub·ber clumsy person
Lub·bock Texan city
Lü·beck West German port
Lu·blin Polish city
lub·ri·cant
lu·bri·cate
lu·bri·ca·tion
lu·bri·ca·tion·al
lu·bri·ca·tive

lu·bri·ca·tor
lu·bric·ity lewdness
lu·bri·cous (*or* ·cious)
Lu·bum·ba·shi Zaïrian city
lu·carne dormer window
lu·cen·cy
lu·cent
Lu·cerne Swiss town
lu·cerne plant
lu·cid
lu·cid·ity (*or* ·cid·ness)
Lu·ci·fer
lu·cif·er·in biochemical compound
Lucina Roman goddess
luck
lucki·ly
lucki·ness
luck·less
luck·less·ness
Luck·now Indian city
lucky (lucki·er, lucki·est)
luc·ra·tive
lu·cra·tive·ly
lu·cre
lu·cu·brate to study
lu·cu·bra·tion
lu·cu·bra·tor
Lud·dite
Lu·dhi·a·na Indian city
lu·di·crous
Lud·low Shropshire town
ludo
Lud·wigs·ha·fen West German city
luff nautical term
luf·fa *US variant spelling of* loofah
Luft·waf·fe German Air Force
lug (lug·ging, lugged)
Lu·gan·da African language
luge toboggan
Lu·ger (*Trademark*)
lug·gage
lugged
lug·ger
lug·ging
lug·sail
lu·gu·bri·ous
lug·worm
luke·warm
lull

lulla·by (*noun, plural* ·bies; *verb* ·bies, ·by·ing, ·bied)
lull·ing·ly
lulu *US* wonderful person or thing
lum·ba·go
lum·bar of loin
lum·ber timber; move awkwardly
lum·ber·er
lum·ber·ing
lum·ber·ing·ly
lumber·jack
lumber·jacket
lumber·yard
lum·bri·cal
lum·bri·ca·lis muscle
lum·bri·coid wormlike
lu·men (*plural* ·mens) unit
lu·men (*plural* ·mina) anatomical duct
lu·men·al (*or* ·min·)
lu·mi·nance
lu·mi·nary (*plural* ·naries)
lu·mi·nesce
lu·mi·nes·cence
lu·mi·nes·cent
lu·mi·nos·ity (*plural* ·ities)
lu·mi·nous
lu·mi·nous·ly
lu·mis·te·rol biochemical compound
lum·me exclamation
lum·mox clumsy person
lump
lump·en stupid
lum·pen·pro·le·tari·at
lum·per *US* stevedore
lump·fish (*plural* ·fish *or* ·fishes)
lumpi·ly
lumpi·ness
lump·ish
lumpy (lumpi·er, lumpi·est)
Luna Roman goddess
luna moth; *compare* lunar
lu·na·cy (*plural* ·cies)
lu·nar of the moon; *compare* luna
lu·nate (*or* ·nat·ed)
lu·na·tic (*or* lu·nati·cal)
lu·na·tion lunar month

lunch

lunch
lunch·eon
lunch·eon·ette *US* café
lunch·er
Lund Swedish city
Lun·dy island
lune maths term
Lü·ne·burg West German city
lu·nette
lung
lunge
lung·er
lung·fish (*plural* ·fish *or* ·fishes)
lung·ful
lun·gi (*or* ·gee) Indian cloth
lung·worm
lung·wort plant
lu·ni·so·lar
lu·ni·tid·al
lu·nu·la (*or* ·nule; *plural* ·lae *or* ·nules)
lu·nu·late (*or* ·lat·ed)
luny (*adj* luni·er, luni·est; *noun, plural* lunies)
Lu·per·ca·lia (*plural* ·lia *or* ·lias) Roman festival
lu·pin (*US* ·pine) plant
lu·pine wolflike; *US spelling of* lupin
lu·pu·lin sedative
Lu·pus constellation
lu·pus skin disease
lur (*or* lure; *plural* lures) musical horn
lurch
lurch·er
lurch·ing·ly
lur·dan stupid
lure
lur·er
Lu·rex (*Trademark*)
lu·rid
lu·rid·ness
lur·ing·ly
lurk
lurk·er
lurk·ing·ly
Lu·sa·ka Zambian capital
Lu·sa·tia East German region
Lu·sa·tian
lus·cious

lus·cious·ness
lush
lush·ly
lush·ness
Lü·shun Chinese port
Lu·si·ta·nia ship
lust
lus·ter *US spelling of* lustre
lust·ful
lust·ful·ly
lust·ful·ness
lusti·ly
lusti·ness
lus·tral
lus·trate purify
lus·tra·tion
lus·tra·tive
lus·tre (*US* ·ter)
lus·tre·less (*US* ·ter·)
lustre·ware (*US* luster·)
lus·trous
lus·trum (*plural* ·trums *or* ·tra) five years
lusty (lusti·er, lusti·est)
lute
lu·teal biology term
lu·tein·iz·ing hor·mone
lu·tenist lute player
lu·teo·lin plant compound
lu·teous greenish-yellow
Lu·tetia *Latin* Paris
lu·tetium (*or* ·tecium) chemical element
Lu·ther·an
Lu·ther·an·ism
Lu·ther·ism
lu·thern dormer window
Lu·tine bell
Lu·ton
lux (*plural* lux) unit
lux·ate dislocate
luxa·tion
Lux·em·bourg
Lux·or Egyptian town
lux·ulia·nite (*or* ·ul·lia·nite) granite
luxu·ri·ance
luxu·ri·ant
luxu·ri·ate
luxu·ria·tion
luxu·ri·ous
luxu·ry (*plural* ·ries)
Lu·zon Philippine island
Ly·all·pur Pakistani city
ly·can·thrope werewolf

270

ly·can·thro·py
ly·cée (*plural* ·cées) French school
Ly·ceum Athenian school
ly·ceum public building
ly·chee *variant spelling of* litchi
lych gate *variant spelling of* lich gate
lych·nis plant
ly·co·pod club moss
ly·co·po·dium type of club moss
lydd·ite explosive
Lydia ancient Asian region
Lyd·ian
lye alkaline solution; *compare* lie
ly·ing
lying-in (*plural* lyings-in)
lyke-wake vigil over corpse
Lyme Re·gis
Lym·ing·ton Hampshire town
lymph
lym·phad·eni·tis
lym·phan·gial
lym·phan·git·ic
lym·phan·gi·tis (*plural* ·gi·des)
lym·phat·ic
lym·phati·cal·ly
lym·pho·blast blood cell
lym·pho·blas·tic
lym·pho·cyte blood cell
lym·pho·cyt·ic
lym·pho·cy·to·sis
lym·pho·cy·tot·ic
lym·phoid
lym·pho·ma (*plural* ·ma·ta *or* ·mas) tumour
lym·pho·ma·toid
lym·pho·poi·esis (*plural* ·eses)
lym·pho·poi·et·ic
lyn·cean resembling a lynx
lynch kill; *compare* linchpin
lynch·er
lynch·ing
lynx (*plural* lynxes *or* lynx)
Lyon French city
Lyon·nais former French province
ly·on·naise cookery term

Ly·on·nesse legendary place
lyo·phil·ic
ly·ophi·lize (*or* ·lise) freeze-dry
lyo·pho·bic
Lyra constellation
ly·rate (*or* rat·ed)
lyre
lyre·bird
lyr·ic
lyri·cal
lyri·cal·ly
lyri·cism
lyri·cist
lyr·ist
lyse biology term
ly·ser·gic acid
ly·sim·eter
ly·sin substance that destroys cells
ly·sine amino acid
ly·sis (*plural* ·ses) biology term
Ly·sol (*Trademark*)
ly·so·so·mal
ly·so·some cell particle
ly·so·zyme enzyme
Lyth·am St. Anne's
lyth·ra·ceous botany term
lyt·ic biology term
lyt·ta (*plural* ·tas *or* ·tae) zoology term

M

ma *Slang* mother
Ma'am title of address for royalty
maar (*plural* maars *or* maare) volcanic crater
Maas·tricht (*or* Maes·) Dutch city
Mab fairy queen
ma·bela ground corn
mac
ma·ca·bre
ma·ca·co (*plural* ·cos) lemur; *compare* macaque
mac·ad·am road surface
maca·da·mia tree
mac·ad·ami·za·tion (*or* ·sa·tion)
mac·ad·am·ize (*or* ·ise)
mac·ad·am·iz·er (*or* ·is·er)
Ma·cao Chinese city
ma·caque monkey; *compare* macaco
maca·ro·ni (*plural* ·nis) pasta
maca·ro·ni (*plural* ·nies) dandy
maca·ron·ic type of verse
maca·roni·cal·ly
maca·roon
Ma·cas·sar *variant spelling of* Makassar
ma·caw
Mac·ca·bean
Mac·ca·bees Apocryphal book
mac·ca·boy (*or* ·co·boy, ·ca·baw) snuff
Mac·cles·field
mace
mace·bearer
ma·cedoine diced vegetables
Mac·edon (*or* ·edo·nia) former kingdom
Mac·edo·nia Yugoslav republic; division of Greece
Mac·edo·nian
Ma·ceió Brazilian port
mac·er macebearer
mac·er·ate
mac·er·at·er (*or* ·era·tor)
mac·era·tion
mac·era·tive
ma·chan tiger-hunting platform
ma·chete
Machia·vel·lian (*or* ·vel·ian)
ma·chico·late fortifications term
ma·chico·la·tion
ma·chin·abil·ity
ma·chin·able (*or* ·chine·)
machi·nate
machi·na·tion
machi·na·tor
ma·chine
machine-gun (*verb*; -gunning, -gunned)
ma·chin·ery (*plural* ·eries)
ma·chin·ist
ma·chis·mo
Mach·meter physics term
Mach num·ber physics term
macho
ma·chree *Irish* my dear
Ma·chu Pic·chu Incan city
Ma·cí·as Ngue·ma Guinean island
Mac·kay Australian port
Mac·ken·zie Canadian district or river
macke·rel (*plural* ·rel *or* ·rels)
Macki·naw coat
mack·in·tosh (*or* mac·in·)
mack·le (*or* mac·ule) printing term; *compare* macle
Maclaurin's se·ries maths term
ma·cle mineral; *compare* mackle
Mâ·con French city; wine
mac·ra·mé
mac·ren·cepha·ly (*or* ·lia) abnormally large brain
macro·bi·ot·ic
macro·cephal·ic (*or* mega·, mega·lo·)
macro·cepha·ly (*or* mega·, mega·lo·) abnormally large head
macro·cli·mate
macro·cli·mat·ic
macro·cli·mati·cal·ly
macro·cosm
macro·cos·mic
macro·cos·mi·cal·ly
macro·cyst

macrocyte

macro·cyte blood cell
macro·cyt·ic
macro·cy·to·sis
macro·eco·nom·ic
macro·eco·nom·ics
macro·evo·lu·tion
macro·evo·lu·tion·ary
macro·gam·ete (*or* mega·)
macro·graph
macro·graph·ic
macro·mo·lec·u·lar
macro·mol·ecule
mac·ron phonetic symbol
macro·nu·cleus (*plural* ·clei)
macro·nu·tri·ent
macro·phage cell
macro·phag·ic
macro·phys·ics
mac·rop·ter·ous having large wings
macro·scop·ic (*or* ·scopi·cal)
macro·scopi·cal·ly
macro·spo·ran·gium (*plural* ·gia) botany term
macro·spore
ma·cru·ral (*or* ·roid, ·rous)
ma·cru·ran crustacean
macu·la (*or* mac·ule; *plural* ·lae *or* ·ules) anatomy term
macu·la lu·tea (*plural* macu·lae lu·teae) spot on retina
macu·lar
macu·la·tion
mac·ule variant of mackle *or* macula
mad (mad·der, mad·dest)
Mada·gas·can
Mada·gas·car
mad·am term of address; conceited girl; brothel keeper
mad·ame (*plural* mes·dames) *French* lady; Mrs
mad·cap
mad·den
mad·den·ing
mad·der plant; dye; more mad
mad·dest

mad·ding *Archaic* mad or maddening
made
Ma·dei·ra
mad·eleine cake
mad·emoi·selle (*plural* mes·de·moi·selles)
mad·house
Madh·ya Pra·desh Indian state
Madi·son US city and avenue
mad·ly
mad·man (*plural* ·men)
mad·ness
Ma·don·na Virgin Mary
Ma·dras Indian port
mad·ras fabric
mad·re·por·al (*or* ·por·ic, ·por·it·ic, ·po·rian)
mad·re·pore coral
Ma·drid
mad·ri·gal
mad·ri·gal·esque
mad·ri·gal·ian
mad·ri·gal·ist
mad·ri·lène consommé
ma·dro·ña (*or* ·ño, ·ne; *plural* ·ñas, ·ños, *or* ·nes) tree
Ma·du·ra Indonesian island
Ma·du·rai Indian city
Ma·du·rese of Madura
ma·du·ro cigar
mad·woman (*plural* ·women)
mad·wort plant
Ma·eba·shi Japanese city
Mael·strom Norwegian whirlpool
mael·strom whirlpool; confusion
mae·nad (*or* me·nad)
mae·nad·ic
maes·to·so musical term
maes·tro (*plural* ·tros *or* ·tri)
Maf·eking South African town
Ma·fia (*or* Maf·fia)
ma·fio·so (*plural* ·sos *or* ·si)
mag
maga·zine
mag·da·len reformed prostitute

Mag·da·lena Colombian river
Mag·da·lenian Palaeolithic culture
Mag·de·burg East German City
Ma·gel·lan strait
ma·gen·ta
mag·got fly larva; *compare* magot
mag·goti·ness
mag·goty
Ma·ghreb (*or* ·ghrib)
Ma·ghre·bi (*or* ·ghri·)
Magi (*sing.* Magus) biblical wise men
magi *plural of* magus
ma·gian
mag·ic (·ick·ing, ·icked)
magi·cal
magi·cal·ly
ma·gi·cian
ma·gilp variant spelling of megilp
Ma·gi·not line
mag·is·te·rial
mag·is·te·rial·ly
mag·is·tery (*plural* ·teries) alchemical substance
mag·is·tra·cy (*or* ·ture; *plural* ·cies *or* ·tures)
mag·is·tral pharmacology term
mag·is·tral·ly (*or* mag·is·trati·cal·ly)
mag·is·trate
mag·is·trate·ship
mag·is·tra·ture variant of magistracy
Mag·le·mo·sian (*or* ·sean) Mesolithic culture
mag·ma (*plural* ·mas *or* ·ma·ta) molten rock
mag·mat·ic
mag·ma·tism
Mag·na Car·ta (*or* Char·ta)
mag·na·nim·ity (*plural* ·ities)
mag·nani·mous
mag·nani·mous·ness
mag·nate
mag·ne·sia magnesium oxide

mag·ne·sian (*or* ·ne·sic, ·ne·sial)
mag·ne·site mineral
mag·ne·sium
mag·net
mag·net·ic
mag·neti·cal·ly
mag·net·ics
mag·net·ism
mag·net·ite mineral
mag·net·it·ic
mag·net·iz·able (*or* ·is·able)
mag·neti·za·tion (*or* ·sa·tion)
mag·net·ize (*or* ·ise)
mag·net·iz·er (*or* ·is·er)
mag·ne·to (*plural* ·tos)
mag·ne·to·chemi·cal
mag·ne·to·chem·is·try
mag·ne·to·elec·tric (*or* ·tri·cal)
mag·ne·to·elec·tric·ity
mag·ne·to·graph
mag·ne·to·hy·dro·dy·nam·ic
mag·ne·to·hy·dro·dy·nam·ics
mag·ne·tom·eter
mag·ne·to·met·ric
mag·ne·tom·etry
mag·ne·to·mo·tive
mag·ne·ton physics unit; *compare* magnetron
mag·ne·to·sphere
mag·ne·to·stric·tion
mag·ne·to·stric·tive
mag·ne·tron microwave generator; *compare* magneton
mag·ni·fi·able
Mag·nifi·cat canticle
mag·ni·fi·ca·tion
mag·nifi·cence
mag·nifi·cent
mag·nifi·co (*plural* ·coes) grandee
mag·ni·fi·er
mag·ni·fy (·fies, ·fy·ing, ·fied)
mag·nilo·quence
mag·nilo·quent
Mag·ni·to·gorsk Soviet city
mag·ni·tude
mag·ni·tu·di·nous
mag·no·lia

mag·no·lia·ceous
mag·num (*plural* ·nums) wine bottle
mag·num opus
mag·nus hitchknot
Magog biblical character
ma·got oriental figurine; *compare* maggot
mag·pie
mag·uey fibre
Magus (*sing. of* Magi)
magus (*plural* magi) Zoroastrian priest; sorcerer
Mag·yar Hungarian
Ma·ha·bha·ra·ta (*or* ·tam, ·tum) Indian poem
Ma·hal·la el Ku·bra Egyptian city
Ma·ha·na·di Indian river
ma·ha·ra·jah (*or* ·ja)
ma·ha·ra·ni (*or* ·nee) maharajah's wife
Ma·ha·rash·tra Indian state
ma·ha·ri·shi Hindu teacher
ma·hat·ma Brahman sage
Ma·ha·ya·na Buddhist school
Mahé Seychelles island
Ma·hi·can (*or* Mo·; *plural* ·cans *or* ·can) American Indian
mah·jong (*or* mah-jongg)
mahl·stick variant spelling *of* maulstick
ma·hoga·ny (*plural* ·nies)
Ma·hom·etan Muslim
ma·ho·nia shrub
ma·hout elephant keeper
Mah·rat·ta *variant spelling of* Maratha
mah·seer fish
Maia mythological character
maid
mai·dan meeting place
maid·en young girl
maiden·hair fern
Maid·en·head Berkshire town
maid·en·head virginity
maid·en·hood
maid·en·li·ness
maid·en·ly
maid·servant
Maid·stone Kent town

maieu·tic (*or* ·ti·cal) philosophy term
Mai·kop Soviet city
mail
mail·able
mail·bag
mail·box
mail·coach
mail·er
mail·sack
mail·shot
maim
maim·er
main
main·brace
Maine US state
Maine-et-Loire French department
Main·land Scottish island
main·land
main·line (*adj, verb*)
main·ly
main·mast
main·sail
main·sheet
main·spring
main·stay
main·stream
main·tain
main·tain·able
main·tain·er
main·te·nance
main·top
main-topmast
main·top·sail
Mainz West German port
ma·ioli·ca *variant spelling of* majolica
mai·son·ette (*or* ·son nette)
maî·tre d'hô·tel (*plural* maî·tres d'hô·tel)
maize cereal; *compare* maze
ma·jes·tic (*or* ·ti·cal)
ma·jes·ti·cal·ly
Maj·es·ty (*plural* ·ties) title for royalty
maj·es·ty dignity
ma·joli·ca (*or* ·ioli·) pottery
ma·jor
Ma·jor·ca
major-domo (*plural* -domos)
ma·jor·ette

majority

ma·jor·ity (*plural* ·ities)
ma·jus·cu·lar
ma·jus·cule printing term
Ma·ka·lu Himalayan mountain range
Ma·kas·ar (*or* ·kas·sar, ·cas·sar) Indonesian port
make (mak·ing, made)
make-believe (*noun*)
make·fast
mak·er
make·shift
make-up (*noun*)
make·weight (*noun*)
Ma·ke·yev·ka Soviet city
Ma·khach·ka·la Soviet port
mak·ing
mako (*plural* makos) shark; tree
Ma·kur·di Nigerian port
Mala·bar Indian region
Ma·la·bo capital of Equatorial Guinea
mal·ab·sorp·tion
Ma·lac·ca Malaysian state
ma·lac·ca walking stick
mala·chite mineral
mala·co·logi·cal
mala·colo·gist
mala·col·ogy study of molluscs
mala·coph·yl·lous having fleshy leaves
mala·cop·te·ryg·ian fish
mala·cos·tra·can crustacean
mala·cos·tra·cous
mal·ad·dress awkwardness
mal·ad·just·ed
mal·ad·just·ment
mal·ad·min·is·ter
mal·ad·min·is·tra·tion
mal·ad·min·is·tra·tor
mala·droit
mala·droit·ness
mala·dy (*plural* ·dies)
mala fide *Latin* in bad faith
Má·la·ga Spanish port; wine
Mala·gasy Madagascan language
ma·la·gueña dance
ma·laise
mala·mute (*or* mal·emute) Eskimo dog

mal·an·ders (*or* mal·lan·, mal·len·) horse disease
Ma·lang Indonesian city
mala·pert saucy
mala·prop·ian
mala·prop·ism
mal·ap·ro·pos
ma·lar of the cheek
ma·laria
ma·lar·ial (*or* ·lar·ian, ·lari·ous)
ma·lar·key (*or* ·ky)
mal·as·simi·la·tion
mal·ate chemistry term
Mala·thi·on (*Trademark*)
Ma·la·tya Turkish city
Ma·la·wi
Ma·la·wian
Ma·lay
Ma·laya
Mala·ya·lam (*or* ·laam) language
Ma·lay·an
Ma·lay·sia
Ma·lay·sian
mal·con·tent
mal de mer *French* sea sickness
Mal·dives
Mal·div·ian (*or* ·di·van)
male
Malé capital of the Maldives
ma·leate chemistry term
mal·edict
mal·edic·tion
mal·edic·tive (*or* ·tory)
mal·efac·tion
mal·efac·tor (*fem* ·tress)
ma·lef·ic
ma·lefi·cence
ma·lefi·cent
ma·leic acid
male·ness
ma·levo·lence
ma·levo·lent
mal·fea·sance illegal act
mal·fea·sant
mal·for·ma·tion
mal·formed
mal·func·tion
mal·gré lui *French* in spite of himself
Mali African republic
Malian

274

mal·ic acid
mal·ice
ma·li·cious
ma·li·cious·ness
ma·lign
ma·lig·nan·cy (*plural* ·cies)
ma·lig·nant
ma·lign·er
ma·lig·nity (*plural* ·nities)
mal·im·print·ed
mal·im·print·ing
ma·lines fabric
ma·lin·ger
ma·lin·ger·er
Ma·lin·ke (*or* ·nin·ke; *plural* ·ke *or* ·kes) African people
mali·son curse
mall
mal·lam (*or* mal·am) Islamic scholar
mal·lard (*plural* ·lard *or* ·lards)
mal·le·abil·ity (*or* ·able·ness)
mal·le·able
mal·lee tree
mal·le·muck bird
mal·leo·lar
mal·leo·lus (*plural* ·li) ankle bone
mal·let
mal·le·us (*plural* ·lei) ear bone
mal·low
malm limestone
Malmö Swedish port
malm·sey wine
mal·nour·ished
mal·nu·tri·tion
mal·oc·clud·ed
mal·oc·clu·sion dentistry term
mal·odor·ous
ma·lo·nic acid
mal·pighia·ceous botany term
Mal·pigh·ian anatomy term
mal·posed
mal·po·si·tion
mal·prac·tice
mal·prac·ti·tion·er
malt
Mal·ta

malt·ase enzyme
malt·ed
Mal·tese (*plural* **·tese**)
mal·tha mineral tar
Mal·thu·sian
Mal·thu·si·an·ism population theory
malti·ness
malt·ing
malt·ose sugar
mal·treat
mal·treat·er
mal·treat·ment
malt·ster
malty (**malti·er, malti·est**)
mal·va·ceous botany term
mal·va·sia wine
Mal·vern
mal·voi·sie wine
mam *Slang* mother
mama (*or* **mam·ma**) mother; *compare* **mamma**
mam·ba snake
mam·bo (*plural* **·bos**) dance
mam·elon hillock
Mam·eluke (*or* **Mama·luke**) Egyptian ruler
ma·mey (*or* **mam·mee**) fruit; *compare* **mammy**
ma·mil·la (*US* **mam·mil·**; *plural* **·lae**) nipple
ma·mil·lary (*US* **mam·mil·**)
ma·mil·late (*or* **·lat·ed**; *US* **mam·mil·**)
mam·ma (*plural* **·mae**) breast; *compare* **mama**
mam·ma variant spelling of **mama**
mam·mal
mam·ma·lian
mam·ma·logi·cal
mam·malo·gist
mam·mal·ogy
mam·ma·ry
mam·mee variant spelling of **mamey**
mam·mif·er·ous
mam·mil·la *US* spelling of **mamilla**
mam·mock *Dialect* shred
mam·mo·gram
mam·mog·ra·phy
mam·mon

mam·mon·ism
mam·mon·ist (*or* **·ite**)
mam·mon·is·tic
mam·moth
mam·my (*or* **·mie**; *plural* **·mies**) mother; *compare* **mamey**
Man (Isle of)
man (*noun, plural* **men**; *verb* **man·ning, manned**)
mana power; *compare* **manna**
mana·cle
Ma·na·do variant spelling of **Menado**
man·age
man·age·abil·ity (*or* **·able·ness**)
man·age·able
man·age·ably
man·age·ment
man·ag·er
man·ag·er·ess
mana·gerial
mana·geri·al·ly
man·ag·ing
Ma·na·gua Nicaraguan capital
mana·kin bird; *compare* **manikin; mannequin**
Ma·na·ma capital of Bahrain
ma·ña·na *Spanish* tomorrow
Ma·nas·sas US town
man-at-arms (*plural* **men-**)
mana·tee sea mammal
mana·toid
Ma·naus (*or* **Ma·náos**) Brazilian port
Manche French department
Man·ches·ter
man·chi·neel tree
Man·chu (*plural* **·chus** *or* **·chu**) Chinese dynasty
Man·chu·ria
Man·chu·rian
man·ci·ple steward
Man·cu·nian native of Manchester
Man·daean
Man·dae·an·ism Iraqi sect
Man·da·lay Burmese city
man·da·mus (*plural* **·muses**) legal term

Man·da·rin language
man·da·rin official; fruit; duck
man·da·tary variant spelling of **mandatory** (*noun*)
man·date
man·da·to·ri·ly
man·da·tory obligatory
man·da·tory (*or* **·tary**; *plural* **·tories** *or* **·taries**) mandate holder
Man·de (*plural* **·de** *or* **·des**) language group
man·di Indian market
man·di·ble
man·dibu·lar
man·dir Hindu temple
man·do·la mandolin
man·do·lin (*or* **·line**)
man·do·lin·ist
man·dor·la art term
man·drake (*or* **man·drago·ra**)
man·drel (*or* **·dril**) spindle
man·drill monkey
man·du·cate eat or chew
mane
man-eater
maned
ma·nège (*or* **·nege**) riding school; *compare* **ménage**
ma·nes Roman deities
ma·neu·ver *US* spelling of **manoeuvre**
man·ful
man·ful·ly
man·ful·ness
man·ga·bey monkey
Man·ga·lore Indian port
man·ga·nate
man·ga·nese
man·gan·ic
Man·gan·in (*Trademark*)
man·ga·nite mineral
man·ga·nous
mange skin disease
man·gel-wur·zel (*or* **·gold-**)
man·ger
mange-tout pea
man·gi·ly
man·gi·ness
man·gle
man·gler

mango

man·go (*plural* ·goes *or* ·gos)
man·go·nel war engine
man·go·steen fruit
man·grove
man·gy (*or* ·gey; ·gi·er, ·gi·est)
man·handle
Man·hat·tan
man·hole
man·hood
man·hour
man·hunt
man·hunter
ma·nia
ma·ni·ac
ma·nia·cal
ma·nia·cal·ly
man·ic
manic-depres·sive
Mani·chae·ism (*or* ·che·) religion
Mani·chee
ma·ni·cot·ti stuffed noodles
mani·cure
mani·cur·ist
mani·fest
mani·fest·able
mani·fes·ta·tion
mani·fes·ta·tion·al
mani·fes·to (*plural* ·toes *or* ·tos)
mani·fold
mani·fold·er
mani·kin (*or* mana·kin, man·ni·kin) dwarf; *compare* manakin; mannequin
Ma·nila Philippine port
ma·nil·la African currency
ma·nille card trump
mani·oc (*or* manio·ca) plant
mani·ple
ma·nipu·labil·ity
ma·nipu·lar
ma·nipu·lat·able (*or* ·lable)
ma·nipu·late
ma·nipu·la·tion
ma·nipu·la·tive
ma·nipu·la·tor
ma·nipu·la·tory
Ma·ni·pur Indian region
Ma·ni·sa Turkish city

Mani·to·ba Canadian province
mani·tou (*or* ·tu; *plural* ·tous, tou, *or* ·tus, ·tu) American Indian spirit
Mani·tou·lin Canadian island
Mani·za·les Colombian city
man·kind
manky (manki·er, manki·est) *Scot* dirty
man·like
man·li·ness
man·ly (·li·er, ·li·est)
man-made
man·na celestial food; *compare* mana
manned
man·ne·quin model; *compare* manakin; manikin
man·ner
man·nered
man·ner·ism
man·ner·ist
man·ner·is·tic (*or* ·ti·cal)
man·ner·is·ti·cal·ly
man·ner·less
man·ner·less·ness
man·ner·li·ness
man·ner·ly
Mann·heim West German city
man·nish
man·nish·ness
man·nit·ic
man·ni·tol plant compound
man·nose sugar
ma·noeu·vrabil·ity (*US* ·neu·)
ma·noeu·vrable (*US* ·neu·)
ma·noeu·vre (*US* ·neu·ver)
ma·noeu·vrer (*US* ·neu·ver·er)
man-of-war (*plural* men-)
ma·nom·eter
mano·met·ric (*or* ·ri·cal)
mano·met·ri·cal·ly
ma·nom·etry
man·or
ma·no·rial
man·power
man·qué unfulfilled
man·rope ship railing

man·sard roof
manse
man·servant (*plural* men·servants)
Mans·field Nottinghamshire town
man·sion
man-sized
man·slaughter
man·sue·tude gentleness
man·ta fish; fabric
man·teau (*plural* ·teaus *or* ·teaux) cloak
man·tel (*or* ·tle) frame round fireplace; *compare* mantle
man·tel·et woman's mantle
man·tel·let·ta vestment
mantel·piece
mantel·shelf (*plural* ·shelves)
mantel·tree lintel over fireplace
man·tic of prophecy
man·ti·cal·ly
man·til·la Spanish scarf
man·tis (*plural* ·tises *or* ·tes)
man·tis·sa maths term
man·tle cloak; *compare* mantel
man·tling
man·tra Hindu psalm
man·trap
Man·tua Italian city
man·tua gown
manu·al
manu·al·ly
ma·nu·brial
ma·nu·brium (*plural* ·bria *or* ·briums) zoology term
manu·fac·tory (*plural* ·tories)
manu·fac·tur·able
manu·fac·tur·al
manu·fac·ture
manu·fac·tur·er
manu·fac·tur·ing
ma·nu·ka tree
Ma·nu·kau New Zealand city
manu·mis·sion
manu·mit (·mit·ting, ·mit·ted) free from slavery
ma·nure

ma·nur·er
ma·nus (*plural* **·nus**) hand
manu·script
Manx
Manx·man (*plural* **·men**)
many
many·plies cow's stomach
many-sided
many-sided·ness
man·za·nil·la sherry
Mao·ism
Mao·ist
Mao·ri (*plural* **·ris** *or* **·ri**)
map (**map·ping, mapped**)
ma·ple
map·pable
Ma·pu·to capital of Mozambique
ma·quette sculptor's model
Ma·quis French Resistance
ma·quis (*plural* **·quis**) shrubby vegetation
mar (**mar·ring, marred**)
mara rodent
mara·bou stork
mara·bout Muslim holy man
ma·ra·bun·ta wasp
ma·raca percussion instrument
Mara·cai·bo Venezuelan port and lake
Ma·ra·cay Venezuelan city
mar·ag·ing steel
Ma·ra·nhão Brazilian state
ma·ras·ca cherry tree
mara·schi·no (*plural* **·nos**) liqueur; cherry
ma·ras·mic
ma·ras·mus
Ma·ra·tha (*or* **Mah·rat·ta**) Indian people
Ma·ra·thi (*or* **Mah·rat·ti**)
Mara·thon Greek plain
mara·thon race
ma·raud
ma·raud·er
mara·vedi (*plural* **·vedis**) coin
mar·ble
mar·bled
mar·bler
mar·bling
mar·bly

Mar·burg West German city
marc brandy
mar·ca·site mineral
mar·ca·siti·cal
mar·cel (**·cel·ling, ·celled**) hair style
mar·ces·cence
mar·ces·cent botany term
March month; *compare* **Marche**
march
Marche former French province; *compare* **March**
march·er
Marches border country
mar·che·sa (*plural* **·se**) wife of marchese
mar·che·se (*plural* **·si**) Italian nobleman
mar·chion·ess wife of marquis or marquess
Mar del Pla·ta Argentine city
Mar·di Gras Shrove Tuesday
mardy *Dialect* spoilt or irritable
mare (*plural* **mares**) female horse
mare (*plural* **ma·ria**) lunar plain
mare clau·sum legal term
mare li·be·rum legal term
ma·rem·ma (*plural* **·me**) marsh
mare's-tail cloud; plant
marg (*or* **marge**) *short for* **margarine**
mar·gar·ic (*or* **·it·ic**) of pearl
mar·ga·rine (*or* **·rin**)
mar·ga·ri·ta cocktail
mar·ga·rite mineral, *compare* **marguerite**
Mar·gate
Mar·gaux wine
mar·gay animal
mar·gin
mar·gin·al
mar·gi·na·lia
mar·gin·al·ity
mar·gin·al·ly
mar·gin·ate
mar·gina·tion
mar·gra·vate

mar·grave German nobleman
mar·gra·vine wife of margrave
mar·gue·rite flower; *compare* **margarite**
mari·achi Mexican street musicians
Mar·ian of the Virgin Mary
Ma·ria·nao Cuban city
Ma·ri·bor Yugoslav city
mari·cul·ture
mari·gold
ma·ri·jua·na (*or* **·hua·**)
ma·rim·ba percussion instrument
ma·ri·na
mari·nade (*noun, verb*)
mari·nate (*verb*)
mari·na·tion
Ma·rin·du·que Philippine island
ma·rine
Mari·ner US space probe
mari·ner seaman
Mari·ola·try (*or* **Mary·**) veneration of Virgin Mary
Mari·ol·ogy (*or* **Mary·**)
mari·on·ette
mari·po·sa plant
Mar·ist member of Christian sect
mar·it·age feudal right
mari·tal
mari·time
Mari·time Alps; Provinces
Mari·tim·er
mar·jo·ram
mark
mark·down (*noun*)
marked
mark·ed·ly
mark·ed·ness
mark·er
mar·ket
mar·ket·abil·ity (*or* **·able·ness**)
mar·ket·able
mar·ket·ably
mar·ket·er
mar·ket·ing
market·place
mar·khor (*or* **·khoor**; *plural* **·khors, ·khor** *or* **·khoors, ·khoor**) goat

marking

mark·ing
mark·ka (*plural* ·kaa)
   Finnish currency
marks·man (*plural* ·men)
marks·man·ship
marks·woman (*plural*
   ·women)
mark-up (*noun*)
marl
mar·la·cious (*or* marly)
Marl·bor·ough
mar·lin (*plural* ·lin *or*
   ·lins) fish
mar·line (*or* ·lin, ·ling)
   nautical rope
mar·line·spike (*or* ·lin·,
   ·ling·)
mar·lite (*or* marl·stone)
marly
mar·ma·lade
Mar·ma·ra (*or* ·mo·)
   Turkish sea
Mar·mite (*Trademark*)
   food
mar·mite cooking pot
mar·mo·real (*or* ·rean) of
   marble
mar·mo·set
mar·mot animal
Marne French river
maro·cain fabric
Maro·nite Syrian Christian
ma·roon
ma·rooned
maro·quin leather
Marprelate tracts
marque brand of car
mar·quee
mar·quess British nobleman
mar·quess·ate
mar·que·try (*or*
   ·que·te·rie; *plural* ·tries
   or ·ries)
mar·quis (*plural* ·quises
   or ·quis) foreign
   nobleman
mar·quis·ate
mar·quise gemstone; wife of
   marquis
mar·qui·sette fabric
Mar·ra·kech (*or* ·kesh)
   Moroccan city
mar·ram grass
Mar·ra·no (*plural* ·nos)
   Iberian Jew
marred

mar·rer
mar·riage
mar·riage·abil·ity (*or*
   ·able·ness)
mar·riage·able
mar·ried
mar·ri·er
mar·ring
mar·ron chestnut
mar·ron gla·cé (*plural*
   mar·rons gla·cés) glazed
   chestnut
mar·row
marrow·bone
marrow·fat pea
mar·ry (·ries, ·ry·ing,
   ·ried)
Mars
Mar·sa·la Sicilian port;
   wine
Mar·seil·laise French
   national anthem
Mar·seille (*or* ·seilles)
   French port
mar·seille (*or* ·seilles)
   fabric
marsh
mar·shal (·shal·ling,
   ·shalled; *US* ·shal·ling,
   ·shaled)
mar·shal·cy (*or* ·shal·ship)
mar·shal·ler (*US* ·shal·er)
Mar·shal·sea former prison
marshi·ness
marsh·land
marsh·mal·low sweet
marsh mal·low plant
marshy (marshi·er,
   marshi·est)
mar·su·pial
mar·su·pia·lian (*or*
   ·su·pian)
mar·su·pium (*plural* ·pia)
   pouch
mart
mar·ta·gon lily
mar·tel·la·to (*or* ·lan·do)
   music term
Mar·tel·lo tower
mar·ten (*plural* ·tens *or*
   ·ten) mammal; *compare*
   martin
mar·ten·site metallurgy
   term
mar·ten·sit·ic
mar·tial

mar·tial·ism
mar·tial·ist
mar·tial·ly
Mar·tian
mar·tin bird; *compare*
   marten
mar·ti·net
mar·ti·net·ish
mar·ti·net·ism
mar·tin·gale
Mar·ti·ni (*Trademark*)
   vermouth
mar·ti·ni (*plural* ·nis)
   cocktail
Mar·ti·ni·can
Mar·ti·nique
Mar·tin·mas
mart·let heraldic swallow
mar·tyr
mar·tyr·dom
mar·tyr·ize (*or* ·ise)
mar·tyri·za·tion (*or*
   ·sa·tion)
mar·tyro·logi·cal (*or*
   ·log·ic)
mar·tyr·olo·gist
mar·tyr·ol·ogy (*plural*
   ·ogies)
mar·tyry (*plural* ·tyries)
   martyr's shrine
mar·vel (·vel·ling, ·velled;
   US ·vel·ing, ·veled)
mar·vel·lous (*US*
   ·vel·ous)
mar·vel·ment
Marx·ian
Marxi·an·ism
Marx·ism
Marxism-Leninism
Marx·ist
Marxist-Leninist
Mary·land
mar·zi·pan
Ma·sai (*plural* ·sais *or*
   ·sai) African people
Ma·san Korean port
Mas·ba·te Philippine island
mas·cara
mas·cle heraldic term
mas·con lunar region
mas·cot
mas·cu·line
mas·cu·lin·ity (*or*
   ·line·ness)

mas·cu·li·ni·za·tion (or
   ·sa·tion)
mas·cu·lin·ize (or ·ise)
ma·ser microwave laser;
   compare mazer
Ma·se·ru capital of Lesotho
mash
mash·er
Mash·had (or Me·shed)
   Iranian city
mashie (or mashy; plural
   mashies) golf club
mas·jid (or mus·) mosque
mask face covering, etc.;
   variant spelling of masque
mas·ka·nonge (or ·ki·)
   variants of muskellunge
masked
mask·er
maso·chism
maso·chist
maso·chis·tic
Ma·son freemason
ma·son stone worker
Mason-Dixon Line
Ma·son·ic
ma·son·ic
ma·soni·cal·ly
ma·son·ry (plural ·ries)
Ma·so·ra (or Ma·so·rah,
   Mas·so·ra, Mas·so·rah)
   Hebrew text
Maso·rete (or
   Mas·so·rete,
   Maso·rite) Hebrew
   scholar
masque (or mask)
   entertainment; compare
   mask
mas·quer (or mask·er)
mas·quer·ade
mas·quer·ad·er
Mass church service
mass
Mas·sa·chu·set (or ·setts;
   plural ·sets, ·set, or
   ·setts) American Indian
Mas·sa·chu·setts US state
mas·sa·cre
mas·sa·crer
mas·sage
mas·sag·er (or ·ist)
mas·sa·sau·ga snake
mas·sé billiards stroke
mass·edly
mas·se·ter muscle

mas·se·ter·ic
mas·seur (fem ·seuse)
mas·si·cot mineral
mas·sif landform; compare
   massive
Mas·sif Cen·tral French
   plateau
mas·sive huge; compare
   massif
mas·sive·ness (or ·siv·ity)
Mas·so·ra (or ·rah) variant
   spellings of Masora
mas·so·thera·peu·tic
mas·so·thera·pist
mas·so·thera·py massage
mass-produce
mass-produc·er
mass-pro·duc·tion
massy (massi·er,
   massi·est) massive
mast
mas·ta·ba (or ·bah)
   pyramid prototype
mas·tec·to·my (plural
   ·mies)
mas·ter
master-at-arms (plural
   masters-)
mas·ter·dom
mas·ter·ful
mas·ter·ful·ly
mas·ter·ful·ness
mas·ter·hood
mas·ter·li·ness
mas·ter·ly
master·mind
master·piece
mas·ter·ship
master·stroke
master·work
mas·tery (plural ·teries)
mast·head
mas·tic resin
mas·ti·cable chewable
mas·ti·cate
mas·ti·ca·tion
mas·ti·ca·tor
mas·ti·ca·tory (plural
   ·tories)
mas·tiff
mas·ti·gopho·ran (or
   ·go·phore) protozoan
mas·ti·tis breast
   inflammation
mas·to·don extinct elephant

mas·toid ear bone
mas·toid·ec·to·my (plural
   ·mies)
mas·toid·itis ear
   inflammation
mas·tur·bate
mas·tur·ba·tion
mas·tur·ba·tor
Ma·su·ria Polish region
Ma·su·rian
mat (mat·ting, mat·ted)
   floor covering; tangle;
   compare matte
mat (or matt, matte;
   mat·ting, mat·ted)
   lacking gloss; compare
   matte
Mata·be·le (plural ·les or
   ·le) African people
Mata·be·le·land
Ma·ta·di Zaïrian port
mata·dor
Mata·mo·ros Mexican port
Mata·pan Greek cape
match
match·board
match·box
match·less
match·less·ness
match·maker
match·mark
match·stick
match·wood
mate
maté (or mate) tea
matelas·sé embossed
mate·lot (or ·lo, ·low)
   Slang sailor
mat·elote (or ·elotte) fish
   stew
ma·ter Slang mother
ma·ter·fa·mili·as
ma·terial
ma·teri·al·ism
ma·teri·al·ist
ma·teri·al·is·tic
ma·teri·al·ity (plural
   ·ities)
ma·teri·ali·za·tion (or
   ·sa·tion)
ma·teri·al·ize (or ·ise)
ma·teri·al·iz·er (or ·is·er)
ma·teri·al·ly
ma·teria medi·ca study of
   drugs

materiel

ma·teri·el (*or* ·téri·) materials and equipment
ma·ter·nal
ma·ter·nal·ism
ma·ter·nal·is·tic
ma·ter·nal·ly
ma·ter·nity
matey (mati·er, mati·est)
matey·ness (*or* mati·ness)
math·emati·cal (*or* ·emat·ic)
math·emati·cal·ly
math·ema·ti·cian
math·emat·ics
Ma·thu·ra Indian city
mati·er
mati·est
Ma·til·da *Austral* bushman's swag
mat·in (*or* mat·tin, mat·in·al) of matins
mati·née
mati·ness *variant spelling of* mateyness
mat·ins (*or* mat·tins)
Mat·lock Derbyshire town
Mato Gros·so (*or* Mat·to Gros·so) Brazilian plateau
ma·tri·arch
ma·tri·ar·chal (*or* ·chic)
ma·tri·ar·chate
ma·tri·ar·chy (*plural* ·chies)
ma·tri·ces *plural of* matrix
mat·ri·cid·al
mat·ri·cide
mat·ri·cli·nous (*or* mat·ro·cli·nous, mat·ro·cli·nal) biology term
ma·tricu·lant
ma·tricu·late
ma·tricu·la·tion
ma·tricu·la·tor
mat·ri·lin·eal
mat·ri·lin·eal·ly
mat·ri·lo·cal living with wife's family
mat·ri·lo·cal·ity
mat·ri·mo·nial
mat·ri·mo·nial·ly
mat·ri·mo·ny (*plural* ·nies)
ma·trix (*plural* ·tri·ces)

mat·ro·cli·nous (*or* ·nal) variants *of* matriclinous
ma·tron
ma·tron·age
ma·tron·al
ma·tron·li·ness
ma·tron·ly
mat·ro·nym·ic *variant spelling of* metronymic
Ma·tsu·ya·ma Japanese port
matt *variant spelling of* mat
mat·ta·more subterranean storehouse
matte smelting material; *variant spelling of* mat
mat·ted
mat·ter
Mat·ter·horn
matter-of-fact (*adj*)
mat·ting
mat·tock agricultural tool
mat·tress
matu·rate
matu·ra·tion
matu·ra·tion·al
ma·tura·tive
ma·ture
ma·tur·ity
ma·tu·ti·nal of morning
(maty) *incorrect spelling of* matey
mat·zo (*or* ·zoh; *plural* ·zos, ·zohs, *or* ·zoth) Jewish biscuit
mat·zoon (*or* mad·) fermented milk
maud plaid shawl
maud·lin
maud·lin·ism
maud·lin·ness
maul
maul·er
maul·stick (*or* mahl·) artist's stick
Mau Mau (*plural* Mau Maus *or* Mau Mau) Kenyan terrorist
Mau·na Kea Hawaiian volcano
Mau·na Loa Hawaiian volcano
maund unit of weight
maun·der behave aimlessly
maun·der·er
Maun·dy money; Thursday

280

Mau·rist French monk
Mau·ri·ta·nia African republic
Mau·ri·ta·nian
Mau·ri·tian
Mau·ri·tius island state
Mau·ser (*Trademark*) gun
mau·so·lean
mau·so·leum (*plural* ·leums *or* ·lea)
mauve
mav·er·ick
ma·vis *Dialect* thrush
ma·vour·neen Irish term of endearment
maw
mawk·ish
mawk·ish·ness
maw·sie *Scot* jersey
maxi (*plural* maxis) long garment
max·il·la (*plural* ·lae) upper jaw
max·il·lar (*or* ·lary)
max·il·li·ped (*or* ·pede) zoology term
max·il·li·ped·ary
max·im
maxi·ma (*plural of* maximum)
maxi·mal
Maxi·mal·ist Soviet radical
maxi·mal·ist activist
maxi·mal·ly
maxi·min maths term
maxi·mi·za·tion (*or* ·sa·tion)
max·im·ize (*or* ·ise)
maxi·miz·er (*or* ·mis·er)
maxi·mum (*plural* ·mums *or* ·ma)
maxi·mus bell-ringing term
maxi·sin·gle
ma·xixe dance
max·well unit
May
may (might)
Maya (*plural* Maya *or* Mayas) American Indian
maya Hindu concept
Ma·yan
may·be (*adv*)
May·day signal
May Day 1 May

Ma·yenne French department
May·fair
May·flower ship
may·flower plant
may·fly (*plural* ·flies)
may·hem (*or* mai·)
May·ing May Day celebration
mayn't may not
Mayo Irish county
Ma·yon Philippine volcano
may·on·naise
mayor
mayor·al
mayor·al·ty (*plural* ·ties)
mayor·ess
mayor·ship
may·pole
may·weed
Ma·zat·lán Mexican port
Maz·da·ism (*or* Maz·deism) religion
maze confusing network; *compare* maize
ma·zer (*or* ·zard, maz·zard) bowl; *compare* maser
ma·zi·ly
ma·zi·ness
ma·zu·ma *US* money
ma·zur·ka (*or* ·zour·)
mazy (·zi·er, ·zi·est) perplexing
maz·zard (*or* ma·zard) *variants of* mazer
Mba·ba·ne capital of Swaziland
Mbu·ji·ma·yi Zaïrian city
McCar·thy·ism anticommunism
McCoy *Slang* genuine thing
McNaughten Rules (*or* McNaghten Rules)
me pronoun; *variant spelling of* mi
mea cul·pa *Latin* my fault
mead drink; *compare* meed
mead·ow
meadow·lark
meadow·sweet
mea·gre (*US* ·ger)
meal
meal·worm
mealy (meali·er, meali·est)

mealy-mouthed
mean (mean·ing, meant) intend; miserly; midpoint; *compare* mien
me·ander
me·ander·er
me·ander·ing·ly
me·androus
mean·ing
mean·ing·ful
mean·ing·ful·ly
mean·ing·ful·ness
mean·ing·less
mean·ing·less·ness
mean·ness
means (*plural* means) method
meant
mean·time
mean·while
meany (*plural* meanies) *Slang* miserly person
mea·sled
mea·sles
mea·sly (·sli·er, ·sli·est)
meas·ur·abil·ity (*or* ·able·ness)
meas·ur·able
meas·ur·ably
meas·ure
meas·ured
meas·ured·ly
meas·ure·less
meas·ure·ment
meas·ur·er
meas·ur·ing
meat
meat·ball
Meath Irish county
meati·ly
meati·ness
mea·tus (*plural* ·tuses *or* ·tus) anatomy term
meaty (meati·er, meati·est)
Mec·ca
Mec·ca·no (*Trademark*)
me·chan·ic
me·chani·cal
me·chani·cal·ly
mecha·ni·cian
me·chan·ics
mecha·nism
mecha·nist
mecha·nis·tic

mecha·nis·ti·cal·ly
mecha·ni·za·tion (*or* ·sa·tion)
mecha·nize (*or* ·nise)
mecha·niz·er (*or* ·nis·er)
mecha·no·thera·py
Mech·elen (*or* ·lin) Belgian city
meck *Dialect* small coin
Meck·len·burg German region
me·co·nium
Med short for Mediterranean
med·al (*verb* ·al·ling, ·alled; *US* ·al·ing, ·aled) award; *compare* meddle
me·dal·lic
me·dal·lion
me·dal·lion·ist
med·al·list (*US* ·al·ist)
Me·dan Indonesian city
med·dle interfere; *compare* medal
med·dler interferer; *compare* medlar
med·dle·some
med·dle·some·ness
med·dling·ly
Mede inhabitant of Media
Medea mythological princess
Me·del·lín Colombian city
Me·dia ancient country
me·dia *plural of* medium, *esp. in communications sense*
me·dia (*plural* ·diae) anatomy and phonetics term
me·dia·cy
me·di·aeval *variant spelling of* medieval
me·dial
me·dial·ly
Me·dian of Medes or Media
me·dian
me·di·ant music term
me·di·as·ti·nal
me·di·as·ti·num (*plural* ·na) anatomy term
me·di·ate
me·dia·tion
me·dia·tive (*or* ·tory, ·to·rial)

mediatization

me·di·a·ti·za·tion (or ·sa·tion)
me·di·a·tize (or ·tise) annex a state
me·di·a·tor
me·di·a·to·ri·al·ly
me·di·a·trix (or ·trice)
med·ic Slang doctor; US spelling of medick
medi·cable
medi·ca·bly
Medi·caid US health assistance
medi·cal
medi·cal·ly
me·dica·ment
medi·ca·men·tal (or ·tary)
Medi·care US health insurance
medi·cate
medi·ca·tion
medi·ca·tive
me·dici·nal
me·dici·nal·ly
medi·cine
med·ick (US ·ic) plant; compare medic
medi·co (plural ·cos)
me·di·eval (or ·aeval)
me·di·eval·ism (or ·aeval·)
me·di·eval·ist (or ·aeval·)
me·di·eval·is·tic (or ·aeval·)
me·di·eval·ly (or ·aeval·)
Me·di·na Saudi Arabian city
me·dio·cre
me·di·oc·rity (plural ·rities)
medi·tate
medi·tat·ing·ly
medi·ta·tion
medi·ta·tive
medi·ta·tive·ness
medi·ta·tor
Medi·ter·ra·nean
me·dium (plural ·dia or ·diums)
med·lar fruit; compare meddler
med·ley
Mé·doc French region; wine
me·dul·la (plural ·las or ·lae)
me·dul·lary (or ·lar)

med·ul·lat·ed
Medusa mythological character
me·du·sa (plural ·sas or ·sae) jellyfish
me·du·san
me·du·soid
Med·way
mee Malaysian noodles
meed Archaic reward; compare mead
meek
meek·ly
meek·ness
meer·kat mongoose
meer·schaum
Mee·rut Indian city
meet (meet·ing, met) come together; compare mete
meet (adj) Archaic fitting; compare mete
meet·er
meet·ing
mega·cephal·ic variant of macrocephalic
mega·cepha·ly variant of macrocephaly
mega·cy·cle
mega·death
mega·ga·mete variant of macrogamete
mega·lith
mega·lith·ic
mega·lo·blast blood cell
mega·lo·blast·ic
mega·lo·car·dia abnormally large heart
mega·lo·cephal·ic variant of macrocephalic
mega·lo·cepha·ly variant of macrocephaly
mega·lo·ma·nia
mega·lo·ma·ni·ac
mega·lo·ma·nia·cal
mega·lopo·lis
mega·lo·poli·tan
mega·lo·saur dinosaur
mega·phone
mega·phon·ic
mega·phoni·cal·ly
mega·pode bird
Mega·ra Greek town
mega·ron (plural ·ra) room
mega·spore botany term

282

mega·spor·ic
mega·spo·ro·phyll
me·gass (or ·gasse) paper
mega·there (or ·ther·ium; plural ·theres or ·ther·ia) extinct sloth
mega·ton
mega·volt
mega·watt
me·gil·lah (plural ·lahs or ·loth) Hebrew scroll
me·gilp (or ma·) oil-painting medium
meg·ohm
me·grim Archaic migraine
Mei·ji period in Japanese history
meio·sis (plural ·ses) cell division; rhetorical device; compare miosis
mei·ot·ic
mei·oti·cal·ly
Meis·sen East German town
Meis·ter·sing·er (plural ·er or ·ers)
Mek·nès Moroccan city
Me·kong Asian river
mel honey
mela·leu·ca shrub
mela·mine
mel·an·cho·lia
mel·an·cho·li·ac
mel·an·chol·ic
mel·an·choli·cal·ly
mel·an·choli·ly
mel·an·choli·ness
mel·an·choly (plural ·cholies)
Mela·nesia
Mela·nesian
mé·lange French mixture
me·lan·ic
mela·nin pigment
mela·nism dark pigmentation; variant of melanosis
mela·nis·tic
mela·nite gemstone
mela·no·cyte melanin cell
mela·noid
mela·no·ma (plural ·mas or ·ma·ta) tumour
mela·no·sis (or ·nism) skin disease
mela·nos·ity

mela·not·ic
mela·nous
mela·phyre rock
mela·to·nin hormone
Melba sauce; toast
Mel·bourne
Mel·bur·nian
Mel·chite Eastern Church member
meld
me·lee (*or* mê·lée)
me·lia·ceous botany term
mel·ic to be sung
meli·lot plant
meli·nite explosive
me·lio·rate ameliorate
me·lio·ra·tion
me·lio·rism
me·lis·ma (*plural* ·ma·ta *or* ·mas) musical term
mel·is·mat·ic
Me·li·to·pol Soviet city
mel·lif·er·ous (*or* ·lif·ic) producing honey
mel·lif·lu·ous (*or* ·lu·ent) sweet-sounding
mel·lif·lu·ous·ness (*or* ·lu·ence)
mel·lo·phone brass instrument
mel·low
mel·low·ness
me·lo·deon accordion
me·lod·ic
me·lodi·cal·ly
me·lo·dious
me·lo·di·ous·ness
melo·dist
melo·dize (*or* ·dise)
melo·diz·er (*or* ·dis·er)
melo·dra·ma
melo·dra·mat·ic
melo·dra·mati·cal·ly
melo·drama·tist
melo·drama·tize (*or* ·tise)
melo·dy (*plural* ·dies)
mel·oid beetle
mel·on
Me·los Greek island
melt (melt·ing, melt·ed, melt·ed *or* mol·ten)
melt·abil·ity
melt·able
melt·age
melt·down

melt·er
melt·ing·ly
mel·ton fabric
Mel·ton Mow·bray
melt·water
Mem·ber an MP
mem·ber
mem·ber·ship
mem·brane
mem·bra·nous (*or* ·bra·na·ceous)
me·men·to (*plural* ·tos *or* ·toes)
me·men·to mori
memo (*plural* memos)
mem·oir
memo·ra·bilia (*sing.* ·rabi·le)
memo·rabil·ity (*or* ·rable·ness)
memo·rable
memo·rably
memo·ran·dum (*plural* ·dums *or* ·da)
me·mo·rial
me·mo·ri·al·ist
me·mo·ri·ali·za·tion (*or* ·sa·tion)
me·mo·ri·al·ize (*or* ·ise)
me·mo·ri·al·iz·er (*or* ·is·er)
memo·riz·able (*or* ·ris·able)
memo·ri·za·tion (*or* ·sa·tion)
memo·rize (*or* ·rise)
memo·riz·er (*or* ·ris·er)
memo·ry (*plural* ·ries)
Mem·phis
Mem·phre·ma·gog North American lake
mem·sa·hib
men
men·ace
men·ac·er
men·ac·ing·ly
me·nad *variant spelling of* maenad
mena·di·one vitamin
Me·na·do (*or* Ma·) Indonesian port
mé·nage household; *compare* manège
mé·nage à trois (*plural* mé·nage à trois)
me·nag·erie

Menai Strait
Me·nam Thai river
mena·qui·none vitamin
men·ar·che start of menstruation
men·ar·cheal (*or* ·chial)
mend
mend·able
men·da·cious
men·da·cious·ness
men·dac·ity (*plural* ·ities) untruthfulness; *compare* mendicancy
men·de·levium chemical element
Men·de·lian
Men·del·ism (*or* ·de·li·an·ism) science of heredity
mend·er
men·di·can·cy (*or* men·dic·ity) begging; *compare* mendacity
men·di·cant
mend·ing
Men·dips
Men·do·za Argentine city
Menelaus mythological king
men·folk
men·ha·den (*plural* ·den) fish
men·hir Bronze Age stone
me·nial
me·nial·ly
mc·nin·geal
me·nin·ges (*sing.* me·ninx) brain membranes
men·in·git·ic
men·in·gi·tis
me·nis·cold
me·nis·cus (*plural* ·ci *or* ·cuses)
meni·sper·ma·ceous botany term
meno musical term
me·nol·ogy (*plural* ·ogies) ecclesiastical calendar
meno·pau·sal (*or* ·sic)
meno·pause
me·no·rah Jewish candelabrum
men·or·rha·gia excessive menstruation
men·or·rhag·ic

Mensa

Men·sa constellation
men·ses (*plural* **·ses**)
  menstruation
Men·she·vik Russian
  socialist
mens rea legal term
men·strual
men·stru·ate
men·strua·tion
men·struous
men·struum (*plural*
  ·struums *or* **·strua**)
  solvent
men·sur·able
men·su·ral
men·su·ra·tion measuring;
  compare **menstruation**
men·su·ra·tion·al
men·su·ra·tive
mens·wear
men·tal
men·tal·ism philosophy
  term
men·tal·is·tic
men·tal·is·ti·cal·ly
men·tal·ity (*plural* **·ities**)
men·tal·ly
men·tha·ceous botany term
men·thol
men·tho·la·ted
men·tion
men·tion·able
men·tion·er
Men·ton French town
men·tor
men·to·rial
menu
meow (*or* **miaou, miaow**)
mepa·crine drug
Meph·is·to·phelean (*or*
  ·phelian)
Mephistopheles (*or*
  Mephisto)
me·phit·ic (*or* **·phiti·cal**)
  poisonous
me·phiti·cal·ly
me·phi·tis foul stench
me·pro·ba·mate
  tranquillizer
mer·bro·min antiseptic
mer·can·tile
mer·can·til·ism
mer·can·til·ist
mer·cap·tan chemical
  compound

mer·cap·tide chemical
  compound
mer·cap·to·pu·rine drug
mer·ce·nari·ly
mer·ce·nari·ness
mer·ce·nary (*plural*
  ·naries)
mer·cer
mer·ceri·za·tion (*or*
  ·sa·tion)
mer·cer·ize (*or* **·ise**)
mer·chan·dise
mer·chan·dis·er
mer·chant
mer·chant·able
mer·chant·man (*plural*
  ·men) ship
Mer·cia Anglo-Saxon
  kingdom
Mer·cian
mer·ci·ful
mer·ci·ful·ly
mer·ci·ful·ness
mer·ci·less
mer·ci·less·ness
mer·cu·rate treat with
  mercury
mer·cu·ra·tion
mer·cu·rial
mer·cu·ri·al·ism mercury
  poisoning
mer·cu·ri·ali·za·tion (*or*
  ·sa·tion)
mer·cu·ri·al·ize (*or* **·ise**)
mer·cu·rial·ly
mer·cu·ri·al·ness (*or*
  ·ri·al·ity)
mer·cu·ric
Mer·cu·ro·chrome
  (*Trademark*)
mer·cu·rous
Mer·cu·ry planet
Mercury Roman god
mer·cu·ry (*or* **·ries**)
mer·cy (*plural* **·cies**)
mere
mere·ly
me·ren·gue dance
mer·etri·cious insincere;
  compare **meritorious**
mer·gan·ser (*plural* **·sers**
  or **·ser**) duck
merge
mer·gence
mer·ger

me·rid·ian
me·ridio·nal
me·ringue
me·ri·no (*plural* **·nos**)
Meri·on·eth·shire former
  Welsh county
me·ri·stem plant tissue
meri·ste·mat·ic
me·ris·tic biology term
mer·it
mer·it·ed·ly
mer·it·less
meri·toc·ra·cy (*plural*
  ·cies)
meri·to·ri·ous
  praiseworthy; *compare*
  meretricious
mer·kin pubic wig
merle *Scot* blackbird
mer·lin falcon
mer·lon part of battlement
mer·maid
mer·man (*plural* **·men**)
mero·blas·tic biology term
mero·blas·ti·cal·ly
mero·crine physiology term
Meroë ancient Sudanese
  city
mero·plank·ton
Mero·vin·gian Frankish
  dynasty
mero·zo·ite biology term
mer·ri·ly
mer·ri·ment
mer·ri·ness
mer·ry (**·ri·er, ·ri·est**)
merry-go-round
merry·maker
merry·making
merry·thought wishbone
Merse Scottish area
Mer·se·burg East German
  city
Mer·sey
Mer·sey·side
Mer·sin Turkish port
Mer·thyr Tyd·fil
Mer·ton London borough
mesa tableland
mé·sal·li·ance *French*
  unsuitable marriage;
  compare **misalliance**
mes·arch botany term
Mesa Verde Colorado
  plateau

mes·cal cactus; alcohol
mes·ca·line (or ·lin) drug
mes·dames plural of madame
mes·de·moi·selles plural of mademoiselle
mes·em·bry·an·themum plant
mes·en·cephal·ic
mes·en·cepha·lon part of brain
mes·en·chy·mal (or ·chyma·tous)
mes·en·chyme embryology term
mes·en·ter·ic
mes·en·teri·tis
mes·en·ter·on (plural ·tera) zoology term
mes·en·ter·on·ic
mes·en·tery (plural ·teries)
mesh
Meshach biblical character
Me·shed variant spelling of Mashhad
meshy
me·sial anatomy term
me·sial·ly
me·sic ecology term; of a meson
mesi·cal·ly
me·sity·lene chemical compound
mes·mer·ic
mes·meri·cal·ly
mes·mer·ism
mes·mer·ist
mes·meri·za·tion (or sa·tion)
mes·mer·ize (or ·ise)
mes·mer·iz·er (or ·is·er)
mesne legal term
meso·ben·thos
meso·blast embryonic tissue
meso·carp botany term
meso·ce·phal·ic
meso·ceph·aly
meso·crat·ic geology term
meso·derm
meso·der·mal (or ·mic)
meso·gas·tric
meso·gas·trium
meso·glea (or ·gloea)
me·sog·na·thism (or ·thy)

me·sog·na·thous
Meso·lith·ic archaeological period
meso·morph
meso·mor·phic of muscular build
meso·mor·phism
meso·mor·phous
meso·mor·phy
me·son elementary particle
meso·neph·ric
meso·neph·ros
meso·pause meteorology term
meso·phyll
meso·phyl·lic (or ·lous)
meso·phyte
meso·phyt·ic
Meso·po·ta·mia
Meso·po·ta·mian
meso·sphere
meso·spher·ic
meso·thelial
meso·thelium
meso·tho·rac·ic
meso·tho·rax (plural ·raxes or ·races)
Meso·zo·ic geological period
mes·quite (or ·quit) tree
mess
mes·sage
mes·sa·line fabric
Mes·sene ancient Greek city
mes·sen·ger
Mes·senia Greek region
Mes·si·ah
mes·si·an·ic (or Mes·)
mes·sieurs plural of monsieur
messi·ly
Mes·si·na Sicilian port
messi·ness
mess·mate
Messrs plural of Mr
mes·suage legal term
messy (messi·er, messi·est)
mes·ter Dialect master
mes·ti·zo (fem ·za; plural ·zos or ·zoes, ·zas) one of mixed parentage
mes·tra·nol synthetic hormone

met
Meta Colombian river
meta·bol·ic
meta·boli·cal·ly
me·tabo·lism
me·tabo·lite
me·tabo·liz·abil·ity (or ·lis·abil·ity)
me·tabo·liz·able (or ·lis·able)
me·tabo·lize (or ·lise)
meta·car·pal
meta·car·pus (plural ·pi) hand bones; compare metatarsus
meta·cen·tre (US ·ter) physics term
meta·cen·tric
meta·chro·mat·ic
meta·chro·ma·tism
meta·cin·nab·a·rite mercury ore
meta·female genetics term
meta·ga·lac·tic
meta·gal·axy (plural ·axies)
met·age official measuring of goods
meta·gen·esis
meta·ge·net·ic (or ·gen·ic)
meta·geneti·cal·ly
me·tag·na·thism
me·tag·na·thous
met·al (verb ·al·ling, ·alled; US ·al·ing, ·aled) substance; compare mettle
meta·lan·guage
me·tal·lic
me·tal·li·cal·ly
met·al·lif·er·ous
met·al·line of metals
met·al·list (US ·al·ist)
met·al·li·za·tion (or ·sa·tion; US met·ali·za·tion)
met·al·lize (or ·lise; US ·al·ize)
me·tal·lo·cene chemical compound
met·al·log·ra·pher (or ·phist)
me·tal·lo·graph·ic
met·al·lo·graphi·cal·ly
met·al·log·ra·phy
met·al·loid

metalloidal

met·al·loi·dal
met·al·lur·gic (*or* ·gi·cal)
met·al·lur·gi·cal·ly
met·al·lur·gist
met·al·lur·gy
metal·work
metal·worker
metal·working
meta·male genetics term
meta·math·emati·cal
meta·math·ema·ti·cian
meta·math·emat·ics
meta·mer chemistry term
me·tam·er·al
meta·mere zoology term
meta·mer·ic
meta·meri·cal·ly
me·tam·er·ism
meta·mor·phic (*or* ·phous)
meta·mor·phism geology term
meta·mor·phose
meta·mor·pho·sis (*plural* ·ses)
meta·neph·ros
meta·phase biology term
meta·phor
meta·phor·ic (*or* ·phori·cal)
meta·phori·cal·ly
meta·phori·cal·ness
meta·phos·phate
meta·phrase literal translation
meta·phrast
meta·phras·tic (*or* ·ti·cal)
meta·phras·ti·cal·ly
meta·phys·ic
Meta·physi·cal denoting poetic group
meta·physi·cal of metaphysics
meta·physi·cal·ly
meta·phy·si·cian (*or* ·physi·cist)
meta·phys·ics
meta·pla·sia
meta·plasm
meta·plas·mic
meta·psy·cho·logi·cal
meta·psy·chol·ogy
meta·so·ma·tism (*or* ·ma·to·sis) geology term
meta·sta·bil·ity

meta·sta·ble
me·tas·ta·sis (*plural* ·ses) medical term
me·tas·ta·size (*or* ·sise)
meta·stat·ic
meta·stati·cal·ly
meta·tar·sal
meta·tar·sus (*plural* ·si) foot bones; *compare* meta carpus
meta·theo·ry study of philosophy
meta·therian marsupial
me·tath·esis (*plural* ·eses) linguistics term
me·tath·esize (*or* ·esise)
meta·thet·ic (*or* ·theti·cal)
meta·tho·rac·ic
meta·tho·rax (*plural* ·raxes *or* ·races)
meta·xy·lem
meta·zo·an
meta·zo·ic
mete allot; *compare* meet
met·em·piri·cal (*or* ·pir·ic)
met·em·piri·cist
met·em·pir·ics
me·tem·psy·cho·sis (*plural* ·ses)
met·en·cephal·ic
met·en·cepha·lon (*plural* ·lons *or* ·la) embryology term
me·teor
me·teor·ic
me·teori·cal·ly
me·teor·ite
me·teor·it·ic
me·teoro·graph
me·teoro·graph·ic (*or* ·graphi·cal)
me·teor·oid
me·teoro·logi·cal (*or* ·log·ic)
me·teoro·logi·cal·ly
me·teor·olo·gist
me·teor·ol·ogy study of weather; *compare* metrology
me·ter instrument; *US* spelling of metre
met·es·trus *US* spelling of metoestrus
meth·ac·ry·late
metha·done (*or* ·don) drug

met·haemo·glo·bin (*US* ·hemo·)
me·thane
metha·nol
me·thinks
me·thio·nine amino acid
meth·od
me·thodi·cal (*or* ·thod·ic)
me·thodi·cal·ly
me·thodi·cal·ness
Meth·od·ism
Meth·od·ist
Meth·od·is·ti·cal·ly
meth·odi·za·tion (*or* ·sa·tion)
meth·od·ize (*or* ·ise)
meth·od·iz·er (*or* ·is·er)
meth·odo·logi·cal
meth·odo·logi·cal·ly
meth·od·olo·gist
meth·od·ol·ogy (*plural* ·ogies)
metho·trex·ate drug
me·thought
meth·ox·ide
Me·thu·se·lah
me·thyl
meth·yl·al chemical compound
me·thyla·mine
meth·yl·ate
meth·yla·tion
meth·yla·tor
me·thyl·do·pa
meth·yl·ene
me·thyl·ic
me·thyl·naph·tha·lene
met·ic ancient Greek alien
me·ticu·lous
me·ticu·lous·ness (*or* ·los·ity)
mé·ti·er profession
Mé·tis (*or* ·tif; *plural* ·tis *or* ·tifs) one of mixed parentage
met·oes·trus (*US* ·es·)
me·tol chemical compound
Me·ton·ic cy·cle
meto·nym
meto·nymi·cal (*or* ·nym·ic)
me·tony·my (*plural* ·mies) linguistics term
met·ope architectural term
me·top·ic of the forehead

me·tral·gia womb pain
me·tre (*US* **·ter**) unit; verse rhythm; *compare* **meter**
met·ric
met·ri·cal
met·ri·cal·ly
met·ri·cate
met·ri·ca·tion
met·rics use of poetic metre
met·ri·fi·er
met·ri·fy (**·fies**, **·fy·ing**, **·fied**)
met·rist
me·tri·tis inflammation of womb
met·ro (*or* **mét·**; *plural* **·ros**)
met·ro·logi·cal
me·trolo·gist
me·trol·ogy (*plural* **·ogies**) study of measurement; *compare* **meteorology**
met·ro·ni·da·zole
met·ro·nome
met·ro·nom·ic of a metronome
met·ro·nym·ic (*or* **mat·**) maternal name
me·tropo·lis (*plural* **·lises**)
met·ro·poli·tan
met·ro·poli·tan·ism
me·tror·rha·gia abnormal bleeding from womb
met·tle courage; *compare* **metal**
met·tle·some
Metz French city
meu plant
meu·nière cookery term
Meurthe-et-Moselle French department
Meuse European river
mew
mewl
mewl·er
mews (*plural* **mews**)
Mexi·cali Mexican city
Mexi·can
Mexi·co
me·zereon shrub
me·zereum (*or* **·zereon**) drug
Me·zières French town

me·zu·zah (*plural* **·zahs** *or* **·zoth**)
mez·za·nine
mez·zo (*plural* **·zos**) musical term
mezzo-relievo (*or* **-rilievo**; *plural* **-relievos** *or* **-rilievos**)
mezzo-soprano (*plural* **-sopranos**)
mez·zo·tint
mi (*or* **me**) musical term
Mi·ami
miaou (*or* **miaow**) variant spellings of **meow**
mi·as·ma (*plural* **·ma·ta** *or* **·mas**)
mi·as·mal (*or* **·mat·ic**, **·mati·cal**, **·mic**)
mica
mi·ca·ceous
Mi·caw·ber feckless person
Mi·caw·ber·ish
mice
mi·cel·lar
mi·celle (*or* **·cell**, **·cel·la**)
Mich·ael·mas
Michi·gan
Michi·gan·der
Michi·gan·ite
Mi·choa·cán Mexican state
mick·ery pool in river bed
mick·ey (*or* **micky**; *as in* take the mickey)
Mick·ey Finn
mick·le *Dialect* much
Mic·mac (*plural* **·macs** *or* **·mac**) American Indian
micro·analy·sis (*plural* **·ses**)
micro·ana·lyst
micro·ana·lyt·ic (*or* **·lyti·cal**)
micro·bal·ance
micro·baro·graph
mi·crobe
mi·cro·bial (*or* **·bic**, **·bian**)
micro·bio·logi·cal (*or* **·log·ic**)
micro·bi·olo·gist
micro·bi·ol·ogy
micro·cephal·ic
micro·cepha·lous
micro·cepha·ly abnormally small skull
micro·chemi·cal

micron

micro·chem·is·try
micro·chip
micro·cir·cuit
micro·cir·cuit·ry
micro·cli·mate
micro·cli·mat·ic
micro·cli·mati·cal·ly
micro·cli·ma·to·log·ic (*or* **·logi·cal**)
micro·cli·ma·tolo·gist
micro·cli·ma·tol·ogy
micro·cline mineral
micro·coc·cus (*plural* **·coc·ci**)
micro·com·put·er
micro·copy (*plural* **·copies**) reduced photographic copy
micro·cosm (*or* **·cos·mos**)
micro·cos·mic (*or* **·cos·mi·cal**)
micro·crys·tal·line
micro·cyte blood cell
micro·cyt·ic
micro·detec·tor
micro·dont (*or* **·don·tous**)
micro·dot
micro·eco·nom·ic
micro·eco·nom·ics
micro·elec·tron·ic
micro·elec·tron·ics
micro·fiche
micro·film
micro·gam·ete
micro·graph
mi·crog·ra·pher
micro·graph·ic
micro·graphi·cal·ly
mi·crog·ra·phy
micro·groove
micro·habi·tat
micro·light
micro·lith
micro·meteor·ite
micro·meteor·ol·ogy
mi·crom·eter measuring instrument
micro·metre (*US* **·meter**) unit of length
micro·met·ric (*or* **·ri·cal**)
mi·crom·etry
micro·minia·turi·za·tion (*or* **·sa·tion**)
mi·cron (*plural* **·crons** *or* **·cra**) unit of length

Micronesia

Micro·nesia
Micro·nesian
micro·nu·cleus (*plural* ·clei)
micro·nu·tri·ent
micro·or·gan·ism
micro·palae·on·to·logi·cal (*or* ·log·ic; *US* ·pale·)
micro·palae·on·tolo·gist (*US* ·pale·)
micro·palae·on·tol·ogy (*US* ·pale·)
micro·para·site
micro·para·sit·ic
micro·phone
micro·phon·ic
micro·pho·to·graph
micro·pho·to·graph·ic
micro·pho·tog·ra·phy
micro·physi·cal
micro·phys·ics
micro·phyte microscopic plant
micro·phyt·ic
micro·print
micro·pro·ces·sor
micro·py·lar
micro·pyle biology term
micro·py·rom·eter
micro·read·er
micro·scope
micro·scop·ic (*or* ·scopi·cal)
micro·scopi·cal·ly
mi·cros·co·pist
mi·cros·co·py
micro·sec·ond
micro·seism
micro·seis·mic (*or* ·mi·cal)
micro·so·mal (*or* ·so·mial, ·so·mic)
micro·some biology term
micro·spo·ran·gium (*plural* ·gia)
micro·spore
micro·spor·ic (*or* ·spo·rous)
micro·sporo·phyll
micro·stoma·tous (*or* mi·cros·to·mous) having small mouth
micro·struc·ture
micro·tome cutting instrument

micro·tom·ic (*or* ·tomi·cal)
mi·croto·mist
mi·croto·my (*plural* ·mies)
micro·ton·al
micro·to·nal·ity
micro·tone musical term
micro·wave
mi·crurgy microscopy technique
mic·tu·rate
mic·tu·ri·tion
mid *Archaic* amid
mid- *prefix denoting* middle
mid·air
Midas legendary king
mid·brain
mid·day
Mid·del·burg Dutch city
mid·den
mid·dle
middle-aged
middle·brow
middle·browism
middle-class (*adj*)
middle-distance (*adj*)
middle-man (*plural* ·men)
Mid·dles·brough
Mid·dle·sex
Mid·dle·ton English town
middle·weight
mid·dling
mid·dy (*plural* ·dies) midshipman
mid·field
Mid·gard Norse mythological place
midge
midg·et
Mid Gla·mor·gan Welsh county
mid·gut
Mid·heav·en astrology term
Midi S France
midi skirt length
Mid·ian biblical character
Midi·an·ite
midi·nette Parisian salesgirl
mid·iron golf club
mid·land inland region
Mid·lands central England
mid·line
Mid·lo·thian former Scottish county

mid·most
mid·night
mid-off
mid-on
mid·point
mid·rash (*plural* ·ra·shim) Jewish biblical commentaries
mid·rib leaf vein
mid·riff
mid·sec·tion
mid·ship
mid·ship·man (*plural* ·men)
mid·ships
midst
mid·sum·mer
mid·term
mid·town *US* town centre
mid·way
mid·week
Mid·west (*or* Mid·dle West) US region
Mid·west·ern
Mid·west·ern·er
mid-wicket
mid·wife (*plural* ·wives)
mid·wife·ry
mid·win·ter
mid·year
mien bearing; *compare* mean
miff *Slang* take offence
mif·fi·ness
mif·fy (·fi·er, ·fi·est)
might
mighti·ly
mighti·ness
mighty (mighti·er, mighti·est)
mi·gnon *French* dainty
mi·gnon·ette plant
mi·graine
mi·grain·ous
mi·grant
mi·grate
mi·gra·tion
mi·gra·tion·al
mi·gra·tor
mi·gra·tory
mih·rab niche in mosque
mi·ka·do (*plural* ·dos)
mike *Slang* microphone
mil unit of length
mi·la·dy (*or* ·la·di; *plural* ·dies)

mil·age *variant spelling of* mileage
Mi·lan
Mil·an·ese (*plural* ·ese)
milch
mild
mil·dew
mil·dewy
mild·ness
mile
mile·age (*or* **mil·age**)
mile·om·eter (*or* **mi·lom·eter**)
mile·post
mil·er
Mi·lesian
mile·stone
Mi·letus old Asian city
mil·foil plant
mili·aria heat rash
mil·iary
mi·lieu (*plural* ·lieus *or* ·lieux)
mili·tan·cy (*or* ·tant·ness)
mili·tant
mili·tari·ly
mili·ta·rism
mili·ta·rist
mili·ta·ris·tic
mili·ta·ris·ti·cal·ly
mili·ta·ri·za·tion (*or* ·sa·tion)
mili·ta·rize (*or* ·rise)
mili·tary (*plural* ·taries)
mili·tate
mili·ta·tion
mi·li·tia
mi·li·tia·man (*plural* ·men)
mil·ium (*plural* **milia**) skin nodule
milk
milk·er
milk·fish (*plural* ·fish *or* ·fishes)
milki·ly
milki·ness
milk·maid
milk·man (*plural* ·men)
milko *Austral* milkman
milk·sop
milk·weed
milk·wort
milky (**milki·er**, **milki·est**)
Milky Way

mill
mill·able
mill·board
mill·dam
milled
mille·feuille pastry
mille·fleurs textile design
mil·le·nar·ian (*or* ·nary)
mil·le·nari·an·ism Christian belief
mil·le·nary (*plural* ·naries) a thousand; *compare* millinery
mil·len·nial
mil·len·ni·al·ist
mil·len·nium (*plural* ·niums *or* ·nia)
mil·le·pede *variant spelling of* millipede
mil·le·pore coral-like organism
mil·ler
mil·ler·ite mineral
mil·lesi·mal denoting a thousandth
mil·let
mil·li·ard thousand million
mil·liary denoting Roman mile
mil·li·bar
mil·lieme Tunisian coin
mil·li·gram (*or* ·gramme)
mil·li·li·tre (*US* ·ter)
mil·li·metre (*US* ·meter)
mil·line unit of advertising copy
mil·li·ner
mil·li·nery hat making; *compare* millenary
mill·ing
mil·lion (*plural* ·lions *or* ·lion)
mil·lion·aire (*or* ·lion·naire)
mil·lion·air·ess
mil·lionth
mil·li·pede (*or* ·le·pede, ·le·ped)
mil·li·sec·ond
mill·pond
mill·race
mill·run
mill·stone
mill·stream
mill·wheel
mill·wright

mi·lord
mi·lom·eter *variant spelling of* mileometer
milque·toast *US* timid person
milt
mil·ter
Mil·ton·ic (*or* ·to·nian) of John Milton
Mil·ton Keynes
Mil·wau·kee *US* port
mim *Dialect* prim
Mi·mas satellite of Saturn
mine
Mimeo·graph (*Trademark*)
mim·er
mi·mesis
mi·met·ic
mi·meti·cal·ly
mim·etite mineral
mim·ic (·ick·ing, ·icked)
mim·ick·er
mim·ic·ry (*plural* ·ries)
miminy-piminy *variant of* niminy-piminy
Mimir Norse giant
mi·mo·sa
mimo·sa·ceous
Min Chinese dialect
mina (*plural* **minae** *or* **minas**) ancient unit
mina *variant spelling of* myna
min·able (*or* **mine·able**)
mi·na·cious threatening
mi·nac·ity
Mina Has·san Tani Moroccan port
mina·ret
mina·ret·ed
Mi·nas Ge·rais Brazilian state
mina·to·ri·ly (*or* ·ri·al·ly)
mina·tory (*or* ·to·rial)
mince
mince·meat
minc·er
Minch Atlantic channel
minc·ing
minc·ing·ly
mind
Min·dan·ao Philippine island
mind·ed
Min·del glaciation period

minder

mind·er
mind·ful
mind·ful·ly
mind·ful·ness
mind·less
mind·less·ness
mind-reader
mind-reading
mine
mine·field
mine·lay·er
min·er one who mines; *compare* minor
min·er·al
min·er·ali·za·tion (*or* ·sa·tion)
min·er·al·ize (*or* ·ise)
min·er·al·iz·er (*or* ·is·er)
min·er·alo·cor·ti·coid hormone
min·er·al·ogi·cal (*or* ·og·ic)
min·er·alo·gist
min·er·al·ogy
min·estro·ne
mine-sweeper
mine-sweeping
Ming
min·gle
Min·gre·lian (*or* Min·grel) Georgian people
min·gy (·gi·er, ·gi·est)
mini (*plural* minis)
minia·ture
minia·tur·ist
minia·turi·za·tion (*or* ·sa·tion)
minia·tur·ize (*or* ·ise)
mini·bus
mini·cab
mini·com·put·er
mini·dress
mini·fi·ca·tion
mini·fy (·fies, ·fy·ing, ·fied)
min·im
mini·ma (*plural of* minimum)
mini·mal
Mini·mal·ist Russian revolutionary
mini·mal·ist advocate of minimal policy
mini·mal·ly

mini·max maths term
mini·mi·za·tion (*or* ·sa·tion)
mini·mize (*or* ·mise)
mini·miz·er (*or* ·mis·er)
mini·mum (*plural* ·mums *or* ·ma)
mini·mus youngest
min·ing
min·ion
mini·pill
(miniscule) *incorrect spelling of* minuscule
mini·skirt
mini·skirted
min·is·ter
min·is·terial
min·is·terial·ly
min·is·te·rium (*plural* ·ria) Lutheran ministers
min·is·trant
mini·stra·tion
min·is·tra·tive
min·is·try (*plural* ·tries)
Mini·track (*Trademark*)
(miniture) *incorrect spelling of* miniature
min·ium red lead
mini·ver fur
mini·vet bird
mink
minke whale
Min·na Nigerian city
Min·ne·apo·lis
min·neo·la hybrid fruit
min·ne·sing·er German minstrel
Min·ne·so·ta
Min·ne·so·tan
min·now (*plural* ·nows *or* ·now)
Mi·no·an of Cretan culture
mi·nor lesser; *compare* miner
Mi·nor·ca
Mi·nor·can
Mi·no·rite friar
mi·nor·ity (*plural* ·ities)
Minos legendary king
Minotaur legendary monster
Minsk Soviet city
min·ster
min·strel
min·strel·sy (*plural* ·sies)
mint

290

mint·age
mint·er
Min·ton porcelain
minty (minti·er, minti·est)
minu·end maths term
minu·et
mi·nus
mi·nus·cu·lar
mi·nus·cule
min·ute 60 seconds
mi·nute very small
min·ute·ly every minute
mi·nute·ly in great detail
Min·ute·man (*plural* ·men)
mi·nute·ness
min·utes record of proceedings
mi·nu·tiae (*sing.* ·tia) trifling details
minx
minx·ish
Mio·cene geological period
mio·sis (*or* myo·) constriction of pupil; *compare* meiosis
mi·ot·ic (*or* my·)
Mi·que·lon French island
mi·ra·bi·le dic·tu Latin wonderful to relate
Mira Ceti star
mi·ra·cid·ial
mi·ra·cid·ium (*plural* ·iia) fluke larva
mira·cle
mi·racu·lous
mira·dor balcony or turret
mi·rage
Mi·ran·da satellite of Uranus
mire
mire·poix vegetable mixture
mir·ky *variant spelling of* murky
mir·ror
mirth
mirth·ful
mirth·ful·ly
mirth·ful·ness
mirth·less
mirth·less·ness
miry
mis·ad·ven·ture
mis·ad·vise

mis·align·ment
mis·al·li·ance unsuitable alliance; compare mésalliance
mis·an·thrope (or ·thro·pist)
mis·an·throp·ic (or ·thropi·cal)
mis·an·thropi·cal·ly
mis·an·thro·pist variant of misanthrope
mis·an·thro·py
mis·ap·pli·ca·tion
mis·ap·ply (·plies, ·ply·ing, ·plied)
mis·ap·pre·hend
mis·ap·pre·hend·ing·ly
mis·ap·pre·hen·sion
mis·ap·pre·hen·sive
mis·ap·pro·pri·ate
mis·ap·pro·pria·tion
mis·be·come (·com·ing, ·came) be unsuitable for
mis·be·got·ten
mis·be·have
mis·be·hav·er
mis·be·hav·iour (US ·ior)
mis·be·lief
mis·cal·cu·late
mis·cal·cu·la·tion
mis·call
mis·car·riage
mis·car·ry (·ries, ·ry·ing, ·ried)
mis·cast (·cast·ing, ·cast)
mis·ce·gena·tion interbreeding
mis·ce·genet·ic
mis·cel·la·nea (plural)
mis·cel·la·neous
mis·cel·la·nist
mis·cel·la·ny (plural ·nies)
mis·chance
mis·chief
mis·chie·vous
mis·chiev·ous·ness
misch met·al
mis·cibil·ity
mis·cible capable of mixing; compare missable
mis·con·ceive
mis·con·ceiv·er
mis·con·cep·tion
mis·con·duct

mis·con·struc·tion
mis·con·strue (·stru·ing, ·strued)
mis·copy (·copies, ·copy·ing, ·cop·ied)
mis·count
mis·cre·ance (or ·an·cy)
mis·cre·ant wrongdoer
mis·cre·ate create badly
mis·crea·tion
mis·cue (·cu·ing, ·cued)
mis·date
mis·deal (·deal·ing, ·dealt)
mis·deal·er
mis·deed
mis·de·mean·ant
mis·de·mean·our (US ·or)
mis·di·rect
mis·di·rec·tion
mis·doubt
mise legal term
mise en scène scenery
mi·ser
mis·er·able
mis·er·able·ness
mis·er·ably
mi·sère call in solo whist
Mis·erere 51st psalm
mis·erere misericord
mis·eri·cord (or ·corde) part of church
mi·ser·li·ness
mi·ser·ly
mis·ery (plural ·eries)
mis·fea·sance legal term
mis·file
mis·fire
mis·fit (·fit·ting, ·fit·ted)
mis·for·tune
mis·give (·giv·ing, ·gave, ·giv·en)
mis·giv·ing
mis·gov·ern
mis·gov·ern·ment
mis·gov·er·nor
mis·guid·ance
mis·guide
mis·guid·ed
mis·guid·er
mis·han·dle
mis·hap
mis·hear (·hear·ing, ·heard)
mis·hit (·hit·ting, ·hit)

mish·mash
Mish·nah (or ·na) Jewish precepts
Mish·na·ic
mis·in·form
mis·in·form·ant (or ·form·er)
mis·in·for·ma·tion
mis·in·ter·pret
mis·in·ter·pre·ta·tion
mis·in·ter·pret·er
mis·join·der legal term
mis·judge
mis·judg·er
mis·judg·ment (or ·judge·)
Mis·kolc Hungarian city
mis·lay (·lay·ing, ·laid)
mis·lay·er
mis·lead (·lead·ing, ·led)
mis·lead·er
mis·man·age
mis·man·age·ment
mis·man·ag·er
mis·match
mis·no·mer
mi·soga·mist marriage hater
mi·soga·my
mi·sogy·nist woman hater
mi·sogy·nous
mi·sogy·ny
mi·solo·gist
mi·sol·ogy hatred of reasoning
miso·neism hatred of anything new
miso·neist
miso·neis·tic
mis·pick·el mineral
mis·place
mis·place·ment
mis·play
mis·plead (·plead·ing, ·plead·ed, ·plead, or ·pled)
mis·plead·ing
mis·print
mis·pri·sion concealment of treason
mis·prize (or ·prise) undervalue
mis·pro·nounce
mis·pro·nun·cia·tion
mis·pro·por·tion

misquotation

mis·quo·ta·tion
mis·quote
mis·read (·read·ing, ·read)
mis·re·mem·ber
mis·re·port
mis·rep·re·sent
mis·rep·re·sen·ta·tion
mis·rep·re·sen·ta·tive
mis·rep·re·sent·er
mis·rule
Miss title of address
miss
miss·able able to be missed; *compare* miscible
mis·sal prayer book
mis·sel thrush *variant spelling of* mistle thrush
mis·shape (·shap·ing, ·shaped *or* ·shap·en)
mis·sile
mis·sile·ry (*or* ·sil·ry)
mis·sing
mis·sion
mis·sion·ary (*plural* ·aries)
mis·sion·er
mis·sis
miss·ish
Mis·sis·sau·ga Canadian town
Mis·sis·sip·pi
Mis·sis·sip·pian
mis·sive
Mis·souri
Mis·sou·rian
mis·spell (·spell·ing, ·spelt *or* ·spelled)
mis·spend (·spend·ing, ·spent)
mis·state
mis·state·ment
mis·sup·pose
missy (*plural* missies)
mist
mis·tak·able (*or* ·take·)
mis·tak·ably (*or* ·take·)
mis·take (·tak·ing, ·took *or* ·tak·en)
mis·tal *Scot* cowshed
Mis·tas·si·ni Canadian lake
mis·teach (·teach·ing, ·taught)
mis·ter
mis·ti·gris joker in poker

misti·ly
mis·time
misti·ness
mis·tle thrush (*or* mis·sel thrush)
mis·tle·toe
mis·took
mis·tral wind; *compare* mistrial
mis·treat
mis·treat·ment
mis·tress
mis·tri·al void trial; *compare* mistral
mis·trust
mis·trust·er
mis·trust·ful
mis·trust·ful·ly
mis·trust·ful·ness
mis·trust·ing·ly
misty (misti·er, misti·est)
mis·under·stand (·stand·ing, ·stood)
mis·us·age
mis·use
mis·us·er
mitch *Dialect* play truant
mite
mi·ter *US spelling of* mitre
Mith·ra·ic
Mith·ra·ism (*or* ·rai·cism)
Mith·ra·ist
Mith·ras (*or* ·ra) Persian god
mith·ri·dat·ic
mith·ri·da·tism immunity to poison
miti·cid·al
miti·cide mite-killing substance
miti·gable
miti·gate
miti·gat·ing
miti·ga·tion
miti·ga·tive (*or* ·tory)
miti·ga·tor
mi·tis malleable iron
mi·to·chon·drial
mi·to·chon·drion (*plural* ·dria) biology term
mi·to·sis (*plural* ·ses) cell division
mi·tot·ic
mi·toti·cal·ly
mi·trail·leuse machine gun

292

mi·tral
mi·tre (*US* ·ter)
mitre·wort (*US* miter·) plant
mitt
mit·ten
mit·ti·mus (*plural* ·muses) legal term
mitz·vah (*plural* ·vahs *or* ·voth)
mix
mix·abil·ity
mix·able
mixed
mix·er
mix·ing
mixo·lyd·ian music term
Mix·tec (*plural* ·tecs *or* ·tec) American Indian
mix·ture
mix-up (*noun*)
Mi·zar star
Mi·zo·ram Indian state
miz·zen (*or* miz·en) nautical term
miz·zen·mast (*or* miz·en·)
miz·zle *Dialect* drizzle
m'lud
mne·mon·ic memory aid
mne·moni·cal·ly
mne·mon·ics
Mnemosyne Greek goddess
mo (*plural* mos) *Slang* moment
moa extinct bird
Moab biblical kingdom
Mo·ab·ite
moan
moan·er
moan·ing·ly
moat ditch; *compare* mote
mob (mob·bing, mobbed)
mob·ber
mob·cap
Mo·bile *US* port
mo·bile
mo·bil·ity
mo·bi·liz·able (*or* ·lis·able)
mo·bi·li·za·tion (*or* ·sa·tion)
mo·bi·lize (*or* ·lise)
mob·oc·ra·cy (*plural* ·cies)

mobo·crat
mobo·crat·ic (*or* ·crati·cal)
mob·ster
Mo·bu·tu African lake
moc·ca·sin
Mo·cha Yemeni port
mo·cha coffee
mock
mock·able
mock·er
mock·ery (*plural* ·eries)
mock-heroic
mock-heroical·ly
mocking·bird
mock·ing·ly
mock-up (*noun*)
mod
mod·al
mo·dal·ity
mo·dal·ly
mode
mod·el (·el·ling, ·elled; *US* ·el·ing, ·eled)
mod·el·ler (*US* ·el·er)
mo·dem computer term
Mo·dena Italian city
mod·er·ate
mod·er·ate·ly
mod·er·ate·ness
mod·era·tion
mod·era·to music term
mod·era·tor
mod·era·tor·ship
mod·ern
mo·derne architectural style
mod·ern·ism
mod·ern·ist
mod·ern·is·tic
mod·ern·is·ti·cal·ly
mo·der·nity (*plural* ·nities)
mod·erni·za·tion (*or* ·sa·tion)
mod·ern·ize (*or* ·ise)
mod·ern·iz·er (*or* ·is·er)
mod·ern·ness
mod·est
mod·est·ly
mod·es·ty (*plural* ·ties)
modge *Dialect* to botch
modi·cum
modi·fi·abil·ity (*or* ·able·ness)
modi·fi·able

modi·fi·ca·tion
modi·fi·ca·tory (*or* ·tive)
modi·fi·er
modi·fy (·fies, ·fy·ing, ·fied)
mo·dil·lion architectural ornament
mo·dio·lus (*plural* ·li) anatomy term
mod·ish
mod·ish·ness
mo·diste (*plural* ·distes) fashionable dressmaker
modu·la·bil·ity
modu·lar
modu·late
modu·la·tion
modu·la·tive (*or* ·tory)
modu·la·tor
mod·ule
modu·lus (*plural* ·li) physics term
mo·dus op·eran·di (*plural* modi op·eran·di) method of working
mo·dus vi·ven·di (*plural* modi vi·ven·di) practical compromise
mo·fette opening in volcano
mog *Slang* cat
Moga·dishu (*or* ·discio) Somali capital
Moga·don (*Trademark*) drug
Moga·dor Moroccan port
mog·gy (*or* ·gie; *plural* ·gies) *Slang* cat
Mo·gi·lev (*or* ·hi·) Soviet city
Mo·gul Muslim ruler
mo·gul important person
mo·hair
Mo·ham·med·an Muslim
Mo·ha·ve (*or* ·ja·; *plural* ·ves *or* ·ve) American Indian
Mo·ha·ve Des·ert (*or* Mo·ja·ve Des·ert)
Mo·hawk (*plural* ·hawks *or* ·hawk) American Indian
Mo·hi·can variant spelling of Mahican
Mo·hock ruffian
Mo·hole geological project
moi·der *Dialect* to bother

mollycoddler

moi·dore coin
moi·ety (*plural* ·eties) half
moire (*noun*) fabric
moi·ré (*adj*) having watered pattern
moist
mois·ten
moist·en·er
moist·ness
mois·ture
mois·tur·ize (*or* ·ise)
mois·tur·iz·er (*or* ·is·er)
Mo·ja·ve variant spelling of Mohave
moke *Slang* donkey
Mok·po South Korean port
mola (*plural* mola *or* molas) fish
mo·lal
mo·lal·ity (*plural* ·ities) chemistry term
mo·lar tooth; chemistry term
mo·lar·ity
mo·las·ses
mold *US spelling of* mould
Mol·da·via
Mol·da·vian
mol·da·vite glass
mold·er *US spelling of* moulder
mole
mo·lecu·lar
mol·ecule
mole·hill
mole·skin
mo·lest
mo·les·ta·tion
mo·lest·er
mo·line heraldic term
Mo·li·se Italian region
moll
mol·li·fi·able
mol·li·fi·ca·tion
mol·li·fi·er
mol·li·fy (·fies, ·fy·ing, ·fied)
mol·li·fy·ing·ly
mol·lusc (*US* ·lusk)
mol·lus·can (*US* ·kan)
mol·lus·coid (*or* ·coi·dal) zoology term
mol·ly (*plural* ·lies) fish
molly·coddle
molly·coddler

Molly Maguire

Molly Maguire Irish secret society member
Mo·loch Semitic god
mo·loch lizard
Mo·lo·kai Hawaiian island
molt US spelling of moult
mol·ten
mol·to musical term
Mo·luc·cas Indonesian islands
moly (plural **molies**) mythological herb; flower
mo·lyb·date
mo·lyb·de·nite mineral
mo·lyb·de·nous
mo·lyb·de·num chemical element
mo·lyb·dic
mo·lyb·dous
mom US mother
Mom·ba·sa Kenyan port
mo·ment
mo·men·tari·ly
mo·men·tary
mo·men·tous
mo·men·tum (plural **·ta** or **·tums**)
Momus Greek god
mona monkey
Mona·can
mona·chal monastic
mona·chism
Mona·co
mon·ad (plural **·ads** or **mona·des**)
mona·del·phous botany term
mo·nad·ic (or **·nadi·cal**)
mon·ad·ism (or **·ad·ol·ogy**) philosophy
mon·ad·is·tic
mo·nad·nock hill
mon·ad·ol·ogy variant of monadism
Mona·ghan Irish county
mon·al (or **·aul**) pheasant
mo·nan·drous botany term
mo·nan·dry
mo·nan·thous botany term
mon·arch
mo·nar·chal (or **·chi·al**)
mo·nar·chic (or **·chi·cal**)
mon·ar·chism
mon·ar·chist
mon·ar·chis·tic
mon·ar·chy (plural **·chies**)
mo·nar·da plant
mon·as·te·rial
mon·as·tery (plural **·teries**)
mo·nas·tic (or **·ti·cal**)
mo·nas·ti·cal·ly
mo·nas·ti·cism
mon·atom·ic (or **mono·**)
mon·aural
mona·zite mineral
Mönchen-Gladbach West German city
Mon·day
mondi·al of the world
Mon·egasque citizen of Monaco
Monel metal (Trademark)
mon·etar·ism
mon·etar·ist
mon·etary
mon·eti·za·tion (or **·sa·tion**)
mon·etize (or **·etise**)
mon·ey (plural **·eys** or **·ies**)
money·changer
mon·eyed (or **mon·ied**)
money·lender
money·lending
money·maker
money·making
money-spinner
money·wort
mon·ger
mon·ger·ing
mon·go (or **goe**; plural **·gos** or **·goes**) Mongolian currency
Mon·gol
Mon·go·lia
Mon·go·lian
Mon·gol·ic
mon·go·lism former name of Down's syndrome
Mon·gol·oid
mon·goose (plural **·gooses**)
mon·grel
mon·grel·ism (or **·ness**)
mon·greli·za·tion (or **·sa·tion**)
mon·grel·ize (or **·ise**)
mon·grel·ly
moni·ker (or **mon·ick·er**) Slang nickname
mo·nili·form
mon·ism
mon·ist
mo·nis·tic
mo·nis·ti·cal·ly
mo·ni·tion warning
moni·tor
moni·to·rial
moni·tor·ship
moni·tory (or **·to·rial**) warning
moni·tress
monk
mon·key
monkey·pot tree
monk·fish (plural **·fish** or **·fishes**)
Mon-Khmer language
monk·hood being a monk
monk·ish
monks·hood plant
Mon·mouth
Mon·mouth·shire former Welsh county
mono (plural **monos**)
mono·ac·id (or **mon·ac·id**, **mono·acid·ic**, **mona·cid·ic**)
mono·atom·ic variant of monatomic
mono·ba·sic
mono·carp botany term
mono·car·pel·lary
mono·car·pic (or **·pous**)
Mo·noc·er·os constellation
mono·cha·sial
mono·cha·sium (plural **·sia**) botany term
mono·chlo·ride
mono·chord acoustic instrument
mono·chro·mat (or **·mate**)
mono·chro·mat·ic (or **mono·chro·ic**)
mono·chro·mati·cal·ly
mono·chro·ma·tism visual defect
mono·chrome
mono·chro·mic (or **·mi·cal**)
mono·chrom·ist
mono·cle
mono·cli·nal

mono·cline geology term
mono·clin·ic crystallography term
mono·cli·nism botany term
mono·cli·nous
mono·coque car or aircraft body
mono·coty·ledon botany term
mono·coty·ledon·ous
mo·noc·ra·cy (plural ·cies)
mono·crat
mono·crat·ic
mo·nocu·lar
mono·cul·ture
mono·cy·clic
mono·cyte blood cell
mono·cyt·ic
mo·nod·ic (or ·nodi·cal)
mono·dist
mono·dra·ma
mono·dra·mat·ic
mono·dy (plural ·dies)
mo·noecious (or ·necious, ·noi·cous) botany term
mono·fila·ment (or ·fil)
mo·noga·mist
mo·noga·mis·tic
mo·noga·mous
mo·noga·my having one spouse; compare monogyny
mono·gen·esis biology term
mono·genet·ic
mono·gen·ic genetics term
mo·nog·enous
mo·nog·eny
mono·gram
mono·gram·matic
mono·grammed
mono·graph
mo·nog·ra·pher
mono·graph·ic
mono·graphi·cal·ly
mo·nogy·nist
mo·nogy·nous
mo·nogy·ny having one female partner; compare monogamy
mono·hull
mono·hy·brid
mono·hy·drate
mono·hy·droxy
mo·nola·ter (or ·trist)

mo·nola·trous
mo·nola·try worship of one god
mono·lay·er
mono·lin·gual
mono·lith
mono·lith·ic
mono·lithi·cal·ly
mono·log·ic (or ·logi·cal)
mono·log·ist
mono·logue (US also ·log)
mo·nol·ogy
mono·ma·nia
mono·ma·ni·ac
mono·ma·nia·cal
mono·mark
mono·mer chemistry term
mono·mer·ic
mo·nom·er·ous botany term
mono·me·tal·lic
mono·met·al·lism
mono·met·al·list
mo·nom·eter verse line
mono·met·ri·cal (or ·met·ric)
mo·no·mial
mono·mo·lecu·lar
mono·mor·phic (or ·phous)
mono·mor·phism
mono·nu·clear
mono·nu·cleo·sis
mono·pet·al·ous
mo·nopha·gous
mo·nopha·gy
mono·pho·bia
mono·pho·bic
mono·phon·ic
mo·nopho·ny
mon·oph·thong
mon·oph·thon·gal
mono·phy·let·ic genetics term
mono·phyl·lous botany term
mono·plane
mono·plegia
mono·plegic
mono·po·dial
mono·po·dium (plural ·dia) botany term
mo·nopo·lism
mo·nopo·list

mo·nopo·lis·tic
mo·nopo·lis·ti·cal·ly
mo·nopo·li·za·tion (or ·sa·tion)
mo·nopo·lize (or ·lise)
mo·nopo·liz·er (or ·lis·er)
Mo·nopo·ly (Trádemark) game
mo·nopo·ly (plural ·lies)
mono·pro·pel·lant
mo·nop·so·nis·tic
mo·nop·so·ny (plural ·nies) economics term
mon·op·te·ros (or ·ron; plural ·roi or ·ra) architectural term
mono·rail
mono·sac·cha·ride
mono·semy having only one meaning
mono·sepa·lous
mono·so·dium glu·ta·mate
mono·some chromosome
mono·so·mic
mono·sper·mous (or ·sper·mal)
mono·stich single-line poem
mono·stich·ic
mono·stich·ous botany term
mono·stome (or mo·nos·to·mous) having one mouth
mo·nos·tro·phe poem
mono·stroph·ic
mono·sty·lous botany term
mono·syl·lab·ic
mono·syl·labi·cal·ly
mono·syl·la·bism
mono·syl·la·ble
mono·theism
mono·theist
mono·theis·tic
mono·theis·ti·cal·ly
mono·tint
mono·tone
mono·ton·ic
mo·noto·nous
mo·noto·ny (plural ·nies)
mono·trema·tous
mono·treme mammal
mo·no·tri·chous (or ·trich·ic) bacteriology term

Monotype

Mono·type (*Trademark*) typesetting machine
mono·type
mono·typ·ic
mono·va·lence (*or* **·len·cy**)
mono·va·lent
mon·ox·ide
Mon·ro·via Liberian capital
Mons Belgian town
mons (*plural* **mon·tes**) anatomy term
Mon·sei·gneur (*plural* **Mes·sei·gneurs**) French title
mon·sieur (*plural* **mes·sieurs**) French gentleman; Mr
Mon·sig·nor (*plural* **·nors** *or* **·nori**) ecclesiastical title
mon·soon
mon·ster
mon·strance receptacle for consecrated Host
mon·stros·ity (*plural* **·ities**)
mon·strous
mon·strous·ness
mon·tage
Mon·ta·gnard (*plural* **·gnards** *or* **·gnard**) mountain people
Mon·tana
mon·tane of mountainous regions
Mon·tau·ban French city
Mont Blanc
mont·bre·tia plant
mon·te gambling game
Mon·te Car·lo
Mon·te·go Bay Jamaican port
mon·teith bowl for cooling wineglasses
Mon·te·ne·grin
Mon·te·ne·gro Yugoslav republic
Mon·te·rey Californian city
mon·te·ro (*plural* **·ros**) hunting cap
Mon·ter·rey Mexican city
Montessori meth·od
Mon·te·vi·deo Uruguayan capital

mont·gol·fier hot-air balloon
Mont·gom·ery US city
month
month·ly (*plural* **·lies**)
mon·ti·cule small hill
Mont·mar·tre
Mont·par·nasse
Mont·pel·lier
Mon·treal
Mon·treuil Parisian suburb
monu·ment
monu·men·tal
monu·men·tal·ly
monu·men·tal·ity
Mon·za Italian city
mon·zo·nite rock
mon·zo·nit·ic
moo
mooch
mooch·er
mood
moodi·ly
moodi·ness
moody (**moodi·er**, **moodi·est**)
Moog syn·the·siz·er (*Trademark*)
moo·lah *Slang* money
mool·vie (*or* **·vi**) Muslim learned man
moon
moon·beam
moon·calf (*plural* **·calves**)
moon·eye fish
moon-faced
moon·fish (*plural* **·fishes** *or* **·fish**)
moon·flower
mooni·ly
mooni·ness
moon·less
moon·light
moon·lighter
moon·light·ing
moon·lit
moon·quake
moon·raker sail
moon·rise
moon·scape
moon·seed
moon·set
moon·shine
moon·shiner *US* whisky smuggler

moon·shot
moon·stone
moon·struck (*or* **·stricken**)
moon·wort
moony (**mooni·er**, **mooni·est**)
Moor African Muslim
moor open ground; attach boat; *compare* **more**
moor·age
moor·cock
moor·fowl
moor·hen
moor·ing
moor·ings
Moor·ish
moor·land
moor·wort shrub
moose (*plural* **moose**)
moot
moot·er
mop (**mop·ping**, **mopped**)
mope
moped *past tense of* **mope**
mo·ped motorcycle
mop·er
mop·ing·ly
mo·poke owl
mopped
mop·pet
mop·ping
mo·quette fabric
mor humus
mora (*plural* **morae** *or* **moras**) prosody term
mo·ra·ceous botany term
Mo·ra·da·bad Indian city
mo·rain·al (*or* **·ic**)
mo·raine glacier debris; *compare* **murrain**
mor·al
mo·rale confidence
mor·al·ism
mor·al·ist
mor·al·is·tic
mor·al·is·ti·cal·ly
mor·al·ity (*plural* **·ities**)
mor·ali·za·tion (*or* **·sa·tion**)
mor·al·ize (*or* **·ise**)
mor·al·iz·er (*or* **·is·er**)
mor·al·iz·ing·ly (*or* **·is·ing·ly**)
mor·al·ly

Mor·ar Scottish loch
mo·rass
mora·to·rium (*plural* **·ria** *or* **·riums**)
mora·tory
Mo·ra·va Czech river
Mo·ra·via
Mo·ra·vian
Mo·ra·vi·an·ism religious movement
Mor·ay former Scottish county
mo·ray (*plural* **·rays**) eel
mor·bid
mor·bid·ity
mor·bid·ness
mor·bif·ic causing disease
mor·bifi·cal·ly
Mor·bi·han French department
mor·bil·li measles
mor·ceau (*plural* **·ceaux**) *French* morsel
mor·cha Indian demonstration
mor·da·cious sarcastic
mor·dac·ity (*or* **·da·cious·ness**)
mor·dan·cy
mor·dant sarcastic; dye fixer
mor·dent musical ornament
Mord·vin (*plural* **·vin** *or* **·vins**) Finnish people
Mor·dvin·ian
more *comparative of* **much**; *compare* **moor**
More·cambe Lancashire town
mo·reen fabric
more·ish (*or* **mor·ish**)
mo·rel edible fungus
Mo·relia Mexican city
mo·rel·lo (*plural* **·los**) cherry
Mo·relos Mexican state
more·over
mo·res customs
Mo·res·co *variant spelling of* **Morisco**
Mo·resque Moorish
Mor·gan horse
mor·ga·nat·ic
mor·ga·nati·cal·ly
mor·gan·ite gemstone

Morgan le Fay legendary character
morgue
mori·bund
mori·bun·dity
mo·ri·on helmet
Mo·ris·co (*or* **·res·**; *plural* **·coes** *or* **·cos**) Spanish Moor
mor·ish *variant spelling of* **moreish**
Mor·mon
Mor·mon·ism
morn morning; *compare* **mourn**
mor·nay cookery term
morn·ing
morning-glory (*plural* **-glories**)
Moro (*plural* **Moros** *or* **Moro**) Muslim people
Mo·roc·can
Mo·roc·co
mo·roc·co leather
mor·on
Mo·ro·ni capital of Comoro Islands
mo·ron·ic
mo·roni·cal·ly
mo·ron·ism (*or* **·ity**)
mo·rose
mo·rose·ly
mo·rose·ness
morph linguistics term
mor·phal·lax·is (*plural* **·laxes**) zoology term
mor·pheme grammatical unit
mor·phem·ic
mor·phemi·cal·ly
Morpheus Greek god
mor·phine (*or* **·phia**)
mor·phin·ism
mor·pho·gen·esis
mor·pho·genet·ic (*or* **·gen·ic**)
mor·pho·log·ic (*or* **·logi·cal**)
mor·pho·logi·cal·ly
mor·pholo·gist
mor·phol·ogy
mor·pho·pho·neme linguistics term
mor·pho·pho·nemic
mor·pho·pho·nemics

mor·pho·sis (*plural* **·ses**) biology term
mor·ris dance
mor·ro (*plural* **·ros**) hill
mor·row
Mors Roman god
Morse code
morse cloak fastening
mor·sel
mort hunting term
mor·tal
mor·tal·ity (*plural* **·ities**)
mor·tal·ly
mor·tar
mortar·board
mort·gage
mort·gage·able
mort·ga·gee
mort·gag·or (*or* **·er**)
mor·tice *variant spelling of* **mortise**
mor·ti·cian *US* undertaker
mor·ti·fi·ca·tion
mor·ti·fi·er
mor·ti·fy (**·fies**, **·fy·ing**, **·fied**)
mor·ti·fy·ing·ly
mor·tise (*or* **·tice**)
mor·tis·er
mort·main legal term
mor·tu·ary (*plural* **·aries**)
moru·la (*plural* **·las** *or* **·lae**) biology term
moru·lar
mor·wong fish
Mo·sa·ic (*or* **·sai·cal**) of Moses
mo·sa·ic (**·ick·ing**, **·icked**)
mo·sai·cist
mos·cha·tel plant
Mos·cow
Mo·selle European river; wine
mo·sey
Mos·lem *variant spelling of* **Muslim**
Mo·so·tho (*plural* **·tho** *or* **·thos**) African people
mosque
mos·qui·to (*plural* **·toes** *or* **·tos**)
moss
moss·back *US* conservative
moss·bunk·er fish

Mossi

Mos·si (*plural* ·**sis** *or* ·**si**) African people
mos·sie bird
mossi·ness
mos·so musical term
moss·trooper
mossy (**mossi·er, mossi·est**)
most
most·ly
Mosul Iraqi city
mote tiny speck; *compare* **moat**
mo·tel
mo·tet
moth
moth·ball
moth-eaten
moth·er
moth·er·hood
mother-in-law (*plural* **mothers-**)
mother·land
moth·er·less
moth·er·li·ness
moth·er·ly
mother-of-pearl
mother·wort plant
moth·proof
mothy (**mothi·er, mothi·est**)
mo·tif theme; *compare* **motive**
mo·tile
mo·til·ity
mo·tion
mo·tion·er
mo·tion·less
mo·tion·less·ness
mo·ti·vate
mo·ti·va·tion
mo·ti·va·tion·al
mo·ti·va·tive
mo·tive reason; causing motion; *compare* **motif**
mo·tive·less
mo·tive·less·ness
mo·tiv·ity
mot juste (*plural* **mots justes**)
mot·ley
mot·mot bird
mo·to·cross motorcycle race
mo·to·neu·ron nerve cell

mo·tor
motor·bike
motor·boat
motor·bus
motor·cade
motor·car
motor·coach
motor·cycle
motor·cyclist
mo·tor·ist
mo·tori·za·tion (*or* ·**sa·tion**)
mo·tor·ize (*or* ·**ise**)
motor·man (*plural* ·**men**)
motor·way
motte castle mound
mott·le
mot·to (*plural* ·**toes** *or* ·**tos**)
mouf·lon (*or* **mouf·flon**) wild sheep
mouil·lé phonetics term
mould (*US* **mold**)
mould·abil·ity (*US* **mold**·)
mould·able (*US* **mold**·)
mould·board (*US* **mold**·) curved blade of plough
mould·er (*US* **mold**·) crumble; one who moulds
mouldi·ness (*US* **moldi**·)
mould·ing (*US* **mold**·)
mould·warp *Dialect* mole
mouldy (*US* **moldy**; **mouldi·er, mouldi·est,** *US* **moldi·er, moldi·est**)
mou·lin glacier shift
Moul·mein (*or* **Maul·main**) Burmese port
moult (*US* **molt**)
moult·er (*US* **molt**·)
mound
mount
mount·able
moun·tain
moun·tain·eer
moun·tain·eer·ing
moun·tain·ous
mountain·top
moun·tebank
moun·tebank·ery
mount·ed
mount·er

Mountie Canadian policeman
mount·ing
Mount Rush·more
mourn grieve; *compare* **morn**
mourn·er
mourn·ful
mourn·ful·ly
mourn·ful·ness
mourn·ing
mouse (*plural* **mice**)
mous·er
mouse·tail plant
mouse·trap
mousi·ness
mous·ing nautical term
mous·sa·ka (*or* **mou·sa**·)
mousse
mousse·line fabric; cookery term
mous·tache (*US* **mus**·)
mousy (*or* **mous·ey**; **mousi·er, mousi·est**)
mouth
mouth·brooder (*or* ·**breeder**) fish
(**mouthe**) *incorrect spelling of* **mouth** (*verb*)
mouth·er
mouth·ful (*plural* ·**fuls**)
mouth·part
mouth·piece
mouth-to-mouth
mouth·wash
mouth·water·ing
mou·ton processed sheepskin
mov·abil·ity (*or* ·**able·ness**)
mov·able (*or in legal contexts* **move**·)
mov·ably
move (**mov·ing, moved**)
move·ables legal term
move·ment
mov·er
movie
Movie·tone (*Trademark*)
mov·ing
mov·ing·ly
Mo·vio·la (*Trademark*)
mow (**mow·ing, mowed, mowed** *or* **mown**)
mow·burnt agricultural term

mow·er
moxa medicinal substance
moxie US courage
Mo·zam·bi·can
Mo·zam·bique (or Mo·çam·)
moz·za·rel·la cheese
moz·zet·ta (or mo·zet·ta) clerical cape
Mr (plural Messrs)
Mrs
Ms
much (more, most)
much·ness
mu·cic acid
mu·cid mouldy
mu·ci·lage
mu·ci·lagi·nous
mu·cin biochemical compound
mu·cin·ous
muck
muck·er
mucki·ly
mucki·ness
muck·le Scot much
muck·rake
muck·rak·er
muck·worm
mucky (mucki·er, mucki·est)
mu·coid (or ·coi·dal)
mu·co·mem·bra·nous
mu·co·poly·sac·cha·ride
mu·co·pro·tein
mu·co·pu·ru·lent
mu·co·sa (plural ·sae) mucous membrane
mu·cos·ity
mu·cous (or ·cose; adj)
mu·cro (plural mu·cro·nes) biology term
mu·cro·nate (or ·nat·ed)
mu·cro·na·tion
mu·cus (noun)
mud (mud·ding, mud·ded)
mud·cat fish
mud·died
mud·di·ly
mud·di·ness
mud·dle
mud·dled·ness
muddle·headed
muddle·headed·ness

mud·dle·ment
mud·dler
mud·dling·ly
mud·dy (adj ·di·er, ·di·est; verb ·dies, ·dy·ing, ·died)
mud·fish (plural ·fish or ·fishes)
mud·guard
mu·dir governor
mud·lark
mud·pack
mu·dra Hindu dance movement
mud·skipper fish
mud·slinger
mud·slinging
mud·stone
muen·ster cheese
mues·li
mu·ez·zin mosque official
muff
muf·fin
muf·fle
muf·fler
Muf·ti (plural ·tis) Muslim legal adviser
muf·ti (plural ·tis) civilian dress
Mu·fu·li·ra Zambian town
mug (mug·ging, mugged)
mug·ger street robber
mug·ger (or ·gar, ·gur) crocodile
mug·gi·ly
mug·gi·ness
mug·gins
mug·gy (·gi·er, ·gi·est)
mug·wort
mug·wump politically neutral person
Mu·ham·mad·an Muslim
Mühl·hau·sen West German city
muk·luk Eskimo boot
mu·lat·to (plural ·tos or ·toes)
mul·berry (plural ·berries)
mulch soil enricher
mulct cheat
mule
mu·leta matador's cape
mu·leteer mule driver

multimedia

mul·ey (or mul·ley) hornless cattle
mul·ga tree
Mül·heim an der Ruhr West German city
mu·li·eb·rity womanhood
mul·ish
mul·ish·ness
Mull Scottish island
mull
mul·lah (or mul·la) Muslim leader
mul·lein (or ·len) plant
mul·ler
mul·let
mul·ley variant spelling of muley
mul·li·gan stew
mul·li·ga·taw·ny
mul·li·on
mul·li·oned
mul·lite mineral
mul·lock Dialect mess
mullo·way fish
Mul·tan Pakistani city
mul·tan·gu·lar (or multi·an·)
mul·teity manifoldness
multi·birth
multi·cel·lu·lar
multi·chan·nel
multi·cide mass murder
multi·col·lin·ear·ity statistics term
multi·col·oured (US ·ored)
multi·di·rec·tion·al
multi·dis·ci·pli·nary
multi·fac·et·ed
multi·fac·to·rial
multi·fari·ous
multi·fid (or mul·tifi·dous)
multi·foil looped design
multi·fold
multi·fo·li·ate
multi·form
multi·for·mity
multi·gravi·da obstetrics term
multi·hull
multi·lami·nar
multi·lat·er·al
multi·lin·gual
multi·media

multimillionaire

multi·mil·lion·aire
multi·na·tion·al
multi·no·mial
multi·nu·clear (*or* ·cleate)
mul·tipa·ra (*plural* ·rae) obstetrics term
multi·par·ity
mul·tipa·rous
multi·par·tite
multi·plane multi-winged aircraft
multi·ple
multiple-choice
multiple·poind·ing Scottish legal term
multi·plet physics term
multi·plex electronics term
multi·plex·er
multi·pli·able
multi·pli·cand number multiplied
multi·pli·cate manifold
multi·pli·ca·tion
multi·pli·ca·tion·al
multi·pli·ca·tive
multi·plic·ity (*plural* ·ities)
multi·pli·er
multi·ply (·plies, ·ply·ing, ·plied)
multi·pro·gram·ming
multi·pur·pose
multi·racial
multi·role
multi·screen
multi·stage
multi·sto·rey
multi·tude
multi·tu·di·nous
multi·va·len·cy
multi·va·lent
multi·vi·bra·tor
mul·ture miller's fee
mum mother; silent
mum (*or* mumm; mum·ming, mummed) act in mummer's play
mum·ble
mum·bler
mum·bling·ly
mum·bo jum·bo (*plural* mum·bo jum·bos)
mum·chance dumbstruck
mum·mer

mum·mery (*plural* ·meries)
mum·mi·fi·ca·tion
mum·mi·fy (·fies, ·fy·ing, ·fied)
mum·my (*plural* ·mies)
mumps
munch
munch·er
mun·dane
mun·dane·ness
mung bean
munga *Austral* food
mun·go (*or* mon·go, mon·goe; *plural* ·gos *or* ·goes) fabric
Mu·nich
mu·nici·pal
mu·nici·pal·ity (*plural* ·ities)
mu·nici·pali·za·tion (*or* ·sa·tion)
mu·nici·pal·ize (*or* ·ise)
mu·nici·pal·ly
mu·nifi·cence (*or* ·cent·ness)
mu·nifi·cent
mu·ni·ment means of defence
mu·ni·ments title deeds
mu·ni·tion
Mun·ster Irish province
Mün·ster West German city
munt·jac (*or* ·jak) deer
muon elementary particle
mu·ral
mu·ral·ist
mur·der
mur·der·er (*fem* ·ess)
mur·der·ous
mur·der·ous·ness
Mu·reş European river
mu·rex (*plural* mu·ri·ces) mollusc
mu·ri·cate (*or* ·cat·ed) biology term
mu·rine of rats and mice
murk (*or* mirk)
murki·ly (*or* mirki·)
murki·ness (*or* mirki·)
murky (*or* mirky; murki·er, murki·est *or* mirki·er, mirki·est)
Mur·mansk Soviet port
mur·mur

300

mur·mur·er
mur·mur·ing
mur·mur·ous
mur·phy (*plural* ·phies) *Dialect* potato
mur·rain cattle disease; *compare* **moraine**
Mur·ray Australian river
murre guillemot
murre·let bird
mur·rhine (*or* ·rine) Roman vase material
Mur·rum·bidgee Australian river
mur·ther *Archaic* murder
mu·sa·ceous botany term
Mus·ca constellation
mus·ca·del (*or* ·delle) variants *of* **muscatel**
mus·ca·dine US grape
mus·ca·rine poisonous alkaloid
Mus·cat capital of Oman
mus·cat grape
mus·ca·tel (*or* ·del, ·delle) wine
mus·cid fly
mus·cle
muscle-bound
mus·cle·man (*plural* ·men)
mus·cly
mus·co·va·do (*or* mus·ca·) raw sugar
Mus·co·vite native of Moscow
mus·co·vite mineral
Mus·co·vy Russian principality; duck
mus·cu·lar
mus·cu·lar·ity
mus·cu·la·ture
muse
muse·ful
mus·eol·ogy museum organization; *compare* musicology
mus·er
mu·sette bagpipe
mu·seum
mush
mushi·ly
mushi·ness
mush·room
mushy (mushi·er, mushi·est)

mu·sic
mu·si·cal
mu·si·cale *US* musical evening
mu·si·cal·ly
mu·si·cal·ness (*or* ·ity)
mu·si·cian
mu·si·cian·ship
mu·si·co·logi·cal
mu·si·colo·gist
mu·si·col·ogy study of music; *compare* museology
mus·jid *variant spelling of* masjid
musk
mus·keg bog
mus·kel·lunge (*or* mas·ka·nonge, ·ki·) fish
mus·ket
mus·ket·eer
mus·ket·ry
muski·ness
musk·melon
musk·rat (*plural* ·rats *or* ·rat)
musky (muski·er, muski·est)
Mus·lim (*or* Mos·lem; *plural* ·lims, ·lim *or* ·lems, ·lem)
Mus·lim·ism (*or* Mos·lem·)
mus·lin
muso *Austral* musician
mus·quash
muss *US* rumple
mus·sel mollusc; *compare* muscle
must
mus·tache *US spelling of* moustache
mus·ta·chio (*plural* ·chi·os)
mus·ta·chi·oed
mus·tang
mus·tard
mus·tee (*or* mes·) person of mixed parentage
mus·te·line of badger family
mus·ter
musth (*or* must) sexual heat in animals
musti·ly
musti·ness
mus·ty (·ti·er, ·ti·est)

mu·tabil·ity (*or* ·table·ness)
mu·table
mu·tably
mu·ta·gen substance causing mutation
mu·ta·gen·ic
mu·tant
mu·tate
mu·ta·tion
mu·ta·tion·al
mu·ta·tis mu·tan·dis
mutch linen cap
mute
mute·ness
mu·ti·cous botany term
mu·ti·late
mu·ti·la·tion
mu·ti·la·tive
mu·ti·la·tor
mu·ti·neer
mu·ti·nous
mu·ti·ny (*noun, plural* ·nies; *verb* ·nies, ·ny·ing, ·nied)
mut·ism
mutt *Slang* fool; cur
mut·ter
mut·ter·er
mut·ter·ing·ly
mut·ton
mutton·chops side whiskers
mut·tony
mu·tu·al
mu·tu·al·ity (*or* ·ness)
mu·tu·al·ize (*or* ·ise)
mu·tu·al·ly
mu·tule architecture term
Mu·zak (*Trademark*)
mu·zhik (*or* mou·jik, mu·jik) Russian peasant
muzz make muzzy
muz·zi·ly
muz·zi·ness
muz·zle
muz·zler
muz·zy (·zi·er, ·zi·est)
my
my·al·gia muscle pain
my·al·gic
mya·lism witchcraft
my·all tree
my·as·thenia muscular weakness
my·as·then·ic

my·celial
my·celium (*plural* ·celia) fungal body
my·celoid
My·cenae ancient Greek city
My·cenaean
my·ceto·ma (*plural* ·mas *or* ·ma·ta) fungal infection
my·ceto·zoan fungus
my·co·bac·te·rium (*plural* ·ria)
my·co·logi·cal (*or* ·log·ic)
my·colo·gist
my·col·ogy study of fungi
my·cor·rhi·za (*or* ·co·rhi·; *plural* ·zae *or* ·zas) botany term
my·cor·rhi·zal (*or* ·co·rhi·)
my·co·sis fungal disease
my·cot·ic
my·dria·sis pupil dilation
myd·ri·at·ic
my·elen·cephal·ic
my·elen·cepha·lon (*plural* ·lons *or* ·la) embryology term
my·elin (*or* ·eline) nerve sheath
my·elin·ic
my·eli·tis
my·eloid
my·elo·ma tumour
my·elo·ma·toid
myia·sis (*plural* ·ses) infestation by fly larvae
my·lo·nite rock
myna (*or* my·nah, mina) bird
Myn·heer Dutch title of address
myo·car·dial
myo·car·dio·graph
myo·car·di·tis
myo·car·dium (*plural* ·dia) heart muscle
myo·gen·ic
myo·glo·bin protein
myo·graph
myo·graph·ic
myo·graphi·cal·ly
my·og·ra·phy
myo·log·ic (*or* ·logi·cal)
my·olo·gist

myology

my·ol·ogy study of muscle diseases
myo·ma (*plural* **·mas** *or* **·ma·ta**) tumour
my·ope
myo·pia
my·op·ic
my·opi·cal·ly
myo·sin protein
myo·sis *variant spelling of* miosis
myo·so·tis (*or* **·sote**) plant
myo·tome anatomy term
myo·to·nia lack of muscle tone
myo·ton·ic
myri·ad
myria·pod invertebrate
myri·apo·dan
myri·apo·dous
my·ri·ca medicinal bark
myr·meco·logi·cal
myr·mecolo·gist
myr·mecol·ogy study of ants
myr·mecopha·gous
myr·meco·phile
myr·mecophi·lous
Myr·mi·don (*plural* **mi·dons** *or* **mido·nes**) mythological race
my·roba·lan fruit
myrrh

myr·ta·ceous
myr·tle
my·self
My·sore Indian city
mys·ta·gog·ic (*or* **·gogi·cal**)
mys·ta·gogi·cal·ly
mys·ta·gogue mystic teacher
mys·ta·go·gy
mys·teri·ous
mys·teri·ous·ness
mys·tery (*plural* **·teries**)
mys·tic
mys·ti·cal
mys·ti·cal·ly
mys·ti·cism
mys·ti·fi·ca·tion
mys·ti·fi·er
mys·ti·fy (**·fies**, **·fy·ing**, **·fied**)
mys·ti·fy·ing·ly
mys·tique
myth
mythi·cal
mythi·cal·ly
mythi·cist (*or* **·ciz·er**, **·cis·er**)
mythi·ci·za·tion (*or* **·sa·tion**)
mythi·cize (*or* **·cise**)
mytho·logi·cal

302

my·tholo·gist
my·tholo·gi·za·tion (*or* **·sa·tion**)
my·tholo·gize (*or* **·gise**)
my·tholo·giz·er (*or* **·gis·er**)
my·thol·ogy (*plural* **·ogies**)
mytho·ma·nia psychiatric term
mytho·ma·ni·ac
mytho·poeia (*or* **·po·esis**) myth making
mytho·poe·ic
mytho·poe·ism
mytho·poe·ist
my·thos (*plural* **·thoi**) group of beliefs
(myxamatosis) *incorrect spelling of* myxomatosis
myx·oedema (*US* **·edema**) thyroid disease
myx·oedem·ic (*US* **·edem·**)
myxo·ma (*plural* **·mas** *or* **·ma·ta**) tumour
myxo·ma·to·sis
myx·oma·tous
myxo·my·cete fungus
myxo·my·cetous
myxo·vi·rus

N

Naafi (*or* **NAAFI**)
nab (**nab·bing**, **nabbed**)
Na·blus (*or* **Nabu·lus**) Jordanian town
na·bob
na·bob·ery (*or* **·ism**)
Nabonidus biblical character
Naboth biblical character
na·celle part of aircraft
na·cre mother-of-pearl
na·cred
na·cre·ous
Na-Dene (*or* **-Déné**) language group
na·dir
nae *Scot* no
nae·void (*US* **ne·**)

nae·vus (*US* **ne·**; *plural* **·vi**) birthmark
nag (**nag·ging**, **nagged**)
Naga (*plural* **Nagas** *or* **Naga**) Indian people
Na·ga·land
na·ga·na (*or* **n'ga·na**) animal disease
Na·ga·no Japanese city
Na·ga·ri Indian script
Na·ga·sa·ki Japanese port
nagged
nag·ger
nag·ging
na·gor antelope
Nagorno-Karabakh Soviet region
Na·go·ya Japanese city

Nag·pur Indian city
Na·huatl (*plural* **·huatl** *or* **·huatls**) American Indian
Na·hua·tlan
nai·ad (*plural* **·ads** *or* **·ades**)
na·if *variant spelling of* naive
nail
nail·brush
nail·er
nail·file
nail·head decorative device
nain·sook fabric
nai·ra Nigerian currency
Nairn former Scottish county
Nai·ro·bi
nais·sant heraldry term

na·ive (*or* ·ïve, ·ïf)
na·ive·ty (*or* ·ive·té, ·ïve·té)
Najd *variant spelling of* Nejd
na·ked
na·ked·ness
na·ker kettledrum
Na·khi·che·van Soviet city
Nal·chik Soviet city
Nama (*or* Na·ma·qua; *plural* Nama, Namas *or* ·qua, ·quas) Hottentot people
nam·able (*or* name·)
Na·man·gan Soviet city
namby-pamby (*plural* -pambies)
nam·dah *variant spelling of* numdah
name
name-dropper
name-dropping
name·less
name·ly
name·plate
name·sake
name·tape
Nam·hoi Chinese city
Na·mibia
Na·mib·ian
Na·mur Belgian province
nan (*or* nanna) *Slang* grandmother
Nan·chang (*or* Nan-ch'ang) Chinese city
Nan·cy French city
nan·cy (*plural* ·cies) effeminate man
Nan·da Devi Himalayan mountain
Nan·ga Par·bat Himalayan mountain
nan·keen (*or* ·kin) fabric
Nan·king (*or* Nan-ching) Chinese port
nanna *variant of* nan
Nan·ning (*or* Nan-ning) Chinese port
nan·ny (*plural* ·nies)
na·no·metre (*US* ·meter)
na·no·plank·ton (*or* nan·no·)
na·no·sec·ond
Nan Shan Chinese mountain range
Nantes French port
Nan·tuck·et US island

Nan·tung Chinese city
Naoise Irish mythological character
nap (nap·ping, napped)
na·palm
nape
naph·tha
naph·tha·lene (*or* ·line, ·lin)
naph·thene
naph·thol
naph·thyl
Na·pier New Zealand port
Na·pier·ian loga·ri·thm
na·pi·form turnip-shaped
nap·kin
Na·ples
na·po·le·on coin
Na·po·leon·ic
nap·pa leather
nappe rock fold
napped
nap·per *Slang* head
nap·pi·ness
nap·ping
nap·py (*noun, plural* ·pies; *adj* ·pi·er, ·pi·est)
Nara Japanese city
Na·ra·yan·ganj Bangladeshi city
nar·ceine (*or* ·ceen) alkaloid
nar·cis·sism (*or* nar·cism)
nar·cis·sist
nar·cis·sis·tic
nar·cis·sus (*plural* ·si *or* ·suses)
nar·co·analy·sis
nar·co·lep·sy
nar·co·lep·tic
nar·co·sis (*plural* ·ses)
nar·co·syn·thesis medical treatment
nar·cot·ic
nar·coti·cal·ly
nar·co·tism
nar·co·ti·za·tion (*or* ·sa·tion)
nar·co·tize (*or* ·tise)
nard medicinal plant
nar·es (*sing.* ·is) nostrils
nar·ghi·le hookah
nar·ial (*or* ·ine)
nark
Nar·ra·gan·set (*or* ·sett; *plural* ·set, ·sets *or*

·sett, ·setts) American Indian
nar·rat·able
nar·rate
nar·ra·tion
nar·ra·tive
nar·ra·tor (*or* ·rat·er)
nar·row
narrow-minded
narrow-minded·ness
nar·row·ness
nar·thex church portico
Nar·vik Norwegian port
nar·whal (*or* ·wal, ·whale) whale
nary *Dialect* not
na·sal
na·sal·ity
na·sali·za·tion (*or* ·sa·tion)
na·sal·ize (*or* ·ise)
na·sal·ly
nas·cence (*or* ·cen·cy)
nas·cent
Nash·ville US city
na·sial
na·si·on anatomy term
na·so·fron·tal
na·so·pha·ryn·geal
na·so·phar·ynx (*plural* ·pha·ryn·ges *or* ·phar·ynxes)
Nas·sau West German region; Bahamian capital
nas·tic botany term
nas·ti·ly
nas·ti·ness
na·stur·tium
nas·ty (*adj* ·ti·er, ·ti·est; *noun, plural* ·ties)
Na·tal South African province; Brazilian port
na·tal of birth
na·tal·ity
na·tant floating
na·ta·tion swimming
na·ta·tion·al
na·ta·tory
na·tes (*sing.* ·tis) buttocks
na·tion
na·tion·al
na·tion·al·ism
na·tion·al·ist
na·tion·al·is·tic
na·tion·al·ity (*plural* ·ities)

nationalization

na·tion·ali·za·tion (*or* ·sa·tion)
na·tion·al·ize (*or* ·ise)
na·tion·al·ly
na·tion·hood
nation-wide
na·tive
na·tiv·ism
na·tiv·ist
na·tiv·is·tic
Na·tiv·ity Christ's birth
na·tiv·ity (*plural* ·ities) birth or origin
NATO
nat·ro·lite mineral
na·tron mineral
nat·ter
nat·ter·jack toad
nat·ti·ly
nat·ti·ness
nat·ty (·ti·er, ·ti·est)
natu·ral
natu·ral·ism artistic movement; *compare* naturism
natu·ral·ist
natu·ral·is·tic
natu·ral·is·ti·cal·ly
natu·rali·za·tion (*or* ·sa·tion)
natu·ral·ize (*or* ·ise)
natu·ral·ly
natu·ral·ness
na·ture
na·tur·ism nudism; *compare* naturalism
na·tur·ist
na·turo·path
na·turo·path·ic
na·tur·opa·thy nature cure
naught *Archaic* nothing; *US spelling of* nought
naugh·ti·ly
naugh·ti·ness
naugh·ty (·ti·er, ·ti·est)
nau·plius (*plural* ·plii) crustacean larva
Nau·ru island republic
Nau·ruan
nau·sea
nau·seate
nau·sea·tion
nau·seous
nau·seous·ness
nautch (*or* nauch) Indian dance
nau·ti·cal

304

nau·ti·cal·ly
nau·ti·loid
nau·ti·lus (*plural* ·luses *or* ·li) mollusc
Nava·ho (*or* ·jo; *plural* ·ho, ·hos *or* ·jo, ·jos) American Indian
na·val of ships; *compare* navel
na·val·ly
nav·ar navigation system
nava·rin mutton stew
Na·varre
nave
na·vel umbilicus; *compare* naval
navi·cert cargo certificate
na·vicu·lar boat-shaped
navi·gabil·ity (*or* ·gable·ness)
navi·gable
navi·gably
navi·gate
navi·ga·tion
navi·ga·tion·al
navi·ga·tor
nav·vy (*plural* ·vies) labourer
navy (*plural* navies)
na·wab Indian prince
Nax·os Greek island
nay no; *compare* neigh
Na·ya·rit Mexican state
Naza·rene inhabitant of Nazareth; Syrian Christian
Naza·reth
Naza·rite (*or* Nazi·) Old Testament ascetic
Naze Essex headland
Nazi (*plural* Nazis)
Na·zi·fy (·fies, ·fy·ing, ·fied)
Na·zism
Ndja·me·na capital of Chad
Ndo·la Zambian city
Neagh Northern Irish lake
Ne·an·der·thal
neap tide
Nea·poli·tan
near
near·by
Ne·arc·tic zoogeographical term
near·ly
near·ness
near·side
near-sighted

near-sighted·ness
neat
neat·en
neath *Archaic* beneath
neat·ness
neat's-foot oil
neb *Dialect* projecting part
Ne·bras·ka
nebu·chad·nez·zar wine bottle
nebu·la (*plural* ·lae *or* ·las)
nebu·lar
nebu·li·za·tion (*or* ·sa·tion)
nebu·lize (*or* ·lise) atomize
nebu·liz·er (*or* ·lis·er)
nebu·los·ity (*plural* ·ities)
nebu·lous
nebu·lous·ness
ne·ces·saries
nec·es·sari·ly
nec·es·sary
ne·ces·si·tar·ian (*or* nec·es·sar·ian)
ne·ces·si·tari·an·ism (*or* nec·es·sari·an·ism) philosophy term
ne·ces·si·tate
ne·ces·sita·tion
ne·ces·si·ta·tive
ne·ces·si·tous
ne·ces·sity (*plural* ·sities)
neck
Neck·ar West German river
neck·band
neck·cloth
neck·er
neck·er·chief
neck·lace
neck·line
neck·piece
neck·tie
neck·wear
nec·ro·bio·sis death of cells
nec·ro·bi·ot·ic
ne-crola·try worship of the dead
nec·ro·logi·cal
ne·crolo·gist
ne·crol·ogy (*plural* ·ogies) list of dead people
nec·ro·man·cer
nec·ro·man·cy
nec·ro·man·tic
nec·ro·philia (*or* ne·crophi·lism)

nec·ro·phili·ac (or ·phile)
nec·ro·phil·ic
nec·ro·phobe
nec·ro·pho·bia
nec·ro·pho·bic
ne·cropo·lis (plural ·lises or ·leis)
nec·rop·sy (plural ·sies)
ne·crose (verb)
ne·cro·sis
ne·crot·ic
ne·croto·my (plural ·mies) dissection of corpse
nec·tar
nec·tar·eous (or ·ous)
nec·tar·ine
nec·ta·ry (plural ·ries)
ned·dy (plural ·dies)
née (or nee) indicating maiden name
need
need·ful
need·ful·ness
needi·ness
nee·dle
needle·cord
needle·craft
needle·fish (plural ·fish or ·fishes)
needle·ful
needle·point
need·less
need·less·ness
needle·woman (plural ·women)
needle·work
need·ments
needn't
needy (needi·er, needi·est)
neep Dialect turnip
ne'er
ne'er-do-well
ne·fari·ous
nefari·ous·ness
ne·gate
ne·ga·tion
nega·tive
nega·tive·ness
negative-raising grammar term
nega·ti·vism
nega·tiv·ist
nega·tiv·is·tic
nega·tiv·ity
ne·ga·tor (or ·gat·er)

ne·ga·to·ry
Neg·ev (or ·eb) Israeli desert
ne·glect
ne·glect·er (or ·glec·tor)
ne·glect·ful
ne·glect·ful·ly
ne·glect·ful·ness
neg·li·gee (or ·gée, ·gé)
neg·li·gence
neg·li·gent
neg·li·gibil·ity (or ·gible·ness)
neg·li·gible
neg·li·gibly
ne·go·tiabil·ity
ne·go·tiable
ne·go·ti·ant
ne·go·ti·ate
ne·go·tia·tion
ne·go·tia·tor
Ne·gress
Ne·gril·lo (plural ·los or ·loes) African Negroid people
Neg·ri Sem·bi·lan Malaysian state
Ne·grit·ic of Negroes or Negritos
Ne·gri·to (plural ·tos or ·toes) Asian Negroid people
ne·gri·tude
Ne·gro (plural ·groes)
Ne·groid
Ne·gro·ism
Ne·gro·phile (or ·phil)
Ne·gro·phobe
Ne·gro·pho·bia
Neg·ro·pont Greek island
Ne·gros Philippine island
ne·gus (plural ·guses) spiced drink
neigh sound of a horse; compare nay
neigh·bour (US ·bor)
neigh·bour·hood (US ·bor·)
neigh·bour·ing (US ·bor·)
neigh·bour·li·ness (US ·bor·)
neigh·bour·ly (US ·bor·)
Neis·se Polish river
nei·ther
Nejd (or Najd) Saudi Arabian province
nek mountain pass

nek·ton minute marine organisms
nek·ton·ic
nel·ly (plural ·lies)
Nel·son Lancashire town; New Zealand port
nel·son wrestling hold
ne·lum·bo (plural ·bos) plant
nema·thel·minth worm
ne·mat·ic chemistry term
nema·to·cyst
nema·to·cys·tic
nema·tode
Nem·bu·tal (Trademark)
Ne·mea ancient Greek valley
Ne·mean
ne·mer·tean (or nem·er·tine) marine worm
ne·mesia plant
Nemesis Greek goddess
nem·esis (plural ·eses) retribution
(nemonic) incorrect spelling of mnemonic
nene goose
neo·an·throp·ic
neo·ars·phena·mine
Neo·cene geological term
neo·clas·si·cal (or ·sic)
neo·clas·si·cism
neo·clas·si·cist
neo·co·lo·nial
neo·co·lo·ni·al·ism
neo·co·lo·ni·al·ist
neo·dym·ium chemical element
Neo·gaea zoogeographical area
Neo·gaean
Neo·gene geological term
neo·im·pres·sion·ism
neo·lith
Neo·lith·ic
neo·logi·cal
neo·logi·cal·ly
ne·olo·gism (or ne·ol·ogy; plural ·gisms or ·ogies)
ne·olo·gist
ne·olo·gis·tic (or ·ti·cal)
ne·olo·gis·ti·cal·ly
ne·olo·gize (or ·gise)
ne·ol·ogy variant of neologism
neo·my·cin antibiotic

neon

neon
neo·na·tal
neo·nate newborn child
neo·phyte novice
neo·phyt·ic
neo·plasm tumour
neo·plas·tic
neo·plas·ti·cism style of painting
neo·plas·ty plastic surgery
Neo-Platonism philosophy
Neo-Platonist
neo·prene synthetic rubber
ne·ot·enous
ne·ot·eny zoology term
neo·ter·ic modern
neo·teri·cal·ly
Neo·tropi·cal zoogeographical term
neo·type
Neo·zo·ic geological term
Ne·pal
Nepa·lese (*plural* ·lese)
Ne·pali
ne·pen·the
ne·pen·thean
ne·per unit
neph·eline (*or* ·elite) mineral
neph·elin·ite rock
neph·elom·eter chemistry apparatus
neph·elom·etry
neph·ew
nepho·gram
nepho·graph
nepho·logi·cal
ne·pholo·gist
ne·phol·ogy study of clouds
nepho·scope
ne·phral·gia kidney pain
ne·phral·gic
ne·phrec·to·my (*plural* ·mies) removal of kidney
ne·phrid·ial
ne·phrid·ium (*plural* ·phridia) excretory organ
neph·rite mineral
ne·phrit·ic of the kidneys
ne·phri·tis
ne·phrol·ogy
neph·ron
ne·phro·sis
ne·phrot·ic
ne·phroto·my (*plural* ·mies)

ne plus ul·tra *Latin* the perfect state
ne·pot·ic (*or* ·tis·tic)
nepo·tism
nepo·tist
Nep·tune planet
Neptune Roman god
Nep·tu·nian
nep·tu·nium chemical element
ne·ral chemistry term
Ne·reid (*plural* ·rei·des) Greek nymph
ne·reis worm
ne·rit·ic ecology term
nero·li oil
ner·vate having leaf veins
nerve
nerve·less
nerve·less·ness
nerve-racking (*or* -wracking)
nervi·ly
nerv·ine soothing the nerves
nervi·ness
nerv·ous
nerv·ous·ness
ner·vure biology term
nervy (nervi·er, nervi·est)
nes·ci·ence ignorance
nes·ci·ent
nesh *Dialect* timid
Ness Scottish lake
ness promontory
nes·sel·rode pudding
nest
nest·er
nes·tle
nes·tler
nest·ling
Nestor mythological character
Nes·to·ri·an·ism theological doctrine
net (net·ting, net·ted) mesh
net (*or* nett; net·ting, net·ted) remaining; earn as profit
net·ball
neth·er
Neth·er·land·er
Neth·er·lands
nether·most
net·su·ke

nett *variant spelling of* net
net·ted
net·ting
net·tle
net·tle·some causing irritation
net·tly
net·ty *Dialect* lavatory
net·work
Neu·châ·tel Swiss city and lake
Neuf·châ·tel French town; cheese
neume (*or* neum) musical symbol
neu·ral
neu·ral·gia
neu·ral·gic
neu·ras·the·nia
neu·ras·then·ic
neu·ras·theni·cal·ly
neu·rec·to·my (*plural* ·mies)
neu·rit·ic
neu·ri·tis
neu·ro·blast embryonic cell
neu·ro·coele embryology term
neu·ro·fi·bril
neu·ro·fi·bril·lar
neu·ro·gen·ic
neu·rog·lia nerve tissue
neu·ro·hy·pophy·sis (*plural* ·ses)
neu·ro·lem·ma (*or* neu·ri·) nerve sheath
neu·ro·logi·cal
neu·rolo·gist
neu·rol·ogy
neu·ro·ma (*plural* ·ma·ta *or* ·mas) tumour
neu·roma·tous
neu·ro·mus·cu·lar
neu·rone (*or* ·ron) nerve cell
neu·ron·ic
neu·ro·path person with nervous disorder
neu·ro·path·ic
neu·ro·pathi·cal·ly
neu·ro·pa·tholo·gist
neu·ro·pa·thol·ogy
neu·ropa·thy disease of nervous system
neu·ro·physio·logi·cal

306

neu·ro·physio·logi·cal·ly
neu·ro·physi·olo·gist
neu·ro·physi·ol·ogy
neu·ro·psy·chi·at·ric
neu·ro·psy·chia·trist
neu·ro·psy·chia·try
neu·rop·ter·an (*or* ·on; *plural* ·ter·ans *or* ·tera) insect
neu·rop·ter·ous (*or* ·ter·an)
neu·ro·sci·ence
neu·ro·sis (*plural* ·ses)
neu·ro·sur·geon
neu·ro·sur·gery
neu·ro·sur·gi·cal
neu·ro·sur·gi·cal·ly
neu·rot·ic
neu·roti·cal·ly
neu·roti·cism
neu·roto·mist
neu·roto·my (*plural* ·mies) nerve surgery
neu·ro·vas·cu·lar
Neuss West German city
neu·ter
neu·tral
neu·tral·ism
neu·tral·ist
neu·tral·ity
neu·trali·za·tion (*or* ·sa·tion)
neu·tral·ize (*or* ·ise)
neu·tral·iz·er (*or* ·is·er)
neu·tral·ly
neu·tret·to (*plural* ·tos) physics term
neu·tri·no (*plural* ·nos) elementary particle
neu·tron
neu·tro·phil (*or* ·phile) blood cell
Neva Soviet river
Ne·va·da
névé mass of ice
nev·er
never·more
never-never
never·the·less
Ne·vis West Indian island
ne·vus *US spelling of* naevus
new
New·ark English town; US port
new·born

New Bruns·wick
New·burg cookery term
New·bury
New·cas·tle Australian port
New·castle-under-Lyme
New·castle-upon-Tyne
new·comer
new·el
new·fan·gled
New·fie *Slang* inhabitant of Newfoundland
New·found·land
New·found·land·er
New·gate former prison
New·ham London borough
New·ha·ven
new·ish
new·ly
newly·wed
New·mar·ket
new·mar·ket gambling game; riding coat
new·ness
New Or·le·ans
New·port Isle of Wight town; Welsh port
news
news·agent
news·cast *US* news broadcast
news·caster
news·hawk
newsi·ness
news·letter
news·paper
news·paper·man (*plural* ·men)
new·speak
news·print
news·reel
news stand
news·worthi·ness
news·worthy
newsy (newsi·er, newsi·est)
newt
New·ton Welsh town
new·ton unit
Newton·abbey Northern Irish town
New·to·nian of Isaac Newton
New Zea·land
New Zea·land·er
next

next-door (*adj*)
nex·us (*plural* nex·us *or* nex·uses)
ngaio (*plural* ngaios) tree
ngo·ma African drum
Ngu·ni language
ngwee Zambian coin
nia·cin vitamin
Ni·aga·ra
Nia·mey capital of Niger
nib (nib·bing, nibbed)
nib·ble
nib·bler
nib·lick golf club
Nica·ra·gua
Nica·ra·guan
nic·co·lite mineral
Nice French city
nice
Ni·cene Creed
nice·ness
ni·cety (*plural* ·ceties)
niche
Ni·chrome (*Trademark*)
nic·ish
nick
nick·el (·el·ling, ·elled; *US* ·el·ing, ·eled)
nick·el·ic
nick·el·if·er·ous
nickel·odeon
nick·el·ous
nick·er
nick·nack *variant spelling of* knickknack
nick·name
Nico·bar Indian islands
Nicol prism
Nico·sia Cypriot capital
ni·co·tia·na plant
nico·tina·mide vitamin
nico·tine
nico·tin·ic
nico·tin·ism
nic·ti·tate (*or* nic·tate) to blink
nic·ti·ta·tion (*or* nic·ta·tion)
ni·dal
niddle-noddle nod rapidly
nide *variant of* nye
ni·dico·lous ornithology term
nidi·fi·cate build nest
nidi·fi·ca·tion

nidifugous

ni·di·fu·gous ornithology term
nidi·fy (·fies, ·fy·ing, ·fied) build nest
nid-nod (-nod·ding, -nod·ded)
ni·dus (*plural* ·di)
niece
ni·el·list
ni·el·lo (*noun, plural* ·li *or* ·los; *verb* ·lo·ing, ·loed) engraving term
Nier·stein·er wine
Nie·tzschean
Nie·tzsche·ism (*or* ·tzschean·ism) philosophy
nieve *Dialect* fist
Niè·vre French department
niff
niffy (niffi·er, niffi·est)
nif·ti·ly
nif·ti·ness
nif·ty (·ti·er, ·ti·est)
Ni·ger
Ni·geria
Ni·gerian
nig·gard
nig·gard·li·ness
nig·gard·ly
nig·ger
nig·gle
nig·gler
nig·gling
nig·gly
nigh
night
night·cap
night·club
night·dress
night·fall
night·gown
night·hawk
nightie (*or* nighty; *plural* nighties)
night·in·gale
night·jar
night·life
night·light
night·long
night·ly
night·mare
night·mar·ish
night·rider
night·shade
night·shirt
night·spot
night-time
night·wear
ni·gres·cence
ni·gres·cent blackish
ni·gro·sine (*or* ·sin) pigment
ni·hil *Latin* nothing
ni·hil·ism
ni·hil·ist
ni·hil·is·tic
ni·hil·ity
Nii·ga·ta Japanese port
Nij·megen Dutch town
Nik·ko Japanese town
Ni·ko·la·yev Soviet city
nil
nil de·spe·ran·dum *Latin* never despair
Nile
nil·gai (*or* ·ghau; *plural* ·gai, ·gais, *or* ·ghau, ·ghaus) antelope
Ni·lot·ic
nim game
nim·ble
nim·ble·ness
nimble-wit *US* clever person
nim·bly
nim·bo·stra·tus (*plural* ·ti)
nim·bus (*plural* ·bi *or* ·buses)
Nîmes French city
niminy-piminy (*or* miminy-)
Nimrod biblical hunter
nin·com·poop
nine
nine·fold
nine·pins
nine·teen
nine·teenth
nine·ti·eth
nine·ty (*plural* ·ties)
Ni·neveh Assyrian capital
Ning·po Chinese port
Ning·sia Hui Chinese region
nin·ny (*plural* ·nies)
ni·non fabric
ninth
nio·bic
nio·bite
nio·bium chemical element
nio·bous
nip (nip·ping, nipped)
nipa palm tree
Nipi·gon Canadian lake
Nip·is·sing Canadian lake
nip·per
nip·pi·ly
nip·ple
nipple-wort plant
Nip·pon
Nip·pon·ese (*plural* ·ese)
Nip·pur Babylonian city
nip·py (·pi·er, ·pi·est)
nir·va·na
nir·va·nic
Niš Yugoslav town
Ni·sha·pur Iranian town
Ni·shi·no·mi·ya Japanese city
nisi legal term
nisi pri·us legal term
ni·sus (*plural* ·sus) striving
nit
ni·ter *US spelling of* nitre
Ni·terói Brazilian port
ni·tid bright
ni·tra·mine
ni·trate
ni·tra·tion
ni·tre (*US* ·ter)
ni·tric containing nitrogen
ni·tride chemical compound
ni·trid·ing metallurgy term
ni·tri·fi·able
ni·tri·fi·ca·tion
ni·tri·fy (·fies, ·fy·ing, ·fied)
ni·trile
ni·trite
ni·tro·bac·te·ria (*sing.* ·rium)
ni·tro·ben·zene
ni·tro·cel·lu·lose
ni·tro·chlo·ro·form
ni·tro·gen
ni·trog·eni·za·tion (*or* ·sa·tion)
ni·trog·en·ize (*or* ·ise)
ni·trog·enous
ni·tro·glyc·er·in (*or* ·ine)
ni·trom·eter
ni·tro·methane
ni·tro·met·ric
ni·tro·par·af·fin

ni·trosa·mine
ni·tro·so (*or* ·syl)
ni·trous
nit·ty (·ti·er, ·ti·est)
nitty-gritty
nit·wit
Niue Pacific island
ni·val of snow
ni·va·tion geology term
niv·eous resembling snow
Ni·ver·nais former French province
nix (*fem* nixie) water sprite
nix·er *Irish* spare-time job
Ni·zam Indian title
ni·zam former Turkish soldier
Njord (*or* Njorth) Norse god
no (*plural* noes *or* nos)
No (*or* Noh) Japanese drama
Noa·chian (*or* No·ach·ic) of Noah
nob *Slang* wealthy person; cribbage term; *compare* knob
no-ball
nob·ble
nob·bler
nob·but *Dialect* nothing but
no·belium chemical element
no·bili·ary
no·bil·ity (*plural* ·ities)
no·ble
no·ble·man (*plural* ·men)
no·ble·ness
no·blesse oblige *French* nobility obliges
noble·woman (*plural* ·women)
no·bly
no·body (*plural* ·bodies)
no·ci·cep·tive causing pain
nock notch on arrow
noc·tam·bu·lism (*or* ·la·tion)
noc·tam·bu·list
noc·ti·lu·ca (*plural* ·cae) protozoan
noc·ti·lu·cence
noc·ti·lu·cent
noc·tu·id moth
noc·tule bat

noc·turn part of Catholic matins; *compare* nocturne
noc·tur·nal
noc·tur·nal·ity
noc·tur·nal·ly
noc·turne musical piece; *compare* nocturn
nocu·ous
nod (nod·ding, nod·ded)
no·dal
no·dal·ity
nod·dle
nod·dy (*plural* ·dies) bird; fool
node
nodi·cal astronomy term
no·dose (*or* ·dous)
no·dos·ity
nodu·lar (*or* ·lose, ·lous)
nod·ule
no·dus (*plural* ·di) problematic situation
Noel (*or* Noël)
no·esis intellectual functioning
no·et·ic
nog
nog·gin measure of spirits
nog·ging building term
Noh *variant spelling of* No
noil textile fibres
noise
noise·less
noise·less·ness
noi·sette
noisi·ly
noisi·ness
noi·some offensive
noi·some·ness
noisy (noisi·er, noisi·est)
no·lens vo·lens *Latin* willing or unwilling
noli-me-tangere warning; plant
nol·le pros·equi legal term
nolo con·ten·de·re legal term
noma medical term
no·mad
no·mad·ic
no·madi·cal·ly
no·mad·ism
no-man's-land
nom·arch

nom·ar·chy (*or* nome; *plural* ·chies *or* nomes) Greek province
nom·bril heraldic term
nom de guerre (*plural* noms de guerre) assumed name
nom de plume (*plural* noms de plume) pen name
nome *variant of* nomarchy
no·men (*plural* nomi·na) ancient Roman's name
no·men·cla·tor inventor of names
no·men·cla·ture
nomi·nal
nomi·nal·ism
nomi·nal·ist
nomi·nal·is·tic
nomi·nal·ly
nomi·nate
nomi·na·tion
nomi·na·tive
nomi·na·tor
nomi·nee
no·mism theology term
no·mis·tic
no·moc·ra·cy (*plural* ·cies) government based on law
nomo·gram (*or* ·graph) type of graph
no·mog·ra·pher
nomo·graph·ic
nomo·graphi·cal
no·mo·graphi·cal·ly
no·mog·ra·phy (*plural* ·phies)
no·mo·logi·cal
no·mo·logi·cal·ly
no·molo·gist
no·mol·ogy science of law
nomo·thet·ic (*or* ·theti·cal) giving laws
no·nage
no·na·genar·ian
nona·gon
non·ago·nal
non·aligned
non·ap·pear·ance
non·at·tend·ance
non·at·tribu·tive
nonce
non·cha·lance
non·cha·lant

non-com

non-com *Slang*
   noncommissioned officer
non·com·bat·ant
non·com·mis·sioned
non·com·mit·tal
non·com·mit·tal·ly
non·com·pli·ance
non com·pos men·tis
   Latin of unsound mind
non·con·cur·rent
non·con·duc·tor
non·con·form·ism
Non·con·form·ist
   dissenting Protestant
non·con·form·ist one who does not conform
Non·con·form·ity (*or* ·ism)
non·con·form·ity
non·con·sti·tu·tion·al
non·con·ta·gious
non·con·tribu·ting
non·con·tribu·tory
non-co-op·era·tion
non-co-op·era·tive
non-co-op·era·tor
non·cor·rod·ing
non·crea·tive
non-de·nomi·na·tion·al
non·de·script
non·dis·junc·tion
non·drink·er
none
non·ed·ible
non·ego philosophy term
non·en·tity (*plural* ·tities)
non·equiva·lence
nones Roman date; canonical hour
non·es·sen·tial
none·such (*or* non·)
non·et
none·the·less
non·ethi·cal
non·event
non·ex·ist·ence
non·ex·ist·ent
non·ex·plo·sive
non·fac·tual
non·fea·sance legal term
non·fer·rous
non·fic·tion
non·fic·tion·al
non·flam·mable
nong *Austral* stupid person

non·har·mon·ic
non·iden·ti·cal
non·idio·mat·ic
no·nil·lion 10^{54}
no·nil·lionth
non-in·dus·trial
non·in·fec·tious
non·in·flam·mable
non·inter·ven·tion
non·inter·ven·tion·al
non·inter·ven·tion·ist
non·in·toxi·cat·ing
non·ir·ri·tant
non·join·der legal term
non·judg·men·tal (*or* ·judge·)
non·ju·ror one refusing to take oath
non li·cet *Latin* unlawful
non·ma·lig·nant
non·medi·cal
non·mem·ber
non·met·al
non·met·al·lic
non·op·er·able
non·op·era·tive
non·pa·reil unsurpassed
non·par·ous never having given birth
non·par·tici·pat·ing
non·par·ti·san (*or* ·zan)
non·par·ty
non·plus (*noun, plural* ·pluses; *verb* ·plusses, ·plus·sing, ·plussed; *US* ·pluses, ·plus·ing, ·plused)
non·poi·son·ous
non·po·liti·cal
non·pro·duc·tive
non·pro·duc·tive·ness
non·pro·duc·tiv·ity
non·pro·gres·sive
non·pro·lif·era·tion
non-pros (-prosses, -prossing, -prossed) legal term
non pro·sequi·tur legal term
non·rep·re·sen·ta·tion·al
non·resi·dence (*or* ·den·cy)
non·resi·dent
non·resi·den·tial
non·re·sis·tant

non·re·stric·tive
non·re·turn·able
non·rig·id
non·sched·uled
non·sec·ta·rian
non·sense
non·sen·si·cal
non·sen·si·cal·ly
non·sen·si·cal·ness (*or* ·ity)
non se·qui·tur
non·slip
non·smok·er
non·spe·cif·ic
non·stand·ard
non·stand·ard·ized (*or* ·ised)
non·start·er
non·sta·tive linguistics term
non·stick
non·stimu·lat·ing
non·stop
non·stra·te·gic
non·striker
non·such *variant spelling of* nonesuch
non·suit
non·swim·mer
non·tech·ni·cal
non·tox·ic
non·typi·cal
non-U
non·un·ion
non·un·ion·ism
non·ver·bal
non·vio·lence
non·vio·lent
non·vot·er
non-White
noo·dle
nook
noon
noon·day
no-one (*or* no one)
noon·ing *US* midday break
noon·time (*or* ·tide)
noose
no·pal cactus
no-par (*adj*)
nope *Slang* no
nor
nor·adrena·line
Nor·dic
Nor·folk
no·ria waterwheel

Nori·cum Celtic Alpine kingdom
nor·ite rock
nork *Austral* breast
norm
Nor·ma constellation
nor·mal
nor·mal·ity (*or esp. US* ·cy)
nor·mali·za·tion (*or* ·sa·tion)
nor·mal·ize (*or* ·ise)
nor·mal·ly
Nor·man
Nor·man·dy
nor·ma·tive
Norn Norse goddess
Norr·kö·ping Swedish port
Norse
Norse·man (*plural* ·men)
north
North·al·ler·ton Yorkshire town
North·amp·ton
North·amp·ton·shire
north·bound
north·country·man (*plural* ·men)
north·east
north·easter
north·easter·ly (*plural* ·lies)
north·eastern
north·eastward
nor·ther·ly (*plural* ·lies)
north·ern
north·ern·er
north·ern·most
north·ing navigation term
north-northeast
north·northwest
North Pole
North·um·ber·land county
North·um·bria region
North·um·brian
north·ward (*adj*)
north·wards (*adv*)
north·west
north·wester
north·wester·ly (*plural* ·lies)
north·western
north·westward
North·wich Cheshire town
Nor·way

Nor·we·gian
Nor·wich
nose
nose·bag
nose·band
nose·bleed
nose-dive (*verb*)
nose·gay
nos·ey *variant spelling of* nosy
nosh
no-side rugby term
nosi·ly
nosi·ness
nos·ing
no·so·co·mial medical term
no·sog·ra·pher
no·so·graph·ic
no·sog·ra·phy written description of disease
noso·logi·cal
noso·logi·cal·ly
no·solo·gist
no·sol·ogy classification of diseases
nos·tal·gia
nos·tal·gic
nos·tal·gi·cal·ly
nos·toc alga
nos·to·log·ic
nos·tol·ogy study of senility
nos·tril
nos·trum quack medicine
nosy (*or* nos·ey; nosi·er, nosi·est)
nosy-parker
not
nota bene *Latin* note well
no·tabil·ity (*plural* ·ities)
no·table
no·table·ness
no·tably
no·tar·ial
no·ta·rize (*or* ·rise)
no·ta·ry (*plural* ·ries)
no·tate
no·ta·tion
no·ta·tion·al
notch
note
note·book
note·case
not·ed
note·let
note·paper
note·worthi·ly

note·worthi·ness
note·worthy
noth·ing
noth·ing·ness
no·tice
no·tice·abil·ity
no·tice·able
no·tice·ably
no·ti·fi·able
no·ti·fi·ca·tion
no·ti·fi·er
no·ti·fy (·fies, ·fy·ing, ·fied)
no-tillage farming system
not·ing
no·tion
no·tion·al
no·tion·al·ly
no·titia ecclesiastical register
no·to·chord zoology term
no·to·chord·al
No·to·gaea zoogeographical term
No·to·gaean
no·to·ri·ety (*or* no·to·ri·ous·ness)
no·to·ri·ous
no·tor·nis bird
no·to·ther·ium (*plural* ·theria) extinct marsupial
no·tour legal term
No·tre Dame
no-trump bridge term
Not·ting·ham
Not·ting·ham·shire
no·tum (*plural* ·ta) entomology term
No·tus mythological wind
not·with·stand·ing
nou·gat
nought (*US* naught) zero; *compare* naught
nou·menon (*plural* ·mena) philosophy term
noun
noun·al
nour·ish
nour·ish·er
nour·ish·ing·ly
nour·ish·ment
nous *Slang* common sense
nou·veau riche (*plural* nou·veaux riches)
nova (*plural* novae *or* novas) star
no·vacu·lite rock
No·va·ra Italian city

Nova

Nova Sco·tia
no·va·tion legal term
nov·el
nov·el·ese
nov·el·ette
nov·el·et·tish
nov·el·ist
nov·el·is·tic
nov·eli·za·tion (*or* ·sa·tion)
nov·el·ize (*or* ·ise)
no·vel·la (*plural* ·las *or* ·le)
nov·el·ty (*plural* ·ties)
No·vem·ber
no·vena (*plural* ·venae) Catholic devotion
Nov·go·rod Soviet city
nov·ice
no·vi·ti·ate (*or* ·ci·ate)
No·vo·caine (*Trademark*)
No·vo·kuz·netsk Soviet city
No·vo·si·birsk Soviet city
now
nowa·days
no·way
Now·el (*or* ·ell) *Archaic* Noel
no·where
nowt *Dialect* nothing
Nox Roman goddess
nox·ious
nox·ious·ness
no·yade execution by drowning
noy·au (*plural* ·aux) liqueur
noz·zle
nth
nu·ance
nub
Nuba (*plural* Nubas *or* Nuba) Sudanese people
nub·bin *US* undeveloped fruit
nub·ble
nub·bly (*or* ·by)
nu·becu·la (*plural* ·lae) small galaxy
Nu·bia
Nu·bian
nu·bile
nu·bil·ity
nu·cel·lar
nu·cel·lus (*plural* ·li) botany term

nu·cha (*plural* ·chae) nape of neck
nu·chal
nu·clear
nu·clease enzyme
nu·cleate
nu·clea·tion
nu·clea·tor
nu·clei *plural of* nucleus
nu·cleic
nu·clein protein
nu·cleo·lar (*or* ·late, ·lat·ed, ·loid)
nu·cleo·lus (*plural* ·li) part of cell nucleus
nu·cleon
nu·cleon·ic
nu·cleoni·cal·ly
nu·cleon·ics branch of physics
nu·cleo·phile
nu·cleo·phil·ic
nu·cleo·plasm
nu·cleo·plas·mic (*or* ·mat·ic)
nu·cleo·pro·tein
nu·cleo·side biochemical compound
nu·cleo·tide biochemical compound
nu·cleus (*plural* ·clei *or* ·cleuses)
nu·clide type of atom
nude
nude·ness
nudge
nudg·er
nu·di·branch mollusc
nu·di·caul (*or* ·cau·lous) botany term
nud·ism
nud·ist
nu·dity (*plural* ·dities)
Nue·vo León Mexican state
nu·ga·tory
nug·gar sailing boat
nug·get
nug·gety
nui·sance
nuke *Slang* nuclear bomb
Nu·ku'a·lo·fa Tongan capital
null
nul·lah Indian stream
nulla-nulla Aboriginal club
nul·li·fi·ca·tion

nul·li·fi·ca·tion·ist
nul·li·fid·ian sceptic
nul·li·fi·er
nul·li·fy (·fies, ·fy·ing, ·fied)
nul·lipa·ra (*plural* ·rae) obstetrics term
nul·lipa·rous
nul·li·pore seaweed
nul·lity (*plural* ·lities)
Nu·man·tia ancient Spanish city
numb
num·bat marsupial
num·ber numeral
numb·er more numb
num·ber·less
number·plate
numb·fish (*plural* ·fish *or* ·fishes)
numb·ness
numb·skull variant spelling *of* numskull
num·dah (*or* nam·) Indian fabric
nu·men (*plural* ·mi·na) Roman deity
nu·mer·able
nu·mer·ably
nu·mera·cy
nu·mer·al
nu·mer·ary of numbers; *compare* nummary
nu·mer·ate
nu·mera·tion
nu·mera·tive
nu·mera·tor
nu·meri·cal (*or* ·mer·ic)
nu·meri·cal·ly
nu·mero·logi·cal
nu·mer·ol·ogy divination by numbers
nu·mer·ous
nu·mer·ous·ness
Nu·midia ancient African country
Nu·mid·ian
nu·mi·nous awe-inspiring
nu·mis·mat·ic
nu·mis·mat·ics (*or* ·ma·tol·ogy)
nu·mis·ma·tist (*or* ·tolo·gist)
num·ma·ry of coins; *compare* numerary
num·mu·lar
num·mu·lite fossil

num·mu·lit·ic
num·skull (or numb·)
nun
nuna·tak mountain peak
Nunc Di·mit·tis canticle
nun·cia·ture
nun·cio (plural ·cios)
nun·cle Dialect uncle
nun·cu·pa·tive legal term
Nun·eaton
nun·hood
nun·like
nun·nery (plural ·neries)
Nupe (plural Nupe or Nupes) Nigerian people
nup·tial
Nu·rem·berg
Nuri (plural Nuris or Nuri) Indo-European people
Nu·ri·stan Afghan region
nurse
nurse·maid
nurse·ry (plural ·ries)
nursery·man (plural ·men)
nurs·ing
nurs·ling (or nurse·) nursed child
nur·tur·able
nur·ture
nur·tur·er
nut (nut·ting, nut·ted)
nu·tant botany term

nu·ta·tion
nu·ta·tion·al
nut·brown
nut·case
nut·cracker
nut·gall
nut·hatch
nut·let
nut·meg
nu·tria coypu fur
nu·tri·ent
nu·tri·ment
nu·tri·tion
nu·tri·tion·al (or ·ary)
nu·tri·tion·ist
nu·tri·tious
nu·tri·tious·ness
nu·tri·tive
nut·shell
nut·ted
nut·ter
nut·ti·ly
nut·ti·ness
nut·ting
nut·ty (·ti·er, ·ti·est)
nut·wood
nux vomi·ca
nuz·zle
nya·la (plural ·la or ·las) antelope
Nyan·ja (plural ·ja or ·jas) African people
Ny·asa·land former name of Malawi

nyc·ta·gi·na·ceous botany term
nyc·ta·lo·pia night blindness
nyc·ti·nas·tic
nyc·ti·nas·ty botany term
nyc·ti·trop·ic
nyc·tit·ro·pism botany term
nyc·to·pho·bia
nyc·to·pho·bic
nye (or nide) flock of pheasants
ny·lon
nymph
nym·pha (plural ·phae) anatomy term
nym·phaea·ceous botany term
nym·phal (or ·phean)
nym·pha·lid butterfly
nymph·et
nymph·like
nym·pho (plural ·phos)
nym·pho·lep·sy (plural ·sies) violent emotion
nym·pho·lept
nym·pho·lep·tic
nym·pho·ma·nia
nym·pho·ma·ni·ac
nym·pho·ma·nia·cal
nys·tag·mic
nys·tag·mus eye condition
nys·ta·tin antibiotic
Nyx Greek goddess

O

O exclamation; used chiefly in religious and poetic contexts
oaf (plural oafs)
oaf·ish
oaf·ish·ness
oak
oak·en
Oak·ham Leicestershire town
Oak·land US port
oakum fibre
oar
oared
oar·fish (plural ·fish or ·fishes)
oar·lock

oars·man (plural ·men)
oars·man·ship
oasis (plural oases)
oast
oast·house
oat
oat·cake
oat·en
oath (plural oaths)
oat·meal
Oaxa·ca Mexican state
oba African chief
Oban Scottish port
ob·bli·ga·to (or ob·li·; plural ·tos or ·ti) musical term
ob·con·ic botany term

ob·cor·date botany term
ob·du·ra·cy (or ·rate·ness)
ob·du·rate
obeah variant of obi
obedi·ence
obedi·ent
obedi·en·tia·ry (plural ·ries) holder of monastic office
obei·sance
obei·sant
ob·elis·cal
ob·elisk
ob·elis·koid
ob·elize (or ·elise)
ob·elus (plural ·eli) text symbol

Oberammergau

Ober·am·mer·gau West German village
Ober·hau·sen West German city
Ober·land Swiss region
Ober·on satellite of Uranus
Oberon fairy king
obese
obesity (*or* obese·ness)
obey
obey·er
ob·fus·cate
ob·fus·ca·tion
ob·fus·ca·tory
obi (*plural* obis *or* obi) Japanese sash
obi (*or* obeah; *plural* obis *or* obeahs) witchcraft
obit obituary; memorial service
obi·ter dic·tum (*plural* obi·ter dic·ta) *Latin* something said in passing
obi·tu·ar·ist
obi·tu·ary (*plural* ·aries)
ob·ject
ob·jec·ti·fi·ca·tion
ob·jec·ti·fy (·fies, ·fy·ing, ·fied)
ob·jec·tion
ob·jec·tion·abil·ity (*or* ·able·ness)
ob·jec·tion·able
ob·jec·tion·ably
ob·jec·tive
ob·jec·tiv·ism
ob·jec·tiv·ist
ob·jec·tiv·is·tic
ob·jec·tiv·is·ti·cal·ly
ob·jec·tiv·ity (*or* ·tive·ness)
ob·jet d'art (*plural* ob·jets d'art)
ob·jet trou·vé (*plural* ob·jets trou·vés) *French* object considered aesthetically
ob·jur·gate scold
ob·jur·ga·tion
ob·jur·ga·tor
ob·jur·ga·tory (*or* ·tive)
ob·lan·ceo·late botany term
ob·last Soviet administrative division
ob·late
ob·la·tion
ob·la·tory (*or* ·tion·al)
ob·li·gable
ob·li·gate
ob·li·ga·tion
ob·li·ga·tion·al
ob·li·ga·tive
ob·li·ga·to *variant spelling of* obbligato
ob·li·ga·tor
ob·liga·to·ri·ly
ob·liga·tory
oblige
ob·li·gee creditor
oblig·er
oblig·ing
ob·li·gor debtor
oblique
oblique·ness
obliqui·tous
obliqui·ty (*plural* ·ties)
oblit·erate
oblit·era·tion
oblit·era·tive
oblit·era·tor
olivi·on
olivi·ous
ob·livi·ous·ness
ob·long
ob·lo·quy (*plural* ·quies)
ob·nox·ious
ob·nox·ious·ness
ob·nu·bil·ate to darken
oboe
obo·ist
obo·lus (*or* obol; *plural* ·li *or* obols) Greek unit; coin
ob·ovate botany term
ob·ovoid botany term
ob·rep·tion obtaining by deceit
ob·scene
ob·scen·ity (*plural* ·ities)
ob·scur·ant
ob·scu·rant·ism
ob·scu·rant·ist
ob·scu·ra·tion
ob·scure
ob·scu·rity (*plural* ·rities)
ob·se·quent
ob·se·quies (*sing.* ·quy)
ob·se·qui·ous
ob·se·qui·ous·ness
ob·serv·able
ob·serv·able·ness (*or* ·abil·ity)
ob·serv·ably
ob·ser·vance
ob·ser·vant
ob·ser·va·tion
ob·ser·va·tion·al
ob·ser·va·tion·al·ly
ob·ser·va·tory (*plural* ·tories)
ob·serve
ob·serv·er
ob·sess
ob·ses·sion
ob·ses·sion·al
ob·ses·sive
ob·ses·sive·ness
ob·sid·ian
ob·so·lesce
ob·so·les·cence
ob·so·les·cent
ob·so·lete
ob·so·lete·ness
ob·sta·cle
ob·stet·ric (*or* ·ri·cal)
ob·stet·ri·cal·ly
ob·ste·tri·cian
ob·stet·rics
ob·sti·na·cy (*plural* ·cies)
ob·sti·nate
ob·sti·pa·tion
ob·strep·er·ous
ob·strep·er·ous·ness
ob·struct
ob·struct·er (*or* ·struc·tor)
ob·struc·tion
ob·struc·tion·al
ob·struc·tion·ism
ob·struc·tion·ist
ob·struc·tive
ob·struc·tive·ness
ob·stru·ent medical term
ob·tain
ob·tain·abil·ity
ob·tain·able
ob·tain·er
ob·tain·ment
ob·tect entomology term
ob·trude
ob·trud·er
ob·tru·sion
ob·tru·sive
ob·tru·sive·ness
ob·tund deaden
ob·tu·rate block up
ob·tu·ra·tion
ob·tu·ra·tor
ob·tuse
ob·tuse·ness
ob·verse
ob·ver·sion

ob·vert logic term
ob·vi·ate
ob·via·tion
ob·vi·ous
ob·vi·ous·ly
ob·vi·ous·ness
ob·vo·lute
ob·vo·lu·tion
ob·vo·lu·tive
oca plant
oca·ri·na musical instrument
oc·ca·sion
oc·ca·sion·al
oc·ca·sion·al·ism philosophical theory
oc·ca·sion·al·ly
Oc·ci·dent Europe and America
oc·ci·dent the west
Oc·ci·den·tal (noun)
oc·ci·den·tal (or Oc·; adj)
Oc·ci·den·tal·ism
Oc·ci·den·tal·ist
oc·ci·den·tali·za·tion (or Oc·, ·sa·tion)
oc·ci·den·tal·ize (or Oc·, ·ise)
oc·ci·den·tal·ly (or Oc·)
oc·cipi·tal
oc·ci·put (plural ·puts or ·cipi·ta) anatomy term
oc·clude
oc·clud·ent
oc·clu·sal
oc·clu·sion
oc·clu·sive
oc·clu·sive·ness
oc·cult
oc·cul·ta·tion astronomy term
oc·cult·ism
oc·cult·ist
oc·cu·pan·cy (plural ·cies)
oc·cu·pant
oc·cu·pa·tion
oc·cu·pa·tion·al
oc·cu·pi·er
oc·cu·py (·pies, ·py·ing, ·pied)
oc·cur (·cur·ring, ·curred)
oc·cur·rence
oc·cur·rent
ocean
ocean·ar·ium (plural ·ar·iums or ·aria)
ocean-going

Oceania Pacific islands
Oce·an·ian
Ocean·ic of Oceania
ocean·ic of the ocean
Ocea·nid (plural Ocea·nids or Oceani·des) Greek nymph
ocean·og·ra·pher
oceano·graph·ic (or ·graphi·cal)
ocean·o·graphi·cal·ly
ocean·og·ra·phy
ocean·ol·ogy
ocel·lar
oc·el·late (or ·lated) having ocelli; compare oscillate; osculate
oc·el·la·tion
ocel·lus (plural ·li) simple eye
oc·elot
och Scot exclamation
ocher US spelling of ochre
och·loc·ra·cy (plural ·cies) mob rule
och·lo·crat
och·lo·crat·ic
och·lo·pho·bia fear of crowds
ochre (US ocher)
ochre·ous (or ochrous, ochry; US ocher·ous or ochery)
ochroid
ock·er Austral boorish person
o'clock
oco·til·lo (plural ·los) tree
oc·rea (or och·; plural ·reae) sheath
oc·re·ate
oc·ta·chord musical instrument
oc·tad
oc·tad·ic
oc·ta·gon (or ·tan·gle)
oc·tago·nal
oc·tago·nal·ly
oc·ta·he·dral
oc·ta·he·drite
oc·ta·he·dron (plural ·drons or ·dra)
oc·tal number system
oc·tam·er·ous
oc·tam·eter
oc·tane

oc·tan·gu·lar
Oc·tans constellation
oc·tant eighth part of circle
oc·tar·chy (plural ·chies)
(octaroon) incorrect spelling of octoroon
oc·ta·va·lent
oc·tave
oc·ta·vo (plural ·vos) book size
oc·ten·nial
oc·ten·nial·ly
oc·tet
oc·til·lion 10^{48}
oc·til·lionth
Oc·to·ber
oc·to·deci·mo (plural ·mos)
oc·to·genar·ian (or oc·tog·enary; plural ·ians or ·enaries)
(octogon) incorrect spelling of octagon
(octohedral) incorrect spelling of octahedral
oc·to·pod
oc·to·pus (plural ·puses)
oc·to·roon
oc·to·syl·lab·ic
oc·to·syl·la·ble
oc·troi duty on goods
oc·tu·ple
ocu·lar
ocu·lar·ist artificial-eye maker
ocu·list ophthalmologist
ocu·lo·mo·tor
oda·lisque (or ·lisk)
odd
odd·ball
odd·ity (plural ·ities)
odd·ly
odd·ment
odd·ness
odd-pinnate botany term
odds-on
ode
Oden·se Danish port
Oder European river
Odes·sa Soviet port
odeum (plural odea) (building for musical performances; compare odium; oidium
Odin (or Othin) Norse god
odi·ous
odi·ous·ness

odium

odium hatred; *compare* odeum; oidium
odom·eter (*or* ho·dom·) *US* mileometer
od·on·tal·gia toothache
od·on·tal·gic
odon·to·blast
odon·to·blas·tic
odon·to·glos·sum orchid
odon·to·graph gear-tooth marking aid
odon·to·graph·ic
od·on·tog·ra·phy
odon·toid
odon·to·logi·cal
od·on·tolo·gist
od·on·tol·ogy science of teeth
od·on·topho·ral (*or* ·toph·or·ous)
odon·to·phore zoology term
odor *US spelling of* odour
odor·if·er·ous
odor·ous
odor·ous·ness
odour (*US* odor)
odour·less (*US* odor·)
Od·ys·sean
Odysseus mythological hero
Od·ys·sey poem
oede·ma (*US* ede·; *plural* ·ma·ta)
oedema·tous (*or* ·tose; *US* edema·)
oedi·pal (*or* ·pean)
Oedipus mythological character
oeil·lade suggestive glance
oeno·logi·cal (*US* eno·)
oenolo·gist (*US* enolo·)
oenol·ogy (*US* enol·) study of wine
oeno·mel drink
Oenone Greek nymph
o'er over
oer·sted unit
oesopha·geal (*US* esopha·)
oesopha·gus (*US* esopha·; *plural* ·gi)
oes·tra·di·ol (*US* es·) hormone
oes·tri·ol (*US* es·) hormone
oes·tro·gen (*US* es·)

oes·tro·gen·ic (*US* es·)
oes·tro·geni·cal·ly (*US* es·)
oes·trone (*US* es·) hormone
oes·trous (*adj*; *US* es·)
oes·trus (*noun*; *US* es·)
oeuvre work of art
of
off
of·fal
Of·fa·ly Irish county
off·beat
off-centre
off·drive (·driving, ·drove, ·driven)
Of·fen·bach West German city
of·fence (*US* ·fense)
of·fend
of·fend·er
of·fen·sive
of·fen·sive·ness
of·fer
of·fer·er (*or* ·fe·ror)
of·fer·ing
of·fer·tory (*plural* ·tories)
off-glide
off·hand
off·handed
off·handed·ly
off·hand·ed·ness
of·fice
of·fic·er
of·fi·cial
of·fi·cial·dom
of·fi·cial·ese
of·fi·cial·ly
of·fi·ci·ant
of·fi·ci·ary (*plural* ·aries) body of officials
of·fi·ci·ate
of·fi·cia·tion
of·fi·cia·tor
of·fi·cious
of·fi·cious·ness
of·fing
of·fish
off-key (*adj*)
off-licence
off-line (*adj*)
off-load
off-peak
off-print
off-putting
off-season (*adj*)
off·set (·set·ting, ·set)

off·shoot
off·shore
off·side
off·spring
off·stage
off-white
oft
of·ten
Oga·den Ethiopian region
Og·bo·mo·sho Nigerian city
og·do·ad group of eight
ogee architectural moulding
og·ham (*or* ogam) ancient writing
ogiv·al
ogive architectural term
ogle
ogler
Ogo·oué (*or* ·we) African river
ogre (*fem* ogress)
ogre·ish
Ogyg·ian prehistoric
oh
Ohio
ohm
ohm·age
ohm·meter
oid·ium (*plural* ·ia) fungal spore
oil
oil·bird
oil·can
oil·cloth
oil·cup
oil·er
oil·field
oil-fired
oili·ly
oili·ness
oil·man (*plural* ·men)
oil·skin
oil·stone
oily (oili·er, oili·est)
oint·ment
Oi·reach·tas Irish parliament
Oita Japanese city
OK (*or* okay; *noun*, *plural* OK's *or* okays; *verb* OK'ing, OK'ed *or* okay·ing, okayed)
oka (*or* oke) Turkish weight
oka·pi (*plural* ·pis *or* ·pi)
okay *variant of* OK

Oka·ya·ma Japanese city
Okee·cho·bee Florida lake
okey-doke (*or* **-dokey**)
Oki·na·wa Japanese island
Ok·la·ho·ma
Okla·ho·man
okra vegetable
okta meteorological unit
old
Old Bai·ley
old·en
Ol·den·burg West German city
old·er
old·fangled
old-fashioned
Old·ham English town
oldie
old·ness
old-time
old-timer
Ol·du·vai Tanzanian gorge
old·wife (*plural* **·wives**) duck; fish
old-world
olé Spanish exclamation
olea·ceous botany term
oleagi·nous oily
olean·der shrub
oleas·ter shrub
oleate chemistry term
olec·ra·nal
olec·ra·non anatomy term
olefine (*or* **olefin**)
olefin·ic
oleic acid
oleo·graph
oleo·graph·ic
oleog·ra·phy
oleo·res·in
oleo·res·in·ous
oleum (*plural* **olea** *or* **oleums**) chemistry term
ol·fac·tion
ol·fac·tory (*plural* **·tories**)
oliba·num frankincense
olid foul-smelling
oli·garch
oli·gar·chic (*or* **·chi·cal**)
oli·gar·chi·cal·ly
oli·gar·chy (*plural* **·chies**)
Oli·go·cene geological period
oli·go·chaete worm
oli·go·clase mineral
oli·gopo·lis·tic

oli·gopo·ly (*plural* **·lies**) economics term
oli·gop·so·nis·tic
oli·gop·so·ny (*plural* **·nies**) economics term
oli·go·sac·cha·ride
oli·go·troph·ic ecology term
oli·got·ro·phy
oli·gu·ret·ic
oli·gu·ria (*or* **·resis**) medical term
olio (*plural* **olios**) miscellany
oli·va·ceous
oli·vary
ol·ive
oliv·en·ite mineral
oli·vine mineral
olla cooking pot
olla po·dri·da Spanish stew
ol·ogy (*plural* **·ogies**) *Slang* branch of knowledge
olo·ro·so (*plural* **·sos**) sherry
Olym·pia
Olym·pi·ad
Olym·pian
Olym·pic
Olym·pus Greek mountain
Om Hindu syllable
oma·dhaun *Irish* fool
Omagh Irish town
Oma·ha US city
Oman Arabian sultanate
Omani
oma·sum (*plural* **·sa**) cow's stomach
Omay·yad (*or* **Umay·**; *plural* **·yads** *or* **·ya·des**) caliph
om·bre (*US* **·ber**) card game
om·buds·man (*plural* **·men**)
Om·dur·man Sudanese city
omega
ome·lette (*or esp. US* **ome·let**)
omen
omen·tal
omen·tum (*plural* **·ta**) anatomy term
omer Hebrew unit
omi·cron Greek letter
omi·nous
omi·nous·ness

omis·sible
omis·sion
omit (**omit·ting**, **omit·ted**)
omit·ter
om·ma·tid·ial
om·ma·tid·ium (*plural* **·tidia**) zoology term
om·mato·phore zoology term
om·ma·topho·rous
om·ni·bus (*plural* **·buses**)
om·ni·com·pe·tence
om·ni·com·pe·tent
om·ni·di·rec·tion·al
om·ni·fari·ous of all sorts
om·nif·ic (*or* **om·nifi·cent**)
om·nipo·tence
om·nipo·tent
om·ni·pres·ence
om·ni·pres·ent
om·ni·range navigation system
om·nis·ci·ence
om·nis·ci·ent
omnium-gather·um assortment
om·ni·vore
om·niv·or·ous
omo·pha·gia (*or* **omoph·agy**) eating raw food
omo·phag·ic (*or* **omopha·gous**)
Omphale mythological queen
om·pha·los sacred object
Omu·ta Japanese city
on
ona·ger (*plural* **·gri** *or* **·gers**) wild ass
ona·gra·ceous botany term
onan·ism
onan·ist
once
once-over
onco·gene
on·co·gen·ic (*or* **on·cog·enous**)
on·co·logi·cal
on·colo·gist
on·col·ogy study of tumours
on·coming
on·cost
on·do·gram
on·do·graph
on·dom·eter
one

Oneida

Onei·da (*plural* **·das** *or* **·da**) US city and lake; American Indian
onei·ric of dreams
onei·ro·crit·ic
onei·ro·criti·cal
one·ness
one-off
oner *Slang* something outstanding
on·er·ous
on·er·ous·ness
one·self
one-sided
one-sidedness
one-step
one-time
one-to-one
one-track
one-upmanship
one-way
on-glide
on·going
on·ion
onion·skin paper
on·iony
Onit·sha Nigerian port
on·looker
on·looking
only
ono·ma·si·ol·ogy
ono·mas·tic
ono·mas·tics study of proper names
ono·mato·poeia
ono·mato·poe·ic (*or* **·po·et·ic**)
ono·mato·poei·cal·ly (*or* **·po·eti·cal·ly**)
on·rush
on·set
on·shore
on·side sports term
on·slaught
on·stage
On·tario
onto
on·to·gen·ic (*or* **·ge·net·ic**)
on·to·geni·cal·ly (*or* **·ge·neti·cal·ly**)
on·tog·eny (*or* **·to·gen·esis**) biology term
on·to·logi·cal
on·to·logi·cal·ly
on·tol·ogy philosophy term
onus (*plural* **onuses**)
onus pro·ban·di burden of proof
on·ward
on·wards
ony·chopho·ran zoology term
ony·mous bearing author's name
onyx gemstone; *compare* oryx
oocyte biology term
oodles
oof *Slang* money
ooga·mous
oog·amy biology term
oogen·esis
ooge·net·ic
oogo·nial
oogo·nium (*plural* **·nia** *or* **·niums**) biology term
ooh exclamation
oolite rock
oolit·ic
oologi·cal
oolo·gist
ool·ogy study of birds' eggs
oolong tea
oomi·ak variant spelling of umiak
oom·pah
oopho·rec·to·my (*plural* **·mies**) removal of ovary
oopho·rit·ic
oopho·ri·tis
oophyte botany term
oophyt·ic
oosperm
oosphere botany term
oospore
oo·spor·ic (*or* **·ous**)
ootheca (*plural* **oothecae**) zoology term
oothecal
ootid zoology term
ooze
oozi·ly
oozi·ness
oozy (**oozi·er**, **oozi·est**)
opac·ity (*plural* **·ities**)
opah fish
opal
opa·lesce
opal·es·cence
opal·es·cent
opal·ine
opaque (**opaqu·ing**, **opaqued**)

318

opaque·ness
open
open-and-shut
open·cast
open-ended
open·er
open-eyed
open-faced
open·handed
open·handed·ness
open·hearted
open·hearted·ness
open·ing
open-minded
open-minded·ness
open-mouthed
open·ness
open·work
op·era
op·er·abil·ity
op·er·able
op·er·and maths term
op·er·ant
op·er·ate
op·er·at·ic
op·er·ati·cal·ly
op·er·at·ics
op·era·tion
op·era·tion·al
op·era·tion·al·ism (*or* **·tion·ism**) science term
op·era·tion·al·ist·ic
op·era·tion·al·ly
op·era·tive
op·era·tive·ness (*or* **·tiv·ity**)
op·era·tize (*or* **·tise**) make into an opera
op·era·tor
oper·cu·lar (*or* **·late**)
oper·cu·lum (*plural* **·la** *or* **·lums**) biology term
op·er·et·ta
op·er·et·tist
op·er·on genetics term
ophi·cleide musical instrument
ophid·ian
ophio·logi·cal
ophi·olo·gist
ophi·ol·ogy study of snakes
Ophir biblical region
ophite rock
ophit·ic
Ophiu·chus constellation
oph·thal·mia
oph·thal·mic

oph·thal·mi·tis
oph·thal·mo·logi·cal
oph·thal·molo·gist
oph·thal·mol·ogy
oph·thal·mo·scope
oph·thal·mo·scop·ic
oph·thal·mos·co·py
opi·ate
opine
opin·ion
opin·ion·at·ed (*or*
 opin·iona·tive)
opin·ion·at·ed·ness
opis·tho·branch zoology
 term
op·is·thog·na·thism
op·is·thog·na·thous
opium
opi·um·ism
Opor·to Portuguese port
opos·sum (*plural* ·sums
 or ·sum)
op·pi·dan urban
op·pi·late to block
op·pi·la·tion
op·po·nen·cy
op·po·nent
op·por·tune
op·por·tune·ness
op·por·tun·ism
op·por·tun·ist
op·por·tun·is·tic
op·por·tu·nity (*plural*
 ·nities)
op·pos·abil·ity
op·pos·able
op·pos·ably
op·pose
op·pos·er
op·pos·ing·ly
op·po·site on the other side
 of; *compare* apposite
op·po·site·ness
Op·po·si·tion parliamentary
 party
op·po·si·tion
op·po·si·tion·al
op·po·si·tion·ist
op·press
op·pres·sing·ly
op·pres·sion
op·pres·sive
op·pres·sive·ness
op·pres·sor
op·pro·bri·ous
op·pro·brium
op·pugn to dispute

op·pug·nant
op·pugn·er
Ops Roman goddess
op·son·ic
op·so·nin
op·so·ni·za·tion (*or*
 ·sa·tion,
 ·soni·fi·ca·tion)
op·so·nize (*or* ·nise,
 ·soni·fy) medical term
opt
op·ta·tive expressing a wish
(opthalmic) *incorrect
 spelling of* ophthalmic
(opthalmology) *incorrect
 spelling of* ophthalmology
op·tic
op·ti·cal
op·ti·cal·ly
op·ti·cian
op·tics
op·ti·mal
op·ti·mal·ly
op·ti·mism
op·ti·mist
op·ti·mis·tic (*or* ·ti·cal)
op·ti·mis·ti·cal·ly
op·ti·mi·za·tion (*or*
 ·sa·tion)
op·ti·mize (*or* ·mise)
op·ti·mum (*plural* ·ma *or*
 ·mums)
op·tion
op·tion·al
op·tion·al·ly
op·tom·eter
op·to·met·ric
op·tom·etrist ophthalmic
 optician
op·tom·etry
opu·lence (*or* ·len·cy)
opu·lent
opun·tia plant
opus (*plural* opuses *or*
 opera)
or
or·ache (*or esp. US*
 or·ach) plant
ora·cle
oracu·lar
ora·cy
Ora·dea Romanian city
oral of the mouth; *compare*
 aural
oral·ly
Oran Algerian port
or·ange

or·ange·ade
Or·ange·ism
Orange·man (*plural*
 ·men) Irish Protestant
or·ang·ery (*plural* ·eries)
orange·wood
orang-utan (*or* -outang)
orate
ora·tion
ora·tor
ora·tori·cal
ora·to·rio (*plural* ·rios)
ora·tory (*plural* ·tories)
orb
or·bicu·lar (*or* ·late,
 ·lat·ed)
or·bicu·lar·ity
or·bit
or·bit·al
orc whale
Or·cad·ian of the Orkneys
or·cein dye
or·chard
or·ches·tra
or·ches·tral
or·ches·tral·ly
or·ches·trate
or·ches·tra·tion
or·ches·tra·tor
or·ches·tri·na (*or* ·on)
 musical instrument
or·chid
or·chi·da·ceous
or·chil (*or* ar·) lichen; dye
or·chis orchid
or·chit·ic
or·chi·tis inflammation of
 testicle
or·ci·nol (*or* or·cin)
 chemical compound
Or·cus Roman god
or·dain
or·dain·er
or·dain·ment
or·deal
or·der
or·der·er
or·der·li·ness
or·der·ly (*plural* ·lies)
or·di·nal
or·di·nance decree; *compare*
 ordnance; ordonnance
or·di·nand
or·di·nari·ly
or·di·nari·ness
or·di·nary (*plural* ·naries)
or·di·nate

ordination

or·di·na·tion
ord·nance weaponry; *compare* ordinance; ordonnance
or·don·nance systematic arrangement; *compare* ordnance; ordinance
Or·do·vi·cian geological period
or·dure excrement
Or·dzho·ni·ki·dze (*or* Or·jo·) Soviet city
ore mineral
öre (*plural* öre) Swedish currency
øre (*plural* øre) Danish or Norwegian currency
oread Greek nymph
Örebro Swedish town
orec·tic of desire
orega·no
Or·egon
Oren·burg Soviet city
Orestes mythological character
orfe fish
or·fray variant spelling of orphrey
or·gan
or·gan·die (*US* ·dy; *plural* ·dies)
or·ga·nelle
or·gan·ic
or·gani·cal·ly
or·gani·cism biological theory
or·gani·cist
or·gani·cis·tic
or·gan·ism
or·gan·is·mal (*or* ·mic)
or·gan·ist
or·gani·za·tion (*or* ·sa·tion)
or·gani·za·tion·al (*or* ·sa·tion·al)
or·gan·ize (*or* ·ise)
or·gan·iz·er (*or* ·is·er)
or·gano·gen·esis
or·gano·genet·ic
or·gano·geneti·cal·ly
or·gano·graph·ic (*or* ·graphi·cal)
or·gan·og·ra·phist
or·gan·og·ra·phy
or·gano·lep·tic
or·gano·logi·cal
or·gan·olo·gist

or·gan·ol·ogy
or·gano·metal·lic
or·ga·non (*or* ·num; *plural* ·na, ·nons, *or* ·nums) philosophy term
or·gano·thera·peu·tic
or·gano·thera·py
or·ga·num (*plural* ·na *or* ·nums) music; *variant spelling of* organon
or·gan·za fabric
or·gan·zine silk thread
or·gasm
or·gas·mic (*or* ·tic)
or·geat barley drink
or·gi·as·tic
orgy (*plural* orgies)
ori·bi (*plural* ·bi *or* ·bis) antelope
ori·el window; *compare* oriole
Ori·ent eastern countries
ori·ent the east; *variant of* orientate
Ori·en·tal (*noun*)
ori·en·tal (*or* Ori·; *adj*)
Ori·en·tal·ism
Ori·en·tal·ist
ori·en·tali·za·tion (*or* Ori·, ·sa·tion)
ori·en·tal·ize (*or* Ori·, ·ise)
ori·en·tal·ly (*or* Ori·)
ori·en·tate (*or* ori·ent)
ori·en·ta·tion
ori·en·ta·tion·al
Ori·en·te Cuban province
ori·en·teer·ing
ori·fice
ori·flamme flag
ori·ga·mi paper folding
ori·ga·num marjoram *or* oregano
ori·gin
origi·nal
origi·nal·ity (*plural* ·ities)
origi·nal·ly
origi·nate
origi·na·tion
origi·na·tor
ori·na·sal phonetics term; *compare* oronasal
Ori·no·co South American river
ori·ole bird; *compare* oriel
Ori·on constellation

320

Orion mythological character
ori·son prayer
Oris·sa Indian state
Ori·ya (*plural* ·ya) Indian people
Ori·za·ba Mexican city
Ork·ney Is·lands (*or* Ork·neys)
orle heraldic term
Or·lé·ans French city
Or·lon (*Trademark*)
or·lop nautical term
Orly Parisian suburb
or·mer mollusc
or·mo·lu decoration
Or·muz variant spelling of Hormuz
or·na·ment
or·na·men·tal
or·na·men·tal·ly
or·na·men·ta·tion
or·nate
or·nate·ness
or·nith·ic of birds
or·ni·thine amino acid
or·ni·this·chian zoology term
or·ni·tho·logi·cal
or·ni·tho·logi·cal·ly
or·ni·tholo·gist
or·ni·thol·ogy
or·ni·tho·man·cy divination from bird behaviour
or·ni·tho·pod dinosaur
or·ni·thop·ter (*or* or·thop·ter) aircraft
or·ni·tho·rhyn·chus platypus
or·ni·thos·co·py divination by bird observation
or·ni·tho·sis
oro·ban·cha·ceous botany term
oro·gen·ic (*or* ·ge·net·ic)
oro·geni·cal·ly (*or* ·geneti·cal·ly)
orog·eny (*or* oro·gen·esis) mountain formation
orog·ra·pher (*or* orolo·gist)
oro·graph·ic (*or* oro·logi·cal)
oro·graphi·cal·ly (*or* oro·logi·cal·ly)

orog·ra·phy (or orol·ogy) mapping mountain relief
oro·ide alloy
orom·eter
Oron·tes Asian river
oro·tund resonant; pompous; compare rotund
or·phan
or·phan·age
or·phari·on lute
Or·phean
Orpheus
Or·phic
Or·phism ancient Greek religion
or·phrey (or ·fray) border on vestment
or·pi·ment mineral
or·pine (or ·pin) plant
or·re·ry (plural ·ries) model of solar system
or·ris (or ·rice) plant
or·ta·nique fruit
or·thi·con electronic device
ortho·cen·tre (US ·ter) maths term
ortho·cephal·ic (or ·cepha·lous) anatomy term
ortho·cepha·ly
ortho·chro·mat·ic
ortho·chro·ma·tism
ortho·clase mineral
ortho·don·tic
ortho·don·tics (or ·don·tla)
or·tho·don·tist
Ortho·dox religion
ortho·dox conforming
ortho·doxy (plural ·doxies)
ortho·ep·ic
ortho·epi·cal·ly
ortho·epy correct pronunciation
ortho·gen·esis
ortho·ge·net·ic
ortho·geneti·cal·ly
ortho·gen·ic medical term
ortho·geni·cal·ly
or·thog·na·thism (or ·thy)
or·thog·na·thous anatomy term
or·thogo·nal
or·thogo·nal·ly
or·thog·ra·pher (or ·phist)

ortho·graph·ic (or ·graphi·cal)
ortho·graphi·cal·ly
or·thog·ra·phy (plural ·phies)
ortho·hy·dro·gen
ortho·mor·phic
ortho·paedic (US ·pedic)
ortho·paedics (US ·pedics)
ortho·paedist (US ·pedist)
ortho·phos·phate
ortho·psy·chi·at·ric
ortho·psy·chia·trist
ortho·psy·chia·try
or·thop·ter variant of ornithopter
or·thop·ter·an (or ·on; plural ·ans or ·tera) insect
or·thop·ter·ous (or ·an)
or·thop·tic
or·thop·tics
or·thop·tist
ortho·rhom·bic crystallography term
ortho·scop·ic
or·thos·ti·chous
or·thos·ti·chy (plural ·chies) botany term
ortho·trop·ic
or·thot·ro·pism
or·thot·ro·pous botany term
or·to·lan bird
orts Dialect scraps
Oru·ro Bolivian city
Or·vie·to Italian town; wine
Or·wel·lian
oryx (plural or·yxes or oryx) antelope; compare onyx
os (plural ossa) bone
os (plural ora) mouth
Osage (plural Osages or Osage) American Indian
Osa·ka Japanese port
Os·car film award
os·cil·late fluctuate regularly; compare ocellate; osculate
os·cil·la·tion
os·cil·la·tor
os·cil·la·tory
os·cil·lo·gram
os·cil·lo·graph

os·cil·lo·graph·ic
os·cil·log·ra·phy
os·cil·lo·scope
os·cine ornithology term
os·ci·tan·cy (or ·tance; plural ·tan·cies or ·tances)
os·ci·tant drowsy
os·cu·lant biology term
os·cu·lar
os·cu·late kiss; maths term; compare ocellate; oscillate
os·cu·la·tion
os·cu·la·tory
os·cu·lum (plural ·la) mouthlike part
Osha·wa Canadian city
Oshog·bo Nigerian city
osier willow tree
Osiris Egyptian god
Oslo
Os·man·li of Ottoman Empire
os·mic
os·mi·ous variant of osmous
os·mi·rid·ium alloy
os·mium metal
os·mom·eter
os·mo·met·ric
os·mo·met·ri·cal·ly
os·mom·etry
os·mose undergo osmosis
os·mo·sis (plural ·ses)
os·mot·ic
os·moti·cal·ly
os·mous (or ·mi·ous)
os·mun·da (or ·mund) fern
Os·na·brück West German city
os·na·burg fabric
os·prey
Ossa Greek mountain
os·sein protein
os·seous bony
Os·sé·tia Soviet region
Os·set·ic (or ·se·tian)
Ossian legendary Irish bard
os·si·cle small bone
os·sicu·lar
os·sif·er·ous
os·si·fi·ca·tion
os·si·fi·er
os·si·frage bird
os·si·fy (·fies, ·fy·ing, ·fied)
os·su·ary (plural ·aries) urn for bones

osteal

os·teal
os·tei·tic
os·tei·tis
Os·tend Belgian port
os·ten·sibil·ity
os·ten·sible
os·ten·sibly
os·ten·sive
os·ten·sory (plural
 ·sories) container for
 Host
os·ten·ta·tion
os·ten·ta·tious
os·teo·ar·thrit·ic
os·teo·ar·thri·tis
os·teo·blast bone cell
os·teo·blas·tic
os·teoc·la·sis medical term
os·teo·clast
os·teo·clas·tic
os·teo·gen·esis
os·teoid
os·teo·logi·cal
os·teo·logi·cal·ly
os·teolo·gist
os·teol·ogy study of bones
os·teo·ma (plural ·ma·ta
 or ·mas) tumour
os·teo·ma·la·cia
os·teo·ma·la·cial (or
 ·lac·ic)
os·teo·my·eli·tis
os·teo·path (or
 ·teopa·thist)
os·teo·path·ic
os·teo·pathi·cal·ly
os·teopa·thy
os·teo·phyte bony
 outgrowth
os·teo·phyt·ic
os·teo·plas·tic
os·teo·plas·ty (plural
 ·ties) bone grafting
os·teo·por·o·sis
os·teo·tome surgical
 instrument
os·teoto·my (plural ·mies)
Os·tia ancient Italian town
os·ti·ary (plural ·aries)
 Catholic official
os·ti·na·to (plural ·tos)
 musical term
os·tio·lar
os·ti·ole pore
os·tium (plural ·tia)
 biology term
ost·ler (or host·ler)

ost·mark East German
 currency
os·to·sis formation of bone
os·tra·cism
os·tra·ciz·able (or ·cis·)
os·tra·cize (or ·cise)
os·tra·ciz·er (or ·cis·er)
os·tra·cod tiny animal
os·tra·co·dan (or ·dous)
os·tra·co·derm extinct fish
Os·tra·va Czech city
os·trich (plural ·triches or
 ·trich)
Os·tro·goth
otal·gia earache
oth·er
other·direct·ed
other·gates Archaic
 otherwise
oth·er·ness
other·where Archaic
 elsewhere
other·wise
other·worldli·ness
other·worldly
otic of the ear
oti·ose futile
oti·os·ity (or ·ose·ness)
oti·tis
oto·cyst
oto·cys·tic
oto·la·ryn·go·logi·cal
oto·lar·yn·golo·gist
oto·lar·yn·gol·ogy
oto·lith
oto·lith·ic
oto·logi·cal
otolo·gist
otol·ogy
oto·scope
oto·scop·ic
ot·ta·va octave
Ot·ta·wa
ot·ter (plural ·ters or ·ter)
Ot·to·man (or Oth·man;
 plural ·mans) Turk;
 Turkish
ot·to·man (plural ·mans)
 sofa
oua·ba·in drug
Ouachi·ta (or Washi·ta)
 US river
Oua·ga·dou·gou capital of
 Burkina Faso
oua·na·niche salmon
oubli·ette dungeon
ouch

Oudh Indian region
ought should; variant
 spelling of aught
Oui·ja (Trademark)
Ouj·da Moroccan city
ounce
our
ours of us
our·selves
Ouse English river
ousel variant spelling of
 ouzel
oust
out
out·age missing goods
out-and-out
out·back
out·bal·ance
out·bid (·bid·ding, ·bid,
 ·bid·den or ·bid)
out·bluff
out·board
out·bound
out·brave
out·break
out·breed (·breed·ing,
 ·bred)
out·build·ing
out·burst
out·cast one cast out
out·caste one with no caste
out·class
out·come
out·crop (·crop·ping,
 ·cropped)
out·cross
out·cry (noun, plural
 ·cries; verb ·cries,
 ·cry·ing, ·cried)
out·date
out·dat·ed
out·dis·tance
out·do (·does, ·do·ing,
 ·did, ·done)
out·door (adj)
out·doors (adv)
out·er
outer·most
out·face
out·fall
out·field
out·field·er
out·fit (·fit·ting, ·fit·ted)
out·fit·ter
out·flank
out·flow
out·foot

out·fox
out·gas (·gas·ses, ·gas·sing, ·gassed)
out·go (·goes, ·go·ing, ·went, ·gone)
out·go·ing (*adj*)
out·go·ings
out·group
out·grow (·grow·ing, ·grew, ·grown)
out·growth
out·gun (·gun·ning, ·gunned)
out·haul
out·house
out·ing
out·jockey
out·land·er
out·land·ish
out·last
out·law
out·law·ry (*plural* ·ries)
out·lay (·lay·ing, ·laid)
out·let
out·li·er
out·line
out·live
out·look
out·ly·ing
out·man (·man·ning, ·manned)
out·ma·noeu·vre (*US* ·ver)
out·match
out·mod·ed
out·num·ber
out-of-doors
out-of-the-way
out·pa·tient
out·point
out·port
out·post
out·pour
out·pour·ing
out·put (·put·ting, ·put *or* ·put·ted)
out·rage
out·ra·geous
out·ra·geous·ness
out·rank
ou·tré unconventional
out·reach
out·ride (·rid·ing, ·rode, ·rid·den)
out·rid·er
out·rig·ger
out·right

out·ri·val (·val·ling, ·valled; *US* ·val·ing, ·valed)
out·run (·run·ning, ·ran, ·run)
out·run·ner
out·rush
out·sell (·sell·ing, ·sold)
out·sert printing term
out·set
out·shine (·shin·ing, ·shone)
out·shoot (·shoot·ing, ·shot)
out·side
out·sid·er
out·size
out·skirts
out·smart
out·sole
out·spo·ken
out·spread (·spread·ing, ·spread)
out·stand (·stand·ing, ·stood)
out·stand·ing (*adj*)
out·stare
out·sta·tion
out·stay
out·stretch
out·strip (·strip·ping, ·stripped)
out·swing
out·swing·er
out·talk
out·think (·think·ing, ·thought)
out·vote
out·ward (*adj*)
out·ward·ly
out·wards (*adv*)
out·wash glacial deposit
out·wear (·wear·ing, ·wore, ·worn)
out·weigh
out·wit (·wit·ting, ·wit·ted)
out·work (·work·ing, ·worked *or* ·wrought)
out·work·er
ouzel (*or* ousel) bird
ouzo (*plural* ouzos) drink
ova *plural of* ovum
oval
oval·ness (*or* ·ity)
ovar·ian
ovari·ec·to·my

ovari·oto·my (*plural* ·mies)
ova·ri·tis
ova·ry (*plural* ·ries)
ovate
ova·tion
ova·tion·al
oven
oven·bird
oven-ready
oven·ware
over
over·abun·dance
over·achieve
over·act
over·ac·tive
over·age
over·all
over·alls
over·am·bi·tious
over·anx·ious
over·arch
over·arm
over·awe
over·bal·ance
over·bear (·bear·ing, ·bore, ·borne)
over·bear·ing·ly
over·bid (·bid·ding, ·bid, ·bid·den *or* ·bid)
over·blown
over·board
over·book
over·boot
over·build (·build·ing, ·built)
over·bur·den
over·call
over·came
over·ca·pac·ity
over·capi·tali·za·tion (*or* ·sa·tion)
over·capi·tal·ize (*or* ·ise)
over·cast
over·cau·tious
over·charge
over·check
over·cloud
over·coat
over·come (·com·ing, ·came, ·come)
over·com·pen·sate
over·com·pen·sa·tion
over·com·pen·sa·tory
over·con·fi·dent
over·cook
over·criti·cal

overcriticize 324

over·criti·cize (*or* ·cise)
over·crop (·crop·ping, ·cropped)
over·crowd
over·crowd·ing
over·cul·ti·vate
over·devel·op
over·devel·op·ment
over·do (·does, ·do·ing, ·did, ·done)
over·dos·age
over·dose
over·draft money
over·draught air current
over·draw (·draw·ing, ·drew, ·drawn)
over·dress
over·drive (·driv·ing, ·drove, ·driv·en)
over·due
over·dye
over·eat (·eat·ing, ·ate, ·eat·en)
over·elabo·rate
over·em·pha·size (*or* ·sise)
over·em·phat·ic
over·en·thu·si·asm
over·en·thu·si·as·tic
over·es·ti·mate
over·es·ti·ma·tion
over·ex·cite
over·ex·pose
over·ex·po·sure
over·feed (·feed·ing, ·fed)
over·fill
over·flight
over·flow (·flow·ing, ·flowed, ·flown)
over·fly (·flies, ·fly·ing, ·flew, ·flown)
over·fold geology term
over·gar·ment
over·gen·er·ous
over·glaze
over·ground
over·grow (·grow·ing, ·grew, ·grown)
over·growth
over·hand
over·hang (·hang·ing, ·hung)
over·haul
over·head
over·heads
over·hear (·hear·ing, ·heard)

over·heat
over·hung
Over·ijs·sel Dutch province
over·in·dulge
over·in·dul·gence
over·in·dul·gent
over·is·sue (·sues, ·su·ing, ·sued)
over·joyed
over·kill
over·land
over·lap (·lap·ping, ·lapped)
over·lay (·lay·ing, ·laid)
over·leaf
over·lie (·ly·ing, ·lay, ·lain)
over·load
over·long
over·look
over·lord
over·ly
over·man (·man·ning, ·manned)
over·man·tel
over·master
over·mat·ter
over·much
over·nice
over·night
over·pass (·pas·sing, ·passed, ·past)
over·pay (·pay·ing, ·paid)
over·pitch
over·play
over·plus excess
over·popu·late
over·popu·la·tion
over·pow·er
over·pow·er·ing
over·print
over·pro·duce
over·pro·duc·tion
over·pro·tect
over·pro·tec·tion
over·pro·tec·tive
over·quali·fied
over·ran
over·rate
over·reach
over·react
over·reac·tion
over·ride (·rid·ing, ·rode, ·rid·den)
over·rid·er
over·riding (*adj*)
over·ripe

over·rode
over·rule
over·run (·run·ning, ·ran, ·run)
over·score cross out
over·seas
over·see (·see·ing, ·saw, ·seen)
over·seer
over·sell (·sell·ing, ·sold)
over·set (·set·ting, ·set) disturb
over·sew (·sew·ing, ·sewed, ·sewn)
over·sexed
over·shad·ow
over·shoe
over·shoot (·shoot·ing, ·shot)
over·side
over·sight
over·sim·pli·fi·ca·tion
over·sim·pli·fy (·fies, ·fy·ing, ·fied)
over·size
over·sized
over·skirt
over·slaugh military term
over·sleep (·sleep·ing, ·slept)
over·soul spiritual essence
over·spend (·spend·ing, ·spent)
over·spill (·spill·ing, ·spilt *or* ·spilled)
over·staff
over·state
over·state·ment
over·stay
over·steer
over·step (·step·ping, ·stepped)
over·strung
over·stuff
over·sub·scribe
overt
over·take (·tak·ing, ·took, ·tak·en)
over·task
over·tax
over-the-counter (*adj*)
over·throw (·throw·ing, ·threw, ·thrown)
over·thrust geological fault
over·time
over·tire
over·tired

over·tone
over·took
over·top (·top·ping, ·topped)
over·trade
over·trick bridge term
over·trump
over·ture
over·turn
over·use
over·view
over·watch
over·ween·ing
over·weigh
over·weight
over·whelm
over·whelm·ing
over·wind (·wind·ing, ·wound)
over·win·ter
over·word repeated word
over·work
over·write (·writ·ing, ·wrote, ·writ·ten)
over·wrought
ovi·du·cal (or ·duc·tal)
ovi·duct
Ovie·do Spanish city
ovif·er·ous
ovi·form egg-shaped
ovine sheeplike
ovi·par·ity
ovipa·rous egg-laying
ovi·pos·it
ovi·po·si·tion
ovi·posi·tor
ovi·sac egg sac
ovoid
ovo·lo (plural ·li) architectural term
ovo·tes·tis (plural ·tes)
ovo·vi·vi·par·ity
ovo·vi·vipa·rous
ovu·lar
ovu·late
ovu·la·tion
ovule
ovum (plural ova)
ow exclamation
owe
ow·el·ty (plural ·ties) legal term
Ower·ri Nigerian town
ow·ing
owl
owl·et
owl·ish
own
own·er
owner-occupier
own·er·ship
owt Dialect anything
ox (plural oxen)
oxa·late chemistry term
ox·al·ic acid
oxa·lis plant
oxa·zine
ox·blood
ox·bow lake
Ox·bridge
oxen plural of ox
ox·eye plant
Ox·fam
Ox·ford
Ox·ford·shire
ox·heart cherry
ox·hide
oxi·dant
oxi·dase enzyme
oxi·date oxidize
oxi·da·tion
oxi·da·tion·al
oxi·da·tion-reduction
oxi·da·tive
ox·ide
oxi·di·met·ric
oxi·dim·ctry
oxi·diz·able chemistry term
oxi·di·za·tion (or ·sa·tion)
oxi·dize (or ·dise)
oxi·diz·er (or ·dis·er)
ox·ime chemical compound
ox·lip plant
Oxo·nian
ox·pecker bird
ox·tail
ox·tongue
oxy·acety·lene
oxy·acid
oxy·cephal·ic (or ·cepha·lous) anatomy term
oxy·cepha·ly
oxy·gen
oxy·gen·ate (or ·ize, ·ise)
oxy·gena·tion
oxy·gen·ic (or ox·yg·enous)
oxy·gen·iz·able (or ·is·able)
oxy·ge·niz·er (or ·is·er)
oxy·hae·mo·glo·bin (US ·he·)
oxy·hy·dro·gen
oxy·mo·ron (plural ·mo·ra) rhetoric term
oxy·salt
oxy·sul·phide (US ·fide)
oxy·tet·ra·cy·cline
oxy·to·cic
oxy·to·cin hormone
oxy·tone linguistics term
oyer legal term
oyez (or oyes) interjection
Oyo Nigerian state
oys·ter
oyster·catcher
Oz Austral Australia
Oza·lid (Trademark)
ozo·cerite (or ·kerite) wax
ozone
ozon·ic (or ozo·nous)
ozo·nif·er·ous
ozo·ni·za·tion (or ·sa·tion)
ozo·nize (or ·nise)
ozo·niz·er (or ·nis·er)
ozo·noly·sis
ozo·no·sphere ozone layer

P

pa Slang father
paca animal
pace
pace·maker
pac·er
pace·setter
pace·way Austral racecourse
pa·cha variant spelling of pasha
pa·chi·si board game
pachy·derm animal
pachy·der·ma·tous
pachy·tene genetics term
Pa·cif·ic ocean, etc.
pa·cif·ic conciliatory

pacifically

pa·cifi·cal·ly
paci·fi·ca·tion
paci·fi·er
paci·fism
paci·fist
paci·fy (·fies, ·fy·ing, ·fied)
pack
pack·able
pack·age
pack·ag·er
pack·ag·ing
pack·er
pack·et
pack·horse
pack·ing
pack·saddle
pack·thread
pact
pad (pad·ding, pad·ded)
pa·dang Malaysian field
pa·dauk (or ·douk) tree
pad·ding
pad·dle
paddle·fish (plural ·fish or ·fishes)
pad·dler
pad·dock
Pad·dy (plural ·dies) Slang Irishman
pad·dy (plural ·dies) rice field; temper
pad·dy·whack
pad·emel·on (or pad·dy·mel·on) wallaby
pad·lock
pa·dre
pa·dro·ne Italian innkeeper
Pad·ua
padua·soy fabric
paean (US also pean) song of praise; compare paeon; pean; peon
pae·di·at·ric (US pe·)
pae·dia·tri·cian (US pe·)
pae·di·at·rics (US pe·)
pae·do·gen·esis biology term
pae·do·genet·ic (or ·gen·ic)
pae·do·logi·cal (US pe·)
pae·dolo·gist (US pe·)
pae·dol·ogy (US pe·)
pae·do·mor·pho·sis biology term
pae·do·phile (US pe·)
pae·do·philia (US pe·)

pa·el·la (plural ·las)
pae·on metrical foot; compare paean; pean; peon
(paeony) incorrect spelling of peony
pa·gan
pa·gan·ism
pa·gan·ist
pa·gan·ist·ic
pa·gan·isti·cal·ly
pa·gani·za·tion (or ·sa·tion)
pa·gan·ize (or ·ise)
pa·gan·iz·er (or ·is·er)
page
pag·eant
pag·eant·ry (plural ·ries)
page·boy
pagi·nal
pagi·nate
pagi·na·tion
pa·go·da
pa·gu·rian (or ·rid) zoology term
Pa·hang Malaysian state
Pa·ha·ri language group
Pah·la·vi Persian language
paid
pai·gle Dialect cowslip
Paign·ton
pail bucket; compare pale
pail·lette sequin
pain hurt; compare pane
pained
pain·ful
pain·ful·ly
pain·ful·ness
pain·killer
pain·less
pain·less·ness
pains·taking
pains·taking·ness
paint
paint·box
paint·brush
paint·er
paint·er·ly
paint·ing
paint·work
painty
pair two similar things; compare pare
pair-oar
pai·sa (plural ·se) Indian coin
Pais·ley Scottish town
pais·ley fabric; pattern

326

pa·jam·as US spelling of pyjamas
pa·keha non-Maori
Pa·ki·stan
Pa·ki·stani
pal (pal·ling, palled) Slang friend; to befriend; compare pall
pal·ace
pala·din
palae·an·throp·ic (US pale·)
Palae·arc·tic zoogeographical region
palae·eth·no·logi·cal (US pale·)
palae·eth·nolo·gist (US pale·)
palae·eth·nol·ogy (US pale·)
palaeo·an·thro·pol·ogy (US paleo·)
palaeo·bo·tani·cal (or ·tan·ic; US paleo·)
palaeo·bota·nist (US paleo·)
palaeo·bota·ny (US paleo·)
Palaeo·cene (US Paleo·) geological epoch
palaeo·cli·ma·tol·ogy (US paleo·)
palaeo·eth·no·bota·ny (US paleo·)
Palaeo·gene (US Paleo·) geology term
palaeo·graph·ic (US paleo·)
palaeo·graphi·cal (US paleo·)
palae·og·ra·phy (US paleo·) study of ancient handwriting
palaeo·lith (US paleo·)
Palaeo·lith·ic (US Paleo·)
palae·on·to·graph·ic (or ·graphi·cal; US pale·)
palae·on·tog·ra·phy (US pale·) description of fossils
palae·on·to·logi·cal (US pale·)
palae·on·tolo·gist (US pale·)
palae·on·tol·ogy (US pale·)

Palaeo·zo·ic (*US* Paleo·)
geological era
palaeo·zoo·logi·cal (*US* paleo·)
palaeo·zo·olo·gist (*US* paleo·)
palaeo·zo·ol·ogy (*US* paleo·)
pal·aes·tra (*plural* ·tras *or* ·trae)
pal·ais dance
pal·an·quin (*or* ·keen)
pal·at·abil·ity (*or* ·able·ness)
pal·at·able
pal·at·ably
pala·tal
pala·tali·za·tion (*or* ·sa·tion)
pala·tal·ize (*or* ·ise) phonetics term
pal·ate roof of mouth; *compare* palette; pallet
pa·la·tial
pa·la·tial·ly
pa·la·tial·ness
Pa·lati·nate German region
pa·lati·nate territory of palatine prince
Pala·tine of the Palatinate; Roman hill
pala·tine
pa·la·ver
pale lacking colour; wooden post; *compare* pail
pa·lea (*plural* ·leae) botany term
pa·lea·ceous
pale·face
pale·ly in a pale way; *compare* paly
Pa·lem·bang Indonesian port
pale·ness
paleo· *US spelling of words beginning with* palaeo·
Pa·ler·mo Sicilian capital
Pal·es·tine
Pal·es·tin·ian
pal·ette (*or* pal·let) artist's board; *compare* palate; pallet
pal·ette knife (*plural* pal·ette knives)
pal·frey
pal·imp·sest manuscript
pal·in·drome

pal·in·drom·ic
pal·ing
pal·in·gen·esis (*plural* ·eses) theology term
pal·in·genet·ic
palin·geneti·cal·ly
pali·node poem
pali·sade
pal·ish
pall coffin cover; to be boring; *compare* pal; pawl
Pal·la·dian architectural term
pal·lad·ic chemistry term
Pal·la·dium statue of Athena
pal·la·dium chemical element
pal·la·dous chemistry term
Pallas Athena; asteroid
pall·bearer
palled *past tense of* pal *or* pall
pal·let straw bed; potter's knife; machine part; *variant spelling of* palette; *compare* palate
pal·leti·za·tion (*or* ·sa·tion)
pal·let·ize (*or* ·ise)
pal·li·asse (*or* pail·lasse)
pal·li·ate
pal·lia·tion
pal·lia·tive
pal·lia·tor
pal·lid
pal·lium (*plural* ·lia *or* ·liums) vestment; anatomy term
Pall Mall
pal·lor
pal·ly (·li·er, ·li·est)
palm
Pal·ma Spanish resort; *compare* Parma
pal·ma·ceous botany term
pal·mar
pal·mate (*or* ·mat·ed)
pal·ma·tion
palm·er pilgrim
pal·mette archaeological ornament
pal·met·to (*plural* ·tos *or* ·toes) palm tree
Pal·mi·ra Colombian city
palm·ist
palm·is·try

panacean

pal·mi·tate chemistry term
pal·mi·tin chemical compound
palmy (palmi·er, palmi·est)
pal·my·ra palm tree
pa·lo·lo (*plural* ·los) worm
Palo·mar Californian mountain
palo·mi·no (*plural* ·nos) horse
pa·loo·ka *US* clumsy person
palp (*or* pal·pus; *plural* palps *or* pal·pi)
pal·pabil·ity (*or* ·pable·ness)
pal·pable
pal·pably
pal·pate examine medically; of palps; *compare* palpitate
pal·pa·tion
pal·pe·bral of the eyelid
pal·pe·brate
pal·pi·tate beat rapidly; *compare* palpate
pal·pi·ta·tion
pal·sied
pal·stave archaeology term
pal·sy (*noun, plural* ·sies; *verb* ·sies, ·sy·ing, ·sied)
pal·ter be insincere
pal·ter·er
pal·tri·ly
pal·tri·ness
pal·try (·tri·er, ·tri·est)
paly heraldic term; *compare* palely
paly·no·logi·cal
paly·nolo·gist
paly·nol·ogy study of pollen
Pa·mirs Asian mountains
pam·pas
pam·pean
pam·per
pam·per·er
pam·pero (*plural* ·peros) wind
pam·phlet
pam·phlet·eer
Pam·phylia ancient Asian region
Pam·plo·na Spanish city
Pan Greek god
pan (pan·ning, panned)
pana·cea
pana·cean

panache

pa·nache
pa·na·da thick sauce
Pana·ma
pana·ma
Pana·ma·nian
Pan-Ameri·can
Pan-Ameri·can·ism
Pan-Arab (or -Arabic)
Pan-Arabism
pana·tela (or pana·tel·la)
Pa·nay Philippine island
pan·cake
pan·chax fish
Pan·chen Lama
pan·chro·mat·ic
pan·chro·ma·tism
pan·cre·as
pan·cre·at·ic
pan·crea·tin
pan·da animal; compare pander
(pandamonium) incorrect spelling of pandemonium
pan·da·na·ceous botany term
pan·da·nus (plural ·nuses) plant
Pandarus mythological character
Pan·dean of Pan
pan·dect treatise
pan·dem·ic
pan·de·mo·ni·ac (or ·mon·ic)
pan·de·mo·nium
pan·der gratify weakness; pimp; compare panda
pan·der·er
pan·dit less common spelling of pundit except as Indian title, as in Pandit Nehru
Pandora mythological character
pan·dora variant of bandora
pan·dour Croatian soldier
pan·dow·dy (plural ·dies) US fruit pie
pan·du·rate (or ·du·ri·form) botany term
pan·dy (plural ·dies) school punishment
pane sheet of glass; compare pain
pan·egyr·ic praise; compare paregoric
pan·egyri·cal
pan·egyr·ist

pan·egy·rize (or ·rise)
pan·el (·el·ling, ·elled; US ·el·ing, ·eled)
pan·el·list
pan·et·to·ne spiced bread
pan·ful (plural ·fuls)
pang
pan·ga knife
Pan·gaea ancient continent
pan·gen·esis heredity theory
pan·genet·ic
pan·geneti·cal·ly
pan·go·lin animal
pan·han·dle
Pan·hel·len·ic
Pan·hel·len·ism
Pan·hel·len·ist
Pan·hel·len·is·tic
pan·ic (·ick·ing, ·icked)
pan·icky
pani·cle botany term
pani·cled
panic-stricken (or -struck)
pa·nicu·late (or ·lat·ed)
pan·jan·drum
pan·mix·is (or ·mixia) genetics term
Pan·mun·jom Korean village
pan·nage pig pasturage
panne fabric
pan·ni·er
pan·ni·kin
pa·no·cha (or pe·nu·che) sugar
pano·plied
pano·ply (plural ·plies)
pan·op·tic (or ·ti·cal)
pan·op·ti·cal·ly
pano·ra·ma
pano·ram·ic
pano·rami·cal·ly
pan·pipes
pan·soph·ic (or ·sophi·cal)
pan·sophi·cal·ly
pan·so·phy universal knowledge
pan·sy (plural ·sies)
pant
pan·ta·lets (or ·lettes) women's drawers
pan·ta·loon pantomime character
pan·ta·loons men's trousers
pan·tech·ni·con

pan·theism
pan·theist
pan·theis·tic (or ·ti·cal)
pan·theis·ti·cal·ly
Pan·the·on Roman temple
pan·the·on temple to all gods
pan·ther (plural ·thers or ·ther)
panties
pan·ti·hose
pan·tile
pan·ti·soc·ra·cy community ruled by all
pan·to (plural ·tos) Slang pantomime
pan·to·graph
pan·tog·ra·pher
pan·to·graph·ic
pan·to·graphi·cal·ly
pan·tog·ra·phy
pan·to·mime
pan·to·mim·ic
pan·to·mim·ist
pan·to·then·ic acid
pan·toum verse form
pan·try (plural ·tries)
pants
pant·suit US trouser suit
panty·waist US childish person
pan·zer
Pao·ting (or Pao-ting) Chinese city
Pao·tow Chinese city
pap
papa
pa·pa·cy (plural ·cies)
pa·pa·in enzyme
pa·pal
pa·pal·ly
pa·pa·vera·ceous botany term
pa·pa·ver·ine alkaloid
pa·paw (or paw·) American fruit
pa·pa·ya West Indian fruit
Pa·pe·ete Tahitian capital
pa·per
paper·back
paper·bark tree
paper·board
paper·boy
paper·clip
paper·cutter
pa·per·er
paper·girl

paper·hanger
paper·hanging
pa·peri·ness
paper·knife (*plural* ·knives)
paper·weight
paper·work
pa·pery
pap·eterie box for papers
Paph·la·go·nia Roman province
Pa·phos Cypriot village
papier-mâché
pa·pil·la (*plural* ·lae)
pa·pil·lary (*or* ·late, ·lose)
pap·il·lo·ma (*plural* ·ma·ta *or* ·mas) tumour
pap·il·lo·ma·to·sis
pap·il·lo·ma·tous
pap·il·lon dog
pap·il·lote paper frill in cookery
pa·pist
pa·pis·ti·cal (*or* ·pis·tic)
pa·pist·ry
pa·poose (*or* pap·poose) American Indian baby
pap·pose (*or* ·pous)
pap·pus (*plural* ·pi) plant hairs
pap·py (·pi·er, ·pi·est) mushy
pap·ri·ka
Pa·puan
Pa·pua New Guinea
papu·lar
pap·ule (*or* papu·la; *plural* ·ules *or* ·lae)
papu·lif·er·ous
papy·ra·ceous
papy·rolo·gist
papy·rol·ogy
pa·py·rus (*plural* ·ri *or* ·ruses)
par accepted standard; *compare* parr
para (*plural* paras *or* para) Yugoslav coin
para (*plural* paras) paratrooper; paragraph
Pará Brazilian state
pa·raba·sis (*pluras* ·ses) speech of Greek chorus
para·bio·sis (*plural* ·ses) union of two individuals
para·bi·ot·ic
para·blast biology term

para·blas·tic
para·ble religious story
pa·rabo·la maths term
para·bol·ic of a parabola
para·bol·ic (*or* ·boli·cal) of parables
para·boli·cal·ly
pa·rabo·list
pa·rabo·li·za·tion (*or* ·sa·tion)
pa·rabo·lize (*or* ·lise)
pa·rabo·loid maths term
pa·rabo·loi·dal
para·brake
pa·ra·ceta·mol
pa·rach·ro·nism error in dating
para·chute
para·chut·ist
Para·clete Holy Ghost
para·clete mediator
pa·rade
pa·rad·er
para·digm
para·dig·mat·ic
para·dise
para·di·sia·cal (*or* ·disi·ac)
para·dos bank behind trench
para·dox
para·doxi·cal
para·doxi·cal·ly
para·drop
par·aes·thesia (*US* ·es·; *plural* ·thesiae) medical term
par·aes·thet·ic (*US* ·es·)
par·af·fin (*or* ·fine)
para·form·al·de·hyde (*or* para·form)
para·gen·esis (*or* ·genesia) geology term
para·genet·ic
para·geneti·cal·ly
para·go·ge (*or* para·gogue) linguistics term
para·gog·ic (*or* ·gogi·cal)
para·gogi·cal·ly
para·gon
para·graph
para·graphia psychiatric term
para·graph·ic (*or* ·graphi·cal)
para·graphi·cal·ly
Para·guay

Para·guay·an
para·hy·dro·gen
Pa·raí·ba Brazilian state
para·keet (*or* par·ra·keet)
para·lan·guage
par·al·de·hyde
para·leip·sis (*or* ·lip·sis; *plural* ·ses) rhetorical device
pa·ra·li·pom·ena supplementary writings
par·al·lac·tic
par·al·lac·ti·cal·ly
par·al·lax
par·al·lel (·lel·ing, ·leled)
par·al·lel·epi·ped (*or* ·lelo·pi·ped)
par·al·lel·ism
par·al·lel·ist
par·al·lelo·gram
pa·ralo·gism invalid argument
pa·ralo·gist
pa·ralo·gis·tic
para·ly·sa·tion (*US* ·za·tion)
para·lyse (*US* ·lyze)
para·lys·er (*US* ·lyz·er)
pa·raly·sis (*plural* ·ses)
para·lyt·ic
para·lyti·cal·ly
para·mag·net·ic
para·mag·net·ism
Para·mari·bo capital of Surinam
para·mat·ta (*or* par·ra·mat·ta) fabric
para·mecium (*plural* ·mecia) protozoan
para·med·ic
para·medi·cal
para·ment (*plural* ·ments *or* ·men·ta) vestment
pa·ram·eter
para·met·ric (*or* ·ri·cal)
para·mili·tary
par·am·ne·sia
para·mo (*plural* ·mos) Andean plateau
para·morph mineralogy term
para·mor·phic (*or* ·phous)
para·mor·phism
para·mount
par·amour
Pa·ra·ná Brazilian state, river, and city

parang

pa·rang knife
para·noia
para·noi·ac
para·noid
para·nor·mal
para·pet
para·pet·ed
par·aph flourish after signature
para·pher·na·lia
para·phrase
para·phras·tic
pa·raphy·sis (*plural* ·ses) botany term
para·plegia
para·plegic
para·po·dium (*plural* ·dia) zoology term
para·prax·is psychology term
para·psy·chol·ogy
Para·quat (*Trademark*)
para·sang Persian unit
para·sele·ne (*plural* ·nae) astronomy term
Pa·ra·shah (*plural* ·shoth) synagogue reading
para·site
para·sit·ic
para·siti·cal·ly
para·siti·cid·al
para·siti·cide
para·sit·ism
para·si·tize (*or* ·tise)
para·si·to·logi·cal
para·si·tol·o·gist
para·sit·ol·ogy
para·sol
pa·ras·ti·chy (*plural* ·chies) botany term
para·sym·pa·thet·ic
para·syn·the·sis linguistics term
para·syn·the·ton (*plural* ·ta)
para·tac·tic
para·tac·ti·cal·ly
para·tax·is linguistics term
para·thi·on insecticide
para·thy·roid
para·troop·er
para·troops
para·ty·phoid
para·vane device on minesweeper
par avion French by plane

para·zo·an (*plural* ·zoans *or* ·zoa) zoology term
par·boil
par·buck·le rope sling
par·cel (·cel·ling, ·celled; *US* ·cel·ing, ·celed)
par·cenary joint heirship
par·cener
parch
parch·ment
par·close church screen
pard *Archaic* leopard
par·da·lote bird
pard·ner *US* partner
par·don
par·don·able
par·don·ably
par·don·er
pare trim; *compare* pair
par·egor·ic medicine; *compare* panegyric
pa·rei·ra medicinal root
pa·ren·chy·ma tissue
par·en·chyma·tous
par·ent
par·ent·age
pa·ren·tal
par·en·ter·al medical term
par·en·ter·ally
pa·ren·thesis (*plural* ·theses)
pa·ren·thesize (*or* ·thesise)
par·en·thet·ic (*or* ·theti·cal)
par·en·theti·cal·ly
par·ent·hood
par·er
par·er·gon (*plural* ·ga) additional work
pa·resis paralysis
par·es·thesia *US* spelling of paraesthesia
pa·ret·ic
par ex·cel·lence *French* beyond comparison
par·fait dessert
par·fleche rawhide
par·get
par·get·ing
par·he·lic (*or* ·he·lia·cal)
par·he·li·on (*plural* ·lia) astronomy term
pa·ri·ah
Parian marble
pari·es (*plural* pa·ri·etes) anatomy term

pa·ri·etal
pari·mutuel (*plural* pari·mutuels *or* paris·mutuels) betting system
par·ing
pari pas·su *Latin* legal term
pari·pin·nate botany term
Par·is French capital
Paris mythological character
par·ish
pa·rish·ion·er
Pa·ris·ian
Pa·risi·enne Parisian woman
pari·son glass mass
pari·syl·lab·ic
par·ity (*plural* ·ities)
park
par·ka coat
par·kin cake
park·ing
par·kin·son·ism
park·land
park·way
parky (parki·er, parki·est)
par·lance
par·lan·do music term
par·lay *US* double up in betting
par·ley discuss
par·ley·er
par·lia·ment (*or* Par·)
Par·lia·men·tar·ian parliamentary supporter in Civil War
par·lia·men·tar·ian
par·lia·men·tari·an·ism (*or* ·tar·ism)
par·lia·men·ta·ry
par·lour (*US* ·lor)
par·lous dangerous
Par·ma Italian city; *compare* Palma
Par·men·tier cookery term
Par·me·san cheese
Par·nas·sian
Par·nas·sus
pa·ro·chial
pa·ro·chi·al·ism
pa·ro·chi·al·ly
pa·rod·ic (*or* ·rodi·cal)
paro·dy (*noun, plural* ·dies; *verb* ·dies, ·dy·ing, ·died)
pa·roi·cous (*or* ·roe·cious) botany term

pa·rol oral
pa·rol·able
pa·role conditional release
pa·rolee
paro·no·ma·sia play on words
paro·no·mas·ti·cal·ly
paro·nym linguistics term
paro·nym·ic (or pa·rony·mous)
Pár·os Greek island
pa·rot·ic near the ear
pa·rot·id gland
paro·ti·tis (or pa·roti·di·tis) mumps
pa·ro·toid poison gland on toad
par·ox·ysm
par·ox·ys·mal (or ·mic)
par·quet
par·quet·ry
parr (plural parrs or parr) salmon; compare par
par·rel (or ·ral) nautical term
par·ri·cid·al
par·ri·cide killing of parent; compare patricide
par·rot
parrot-fashion
parrot·fish (plural ·fish or ·fishes)
par·ry (verb ·ries, ·ry·ing, ·ried; noun, plural ·ries)
pars·able
parse
par·sec unit
Par·see
Par·see·ism Indian religion
pars·er
par·si·mo·ni·ous
par·si·mo·ny
pars·ley
pars·nip
par·son
par·son·age
part
par·take (·tak·ing, ·took, ·tak·en)
par·tak·er
par·tan Scot crab
part·ed
par·terre garden
par·theno·car·pic (or ·pous)

par·theno·car·py botany term
par·theno·genesis
par·theno·genet·ic
par·theno·geneti·cal·ly
Par·the·non Greek temple
Parthenope mythological character
Par·thia ancient Asian country
Par·thian
par·tial
par·tial·ity (plural ·ities)
par·tial·ly
par·tial·ness
part·ible
par·tici·pant
par·tici·pate
par·tici·pa·tion (or ·tici·pance)
par·tici·pa·tor
par·ti·cipi·al
par·ti·ci·ple
par·ti·cle
parti-coloured (US -colored)
par·ticu·lar
par·ticu·lar·ism
par·ticu·lar·ist
par·ticu·lar·is·tic
par·ticu·lar·ity (plural ·ities)
par·ticu·lari·za·tion (or ·sa·tion)
par·ticu·lar·ize (or ·ise)
par·ticu·lar·iz·er (or ·is·er)
par·ticu·late (adj)
part·ing
par·ti pris French preconceived opinion
par·ti·san (or ·zan)
par·ti·san·ship (or ·zan·ship)
par·ti·ta musical piece
par·tite divided
par·ti·tion
par·ti·tion·er (or ·ist)
par·ti·tive
part·let shawl
part·ly
part·ner
part·ner·ship
par·ton physics term
par·took
par·tridge (plural ·tridges or ·tridge)

part-time (adj)
part-timer
par·tu·ri·ent of childbirth
par·tu·ri·fa·cient
par·tu·ri·tion
par·ty (plural ·ties)
pa·ru·lis (plural ·li·des) gumboil
pa·rure set of jewels
par·venu (fem ·venue)
par·vis (or ·vise) church porch
Pasa·dena US city
Pa·sar·ga·dae ancient Persian city
Pa·say Philippine city
pas·cal unit
pas·chal of Easter
Pas-de-Calais French department
pas de deux (plural pas de deux) ballet sequence
pash Slang infatuation
Pa·sha Turkish title
pa·sha (or ·cha) Ottoman governor
pa·sha·lik (or ·lic) province of pasha
Pash·to (or Push·tu) language
paso do·ble (plural paso do·bles or pasos do·bles) dance
pasque·flow·er
pas·quin·ade (or pas·quil) satire
pas·quin·ad·er
pass
pass·able able to be passed; compare passible
pass·ably
pas·sa·ca·glia musical piece
pas·sade dressage term
pas·sage
passage·way
pas·sant heraldic term
pass·book
pas·sé out-of-date
passed past tense of pass; compare past
passe·men·terie decorative trimming
pas·sen·ger
passe-partout picture mounting
passe·pied dance

passer-by

passer-by (*plural* passers-by)
pas·ser·ine ornithology term
pas seul dance sequence
pas·sibil·ity
pas·sible sensitive; *compare* passable
pas·si·flo·ra·ceous botany term
pas·sim *Latin* throughout
pass·ing
Pas·sion Christ's sufferings
pas·sion
pas·sion·al
pas·sion·ate
pas·sion·ate·ness
passion-flower
pas·sion·less
pas·sion·less·ness
Passion-tide
pas·sive
pas·sive·ness (*or* pas·siv·ity)
pas·siv·ism
pas·siv·ist
pass·key
Pass·over
pass·port
(passtime) *incorrect spelling of* pastime
pas·sus (*plural* ·sus *or* ·suses) part of poem
pass·word
past
pas·ta
paste
paste·board
pas·tel drawing crayon; *compare* pastille
pas·tel·list (*or* ·tel·ist)
pas·tern part of horse's foot
paste-up
pas·teur·ism rabies treatment
pas·teuri·za·tion (*or* ·sa·tion)
pas·teur·ize (*or* ·ise)
pas·teur·iz·er (*or* ·is·er)
pas·tic·cio (*plural* ·cios) pasticche
pas·tiche artistic medley; *compare* postiche
pas·tille (*or* ·til) lozenge; *compare* pastel
pasti·ly
pas·time

pasti·ness
pas·tis alcoholic drink
pas·tor
pas·to·ral of shepherds or pastors
pas·to·rale (*plural* ·rales *or* ·ra·li) musical piece
pas·to·ral·ly
pas·tor·ate
pas·tra·mi smoked beef
pas·try (*plural* ·tries)
pas·tur·age
pas·ture
(pasturize) *incorrect spelling of* pasteurize
pasty (*noun, plural* pasties; *adj* pasti·er, pasti·est) a pastry; pale
pat (pat·ting, pat·ted)
pa·ta·gium (*plural* ·gia) zoology term
Pata·go·nia South American region
patch
patch·able
patch·er
patchi·ly
patchi·ness
patchou·li (*or* pachou·li, patchou·ly) perfume
patch·work
patchy (patchi·er, patchi·est)
pate the head
pâté food; *compare* pattée
pâté de foie gras (*plural* pâtés de foie gras)
pa·tel·la (*plural* ·lae) kneecap
pa·tel·lar
pa·tel·late
pa·tel·li·form
pat·en (*or* ·in, ·ine) plate for Eucharist; *compare* patten
pa·ten·cy
pa·tent
pa·tent·able
pa·tentee
pa·tent·ly
pa·ten·tor
pa·ter *Slang* father
pa·ter·fa·mili·as (*plural* pa·tres·fa·mili·as) male head of family
pa·ter·nal
pa·ter·nal·ism

332

pa·ter·nal·ist
pa·ter·nal·is·tic
pa·ter·nal·is·ti·cal·ly
pa·ter·nal·ly
pa·ter·nity
Pat·er·nos·ter Lord's Prayer
pat·er·nos·ter rosary beads; fishing tackle; lift
Pat·er·son US city
path
Pa·than Afghan or Pakistani Muslim
pa·thet·ic
pa·theti·cal·ly
path·finder
path-finding
patho·gen (*or* ·gene)
patho·gen·esis (*or* pa·thog·eny)
patho·genet·ic of disease
patho·gen·ic causing disease
path·og·no·mon·ic indicating disease
path·og·no·moni·cal·ly
path·og·no·my study of emotions
patho·logi·cal (*or* ·log·ic)
patho·logi·cal·ly
pa·tholo·gist
pa·thol·ogy (*plural* ·ogies)
pa·thos
path·way
Pa·tia·la Indian city
pa·tience
pa·tient
pa·tient·ly
pati·na
pa·tio (*plural* ·tios)
pa·tis·serie
Pat·mos Greek island
Pat·na Indian city; rice
pat·ois (*plural* pat·ois) dialect
Pa·tras Greek port
pa·trial
pa·tri·arch
pa·tri·ar·chal
pa·tri·ar·chate
pa·tri·ar·chy (*plural* ·chies)
pa·tri·cian
pa·tri·ci·ate rank of patrician
pat·ri·cid·al

pat·ri·cide killing one's father; *compare* **parricide**
pat·ri·cli·nous (*or* ·ro·cli·nous, ·ro·cli·nal) resembling male parent
pat·ri·lin·eal (*or* ·ear)
pat·ri·lo·cal living with husband's family
pat·ri·mo·nial
pat·ri·mo·ny (*plural* ·nies)
pa·tri·ot
pat·ri·ot·ic
pat·ri·ot·ism
pa·tris·tic (*or* ·ti·cal)
pa·tris·ti·cal·ly
pa·trol (·trol·ling, ·trolled)
pa·trol·ler
patrol·man (*plural* ·men)
pa·trol·ogy writings of Church Fathers
pa·tron
pat·ron·age
pa·tron·al
pa·tron·ess
pat·ron·ize (*or* ·ise)
pat·ron·iz·er (*or* ·is·er)
pat·ron·iz·ing·ly (*or* ·is·ing·ly)
pat·ro·nym·ic
pat·ted
pat·tée type of cross; *compare* pâté
pat·ten wooden clog; *compare* paten
pat·ter
pat·tern
pat·ting
pat·ty (*plural* ·ties)
patu·lous
paua shellfish
pau·cal linguistics term
pau·city
paul·dron armour plate
Paul·ine of St Paul
pau·low·nia tree
paunch
paunchi·ness
paunchy (paunchi·er, paunchi·est)
pau·per
pau·per·ism
pau·per·ize (*or* ·ise)
pause
paus·er
paus·ing·ly
pav·age paving tax

pa·vane (*or* pa·van) dance
pave
pavé paved surface
pave·ment
pa·vil·ion
pav·ing
pav·ior (*or* ·iour) one who paves
pav·is (*or* ·ise) shield
Pav·lo·va meringue cake
pavo·nine of peacocks
paw
pawky (pawki·er, pawki·est) *Scot* drily witty
pawl part of ratchet; *compare* **pall**
pawn
pawn·age
pawn·broker
pawn·broking
Paw·nee (*plural* ·nees *or* ·nee) American Indian
pawn·shop
paw·paw variant spelling of **papaw**
pax
pax·wax *Dialect* ligament
pay (pay·ing, paid)
pay·able
pay·day
payee
pay·er
pay·load
pay·master
pay·ment
pay·nim *Archaic* heathen
pay-off (*noun*)
pay·ola *US* bribe
pay·phone
pay·roll
pea
peace
peace·able
peace·able·ness
peace·ful
peace·ful·ly
peace·ful·ness
peace·maker
peace·time
peach
peachi·ness
peachy (peachi·er, peachi·est)
pea·cock (*plural* ·cocks *or* ·cock)

pea·fowl (*plural* ·fowls *or* ·fowl)
pea·hen
peak summit; to sicken; *compare* **peek**; **peke**
peaked
peaky (peaki·er, peaki·est)
peal loud sound; *compare* **peel**
pean heraldic term; *US variant spelling of* **paean**; *compare* **paeon**; **peon**
pea·nut
pear
pearl jewel; *compare* **purl**
pearl·er
pearl·ite steel constituent; *variant spelling of* **perlite**
pearl·it·ic
pearl·ized (*or* ·ised)
pearly (*adj* pearli·er, pearli·est; *noun*, *plural* pearlies)
pear·main apple
peas·ant
peas·ant·ry
pease *Dialect* pea
pea·shooter
pea·soup·er *Slang* fog
peat
peaty
peau de soie fabric
peb·ble
pebble-dash
peb·bling
peb·bly
pe·can nut; *compare* **pekan**
pec·ca·bil·ity
pec·cable liable to sin
pec·ca·dil·lo (*plural* ·los *or* ·loes)
pec·can·cy
pec·cant
pec·ca·ry (*plural* ·ries *or* ·ry) piglike animal
pec·ca·vi (*plural* ·vis) confession of guilt
peck
peck·er
peck·ing
peck·ish
pec·tase enzyme
pec·tate
pec·ten (*plural* ·tens *or* ·ti·nes) zoology term; *compare* **pectin**

pectic

pec·tic of pectin; *compare* **peptic**
pec·tin gelling substance; *compare* **pecten**
pec·ti·nate (*or* **·nat·ed**) comb-shaped
pec·ti·na·tion
pec·tin·ous
pec·tiz·able (*or* **·tis·able**)
pec·ti·za·tion (*or* **·sa·tion**)
pec·tize (*or* **·tise**) jellify
pec·to·ral
pecu·late embezzle
pecu·la·tion
pecu·la·tor
pe·cu·liar
pe·cu·li·ar·ity (*plural* **·ities**)
pe·cu·ni·ari·ly
pe·cu·ni·ary
peda·gog·ic (*or* **·gogi·cal**)
peda·gogi·cal·ly
peda·gog·ics
peda·gog·ism (*or* **·gogu·ism**)
peda·gogue (*or* **·gog**)
peda·go·gy
ped·al (**·al·ling**, **·alled**; *US* **·dal·ing**, **·daled**) foot lever; operate pedals; *compare* **peddle**
pe·dal of the foot
pe·dal·fer soil
ped·al·ler (*US* **·al·er**) one who pedals; *compare* **peddler; pedlar**
peda·lo (*plural* **·los** *or* **·loes**) pedal boat
ped·ant
pe·dan·tic
ped·ant·ry (*plural* **·ries**)
ped·ate biology term
pe·dati·fid botany term
ped·dle sell; *compare* **pedal**
ped·dler drugs seller; *US* spelling of **pedlar**
ped·er·ast (*or* **paed·**)
ped·er·as·tic (*or* **paed·**)
ped·er·as·ty (*or* **paed·**)
ped·es·tal
pe·des·trian
pe·des·tria·ni·za·tion (*or* **·sa·tion**)
pe·des·tri·an·ize (*or* **·ise**)
Pedi African people
pe·di·at·rics *US* spelling of **paediatrics**

pedi·cab tricycle cab
pedi·cel flower stalk
pedi·cle small stalk
pe·dicu·lar of lice or pedicles
pe·dicu·late zoology term
pe·dicu·lo·sis infestation with lice
pe·dicu·lous
pedi·cure
pedi·form
pedi·gree
pedi·greed
pedi·ment
pedi·ment·al
pedi·palp zoology term
ped·lar (*US* **ped·dler**) hawker; *compare* **peddler**
pedo·cal soil
pe·do·logi·cal
pe·dolo·gist
pe·dol·ogy study of soils
pe·dom·eter
pe·dun·cle flower stalk
pe·dun·cu·lar
pe·dun·cu·late (*or* **·lat·ed**)
pe·dun·cu·la·tion
pee (**pee·ing**, **peed**)
Pee·bles former Scottish county
peek peep; *compare* **peak; peke**
peeka·boo
peel rind; to be shed; fortified tower; *compare* **peal**
peel·er
peelie-wally *Scot* unwell
peel·ing
peen part of hammer
peep
peep·er
peep·hole
peep·show
pee·pul (*or* **pi·pal**) sacred tree
peer a noble; an equal; to look; *compare* **pier**
peer·age
peer·ess
peer·less
peeve *Slang* irritate
peev·ers *Scot* hopscotch
peev·ish
peev·ish·ness
pee·wee *variant spelling of* **pewee**

334

pee·wit (*or* **pe·wit**) lapwing
peg (**peg·ging**, **pegged**)
Pega·sus mythological horse; constellation
peg·board
peg·ma·tite rock
peg·ma·tit·ic
peign·oir
pejo·ra·tion
pe·jo·ra·tive
pek·an animal; *compare* **pecan**
peke *Slang* Pekingese dog; *compare* **peak; peek**
Pe·kin duck
Pe·king Chinese capital
Pe·king·ese (*or* **·kin·**) dog; of Peking
pe·koe tea
pel·age
Pe·la·gi·an·ism Christian doctrine
pe·lag·ic of open sea
pel·ar·go·nium
Pe·lée West Indian volcano
pel·er·ine cape
Peleus mythological character
pelf *Slang* money
pel·ham horse's bit
peli·can
Pe·li·on Greek mountain
pe·lisse
pe·lite rock
pe·lit·ic
Pel·la ancient Greek city
pel·la·gra
pel·la·grous
pel·let
pel·li·cle
pel·licu·lar
pel·li·tory (*plural* **·tories**) plant
pell-mell
pel·lu·cid
pel·lu·cid·ity (*or* **·ness**)
Pel·man·ism memory training
pel·man·ism card game
pel·met
Pelo·pon·nese
Pelo·pon·ne·sian
Pelops mythological character
pe·lo·ria botany term
pe·lo·rus (*plural* **·ruses**) gyrocompass

pe·lo·ta ball game
Pe·lo·tas Brazilian port
pelt
pel·tast ancient Greek soldier
pel·tate botany term
pel·ta·tion
pelt·er
Peltier ef·fect
pelt·ry (*plural* ·ries) animal pelts
pel·vic
pel·vis (*plural* ·vises *or* ·ves)
Pem·ba Tanzanian island
Pem·broke
Pem·broke·shire former Welsh county
pem·mi·can (*or* pemi·can) food
pem·phi·gus skin disease
pen (pen·ning, penned) writing tool; write
pen (pen·ning, penned *or* pent) enclosure; enclose
pe·nal
pe·nali·za·tion (*or* ·sa·tion)
pe·nal·ize (*or* ·ise)
pen·al·ty (*plural* ·ties)
pen·ance
Pe·nang Malaysian state
pe·na·tes Roman gods
pence
pen·cel (*or* ·sel, ·sil) small flag; *compare* pencil
pen·chant
Pen·chi (*or* ·ki) Chinese city
pen·cil (·cil·ling, ·cilled; *US* ·cil·ing, ·ciled) writing tool, etc.; *compare* pencel
pen·cil·ler (*US* ·cil·er)
pend
pen·dant necklace
pen·dent dangling
pen·den·te lite legal term
pen·den·tive architectural term
pend·ing
pen·dragon leader of ancient Britons
pen·du·lous
pen·du·lum
pe·neplain (*or* ·neplane) flat land

pe·ne·pla·na·tion
pen·etrabil·ity
pen·etrable
pen·etra·lia innermost parts
pen·etra·lian
pen·etrance
pen·etrant
pen·etrate
pen·etra·tion
pen·etra·tor
Peng·pu (*or* Pang-fou) Chinese city
pen·guin
peni·cil·late biology term
peni·cil·la·tion
peni·cil·lin antibiotic
peni·cil·lium (*plural* ·liums *or* ·lia) mould
pe·nile of the penis
pe·nil·li·on (*sing.* pe·nill) Welsh sung poetry
pen·in·su·la
pen·in·su·lar
pe·nis (*plural* ·nises *or* ·nes)
peni·tence
peni·tent
peni·ten·tial
peni·ten·tia·ry (*plural* ·ries)
pen·knife (*plural* ·knives)
pen·man (*plural* ·men)
pen·man·ship
pen·na (*plural* ·nae) feather
pen·nant ship's flag; *compare* pennon
pen·nate (*or* ·nat·ed)
penned
pen·nies
pen·ni·less
pen·ni·less·ness
Pen·nine
Pen·nines
pen·ning
pen·ni·nite mineral
pen·non long flag; *compare* pennant
Penn·syl·va·nia
Penn·syl·va·nian
pen·nul·ti·mate
pen·ny (*plural* pen·nies *or* pence)
pen·ny·cress
penny-pincher
penny-pinching
penny·royal plant

penny·weight
penny-wise
penny·wort plant
penny·worth
pe·no·logi·cal (*or* poe·)
pe·nolo·gist (*or* poe·)
pe·nol·ogy (*or* poe·)
Pen·rith Cumbrian town
pen·sile ornithology term
pen·sil·ity (*or* ·sile·ness)
pen·sion
pen·sion·able
pen·sion·ary (*plural* ·aries)
pen·sion·er
pen·sive
pen·sive·ness
pen·stock water channel
pent
pen·ta·chlo·ro·phe·nol
pen·ta·cle variant of pentagram
pen·tad group of five
pen·ta·dac·tyl
Pen·ta·gon US defence headquarters
pen·ta·gon five-sided polygon
pen·tago·nal
pen·ta·gram (*or* ·cle) magical symbol
pen·ta·he·dron (*plural* ·drons *or* ·dra)
pen·tam·er·ous botany term
pen·tam·eter verse line
pen·tane organic compound
pen·tan·gu·lar
pen·ta·no·ic acid
pen·ta·prism
pen·ta·quine drug
pen·tar·chi·cal
pen·tar·chy (*plural* ·chies) government by five
pen·ta·stich five-line poem
Pen·ta·teuch Old Testament books
pen·tath·lete
pen·tath·lon
pen·ta·ton·ic musical term
pen·ta·va·lent
Pen·tecost
Pen·tecos·tal
pen·tene organic compound
pent·house
pen·ti·men·to (*plural* ·ti) art term

pentlandite

pent·land·ite mineral
pen·to·bar·bi·tone (*US* ·tal)
pen·tode electronic valve
pen·tom·ic military term
pen·to·san biochemical compound
pen·tose sugar
Pen·to·thal (*Trademark*)
pent·ox·ide
pent·ste·mon (*or* pen·ste·mon) plant
pent-up
pen·tyl chemistry term
pentylene·tetrazol
pe·nu·che variant of panocha
pen·ult (*or* pe·nul·ti·ma)
pe·nul·ti·mate
pe·num·bra (*plural* ·brae *or* ·bras)
pe·num·bral (*or* ·brous)
pe·nu·ri·ous
penu·ry
Pen·za Soviet city
Pen·zance
peon Indian worker; debtor; *compare* paean; paeon; pean
pe·on·age (*or* pe·on·ism)
peo·ny (*plural* ·nies)
peo·ple
Peo·ria US port
pep (pep·ping, pepped)
pep·lum (*plural* ·lums *or* ·la) ruffle
pepo (*plural* pepos) botany term
pep·per
pepper·corn
pepper·grass
pepper·mint
pepper·wort
pep·pery
pep·py (·pi·er, ·pi·est)
pep·sin (*or* ·sine) enzyme
pep·si·nate
pep·sino·gen enzyme
pep·tic of digestion; *compare* pectic
pep·ti·dase enzyme
pep·tide protein
pep·tiz·able (*or* ·tis·able)
pep·ti·za·tion (*or* ·sa·tion)
pep·tize (*or* ·tise)
pep·tiz·er (*or* ·tis·er)

pep·tone product of digestion
pep·to·ni·za·tion (*or* ·sa·tion)
pep·to·nize (*or* ·nise)
pep·to·niz·er (*or* ·nis·er)
Pe·quot (*plural* ·quot *or* ·quots) American Indian
per
per·acid
pera·cid·ity
per·ad·ven·ture Archaic by chance
Pe·raea ancient Palestinian region
Pe·rak Malaysian state
per·am·bu·late
per·am·bu·la·tion
per·am·bu·la·tor
per·am·bu·la·tory
per an·num
per·bo·rate chemistry term
per·cale sheet fabric
per·ca·line lining fabric
per capi·ta
per·ceiv·abil·ity
per·ceiv·able
per·ceive
per·ceiv·er
per cent
per·cent·age
per·cen·tile
per·cept object of perception
per·cep·tibil·ity (*or* ·tible·ness)
per·cep·tible
per·cep·tibly
per·cep·tion
per·cep·tion·al
per·cep·tive
per·cep·tivi·ty (*or* ·tive·ness)
per·cep·tual
perch (*plural (for fish)* perch *or* perches)
per·chance
perch·er
Per·cheron horse
per·chlo·rate
per·chlo·ride
per·cipi·ence
per·cipi·ent
per·coid (*or* ·coi·dean) zoology term
per·co·late
per·co·la·tion

per·co·la·tive
per·co·la·tor
per·cuss
per·cus·sion
per·cus·sion·ist
per·cus·sive
per·cus·sor
per·cu·ta·neous
per diem *Latin* every day
per·di·tion
per·egri·nate
per·egri·na·tion
per·egri·na·tor
per·egrine
Pe·rei·ra Colombian city
pe·rei·ra medicinal bark
per·emp·to·ri·ly
per·emp·to·ri·ness
per·emp·tory
pe·ren·nate botany term
pe·ren·na·tion
per·en·nial
per·en·nial·ly
per·fect
per·fect·er
per·fect·ibil·ity
per·fect·ible
per·fec·tion
per·fec·tion·ism
per·fec·tion·ist
per·fec·tive
per·fec·to (*plural* ·tos) cigar
per·fer·vid ardent
per·fidi·ous
per·fidi·ous·ness
per·fi·dy (*plural* ·dies)
per·fo·li·ate botany term
per·fo·li·a·tion
per·fo·rable
per·fo·rate
per·fo·ra·tion
per·fo·ra·tive (*or* ·tory)
per·fo·ra·tor
per·force
per·form
per·form·able
per·for·mance
per·for·ma·tive
per·form·er
per·form·ing
per·fume
per·fum·er
per·fum·ery (*plural* ·eries)
per·func·to·ri·ly
per·func·to·ri·ness

per·func·tory
per·fuse
per·fu·sion
per·fu·sive
Per·ga·mum ancient Asian city
per·go·la
per·haps
peri (*plural* peris) fairy
peri·anth petals of flower
peri·apt amulet
peri·blem plant tissue
peri·car·dit·ic
peri·car·di·tis
peri·car·dium (*plural* ·dia)
peri·carp botany term
peri·car·pial (*or* ·pic)
peri·chon·drium (*plural* ·dria) anatomy term
peri·clase mineral
peri·clas·tic
peri·cli·nal botany term
peri·cline mineral
pe·rico·pe church reading
peri·cra·nial
peri·cra·nium (*plural* ·nia)
peri·cy·cle plant tissue
peri·cy·clic
peri·cyn·thi·on point in lunar orbit
peri·derm botany term
peri·derm·al (*or* ·ic)
pe·rid·ium (*plural* ·ridia) botany term
peri·dot gemstone
peri·do·tite rock
peri·do·tit·ic
peri·gean (*or* ·geal)
peri·gee point in lunar orbit
peri·gon maths term
Peri·gor·dian Palaeolithic culture
pe·rigy·nous botany term
pe·rigy·ny
peri·he·lion (*plural* ·lia) point in planet's orbit
per·il
peri·lous
peri·lous·ness
peri·lune point in lunar orbit
peri·lymph anatomy term
pe·rim·eter
peri·met·ric (*or* ·ri·cal, pe·rim·etral)
peri·met·ri·cal·ly
pe·rim·etry

peri·morph mineralogy term
peri·mor·phic (*or* ·phous)
peri·mor·phism
peri·mys·ium anatomy term
peri·na·tal
peri·neal
peri·neph·rium (*plural* ·ria) anatomy term
peri·neum (*plural* ·nea) vaginal area
peri·neu·ri·tic
peri·neu·ri·tis
peri·neu·rium nerve tissue
pe·ri·od
pe·rio·date chemistry term
pe·ri·od·ic
peri·od·ic acid
pe·ri·odi·cal
pe·ri·odi·cal·ly
pe·rio·dic·ity (*plural* ·ities)
perio·don·tal
perio·don·tic
perio·don·ti·cal·ly
perio·don·tics
perio·don·tol·ogy branch of dentistry
peri·onych·ium (*plural* ·onychia) anatomy term
peri·os·teum (*plural* ·tea) bone tissue
peri·os·tit·ic
peri·os·ti·tis
peri·otic around the ear
perl·pa·tet·ic
peri·pa·teti·cal·ly
peri·peteia (*or* ·petia, pe·rip·ety) drama term
peri·peteian (*or* ·petian)
pe·riph·er·al
pe·riph·er·al·ly
pe·riph·ery (*plural* ·eries)
pe·riph·ra·sis (*plural* ·ses) circumlocution
peri·phras·tic
peri·phras·ti·cal·ly
pe·riphy·ton aquatic organisms
pe·rip·teral
pe·rique tobacco
peri·sarc zoology term
peri·sar·cal (*or* ·cous)
peri·scope
peri·scop·ic
peri·scopi·cal·ly
per·ish

per·ish·abil·ity (*or* ·able·ness)
per·ish·able
per·ish·er
per·ish·ing
peri·sperm botany term
peri·sperm·al
peri·spo·menon linguistics term
pe·ris·so·dac·tyl (*or* ·tyle) zoology term
pe·ris·so·dac·ty·lous
peri·stal·sis (*plural* ·ses)
peri·stal·tic
peri·stal·ti·cal·ly
peri·sto·mal (*or* ·mial)
peri·stome botany term
peri·sty·lar
peri·style colonnade
peri·thecium (*plural* ·thecia) botany term
peri·to·neal
peri·to·neum (*plural* ·nea *or* ·niums)
peri·to·nit·ic
peri·to·ni·tis
peri·track taxiway
pe·rit·ri·cha (*sing.* peri·trich) biology term
pe·rit·ri·chous
peri·wig
peri·win·kle
(perjorative) *incorrect spelling of* pejorative
per·jure
per·jur·er
per·jury (*plural* ·juries)
perk
perki·ly
perki·ness
perky (perki·er, perki·est)
Per·lis Malaysian state
per·lite (*or* pearl·) filler and soil-conditioner; *compare* pearlite
per·lit·ic (*or* pearl·)
per·lo·cu·tion
per·lo·cu·tion·ary
Perm Soviet port
perm
per·ma·frost
perm·al·loy
per·ma·nence
per·ma·nen·cy (*plural* ·cies)
per·ma·nent

permanganate

per·man·ga·nate
per·me·abil·ity (*plural* ·ities)
per·me·able
per·me·ance
per·me·ant
per·me·ate
per·mea·tion
per·mea·tive
per·mea·tor
per men·sem *Latin* every month
Per·mian geological period
per·mis·sibil·ity
per·mis·sible
per·mis·sion
per·mis·sive
per·mis·sive·ness
per·mit (·mit·ting, ·mit·ted)
per·mit·ter
per·mit·tiv·ity (*plural* ·ities) physics term
per·mu·ta·tion
per·mu·ta·tion·al
per·mute
Per·nam·bu·co Brazilian state
per·ni·cious
per·ni·cious·ness
per·nick·eti·ness
per·nick·ety
Per·nod (*Trademark*)
pe·ro·neal of the outer leg
pero·rate
pero·ra·tion
pe·roxi·dase enzyme
per·ox·ide
per·pend (*or* ·pent) wall stone
per·pen·dicu·lar
per·pen·dicu·lar·ity
per·pe·trate
per·pe·tra·tion
per·pe·tra·tor
per·pet·ual
per·pet·ual·ly
per·petu·ate
per·petua·tion
per·pe·tu·ity (*plural* ·ities)
Per·pi·gnan French town
per·plex
per·plex·ity (*plural* ·ities)
per·qui·site
Per·rier (*Trademark*)
per·ron flight of steps
per·ry (*plural* ·ries) pear wine
per·salt chemical compound
per se *Latin* in itself
perse greyish-blue
per·secute
per·secu·tion
per·secu·tive (*or* ·tory)
per·secu·tor
Per·seid meteor shower
Persephone mythological character
Per·sepo·lis capital of ancient Persia
Perseus mythological character
Per·seus constellation
per·sever·ance
per·se·ver·ant
per·sev·era·tion psychology term
per·severe
Per·sia
Per·sian
per·si·caria plant
per·si·ennes Persian blinds
per·si·flage
per·sim·mon fruit
Per·sis ancient Persian region
per·sist
per·sis·tence (*or* ·ten·cy)
per·sis·tent
per·sist·er
per·son (*plural* ·sons)
per·so·na (*plural* ·nae)
per·son·able
per·son·able·ness
per·son·age
per·so·na gra·ta (*plural* per·so·nae gra·tae)
per·son·al
per·son·al·ism
per·son·al·ist
per·son·al·is·tic
per·son·al·ity (*plural* ·ities)
per·son·ali·za·tion (*or* ·sa·tion)
per·son·al·ize (*or* ·ise)
per·son·al·ly
per·son·al·ty (*plural* ·ties) personal property
per·so·na non gra·ta (*plural* per·so·nae non gra·tae)
per·son·ate
per·sona·tion
per·sona·tive
per·sona·tor
per·soni·fi·able
per·soni·fi·ca·tion
per·soni·fy (·fies, ·fy·ing, ·fied)
per·son·nel
per·spec·tive
Per·spec·tiv·ism philosophical doctrine
Per·spex (*Trademark*)
per·spi·ca·cious perceptive; *compare* perspicuous
per·spi·cac·ity (*or* ·ca·cious·ness)
per·spi·cu·ity (*or* ·spicu·ous·ness)
per·spicu·ous lucid; *compare* perspicacious
per·spi·ra·tion
per·spir·atory
per·spire
per·spir·ing·ly
per·suad·abil·ity (*or* per·sua·si·bil·ity)
per·suad·able (*or* per·sua·sible)
per·suade
per·suad·er
per·sua·sion
per·sua·sive
per·sua·sive·ness
(persue) incorrect spelling of pursue
pert
per·tain
Perth
per·ti·na·cious
per·ti·nac·ity (*or* ·na·cious·ness)
per·ti·nence
per·ti·nent
pert·ness
per·turb
per·turb·able
per·turb·ably
per·tur·ba·tion
per·turb·ing·ly
per·tus·sis whooping cough
Peru
Pe·ru·gia Italian city
pe·ruke wig
pe·rus·al
pe·ruse
pe·rus·er
Pe·ru·vian

per·vade
per·vad·er
per·va·sion
per·va·sive
per·va·sive·ness
per·verse
per·verse·ness
per·ver·sion
per·ver·sity (*plural* ·sities)
per·ver·sive
per·vert
per·vert·ed
per·vert·ed·ly
per·vert·ed·ness
per·vert·er
per·ver·tible
per·vi·ous
per·vi·ous·ness
pes (*plural* pedes) foot
Pe·sach (*or* ·sah) Passover
pe·sade dressage term
Pe·sca·ra Italian city
pe·seta Spanish currency
pe·sewa Ghanaian currency
Pesha·war Pakistani city
Pe·shit·ta (*or* ·shi·to) Syriac Bible
pesky (peski·er, peski·est)
peso (*plural* pesos) coin
pe·soni·fi·er
pes·sa·ry (*plural* ·ries)
pes·si·mism
pes·si·mist
pes·si·mis·tic (*or* ·ti·cal)
pes·si·mis·ti·cal·ly
pest
pes·ter
pes·ter·er
pes·ter·ing·ly
pest·hole
pes·ti·cid·al
pes·ti·cide
pes·tif·er·ous
pes·ti·lence
pes·ti·lent
pes·ti·len·tial
pes·tle
pet (pet·ting, petted)
pet·al
pet·al·if·er·ous (*or* ·al·ous)
pet·al·ine
pet·alled (*US* ·aled)
petal-like
peta·lod·ic
pet·alo·dy botany term
pet·al·oid

pe·tard
pet·cock valve on steam boiler
pe·techia (*plural* ·techiae) red spot on skin
pe·techial
pe·ter
Pe·ter·bor·ough
Pe·ter·lee Durham town
Pe·ter·loo massacre
peter·man (*plural* ·men) *Slang* safe-breaker
Pe·ters·burg US city; *compare* St Petersburg
pe·ter·sham ribbon
pethi·dine
petio·late (*or* ·la·ted)
peti·ole leaf stalk
pe·tio·lule
pet·it of lesser importance; small; *compare* petite
pe·tit bour·geois (*plural* pe·tits bour·geois)
pe·tite small and dainty; *compare* petit
pet·ite bour·geoisie
pet·it four (*plural* pet·its fours) small cake
pe·ti·tion
pe·ti·tion·ary
pe·ti·tion·er
pet·it mal epilepsy
pet·it point needlework stitch
pe·tits pois French peas
Pet·ra ancient city
pet·rel bird; *compare* petrol
Pe·tri dish
pet·ri·fac·tion (*or* pet·ri·fi·ca·tion)
pe·tri·fi·er
pet·ri·fy (·fies, ·fy·ing, ·fied)
Pe·trine of St Peter
pet·ro·chemi·cal
pet·ro·chem·is·try
pet·ro·dol·lar
pet·ro·glyph prehistoric rock carving
Pet·ro·grad *former name of* Leningrad
pe·trog·ra·pher
pet·ro·graph·ic (*or* ·graphi·cal)
pet·ro·graphi·cal·ly
pe·trog·ra·phy classification of rocks

pet·rol fuel; *compare* petrel
pet·ro·la·tum petroleum jelly
pe·tro·leum
pe·trol·ic of petroleum
pet·ro·logi·cal
pe·trolo·gist
pe·trol·ogy (*plural* ·ogies) study of rocks
pet·ro·nel firearm
Pe·tro·pav·lovsk Soviet city
Pe·tró·po·lis Brazilian city
pe·tro·sal anatomy term
pet·rous
Pe·tro·za·vodsk Soviet city
pet·ter
pet·ti·coat
pet·ti·fog (·fog·ging, ·fogged)
pet·ti·fog·ger
pet·ti·fog·gery
pet·ti·ly
pet·ting
pet·tish
pet·tish·ness
pet·ti·toes pigs' trotters
pet·ty (·ti·er, ·ti·est)
petu·lance (*or* ·lan·cy)
petu·lant
pe·tu·nia
pe·tun·tse (*or* ·tze) mineral
pew
pe·wee (*or* pee·) bird
pe·wit variant spelling of peewit
pew·ter
pew·ter·er
pe·yo·te cactus
pfen·nig (*plural* ·nigs *or* ·ni·ge) German coin
Pforz·heim West German city
Phaedra wife of Theseus
Phaëthon mythological character
phae·ton horse-drawn carriage
phage virus
phag·edae·na (*or esp. US* ·edena) ulcer
phago·cyte
phago·cyt·ic
phago·cy·to·sis
phago·ma·nia compulsive eating
phago·ma·ni·ac

phagophobia

phago·pho·bia
phago·pho·bic
phal·ange *variant of* phalanx
pha·lan·geal anatomy term
pha·lan·ger marsupial
pha·lan·ges *plural of* phalanx
phal·an·stery (*plural* ·steries)
phal·anx (*plural* phal·anxes *or* pha·lan·ges) battle formation; compact group
phal·anx (*or* ·ange; *plural* pha·lan·ges) finger or toe bone
phala·rope bird
phal·lic
phal·li·cism (*or* phal·lism)
phal·li·cist (*or* phal·list)
phal·lus (*plural* ·li *or* ·luses)
phan·ero·crys·tal·line
phan·ero·gam botany term
phan·ero·gam·ic (*or* ·er·oga·mous)
pha·nero·phyte botany term
Pha·nero·zo·ic biology term
phan·tasm
phan·tas·ma·go·ria (*or* ·gory)
phan·tas·ma·go·ric (*or* ·ri·cal)
phan·tas·ma·go·ri·cal·ly
phan·tas·mal (*or* ·mic)
phan·tom
phar·aoh (*or* Phar·)
phar·aon·ic (*or* Phar·)
Phari·sa·ic (*or* ·sai·cal)
Phari·see
phar·ma·ceu·ti·cal (*or* ·tic)
phar·ma·ceu·tics
phar·ma·cist (*or* ·ma·ceu·tist)
phar·ma·co·dy·nam·ic
phar·ma·co·dy·nam·ics
phar·ma·cog·no·sist
phar·ma·cog·nos·tic
phar·ma·cog·no·sy branch of pharmacology
phar·ma·co·logi·cal
phar·ma·colo·gist
phar·ma·col·ogy
phar·ma·co·poeia

phar·ma·co·poe·ial (*or* ·poe·ic)
phar·ma·co·poe·ist
phar·ma·cy (*plural* ·cies)
Pha·ros Greek lighthouse
phar·yn·geal (*or* pha·ryn·gal)
phar·yn·gi·tis
phar·yn·go·logi·cal
phar·yn·golo·gist
phar·yn·gol·ogy
pha·ryn·go·scope
pha·ryn·go·scop·ic
phar·yn·gos·co·py
phar·yn·goto·my (*plural* ·mies)
phar·ynx (*plural* pha·ryn·ges *or* phar·ynxes)
phase
pha·sic (*or* phaseal)
phas·mid insect
phat·ic of conversation
pheas·ant
phel·lem
phel·lo·derm
phel·lo·der·mal
phel·lo·gen
phel·lo·genet·ic (*or* ·gen·ic)
phe·na·caine anaesthetic
phe·nac·etin analgesic
phena·cite (*or* ·kite) mineral
phe·nan·threne
phena·zine
phe·net·ic biology term
phe·neti·dine
phen·etole
phen·for·min drug
phe·no·bar·bi·tone (*US* ·tal)
phe·no·copy (*plural* ·copies) biology term
phe·no·cryst geology term
phe·nol
phe·no·late disinfect
phe·nol·ic
phe·no·logi·cal
phe·nolo·gist
phe·nol·ogy study of phenomena
phenol·phthalein
phe·nom·ena *plural of* phenomenon
phe·nom·enal
phe·nom·enal·ism

phe·nom·enal·ist
phe·nom·enal·is·ti·cal·ly
phe·nom·enal·ly
phe·nom·eno·logi·cal
phe·nom·enol·ogy
phe·nom·enon (*plural* ·ena *or* ·enons)
phe·no·thia·zine
phe·no·type biology term
phe·no·typ·ic (*or* ·typi·cal)
phe·no·typi·cal·ly
phe·nox·ide
phe·nyl
phenyl·alanine
phenyl·keton·uria
phero·mone chemical in animals
phew
phial
Phi Beta Kap·pa US academic society
Phila·del·phia
phila·del·phus shrub
Phi·lae Egyptian island
phi·lan·der
phi·lan·der·er
phil·an·throp·ic (*or* ·thropi·cal)
phi·lan·thro·pist (*or* phil·an·thrope)
phi·lan·thro·py (*plural* ·pies)
phil·an·thropi·cal·ly
phila·tel·ic
phila·teli·cal·ly
phi·lat·elist
phi·lat·ely
phil·har·mon·ic
phil·hel·lene (*or* ·len·ist) lover of Greece
phil·hel·len·ism
Phi·lip·pi ancient Macedonian city
phi·lip·pic bitter speech
Phil·ip·pine
Phil·ip·pines
Phil·is·tine
Phil·is·tin·ism
phil·lu·men·ist collector of matchbox labels
philo·den·dron (*plural* ·drons *or* ·dra) plant
phi·logy·ny fondness for women
philo·logi·cal
phi·lolo·gist (*or* ·ger)
phi·lol·ogy

philo·mel (*or* ·mela)
  nightingale
Philomela mythological
  princess
phi·loso·pher
philo·soph·ic
philo·sophi·cal (*or*
  ·soph·ic)
philo·sophi·cal·ly
philo·sophi·cal·ness
phi·loso·phi·za·tion (*or*
  ·sa·tion)
phi·loso·phize (*or* ·phise)
phi·loso·phiz·er (*or*
  ·phis·er)
phi·loso·phy (*plural*
  ·phies)
phil·tre (*US* ·ter) love
  potion; *compare* filter
phi·mo·sis medical term
phi-phenom·enon (*plural*
  ·ena) psychology term
phiz *Slang* face
phle·bit·ic
phle·bi·tis
phlebo·scle·ro·sis
phlebo·tom·ic (*or*
  ·tomi·cal)
phle·boto·mist
phle·boto·mize
phle·boto·my (*plural*
  ·mies) incision into vein
phlegm
phleg·mat·ic (*or* ·mati·cal)
phleg·mati·cal·ly
phleg·mati·cal·ness (*or*
  ·mat·ic·ness)
phlo·em plant tissue
phlo·gis·tic
phlo·gis·ton
phlogo·pite mineral
phlox (*plural* phlox *or*
  phloxes)
phlyc·ten (*or* ·te·na;
  plural ·tens *or* ·nae)
  blister
Phnom Penh (*or* Pnom
  Penh) Cambodian capital
pho·bia
pho·bic
Pho·bos satellite of Mars
pho·cine of seals
Pho·cis region of ancient
  Greece
pho·co·melia (*or*
  ·com·ely)
Phoe·be satellite of Saturn

phoe·be bird
Phoebus Apollo
Phoe·ni·cia
Phoe·ni·cian
Phoe·nix US city
phoe·nix legendary bird
phon unit
pho·nate utter speech
pho·na·tion
pho·na·tory
phone
phone-in (*noun*)
pho·neme linguistics term
pho·nemic
pho·nemi·cal·ly
pho·nemics
pho·net·ic
pho·neti·cal·ly
pho·neti·cian
pho·net·ics
pho·net·ist
pho·ney (*or* ·ny; *adj*
  ·ni·er, ·ni·est; *noun,
  plural* ·neys *or* ·nies)
pho·ney·ness (*or* ·ni·)
phon·ic
phoni·cal·ly
phon·ics teaching method
pho·ni·ness *variant spelling
  of* phoneyness
pho·no·gram
pho·no·gram·ic (*or*
  ·gram·mic)
pho·no·graph
pho·nog·ra·pher (*or*
  ·phist)
pho·nog·ra·phy
pho·no·lite rock
pho·no·lit·ic
pho·no·logi·cal
pho·nolo·gist
pho·nol·ogy (*plural*
  ·ogies)
pho·nom·eter
pho·no·met·ric (*or* ·ri·cal)
pho·non physics term
pho·no·scope
pho·no·tac·tics branch of
  linguistics
pho·no·type
pho·no·typ·ic (*or*
  ·typi·cal)
pho·no·typ·ist (*or* ·typ·er)
pho·no·typy phonetic
  transcription
pho·ny *variant spelling of*
  phoney

phoo·ey
phos·gene poisonous gas
phos·ge·nite mineral
phos·pha·tase enzyme
phos·phate
phos·phat·ic
phos·pha·tide biochemical
  compound
phos·pha·ti·za·tion (*or*
  ·sa·tion)
phos·pha·tize (*or* ·tise)
phos·pha·tu·ria
phos·pha·tu·ric
phos·phene physiology
  term; *compare* phosphine
phos·phide
phos·phine gas; *compare*
  phosphene
phos·phite
phos·pho·crea·tine (*or*
  ·tin)
phos·pho·lip·id
phos·pho·pro·tein
phos·phor
phos·pho·rate
phos·pho·resce
phos·pho·res·cence
phos·pho·res·cent
phos·phor·ic
phos·pho·rism
phos·pho·rite mineral
phos·pho·rit·ic
phos·phoro·scope
phos·pho·rous (*adj*)
phos·pho·rus (*noun*)
phos·phory·lase enzyme
phot unit
pho·tic of light
pho·to (*plural* ·tos)
photo·ac·tin·ic
photo·ac·tive
photo·auto·troph·ic
  biology term
photo·bath·ic biology term
photo·cath·ode
photo·cell
photo·chemi·cal
photo·chem·ist
photo·chem·is·try
photo·com·pose
photo·com·pos·er
photo·com·po·si·tion
photo·con·duc·tion
photo·con·duc·tiv·ity
photo·con·duc·tor
photo·copi·er

photocopy

photo·copy (*noun, plural* ·copies; *verb* ·copies, ·copy·ing, ·cop·ied)
photo·cur·rent
photo·dis·in·te·gra·tion
photo·dy·nam·ic
photo·dy·nam·ics
photo·elas·tic·ity
photo·elec·tric (*or* ·tri·cal)
photo·elec·tri·cal·ly
photo·elec·tric·ity
photo·elec·tron
photo·elec·tro·type
photo·emis·sion
photo·emis·sive
photo·en·grave
photo·en·grav·er
photo·en·grav·ing
Photo·fit (*Trademark*)
photo·flash
photo·flood tungsten lamp
photo·fluo·rog·ra·phy
photo·gen·ic
photo·geni·cal·ly
photo·geol·ogy
photo·gram type of photograph
photo·gram·met·ric
photo·gram·metrist
photo·gram·metry
photo·graph
pho·tog·ra·pher
photo·graph·ic
photo·graphi·cal·ly
pho·tog·ra·phy
photo·gra·vure
photo·jour·nal·ism
photo·jour·na·list
photo·jour·na·lis·tic
photo·ki·nesis
photo·ki·net·ic
photo·ki·neti·cal·ly
photo·litho·graph
photo·li·thog·ra·pher
photo·li·thog·ra·phy
pho·to·lu·mi·nes·cence
pho·to·lu·mi·nes·cent
pho·toly·sis
photo·lyt·ic
photo·map (·map·ping, ·mapped)
photo·mechani·cal
pho·tom·eter
photo·met·ric
photo·met·ri·cal·ly
pho·tom·etrist
pho·tom·etry

photo·micro·graph
photo·mi·crog·ra·pher
photo·micro·graph·ic
photo·micro·graphi·cal·ly
photo·mi·crog·ra·phy
photo·mon·tage
photo·multi·pli·er
photo·mu·ral
pho·ton
photo·nas·tic
photo·nas·ty botany term
photo·neu·tron
photo·nu·cle·ar
photo-offset
photo·peri·od
photo·peri·od·ic
photo·peri·odi·cal·ly
photo·peri·od·ism biology term
pho·tophi·lous botany term
pho·tophi·ly
photo·pho·bia
photo·pho·bic
photo·phore light-producing organ
photo·pia day vision
pho·top·ic
photo·poly·mer
photo·recep·tor
photo·recon·nais·sance
photo·sen·si·tive
photo·sen·si·tiv·ity
photo·sen·si·ti·za·tion (*or* ·sa·tion)
photo·sen·si·tize (*or* ·tise)
photo·set (·set·ting, ·set)
photo·set·ter
photo·sphere surface of sun
photo·spher·ic
Photo·stat (*Trademark*) machine
photo·stat (*noun, verb*) photocopy
photo·stat·ic
photo·syn·the·sis
photo·syn·the·size
photo·syn·thet·ic
photo·syn·theti·cal·ly
photo·tac·tic
photo·tax·is (*or* ·taxy) biology term
photo·tele·graph·ic
photo·tele·graphi·cal·ly
photo·teleg·ra·phy
photo·thera·peu·tic
photo·thera·peu·ti·cal·ly

photo·thera·py (*or* ·peu·tics)
photo·ther·mic (*or* ·mal)
photo·ther·mi·cal·ly (*or* ·mal·ly)
photo·ton·ic
pho·toto·nus botany term
photo·to·pog·ra·phy
photo·tran·sis·tor
photo·trop·ic
pho·tot·ro·pism botany term
photo·tube
photo·type
photo·type·set·ting
photo·typ·ic
photo·typi·cal·ly
photo·ty·pog·ra·phy
photo·vol·ta·ic
photo·zin·co·graph
photo·zin·cog·ra·phy
phras·al
phrase
phra·seo·gram symbol
phra·seo·graph phrase
phra·seo·graph·ic
phra·seog·ra·phy
phra·seo·logi·cal
phra·seolo·gist
phra·seol·ogy (*plural* ·ogies)
phras·ing
phra·tric anthropology term
phra·try (*plural* ·tries)
phre·at·ic geography term
phren·ic of the diaphragm
phre·net·ic *obsolete spelling of* frenetic
phreno·logi·cal
phre·nolo·gist
phre·nol·ogy study of head bumps
Phrygia ancient Asian country
Phryg·ian
phtha·lein
phthal·ic acid
phthalo·cya·nine
phthi·ria·sis infestation with lice; *compare* pthisis
phthi·sic
phthisi·cal
phthi·sis wasting disease; *compare* phthiriasis
phut
phy·co·logi·cal
phy·colo·gist

342

phy·col·ogy study of algae
phy·co·my·cete fungus
phy·co·my·cetous
phy·lac·tery (plural
  ·teries) case for Hebrew
  texts
phy·le (plural ·lae) ancient
  Greek tribe
phy·let·ic (or
  phy·lo·genet·ic) biology
  term
phy·leti·cal·ly (or
  phy·lo·geneti·cal·ly)
phyl·lite rock
phyl·lit·ic
phyl·lo·clade (or ·clad)
  botany term
phyl·lode botany term
phyl·lo·dial
phyl·loid leaflike
phyl·lome botany term
phyl·lom·ic
phyl·lo·qui·none vitamin
phyl·lo·tax·is (or ·taxy;
  plural ·taxes or taxies)
phyl·lox·era (plural ·erae
  or ·eras) vine pest
phy·lo·gen·ic (or
  ·genet·ic)
phy·log·eny (or
  ·lo·gen·esis; plural
  ·nies or ·eses) biology
  term
phylo·tac·tic
phy·lum (plural ·la)
physi·at·ric (or ·ri·cal)
physi·at·rics US
  physiotherapy
phys·ic (·ick·ing, ·icked)
physi·cal
physi·cal·ism philosophical
  doctrine
physi·cal·ist
physi·cal·is·tic
physi·cal·ly
physi·cal·ness
phy·si·cian
physi·cist
physi·co·chemi·cal
phys·ics
physio·crat
physio·crat·ic
physi·og·nom·ic (or
  ·nomi·cal)
physi·og·nomi·cal·ly
physi·og·no·mist

physi·og·no·my (plural
  ·mies)
physi·og·ra·pher
physio·graph·ic (or
  ·graphi·cal)
physi·og·ra·phy physical
  geography
physio·logi·cal
physio·logi·cal·ly
physi·olo·gist
physi·ol·ogy
(physionomy) incorrect
  spelling of physiognomy
physio·thera·pist
physio·thera·py
phy·sique
phy·so·clis·tous zoology
  term
phy·so·stig·mine (or ·min)
  drug
phy·sos·to·mous zoology
  term
phyto·gen·esis (or
  phy·tog·eny) botany
  term
phyto·genet·ic
phyto·geneti·cal·ly
phyto·gen·ic
phyto·geog·ra·pher
phyto·geog·ra·phy
phy·tog·ra·phy
phyto·hor·mone
phy·tol·ogy
phy·ton botany term
phyto·patho·logi·cal
phyto·pa·tholo·gist
phyto·pa·thol·ogy
phy·topha·gous
phy·topha·gy
phyto·plank·ton
phyto·plank·ton·ic
phyto·so·clo·logi·cal
phyto·so·ci·olo·gist
phyto·so·ci·ol·ogy
phyto·tox·in
phyto·tron botanical
  apparatus
pi (plural pis) Greek letter
Pia·cen·za Italian town
pi·acu·lar making
  atonement
pi·affe dressage term
pia ma·ter brain membrane
pia·nism
pia·nis·si·mo
pia·nist
pia·nis·tic

pi·ano (plural ·anos)
pi·ano·for·te
Pia·no·la (Trademark)
pi·as·sa·va (or ·ba) palm
  tree
pi·as·tre (or esp. US ·ter)
  currency
Piauí Brazilian state
pi·az·za
pi·broch bagpipe music
pica printer's measure;
  eating dirt; compare pika
pica·dor
Pic·ar·dy French region
pica·resque of type of
  fiction; compare
  picturesque
pica·roon (or picka·)
  adventurer
pica·yune US of little value
Pic·ca·dil·ly
pic·ca·lil·li pickle
pic·ca·nin·ny (or picka·;
  plural ·nies) Negro child
pic·co·lo (plural ·los)
pice (plural pice) coin
pic·eous of pitch
pichi·ci·ego (plural ·egos)
  animal
pick
picka·back variant of
  piggyback
pick·able
pick·axe (US ·ax)
pick·er
pick·er·el (plural ·el or
  ·els) fish
pickerel·weed
pick·et
pick·et·er
pick·et·ing
pick·ings
pick·le
pick·led
pick·ler
pick·lock
pick-me-up
pick·pocket
pick-up (noun)
Pick·wick·ian
picky
pic·nic (·nick·ing,
  ·nicked)
pic·nick·er
pico·line chemical
  compound
pico·lin·ic

picot

pi·cot pattern of loops
pico·tee carnation
pic·rate chemistry term
pic·ric acid
pic·rite rock
pic·ro·tox·in
Pict
Pict·ish
pic·to·graph
pic·to·rial
pic·to·rial·ly
pic·ture
pic·tur·esque strikingly pleasing; compare picaresque
pic·tur·esque·ness
pic·ul unit
pid·dle
pid·dling
pid·dock mollusc
pidg·in language; compare pigeon
pie
pie·bald
piece
pièce de ré·sis·tance (plural pièces de ré·sis·tance)
piece-dyed
piece·meal
piec·er
piece·work
pie·crust
pied multi-coloured
pied-à-terre (plural pieds-à-terre)
Pied·mont Italian region
pied·mont at mountain base
pied·mont·ite mineral
pie-eyed
pie·man (plural ·men)
pier landing place; pillar; compare peer
pierc·able
pierce
pierc·er
pierc·ing
pierc·ing·ly
Pi·erian
Pi·eri·des Muses
pi·eri·dine zoology term
Pi·er·rot pantomime clown
pi·età religious painting
Pie·ter·mar·itz·burg South African city
pi·ety (plural ·eties)
pi·ezo·chem·is·try

pi·ezo·elec·tric
pi·ezo·elec·tri·cal·ly
pi·ezo·elec·tric·ity
pi·ezom·eter
pi·ezo·met·ric
pi·ezo·met·ri·cal·ly
pif·fle
pig (pig·ging, pigged)
pi·geon bird; compare pidgin
pigeon·hole
pigeon-toed
pig·face plant
pig·fish (plural ·fish or ·fishes)
pig·gery (plural ·geries)
pig·gin small bucket
pig·gish
pig·gish·ness
pig·gy (noun, plural ·gies; adj ·gi·er, ·gi·est)
piggy·back (or picka·back)
pig-headed
pig-headed·ness
pig·let
pig·like
pig·meat
pig·ment
pig·men·tary
pig·men·ta·tion
pig·ment·ed
pig·my variant spelling of pygmy
pig·nut
pig·skin
pig·stick
pig·stick·er
pig·stick·ing
pig·sty (plural ·sties)
pig·swill
pig·tail
pig·tailed
pig·weed
pika animal; compare pica
pike
pike·let crumpet
pike·perch (plural ·perch or ·perches) fish
pik·er
pike·staff
pil·af (or ·aff) variant of pilau
pi·las·ter
pi·lau (or pil·af, pil·aff) rice dish
pilch Archaic infant's garment

pil·chard
pile
pi·leate (or ·leat·ed) biology term
pile-driver
pi·leous of hair
piles
pi·leum (plural ·lea) top of bird's head
pile-up (noun)
pi·leus (plural ·lei) mushroom cap
pile·wort
pil·fer
pil·fer·age
pil·fer·er
pil·garlic Dialect pitiful person
pil·grim
pil·grim·age
pili (plural pilis) tree
pi·li plural of pilus
pi·lif·er·ous
pili·form
pil·ing
pill
pil·lage
pil·lag·er
pil·lar
pill·box
pil·lion
pil·li·winks instrument of torture
pil·lo·ry (noun, plural ·ries; verb ·ries, ·ry·ing, ·ried)
pil·low
pillow·case (or ·slip)
pi·lo·car·pine (or ·pin) drug
pi·lose biology term
pi·lot
pi·lot·age
Pils·ner (or Pil·sen·er) beer
Pilt·down man
pilu·lar
pil·ule
pi·lus (plural ·li) a hair
pi·men·to (plural ·tos) spice
pi·mien·to (plural ·tos) sweet pepper
pimp
pim·per·nel
pim·ple
pim·pled

pim·pli·ness
pim·ply (·pli·er, ·pli·est)
pin (pin·ning, pinned)
pi·na·ceous botany term
pina·fore
pi·nas·ter pine tree
pin·ball
pince-nez (*plural* pince-nez)
pin·cer
pin·cers tool
pinch
pinch·beck imitation gold
pinch·cock clamp
pinch·penny (*plural* ·pennies)
pin·cushion
Pin·dar·ic ode
pind·ling *Dialect* peevish
Pin·dus Greek mountain range
pine
pin·eal gland
pine·apple
pi·nene chemical compound
pi·nery (*plural* ·neries)
pi·netum (*plural* ·neta) plantation
pin·feather
pin·fish (*plural* ·fish *or* ·fishes)
pin·fold
ping
ping·er
pin·go (*plural* ·gos) landform
Ping-Pong (*Trademark*) (*or* ping-pong)
pin·guid fatty
pin·guid·ity (*or* ·ness)
pin·head
pin·hole
pin·ion
pin·ite mineral
pink
pink·eye
pinkie (*or* pinky) *US* little finger
pink·ish
pink·root
pinky pinkish; *variant spelling of* pinkie
pin·na (*plural* ·nae *or* ·nas) biology term
pin·nace boat
pin·na·cle

pin·nate (*or* ·nat·ed) feather-like
pin·nati·fid botany term
pin·na·tion
pin·nati·par·tite botany term
pin·nati·ped ornithology term
pin·nati·sect botany term
pinned
pin·ner
pin·ning
pin·ni·ped (*or* ·pedian) zoology term
pin·nu·lar
pin·nule (*or* ·nu·la; *plural* ·nules *or* ·nu·lae)
pin·ny (*plural* ·nies) *Slang* pinafore
pi·noch·le (*or* ·nuch·le, ·noc·le) card game
pi·no·le flour
pin·point
pin·prick
pin·stripe
pint
pin·ta skin disease
pin·ta·dera Neolithic stamp
pin·tail (*plural* ·tails *or* ·tail) duck
pin·tle hinge pin
pin·to (*plural* ·tos) piebald horse
pin-up (*noun*)
pin·wheel
pin·work
pin·worm
pinx·it *Latin* painted (*inscription on painting*)
piny (*or* piney; pini·er, pini·est)
pio·let ice axe
pion physics term
pio·neer
pi·ous
pi·ous·ness
pip (pip·ping, pipped)
pipa toad
pip·age
pi·pal *variant spelling of* peepul
pipe
pipe·clay
pipe·fish (*plural* ·fish *or* ·fishes)
pipe·fitting
pipe·line

pip·er
pip·era·ceous botany term
pi·pera·zine drug
pi·peri·dine organic compound
pip·er·ine alkaloid
pip·ero·nal fragrant compound
pipe·stone
pi·pette
pipe·wort
pip·ing
pipi·strelle bat
pip·it bird
pip·kin small pot
pipped
pip·pin apple
pip·ping
pip·sis·sewa plant
pip·squeak
pi·quan·cy (*or* ·quant·ness)
pi·quant
pique (piqu·ing, piqued)
pi·qué fabric
pi·quet card game
pi·ra·cy (*plural* ·cies)
Pi·rae·us (*or* Pei·) Greek port
pi·ra·nha (*or* ·na)
pi·rate
pi·rat·ic (*or* ·rati·cal)
pi·rati·cal·ly
pirn fishing rod
pi·rog (*plural* ·ro·gi) pie
pi·rogue (*or* pi·ra·gua) canoe
pirou·ette
Pisa
pis al·ler *French* a last resort
pis·ca·ry (*plural* ·ries) fishing place
pis·ca·to·rial (*or* ·tory)
Pi·sces constellation; sign of zodiac
pis·ci·cul·tur·al
pis·ci·cul·ture
pis·ci·cul·tur·ist
pis·ci·na (*plural* ·nae *or* ·nas) basin in church
pis·cine
pis·civo·rous
pi·shogue *Irish* sorcery
pisi·form pealike
pis·mire *Dialect* ant
pi·so·lite rock

piss
pis·ta·chio (*plural* ·chios)
pis·ta·reen coin
piste skiing slope
pis·til flower part; *compare* pistol
pis·til·late
pis·tol (·tol·ling, ·tolled; US ·tol·ing, ·toled) gun; *compare* pistil
pis·tole coin
pis·to·leer soldier
pis·ton
pit (pit·ting, pit·ted)
pita fibre; *compare* pitta
pita·pat (·pat·ting, ·pat·ted)
Pit·cairn Pacific island
pitch
pitch-black
pitch·blende mineral
pitch-dark
pitch·er
pitch·fork
pitchi·ness
pitch·om·eter nautical term
pitch·stone
pitchy (pitchi·er, pitchi·est)
pit·eous
pit·eous·ness
pit·fall
pith
pit·head
pith·ecan·thro·pine (*or* ·poid)
pith·ecan·thro·pus (*plural* ·pi) apelike man
pithi·ly
pithi·ness
pi·thos (*plural* ·thoi) oil container
pithy (pithi·er, pithi·est)
piti·able
piti·able·ness
piti·ably
piti·ful
piti·ful·ly
piti·ful·ness
piti·less
piti·less·ness
pit·man (*plural* ·men)
pi·ton mountaineering spike
pit·saw
pit·ta flat bread; *compare* pita
pit·tance

pitter-patter
Pitts·burgh US port
pi·tui·tary (*plural* ·taries)
pitu·ri shrub
pity (*noun, plural* pities; *verb* pities, pity·ing, pit·ied)
pity·ing·ly
pity·ria·sis (*plural* ·ses) skin disease
Piu·ra Peruvian city
piv·ot
piv·ot·al
pix *Slang* pictures; *compare* pyx
pixie (*or* pixy; *plural* pixies)
pixi·lat·ed US eccentric
pize *Dialect* to hit
piz·za
piz·ze·ria
piz·zi·ca·to (*plural* ·ti *or* ·tos)
plac·abil·ity (*or* ·able·ness)
plac·able easily placated; *compare* placeable
plac·ard
pla·cate
pla·ca·tion
placa·tory (*or* ·tive)
place position; *compare* plaice
place·able easily placed; *compare* placable
pla·cebo (*plural* ·cebos *or* ·ceboes)
place·ment
pla·cen·ta (*plural* ·tas *or* ·tae)
pla·cen·tal (*or* ·tate)
plac·en·ta·tion
plac·er
pla·cet vote of assent
plac·id
pla·cid·ity (*or* ·ness)
plac·ing
plack·et dressmaking term
placo·derm extinct fish
plac·oid platelike
(plad) *incorrect spelling of* plaid
pla·fond ceiling; card game
pla·gal musical term
plage astronomy term
pla·gia·rism
pla·gia·rist

pla·gia·ris·tic
pla·gia·rize (*or* ·rise)
pla·gia·riz·er (*or* ·ris·er)
pla·gio·clase mineral
pla·gio·cli·max ecology term
pla·gi·ot·ro·pism botany term
plague (plagu·ing, plagued)
plagu·er
pla·gui·ly
pla·guy (*or* ·guey)
plaice (*plural* plaice *or* plaices) fish; *compare* place
plaid tartan cloth
plain simple; unattractive; treeless region; *compare* plane
plain·chant
plain·ish rather plain; *compare* planish
plain-laid describing rope
plain·ness
plains·man (*plural* ·men)
plain·song
plain-spoken
plaint
plain·tiff legal term
plain·tive melancholy
plain·tive·ness
plait braid; *compare* plat
plan (plan·ning, planned)
pla·nar
pla·nar·ian flatworm
pla·na·tion erosion of land
planch·et blank coin
plan·chette board for spirit messages
plane aircraft; level; tool; tree; *compare* plain
plan·er
plan·et
plan·etar·ium (*plural* ·iums *or* ·taria)
plan·etary (*plural* ·etaries)
plan·etesi·mal small planetary body
plan·et·oid asteroid
plan·etoid·al
plan·form silhouette
plan·gen·cy
plan·gent
pla·nim·eter
plani·met·ric (*or* ·ri·cal)

pla·nim·etry
plan·ish to smooth; *compare*
    plainish
plan·ish·er
plani·sphere
plani·spher·ic
plank
plank·ing
plank-sheer nautical term
plank·ton
plank·ton·ic
planned
plan·ner
plan·ning
plano-concave
plano-convex
plano·gam·ete
pla·no·graph·ic
pla·no·graphi·cal·ly
pla·nog·ra·phy printing
    process
pla·nom·eter
pla·no·met·ric
pla·nom·etry
pla·no·sol soil
plant
plant·able
plan·tain weed; cooking
    banana
plan·tar of sole of foot
plan·ta·tion
plant·er
plan·ti·grade zoology term
planu·la (*plural* ·lae) larva
planu·lar
plaque
plash
plashy (plashi·er,
    plashi·est)
plasm protoplasm
plas·ma blood fluid; physics
    term
plas·ma·gel jelly-like
    protoplasm
plas·ma·gene
plas·ma·gen·ic
plas·ma·sol fluid
    protoplasm
plas·min enzyme
plas·mo·des·ma (*or*
    ·desm; *plural*
    ·des·ma·ta *or* ·desms)
    botany term
plas·mo·dium (*plural* ·dia)
    biology term; malaria
    parasite
plas·mo·lyse (*US* ·lyze)

plas·moly·sis
plas·mo·lyt·ic
plas·mo·lyti·cal·ly
plas·mon biology term
plas·mo·some
Plas·sey Indian battle site
plas·ter
plaster·board
plas·tered
plas·ter·er
plas·ter·ing
plas·tic
plas·ti·cal·ly
Plas·ti·cine (*Trademark*)
plas·tic·ity
plas·ti·ci·za·tion (*or*
    ·sa·tion)
plas·ti·cize (*or* ·cise)
plas·ti·ciz·er (*or* ·cis·er)
plas·tid cell structure
plas·tom·eter plasticity
    measurer
plas·to·met·ric
plas·tom·etry
plas·tral
plas·tron
plat small plot; *compare* plait
plat·an plane tree; *compare*
    platen
plat du jour (*plural* plats
    du jour)
plate
plat·eau (*plural* ·eaus *or*
    ·eaux)
plat·ed
plate·ful (*plural* ·fuls)
plate·layer
plate·let
plate·mark hallmark
plat·en printing plate;
    typewriter roller; *compare*
    platan
plat·er
plat·form
plati·na alloy
plat·ing
pla·tin·ic
plati·nif·er·ous
plat·ini·rid·ium alloy
plati·ni·za·tion (*or*
    ·sa·tion)
plati·nize (*or* ·nise)
plati·no·cya·nide
plati·noid
plati·no·type photographic
    process
plati·nous

plati·num
platinum-blond (*fem*
    -blonde)
plati·tude
plati·tu·di·nize (*or* ·nise)
plati·tu·di·niz·er (*or*
    ·nis·er)
plati·tu·di·nous
Pla·ton·ic of Plato
pla·ton·ic nonerotic
pla·toni·cal·ly
Pla·to·nism
Pla·to·nize (*or* ·nise)
pla·toon
Platte US river
plat·ter
platy (plati·er, plati·est)
platy (*plural* platy, platys,
    or platies) fish
platy·hel·minth flatworm
platy·hel·min·thic
platy·pus (*plural* ·puses)
plat·yr·rhine (*or* ·rhin·ian)
    zoology term
plau·dit
plau·sibil·ity (*or*
    ·sible·ness)
plau·sible
plau·sibly
plau·sive approving
play
pla·ya lake
play·able
play-act
play-actor
play·back
play·bill
play·boy
play·er
play·fellow
play·ful
play·ful·ly
play·ful·ness
play goer
play·ground
play·group
play·house
play·let
play·mate
play-off (*noun*)
play·pen
play·room
play·school
play·suit
play·thing
play·time
play·wright

plaza

pla·za
plea
pleach make hedge
plead (plead·ing,
  plead·ed, plead or
  pled)
plead·able
plead·er
pleas·able
pleas·ance secluded garden
pleas·ant
pleas·ant·ness
pleas·ant·ry (*plural* ·ries)
please
pleased
pleas·ed·ly
pleas·er
pleas·ing
pleas·ing·ness
pleas·ur·able
pleas·ur·able·ness
pleas·ur·ably
pleas·ure
pleas·ure·ful
pleas·ure·less
pleat
pleat·er
pleb
pleb·by (·bi·er, ·bi·est)
ple·beian
ple·beian·ism
plebi·scite
plec·tog·nath fish
plec·trum (*or* ·tron;
  plural ·tra, ·trums, *or*
  ·trons)
pledge
pledgee
pledg·er (*or esp. in legal
  contexts* ·or)
pledg·et bandaging pad
plei·ad talented group
Pleia·des constellation
Pleiades (*sing.* Pleiad)
  mythological characters
plein-air art term
plei·ot·ro·pism genetics
  term
Pleis·to·cene geological
  epoch
ple·na·ri·ly
ple·na·ry
ple·nipo·tent
pleni·po·ten·ti·ary (*plural*
  ·aries)
pleni·tude abundance
plen·teous

plen·teous·ness
plen·ti·ful
plen·ti·ful·ly
plen·ti·ful·ness
plen·ty (*plural* ·ties)
ple·num (*plural* ·nums *or*
  ·na)
pleo·chro·ic
ple·och·ro·ism chemistry
  term
pleo·mor·phic
pleo·mor·phism (*or* ·phy)
  biology term
pleo·nasm use of
  superfluous words
pleo·nas·tic
pleo·nas·ti·cal·ly
ple·sio·saur
ples·sor *variant of* plexor
pletho·ra
ple·thys·mo·graph
pleu·ra (*plural* ·rae)
  membrane round lungs;
  plural of pleuron
pleu·ral
pleu·ri·sy
pleu·rit·ic
pleu·ro·dont zoology term
pleu·ro·dy·nia pain between
  ribs
pleu·ron (*plural* ·ra)
  zoology term; *compare*
  pleura
pleu·ro·pneu·mo·nia
pleu·roto·my (*plural*
  ·mies)
pleus·ton floating algae
plew (*or* plue, plu) beaver
  skin
plexi·form
Plexi·glass (*Trademark*)
plex·or (*or* ples·sor)
  medical hammer
plex·us (*plural* ·uses *or*
  ·us) network
pli·abil·ity (*or* able·ness)
pli·able
pli·an·cy (*or* ·ant·ness)
pli·ant
pli·ca (*plural* ·cae)
  anatomy term
pli·cal
pli·cate (*or* ·cat·ed)
  pleated
pli·cate·ness
pli·ca·tion (*or* plica·ture)
plié ballet posture

348

pli·er (*or* ply·) one who
  plies
pli·ers tool
plight
plight·er
plim·soll (*or* ·sole)
Plim·soll line
plinth
Plio·cene (*or* Pleio·cene)
  geological epoch
plis·sé fabric with wrinkled
  finish
ploat *Dialect* thrash
plod (plod·ding, plod·ded)
plod·der
plod·ding·ly
plod·ding·ness
plodge *Dialect* wade
Plo·eş·ti Romanian city
plonk
plonk·er *Slang* idiot
plonko *Austral* alcoholic
plop (plop·ping, plopped)
plo·sion phonetics term
plo·sive phonetics term
plot (plot·ting, plot·ted)
plot·ter
Plough group of stars
plough (*US* plow)
plough·boy (*US* plow·)
plough·er (*US* plow·)
plough·man (*US* plow·;
  plural ·men)
plough·man·ship (*US*
  plow·)
plough·share (*US* plow·)
plough·staff (*US* plow·)
Plov·div Bulgarian city
plov·er
plow *US spelling of* plough
ploy
pluck
pluck·er
plucki·ly
plucki·ness
plucky (plucki·er,
  plucki·est)
plug (plug·ging, plugged)
plug-board
plum fruit; *compare* plumb
plum·age
plu·mate (*or* ·mose)
plumb work as plumber;
  experience misery;
  compare plum
plumb·able

plum·bagi·na·ceous botany term
plum·ba·go (*plural* ·gos) graphite; plant
plum·beous of lead
plumb·er
plumb·ery (*plural* ·eries)
plum·bic chemistry term
plum·bi·con TV camera tube
plum·bif·er·ous
plumb·ing
plum·bism lead poisoning
plum·bous chemistry term
plum·bum lead
plume
plum·met
plum·my (·mi·er, ·mi·est)
plump
plump·er
plump·ness
plu·mule
plumy (plumi·er, plumi·est)
plun·der
plun·der·able
plun·der·age
plun·der·er
plun·der·ous
plunge
plung·er
plunk
plu·per·fect grammar term
plu·ral
plu·ral·ism
plu·ral·ist
plu·ral·ity (*plural* ·ities)
plu·rali·za·tion (*or* ·sa·tion)
plu·ral·ize (*or* ·ise)
plu·ral·iz·er (*or* ·is·er)
plu·ral·ly
plus
plush
plush·ness
plushy (plushi·er, plushi·est)
Pluto Greek god
Plu·to planet
plu·toc·ra·cy (*plural* ·cies)
plu·to·crat
plu·to·crat·ic (*or* ·crati·cal)
plu·to·crati·cal·ly
plu·ton geology term
Plu·to·nian infernal
plu·ton·ic geology term

plu·to·nium
plu·vial of rain
plu·vi·om·eter
plu·vio·met·ric
plu·vio·met·ri·cal·ly
plu·vi·om·etry
plu·vi·ous (*or* ·ose)
ply (*verb* plies, ply·ing, plied; *noun, plural* plies)
ply·er *variant spelling of* plier
Plym·outh
ply·wood
Plzeň Czech city
pneu·ma philosophy term
pneu·mat·ic
pneu·mati·cal·ly
pneu·mat·ics branch of physics
pneu·ma·tol·ogy branch of theology
pneu·ma·toly·sis geology term
pneu·ma·tom·eter
pneu·ma·tom·etry
pneu·mato·phore biology term
pneu·mo·ba·cil·lus (*plural* ·li)
pneu·mo·coc·cus (*plural* ·coc·ci)
pneu·mo·co·nio·sis
pneu·mo·dy·nam·ics pneumatics
pneu·mo·en·cepha·lo·gram
pneu·mo·gas·tric
pneu·mo·graph
pneu·mo·nec·to·my (*or* pneu·mec·to·my; *plural* ·mies)
pneu·mo·nia
pneu·mon·ic
pneu·mon·it·is
pneu·mo·tho·rax
Po Italian river
po (*plural* pos) chamber pot
poa·ceous botany term
poach
poach·er
poach·ing
po·chard (*plural* ·chards *or* ·chard) duck
pock
pock·et
pock·et·able
pocket·book

pock·et·ful (*plural* ·fuls)
pocket·knife (*plural* ·knives)
pock·mark
poco musical term
po·co·cu·ran·te indifferent
pod (pod·ding, pod·ded)
po·dag·ra gout
po·dag·ral (*or* ·ric, ·ri·cal, ·rous)
pod·dy (*plural* ·dies) *Austral* hand-fed calf
po·des·ta Italian magistrate
podgi·ly
podgi·ness
podgy (podgi·er, podgi·est)
po·dia·try *US* chiropody
po·dium (*plural* ·diums *or* ·dia)
Po·dolsk Soviet city
podo·phyl·lin medicinal resin
pod·zol (*or* ·sol)
pod·zol·ic (*or* ·sol·ic)
poem
po·esy (*plural* ·esies)
poet
po·et·as·ter inferior poet
po·et·ess
po·et·ic (*or* ·eti·cal)
po·eti·cal·ly
po·eti·cize (*or* po·et·ize, po·eti·cise, po·et·ise)
po·et·ics
poet lau·reate (*plural* poets lau·reate)
po·et·ry
po-faced
pogge fish
po·go·nia orchid
pog·rom
Po·hai inlet of Yellow Sea
poi Hawaiian food
poign·an·cy
poign·ant
poi·ki·lo·ther·mic (*or* ·mal) cold-blooded
poi·ki·lo·ther·mism (*or* ·my)
poi·lu French soldier
poin·cia·na tree
poin·set·tia house plant
point
point-blank
pointe ballet term
point·ed

pointedly

point·ed·ly
point·ed·ness
Pointe-Noire Congolese port
point·er
poin·til·lism painting technique
poin·til·list
point·ing
point·less
point·less·ness
points·man (plural ·men)
point-to-point
poise
poised
poi·son
poi·son·er
poi·son·ous
poi·son·ous·ness
Poi·tiers French town
Poi·tou former French province
poke
poke·berry (plural ·berries)
pok·er
poke·weed
poki·ly
poki·ness
poky (poki·er, poki·est)
Po·land
po·lar
po·lar·im·eter
po·lari·met·ric
po·lar·im·etry
Po·la·ris North Star; missile
po·lari·scope
po·lar·ity (plural ·ities)
po·lar·iz·able (or ·is·able)
po·lari·za·tion (or ·sa·tion)
po·lar·ize (or ·ise)
po·lar·iz·er (or ·is·er)
po·lar·og·ra·phy
Po·lar·oid (Trademark)
pol·der reclaimed land
Pole Polish native; star
pole
pole-axe (US ·ax)
pole·cat (plural ·cats or ·cat)
pol·emarch ancient Greek official
po·lem·ic
po·lemi·cal
po·lemi·cal·ly
po·lemi·cist (or ·emist)

po·lem·ics
pol·emo·nia·ceous botany term
po·len·ta Italian porridge
pol·er
pole-vault (verb)
po·leyn armour
po·lice
police·man (plural ·men)
police·woman (plural ·women)
poli·cy (plural ·cies)
policy·holder
po·lio
po·lio·my·eli·tis
pol·is (plural ·eis) Greek city-state
Po·lish
pol·ish
pol·ish·er
Pol·it·bu·ro
po·lite
po·lite·ness
poli·tesse French formal politeness
poli·tic shrewd
po·liti·cal of politics
po·liti·cal·ly
poli·ti·cian
po·liti·cize (or ·cise)
poli·tick·ing political canvassing
po·liti·co (plural ·cos) Slang politician
poli·tics
pol·ity (plural ·ities)
pol·je geography term
pol·ka (noun, plural ·kas; verb ·kas, ·ka·ing, ·kaed)
poll
pol·lack (or ·lock; plural ·lacks, ·lack or ·locks, ·lock) fish
pol·lan fish; compare pollen
pol·lard
polled
pol·len plant product; compare pollan
pol·lex (plural ·li·ces) thumb
pol·li·cal
pol·li·nate (or ·lenate)
pol·li·na·tion (or ·lena·tion)
pol·li·na·tor (or ·lena·tor)
poll·ing

350

pol·lin·ic of pollen
pol·li·nif·er·ous (or ·lenif·er·ous)
pol·lin·ium (plural ·linia)
pol·lino·sis (or ·leno·) hay fever
pol·li·wog (or ·ly·) Slang sailor; tadpole
poll·ster
pol·lu·cite mineral
pol·lu·tant
pol·lute
pol·lut·er
pol·lu·tion
Pollux star; mythological character
polo
polo·naise
po·lo·nium radioactive element
po·lo·ny (plural ·nies) sausage
Pol·ta·va Soviet city
pol·ter·geist
pol·troon
poly (plural polys) Slang polytechnic
polya·del·phous botany term
poly·am·ide
poly·an·drous
poly·an·dry
poly·an·thus (plural ·thuses)
poly·atom·ic
poly·ba·sic
poly·ba·site mineral
poly·car·pel·lary
poly·car·pic (or ·pous) botany term
poly·carpy
poly·cen·trism political theory
poly·chaete worm
poly·chae·tous
poly·cha·sium (plural ·sia) botany term
poly·chro·mat·ic (or ·mic, ·mous)
poly·chro·ma·tism
poly·chrome
poly·chro·my
poly·clin·ic hospital
poly·con·ic maths term
poly·coty·ledon
poly·coty·ledon·ous
poly·cy·clic

poly·cy·thae·mia (*US* ·themia)
poly·dac·tyl
poly·dac·ty·lous
poly·dem·ic ecology term
poly·dip·sia
poly·dip·sic
poly·em·bry·on·ic
poly·em·bry·ony
poly·es·ter
po·lyga·la plant
poly·ga·la·ceous
po·lyga·mist
po·lyga·mous
po·lyga·my
poly·gene genetics term
poly·gen·ic
poly·gen·esis biology term
poly·genet·ic
poly·geneti·cal·ly
poly·glot
poly·glot·ism (*or* ·glot·tism)
poly·gon
poly·go·naceous botany term
po·lygo·nal
po·lygo·num plant
poly·graph lie detector
poly·graph·ic
poly·graphi·cal·ly
po·lygy·nist
po·lygy·nous
po·lygy·ny
poly·he·dral
poly·he·dron (*plural* ·drons *or* ·dra)
poly·hy·droxy (*or* ·dric)
poly·iso·prene
poly·math
poly·math·ic
poly·mer
poly·mer·ic
po·lym·er·ism
po·lym·eri·za·tion (*or* ·sa·tion)
poly·mer·ize (*or* ·ise)
po·lym·er·ous
poly·morph
poly·mor·phism
poly·mor·pho·nu·clear
poly·mor·phous (*or* ·phic)
poly·myx·in antibiotic
Poly·nesia
Poly·nesian
poly·neu·ri·tis

Polynices mythological character
poly·no·mial
poly·nu·clear (*or* ·cleate)
poly·nu·cleo·tide
po·lyn·ya arctic water
poly·ony·mous having several names
pol·yp
poly·pary (*or* ·par·ium; *plural* ·paries *or* ·paria) zoology term
poly·pep·tide
poly·pet·al·ous
poly·pha·gia
pol·ypha·gous
poly·phase
poly·phone linguistics term
poly·phon·ic
poly·phoni·cal·ly
po·lypho·nous
po·lypho·ny (*plural* ·nies) musical term
poly·phy·let·ic biology term
poly·phy·leti·cal·ly
poly·phyo·dont zoology term
poly·ploid genetics term; *compare* polypoid
poly·ploi·dal (*or* ·dic)
poly·ploi·dy
poly·pod many-legged animal
po·lypo·dous
poly·po·dy (*plural* ·dies) fern
poly·poid of a polyp; *compare* polyploid
poly·pro·pyl·ene
poly·pro·to·dont zoology term
pol·yp·tych altarpiece
poly·pus (*plural* ·pi) pathological polyp
poly·rhythm
poly·rhyth·mic
poly·sac·cha·ride (*or* ·rose)
poly·semous
poly·semy ambiguity
poly·sep·al·ous
poly·so·mic genetics term
poly·sty·rene
poly·sul·phide (*US* ·fide)
poly·syl·lab·ic (*or* ·labi·cal)
poly·syl·labi·cal·ly

poly·syl·la·ble
poly·syl·lo·gism
poly·syn·deton grammar term
poly·syn·the·sis
poly·syn·the·sism
poly·syn·thet·ic
poly·tech·nic
poly·tet·ra·fluo·ro·ethy·lene
poly·theism
poly·theist
poly·theis·tic
poly·theis·ti·cal·ly
poly·thene
poly·to·nal
poly·to·nal·ist
poly·to·nal·ity (*or* ·ism)
poly·troph·ic biology term
poly·typ·ic (*or* ·typi·cal)
poly·un·satu·rat·ed
poly·urethane (*or* ·urethan)
poly·uria
poly·ur·ic
poly·va·len·cy
poly·va·lent
poly·vi·nyl
Polyxena mythological princess
poly·zoan aquatic organism
poly·zo·ar·ium (*plural* ·aria)
poly·zo·ic
pom *short for* pommy
pom·ace pulped apples
po·ma·ceous botany term
po·made hair oil
po·man·der
pome fruit of apple
pom·egran·ate
pom·elo (*plural* ·elos) grapefruit
Pom·era·nia European region
Pom·era·nian
pom·fret liquorice sweet
pomi·cul·ture
pom·if·er·ous
pom·mel part of saddle; *less common spelling of* pummel
pom·my (*plural* ·mies) *Austral* English person
pomo·logi·cal
pom·olo·gist
pom·ol·ogy fruit cultivation
Po·mo·na Roman goddess
pomp

pom·pa·dour hairstyle
pom·pa·no (*plural* **·no** *or* **·nos**) fish
Pom·peii
Pom·pei·ian
Pom·pey *Slang* Portsmouth
pom-pom cannon
pom·pon (*or* **·pom**) globular tuft, flower, etc.
pom·pos·ity (*plural* **·ities**)
pomp·ous
pomp·ous·ness
Pon·ce Puerto Rican port
ponce
pon·cho (*plural* **·chos**)
pond
pon·der
pon·der·abil·ity
pon·der·able
pon·der·er
pon·der·ous
Pon·di·cher·ry Indian territory
Pon·do·land South African region
pond-skater insect
pond·weed
pone maize bread
pong
pon·gee fabric
pon·gid ape
pon·iard dagger
pons (*plural* **pon·tes**) anatomy term
pons asi·no·rum geometry theorem
pons Va·ro·lii (*plural* **pon·tes Va·ro·lii**) part of brain
pont river ferry
Pont·char·train US lake
Pon·te·fract
Pon·tia·nak Indonesian port
Pon·tic of the Black Sea
pon·ti·fex (*plural* **·tifi·ces**)
pon·tiff
pon·tifi·cal
pon·tifi·cals bishop's robes
pon·tifi·cate
pon·tine of bridges
pon·to·nier bridge builder
pon·toon
Pon·ty·pool Welsh town
Pon·ty·pridd Welsh town
pony (*plural* **ponies**)
pony·tail

pooch
pood unit of weight
poo·dle
poof (*or* **poove**) *Slang* homosexual; *compare* **pouf**
pooh
Pooh-Bah pompous official
pooh-pooh
pool
Poole Dorset port
pools gambling system
poon tree
Poo·na (*or* **Pune**) Indian city
poop
poor needy; unfortunate; *compare* **pore**; **pour**
poor·house
poor·ly
poor·ness
pop (**pop·ping, popped**)
pop·corn
pope
pope·dom
pop·ery
pop-eyed
pop·gun
pop-in·jay
pop·ish
pop·ish·ness
pop·lar
pop·lin
pop·lit·eal anatomy term
Po·po·ca·té·petl Mexican volcano
pop·over
pop·pa·dom (*or* **·dum**) Indian bread
popped
pop·per
pop·pet
pop·ping
pop·ple
pop·py (*plural* **·pies**)
poppy·cock
poppy·head
Pop·si·cle (*Trademark*)
pop·sy (*plural* **·sies**)
popu·lace
popu·lar
popu·lar·ity
popu·lari·za·tion (*or* **·sa·tion**)
popu·lar·ize (*or* **·ise**)
popu·lar·iz·er (*or* **·is·er**)
popu·late
popu·la·tion

Popu·list member of US political party
popu·lous
popu·lous·ness
por·bea·gle shark
porce·lain
por·cel·la·neous
porch
por·cine
por·cu·pine
pore examine; small hole; *compare* **poor**; **pour**
por·gy (*plural* **·gy** *or* **·gies**) fish
po·rif·er·an a sponge
po·rif·er·ous
Po·ri·rua New Zealand city
po·rism mathematical proposition
pork
pork·er
porki·ness
pork·pie
porky (**porki·er, porki·est**)
por·noc·ra·cy (*plural* **·cies**) government by prostitutes
por·nog·ra·pher
por·no·graph·ic
por·no·graphi·cal·ly
por·nog·ra·phy
poro·mer·ic chemistry term
po·ros·ity (*plural* **·ities**)
po·rous
po·rous·ness
por·phy·ria disease
por·phy·rin pigment
por·phy·rit·ic geology term
por·phy·rog·enite prince
por·phy·roid geology term
por·phy·rop·sin pigment
por·phy·ry (*plural* **·ries**) rock
por·poise (*plural* **·poise** *or* **·poises**)
por·ridge
por·rin·ger dish
Porsena legendary king
port
port·abil·ity (*or* **·able·ness**)
port·able
Por·ta·down Northern Irish town
por·tage
por·tal

por·ta·men·to (*plural* ·ti) musical term
por·ta·tive portable
Port-au-Prince Haitian capital
port·cul·lis
porte-cochere covered entrance
por·tend
por·tent
por·ten·tous
por·ten·tous·ness
por·ter
por·ter·age
porter·house
port·fire
port·fo·lio (*plural* ·lios)
Port Har·court Nigerian port
port·hole
por·ti·co (*plural* ·coes *or* ·cos)
por·ti·ère door curtain
por·tion
Port·land
Port·laoise Irish town
port·li·ness
port·ly (·li·er, ·li·est)
port·man·teau (*plural* ·teaus *or* ·teaux)
Port Mores·by capital of New Guinea
Pôr·to Ale·gre Brazilian port
Por·to Novo capital of Benin
por·trait
por·trait·ist
por·trai·ture
por·tray
por·tray·able
por·tray·al
por·tray·er
port·ress
Port Said Egyptian port
Port-Salut cheese
Ports·mouth
Port Tal·bot Welsh port
Por·tu·gal
Por·tu·guese (*plural* ·guese)
por·tu·laca plant
por·tu·la·ca·ceous
pose
Poseidon Greek god
pos·er one who poses; problem

po·seur affected person
posh
pos·it postulate; *compare* posset
posi·tif organ keyboard
po·si·tion
po·si·tion·al
posi·tive
posi·tive·ly
posi·tive·ness
posi·tiv·ism
posi·tiv·ist
posi·tiv·is·tic
posi·tiv·is·ti·cal·ly
posi·tron physics term
posi·tro·nium physics term
po·sol·ogy branch of medicine
pos·se
pos·sess
pos·sessed
pos·ses·sion
pos·ses·sive
pos·ses·sive·ness
pos·ses·sor
pos·ses·so·ry
pos·set hot drink; *compare* posit
pos·sibil·ity (*plural* ·ities)
pos·sible
pos·sibly
pos·sum *Slang* opossum; phalanger
post
post·age
post·al
post·ax·ial
post·bag
post-bellum after war
post·box
post·boy
post·card
post·ca·val anatomy term
post chaise
post·code
post·coit·al
post·date
post·di·lu·vial
post·di·lu·vian
post·doc·tor·al
post·er
poste res·tante
pos·teri·or
pos·ter·ity
pos·tern
post·fix add to the end
post-free

post·gla·cial
post·gradu·ate
post·haste
post·hu·mous
post·hyp·not·ic
pos·tiche architectural term; *compare* pastiche
pos·ti·cous posterior
pos·til marginal note
pos·til·ion (*or* ·til·lion)
post·im·pres·sion·ism
post·im·pres·sion·ist
post·ing
post·limi·ny (*or* ·li·min·ium; *plural* ·nies *or* ·minia) legal term
post·lude concluding music
post·man (*plural* ·men)
post·mark
post·master
post·me·rid·ian (*adj*)
post me·rid·iem *Latin* after noon
post·mil·len·nial
post·mor·tem
post·na·tal
post·nup·tial
post-obit legal term
post·op·era·tive
post·paid
post·par·tum after childbirth
post·pon·able
post·pone
post·pone·ment
post·pon·er
post·po·si·tion
post·po·si·tion·al
post·posi·tive
post·pran·dial
post·script
po_·tu·lan·cy (*or* ·lant·ship)
pos·tu·lant
pos·tu·late
pos·tu·la·tion
pos·tu·la·tor
pos·tur·al
pos·ture
pos·tur·er
post·war
posy (*plural* posies)
pot (pot·ting, pot·ted)
pot·abil·ity (*or* ·able·ness)
po·table drinkable
po·tage *French* soup; *compare* pottage

potamic

po·tam·ic
po·ta·mol·ogy study of rivers
pot·ash
po·tas·sic
po·tas·sium
po·ta·tion drinking
po·ta·to (*plural* ·toes)
pot·au·feu French stew
pot·bel·lied
pot·belly (*plural* ·bellies)
pot·boiler
pot·boy (*or* pot·man; *plural* ·boys *or* ·men)
potch *Austral* inferior opal
po·teen *Irish* illicit whiskey
po·ten·cy (*or* ·tence; *plural* ·ten·cies *or* ·tences)
po·tent
po·ten·tate ruler; *compare* potentiate
po·ten·tial
po·ten·ti·al·ity (*plural* ·ities)
po·ten·tial·ly
po·ten·ti·ate increase effectiveness; *compare* potentate
po·ten·til·la
po·ten·ti·om·eter
po·tent·ness
pot·ful (*plural* ·fuls)
pot·head *Slang* cannabis user
poth·er
pot·herb
pot·hole
pot·holer
pot·hol·ing
pot·hook
pot·house
pot·hunter
po·tiche (*plural* ·tiches) tall vase
po·tion
Potiphar biblical character
pot·latch ceremonial feast
pot·luck
Po·to·mac US river
pot·pie stew pie
pot·pour·ri (*plural* ·ris)
Pots·dam East German city
pot·sherd (*or* ·shard)
pot·stone
pot·tage thick soup; *compare* potage

pot·ted
pot·ter
pot·ter·er
Pot·teries Staffordshire region
pot·tery (*plural* ·teries)
pot·ting
pot·to (*plural* ·tos) animal
pot·ty (*adj* ·ti·er, ·ti·est; *noun, plural* ·ties)
pouch
pouched
pouchy
pouf (*or* pouffe) cushion seat; *compare* poof
pou·lard (*or* ·larde) spayed hen
poult young chicken
poul·ter·er
poul·tice
poul·try
poultry·man (*plural* ·men)
pounce
pound
pound·age
pound·al unit
pound·er
pour flow; *compare* poor; pore
pour·boire French tip
pour·er
pour·par·ler French informal conference
pour·point doublet
pous·sette country dance
pous·sin spring chicken
pout
pout·er
pout·ing·ly
pov·er·ty
poverty-stricken
pow exclamation
pow·an fish
pow·der
pow·der·er
pow·dery
pow·er
power·boat
pow·er·ful
pow·er·ful·ly
pow·er·ful·ness
power·house
pow·er·less
pow·er·less·ness
pow·wow
Pow·ys Welsh county

pox
poxy
Po·yang Chinese lake
Poz·nań Polish city
poz·zuo·la·na (*or* ·zo·) volcanic ash
prac·ti·cabil·ity (*or* ·cable·ness)
prac·ti·cable
prac·ti·cably
prac·ti·cal
prac·ti·cal·ity (*or* ·cal·ness)
prac·ti·cal·ly
prac·tice (*noun*)
prac·tise (*US* ·tice; *verb*)
prac·tised (*US* ·ticed)
prac·ti·tion·er
prae·dial (*or* pre·) of land
prae·di·al·ity (*or* pre·)
prae·mu·ni·re legal term
prae·no·men Roman's first name
Prae·se·pe star cluster
prae·sid·ium variant spelling *of* presidium
prae·tor (*or* pre·) Roman magistrate
prag·mat·ic
prag·mati·cal·ly
prag·mat·ics (*sing.*)
prag·ma·tism
prag·ma·tist
prag·ma·tis·tic
Prague
prai·rie
praise acclaim; *compare* prase
prais·er
praise·worthi·ly
praise·worthi·ness
praise·worthy
pra·line
prall·triller musical term
pram
prance
pranc·er
pranc·ing·ly
pran·dial
prang
prank
prank·ish
prank·ster
prase quartz; *compare* praise
pra·seo·dym·ium chemical element
prat *Slang* idiot

prate chatter
prat·er
prat·in·cole bird
prat·ing·ly
pra·tique permission to use port
Pra·to Italian city
prat·tle
prat·tler
prat·tling·ly
prau *variant of* proa
prawn
prawn·er
prax·is (*plural* prax·ises *or* praxes) practice
pray utter prayer; *compare* prey
prayer petition
pray·er one who prays
prayer·ful
prayer·ful·ly
preach
preach·er
preachi·fi·ca·tion
preachi·fy (·fies, ·fy·ing, ·fied)
preach·ment
pre·ad·am·ite
pre·ad·ap·ta·tion
pre·ado·les·cence
pre·ado·les·cent
pre·am·ble
pre·am·bu·lar (*or* ·la·tory, ·lary)
pre·am·pli·fi·er
pre·ar·range
pre·ar·ranged
pre·ar·range·ment
pre·ar·rang·er
pre·ax·ial
preb·end
pre·ben·dal
preb·en·dary (*plural* ·daries)
Pre·cam·brian geological term
pre·can·cel (·cel·ling, ·celled; *US* ·cel·ing, ·celed)
pre·can·cel·la·tion
pre·cari·ous
pre·cari·ous·ness
pre·cast (·cast·ing, ·cast)
preca·tory (*or* ·tive)
pre·cau·tion
pre·cau·tion·ary (*or* ·tion·al)

pre·cau·tious
pre·cede come before; *compare* proceed
prec·edence
prec·edent
prec·eden·tial
pre·ced·ing
pre·cen·tor cleric; *compare* preceptor
pre·cen·to·rial
pre·cept
pre·cep·tive
pre·cep·tor teacher; *compare* precentor
pre·cep·tor·ate
pre·cep·to·rial (*or* ·to·ral)
pre·cep·tor·ship
pre·cep·tress
pre·cess
pre·ces·sion rotation; motion of equinoxes; *compare* procession
pre·ces·sion·al
pre·cinct
pre·ci·os·ity (*plural* ·ities) affectation
pre·cious
pre·cious·ness
preci·pice
preci·piced
pre·cipi·tance (*or* ·tan·cy)
pre·cipi·tant
pre·cipi·tate
pre·cipi·ta·tion
pre·cipi·ta·tive
pre·cipi·ta·tor
pre·cipi·tin antibody
pre·cipi·tous
pre·cipi·tous·ness
pre·cis (*or* pré·; *plural* ·cis)
pre·cise
pre·cise·ness
pre·ci·sian strict observer of rules; *compare* precision
pre·ci·sian·ism
pre·ci·sion accuracy; *compare* precisian
pre·ci·sion·ism
pre·ci·sion·ist
pre·clini·cal
pre·clud·able
pre·clude
pre·clu·sion
pre·clu·sive
pre·co·cial ornithology term
pre·co·cious

pre·co·cious·ness (*or* pre·coc·ity)
pre·cog·ni·tion
pre·cog·ni·tive
pre·con·ceive
pre·con·cep·tion
pre·con·cert
pre·con·demn
pre·con·di·tion
pre·co·ni·za·tion (*or* ·sa·tion)
pre·co·nize (*or* ·nise) announce publicly
pre·con·scious
pre·con·scious·ness
pre·con·tract
pre·cook
pre·criti·cal
pre·cur·sor
pre·cur·sory (*or* ·sive)
pre·da·cious (*or* ·ceous) predatory
pre·da·cious·ness (*or* ·ceous·ness, pre·dac·ity)
pre·date precede
pre·da·tion predatory action
preda·tor
preda·to·ri·ly
preda·to·ri·ness
preda·tory
pre·de·cease
pre·de·ces·sor
pre·del·la (*plural* ·le) altar platform; painting
pre·des·ti·nar·ian
pre·des·ti·nari·an·ism
pre·des·ti·nate predestined; *variant of* predestine
pre·des·ti·na·tion
pre·des·tine (*or* ·ti·nate)
pre·de·ter·mi·nate
pre·de·ter·mi·na·tion
pre·de·ter·mi·na·tive
pre·de·ter·mine
pre·de·ter·min·er
pre·dial *variant spelling of* praedial
predi·cabil·ity (*or* ·cable·ness)
predi·cable affirmable
pre·dica·ment
predi·cant of preaching
predi·cate
predi·ca·tion
pre·dica·tive
predi·ca·tory of preaching

predict

pre·dict
pre·dict·abil·ity (or ·able·ness)
pre·dict·able
pre·dict·ably
pre·dic·tion
pre·dic·tive
pre·dic·tive·ly
pre·dic·tor
pre·di·gest
pre·di·ges·tion
pre·di·lec·tion
pre·dis·pos·al
pre·dis·pose
pre·dis·po·si·tion
pred·ni·sone drug
pre·domi·nance (or ·nan·cy)
pre·domi·nant
pre·domi·nate
pre·domi·na·tion
pre·domi·na·tor
pre-eclamp·sia
pree·mie (or pre·mie) US premature baby
pre-eminence
pre-eminent
pre-empt
pre-emption
pre-emptive
pre-emptor
pre-emptory
preen
preen·er
pre-exist
pre-exist·ence
pre·fab
pre·fab·ri·cate
pre·fab·ri·ca·tion
pre·fab·ri·ca·tor
pref·ace
pref·ac·er
prefa·to·ri·ly (or ·ri·al·ly)
prefa·tory (or ·to·rial)
pre·fect
pre·fec·to·rial
pre·fec·tur·al
pre·fec·ture
pre·fer (·fer·ring, ·ferred)
pref·er·abil·ity (or ·able·ness)
pref·er·able
pref·er·ably
pref·er·ence
pref·er·en·tial
pref·er·en·tial·ly
pref·er·en·ti·al·ity

pre·fer·ment
pre·fer·rer
pre·figu·ra·tion
pre·figu·ra·tive
pre·figu·ra·tive·ness
pre·fig·ure
pre·fig·ure·ment
pre·fix
pre·fix·al
pre·flight
pre·form
pre·for·ma·tion
pre·fron·tal anatomy term
pre·gla·cial
preg·nabil·ity
preg·nable
preg·nan·cy (plural ·cies)
preg·nant
pre·heat
pre·hen·sile
pre·hen·sion
pre·his·to·rian
pre·his·tor·ic (or ·tori·cal)
pre·his·tori·cal·ly
pre·his·to·ry (plural ·ries)
pre·homi·nid
pre·ignition
pre·judge
pre·judg·er
pre·judg·ment (or ·judge·ment)
preju·dice
preju·di·cial
prela·cy (plural ·cies)
prel·ate
pre·lat·ic
prela·tism
prela·tist
prela·ture
pre·lect to lecture
pre·lec·tion
pre·lec·tor
pre·lexi·cal grammar term
pre·limi·nari·ly
pre·limi·nary (plural ·naries)
pre·lims front matter of book; first exams
pre·lit·era·cy
pre·lit·er·ate
prel·ude
pre·lud·er
pre·lu·di·al
pre·lu·sion
pre·lu·sive (or ·so·ry)
pre·mari·tal
prema·ture

prema·tur·ity (or ·ture·ness)
pre·max·il·la (plural ·lae) bone
pre·max·il·lary
pre·med short for premedical; premedication
pre·medi·cal
pre·medi·ca·tion
pre·medi·tate
pre·medi·tat·ed·ly
pre·medi·ta·tion
pre·medi·ta·tive
pre·medi·ta·tor
pre·men·stru·al
prem·ier first in importance
premi·ere first performance
prem·ier·ship
prem·ise state as premiss; variant spelling of premiss
prem·ises land and buildings
prem·iss (or ·ise) logical statement
pre·mium
pre·mo·lar
premo·ni·tion
pre·moni·tory
pre·morse biology term
pre·mu·ni·tion immunity
pre·na·tal
pre·nomi·nal
pre·oc·cu·pa·tion (or ·pan·cy)
pre·oc·cu·py (·pies, ·py·ing, ·pied)
pre·or·dain
pre·or·di·na·tion
prep Slang homework; preparatory school
pre·pack
pre·pack·age
prepaid
prepa·ra·tion
pre·para·tive
pre·para·to·ri·ly
pre·para·tory
pre·pare
pre·par·ed·ly
pre·par·ed·ness
pre·pay (·pay·ing, ·paid)
pre·pay·able
pre·pay·ment
pre·pense premeditated
pre·pon·der·ance (or ·an·cy)
pre·pon·der·ant

pre·pon·der·ate
pre·pon·der·at·ing·ly
pre·pon·dera·tion
prepo·si·tion
prepo·si·tion·al
pre·posi·tive linguistics term
pre·posi·tor (*or* ·pos·tor) prefect
pre·pos·sess
pre·pos·sess·ing
pre·pos·sess·ing·ness
pre·pos·ses·sion
pre·pos·ter·ous
pre·pos·ter·ous·ness
pre·po·ten·cy
pre·po·tent
pre·puce foreskin
pre·pu·tial
Pre-Raphael·ite
pre·re·cord
pre·requi·site
pre·roga·tive
pre·sa (*plural* ·se) musical term
pres·age
pre·sage·ful
pre·sag·er
pres·byo·pia
pres·by·op·ic
pres·by·ter church elder
pres·by·ter·al
pres·byt·er·ate
pres·by·ter·ial
Pres·by·ter·ian Church
pres·by·ter·ian of government by presbyters
Pres·by·teri·an·ism
pres·by·teri·an·is·tic
pres·by·tery (*plural* ·teries)
pre·school
pres·ci·ence forcknowledge
pres·ci·ent
pre·scribe give ruling; order use of drug; *compare* proscribe
pre·scrib·er
pre·script
pre·scrip·tibil·ity
pre·scrip·tible
pre·scrip·tion
pre·scrip·tive
pre·scrip·tiv·ism
pres·ence
pres·ent the time now; in existence now

pre·sent gift; to give
pre·sent·able
pre·sent·ably
pre·sent·able·ness (*or* ·abil·ity)
pres·en·ta·tion
pres·en·ta·tion·al
pres·en·ta·tion·ism philosophy term
pres·en·ta·tion·ist
pre·senta·tive
pre·senta·tive·ness
present-day (*adj*)
pres·en·tee
pre·sent·er
pre·sen·tient
pre·sen·ti·ment
pres·ent·ly
pre·sent·ment
pre·serv·abil·ity
pre·serv·able
pres·er·va·tion
pre·serva·tive
pre·serve
pre·serv·er
pre·set (·set·ting, ·set)
pre·set·ter
pre·shrunk
pre·side
presi·den·cy (*plural* ·cies)
presi·dent
president-elect
presi·den·tial
pre·sid·er
pre·sidio (*plural* ·sidios) military establishment
pre·sid·ium (*or* prae·; *plural* ·iums *or* ·ia) Communist committee
pre·sig·ni·fy (·fies, ·fy·ing, ·fied)
press
press·er one that presses; *compare* pressor
press-gang (*verb*)
press·ing
press·ing·ness
press·man (*plural* ·men)
press·mark code on library book
pres·sor (*adj*) increasing blood pressure; *compare* presser
press·room
press-up (*noun*)
pres·sure

pres·suri·za·tion (*or* ·sa·tion)
pres·sur·ize (*or* ·ise)
pres·sur·iz·er (*or* ·is·er)
press·work
pres·ti·digi·ta·tion
pres·ti·digi·ta·tor
pres·tige
pres·tig·ious
pres·tig·ious·ness
pres·tis·si·mo (*plural* ·mos) musical term
pres·to (*plural* ·tos)
Pres·ton Lancashire town
Pres·ton·pans Scottish battle site
pre·stress
Prest·wich Scottish town
pre·sum·able
pre·sum·ably
pre·sume
pre·sum·ed·ly
pre·sum·er
pre·sum·ing·ly
pre·sump·tion
pre·sump·tive
pre·sump·tive·ness
pre·sump·tu·ous
pre·sump·tu·ous·ness
pre·sup·pose
pre·sup·po·si·tion
pre·tence (*US* ·tense)
pre·tend
pre·tend·ed·ly
pre·tend·er
pre·ten·sion
pre·ten·tious
pre·ten·tious·ness
pret·er·ite (*or* ·it) grammar term
pret·eri·tion act of omitting
pre·teri·tive grammar term
pre·ter·natu·ral
pre·ter·natu·ral·ism
pre·ter·natu·ral·ness (*or* ·ral·ity)
pre·test
pre·text
Pre·to·ria
pret·ti·fy (·fies, ·fy·ing, ·fied)
pret·ti·ly
pret·ti·ness
pret·ty (*adj* ·ti·er, ·ti·est; *verb* ·ties, ·ty·ing, ·tied)
pret·zel biscuit
pre·vail

prevailer

pre·vail·er
pre·vail·ing
pre·vail·ing·ly
preva·lence (*or* ·lent·ness)
preva·lent
pre·vari·cate
pre·vari·ca·tion
pre·vari·ca·tor
pre·ve·ni·ent preceding
pre·vent
pre·vent·able
pre·vent·ably
pre·ven·ta·tive variant of preventive
pre·vent·er
pre·ven·tion
pre·ven·tive (*or* ·ta·tive)
pre·ven·tive·ness (*or* ·ta·tive·ness)
pre·view (*or* ·vue)
pre·vi·ous
pre·vi·ous·ly
pre·vi·ous·ness
pre·vi·sion
pre·vo·cal·ic coming before a vowel
pre·war
prey victim; to hunt; victimize; *compare* pray
prey·er
Priam mythological king
pri·ap·ic of Priapus
pria·pism medical term
Priapus fertility god
price
price·less
price·less·ness
pricey (*or* pricy; prici·er, prici·est)
prick
prick·er
prick·et
prick·le
prick·li·ness
prick·ly (·li·er, ·li·est)
pricy variant spelling of pricey
pride
pride·ful
prie-dieu kneeling desk
pri·er (*or* pry·) one who pries; *compare* prior
priest
priest·craft
priest·ess
priest-hole

priest·hood
priest·li·ness
priest·ly (·li·er, ·li·est)
priest-ridden
prig
prig·gery (*or* prig·gish·ness)
prig·gish
prig·gism
prill
prim (*adj* prim·mer, prim·mest; *verb* prim·ming, primmed)
pri·ma bal·leri·na
pri·ma·cy (*plural* ·cies)
pri·ma don·na (*plural* pri·ma don·nas)
pri·mae·val variant spelling of primeval
pri·ma fa·cie
pri·mal
pri·ma·quine drug
pri·mari·ly
pri·ma·ry (*plural* ·ries)
pri·mate
pri·ma·tial
pri·ma·tol·ogy branch of zoology
prime
prime·ness
pri·mer introductory text
prim·ero one that primes
pri·mero card game
pri·meval (*or* ·mae·val)
pri·meval·ly
primi·gravi·da (*plural* ·das *or* ·dae) obstetrics term
pri·mine botany term
prim·ing
pri·mipa·ra (*or* uni·; *plural* ·ras *or* ·rae) obstetrics term
primi·par·ity
pri·mipa·rous
primi·tive
primi·tive·ness
primi·tiv·ism
primi·tiv·ist
primi·tiv·is·tic
prim·ness
pri·mo (*plural* ·mos *or* ·mi)
pri·mo·geni·tary
pri·mo·geni·tor
pri·mo·geni·ture
pri·mor·dial
pri·mor·dium (*plural* ·dia)

358

primp
prim·rose
primu·la
primu·la·ceous
pri·mum mo·bi·le Latin prime mover
Pri·mus (*Trademark*) stove
pri·mus presiding bishop
prince
prince·dom
prince·li·ness
prince·ling
prince·ly (·li·er, ·li·est)
prin·cess
Prince·ton US town
prin·ci·pal foremost; head person; *compare* principle
prin·ci·pal·ity (*plural* ·ities)
prin·ci·pal·ly
Prín·ci·pe island
prin·cip·ium (*plural* ·cipia) fundamental principle
prin·ci·ple standard; *compare* principal
prin·ci·pled
prink
prink·er
print
print·abil·ity (*or* ·able·ness)
print·able
print·er
print·ing
print·maker
print·out
pri·or abbot's deputy; *compare* prier
pri·or·ate
pri·or·ess
pri·or·ity (*plural* ·ities)
pri·ory (*plural* ·ories)
pris·age duty on wine
prise (*or* prize) force open; *compare* prize
prism
pris·mat·ic
pris·ma·toid geometric solid
pris·ma·toid·al
pris·moid
pris·moid·al
pris·on
pris·on·er
pris·si·ly
pris·si·ness

pris·sy (·si·er, ·si·est)
pris·tine
prithee
pri·va·cy (*plural* ·cies)
pri·vate
pri·va·teer
pri·va·tion
priva·tive
priv·et
privi·lege
privi·leged
privi·ly
priv·ity (*plural* ·ities) legal relationship
privy (*noun, plural* privies; *adj* privi·er, privi·est) lavatory; secret
prize award; *variant spelling of* prise
prize·fight
prize·fighter
pro (*plural* pros)
proa (*or* prau) boat
pro·ac·tive
pro-am professional and amateur
proba·bil·ism
prob·abil·ist
prob·abil·is·tic
prob·abil·ity (*plural* ·ities)
prob·able
prob·ably
pro·band person in genealogical study
pro·bang surgical instrument
pro·bate
pro·ba·tion
pro·ba·tion·al (*or* ·tion·ary)
pro·ba·tion·er
pro·ba·tive (*or* ·tory)
probe
probe·able
prob·er
pro·bity
prob·lem
prob·lem·at·ic (*or* ·ati·cal)
prob·lem·ati·cal·ly
pro bono pub·li·co *Latin* for the public good
pro·bos·cid·ean (*or* ·ian) zoology term
pro·bos·cis (*plural* ·cises *or* ·ci·des)
pro·caine
pro·cam·bial

pro·cam·bium botany term
pro·carp botany term
pro·ca·thedral church
pro·cedur·al
pro·cedure
pro·ceed carry on; *compare* precede
pro·ceed·er
pro·ceed·ing
pro·ceed·ings
pro·ceeds (*noun*)
proc·eleus·mat·ic prosody term
pro·cephal·ic anatomy term
pro·cess
pro·ces·sion
pro·ces·sion·al
pro·ces·sor
process-server
pro·chro·nism dating error
pro·claim
proc·la·ma·tion
pro·clama·tory
pro·clit·ic linguistics term
pro·cliv·ity (*plural* ·ities)
Procne mythological princess
pro·con·sul
pro·con·su·lar
pro·con·su·late (*or* ·sul·ship)
pro·cras·ti·nate
pro·cras·ti·na·tion
pro·cras·ti·na·tor
pro·creant (*or* ·crea·tive)
pro·cre·ate
pro·crea·tion
pro·crea·tor
Pro·crus·tean
Procrustes mythological robber
pro·cryp·tic zoology term
pro·cryp·ti·cal·ly
proc·to·logi·cal
proc·tolo·gist
proc·tol·ogy branch of medicine
proc·tor
proc·to·rial
proc·to·scope
proc·to·scop·ic
proc·tos·co·py
pro·cum·bent
pro·cur·able
procu·ra·tion
procu·ra·tor

procu·ra·tor fis·cal Scottish legal officer
procu·ra·tory
pro·cure
pro·cure·ment (*or* ·cur·ance, ·cur·al)
pro·cur·er (*fem* ·ess)
prod (prod·ding, prod·ded)
prod·der
prodi·gal
prodi·gal·ity (*plural* ·ities)
prodi·gal·ly
pro·di·gious
pro·di·gious·ness
prodi·gy (*plural* ·gies)
pro·dro·mal (*or* ·drom·ic)
pro·drome symptom of disease
pro·duce
pro·duc·er
pro·duc·ibil·ity
pro·duc·ible
prod·uct
pro·duc·tion
pro·duc·tion·al
pro·duc·tive
prod·uc·tiv·ity (*or* ·tive·ness)
pro·em preface
pro·emial
prof *Slang* professor
profa·na·tion
pro·fana·to·ry
pro·fane
pro·fane·ness
pro·fan·er
pro·fan·ity (*plural* ·ities)
pro·fess
pro·fess·ed·ly
pro·fes·sion
pro·fes·sion·al
pro·fes·sion·al·ism
pro·fes·sion·al·ist
pro·fes·sion·al·ly
pro·fes·sor
prof·es·so·rial
prof·es·sor·iate (*or* ·so·rate)
pro·fes·sor·ship
prof·fer
prof·fer·er
pro·fi·cien·cy (*plural* ·cies)
pro·fi·cient
pro·file
prof·it

profitability

prof·it·abil·ity
prof·it·able
prof·it·ably
profi·teer
prof·it·er
pro·fit·er·ole
prof·it·less
profit-sharing
prof·li·ga·cy
prof·li·gate
prof·lu·ent flowing smoothly
pro-form grammar term
pro for·ma *Latin* as prescribed
pro·found
pro·found·ly
pro·found·ness
pro·fun·dity (*plural* ·dities)
pro·fuse
pro·fuse·ly
pro·fuse·ness
pro·fu·sion
prog (prog·ging, progged) *Slang* prowl
pro·geni·tive
pro·geni·tive·ness
pro·geni·tor
prog·eny (*plural* ·enies)
pro·ges·ta·tion·al before pregnancy
pro·ges·ter·one hormone
pro·ges·to·gen (*or* pro·ges·tin) synthetic progesterone
pro·glot·tis (*or* ·tid; *plural* ·glot·ti·des) tapeworm segment
prog·na·thism
prog·na·thous (*or* ·nath·ic)
prog·no·sis (*plural* ·ses)
prog·nos·tic
prog·nos·ti·cate
prog·nos·ti·ca·tion
prog·nos·ti·ca·tive
prog·nos·ti·ca·tor
pro·gram *US spelling of* programme
pro·gram (·gram·ming, ·grammed) computer term
pro·gram·ma·ble
pro·gram·mat·ic
pro·gramme (*US* ·gram; ·gram·ming,

·grammed; *US* ·gram·ing, ·gramed)
pro·gram·mer
pro·gress
pro·gres·sion
pro·gres·sion·al
Pro·gres·sive political party
pro·gres·sive
pro·gres·sive·ness
pro·gres·siv·ism
pro·gres·siv·ist
pro·hib·it
pro·hib·it·er (*or* ·hibi·tor)
pro·hi·bi·tion
pro·hi·bi·tion·ary
pro·hi·bi·tion·ism
pro·hi·bi·tion·ist
pro·hibi·tive (*or* ·tory)
pro·hibi·tive·ness
proj·ect
pro·jec·tile
pro·jec·tion
pro·jec·tion·al
pro·jec·tion·ist
pro·jec·tive
pro·jec·tor
pro·jet draft treaty
Pro·kop·yevsk Soviet city
pro·lac·tin hormone
pro·la·mine plant protein
pro·lapse
pro·late spheroidal
pro·late·ness
prole
pro·leg zoology term
pro·legom·enal
pro·legom·enon (*plural* ·ena) critical introduction
pro·lep·sis (*plural* ·ses) rhetorical device
pro·lep·tic
pro·lep·ti·cal·ly
pro·letar·ian (*or* ·letary; *plural* ·ians *or* ·letaries)
pro·letar·ian·ism
pro·letar·ian·ness
pro·letari·at
pro·lif·er·ate
pro·lif·era·tion
pro·lif·era·tive
pro·lif·er·ous
pro·lif·ic
pro·lifi·cal·ly
pro·lif·ic·ness (*or* ·lifi·ca·cy)
pro·line amino acid

pro·lix long-winded
pro·lix·ity (*or* ·ness)
pro·locu·tor Anglican official
pro·logue (*US also* ·log; ·logu·ing, ·logued; *US also* ·log·ing, ·loged)
pro·long
pro·lon·ga·tion
pro·long·er
pro·long·ment
pro·lu·sion preliminary essay
pro·lu·so·ry
prom
prom·enade
prom·enad·er
Pro·methean
Prometheus mythological character
pro·methium radioactive element
promi·nence
promi·nent
promi·nent·ness
promis·cu·ity (*plural* ·ities)
pro·mis·cu·ous
pro·mis·cu·ous·ness
prom·ise
promi·see
prom·is·er (*or in legal contexts* promi·sor)
prom·is·ing
prom·is·sory
prom·on·tory (*plural* ·tories)
pro·mot·able
pro·mote
pro·mot·er
pro·mo·tion
pro·mo·tion·al
pro·mo·tive
pro·mo·tive·ness
prompt
prompt·book
prompt·er
promp·ti·tude
prompt·ness
prom·ul·gate
prom·ul·ga·tion
prom·ul·ga·tor
pro·my·celium (*plural* ·celia) botany term
pro·nate
pro·na·tion
pro·na·tor muscle

prone
prone·ness
pro·neph·ric
pro·neph·ros (*plural* ·roi or ·ra) zoology term
prong
prong·horn deer
pro·nomi·nal of a pronoun
pro·nomi·nali·za·tion (*or* ·sa·tion)
pro·nomi·nal·ize (*or* ·ise)
pro·noun
pro·nounce
pro·nounce·able
pro·nounced
pro·nounc·ed·ly
pro·nounce·ment
pro·nounc·er
pron·to
pro·nu·clear
pro·nu·cleus (*plural* ·clei)
pro·nun·cia·men·to (*plural* ·tos) manifesto
pro·nun·cia·tion
pro-oestrus (*US* pro·es·trus)
proof
proof·read (·read·ing, ·read)
proof·reader
prop (prop·ping, propped)
pro·pae·deu·tic preparatory instruction
pro·pae·deu·ti·cal
propa·gabil·ity (*or* ·gable·ness)
propa·gable
propa·gan·da
propa·gan·dism
propa·gan·dist
propa·gan·dize (*or* ·dise)
propa·gate
propa·ga·tion
propa·ga·tion·al
propa·ga·tive
propa·ga·tor
propa·gule (*or* pro·pagu·lum; *plural* ·gules *or* ·la) botany term
pro·pane
pro·pa·roxy·tone grammar term
pro pa·tria *Latin* for one's country
pro·pel (·pel·ling, ·pelled)

pro·pel·lant (*or* ·lent; *noun*)
pro·pel·lent (*adj*)
pro·pel·ler
pro·pene chemical compound
pro·pen·sity (*plural* ·sities)
prop·er
prop·er·ly
prop·er·ness
prop·er·tied
prop·er·ty (*plural* ·ties)
pro·phage virus
pro·phase biology term
proph·ecy (*plural* ·ecies)
proph·esi·able
proph·esi·er
proph·esy (·esies, ·esy·ing, ·esied)
proph·et (*fem* ·et·ess)
pro·phet·ic
pro·pheti·cal·ly
prophy·lac·tic
prophy·lax·is
pro·pin·quity
pro·pio·nate
pro·pi·on·ic acid
pro·pi·ti·able
pro·pi·ti·ate
pro·pi·tia·tion
pro·pi·tia·tious appeasing; *compare* propitious
pro·pi·tia·tive
pro·pi·tia·tor
pro·pi·tious favourable; *compare* propipiatious
pro·pi·tious·ness
prop·jet
propo·lis substance collected by bees
pro·po·nent
pro·por·tion
pro·por·tion·abil·ity
pro·por·tion·able
pro·por·tion·al
pro·por·tion·al·ity
pro·por·tion·al·ly
pro·por·tion·ate
pro·por·tion·ate·ness
pro·por·tion·ment
pro·po·sable
pro·po·sal
pro·pose
pro·pos·er
propo·si·tion
propo·si·tion·al

proselytizer

pro·posi·tus (*plural* ·ti) legal term
pro·pound
pro·pound·er
pro·prae·tor provincial praetor
pro·prano·lol
pro·pri·etari·ly
pro·pri·etary
pro·pri·etor (*fem* ·etress)
pro·pri·etor·ial
pro·pri·ety (*plural* ·eties)
pro·prio·cep·tive
pro·prio·cep·tor nerve ending
prop·to·sis (*plural* ·ses) medical term
pro·pul·sion
pro·pul·sive (*or* ·sory)
pro·pyl chemistry term
propy·laeum (*or* ·lon; *plural* ·laea *or* ·lons, ·la) temple portico
pro·pyl·ene propene
propy·lite geology term
pro rata
pro·rate
pro·ra·tion
pro·ro·ga·tion
pro·rogue
pro·sa·ic
pro·sai·cal·ly
pro·sa·ic·ness
pro·sa·ism (*or* ·sai·cism) prosaic style
pro·scenium (*plural* ·scenia *or* ·sceniums)
pro·sciut·to Italian ham
pro·scribe prohibit; *compare* prescribe
pro·scrip·tion
pro·scrip·tive
pro·scrip·tive·ness
prose
pro·sec·tor dissector
pros·ecut·able
pros·ecute
pros·ecu·tion
pros·ecu·tor
pros·elyte
pros·elyt·ic
pros·elyt·ism
pros·elyti·za·tion (*or* ·sa·tion)
pros·elyt·ize (*or* ·ise)
pros·elyt·iz·er (*or* ·is·er)

prosencephalon

pros·en·ceph·a·lon (*plural* ·la) anatomy term
pros·en·chy·ma plant tissue
pros·en·chy·ma·tous
Proserpina Roman goddess
prosi·ly
pro·sim·ian zoology term
prosi·ness
pro·sod·ic
proso·dist
proso·dy
proso·po·poeia (*or* ·peia) rhetorical device
proso·po·poeial (*or* ·peial)
pros·pect
pro·spec·tive
pro·spec·tor
pro·spec·tus (*plural* ·tuses)
pros·per
pros·per·ity (*plural* ·ities)
pros·per·ous
pros·per·ous·ness
pros·ta·glan·din hormone-like compound
pros·tate gland; *compare* prostrate
pros·ta·tec·to·my (*plural* ·mies)
pros·tat·ic
pros·ta·ti·tis
pros·the·sis (*plural* ·ses) artificial body part; *compare* prothesis
pros·thet·ic
pros·theti·cal·ly
pros·thet·ics
pros·tho·don·tics branch of dentistry
pros·tho·don·tist
pros·ti·tute
pros·ti·tu·tion
pros·ti·tu·tor
pro·sto·mium (*plural* ·mia) zoology term
pros·trate face down; *compare* prostate
pros·tra·tion
pro·style architectural term
prosy (prosi·er, prosi·est)
pro·tac·tin·ium radioactive element
pro·tago·nism
pro·tago·nist
pro·ta·mine protein
pro·tan·drous botany term
pro·tan·dry

pro·ta·no·pia red blindness
pro·ta·nop·ic
prota·sis (*plural* ·ses) conditional clause
pro·tea shrub
pro·tean variable
pro·tease enzyme
pro·tect
pro·tec·tion
pro·tec·tion·ism
pro·tec·tion·ist
pro·tec·tive
pro·tec·tive·ness
pro·tec·tor
pro·tec·to·ral
pro·tec·tor·ate
pro·tec·tory (*plural* ·tories) institution for children
pro·tec·tress
pro·té·gé (*fem* ·gée)
pro·tein
pro·teina·ceous (*or* ·tein·ic, ·tei·nous)
pro·tein·ase enzyme
pro tem (*or* pro tem·po·re) temporarily
pro·teoly·sis
pro·teo·lyt·ic
pro·teose biochemical compound
Pro·tero·zo·ic geology term
pro·test
Prot·es·tant religion
pro·test·ant protester
Prot·es·tant·ism
pro·tes·ta·tion
pro·test·er
pro·test·ing·ly
Proteus Greek god
pro·tha·la·mi·on (*or* ·mium; *plural* ·mia) marriage song
pro·thal·lic (*or* ·lial)
pro·thal·lus (*or* ·lium; *plural* ·li *or* ·lia) botany term
proth·esis linguistics term; *compare* prosthesis
pro·thet·ic
pro·theti·cal·ly
pro·thono·tar·ial (*or* pro·tono·)
pro·tho·no·tary (*or* proto·no·tary; *plural* ·taries)

pro·tho·rax (*plural* ·raxes *or* ·ra·ces)
pro·throm·bin
pro·tist microscopic organism
pro·tium isotope of hydrogen
proto·chor·date zoology term
proto·col
pro·togy·nous
pro·togy·ny biology term
proto·his·tor·ic
proto·his·to·ry
proto·hu·man
proto·lan·guage
proto·lith·ic of the Stone Age
proto·mor·phic primitive
pro·ton
proto·nema (*plural* ·ne·ma·ta) botany term
proto·ne·mal (*or* ·nema·tal)
proto·path·ic
pro·topa·thy physiology term
proto·plasm
proto·plas·mic (*or* ·mal, ·mat·ic)
proto·plast
proto·plas·tic
Proto·semit·ic language
proto·star
proto·stele botany term
proto·stelic
proto·therian zoology term
proto·troph·ic biology term
proto·ty·pal (*or* ·typ·ic, ·typi·cal)
proto·type
pro·tox·ide
proto·xy·lem
proto·zoan (*or* ·zo·on; *plural* ·zoans *or* ·zoa)
proto·zo·ologi·cal
proto·zo·olo·gist
proto·zo·ol·ogy
pro·tract
pro·tract·ed·ly
pro·tract·ed·ness
pro·trac·tile (*or* ·tract·ible)
pro·trac·tion
pro·trac·tive
pro·trac·tor
pro·trud·able

pro·trude
pro·tru·dent
pro·tru·sile
pro·tru·sion
pro·tru·sive
pro·tru·sive·ness
pro·tu·ber·ance (*or*
  ·an·cy; *plural* ·ances *or*
  ·an·cies)
pro·tu·ber·ant
pro·tyle (*or* ·tyl) chemistry
  term
proud
proud·ness
proust·ite mineral
prov·abil·ity
prov·able
prove (prov·ing, proved,
  proved *or* prov·en)
prov·enance (*or*
  ·veni·ence)
Pro·ven·çal of Provence
Pro·ven·çale cookery term
Pro·vence
prov·en·der
prov·en·ly
pro·ven·tricu·lar
pro·ven·tricu·lus (*plural*
  ·li) zoology term
prov·erb
pro·ver·bial
pro·ver·bial·ly
pro·vide
Provi·dence US port
provi·dence
provi·dent
provi·den·tial
provi·den·tial·ly
pro·vid·er
prov·ince
pro·vin·cial
pro·vin·cial·ism
pro·vin·ci·al·ity
pro·virus
pro·vi·sion
pro·vi·sion·al (*or* ·ary)
pro·vi·sion·al·ly
pro·vi·sion·er
pro·vi·sions
pro·vi·so (*plural* ·sos *or*
  ·soes)
pro·vi·so·ri·ly
pro·vi·sory
pro·vita·min
Pro·vo (*plural* ·vos)
  Provisional IRA member
provo·ca·tion

pro·voca·tive
pro·voca·tive·ness
pro·voke
pro·vok·ing·ly
pro·vo·lo·ne cheese
prov·ost
prow
prow·ess
prowl
prowl·er
Proxi·ma star
proxi·mal anatomy term
proxi·mal·ly
proxi·mate nearest
proxi·mate·ness
proxi·ma·tion
prox·im·ity
proxi·mo next month
proxy (*plural* proxies)
prude
pru·dence
pru·dent
pru·den·tial
pru·dent·ness
prud·ery (*plural* ·eries)
prud·ish
prud·ish·ness
prui·nose botany term
prun·able
prune
pru·nel·la (*or* ·nelle,
  ·nel·lo) fabric
pru·nelle liqueur
prun·er
pru·ri·ence
pru·ri·ent lewd; *compare*
  purulent
pru·ri·go skin disease
pru·rit·ic
pru·ri·tus itching
Prus·sia
Prus·sian
prus·si·ate cyanide
prus·sic acid
pry (*verb* pries, pry·ing,
  pried; *noun, plural*
  pries)
pry·er variant spelling of
  prier
pryta·neum (*plural* ·nea)
  ancient Greek town hall
psalm
psalm·ic
psalm·ist
psalm·od·ic
psalmo·dist
psalmo·dy (*plural* ·dies)

psychiatry

Psalms Old Testament book
Psal·ter (*or* psal·) psalm
  book
psal·ter·ium (*plural* ·teria)
  cow's stomach
psal·tery (*plural* ·teries)
  musical instrument
pse·phite rock
pse·phit·ic
psepho·logi·cal
psepho·logi·cal·ly
pse·pholo·gist
pse·phol·ogy study of
  elections
pseud *Slang* pretentious
  person
pseud·axis botany term
Pseud·epig·ra·pha Jewish
  writings
pseu·do *Slang* pretended
pseudo·carp botany term
pseudo·morph geology
  term
pseudo·mor·phic (*or*
  ·phous)
pseudo·mor·phism
pseudo·mu·tu·al·ity
  (*plural* ·ities) psychology
  term
pseudo·nym
pseudo·nym·ity
pseu·dony·mous
pseudo·po·dium (*plural*
  ·dia) biology term
pshaw exclamation
psi Greek letter
psilo·cy·bin hallucinogen
psi·lom·elane mineral
psit·ta·cine of parrots
psit·ta·co·sis
Pskov Soviet city
pso·as muscle
pso·ra·lea plant
pso·ria·sis skin disease
pso·ri·at·ic
psych *Slang* deduce; prepare
Psyche mythological
  character
psy·che human mind
psychedelia
psychedel·ic (*or* psycho·)
psychedeli·cal·ly (*or*
  psycho·deli·)
psy·chi·at·ric
psy·chi·at·ri·cal·ly
psy·chia·trist
psy·chia·try

psy·chic telepathic
psy·chi·cal
psy·cho (*plural* ·chos) *Slang* psychopath
psycho·acous·tics
psycho·ac·tive
psycho·ana·lyse (*US* ·lyze)
psycho·analy·sis
psycho·ana·lyst
psycho·ana·lyt·ic (*or* ·lyti·cal)
psycho·ana·lyti·cal·ly
psycho·bio·logi·cal
psycho·bi·olo·gist
psycho·bi·ol·ogy
psycho·chemi·cal
psycho·dra·ma
psycho·dra·mat·ic
psycho·dy·nam·ic
psycho·dy·nami·cal·ly
psycho·dy·nam·ics
psycho·gen·esis
psycho·genet·ic
psycho·geneti·cal·ly
psycho·gen·ic
psycho·geni·cal·ly
psy·chog·no·sis
psy·chog·nos·tic
psycho·graph
psycho·graph·ic
psy·chog·ra·phy
psycho·his·to·ry (*plural* ·ries)
psycho·ki·nesis
psycho·ki·net·ic
psycho·lin·guist
psycho·lin·guis·tic
psycho·lin·guis·tics
psycho·logi·cal
psycho·logi·cal·ly
psy·cholo·gism belief in psychology
psy·cholo·gist
psy·cholo·gist·ic
psy·cholo·gize (*or* ·gise)
psy·chol·ogy (*plural* ·ogies)
psycho·met·ric (*or* ·ri·cal)
psycho·met·ri·cal·ly
psycho·metri·cian (*or* psy·chom·etrist)
psycho·met·rics (*or* psy·chom·etry) testing mental processes
psycho·mo·tor

psycho·neu·ro·sis (*plural* ·ses)
psycho·neu·rot·ic
psycho·path
psycho·path·ic
psycho·path·ical·ly
psycho·patho·logi·cal
psycho·pa·tholo·gist
psycho·pa·thol·ogy
psy·chopa·thy
psycho·phar·ma·co·logi·cal
psycho·phar·ma·colo·gist
psycho·phar·ma·col·ogy
psycho·physi·cal
psycho·phys·ics
psycho·physio·logi·cal
psycho·physi·olo·gist
psycho·physi·ol·ogy
psycho·sex·ual
psycho·sexu·al·ity
psy·cho·sis (*plural* ·ses)
psycho·so·cial
psycho·so·mat·ic
psycho·sur·gery
psycho·sur·gi·cal
psycho·tech·ni·cal
psycho·tech·ni·cian
psycho·tech·nics
psycho·thera·peu·tic
psycho·thera·peu·ti·cal·ly
psycho·thera·pist
psycho·thera·py
psycho·trop·ic
psy·chot·ic
psy·choti·cal·ly
psy·choto·mi·met·ic
psy·chrom·eter humidity meter
psy·chro·phil·ic biology term
psyl·lid (*or* ·la) insect
Ptah Egyptian god
ptar·mi·gan (*plural* ·gans *or* ·gan) bird
pteri·do·logi·cal
pteri·dolo·gist
pteri·dol·ogy study of ferns
pteri·do·phyte
pteri·do·phyt·ic (*or* ·dophy·tous)
pteri·do·sperm extinct plant
ptero·dac·tyl
ptero·pod mollusc
ptero·saur
ptery·goid anatomy term

ptery·la (*plural* ·lae) ornithology term
pti·san grape juice
pto·choc·ra·cy (*plural* ·cies) government by the poor
Ptol·emae·us moon crater
Ptol·ema·ic
Ptol·ema·ist
pto·maine (*or* ·main) chemical compound
pto·sis (*plural* ·ses) drooping of eyelid
ptya·lin enzyme
ptya·lism excessive salivation
pub (pub·bing, pubbed)
pu·ber·ty
pu·beru·lent downy
pu·bes (*plural* ·bes) pubic region; *plural of* pubis
pu·bes·cence
pu·bes·cent
pu·bic
pu·bis (*plural* ·bes) hip bone
pub·lic
pub·li·can
pub·li·ca·tion
pub·li·cist
pub·lic·ity
pub·li·cize (*or* ·cise)
pub·lic·ly
public-spirit·ed
pub·lish
pub·lish·able
pub·lish·er
puc·coon plant
puce
puck
puck·er
puck·ish
puck·ish·ness
pud·ding
pud·dle
pud·dler
pud·dling
pud·dly
pu·den·cy modesty
pu·den·dal
pu·den·dum (*plural* ·da)
pudgi·ly
pudgi·ness
pudgy (pudgi·er, pudgi·est)
Pue·bla Mexican city

Pueb·lo (*plural* ·lo *or* ·los) American Indian
pueb·lo (*plural* ·los) village
pu·er·ile
pu·er·il·ism
pu·er·il·ity (*plural* ·ities)
pu·er·per·al
pu·er·per·ium period after childbirth
Puer·to Ri·can
Puer·to Rico
puff
puff·ball
puff·bird
puff·er
puff·ery (*plural* ·eries) exaggerated praise
puffi·ly
puf·fin
puffi·ness
puffy (puffi·er, puffi·est)
pug (pug·ging, pugged) dog; knead clay
pug·gish
pu·gi·lism
pu·gi·list
pu·gi·lis·tic
pu·gi·lis·ti·cal·ly
pug·na·cious
pug·nac·ity (*or* ·na·cious·ness)
pug-nosed
puis·ne legal term
pu·is·sance *Archaic* power; showjumping event
pu·is·sant
puke
puk·ka
pul (*plural* puls *or* puli) Afghan coin
pul·chri·tude
pul·chri·tudi·nous
pule to whimper
pul·er
pull
pul·let
pul·ley
pull-in (*noun*)
Pull·man (*plural* ·mans) rail coach
pull-out (*noun*)
pull·over
pul·lu·late breed rapidly
pul·lu·la·tion
pul·mo·nary
pul·mo·nate

pul·mon·ic
Pul·motor (*Trademark*)
pulp
pulpi·ness
pul·pit
pulp·wood
pulpy (pulpi·er, pulpi·est)
pul·que alcoholic drink
pul·sar star
pul·sate
pul·sa·tile
pul·sa·til·ity
pul·sa·tion
pul·sa·tive
pul·sa·tor
pul·sa·tory
pulse
pulse·jet
pul·sim·eter (*or* ·som·)
pul·ver·able
pul·veri·za·tion (*or* ·sa·tion)
pul·ver·ize (*or* ·ise)
pul·ver·iz·er (*or* ·is·er)
pul·veru·lence
pul·veru·lent of dust
pul·vil·lus (*plural* ·li) zoology term
pul·vi·nate (*or* ·nat·ed)
pul·vi·nus (*plural* ·ni) botany term
puma
pum·ice
pu·mi·ceous
pum·mel (*or* pom·; ·mel·ling, ·melled; *US* ·mel·ing, ·meled) to pound; *compare* pommel
pump
pum·per·nick·el
pump·kin
pumpkin·seed
pun (pun·ning, punned)
punce *Dialect* kick
punch
punch·ball
punch·board
punch·bowl
punch-drunk
pun·cheon
punch·er
Pun·chi·nel·lo (*plural* ·los *or* ·loes) clown
punch-up (*noun*)
punchy (punchi·er, punchi·est)
punc·tate (*or* ·tat·ed)

punc·ta·tion
punc·tilio (*plural* ·tilios) etiquette
punc·tili·ous
punc·tili·ous·ness
punc·tu·al
punc·tu·al·ity
punc·tu·al·ly
punc·tu·ate
punc·tua·tion
punc·tua·tor
punc·tum (*plural* ·ta) anatomy term
punc·tur·able
punc·ture
punc·tur·er
pun·dit (*or* pan·) expert; learned Hindu; *compare* pandit
pung *US* sleigh
pun·gen·cy
pun·gent
Pu·nic of Carthage
puni·ness
pun·ish
pun·ish·abil·ity
pun·ish·able
pun·ish·er
pun·ish·ing·ly
pun·ish·ment
pu·ni·tive (*or* ·tory)
pu·ni·tive·ness
Pun·jab
Pun·ja·bi (*or* Pan·)
punk
pun·ka (*or* ·kah) palm-leaf fan
punned
pun·ner
pun·net
pun·ning
pun·ster
punt
punt·er
pun·ty (*plural* ·ties) glass-blowing rod
puny (pu·ni·er, pu·ni·est)
pup (pup·ping, pupped)
pupa (*plural* pupae *or* pupas)
pu·pal
pu·par·ial
pu·par·ium (*plural* ·paria)
pu·pate
pu·pa·tion
pu·pil
pu·pil·lage (*US* ·pil·age)

pupillary

pu·pil·lary (or ·pi·lary)
pu·pipa·rous entomology term
pup·pet
pup·pet·eer
pup·pet·ry
pup·ping
Pup·pis constellation
pup·py (plural ·pies)
pup·py·hood
pup·py·ish
Pu·ra·na Sanskrit writings
Pur·beck Dorset peninsula; marble
pur·blind
pur·chasa·bil·ity
pur·chas·able
pur·chase
pur·chas·er
pur·dah (or pur·da, par·dah)
pure
pure·bred
pu·ree (or puri) Indian bread
pu·rée (·rée·ing, ·reed) pulped food
pure·ly
pure·ness
pur·fle ornamental band
pur·ga·tion
pur·ga·tive
pur·ga·to·rial
pur·ga·tory
purge
purg·er
Puri Indian port
pu·ri·fi·ca·tion
pu·ri·fi·ca·tor Communion cloth
pu·rifi·ca·tory
pu·ri·fi·er
pu·ri·fy (·fies, ·fy·ing, ·fied)
Pu·rim Jewish holiday
pu·rine (or ·rin) biochemical compound
pur·ism
pur·ist
pu·rist·ic
pu·ris·ti·cal·ly
Pu·ri·tan extreme Protestant
pu·ri·tan strictly moral person
pu·ri·tani·cal (or ·tan·ic)
pu·ri·tani·cal·ness
Pu·ri·tan·ism

pu·ri·tan·ism
pu·rity
purl knitting stitch; compare pearl
pur·ler headlong fall
pur·lieu outlying area
pur·lin (or ·line) roof beam
pur·loin
pur·loin·er
pur·ple
pur·ple·ness
pur·plish
pur·port
pur·pose
pur·pose·ful
pur·pose·ful·ly determinedly; compare purposely
pur·pose·ful·ness
pur·pose·less
pur·pose·less·ness
pur·pose·ly intentionally; compare purposefully
pur·pos·ive
pur·pos·ive·ness
pur·pu·ra disease
pur·pure heraldic purple
pur·pu·rin biological dye
purr
purse
purs·er
purs·lane plant
pur·su·ance
pur·su·ant
pur·sue (·su·ing, ·sued)
pur·su·er
pur·suit
pur·sui·vant heraldic officer
pursy short-winded
pu·ru·lence (or ·len·cy)
pu·ru·lent of pus; compare prurient
pur·vey
pur·vey·ance
pur·vey·or
pur·view scope
pus matter from wound; compare puss
Pu·san South Korean port
push
push·chair
push·er
pushi·ly
pushi·ness
push·ing
push·ing·ly
push·ing·ness

push·over
push-pull
push·rod
Push·tu variant of Pashto
push-up US press-up
pushy (pushi·er, pushi·est)
pu·sil·la·nim·ity
pu·sil·lani·mous
puss Slang cat; compare pus
pus·sy (·si·er, ·si·est) full of pus
pussy (or pussy·cat; plural pussies or ·cats)
pussy·foot
pus·tu·lant
pus·tu·lar
pus·tu·late
pus·tu·la·tion
pus·tule
put (put·ting, put) to place, etc.; compare putt
pu·ta·men (plural ·tami·na) botany term
pu·ta·tive
put-down (noun)
put·log (or ·lock) scaffold beam
put-on (noun)
pu·tre·fac·tion
pu·tre·fac·tive (or ·fa·cient)
pu·tre·fi·able
pu·tre·fi·er
pu·tre·fy (·fies, ·fy·ing, ·fied)
pu·tres·cence
pu·tres·cent
pu·tres·cine organic compound
pu·trid
pu·trid·ity (or ·trid·ness)
(putrify) incorrect spelling of putrefy
Putsch German uprising
putt golf stroke; compare put
put·tee (or ·ty; plural ·tees or ·ties) leg cloth
putt·er golf club
put·ter placer
putt·ing golf stroke
put·ting placing
put·to (plural ·ti) boy cupid
put·ty (noun, plural ·ties; verb ·ties, ·ty·ing, ·tied)
putty·root

put-up (*adj*)
Puy de Dôme French department
puz·zle
puz·zle·ment
puz·zler
puz·zling·ly
pya Burmese coin
py·aemia (*US* ·emia) blood poisoning
py·aemic (*US* ·emic)
pyc·nid·ium (*plural* ·nidia) botany term
pyc·nom·eter density measurer
pyc·no·met·ric
Pyd·na ancient Macedonian town
pye-dog (*or* pie-)
py·elit·ic
py·eli·tis kidney disease
py·elo·gram
py·elo·graph·ic
py·elog·ra·phy
py·elo·nephri·tis
py·emia *US spelling of* pyaemia
py·gid·ial
py·gid·ium (*plural* ·gidia) zoology term
Pygmalion mythological king
Pyg·my (*or* Pig·; *plural* ·mies) African race
pyg·my (*or* pig·; *plural* ·mies) dwarf
py·ja·ma (*US* pa·; *adj*)
py·ja·mas (*US* pa·)
pyk·nic squat
py·lon
py·lo·rec·to·my (*plural* ·mies)
py·lo·ric
py·lo·rus (*plural* ·ri) stomach opening
pyo·der·ma skin disease
pyo·gen·esis
pyo·gen·ic causing pus; *compare* pyrogenic
py·oid
Pyong·yang capital of North Korea
py·or·rhoea (*US* ·rhea) gum disease
py·or·rhoeal (*or* ·rhoe·ic; *US* ·rheal *or* ·rhe·ic)
pyo·sis pus formation

py·ra·can·tha shrub
pyra·lid moth
pyra·mid
py·rami·dal (*or* pyra·midi·cal, pyra·mid·ic)
Pyramus legendary lover
py·ran chemical compound
py·ra·nom·eter solarimeter
py·rar·gy·rite mineral
py·ra·zole chemical compound
pyre
py·rene chemical compound; botany term
Pyr·enean
Pyr·enees
Py·ré·nées At·lan·tiques French department
Py·ré·nées-Orientales French department
pyr·enoid protein granule
py·rethrin insecticide
py·rethrum plant
py·ret·ic of fever
Py·rex (*Trademark*)
py·rexia fever
py·rex·ial (*or* ·rex·ic)
pyr·he·li·om·eter
pyr·he·lio·met·ric
pyri·dine chemical compound
pyri·dox·al biochemical compound
pyri·doxa·mine
pyri·dox·ine
pyri·form pear-shaped
py·rimi·dine biochemical compound
py·rite mineral
py·ri·tes (*plural* ·tes) mineral
py·rit·ic (*or* ·ti·tous)
pyro·cat·echol (*or* ·echin)
pyro·chemi·cal
pyro·clas·tic geology term
pyro·con·duc·tiv·ity
pyro·elec·tric
pyro·elec·tric·ity
pyro·gal·late
pyro·gal·lic
pyro·gal·lol
pyro·gen
pyro·gen·ic (*or* py·rog·enous) causing heat or fever; *compare* pyogenic

py·rog·nos·tics
py·rog·ra·pher
pyro·graph·ic
py·rog·ra·phy (*plural* ·phies) design by burning
pyro·lig·ne·ous (*or* ·lig·nic)
pyro·lit·ic
pyro·lu·site mineral
py·roly·sis chemical reaction
pyro·man·cer
pyro·man·cy divination by fire
pyro·ma·nia
pyro·ma·ni·ac
pyro·ma·nia·cal
pyro·man·tic
pyro·met·al·lur·gy
py·rom·eter
pyro·met·ric (*or* ·met·ri·cal)
pyro·met·ri·cal·ly
py·rom·etry
pyro·mor·phite mineral
py·rone chemical compound
py·rope garnet
pyro·phor·ic
pyro·phos·phate
pyro·pho·tom·eter
pyro·pho·tom·etry
pyro·phyl·lite mineral
pyro·sis heartburn
pyro·stat
pyro·stat·ic
pyro·sul·phate (*US* ·fate)
pyro·tech·nic (*or* ·ni·cal)
pyro·tech·nics
py·rox·ene mineral
py·rox·en·ic
py·rox·enite rock
py·roxy·lin constituent of plastics
Pyrrha mythological character
Pyr·rhic of Pyrrhus
pyr·rhic prosody term
pyr·rho·tite (*or* ·tine) mineral
pyr·rhu·loxia bird
pyr·role biochemical compound
pyr·rol·ic
pyr·roli·dine
pyr·ru·vic acid
Py·thago·rean

Pythia

Pythia mythological priestess
Pyth·ian
py·thon
py·thon·ess female soothsayer
py·thon·ic
pyu·ria medical term
pyx container for Eucharist; *compare* **pix**
pyx·id·ium (*plural* ·idia) botany term
pyxie shrub
pyx·is (*plural* **pyxi·des**) box

Q

Qair·wan Tunisian city
Qa·tar Arabian state
Qa·ta·ri
Qeshm (*or* **Qishm**) Iranian island
qin·tar (*or* ·**dar**) Albanian coin
qua in the capacity of
quack
quack·ery (*plural* ·**eries**)
quack·sal·ver quack doctor
quad quadrangle; quadruplet; *compare* **quod**
quad·ra·gesi·ma
Quad·ra·gesi·ma
Quad·ra·gesi·mal
quad·ran·gle
quad·ran·gu·lar
quad·rant
quad·ran·tal
quad·ra·phon·ic (*or* ·**ro**·)
quad·ra·phon·ics (*or* ·**ro**·)
quad·rat ecology term
quad·rate cube; bone
quad·rat·ic
quad·rat·ics branch of algebra
quad·ra·ture maths term
quad·ren·nial
quad·ren·nial·ly
quad·ren·nium (*plural* ·**niums** *or* ·**nia**)
quad·ric maths term
quad·ri·cen·ten·nial
quad·ri·ceps (*plural* ·**cepses**) muscle
quad·ri·cipi·tal
quad·ri·fid botany term
quad·ri·ga (*plural* ·**gas** *or* ·**gae**) chariot
quad·ri·lat·er·al
quad·rille dance
quad·ril·lion 10^{24}
quad·ril·lionth
quad·ri·no·mial
quad·ri·par·tite
quad·ri·plegia
quad·ri·plegic
quad·ri·sect
quad·ri·sec·tion
quad·ri·va·len·cy (*or* ·**lence**)
quad·ri·va·lent
quad·riv·ial having four roads meeting
quad·riv·ium medieval branch of learning
quad·roon
quad·ru·ma·nous zoology term
quad·ru·ped
quad·ru·ped·al
quad·ru·ple
quad·ru·plet
quad·ru·plex fourfold
quad·ru·pli·cate
quad·ru·pli·ca·tion
quad·ru·plic·ity (*plural* ·**ities**)
quaes·tor (*or* **ques**·) Roman magistrate
quaff
quaff·er
quag·ga (*plural* ·**gas** *or* ·**ga**) extinct horse
quag·gy (·**gi·er**, ·**gi·est**) marshy
quag·mire
qua·hog clam
quail (*plural* **quails** *or* **quail**)
quaint
quaint·ness
quake
Quak·er
Quak·er·ism
quaki·ly
quaki·ness
quaky (**quaki·er**, **quaki·est**)
qua·le (*plural* ·**lia**) philosophy term
quali·fi·able
quali·fi·ca·tion
quali·fi·ca·tory
quali·fied
quali·fi·er
quali·fy (·**fies**, ·**fy·ing**, ·**fied**)
quali·fy·ing·ly
quali·ta·tive
qual·ity (*plural* ·**ities**)
qualm
qualm·ish
quam·ash plant
quan·da·ry (*plural* ·**ries**)
quan·dong (*or* ·**dang**, ·**tong**) fruit tree
quango (*plural* **quangos**)
quant punting pole
quan·tal
quan·tic maths term
quan·ti·fi·able
quan·ti·fi·ca·tion
quan·ti·fi·er
quan·ti·fy (·**fies**, ·**fy·ing**, ·**fied**)
quan·ti·ta·tive (*or* **quan·ti·tive**)
quan·tity (*plural* ·**tities**)
quan·ti·za·tion (*or* ·**sa·tion**)
quan·tize (*or* ·**tise**)
quan·tum (*plural* ·**ta**)
qua·qua·ver·sal geology term
quar·an·tine
quare *Irish* remarkable
quark
quar·rel (·**rel·ling**, ·**relled**; *US* ·**rel·ing**, ·**reled**)
quar·rel·ler (*US* ·**rel·er**)
quar·rel·some
quar·rian bird

quar·ri·er (or
 quarry·man; plural ·ers
 or ·men)
quar·ry (noun, plural
 ·ries; verb ·ries, ·ry·ing,
 ·ried)
quart
quar·tan every third day
quar·ter
quar·ter·age quarterly
 payment
quarter·back
quarter-bound
quarter·deck
quar·tered
quarter·final
quarter-hour
quar·ter·ing
quarter·light window
quar·ter·ly (plural ·lies)
quarter·master
quar·tern measure of weight
quar·ters
quarter·saw (·saw·ing,
 ·sawed, ·sawed or
 ·sawn)
quarter·staff (plural
 ·staves)
quar·tet (or ·tette)
quar·tic maths term
quar·tile
quar·to (plural ·tos)
quartz
quartz·if·er·ous
quartz·ite
qua·sar
quash
quas·sia tree
qua·ter·cen·te·nary
 (plural ·naries)
Qua·ter·nary geological
 period
qua·ter·nary (plural
 ·naries) of four; fourth
qua·ter·ni·on maths term
qua·ter·ni·ty (plural ·ties)
 group of four
quat·rain
qua·tre playing card
quatre·foil
quat·tro·cen·to 15th
 century
qua·ver
qua·ver·er
qua·ver·ing·ly
qua·very (or ·ver·ous)
quay

quay·age
quay·side
quea·si·ly
quea·si·ness
quea·sy (·si·er, ·si·est)
Que·bec
Qué·be·cois (plural ·cois)
que·bra·cho (plural ·chos)
 tree
Quech·ua (or Kech·ua;
 plural ·uas or ·ua)
 American Indian
Quech·uan (or Kech·)
queen
queen·cake
queen·dom
queen·li·ness
queen·ly (·li·er, ·li·est)
Queens New York borough
Queens·ber·ry rules
Queens·land
queer
queer·ness
quell
quell·er
quel·que·chose
 insignificant thing
quench
quench·able
quench·er
que·nelle dumpling
quer·cetin (or ·ci·tin)
 pigment
quer·cine of the oak
Que·réta·ro Mexican state
que·rist questioner
quern stone hand mill
queru·lous
queru·lous·ness
que·ry (noun, plural ·ries;
 verb ·ries, ·ry·ing,
 ·ried)
quest
quest·er
quest·ing·ly
ques·tion
ques·tion·able
ques·tion·able·ness (or
 ·abil·ity)
ques·tion·ably
ques·tion·ary
ques·tion·er
ques·tion·ing
ques·tion·less
ques·tion·naire
Quet·ta Pakistani city
quet·zal bird

Quet·zal·coa·tl Aztec god
queue (queu·ing, queued)
 line; pigtail; compare cue
Que·zon City Philippine
 capital
quib·ble
quib·bler
quib·bling·ly
Qui·beron French
 peninsula
quiche
quick
quick·en
quick-freeze (-freezing,
 -froze, -frozen)
quickie
quick·lime
quick·ly
quick·ness
quick·sand
quick·set hedge
quick·silver
quick·step (·step·ping,
 ·stepped)
quick-tempered
quick-witted
quick-witted·ness
quid
quid·dity (plural ·dities)
quid·nunc gossipmonger
quid pro quo (plural quid
 pro quos)
qui·es·cence (or ·cen·cy)
qui·es·cent
qui·et
qui·et·en
qui·et·ism form of
 mysticism
qui·et·ness
qui·etude
qui·etus (plural ·ctuses)
quiff
quill
quil·lai tree
quill·wort
Quil·mes Argentine city
quilt
quilt·er
quilt·ing
quin
qui·na·ry (noun, plural
 ·ries) consisting of five
qui·nate composed of five
 parts
quince
quin·cen·te·nary (plural
 ·naries)

quincuncial

quin·cun·cial
quin·cunx arrangement of five
quin·deca·gon 15-sided figure
quin·deca·plet group of 15
quin·de·cen·nial
Qui Nhong Vietnamese port
quini·dine
qui·nine
quin·ol
quino·line
qui·none
quino·noid (or quin·oid)
quin·qua·genar·ian
Quin·qua·gesi·ma
quin·que·fo·li·ate
quin·quen·nial
quin·quen·nial·ly
quin·quen·nium (plural ·nia)
quin·que·par·tite
quin·que·reme ship
quin·que·va·len·cy (or ·lence)
quin·que·va·lent
quin·sy
quint organ stop; piquet term
quin·tain tilting target
quin·tal unit of weight
quin·tan recurring every fourth day
quin·tes·sence
quin·tes·sen·tial
quin·tes·sen·tial·ly
quin·tet (or ·tette)

quin·tic maths term
quin·tile astrology term
quin·til·lion (plural ·lions or ·lion) 10^{30}
quin·til·lionth
quin·tu·ple
quin·tu·plet
quin·tu·pli·cate
quin·tu·pli·ca·tion
quip (·quip·ping, ·quipped)
quip·ster
quire set of paper; compare choir
Quiri·nal Roman hill
Quirinus Roman god
quirk
quirki·ly
quirki·ness
quirky (quirki·er, quirki·est)
quirt whip
quis·ling
quist Dialect wood pigeon
quit (quit·ting, quit·ted or quit)
quitch grass
quit·claim legal term
quite
Qui·to Ecuadorian capital
quits
quit·tance
quit·ter one that quits
quit·tor horse's foot infection
quiv·er
quiv·er·er
quiv·er·ful

quiv·er·ing·ly
quiv·ery
qui vive French attentive
quix·ot·ic (or ·oti·cal)
quix·oti·cal·ly
quixo·tism
quiz (noun, plural quiz·zes; verb quiz·zes, quiz·zing, quizzed)
quiz·master
quiz·zer
quiz·zi·cal
quiz·zi·cal·ity
quiz·zi·cal·ly
quod Slang jail; compare quad
quod erat de·mon·stran·dum Latin which was to be proved
quod·li·bet piece of music
quod·li·beti·cal
quod·li·beti·cal·ly
quoin (or coign, coigne) cornerstone
quoit
quoits
quok·ka wallaby
quon·dam former
quor·um
quo·ta
quot·abil·ity
quot·able
quo·ta·tion
quote
quoth Archaic said
quo·tid·ian daily
quo·tient
quo war·ran·to legal term

R

Ra (or Re) Egyptian god
Ra·bat Moroccan capital
ra·ba·to (or re·; plural ·tos) collar
rab·bet variant of rebate
rab·bi (or ·bin; plural ·bis or ·bins)
rab·bin·ate office of rabbi
Rab·bin·ic language
rab·bini·cal (or ·bin·ic)
rab·bin·ism
rab·bit note Welsh rabbit (or rarebit)

rab·bit·er
rabbit·fish (plural ·fish or ·fishes)
rab·bit·ry (plural ·ries)
rab·bity
rab·ble
rab·bler
rabble-rouser
rabble-rousing
Rab·elai·sian
rabi Indian crop
rab·id
ra·bid·ity (or rab·id·ness)

ra·bies
rac·coon (or ra·coon)
race
race·card
race·course
race·go·er
race·horse
ra·ceme botany term
ra·cemic chemistry term
rac·emism
rac·emi·za·tion (or ·sa·tion)
rac·emize

rac·emose (*or* ·emous) botany term
rac·er
race·track
ra·chial (*or* ·chid·ial, rha·)
ra·chis (*or* rha·; *plural* ·chises *or* ·chi·des) biology term
ra·chit·ic
ra·chi·tis rickets
Rach·man·ism exploitation of tenants
ra·cial
ra·cial·ly
raci·ly
raci·ness
rac·ing
rac·ism (*or* ra·cial·ism)
rac·ist (*or* ra·cial·ist)
rack frame; toothed bar; to strain; etc.; *compare* wrack
rack (*or* wrack) destruction, *esp. in* rack and ruin
rack-and-pinion
rack·er
rack·et disturbance; dishonest practice
rack·et (*or* rac·quet) bat
rack·et·eer
rack·ets game
rack·ety
rack-rent
rack-renter
rac·on·teur
ra·coon variant spelling of raccoon
rac·quet variant spelling of racket
racy (raci·er, raci·est)
rad unit
ra·dar
radar·scope
rad·dle
rad·dled
ra·dial
ra·dial·ly
radial-ply
ra·dian unit
ra·di·ance (*or* ·an·cy; *plural* ·ances *or* ·an·cies)
ra·di·ant
ra·di·ate
ra·dia·tion
ra·dia·tion·al
ra·dia·tive (*or* ·tory)

ra·dia·tor
radi·cal basic; extreme; chemistry term; *compare* radicle
radi·cal·ism
radi·cal·is·tic
radi·cal·is·ti·cal·ly
radi·cal·ly
radi·cal·ness
radi·cand maths term
radi·cel tiny root
radi·ces *plural of* radix
radi·cle embryonic plant root; *compare* radical
ra·dii *plural of* radius
ra·dio (*noun, plural* ·dios; *verb* ·dios, ·dio·ing, ·di·oed)
radio·ac·ti·vate
radio·ac·ti·va·tion
radio·ac·tive
radio·ac·tiv·ity
radio·bio·logi·cal
radio·bi·olo·gist
radio·bi·ol·ogy
radio·car·bon
radio·chemi·cal
radio·chem·ist
radio·chem·is·try
radio·com·mu·ni·ca·tion
radio·el·ement
radio·gen·ic
radio·gram
radio·graph
ra·di·og·ra·pher
radio·graph·ic
ra·di·og·ra·phy
radio·iso·tope
radio·iso·top·ic
radio·lar·ian marine organism
radio·lo·ca·tion·al
radio·logi·cal
ra·di·olo·gist
ra·di·ol·ogy
radio·lu·cent
radio·lu·mi·nes·cence
radio·lu·mi·nes·cent
ra·di·oly·sis
ra·di·om·eter
radio·met·ric
ra·di·om·etry
ra·dio·mi·crom·eter
radio·nu·clide
radio·pac·ity (*or* radio-opacity)

radio·paque (*or* radio-opaque) impervious to X-rays
radio·phone
radio·phon·ic
radio·phoni·cal·ly
ra·di·opho·ny
radio·scope
radio·scop·ic
radio·scopi·cal·ly
ra·di·os·co·py
radio·sen·si·tive
radio·sen·si·tiv·ity
radio·sonde meteorological device
radio·tele·gram
radio·tele·graph
radio·tele·graph·ic
radio·tele·graphi·cal·ly
radio·teleg·ra·phy
radio·telem·etry
radio·tele·phone
radio·tele·phon·ic
radio·telepho·ny
radio·tele·type
radio·thera·peu·tic
radio·thera·peu·ti·cal·ly
radio·thera·pist
radio·thera·py
radio·thermy
radio·tox·ic
rad·ish
ra·dium radioactive element
ra·dius (*plural* ·dii *or* ·di·uses)
ra·dix (*plural* ·di·ces *or* ·dixes) maths or biology term
Rad·nor·shire former Welsh county
Ra·dom Polish city
ra·dome radar antenna's housing
ra·don radioactive element
radu·la (*plural* ·lae) zoology term
radu·lar
raff *Dialect* rubbish
raf·fia (*or* raphia)
raf·fi·nate chemistry term
raf·fi·nose sugar
raff·ish
raff·ish·ness
raf·fle
raf·fler
raf·fle·sia plant
raft

rafter

raft·er
rag (rag·ging, ragged)
raga musical term
raga·muf·fin
rag·bag
rage
ragged teased
rag·ged tattered
rag·ged·ness
rag·gedy
raggle-taggle
ragi (or rag·gee, rag·gy) cereal
rag·lan
rag·man (plural ·men)
ra·gout stew
rag·tag
rag·time
rag·weed
rag·worm
rag·wort
raid
raid·er
rail
rail·car
rail·er
rail·head
rail·ing
rail·lery (plural ·leries)
rail·road
rail·way
rail·way·man (plural ·men)
rai·ment
rain
rain·band
rain·bird
rain·bow
rain·check
rain·coat
rain·drop
rain·fall
Rai·ni·er US mountain
raini·ly
raini·ness
rain·maker
rain·making
rain·out radioactive fallout
rain·proof
rain·storm
rain·water
rain·wear
rainy (raini·er, raini·est)
rais·able (or raise·)
raise elevate; compare raze
rais·er
rai·sin

rais·ing
rai·siny
rai·son d'être (plural rai·sons d'être)
raj
ra·jah (or raja)
Ra·ja·sthan Indian state
Raj·kot Indian city
Raj·put (or ·poot) Indian clan
Ra·jya Sa·bha chamber of Indian parliament
rake
rake-off (noun)
rak·er
raki (or ra·kee) drink
rak·ish
rak·ish·ly
rak·ish·ness
rale (or râle) medical term
Ra·leigh US city
ral·len·tan·do musical term
ral·li·er
ral·line ornithology term
ral·ly (verb ·lies, ·ly·ing, ·lied; noun, plural ·lies)
ral·ly·cross
ram (ram·ming, rammed)
Rama Hindu hero
Ramachandra mythological character
Rama·dan (or Rhama·dhan, Rama·zan) period in Muslim year
Ra·mat Gan Israeli city
ram·ble
ram·bler
ram·bling
Ram·bouil·let sheep
ram·bunc·tious Slang boisterous
ram·bu·tan fruit
ram·ekin (or ·equin)
ram·en·ta·ceous
ra·men·tum (plural ·ta) fern scale
ramie (or ramee) fibre
rami·fi·ca·tion
rami·form
rami·fy (·fies, ·fy·ing, ·fied)
Ra·mil·lies Belgian battle site
ram·jet
rammed
ram·mer

ram·ming
ram·mish (or ram·my)
ra·mose (or ·mous) branched
ra·mos·ity
ramp
ram·page
ram·pa·geous
ram·pa·geous·ness
ram·pag·er
ram·pan·cy
ram·pant
ram·part
ram·pi·on plant
Ram·pur Indian city
ram·rod
Rams·gate
ram·shack·le
ram·sons plant
ram·til plant
ramu·lose (or ·lous)
ra·mus (plural rami) biology term
ran
rance marble
ranch
ranch·er
ran·che·ro (plural ·ros) US rancher
Ran·chi Indian city
ran·cid
ran·cid·ness (or ·ity)
ran·cor·ous
ran·cor·ous·ness
ran·cour (US ·cor)
rand
ran·dan boat
randi·ly
randi·ness
ran·dom
ran·domi·za·tion (or ·sa·tion)
ran·dom·ize (or ·ise)
ran·dom·ness
randy (randi·er, randi·est)
rang
range
range·finder
Rang·er senior Guide
rang·er
rangi·ly
rangi·ness
Ran·goon Burmese capital
rangy (rangi·er, rangi·est)
rani (or ra·nee) Indian queen or princess

rank
rank·er
Rankine scale
rank·ing
ran·kle
rank·ness
ran·sack
ran·sack·er
ran·som
ran·som·er
rant
rant·er
rant·ing·ly
ra·nun·cu·la·ceous botany term
ra·nun·cu·lus (*plural* ·luses *or* ·li) plant
rap (rap·ping, rapped) strike; *compare* wrap
ra·pa·cious
ra·pac·ity (*or* ·pa·cious·ness)
Rapa Nui Easter Island
rape
rape·seed
Rapha·el·esque
ra·phe (*plural* ·phae) botany term
raphia *variant spelling of* raffia
ra·phide (*or* ra·phis; *plural* raphi·des) botany term
rap·id
ra·pid·ity (*or* rap·id·ness)
rap·ids
ra·pi·er
rap·ine (*noun*)
rap·ist
rap·pa·ree Irish soldier
rapped *past tense of* rap; *compare* rapt
rap·pee snuff
rap·pel (·pel·ling, ·pelled) mountaineering technique
rap·per
rap·ping
rap·port harmony
rap·por·teur preparer of report
rap·proche·ment
rap·scal·lion
rapt engrossed; *compare* rapped
rap·tor bird of prey
rap·to·rial
rap·ture

rap·tur·ous
rap·tur·ous·ness
rara avis (*plural* ra·rae aves) *Latin* unusual person or thing
rare
rare·bit *variant of* (Welsh) rabbit
rar·efac·tion (*or* ·efi·ca·tion)
rar·efac·tion·al (*or* ·efac·tive)
rar·efi·able
rar·efi·er
rar·efy (·fies, ·fy·ing, ·fied)
rare·ly
rare·ripe *US* ripening early
rar·ing
rar·ity (*plural* ·ities)
Ra·ro·ton·ga Pacific island
ras·bo·ra fish
ras·cal
ras·cal·ity (*plural* ·ities)
ras·cal·ly
rase *variant spelling of* raze
rash
rash·er
rash·ness
Rasht (*or* Resht) Iranian city
ra·so·rial zoology term
rasp
ras·pa·tory (*plural* ·tories) surgical instrument
rasp·berry (*plural* ·berries)
rasp·er
rasp·ing (*or* raspy)
rasse civet; *compare* wrasse
Ras·ta·far·ian (*or* Ras·ta)
ras·ter electronics term
rat (rat·ting, rat·ted)
ra·ta tree
rat·abil·ity (*or* ·able·ness, rate·)
rat·able (*or* rate·)
rat·ably (*or* rate·)
rata·fia (*or* ·fee) liqueur; biscuit
ra·tal ratable value
ra·tan *variant spelling of* rattan
rata·tat-tat (*or* rata·tat)
ra·ta·touille vegetable stew
rat·bag
ratch·et

rate
rate·able *variant spelling of* ratable
ra·tel animal
rate·payer
rat·fink
rat·fish (*plural* ·fish *or* ·fishes)
rathe (*or* rath) *Archaic* blossoming early
ra·ther
rati·fi·able
rati·fi·ca·tion
rati·fi·er
rati·fy (·fies, ·fy·ing, ·fied)
ra·tine (*or* ra·teen, rat·teen, rati·né) cloth
rat·ing
ra·tio (*plural* ·tios)
ra·ti·oci·nate argue logically
ra·ti·oci·na·tion
ra·ti·oci·na·tor
ra·tion
ra·tion·al using reason
ra·tion·ale basis
ra·tion·al·ism
ra·tion·al·ist
ra·tion·al·is·tic
ra·tion·al·is·ti·cal·ly
ra·tion·al·ity (*plural* ·ities)
ra·tion·ali·za·tion (*or* ·sa·tion)
ra·tion·al·ize (*or* ·ise)
ra·tion·al·iz·er (*or* ·is·er)
ra·tion·al·ly
ra·tions
Rat·is·bon Regensburg
rat·ite flightless bird
Rat·lam Indian city
rat·line (*or* ·lin) nautical term
ra·toon (*or* rat·toon) new shoot
rats·bane
rat·tail fish; horse; file
rat·tan (*or* ra·tan)
rat·ted
rat·ter
rat·ti·ly
rat·ti·ness
rat·ting
rat·tish
rat·tle
rattle·box
rat·tler
rattle·snake
rattle·trap

rattling

rat·tling
rat·tly (·tli·er, ·tli·est)
rat·trap
rat·ty (·ti·er, ·ti·est)
rau·cous
rau·cous·ness (or rau·city)
raun·chy (·chi·er, ·chi·est)
rau·wol·fia drug
rav·age
rav·age·ment
rav·ag·er
rave
rav·el (·el·ling, ·elled; US ·el·ing, ·eled)
rave·lin fortification
rav·el·ler (US ·el·er)
rav·el·ly
ra·ven bird
rav·en to plunder
rav·en·er
rav·en·ing
Ra·ven·na Italian city
rav·en·ous
rav·en·ous·ness
rav·er
rave-up
ra·vine
rav·ing
ra·vio·li
rav·ish
rav·ish·er
rav·ish·ing
rav·ish·ment
raw
Ra·wal·pin·di
raw·boned
raw·hide
ra·win·sonde meteorological balloon
raw·ness
ray
ray·less
ray·let
ray·on
raze (or rase) destroy; compare raise
razee ship
raz·er (or ras·) demolisher; compare razor
ra·zoo Austral small sum of money
ra·zor shaver; compare razer
razor·back whale
razor·bill
razor-cut (-cutting, -cut)
razz Slang deride

razz·ma·tazz (or razzle-dazzle)
re concerning
re·ab·sorb
reach
reach·able
reach·er
re·act act in response
re·act act again
re·ac·tance physics term
re·ac·tant
re·ac·tion
re·ac·tion·al
re·ac·tion·ary (plural ·aries)
re·ac·tion·ism
re·ac·ti·vate
re·ac·ti·va·tion
re·ac·tive
re·ac·tiv·ity (or ·tive·ness)
re·ac·tor
read (read·ing, read)
read·abil·ity (or ·able·ness)
read·able
read·ably
re·ad·dress
read·er
read·er·ship
read·ily
readi·ness
Read·ing
re·adjust
re·adjust·able
re·adjust·er
re·adjust·ment
re·admis·sion
re·admit (·admit·ting, ·admit·ted)
re·admit·tance
read-out (noun)
ready (adj readi·er, readi·est; verb readies, ready·ing, readied)
ready-made
ready-mix
ready-to-wear
ready-witted
re·affirm
re·affir·ma·tion (or ·affirm·ance)
re·affor·est (or ·for·est)
re·affor·esta·tion (or ·for·esta·tion)
re·agent
real actual

real (plural reals or rea·les) Spanish coin
real (plural reis) Portuguese coin
re·al·gar mineral
re·align
re·align·ment
re·al·ism
re·al·ist
re·al·is·tic
re·al·is·ti·cal·ly
re·al·ity (plural ·ities)
re·al·iz·able (or ·is·able)
re·al·iz·ably (or ·is·ably)
re·ali·za·tion (or ·sa·tion)
re·al·ize (or ·ise)
re·al·iz·er (or ·is·er)
re·allo·cate
re·allo·ca·tion
re·al·ly
realm
Re·al·po·li·tik German opportunistic politics
re·al·tor US estate agent
re·al·ty real property
ream
ream·er
re·ani·mate
re·ani·ma·tion
reap
reap·able
reap·er
re·appear
re·appear·ance
re·apply (·applies, ·apply·ing, ·applied)
re·appoint
re·appoint·ment
re·appor·tion
re·apprais·al
re·appraise
rear
rear·er
rear-guard
re·arm
rear·most
re·arrange
re·arrange·ment
re·arrang·er
rear·ward (adj)
rear·wards (adv)
rea·son
rea·son·able
rea·son·able·ness (or ·abil·ity)
rea·son·ably
rea·soned

rea·son·er
rea·son·ing
re·as·sem·ble
re·assur·ance
re·assure
re·assur·er
re·assur·ing
rea·ta *variant spelling of* riata
re·awak·en
reb *US* Confederate soldier
re·bar·ba·tive
re·bat·able (*or* ·bate·)
re·bate refund
re·bate (*or* rab·bet) carpentry term
re·bat·er
re·bec (*or* ·beck) musical instrument
re·bel (·bel·ling, ·belled)
re·bel·lion
re·bel·lious
re·bel·lious·ness
re·birth
re·born
re·bound
re·buff
re·build (·build·ing, ·built)
re·buk·able
re·buke
re·buk·er
re·buk·ing·ly
re·bus (*plural* ·buses) picture puzzle
re·but (·but·ting, ·but·ted)
re·but·table
re·but·tal
re·but·ter
rec *Slang* recreation ground
re·cal·ci·trance (*or* ·tran·cy)
re·cal·ci·trant
re·cal·esce
re·ca·les·cence chemistry term
re·ca·les·cent
re·call
re·call·able
re·cant
re·can·ta·tion
re·cant·er
re·cap (·cap·ping, ·capped)
re·capi·tali·za·tion (*or* ·sa·tion)
re·capi·tal·ize (*or* ·ise)
re·ca·pitu·late
re·ca·pitu·la·tion

re·ca·pitu·la·tive (*or* ·tory)
re·cap·tion legal term
re·cap·ture
re·cast (·cast·ing, ·cast)
rec·ce (·ce·ing, ·ced *or* ·ceed) *Slang* reconnoitre; reconnaissance
re·cede withdraw
re-cede restore
re·ceipt
re·ceipt·or
re·ceiv·able
re·ceive
re·ceiv·er
re·ceiv·er·ship
re·cen·sion literary revision
re·cent
re·cent·ness (*or* ·cen·cy)
re·cept psychology term
re·cep·ta·cle
re·cep·tion
re·cep·tion·ist
re·cep·tive
re·cep·tiv·ity (*or* ·tive·ness)
re·cep·tor
re·cess
re·ces·sion
re·ces·sion·al
re·ces·sive
re·ces·sive·ness
Rech·abite teetotaller
re·charge
ré·chauf·fé warmed-up food
re·cher·ché exquisite; rare
re·chris·ten
re·cidi·vism
re·cidi·vist
re·cidi·vis·tic (*or* ·cidi·vous)
(**recieve**) *incorrect spelling of* receive
Re·ci·fe Brazilian port
reci·pe
re·cipi·ence
re·cipi·ent
re·cip·ro·cal
re·cip·ro·cal·ity (*or* ·ness)
re·cip·ro·cal·ly
re·cip·ro·cate
re·cip·ro·ca·tion
re·cip·ro·ca·tive (*or* ·tory)
re·cip·ro·ca·tor
reci·proc·ity
re·ci·sion cancellation
re·cit·able
re·cit·al

reci·ta·tion
reci·ta·tive (*or* ·ta·ti·vo)
re·cite
re·cit·er
reck·less
reck·less·ness
Reck·ling·hau·sen West German city
reck·on
reck·on·er
reck·on·ing
re·claim
re·claim·able
re·claim·ant (*or* ·er)
rec·la·ma·tion
ré·clame acclaim
re·clin·able
rec·li·nate bent backwards
rec·li·na·tion
re·cline
re·clin·er
re·clothe
re·cluse
re·clu·sion
re·clu·sive
rec·og·ni·tion
rec·og·ni·tion·al (*or* ·ni·tive, ·ni·tory)
rec·og·niz·abil·ity (*or* ·nis·)
rec·og·niz·able (*or* ·nis·)
rec·og·niz·ably (*or* ·nis·)
re·cog·ni·zance (*or* ·sance)
rec·og·nize (*or* ·nise)
rec·og·ni·zee (*or* ·see)
rec·og·niz·er (*or* ·nis·er *or in legal contexts* ·ni·zor, ·ni·sor)
re·coil
re·coil·er
re·coil·ing·ly
re·coil·less
rec·ol·lect
rec·ol·lec·tion
rec·ol·lec·tive
re·com·bi·nant
re·com·bi·na·tion
re·com·bine
re·com·mence
re·com·mence·ment
rec·om·mend
rec·om·mend·able
rec·om·men·da·tion
rec·om·menda·tory
rec·om·mend·er

recommit

re·com·mit (·mit·ting, ·mit·ted)
re·com·mit·ment (or ·mit·tal)
rec·om·pen·sable
rec·om·pense
rec·om·pens·er
re·com·pose
re·com·po·si·tion
rec·on·cil·abil·ity (or ·able·ness)
rec·on·cil·able
rec·on·cil·ably
rec·on·cile
rec·on·cile·ment
rec·on·cil·er
rec·on·cilia·tion
rec·on·cilia·tory
rec·on·cil·ing·ly
re·con·dite
re·con·dite·ness
re·con·di·tion
re·con·di·tion·er
re·con·nais·sance (or ·nois·sance)
rec·on·noi·tre (US ·ter)
rec·on·noi·trer (US ·ter·er)
re·con·sid·er
re·con·sid·era·tion
re·con·stitu·ent
re·con·sti·tute
re·con·sti·tut·ed
re·con·sti·tu·tion
re·con·struct
re·con·struc·tible
re·con·struc·tion
re·con·struc·tive (or ·tion·al)
re·con·struc·tor
re·con·vene
re·con·ver·sion
re·con·vert
rec·ord (noun)
re·cord (verb)
re·cord·able
record-changer
re·cord·er
re·cord·ing
record-player
re·count relate
re·count count again
re·count·al
re·coup
re·coup·able
re·coup·ment
re·course

re·cov·er regain
re-cover cover again
re·cov·er·abil·ity
re·cov·er·able
re·cov·er·er
re·cov·ery (plural ·eries)
re-create
re-creation new creation
rec·rea·tion enjoyment
rec·rea·tion·al
re-creator
rec·re·ment waste matter
rec·re·men·tal
re-crimi·nate
re·crimi·na·tion
re·crimi·na·tive (or ·tory)
re·crimi·na·tor
re·cru·desce
re·cru·des·cence
re·cruit
re·cruit·able
re·cruit·er
re·cruit·ment
re·crys·tal·li·za·tion (or ·sa·tion)
re·crys·tal·lize (or ·lise)
rec·ta plural of rectum
rec·tal
rec·tan·gle
rec·tan·gu·lar
rec·tan·gu·lar·ity
rec·ti plural of rectus
rec·ti·fi·able
rec·ti·fi·ca·tion
rec·ti·fi·er
rec·ti·fy (·fies, ·fy·ing, ·fied)
rec·ti·lin·ear (or ·eal)
rec·ti·tude
rec·to (plural ·tos) right-hand page
rec·to·cele hernia
rec·tor
rec·tor·ate
rec·tor·ial
rec·tor·ship
rec·tory (plural ·tories)
rec·trix (plural ·tri·ces) tail feather
rec·tum (plural ·tums or ·ta) part of intestine
rec·tus (plural ·ti) muscle
re·cum·bence (or ·ben·cy)
re·cum·bent
re·cu·per·ate
re·cu·pera·tion
re·cu·pera·tive

376

re·cu·pera·tor
re·cur (·cur·ring, ·curred)
re·cur·rence
re·cur·rent
re·cur·ring·ly
re·cur·sion returning
re·curve
recu·sance (or ·san·cy)
recu·sant insubordinate
re·cy·cle
red (red·der, red·dest) colour; variant spelling of redd
re·dact prepare for publication
re·dac·tion
re·dac·tion·al
re·dac·tor
re·dan fortification
red-blooded
red·breast
red·brick
red·bud tree
red·bug
red·cap
red·coat
red·cur·rant
redd (or red; red·ding, redd or red·ded) Dialect to tidy
red·den
red·dish
Red·ditch
red·dle variant spelling of ruddle
re·deco·rate
re·deem
re·deem·abil·ity
re·deem·able (or re·demp·tible)
re·deem·ably
re·deem·er
re·deem·ing
re·deliv·er
re·deliv·ery
re·demand
re·demand·able
re·demp·tion
re·demp·tion·al (or ·tive, ·tory)
re·demp·tion·er emigrant to America
Re·demp·tor·ist Catholic missionary
re·deploy
re·deploy·ment
re·de·sign

re·devel·op
re·devel·op·er
re·devel·op·ment
red·eye
red-faced
red·fin fish
red·fish (*plural* ·fish *or* ·fishes)
red-handed
red·head
red-headed
red-hot
re·dia (*plural* ·diae) zoology term
re·dial (·dial·ling, ·dialled; *US* ·dial·ing, ·dialed)
Re·dif·fu·sion (*Trademark*)
red·in·gote overcoat
red·in·te·grate renew
red·in·te·gra·tion
red·in·te·gra·tive
re·di·rect
re·di·rec·tion
re·dis·count
re·dis·cov·er
re·dis·cov·ery (*plural* ·eries)
re·dis·trib·ute
re·dis·tri·bu·tion
red·neck
red·ness
redo (re·does, ·do·ing, ·did, ·done)
redo·lence (*or* ·len·cy)
redo·lent
re·dou·ble
re·doubt fortification
re·doubt·able
re·doubt·able·ness
re·doubt·ably
re·dound affect
redo·wa folk dance
re·dox chemistry term
red·poll bird
re·draft
re·draw (·drawing, ·drew, ·drawn)
re·dress put right
re·dress dress again
re·dress·able (*or* ·ible)
re·dress·er (*or* ·dres·sor)
red·root plant
red·shank bird
red·skin
red·start bird
re·duce

re·duc·er
re·duc·ibil·ity
re·duc·ible
re·duc·tase enzyme
re·duc·tio ad ab·sur·dum
re·duc·tion
re·duc·tion·al (*or* ·tive)
re·dun·dan·cy (*plural* ·cies)
re·dun·dant
re·du·pli·cate
re·du·pli·ca·tion
re·du·pli·ca·tive
re·du·vi·id insect
red·ware seaweed
red·wing bird
red·wood
re-echo (-echoes, -echoing, -echoed)
reed
reed·buck (*plural* ·bucks *or* ·buck) antelope
reedi·ness
reed·ing moulding
reed·ling bird
re-educate
re-education
reedy (reedi·er, reedi·est)
reef
reef·er
reek
reek·ing·ly
reeky
reel
reel·able
reel·ably
re-elect
re-election
reel·er
re-em·ploy
re-em·ploy·ment
reen (*or* rean) *Dialect* ditch
re-enact
re-enforce enforce again; *compare* reinforce
re-enforce·ment
re-enforc·er
re-enter
re-entrance
re-entrant
re-entry (*plural* -entries)
reeve (reev·ing, reeved *or* rove) nautical term; bird; medieval official
re-examin·able
re-examina·tion
re-examine

re-examin·er
re-export
re-exporta·tion
re-export·er
ref *Slang* referee
re·face
re·fash·ion
re·fec·tion
re·fec·tory (*plural* ·tories)
re·fer (·fer·ring, ·ferred)
ref·er·able (*or* re·fer·rable)
ref·eree (·eree·ing, ·ereed)
ref·er·ence
ref·er·enc·er
ref·er·en·dum (*plural* ·dums *or* ·da)
ref·er·ent
ref·er·en·tial of a reference; *compare* reverential
re·fer·ral
re·fer·rer
re·fill
re·fill·able
re·fin·able
re·fi·nance
re·fine
re·fined
re·fine·ment
re·fin·er
re·fin·ery (*plural* ·eries)
re·fin·ish
re·fin·ish·er
re·fit (·fit·ting, ·fit·ted)
re·flate
re·fla·tion
re·flect
re·flec·tance
re·flect·ing·ly
re·flec·tion (*or* ·flex·lon)
re·flec·tlon·al (*or* ·flex·ion·al)
re·flec·tive contemplative; able to reflect; *compare* reflexive
re·flec·tive·ness (*or* ·tiv·ity)
re·flec·tor
re·flet lustre
re·flex
re·flex·ion variant spelling of reflection
re·flex·ive grammar term; *compare* reflective
re·flex·ive·ness (*or* ·iv·ity)
re·flex·ol·ogy therapy

reflux

re·flux
re·form improve
re-form form again
re·form·able
Ref·or·ma·tion religious movement
ref·or·ma·tion
re-formation
ref·or·ma·tion·al
re·forma·tive
re·forma·tory (plural ·tories)
re·formed
re·form·er
re·form·ism
re·form·ist
re·fract
re·fract·able
re·frac·tion
re·frac·tion·al
re·frac·tive
re·frac·tive·ness (or ·tiv·ity)
re·frac·tom·eter
re·frac·to·met·ric
re·frac·tom·etry
re·frac·tor
re·frac·to·ri·ly
re·frac·to·ri·ness
re·frac·tory (plural ·tories)
re·frain
re·frain·er
re·frain·ment
re·fran·gibil·ity (or ·gible·ness)
re·fran·gible
re·freeze (·freez·ing, ·froze, ·fro·zen)
re·fresh (or ·fresh·en)
re·fresh·er
re·fresh·ful
re·fresh·ing
re·fresh·ment
re·frig·er·ant
re·frig·er·ate
re·frig·era·tion
re·frig·era·tive (or ·tory)
re·frig·era·tor
re·frin·gen·cy (or ·gence)
re·frin·gent
re·froze
re·fu·el (·el·ling, ·elled; US ·el·ing, ·eled)
ref·uge
refu·gee
refu·gee·ism
re·fu·gium (plural ·gia)
re·ful·gence (or ·gen·cy)
re·ful·gent shining
re·fund give back money
re·fund replace bond issue
re·fund·able
re·fund·er
re·fur·bish
re·fur·bish·ment
re·fus·able
re·fus·al
re·fuse decline
ref·use rubbish
re·fus·er
refu·tabil·ity
refu·table
refu·ta·tion
re·fute
re·fut·er
re·gain
re·gain·able
re·gain·er
re·gal royal
re·gale amuse
re·gale·ment
re·ga·lia
re·gal·ity (plural ·ities)
re·gal·ly
re·gard
re·gard·able
re·gar·dant heraldic term
re·gard·ful
re·gard·ing
re·gard·less
re·gards
re·gat·ta
re·ge·late
re·ge·la·tion physics term
Re·gen·cy historical period
re·gen·cy (plural ·cies) rule by regent
re·gen·er·able
re·gen·era·cy
re·gen·er·ate
re·gen·era·tion
re·gen·era·tive
re·gen·era·tor
Re·gens·burg West German city
re·gent
re·gent·al
re·gent·ship
reg·gae
Reg·gio di Ca·la·bria Italian port
Reg·gio nell'Emilia Italian city
regi·cid·al
regi·cide
re·gime (or ré·gime) administration
regi·men course of treatment
regi·ment
regi·men·tal
regi·men·tals military dress
regi·men·ta·tion
Re·gi·na the queen; Canadian city
re·gion
re·gion·al
re·gion·al·ism
re·gion·al·ist
re·gion·al·ly
reg·is·ter
reg·is·ter·er
reg·is·trable
reg·is·trant
reg·is·trar
reg·is·trar·ship
reg·is·tra·tion
reg·is·tra·tion·al
reg·is·try (plural ·tries)
Re·gius pro·fes·sor
reg·let
reg·nal of a sovereign
reg·nant reigning
rego·lith
re·gorge
rego·sol soil
re·grate buy up for profit
re·grat·er
re·gress
re·gres·sion
re·gres·sive
re·gres·sive·ness
re·gres·sor
re·gret (·gret·ting, ·gret·ted)
re·gret·ful
re·gret·ful·ly
re·gret·ful·ness
re·gret·table
re·gret·tably
re·gret·ter
re·group
re·growth
regu·lable
regu·lar
regu·lar·ity (plural ·ities)
regu·lari·za·tion (or ·sa·tion)
regu·lar·ize (or ·ise)
regu·late

regu·la·tion
regu·la·tive (*or* ·tory)
regu·la·tor
regu·line
regu·lus (*plural* ·luses *or* ·li) impure metal
re·gur·gi·tant
re·gur·gi·tate
re·gur·gi·ta·tion
re·ha·bili·tate
re·ha·bili·ta·tion
re·ha·bili·ta·tive
re·hash
re·hear (·hear·ing, ·heard)
re·hears·al
re·hearse
re·hears·er
re·heat
re·heat·er
re·ho·bo·am wine bottle
re·house
Reich *German* kingdom or republic
Reichs·mark (*plural* ·marks *or* ·mark) currency
Reichs·tag German assembly
rei·fi·ca·tion
rei·fier
rei·fy (·fies, ·fy·ing, ·fied) make real
Rei·gate
reign rule; *compare* rein
re·im·burs·able
re·im·burse
re·im·burse·ment
re·im·burs·er
re·im·port
re·im·por·ta·tion
re·im·pose
re·im·po·si·tion
re·im·pres·sion
Reims (*or* Rheims) French city
rein long strap; *compare* reign
re·incar·nate
re·incar·na·tion
re·incar·na·tion·ist
rein·deer (*plural* ·deer *or* ·deers)
re·inforce strengthen; *compare* re-enforce
re·inforce·ment
re·install
re·in·stal·la·tion

re·instate
re·instate·ment
re·insta·tor
re·insur·ance
re·insure
re·insur·er
re·intro·duce
re·intro·duc·tion
re·invest
re·invest·ment
re·issu·able
re·issue (·issu·ing, ·issued)
re·issu·er
re·it·er·ant
re·it·er·ate
re·it·era·tion
re·it·era·tive
re·ject
re·ject·able
re·ject·er (*or* ·jec·tor)
re·jec·tion
re·jec·tive
re·jig (·jig·ging, ·jigged) re-equip
re·joice
re·joic·er
re·joic·ing
re·join
re·join·der
re·ju·venate (*or* ·venize, ·venise)
re·ju·vena·tion
re·ju·vena·tor
re·ju·venesce
re·ju·venes·cence
re·ju·venes·cent
re·kin·dle
re·la·bel (·bel·ling, ·belled; *US* ·bel·ing, ·beled)
re·lapse
re·laps·er
re·lat·able
re·late
re·lat·ed
re·lat·ed·ness
re·lat·er one that relates; *compare* relator
re·la·tion
re·la·tion·al
re·la·tion·ship
rela·tive
rela·tive·ly
rela·tiv·ism
rela·tiv·ist
rela·tiv·is·tic

rela·tiv·is·ti·cal·ly
rela·tiv·ity
re·la·tor legal term; *compare* relater
re·la·tum (*plural* ·ta) logic term
re·lax
re·lax·able
re·lax·ant
re·laxa·tion
re·lax·ed·ly
re·lax·er
re·lax·in hormone
re·lay convey
re·lay (-laying, -laid) lay again
re·lease
re·leas·er
rel·ega·table
rel·egate
rel·ega·tion
re·lent
re·lent·less
re·lent·less·ness
re·let (·let·ting, ·let)
rel·evance (*or* ·evan·cy)
rel·evant
re·li·abil·ity (*or* ·able·ness)
re·li·able
re·li·ably
re·li·ance
re·li·ant
rel·ic object from past
rel·ict biology term; widow
re·lief
re·liev·able
re·lieve
re·liev·er
re·li·gion
re·li·gion·ism
re·ligi·ose
re·ligi·os·ity
re·li·gious
re·li·gious·ness
re·line
re·lin·quish
re·lin·quish·er
re·lin·quish·ment
reli·quary (*plural* ·quaries)
re·liquiae fossil remains
rel·ish
rel·ish·able
rel·ish·ing·ly
re·liv·able
re·live

reload

re·load
re·lo·cate
re·lo·ca·tion
re·luc·tance (*or* ·tan·cy)
re·luc·tant
rel·uc·tiv·i·ty (*plural* ·ities)
 physics term
rely (re·lies, rely·ing,
 re·lied)
re·made
re·main
re·main·der
remainder·man (*plural*
 ·men) legal term
re·mains
re·make (·mak·ing,
 ·made)
re·mand
re·mand·ment
rema·nence physics term
re·mark
re·mark·able
re·mark·able·ness (*or*
 ·abil·ity)
re·mark·ably
re·mark·er
re·marque (*or* ·mark)
 mark on engraved plate
re·mar·riage
re·mar·ry (·ries, ·ry·ing,
 ·ried)
re·match
re·medi·able
re·medi·ably
re·medial
re·medial·ly
rem·edi·less
rem·edy (*noun, plural*
 ·edies; *verb* ·edies,
 ·edy·ing, ·edied)
re·mem·ber
re·mem·ber·er
re·mem·brance
Re·mem·branc·er
 Exchequer official
re·mex (*plural* remi·ges)
 flight feather
re·mig·ial
re·mind
re·mind·er
re·mind·ful
remi·nisce
remi·nis·cence
remi·nis·cent
re·mise legal term
re·miss negligent

re·mis·sibil·ity (*or*
 ·sible·ness)
re·mis·sible
re·mis·sion (*or* ·mit·tal)
re·mis·sive
re·miss·ness
re·mit (·mit·ting, ·mit·ted)
re·mit·table
re·mit·tal
re·mit·tance payment
re·mit·tee
re·mit·tence (*or* ·ten·cy)
 diminution
re·mit·tent
re·mit·ter (*or* ·tor)
rem·nant
re·mod·el (·el·ling, ·elled)
re·mod·el·ler
re·mon·eti·za·tion (*or*
 ·sa·tion)
re·mon·etize (*or* ·etise)
re·mon·strance
re·mon·strant
re·mon·strate
re·mon·stra·tion
re·mon·stra·tive
re·mon·stra·tor
re·mon·tant
rem·on·toir (*or* ·toire)
 device in clock
remo·ra fish
re·morse
re·morse·ful
re·morse·ful·ly
re·morse·ful·ness
re·morse·less
re·morse·less·ness
re·mote
remote-controlled
re·mote·ness
re·mould (*US* ·mold)
re·mount
re·mov·abil·ity (*or*
 ·able·ness)
re·mov·able
re·mov·ably
re·mov·al
re·mov·al·ist *Austral*
 furniture remover
re·move
re·mov·er
Rem·scheid West German
 city
re·mu·ner·abil·ity
re·mu·ner·able
re·mu·ner·ate
re·mu·nera·tion

re·mu·nera·tive
re·mu·nera·tor
Re·nais·sance historical
 period
re·nais·sance (*or*
 ·nas·cence) revival
re·nal
re·name
re·nas·cent
Ren·ault (*Trademark*)
rend (rend·ing, rent)
rend·er (*noun*)
ren·der (*verb*)
rend·er·able submittable;
 compare rendible
rend·er·er
ren·der·ing
ren·dez·vous (*plural*
 ·vous)
rend·ible tearable; *compare*
 renderable
ren·di·tion
ren·dzi·na soil
ren·egade
re·nege (*or* ·negue)
re·neg·er (*or* ·negu·er)
re·nego·ti·able
re·nego·ti·ate
re·nego·tia·tion
re·new
re·new·abil·ity
re·new·able
re·new·al
re·new·edly
re·new·er
Ren·frew Scottish town
reni·form kidney-shaped
re·nin kidney enzyme;
 compare rennin
Rennes French city
ren·net
ren·nin milk-coagulating
 enzyme; *compare* renin
Reno US city
re·nounce
re·nounce·ment
re·nounc·er
reno·vate
reno·va·tion
reno·va·tive
reno·va·tor
re·nown
re·nowned
re·nown·edly
rens·selaer·ite mineral
rent
rent·abil·ity

rent·able
rent·al
rente *French* type of income
rent·er
rent-free
ren·tier one living on rentes
rent-roll
re·num·ber
re·nun·cia·tion
re·nun·cia·tive (*or* ·tory)
ren·voi legal term
re·oc·cu·pa·tion
re·oc·cu·py (·pies, ·py·ing, ·pied)
re·open
re·or·der
re·or·gani·za·tion (*or* ·sa·tion)
re·or·gan·ize (*or* ·ise)
re·or·gan·iz·er (*or* ·is·er)
rep *Slang* representative; repertory
rep (*or* repp) fabric
re·paint
re·pair
re·pair·able able to be repaired; *compare* reparable
re·pair·er
re·pair·man (*plural* ·men)
re·pand having a wavy margin
repa·rabil·ity
repa·rable able to be made good; *compare* repairable
repa·rably
repa·ra·tion
re·para·tive (*or* ·tory)
rep·ar·tee
rep·ar·ti·tion
re·past
re·pat·ri·ate
re·pat·ria·tion
re·pay (·pay·ing, ·paid)
re·pay·able
re·pay·ment
re·peal
re·peal·able
re·peal·er
re·peat
re·peat·abil·ity
re·peat·able
re·peat·ed
re·peat·ed·ly
re·peat·er
rep·echage contest for runners-up

re·pel (·pel·ling, ·pelled)
re·pel·lence (*or* ·len·cy)
re·pel·lent
re·pel·ler
re·pel·ling·ly
re·pel·ling·ness
re·pent
re·pent·ance
re·pent·ant
re·pent·er
re·peo·ple
re·per·cus·sion
re·per·cus·sive
rep·er·toire
rep·er·to·rial
rep·er·tory (*plural* ·tories)
rep·etend repeated digit
ré·pé·ti·teur opera-singer coach
rep·eti·tion
rep·eti·tious
rep·eti·tious·ness
re·peti·tive
re·peti·tive·ness
re·phrase
re·pine
re·place
re·place·abil·ity
re·place·able
re·place·ment
re·plac·er
re·plan (·plan·ning, ·planned)
re·plant
re·play
re·plen·ish
re·plen·ish·er
re·plen·ish·ment
re·plete
re·plete·ness
re·ple·tion
re·ple·tive
re·plevi·able (*or* ·plev·is·able)
re·plev·in legal term
re·plevy (*verb* ·plevies, ·plevy·ing, ·plev·ied; *noun, plural* ·plevies) legal term
rep·li·ca
rep·li·cate
rep·li·ca·tion
rep·li·ca·tive
re·pli·er
re·ply (*verb* ·plies, ·ply·ing, ·plied; *noun, plural* ·plies)

re·point
re·pone legal term
re·port
re·port·able
re·port·age
re·port·ed·ly
re·port·er
re·pos·al
re·pose
re·pos·ed·ly
re·pose·ful
re·pose·ful·ly
re·pose·ful·ness
re·pos·er
re·pos·it put away
re·po·si·tion
re·posi·tory (*plural* ·tories)
re·pos·sess
re·pos·ses·sion
re·pos·ses·sor
re·pot (·pot·ting, ·pot·ted)
re·pous·sé raised design
repp *variant spelling of* rep
rep·re·hend
rep·re·hend·able
rep·re·hend·er
rep·re·hen·sibil·ity (*or* ·sible·ness)
rep·re·hen·sible
rep·re·hen·sibly
rep·re·hen·sion
rep·re·hen·sive
rep·re·hen·sory
rep·re·sent correspond to
re-present present again
rep·re·sent·abil·ity
rep·re·sent·able
rep·re·sen·ta·tion
rep·re·sen·ta·tion·al
rep·re·sen·ta·tion·al·ism philosophy term
rep·re·sen·ta·tion·al·is·tic
rep·re·senta·tive
rep·re·senta·tive·ness
re·press restrain
re-press press again
re·press·er (*or* ·pres·sor)
re·press·ible
re·pres·sion
re·pres·sive
re·pres·sive·ness
re·priev·able
re·prieve
re·priev·er
rep·ri·mand
rep·ri·mand·er

reprimandingly

rep·ri·mand·ing·ly
re·print
re·print·er
re·pris·al
re·prise
re·pro (*plural* ·pros)
re·proach
re·proach·able
re·proach·ably
re·proach·er
re·proach·ful
re·proach·ful·ly
re·proach·ful·ness
re·proach·ing·ly
rep·ro·ba·cy (*or* ·bate·ness)
rep·ro·bate
rep·ro·bat·er
rep·ro·ba·tion
rep·ro·ba·tive (*or* ·tion·ary)
re·pro·duce
re·pro·duc·er
re·pro·duc·ibil·ity
re·pro·duc·ible
re·pro·duc·tion
re·pro·duc·tive
re·pro·duc·tive·ness
rep·ro·graph·ic
re·prog·ra·phy
re·proof rebuke
re-proof renew texture
re·prov·able
re·prov·al
re·prove
re·prov·er
re·prov·ing·ly
re·pro·vi·sion
rep·tant
rep·tile
rep·til·ian
rep·ti·loid
re·pub·lic
Re·pub·li·can political party
re·pub·li·can of a republic
re·pub·li·can·ism
re·pub·li·cani·za·tion (*or* ·sa·tion)
re·pub·li·can·ize (*or* ·ise)
re·pub·li·ca·tion
re·pub·lish
re·pub·lish·able
re·pub·lish·er
re·pu·di·able
re·pu·di·ate
re·pu·di·a·tion

re·pu·dia·tive
re·pu·dia·tor
re·pu·dia·tory
re·pugn oppose
re·pug·nance (*or* ·nan·cy; *plural* ·nances *or* ·nan·cies)
re·pug·nant
re·pulse
re·puls·er
re·pul·sion
re·pul·sive
re·pul·sive·ness
repu·tabil·ity (*or* ·table·ness)
repu·table
repu·tably
repu·ta·tion
re·pute
re·put·ed
re·put·ed·ly
re·quest
re·quest·er
requi·em
requi·es·cat prayer
re·quir·able
re·quire
re·quire·ment
re·quir·er
requi·site
requi·si·tion
requi·si·tion·ary
requi·si·tion·er (*or* ·ist)
re·quit·able
re·quit·al
re·quite
re·quite·ment
re·quit·er
re·ra·dia·tion
re·read (·read·ing, ·read)
rere·dos
rere·mouse *Dialect* bat
re·route (·route·ing *or* ·rout·ing, ·routed)
re·run (·run·ning, ·ran, ·run)
re·sal·able (*or* ·sale·)
re·sale
re·scind
re·scind·able
re·scind·er
re·scind·ment
re·scis·sible rescindable
re·scis·sion
re·scis·sory able to rescind
re·script
res·cu·able

382

res·cue (·cu·ing, ·cued)
res·cu·er
re·search
re·search·able
re·search·er
re·seat
re·seau (*plural* ·seaux *or* ·seaus) lace mesh
re·sect remove surgically
re·sec·tion
re·sec·tion·al
res·eda plant
re·sell (·sell·ing, ·sold)
re·sem·blance
re·sem·blant
re·sem·ble
re·sem·bler
re·sent
re·sent·ful
re·sent·ful·ly
re·sent·ful·ness
re·sent·ment
re·ser·pine drug
re·serv·able
re·servable
res·er·va·tion
re·serve set aside, etc.
re·serve serve again
re·served
re·serv·ed·ly
re·serv·ed·ness
re·serv·er
re·serv·ist
res·er·voir
re·set (·set·ting, ·set)
re·set·ter
re·set·tle
re·set·tle·ment
re·shape
re·ship (·ship·ping, ·shipped)
re·ship·ment
Resht *variant spelling of* Rasht
re·shuf·fle
re·side
resi·dence
resi·den·cy (*plural* ·cies)
resi·dent
resi·den·tial
resi·den·tiary (*plural* ·tiaries)
resi·dent·ship
re·sid·er
re·sid·ual
re·sidu·ary
resi·due

re·sid·uum (*plural* ·sidua)
re·sign give up
re·sign sign again
res·ig·na·tion
re·signed
re·sign·ed·ly
re·sign·ed·ness
re·sign·er
re·sile spring back
re·sile·ment
re·sili·ence (*or* ·en·cy)
re·sili·ent
res·in gumlike substance; *compare* rosin
res·in·ate
res·in·if·er·ous
res·in·oid
res·in·ous
res·in·ous·ness
resi·pis·cence acknowledgment of error
re·sist
Re·sist·ance French organization
re·sist·ance
re·sist·ant (*or* ·sis·tive)
Re·sis·ten·cia Argentine city
re·sist·er opposer; *compare* resistor
re·sist·ibil·ity (*or* ·ible·ness)
re·sist·ible
re·sist·ibly
re·sist·ing·ly
re·sis·tive·ness (*or* ·tiv·ity)
re·sis·tiv·ity electrical property
re·sist·less
re·sis·tor electrical component; *compare* resister
re·sit (·sit·ting, ·sat)
res·na·tron electronic valve
re·sole
re·sol·ubil·ity (*or* ·uble·ness)
re·sol·uble resolvable
re·soluble able to be dissolved again
reso·lute
reso·lute·ness
reso·lu·tion
reso·lu·tion·er (*or* ·ist)
re·solv·abil·ity (*or* ·able·ness)

re·solv·able
re·solve
re·solved
re·solv·ed·ness
re·sol·vent
re·solv·er
reso·nance
reso·nant
reso·nate
reso·na·tion
reso·na·tor
re·sorb
re·sorb·ent
res·or·cin·ol chemical compound
re·sorp·tion
re·sorp·tive
re·sort holiday town; to use
re-sort sort again
re·sort·er
re·sound echo
re·sound sound again
re·sound
re·sound·ing
re·sound·ing·ly
re·source
re·source·ful
re·source·ful·ly
re·source·ful·ness
re·source·less
re·spect
re·spect·abil·ity (*plural* ·ities)
re·spect·able
re·spect·ably
re·spect·er
re·spect·ful
re·spect·ful·ly
re·spect·ful·ness
re·spect·ing
re·spec·tive
re·spec·tive·ly
re·spir·abil·ity
res·pir·able
res·pi·ra·tion
res·pi·ra·tion·al
res·pi·ra·tor
re·spira·tory
re·spire
res·pite
re·splend·ence (*or* ·en·cy)
re·splend·ent
re·spond
re·spond·ence (*or* ·en·cy)
re·spond·ent legal term
re·spond·er
re·sponse

restrictively

re·spons·er (*or* ·spon·sor) radio receiver
re·spon·sibil·ity (*plural* ·ities)
re·spon·sible
re·spon·sible·ness
re·spon·sibly
re·spon·sive
re·spon·sive·ly
re·spon·sive·ness
re·spon·so·ry (*plural* ·ries)
re·spray
res pu·bli·ca *Latin* the state
rest
re·state
re·state·ment
res·tau·rant
res·tau·ra·teur
rest·er
rest·ful
rest·ful·ly
rest·ful·ness
rest·harrow plant
res·ti·form
rest·ing
res·ti·tu·tion
res·ti·tu·tive (*or* ·tory)
res·tive
res·tive·ly
res·tive·ness
rest·less
rest·less·ly
rest·less·ness
re·stock
re·stor·able
Res·to·ra·tion historical period
res·to·ra·tion
res·to·ra·tion·ism theological belief
re·stora·tive
re·store
re·stor·er
re·strain
re·strain·able
re·strain·ed·ly
re·strain·er
re·strain·ing·ly
re·straint
re·strict
re·strict·ed·ly
re·strict·ed·ness
re·stric·tion
re·stric·tion·ist
re·stric·tive
re·stric·tive·ly

restrictiveness

re·stric·tive·ness
re·struc·ture
re·style
re·sult
re·sult·ant
re·sum·able
re·sume restart
ré·su·mé summary
re·sump·tion
re·sump·tive
re·su·pi·nate botany term
re·su·pi·na·tion
re·sur·face
re·surge
re·sur·gence
re·sur·gent
res·ur·rect
Res·ur·rec·tion rising of Christ
res·ur·rec·tion revival
res·ur·rec·tion·al
res·ur·rec·tion·ary
res·ur·rec·tion·ism
res·ur·rec·tion·ist
re·sus·ci·table
re·sus·ci·tate
re·sus·ci·ta·tion
re·sus·ci·ta·tive
re·sus·ci·ta·tor
ret (ret·ting, ret·ted) soak fibre
re·ta·ble altar screen
re·tail
re·tail·er
re·tain
re·tain·abil·ity (or ·able·ness)
re·tain·able
re·tain·er
re·tain·ment
re·take (·tak·ing, ·took, ·tak·en)
re·tak·er
re·tali·ate
re·talia·tion
re·talia·tive (or ·tory)
re·talia·tor
re·tard
re·tard·ant
re·tard·ate retarded person
re·tar·da·tion (or ·tard·ment)
re·tarda·tive (or ·tory)
re·tard·ed
re·tard·er
re·tard·ing·ly
retch vomit; *compare* wretch
rete (*plural* re·tia) anatomy term
re·tell (·tell·ing, ·told)
re·tene chemical compound
re·ten·tion
re·ten·tive
re·ten·tive·ly
re·ten·tive·ness
re·ten·tiv·ity
re·think (·think·ing, ·thought)
re·tial of a rete
re·ti·ar·ius (*plural* ·arii) gladiator
reti·cence
reti·cent
reti·cle (*or* ·cule) grid; *compare* reticule
re·ticu·lar
re·ticu·late
re·ticu·la·tion
reti·cule woman's bag; *variant of* reticle
re·ticu·lo·cyte
re·ticu·lo·en·do·the·lial anatomy term
re·ticu·lum (*plural* ·la) network; cow's stomach
reti·na (*plural* ·nas *or* ·nae)
reti·nacu·lar
reti·nacu·lum (*plural* ·la) biology term
reti·nal
reti·nene biochemical compound
reti·nite resin
reti·ni·tis
reti·nol biochemical compound
reti·no·scop·ic
reti·no·scopi·cal·ly
reti·nos·co·pist
reti·nos·co·py ophthalmic procedure
reti·nue
reti·nued
re·tire
re·tire·ment
re·tir·er
re·tir·ing
re·tir·ing·ly
re·tool
re·tor·sion reprisal
re·tort
re·tort·er
re·tor·tion retorting
re·touch
re·touch·able
re·touch·er
re·trace
re·trace·able
re·trace·ment
re·tract
re·tract·abil·ity (or ·ibil·)
re·tract·able (or ·ible)
re·trac·tile
re·trac·til·ity
re·trac·tion
re·trac·tive
re·trac·tor
re·train
re·tread (·tread·ing, ·tread·ed) remould
re·tread (-tread·ing, -trod, -trod·den or -trod) tread again
re·treat
re·treat·al
re·trench
re·trench·able
re·trench·ment
re·tri·al
ret·ri·bu·tion
re·tribu·tive (or ·tory)
re·tribu·tive·ly
re·triev·abil·ity
re·triev·able
re·triev·ably
re·triev·al
re·trieve
re·triev·er
ret·ro (*plural* ·ros) *Slang* retrorocket
retro·act
retro·ac·tion
retro·ac·tive
retro·ac·tive·ly
retro·ac·tiv·ity (or ·tive·ness)
retro·cede give back
retro·ces·sion (or ·ced·ence)
retro·ces·sive (or ·ced·ent)
retro·choir space behind altar
retro·fire

retro·fit (·fit·ting, ·fit·ted) equip with extra parts
retro·flex (or ·flexed)
retro·flex·ion (or ·flec·tion)
retro·gra·da·tion
retro·gra·da·tory
retro·grade
retro·gress
retro·gres·sion
retro·gres·sive
retro·gres·sive·ly
retro·ject throw backwards
retro·len·tal anatomy term
retro-operative
retro·pack
retro·rock·et
re·trorse pointing backwards
retro·spect
retro·spec·tion
retro·spec·tive
retro·spec·tive·ly
retro·spec·tive·ness
re·trous·sé
retro·verse
retro·ver·sion
retro·vert·ed
re·try (·tries, ·try·ing, ·tried)
ret·si·na
re·turn
re·turn·abil·ity
re·turn·able
re·turn·er
re·tuse botany term
re·type
re·uni·fi·ca·tion
re·uni·fy (·fies, ·fy·ing, ·fied)
Réu·nion French island
re·union
re·union·ism
re·union·ist
re·union·is·tic
re·unit·able
re·unite
re·unit·er
re·up·hol·ster
re·us·abil·ity (or ·able·ness)
re·us·able
re·use
re·uti·li·za·tion (or ·sa·tion)

re·uti·lize (or ·lise)
rev (rev·ving, revved)
re·val·ori·za·tion (or ·sa·tion)
re·val·or·ize (or ·ise) revalue
re·valua·tion
re·value (·valu·ing, ·valued)
re·vamp
re·vamp·er
re·vamp·ing
re·vanch·ism foreign policy
re·vanch·ist
re·veal
re·veal·abil·ity
re·veal·able
re·veal·ed·ly
re·veal·er
re·veal·ing
re·veal·ing·ly
re·veal·ment
re·veg·etate grow again
re·veg·eta·tion
re·veil·le
rev·el (·el·ling, ·elled; US ·el·ing, ·eled)
rev·ela·tion
rev·ela·tion·al
rev·ela·tion·ist believer in divine revelation
rev·el·ler (US ·el·er)
rev·el·ment
rev·el·rous
rev·el·ry (plural ·ries)
rev·enant
re·venge
re·venge·ful
re·venge·ful·ly
re·veng·er
re·veng·ing·ly
rev·enue
rev·enued
rev·enu·er US revenue officer
re·ver·able
re·ver·ber·ant
re·ver·ber·ate
re·ver·bera·tion
re·ver·bera·tive
re·ver·bera·tor
re·ver·bera·tory (plural ·tories)
re·vere
rev·er·ence

rev·er·enc·er
rev·er·end deserving reverence; clergyman
rev·er·ent feeling reverence
rev·er·en·tial showing reverence; compare referential
rev·er·en·tial·ly
rev·er·ent·ly
rev·er·ent·ness
re·ver·er
rev·erie (or ·ery; plural ·eries)
re·vers (plural ·vers) lapel
re·ver·sal
re·verse
re·vers·er
re·ver·si board game
re·vers·ibil·ity (or ·ible·ness)
re·vers·ible
re·vers·ibly
re·ver·sion
re·ver·sion·ary (or ·al)
re·ver·sion·er legal term
re·vert
re·vert·er
re·vert·ible
re·ver·tive
re·vest restore power
re·vet (·vet·ting, ·vet·ted) face with stones
re·vet·ment
re·view survey; critical opinion; compare revue
re·view·able
re·view·al
re·view·er
re·vile
re·vile·ment
re·vil·er
re·vil·ing·ly
re·vis·abil·ity
re·vis·able
re·vis·al
re·vise
re·vis·er (or ·or)
re·vi·sion
re·vi·sion·al (or ·ary)
re·vi·sion·ism
re·vi·sion·ist
re·vi·so·ry
re·vi·tali·za·tion (or ·sa·tion)
re·vi·tal·ize (or ·ise)

revivability

re·viv·abil·ity
re·viv·able
re·viv·ably
re·viv·al
re·viv·al·ism
re·viv·al·ist
re·viv·al·is·tic
re·vive
re·viv·er
re·vivi·fi·ca·tion
re·vivi·fy (·fies, ·fy·ing, ·fied)
re·viv·ing·ly
revi·vis·cence *revival*
revi·vis·cent
revo·cabil·ity (*or* ·cable·ness)
revo·cable (*or* re·vok·able)
revo·cably
revo·ca·tion
re·voca·tive (*or* revo·ca·tory)
re·voice
re·vok·able *variant spelling of* revocable
re·voke
re·vok·er
re·vok·ing·ly
re·volt
re·volt·er
re·volt·ing
re·volt·ing·ly
revo·lute *botany term*
revo·lu·tion
revo·lu·tion·ari·ly
revo·lu·tion·ary (*plural* ·aries)
revo·lu·tion·ist
revo·lu·tion·ize (*or* ·ise)
revo·lu·tion·iz·er (*or* ·is·er)
re·volv·able
re·volve
re·volv·er
re·volv·ing
re·volv·ing·ly
re·vue *entertainment; compare* review
re·vul·sion
re·vul·sion·ary
re·vul·sive
re·ward
re·ward·able
re·ward·er

re·ward·ing
re·wind (·wind·ing, ·wound)
re·wind·er
re·wir·able
re·wire
re·word
re·work
re·write (·writ·ing, ·wrote, ·writ·ten)
Rex *the king*
Rey·kja·vik *Icelandic capital*
Rey·no·sa *Mexican city*
rhab·do·man·cy *water divining*
rhab·do·man·tist (*or* ·man·cer)
rhab·do·myo·ma (*plural* ·mas *or* ·ma·ta) *tumour*
Rhae·tia *Roman province*
Rhae·tian
Rhae·tic (*or* **Rhe·tic**) *geology term*
rham·na·ceous *botany term*
rhap·sod·ic
rhap·sodi·cal·ly
rhap·so·dist
rhap·so·dis·tic
rhap·so·dize (*or* ·dise)
rhap·so·dy (*plural* ·dies)
rhata·ny (*plural* ·nies) *shrub*
rhea *bird*
rhe·bok (*or* ree·; *plural* ·boks *or* ·bok) *antelope*
Rheims *variant spelling of* **Reims**
Rhe·mish *of Reims*
Rhen·ish *of the Rhine*
rhe·nium *chemical element*
rheo·base *physiology term*
rheo·logi·cal
rhe·olo·gist
rhe·ol·ogy *branch of physics*
rhe·om·eter
rheo·met·ric
rhe·om·etry
rheo·stat
rheo·stat·ic
rheo·tac·tic
rheo·tax·is *biology term*
rheo·trop·ic
rhe·ot·ro·pism *botany term*

rhe·sus
rhe·tor *teacher of rhetoric*
rheto·ric
rhe·tori·cal
rhe·tori·cal·ly
rhe·tori·cian
rheum
rheu·mat·ic
rheu·mati·cal·ly
rheu·mat·ics
rheu·ma·tism
rheu·ma·toid (*or* ·toi·dal)
rheu·ma·tolo·gist
rheu·ma·tol·ogy
rheumy
Rheydt *West German town*
rhigo·lene *anaesthetic*
rhi·nal *of the nose*
Rhine
Rhine·land
Rhineland-Pala·ti·nate *West German state*
rhi·nen·cephal·ic
rhi·nen·cepha·lon (*plural* ·lons *or* ·la) *anatomy term*
rhine·stone
rhi·ni·tis
rhi·no (*plural* ·nos *or* ·no)
rhi·noc·er·os (*plural* ·oses *or* ·os)
rhi·no·cerot·ic
rhi·no·logi·cal
rhi·nolo·gist
rhi·nol·ogy *branch of medicine*
rhi·no·plas·tic
rhi·no·plas·ty *plastic surgery of nose*
rhi·no·scop·ic
rhi·nos·co·py
rhi·zo·bium (*plural* ·bia) *bacterium*
rhi·zo·car·pous *botany term*
rhi·zo·cepha·lan *zoology term*
rhi·zo·cepha·lous
rhi·zo·gen·ic (*or* ·zo·genet·ic, ·zog·enous)
rhi·zoid *rootlike part*
rhi·zoi·dal
rhi·zoma·tous
rhi·zome

rhi·zo·morph
rhi·zo·mor·phous
rhi·zo·pod protozoan
rhi·zopo·dan
rhi·zopo·dous
rhi·zo·pus fungus
rhi·zo·sphere
rhi·zoto·my (*plural* ·mies) surgery
rho Greek letter
rho·da·mine dye
Rhode Is·land
Rhodes
Rho·desia
Rho·desian
Rho·dian of Rhodes
rho·dic
rho·di·nal oil
rho·dium chemical element
rho·do·chro·site mineral
rho·do·den·dron
rhodo·lite gemstone
rhodo·nite mineral
rho·dop·sin retinal pigment
rhomb rhombus; *compare* rhumb
rhom·ben·cepha·lon anatomy term
rhom·bic (*or* ·bi·cal)
rhom·bo·he·dral
rhom·bo·he·dron (*plural* ·drons *or* ·dra)
rhom·boid
rhom·boi·dal
rhom·bus (*plural* ·buses *or* ·bi) geometric figure
rhon·chal (*or* ·chial)
rhon·chus (*plural* ·chi) breathing sound
Rhon·dda
Rhône
rho·ta·cism phonetics term
rho·ta·cist
rho·ta·cis·tic
rho·tic
rhu·barb
rhumb navigation term; *compare* rhomb; rum
rhum·ba *variant spelling of* rumba
rhum·ba·tron
rhyme identical-sounding word; verse; *compare* rime
rhyme·ster (*or* rhym·er)

rhyn·cho·cephal·ian zoology term
rhyo·lite rock
rhyo·lit·ic
rhythm
rhyth·mic (*or* ·mi·cal)
rhyth·mi·cal·ly
rhyth·mic·ity
rhyth·mics
rhy·ton (*plural* ·ta) drinking vessel
ria inlet
rial currency
Ri·al·to Venetian island
ri·al·to (*plural* ·tos) market
ria·ta (*or* rea·ta) lasso
rib (rib·bing, ribbed)
rib·ald
rib·ald·ry
rib·and (*or* rib·band) award
Rib·ble English river
rib·bon
ribbon·fish (*plural* ·fish *or* ·fishes)
ribbon·wood
Ri·bei·rão Pré·to Brazilian city
ri·bo·fla·vin (*or* ·vine) vitamin
ri·bo·nu·clease enzyme
ri·bo·nu·cleic acid
ri·bose sugar
ri·bo·so·mal
ri·bo·some part of cell
rib·wort
rice
rice·bird
ric·er US sieve
ri·cer·ca·re (*or* ri·cer·car; *plural* ·ca·ri *or* ·cars) musical term
rich
riches
Rich·mond
rich·ness
Richter scale
ri·cin protein
ric·ino·leic acid
rick
rick·eti·ness
rick·ets
rick·ett·sia (*plural* ·siae *or* ·sias) pathogenic microorganism

rick·ett·sial
rick·ety
rick·rack (*or* ric·rac) braid
rick·shaw (*or* ·sha)
rico·chet (·chet·ing, ·chet·ed *or* ·chet·ting, ·chet·ted)
ri·cot·ta cheese
ric·tal
ric·tus (*plural* ·tus *or* ·tuses) gape
rid (rid·ding, rid *or* rid·ded)
rid·able (*or* ride·)
rid·dance
rid·den
rid·der
rid·dle
rid·dler
ride (rid·ing, rode, rid·den)
ride·able *variant spelling of* ridable
rid·er
rid·er·less
ridge
ridge·ling (*or* ridg·ling, rid·gel) veterinary term
ridge·pole (*or* ·tree) roof timber
ridge·way
ridgy
ridi·cule
ridi·cul·er
ri·dicu·lous
ri·dicu·lous·ly
ri·dicu·lous·ness
rid·ing
ri·dot·to (*plural* ·tos) musical entertainment
ries·ling wine
Rif (*or* Riff; *plural* Rifs, Riffs, Rifis *or* Rif, Riff) Moroccan people
rife
rife·ness
riff jazz term
rif·fle
rif·fler
riff·raff
ri·fle
rifle·bird
rifle·man (*plural* ·men)
ri·fler
ri·fle·ry

rifling

ri·fling
rift
rig (rig·ging, rigged)
Riga Soviet port
riga·doon (or ri·gau·don) dance
ri·ga·to·ni pasta
rig·ger
rig·ging
right
right·able
right-angled
right·en
right·eous
right·eous·ly
right·eous·ness
right·er
right·ful
right·ful·ly
right·ful·ness
right-hand (adj)
right-handed
right-handed·ness
right-hander
right·ish
right·ism
right·ist
right·ly
right-minded
right-minded·ly
right-minded·ness
right·ness
right·ward (adj)
right·wards (adv)
right-winger
rig·id
ri·gidi·fy (·fy·ing, ·fied)
ri·gid·ity (or ·ness)
rig·id·ly
rig·ma·role (or riga·)
ri·gor medical term; compare rigour
rig·or US spelling of rigour
rig·or·ism
rig·or·ist
rig·or·is·tic
rig·or mor·tis
rig·or·ous
rig·or·ous·ly
rig·or·ous·ness
rig·our (US ·or) harshness; compare rigor
Rig-Veda Hindu poetry
Ri·je·ka Yugoslav port
Rijks·museum

rile
rill stream; channel
rill (or rille) moon valley
ril·let
rim (rim·ming, rimmed)
rime frost; less common spelling of rhyme
rim-fire
Ri·mi·ni
rimmed
rim·ming
ri·mose botany term
ri·mos·ity
rim·rock
rimy (rimi·er, rimi·est)
rind
rinder·pest
ring (ring·ing, rang, rung) produce sound
ring (ring·ing, ringed) circular band; to encircle
ring·bolt
ring·bone
ring·dove
ring-dyke
rin·gent botany term
ring·er
ring·git Malaysian currency
ring·hals (plural ·hals or ·halses) snake
ring·ing
ring·leader
ring·let
ring·master
ring-necked
ring·side
ring·tail animal
ring-tailed
ring·worm
rink
rins·abil·ity (or ·ibil·ity)
rins·able (or ·ible)
rinse
rins·er
Rio de Ja·nei·ro
Rio Grande
Rio Gran·de do Nor·te Brazilian state
Rio Gran·de do Sul Brazilian state
riot
ri·ot·er
ri·ot·ous
ri·ot·ous·ly
ri·ot·ous·ness

rip (rip·ping, ripped)
ri·par·ian of a river bank
rip·cord
ripe
ripe·ly
rip·en
rip·en·er
ripe·ness
ri·pieno (plural ·pienos) musical term
rip-off (noun)
Rip·on
ri·poste (or ·post)
rip·pable
ripped
rip·per
rip·ping
rip·ple
rip·pler
rip·plet
rip·pling·ly
rip·ply
rip-roaring
rip·saw
rip·snorter
rip·tide
rise (ris·ing, rose, ris·en)
ris·er
ris·ibil·ity (plural ·ities)
ris·ible laughable
ris·ibly
ris·ing
risk
risk·er
risk·ily
riski·ness
risky (riski·er, riski·est) involving risk; compare risqué
Ri·sor·gi·men·to political movement
ri·sot·to (plural ·tos)
ris·qué improper; compare risky
Riss glaciation
ris·sole
ri·tar·dan·do musical term
rite
ri·tenu·to musical term
ri·tor·nel·lo musical term
ritu·al
ritu·al·ism
ritu·al·ist
ritu·al·is·tic
ritu·al·is·ti·cal·ly

ritu·al·ize (or ·ise)
ritu·al·ly
ritzy (ritzi·er, ritzi·est)
ri·val (·val·ling, ·valled;
    US ·val·ing ·valed)
ri·val·rous
ri·val·ry (plural ·ries)
rive (riv·ing, rived, rived
    or riv·en)
riv·er
river·bed
river·head
riv·er·ine
River·side US city
river·side
riv·et
riv·et·er
Rivi·era
ri·vi·ère necklace
rivu·let
rix-dollar
Ri·yadh Saudi Arabian
    capital
ri·yal currency
roach nautical term; Slang
    cockroach
roach (plural roach or
    roaches) fish
road
road·bed
road·block
road·holding
road·house
road·roller
road·runner bird
road·stead
road·ster
road·way
road·work sports training
road·works road repairs
road·worthi·ness
road·worthy
roam
roam·er
roan
Roa·noke US island
roar
roar·er
roar·ing
roast
roast·er
roast·ing
rob (rob·bing, robbed)
roba·lo (plural ·los or ·lo)
    fish

rob·and (or rob·bin)
    nautical term
rob·ber
rob·bery (plural ·beries)
rob·bin variant of roband;
    compare robin
rob·bing
robe
rob·in bird; compare robbin
ro·binia tree
ro·ble oak
ro·bor·ant fortifying
ro·bot
ro·bot·ics
ro·bot·ism (or ·bot·ry)
ro·bust
ro·bust·ness
roc legendary bird; compare
    rock
ro·caille decorative work
roc·am·bole plant
Roch·dale Lancashire town
Roch·es·ter Kent city; US
    city
roch·et bishop's surplice
rock hard mass; sway;
    compare roc
rocka·bil·ly
rock-and-roll (or rock-
    'n'- roll)
rock-and-roller (or rock-
    'n'-roller)
rock-bottom (adj)
rock-bound
rock·er
rock·ery (plural ·eries)
rock·et
rock·et·eer (or ·er) rocket
    engineer
rock·et·ry
rock·fish (plural ·fish or
    ·fishes)
Rock·ford US city
Rockies Rocky Mountains
rocki·ly
rocki·ness
rock·like
rock·ling (plural ·lings or
    ·ling) fish
rock·oon exploratory rocket
rock·rose
rock·shaft
rock·weed
rocky (rocki·er, rocki·est)
Rocky Moun·tains

ro·co·co
rod
rode
ro·dent
ro·denti·cide
ro·deo (plural ·deos)
rod·like
rodo·mon·tade boastful
    talk
roe fish ovary or testis; deer;
    compare row
roe·buck (plural ·bucks
    or ·buck)
roent·gen (or rönt·)
    radiation unit
roent·geno·gram (or
    ·graph, rönt·) US X-ray
    photograph
roent·gen·ol·ogy (or
    rönt·) radiology
ro·ga·tion
roga·tory
rog·er
rogue
ro·guery (plural ·gueries)
ro·guish
ro·guish·ly
ro·guish·ness
roil
roily (roili·er, roili·est)
    cloudy
rois·ter
roist·er·er
roist·er·ous
role (or rôle)
role-playing
roll
roll·away mounted on
    rollers
roll·bar
roll·er
rol·lick
rol·lick·ing
rol·lick·some (or ·licky)
roll·ing
roll·mop
roll·neck
roll-on (noun, adj)
Rolls Royce
    (Trademark)
roll-top
roll·way
roly-poly (plural -polies)
Rom (plural Roma) male
    gipsy

Romagna

Ro·ma·gna Italian region
Ro·ma·ic language
ro·maine *US* cos lettuce
ro·ma·ji alphabet
Ro·man of Rome
ro·man type style
Ro·mance language
ro·mance love affair
Roma·nes Romany language
Ro·man·esque art style
Ro·ma·nia (*or* **Ru·**)
Ro·ma·nian (*or* **Ru·**)
Ro·man·ism Roman Catholicism
Ro·man·ist
Ro·man·ize (*or* **·ise**)
Ro·ma·no cheese
Romanov Russian dynasty
Ro·mansch (*or* **·mansh**) Swiss language
ro·man·tic
ro·man·ti·cal·ly
ro·man·ti·cism
ro·man·ti·cist
ro·man·ti·ci·za·tion (*or* **·sa·tion**)
ro·man·ti·cize (*or* **·cise**)
Roma·ny (*or* **Rom·ma·ny**; *plural* **·nies**)
Rome
Romeo (*plural* **Romeos**)
romp
romp·er
romp·ers baby garment
romp·ing·ly
ron·deau (*plural* **·deaux**) poem; *compare* **rondo**
ron·del (*or* **roun·del**) poem
ron·delet poem
ron·do (*plural* **·dos**) musical work; *compare* **rondeau**
ron·dure curvature
rone *Scot* drainpipe
Ro·neo (*Trademark*; *verb* **·neos**, **·neo·ing**, **·neod**; *noun*, *plural* **·neos**)
rong·geng Malay dance
rönt·gen *variant spelling of* **roentgen**
roo *Austral* kangaroo
rood
Roo·depoort South African city

roof (*plural* **roofs**)
roof·ing
roof·less
roof·tree
rook
rook·ery (*plural* **·eries**)
rookie *Slang* new recruit
room
room·er
room·ette *US* rail sleeper
room·ful (*plural* **·fuls**)
roomi·ly
roomi·ness
room·mate
roomy (**roomi·er**, **roomi·est**)
roor·back *US* false report
roose *Dialect* to praise
roost
roost·er
root
root·age
root·er
rooti·ness
root·le
root·less
root·let
root·like
root·stock
rooty
rop·able (*or* **rope·**)
rope
rope·walk
ropi·ly
ropi·ness
ropy (**ropi·er**, **ropi·est**)
roque *US* game
Roque·fort cheese
roque·laure cloak
ro·quet croquet term
ror·qual whale
Rorschach test
rort *Austral* party
rorty
ros·ace rose window
ro·sa·ceous botany term
ro·sani·line (*or* **·lin**) dye
ro·sar·ian rose grower
Ro·sa·rio Argentine port
ro·sar·ium (*plural* **·sar·iums** *or* **·saria**) rose garden
ro·sary (*plural* **·saries**) prayer beads; *compare* **rosery**

Ros·com·mon Irish county
rosé wine
rose
ro·seate
rose·bay plant
rose·bud
rose·bush
rose·fish (*plural* **·fish** *or* **·fishes**)
rose·hip
ro·sel·la parrot
ro·sema·ling decoration
rose·mary (*plural* **·maries**)
ro·seo·la skin rash
ro·seo·lar
rose-root plant
ro·sery (*plural* **·series**) rose garden; *compare* **rosary**
Ro·set·ta Egyptian town
ro·sette
rose·wood
Rosh Ha·sha·nah (*or* **Rosh Ha·sha·na**) Jewish New Year
Ro·si·cru·cian
Ro·si·cru·cian·ism
rosi·ly
ros·in type of resin
Ros·in·ante old horse
rosi·ness
rosin·weed
ros·iny
ros·tel·late (*or* **·lar**)
ros·tel·lum (*plural* **·la**) biology term
ros·ter
Ros·tock East German port
Ros·tov Soviet port
ros·tral (*or* **·trate**, **·trat·ed**)
ros·trum (*plural* **·trums** *or* **·tra**)
rosy (**rosi·er**, **rosi·est**)
rot (**rot·ting**, **rot·ted**)
rota
Ro·ta·me·ter (*Trademark*)
Ro·tar·ian
Ro·ta·ry association
ro·ta·ry (*plural* **·ries**)
ro·tat·able
ro·tate
ro·ta·tion

ro·ta·tion·al
ro·ta·tive
ro·ta·tor
ro·ta·tory
rote
ro·tenone insecticide
rot·gut
Roth·er·ham Yorkshire town
Rothe·say Scottish town
roti bread
ro·ti·fer minute organism
ro·tif·er·al (or ·ous)
ro·tis·serie
rotl (plural rotls or ar·tal) unit of weight
ro·to·gra·vure printing process
ro·tor
Ro·to·rua New Zealand city
rot·ted
rot·ten
rot·ten·ly
rot·ten·ness
rotten·stone
rot·ter
Rot·ter·dam
rot·ting
Rott·wei·ler dog
ro·tund stout; compare orotund
ro·tun·da building
ro·tun·dity (or ·tund·ness)
Rou·balx French city
rou·ble (or ru·)
rouche variant spelling of ruche
roué
Rou·en French city
rouge
rouge et noir card game
rough
rough·age
rough-and-readi·ness
rough-and-ready
rough-and-tumble
rough·cast (cast·ing, ·cast)
rough·cast·er
rough-dry (-dries, -dry·ing, -dried)
rough·en
rough-hew (-hewing, -hewed, -hewed or -hewn)
rough·house
rough·ish
rough·ly
rough·neck
rough·ness
rough·rider
rough·shod
rough-spoken
rou·lade
rou·leau (plural ·leaux or ·leaus)
rou·lette
round
round·about (noun, adj)
round-arm cricketing term
round·ed
round·ed·ness
roun·del
roun·de·lay dance
round·er
round·ers
Round·head Parliamentarian
round·house
round·ish
round·ly
round·ness
round-shouldered
rounds·man (plural ·men)
round·up (noun)
round·worm
roup Dialect auction; bird disease
roupy
rouse
rous·edness
rous·er
rous·ing
rous·ing·ly
Rous·sil·lon former French province
roust
roust·about
rout defeat
route road; course
route·march
rout·er
rou·tine
rou·tine·ly
rou·tin·ism
rou·tin·ist
roux (plural roux) fat-and-flour paste; compare rue
rove

rove-over prosody term
rov·er
row line; propel boat; compare roe
ro·wan
row·boat
row·di·ly
row·di·ness (or ·dy·ism)
row·dy (·di·er, ·di·est)
row·el (·el·ling, ·elled; US ·el·ing, ·eled) spur wheel
row·er
row·lock
roy·al
roy·al·ism
roy·al·ist
roy·al·is·tic
roy·al·ly
roy·al·ty (plural ·ties)
roz·zer Slang policeman
rub (rub·bing, rubbed)
ru·bái·yát Persian verse form
Rub' al Kha·li Arabian desert
ru·ba·to (plural ·tos) musical term
rubbed
rub·ber
rub·ber·ize (or ·ise)
rubber·neck Slang inquisitive person
rubber-stamp (verb)
rub·bery
rub·bing
rub·bish
rub·bishy
rub·ble
rubble·work
rub·bly
rube US country bumpkin
ru·befa·cient
ru·befac·tion
ru·befy (·befies, ·befy·ing, ·befied) make red
ru·bel·la German measles; compare rubeola
ru·bel·lite gemstone
ru·beo·la measles; compare rubella
ru·beo·lar
ru·bes·cence
ru·bes·cent
ru·bia·ceous botany term

Rubicon

Ru·bi·con
ru·bi·cund
ru·bi·cun·dity
ru·bid·ic
ru·bid·ium radioactive element
ru·bigi·nous (*or* ·nose) rust-coloured
ru·bi·ous dark red
ru·bric
ru·bri·cal
ru·bri·cate
ru·bri·ca·tion
ru·bri·ca·tor
ru·bri·cian
ruby (*plural* rubies)
ruche (*or* rouche)
ruch·ing
ruck
ruck·sack
ruck·us (*plural* ·uses) uproar
ruc·tion
ru·da·ceous geology term
rud·beckia plant
rudd (*plural* rudd *or* rudds) fish
rud·der
rudder·head
rudder·less
rudder·post
rud·di·ly
rud·di·ness
rud·dle (*or* rad·, red·) red dye
rud·dock *Dialect* robin
rud·dy (·di·er, ·di·est)
rude
rude·ly
rude·ness (*or* ru·dery)
ru·deral botany term
Ru·des·heim·er wine
ru·di·ment
ru·di·men·ta·ril·ly (*or* ·men·tal·ly)
ru·di·men·ta·ry (*or* ·men·tal)
rud·ish
rue (ru·ing, rued) regret; plant; *compare* roux
rue·ful
rue·ful·ly
rue·ful·ness
ru·fes·cence
ru·fes·cent

ruff raised collar; bird; cards term
ruffe (*or* ruff) fish
ruf·fian
ruf·fi·an·ism
ruf·fi·an·ly
ruf·fle
ruf·fler
ruf·fly
ru·fous
rug
ruga (*plural* rugae) anatomy term
Rug·by Warwickshire town
rug·by football
rug·ged
rug·ged·ize (*or* ·ise) make durable
rug·ged·ly
rug·ged·ness
rug·ger
ru·gose (*or* ·gous, ·gate)
ru·gos·ity
Ruhr West German river
ruin
ru·in·able
ru·ina·tion
ru·in·er
ru·ing
ru·in·ous
Ruis·lip
rul·able
rule
rul·er
rul·ing
rum (rum·mer, rum·mest) spirit; *Slang* odd; *compare* rhumb
Ru·ma·nia variant spelling of Romania
rum·ba (*or* rhum·)
rum·ble
rum·bler
rum·bling·ly
rum·bly
rum·bus·tious
rum·bus·tious·ly
rum·bus·tious·ness
Ru·melia part of Ottoman empire
ru·men (*plural* ·mens *or* ·mi·na) cow's stomach
ru·mi·nant
ru·mi·nate
ru·mi·nat·ing·ly

ru·mi·na·tion
ru·mi·na·tive
ru·mi·na·tor
rum·mage
rum·mag·er
rum·mer drinking glass
rum·my
ru·mour (*US* ·mor)
rump
rum·ple
rum·ply
rum·pus (*plural* ·puses)
run (run·ning, ran, run)
run·about (*noun*)
run·away (*noun*, *adj*)
runch plant
run·ci·nate botany term
Run·corn Cheshire town
run·dle ladder rung
run·down (*noun*)
run·down (*adj*)
rune
rung
ru·nic
run·nel (*or* ·let)
run·ner
runner-up (*plural* runners-up)
run·ning
run·ny (·ni·er, ·ni·est)
Run·ny·mede
run·off (*noun*)
run-of-the-mill
run-on (*noun*)
runt
runti·ness
runt·ish
runt·ish·ness
runty
run-up (*noun*)
run·way
ru·pee
ru·pi·ah (*plural* ·ah *or* ·ahs) Indonesian currency
rup·tur·able
rup·ture
ru·ral
ru·ral·ism
ru·ral·ist (*or* ·ite)
ru·ral·ity
ru·rali·za·tion (*or* ·sa·tion)
ru·ral·ize (*or* ·ise)
ru·ral·ly
Ru·ri·ta·nia fictional kingdom

Ru·ri·ta·nian
Ruse Bulgarian city
ruse
rush
rush·er
rushi·ness
rushy (rushi·er, rushi·est)
rusk
rus·set
rus·set·ish (*or* ·sety)
Rus·sia
Rus·sian
Rus·sian·ize (*or* ·ise)
Russ·ky (*or* ·ki; *plural* ·kies *or* ·kis) *Slang* a Russian
Rus·so·phile (*or* ·phil)
Rus·so·phobe
Rus·so·pho·bia
Rus·so·pho·bic
rust
rus·tic
rus·ti·cal·ly
rus·ti·cate
rus·ti·ca·tion
rus·ti·ca·tor
rus·tic·ity
rusti·ly
rusti·ness
rus·tle
rus·tler
rus·tling·ly
rust·proof
rusty (rusti·er, rusti·est)
rut (rut·ting, rut·ted)
ru·ta·ba·ga *US* swede
ru·ta·ceous botany term
Ru·the·nia Soviet region
Ru·the·nian
ru·then·ic
ru·the·nious
ru·the·nium chemical element
ruth·er·ford unit
ruth·ful
ruth·less
ruth·less·ly
ruth·less·ness
ru·ti·lat·ed mineralogy term
ru·tile mineral
Rut·land former English county
rut·ted
rut·ti·ly
rut·ti·ness
rut·ting
rut·tish of an animal in rut
rut·tish·ness
rut·ty (·ti·er, ·ti·est) full of ruts
Ru·wen·zo·ri African mountains
Rwan·da African republic
Rya·zan Soviet city
Ry·binsk Soviet city
Ry·dal Cumbrian village
rye
rye-brome plant
rye-grass
ryo·kan Japanese inn
ryot Indian peasant

S

Saab (*Trademark*)
Saar European river
Saar·brück·en West German city
Saar·land West German state
Saba West Indian island
Sa·ba·dell Spanish town
saba·dil·la plant
Sa·bah Malaysian state
sa·ba·yon dessert
Sab·ba·tar·ian observer of Sabbath
Sab·bath seventh day
sab·bath (*or* ·bat) rest period
Sab·bati·cal (*or* ·bat·ic) of the Sabbath
sab·bati·cal (*noun*) academic leave
Sa·bel·lian language
sa·ber *US spelling of* sabre
sa·bin unit
Sab·ine
sa·ble (*plural* ·bles *or* ·ble)
sab·ot
sabo·tage
sabo·teur
sa·bra Israeli-born Jew
sa·bre (*US* ·ber)
sa·bre·tache (*US* ·ber·) leather case
sabu·los·ity
sabu·lous (*or* ·lose) gritty
sac biological pouch; *compare* sack
saca·ton grass
sac·cate
sac·cha·rase enzyme
sac·cha·rate chemical compound
sac·cha·ride sugar
sac·chari·fi·ca·tion
sac·chari·fy (·fies, ·fy·ing, ·fied)
sac·cha·rim·eter
sac·cha·rin sugar
sac·cha·rine sugary
sac·cha·rin·ity
sac·cha·ri·za·tion (*or* ·sa·tion)
sac·cha·rize (*or* ·rise)
sac·cha·roid (*or* ·roi·dal) geology term
sac·cha·rom·eter
sac·cha·rose
sac·cu·late (*or* ·lat·ed, ·lar)
sac·cu·la·tion
sac·cule (*or* ·cu·lus)
sac·er·do·tal
sac·er·do·tal·ism
sa·chet
sack bag; to plunder, etc.; *compare* sac
sack·but
sack·cloth
sack·er
sack·ful (*plural* ·fuls)
sack·ing
sack·like
sa·cral of sacred rites or the sacrum

sacrament

sac·ra·ment
sac·ra·men·tal
sac·ra·men·tal·ism
sac·ra·men·tal·ist
sac·ra·men·tal·ity (*or* ·ness)
sac·ra·men·tal·ly
Sac·ra·men·tar·ian theology term
Sac·ra·men·to US port
sa·crar·ium (*plural* ·craria) church sanctuary
sa·cred
sa·cred·ness
sac·ri·fice
sac·ri·fice·able
sac·ri·fic·er
sac·ri·fi·cial
sac·ri·fi·cial·ly
sac·ri·fic·ing
sac·ri·lege
sac·ri·legious
sac·ri·legious·ness
sac·ri·legist
sac·ris·tan (*or* sac·rist)
sac·ris·ty (*plural* ·ties)
sa·cro·ili·ac anatomy term
sac·ro·sanct
sac·ro·sanc·tity (*or* ·sanct·ness)
sa·crum (*plural* ·cra) bone
sad (sad·der, sad·dest)
sad·den
sad·den·ing
sad·der
sad·dest
sad·dle
saddle·back
saddle·bag
saddle·bill
saddle·bow
saddle·cloth
sad·dler
sad·dlery (*plural* ·dleries)
saddle·tree saddle frame
Sad·du·cean
Sad·du·cees
sad·iron heavy iron
sad·ism
sad·ist
sa·dis·tic
sa·dis·ti·cal·ly
sad·ly
sad·ness
sado·maso·chism

sado·maso·chist
sado·maso·chis·tic
Sa·do·wa battle site
sa·fa·ri (*plural* ·ris)
safe
safe-conduct
safe-deposit (*or* safety-)
safe·guard
safe·keeping
safe·light photography term
safe·ness
safe·ty (*plural* ·ties)
saf·fian tanned leather
saf·flow·er
saf·fron
Sa·fid Rud Iranian river
saf·ra·nine (*or* ·nin) dye
saf·role plant oil
sag (sag·ging, sagged)
saga
sa·ga·cious
sa·ga·cious·ness
sa·gac·ity
saga·more American Indian chief
sage
sage·brush shrub
sag·gar (*or* ·ger) pottery-firing box
sagged
sag·ging
Sa·git·ta constellation
sag·it·tal
Sag·it·ta·rian
Sag·it·ta·rius
sag·it·tate (*or* sa·git·ti·form)
sago (*plural* sagos)
Sa·guache US mountain range
sa·gua·ro (*or* ·hua·; *plural* ·ros) cactus
Sa·hap·tin (*or* ·tan; *plural* ·tins, ·tin *or* ·tans, ·tan) American Indian
Sa·ha·ra
Sa·har·an
Sa·ha·ran·pur Indian town
Sa·hel African region
sa·hib (*or* ·heb)
said
Sai·da Lebanese port
sai·ga antelope
Sai·gon
sail

394

sail·able
sail·cloth
sail·er sailing vessel; *compare* sailor
sail·fish (*plural* ·fish *or* ·fishes)
sail·ing
sail·or seaman; *compare* sailer
sail·or·ly
sail·plane
sain·foin plant
saint
St Al·bans
St An·drews
St Aus·tell Cornish town
St Ber·nard dog
saint·ed
Sainte Foy suburb of Quebec
Saint-Émilion wine
St-Étienne French town
St Gall Swiss town
St George's capital of Grenada
St He·le·na Atlantic island
St Hel·ens Merseyside town
St Hel·ier Jersey town
saint·hood
St Ives
St John Canadian city
St John's Canadian city; Antiguan port
St Kil·da Hebridean island
St Kitts West Indian island
St Law·rence North American river
St Leg·er horse race
saint·li·ly
saint·li·ness
St Lou·is US city
St Lu·cia West Indian island
saint·ly
St Mo·ritz Swiss resort
St Paul US city
saint·pau·lia plant
St Pe·ters·burg former name of Leningrad; *compare* Pe·ters·burg
St Vitus's dance
Sai·pan Pacific island
Saïs Egyptian city
saithe fish

Sai·va Hindu
Sa·kai Japanese port
sake benefit
sake (or saké, saki) Japanese liquor; compare saki
sa·ker falcon
Sa·kha·lin (or ·ghal·ien) Soviet island
saki monkey; compare sake
Sak·tas Hindu sect
Sa·kya·mu·ni title of Buddha
sal salt
sa·laam Muslim greeting
sal·able variant spelling (esp. US) of saleable
sa·la·cious
sa·la·cious·ness (or ·lac·ity)
sal·ad
Sala·man·ca Spanish city
sala·man·der amphibian
sala·man·drine
Sa·lam·bria Greek river
sa·la·mi sausage; compare salmi
Sala·mis Greek island
sala·ried
sala·ry (noun, plural ·ries; verb ·ries, ·ry·ing, ·ried)
sal·chow ice-skating jump
sale
sale·abil·ity (or ·able·ness)
sale·able (or esp. US sal·able)
sale·ably
Sa·lem Indian city; US city
sal·ep dried orchid tuber
sal·era·tus sodium bicarbonate
Sa·ler·no Italian port
sale·room
sales·clerk
sales·man (plural ·men)
sales·man·ship
sales·room
sales·woman (plural ·women)
Sal·ford
Sa·lian Frankish
Sal·ic of Frankish law
sal·ic geology term
sali·ca·ceous botany term

sa·li·cin (or ·cine) drug
sa·li·cion·al (or sa·li·cet) organ stop
sali·cor·nia plant
sa·licy·late
sali·cyl·ic acid
sa·li·ence (or ·en·cy)
sa·li·ent
sa·li·en·tian amphibian
sa·li·ent·ness
sa·lif·er·ous containing salt
sali·fi·able
sali·fi·ca·tion
sali·fy (·fies, ·fy·ing, ·fied) mix with salt
sal·im·eter
sali·met·ric
sal·im·etry
sa·lina salt lake
sa·line containing salt
sa·lin·ity
sali·nom·eter
sali·no·met·ric
sali·nom·etry
Salis·bury
Sa·lish (or ·lish·an) language
sa·li·va
sali·vary
sali·vate
sali·va·tion
sal·lee tree
sal·let (or sal·et, sa·lade) helmet
sal·li·er
sal·low
sal·low·ness
sal·ly (noun, plural ·lies; verb ·lies, ·ly·ing, ·lied)
Sal·ly Lunn cake
sal·ma·gun·di salad
sal·ma·naz·ar wine bottle
sal·mi (or ·mis; plural ·mis) French stew; compare salami
salm·on (plural ·ons or ·on)
salmon·berry (plural ·berries)
sal·mo·nel·la (plural ·lae) bacterium
sal·mo·nel·lo·sis
sal·mo·noid
sal·ol chemical compound

sa·lon reception room; beauty establishment, etc.; compare saloon
Sa·lo·ni·ka Greek port
sa·loon large room; pub bar; compare salon
sa·loop aromatic infusion
salo·pette skiing garment
sal·pa (plural ·pas or ·pae) marine organism
sal·pi·con chopped food
sal·pi·form
sal·pi·glos·sis plant
sal·pin·gec·to·my (plural ·mies)
sal·pin·gian
sal·pin·gi·tic
sal·pin·git·is
sal·pinx (plural ·pin·ges) Fallopian tube
sal·si·fy (plural ·fies) vegetable
salt
Sal·ta Argentine city
sal·tant biology term
sal·ta·rel·lo (plural ·li or ·los) dance
sal·ta·tion biology term
sal·ta·to·rial (or sal·ta·tory) adapted for jumping
salt·box
salt·bush
salt·cellar
salt·ed
salt·er
salt·ern saltworks
salt·fish
sal·ti·grade moving by jumps
Sal·til·lo Mexican state
salti·ly
salti·ness
sal·tire (or ·tier) heraldic term
salt·ness
salt·pan
salt·pe·tre (US ·ter)
salt·pot
sal·tus (plural ·tuses) break in sequence
salt·water
salt·works
salt·wort
salty (salti·er, salti·est)
sa·lu·bri·ous

salubriousness

sa·lu·bri·ous·ness (*or* ·bri·ty)
Sa·lu·ki dog
salu·tari·ly
salu·tari·ness
salu·tary beneficial; *compare* salutatory
salu·ta·tion
sa·lu·ta·to·ri·ly
sa·lu·ta·tory welcoming; *compare* salutary
sa·lute
sa·lut·er
sal·vabil·ity (*or* ·vable·ness)
salv·able
sal·vably
Sal·va·dor Brazilian port
Sal·va·do·rian
sal·vage rescue; *compare* selvage
sal·vage·able
sal·vag·er
sal·va·tion
sal·va·tion·al
sal·va·tion·ism
sal·va·tion·ist member of evangelical sect
salve
sal·ver tray; *compare* salvor
sal·ver·form botany term
sal·via plant
sal·vo (*plural* ·vos *or* ·voes) gun fire
sal·vo (*plural* ·vos) provisos
sal vola·ti·le
sal·vor one who salvages; *compare* salver
Sal·ween Asian river
Sal·yut Soviet space station
Salz·burg
Salz·git·ter West German city
sa·ma·ra botany term
Sa·maria Palestinian region
Sa·mari·tan
Sa·mari·tan·ism
sa·mar·ium chemical element
Sa·mar·kand
sa·mar·skite mineral
sam·ba (*plural* ·bas) dance
sam·bar (*or* ·bur; *plural* ·bars, ·bar *or* ·burs, ·bur) deer

same
same·ness
Sa·mian of Samos
sami·sen musical instrument
sam·ite fabric
sa·mi·ti (*or* ·thi) Indian political association
Sam·nite
Sam·ni·um ancient Italian city
Sa·moa Pacific islands
Sa·mo·an
Sa·mos Greek island
Samo·thrace Greek island
samo·var
Samo·yed (*plural* ·yed *or* ·yeds) Siberian people; dog
sam·pan boat
sam·phire plant
sam·ple
sam·pler
sam·pling
Sam·sun Turkish port
samu·rai (*plural* ·rai)
San language group
San'a (*or* Sa·naa) capital of North Yemen
San An·to·nian
San An·to·nio US city
sana·to·rium (*US* sani·ta·; *plural* ·riums *or* ·ria)
san·be·ni·to (*plural* ·tos) garment
San Ber·nar·di·no US city
sanc·ti·fi·able
sanc·ti·fi·ca·tion
sanc·ti·fi·er
sanc·ti·fy (·fies, ·fy·ing, ·fied)
sanc·ti·mo·ni·ous
sanc·ti·mo·ni·ous·ness
sanc·ti·mo·ny
sanc·tion
sanc·tion·able
sanc·tion·er
sanc·ti·tude
sanc·tity (*plural* ·tities)
sanc·tu·ary (*plural* ·aries)
sanc·tum (*plural* ·tums *or* ·ta)
Sanc·tus hymn
sand

396

san·dal
san·dalled (*US* ·daled)
sandal·wood
san·da·rac (*or* ·rach) tree
sand·bag (*verb* ·bag·ging, ·bagged)
sand·bag·ger
sand·bank
sand·blast
sand·blast·er
sand-blind
sand-blindness
sand·box
sand-cast (-casting, -cast)
sand·er
sand·er·ling bird
sand·fly (*plural* ·flies)
sand·grouse
san·dhi (*plural* ·dhis) linguistics term
sand·hog *US* underground worker
Sand·hurst
San Di·ego US port
sandi·ness
sand·man (*plural* ·men)
sand·paper
sand·piper
sand·pit
San·dring·ham
sand·soap
sand·stone
sand·storm
sand·wich
sand·worm
sand·wort
sandy (sandi·er, sandi·est)
sane
sane·ness
San Fernando Trinidadian port
San·for·ize (*or* ·ise; *Trademark*)
San Fran·cis·can
San Fran·cis·co
sang
san·ga·ree spiced drink
sang-froid
San·graal (*or* ·greal) Holy Grail
san·gria drink
san·gui·naria drug; plant
san·gui·nari·ly
san·gui·nari·ness

san·gui·nary
san·guine
san·guine·ness (or
·guin·ity)
san·guin·eous
san·guino·len·cy
san·guino·lent containing
  blood
San·hed·rin Jewish tribunal
sani·cle plant
sa·ni·es discharge from
  wound
sani·tar·ian of sanitation
san·itari·ly
sani·tari·ness
sani·ta·rium US spelling of
  sanatorium
sani·tary
sani·ta·tion
sani·tize (or ·tise)
san·ity
San Jose Californian city
San José Costa Rican
  capital
San Juan Puerto Rican
  capital
sank
San Luis Po·to·sí Mexican
  state
San Mari·nese (or
  Sam·mari·nese)
San Ma·ri·no European
  republic
sann·ya·si Brahman
  mendicant
San Sal·va·dor capital of
  El Salvador
sans-culotte
San Se·bas·tián Spanish
  port
san·ser·if (or sans serif)
san·se·vieria plant
San·skrit
San·skrit·ic
San·skrit·ist
sans ser·if variant spelling of
  san·ser·if
San Ste·fa·no Turkish
  village
San·ta Ana El Salvador
  city; Californian city
San·ta Ca·ta·ri·na
  Brazilian state
San·ta Cla·ra Cuban city
Santa Claus

San·ta Cruz Argentine
  province; Bolivian city
San·ta Cruz de Te·ne·rife
  Tenerife port
San·ta Fe Mexican city;
  Argentine port
san·ta·la·ceous botany
  term
San·ta Maria Brazilian city
San·ta Mar·ta Colombian
  port
San·tan·der Spanish port
San·ta·rém Brazilian port
San·tee US river
San·tia·go Chilean capital
San·tia·go de Cuba Cuban
  port
San·tia·go del Es·te·ro
  Argentine city
San·to Do·min·go capital
  of Dominican Republic
san·toni·ca plant
san·to·nin
San·tos Brazilian port
São Luís (or São Luíz)
  Brazilian port
Saône-et-Loire French
  department
São Pau·lo Brazilian port
São Tomé e Prín·ci·pe
  island republic
sap (sap·ping, sapped)
sapa·jou monkey
sa·pele tree
sa·phe·na (plural ·nae)
  vein
sa·phe·nous
(saphire) incorrect spelling
  of sapphire
sap·id palatable
sa·pid·ity (or ·ness)
sa·pi·ence (or ·en·cy)
  wisdom
sa·pi·ent
sa·pi·en·tial
sap·in·da·ceous botany
  term
sap·less
sap·ling
sapo·dil·la fruit
sapo·na·ceous soapy
sa·poni·fi·able
sa·poni·fi·ca·tion
sa·poni·fi·er
sa·poni·fy (·fies, ·fy·ing,
  ·fied)

sapo·nin plant compound
sapo·nite mineral
sa·po·ta fruit
sapo·ta·ceous
sap·pan·wood (or sap·an·)
sapped
sap·per
Sap·phic verse form; of
  Sappho
sap·phire
sap·phir·ine mineral
sap·pi·ly
sap·pi·ness
sap·ping
Sap·po·ro Japanese city
sap·py (·pi·er, ·pi·est)
sa·prae·mia (US ·pre·)
  blood poisoning
sa·prae·mic (US ·pre·)
sap·robe organism
  inhabiting foul water
sap·ro·bic
sap·ro·gen·ic (or ·ous)
sap·ro·genic·ity
sap·ro·lite geological
  deposit
sap·ro·lit·ic
sap·ro·pel sludge
sap·ro·pel·ic
sa·propha·gous feeding on
  decaying matter
sap·ro·phyte
sap·ro·phyt·ic
sap·ro·phyti·cal·ly
sap·ro·zo·ic
sap·sa·go cheese
sap·sucker bird
sap·wood
sara·band (or ·bande)
Sara·cen
Sara·cen·ic (or ·ceni·cal)
Sara·gos·sa Spanish city
Sa·ra·jevo (or Se·)
  Yugoslav city
sa·ran resin
Sa·ransk Soviet city
Sa·ra·tov Soviet city
Sa·ra·wak Malaysian state
sar·casm
sar·cas·tic
sar·cas·ti·cal·ly
sar·co·carp botany term
sar·coid
sar·co·ma (plural ·mas or
  ·ma·ta)

sarcomatoid

sar·co·ma·toid (*or* ·tous)
sar·co·ma·to·sis
sar·copha·gus (*plural* ·gi *or* ·guses)
sar·cous muscular or fleshy
sard gemstone
sar·dine (*plural* ·dine *or* ·dines)
Sar·dinia
Sar·din·ian
Sar·dis (*or* ·des) ancient Asian city
sar·di·us biblical gemstone
sar·don·ic
sar·doni·cal·ly
sar·doni·cism
sar·don·yx gemstone
Sar·gas·so sea
sar·gas·so (*plural* ·sos) seaweed
sar·gas·sum seaweed
sarge *Slang* sergeant
Sar·go·dha Pakistani city
sari (*plural* ·ris)
Sark Channel island
sar·men·tose (*or* ·tous, ·ta·ceous) botany term
Sar·nia Canadian port
sa·rong
sa·ron·ic
sa·ros cycle of eclipses
sar·panch Indian leader
sar·ra·cenia plant
sar·ra·cenia·ceous
sar·sa·pa·ril·la
sar·sen boulder
Sarthe French department
sar·tor tailor
sar·to·rial
sar·to·rius (*plural* ·to·rii) muscle
Sar·um Salisbury
Sa·sebo Japanese port
sash
Sas·katch·ewan
Sas·ka·toon Canadian city
sas·ka·toon fruit
(sarsparilla) *incorrect spelling of* sarsaparilla
sass *US* insolent
sas·sa·by (*plural* ·bies) antelope
sas·sa·fras tree; oil

Sas·sa·nid (*plural* ·sa·nids *or* ·sani·dae) member of Persian dynasty
Sas·sa·ri Sardinian city
Sas·se·nach
sas·si·ly
sas·si·ness
sas·sy (·si·er, ·si·est) saucy
sas·sy (*or* sass·wood, sas·sy wood) tree
sa·stru·ga (*or* zas·tru·) ridge on snowfield
sat
sa·tai (*or* ·tay) Indonesian food
Satan
sa·tang (*plural* ·tang) Thai coin
sa·tan·ic (*or* ·tani·cal)
sa·tani·cal·ly
sa·tani·cal·ness
Sa·tan·ism
Sa·tan·ist
satch·el
sate
sa·teen imitation satin
sat·el·lite
sat·el·lit·ium astrology term
sa·tem linguistics term
sa·ti·abil·ity (*or* ·able·ness)
sa·ti·able
sa·ti·ably
sa·ti·ate
sa·tia·tion
sa·ti·ety
sat·in
sati·net (*or* ·nette) imitation satin
satin·wood
sat·iny
sat·ire parody; *compare* satyr
sa·tir·ic
sa·tiri·cal (*or* ·tir·ic)
sa·tiri·cal·ly
sa·tiri·cal·ness
sati·rist
sati·ri·za·tion (*or* ·sa·tion)
sati·rize (*or* ·rise)
sati·riz·er (*or* ·ris·er)
sat·is·fac·tion
sat·is·fac·tion·al
sat·is·fac·to·ri·ly
sat·is·fac·to·ri·ness

sat·is·fac·tory
sat·is·fi·able
sat·is·fi·er
sat·is·fy (·fies, ·fy·ing, ·fied)
sat·is·fy·ing·ly
sa·trap Persian governor
sa·trapy (*plural* ·trapies)
Sa·tsu·ma Japanese province; porcelain
sat·su·ma fruit
satu·rabil·ity
satu·rable
satu·rant
satu·rate
satu·rat·ed
satu·rat·er (*or* ·ra·tor)
satu·ra·tion
Sat·ur·day
Sat·urn planet
Saturn Roman god
Sat·ur·na·lia (*plural* ·lia *or* ·lias) ancient festival
Sa·tur·nian
sa·tur·ni·id moth
sat·ur·nine
sat·ur·nine·ness (*or* ·nin·ity)
sat·ur·nism lead poisoning
sat·ya·gra·hi nonviolent protester
sa·tyr goatlike deity; lustful man; *compare* satire
saty·ria·sis (*or* sa·tyro·ma·nia)
sa·tyr·ic (*or* ·tyri·cal)
sa·ty·rid butterfly
sauce
sauce·pan
sau·cer
sau·cer·ful (*plural* ·fuls)
sau·ci·ly
sau·ci·ness
saucy (·ci·er, ·ci·est)
Sau·di (*or* Sau·di Ara·bian)
Sau·di Ara·bia
sau·er·bra·ten beef dish
sau·er·kraut
sau·ger fish
Sault Ste Ma·rie Canadian city; US city
sau·na
saun·ter
saun·ter·er

sau·rian lizard-like
saur·is·chian dinosaur
sau·ro·pod dinosaur
sau·ropo·dous
sau·ry (*plural* ·ries) fish
sau·sage
sau·té (·té·ing *or* ·tée·ing, ·téed)
Sau·ternes wine
Sava (*or* Save) Yugoslav river
sav·able (*or* save·able)
sav·able·ness (*or* save·)
sav·age
sav·age·ness
sav·age·ry (*plural* ·ries)
Sa·vaii Samoan island
sa·van·na (*or* ·nah)
Sa·van·nah US port
sa·vant (*fem* ·vante) learned person
sa·vate form of boxing
save
save·able *variant spelling of* savable
save-all
sav·eloy
sav·er
sav·in (*or* ·ine) shrub
sav·ing
sav·ings
Sav·iour (*US* ·ior) Christ
sav·iour (*US* ·ior) rescuer
Sa·voie French department
savoir-faire
sa·vor·ous
sa·vory (*plural* ·vories) plant; *US spelling of* savoury
sa·vour (*US* ·vor)
sa·vouri·ness (*US* ·vori·)
sa·vour·ing·ly (*US* ·vor·)
sa·voury (*US* ·vory; *plural* ·vouries)
Sa·voy French region
sa·voy cabbage
Sa·voy·ard of Savoy
sav·vy (·vies, ·vy·ing, ·vied)
saw (saw·ing, sawed, sawed *or* sawn)
saw·bill
saw·bones
saw·der flatter
saw·dust

sawed
saw·er one that saws; *compare* sawyer
saw·fish (*plural* ·fish *or* ·fishes)
saw·fly (*plural* ·flies)
saw·horse
saw·ing
saw·mill
sawn
sawn-off
saw·tooth
saw·yer professional timber sawer; *compare* sawer
sax axe
saxe blue
sax·horn
sax·ico·lous (*or* saxa·tile) biology term
saxi·fra·ga·ceous
saxi·frage
Sax·on
Saxo·ny German region
saxo·ny yarn
saxo·phone
saxo·phon·ic
sax·opho·nist
sax·tuba
say (say·ing, said)
say·er
say-so
say·yid (*or* say·id, said) Muslim title
saz·erac cocktail
scab (scab·bing, scabbed)
scab·bard
scab·bi·ly
scab·bi·ness
scab·ble shape roughly
scab·by (·bi·er, ·bi·est)
sca·bies
sca·bi·et·ic
sca·bi·ous scabby; plant
sca·brous scaly; salacious
scad fish
scads *US* many
Sca·fell Pike Cumbrian mountain
scaf·fold
scaf·fold·er
scaf·fold·ing
scag (scag·ging, scagged) *Dialect* to tear
scaglio·la imitation marble
scal·able

scal·able·ness
scal·ably
scal·age *US* price reduction
sca·lar maths term; *compare* scaler
sca·lare fish
sca·lari·form
scala·wag *variant spelling of* scallywag
scald
scald·fish (*plural* ·fish *or* ·fishes)
scale
scale·board veneer
sca·lene maths term
sca·lenus (*plural* ·leni) muscle
scal·er one that scales; *compare* scalar
scales
scali·ness
scall scalp disease
scal·lion small onion
scal·lop
scal·lop·er
scal·ly·wag (*or* scala·wag)
sca·lop·pi·ne (*or* ·ni) Italian dish
scalp
scal·pel
scal·pel·lic
scalp·er
scalp·ing
scaly (scali·er, scali·est)
scam·mo·ni·ate
scam·mo·ny (*plural* ·nies) plant; medicinal resin
scamp
scamp·er
scam·per·er
scam·pi
scamp·ish
scan (scan·ning, scanned)
scan·dal
scan·dali·za·tion (*or* ·sa·tion)
scan·dal·ize (*or* ·ise)
scan·dal·iz·er (*or* ·is·er)
scandal-monger
scan·dal·ous
scan·dal·ous·ness
Scan·da·roon pigeon
scan·dent climbing
Scan·dian Scandinavian
scan·dic of scandium

Scandinavia

Scan·di·na·via
Scan·di·na·vian
scan·dium chemical element
scan·ner
scan·sion
scan·so·rial adapted for climbing
scant
scanti·ly
scanti·ness
scant·ling rafter
scant·ness
scanty (scanti·er, scanti·est)
Scapa Flow naval base
scape biology term
scape·goat
scape·grace
scapho·pod mollusc
scapo·lite mineral
scap·ose botany term
scapu·la (*plural* ·lae *or* ·las) shoulder bone
scapu·lar of scapula; part of monk's habit
scar (scar·ring, scarred)
scar·ab beetle
scara·bae·id (*or* ·baean)
scara·bae·oid (*or* scara·boid)
scara·bae·us (*plural* ·bae·uses *or* ·baei) scarab
Scar·borough
scarce
scarce·ly
scarce·ment wall ledge
scarce·ness
scar·city (*plural* ·cities)
scare
scare·crow
scare·monger
scar·er
scarf (*plural* scarfs *or* scarves)
scarf·skin outer skin layer
scari·fi·ca·tion
scari·fi·ca·tor surgical instrument
scari·fi·er
scari·fy (·fies, ·fy·ing, ·fied)
scar·ing·ly
scari·ous (*or* ·ose) botany term

scar·la·ti·na scarlet fever
scar·la·ti·nal (*or* ·nous)
scar·let
scarp
scarp·er
scary (scari·er, scari·est)
scat (scat·ting, scat·ted)
scathe
scath·ing
scato·logi·cal (*or* ·log·ic)
sca·tolo·gist
sca·tol·ogy study of excrement
scat·ter
scat·ter·able
scatter·brain
scatter·brained
scat·ter·er
scatter-gun
scat·ter·ing
scat·ti·ly
scat·ti·ness
scat·ty (·ti·er, ·ti·est)
scaup duck
scav·enge
scav·en·ger
sce·nario (*plural* ·narios)
sce·nar·ist
scend (*or* send; scend·ing, scend·ed *or* send·ing, sent) nautical term
scene
scen·ery (*plural* ·eries)
sce·nic
sce·ni·cal·ly
sce·nog·raph·er
sce·no·graph·ic (*or* ·graphi·cal)
sce·no·graphi·cal·ly
sce·nog·ra·phy depicting in perspective
scent
scented
scent·less
scep·tic (*US* skep·) doubter; *compare* septic
scep·ti·cal (*US* skep·)
scep·ti·cal·ly (*US* skep·)
scep·ti·cal·ness (*US* skep·)
scep·ti·cism (*US* skep·)
scep·tre (*US* ·ter)
scep·tred (*US* ·tered)
Schaer·beek Belgian city

400

Schaff·hau·sen Swiss town
schap·pe yarn or fabric
schedu·lar
sched·ule
scheel·ite mineral
Scheldt European river
sche·ma (*plural* ·ma·ta)
sche·mat·ic
sche·mati·cal·ly
sche·ma·tism
sche·ma·ti·za·tion (*or* ·sa·tion)
sche·ma·tize (*or* ·tise)
scheme
schem·er
schem·ing
schem·ing·ly
scher·zan·do (*plural* ·di *or* ·dos) musical term
scher·zo (*plural* ·zos *or* ·zi)
schil·ler metallic lustre
schil·ling Austrian currency
schip·per·ke dog
schism
schis·mat·ic (*or* ·mati·cal)
schis·mati·cal·ly
schis·mati·cal·ness
schist rock
schis·tose
schis·tos·ity
schis·to·some blood parasite
schis·to·so·mia·sis
schizo (*plural* schizos)
schizo·carp botany term
schizo·car·pous (*or* ·pic)
schizo·gen·esis biology term
schizo·genet·ic
schi·zogo·ny zoology term
schiz·oid
schizo·my·cete biology term
schizo·my·cet·ic
schizo·my·cetous
schi·zont zoology term
schizo·phre·nia
schizo·phren·ic
schizo·phy·ceous
schizo·phyte
schizo·phyt·ic
schizo·pod crustacean
schizo·thy·mia psychology term

schizo·thy·mic
schle·miel *US* clumsy
schlep (schlep·ping, schlepped) *US* drag
Schleswig-Holstein West German state
schlie·ren physics term
schlie·ric
schlock *US* inferior goods
schmaltz (*or* schmalz) sentimentality
schmaltzy
schmooze *US* chat
schnapps (*or* schnaps)
schnau·zer dog
schnecke (*plural* schneck·en) *US* bread roll
schnit·zel
schnook *US* stupid person
schnor·rer *US* professional beggar
schnoz·zle *Slang* nose
scho·la can·to·rum (*plural* schol·ae can·to·rum) choir
schol·ar
schol·ar·li·ness
schol·ar·ly
schol·ar·ship
scho·las·tic
scho·las·ti·cal
scho·las·ti·cal·ly
scho·las·ti·cate Jesuit's probation period
scho·las·ti·cism
scho·li·ast
scho·li·as·tic
scho·lium (*plural* ·lia) marginal note
school
school·boy
school·child (*plural* ·children)
school·girl
school·fellow
school·house
schoolie *Austral* schoolteacher
school·ing
school·marm
school·marm·ish
school·master
school·master·ship
school·mate

school·mistress
school·mistressy
school·teacher
schoon·er
schorl mineral
schor·la·ceous
schot·tische dance
schuss ski run
schwa (*or* shwa) unstressed vowel sound
Schwa·ben West German region
Schwe·rin East German city
Schwyz Swiss town
sci·aenid (*or* ·aenoid) fish
sci·ama·chy (*or* ·oma·, ski·) fight with imaginary enemy
sci·at·ic
sci·ati·ca
sci·ence
sci·en·ter legal term
sci·en·tial knowledgeable
sci·en·tif·ic
sci·en·tifi·cal·ly
sci·en·tism
sci·en·tist
sci·en·tis·tic
Sci·en·tolo·gist
Sci·en·tol·ogy religious cult
sci-fi
scili·cet that is
scil·la plant
Scil·lo·nian
Scil·ly Isles (*or* Scil·lies)
scimi·tar (*or* simi·)
scin·coid (*or* ·coid·ian) skinklike
scin·tig·ra·phy medical technique
scin·til·la minute amount
scin·til·late
scin·til·lat·ing·ly
scin·til·la·tion
scin·til·la·tor physics term
scin·til·lom·eter
scio·man·cer
scio·man·cy divination through ghosts
scio·man·tic
sci·on descendant; plant graft
scir·rhoid
scir·rhos·ity

scir·rhous (*adj*)
scir·rhus (*plural* ·rhi *or* ·rhuses) cancerous growth; *compare* cirrus
scis·sel waste metal
scis·sile divisible
scis·sion
scis·sor
scis·sors
sciu·rine of squirrels
sciu·roid
sclaff golf stroke
sclaff·er
scle·ra eyeball covering
scle·ren·chy·ma plant tissue
scle·ren·chyma·tous
scle·rite zoology term
scle·rit·ic
scle·ri·tis (*or* ·ro·ti·tis) eye inflammation
scle·ro·der·ma skin disease
scle·ro·der·ma·tous
scle·roid
scle·ro·ma (*plural* ·ma·ta) hard tissue
scle·rom·eter geology apparatus
sclero·met·ric
scle·ro·phyll botany term
scle·ro·pro·tein
scle·ro·sal
scle·rosed
scle·ro·sis (*plural* ·ses)
scle·rot·ic
scle·ro·ti·oid (*or* ·ro·tial)
scle·ro·tium (*plural* ·tia) fungal tissue
scle·roto·my (*plural* ·mies) eye surgery
scle·rous
scoff
scoff·er
scoff·ing·ly
scoff·law *US* habitual lawbreaker
scold
scold·able
scold·er
scold·ing
scold·ing·ly
scol·ecite mineral
sco·lex (*plural* sco·leces *or* scoli·ces) tapeworm head

scoliosis

sco·lio·sis (*or* **·lio·ma**) spinal curvature
sco·li·ot·ic
(scollop) *incorrect spelling of* scallop
scolo·pen·drid centipede
scolo·pen·drine
scom·broid fish
sconce
Scone Scottish site of coronation stone
scone cake
scoop
scoop·er
scoot
scoot·er
scop Anglo-Saxon minstrel
scope
sco·pola·mine drug
sco·po·line sedative
scopu·la (*plural* **·las** *or* **·lae**) zoology term
scopu·late
scor·bu·tic (*or* **·ti·cal**) having scurvy
scorch
scorch·er
scorch·ing
score
score·board
score·card
scor·er
sco·ria (*plural* **·riae**) solid lava; slag
sco·ria·ceous
sco·ri·fi·ca·tion
sco·ri·fi·er
sco·ri·fy (**·fies, ·fy·ing, ·fied**)
scorn
scorn·er
scorn·ful
scorn·ful·ly
scorn·ful·ness
scorn·ing·ly
scor·pae·nid fish
scor·pae·noid
scor·per (*or* **scau·**) chisel
Scor·pi·an of Scorpio
Scor·pio sign of zodiac
scor·pi·oid
Scor·pi·on Scorpius
scor·pi·on arachnid
Scor·pius constellation
Scot

Scotch whisky; eggs; broth; *its use as a synonym for* **Scottish** *or* **Scots** *is regarded as incorrect*
scotch
sco·ter (*plural* **·ters** *or* **·ter**) duck
scot-free
sco·tia architectural moulding
Scot·land
sco·to·ma (*plural* **·mas** *or* **·ma·ta**) visual defect
sco·toma·tous
sco·to·pia night vision
sco·top·ic
Scots
Scots·man (*plural* **·men**)
Scots·woman (*plural* **·women**)
Scot·ti·cism
Scot·tie (*or* **Scot·ty**; *plural* **·ties**)
Scot·tish
scoun·drel
scoun·drel·ly
scour
scour·er
scourge
scourg·er
scourg·ing·ly
Scouse Liverpudlian
scouse *Dialect* stew
scout
scout·er
scout·master
scow boat
scowl
scowl·er
scowl·ing·ly
Scrab·ble (*Trademark*) game
scrab·ble
scrab·bler
scrag (**scrag·ging, scragged**)
scrag·gi·ly
scrag·gi·ness
scrag·gly (**·gli·er, ·gli·est**) untidy
scrag·gy (**·gi·er, ·gi·est**) scrawny
scram (**scram·ming, scrammed**)
scramb (*or* **scram**) *Dialect* scratch

scram·ble
scram·bler
scran *Slang* food
Scran·ton US city
scrap (**scrap·ping, scrapped**)
scrap·able
scrap·book
scrape
scrap·er
scrap·er·board
scrap·heap
scrap·pi·ly
scrap·pi·ness
scrap·py (**·pi·er, ·pi·est**)
scratch
scratch·er
scratchi·ly
scratchi·ness
scratchy (**scratchi·er, scratchi·est**)
scrawl
scrawl·er
scrawly
scrawni·ly
scrawni·ness
scrawny (**scrawni·er, scrawni·est**)
screak *Dialect* screech
scream
scream·er
scree
screech
screech·er
screechy
screed
screen
screen·able
screen·er
screen·ings sifted refuse
screen·play
screw
screw·ball
screw·driver
screw·er
screw·worm
screwy (**screwi·er, screwi·est**)
scrib·al of scribes
scrib·ble
scrib·bler
scrib·bly
scribe
scrib·er tool
scrim fabric

scrim·mage struggle; compare **scrummage**
scrim·mag·er
scrimp
scrimpi·ly
scrimpi·ness
scrimpy (**scrimpi·er, scrimpi·est**)
scrim·shank *Slang* shirk work
scrim·shaw sailors' carving
scrip certificate
script
scrip·to·rium (*plural* ·**riums** *or* ·**ria**)
scrip·tur·al
scrip·ture sacred book
Scrip·tures Bible
script·writer
script·writing
scrive·ner
scro·bicu·late (*or* ·**lat·ed**) biology term
scrod *US* young cod
scrofu·la
scrofu·lous
scroll
scroll·work
scroop *Dialect* creak
scrophu·laria·ceous botany term
scro·tal
scro·tum (*plural* ·**ta** *or* ·**tums**)
scrouge *Dialect* to crowd
scrounge
scroung·er
scrub (**scrub·bing, scrubbed**)
scrub·ber
scrub·bi·ness
scrub·by (·**bi·er,** ·**bi·est**)
scrub·land
scruff
scruffi·ly
scruffi·ness
scruffy (**scruffi·er, scruffi·est**)
scrum (**scrum·ming, scrummed**)
scrum·mage rugby scrum; compare **scrimmage**
scrum·mag·er
scrump *Dialect* steal apples
scrump·tious

scrump·tious·ness
scrumpy cider
scrunch
scru·ple
scru·pu·lous
scru·pu·lous·ness
scru·ta·tor examiner
scru·ti·neer
scru·ti·nize (*or* ·**nise**)
scru·ti·niz·er (*or* ·**nis·er**)
scru·ti·niz·ing·ly (*or* ·**nis·ing·ly**)
scru·ti·ny (*plural* ·**nies**)
scry (**scry·ing, scried**) crystal-gaze
scu·ba
scud (**scud·ding, scud·ded**)
scuff
scuf·fle
scull oar; compare **skull**
scull·er
scul·lery (*plural* ·**leries**)
scul·lion
scul·pin (*plural* ·**pin** *or* ·**pins**) fish
sculp·sit *Latin* sculptured (*inscription on sculpture*)
sculpt
sculp·tor (*fem* ·**tress**)
sculp·tur·al
sculp·tur·al·ly
sculp·ture
sculp·tur·esque
scum (**scum·ming, scummed**)
scum·ble art term
scum·mer
scum·my (·**mi·er,** ·**mi·est**)
scun·cheon part of door jamb; compare **scutcheon**
scunge *Austral* borrow
scungy (**scungi·er, scungi·est**) *Austral* miserable
scun·ner *Scot* aversion
Scun·thorpe
scup fish
scup·per ship's drain
scup·per·nong wine
scurf
scurfy
scur·ril·ity
scur·ril·ous
scur·ri·lous·ness

scur·ry (*verb* ·**ries,** ·**ry·ing,** ·**ried**; *noun, plural* ·**ries**)
scur·vi·ly
scur·vi·ness
scur·vy (·**vi·er,** ·**vi·est**)
scut tail
scu·tage feudal payment
Scu·ta·ri Albanian town; Turkish town
scu·tate biology term
scu·ta·tion
scutch separate fibres
scutch·eon escutcheon; compare **scuncheon**
scute zoology term
scu·tel·lar
scu·tel·late
scu·tel·la·tion
scu·tel·lum (*plural* ·**la**) biology term
scu·ti·form shield-shaped
scut·ter
scut·tle
scuttle·butt ship's drinking fountain
scu·tum (*plural* ·**ta**) zoology term; Roman shield
Scylla sea monster
scy·phi·form cup-shaped
scy·phis·to·ma (*plural* ·**mae** *or* ·**mas**) zoology term
scy·pho·zo·an jellyfish
scy·phus (*plural* ·**phi**) drinking cup
scythe
Scythia ancient Asian region
Scyth·ian
sea
sea·bed
sea·board
sea·borne
sea·coast
sea·cock
sea·dog
sea·farer
sea·faring
sea·food
sea·front
sea·girt
sea·going
sea·gull

seal

seal device; to close; animal; compare seel
seal·able
sea-lane
seal·ant
sealed-beam
seal·er
seal·ery (*plural* ·eries)
sea·lion
seal-point Siamese cat
seal·skin
Sealy·ham terrier
seam
sea·man (*plural* ·men) sailor; compare semen
sea·man·ly
sea·man·ship
sea·mark
seam·er
seami·ness
seam·less
sea·mount underwater mountain
seam·stress (*or* semp·)
seamy (seami·er, seami·est)
Sean·ad Éire·ann Irish parliament
se·ance
sea·plane
sea·port
sea·quake
sear scorch; gun part; compare seer; sere
search
search·able
search·er
search·ing
search·ing·ly
search·light
sear·ing
sea·scape
sea·shell
sea·shore
sea·sick
sea·sick·ness
sea·side
sea·son
sea·son·able
sea·son·able·ness
sea·son·ably
sea·son·al
sea·son·al·ly
sea·son·al·ness
sea·soned·ly

sea·son·er
sea·son·ing
seat
seat·ed
seat·er
seat·ing
Se·at·tle
sea·wan (*or* se·wan) shell beads
sea·ward (*adj*)
sea·wards (*adv*)
sea·ware seaweed
sea·water
sea·way
sea·weed
sea·worthiness
sea·worthy
se·ba·ceous
Se·bas·to·pol variant spelling *of* Sevastopol
se·bif·er·ous biology term
seb·or·rhoea (*US* ·rhea)
seb·or·rhoeal (*or* ·rhoe·ic; *US* ·rheal *or* ·rhe·ic)
se·bum oily secretion
sec short *for* second *or* secant; dry (*of wine*)
se·cant
seca·teurs
sec·co (*plural* ·cos) wall painting
se·cede withdraw
se·ced·er
se·ces·sion
se·ces·sion·al
se·ces·sion·ism
se·ces·sion·ist
se·clude
se·clud·ed sheltered; compare seclusive
se·clud·ed·ness
se·clu·sion
se·clu·sive reclusive; compare secluded
se·clu·sive·ness
sec·ond unit of time; following first
se·cond transfer
sec·ond·ari·ly
sec·ond·ari·ness
sec·ond·ary (*plural* ·aries)
second-best (*adj*)
second-class (*adj*)
se·conde fencing position
sec·ond·er

second-floor (*adj*)
second-hand
se·cond·ment
se·con·do (*plural* ·di) part in piano duet
second-rate
second-rater
second-sighted
se·cre·cy (*plural* ·cies)
se·cret
sec·re·taire writing desk
sec·re·tar·ial
sec·re·tari·at
sec·re·tary (*plural* ·taries)
sec·retary-general (*plural* sec·re·taries-general)
sec·re·tary·ship
se·crete
se·cre·tin hormone
se·cre·tion
se·cre·tion·ary
se·cre·tive
se·cre·tive·ness
se·cre·tory
sect
sec·tar·ian
sec·tari·an·ism
sec·tary (*plural* ·taries) member of sect
sec·tile easily sliced
sec·til·ity
sec·tion
sec·tion·al
sec·tion·al·ism
sec·tion·al·ist
sec·tion·ali·za·tion (*or* ·sa·tion)
sec·tion·al·ize (*or* ·ise)
sec·tion·al·ly
sec·tor
sec·tor·al
sec·to·rial
secu·lar
secu·lar·ism
secu·lar·ist
secu·lar·is·tic
secu·lar·ity (*plural* ·ities)
secu·lari·za·tion (*or* ·sa·tion)
secu·lar·ize (*or* ·ise)
secu·lar·iz·er (*or* ·is·er)
se·cund botany term
sec·un·dine botany term
sec·un·dines (*plural*) afterbirth

se·cur·able
se·cure
se·cure·ment
se·cure·ness
se·cur·er
se·cu·ri·ty (*plural* ·rities)
se·dan
se·date
se·date·ness
se·da·tion
seda·tive
sed·en·tari·ly
sed·en·tari·ness
sed·en·tary
Se·der Jewish meal
sedge
Sedge·moor English battle site
sedgy
se·di·lia (*sing.* ·le) church seats
sedi·ment
sedi·men·tari·ly
sedi·men·tary (*or* ·tal)
sedi·men·ta·tion
sedi·men·tol·ogy
sedi·men·tous
se·di·tion
se·di·tion·ary (*plural* ·aries)
se·di·tious
se·di·tious·ness
se·duce
se·duc·er
se·duc·ible (*or* ·duce·able)
se·duc·ing·ly
se·duc·tion
se·duc·tive
se·duc·tive·ness
se·duc·tress
se·du·lity
sedu·lous
sedu·lous·ness
se·dum plant
see (see·ing, saw, seen)
see·able
See·beck philately term
seed
seed·bed
seed·cake
seed·case
seed·er
seedi·ly
seedi·ness
seed·less

seed·ling
seedy (seedi·er, seedi·est)
see·ing
seek (seek·ing, sought)
seek·er
seel falconry term; *compare* seal
seem
seem·er
seem·ing
seem·ing·ly
seem·li·ness
seem·ly (·li·er, ·li·est)
seen
seep
seep·age
seer prophet; *compare* sear; sere
seer·sucker
see·saw
seethe
seeth·ing·ly
seg·ment
seg·men·tal
seg·men·tary
seg·men·ta·tion
se·gno (*plural* ·gni) musical term
Se·go·via Spanish town
seg·re·gable
seg·re·gate
seg·re·ga·tion
seg·re·ga·tion·al
seg·re·ga·tion·ist
seg·re·ga·tive
seg·re·ga·tor
se·gui·dil·la dance
seiche water movement
(seige) *incorrect spelling of* siege
sei·gneur
sei·gneu·rial
sei·gneury (*plural* ·gneuries)
sei·gnior·age
Seine French river
seine fishing net
Seine-et-Marne French department
Seine-Maritime French department
Seine-Saint-Denis French department
seis·able

seise legal term; *compare* seize
seis·er
sei·sin legal term
seism earthquake
seis·mic (*or* ·mal, ·mi·cal)
seis·mi·cal·ly
seis·mism
seis·mo·gram
seis·mo·graph
seis·mog·ra·pher
seis·mo·graph·ic
seis·mog·ra·phy
seis·mo·log·ic (*or* ·logi·cal)
seis·molo·gist
seis·mol·ogy
seis·mo·scope
seis·mo·scop·ic
(seive) *incorrect spelling of* sieve
seiz·able
seize grasp; *compare* seise
seiz·er
seiz·ing
sei·zure
se·jant (*or* ·jeant) heraldic term
Sejm Polish legislature
Sek·on·di Ghanaian port
se·la·chian zoology term
sela·gi·nel·la moss
Se·lan·gor Malaysian state
sel·dom
se·lect
se·lec·tion
se·lec·tive
se·lec·tive·ness
se·lec·tiv·ity
se·lect·ness
se·lec·tor
sel·enate
se·lenic
se·leni·ous (*or* ·lenous)
sel·enite mineral
se·lenium chemical element
se·leno·graph
se·lenog·ra·pher (*or* ·phist)
se·leno·graph·ic (*or* ·graphi·cal)
se·leno·graphi·cal·ly
se·lenog·ra·phy mapping moon's surface
se·lenolo·gist

selenology

se·lenol·ogy study of moon
se·leno·mor·phol·ogy
Se·leu·cid (*plural* ·cids *or* ·cidae) member of Hellenistic dynasty
self (*plural* selves)
self-abasement
self-abnega·tion
self-absorbed
self-absorp·tion
self-abuse
self-action
self-actuali·za·tion
self-addressed
self-aggran·dize·ment
self-analy·sis
self-analyti·cal
self-anneal·ing
self-annihi·la·tion
self-appoint·ed
self-assertion
self-assertive
self-assurance
self-assured
self-aware
self-aware·ness
self-cater·ing
self-centred (*US* -centered)
self-centred·ness (*US* -centered·ness)
self-coloured (*US* -colored)
self-concept
self-confessed
self-confidence
self-confident
self-conscious
self-conscious·ness
self-contained
self-contra·dic·tion
self-contra·dic·tory
self-control
self-controlled
self-deception (*or* -deceit)
self-deceptive
self-defence
self-denial
self-denying
self-discipline
self-disciplined
self-educat·ed
self-employed
self-efface·ment

self-effacing
self-esteem
self-evident
self-evidence
self-feeder
self-fertile
self-fertili·za·tion (*or* ·sa·tion)
self-fertilized (*or* -fertilised)
self-govern·ment
self·heal plant
self-help
self·hood
self-image
self-import·ance
self-import·ant
self-imposed
self-improve·ment
self-induced
self-induct·ance
self-induction
self-inductive
self-indulgence
self-indulgent
self-inflict·ed
self-inflic·tion
self-interest
self·ish
self·ish·ness
self-justifi·ca·tion
self-justify·ing
self-knowledge
self·less
self·less·ness
self-liquidat·ing
self-loading
self-made
self-opin·ion·at·ed (*or* -opinioned)
self-pity
self-pitying
self-pollinat·ed
self-pollina·tion
self-portrait
self-possessed
self-posses·sion
self-preser·va·tion
self-propelled
self-protec·tion
self-raising
self-regard
self-reliance
self-reliant
self-reproach

self-reproach·ful
self-respect
self-respect·ing
self-restraint
self-righteous
self-righteous·ness
self-rule
self-sacrifice
self-sacrific·ing
self·same
self-satisfac·tion
self-satisfied
self-sealing
self-seeker
self-seeking
self-service
self-starter
self-styled
self-sufficiency
self-sufficient (*or* -suffic·ing)
self-taught
self-willed
self-winding
Sel·juk (*or* ·ju·kian) member of Turkish dynasty
Sel·kirk former Scottish county
sell (sell·ing, sold)
sell·er
selling-plater type of racehorse
Sel·lo·tape (*Trademark*)
sell·out (*noun*)
Selt·zer mineral water
sel·va forest
sel·vage (*or* ·vedge) edge of fabric; *compare* salvage
selves *plural of* self
se·man·tic
se·man·ti·cal·ly
se·man·ti·cist
se·man·tics
sema·phore
sema·phor·ic (*or* ·phori·cal)
sema·phori·cal·ly
Se·ma·rang (*or* Sa·) Indonesian port
se·ma·sio·logi·cal
se·ma·sio·logi·cal·ly
se·ma·si·olo·gist
se·ma·siol·ogy semantics
se·mat·ic zoology term

sema·tol·ogy semantics
sem·blance
semé (or se·mée) heraldry term
sem·eme linguistics term
se·men ejaculated fluid; compare seaman
se·mes·ter
se·mes·tral
semi (plural semis)
semi·an·nual
semi·an·nu·al·ly
semi·aquat·ic
semi·ar·id
semi·arid·ity
semi·auto·mat·ic
semi·auto·mati·cal·ly
Semi-Bantu African language
semi·bold printing term
semi·breve
semi·cen·ten·nial
semi·cir·cle
semi·cir·cu·lar
semi·co·lon
semi·con·duc·tion
semi·con·duc·tor
semi·con·scious
semi·con·scious·ness
semi·de·tached
semi·di·am·eter
semi·di·ur·nal
semi·dome
semi·el·lip·ti·cal
semi·fi·nal
semi·fi·nal·ist
semi·flu·id
semi·flu·id·ic
semi·flu·id·ity
semi·lit·er·ate
semi·lu·nar
semi·month·ly
semi·nal
semi·nal·ity
semi·nal·ly
semi·nar
semi·nar·ial
semi·nar·ian student at seminary
semi·nary (plural ·naries)
semi·nif·er·ous transporting semen
Semi·nole (plural ·noles or ·nole) American Indian

se·mi·ol·ogy (or ·mei·)
se·mi·ot·ic (or ·mei·)
se·mi·ot·ics (or ·mei·) study of symbols
Se·mi·pa·la·tinsk Soviet city
semi·pal·mate (or ·mat·ed) zoology term
semi·para·sit·ic
semi·para·sit·ism
semi·per·meabil·ity
semi·per·meable
semi·porce·lain
semi·precious
semi·pro (plural ·pros)
semi·pro·fes·sion·al
semi·qua·ver
Se·mira·mis legendary queen
semi·rig·id
semi·skilled
semi·sol·id
Se·mite (or Shem·ite)
Se·mit·ic (or She·)
Se·mit·ics study of Semitic languages
Semi·tist
semi·ton·al·ly
semi·tone
semi·ton·ic
semi·trail·er
semi·tropi·cal
semi·trop·ics
semi·vit·reous
semi·vo·cal (or ·cal·ic)
semi·vow·el
semi·week·ly
semi·year·ly
semo·li·na
sem·per fi·de·lis Latin always faithful
sem·per pa·ra·tus Latin always prepared
sem·pi·ter·nal everlasting
sem·pi·ter·nity
sem·pli·ce musical term
sem·pre musical term
semp·stress variant spelling of seamstress
sen (plural sen) Oriental currency
sen·ar·mon·tite mineral
sen·ary of six
Sen·ate senate of USA, ancient Rome, etc.

sen·ate legislative body
sena·tor
sena·to·rial
send (send·ing, sent)
send·able
Sen·dai Japanese city
sen·dal fabric
send·er
send·off
send-up (noun)
Sen·eca (plural ·ecas or ·eca) American Indian
sen·ega plant
Sen·egal
Sen·ega·lese
Sen·egam·bia African region
se·nes·cence
se·nes·cent
sen·eschal medieval steward
sen·hor (plural ·hors or ·hores) Portuguese man; Mr
sen·hora Portuguese woman; Mrs
sen·hor·ita Portuguese young woman; Miss
se·nile
se·nil·ity
sen·ior
sen·ior·ity (plural ·ities)
Sen·lac battle site
sen·na
Sen·nar Sudanese region
sen·net fanfare
sen·nit braided cordage
se·ñor (plural ·ñors or ·ñores) Spanish man; Mr
se·ño·ra Spanish woman; Mrs
se·ño·ri·ta Spanish young woman; Miss
sen·sate (·sat·ed)
sen·sa·tion
sen·sa·tion·al
sen·sa·tion·al·ly
sen·sa·tion·al·ism
sen·sa·tion·al·ist
sen·sa·tion·al·is·tic
sense
sense·less
sense·less·ness
sen·si·bilia what can be sensed

sensibility

sen·sibil·ity (*plural* ·ities)
sen·sible
sen·sible·ness
sen·sibly
sen·sil·lum (*plural* ·la) zoology term
sen·si·tive
sen·si·tive·ness
sen·si·tiv·ity (*plural* ·ities)
sen·si·ti·za·tion (*or* ·sa·tion)
sen·si·tize (*or* ·tise)
sen·si·tiz·er (*or* ·tis·er)
sen·si·tom·eter
sen·si·tom·etry
sen·sor sensing device; *compare* censor
sen·so·ri·mo·tor (*or* sen·so·mo·tor) physiology term
sen·so·rium area of brain
sen·so·ry (*or* ·rial)
sen·sual gratifying the senses; *compare* censual; sensuous
sen·su·al·ism
sen·su·al·ist
sen·su·al·ity (*plural* ·ities)
sen·su·al·ly
sen·su·al·ness
sen·su·ous pleasing to the senses; *compare* sensual
sen·su·ous·ness
sent
sen·tence
sen·ten·tial
sen·ten·tious
sen·ten·tious·ness
sen·tience (*or* ·tien·cy)
sen·ti·ent
sen·ti·ment
sen·ti·ment·al
sen·ti·men·tal·ism
sen·ti·men·tal·ist
sen·ti·men·tal·ity (*plural* ·ities)
sen·ti·men·tali·za·tion (*or* ·sa·tion)
sen·ti·men·tal·ize (*or* ·ise)
sen·ti·men·tal·ly
sen·ti·nel
sen·try (*plural* ·tries)
Se·nus·si (*or* ·nu·si; *plural* ·sis) member of Muslim sect

sen·za musical term
Seoul capital of South Korea
sep·al
se·palled (*or* ·pal·ous)
se·pa·loid (*or* ·line)
sepa·rabil·ity (*or* ·rable·ness)
sepa·rable
sepa·rate
sepa·rate·ness
sepa·ra·tion
sepa·ra·tism
sepa·ra·tist (*or* ·ra·tion·ist)
sepa·ra·tis·tic
sepa·ra·tive
sepa·ra·tive·ness
sepa·ra·tor
sepa·ra·trix (*plural* ·trices) oblique stroke
Se·phar·di (*plural* ·dim) Iberian Jew
Se·phar·dic
se·pia
se·pio·lite mineral
se·poy Indian soldier
sep·sis
sept clan
sep·ta *plural of* septum
sep·tal
sep·tar·ian
sep·tar·ium (*plural* ·ia) geology term
sep·tate
sep·ta·va·lent *variant spelling of* septivalent
Sep·tem·ber
Sep·tem·brist French revolutionary
sep·te·nary (*plural* ·naries)
sep·ten·nial
sep·ten·nium (*plural* ·niums *or* ·nia)
sep·tet (*or* ·tette)
sep·tic putrefying; *compare* sceptic
sep·ti·cae·mia (*US* ·cemia)
sep·ti·cae·mic (*US* ·cemic)
sep·ti·cal·ly
sep·ti·cid·al botany term
sep·tic·ity
sep·tif·ra·gal botany term

sep·ti·lat·er·al
sep·til·lion (*plural* ·lion *or* ·lions) 10^{42}
sep·til·lionth
sep·time fencing position
sep·ti·va·lent (*or* ·ta·)
sep·tua·genar·ian
Sep·tua·gesi·ma third Sunday before Lent
Sep·tua·gint Greek Old Testament
sep·tum (*plural* ·ta)
sep·tu·ple
sep·tup·let
sep·tu·pli·cate
se·pul·chral
se·pul·chral·ly
sep·ul·chre (*US* ·cher)
sep·ul·ture burial
se·qua·cious in sequence
se·quac·ity
se·quel
se·quela (*plural* ·quelae) medical term
se·quence
se·quenc·er electronic device
se·quent
se·quen·tial
se·quen·ti·al·ity
se·quen·tial·ly
se·ques·ter
se·ques·trable
se·ques·tral
se·ques·trant
se·ques·trate
se·ques·tra·tion
se·ques·tra·tor
se·ques·trum (*plural* ·tra) medical term
se·quin
se·quined
se·quoia
ser (*or* seer) Indian unit
sera *plural of* serum
sé·rac ice pinnacle
se·ra·glio (*plural* ·glios)
se·rail harem
Se·rang Indonesian island
ser·aph (*plural* ·aphs *or* ·aphim) angel; *compare* serif
se·raph·ic (*or* ·raphi·cal)
Sera·pis Egyptian god
Serb a Serbian

Ser·bia Yugoslav republic
Ser·bian
Serbo-Croat (*or* **-Croa·tian**) language
ser·dab chamber in Egyptian tomb
sere ecology term; *compare* **cere; sear; seer**
sere (*or* **sear**) withered; *compare* **cere; sear; seer**
se·rein tropical rain
ser·enade
ser·enad·er
se·rena·ta cantata
ser·en·dip·ity
se·rene
se·rene·ness
se·ren·ity (*plural* **·ities**)
serf medieval peasant; *compare* **surf**
serf·dom (*or* **·hood**)
serge fabric; *compare* **surge**
ser·gean·cy (*or* **·geant·ship**)
ser·geant
Ser·gi·pe Brazilian state
se·rial story in instalments; in series; *compare* **cereal**
se·rial·ism
se·riali·za·tion (*or* **·sa·tion**)
se·rial·ize (*or* **·ise**)
se·rial·ly
se·ri·ate
se·ria·tim in a series
se·ri·ceous
seri·cin protein in silk
seri·cul·tur·al
seri·cul·ture silkworm rearing
seri·cul·tur·ist
seri·ema bird
se·ries (*plural* **·ries**)
series-wound electrical term
ser·if (*or* **·iph**) printing term; *compare* **seraph**
seri·graph silk-screen print
se·rig·ra·phy
ser·in bird
ser·ine amino acid
se·rin·ga rubber tree; *compare* **syringa**
se·rio·com·ic (*or* **·comi·cal**)
se·rio·comi·cal·ly
se·ri·ous grave; *compare* **serous**
se·ri·ous·ly
se·ri·ous·ness
ser·jeant at law
ser·mon
ser·mon·ic
ser·moni·cal
ser·mon·ize (*or* **·ise**)
ser·mon·iz·er (*or* **·is·er**)
se·ro·log·ic (*or* **·logi·cal**)
se·rolo·gist
se·rol·ogy study of serums
se·ro·sa membrane
se·rosi·ty (*or* **·rous·ness**)
se·roti·nal (*or* **·nous**)
sero·tine bat
sero·to·nin biochemical compound
se·rous of serum; *compare* **serious**
ser·ow antelope
ser·pent
ser·pen·tine
ser·pigi·nous
ser·pi·go skin disease
ser·pu·lid worm
ser·ra·nid (*or* **·noid**) fish
ser·rate
ser·rat·ed
ser·ra·tion (*or* **·ture**)
ser·ried
ser·ri·form
ser·ru·late (*or* **·lat·ed**)
ser·ru·la·tion notch
ser·tu·lar·ian zoology term
se·rum (*plural* **·rums** *or* **·ra**)
serv·able (*or* **serve·**)
ser·val (*plural* **·vals** *or* **·val**) animal
serv·ant
serve
serv·er
serv·ery (*plural* **·eries**)
ser·vice
ser·vice·abil·ity (*or* **·able·ness**)
ser·vice·able
ser·vice·ably
ser·vice·berry (*plural* **·berries**)
ser·vice·man (*plural* **·men**)
ser·vi·ette

settlement

ser·vile
ser·vil·ity (*or* **·vile·ness**)
serv·ing
ser·vi·tor
ser·vi·tude
ser·vo (*plural* **·vos**)
ser·vo·mechani·cal
ser·vo·mecha·nism
ser·vo·mo·tor
sesa·me
sesa·moid bone
Se·so·tho language
ses·qui·al·te·ra organ stop
ses·qui·car·bon·ate
ses·qui·cen·ten·nial
ses·qui·ox·ide
ses·qui·peda·lian (*or* **·quip·edal**) using long words
ses·qui·peda·li·an·ism
ses·sile
ses·sil·ity
ses·sion meeting; *compare* **cession**
ses·sion·al
ses·sion·al·ly
ses·terce (*or* **·ter·tius**; *plural* **·terces** *or* **·tia**) Roman coin
ses·ter·tium (*plural* **·tia**) Roman coin
ses·tet six-line verse; *compare* **sextet**
ses·ti·na verse form
Ses·tos ancient Turkish town
set (**set·ting, set**)
seta (*plural* **setae**) small bristle
se·ta·ceous
se·tal
set·back
se·ti·form
set·line
set-off printing term
se·tose bristly
set·screw
sett (*or* **set**) paving slab; badger's den
set·tee
set·ter
set·ting
set·tle
set·tle·able
set·tle·ment

settler

set·tler (*or in legal contexts* ·tlor)
set-to (*noun, plural* -tos)
set-up (*noun*)
Se·van Soviet lake
Se·vas·to·pol (*or* ·bas·) Soviet port
sev·en
sev·en·fold
sev·en·teen
sev·en·teenth
sev·enth
sev·en·ti·eth
sev·en·ty (*plural* ·ties)
sev·er
sev·er·able
sev·er·al
sev·er·al·ly
sev·er·al·ty (*plural* ·ties) separateness
sev·er·ance
se·vere
se·vere·ness
se·ver·ity (*plural* ·ities)
Sev·ern British river
Se·ville Spanish port
Sèvres porcelain
sew (sew·ing, sewed, sewn *or* sewed) to stitch; *compare* sow
sew·age waste matter
sew·er sewage drain; one who sews; *compare* suer
sew·er·age system of sewers
sew·ing
sewn
sex
sexa·genar·ian
sex·ag·enary (*plural* ·enaries)
Sexa·gesi·ma second Sunday before Lent
sexa·gesi·mal of 60
sex·cen·te·nary (*plural* ·naries)
sex·en·nial
sexi·ly
sexi·ness
sex·ism
sex·ist
sexi·va·lent (*or* sexa·)
sex·less
sex·less·ness
sex·olo·gist
sex·ol·ogy
sex·par·tite
sex·pot
sext canonical hour
sex·tant
sex·tet (*or* ·tette) group of six; *compare* sestet
sex·tile
sex·til·lion (*plural* ·lions *or* ·lion) 10^{36}
sex·til·lionth
sex·to·deci·mo (*plural* ·mos)
sex·ton
sex·tu·ple
sex·tup·let
sex·tu·pli·cate
sex·ual
sexu·al·ity
sex·ual·ly
sexy (sexi·er, sexi·est)
Sey·chelles
Sfax Tunisian port
sfor·zan·do (*or* ·za·to) musical term
sfu·ma·to art term
sgraf·fi·to (*plural* ·ti) art term
shab·bi·ly
shab·bi·ness
shab·by (·bi·er, ·bi·est)
shack
shack·le
shack·ler
shad (*plural* shad *or* shads) fish
shad·bush
shad·dock fruit
shade
shadi·ly
shadi·ness
shad·ing
sha·doof (*or* ·duf) water-raising device
shad·ow
shadow-box
shadow-boxing
shad·ow·er
shad·ow·graph
shad·owi·ness
shad·owy
Shadrach biblical character
shady (shadi·er, shadi·est)
shaft
shaft·ing

410

shag (shag·ging, shagged)
shag·bark (*or* shell·bark)
shag·gi·ly
shag·gi·ness
shag·gy (·gi·er, ·gi·est)
sha·green
shah
shah·dom
Shah·ja·han·pur Indian city
shak·able (*or* shake·)
shake (shak·ing, shook, shak·en)
shake·down (*noun*)
shak·er
Shak·ers US sect
Shake·spear·ean (*or* ·ian)
Shake·spear·ea·na
shake-up (*noun*)
Shakh·ty Soviet city
shaki·ly
shaki·ness
shako (*or* shacko; *plural* shakos *or* shackos) military headdress
shaky (shaki·er, shaki·est)
shale
shall (should)
shal·loon fabric
shal·lop boat
shal·lot
shal·low
shal·low·ness
sha·lom Jewish greeting; *compare* slalom
shalt
shaly
sham (sham·ming, shammed)
sham·able (*or* shame·)
sham·an priest
sham·an·ism
Sha·mash Assyrian god
sham·ble
sham·bles
sham·bol·ic
shame
shame·faced
shame·faced·ness
shame·ful
shame·ful·ly
shame·ful·ness
shame·less
shame·less·ness

sham·mer
sham·my (*plural* **·mies**) leather
sham·poo (*noun, plural* **·poos**; *verb* **·poos,** **·poo·ing, ·pooed**)
sham·poo·er
sham·rock
Shan (*plural* **Shans** or **Shan**) Mongoloid people
shan·dry·dan cart
shan·dy (*plural* **·dies**)
shan·dy·gaff *US* shandy
Shang Chinese dynasty
Shang·hai Chinese port
shang·hai (**·hais, ·hai·ing, ·haied**) kidnap
Shangri-la
shank
Shan·non Irish river
shan·ny (*plural* **·nies**) fish
Shan·si Chinese province
shan't shall not
Shan·tung Chinese province
shan·tung silk
shan·ty (*plural* **·ties**) hut
shan·ty (*or* **shan·tey, chan·ty;** *US* **chan·tey;** *plural* **·ties** *or* **·teys**) sea song
shanty·town
shap·able (*or* **shape·**)
shape
shape·less
shape·less·ness
shape·li·ness
shape·ly (**·li·er, ·li·est**)
shap·er
shar·able (*or* **share·**)
shard (*or* **sherd**)
share
share·crop (**·crop·ping, ·cropped**)
share·crop·per
share·holder
share-out (*noun*)
shar·er
sha·ria (*or* **she·**) Islamic doctrines
shark
shark·skin
Sha·ron Israeli plain
sharp
sharp·en
sharp·en·er

sharp·er
sharp-eyed
sharp·ish
sharp·ness
sharp-set
sharp·shooter
sharp-sighted
sharp-sighted·ness
sharp-tongued
sharp-witted
sharp-witted·ness
shash·lik (*or* **·lick**) kebab
shat·ter
shat·ter·er
shat·ter·ing·ly
shatter·proof
shav·able (*or* **shave·**)
shave (**shav·ing, shaved, shaved** *or* **shav·en**)
shav·er
Sha·vian of G. B. Shaw
shav·ing
shawl
shawm musical instrument
Shaw·nee (*plural* **·nees** *or* **·nee**) American Indian
she
shea tree
shead·ing Manx region
sheaf (*plural* **sheaves**)
shear (**shear·ing, sheared, sheared** *or* **shorn**) cut; deformation; *compare* **sheer**
shear·er
shear·legs *variant spelling of* **sheerlegs**
shear·ling
shears
shear·water bird
sheat·fish (*plural* **·fish** *or* **·fishes**)
sheath (*noun; plural* **sheaths**)
sheath·bill
sheathe (*verb*)
sheath·ing
sheave bind in sheaves; grooved wheel
She·ba ancient kingdom
she·bang *Slang* situation
she·been (*or* **·bean**) illegal drinking place
She·chem ancient Jordanian town

shelterer

shed (**shed·ding, shed**)
she'd she had; she would
shed·able (*or* **shed·dable**)
shed·der
sheen
sheeny
sheep (*plural* **sheep**)
sheep·cote
sheep-dip
sheep·dog
sheep·fold
sheep·ish
sheep·ish·ness
sheep·shank knot
sheeps·head (*plural* **·head** *or* **·heads**) fish
sheep·shearer
sheep·shearing
sheep·skin
sheep·walk grazing land
sheer steep; transparent; absolutely; deviate; *compare* **shear**
sheer·legs (*or* **shear·**) lifting device
Sheer·ness English port
sheer·ness
sheet
sheet·ing
Shef·field
sheik (*or* **sheikh**)
sheik·dom (*or* **sheikh·**)
shei·la *Austral* girl
shek·el
shel·duck (*or* **·drake;** *plural* **·ducks, ·duck** *or* **·drakes, ·drake**)
shelf (*plural* **shelves**)
shell
she'll she will
shel·lac (**·lack·ing, ·lacked**)
shell·back experienced sailor
shell·fire
shell·fish (*plural* **·fish** *or* **·fishes**)
shell-less
shell-like
shell·proof
shell-shocked
Shel·ta tinkers' language
shel·ter
shel·ter·er

sheltie

shel·tie (*or* ·ty; *plural* ·ties) dog; pony
shelve (*verb*)
shelv·er
shelv·ing
She·ma Jewish doctrine
she·moz·zle
Shen·an·do·ah US river; national park
she·nani·gan
Shen·si Chinese province
Shen·yang Chinese city
She·ol abode of the dead
shep·herd
shep·herd·ess
shepherd's-purse
Shep·pey (Isle of)
sher·ardi·za·tion (*or* ·sa·tion)
sher·ard·ize (*or* ·ise)
Sheraton furniture
sher·bet
Sher·brooke Canadian city
sherd variant spelling of shard
she·rif (*or* ·reef) Muslim ruler
sher·iff officer
Sher·pa (*plural* ·pas *or* ·pa)
sher·ry (*plural* ·ries)
sher·wa·ni Indian coat
she's she is
Shet·land
shew·bread (*or* show·) biblical bread
Shi·ah Muslim sect
shiai judo contest
shib·bo·leth
shick·er *Austral* alcoholic drink
shied
shield
shield·er
shiel·ing *Scot* hut; pasture
shi·er (*adj*) variant spelling of shyer
shi·est variant spelling of shyest
shift
shift·er
shifti·ly
shifti·ness
shift·ing·ly
shift·less

shift·less·ness
shifty (shifti·er, shifti·est)
shi·gel·la bacterium
Shih·chia·chuang (*or* ·kia·chwang) Chinese city
shih-tzu dog
Shi·ism
Shi·ite adherent of Shiah
shi·kar (·kar·ring, ·karred) hunt game
shi·ka·ri (*or* ·ree; *plural* ·ris *or* ·rees) hunter
Shi·ko·ku Japanese island
shil·lelagh (*or* shil·la·la) Irish cudgel
shil·ling
Shil·long Indian city
shilly·shalli·er
shilly·shally (·shallies, ·shally·ing, ·shallied)
Shi·loh biblical city
shi·ly less common spelling of shyly
shim (shim·ming, shimmed)
shim·mer
shim·mer·ing·ly
shim·mery
shim·my (*noun, plural* ·mies; *verb* ·mies, ·my·ing, ·mied) dance
Shi·mo·no·seki Japanese port
shin (shin·ning, shinned)
shin·bone
shin·dig (*or* ·dy; *plural* ·digs *or* ·dies)
shine (shin·ing, shone)
shin·er
shin·gle
shin·gler
shin·gles
shin·gly
shini·ness
Shin·to Japanese religion
Shin·to·ism
Shin·to·ist
shin·ty (*US* ·ny; *plural* ·ties *or* ·nies) hockey
shiny (shini·er, shini·est)
ship (ship·ping, shipped)
ship·able
ship·board
ship·builder
ship·building

412

ship·load
ship·master (*or* ·man; *plural* ·masters *or* ·men)
ship·mate
ship·ment
ship·owner
ship·per
ship·ping
ship-rigged
ship·shape
ship·way
ship·worm
ship·wreck
ship·wright
ship·yard
shi·ra·lee *Austral* swagman's bundle
Shi·raz Iranian city
Shi·ré African river
shire
shirk
shirk·er
shirr
shirr·ing
shirt
shirti·ly
shirti·ness
shirt·ing
shirt·sleeve
shirt-tail
shirt·waister
shirty (shirti·er, shirti·est)
shit (shit·ting, shit·ted *or* shit)
shit·tah (*plural* ·tim *or* ·tahs) biblical tree
Shit·tim biblical place
shit·ty
Shiva variant spelling of Siva
shive cork
shiv·er
shiv·er·er
shiv·er·ing·ly
shiv·ery
Shi·zuo·ka Japanese city
Shluh (*plural* Shluhs *or* Shluh) African people
Shoa Ethiopian province
shoal
shoali·ness
shoaly
shoat (*or* shote) weaned piglet

shock
shock·abil·ity
shock·able
shock·er
shock·headed
shock·ing
shock·ing·ness
shock·proof
shod
shod·di·ly
shod·di·ness
shod·dy (·di·er, ·di·est)
shoe (shoe·ing, shod) footwear; *compare* shoo
shoe·bill
shoe·black
shoe·horn
shoe·lace
shoe·maker
shoe·making
shoe·shine
shoe·string
shoe·tree
sho·far (*or* ·phar; *plural* ·fars, ·phars *or* ·froth, ·phroth) Jewish horn
sho·gun Japanese leader
sho·gun·ate
sho·ji (*plural* ·ji *or* ·jis) paper screen
Sho·la·pur Indian city
Sho·na (*plural* ·na *or* ·nas) African people
shone
shoo (shoos, shoo·ing, shooed) chase off; *compare* shoe
shook
shoon *Scot* shoes
shoot (shoot·ing, shot)
shoot·er
shoot-out (*noun*)
shop (shop·ping, shopped)
shop·girl
shop·keeper
shop·keeping
shop·lifter
shop·lifting
shop·per
shop·ping
shop·soiled (*US* ·worn)
shop·talk
shop·walker
shop·worn *US* shopsoiled

shor·an radar system
shore
shore·less
shore·line
shore·ward (*adj*)
shore·wards (*adv*)
shor·ing
shorn
short
short·age
short·bread
short·cake
short-change
short-changer
short-circuit (*verb*)
short·coming
short·en
short·en·er
short·en·ing
short·fall
short-haired
short·hand
short-handed
short-handed·ness
short·horn cattle
shortie (*or* shorty; *plural* shorties)
short·ish
short-list (*verb*)
short-lived
short·ly
short·ness
short-range
shorts
short-sighted
short-sighted·ness
short-spoken
short-tempered
short-term (*adj*)
short-waisted
short-winded
shorty *variant spelling of* shortie
Sho·sho·ne (*or* ·ni; *plural* ·nes, ·ne *or* ·nis, ·ni) American Indian
Sho·sho·nean (*or* ·nian)
shot
shote *variant spelling of* shoat
shot·gun (·gun·ning, ·gunned)
shot-putter
shott (*or* chott) salt lake
shot·ten recently spawned

should
shoul·der
shouldn't
shouse *Austral* lavatory
shout
shout·er
shove
shov·el (·el·ling, ·elled; *US* ·el·ing, ·eled)
shov·el·er duck; *compare* shoveller
shovel·ful (*plural* ·fuls)
shovel·head shark
shov·el·ler (*US* ·el·er) one who shovels; *compare* shoveler
shovel·nose fish
shov·er
show (show·ing, showed, shown *or* showed)
show·biz
show·boat
show·case
showd *Scot* rock
show·down
show·er
shower·proof
show·ery
show·girl
showi·ly
showi·ness
show·ing
show·jumper
show·jumping
show·man (*plural* ·men)
show·man·ship
shown
show-off (*noun*)
show·piece
show·place
show·room
showy (showi·er, showi·est)
shrank
shrap·nel
shred (shred·ding, shred·ded *or* shred)
shred·der
Shreve·port US city
shrew
shrewd
shrewdie *Austral* shrewd person
shrewd·ness
shrew·ish

shrewishness

shrew·ish·ness
Shrews·bury
shriek
shriek·er
shrie·val of a sheriff
shriev·al·ty (*plural* ·ties)
shrift
shrike
shrill
shrill·ness
shrilly
shrimp
shrimp·er
shrine
shrink (shrink·ing, shrank *or* shrunk, shrunk *or* shrunk·en)
shrink·able
shrink·age
shrink·er
shrink·ing·ly
shrink-wrap (-wrapping, -wrapped)
shrive (shriv·ing, shrove *or* shrived, shriv·en *or* shrived)
shriv·el (·el·ling, ·elled; *US* ·el·ing, ·eled)
shriv·er
shroff detector of counterfeit money
Shrop·shire
shroud
shroud-laid
shrove
Shrove·tide
shrub
shrub·bery (*plural* ·beries)
shrub·bi·ness
shrub·by (·bi·er, ·bi·est)
shrug (shrug·ging, shrugged)
shrunk
shrunk·en
shuck
shuck·er
shucks exclamation
shud·der
shud·der·ing·ly
shud·dery
shuf·fle
shuffle·board
shuf·fler
shug·gy (*plural* ·gies) *Dialect* swing
shul (*or* schul; *plural* shuln *or* schuln) synagogue
shun (shun·ning, shunned)
shun·nable
shun·ner
shunt
shunt·er
shunt-wound electrical term
shush
shut (shut·ting, shut)
shut·down (*noun*)
shut·eye
shut-off (*noun*)
shut·out (*noun*)
shut·ter
shut·ter·ing
shut·tle
shuttle·cock
shy (*adj* shy·er, shy·est *or* shi·er, shi·est; *verb* shies, shy·ing, shied; *noun, plural* shies)
shy·er (*noun*)
Shy·lock heartless creditor
shy·ly
shy·ness
shy·ster
Si (*or* Hsi) Chinese river
sial part of earth's crust
si·ala·gog·ic (*or* ·alo·) stimulating salivation
si·ala·gogue (*or* ·alo·)
si·al·ic
Si·al·kot Pakistani city
sia·loid saliva-like
Siam *former name of* Thailand
sia·mang ape
Sia·mese (*plural* ·mese)
Sian (*or* Hsian) Chinese city
Siang (*or* Hsiang) Chinese river
Siang·tan Chinese city
sib (*or* sibb) kin
Si·beria
Si·berian
sibi·lance (*or* ·lan·cy)
sibi·lant
sibi·late
sibi·la·tion
Si·biu Romanian town
sib·ling
sib·yl prophetess
sib·yl·line (*or* si·byl·lic)
sic *Latin* thus; *indicates the deliberate inclusion of a questionable word in text*
sic·ca·tive drying agent
sice *variant spelling of* syce
Si·cil·ian
Sici·ly
sick
sick·bay
sick·bed
sick·en
sick·en·er
sick·en·ing
sick·en·ing·ly
sick·le
sickle·bill
sick·li·ness
sick·ly (·li·er, ·li·est)
sick·ness
sic pas·sim *Latin* thus everywhere; *indicates a word in text is the same throughout*
Sicy·on ancient Greek city
side
side·band electronics term
side·board
side·boards (*or esp. US* ·burns)
side·car
side-dress
side·kick
side·light
side·line
side·long
si·dereal of stars
si·der·ite mineral
si·der·it·ic
si·dero·lite meteorite
si·der·osis disease
si·dero·stat astronomical instrument
si·dero·stat·ic
sid·er·ot·ic
side-saddle
side·show
side·slip (·slip·ping, ·slipped)
sides·man (*plural* ·men)
side-splitting

side·step (·step·ping,
  ·stepped)
side·step·per
side·stroke
side·swipe
side·swip·er
side·track
side·walk US pavement
side·wall
side·ward (adj)
side·wards (adv)
side·ways
side·wheel
side·wheeler boat
side·winder snake
Sidi-bel-Abbès Algerian
  city
sid·ing
si·dle
si·dler
Si·don Phoenician city
siè·cle French century
siege
sie·mens (plural ·mens)
  unit
Si·ena Italian city
si·en·na pigment
si·er·ra
Si·er·ra Leo·ne
Si·er·ra Le·on·ean
Si·er·ra Ma·dre Mexican
  mountains
si·er·ran
Si·er·ra Ne·va·da US
  mountains
si·es·ta
sieve
(sieze) incorrect spelling of
  seize
si·fa·ka animal
sift
sift·er
sift·ings
sigh
sigh·er
sight vision; compare site
sight·able
sight·ed
sight·er
sight·less
sight·less·ness
sight·li·ness
sight·ly (·li·er, ·li·est)
sight-read (-reading,
  -read)

sight-reader
sight·screen
sight·see (·see·ing, ·saw,
  ·seen)
sight·seer
sig·la list of symbols
sig·los (plural ·loi) coin
sig·ma Greek letter
sig·mate
sig·ma·tion
sig·moid (or ·moi·dal)
sig·moido·scope medical
  instrument
sig·moido·scop·ic
sig·moid·os·co·py
sign
sig·nal (·nal·ling, ·nalled;
  US ·nal·ling, ·naled)
sig·nal·ize (or ·ise)
sig·nal·ler (US ·nal·er)
sig·nal·ly
sig·nal·man (plural ·men)
sig·na·tory (plural ·tories)
sig·na·ture
sign·board
sign·er
sig·net seal on ring; compare
  cygnet
sig·ni·fi·able
sig·nifi·cance
sig·nifi·cant
sig·nifi·cant·ly
sig·ni·fi·ca·tion
sig·nifi·ca·tive
sig·nifi·ca·tive·ness
sig·ni·fi·er
sig·ni·fy (·fies, ·fy·ing,
  ·fied)
si·gnor (plural ·gnors or
  ·gnori) Italian man; Mr
si·gno·ra (plural ·ras or
  ·re) Italian woman; Mrs
si·gno·re (plural ·ri)
  Italian man; Sir
si·gnori·na (plural ·nas or
  ·ne) Italian young
  woman; Miss
sign·post
Sigurd Norse hero
sika deer
sike Dialect small stream
Sikh
Sikh·ism
Sik·kim Indian state
Sik·ki·mese

siltation

si·lage
Si·las·tic (Trademark)
sild fish
sile Dialect rain
si·lence
si·lenc·er
si·lent
si·lent·ly
si·lent·ness
Silenus Greek satyr
Si·lesia European region
si·lesia fabric
si·lex heat-resistant glass
sil·hou·ette
sili·ca mineral; compare
  silicon; silicone
sili·cate
si·li·ceous (or ·cious)
si·lic·ic
sili·cide chemical compound
sili·cif·er·ous
si·lici·fi·ca·tion
si·lici·fy (·fies, ·fy·ing,
  ·fied)
sili·cle (or si·licu·la,
  sili·cule) botany term
sili·con chemical element;
  compare silica; silicone
sili·cone polymer; compare
  silica; silicon
sili·co·sis disease
si·licu·lose
si·li·qua (or ·lique; plural
  ·li·quae, ·li·quas, or
  ·liques) botany term
sili·qua·ceous
silk
silka·line (or ·lene) fabric
silk·en
silki·ly
silki·ness
silk·worm
silky (silki·er, silki·est)
sill
sil·la·bub variant spelling of
  syllabub
sil·li·ly
sil·li·ma·nite mineral
sil·li·ness
sil·ly (adj ·li·er, ·li·est;
  noun, plural ·lies)
silo (plural silos)
si·lox·ane
silt
sil·ta·tion

silty 416

silty
Si·lu·res ancient Britons
Si·lu·rian geological period; of Silures
si·lu·rid fish
sil·va *variant spelling of* sylva
sil·van *variant spelling of* sylvan
Silvanus (*or* Sylvanus) Roman god
sil·ver
sil·ver·er
silver·fish (*plural* ·fish *or* ·fishes)
sil·veri·ness
sil·ver·ing
silver·point drawing technique
silver·side
silver·smith
silver·ware
silver·weed
sil·very
sil·vi·cul·tur·al
sil·vi·cul·ture tree cultivation
sil·vi·cul·tur·ist
s'il vous plaît *French* please
sima layer of earth's crust
sima·rou·ba (*or* ·ru·) tree
sima·rou·ba·ceous (*or* ·ru·)
Sim·fero·pol Soviet city
sim·ian (*or* simi·ous)
simi·lar
simi·lar·ity (*plural* ·ities)
simi·lar·ly
simi·le (*plural* ·les)
si·mili·tude
simi·ous *variant of* simian
sim·mer
sim·mer·ing·ly
sim·nel cake
si·mo·ni·ac practiser of simony
si·mo·nia·cal
si·mo·nia·cal·ly
si·mon·ist
si·mo·ny
si·moom (*or* ·moon) wind
simp *US* simpleton
sim·pa·ti·co
sim·per
sim·per·er
sim·per·ing·ly

sim·ple
simple-minded
simple-minded·ly
simple-minded·ness
sim·ple·ness
sim·ple·ton
sim·plex
sim·pli·ci·den·tate zoology term
sim·plic·ity (*plural* ·ities)
sim·pli·fi·ca·tion
sim·pli·fi·ca·tive
sim·pli·fi·er
sim·pli·fy (·fies, ·fy·ing, ·fied)
sim·plism
sim·plis·tic
sim·plis·ti·cal·ly
Sim·plon Pass
simp·ly
Simp·son Australian desert
simu·la·crum (*plural* ·cra)
simu·lant
simu·lar
simu·late
simu·lated
simu·la·tion
simu·la·tive
simu·la·tor
sim·ul·cast radio-TV broadcast
sim·ul·ta·neous
sim·ul·ta·neous·ly
sim·ul·ta·neous·ness (*or* ·ta·neity)
sin (sin·ning, sinned)
Si·nai Egyptian peninsula
Si·na·it·ic (*or* Si·na·ic)
Si·na·loa Mexican state
sin·an·thro·pus primitive man
sina·pism mustard plaster
Sin·ar·quist Mexican fascist
since
sin·cere
sin·cere·ly
sin·cer·ity (*or* ·cere·ness)
sin·cipi·tal
sin·ci·put (*plural* ·ci·puts *or* ·cipi·ta) part of skull
Sind Pakistani province
Sin·dhi (*plural* ·dhi *or* ·dhis)
sine trigonometry term; *Latin* without

si·necure
si·necur·ism
si·necur·ist
sine die *Latin* without a day fixed
sine qua non *Latin* essential requirement
sin·ew
sin·ewi·ness
sin·ewy
sin·fo·nia (*plural* ·nie) symphony
sin·fo·niet·ta
sin·ful
sin·ful·ly
sin·ful·ness
sing (sing·ing, sang, sung)
sing·able
Sin·ga·pore
Sin·ga·po·rean
singe (singe·ing, singed)
sing·er
sing·ing·ly
sin·gle
single-acting
single-action
single-blind
single-breasted
single-cross
single-decker
single-handed
single-minded
single-minded·ness
single·ness
single-phase
sin·gles tennis match
single-space (*verb*)
single·stick wooden sword
sin·glet
sin·gle·ton
single-track (*adj*)
sin·gly
sing·song
sin·gu·lar
sin·gu·lar·ity (*plural* ·ities)
sin·gu·lari·za·tion (*or* ·sa·tion)
sin·gu·lar·ize (*or* ·ise)
sin·gu·lar·ly
sin·gu·lar·ness
sin·gul·tus hiccup
sinh trigonometry term

Sin·hai·lien (or Hsin-hai-lien) Chinese city
Sin·ha·lese (or ·gha·; plural ·leses or ·lese) Sri Lankan
Si·ning (or Hsi·ning) Chinese city
sin·is·ter
sin·is·ter·ly
sin·is·ter·ness
sin·is·tral of the left side
sin·is·tral·ly
sin·is·tro·dex·tral
sin·is·tror·sal
sin·is·trorse spiralling right to left
sin·is·trous
Si·nit·ic language group
sink (sink·ing, sank or sunk, sunk or sunk·en)
sink·able
sink·er
sink·hole
Sinkiang-Uighur Chinese region
sink·ing
sin·less
sin·less·ness
sinned
sin·ner
Sinn Fein
Sinn Fein·er
Sinn Fein·ism
sin·ning
Si·no·logi·cal
Si·nolo·gist
Si·no·logue
Si·nol·ogy study of Chinese
Sino-Tibetan
sin·ter silicaceous deposit
sinu·ate (or ·at·ed) botany term
Si·nŭi·ju North Korean port
sinu·os·ity (or sinua·tion; plural ·ities or ·tions)
sinu·ous
sinu·ous·ly
sinu·ous·ness
si·nus (plural ·nuses)
si·nusi·tis
si·nus·oid maths term
si·nusoi·dal
Siouan
Sioux (plural Sioux)
sip (sip·ping, sipped)

si·phon (or sy·)
si·phon·age
si·phon·al (or ·ic)
si·pho·no·phore marine animal
si·pho·nopho·rous
si·phono·stele botany term
si·pho·no·stelic
Si·ple Antarctic mountain
sipped
sip·per
sip·pet small piece
sip·ping
sir
sir·dar leader
sire
si·ren
si·renian zoology term
Si·ret European river
Sir·ius star
sir·loin
si·roc·co (plural ·cos) wind
sir·rah archaic term of address
sir·ree US exclamation
sir·up US variant spelling of syrup
sir·vente verse form
sis
si·sal
Sisera biblical character
sis·kin bird
sis·sy (plural ·sies)
sis·sy·ish
sis·ter
sis·ter·hood
sister-in-law (plural sisters-)
sis·ter·li·ness
sis·ter·ly
Sis·tine chapel
sis·troid maths term
sis·trum (plural ·tra) musical instrument
Sisy·phean
Sisyphus mythological king
sit (sit·ting, sat)
si·tar musical instrument
si·tar·ist
sit·com
site place; compare sight
sit·fast sore on horse
sit-in (noun)
si·tol·ogy study of nutrition

si·tos·ter·ol soya-bean extract
sit·ter
sit·ting
situ·ated (or esp. in legal contexts ·ate)
situa·tion
situa·tion·al
situ·la (plural ·lae) Iron Age container
si·tus (plural ·tus) anatomical location
sitz·kreig
sitz·mark skiing term
Siva (or Shiva) Hindu god
Si·va·ism
Si·va·ist
Si·vas Turkish city
si·wash Canadian sweater
six
six·ain six-line poem
six·fold
six-footer
six·mo (plural ·mos) book size
six·pence
six·penny
sixte fencing position
six·teen
six·teen·mo (plural ·mos) book size
six·teenth
sixth
sixth-former
six·ti·eth
six·ty (plural ·ties)
siz·able (or size·)
siz·able·ness (or size·)
siz·ably (or size·)
siz·ar maintained student
si·zar·ship
size
sized
siz·er
siz·zle
siz·zler
sjam·bok whip
Ska·gen variant of Skaw
Skag·er·rak Scandinavian channel
skald (or scald) Scandinavian bard
skat card game
skate (noun, verb) sport

skate

skate (*plural* skate *or* skates) fish
skate·board
skate·board·er
skat·er
skat·ing
skat·ole organic compound
Skaw (*or* Ska·gen) Danish cape
skean dagger
ske·dad·dle
skeet clay-pigeon shooting
skeg nautical term
skein
skel·etal
skel·etal·ly
skel·eton
skel·eton·ize (*or* ·ise)
skelf *Dialect* wood splinter
skel·ly (*plural* ·lies) fish
Skel·mers·dale Merseyside town
skelp *Dialect* slap; metal tube
sken (sken·ing, skenned) *Dialect* squint
skep beehive
skep·tic *US spelling of* sceptic
sker·rick *US* small fragment
sker·ry (*plural* ·ries) *Scot* small island
sket (sket·ting, sket·ted) *Welsh* splash
sketch
sketch·able
sketch·book
sketch·er
sketchi·ly
sketchi·ness
sketchy (sketchi·er, sketchi·est)
skew
skew·back
skew·bald
skew·er long pin; *compare* skua
skew·ness
skew·whiff
ski (*verb* skis, ski·ing, skied *or* ski'd; *noun*, *plural* skis)
ski·able
skia·scope eye-examining instrument
ski·as·co·py
ski·bob
ski·bob·ber
ski·bob·bing
skid (skid·ding, skid·ded)
skid·lid *Slang* crash helmet
skid·pan
skid·proof
skid·way *US* platform for logs
skied
ski·er one who skis; *compare* skyer
skiff
skif·fle
ski·ing
ski·jor·er
ski·jor·ing snow sport
skil·ful (*US* skill·)
skil·ful·ly (*US* skill·)
skil·ful·ness (*US* skill·)
skill
skilled
skil·let
skill·ful *US spelling of* skilful
skil·ling coin
skil·lion *Austral* lean-to
skil·ly thin soup
skim (skim·ming, skimmed)
skim·mer
skim·mia shrub
skim·mings
skimp
skimpi·ly
skimpi·ness
skimpy (skimpi·er, skimpi·est)
skin (skin·ning, skinned)
skin-deep
skin-diver
skin·flint
skin·ful
skin·head
skink lizard
skin·less
skinned
skin·ner
skin·ni·ness
skin·ning
skin·ny (·ni·er, ·ni·est)
skint
skin·tight
skip (skip·ping, skipped)
skip·jack (*plural* ·jacks *or* ·jack) fish
ski·plane
skip·per
skip·pet box for document
skip·ping
skipping-rope
Skip·ton Yorkshire town
skirl *Dialect* play bagpipes
skir·mish
skir·mish·er
skirr move rapidly
skir·ret plant
skirt
skirt·er *Austral* fleece trimmer
skirt·ing
skit
skite *Austral* boast
skit·ter
skit·tish
skit·tish·ly
skit·tish·ness
skit·tle
skive
skiv·er
skiv·vy (*noun*, *plural* ·vies; *verb* ·vies, ·vy·ing, ·vied)
skoal drinking toast
skoki·aan South African liquor
Skop·je Yugoslav city
(skrimshank) incorrect spelling of scrimshank
skua bird; *compare* skewer
skul·dug·gery
skulk
skulk·er
skull head bones; *compare* scull
skull·cap
skunk (*plural* skunk *or* skunks)
sky (*noun*, *plural* skies; *verb* skies, sky·ing, skied)
sky·dive (·div·ing, ·dived (*US* dove), dived)
sky·div·er
Skye Scottish island
sky·er one who skies; *compare* skier
sky-high
sky·jack
sky·jack·er
Sky·lab *US* space station

sky·lark
sky·lark·er
sky·light
sky·line
sky·rocket
Sky·ros (or Scy·) Greek island
sky·sail
sky·scape
sky·scraper
sky·wards (or esp. US ·ward)
sky·writer
sky·writing
slab (slab·bing, slabbed)
slab·ber Dialect slobber
slack
slack·en
slack·er
slack·ness
slacks
slag (slag·ging, slagged)
slag·gy
slain
slais·ter Scot confused mess
slak·able (or slake·)
slake
slak·er
sla·lom skiing race; compare shalom
slam (slam·ming, slammed)
slan·der
slan·der·er
slan·der·ous
slan·der·ous·ness
slang
slangi·ly
slangi·ness
slangy
slant
slant·ing
slant·ing·ly (or slant·ly)
slant·wise (or ·ways)
slap (slap·ping, slapped)
slap-bang
slap·dash
slap·happy (·happier, ·happiest)
slap·jack card game
slap·per
slap·shot ice hockey shot
slap·stick
slap-up (adj)
slash

slash·er
slash·ing·ly
slat (slat·ting, slat·ted)
slate
slat·er
slath·er Slang large quantity
slati·ness
slat·ing
slat·tern
slat·tern·li·ness
slat·tern·ly
slaty (slati·er, slati·est)
slaugh·ter
slaugh·ter·er
slaughter·house
slaughter·man (plural ·men)
slaugh·ter·ous
Slav
slave
slave-drive (-driving, -drove, -driven)
slave-driver
slav·er
slav·er·er
slav·ery
slav·ey servant
Slav·ic variant of Slavonic
slav·ish
slav·ish·ly
slav·ish·ness
slav·oc·ra·cy (plural ·cies) domination by slaveholders
Sla·vo·nla Yugoslav region
Sla·vo·nian
Sla·von·ic (or Slav·ic) language
Slavo·phile (or ·phil)
Sla·vophi·lism
slay (slay·ing, slew, slain) kill; compare sleigh
slay·er
sleave tangled thread; compare sleeve
slea·zi·ly
slea·zi·ness
slea·zy (·zi·er, ·zi·est)
sled (sled·ding, sled·ded) variant (esp. US) of sledge
sled·der
sledge (or esp. US sled)
sledge-hammer
sleek
sleek·ness

Sligo

sleep (sleep·ing, slept)
sleep·er
sleepi·ly
sleepi·ness
sleep·less
sleep·less·ly
sleep·less·ness
sleep·walk
sleep·walk·er
sleep·walk·ing
sleepy (sleepi·er, sleepi·est)
sleepy·head
sleet
sleety
sleeve covering; compare sleave
sleeve·less
sleev·ing wire insulation
sleigh sledge; compare slay
sleigh·er
sleight trick; compare slight
slen·der
slen·der·ize (or ·ise)
slen·der·ness
slept
sleuth
sleuth·hound
slew past tense of slay
slew (US also slue) twist
slice
slice·able
slic·er
slick
slick·en·side geology term
slick·er
slick·ly
slick·ness
slid
slid·able
slide (slid·ing, slid or slid·den)
slide-action
slid·er
slid·ing
sli·er variant spelling of slyer
sli·est variant spelling of slyest
slight small; snub; compare sleight
slight·ing
slight·ing·ly
slight·ly
slight·ness
Sli·go Irish county

slily
sli·ly *variant spelling of* **slyly**
slim (*adj* **slim·mer,
slim·mest**; *verb*
slim·ming, slimmed)
slime
slimi·ly
slimi·ness
slim·mer
slim·ming
slim·ness
slim·sy *US* frail
slimy (**slimi·er, slimi·est**)
sling (**sling·ing, slung**)
sling·back
sling·er
sling·shot
slink (**slink·ing, slunk**)
slinki·ly
slinki·ness
slink·ing·ly
slinky (**slinki·er,
slinki·est**)
slip (**slip·ping, slipped**)
slip·case
slip·knot
slip·noose
slip-on (*adj, noun*)
slip·over
slip·page
slip·per
slip·pered
slip·peri·ness
slipper·wort
slip·pery
slip·pi·ness
slip·ping·ly
slip·py (**·pi·er, ·pi·est**)
slip·sheet
slip·shod
slip·shoddi·ness (*or*
·shod·ness)
slip·slop
slip·stream
slip-up (*noun*)
slip·way
slit (**slit·ting, slit**)
slith·er
slith·ery
slit·ter
sliv·er
sliv·er·er
slivo·vitz plum brandy
slob
slob·ber
slob·ber·er

slob·bery
sloe fruit; *compare* **slow**
sloe-eyed
slog (**slog·ging, slogged**)
slo·gan
slo·gan·eer
slog·ger
sloop
sloop-rigged
sloot ditch
slop (**slop·ping, slopped**)
slope
slop·er
slop·ing
slop·ing·ly
slop·pi·ly
slop·pi·ness
slop·py (**·pi·er, ·pi·est**)
slops
slop·work
slop·worker
slosh
sloshy
slot (**slot·ting, slot·ted**)
sloth
sloth·ful
sloth·ful·ly
sloth·ful·ness
slot·ter
slouch
slouch·er
slouchi·ly
slouchi·ness
slouch·ing·ly
slouchy
Slough Berkshire town
slough bog; to shed
sloughy
Slo·vak (*or* **·vak·ian**)
Slo·vakia Czech region
slov·en
Slo·vene (*or* **·venian**)
Slo·venia Yugoslav republic
slov·en·li·ness
slov·en·ly
slow not fast, etc.; *compare*
sloe
slow·coach
slow·down
slow·ly
slow·ness
slow·poke *US* slowcoach
slow-witted
slow·worm

420
slub (**slub·bing, slubbed**)
lump in yarn; twist fibre
slub·ber·de·gul·lion
slovenly person
sludge
sludgy
slue (**slu·ing, slued**) *US*
variant spelling of **slew**
slug (**slug·ging, slugged**)
sluga·bed
slug·gard
slug·gard·li·ness
slug·gard·ly
slug·ger
slug·gish
slug·gish·ness
sluice
sluice·gate
slum (**slum·ming,
slummed**)
slum·ber
slum·ber·er
slum·ber·ing·ly
slum·ber·less
slum·ber·ous
slum·ber·ous·ness
slum·mer
slum·my (**·mi·er, ·mi·est**)
slump
slung
slunk
slur (**slur·ring, slurred**)
slurp
slur·ry (*plural* **·ries**)
slush
slushi·ness
slushy
slut
slut·tish
slut·tish·ness
sly (**sly·er, sly·est** *or*
sli·er, sli·est)
sly·ly (*or* **sli·**)
sly·ness
slype passageway in
cathedral
smack
smack·er
small
small·boy steward's
assistant
small·holder
small·holding
small·ish
small-minded

small-minded·ly
small-minded·ness
small·ness
small·pox
smalls underwear
small-scale
smalt blue glass; pigment
smalt·ite mineral
smal·to (*plural* ·tos *or* ·ti) mosaic pieces
sma·rag·dite mineral
smarm
smarmy (smarmi·er, smarmi·est)
smart
smart·en
smartie clever person
smart·ing·ly
smart·ish
smart·ness
smash
smash·able
smash·er
smash·ing
smash-up (*noun*)
smat·ter
smat·ter·er
smat·ter·ing
smaze *US* smoky haze
smear
smear·er
smeari·ness
smeary (smeari·er, smeari·est)
smec·tic chemistry term
smeg·ma sebum
smell (smell·ing, smelt *or* smelled)
smelli·ness
smelly (smelli·er, smelli·est)
smelt (*plural* smelt *or* smelts) extract metal; fish
smel·ter
smelt·ery (*plural* ·eries)
smew duck
smid·gen (*or* ·gin)
smi·la·ca·ceous botany term
smi·lax shrub
smile
smil·er
smil·ing·ly
smil·ing·ness

smirch
smirch·er
smirk
smirk·er
smirk·ing·ly
smit (*or* smit·tle) *Dialect* infection
smite (smit·ing, smote, smit·ten *or* smit)
smit·er
smith
smith·er·eens
smith·ery (*plural* ·eries)
Smith·so·nian US museum
smith·son·ite mineral
smithy (*plural* smithies)
smit·ten
smock
smock·ing
smog
smog·gy
smok·able (*or* smoke·)
smoke
smoke·house
smoke·jack spit-turning device
smoke·less
smok·er
smoke·stack
smoki·ly
smoki·ness
smok·ing
smo·ko (*or* smoke·ho; *plural* ·kos *or* ·hos) *Austral* teabreak
smoky (smoki·er, smoki·est)
smol·der *US spelling of* smoulder
Smo·lensk Soviet city
smolt young salmon
smooch
smoodge *Austral* smooch
smooth
smooth·able
smooth·bore
smooth·en
smooth·er
smooth-faced
smoothie
smooth·ness
smooth-spoken
smooth-tongued

smor·gas·bord Scandinavian hors d'oeuvres
smote
smoth·er
smoth·ery
smoul·der (*US* smol·)
smri·ti Hindu literature
smudge
smudgi·ly (*or* smudg·ed·ly)
smudgi·ness
smudgy (smudgi·er, smudgi·est)
smug (smug·ger, smug·gest)
smug·gle
smug·gler
smug·gling
smug·ly
smug·ness
smut (smut·ting, smut·ted)
smutch smudge
smutchy
smut·ti·ly
smut·ti·ness
smut·ty (·ti·er, ·ti·est)
Smyr·na ancient Asian city
snack
snack·ette snack bar
snaf·fle
sna·fu (·fues, ·fu·ing, ·fued) *US* chaos; make chaotic
snag (snag·ging, snagged)
snaggle·tooth (*plural* ·teeth)
snag·gy
snail
snail-like
snake
snake·bite
snake·like
snake·mouth orchid
snake·root
snake·skin
snaki·ly
snaki·ness
snaky (snaki·er, snaki·est)
snap (snap·ping, snapped)
snap·back
snap·dragon

snappable 422

snap·pable
snap·per
snap·pi·ly
snap·pi·ness
snap·ping·ly
snap·py (·pi·er, ·pi·est)
snap·shot
snare
snar·er
snar·ing·ly
snarl
snarl·er
snarl·ing·ly
snarl-up (*noun*)
snarly
snatch
snatch·er
snatchi·ly
snatchy (snatchi·er, snatchi·est) spasmodic
snath (*or* snathe) scythe handle
snaz·zi·ly
snaz·zi·ness
snaz·zy (·zi·er, ·zi·est)
sneak
sneak·ers shoes
sneaki·ly
sneaki·ness
sneak·ing
sneak·ing·ly
sneak·ing·ness
sneaky (sneaki·er, sneaki·est)
sneck wall stone; latch
sned (sned·ding, sned·ded) *Dialect* to prune
sneer
sneer·er
sneer·ing
sneer·ing·ly
sneeze
sneez·er
sneeze·wort
sneezy
snib *Scot* door fastening
snick
snick·er
snick·et *Dialect* passageway
snide
snide·ness
sniff
sniff·er
sniffi·ly

sniffi·ness
sniff·ing·ly
snif·fle
snif·fler
snif·fy (·fi·er, ·fi·est)
snif·ter
snig·ger
snig·ger·ing·ly
snig·gle catch eels
snig·gler
snip (snip·ping, snipped)
snipe (*plural* snipe *or* snipes) bird; to attack
snipe·fish (*plural* ·fish *or* ·fishes)
snip·er
sniper·scope
snip·pet
snip·pi·ly
snip·pi·ness (*or* ·peti·ness)
snip·py (·pi·er, ·pi·est)
snips shears
snitch
sniv·el (·el·ling, ·elled; *US* ·el·ing, ·eled)
sniv·el·ler (*US* ·el·er)
sniv·el·ly
snob
snob·bery
snob·bish
snob·bish·ness (*or* ·bism)
Sno-Cat (*Trademark*)
snog (snog·ging, snogged)
snood
snook rude gesture
snook (*plural* snook *or* snooks) fish
snook·er
snoop
snoop·er
snooper·scope
snoopy
snoot *Slang* nose
snooti·ly
snooti·ness
snooty (snooti·er, snooti·est)
snooze
snooz·er
snoozy
snore
snor·er
snor·kel

snort
snort·er
snort·ing·ly
snot
snot·ti·ly
snot·ti·ness
snot·ty (*noun, plural* ·ties; *adj* ·ti·er, ·ti·est)
snout
snout·ed
snout·like
snow
snow·ball
snow·ball·ing
snow·berry (*plural* ·berries)
snow·bird
snow·blind
snow·blind·ness
snow·blink reflection from snow
snow·bound
snow·cap
snow·capped
Snow·don
Snow·donia
snow·drift
snow·drop
snow·fall
snow·field
snow·flake
snowi·ly
snowi·ness
snow·man (*plural* ·men)
snow·mobile
snow·plough
snow·shed
snow·shoe (·shoe·ing, ·shoed)
snow·sho·er
snow·storm
snow-white
snowy (snowi·er, snowi·est)
snub (snub·bing, snubbed)
snub·ber
snub·bing·ly
snub·by
snub-nosed
snuff
snuff·box
snuf·fer
snuffi·ness
snuff·ing·ly

snuf·fle
snuf·fler
snuf·fly
snuffy (snuffi·er, snuffi·est) unpleasant
snug (adj snug·ger, snug·gest; verb snug·ging, snugged)
snug·gery (plural ·geries)
snug·gle
snug·ness
snye river channel
so
soak
soak·age
soak·er
soak·ing
soak·ing·ly
so-and-so (plural so-and-sos)
soap
soap·bark
soap·berry (plural ·berries)
soap·box
soapi·ly
soapi·ness
soap·less
soapo·lal·lie drink
soap·stone (or ·rock)
soap·suds
soap·sudsy
soap·wort
soapy (soapi·er, soapi·est)
soar
soar·er
soar·ing·ly
sob (sob·bing, sobbed)
sob·ber
sob·bing·ly
so·beit Archaic provided that
so·ber
so·ber·ing·ly
so·ber·ness
so·bri·ety
so·bri·quet (or sou·)
soc·age legal term
soc·ag·er
so-called (adj)
soc·cer
So·che (or So-ch'e) Chinese town
So·chi Soviet city

so·cia·bil·ity (or ·ble·ness)
so·cia·ble
so·cia·bly
so·cial
so·cial·ism
so·cial·ist
so·cial·is·tic
so·cial·is·ti·cal·ly
so·cial·ite
so·ci·al·ity (plural ·ities)
so·cial·iz·able (or ·is·able)
so·ciali·za·tion (or ·sa·tion)
so·cial·ize (or ·ise)
so·cial·iz·er (or ·is·er)
so·cial·ly
so·cial·ness
so·ci·etal
so·ci·ety (plural ·eties)
So·cin·ian
So·cini·an·ism religious doctrine
so·cio·biolo·gy
so·cio·eco·nom·ic
so·cio·eco·nomi·cal·ly
so·cio·lin·guist
so·cio·lin·guis·tic
so·cio·lin·guis·tics
so·cio·logi·cal
so·ci·olo·gist
so·ci·ol·ogy
so·cio·met·ric
so·ci·om·etrist
so·ci·om·etry
so·cio·path
so·cio·path·ic
so·ci·opa·thy
so·cio·po·liti·cal
sock
sock·dolo·ger (or ·dola·) US decisive blow
sock·et
sock·eye salmon
so·cle plinth
soc·man (or soke·; plural ·men) tenant
So·crat·ic (or ·crati·cal)
sod (sod·ding, sod·ded)
soda
so·da·lite mineral
so·dal·ity (plural ·ities) Catholic society
so·da·mide chemical compound
sod·den

sod·den·ness
sod·ding
so·dium
Sod·om biblical city
sodo·mite
sodo·mize (or ·mise)
sodo·my
so·ever
sofa
so·far marine locating system
sof·fit architectural term
So·fia Bulgarian capital
soft
sof·ta Muslim student
soft·ball
soft-boiled
sof·ten
sof·ten·er
soft-finned
soft-headed
soft·hearted
soft-hearted·ness
softie variant spelling of softy
soft·ness
soft-pedal (-pedalling, -pedalled; US -pedaling, -pedaled)
soft-soap (verb)
soft-spoken
soft·ware
soft·wood
softy (or softie; plural softies)
sog·gi·ly
sog·gi·ness
sog·gy (·gi·er, ·gi·est)
soh (or so) musical note
Soho
soi-disant French so-called
soi·gné (fem ·gnée) well-groomed
soil
soil·age green fodder
soil·less
soi·ree
so·journ
so·journ·er
soke legal term
sol colloid
sol (plural sols or so·les) Peruvian currency
sol·ace
sol·ac·er
sola·na·ceous botany term

solander

so·lan·der botanical box
so·la·num plant
so·lar
so·lar·im·eter
so·lar·ium (plural ·laria or ·lar·iums)
so·lari·za·tion (or ·sa·tion)
so·lar·ize (or ·ise)
sold
sol·dan Archaic sultan
sol·der
sol·der·able
sol·der·er
sol·dier
sol·dier·li·ness
sol·dier·ly
sol·diery (plural ·dieries)
sole only; underside of foot or shoe; compare soul
sole (plural sole or soles) fish; compare soul
sol·ecism
sol·ecist
sol·ecis·tic (or ·ti·cal)
sole·ly
sol·emn
so·lem·ni·fi·ca·tion
so·lem·ni·fy (·fies, ·fy·ing, ·fied)
so·lem·nity (plural ·nities)
sol·em·ni·za·tion (or ·sa·tion)
sol·em·nize (or ·nise)
sol·em·niz·er (or ·nis·er)
sol·emn·ness (or ·em·ness)
so·leno·don animal
so·lenoid
so·lenoi·dal
So·lent English strait
sol-fa musical system
sol·fa·ta·ra volcanic vent
sol·fa·ta·ric
sol·feg·gio (or ·fège; plural ·feg·gi, ·feg·gios, or ·fèges) musical term
sol·fe·ri·no reddish-purple
soli musical term
so·lic·it
so·lici·ta·tion
so·lici·tor

So·lici·tor Gen·er·al (plural So·lici·tors Gen·er·al)
so·lici·tor·ship
so·lici·tous
so·lici·tous·ly
so·lici·tous·ness
so·lici·tude
sol·id
soli·da·go (plural ·gos) plant
soli·dar·ity (plural ·ities)
soli·dary united by interests
so·lidi·fi·able
so·lidi·fi·ca·tion
so·lidi·fi·er
so·lidi·fy (·fies, ·fy·ing, ·fied)
so·lid·ity
sol·id·ness
solid-state (adj)
soli·dus (plural ·di) oblique stroke in text
soli·fid·ian religious term
soli·fluc·tion (or ·flux·ion) soil movement
So·li·hull English town
so·lilo·quist (or ·quiz·er, ·quis·er)
so·lilo·quize (or ·quise)
so·lilo·quy (plural ·quies)
So·ling·en West German city
sol·ip·sism
sol·ip·sist
sol·ip·sis·tic
soli·taire game; gem
soli·tari·ly
soli·tari·ness
soli·tary (plural ·taries)
soli·tude
soli·tu·di·nous
sol·ler·et part of armour
sol·mi·za·tion (or ·sa·tion) musical term
solo (plural solos or soli)
so·lo·ist
Solo·mon Is·lands
sol·on·chak soil
solo·netz (or ·nets) soil
So·lo·thurn Swiss town
sol·stice
sol·sti·tial
sol·ubil·ity (plural ·ities)
solu·bil·ize (or ·ise)

sol·uble
sol·uble·ness
sol·ubly
so·lum (plural ·lums or ·la) soil layer
so·lute
so·lu·tion
So·lu·trean Palaeolithic culture
solv·abil·ity (or ·able·ness)
solv·able
solv·ate
solva·tion
Solvay pro·cess
solve
sol·ven·cy
sol·vent
solv·er
sol·voly·sis chemistry term
Sol·way Firth
soma (plural soma·ta or somas) biology term
So·ma·li (plural ·lis or ·li)
So·ma·lia African republic
So·ma·lian
So·ma·li·land former African region
so·mat·ic of the body
so·mati·cal·ly
so·ma·to·log·ic (or ·logi·cal)
so·ma·tolo·gist
so·ma·tol·ogy
so·ma·to·plasm
so·ma·to·plas·tic
so·ma·to·pleu·ral (or ·ric)
so·ma·to·pleure embryonic tissue
so·ma·to·type
som·bre (US ·ber)
som·bre·ly (US ·ber·)
som·bre·ness (US ·ber·)
som·brero (plural ·breros)
som·brous
some
some·body (plural ·bodies)
some·day
some·how
some·one
some·place
som·er·sault (or sum·mer·sault)

Som·er·set
some·thing
some·time (*adv, adj*)
some·times
some·way
some·what
some·where
some·wise somehow
so·mi·tal (*or* ·mit·ic)
so·mite embryonic tissue
Somme French river
som·melier wine steward
som·nam·bu·lance
som·nam·bu·lant
som·nam·bu·late
som·nam·bu·la·tion
som·nam·bu·la·tor
som·nam·bu·lism
som·nam·bu·list
som·nam·bu·lis·tic
som·nilo·quy (*plural* ·quies) talking in one's sleep
som·no·lence (*or* ·len·cy)
som·no·lent
son
so·nance
so·nant phonetics term
so·nant·al (*or* ·nan·tic)
so·nar
so·na·ta
sona·ti·na
son·dage archaeological trench
sonde observing device
sone unit
son et lu·mi·ère
song
song·bird
song·ful
song·ful·ly
song·ful·ness
Son·ghai (*plural* ·ghai *or* ·ghais) African people
song·ster (*fem* ·stress)
song·writer
son·ic
so·nif·er·ous
son-in-law (*plural* sons-)
son·net
son·net·eer
son·ny (*plural* ·nies)
so·no·buoy
So·no·ra Mexican state
son·or·ant phonetics term

so·nor·ity
so·no·rous
so·no·rous·ness
Soo·chow (*or* Su-chou) Chinese city
sook *Dialect* coward
soon
soon·er
soot
sooth *Archaic* truth
soothe
sooth·er
sooth·ing
sooth·ing·ly
sooth·say (·say·ing, ·said)
sooth·say·er
sooti·ly
sooti·ness
sooty (sooti·er, sooti·est)
sop (sop·ping, sopped)
soph·ism
soph·ist
soph·ist·er second-year undergraduate
so·phis·tic (*or* ·ti·cal)
so·phis·ti·cal·ly
so·phis·ti·cate
so·phis·ti·cat·ed
so·phis·ti·ca·tion
so·phis·ti·ca·tor
soph·ist·ry (*plural* ·ries)
sopho·more *US* second-year student
So·phy (*or* So·phi; *plural* ·phies) title of Persian kings
so·por stupor
sopo·rif·er·ous
sopo·rif·ic
sopo·rifi·cal·ly
sopped
sop·pi·ly
sop·pi·ness
sop·ping
sop·py (·pi·er, ·pi·est)
so·pra·ni·no (*plural* ·nos)
so·pra·no (*plural* ·nos *or* ·ni)
sora bird
sorb tree
sor·befa·cient causing absorption
sor·bet
sorb·ic acid
sor·bi·tol

Sor·bonne French university
sor·bose sugar
sor·cer·er (*fem* ·ess)
sor·cer·ous
sor·cery (*plural* ·ceries)
sor·did
sor·did·ness
sor·di·no (*plural* ·ni) musical term
sore
so·redium (*plural* ·redia) botany term
sore·head *US* peevish person
sore·ly
sore·ness
sor·ghum cereal crop
sor·go (*or* ·gho; *plural* ·gos *or* ·ghos) fodder crop
sori *plural of* sorus
sori·cine shrewlike
so·ri·tes logic term
so·riti·cal (*or* ·rit·ic)
sorn *Scot* scrounge hospitality
So·ro·ca·ba Brazilian city
so·ror·ate marriage custom
so·rori·cid·al
so·rori·cide
so·ror·ity (*plural* ·ities)
so·ro·sis (*plural* ·ses) botany term
sorp·tion adsorption or absorption
sor·rel
Sor·ren·to Italian port
sor·ri·ly
sor·ri·ness
sor·row
sor·row·er
sor·row·ful
sor·row·ful·ly
sor·row·ful·ness
sor·ry (·ri·er, ·ri·est)
sort
sort·able
sort·er
sor·tie (·tie·ing, ·tied)
sor·ti·lege divination by drawing lots
sor·ti·tion casting lots
so·rus (*plural* ·ri) spore-producing structure

Sosnowiec

Sos·no·wiec Polish town
so-so
sos·te·nu·to musical term
sot
so·te·ri·ol·ogy doctrine of salvation
So·thic of Sirius
So·tho (*plural* ·**tho** *or* ·**thos**) African people
sot·tish
sot·to voce
sou coin
sou·bise onion sauce
sou·brette pert girl
sou·bri·quet *variant spelling of* **sobriquet**
sou·chong tea
Sou·dan *French* Sudan
souf·fle medical term
souf·flé light dish
sough sighing sound
sought
soul spirit; *compare* **sole**
soul-destroy·ing
soul·ful
soul·ful·ly
soul·ful·ness
soul·less
soul·less·ly
soul·less·ness
soul-searching
sound
sound·able
sound·box
sound·er
sound·ing
sound·less
sound·less·ness
sound·ly
sound·ness
sound·post musical term
sound·proof
sound·track
soup
soup·çon *French* slight amount
soup·fin shark
soupy (**soupi·er, soupi·est**)
sour
source
sour·dine organ stop
sour·ish
sour·ly
sour·ness

sour·puss
sour·sop fruit
sou·sa·phone
sou·sa·phon·ist
souse
sous·lik (*or* **sus·**) animal
Sousse Tunisian port
sou·tache braid
sou·tane cassock
sout·er *Scot* cobbler
sou·ter·rain underground chamber
south
South·amp·ton
south·bound
South·down sheep
south·east
south·easter
south·easter·ly (*plural* ·**lies**)
south·eastern
south·eastern·most
south·eastward (*adj*)
south·eastwards (*adv*)
South·end
south·er
south·er·li·ness
south·er·ly (*plural* ·**lies**)
south·ern
south·ern·er
south·ern·most
southern·wood
south·ing navigation term
south·paw
South Pole
South·port
south-southeast
south-southwest
south·ward (*adj*)
south·wards (*adv*)
South·wark London borough
south·west
south·wester strong wind
south·wester·ly (*plural* ·**lies**)
south·western
south·western·most
south·westward (*adj*)
south·westwards (*adv*)
sou·venir
sou'·west·er hat
sov·er·eign
sov·er·eign·ty (*plural* ·**ties**)

So·vi·et of the USSR
so·vi·et a Soviet council
so·vi·et·ism
so·vi·et·ist
so·vi·et·is·tic
so·vi·eti·za·tion (*or* ·**sa·tion**)
so·vi·et·ize (*or* ·**ise**)
sov·khoz (*plural* ·**kho·zy**) state farm
sov·ran *Poetic* sovereign
sow female pig
sow (**sow·ing, sowed, sown** *or* **sowed**) plant seed; *compare* **sew**
sow·bread plant
sow·er
So·we·to South African suburb
sow·ing
sown
soya bean (*US* **soy·bean**)
soy sauce
So·yuz Soviet spacecraft
soz·zled
spa mineral spring; *compare* **spar**
space
space·band printing term
space-bar
space·craft
space·less
space·man (*plural* ·**men**)
space·port
spac·er
space·ship
space·suit
space-time physics term
space·walk
space·woman (*plural* ·**women**)
spac·ing
spa·cious roomy; *compare* **specious**
spa·cious·ness
spade
spade·fish (*plural* ·**fish** *or* ·**fishes**)
spade·ful (*plural* ·**fuls**)
spad·er
spade·work
spa·di·ceous
spa·dix (*plural* ·**di·ces**) botany term
spae *Scot* foretell

spa·ghet·ti
Spain
spake
spall rock splinter
spalla·tion nuclear reaction
spal·peen *Irish* rascal
Spam (*Trademark*)
span (**span·ning, spanned**)
span·cel (**·cel·ling, ·celled;** *US* **·cel·ing, ·celed**) fettering rope
span·drel (*or* **·dril**) architectural term
spang *US* exactly
span·gle
span·gly
Span·iard
span·iel
Span·ish
Spanish-American
spank
spank·er
spank·ing
span·ner
spar (**spar·ring, sparred**) fight; nautical gear; mineral; *compare* **spa**
spar·able small nail
spare
spare·ly
spare·ness
spar·er
spare·rib
sparge sprinkle
spar·id (*or* **·oid**) fish
spar·ing frugal; *compare* **sparring**
spar·ing·ly
spar·ing·ness
spark
spar·kle
spar·kler
spar·ling (*plural* **·lings** *or* **·ling**) fish
spar·ring fighting; *compare* **sparing**
spar·row
sparrow·grass *Dialect* asparagus
sparrow·hawk
spar·ry geology term
sparse
sparse·ly
sparse·ness (*or* **spar·sity**)

Spar·ta
Spar·tan
Spar·tan·ism
spar·teine alkaloid
spasm
spas·mod·ic (*or* **·modi·cal**)
spas·modi·cal·ly
spas·tic
spas·ti·cal·ly
spat *past tense of* **spit**
spat (**spat·ting, spat·ted**) quarrel
spatch·cock
spate
spa·tha·ceous
spathe botany term
spathed
spath·ic (*or* **·ose**) mineralogy term
spa·tial (*or* **·cial**)
spa·ti·al·ity
spa·tial·ly
spa·tio·tem·por·al
spat·ter
spatu·la
spatu·lar
spatu·late
spav·in
spav·ined
spawn
spawn·er
spay
speak (**speak·ing, spoke, spo·ken**)
speak·able
speak·easy (*plural* **·easies**)
speak·er
speak·er·ship
speak·ing
spear
spear·er
spear·head
spear·mint
spear·wort
spec speculation
spe·cial
spe·cial·ism
spe·cial·ist
spe·cial·is·tic
spe·ci·al·ity (*US* **·ty;** *plural* **·ities**) special skill; *compare* **specialty**
spe·ciali·za·tion (*or* **·sa·tion**)

spectrophotometric

spe·cial·ize (*or* **·ise**)
spe·cial·ly
spe·cial·ness
spe·cial·ty (*plural* **·ties**) legal term; medical speciality; *US* spelling of **speciality**
spe·cia·tion biology term
spe·cie coin money
spe·cies (*plural* **·cies**)
speci·fi·able
spe·cif·ic
spe·cifi·cal·ly
speci·fi·ca·tion
speci·fi·ca·tive
speci·fic·ity
speci·fi·er
speci·fy (**·fies, ·fy·ing, ·fied**)
speci·men
spe·ci·os·ity (*plural* **·ities**)
spe·cious deceptively plausible; *compare* **spacious**
spe·cious·ly
spe·cious·ness
speck
speck·le
specs *Slang* spectacles
spec·ta·cle
spec·ta·cled
spec·ta·cles
spec·tacu·lar
spec·tacu·lar·ly
spec·ta·tor
spec·tra *plural of* **spectrum**
spec·tral
spec·tral·ity (*or* **·tral·ness**)
spec·tral·ly
spec·tre (*US* **·ter**)
spec·tro·bo·lom·eter
spec·tro·holo·met·ric
spec·tro·graph
spec·tro·graph·ic
spec·tro·graphi·cal·ly
spec·trog·ra·phy
spec·tro·he·lio·graph
spec·tro·he·lio·graph·ic
spec·tro·he·lio·scope
spec·tro·he·lio·scop·ic
spec·trom·eter
spec·tro·met·ric
spec·trom·etry
spec·tro·pho·tom·eter
spec·tro·photo·met·ric

spectrophotometry

spec·tro·pho·tom·e·try
spec·tro·scope
spec·tro·scop·ic (or ·scopi·cal)
spec·tro·scopi·cal·ly
spec·tros·co·pist
spec·tros·co·py
spec·trum (plural ·tra)
specu·lar
specu·late
specu·la·tion
specu·la·tive
specu·la·tive·ly
specu·la·tive·ness
specu·la·tor
specu·lum (plural ·la or ·lums)
sped
speech
speechi·fi·ca·tion
speechi·fi·er
speechi·fy (·fies, ·fy·ing, ·fied)
speech·less
speech·less·ly
speech·less·ness
speed (speed·ing, sped or speed·ed)
speed·boat
speed·er
speedi·ly
speedi·ness
speedo (plural speedos) *Slang* speedometer
speed·om·eter
speed·ster
speed·way
speed·well
Speed·writing (*Trademark*)
speedy (speedi·er, speedi·est)
speel *Dialect* wood splinter; compare **spiel**
speiss smelting term
spe·laean (or ·lean) of caves
spe·leo·logi·cal (or ·laeo·)
spe·leolo·gist (or ·laeolo·)
spe·leol·ogy (or ·laeol·) study of caves
spelk *Dialect* wood splinter
spell (spell·ing, spelt or spelled)
spell·able

spell·bind (·bind·ing, ·bound)
spell·bind·er
spell·bound
spell·er
spell·ing
spelt wheat; *past tense of* spell
spel·ter impure zinc
spe·lunk·er cave explorer
spe·lunk·ing
spence *Dialect* larder
spen·cer short coat; vest
Spen·cer Gulf
spend (spend·ing, spent)
spend·able
spend·er
spend·thrift
Spen·serian of the poet Spenser
spent
spe·os temple
sperm (plural sperm or sperms)
sper·ma·ceti waxy substance
sper·mary (plural ·maries) sperm-producing organ
sper·ma·the·ca
sper·ma·the·cal
sper·mat·ic
sper·ma·tid immature sperm
sper·ma·tium (plural ·tia)
sper·mato·cyte
sper·mato·gen·esis
sper·ma·to·genet·ic
sper·mato·go·nial
sper·mato·go·nium (plural ·nia)
sper·ma·topho·ral
sper·mato·phore
sper·ma·to·phyte seed plant
sper·ma·to·phyt·ic
sper·ma·tor·rhoea (*US* ·rhea)
sper·ma·to·zo·al (or ·an, ·ic)
sper·ma·to·zo·id botany term
sper·ma·to·zo·on (plural ·zoa)
sper·mic
sper·mi·ci·dal

sper·mi·cide
sperm·ine biochemical compound
sper·mio·gen·esis
sper·mio·genet·ic
sper·mo·go·nium (plural ·nia)
sper·mo·phile animal
sper·mous
sperry·lite mineral
spes·sar·tite mineral
spew
spew·er
Spey Scottish river
sphag·nous
sphag·num
sphal·er·ite mineral
sphene mineral
sphe·nic wedge-shaped
sphe·no·don lizard
sphe·noid (*noun*) bone
sphe·noid (or ·noi·dal; *adj*) wedge-shaped
spher·al
sphere
spheri·cal (or spher·ic)
spheri·cal·ly
spheri·cal·ness
sphe·ric·ity
spher·ics (*US* sfer·ics) atmospherics
sphe·roid
sphe·roi·dal
sphe·roi·dic·ity
sphe·rom·eter
spheru·lar
spher·ule tiny sphere
spheru·lite geology term
spheru·lit·ic
sphery *Poetic* spherelike; starlike
sphinc·ter
sphinc·ter·al
sphin·go·my·elin
sphin·go·sine
Sphinx mythological monster
sphinx (plural sphinxes or sphin·ges) Egyptian statue
sphra·gis·tic
sphra·gis·tics study of seals
sphyg·mic of the pulse
sphyg·mo·graph
sphyg·mo·graph·ic

sphyg·mog·ra·phy
sphyg·moid
sphyg·mo·ma·nom·eter
Spi·ca star
spi·ca (*plural* ·cae *or* ·cas) spiral bandage
spi·cate botany term
spic·ca·to musical term
spice
spice·berry (*plural* ·berries)
spice·bush
spic·er
spic·ery (*plural* ·eries)
spici·ly
spici·ness
spick-and-span (*or* spic-)
spicu·late
spic·ule
spicu·lum (*plural* ·la)
spicy (spici·er, spici·est)
spi·der
spider·man (*plural* ·men)
spider·wort
spi·dery
spied
spie·gelei·sen pig iron
spiel *Slang* glib talk; *compare* speel
spiel·er
spif·fing
spif·fy (·fi·er, ·fi·est) *US* smart
spif·li·cate *Slang* destroy
spig·nel plant
spig·ot cask stopper
spike
spike·let grass flower
spike·nard plant
spike-rush plant
spiki·ly
spiki·ness
spiky (spiki·er, spiki·est)
spile heavy stake
spill (spill·ing, spilt *or* spilled)
spill·age
spill·er
spil·li·kin (*or* spili·) thin strip
spil·li·kins game
spill·way
spilt
spin (spin·ning, spun)
spi·na bi·fi·da
spin·ach
spi·nal
spi·nal·ly
spin·dle
spin·dling
spin·dly (·dli·er, ·dli·est)
spin·drift (*or* spoon·) sea spray
spin-dry (-dries, -drying, -dried)
spin-dryer
spine
spine-chiller
spine-chilling
spi·nel mineral
spine·less
spine·less·ness
spi·nes·cence
spi·nes·cent
spin·et
spi·nif·er·ous (*or* ·nig·)
spini·fex plant
spini·ness
spin·na·ker racing sail
spin·ner
spin·ner·et zoology term
spin·ney
spin·ning
spin-off
spi·nose
spi·nos·ity
spi·nous
Spi·no·zism philosophical system
spin·ster
spin·ster·hood
spin·ster·ish
spin·tha·ri·scope physics apparatus
spi·nule
spi·nu·lose
spiny (spini·er, spini·est)
spiny-finned
spira·cle respiratory aperture
spi·racu·lar
spi·racu·late
spi·raea shrub
spi·ral (·ral·ling, ·ralled; *US* ·ral·ing, ·ralled)
spi·ral·ly
spi·rant phonetics term
spire
spi·reme cytology term
spi·rif·er·ous
spi·ril·lar
spi·ril·lum (*plural* ·la) bacterium
spir·it
spir·it·ed
spir·it·ed·ly
spir·it·ed·ness
spir·it·less
spir·it·less·ness
spi·ri·to·so musical term
spiri·tous *variant of* spirituous
spir·itu·al
spir·itu·al·ism
spir·itu·al·ist
spir·itu·al·ity (*plural* ·ities)
spir·itu·ali·za·tion (*or* ·sa·tion)
spir·itu·al·ize (*or* ·ise)
spir·itu·al·iz·er (*or* ·is·er)
spir·itu·al·ly
spir·itu·al·ness
spir·itu·el (*fem* ·elle) witty
spir·itu·os·ity (*or* ·ous·ness)
spir·itu·ous (*or* spiri·tous) alcoholic
spir·ket·ting nautical term
spi·ro·chaete bacterium
spi·ro·chae·to·sis
spi·ro·graph medical apparatus
spi·ro·graph·ic
spi·ro·gy·ra alga
spi·roid
spi·rom·eter
spi·ro·met·ric
spi·rom·etry
spi·ro·no·lac·tone drug
spirt *variant spelling of* spurt
spiru·la mollusc
spiry
spit (spit·ting, spat *or* spit) expectorate
spit (spit·ting, spit·ted) pointed rod; pierce
spitch·cock
spite
spite·ful
spite·ful·ly
spite·ful·ness
spit·fire
Spit·head

spitsticker

spit·sticker wood-engraving tool
spit·ter
spit·tle
spittle·bug
spit·toon
spitz dog
spiv
spiv·vy
splake trout
splanch·nic visceral
splash
splash·back
splash·board
splash·down
splash·er
splashi·ly
splashi·ness
splashy (splashi·er, splashi·est)
splat
splat·ter
splay
splay·foot
splay·footed·ly
spleen
spleen·ish (*or* spleeny)
spleen·wort
splen·did
splen·did·ness
splen·dif·er·ous
splen·dor·ous (*or* ·drous)
splen·dour (*US* ·dor)
sple·nec·to·my (*plural* ·mies) removal of spleen
sple·net·ic (*or* ·neti·cal) peevish
sple·neti·cal·ly
sple·nial of the splenius
splen·ic of the spleen
sple·ni·tis
sple·nius (*plural* ·nii) muscle
sple·no·mega·ly
splice
splic·er
spline machine part
splint
splin·ter
splin·tery
Split Yugoslav port
split (split·ting, split)
split-level
splits gymnastic act
split·ter
split·ting
splodge
splodgy
splore *Scot* revel
splotch
splotchy
splurge
splut·ter
splut·ter·er
splut·tery
spode porcelain
spodu·mene mineral
spoil (spoil·ing, spoilt *or* spoiled)
spoil·age
spoil·er
spoil·five card game
spoils
spoil·sport
Spo·kane US city
spoke
spo·ken
spoke·shave
spokes·man (*plural* ·men)
spokes·woman (*plural* ·women)
spo·li·ate despoil
spo·lia·tion
spo·lia·tory
spon·da·ic (*or* ·dai·cal)
spon·dee metrical foot
spon·du·lix (*or* ·licks) *Slang* money
spon·dy·li·tis spinal disorder
sponge
sponge·able
spong·er
spon·gi·ly
spon·gin
spon·gi·ness
spon·gio·blast nerve cell
spon·gio·blas·tic
spon·gy (·gi·er, ·gi·est)
spon·sion sponsorship
spon·son support on boat
spon·sor
spon·so·rial
spon·sor·ship
spon·ta·neity (*plural* ·neities)
spon·ta·neous
spon·ta·neous·ly
spon·ta·neous·ness
spon·toon short pike
spoof
spoof·er
spook
spooki·ly
spooki·ness
spook·ish
spooky (spooki·er, spooki·est)
spool
spoon
spoon·bill
spoon·er·ism
spoon-feed (·feeding, -fed)
spoon·ful (*plural* ·fuls)
spoony (spooni·er, spooni·est) amorous
spoor animal trail; *compare* spore
spoor·er
Spora·des Greek islands
spo·rad·ic (*or* ·radi·cal)
spo·radi·cal·ly
spo·radi·cal·ness
spo·ran·gial
spo·ran·gium (*plural* ·gia)
spore reproductive body; *compare* spoor
spo·ro·carp
spo·ro·cyst
spo·ro·cyte
spo·ro·gen·esis
spo·rog·enous
spo·ro·go·nial
spo·ro·go·nium (*plural* ·nia)
spo·rogo·ny
spo·ro·phore
spo·ro·phyll (*or* ·phyl)
spo·ro·phyte
spo·ro·phyt·ic
spo·ro·zo·an
spo·ro·zo·ite
spor·ran
sport
sport·er
sporti·ly
sporti·ness
sport·ing
sport·ing·ly
spor·tive
spor·tive·ly
spor·tive·ness
sports·cast
sports·caster

sports·man (*plural* ·men)
sportsman-like
sports·man·ly
sports·man·ship
sports·wear
sports·woman (*plural* ·women)
sporty (sporti·er, sporti·est)
sporu·late produce spores
sporu·la·tion
spor·ule
spot (spot·ting, spot·ted)
spot·less
spot·less·ness
spot·light (·light·ing, ·lit *or* ·light·ed)
spot-on
spot·table
spot·ted
spot·ter
spot·ti·ly
spot·ti·ness
spot·ty (·ti·er, ·ti·est)
spot-weld
spot-welder
spous·al marriage ceremony
spouse
spout
spout·er
sprag
sprain
sprang
sprat
sprawl
sprawl·er
sprawl·ing
sprawly
spray
spray·er
spread (spread·ing, spread)
spread·able
spread-eagle
spread·er
sprech·stimme *German* musical term
spree
sprig (sprig·ging, sprigged)
sprig·ger
sprig·gy
spright·li·ness
spright·ly (·li·er, ·li·est)

spring (spring·ing, sprang *or* sprung, sprung)
spring·board
Spring·bok South African athlete
spring·bok (*or* ·buck; *plural* ·bok, boks *or* ·buck, ·bucks) antelope
spring-clean
spring-cleaning
springe snare
spring·er
Spring·field US city
spring·haas (*plural* ·haas, ·ha·se) animal
spring·head
springi·ly
springi·ness
spring·ing
spring·let
Springs South African city
spring·tail
spring·time
spring·wood
springy (springi·er, springi·est)
sprin·kle
sprin·kler
sprin·kling
sprint
sprint·er
sprit nautical term
sprite
sprit·sail
sprock·et
sprout
spruce
spruce·ly
spruce·ness
sprue disease
spru·ik *Austral* speak in public
sprung
spry (spri·er, spri·est)
spry·ly
spry·ness
spud (spud·ding, spud·ded)
spume froth
spu·mes·cence
spu·mes·cent
spu·mo·ne (*or* ·ni; *plural* ·ni) ice cream
spu·mous (*or* spumy)
spun

spunk
spunki·ly
spunki·ness
spunky (spunki·er, spunki·est)
spur (spur·ring, spurred)
spurge plant
spu·ri·ous
spu·ri·ous·ly
spu·ri·ous·ness
spurn
spurn·er
spur·ri·er spur maker
spur·ry (*or* ·rey; *plural* ·ries) plant
spurt (*or* spirt)
sput·nik Soviet satellite
sput·ter
sput·ter·er
spu·tum (*plural* ·ta)
spy (*noun, plural* spies; *verb* spies, spy·ing, spied)
spy·glass
spy·ing
squab (*plural* squabs *or* squab) young pigeon
squab·ble
squab·bler
squab·by (·bi·er, ·bi·est)
squac·co (*plural* ·cos) heron
squad
squad·die (*or* ·dy; *plural* ·dies) *Slang* soldier
squad·ron
squa·lene biochemical compound
squal·id
squa·lid·ity (*or* squal·id·ness)
squall
squall·er
squal·ly
squal·or
squa·ma (*plural* ·mae) scale
squa·mate
squa·ma·tion
squa·mo·sal bone
squa·mous (*or* ·mose)
squa·mous·ness (*or* ·mose)
squamu·lose covered with small scales

squander

squan·der
squan·der·er
squan·der·ing·ly
square
square·ly
square·ness
squar·er
square-rigger
squar·ish
squar·rose *biology term*
squash
squash·er
squashi·ly
squashi·ness
squashy (squashi·er, squashi·est)
squat (squat·ting, squat·ted)
squat·ness
squat·ter
squat·toc·ra·cy *Austral* rich farmers
squaw
squawk
squawk·er
squeak
squeak·er
squeaki·ly
squeaki·ness
squeaky
squeal
squeal·er
squeam·ish
squeam·ish·ness
squee·gee (*or* squil·; ·gee·ing, ·geed)
squeez·able
squeeze
squeez·er
squelch
squelch·er
squelch·ing·ly
sque·teague (*plural* ·teague *or* ·teagues) fish
squib (squib·bing, squibbed)
squid (*plural* squid *or* squids)
squif·fy (·fi·er, ·fi·est)
squig·gle
squig·gler
squig·gly
squill plant

squil·la (*plural* ·las *or* ·lae) shrimp
squinch architectural support
squint
squint·er
squinty
squire
squire·ar·chy (*or* squir·ar·chy; *plural* ·chies)
squirm
squirm·er
squirm·ing·ly
squirmy
squir·rel
squirrel·fish (*plural* ·fish *or* ·fishes)
squirt
squirt·er
squish
squishy (squishi·er, squishi·est)
squit *Slang* insignificant person
squiz (*plural* squizzes) *Austral* inquisitive glance
Sri Lan·ka
Sri Lan·kan
Sri·na·gar Indian city
St *abbrev. for* Saint; *all entries preceded by* St *are listed in the section of this dictionary following the entry* saint
stab (stab·bing, stabbed)
Sta·bat Ma·ter hymn
stab·ber
sta·bile arts term
sta·bil·ity (*plural* ·ities)
sta·bi·li·za·tion (*or* ·sa·tion)
sta·bi·lize (*or* ·lise)
sta·bi·li·zer (*or* ·ser)
sta·ble
stable·boy
stable·man (*plural* ·men)
sta·ble·ness
sta·bling
sta·bly
stac·ca·to
stack
stack·er
stac·te biblical spice
stad·dle prop
staddle·stone

432

stad·hold·er (*or* stadt·) Dutch ruler
sta·di·om·eter
sta·dium (*plural* ·diums *or* ·dia)
staff (*plural* staffs) personnel
staff (*plural* staffs *or* staves) pole
staff (*or* stave; *plural* staffs *or* staves) musical term
Staf·fa Scottish island
staff·er *Slang* staff member
staff·man (*plural* ·men)
Staf·ford
Staf·ford·shire
stag
stage
stage·coach
stage·craft
stage·hand
stage-manage
stag·er
stag·fla·tion economics term
stag·gard deer
stag·ger
stagger·bush
stag·ger·er
stag·ger·ing
stag·ger·ing·ly
stag·gers horse disease
stag·hound
stagi·ly
stagi·ness
stag·ing
Sta·gi·ra ancient Macedonian city
stag·nan·cy (*or* ·nance)
stag·nant
stag·nate
stag·na·tion
stagy (stagi·er, stagi·est) theatrical
staid sedate; *compare* stayed
staid·ness
stain
stain·abil·ity
stain·able
stain·er
Staines Surrey town
stain·less
stair step; *compare* stare
stair·case

stair·head
stairs
stair·way
stair·well
stake stick; money; compare
    steak
stake·out
sta·lac·ti·form
stal·ac·tite downward
    projection in cave
stal·ac·tit·ic (or ·titi·cal)
sta·lag German prison camp
stal·ag·mite upward
    projection in cave
stal·ag·mit·ic (or ·miti·cal)
stale
stale·ly
stale·mate
stale·ness
Sta·lin·ism
Sta·lin·ist
stalk
stalked
stalk·er
stalki·ly
stalki·ness
stalk·like
stalky (stalki·er,
    stalki·est)
stall
stall-feed (-feeding, -fed)
stal·lion
stal·wart
stal·wart·ness
Stam·bul (or ·boul) part of
    Istanbul
sta·men (plural sta·mens
    or stami·na)
Stam·ford US city
stami·na
stami·nal
stami·nate having stamens
stami·nif·er·ous
stami·node (or ·no·dium;
    plural ·nodes or
    ·no·dia) botany term
stami·no·dy
stam·mel fabric
stam·mer
stam·mer·er
stam·mer·ing·ly
stamp
stam·pede
stam·ped·er
stamp·er

stance
stanch (or staunch) check
    blood flow; compare
    staunch
stanch·able (or staunch·)
stanch·er (or staunch·)
stan·chion
stand (stand·ing, stood)
stand·ard
standard-bearer
stand·ardi·za·tion (or
    ·sa·tion)
stand·ard·ize (or ·ise)
stand·ard·iz·er (or ·is·er)
stand-by (noun; plural
    -bys)
standee one who stands
stand·er
stand-in (noun)
stand·ing
stand·ish inkstand
stand·offish
stand·pipe
stand·point
stand·still
stang Dialect throb with
    pain
stan·hope carriage
stank
Stan·ley capital of Falkland
    Islands
Stan·na·ries English district
stan·na·ry (plural ·ries)
    tin mine
stan·nic chemistry term
stan·nif·er·ous
stan·nite mineral
stan·nous chemistry term
stan·za
stan·zaed
stan·za·ic
sta·pedial
sta·pelia plant
sta·pes (plural ·pes or
    ·pedes) ear bone
staphy·lo·coc·cal
staphy·lo·coc·cus (plural
    ·coc·ci)
staphy·lo·plas·tic
staphy·lo·plas·ty palate
    surgery
staphy·lor·rhaph·ic
staphy·lor·rha·phy repair
    of cleft palate
sta·ple

sta·pler
star (star·ring, starred)
star-apple
Sta·ra Za·go·ra Bulgarian
    city
star·board
starch
starch·er
starchi·ly
starchi·ness
starch-reduced
starchy (starchi·er,
    starchi·est)
star-crossed
star·dom
star·dust
stare look at; compare stair
star·er
star·fish (plural ·fish or
    ·fishes)
star·flower
star·gaze
star·gaz·er
star·gaz·ing
stark
stark·ness
star·less
star·let
star·light
star·like
star·ling
star·lit
star-of-Bethlehem plant
starred
star·ri·ly
star·ri·ness
star·ry (·ri·er, ·ri·est)
starry-eyed
star-spangled
start
start·er
star·tle
star·tler
star·tling
star·tling·ly
star·va·tion
starve
starve·ling
starv·er
starv·ing
star·wort
stash
sta·sis stagnation
stat·able (or state·)
sta·tant heraldic term

state

state
state·craft
state·hood
State·house *US* state capitol
state·less
state·less·ness
state·li·ness
state·ly (·li·er, ·li·est)
state·ment
Stat·en Is·land
sta·ter one who states; ancient coin; *compare* stator
state·room
States the USA
state·side
states·man (*plural* ·men)
statesman-like (*or* states·man·ly)
states·man·ship
states·woman (*plural* ·women)
stat·ic
stati·cal
stati·cal·ly
stat·ice plant
stat·ics
sta·tion
sta·tion·ari·ly
sta·tion·ari·ness
sta·tion·ary not moving; *compare* stationery
sta·tion·er
sta·tion·ery writing materials; *compare* stationary
station·master
stat·ism state control
stat·ist
sta·tis·tic
sta·tis·ti·cal
sta·tis·ti·cal·ly
stat·is·ti·cian
sta·tis·tics
sta·tive linguistics term
stato·blast zoology term
stato·cyst zoology term
stato·lith biology term
stato·lith·ic
sta·tor part of machine; *compare* stater
stato·scope aircraft instrument
statu·ary (*plural* ·aries)

statue
stat·ued
statu·esque
statu·esque·ly
statu·esque·ness
statu·ette
stat·ure
sta·tus (*plural* ·tuses)
sta·tus quo
statu·table
stat·ute
statu·to·ri·ly
statu·tory
staunch loyal; variant spelling of stanch
staunch·ness
stau·ro·lite mineral
stau·ro·lit·ic
stau·ro·scope
stau·ro·scopi·cal·ly
Sta·vang·er Norwegian port
stave (stav·ing, staved *or* stove) wooden strip; to crush; variant spelling of staff
staves (*noun*) *plural of* staff *or* stave
staves·acre plant
Stav·ro·pol Soviet city
stay
stayed *past tense of* stay; *compare* staid
stay·er
stays boned corsets
stay·sail
stead
stead·fast (*or* sted·)
stead·fast·ness (*or* sted·)
steadi·ly
steadi·ness
steady (*adj* steadi·er, steadi·est; *verb* stead·ies, steady·ing, stead·ied)
steady·ing·ly
steak meat; *compare* stake
steak·house
steal (steal·ing, stole, sto·len)
steal·er
stealth
stealth·ful
stealthi·ly
stealthi·ness

stealthy (stealthi·er, stealthi·est)
steam
steam·boat
steam-boiler
steam-chest
steam-engine
steam·er
steamie *Scot* public washhouse
steami·ly
steami·ness
steam·roller
steam·ship
steam-shovel
steam·tight
steam·tight·ness
steamy (steami·er, steami·est)
ste·ap·sin enzyme
stea·rate
ste·aric
stea·rin (*or* ·rine) biochemical compound
stea·rop·tene
stea·tite mineral
stea·tit·ic
stea·toly·sis digestive process
stea·to·py·gia (*or* ·ga) excessively fat buttocks
stea·to·pyg·ic (*or* ·py·gous)
stea·tor·rhoea (*US* ·rhea)
steed
steel alloy; *compare* stele
steel·head (*plural* ·heads *or* ·head) fish
steeli·ness
steel·work
steel·worker
steel·working
steel·works
steely (steeli·er, steeli·est)
steel·yard
steen·bok variant spelling of steinbok
steep
steep·en
steep·er
steep·ish
stee·ple
steeple-chase
steeple·chas·er

steeple·jack
steep·ness
steer guide; bullock;
    compare stere
steer·able
steer·age
steer·age·way
steer·er
steer·ing
steers·man (*plural* ·men)
steeve nautical term
stego·don (*or* ·dont)
    extinct mammal
stego·myia mosquito
stego·saur (*or* ·saur·us)
stein beer mug
stein·bok (*or* steen·;
    plural ·boks *or* ·bok)
    antelope
ste·lar of a stele; *compare*
    stellar
ste·le (*or* ·la; *plural* ·lae
    or ·les) stone slab
stele plant tissue; *compare*
    steel
stel·lar of stars; *compare*
    stelar
stel·lara·tor physics
    apparatus
stel·late (*or* ·lat·ed)
stel·lif·er·ous
stel·li·form
stel·li·fy (·fies, ·fy·ing,
    ·fied) change into a star
Stel·lite (*Trademark*)
stel·lu·lar
stem (stem·ming,
    stemmed)
stem·head
stem·ma family tree
stem·mer
stem·son nautical term
stem·ware stemmed glasses
stem-winder
stench
sten·cil (·cil·ling, ·cilled;
    US ·cil·ing, ·ciled)
sten·cil·ler (*US* ·cil·er)
Sten gun
steno (*plural* stenos) *US*
    shorthand typist
steno·graph
ste·nog·ra·pher *US*
    shorthand typist
steno·graph·ic (*or*
    ·graphi·cal)
ste·nog·ra·phy
steno·ha·line
steno·pet·al·ous
ste·nopha·gous
steno·phyl·lous
ste·no·sis (*plural* ·ses)
steno·ther·mal
ste·not·ic
steno·trop·ic (*or* ·top·)
    ecology term
Steno·type (*Trademark*)
steno·typ·ic
steno·typ·ist
steno·typy form of
    shorthand
sten·tor loud person;
    microscopic animal
sten·to·rian
step (step·ping, stepped)
    motion of foot; stage; etc.;
    compare steppe
step·brother
step·child (*plural*
    ·children)
step·daughter
step·father
stepha·no·tis
step·ladder
step·mother
step-parent
steppe grassy plain; *compare*
    step
step·per
Steppes Eurasian grasslands
step·sister
step·son
step·wise
ste·ra·dian unit
ster·co·ra·ceous of dung
ster·co·rico·lous
ster·cu·lia·ceous botany
    term
stere unit; *compare* steer
ste·reo (*plural* ·reos)
ste·reo·bate foundation of
    building
ste·reo·chem·is·try
ste·reo·chrome
ste·reo·chro·my wall
    painting
ste·reo·gram
ste·reo·graph
ste·reo·graph·ic (*or*
    ·graphi·cal)
ste·reog·ra·phy
ste·reo·iso·mer
ste·reo·isom·er·ism
ste·reo·iso·met·ric
ste·reo·met·ric
ste·reo·met·ri·cal
ste·reom·etry
ste·reo·phon·ic
ste·reo·phoni·cal·ly
ste·reoph·ony
ste·reop·sis stereoscopic
    vision
ste·reop·ti·con type of
    projector
ste·reo·scope
ste·reo·scop·ic (*or*
    ·scopi·cal)
ste·reo·scopi·cal·ly
ste·reos·co·pist
ste·reos·co·py
ste·reo·spe·cif·ic
ste·reo·tac·tic (*or* ·ti·cal)
ste·reo·tac·ti·cal·ly
ste·reo·tax·is biology term
ste·reot·omy
ste·reo·trop·ic
ste·reot·ro·pism botany
    term
ste·reo·type
ste·reo·typ·er (*or* ·ist)
ste·reo·typ·ic (*or*
    ·typi·cal)
ste·reo·typy
ste·reo·vi·sion
ste·ric (*or* ·ri·cal)
    chemistry term
ste·ri·cal·ly
ster·ig·ma (*plural* ·ma·ta)
    botany term
steri·lant
ster·ile
ste·ril·ity
steri·liz·able (*or* ·lis·able)
steri·li·za·tion (*or*
    ·sa·tion)
steri·lize (*or* ·lise)
steri·liz·er (*or* ·lis·er)
ster·let fish
ster·ling
stern
ster·nal of the sternum
stern·most
stern·ness
stern·post
stern·son nautical term

ster·num (*plural* ·na *or*
  ·nums) breastbone
ster·nu·ta·tion sneezing
ster·nu·ta·tive
ster·nu·ta·tor
ster·nu·ta·tory (*plural*
  ·tories)
stern·wards (*or esp. US*
  ·ward)
stern·way
ster·oid
ster·oi·dal
ster·ol biochemical
  compound
ster·tor noisy breathing
ster·to·rous
ster·to·rous·ness
stet (stet·ting, stet·ted)
stetho·scope
stetho·scop·ic
ste·thos·co·py
stet·son
ste·vedore
Ste·ven·age Hertfordshire
  town
Ste·ven·graph (*or* ·vens·)
  silk picture
stew
stew·ard
stew·ard·ess
stew·ard·ship
stewed
sthen·ic strong
stib·ine poisonous gas
stib·nite mineral
stich line of poetry; *compare*
  stitch
stich·ic
stichi·cal·ly
sticho·met·ric (*or* ·ri·cal)
sti·chom·etry
sticho·mythia (*or*
  sti·chomy·thy) drama
  term
stick (stick·ing, stuck)
stick·er
stick·ful (*plural* ·fuls)
sticki·ly
sticki·ness
stick·le argue
stickle·back
stick·ler
stick·seed
stick·tight plant
stick-up (*noun*)

stick·weed
sticky (sticki·er,
  sticki·est)
sticky·beak *Austral*
  inquisitive person
stiff
stiff·en
stiff·en·er
stiff·ness
sti·fle
sti·fler
sti·fling
sti·fling·ly
stig·ma (*plural* ·mas)
  mark; flower part
stig·ma (*plural* ·ma·ta)
  crucifixion mark
stig·mas·ter·ol biochemical
  compound
stig·mat·ic (*or* ·mati·cal)
stig·ma·tism
stig·ma·tist
stig·ma·ti·za·tion (*or*
  ·sa·tion)
stig·ma·tize (*or* ·tise)
stig·ma·tiz·er (*or* ·tis·er)
stil·bene
stil·bite mineral
stil·boes·trol (*US* ·bes·)
stile steps over fence;
  compare style
sti·let·to (*noun, plural*
  ·tos; *verb* ·toes,
  ·toe·ing, ·toed)
still
stil·lage platform
still·birth
still·born
still life (*plural* still lifes)
  picture
stil·li·cide legal term
still·ness
stilt
stilt·ed
stilt·ed·ness
Stil·ton cheese
stimu·lable
stimu·lant
stimu·late
stimu·lat·ing·ly
stimu·la·tion
stimu·la·tive
stimu·la·tor (*or* ·lat·er)
stimu·lus (*plural* ·li)
sting (sting·ing, stung)

sting·er
stin·gi·ly
stin·gi·ness
sting·ing·ly
stin·go beer
sting·ray
stin·gy (·gi·er, ·gi·est)
stink (stink·ing, stank *or*
  stunk)
stink·er
stink·horn fungus
stink·ing·ly
stink·ing·ness
stink·pot
stink·stone
stink·weed
stink·wood
stint
stint·er
stipe plant stalk
sti·pel small leaflike
  structure; *compare* stipple
sti·pel·late
sti·pend
sti·pen·di·ary (*plural*
  ·aries)
sti·pes (*plural* stipi·tes)
  zoology term
sti·pi·form (*or* stipi·ti·)
stipi·tate
stip·ple dot or fleck;
  compare stipel
stip·pler
stip·pling
stipu·lable
stipu·lar
stipu·late
stipu·la·tion
stipu·la·tor
stipu·la·tory
stip·ule leaflike structure
stir (stir·ring, stirred)
stirk heifer
Stir·ling Scottish town
stirps (*plural* stir·pes) line
  of descendants
stir·rable
stir·rer
stir·ring
stir·ring·ly
stir·rup
stitch needlework link;
  compare stich
stitch·er
stitch·ing

stitch·wort
stithy (*plural* stithies)
　Dialect forge
sti·ver coin
stoa (*plural* stoae *or* stoas) covered walk
stoat
stob *Dialect* stump
sto·chas·tic statistics term
sto·chas·ti·cal·ly
stock
stock·ade
stock·breeder
stock·breeding
stock·broker
stock·bro·ker·age (*or* ·broking)
stock·er
stock·fish (*plural* ·fish *or* ·fishes)
stock·holder
stock·holding
Stock·holm
stocki·ly
stocki·ness
stocki·net
stock·ing
stock·inged
stock·ish stupid
stock·ist
stock·jobber
stock·jobbery (*or* ·jobbing)
stock·man (*plural* ·men)
stock·plle
stock·pil·er
Stock·port English town
stock·pot
stock·room
stocks instrument of punishment
stock·still
stock·taking
Stock·ton English town; US port
stocky (stocki·er, stocki·est)
stock·yard
stodge
stodgi·ly
stodgi·ness
stodgy (stodgi·er, stodgi·est)
sto·gy (*or* sto·gey; *plural* ·gies) *US* cigar

Sto·ic philosopher
sto·ic self-controlled person
stoi·cal
stoi·cal·ly
stoi·cal·ness
stoi·chio·logi·cal
stoi·chi·ol·ogy branch of biology
stoi·chio·met·ric
stoi·chi·om·etry branch of chemistry
stoi·cism
stoke
stoke·hold
stoke·hole
Stoke Mandeville Buckinghamshire town
stok·er
stokes (*or* stoke; *plural* stokes) unit
stole long shawl; *past tense of* steal
stol·en
stol·id
sto·lid·ity (*or* stol·id·ness)
stol·len bread
sto·lon stem
sto·loni·fer·ous
sto·ma (*plural* ·ma·ta)
stom·ach
stomach·ache
stom·ach·er
sto·mach·ic
sto·machi·cal
stom·achy
sto·ma·tal (*or* stoma·tous)
sto·mat·ic of the mouth
sto·ma·ti·tic
sto·ma·ti·tis
sto·ma·tol·ogy
stoma·to·plas·ty
stoma·to·pod crustacean
sto·mo·daeal (*or* ·deal)
sto·mo·daeum (*or* ·deum) embryonic mouth cavity
stomp
stomp·er
ston·able (*or* stone·)
stone
stone-blind
stone·chat bird
stone·crop plant
stone·cutter
stone·cutting
stoned

stone·fish (*plural* ·fish *or* ·fishes)
stone·fly (*plural* ·flies)
stone·ground
Stone·henge
stone·less
stone-lily fossil
stone·mason
stone·mason·ry
ston·er
stone·wall
stone·wall·er
stone·ware
stone·work
stone·worker
stone·wort alga
stoni·ly
stoni·ness
stonk bombard with artillery
stony (*or* stoney; stoni·er, stoni·est)
stony-broke
stony-hearted
stony-hearted·ness
stood
stooge
stook
stook·er
stool
stoop bend body; *compare* stoup; stupe
stoop·er
stoop·ing·ly
stop (stop·ping, stopped)
stop·cock
stope mine excavation
stop·gap
stop-go economics term
stop·ing geology term
stop·light
stop·over (*noun*)
stop·pable
stop·page
stop·per
stop·ping
stops card game
stop·watch
stor·able
stor·age
sto·rax plant; drug
store
store·house
store·keeper
store·keeping
store·room

storey

sto·rey (*plural* ·reys *or* ·ries) level; *compare* story
sto·reyed multilevelled
sto·ried recorded
stork
storks·bill plant
storm
storm·bound
stormi·ly
stormi·ness
storm·proof
storm-trooper
stormy (stormi·er, stormi·est)
Stor·no·way Scottish port
Stor·ting (*or* ·thing) Norwegian parliament
sto·ry (*plural* ·ries) tale; *compare* storey
story·book
story·teller
story·telling
stoss geology term
stot (stot·ting, stot·ted) *Scot* bounce
sto·tin·ka (*plural* ·ki) Bulgarian coin
sto·tious *Irish* drunk
stot·ter *Scot* good-looking woman
stound *Dialect* short period
stoup basin for holy water; drinking mug; *compare* stoop; stupe
stour *Dialect* turmoil
Stour·bridge English town
stout
stout·hearted
stout·hearted·ness
stout·ish
stout·ness
stove
stove·pipe
stove·pipes tight trousers
stov·er
stow
stow·age
stow·away
stra·bis·mal (*or* ·mic, ·mi·cal)
stra·bis·mus squint
strad·dle
strad·dler
Stradi·var·ius violin
strafe

straf·er
strag·gle
strag·gler
strag·gling·ly
strag·gly (·gli·er, ·gli·est)
straight not curved; directly; *compare* strait
straight·away
straight·edge
straight·en put straight; *compare* straiten
straight·en·er
straight-faced
straight·forward
straight·forward·ness
straight·ness
strain
strained
strained·ness
strain·er
strain·ing·ly
strait sea channel; difficulty; *compare* straight
strait·en embarrass financially; *compare* straighten
strait·jacket (*or* straight·)
strait-laced (*or* straight-)
strait·ness
strake metal part of wheel
stra·mo·nium drug
Strand London street
strand
stranded
strange
strange·ness
stran·ger
stran·gle
strangle·hold
stran·gler
stran·gles horse disease
stran·gu·late
stran·gu·la·tion
stran·gu·ry painful urination
Stran·raer Scottish port
strap (strap·ping, strapped)
strap·hanger
strap·hanging
strap·less
strap·pa·do (*plural* ·does) torture
strap·per
strap·ping

Stras·bourg French city
strass imitation gem
stra·ta *plural of* stratum
strata·gem
stra·tal
stra·tegic (*or* ·tegi·cal)
stra·tegi·cal·ly
stra·tegics military strategy
strat·egist
strat·egy (*plural* ·egies)
Stratford-on-Avon
strath *Scot* glen
Strath·clyde Scottish region
strath·spey dance
stra·ticu·late geology term
stra·ticu·la·tion
strati·fi·ca·tion
strati·form
strati·fy (·fies, ·fy·ing, ·fied)
stra·tig·ra·pher (*or* ·phist)
strati·graph·ic (*or* ·graphi·cal)
stra·tig·ra·phy study of rock strata
stra·toc·ra·cy (*plural* ·cies) military rule
strato·crat
strato·crat·ic
strato·cu·mu·lus (*plural* ·li)
strato·pause meteorology term
strato·sphere
strato·spher·ic (*or* ·spheri·cal)
stra·tum (*plural* ·ta *or* ·tums) layer
stra·tus (*plural* ·ti) cloud
stra·vaig *Scot* wander
straw
straw·berry (*plural* ·berries)
straw·board
straw·flower
strawy
stray
stray·er
strays electronics term
streak
streaked
streak·er
streaki·ly
streaki·ness
streak·ing

streaky (streaki·er,
    streaki·est)
stream
stream·er
stream·line
stream·lined
street
street·car
street·light (or ·lamp)
street·walker
street·walking
stre·lit·zia plant
strength
strength·en
strength·en·er
strenu·os·ity (or
    ·ous·ness)
strenu·ous
strep·to·coc·cal (or ·cic)
strep·to·coc·cus (plural
    ·coc·ci)
strep·to·ki·nase drug
strep·to·my·cin antibiotic
strep·to·thri·cin antibiotic
stress
stress·ful
stress·ful·ly
stretch
stretch·abil·ity
stretch·able
stretch·er
stretcher-bearer
stretchi·ness
stretchy (stretchi·er,
    stretchi·est)
stret·to (plural ·tos or ·ti)
    musical term
streu·sel pastry topping
strew (strew·ing, strewed,
    strewn or strewed)
strew·er
strewth exclamation
stria (plural striae)
stri·ate (or ·at·ed)
stria·tion
strick textile fibres
strick·en
strick·le
strict
strict·ness
stric·ture
stride (strid·ing, strode,
    strid·den)
stri·dence (or ·den·cy)
stri·dent

stri·dor wheezing sound
stridu·late zoology term
stridu·la·tion
stridu·la·tor
stridu·la·tory
stridu·lous (or ·lant)
stridu·lous·ness (or
    stridu·lance)
strife
strigi·form ornithology term
strig·il body scraper
stri·gose biology term
strik·able
strike (strik·ing, struck)
strike-bound
strike·breaker
strike·breaking
strik·er
strik·ing
strik·ing·ness
string (string·ing, strung)
string·board
stringed
strin·gen·cy
strin·gen·do musical term
strin·gent
string·er
string·halt veterinary term
stringi·ly
stringi·ness
string·piece
stringy (stringi·er,
    stringi·est)
strip (strip·ping, stripped)
stripe
strip·er
strip·ling lad
strip·per
strip·tease
stripy (stripi·er stripi·est)
strive (striv·ing, strove,
    striv·en)
striv·er
strobe lighting
stro·bic spinning
stro·bi·la (plural ·lae)
    body of tapeworm
stro·bi·la·ceous
stro·bi·la·tion
stro·bi·lus (or stro·bile;
    plural ·li, ·luses or
    ·biles) plant cone
stro·bo·scope
stro·bo·scop·ic (or
    ·scopi·cal)

stro·bo·scopi·cal·ly
strode
stroga·noff
stroke
stroll
stroll·er
stro·ma (plural ·ma·ta)
    biology term
stro·mat·ic (or ·ma·tous)
stro·mato·lite rock
stro·mato·lit·ic
Strom·bo·li volcanic island
strong
strong-arm
strong·box
strong·hold
strong·ly
strong·man (plural ·men)
strong-minded
strong-minded·ness
strong·ness
strong·room
strong-willed
stron·gyle (or ·gyl)
    parasitic worm
strontia strontium
    compound
stron·ti·an·ite (or
    stron·tian) mineral
stron·tium chemical
    element
strop (strop·ping,
    stropped)
stro·phan·thin drug
stro·phan·thus tree
stro·phe prosody term
stroph·ic (or strophi·cal)
strop·pi·ly
strop·pi·ness
strop·py (·pi·er, ·pi·est)
Stroud English town
stroud fabric
strove
struck
struc·tur·al
struc·tur·al·ism
struc·tur·al·ist
struc·tur·al·ly
struc·ture
struc·ture·less
stru·del
strug·gle
strug·gler
strug·gling·ly

strum

strum (strum·ming, strummed)
stru·ma (*plural* ·mae) swelling
stru·mat·ic (*or* stru·mous, stru·mose)
strum·mer
strum·pet
strung
strut (strut·ting, strut·ted)
stru·thi·ous ostrich-like
strut·ter
strut·ting·ly
strych·nic
strych·nine
strych·nin·ism
stub (stub·bing, stubbed)
stub·bi·ly
stub·bi·ness
stub·ble
stub·bled
stub·bly
stub·born
stub·born·ness
stub·by (·bi·er, ·bi·est)
stuc·co (*noun, plural* ·coes *or* ·cos; *verb* ·coes *or* ·cos, ·co·ing, ·coed)
stuck
stud (stud·ding, stud·ded)
stud·book
stud·ding
studding·sail
stu·dent
stu·dent·ship
stud·horse
stud·ied
stud·ied·ly
stud·ied·ness
stu·dio (*plural* ·dios)
stu·di·ous
stu·di·ous·ness
stud·work
study (*noun, plural* studies, *verb* stud·ies, study·ing, stud·ied)
stuff
stuffed
stuff·er
stuf·fi·ly
stuffi·ness
stuff·ing
stuffy (stuffi·er, stuffi·est)

stull mining prop
stul·ti·fi·ca·tion
stul·ti·fi·er
stul·ti·fy (·fies, ·fy·ing, ·fied)
stum (stum·ming, stummed) wine-making term
stum·ble
stum·bler
stum·bling·ly
stu·mer *Slang* forgery
stump
stump·er
stumpi·ness
stumpy (stumpi·er, stumpi·est)
stun (stun·ning, stunned)
stung
stunk
stun·ner
stun·ning
stun·ning·ly
stunt
stunt·ed
stunt·ed·ness
stupe medical compress; *compare* stoop; stoup
stu·pefa·ci·ent (*or* ·pefac·tive)
stu·pefac·tion
stu·pefi·er
stu·pefy (·pefies, ·pefy·ing, ·pefied)
stu·pefy·ing·ly
stu·pen·dous
stu·pen·dous·ness
stu·pid
stu·pid·ity (*plural* ·ities)
stu·pid·ness
stu·por
stu·por·ous
stur·di·ly
stur·di·ness
stur·dy (·di·er, ·di·est)
stur·geon
Stur·mer apple
stut·ter
stut·ter·er
stut·ter·ing·ly
Stutt·gart West German city
sty (*noun, plural* sties, *verb* sties, sty·ing, stied) pig's pen

440

sty (*or* stye; *plural* sties *or* styes) inflamed eye spot
Styg·ian of the Styx
stylar
style form; elegance; flower part; *compare* stile
style·book
styl·er
sty·let
sty·li·form
styl·ish
styl·ish·ness
styl·ist
sty·lis·tic
sty·lis·ti·cal·ly
sty·lite recluse
styli·za·tion (*or* ·sa·tion)
styl·ize (*or* ·ise)
styl·iz·er (*or* ·is·er)
sty·lo·bate architectural term
sty·lo·graph
sty·lo·graph·ic (*or* ·graphi·cal)
sty·lo·graphi·cal·ly
sty·log·ra·phy engraving
sty·loid
sty·lo·lite geology term
sty·lo·lit·ic
sty·lo·pize (*or* ·pise) parasitize with stylops
sty·lo·po·dium (*plural* ·dia) botany term
sty·lops (*plural* ·lo·pes) insect
sty·lo·stix·is acupuncture
sty·lus (*plural* ·li *or* ·luses)
sty·mie (*or* ·my; *verb* ·mies, ·mie·ing, ·mied *or* ·mies, ·my·ing, ·mied; *noun, plural* ·mies)
styp·sis
styp·tic
styp·ti·cal
styp·tic·ity
sty·ra·ca·ceous
sty·rax tree
sty·rene organic compound
Styria Austrian province
Styx mythological river
su·abil·ity
su·able
Sua·kin Sudanese port

suave
suave·ly
suav·ity (or suave·ness)
sub (sub·bing, subbed)
sub·ac·etate
sub·acid
sub·acid·ity (or ·acid·ness)
sub·acute medical term
sub·acute·ly
sub·agent
su·bah Mogul province
sub·al·pine
sub·al·tern
sub·al·ter·nate botany term
sub·al·ter·na·tion
sub·ant·arc·tic
sub·aquat·ic
sub·aque·ous
sub·arc·tic
sub·ar·id
sub·as·sem·bly (plural ·blies)
sub·atom·ic
sub·audi·tion
sub·auricu·lar
sub·ax·il·la·ry
sub·base pedestal base
sub·base·ment
sub·bass (or ·base) organ stop
sub·cali·bre
sub·car·ti·lagi·nous
sub·ce·les·tial
sub·cep·tion subliminal perception
sub·chlo·ride
sub·class
sub·cla·vian
sub·cli·mac·tic
sub·cli·max
sub·com·mit·tee
sub·con·scious
sub·con·scious·ness
sub·con·ti·nent
sub·con·ti·nen·tal
sub·con·tract
sub·con·trac·tor
sub·con·tra·ry (plural ·ries)
sub·cor·tex (plural ·tices)
sub·cor·ti·cal
sub·cul·tur·al
sub·cul·ture
sub·cu·ta·neous

sub·dea·con
sub·dea·con·ate
sub·de·lir·ium (plural ·lir·iums or ·liria)
sub·di·aco·nal
sub·di·aco·nate subdeacon's rank
sub·di·vide
sub·di·vid·er
sub·di·vi·sion
sub·di·vi·sion·al
sub·domi·nant
sub·du·able
sub·du·al
sub·duct
sub·duc·tion
sub·due (·dues, ·du·ing, ·dued)
sub·dued·ly
sub·dued·ness
sub·edit
sub·edi·tor
sub·equa·to·rial
su·ber·in plant substance
su·beri·za·tion (or ·sa·tion)
su·ber·ize (or ·ise)
su·ber·ose (or ·bereous, ·ber·ic) of cork
sub·fami·ly (plural ·lies)
sub·floor
sub·fusc drab; academic dress
sub·ge·ner·ic
sub·ge·nus (plural ·gen·era or ·ge·nuses)
sub·gla·cial
sub·gla·cial·ly
sub·group
sub·head·ing (or ·head)
sub·hu·man
sub·in·dex (plural ·dices or ·dexes)
sub·in·feu·date
sub·in·feu·da·tion
sub·in·feu·da·tory (plural ·tories)
sub·ir·ri·gate
sub·ir·ri·ga·tion
su·bi·to musical term
sub·ja·cen·cy
sub·ja·cent
sub·ject
sub·ject·abil·ity
sub·ject·able

submersible

sub·jec·ti·fi·ca·tion
sub·jec·ti·fy (·fies, ·fy·ing, ·fied)
sub·jec·tion
sub·jec·tive
sub·jec·tive·ly
sub·jec·tiv·ism
sub·jec·tiv·ist
sub·jec·ti·vis·tic
sub·jec·ti·vis·ti·cal·ly
sub·jec·tiv·ity (or ·tive·ness)
subject-raising
sub·join
sub·join·der
sub ju·di·ce
sub·ju·gable
sub·ju·gate
sub·ju·ga·tion
sub·ju·ga·tor
sub·junc·tion
sub·junc·tive
sub·king·dom
sub·lease
sub·les·see
sub·les·sor
sub·let (·let·ting, ·let)
sub·lieu·ten·an·cy
sub·lieu·ten·ant
sub·li·mable
sub·li·mate
sub·li·ma·tion
sub·lime
sub·lime·ly
sub·limi·nal
sub·limi·nal·ly
sub·lim·ity (plural ·ities)
sub·lin·gual
sub·lit·to·ral near seashore
sub·lu·nary between moon and earth
sub·machine-gun
sub·mar·gin·al
sub·ma·rine
sub·ma·rin·er
sub·max·il·lary of lower jaw
sub·me·di·ant musical term
sub·men·tal beneath the chin
sub·merge (or ·merse)
sub·mers·ibil·ity (or ·merg·)
sub·mers·ible (or ·merg·)

submersion

sub·mer·sion (*or* ·merg·ence)
sub·micro·scop·ic
sub·micro·scopi·cal·ly
sub·miss *Archaic* docile
sub·mis·sion
sub·mis·sive
sub·mis·sive·ly
sub·mis·sive·ness
sub·mit (·mit·ting, ·mit·ted)
sub·mit·table (*or* ·mis·sible)
sub·mit·tal
sub·mit·ter
sub·mit·ting·ly
sub·mon·tane
sub·mu·co·sa (*plural* ·sae)
sub·mul·ti·ple
sub·nor·mal
sub·nor·mal·ity
sub·nor·mal·ly
sub·ocean·ic
sub·or·bi·tal
sub·or·der
sub·or·di·nal
sub·or·di·nary (*plural* ·naries) heraldic term
sub·or·di·nate
sub·or·di·nate·ly
sub·or·di·nate·ness
sub·or·di·na·tion
sub·or·di·na·tive
sub·orn
sub·or·na·tion
sub·or·na·tive
sub·orn·er
sub·ox·ide
sub·phy·lar
sub·phy·lum (*plural* ·la)
sub·plot
sub·poe·na (·nas, ·na·ing, ·naed)
sub·popu·la·tion
sub·prin·ci·pal
sub·re·gion
sub·re·gion·al
sub·rep·tion concealment of facts
sub·rep·ti·tious
sub·ro·gate legal term
sub·ro·ga·tion
sub rosa *Latin* in secret
sub·rou·tine
sub·scapu·lar
sub·scribe
sub·scrib·er
sub·script
sub·scrip·tion
sub·scrip·tive
sub·sec·tion
sub·se·quence
sub·se·quent
sub·serve
sub·ser·vience (*or* ·vi·en·cy)
sub·ser·vi·ent
sub·set
sub·shrub
sub·side
sub·sid·ence
sub·sid·er
sub·sidi·ari·ly
sub·sidi·ari·ness
sub·sidi·ary (*plural* ·aries)
sub·si·diz·able (*or* ·dis·able)
sub·si·di·za·tion (*or* ·sa·tion)
sub·si·dize (*or* ·dise)
sub·si·diz·er (*or* ·dis·er)
sub·si·dy (*plural* ·dies)
sub·sist
sub·sist·ence
sub·sist·ent
sub·sist·er
sub·sist·ing·ly
sub·so·cial
sub·soil
sub·soil·er
sub·so·lar
sub·son·ic
sub·soni·cally
sub·spe·cies (*plural* ·cies)
sub·spe·cif·ic
sub·spe·cifi·cal·ly
sub·stage
sub·stance
sub·stand·ard
sub·stan·tial
sub·stan·tial·ism
sub·stan·tial·ist
sub·stan·ti·al·ity (*or* ·tial·ness)
sub·stan·tial·ly
sub·stan·ti·ate
sub·stan·tia·tion
sub·stan·tia·tive
sub·stan·tia·tor
sub·stan·ti·val grammar term
sub·stan·ti·val·ly
sub·stan·tive
sub·stan·tive·ly
sub·stan·tive·ness
sub·stan·ti·vi·za·tion (*or* ·sa·tion)
sub·stan·tiv·ize (*or* ·ise)
sub·sta·tion
sub·stitu·ent
sub·sti·tuta·bil·ity
sub·sti·tut·able
sub·sti·tute
sub·sti·tu·tion
sub·sti·tu·tive
sub·strate
sub·stra·tive (*or* ·tal)
sub·stra·tum (*plural* ·stra·ta)
sub·struc·tur·al (*or* ·tion·al)
sub·struc·ture (*or* ·tion)
sub·sum·able
sub·sume
sub·sump·tion
sub·sump·tive
sub·tan·gent
sub·tem·per·ate
sub·ten·an·cy (*plural* ·cies)
sub·ten·ant
sub·tend
sub·ter·fuge
sub·ter·ra·nean
sub·ter·res·trial
sub·tili·za·tion (*or* ·sa·tion)
sub·til·ize (*or* ·ise) refine
sub·til·iz·er (*or* ·is·er)
sub·ti·tle
sub·titu·lar
sub·tle
sub·tle·ness
sub·tler more subtle; *compare* sutler
sub·tle·ty (*plural* ·ties)
sub·tly
sub·ton·ic musical note
sub·tor·rid
sub·to·tal (·tal·ling, ·talled; *US* ·tal·ing, ·taled)
sub·tract
sub·tract·er

sub·trac·tion
sub·trac·tive
sub·tra·hend number subtracted
sub·tropi·cal
sub·trop·ics
sub·type
sub·typi·cal
su·bu·late awl-shaped
sub·urb
sub·ur·ban
sub·ur·ban·ite
sub·ur·bani·za·tion (or ·sa·tion)
sub·ur·ban·ize (or ·ise)
sub·ur·bia
sub·vene
sub·ven·tion
sub·ven·tion·ary
sub·ver·sion
sub·ver·sive
sub·ver·sive·ly
sub·ver·sive·ness
sub·vert
sub·vert·er
sub·way
sub·zero
suc·ce·da·neous
suc·ce·da·neum (plural ·nea) substitute drug
suc·ceed
suc·ceed·able
suc·ceed·er
suc·ceed·ing·ly
suc·cen·tor cathedral cleric
suc·cess
suc·cess·ful
suc·cess·ful·ly
suc·cess·ful·ness
suc·ces·sion
suc·ces·sion·al
suc·ces·sive
suc·ces·sive·ly
suc·ces·sive·ness
suc·ces·sor
suc·ces·sor·al
suc·cin·ate chemical compound
suc·cinct
suc·cinct·ness
suc·cin·ic of amber; chemistry term
suc·cory (plural ·cories) chicory

suc·co·tash US mixed vegetables
suc·cour (US ·cor)
suc·cour·able (US ·cor·)
suc·cour·er (US ·cor·)
suc·cu·bus (plural ·bi) female demon
suc·cu·lence (or ·len·cy)
suc·cu·lent
suc·cumb
suc·cumb·er
suc·cur·sal subsidiary
suc·cuss
suc·cus·sion
suc·cus·sive
such
such·like
Su·chou variant spelling of Soochow
Sü·chow (or Hsü-chou) Chinese city
suck
suck·er
sucker·fish (or suck·fish; plural ·fish or ·fishes)
suck·le
suck·ler
suck·ling
su·crase enzyme
su·crose sugar
suc·tion
suc·tion·al
suc·to·rial
Su·dan
Su·da·nese (plural ·nese)
Su·dan·ic
su·dar·ium (plural ·daria) face cloth
su·da·to·rium (or ·tory; plural ·to·ria or ·tories) steam-bath room
Sud·bury Canadian city
sudd water weed
sud·den
sud·den·ness
Su·deten·land Czech region
Su·detes (or Su·deten) European mountains
su·dor sweat
su·dor·al
su·dor·if·er·ous
su·dor·if·ic
suds
sudsy
sue (su·ing, sued)

(sueable) incorrect spelling of suable
suede
suer one who sues; compare sewer
suet
su·ety
Suez
suf·fer
suf·fer·able
suf·fer·ance
suf·fer·er
suf·fer·ing
suf·fice
suf·fic·er
suf·fi·cien·cy (plural ·cies)
suf·fi·cient
suf·fix
suf·fix·al
suf·fix·ion
suf·fo·cate
suf·fo·cat·ing·ly
suf·fo·ca·tion
suf·fo·ca·tive
Suf·folk
suf·fra·gan assistant bishop
suf·fra·gan·ship
suf·frage
suf·fra·gette
suf·fra·get·tism
suf·fra·gism
suf·fra·gist
suf·fru·ti·cose botany term
suf·fu·mi·gate
suf·fu·mi·ga·tion
suf·fuse
suf·fu·sion
suf·fu·sive
Sufi (plural Sufis) Muslim mystic
Su·fic
Su·fism
Su·fis·tic
sug·ar
sug·ari·ness
sugar·plum
sug·ary
sug·gest
sug·gest·er
sug·gest·ibil·ity
sug·gest·ible
sug·gest·ible·ness
sug·gest·ing·ly
sug·ges·tion

suggestive

sug·ges·tive
sug·ges·tive·ly
sug·ges·tive·ness
sui·cid·al
sui·cid·al·ly
sui·cide
sui gen·er·is unique
su·int substance in fleece
suit clothes; set of cards; petition; to be appropriate; *compare* suite
suit·abil·ity (or ·able·ness)
suit·able
suit·ably
suit·case
suite set of rooms; furniture; musical piece; *compare* suit
suit·ing
suit·or
Su·khu·mi Soviet port
su·ki·ya·ki Japanese dish
Su·la·we·si Indonesian island
sul·cate
sul·ca·tion
sul·cus (*plural* ·ci) groove
sul·fur *US spelling of* sulphur; *note all words starting* sulph- *have the US spelling* sulf-
sulk
sulk·er
sulki·ly
sulki·ness
sulky (*adj* sulki·er, sulki·est; *noun, plural* sulkies) sullen; vehicle
sul·lage sewage
sul·len
sul·len·ness
sul·li·able
sul·ly (·lies, ·ly·ing, ·lied)
sul·pha (*US* ·fa) class of drugs; *compare* sulphur
sul·pha·dia·zine (*US* ·fa·)
sul·pha·nila·mide (*US* ·fa·)
sul·phate (*US* ·fate)
sul·pha·thia·zole (*US* ·fa·)
sul·pha·tion (*US* ·fa·)
sul·phide (*US* ·fide)
sul·phi·soxa·zole (*US* ·fi·)
sul·phite (*US* ·fite)
sul·phit·ic (*US* ·fit·)

sul·phona·mide (*US* ·fona·) sulpha drug
sul·pho·nate (*US* ·fo·)
sul·phone (*US* ·fone)
sul·phon·me·thane (*US* ·fon·)
sul·phur (*US* ·fur) chemical element; *compare* sulpha
sul·phur·ate (*US* ·fur·)
sul·phu·ra·tion (*US* ·fu·)
sul·phu·reous (*US* ·fu·)
sul·phu·reous·ness (*US* ·fu·)
sul·phu·ret (*US* ·fu·; ·ret·ting, ·ret·ted, *US* ·ret·ing, ·ret·ed)
sul·phu·ric (*US* ·fu·)
sul·phu·ri·za·tion (*or* ·sa·tion; *US* ·fu·ri·za·tion)
sul·phu·rize (*or* ·rise; *US* ·fu·rize)
sul·phur·ous (*US* ·fur·)
sul·phur·ous·ness (*US* ·fur·)
sul·phur·yl (*US* ·fur·)
sul·tan
sul·tana
sul·tan·ate
sul·tan·ic
sul·tri·ly
sul·tri·ness
sul·try (·tri·er, ·tri·est)
Sulu Philippine archipelago
sum (sum·ming, summed)
su·mach (*or* ·mac) shrub
Su·ma·tra
Su·ma·tran
Su·mer Babylonian region
Su·me·rian
sum·ma (*plural* ·mae) medieval compendium
sum·ma cum lau·de highest achievement in examination
sum·mand part of a sum
sum·mari·ly
sum·mari·ness
sum·ma·riz·able (*or* ·ris·able)
sum·ma·ri·za·tion (*or* ·sa·tion)
sum·ma·rize (*or* ·rise)
sum·ma·riz·er (*or* ·ris·er)

444

sum·mary (*plural* ·maries) brief account; *compare* summery
sum·ma·tion
sum·ma·tion·al
sum·mer
summer·house
sum·meri·ness
sum·mer·sault variant spelling of somersault
summer·time
summer·wood
sum·mery like summer; *compare* summary
summing-up (*plural* summings-)
sum·mit
sum·mit·al
sum·mit·ry
sum·mon (*verb*)
sum·mon·able
sum·mons (*noun, plural* ·monses; *verb* ·mons, ·mons·ing, ·monsed)
sum·mum bon·um *Latin* highest good
Sumo wrestling
sump
sump·tua·ry
sump·tu·ous
sump·tu·ous·ness (*or* ·tu·os·ity)
sun (sun·ning, sunned)
sun·bake *Austral* sunbathing
sun·baked
sun·bathe
sun·bather
sun·beam
sun·bird
sun·bonnet
sun·bow
sun·burn
sun·burnt (*or* ·burned)
sun·burst
sun·dae dessert
Sun·da Is·lands
Sun·day
sun·der
sun·der·able
sun·der·ance
sun·der·er
Sun·der·land
sun·dew
sun·dial

sun·dog small rainbow
sun·down
sun·dress
sun·dried
sun·dry (*plural* **·dries**)
sun·fast
sun·fish (*plural* **·fish** *or* **·fishes**)
sun·flower
sung
Sun·ga·ri Chinese river
sun·glass burning glass
sun·glasses spectacles
sun·glow
sun·god
sun·grebe bird
sun·hat
sunk
sunk·en
sun·less
sun·less·ness
sun·light
sun·lit
sunn fibre
Sun·na Islamic law
sunned
Sun·ni (*plural* **·ni**) Muslim sect
sun·ni·ly
sun·ni·ness
sun·ning
Sun·nite Muslim
sun·ny (**·ni·er**, **·ni·est**)
sun·ray pleats
sun·rise
sun·roof
sun·set
sun·shade
sun·shine
sun·shiny
sun·spot
sun·spotted
sun·star starfish
sun·stroke
sun·suit
sun·tan
sun·tanned
sun·trap
sun·wards (*or esp. US* **·ward**)
sun·wise
sup (**sup·ping, supped**)
su·per
super·abil·ity (*or* **·able·ness**)

super·able
super·ably
super·abound
super·abun·dance
supera·bun·dant
super·add
super·ad·di·tion
super·ad·di·tion·al
super·an·nu·ate
super·an·nu·at·ed
super·an·nua·tion
su·perb
super·ba·zaar Indian store
su·perb·ness
super·cal·en·der
super·car·go (*plural* **·goes**)
(supercede) *incorrect spelling of* **supersede**
super·charge
super·char·ger
super·cili·ary of the eyebrow
super·cili·ous
super·cili·ous·ness
super·class
super·co·lum·nar
super·con·duc·tion
super·con·duc·tive (*or* **·duct·ing**)
super·con·duc·tiv·ity
super·con·duc·tor
super·cool (*verb*)
super-duper
super·ego (*plural* **·egos**)
super·el·eva·tion
super·emi·nence
super·emi·nent
super·eroga·tory superfluous
super·fami·ly (*plural* **·lies**)
super·fe·cun·da·tion
super·fe·tate
super·fe·ta·tion physiology term
super·fi·cial
super·fi·ci·al·ity (*or* **·cial·ness**)
super·fi·cial·ly
super·fine
super·fix linguistics term
super·fluid
super·flu·id·ity
super·flu·ity
super·flu·ous

super·flu·ous·ness
super·gi·ant
super·gla·cial
super·heat (*verb*)
super·he·ro (*plural* **·roes**)
super·het·ero·dyne radio receiver
super·high·way *US* fast dual carriageway
super·hu·man
super·hu·man·ity (*or* **·man·ness**)
super·im·pose
super·im·po·si·tion
super·in·cum·bence (*or* **·ben·cy**)
super·in·cum·bent
super·in·duce
super·induce·ment
super·in·duc·tion
super·in·tend
super·in·tend·ence
super·in·tend·en·cy (*plural* **·cies**) office of superintendent
super·in·ten·dent
Su·peri·or *US* lake
su·peri·or
su·peri·or·ity
super·ja·cent
super·la·tive
super·la·tive·ly
super·la·tive·ness
super·lun·ar
super·lun·ary
super·man (*plural* **·men**)
super·mar·ket
super·nal celestial
super·nal·ly
super·na·tant
super·na·ta·tion
super·natu·ral
super·natu·ral·ism
super·natu·ral·ist
super·natu·ral·is·tic
super·natu·ral·ly
super·natu·ral·ness
super·nor·mal
super·nor·mal·ity (*or* **·ness**)
super·nor·mal·ly
super·no·va (*plural* **·vae** *or* **·vas**)
super·nu·mer·ary (*plural* **·aries**)

superorder

super·or·der
super·ordi·nal
super·or·di·nate
super·ox·ide
super·phos·phate
super·physi·cal
super·pos·able
super·pose
super·po·si·tion
super·pow·er
super·satu·rat·ed chemistry term
super·satu·ra·tion
super·scribe
super·script
super·scrip·tion
super·sed·able
super·sede
super·sed·ence
super·sed·er
super·se·dure
super·sen·sible (or ·sory)
super·ses·sion
super·sex genetics term
super·son·ic
super·soni·cal·ly
super·son·ics
super·star
super·sti·tion
super·sti·tious
super·sti·tious·ness
super·store
super·stra·tum (plural ·ta or ·tums)
super·struct build on another structure
super·struc·tur·al
super·struc·ture
super·tank·er
super·tax
super·ton·ic musical note
super·vene
super·veni·ent
super·ven·tion (or ·veni·ence)
super·vise
super·vi·sion
super·vi·sor
super·vi·sory
su·pi·nate
su·pi·na·tion
su·pi·na·tor muscle
su·pine
su·pine·ly
su·pine·ness
su·plex wrestling hold
supped
sup·per
sup·ping
sup·plant
sup·plan·ta·tion
sup·plant·er
sup·ple
supple·jack plant
sup·ple·ly variant spelling of supply
sup·plement
sup·plemen·tal
sup·ple·men·ta·ri·ly (or ·tal·ly)
sup·plemen·ta·ry (plural ·ries)
sup·plemen·ta·tion
sup·plement·er
sup·ple·ness
sup·pletion linguistics term
sup·pletive
sup·pleto·ri·ly
sup·pletory
sup·pli·able
sup·pli·ance (or ·an·cy)
sup·pli·ant
sup·pli·cant (or ·pli·ant)
sup·pli·cate
sup·pli·ca·tion
sup·pli·ca·tory
sup·pli·er
sup·ply (noun, plural ·plies; verb ·plies, ·ply·ing, ·plied)
sup·ply (or sup·ple·ly) in a supple way
sup·port
sup·port·abil·ity (or ·able·ness)
sup·port·ably
sup·port·able
sup·port·er
sup·port·ing
sup·port·ive
sup·pos·able
sup·pose
sup·posed
sup·pos·ed·ly
sup·pos·er
sup·po·si·tion
sup·po·si·tion·al
sup·po·si·tious (or ·posi·ti·tious)
sup·po·si·tious·ness (or ·posi·ti·tious·ness)
sup·posi·tive involving supposition
sup·posi·tory (plural ·tories)
sup·press
sup·press·ible
sup·pres·sion
sup·pres·sive
sup·pres·sor (or ·press·er)
sup·pu·rate
sup·pu·ra·tion
sup·pu·ra·tive
su·pra above
supra·glot·tal
supra·lap·sar·ian theology term
supra·limi·nal
supra·mo·lecu·lar
supra·na·tion·al
supra·na·tion·al·ism
supra·or·bit·al
supra·re·nal
supra·seg·men·tal
su·prema·cist
su·prema·cy
Su·prema·tism cubist art
su·prema·tism
Su·prema·tist
su·preme
su·prême cookery term
su·preme·ly
su·preme·ness
su·prem·ity
su·pre·mo (plural ·mos)
sura Koran chapter
Su·ra·ba·ya (or ·ja, Soe·ra·ba·ja) Indonesian port
su·rah fabric
Su·ra·kar·ta Indonesian town
su·ral anatomy term
Su·rat Indian port
su·rat fabric
sur·base architectural term
sur·base·ment
sur·cease
sur·charge
sur·charg·er
sur·cin·gle horse's girth; cassock belt
sur·coat
sur·cu·lose bearing suckers

surd maths term
sure
sure-fire
sure-footed
sure-footed·ly
sure-footed·ness
sure·ly
sure·ness
sure·ty (*plural* ·ties)
surf breaking waves; *compare* serf
surf·able
sur·face
surface-active
sur·fac·er
sur·fac·tant
surf·bird
surf·board
surf·boat
surf·caster
surf·casting shore-fishing
sur·feit
sur·feit·er
surf·er
surfie *Austral* surfer
surf·ing
surf·like
surf·perch fish
surf·rider
surfy
surge rush; *compare* serge
sur·geon
sur·geon·cy (*plural* ·cies)
surgeon·fish (*plural* ·fish *or* ·fishes)
surg·er
sur·gery (*plural* ·geries)
sur·gi·cal
sur·gi·cal·ly
su·ri·cate animal
Su·ri·nam South American republic
sur·jec·tion
sur·jec·tive
sur·li·ly
sur·li·ness
sur·ly (·li·er, ·li·est)
sur·mis·able
sur·mise
sur·mis·ed·ly
sur·mis·er
sur·mount
sur·mount·able
sur·mount·able·ness
sur·mount·er

sur·name
sur·pass
sur·pass·able
sur·pas·sing
sur·pass·ing·ly
sur·pass·ing·ness
sur·plice vestment
sur·pliced
sur·plus (*plural* ·pluses) excess
sur·plus·age
sur·print overprint
sur·prise
sur·pris·ed·ly
sur·pris·er
sur·pris·ing
sur·pris·ing·ly
sur·pris·ing·ness
sur·ra animal disease
sur·re·al
sur·re·al·ism
sur·re·al·ist
sur·re·al·is·tic
sur·re·al·is·ti·cal·ly
sur·re·but·tal
sur·re·but·ter
sur·re·join·der
sur·ren·der
sur·ren·der·er
sur·rep·ti·tious
sur·rep·ti·tious·ness
Sur·rey English county
sur·rey carriage
sur·ro·gate
sur·ro·gate·ship
sur·ro·ga·tion
sur·round
sur·round·ing
sur·round·ings
sur·tax
sur·tout overcoat
sur·veil·lance
sur·veil·lant
sur·vey
sur·vey·able
sur·vey·ing
sur·vey·or
sur·vey·or·ship
sur·viv·abil·ity
sur·viv·able
sur·viv·al
sur·vive
sur·vi·vor
Susa ancient Persian city

sus·cep·tance magnetic property
sus·cep·tibil·ity (*plural* ·ities)
sus·cep·tible
sus·cep·tibly
sus·cep·tible·ness
sus·cep·tive
sus·cep·tiv·ity (*or* ·tive·ness)
su·shi Japanese food
sus·lik variant spelling of souslik
sus·pect
sus·pect·er
sus·pend
sus·pend·er
sus·pend·ibil·ity
sus·pend·ible (*or* ·pens·)
sus·pense
sus·pense·ful
sus·pen·sion
sus·pen·sive
sus·pen·sive·ness
sus·pen·soid chemistry term
sus·pen·sor
sus·pen·so·ry (*plural* ·ries)
sus·pi·cion
sus·pi·cion·al
sus·pi·cious
sus·pi·cious·ness
sus·pi·ra·tion
sus·pire sigh
Sus·que·han·na US river
suss
Sus·sex
sus·tain
sus·tain·able
sus·tain·ed·ly
sus·tain·er
sus·tain·ing·ly
sus·tain·ment
sus·te·nance
sus·ten·tacu·lar supporting
sus·ten·ta·tion nourishment
sus·ten·tion
su·sur·rant
su·sur·rate
su·sur·ra·tion (*or* su·sur·rus)
Suth·er·land former Scottish county
Sut·lej Asian river

sutler

sut·ler provisioner; *compare* subtler
su·tra Sanskrit sayings
sut·tee Hindu custom
Sut·ton Cold·field English town
su·tur·al
su·ture
Suva Fijian capital
Su·wan·nee (*or* Swa·nee) US river
su·ze·rain
su·ze·rain·ty (*plural* ·ties)
Sval·bard Norwegian archipelago
svelte
Sverd·lovsk Soviet city
swab (swab·bing, swabbed)
swab·ber
Swa·bia former German duchy
Swa·bian
swacked *Slang* intoxicated
swad·dle
swag (swag·ging, swagged)
swage tool
swag·er
swag·ger
swag·ger·er
swag·ger·ing·ly
swag·man (*plural* ·men)
Swa·hi·li (*plural* ·lis *or* ·li)
Swa·hi·lian
swain
swal·low
swal·low·able
swal·low·er
swallow·tail
swallow·wort
swam
swa·mi (*plural* ·mies *or* ·mis) Hindu title
swamp
swamp·land
swampy (swampi·er, swampi·est)
swan (swan·ning, swanned)
Swa·nee variant spelling of Suwannee
swan·herd
swank
swanki·ly

swanki·ness
swanky (swanki·er, swanki·est)
swan·like
swan·nery (*plural* ·neries)
swan's-down
Swan·sea
swan·skin
swan-upping
swap (*or* swop; swap·ping, swapped *or* swop·ping, swopped)
swap·per (*or* swop·)
swa·raj Indian self-government
sward (*or* swarth) turf; *compare* sword
swarf metal off-cuttings
swarm
swarthi·ly
swarthi·ness
swarthy (swarthi·er, swarthi·est)
swash splash
swash·buck·ler
swash·buck·ling
swash·ing·ly
swas·ti·ka
swat (swat·ting, swat·ted) hit; *compare* swot
swatch
swath (*or* swathe; *noun*)
swath·able (*or* swathe·)
swathe (*verb*)
Swa·tow Chinese port
swats *Dialect* beer
swat·ter
sway
sway·able
sway-back
sway·er
sway·ing·ly
Swa·zi (*plural* ·zis *or* ·zi)
Swa·zi·land
swear (swear·ing, swore, sworn)
swear·er
swear·ing·ly
swear·word
sweat (sweat·ing, sweat *or* sweat·ed)
sweat·band
sweat·box
sweat·er
sweati·ly

sweati·ness
sweat·shop
sweaty (sweati·er, sweati·est)
Swede native of Sweden
swede vegetable
Swe·den
Swe·den·bor·gi·an·ism (*or* ·bor·gism) religious movement
Swe·dish
swee·ny veterinary term
sweep (sweep·ing, swept)
sweep·back
sweep·er
sweep·ing
sweep·ing·ly
sweep·ing·ness
sweep·ings
sweep·stake
sweet
sweet·bread
sweet·brier
sweet·en
sweet·en·er
sweet·en·ing
sweet·heart
sweetie
sweetie·wife (*plural* ·wives) *Scot* talkative woman
sweet·ish
sweet·meal
sweet·meat
sweet·ness
sweet·shop
sweet·sop fruit
swell (swell·ing, swelled, swol·len *or* swelled)
swell·fish (*plural* ·fish *or* ·fishes)
swell·ing
swel·ter
swel·ter·ing
swel·ter·ing·ly
swept
swept·back
swept·wing
swerv·able
swerve
swerv·er
swerv·ing·ly
swift
swift·er nautical term
swiftie *Austral* a trick

swift·let bird
swift·ness
swig (swig·ging, swigged)
swig·ger
swill
swill·er
swim (swim·ming, swam, swum)
swim·mable
swim·mer
swim·mer·et zoology term
swim·ming·ly
swim·suit
swin·dle
swin·dler
swin·dling·ly
Swin·don
swine (plural swines)
swine·herd
swine·pox
swing (swing·ing, swung)
swing·boat
swinge (swinge·ing, swinged) punish
swing·er
swing·ing
swin·gle flax-beating instrument
swing·om·eter
swing-wing
swin·ish
swin·ish·ness
swink Dialect toil
swipe
swipes Slang beer
swip·ple (or swi·ple) part of flail
swirl
swirl·ing·ly
swirly
swish
swish·er
swish·ing·ly
swishy
Swiss
switch
switch·back
switch·board
switch·er
switch·eroo US unexpected change
switch·girl Austral switchboard operator
switch-over (noun)
swith·er Scot hesitate

Switz·er a Swiss
Swit·zer·land
swiv·el (·el·ling, ·elled; US ·el·ing, ·eled)
swiv·et Dialect excitement
swizz Slang disappointment
swiz·zle
swol·len
swol·len·ness
swoon
swoon·ing·ly
swoop
swoosh
swop variant spelling of swap
sword weapon; compare sward
sword·bill
sword·craft
sword·fish (plural ·fish or ·fishes)
sword·like
sword·play
swords·man (plural ·men)
swords·man·ship
sword·stick
sword·tail fish
swore
sworn
swot (swot·ting, swot·ted) study; compare swat
swound Dialect swoon
swum
swung
swy Austral gambling game
Syba·ris ancient Greek colony
Syba·rite
syba·rite lover of luxury
syba·rit·ic (or ·riti·cal)
syba·riti·cal·ly
(sybil) incorrect spelling of sibyl
syca·mine mulberry
syca·more
syce (or sice, saice) Indian servant
sy·cee silver ingots
sy·co·nium (plural ·nia) botany term
syco·phan·cy
syco·phant
syco·phan·tic
syco·phan·ti·cal·ly
sy·co·sis skin disease

Syd·ney Australian city; Canadian port
Sy·ene ancient Egyptian town
sy·enite rock
sy·enit·ic
Syk·tyv·kar Soviet city
syl·la·bary (plural ·baries)
syl·lab·ic
syl·labi·cal·ly
syl·labi·cate syllabify
syl·labi·fi·ca·tion (or ·labi·ca·tion)
syl·labi·fy (·fies, ·fy·ing, ·fied)
syl·la·bism
syl·la·ble
syl·labo·gram
syl·lab·og·ra·phy
syl·la·bub (or sil·)
syl·la·bus (plural ·buses or ·bi)
syl·lep·sis (plural ·ses) linguistics term
syl·lep·tic
syl·lep·ti·cal·ly
syl·lo·gism
syl·lo·gis·tic
syl·lo·gis·ti·cal
syl·lo·gis·ti·cal·ly
syl·lo·gi·za·tion (or ·sa·tion)
syl·lo·gize (or ·gise)
syl·lo·giz·er (or ·gis·er)
sylph
sylph·ic (or ·id)
sylph·like (or ·ish)
syl·va (or sil·; plural ·vas or ·vae) trees
syl·van (or sil·)
syl·van·ite mineral
Sylvanus variant spelling of Silvanus
syl·vat·ic (or ·ves·tral) occurring in a wood
syl·vite (or ·vine) mineral
sym·bi·ont
sym·bi·on·tic
sym·bio·sis
sym·bi·ot·ic (or ·oti·cal)
sym·bi·oti·cal·ly
sym·bol (·bol·ling, ·bolled; US ·bol·ing, ·boled) thing representing something; compare cymbal

symbolic

sym·bol·ic (*or* ·boli·cal)
sym·boli·cal·ly
sym·boli·cal·ness
sym·bol·ism
sym·bol·ist
sym·bol·is·tic (*or* ·ti·cal)
sym·bol·is·ti·cal·ly
sym·boli·za·tion (*or* ·sa·tion)
sym·bol·ize (*or* ·ise)
sym·bo·logi·cal
sym·bolo·gist
sym·bol·ogy
sym·met·al·lism economic doctrine
sym·met·ri·cal
sym·met·ri·cal·ly
sym·met·ri·cal·ness
sym·me·tri·za·tion (*or* ·sa·tion)
sym·me·trize (*or* ·trise)
sym·me·try (*plural* ·tries)
sym·pa·thec·to·my (*plural* ·mies) nerve surgery
sym·pa·thet·ic (*or* ·theti·cal)
sym·pa·theti·cal·ly
sym·pa·thin hormone
sym·pa·thize (*or* ·thise)
sym·pa·thiz·er (*or* ·this·er)
sym·pa·thiz·ing·ly (*or* ·this·ing·ly)
sym·pa·tho·lyt·ic pharmacology term
sym·pa·tho·mi·met·ic pharmacology term
sym·pa·thy (*plural* ·thies)
sym·pat·ric biology term
sym·pat·ri·cal·ly
sym·pet·al·ous
sym·phile entomology term
sym·phon·ic
sym·phoni·cal·ly
sym·pho·ni·ous
sym·pho·nist
sym·pho·ny (*plural* ·nies)
sym·phys·ial (*or* ·eal)
sym·physi·cal·ly (*or* ·phyti·)
sym·phy·sis (*plural* ·ses) anatomy term
sym·phys·tic (*or* ·phyt·ic)
sym·po·dial

sym·po·dium (*plural* ·dia) botany term
sym·po·si·ac
sym·po·sium (*plural* ·siums *or* ·sia)
symp·tom
symp·to·mat·ic (*or* ·mati·cal)
symp·to·mati·cal·ly
symp·toma·tol·ogy
syn·aer·esis *variant spelling of* syneresis
syn·aes·the·sia (*US* ·es·) medical term
syn·aes·thet·ic (*US* ·es·)
syna·gogi·cal (*or* ·gog·al)
syna·gogue
syna·lepha (*or* ·loepha) linguistics term
syn·apse nerve-cell junction
syn·ap·sis (*plural* ·ses) stage of meiosis
syn·ap·tic (*or* ·ti·cal)
syn·ap·ti·cal·ly
syn·ar·chy (*plural* ·chies) joint rule
syn·ar·thro·dial
syn·ar·thro·sis (*plural* ·ses) anatomy term
sync *Slang* synchronize; synchrony
syn·carp botany term
syn·car·pous
syn·car·py
syn·chro (*plural* ·chros) electrical device
syn·chro·cy·clo·tron
syn·chro·flash camera mechanism
syn·chro·mesh
syn·chron·ic
syn·chroni·cal·ly
syn·chro·nism
syn·chro·nis·tic (*or* ·ti·cal)
syn·chro·nis·ti·cal·ly
syn·chro·ni·za·tion (*or* ·sa·tion)
syn·chro·nize (*or* ·nise)
syn·chro·niz·er (*or* ·nis·er)
syn·chro·nous
syn·chro·nous·ness
syn·chrony
syn·chro·scope (*or* ·chrono·)
syn·chro·tron

450

syn·clas·tic maths term
syn·cli·nal
syn·cline geology term
syn·cli·no·rium (*plural* ·ria)
Syn·com communications. satellite
syn·co·pate
syn·co·pa·tion
syn·co·pa·tor
syn·co·pe
syn·cop·ic (*or* ·co·pal)
syn·cret·ic (*or* ·cre·tis·tic)
syn·cre·tism
syn·cre·tist
syn·cre·ti·za·tion (*or* ·sa·tion)
syn·cre·tize (*or* ·tise) combine differing beliefs
syn·cyt·ial
syn·cyt·ium (*plural* ·cytia) zoology term
syn·dac·tyl
syn·dac·tyly (*or* ·tyl·ism)
syn·de·sis linguistics term
syn·des·mo·sis (*plural* ·ses) anatomy term
syn·des·mot·ic
syn·det·ic (*or* ·deti·cal)
syn·deti·cal·ly
syn·de·ton
syn·dic business agent
syn·di·cal
syn·di·cal·ism
syn·di·cal·ist
syn·di·cal·is·tic
syn·di·cate
syn·di·ca·tion
syn·dic·ship
syn·dio·tac·tic chemistry term
syn·drome
syn·drom·ic
syne *Scot* since
syn·ec·do·che figure of speech
syn·ec·doch·ic (*or* ·dochi·cal)
syn·ec·dochi·cal·ly
syn·eco·log·ic (*or* ·logi·cal)
syn·eco·logi·cal·ly
syn·ecol·ogy
syn·ec·tics problem solving

syn·er·esis (or ·aer·) chemistry or phonetics term
syn·er·get·ic (or ·gis·tic)
syn·er·geti·cal·ly (or ·gis·ti·)
syn·er·gic
syn·er·gism acting together
syn·er·gist
syn·er·gis·tic
syn·er·gy (plural ·gies)
syn·esis linguistics term
syn·es·the·sia US spelling of synaesthesia
syn·gam·ic (or ·ga·mous)
syn·ga·my (or ·gen·esis) biology term
syni·zesis phonetics or biology term
syn·kary·on biology term
syn·kary·on·ic
syn·od
syn·od·al (or ·odi·cal)
syn·od·ic
syn·oecious (or syn·ecious, synoi·cous) botany term
syn·oekete (or ·oecete) zoology term
syno·nym
syno·nym·ic (or ·nymi·cal)
syno·nym·ity
syn·ony·mize (or ·mise)
syn·ony·mous
syn·ony·mous·ness
syn·ony·my (plural ·mies)
syn·op·sis (plural ·ses)
syn·op·tic
syn·op·ti·cal·ly
syn·op·tist
syno·via fluid in joint
syno·vial
syno·vit·ic
syno·vi·tis

syn·sep·al·ous botany term
syn·tac·tic (or ·ti·cal)
syn·tac·ti·cal·ly
syn·tac·tics study of symbols
syn·tag·ma (or syn·tagm; plural ·tag·ma·ta or ·tagms) linguistics term
syn·tax
syn·the·sis (plural ·ses)
syn·the·sist
syn·the·si·za·tion (or ·sa·tion)
syn·the·size (or ·sise)
syn·the·siz·er (or ·sis·er)
syn·thet·ic
syn·theti·cal
syn·theti·cal·ly
syn·the·tism art term
syn·the·tist
syn·ton·ic psychology term
syn·toni·cal·ly
sy·pher woodworking term; compare cipher
sy·pher·ing
syphi·lis
syphi·lit·ic
syphi·liti·cal·ly
syphi·loid
syphi·lolo·gist
syphi·lol·ogy
syphi·lo·ma (plural ·mas or ·ma·ta) tumour
sy·phon variant spelling of siphon
Sy·ra·cuse Italian port; US city
Syria
Syri·ac
Syr·ian
sy·rin·ga ornamental shrub; compare seringa
sy·ringe
sy·rin·geal

sy·rin·go·my·elia disease
sy·rin·go·my·el·ic
syr·inx (plural sy·rin·ges or syr·inx·es) zoology term
syr·phid fly
syr·up (US also sir·)
syr·upy
sys·sar·co·sis (plural ·ses) anatomy term
sys·sar·cot·ic
sys·tal·tic of heartbeat
sys·tem
sys·tem·at·ic methodical; compare systemic
sys·tem·ati·cal·ly
sys·tem·ati·cal·ness
sys·tem·at·ics
sys·tema·tism
sys·tema·tist
sys·tema·ti·za·tion (or ·sa·tion)
sys·tema·tize (or ·tise)
sys·tema·tiz·er (or ·tis·er)
sys·tema·tol·ogy
sys·tem·ic affecting whole body; compare systematic
sys·temi·cal·ly
sys·temi·za·tion (or ·sa·tion) systematization
sys·tem·iz·er (or ·is·er)
sys·to·le
sys·tol·ic
Syz·ran Soviet port
syzy·geti·cal·ly
sy·zyg·ial (or syzy·get·ic, syzy·gal)
syzy·gy (plural ·gies) astronomy term
Szcze·cin Polish port
Sze·chwan Chinese province
Sze·ged Hungarian city

T

ta Slang thank you
Taal Philippine volcano
tab (tab·bing, tabbed)
taba·nid fly
tab·ard

taba·ret fabric
Ta·bas·co Mexican state; (Trademark) sauce
tabbed
tab·bing

tab·by (plural ·bies)
tab·er·nac·le
tab·er·nacu·lar
ta·bes wasting
ta·bes·cence

tabescent

ta·bes·cent
tab·la·ture musical notation
ta·ble
tab·leau (*plural* ·leaux *or* ·leaus)
table·cloth
ta·ble d'hôte (*plural* ta·bles d'hôte)
table·land
table·spoon
table·spoon·ful (*plural* ·fuls)
tab·let
table-turning
table·ware
tab·loid
ta·boo (*or* tabu; *plural* ·boos *or* ·bus)
ta·bor (*or* ·bour) drum
tabo·ret (*or* tabou·) stool
tabo·rin (*or* tabou·) drum
Ta·briz Iranian city
tabu·lable
tabu·lar
tabu·lar·ize
tabu·late
tabu·la·tion
tabu·la·tor
taca·ma·hac (*or* tac·ma·hack) gum
ta·cet musical term
tache *Archaic* buckle; *Slang* moustache
tach·eom·eter (*or* ta·chym·) surveying instrument; *compare* tachometer
tacheo·met·ric (*or* ·ri·cal, tachy·)
tacheo·met·ri·cal·ly (*or* tachy·)
tach·eom·etry (*or* ta·chym·)
tachi·na fly
ta·chis·to·scope
ta·chis·to·scop·ic
ta·chis·to·scopi·cal·ly
tacho·graph speed-recording device
ta·chom·eter speed-measuring device; *compare* tacheometer
tacho·met·ric (*or* ·ri·cal)
tacho·met·ri·cal·ly
ta·chom·etry

tachy·car·dia rapid heartbeat
tachy·car·di·ac
ta·chyg·ra·pher (*or* ·phist)
tachy·graph·ic (*or* ·graphi·cal)
ta·chyg·ra·phy shorthand
tachy·lyte (*or* ·lite) basalt
tachy·lyt·ic (*or* ·lit·)
ta·chym·eter *variant of* tacheometer
ta·chym·etry *variant of* tacheometry
tachy·on physics term
tachy·phy·lax·is medical term
tac·it
tac·it·ness
taci·turn
taci·tur·nity
tack
tack·er
tack·et *Dialect* hobnail
tacki·ly
tacki·ness
tack·le
tack·ler
tacky (tacki·er, tacki·est)
tac·node maths term
taco (*plural* tacos) Mexican food
Ta·co·ma US port
taco·nite rock
tact
tact·ful
tact·ful·ly
tact·ful·ness
tac·tic
tac·ti·cal
tac·ti·cal·ly
tac·ti·cian
tac·tics
tac·tile
tac·til·ity
tact·less
tact·less·ness
tac·tual
tad *US* boy
tad·pole
Ta·dzhik (*plural* ·dzhiks *or* ·dzhik) Muslim people
Ta·dzhiki·stan Soviet republic
Tae·gu South Korean city
Tae·jon South Korean city

tae·nia (*or esp. US* te·; *plural* ·niae) band; architectural term; *compare* tinea
tae·nia (*US also* te·; *plural* ·niae) tapeworm; *compare* tinea
tae·nia·cide (*US also* te·)
tae·nia·fuge (*US also* te·)
tae·nia·sis (*US also* te·)
taf·fe·ta
taff·rail ship's rail
Taf·fy (*plural* ·fies) *Slang* Welshman
taf·fy (*plural* ·fies) *US* sweet
tafia (*or* taf·fia) rum
Ta·fi·lelt (*or* Ta·fi·la·let) oasis
tag (tag·ging, tagged)
Ta·ga·log (*plural* ·logs *or* ·log) Philippine people
Ta·gan·rog Soviet port
tag·gers tin-coated iron sheet
tag·ging
ta·glia·tel·le pasta
tag·meme linguistics term
tag·mem·ic
tag·mem·ics
Ta·gus European river
ta·hi·na sesame paste
Ta·hi·ti
Ta·hi·tian
tahr animal
tah·sil·dar Indian tax collector
Tai·chung (*or* T'ai-chung) Chinese city
tai·ga subarctic forests
tail appendage; *compare* tale
tail·back
tail·board
tail·ender
tail·gate
tail·ing
taille (*plural* tailles) French tax
tail·less
tail·light (*or* ·lamp)
tail·like
tai·lor
tailor·bird
tailor-made
tail·piece
tail·pipe

tail·plane
tail·race
tails tail coat
tail·skid
tail·spin
tail·stock
tail·wind
tain mirror backing
Tai·nan (or T'ai-nan) Chinese city
taint
tai·pan snake
Tai·pei (or T'ai-pei) Taiwanese capital
Tai·wan
Tai·wan·ese
Tai·yuan (or T'ai-yüan) Chinese city
taj Muslim cap
Taj Ma·hal
taka Bangladeshi currency
tak·able (or take·able)
ta·ka·he bird
Taka·mat·su Japanese port
take (tak·ing, took, tak·en)
take·away
tak·en
take·off
take·over
tak·er
tak·in animal
tak·ing
tak·ing·ness
tak·ings
Ta·ko·ra·di Ghanaian port
tala·poin monkey
ta·laria winged sandals
talc (talck·ing, talcked or talc·ing, talced)
Tal·ca·hua·no Chilean city
talc·ose (or tal·cous)
tal·cum
tale story; compare tail
tal·ent
tal·ent·ed
ta·les legal term
ta·les·man (plural ·men)
tali·grade zoology term
tali·on legal term
tali·ped
tali·pes club foot
tali·pot palm tree
tal·is·man (plural ·mans)
tal·is·man·ic

talk
talka·bil·ity
talk·able
talka·tive
talka·tive·ly
talka·tive·ness
talk·er
talkie
talking-to (plural -tos)
tall
tal·lage historical tax
Tal·la·has·see US city
tall·boy
tal·li·er
Tal·linn (or ·lin) Soviet port
tall·ish
tal·lith (plural ·lai·sim, ·lithes or ·li·toth) prayer shawl
tall·ness
tal·low
tally-ho (verb -hos, -hoing, -hoed; noun, plural -hos)
hoing, -hoed; noun, plural -hos)
tally·man (plural ·men)
Tal·mud Jewish literature
Tal·mud·ic (or ·mudi·cal)
Tal·mud·ism
Tal·mud·ist
tal·on
ta·loned
ta·luk (or ·lu·ka, ·loo·ka) Indian district
ta·lus (plural ·li) anklebone
ta·lus (plural ·luses) scree
tam·abil·ity (or tame·)
tam·able (or tame·)
tam·able·ness (or tame·)
ta·ma·le Mexican food
ta·man·dua (or ·du) animal
tama·rack tree
ta·ma·rau (or ·rao) cattle
tama·rin monkey
tama·rind (or ·rin·do; plural ·rinds or ·rin·dos) tree, fruit
tama·risk tree
ta·ma·sha Indian entertainment
Ta·mau·li·pas Mexican state

tangential

Tam·bo·ra Indonesian volcano
tam·bour
tam·boura musical instrument
tam·bou·rin dance
tam·bou·rine musical instrument
tam·bou·rin·ist
Tam·bov Soviet city
tame
tame·able variant spelling of tamable
tame·ness
tam·er
Tam·il (plural ·ils or ·il) Asian people
Tam·il Nadu Indian state
tam·is (plural ·ises) straining cloth
Tam·ma·ny Hall US political party organization
tam·my (plural ·mies)
tam-o'-shanter
tamp
Tam·pa Florida resort
tam·per
Tam·pe·re Finnish city
tam·per·er
Tam·pi·co Mexican port
tamp·ing Welsh angry
tam·pi·on (or tom·) gun plug
tam·pon medical plug
tam·pon·ade
tam-tam gong; compare tom-tom
tan (tan·ning, tanned)
Tana Ethiopian lake
tana lemur
tana·ger bird
Tana·na Alaskan river
tan·bark
tan·dem
tan·doori
Tang Chinese dynasty
tang
Tan·ga Tanzanian port
Tan·gan·yi·ka African lake
tan·ge·lo (plural ·los) hybrid fruit
tan·gen·cy
tan·gent
tan·gen·tial

tangentiality

tan·gen·ti·al·ity
tan·gen·tial·ly (or ·tal·ly)
Tan·ge·rine of Tangier
tan·ge·rine fruit
tan·gibil·ity (or ·gible·ness)
tan·gible
Tan·gier Moroccan port
tangi·ness
tan·gle
tan·gle·ment
tan·gler
tan·gly
tan·go (noun, plural ·tos; verb ·goes, ·go·ing, ·goed)
tan·go·ist
tan·gram puzzle
Tang·shan Chinese city
tangy (tangi·er, tangi·est)
tanh maths term
Ta·nis ancient Egyptian city
tan·ist heir of Celtic chieftain
Tan·jore Indian city
tank
tan·ka (plural ·kas or ·ka) Japanese verse
tank·age
tank·ard
tank·er
tank·ful (plural ·fuls)
tan·nage
tan·nate
tanned
tan·ner
tan·nery (plural ·neries)
tan·nic
tan·nin
tan·ning
Tan·noy (Trademark)
tan·sy (plural ·sies) plant
Tan·ta Egyptian city
tan·ta·late
tan·tal·ic
tan·ta·lite mineral
tan·ta·li·za·tion (or ·sa·tion)
tan·ta·lize (or ·lise)
tan·ta·liz·er (or ·lis·er)
tan·ta·liz·ing·ly (or ·lis·ing·ly)
tan·ta·lous chemistry term; compare tantalus
tan·ta·lum chemical element

Tantalus mythological king
tan·ta·lus case for bottles; compare tantalous
tan·ta·mount
tan·ta·ra fanfare
tan·tivy (plural ·tivies) hunting cry
tan·to musical term
Tan·tra Sanskrit books
Tan·tric
Tan·trism
Tan·trist
tan·trum
Tan·za·nia
Tan·za·nian
Tao·ism Chinese philosophy
Tao·ist
tap (tap·ping, tapped)
tapa mulberry bark
tap-dance (verb)
tap-dancer
tapa·der·a stirrup covering
tape
ta·per
ta·per·er
ta·per·ing·ly
tap·es·tried
tap·es·try (plural ·tries)
ta·petal
ta·petum (plural ·peta) biology term
tape·worm
tap·hole
tapio·ca
ta·pir (plural ·pirs or ·pir) animal
tap·is (plural tap·is) carpet
tap·pable
tapped
tap·per
tap·pet
tap·ping
tappit-hen
tap·room
tap·root
tap·ster
tar (tar·ring, tarred)
ta·ra·did·dle variant spelling of tarradiddle
ta·ra·ma·sa·la·ta
ta·ran·tass Russian carriage
tar·an·tel·la dance; compare tarantula
tar·ant·ism nervous disorder
Ta·ran·to Italian port

ta·ran·tu·la (plural ·las or ·lae) spider; compare tarantella
ta·raxa·cum plant
tar·boosh (or ·bush, ·bouche) Muslim cap
Tar·de·noi·sian Mesolithic culture
tar·di·grade minute animal
tar·di·ly
tar·di·ness
tar·dy (·di·er, ·di·est)
tare plant; weight of goods container; compare tear
tar·get
tar·iff
Ta·rim Chinese river
tar·la·tan fabric
tar·mac (·mack·ing, ·macked)
tarn lake
tar·nal US damned
tar·na·tion
Tarn-et-Garonne French department
tar·nish
tar·nish·able
tar·nish·er
taro (plural taros) plant
ta·rot card
tarp Austral tarpaulin
tar·pan extinct horse
tar·pau·lin
Tar·pe·ian Rock
tar·pon (plural ·pons or ·pon) fish
tar·ra·did·dle (or ta·ra·)
tar·ra·gon
Tar·ra·sa Spanish city
tarred
tar·ri·ness
tar·ring
tar·ry (verb ·ries, ·ry·ing, ·ried; adj ·ri·er, ·ri·est)
tar·sal
tar·si·er animal
tar·so·meta·tar·sal
tar·so·meta·tar·sus (plural ·si)
Tar·sus Turkish city
tar·sus (plural ·si) ankle bones
tart
tar·tan

Tar·tar *variant spelling of* **Tatar**
tar·tar deposit on teeth; fearsome person; sauce; chemical substance
tar·tar·ic
tar·tari·za·tion (*or* **·sa·tion**)
tar·tar·ize (*or* **·ise**)
tar·tar·ous of tartar
Tar·ta·rus Hades
Tar·ta·ry *variant spelling of* **Tatary**
tart·let
tart·ness
tar·trate
tarty
Tar·zan
Tash·kent Soviet city
ta·sim·eter temperature-change measurer
tasi·met·ric
ta·sim·etry
task
task·er
task·master (*fem* **·mistress**)
task·work
Tas·ma·nia
Tas·ma·nian
Tas·man Sea
Tass Soviet news agency
tass *Dialect* cup
tas·sel (**·sel·ling, ·selled;** *US* **·sel·ing, ·seled**)
tas·sel·ly
tas·set piece of armour
tast·able
taste
taste·ful
taste·ful·ly
taste·ful·ness
taste·less
taste·less·ness
tast·er
tasti·ly
tasti·ness
tasty (**tasti·er, tasti·est**)
tat (**tat·ting, tat·ted**)
ta-ta *Slang* goodbye
Ta·tar (*or* **Tar·tar**) Mongoloid people
Ta·tar·ian (*or* **Tar·tar·ian, Ta·tar·ic, Tar·tar·ic**)

Ta·ta·ry (*or* **Tar·ta·ry**) historical region
ta·ter *Dialect* potato
Tat·ler journal; *compare* **tattler**
tatou·ay armadillo
Ta·tra mountain range
tat·ted
tat·ter
tat·ter·de·mal·ion
tat·ter·sall fabric
tat·ting
tat·tle
tat·tler one who tattles; *compare* **Tatler**
tattle·tale
tat·tling·ly
tat·too (*noun, plural* **·toos;** *verb* **toos, ·too·ing, ·tooed**)
tat·too·ist (*or* **·er**)
tat·ty (**·ti·er, ·ti·est**)
tatty-peelin *Scot* pretentious
tau Greek letter; *compare* **taw**
taught past tense of teach; *compare* **taut**
taunt
taunt·er
taunt·ing·ly
Taun·ton Somerset town
taupe brownish grey
Tau·ranga New Zealand port
Tau·rean
tau·rine bull-like; biochemical compound
tau·ro·ma·chian
tau·roma·chy bullfighting
Tau·rus constellation; sign of zodiac
taut tight; *compare* **taught**
taut·en
taut·ness
tau·tog fish
tau·to·logi·cal (*or* **·to·log·ic, ·tolo·gous**)
tau·to·logi·cal·ly
tau·tolo·gize (*or* **·gise**)
tau·tol·ogy (*plural* **·gies**)
tau·to·mer chemistry term
tau·to·mer·ic
tau·tom·er·ism
tau·to·nym biology term

tau·to·nym·ic (*or* **·tony·mous**)
tau·tony·my
Ta·vel wine
tav·ern
tav·ern·er
taw marble; tanning term; *compare* **tau**
taw·dri·ly
taw·dri·ness
taw·dry (**·dri·er, ·dri·est**)
taw·er
taw·ny (*or* **·ney**)
tawse (*or* **taws**) leather strap
tax
tax·abil·ity (*or* **·able·ness**)
tax·able
taxa·ceous botany term
taxa·tion
taxa·tion·al
tax·deduct·ible
tax·eme linguistics term
tax·er
taxi (*noun, plural* **taxis** *or* **taxies;** *verb* **taxies, taxi·ing, tax·ied**)
taxi·cab
taxi·der·mal (*or* **·mic**)
taxi·der·mist
taxi·der·my
taxi·meter
tax·ing·ly
taxi·plane
tax·is biology term; surgical process
taxis (*or* **taxies**) *plural of* **taxi**
taxi·way
tax·man (*plural* **·men**)
tax·on (*plural* **taxa**) biology term
taxo·nom·ic (*or* **·nomi·cal**)
taxo·nomi·cal·ly
tax·ono·mist (*or* **·mer**)
tax·ono·my
tax·payer
tax·paying
Tay Scottish river
tay *Irish* tea
tay·ra animal
Tay·side Scottish region
taz·za wine cup

Tbilisi

Tbi·li·si (*or* Tif·lis) Soviet city
te (*or* ti) musical term; *compare* tea; tee
tea beverage; *compare* te; tee
tea·ber·ry (*plural* ·ber·ries)
tea·cake
tea·cart
teach (teach·es, teach·ing, taught)
teach·able
teach·er
teach-in
teach·ing
tea·cup
tea·cup·ful (*plural* ·fuls)
tea·house
teak
tea·ket·tle
teal (*plural* teals *or* teal) duck
team group; *compare* teem
tea-maker
team-mate
team·ster
team·work
tea·pot
tea·poy table with tripod base
tear (tear·ing, tore, torn) rip; *compare* tare
tear drop from eye; *compare* tier
tear·able
tear·er
tear·ful
tear·ful·ly
tear·ful·ness
tear·ing
tear·ing·ly
tear-jerker
tear·less
tea·room
tease
tea·sel (*or* ·zel, ·zle; ·sel·ling, ·selled; *US* ·sel·ing, ·seled)
teas·er
tea·shop
teas·ing·ly
tea·spoon
tea·spoon·ful (*plural* ·fuls)
teat

techi·ly variant spelling of tetchily
techi·ness variant spelling of tetchiness
tech·ne·tium chemical element
tech·nic variant of **technique**
tech·ni·cal
tech·ni·cal·ity (*plural* ·ities)
tech·ni·cal·ly
tech·ni·cian
Tech·ni·col·or (*Trademark*)
tech·nics study of industry
tech·nique (*or* ·nic)
tech·noc·ra·cy (*plural* ·cies)
tech·no·crat
tech·no·crat·ic
tech·nog·ra·phy
tech·no·logi·cal
tech·no·logi·cal·ly
tech·nolo·gist
tech·nol·ogy (*plural* ·ogies)
tech·no·struc·ture
techy variant spelling of tetchy
tec·ton·ic
tec·toni·cal·ly
tec·ton·ics
tec·tri·cial
tec·trix (*plural* ·tri·ces) feather
ted (ted·ding, ted·ded) shake out hay
ted·der
ted·dy (*plural* ·dies)
Te Deum
te·di·ous
te·di·ous·ness
te·dium
tee (tee·ing, teed) golf term; T-shaped part; *compare* te; tea
teem abound; *compare* **team**
teem·ing
teen
teen·age
teen·aged
teen·ager
tee·ny (·ni·er, ·ni·est)
teeny·bopper
Tees English river

Tees·side
tee·ter
teeth plural of **tooth**
teethe (*verb*)
teeth·ing
tee·to·tal
tee·to·tal·ism
tee·to·tal·ler (*US* ·tal·er)
tee·to·tum spinning top
tef (*or* teff) grass
Tef·lon (*Trademark*)
teg sheep
teg·men (*plural* ·mi·na) zoology term
teg·mi·nal
Te·gu·ci·gal·pa Honduran capital
tegu·lar of a tile
tegu·lar·ly
Teh·ran (*or* Te·he·ran)
Te·huan·tepec Mexican region
tek·tite
tela (*plural* telae) weblike structure
tel·aes·the·sia (*US* ·es·) paranormal perception
tel·aes·thet·ic (*US* ·es·)
tela·mon (*plural* ·mones) supporting pillar
tel·an·gi·ec·ta·sis (*or* ·sia; *plural* ·ses) medical term
tel·an·gi·ec·tat·ic
Tel·auto·graph (*Trademark*)
tel·auto·graph·ic
tel·autog·ra·phy
Tel Aviv
tele·cast (·cast·ing, ·cast *or* ·cast·ed)
tele·cast·er
tele·com·mu·ni·ca·tion
tele·com·mu·ni·ca·tions
tel·edu badger
te·le·ga cart
tele·gen·ic
tel·eg·no·sis parapsychology term
tel·eg·nos·tic
tel·egon·ic
Telegonus son of Odysseus
te·lego·ny genetics term
tele·gram
tele·graph
te·leg·ra·pher (*or* ·phist)

tele·graph·ic
tele·graphi·cal·ly
te·leg·ra·phy
tele·ki·ne·sis
tele·ki·net·ic
Telemachus son of Odysseus
tel·emark skiing term
te·lem·eter
tele·met·ric (*or* ·ri·cal)
tele·met·ri·cal·ly
te·lem·etry
tel·en·cephal·ic
tel·en·cepha·lon anatomy term
teleo·logi·cal (*or* ·log·ic)
teleo·logi·cal·ly
tele·olo·gism
tele·olo·gist
tele·ol·ogy
tel·eost fish
tele·path·ic
tele·pathi·cal·ly
te·lepa·thist
te·lepa·thize (*or* ·thise)
te·lepa·thy
tele·phone
tele·phon·er
tele·phon·ic
te·lepho·nist
te·lepho·ny
tele·photo·graph·ic
tele·pho·tog·ra·phy
tele·photo
tele·play
tele·print·er
tele·prompt·er
Tele·ran (*Trademark*) navigational aid
tele·scope
tele·scop·ic
tele·scopi·cal·ly
te·les·co·py
tele·script
tele·sis
tele·spec·tro·scope
tele·ste·reo·scope
tel·es·the·sia *US spelling of* telaesthesia
te·les·tich poem
tele·thon
tele·tran·scrip·tion
tele·tube *short for* television tube
Tele·type (*Trademark*)

Tele·type·set·ter (*Trademark*)
tele·type·set·ting
te·leu·to·spore
te·leu·to·spor·ic
tele·vise
tele·vi·sion
tele·vi·sion·al
tele·vi·sion·ary
tele·writ·er
tel·ex
Tel·ford Shropshire town
tel·geni·cal·ly
te·lial
tel·ic purposeful
te·lio·spore
te·lium (*plural* ·lia) fungal structure
tell (tell·ing, told)
tell·able
Tell el Amar·na Egyptian ruins
tell·er
tell·ing
tell·ing·ly
tell·tale
tel·lu·rate chemistry term
tel·lu·rian of the earth
tel·lu·ric
tel·lu·ride chemical compound
tel·lu·ri·on (*or* ·lu·rian) model of earth
tel·lu·rite
tel·lu·rium chemical element
tel·lu·rize (*or* ·rise)
tel·lu·rom·eter surveying instrument
tel·lu·rous
tel·ly (*plural* tel·lies)
telo·phase biology term
telo·pha·sic
tel·pher (*or* ·fer)
tel·pher·age (*or* ·fer·) transport system
tel·pher·ic (*or* ·fer·)
tel·son zoology term
tel·son·ic
Tel·star satellite
Te·luk·be·tung (*or* **Te·loek·be·toeng**) Indonesian port
Tema Ghanaian port
tem·er·ari·ous

te·mer·ity
temp
tem·per
tem·pera painting medium
tem·per·abil·ity
tem·per·able
tem·pera·ment
tem·pera·men·tal
tem·pera·men·tal·ly
tem·per·ance
tem·per·ate
tem·per·ate·ly
tem·per·ate·ness
tem·pera·ture
tem·per·er
tem·pest
tem·pes·tu·ous
tem·pes·tu·ous·ness
Tem·plar member of religious order
tem·plate (*or* ·plet)
tem·ple
tem·po (*plural* ·pos *or* ·pi)
tem·po·ral of time or the temples
tem·po·ral·ity
tem·po·ral·ly of time
tem·po·rari·ly not permanently
tem·po·rari·ness
tem·po·rary (*plural* ·raries)
tem·po·ri·za·tion (*or* ·sa·tion)
tem·po·rize (*or* ·rise)
tem·po·riz·er (*or* ·ris·er)
tempt
tempt·able
temp·ta·tion
tempt·er
tempt·ing
tempt·ing·ly
tempt·ress
tem·pu·ra Japanese food
Te·mu·co Chilean city
ten
ten·abil·ity (*or* ·able·ness)
ten·able
ten·ably
ten·ace bridge term
te·na·cious
te·na·cious·ness
te·nac·ity
te·nacu·lum (*plural* ·la) surgical instrument

tenaille

te·naille fortification
ten·an·cy (*plural* ·cies)
ten·ant
ten·ant·able
ten·ant·ry
tench (*plural* tench)
tend
ten·den·cy (*plural* ·cies)
ten·den·tious (*or* ·cious)
ten·den·tious·ness (*or* ·cious·)
ten·der
ten·der·able
ten·der·er
tender·foot (*plural* ·foots *or* ·feet)
tender·hearted
tender·hearted·ness
ten·deri·za·tion (*or* ·sa·tion)
ten·der·ize (*or* ·ise)
ten·der·iz·er (*or* ·is·er)
ten·der·loin
ten·der·ness
ten·din·itis inflammation of tendon
ten·di·nous of tendons
ten·don
ten·dril
ten·dril·lar (*or* ·ous)
ten·ebrism style of painting
ten·ebrist
ten·ebros·ity
ten·ebrous (*or* te·neb·ri·ous)
Ten·edos Greek island
ten·ement
ten·emen·tal (*or* ·tary)
ten·ement·ed
Ten·erife
te·nes·mic
te·nes·mus medical term
ten·et belief
ten·fold
Ten·gri Nor Chinese lake
te·nia *variant spelling* (*esp. US*) *of* taenia
ten·ner
Ten·nes·sean
Ten·nes·see
ten·nis
ten·no (*plural* ·no *or* ·nos) Japanese emperor
ten·on
ten·on·er

ten·or
teno·rite mineral
te·nor·rha·phy (*plural* ·phies) tendon surgery
te·noto·mist
te·noto·my (*plural* ·mies) incision into tendon
ten·pin
ten·pins
ten·rec animal
tense
tense·ly
tense·ness
ten·sibil·ity (*or* ·sible·ness)
ten·sible
ten·sile
ten·sil·ity (*or* ·sile·ness)
ten·sim·eter device measuring vapour pressure
ten·si·om·eter device measuring tensile strength
ten·sion
ten·sion·al
ten·sive
ten·sor
ten·so·rial
tent
ten·ta·cle
ten·ta·cled
ten·tacu·lar
tent·age tents
ten·ta·tion mechanical process
ten·ta·tive
ten·ta·tive·ness
tent·ed
ten·ter
tenter·hook
tenth
tenu·ity
tenu·ous
tenu·ous·ness
ten·ure
tenu·rial
te·nu·to musical term
teo·cal·li (*plural* ·lis) Aztec pyramid
teo·sin·te grass
te·pal botany term
te·pee (*or* tee·) tent
tep·efac·tion
tep·efy (·efies, ·efy·ing, ·efied) make tepid
teph·rite rock

teph·rit·ic
Te·pic Mexican city
tep·id
te·pid·ity (*or* tep·id·ness)
te·qui·la
Te·rai Indian marshland
ter·aph (*plural* ·aphim) biblical god
tera·tism malformed fetus
tera·to·gen
tera·to·gen·ic causing fetal deformity
tera·toid
tera·to·log·ic (*or* ·logi·cal)
tera·tolo·gist
tera·tol·ogy study of fetal abnormalities
tera·to·ma (*plural* ·mas *or* ·ma·ta)
ter·bic
ter·bium chemical element
terce (*or* tierce) canonical hour
ter·cel (*or* tier·cel) male falcon
ter·cen·te·nary (*or* ·cen·ten·nial; *plural* ·naries *or* ·nials)
ter·cet verse
ter·ebene
te·reb·ic acid
ter·ebinth tree
ter·ebin·thine
te·re·do (*plural* ·dos *or* ·di·nes) mollusc
Te·re·si·na Brazilian port
te·rete botany term
ter·gal
ter·gi·ver·sate
ter·gi·ver·sa·tion
ter·gi·ver·sa·tor (*or* ·ver·sant)
ter·gi·ver·sa·tory
ter·gum (*plural* ·ga) zoology term
teri·ya·ki Japanese food term
ter·ma·gan·cy
ter·ma·gant
ter·mi·nabil·ity (*or* ·nable·ness)
ter·mi·nable
ter·mi·nal
ter·mi·nal·ly
ter·mi·nate

ter·mi·na·tion
ter·mi·na·tion·al
ter·mi·na·tive
ter·mi·na·tor
ter·mi·na·tory
ter·mi·no·logi·cal
ter·mi·nolo·gist
ter·mi·nol·ogy (*plural* ·ogies)
ter·mi·nus (*plural* ·ni *or* ·nuses)
ter·mi·tar·ium (*plural* ·taria) termite nest
ter·mite
ter·mit·ic
term·less
ter·mor (*or* ·mer) legal term
tern bird; *compare* terne; turn
ter·na·ry (*plural* ·ries)
ter·nate botany term
terne alloy; *compare* tern; turn
Ter·ni Italian city
ter·pene
ter·pe·nic
ter·pin·eol
Terpsichore Greek Muse
Terp·si·cho·rean (*or* ·real)
ter·ra land
ter·race
ter·ra·cot·ta
ter·ra fir·ma
ter·rain surroundings; *compare* terrane
Ter·ra·my·cin (*Trademark*)
ter·rane rock formation; *compare* terrain
ter·ra·pin
ter·rar·ium (*plural* ·rar·iums *or* ·raria) biological container
ter·raz·zo
ter·rene earthly; *compare* terrine; tureen
terre·plein top of rampart
ter·res·trial
ter·res·tri·al·ly
ter·ret harness ring
terre-verte painting pigment
ter·ri·ble
ter·ri·ble·ness

ter·ri·bly
ter·rico·lous living in soil
ter·ri·er
ter·rif·ic
ter·rifi·cal·ly
ter·ri·fi·er
ter·ri·fy (·fies, ·fy·ing, ·fied)
ter·ri·fy·ing·ly
ter·rig·enous of the earth
ter·rine dish; food; *compare* terrene; tureen
ter·ri·to·rial
ter·ri·to·ri·al·ism
ter·ri·to·ri·al·ist
ter·ri·to·ri·al·ity
ter·ri·to·ri·ali·za·tion (*or* ·sa·tion)
ter·ri·to·ri·al·ize (*or* ·ise)
ter·ri·to·rial·ly
ter·ri·tory (*plural* ·tories)
ter·ror
ter·ror·ful
ter·ror·ism
ter·ror·ist
ter·ror·is·tic
ter·rori·za·tion (*or* ·sa·tion)
ter·ror·ize (*or* ·ise)
ter·ror·iz·er (*or* ·is·er)
terror-stricken (*or* -struck)
ter·ry (*plural* ·ries) towelling
terse
terse·ly
terse·ness
ter·tial ornithology term
ter·tian recurring every other day
Ter·tiary geological period
ter·tiary (*plural* ·tiaries)
ter·tium quid a third unknown thing
ter·va·lent *variant of* trivalent
Tery·lene (*Trademark*)
ter·zet·to (*plural* ·tos *or* ·ti) vocal trio
tes·la unit; coil
tes·sel·late
tes·sel·la·tion
tes·sera (*plural* ·serae) mosaic tile

tes·ser·act four-dimensional figure
tes·ser·al
tes·si·tu·ra musical term
test
tes·ta (*plural* ·tae) seed coat
test·abil·ity
test·able
tes·ta·ceous
tes·ta·cy
tes·ta·ment
tes·ta·men·tal
tes·ta·men·tary
tes·tate
tes·ta·tor (*fem* ·trix)
test-drive (*verb* -driving, -drove, -driven)
test·er one who tests
tes·ter canopy; coin
tes·tes *plural of* testis
tes·ti·cle
tes·ticu·lar
tes·ticu·late
tes·ti·fi·ca·tion
tes·ti·fi·er
tes·ti·fy (·fies, ·fy·ing, ·fied)
testi·ly
tes·ti·mo·nial
tes·ti·mo·ny (*plural* ·nies)
testi·ness
test·ing
test·ing·ly
tes·tis (*plural* ·tes)
tes·ton (*or* ·toon) coin
tes·tos·ter·one hormone
tes·tu·di·nal (*or* ·nary) of tortoises
tes·tu·do (*plural* ·di·nes) Roman military manoeuvre
tes·ty (·ti·er, ·ti·est)
te·tan·ic
te·tani·cal·ly
teta·ni·za·tion (*or* ·sa·tion)
teta·nize (*or* ·nise)
teta·nus
teta·ny
te·tar·to·he·dral·ism (*or* te·to·he·drism)
te·tar·to·he·dral
tetchi·ly (*or* techi·)
tetchi·ness (*or* techi·)

tetchy

tetchy (*or* techy; tetchi·er, tetchi·est *or* techi·er, techi·est)
tête-à-tête (*plural* -têtes *or* -tête)
tête-bêche philately term
teth·er
tet·ra (*plural* ·ra *or* ·ras) fish
tetra·ba·sic
tetra·ba·sic·ity
tetra·brach metrical foot
tetra·bran·chi·ate zoology term
tetra·chlo·ride
tetra·chord musical term
tetra·chor·dal
te·trac·id chemistry term
tetra·cy·cline
tet·rad
te·trady·mite mineral
tetra·dy·na·mous botany term
tetra·ethyl
te·trago·nal
tetra·gram
tetra·he·dral
tetra·he·drite mineral
tetra·he·dron (*plural* ·drons *or* ·dra)
te·tral·ogy (*plural* ·ogies) set of four
te·tram·er·ism
te·tram·er·ous biology term
tetra·methyl·diar·sine
tetra·ple·gia
tetra·ploid genetics term
tetra·ploidy
tetra·pod
tetra·pod·ic
te·trapo·dy (*plural* ·dies) metrical unit
te·trap·ter·ous four-winged
te·trarch
te·trarch·ate
te·trar·chic (*or* ·chi·cal)
te·trar·chy (*plural* ·chies)
tetra·spore
tetra·spor·ic (*or* ·ous)
tetra·stich four-line poem
tetra·stich·ic (*or* tetras·ti·chal)
te·tras·ti·chous botany term

tetra·syl·lab·ic (*or* ·labi·cal)
tetra·syl·la·ble
tetra·tom·ic
tetra·va·len·cy
tetra·va·lent
tet·rode electronic valve
te·trox·ide
tet·ryl
tet·ter skin eruption
Te·tuán Moroccan city
Teucer mythological character
Teu·ton ancient German
Teu·ton·ic
Teu·ton·ism
Teu·ton·ize (*or* ·ise)
Tewkes·bury
Tex·an
Tex·as
text
text·book
tex·tile
tex·tu·al of text; *compare* textural
tex·tu·al·ism
tex·tu·al·ist
tex·tu·al·ly
tex·tu·ary (*plural* ·aries)
tex·tur·al of texture; *compare* textual
tex·tur·al·ly
tex·ture
Thai (*plural* Thais *or* Thai)
Thai·land
thala·men·cephal·ic
thala·men·cepha·lon (*plural* ·lons *or* ·la) anatomy term
tha·lam·ic
tha·lami·cal·ly
thala·mus (*plural* ·mi) part of brain
tha·las·sic of the sea
thal·as·soc·ra·cy (*or* ·at·toc·)
tha·ler (*or* ta·; *plural* ·ler *or* ·lers) coin
tha·lido·mide
thal·lic
thal·lium chemical element
thal·loid
thal·lo·phyte
thal·lo·phyt·ic

460

thal·lous of thallium
thal·lus (*plural* ·li *or* ·luses) botany term
thal·weg (*or* tal·) geography term
Thames
than
thana·top·sis
Thanatos personification of death
thane (*or* thegn)
Than·et
Than·ja·vur Indian city
thank
thank·ful
thank·ful·ly
thank·ful·ness
thank·less
thank·less·ness
thanks·giving
Thap·sus battle site
Thá·sos Greek island
that
thatch
thatch·er
Thatch·er·ism
Thatch·er·ite supporter of Margaret Thatcher
thatch·ing
thau·ma·tol·ogy study of miracles
thau·ma·trope
thau·ma·tropi·cal
thau·ma·turge miracle performer
thau·ma·tur·gic
thau·ma·tur·gy
thaw
thaw·er
thea·ceous botany term
the·an·throp·ic
the·an·thro·pism
the·an·thro·pist
the·ar·chic
the·ar·chy (*plural* ·chies) government by gods
thea·tre (*US* ·ter)
theatre·goer (*US* theater·)
the·at·ri·cal
the·at·ri·cal·ity (*or* ·cal·ness)
the·at·ri·cal·ly
the·at·ri·cals dramatic entertainments

the·at·rics exaggerated mannerisms
the·ba·ine drug
The·ban
Thebes
the·ca (*plural* **·cae**) biology term
the·cal (*or* **·cate**)
the·co·dont extinct reptile
thee
theft
thegn *variant spelling of* **thane**
the·ine stimulant in tea
their of them; *compare* **there; they're**
theirs
the·ism
the·ist
the·is·tic (*or* **·ti·cal**)
the·is·ti·cal·ly
them
the·mat·ic
the·mati·cal·ly
theme
Themis Greek goddess
them·selves
then
the·nar palm of hand
the·nard·ite mineral
thence
thence·forth
thence·forward (*or* **·forwards**)
theo·bro·mine
theo·cen·tric theology term
theo·cen·tric·ity
theo·cen·trism (*or* **·tri·cism**)
the·oc·ra·cy (*plural* **·cies**)
the·oc·ra·sy mingling of deities
theo·crat
theo·crat·ic (*or* **·crati·cal**)
theo·crati·cal·ly
the·odi·cy (*plural* **·cies**) branch of theology
the·odo·lite
the·odo·lit·ic
the·ogo·ny (*plural* **·nies**) origin of the gods
theo·lo·gian
theo·logi·cal
theo·logi·cal·ly
the·olo·gist

the·olo·gi·za·tion (*or* **·sa·tion**)
the·olo·gize (*or* **·gise**)
the·olo·giz·er (*or* **·gis·er**)
the·ol·ogy (*plural* **·ogies**)
the·oma·chy (*plural* **·chies**) battle among the gods
theo·man·cy
theo·ma·nia
theo·ma·niac
the·ono·my being governed by God
the·opa·thy religious emotion
the·opha·gy (*plural* **·gies**)
the·opha·ny (*plural* **·nies**) manifestation of deity
Theophi·lus moon crater
theo·pho·bia
theo·pho·bi·ac
theo·phyl·line
the·or·bo (*plural* **·bos**) musical instrument
theo·rem
theo·remat·ic (*or* **·rem·ic**)
theo·remati·cal·ly
theo·reti·cal (*or* **·ret·ic**)
theo·reti·cal·ly
theo·reti·cian
theo·ret·ics
theo·rist
theo·ri·za·tion (*or* **·sa·tion**)
theo·rize (*or* **·rise**)
theo·riz·er (*or* **r·is·er**)
theo·ry (*plural* **·ries**)
theo·soph·ic (*or* **·sophi·cal**)
theo·sophi·cal·ly
the·oso·phism
the·oso·phist
the·oso·phy
thera·peu·tic
thera·peu·ti·cal·ly
thera·peu·tics
thera·pist
the·rap·sid extinct reptile
thera·py (*plural* **·pies**)
there in that place; *compare* **their; they're**
there·abouts (*or* **·about**)
there·after
there·at
there·by

there·fore
there·from
there·in
there·in·after
there·into
there·of
there·on
there·to
there·to·fore
there·under
there·upon
there·with (*or* **·with·al**)
the·ri·an·throp·ic part animal, part human
the·rian·thro·pism
the·rio·morph
the·rio·mor·phic (*or* **·phous**) in animal form
therm unit
ther·mae public baths
therm·aes·the·sia (*US* **·es·**) sensitivity to temperature
ther·mal
ther·mal·ly
ther·mal·ize (*or* **·ise**)
ther·mic
ther·mi·on
ther·mi·on·ic
ther·mi·on·ics
ther·mis·tor
Ther·mit (*or* **·mite**; *Trademark*)
ther·mite pro·cess
ther·mo·baro·graph
ther·mo·chemi·cal
ther·mo·chemi·cal·ly
ther·mo·chem·ist
ther·mo·chem·is·try
ther·mo·cline
ther·mo·cou·ple
ther·mo·dy·nam·ic (*or* **·nami·cal**)
ther·mo·dy·nami·cal·ly
ther·mo·dy·nam·ics
ther·mo·elec·tric (*or* **·tri·cal**)
ther·mo·elec·tri·cal·ly
ther·mo·elec·tric·ity
ther·mo·elec·tron
ther·mo·gen·esis
ther·mog·enous (*or* **·mo·genet·ic**)
ther·mo·gram
ther·mo·graph

thermographer

ther·mog·ra·pher
ther·mo·graph·ic
ther·mog·ra·phy
ther·mo·junc·tion
ther·mo·la·bile
ther·mo·lu·mi·nes·cence
ther·mo·lu·mi·nes·cent
ther·moly·sis
ther·mo·lyt·ic
ther·mo·mag·net·ic
ther·mom·eter
ther·mo·met·ric (or ·ri·cal)
ther·mo·met·ri·cal·ly
ther·mom·etry
ther·mo·nu·clear
ther·mo·phile (or ·phil) organism thriving in warmth
ther·mo·phil·ic (or ·phil·ous)
ther·mo·pile radiant-energy detector
ther·mo·plas·tic
ther·mo·plas·tic·ity
Ther·mopy·lae battle site
Ther·mos (*Trademark*)
ther·mo·scope
ther·mo·scop·ic (or ·scopi·cal)
ther·mo·scopi·cal·ly
ther·mo·set·ting
ther·mo·si·phon
ther·mo·sphere atmospheric layer
ther·mo·sta·bil·ity
ther·mo·stable
ther·mo·stat
ther·mo·stat·ic
ther·mo·stati·cal·ly
ther·mo·stat·ics
ther·mo·tac·tic
ther·mo·tax·is biology term
ther·mo·ten·sile
ther·mo·thera·py
ther·mo·trop·ic
ther·mo·tro·pism botany term
the·roid beastlike
the·ro·pod dinosaur
the·ropo·dan
the·sau·rus (*plural* ·ri *or* ·ruses)
these

Theseus mythological character
the·sis (*plural* ·ses)
Thespian
Thes·sa·li·an
Thes·sa·lo·nian
Thes·sa·lo·ni·ca ancient Thessaloníki
Thes·sa·lo·ní·ki Greek port
Thes·sa·ly Greek region
the·ta
thet·ic of metrical stress
theti·cal·ly
Thetis Greek goddess
the·urg·ic (or ·ur·gi·cal)
the·ur·gi·cal·ly
the·ur·gist
the·ur·gy (*plural* ·gies) divine intervention
thew muscle
they
they'd they would; they had
they'll they will; they shall
they're they are; *compare* their; there
they've they have
thia·mine (or ·min) vitamin
thia·zine
thia·zole (or ·zol)
thick
thick-and-thin
thick·en
thick·en·er
thick·en·ing
thick·et
thick·head
thick·headed·ness
thick·leaf (*plural* ·leaves) plant
thick·ly
thick·ness
thick·set
thick-skinned
thick-witted
thick-witted·ness
thief (*plural* thieves)
thieve
thiev·ery (*plural* ·eries)
thiev·ing
thiev·ing·ly
thiev·ish
thiev·ish·ness
thigh
thigh·bone

462

thig·mo·tac·tic
thig·mo·tax·is biology term
thig·mo·trop·ic
thig·mot·ro·pism botany term
thim·ble
thim·ble·ful (*plural* ·fuls)
thimble·rig game
thimble·weed
thimble·wit *US* dunce
thi·mero·sal antiseptic
thin (*adj* thin·ner, thin·nest; *verb* thin·ning, thinned)
thine
thin-film electronics term
thing
thingu·ma·bob (or thinga·)
thingu·ma·jig (or thinga·)
think (think·ing, thought)
think·able
think·er
think·ing
think-tank
thin·ner
thin·ness
thin·nish
thin-skinned
thio·cya·nate
thio·cy·an·ic acid
thio-ether
thiol
thi·on·ic of sulphur
thio·nine (or ·nin)
thio·nyl
thio·pen·tone (*US* ·tal)
thio·phen (or ·phene)
thio·sina·mine
thio·sul·phate (*US* ·fate)
thio·sul·phur·ic acid (*US* ·fur·)
thio·ura·cil
thio·urea
third
third-rate
third·stream jazz
thirl *Dialect* to drill
Thirl·mere Cumbrian lake
thirst
thirst·er
thirsti·ly
thirsti·ness
thirsty (thirsti·er, thirsti·est)

thir·teen
thir·teenth
thir·ti·eth
thir·ty (*plural* ·ties)
this
this·tle
thistle·down
this·tly
thith·er (*or* ·er·ward)
thither·to
thixo·trop·ic
thix·ot·ro·py chemistry term
thole (*or* thole·pin)
tho·los (*plural* ·loi) tomb
Tho·mism doctrine of Thomas Aquinas
Tho·mist
Thon·bu·ri Thai city
thong
Thor Norse god
tho·rac·ic (*or* ·ra·cal)
tho·ra·co·plas·ty (*plural* ·ties) surgery
thora·coto·my (*plural* ·mies)
thor·ax (*plural* thor·axes *or* tho·ra·ces)
tho·ria chemical compound
tho·ria·nite mineral
tho·ric
tho·rite mineral
tho·rium radioactive element
thorn
thorn·back fish
thorn·bill
thorni·ly
thorni·ness
thorny (thorni·er, thorni·est)
tho·ron radioisotope of radon
thor·ough
Thorough·bred horse
thorough·bred purebred
thorough·fare
thorough·going
thor·ough·ly
thor·ough·ness
thorough·paced
thorough·pin swollen hock
those
Thoth Egyptian god
thou

though
thought
thought·ful
thought·ful·ly
thought·ful·ness
thought·less
thought·less·ness
thought-out
thou·sand
thou·sandth
Thrace Balkan region
thrall
thrall·dom
thrash
thrash·er
thrash·ing
thrawn *Dialect* crooked
thread
thread·bare
thread·er
thread·fin (*plural* ·fin *or* ·fins) fish
threadi·ness
Thread·needle Street
thread·worm
thready (threadi·er, threadi·est)
threap (*or* threep) *Dialect* to scold
threat
threat·en
threat·en·er
threat·en·ing
three
three-dimension·al
three·fold
three-legged
three-phase
three-piece
three-ply
three-quarter (*adj*)
three-quarters
three·score
three·some
three-wheeler
threm·ma·tol·ogy science of breeding
threno·dy (*or* thre·node; *plural* ·dies *or* ·nodes) ode of lamentation
threo·nine amino acid
thresh
thresh·er
thresh·old
threw

thrice
thrift
thrifti·ly
thrifti·ness
thrift·less
thrift·less·ness
thrifty (thrifti·er, thrifti·est)
thrill
thrill·er
thrill·ing
thrips (*plural* thrips) insect
thrive (thriv·ing, thrived *or* throve, thrived *or* thriv·en)
throat
throati·ly
throati·ness
throat·lash (*or* ·latch) bridle strap
throaty (throati·er, throati·est)
throb (throb·bing, throbbed)
throe violent pang; *compare* throw
throm·bin enzyme
throm·bo·cyte
throm·bo·cyt·ic
throm·bo·em·bo·lism
throm·bo·gen protein
throm·bo·phle·bi·tis
throm·bo·plas·tic
throm·bo·plas·tin
throm·bose (*verb*)
throm·bo·sis
throm·bot·ic
throm·bus (*plural* ·bi) blood clot
throne
throng
thros·tle thrush
throt·tle
throt·tler
through
through·out
through·put
through·way
throw (throw·ing, threw, thrown) cast; *compare* throe
throw·away (*adj, noun*)
throw·back
throw·er

thrown

thrown
throw·ster yarn spinner
thrum (thrum·ming, thrummed)
thrum·mer
thrush
thrust
thrust·er
thud (thud·ding, thud·ded)
Thug Indian assassin
thug
thug·gee practices of Thugs
thug·gery
thug·gish
thu·ja (or ·ya) tree
Thule ancient northern land; Eskimo settlement
thu·lium chemical element
thumb
thumb·nail
thumb·nut
thumb·print
thumb·screw
thumb·stall
thumb·tack US drawing pin
thump
thump·er
thump·ing
thun·der
thunder·bird
thunder·bolt
thunder·clap
thunder·cloud
thun·der·er
thunder·head cloud
thun·der·ing
thun·der·ous
thunder·shower
thunder·stone
thunder·storm
thunder·struck (or ·stricken)
thun·dery
Thur·gau Swiss canton
thu·ri·ble incense container
thu·ri·fer thurible carrier
Thu·rin·gia German region
Thu·rin·gian
Thurs·day
thus
thwack
thwack·er
thwart
thwart·er

thy
Thyestes mythological character
thy·la·cine animal
thyme herb
thym·elaea·ceous botany term
thym·ic
thy·mi·dine
thy·mine
thy·mol
thy·mus (plural ·muses or ·mi)
thymy of thyme
thy·ra·tron
thy·ris·tor
thy·ro·cal·ci·ton·in hormone
thy·roid
thy·roid·ec·to·my (plural ·mies)
thy·roidi·tis
thy·ro·toxi·co·sis
thy·ro·tro·pin (or ·phin) hormone
thy·rox·ine (or ·in) hormone
thyrse (plural therses) botany term
thyr·soid
thyr·sus (plural ·si) Bacchus' staff
thysa·nu·ran insect
thy·self
ti plant; variant spelling of te
Tia Ma·ria (Trademark)
ti·ara
ti·ar·aed
Ti·ber
Ti·bes·ti African mountains
Ti·bet
Ti·bet·an
tibia (plural tibiae or tibias)
tib·ial
tic twitch; compare tick
ti·cal (plural ·cals or ·cal)
tic dou·lou·reux neuralgia
Ti·ci·no Swiss canton; river
tick parasite; compare tic
tick·er
tick·et
tick·ing
tick·le
tick·ler

464

tick·lish
tick·lish·ness
tick·ly
tick·tack
tick-tack-toe US noughts and crosses
tick·tock
Ti·con·dero·ga US battle site
tid·al
tid·al·ly
tid·bit US spelling of titbit
tid·dler
tid·dly
tiddly·winks
tide
tide·mark
tide·water
tide·way
ti·di·ly
ti·di·ness
tid·ings
tidy (adj tidi·er, tidi·est; verb ti·dies, tidy·ing, ti·died; noun, plural ti·dies)
tie (ty·ing, tied)
tie·back US curtain fastening
tie·breaker (or ·break)
tied
tie-dyeing
tie-dyed
tie·man·nite mineral
Tien·tsin (or T'ien-ching) Chinese city
tie·pin
tier layer; compare tear
tierce fencing position; variant spelling of terce
tiered
Tier·ra del Fue·go South American archipelago
tiff
tif·fa·ny (plural ·nies) fabric
tif·fin meal
Tif·lis variant spelling of Tbilisi
ti·ger
ti·ger·ish
tiger's-eye (or tiger·eye) gemstone
tight
tight·en

tight·en·er
tight·fisted
tight·knit
tight-lipped
tight·ness
tight·rope
tights
tight·wad
tig·lic acid
ti·gon (*or* tig·lon) animal
Ti·gré Ethiopian province
ti·gress
Ti·gri·nya Ethiopian language
Ti·gris Asian river
Ti·jua·na Mexican city
tike *variant spelling of* tyke
tiki Maori amulet
ti·lapia fish
Til·burg Dutch city
Til·bury Essex region
til·bury (*plural* ·buries) carriage
til·de phonetic symbol
tile
tile·fish (*plural* ·fish *or* ·fishes)
til·er
tilia·ceous botany term
til·ing
till
till·able
till·age
til·land·sia plant
till·er
til·li·cum *US* friend
Til·sit Soviet town
tilt
tilt·er
tilth
tilt·yard
Tima·ru New Zealand port
tim·bal (*or* tym·) kettledrum
tim·bale pie
tim·ber wood; *compare* timbre
timber·head
tim·ber·ing
timber·land
timber·work
timber·yard
tim·bre tone quality; *compare* timber
tim·brel tambourine

Tim·buk·tu Malian town
time
time·able
time·card
time-consum·ing
time-honoured
time·keeper
time·keeping
time·lag
time·less
time·less·ness
time·li·ness
time·ly (·li·er, ·li·est)
time·ous *Scot* timely
time·piece
tim·er
time·saver
time·saving
time·server
time·serving
time·table
time·work
time·worker
time·worn
tim·id
ti·mid·ity (*or* tim·id·ness)
tim·ing
Ti·mi·şoa·ra Romanian city
ti·moc·ra·cy (*plural* ·cies) political system
Ti·mor Indonesian island
tim·or·ous
tim·or·ous·ness
timo·thy grass
tim·pa·ni (*or* tym·; *sing.* ·no) kettledrums; *compare* tympanum
tim·pa·nist (*or* tym·)
timps *short for* timpani
tin (tin·ning, tinned)
tina·mou bird
tin·cal borax
tinct tinted
tinc·to·rial of dyeing
tinc·ture
tin·der
tinder·box
tin·dery
tine
tinea ringworm; *compare* taenia
tin·eal
tin·eid moth
tin·foil
ting

ting-a-ling
tinge (tinge·ing *or* ting·ing, tinged)
tin·gle
tin·gler
tin·gling·ly
tin·gly
ti·ni·ly
ti·ni·ness
tink·er
tink·er·er
tin·kle
tin·kling
tin·kly
tin liz·zie *Slang* decrepit car
tinned
tin·ni·ly
tin·ni·ness
tin·ning
tin·ni·tus ringing in ears
tin·ny (·ni·er, ·ni·est)
tin-plate (*verb*)
tin·pot *Slang* inferior
tin·sel (·sel·ling, ·selled; *US* ·sel·ing, ·seled)
tin·smith
tint
Tin·tag·el
tint·ed
tin·tin·nabu·lar (*or* ·lary, ·lous)
tin·tin·nabu·la·tion
tin·tin·nabu·lum (*plural* ·la) bell
tin·type photographic print
tin·ware
tin·work
tiny (tini·er, tini·est)
tip (tip·ping, tipped)
tip·cat game
tip-off (*noun*)
tip·pable
tipped
tip·per
Tip·per·ary
tip·pet cape
tip·ping
tip·ple
tip·pler
tip·si·ly
tip·si·ness
tip·staff
tip·ster
tip·sy (·si·er, ·si·est)
tip·toe (·toe·ing, ·toed)

tiptop 466

tip·top
ti·rade
Ti·ra·na (*or* ·në) Albanian capital
tire exhaust; *US spelling of* tyre
tire·less
tire·less·ness
tire·some
tire·some·ness
Ti·rich Mir Pakistani mountain
tir·ing
tiro *variant spelling of* tyro
Ti·rol *variant spelling of* Tyrol
Ti·ros US satellite
Ti·ru·nel·veli Indian city
'tis
ti·sane
tis·sue
tit
Ti·tan Greek god; satellite of Saturn
ti·tan·ate chemistry term
Ti·tan·esque
Ti·ta·nia satellite of Uranus
ti·tan·ic huge; chemistry term
ti·tani·cal·ly
ti·tan·if·er·ous
Ti·tan·ism spirit of rebellion
ti·tan·ite mineral
ti·ta·nium chemical element
ti·tano·saur
ti·tano·there extinct mammal
ti·tan·ous
tit·bit (*US* tid·)
ti·ter *US spelling of* titre
tith·able
tithe
tith·er
tith·ing
Tithonus mythological character
titi (*plural* titis) monkey
tit·il·late
tit·il·lat·ing
tit·il·la·tion
tit·il·la·tive
titi·vate (*or* tit·ti·)
titi·va·tion (*or* tit·ti·)
titi·va·tor (*or* tit·ti·)
tit·lark

ti·tle
ti·tled
title·holder
tit·man (*plural* ·men) small piglet
tit·mouse (*plural* ·mice)
Ti·to·grad Yugoslav city
Ti·to·ism
Ti·to·ist
ti·trant chemistry term
ti·trat·able
ti·trate
ti·tra·tion
ti·tre (*US* ·ter)
tit·ter
tit·ter·er
tit·tle
tittle-tattle
tittle-tattler
tit·tup (·tup·ping, ·tupped)
titu·ba·tion medical term
titu·lar (*or* ·lary; *plural* ·lars *or* ·laries)
Tiv (*plural* Tivs *or* Tiv) African people
Tivo·li Italian town
tiz·zy (*plural* ·zies)
Tlax·ca·la Mexican state
Tlin·git (*plural* ·gits *or* ·git) American Indian
tme·sis linguistics term
to
toad
toad·fish (*plural* ·fish *or* ·fishes)
toad·flax
toad·ish (*or* ·like)
toad·stone
toad·stool
toady (noun, *plural* toadies; verb toadies, toady·ing, toad·ied)
toady·ism
to-and-fro (*adj*)
toast
toast·er
toast·master (*fem* ·mistress)
to·bac·co (*plural* ·cos *or* ·coes)
to·bac·co·nist
To·ba·go West Indian island
to·bog·gan
to·bog·gan·er (*or* ·ist)

To·bruk Libyan port
toby jug
toc·ca·ta
To·char·ian (*or* ·khar·) language
to·col·ogy (*or* ·kol·) obstetrics
to·coph·er·ol vitamin
toc·sin alarm bell; *compare* toxin
tod
to·day
tod·dle
tod·dler
tod·dy (*plural* ·dies)
to-do (*plural* -dos)
tody (*plural* todies) bird
toe (toe·ing, toed)
toea coin
toe·cap
toed
toe·hold
toe-in
toe·ing
toe·nail
toey *Austral* nervous
toff
tof·fee (*or* ·fy; *plural* ·fees *or* ·fies)
toft homestead
tog (tog·ging, togged)
toga
to·geth·er
to·geth·er·ness
togged
tog·gery clothes
tog·ging
tog·gle
Tog·li·at·ti Soviet city
Togo African republic
To·go·lese
to·he·roa mollusc
toil
toile fabric
toil·er
toi·let lavatory
toi·let·ry (*plural* ·ries)
toi·lette act of dressing
toil·some (*or* ·ful)
toil·some·ness
To·kay wine
to·kay lizard
to·ken
to·ken·ism

toparchy

toko·loshe mythical creature
To·kyo
tola unit of weight
to·lan (or ·lane) organic compound
tol·bu·ta·mide drug
told
tole metal ware
To·le·do Spanish city; US city
tol·er·able
tol·er·able·ness (or ·abil·ity)
tol·er·ably
tol·er·ance
tol·er·ant
tol·er·ate
tol·era·tion
tol·era·tion·ism
tol·era·tion·ist
tol·era·tive
tol·era·tor
toli·dine
toll
toll·booth (or tol·)
toll·gate
toll·house
Tol·pud·dle Dorset town; martyrs
Tol·tec (plural ·tecs or ·tec) American Indian
tolu·ate chemical compound
To·lu·ca Mexican city
tolu·ene
to·lu·ic acid
to·lui·dine
tolu·yl
tol·yl
tom male animal
toma·hawk
tom·al·ley lobster liver
to·man coin
to·ma·to (plural ·toes)
tomb
tom·bac (or tam·) alloy
tomb·like
tom·bo·la lottery
tom·bo·lo (plural ·los) sand bar
tom·boy
tom·boy·ish
tomb·stone
tom·cat
tome book

to·men·tose
to·men·tum (plural ·ta) biology term
tom·fool
tom·fool·ery (plural ·eries)
tom·my (plural ·mies)
tommy·rot
tomo·gram
to·mog·ra·phy X-ray technique
to·mor·row
tom·pi·on variant spelling of tampion
Tomsk Soviet city
tom·tit
tom-tom drum; compare tam-tam
ton imperial weight; compare tonne; tun
ton·al
to·nal·ity (plural ·ities)
ton·al·ly
Ton·bridge Kent town; compare Tunbridge Wells
ton·do (plural ·di) circular painting
tone
tone-deaf
tone·less
tone·less·ness
ton·eme linguistics term
ton·er
to·net·ic linguistics term
tong
Tonga Pacific kingdom
Ton·ga (plural ·gas or ·ga) African people
Tong·an
tongs
tongue (tongu·ing, tongued)
tongue-tied
ton·ic
toni·cal·ly
to·nic·ity
to·night
ton·ing
tonk Austral effeminate man
ton·ka tree; bean
Ton·kin (or Tong·king) Chinese gulf
Ton·le Sap Cambodian lake
ton·nage (or tun·)

tonne metric weight; compare ton; tun
ton·neau (plural ·neaus or ·neaux)
to·nom·eter
tono·met·ric
to·nom·etry
ton·sil
ton·sil·lar (or ·lary)
ton·sil·lec·to·my (plural ·mies)
ton·sil·lit·ic
ton·sil·li·tis
ton·sil·loto·my (plural ·mies)
ton·so·rial
ton·sure
ton·tine annuity scheme
to·nus muscle tone
too
toodle-oo
took
tool
tool·er
tool·ing
tool·less
tool-maker
tool-making
toon tree
toot
toot·er
tooth (plural teeth)
tooth·ache
tooth·brush
toothed
toothi·ly
toothi·ness
tooth·less
tooth·paste
tooth·pick
tooth·some
tooth·some·ness
tooth·wort
toothy (tooth·ier, toothi·est)
too·tle
too·tler
toots (or toot·sie) term of endearment
toot·sy (or tootsy-wootsy; plural ·sies or -wootsies) Slang foot
top (top·ping, topped)
top·arch ruler
top·ar·chy

topaz 468

to·paz
to·pazo·lite gemstone
top·coat
top-dress (*verb*)
tope
to·pee (*or* topi; *plural* ·pees *or* topis) tropical helmet
To·pe·ka US city
top·er
top-flight (*adj*)
top·gal·lant ship's mast
top-heavily
top-heaviness
top-heavy
To·phet (*or* ·pheth) biblical place
to·phus (*plural* ·phi) gout stone
topi *variant spelling of* topee
to·pi·ar·ian
to·pia·rist
to·pi·ary
top·ic
topi·cal
topi·cal·ity
topi·cal·ly
top·knot
top·less
top·less·ness
top-level (*adj*)
top·lofty haughty
top·mast
top·min·now (*plural* ·now *or* ·nows) fish
top·most
top·notch
top·notcher
to·pog·ra·pher
topo·graph·ic (*or* ·graphi·cal)
topo·graphi·cal·ly
to·pog·ra·phy (*plural* ·phies) mapping; *compare* topology
topo·logic (*or* ·logi·cal)
topo·logi·cal·ly
to·polo·gist
to·pol·ogy branch of geometry; *compare* topography
topo·nym
topo·nym·ic (*or* ·nymi·cal)
to·pony·my

top·os (*plural* ·oi) basic concept
topo·type
topped
top·per
top·ping
top·ple
top·sail
top-secret (*adj*)
top-shell mollusc
top·side
top·soil
top·spin
topsy-turvy
toque (*or* to·quet) hat
tor hill; *compare* torr
To·rah Jewish writings
Tor·bay Devon town
tor·bern·ite mineral
torch
torch·bearer
tor·chère candelabrum stand
tor·chier (*or* ·chiere) lamp
torch·light
torch·lit
tor·chon lace
torch·wood
tore
torea·dor
to·re·ro (*plural* ·ros) bullfighter
to·reu·tic
to·reu·tics metalworking
tori *plural of* torus
tor·ic
to·rii (*plural* ·rii) gateway
tor·ment
tor·ment·ed·ly
tor·men·til plant
tor·ment·ing·ly
tor·men·tor (*or* ·ment·er)
torn
tor·nad·ic
tor·na·do (*plural* ·does *or* ·dos) storm; *compare* tournedos
to·roid geometry term
to·roi·dal
to·roi·dal·ly
To·ron·to
To·ron·to·nian
to·rose (*or* ·rous) biology term

tor·pe·do (*noun, plural* ·does; *verb* ·does, ·do·ing, ·doed)
tor·pid
tor·pid·ity (*or* ·ness)
tor·por
tor·por·if·ic
tor·quate
Tor·quay
torque metal collar; mechanical force
tor·ques zoology term
torr unit; *compare* tor
Tor·rance US city
tor·re·fac·tion (*or* ·ri·)
tor·re·fy (*or* ·ri·; ·fies, ·fy·ing, ·fied) roast
tor·rent
tor·ren·tial
tor·ren·tial·ly
Tor·re·ón Mexican city
Tor·ri·cel·lian physics term
tor·rid
tor·rid·ity (*or* ·ness)
tor·sade ornament on hat
tor·si·bil·ity
tor·sion
tor·sion·al
torsk (*plural* torsks *or* torsk) fish
tor·so (*plural* ·sos *or* ·si)
tort legal term
torte cake
tor·tel·li·ni pasta
tort·feasor legal term
tor·ti·col·lar
tor·ti·col·lis wryneck
tor·til·la Mexican pancake
tor·tious legal term; *compare* tortuous; torturous
tor·toise
tortoise·shell
tor·to·ni ice cream
tor·tri·cid moth
tor·tu·os·ity (*plural* ·ities)
tor·tu·ous twisting; devious; *compare* tortious; torturous
tor·tu·ous·ness
tor·ture
tor·tured·ly
tor·tur·er
tor·ture·some
tor·tur·ing·ly

tor·tur·ous causing pain; compare tortious; tortuous
To·ruń Polish city
to·rus (plural ·ri)
Tory (plural Tories)
To·ry·ism
tosh
toss
toss·er
toss·pot Archaic drinker
tot (tot·ting, tot·ted)
to·tal (·tal·ling, ·talled; US ·tal·ing,·taled)
to·tali·tar·ian
to·tali·tar·ian·ism
to·tal·ity (plural ·ities)
to·tali·za·tion (or ·sa·tion)
to·tali·za·tor (or ·sa·tor) betting machine
to·tal·ize (or ·ise)
to·tal·iz·er (or ·is·er)
to·tal·ly
to·ta·quine drug
tote
to·tem
to·tem·ic
to·temi·cal·ly
to·tem·ism
to·tem·ist
to·tem·is·tic
tot·er
to·ti·pal·mate
to·ti·pal·ma·tion
to·tipo·ten·cy
to·tipo·tent zoology term
tot·ted
tot·ter
tot·ter·er
tot·tery
tot·ting
tou·can
touch
touch·able
touch·down
tou·ché acknowledgment
touch·er
touchi·ly
touchi·ness
touch·ing
touch·ing·ly
touch·line
touch·mark
touch·stone
touch-type
touch-typist

touch·wood
touchy (touchi·er, touchi·est)
tough
tough·en
tough·en·er
toughie
tough·ish
tough·ness
Tou·lon French town
Tou·louse French city
tou·pee hairpiece
tour
tou·ra·co (or tu·; plural ·cos) bird
Tou·raine French region
Tou·rane Vietnamese port
tour·bil·lion whirlwind
tour de force (plural tours de force)
tour·er
tour·ism
tour·ist
tour·is·tic
tour·isty
tour·ma·line
tour·ma·lin·ic
tour·na·ment
tour·nedos (plural ·nedos) steak; compare tornado
tour·ney
tour·ni·quet
Tours French town
tou·sle
tous-les-mois plant
tout Slang solicit
tout à fait French completely
tout en·sem·ble French all in all
tout le monde French everyone
to·va·risch (·rich or ·rish) Russian term of address
tow
tow·age
to·ward (adj)
to·wards (prep.)
tow·bar
tow·boat
tow·el (·el·ling, ·elled; US ·el·ing, ·eled)
tow·el·ling (US ·el·ing)
tow·er

tow·er·ing
tow-haired
tow·head
tow·hee bird
tow·line
town
townee
town·hall
town·scape
town·ship
towns·man (plural ·men)
towns·people (or ·folk)
towns·woman (plural ·women)
tow·path
tow·rope
tox·aemia (US ·emia)
tox·aemic (US ·emic)
tox·al·bu·min
toxa·phene
tox·ic
toxi·cal·ly
toxi·cant poison
tox·ic·ity
toxi·co·gen·ic
toxi·co·logi·cal (or ·log·ic)
toxi·co·logi·cal·ly
toxi·colo·gist
toxi·col·ogy
toxi·co·sis
tox·in poison; compare tocsin
tox·oid
tox·ophi·lite archer
tox·ophi·lit·ic
tox·ophi·ly
toxo·plas·mic
toxo·plas·mo·sis
toy
To·ya·ma Japanese city
toy·er
tra·beated (or ·beate) architectural term
tra·bea·tion
tra·becu·la (plural ·lae) anatomy term
tra·becu·lar (or ·late)
Trab·zon Turkish port
trace
trace·abil·ity (or ·able·ness)
trace·able
trace·less
trac·er
trac·ery (plural ·eries)

trachea

tra·chea (*plural* ·cheae)
tra·cheal
tra·che·ate
tra·che·id (*or* ·ide) plant cell
tra·chei·dal
tra·che·itis
tra·cheo·phyte botany term
tra·che·osto·my (*plural* ·mies)
tra·che·oto·mist
tra·che·oto·my (*plural* ·mies)
tra·cho·ma eye disease
tra·choma·tous
tra·chyte rock
tra·chyt·ic
trachy·toid
trac·ing
track
track·able
track·er
track·less
track·suit
tract
trac·tabil·ity (*or* ·table·ness)
trac·table
trac·tably
Trac·tar·ian
Trac·tari·an·ism religious movement
trac·tate treatise
trac·tile ductile
trac·til·ity
trac·tion
trac·tion·al
trac·tive
trac·tor
trad *Slang* traditional jazz
trad·able (*or* trade·)
trade
trade-in (*noun*)
trade·mark
trade-off (*noun*)
trad·er
trad·es·can·tia plant
trades·man (*plural* ·men)
trades·people (*or* ·folk)
trades·woman (*plural* ·women)
trade union (*plural* trade unions) *note* Trades Union Congress
trad·ing

tra·di·tion
tra·di·tion·al
tra·di·tion·al·ism
tra·di·tion·al·ist
tra·di·tion·al·is·tic
tra·di·tion·ally
tra·di·tion·ist
tradi·tor (*plural* ·to·res *or* ·tors) Christian betrayer
tra·duce
tra·duce·ment
tra·duc·er
tra·du·cian·ism theology term
tra·du·cian·ist (*or* ·du·cian)
tra·du·cian·is·tic
tra·duc·ible
Tra·fal·gar
traf·fic (·fick·ing, ·ficked)
traf·fi·ca·tor car indicator
traf·fick·er
traga·canth plant
tra·gal
tra·gedian (*fem* ·gedi·enne)
trag·edy (*plural* ·edies)
trag·ic (*or* tragi·cal)
tragi·cal·ly
tragi·com·edy (*plural* ·edies)
tragi·com·ic (*or* ·comi·cal)
tragi·comi·cal·ly
trago·pan bird
tra·gus (*plural* ·gi) part of ear
trail
trail·blazer
trail·blazing
trail·er
trail·ing·ly
trail·less
train
train·able
train·band English militia
train·bearer
trainee
train·er
train·ing
traipse
trait characteristic
trai·tor
trai·tor·ous
trai·tor·ous·ness
trai·tress

tra·ject *Archaic* transport
tra·jec·tile
tra·jec·tion
tra·jec·tory (*plural* ·tories)
tra-la
Tra·lee Irish town
tram (tram·ming, trammed)
tram·car
tram·line
tram·mel (·el·ling, ·elled; *US* ·el·ing, ·eled)
tram·mel·ler (*US* ·mel·er)
tram·mie *Austral* tram driver
tra·mon·tane (*or* trans·) across mountains
tramp
tramp·er
tramp·ish
tramp·ish·ness
tram·ple
tram·pler
tram·po·line
tram·po·lin·er (*or* ·ist)
tram·way
trance
trance·like
tranche
tran·nie *Slang* transistor radio
tran·quil
tran·quil·lity
tran·quil·li·za·tion (*or* ·sa·tion; *US* ·quili·za·tion)
tran·quil·lize (*or* ·lise; *US* ·quil·ize)
tran·quil·liz·er (*US* ·quil·iz·er)
tran·quil·ly
tran·quil·ness
trans·act
trans·ac·ti·nide
trans·ac·tion
trans·ac·tion·al
trans·ac·tor
trans·al·pine
trans·at·lan·tic
Trans·cau·ca·sia Soviet region
Trans·cau·ca·sian
trans·ceiv·er
trans·cend

tran·scend·ence (or
    ·en·cy)
trans·cend·ent
tran·scen·den·tal
tran·scen·den·tal·ism
tran·scen·den·tal·ist
tran·scen·den·tal·ity
tran·scen·den·tal·ly
tran·scend·ent·ness
trans·con·ti·nen·tal
trans·con·ti·nen·tal·ly
tran·scrib·able
tran·scribe
tran·scrib·er
tran·script
tran·scrip·tion
tran·scrip·tion·al (or
    ·scrip·tive)
trans·cul·tura·tion
trans·cur·rent
trans·duc·er
trans·duc·tion
tran·sect
tran·sec·tion
tran·sept
tran·sep·tal
trans·eunt philosophy term
trans·fer (·fer·ring,
    ·ferred)
trans·fer·abil·ity
trans·fer·able (or
    ·fer·rable)
trans·fer·ase enzyme
trans·feree
trans·fer·ence
trans·fer·en·tial
trans·fer·rer (or in legal
    contexts ·fer·or)
trans·fer·rin biochemical
    compound
trans·figu·ra·tion
trans·fig·ure
trans·fig·ure·ment
trans·fi·nite
trans·fix (·fix·ing, fixed
    or ·fixt)
trans·fix·ion
trans·form
trans·form·able
trans·for·ma·tion
trans·for·ma·tion·al
trans·forma·tive
trans·form·er
trans·form·ism
    evolutionary theory
trans·form·ist
trans·fuse
trans·fus·er
trans·fus·ible (or ·able)
trans·fu·sion
trans·fu·sive
trans·gress
trans·gress·ible
trans·gress·ing·ly
trans·gres·sion
trans·gres·sive
trans·gres·sor
tran·ship variant spelling of
    transship
trans·hu·mance migration
    of livestock
trans·hu·mant
tran·si·ence (or ·en·cy,
    ·ent·ness)
tran·si·ent
trans·il·lu·mi·nate
trans·il·lu·mi·na·tion
trans·il·lu·mi·na·tor
tran·sis·tor
tran·sis·tori·za·tion (or
    ·sa·tion)
tran·sis·tor·ize (or ·ise)
trans·it
tran·sit·able
tran·si·tion
tran·si·tion·al (or ·ary)
tran·si·tion·al·ly
tran·si·tive
tran·si·tive·ness (or
    ·tiv·ity)
tran·si·to·ri·ly
tran·si·to·ri·ness
tran·si·tory
Trans-Jordan
Trans-Jordanian
Trans·kei South African
    republic
Trans·kei·an
trans·lat·abil·ity (or
    ·able·ness)
trans·lat·able
trans·late
trans·la·tion
trans·la·tion·al
trans·la·tor
trans·la·to·rial
trans·lit·er·ate
trans·lit·era·tion
trans·lit·era·tor
trans·lo·cate
trans·lo·ca·tion
trans·lu·cence (or
    ·cen·cy)
trans·lu·cent
trans·lu·nar (or ·nary)
trans·mi·grant
trans·mi·grate
trans·mi·gra·tion
trans·mi·gra·tion·al
trans·mi·gra·tive
trans·mi·gra·tor
trans·mi·gra·tory
trans·mis·sibil·ity
trans·mis·sible
trans·mis·sion
trans·mis·sive
trans·mis·sive·ness
trans·mis·siv·ity
trans·mit (·mit·ting,
    ·mit·ted)
trans·mit·table (or ·tible)
trans·mit·tal
trans·mit·tance
trans·mit·tan·cy physics
    term
trans·mit·ter
trans·mog·ri·fi·ca·tion
trans·mog·ri·fy (·fies,
    ·fy·ing, ·fied)
trans·mon·tane variant of
    tramontane
trans·mun·dane beyond
    this world
trans·mut·able
trans·mut·ably
trans·mu·ta·tion
trans·mu·ta·tion·al (or
    ·ta·tive)
trans·mu·ta·tion·ist
trans·mute
trans·mut·er
trans·ocean·ic
tran·som
tran·son·ic of the sound
    barrier
trans·pa·cif·ic
trans·pa·dane
trans·par·en·cy (plural
    ·cies)
trans·par·ent
trans·par·ent·ness
tran·spicu·ous transparent
trans·pierce
trans·spir·able
tran·spi·ra·tion

transpiratory

tran·spira·tory
tran·spire
trans·plant
trans·plant·able
trans·plan·ta·tion
trans·plant·er
trans·po·lar
tran·spond·er (or ·spon·dor)
trans·pon·tine across a bridge
trans·port
trans·port·abil·ity
trans·port·able
trans·por·ta·tion
trans·port·ed·ly
trans·port·er
trans·port·ive
trans·pos·abil·ity
trans·pos·able
trans·pos·al
trans·pose
trans·pos·er
trans·po·si·tion
trans·po·si·tion·al (or ·posi·tive)
trans·sexu·al
trans·sex·ual·ism
trans·ship (or tran·ship; ·ship·ping, ·shipped)
trans·ship·ment (or tran·ship·)
Trans-Siberian Rail·way
tran·sub·stan·tial
tran·sub·stan·ti·ate
tran·sub·stan·tia·tion
tran·sub·stan·tia·tion·al·ist
tran·su·date
tran·su·da·tion
tran·su·da·tory
tran·sude
transu·ran·ic (or ra·nian, ·ra·nium) chemistry term
Trans·vaal
Trans·vaal·er
Trans·vaal·ian
trans·valu·ation
trans·value (·valu·ing, ·valued)
trans·valu·er
trans·ver·sal
trans·ver·sal·ly
trans·verse
trans·verse·ly
trans·verse·ness

trans·ves·tism (or ·ti·tism)
trans·ves·tite
Transylvania
Transylvanian
trap (trap·ping, trapped)
tra·peze
tra·pezial
tra·pezium (plural ·peziums or ·pezia)
tra·pezius (plural ·peziuses) muscle
tra·pezo·he·dral
tra·pezo·he·dron (plural ·drons or ·dra)
trap·ezoid
trap·per
trap·pings
Trap·pist monk
trap·rock
traps belongings
trap·shooter
trap·shooting
tra·pun·to (plural ·tos) quilting
trash
trashi·ly
trashi·ness
trashy (trashi·er, trashi·est)
trass rock
trat·to·ria
trau·ma (plural ·mas, ·ma·ta)
trau·mat·ic
trau·mati·cal·ly
trau·ma·tism
trau·ma·ti·za·tion (or ·sa·tion)
trau·ma·tize (or ·tise)
trav·ail
trave horse-shoeing cage; crossbeam
trav·el (·el·ling, ·elled; US ·el·ing, ·eled)
trav·el·ler (US ·el·er)
trav·elogue (US also ·elog)
tra·vers·able
tra·vers·al
trav·erse
tra·vers·er
trav·er·tine (or ·tin) rock
trav·es·ty (noun, plural ·ties; verb ·ties, ·ty·ing, ·tied)

472

tra·vois (plural ·vois) sledge
trawl
trawl·er
tray receptacle; compare trey
tray·mobile Austral trolley
treach·er·ous
treach·er·ous·ness
treach·ery (plural ·eries)
trea·cle
trea·cli·ness
trea·cly
tread (tread·ing, trod, trod·den or trod)
tread·er
trea·dle
trea·dler
tread·mill
trea·son
trea·son·able (or ·ous)
trea·son·able·ness
trea·son·ably
treas·ur·able
treas·ure
treas·ur·er
treas·ur·er·ship
treasure-trove
Treas·ury government department
treas·ury (plural ·uries)
treat
treat·able
treat·er
trea·tise
treat·ment
trea·ty (plural ·ties)
Trebi·zond former name of Trabzon
tre·ble
Tre·blin·ka concentration camp
tre·bly
trebu·chet (or tre·buck·et) weapon
tre·cen·tist
tre·cen·to 14th century
tree (tree·ing, treed)
tree·hopper insect
tree·less
tree·less·ness
tre·en wooden
tree·nail (or tre·nail, trun·nel) dowel
treen·ware
tre·foil

tre·ha·la sugary substance
tre·ha·lose
treil·lage trellis
trek (trek·king, trekked)
trek·ker
trel·lis
trellis·work
trema·tode parasite
trem·ble
trem·bler
trem·bling·ly
trem·bly
tre·men·dous
tre·men·dous·ness
tremo·lite mineral
tremo·lo (plural ·los)
trem·or
trem·or·ous
tremu·lant musical term
tremu·lous
tremu·lous·ness
trench
trench·an·cy
trench·ant
trench·er
trencher·man (plural ·men) hearty eater
trend
trendi·ly
trendi·ness
trendy (adj trendi·er, trendi·est; noun, plural trendies)
Treng·ga·nu Malaysian state
Trent English river
Trentino-Alto Adi·ge Italian region
Tren·ton US city
tre·pan (·pan·ning, panned) surgical instrument
tre·pang sea cucumber
trephi·na·tion
tre·phine surgical instrument
trepi·da·tion
trepo·nema (or ·neme; plural ·nemas, ·nema·ta, or ·nemes) bacterium
trepo·nema·tous
tres·pass
tres·pass·er
tress

tres·sure heraldic term
tressy
tres·tle
trestle·tree
trestle·work
tret commerce term
tre·val·ly fish
trews trousers
trey card or dice thrown; compare tray
tri·able
tri·able·ness
tri·ac·id
Tri·ad Chinese secret society
tri·ad
tri·ad·ic
tri·ad·ism
tri·age
tri·al
tri·an·gle
tri·an·gu·lar
tri·an·gu·lar·ity
tri·an·gu·late
tri·an·gu·la·tion
Tri·an·gu·lum constellation
tri·ar·chy (plural ·chies)
Trias geology term
Tri·as·sic
tri·ath·lon
tri·atom·ic
tri·atomi·cal·ly
tri·ax·ial
tria·zine (or ·zin)
tria·zole
tria·zol·ic
trib·ade lesbian
tri·bad·ic
trib·ad·ism
trib·al
trib·al·ism
trib·al·ist
trib·al·ly
tri·ba·sic
tribe
tribes·man (plural ·men)
trib·let spindle
tri·bo·elec·tric
tri·bo·elec·tric·ity
tri·bol·ogy study of friction
tri·bo·lu·mi·nes·cence
tri·bo·lu·mi·nes·cent
tri·brach metrical foot
tri·brach·ic (or ·brach·ial)
tri·bro·mo·etha·nol
tribu·la·tion

trichroism

tri·bu·nal
tribu·nary
tribu·nate (or trib·une·ship)
trib·une
tribu·tari·ly
tribu·tary (plural ·taries)
trib·ute
trice
tri·cen·ten·ary (plural ·aries)
tri·cen·ten·nial
tri·ceps (plural ·cepses or ·ceps)
tri·cera·tops
tri·chia·sis eye condition
tri·chi·na (plural ·nae) parasite
trichi·nia·sis variant of trichinosis
trichi·ni·za·tion (or ·sa·tion)
trichi·nize (or ·nise)
Trichi·nopo·ly Indian city
trichi·no·sis (or ·nia·) parasitic disease
trichi·nous
trich·ite crystal
tri·chit·ic
tri·chlo·ride
tri·chlo·ro·acetic acid
tri·chlo·ro·phenoxy·acetic acid
tricho·cyst zoology term
tricho·cys·tic
tricho·gyne botany term
tricho·gyn·ial (or ·ic)
trich·oid
tri·cholo·gist
tri·chol·ogy study of hair
tri·chome plant structure
tri·chom·ic
tricho·mon·ad parasite
tricho·mona·dal (or ·mon·al)
tricho·mo·nia·sis
tri·chop·ter·an insect
tri·cho·sis hair disease
tricho·tom·ic (or ·choto·mous)
tri·choto·my (plural ·mies)
tri·chro·ic
tri·chro·ism crystallography term

trichromat

tri·chro·mat
tri·chro·mat·ic (*or* ·chro·mic)
tri·chro·ma·tism
trick
trick·er
trick·ery (*plural* ·eries)
tricki·ly
tricki·ness
trick·ing·ly
trick·le
trick·ling·ly
trick·ly
tricki·si·ness
trick·ster
trick·sy (·si·er, ·si·est) mischievous
tricky (tricki·er, tricki·est)
tri·clin·ic crystallography term
tri·clin·i·um (*plural* ·ia) Roman dining room
tri·col·our (*US* ·or)
tri·col·oured (*US* ·ored)
tri·corn (*or* ·corne) hat
tri·cos·tate biology term
tri·cot fabric
tri·co·tine fabric
tri·crot·ic medical term
tri·crot·ism
tric·trac (*or* trick·track) board game
tri·cus·pid
tri·cus·pi·dal
tri·cy·cle
tri·cy·clic chemistry term
tri·cy·clist
tri·dac·tyl (*or* ·tyl·ous)
tri·dent
tri·den·tate (*or* ·tal)
Tri·den·tine of Council of Trent
tri·di·men·sion·al
tri·di·men·sion·al·ity
trid·uum prayer days
tried
tri·en·nial
tri·en·nial·ly
tri·en·ni·um (*plural* ·niums *or* ·nia)
Trier West German city
tri·er one who tries
tri·er·ar·chy (·chies)
Tri·este Italian port

trif·fid fictional plant
tri·fid three-lobed
tri·fle
tri·fler
tri·fling
tri·fo·cal
tri·fo·li·ate (*or* ·at·ed)
tri·fo·lium plant
tri·fo·rial
tri·fo·rium (*plural* ·ria) part of church
tri·fur·cate (*or* ·cat·ed)
tri·fur·ca·tion
trig (trig·ging, trigged) *Dialect* neat; wedge
tri·gemi·nal anatomy term
trig·ger
trigger·fish (*plural* ·fish *or* ·fishes)
tri·glyc·er·ide
tri·glyph architectural term
tri·glyph·ic
tri·gon harp
trigo·nal crystallography term
trigo·no·met·ric (*or* ·ri·cal)
trigo·no·met·ri·cal·ly
trigo·nom·etry
trigo·nous botany term
tri·graph phonetics term
tri·graph·ic
tri·he·dral
tri·he·dron (*plural* ·drons *or* ·dra)
tri·hy·drate
tri·hy·dric (*or* ·droxy)
tri·io·do·thy·ro·nine
trike *Slang* tricycle
tri·lat·er·al
tri·lat·er·al·ly
tri·lat·era·tion surveying method
tril·by (*plural* ·bies)
tri·lem·ma
tri·lin·ear
tri·lin·gual
tri·lin·gual·ism
tri·lin·gual·ly
tri·lit·er·al
tri·lith·ic
tri·lith·on (*or* tri·lith)
trill
tril·lion
tril·lionth

474

tril·lium plant
tri·lo·bate three-lobed
tri·lo·bite fossil
tri·locu·lar
tril·ogy (*plural* ·gies)
trim (*adj* trim·mer, trim·mest; *verb* trim·ming, trimmed)
tri·ma·ran
tri·mer chemistry term
trim·er·ous
tri·mes·ter
tri·mes·tral (*or* ·trial)
trim·eter verse line
tri·metha·di·one
tri·met·ric (*or* ·ri·cal)
tri·met·ro·gon aerial photography
trim·ly
trim·mer
trim·ming
trim·ness
tri·mo·lecu·lar
tri·month·ly
tri·morph
tri·mor·phic (*or* ·phous)
tri·mor·phism
Tri·mur·ti Hindu gods
tri·nal
tri·na·ry consisting of three
Trin·co·ma·lee Sri Lankan port
trine astrology term
Trini·dad
Trini·dad·ian
Trini·tar·ian believer in the Trinity
Trini·tar·ian·ism
tri·ni·tro·ben·zene
tri·ni·tro·cre·sol
tri·ni·tro·glyc·er·in
tri·ni·tro·phe·nol
tri·ni·tro·tolu·ene (*or* ·ol)
Trin·ity God
trini·ty (*plural* ·ities)
trin·ket
trin·ket·ry
tri·nocu·lar
tri·no·mial
trio (*plural* trios)
tri·ode electronic valve
tri·oecious (*or* ·ecious) botany term
trio·elein
tri·ol

trio·let verse form
tri·ose
tri·ox·ide
trip (trip·ping, tripped)
tri·pal·mi·tin
tri·par·tite
tri·par·tite·ly
tri·par·ti·tion
tripe
trip·hammer
tri·phe·nyl·me·thane
tri·phibi·ous
triph·thong vowel sound
triph·thong·al
triphy·lite mineral
tri·pin·nate botany term
tri·plane
tri·ple
tri·plet
triple·tail (plural ·tail or ·tails) fish
triple-tongue musical term
Tri·plex (Trademark)
trip·li·cate
trip·li·ca·tion
tri·plic·ity (plural ·ities) group of three
trip·lo·blas·tic
trip·loid biology term
trip·loidy
triply
tri·pod
tripo·dal
tripo·dy (plural ·dies) metrical unit
Tripo·li Libyan capital
tripo·li rock
Tripo·li·ta·nia Libyan region
Tripo·li·ta·nian
trip·pos
trip·per
trip·pet
trip·ping·ly
trip·tane
trip·ter·ous
Triptolemus mythological character
trip·tych altarpiece; compare tryptic
trip·tyque customs permit
Tripu·ra Indian state
trip·wire
tri·que·trous
tri·ra·di·ate

tri·reme
tri·sac·cha·ride
tri·sect
tri·sec·tion
tri·sec·tor
tri·se·rial
tris·kai·deka·pho·bia fear of number 13
tris·kai·deka·pho·bic
tris·keli·on (or ·kele) symbol
tris·mic
tris·mus lockjaw
tris·oc·ta·he·dral
tris·oc·ta·he·dron (plural ·drons or ·dra)
tri·some genetics term
tri·so·mic
tri·somy
Tris·tan da Cu·nha South Atlantic islands
tris·tich three-line poem
tris·tich·ic
tris·ti·chous
tri·sul·phide
tri·syl·la·ble
tri·syl·lab·ic (or ·labi·cal)
tri·tano·pia blue blindness
tri·tan·op·ic
trite
trite·ly
trite·ness
tri·the·ism belief in Trinity
tri·the·ist
triti·ate chemistry term
tritia·tion
triti·ca·le hybrid cereal
triti·cum cereal grass
trit·ium isotope of hydrogen
Tri·ton satellite of Neptune
Tri·ton Greek god
tri·ton mollusc
tri·tone musical term
tritu·rable
tritu·rate grind
tritu·ra·tion
tritu·ra·tor
tri·umph
tri·um·phal
tri·um·phal·ly
tri·um·phant
tri·umph·er
tri·um·vir (plural ·virs or ·vi·ri)

tri·um·vi·ral
tri·um·vi·rate
tri·une three in one
tri·unity
tri·va·len·cy
tri·va·lent (or ter·)
Tri·van·drum Indian city
triv·et
trivia (plural)
triv·ial
trivi·al·ity (plural ·ities)
trivi·ali·za·tion (or ·sa·tion)
trivi·al·ize (or ·ise)
trivi·al·ly
trivi·al·ness
tri·week·ly (plural ·lies)
Tro·as Trojan region
troat bellow
tro·car surgical instrument
tro·cha·ic of a trochee
tro·chai·cal·ly
tro·chal zoology term
tro·chan·ter anatomy term
troche lozenge
tro·chee metrical foot
trochi·lus hummingbird
troch·lea (plural ·leae) anatomy term
troch·le·ar
tro·choid
tro·choi·dal
trocho·phore (or ·sphere) zoology term
trod
trod·den
trog (trog·ging, trogged) stroll
trog·lo·dyte
trog·lo·dyt·ic (or ·dyti·cal)
tro·gon bird
troi·ka
Troilus mythological character
Tro·jan
troll
trol·ley
trol·lop
trom·bi·dia·sis mite infestation
trom·bone
trom·bon·ist
trom·mel
trompe forge apparatus

trompe l'oeil

trompe l'oeil (*plural* **trompe l'oeils**) painting illusion
tro·na mineral
Trond·heim Norwegian port
troop large group; move in group; *compare* **troupe**
troop·er
troops
troop·ship
troost·ite mineral
tro·paeo·lin
tro·paeo·lum (*plural* **·lums** *or* **·la**) plant
trope figure of speech; liturgical interpolation
troph·al·lac·tic
troph·al·lax·is
troph·ic of nutrition
trophi·cal·ly
tropho·blast embryonic membrane
tropho·blas·tic
tropho·zo·ite zoology term
tro·phy (*plural* **·phies**)
trop·ic line of latitude
tro·pic of a tropism
tropi·cal
tropi·cal·ity
tropi·cali·za·tion (*or* **·sa·tion**)
tropi·cal·ize (*or* **·ise**)
tropi·cal·ly
tropic·bird
trop·ics
tro·pism biology term
tropo·log·ic (*or* **·logi·cal**)
tro·pol·ogy (*plural* **·ogies**) use of tropes
tropo·pause atmospheric layer
tro·pophi·lous
tropo·phyte
tropo·phyt·ic
tropo·sphere atmospheric layer
tropo·spher·ic
trop·po musical term
Tros·sachs Scottish valley
trot (**trot·ting, trot·ted**)
troth
trot·line
Trot·sky·ism
Trot·sky·ite (*or* **·ist**)
trot·ter
tro·tyl TNT
trou·ba·dour
trou·ble
trou·bled·ly
trouble·maker
trouble·making
trou·bler
trouble·shooter
trou·ble·some
trou·ble·some·ness
trou·bling·ly
trou·blous
trou-de-loup (*plural* **trous-de-loup**) pit for defence
trough
trounce
troupe group of performers; *compare* **troop**
troup·er
trou·pial bird
trouse Irish breeches
trou·sered
trou·sers
trous·seau (*plural* **·seaux** *or* **·seaus**)
trout (*plural* **trout** *or* **trouts**)
trou·vère (*or* **·veur**) medieval poet
trove
tro·ver legal term
Trow·bridge Wiltshire town
trow·el (**·el·ling, ·elled;** *US* **·el·ing, ·eled**)
trow·el·ler (*US* **·el·er**)
Troy
tru·an·cy
tru·ant
truce
Tru·cial States
truck
truck·age *US* conveyance by lorry
truck·er
truckie *Austral* truck driver
truck·ing
truck·le
truck·ler
truck·load
trucu·lence (*or* **·len·cy**)
trucu·lent
trudge
trudg·en swimming stroke
trudg·er
true (*adj* **tru·er, tru·est;** *verb* **tru·ing, trued**)
true-blue
true-born
true-life (*adj*)
true·love
true·ness
truf·fle
trug
tru·ism
tru·is·tic (*or* **·ti·cal**)
Trujillo Peruvian city
tru·ly
tru·meau (*plural* **·meaux**) architectural term
trump
trump·ery (*plural* **·eries**)
trum·pet
trum·pet·er
trumpet·weed
trun·cate
trun·cat·ed
trun·ca·tion
trun·cheon
trun·dle
trunk
trunk·fish (*plural* **·fish** *or* **·fishes**)
trunk·ful (*plural* **·fuls**)
trunks
trun·nion pivot
Tru·ro Cornish town
truss
truss·er
truss·ing
trust
trust·abil·ity
trust·able
trus·tee (**·tee·ing, ·teed**)
trus·tee·ship
trust·er
trust·ful (*or* **·ing**)
trust·ful·ly (*or* **·ing·ly**)
trust·ful·ness (*or* **·ing·**)
trusti·ly
trusti·ness
trust·worthi·ly
trust·worthi·ness
trust·worthy
trusty (**trusti·er, trusti·est**)
truth
truth·ful
truth·ful·ly

truth·ful·ness
truth-function logic term
truth-value logic term
try (*verb* tries, try·ing, tried; *noun, plural* tries)
(tryer) *incorrect spelling of* trier
try·ing·ly
try·ing·ness
try·ma (*plural* ·ma·ta) botany term
try-on (*noun*)
try-out (*noun*)
trypa·no·so·mal (*or* ·som·ic)
trypa·no·some parasite
trypa·no·so·mia·sis sleeping sickness
try·par·sa·mide
tryp·sin enzyme
tryp·sino·gen enzyme
tryp·tic of trypsin; *compare* triptych
tryp·to·phan amino acid
try·sail
tryst
tryst·er
tsar (*or* czar)
tsar·dom (*or* czar·)
tsar·evitch (*or* czar·)
tsa·ri·na (*or* ·rit·sa, cza·)
tsar·ism (*or* czar·)
tsar·ist (*or* czar·)
Tse·li·no·grad Soviet city
tset·se (*or* tzet·ze)
Tshi·lu·ba African language
Tsi·nan (*or* Chi·nan, Chi·nan) Chinese city
Tsing·hai (*or* Ching·hai, Ch'ing-hai) Chinese province
Tsing·tao (*or* Ching·tao, Ch'ing-tao) Chinese port
Tson·ga (*plural* ·ga *or* ·gas) African people
tsu·na·mi tidal wave
Tsu·shi·ma Japanese islands
tsu·tsu·ga·mu·shi dis·ease
Tswa·na (*plural* ·na *or* ·nas) African people
Tua·reg (*plural* ·reg *or* ·regs) Berber people
tuart tree
tua·ta·ra reptile
tub (tub·bing, tubbed)

tuba (*plural* tubas *or* tubae) musical instrument; *compare* tuber
tu·bal
Tubal-cain biblical character
tu·bate
tubbed
tub·bi·ness
tub·bing
tub·by (·bi·er, ·bi·est)
tube
tube·less
tu·ber underground plant stem; *compare* tuba
tu·ber·cle
tu·ber·cu·lar
tu·ber·cu·late covered with nodules
tu·ber·cu·la·tion
tu·ber·cu·lin
tu·ber·cu·lo·sis
tu·ber·cu·lous
tu·ber·ose plant; *compare* tuberous
tu·ber·os·ity (*plural* ·ities)
tu·ber·ous (*or* ·ose) having tubers; *compare* tuberose
tu·bi·fex (*plural* ·fex *or* ·fexes) worm
tu·bi·form
tub·ing
tub-thumper
tubu·lar
tu·bu·lar·ity
tu·bu·late
tu·bu·la·tion
tu·bu·la·tor
tu·bule
tu·bu·li·flo·rous botany term
tu·bu·lous
Tu·ca·na constellation
tu·chun Chinese governor
tuck
tuck·er
tuck·et flourish on trumpet
tu·co·tu·co (*or* tu·cu·tu·cu) animal
Tuc·son US city
Tu·cu·mán Argentine city
Tu·dor
Tues·day
tufa soft rock
tuff hard rock

tuffa·ceous
tuf·fet
tuft
tuft·ed
tuft·er
tufty
tug (tug·ging, tugged)
tug·ger
tu·grik (*or* ·ghrik) Mongolian currency
tui bird
Tui·ler·ies French palace
tui·tion
tui·tion·al (*or* ·ary)
tu·la·rae·mia (*US* ·re·) disease
tu·la·rae·mic (*US* ·remic)
tu·lip
tulip·wood
tulle fabric
Tul·sa US city
tum *Slang* stomach
tum·ble
tumble-down
tumble-drier
tumble·home nautical term
tum·bler
tum·bler·ful (*plural* ·fuls)
tumble·weed
tum·brel (*or* ·bril)
tu·mefa·ci·ent
tu·mefac·tion
tu·mefy (·mefies, ·mefy·ing, ·mefied) swell
tu·mes·cence
tu·mes·cent
tu·mid
tu·mid·ity (*or* ·ness)
tum·my (*plural* ·mies)
tu·mor·ous (*or* ·mor·al)
tu·mour (*US* ·mor)
tump *Dialect* small mound
tu·mu·lar
tu·mu·lose (*or* ·lous)
tu·mu·los·ity
tu·mult
tu·mul·tu·ous
tu·mul·tu·ous·ness
tu·mu·lus (*plural* ·li) burial mound
tun (tun·ning, tunned) cask; *compare* ton; tonne
tuna (*plural* tuna *or* tunas)

tunable

tun·able (or tune·)
Tun·bridge Wells Kent town; compare Tonbridge
tun·dra
tune
tune·ful
tune·ful·ly
tune·ful·ness
tune·less
tune·less·ness
tun·er
tune·smith
tung·sten
tung·stic
tung·stite mineral
Tun·gus (plural ·guses or ·gus) Mongoloid people
Tun·gu·sian
Tun·gus·ic language
tu·nic
tu·ni·ca (plural ·cae) anatomy term
tu·ni·cate marine animal
tu·ni·cle vestment
tun·ing musical term
Tu·nis Tunisian capital
Tu·ni·sia
Tu·ni·sian
tun·nage variant spelling of tonnage
tun·nel (·nel·ling, ·nelled; US ·nel·ing, ·neled)
tun·nel·ler (US ·nel·er)
tun·ny (plural ·nies or ·ny) tuna fish
tup (tup·ping, tupped)
tu·pelo (plural ·pelos) tree
Tupi (plural ·pis or ·pi) South American Indian
tupped
tup·pence variant spelling of twopence
tup·pen·ny variant spelling of twopenny
tup·ping
tuque cap
tur·ban
tur·baned
tur·ba·ry (plural ·ries) peat-cutting area
tur·bel·lar·ian flatworm
tur·bid opaque; muddy; compare turgid
tur·bi·dim·eter
tur·bid·ity (or ·ness)

tur·bi·nate (or ·nal) scroll-shaped
tur·bi·na·tion
tur·bine
tur·bit pigeon
tur·bo·car
tur·bo·charg·er
turbo-electric
tur·bo·fan
tur·bo·gen·era·tor
tur·bo·jet
tur·bo·prop
tur·bo·super·charg·er
tur·bot (plural ·bot or ·bots)
tur·bu·lence (or ·len·cy)
tur·bu·lent
turd
tur·dine of thrushes
tu·reen soup dish; compare terrene; terrine
turf (plural turfs or turves)
turfi·ness
turfy (turfi·er, turfi·est)
tur·ges·cence (or ·cen·cy)
tur·ges·cent
tur·gid swollen; pompous; compare turbid
tur·gid·ity (or ·ness)
tur·gite mineral
tur·gor biology term
Tu·rin Italian city
Turing ma·chine
turi·on plant bud
Turk
Tur·ke·stan variant spelling of Turkistan
Tur·key
tur·key (plural ·keys or ·key)
Tur·ki of Turkic
Tur·kic language
Turk·ish
Tur·ki·stan (or ·ke·) Asian region
Turk·men language
Turk·meni·stan Soviet republic
Turko·man (or Turk·man; plural ·mans or ·men) Asian people
Tur·ku Finnish city
tur·mer·ic

478

tur·moil
turn move; compare tern; terne
turn·able
turn·about
turn·around
turn·buckle
turn·coat
turn·er
turn·ery (plural ·eries) lathe work
turn·ing
tur·nip
turn·key
turn-off (noun)
turn-on (noun)
turn-out (noun)
turn-over (noun)
turn·pike
turn-round (noun)
turn·sole plant
turn·stile
turn·stone bird
turn·table
turn-up (noun)
tur·pen·tine
tur·peth plant
tur·pi·tude
turps turpentine
tur·quoise
tur·ret
tur·ret·ed
tur·ricu·late (or ·la·ted)
tur·tle
turtle·back part of ship
turtle·dove
turtle·neck
tur·tler
Tus·can
Tus·ca·ny
Tus·ca·ro·ra (plural ·ras or ·ra) American Indian
tusche lithographic substance
Tus·cu·lum ancient city
tush
tusk
tusk·er
tusk·like
tus·sah (or tus·sore) silk
tus·sal
tus·sis cough
tus·sive
tus·sle
tus·sock

tus·socky
tus·sore *variant spelling of* tussah
tut (tut·ting, tut·ted)
tu·tee
tu·telage
tu·telary (*or* ·telar; *plural* ·telaries *or* ·telars)
tu·ti·or·ism Catholic doctrine
tu·ti·or·ist
tu·tor
tu·tor·age (*or* ·ship)
tu·to·rial
tu·to·rial·ly
tut·san shrub
tut·ti musical term
tutti-frutti ice cream
tut·ty polishing powder
tutu ballet skirt
Tuvalu Pacific state
tu-whit tu-whoo
tux·edo (*plural* ·dos)
tu·yère (*or* twy·er) blast-furnace nozzle
twad·dle
twad·dler
twain
twang
twangy
'twas
tway·blade orchid
tweak
twee
Tweed Scottish river
tweed fabric
tweedy (tweedi·er, tweedi·est)
tweeny (*plural* tweenies) *Slang* maid
tweet
tweet·er loudspeaker
tweeze
twee·zers
twelfth
Twelfth·tide Epiphany
twelve
twelve·mo (*plural* ·mos) paper size
twelve·month
twelve-tone musical term
twen·ti·eth
twen·ty (*plural* ·ties)
'twere
twerp

Twi (*plural* Twi *or* Twis) language or people
twi·bill (*or* ·bil) tool
twice
twice-laid
Twick·en·ham
twid·dle
twid·dler
twig (twig·ging, twigged)
twig·gy (·gi·er, ·gi·est)
twi·light
twi·lit
twill
twin (twin·ning, twinned)
twine
twin·er
twin·flower
twinge (twinge·ing *or* twing·ing, twinged)
twink
twin·kle
twin·kler
twin·kling·ly
twirl
twirl·er
twist
twist·abil·ity
twist·able
twist·ed·ly
twist·er
twist·ing·ly
twisty (twisti·er, twisti·est)
twit (twit·ting, twit·ted)
twitch
twitch·er
twitchi·ly
twitchi·ness
twitch·ing·ly
twitchy (twitchi·er, twitchi·est)
twite bird
twit·ter
twit·ter·er
twit·tery
twixt
two (*plural* twos)
two-by-four
two-dimen·sion·al
two-dimen·sion·al·ity
two-dimen·sion·al·ly
two-edged
two-faced
two-facedly
two-facedness

two·fold
two-handed
two-handed·ly
two·pence (*or* tup·pence)
two·pen·ny (*or* tup·pen·ny)
two-phase
two-piece
two-ply (*plural* -plies)
two-seater
two-sided
two·some
two-step
two-stroke
two-time
two-timer
two-tone
two-way
Ty·burn
Tyche Greek goddess
tych·ism philosophy term
Ty·cho moon crater
ty·coon
ty·ing
tyke (*or* tike)
ty·lo·pod zoology term
ty·lo·sis botany term
tym·pan printing term
tym·pa·ni *variant spelling of* timpani
tym·pan·ic
tym·pa·nist *variant spelling of* timpanist
tym·pa·ni·tes (*or* ·pa·ny) abdominal distension
tym·pa·nit·ic
tym·pa·ni·tis
tym·pa·num (*plural* ·nums *or* ·na) part of ear; architectural term; *compare* timpani
tym·pa·ny *variant of* tympanites
Tyne English river
Tyne and Wear English county
Tyne·side
Tyn·wald Manx Parliament
type
type·bar
type·case
type·cast (·cast·ing, ·cast)
type·cast·er
type·face
type-high

typescript

type·script
type·set (·set·ting, ·set)
type·set·ter
type·write (·writ·ing, ·wrote, ·writ·ten)
type·writ·er
typh·li·tic
typh·li·tis intestinal disorder
typh·lol·ogy study of blindness
ty·pho·gen·ic causing typhoid
ty·phoid
ty·phoi·dal
ty·phoi·din
ty·phon·ic
ty·phoon
ty·phous (adj)
ty·phus (noun)
typi·cal (or typ·ic)
typi·cal·ly
typi·cal·ness (or ·ity)
typi·fi·ca·tion
typi·fi·er
typi·fy (·fies, ·fy·ing, ·fied)
typ·ing

typ·ist
typo (plural typos)
ty·pog·ra·pher
ty·po·graphi·cal (or ·graph·ic)
ty·po·graphi·cal·ly
ty·pog·ra·phy
ty·po·logi·cal (or ·log·ic)
ty·pol·o·gist
ty·pol·ogy theology term
ty·poth·etae US printers
ty·ra·mine
ty·ran·ni·cal (or ran·nic)
ty·ran·ni·cal·ly
ty·ran·ni·cal·ness
ty·ran·ni·cid·al
ty·ran·ni·cide
tyr·an·nize (or ·nise)
tyr·an·niz·er (or ·nis·er)
tyr·an·niz·ing·ly (or ·nis·ing·ly)
ty·ran·no·saur (or ·saur·us)
tyr·an·nous
tyr·an·nous·ness
tyr·an·ny (plural ·nies)

480

ty·rant
Tyre Lebanese port
tyre (US tire) wheel ring; compare tire
Tyr·ian
tyro (or tiro; plural tyros or tiros) novice
ty·ro·ci·dine antibiotic
Ty·rol (or Ti·) Austrian province
Tyro·lese (or ·lean)
Ty·ro·li·enne dance
Ty·rone Irish county
ty·ron·ic (or ti·)
ty·ro·si·nase enzyme
ty·ro·sine amino acid
ty·ro·thri·cin antibiotic
Tyr·rhe·nian Sea
Tyu·men Soviet port
tzar less common spelling of tsar
Tzi·gane gipsy
tzet·ze variant spelling of tsetse
Tzu·po (or Tze·po) Chinese city

U

ubi·ety being in particular place
ubiqui·tar·ian Lutheran
ubiqui·tous
ubiquity (or ubiqui·tous·ness)
ubi su·pra Latin where mentioned above
U-boat
Udai·pur Indian city
udal legal term
ud·der
Udi·ne Italian city
udo (plural udos) plant
Uf·fizi Italian art gallery
UFO (plural UFOs)
ufol·ogy study of UFOs
Ugan·da
Ugan·dan
Uga·rit·ic language
ugli (plural uglis or uglies) fruit
ug·li·fi·ca·tion

ug·li·fi·er
ug·li·fy (·fies, ·fy·ing, ·fied)
ug·li·ly
ug·li·ness
ugly (ug·li·er, ug·li·est)
Ugrian Asian people
Ugric language
uh·lan Polish lancer
uhu·ru African national independence
Uigur (or Uighur; plural Uigur, Uigurs or Uighur, Uighurs) Mongoloid people
Uigu·rian (or ·ric, Uighu·)
uin·ta·there extinct mammal
uit·land·er South African foreigner
Uj·jain Indian city
ukase tsar's edict

uke·lele variant spelling of ukulele
uki·yoe (or ukiyo-e) Japanese art
Ukraine
Ukrain·ian
uku·lele (or uke·)
Ulan Ba·tor Mongolian capital
Ulan-Ude Soviet city
ul·cer
ul·cer·ate
ul·cera·tion
ul·cera·tive
ul·cer·ous
ulema Muslim scholar
ul·lage
ul·laged
Ulls·wa·ter
ul·ma·ceous botany term
ulna (plural ulnae or ulnas) arm bone
ul·nar

ulot·ri·chous curly haired
ulot·ri·chy
Ul·ster Northern Ireland
ul·ster overcoat
Ul·ster·man (*plural* ·men)
ul·te·ri·or
ul·ti·ma final syllable
ul·ti·mate
ul·ti·mate·ly
ul·ti·ma·tum (*plural* ·tums or ·ta)
ul·ti·mo last month
ul·ti·mo·geni·ture legal term
ul·tra
ultra·cen·trifu·gal
ultra·cen·trifu·ga·tion
ultra·cen·tri·fuge
ultra·con·ser·va·tive
ultra·fiche
ultra·fil·ter
ultra·fil·tra·tion
ultra·high
ultra·ism extreme philosophy
ultra·ist
ultra·is·tic
ultra·ma·rine colour
ultra·mi·crom·eter
ultra·micro·scope
ultra·micro·scop·ic
ultra·mi·cros·co·py
ultra·mod·ern
ultra·mod·ern·ism
ultra·mod·ern·ist
ultra·mod·ern·is·tic
ultra·mon·tane beyond the mountains
ultra·mon·ta·nism religious doctrine
ultra·mon·tan·ist
ultra·mun·dane beyond this world
ultra·na·tion·al
ultra·na·tion·al·ism
ultra·na·tion·al·ist
ultra·na·tion·al·is·tic
ultra·short
ultra·son·ic
ultra·soni·cal·ly
ultra·son·ics
ultra·sound
ultra·struc·tur·al
ultra·struc·ture
ultra·vio·let

ul·tra vi·res legal term
ultra·vi·rus
ulu·lant
ulu·late wail
ulu·la·tion
Ul·ya·novsk Soviet city
Umay·yad *variant spelling of* Omayyad
um·bel botany term
um·bel·late (*or* ·lar, ·lat·ed)
um·bel·lif·er·ous
um·bel·lu·late
um·bel·lule
um·ber pigment
um·bili·cal
um·bili·cate
um·bili·ca·tion
um·bili·cus (*plural* ·ci) navel
um·bili·form
umbo (*plural* um·bo·nes *or* umbos) small hump
um·bo·nate (*or* ·bo·nal, ·bon·ic)
um·bra (*plural* ·brae) shadow
um·brage
um·bra·geous shady
um·bral
um·brel·la
Um·bria Italian region
Um·brian
Um·bri·el satellite of Uranus
umi·ak (*or* oomi·) Eskimo boat
um·laut
um·pire
um·pire·ship (*or* ·pir·age)
ump·teen
ump·teenth
Um·ta·li Zimbabwean city
un·abashed
un·abat·ed
un·able
un·abridged
un·ab·sorbed
un·ac·cent·ed
un·ac·cep·table
un·ac·claimed
un·ac·com·mo·dat·ed
un·ac·com·mo·dat·ing
un·ac·com·pa·nied
un·ac·com·plished

un·ac·count·able
un·ac·count·able·ness (*or* ·abil·ity)
un·ac·count·ably
un·ac·count·ed
un·ac·counted-for
un·ac·cus·tomed
un·ack·nowl·edged
un·ac·quaint·ed
un·ad·mit·ted
un·adopt·ed
un·adorned
un·adul·ter·at·ed
un·ad·ven·tur·ous
un·ad·vised
un·ad·vis·ed·ly
un·ad·vis·ed·ness
un·af·fect·ed
un·afraid
un·aid·ed
un·aimed
un·aired
un·al·loyed pure
un·al·ter·able
un·al·ter·ably
un·al·tered
un·am·bigu·ous
un·am·bi·tious
un-Ameri·can
una·nim·ity (*or* unani·mous·ness)
unani·mous
un·an·nounced
un·an·swer·able
un·an·swered
un·ap·peal·able legal term
un·ap·peased
un·ap·pre·ciat·ed
un·ap·pre·cia·tive
un·ap·proach·able
un·ap·pro·pri·at·ed
un·apt inapt
un·apt·ness
un·argu·able
un·arm
un·armed
unary consisting of single element
un·ashamed
un·asham·ed·ly
un·asham·ed·ness
un·asked
un·as·sail·able
un·as·sist·ed
un·as·sumed

un·as·sum·ing
un·atoned
un·at·tached
un·at·tain·able
un·at·tend·ed
un·at·test·ed
un·at·trac·tive
un·authen·ti·cat·ed
un·author·ized
un·avail·able
un·avail·ing
un·avoid·abil·ity (or ·able·ness)
un·avoid·able
un·avoid·ably
un·aware
un·aware·ness
un·awares (adv)
un·backed
un·bal·ance
un·bal·anced
un·bal·las·ted
un·bar (·bar·ring, ·barred)
un·bear·able
un·bear·able·ness
un·bear·ably
un·beat·able
un·beat·en
un·be·com·ing
un·be·com·ing·ness
un·be·fit·ting
un·be·known (or ·knownst)
un·be·lief
un·be·liev·abil·ity (or ·able·ness)
un·be·liev·able
un·be·liev·ably
un·be·liev·er
un·be·liev·ing
un·be·liev·ing·ly
un·belt
un·bend (·bend·ing, ·bent)
un·bend·able
un·bend·ing
un·bend·ing·ness
un·bent
un·bi·ased (or ·assed)
un·bi·ased·ly (or ·assed·)
un·bi·ased·ness (or ·assed·)
un·bid·den
un·bind (·bind·ing, ·bound)

un·birth·day
un·blem·ished
un·blessed
un·bless·ed·ness
un·blink·ing
un·block
un·blush·ing
un·bolt
un·bolt·ed
un·boned
un·bon·net remove hat
un·born
un·bos·om relieve by disclosing
un·bound released
un·bound·ed unlimited
un·bowed
un·brace relax
un·break·able
un·bred
un·bri·dle
un·bri·dled
un-Brit·ish
un·bro·ken
un·brushed
un·buck·le
un·bur·den
un·bur·ied
un·but·ton
un·caged
uncalled-for
un·can·ni·ly
un·can·ny (·ni·er, ·ni·est)
un·cap (·cap·ping, ·capped)
uncared-for
un·car·ing
un·ceas·ing
un·ceas·ing·ness
un·cer·emo·ni·ous
un·cer·emo·ni·ous·ness
un·cer·tain
un·cer·tain·ness
un·cer·tain·ty (plural ·ties)
un·chain
un·chal·lenge·able
un·chal·lenged
un·changed
un·chang·ing
un·chap·er·oned
un·charged
un·chari·table
un·chari·tably
un·chari·table·ness

un·chart·ed not mapped
un·char·tered not authorized
un·chaste
un·chaste·ness (or ·chas·tity)
un·checked
un·chris·tian
un·church excommunicate
un·cial type of capital letter
un·ci·form hook-shaped
un·ci·na·ria·sis hookworm disease
un·ci·nate
un·ci·nus (plural ·ni) small hook
un·cir·cum·cised
un·civ·il
un·ci·vil·ity (or ·civ·il·ness)
un·civi·lized (or ·lised)
un·civil·ly
un·clad
un·claimed
un·clasp
un·clas·si·fied
un·cle
un·clean
un·cleaned
un·clean·li·ness
un·clean·ly
un·clean·ness
un·clear
un·clench
un·clip (·clip·ping, ·clipped)
un·cloak
un·clog (·clog·ging, ·clogged)
un·close
un·clothe (·cloth·ing, ·clothed or ·clad)
un·clothed
un·cloud·ed
un·clut·tered
unco Scot strange
un·coil
un·coined
un·com·fort·able
un·com·fort·ably
un·com·mer·cial
un·com·mit·ted
un·com·mon
un·com·mon·ly
un·com·mon·ness

un·com·mu·ni·ca·tive
un·com·pen·sat·ed
un·com·peti·tive
un·com·plain·ing
un·com·plet·ed
un·com·pli·cat·ed
un·com·pli·men·ta·ry
un·com·pro·mis·ing
un·com·pro·mis·ing·ness
un·con·cealed
un·con·cern
un·con·cerned
un·con·cern·ed·ly
un·con·cern·ed·ness
un·con·clud·ed
un·con·di·tion·al
un·con·di·tion·al·ly
un·con·di·tion·al·ness (*or* ·ity)
un·con·di·tioned
un·con·fined
un·con·firmed
un·con·form·abil·ity (*or* ·able·ness)
un·con·form·able
un·con·form·ity (*plural* ·ities)
un·con·gen·ial
un·con·gen·ial·ly
un·con·nect·ed
un·con·nect·ed·ness
un·con·quer·able
un·con·quered
un·con·scion·able
 unscrupulous; excessive
un·con·scious
un·con·scious·ness
un·con·sent·ing
un·con·sti·tu·tion·al
un·con·sti·tu·tion·al·ity
un·con·sti·tu·tion·al·ly
un·con·strained
un·con·sum·mat·ed
un·con·tami·nat·ed
un·con·test·ed
un·con·trol·labil·ity (*or* ·lable·ness)
un·con·trol·lable
un·con·trol·lably
un·con·ven·tion·al
un·con·ven·tion·al·ity
un·con·ven·tion·al·ly
un·con·vert·ed
un·con·vinced
un·con·vinc·ing

un·cooked
un·co·opera·tive
un·co·ordi·nat·ed
un·cork
un·cor·rected
un·cor·robo·rat·ed
un·cor·rupt·ed
un·count·able
un·count·ed
un·cou·ple
un·couth
un·cov·enant·ed
un·cov·er
un·cov·ered
un·criti·cal
un·criti·cal·ly
un·cross
un·crowned
unc·tion
unc·tu·os·ity (*or* ·tu·ous·ness)
unc·tu·ous
un·cul·ti·vat·ed
un·curbed
un·cured
un·curl
un·curt·ained
un·cus (*plural* unci) hooked structure
un·cut
un·dam·aged
un·damped
un·dat·ed
un·daunt·ed
un·deca·gon eleven-sided polygon
un·de·ceiv·able
un·de·ceive
un·de·ceiv·er
un·de·cid·ed
un·de·cid·ed·ness
un·de·clared
un·de·feat·ed
un·de·fend·ed
un·de·filed
un·de·mand·ing
un·demo·crat·ic
un·demo·crati·cal·ly
un·de·mon·stra·tive
un·de·ni·able
un·de·ni·ably
un·der
under·achieve
under·achieve·ment
under·achiev·er

under·act
under·age
under·arm
under·belly (*plural* ·bellies)
under·bid (·bid·ding, ·bid)
under·bid·der
under·body (*plural* ·bodies)
under·bred
under·breeding
under·brush *US* undergrowth
under·buy (·buy·ing, ·bought)
under·capi·tal·ize (*or* ·ise)
under·carriage
under·cart undercarriage
under·charge
under·clay
under·clothes (*or* ·cloth·ing)
under·coat
under·cook
under·cov·er
under·croft underground chamber
under·cur·rent
under·cut (·cut·ting, ·cut)
under·de·vel·op
under·de·vel·op·ment
under·do (·does, ·do·ing, ·did, ·done)
under·dog
under·done
under·drain
under·drain·age
under·dressed
under·em·ployed
under·em·ploy·ment
under·es·ti·mate
under·es·ti·ma·tion
under·ex·pose
under·ex·po·sure
under·feed (·feed·ing, ·fed)
under·felt
under·floor
under·foot
under·fur
under·gar·ment
under·gird (·gird·ing, ·gird·ed *or* ·girt) strengthen from below
under·glaze

undergo

under·go (·goes, ·go·ing, ·went, ·gone)
under·go·er
under·gone
under·gradu·ate
under·ground
under·grown
under·growth
under·hand
under·hand·ed
under·hand·ed·ly
under·hand·ed·ness
under·hung
under·laid
under·lain
under·lay (·lay·ing, ·laid) to place under
under·let (·let·ting, ·let)
under·let·ter
under·lie (·ly·ing, ·lay, ·lain) to lie under
under·li·er
under·line
under·ling
under·ly·ing
under·manned
under·men·tioned
under·mine
under·min·er
under·min·ing·ly
under·most
under·named
under·neath
under·nour·ish
under·nour·ished
under·nour·ish·ment
under·paid
under·paint·ing
under·pants
under·pass
under·pay (·pay·ing, ·paid)
under·pay·ment
under·pin (·pin·ning, ·pinned)
under·pin·nings
under·play
under·plot subplot
under·price
under·privi·leged
under·pro·duc·tion
under·proof less than proof spirit
under·prop (·prop·ping, ·propped)
under·quote
under·rate
under·ripe
under·score
under·sea
under·seal
under·sec·re·tary (*plural* ·taries)
under·sec·re·tary·ship
under·sell (·sel·ling, ·sold)
under·sell·er
under·set (·set·ting, ·set)
under·sexed
under·sher·iff
under·shirt
under·shoot (·shoot·ing, ·shot)
under·side
under·signed
under·sized
under·skirt
under·slung
under·soil
under·sold
under·spend (·spend·ing, ·spent)
under·staffed
under·stand (·stand·ing, ·stood)
under·stand·able
under·stand·ably
under·stand·ing
under·stand·ing·ly
under·state
under·state·ment
under·stock
under·stood
under·study (*noun, plural* ·studies; *verb* ·studies, ·study·ing, ·stud·ied)
under·sur·face
under·take (·tak·ing, ·took, ·tak·en)
under·tak·er
under·tak·ing
under·thrust geological fault
under·tint
under·tone
under·took
under·tow
under·trick bridge term
under·trump
under·valu·ation
under·value (·valu·ing, ·val·ued)
under·valu·er
under·vest
under·wa·ter
under·wear
under·weight
under·went
under·wing moth
under·world
under·write (·writ·ing, ·wrote, ·writ·ten)
under·writ·er
un·des·cend·ed
un·de·served
un·de·serv·ing
un·de·sign·ing
un·de·sir·abil·ity (*or* ·able·ness)
un·de·sir·able
un·de·sir·ably
un·de·sired
un·de·tect·ed
un·de·ter·mined
un·de·terred
un·de·vel·oped
un·de·vi·at·ing
un·di·ag·nosed
un·did
un·dies
un·dif·fer·en·ti·at·ed
un·di·gest·ed
un·dig·ni·fied
un·di·lut·ed
un·dim·in·ished
un·dimmed
un·dine water spirit
un·di·rect·ed
un·dis·ci·plined
un·dis·closed
un·dis·cov·ered
un·dis·crimi·nat·ing
un·dis·guised
un·dis·put·ed
un·dis·solved
un·dis·tin·guished
un·dis·trib·ut·ed logic term
un·dis·turbed
un·di·vid·ed
undo (un·does, un·do·ing, un·did, un·done)
un·do·er
un·do·ing
un·done
un·doubt·ed

un·doubt·ed·ly
un·dreamed (*or* ·dreamt)
un·dress
un·drink·able
un·due
un·du·lance
un·du·lant
un·du·late
un·du·la·tion
un·du·la·tor
un·du·la·tory
un·du·ly
un·dy·ing
un·earned
un·earth
un·earth·li·ness
un·earth·ly
un·ease
un·easi·ly
un·easi·ness
un·easy
un·eat·able
un·eat·en
un·eco·nom·ic
un·eco·nomi·cal
un·eco·nomi·cal·ly
un·ed·it·ed
un·edu·cat·ed
un·elect·able
un·emo·tion·al
un·emo·tion·al·ly
un·em·ploy·abil·ity
un·em·ploy·able
un·em·ployed
un·em·ploy·ment
un·end·ing
un·en·gaged
un-Eng·lish
un·en·light·ened
un·en·ter·pris·ing
un·en·thu·si·as·tic
un·en·thu·si·asti·cal·ly
un·en·vi·able
un·equal
un·equalled (*US* ·equaled)
un·equal·ly
un·equivo·cal
un·equivo·cal·ly
un·equivo·cal·ness
un·err·ing
un·err·ing·ly
un·es·sen·tial *less common word for* inessential
un·ethi·cal

un·ethi·cal·ly
un·even
un·even·ness
un·event·ful
un·event·ful·ly
un·ex·am·pled
un·ex·cep·tion·able
  beyond criticism
un·ex·cep·tion·able·ness (*or* ·abil·ity)
un·ex·cep·tion·al ordinary
un·ex·cit·ing
un·ex·pec·ted
un·ex·pec·ted·ly
un·ex·pect·ed·ness
un·ex·pe·ri·enced
un·ex·pired
un·ex·plain·able *less common word for* inexplicable
un·ex·plained
un·ex·plod·ed
un·ex·plored
un·ex·posed
un·ex·pressed
un·ex·pres·sive
un·ex·pres·sive·ness
un·ex·pur·gat·ed
un·fad·ing
un·fail·ing
un·fair
un·fair·ness
un·faith·ful
un·faith·ful·ly
un·faith·ful·ness
un·fa·mil·iar
un·fa·mili·ar·ity
un·fash·ion·able
un·fash·ion·ably
un·fas·ten
un·fa·thered
un·fath·om·able
un·fath·omed
un·fa·vour·able (*US* ·vor·)
un·fa·vour·able·ness (*US* ·vor·)
un·fa·vour·ably (*US* ·vor·)
un·fed
un·feel·ing
un·feel·ing·ness
un·feigned
un·feigned·ly
un·femi·nine
un·fenced
un·fer·til·ized (*or* ·ised)

un·fet·ter
un·fil·ial
un·filled
un·fin·ished
un·fit
un·fit·ness
un·fit·ted
un·fit·ting
un·fix
un·flag·ging
un·flap·pabil·ity (*or* ·pable·ness)
un·flap·pable
un·flat·ter·ing
un·fledged
un·flinch·ing
un·flinch·ing·ness
un·flust·ered
un·fo·cused
un·fold
un·fold·er
un·forced
un·fore·see·able
un·fore·seen
un·for·get·table
un·for·giv·able
un·for·giv·en
un·for·giv·ing
un·for·got·ten
un·formed
un·for·tu·nate
un·for·tu·nate·ly
un·for·tu·nate·ness
un·found·ed
un·found·ed·ness
un·framed
un·freeze (·freez·ing, ·froze, ·fro·zen)
un·fre·quent·ed
un·friend·li·ness
un·friend·ly (·li·er, ·li·est)
un·frock
un·froze
un·fro·zen
un·fruit·ful
un·fruit·ful·ly
un·fruit·ful·ness
un·ful·filled
un·furl
un·fur·nished
un·gain·li·ness
un·gain·ly (·li·er, ·li·est)
Un·ga·va Canadian region
un·gen·er·ous
un·gen·tle·man·ly

un-get-at-able

un-get-at-able
un-glazed
un-god-li-ness
un-god-ly (·li·er, ·li·est)
un-gov-ern-able
un-gov-ern-able-ness
un-gov-ern-ably
un-grace-ful
un-grace-ful-ly
un-gra-cious
un-gram-mati-cal
un-grate-ful
un-grate-ful-ly
un-grate-ful-ness
un-grudg-ing
un-gual (*or* ·gu·lar) of finger- or toenails
un-guard-ed
un-guard-ed-ness
un-guent ointment
un-guen-tary
un-guicu-late biology term
un-gui-nous greasy
un-guis (*plural* ·gues) claw or hoof
un-gu-la (*plural* ·lae) maths term
un-gu-lar
un-gu-late hoofed mammal
un-gu-li-grade walking on hooves
un-hair
un-hal-lowed
un-ham-pered
un-hand
un-hand-some
un-hand-some-ness
un-hap-pi-ly
un-hap-pi-ness
un-hap-py (·pi·er, ·pi·est)
un-harmed
un-har-ness
un-healthi-ly
un-healthi-ness
un-healthy (·healthi·er, ·healthi·est)
un-heard
unheard-of
un-heed-ed
un-heed-ing
un-helm remove the helmet of
un-help-ful
un-help-ful-ly
un-her-ald-ed

un-hesi-tat-ing
un-hid-den
un-hinge
un-ho-li-ness
un-ho-ly (·li·er, ·li·est)
un-hon-oured (*US* ·ored)
un-hook
unhoped-for
un-horse
un-hur-ried
un-hurt
un-hy-gien-ic
un-hy-gieni-cal-ly
un-hy-phen-at-ed
uni *Austral* university
Uni-at (*or* ·ate) Eastern Church
Uni-at-ism
uni-ax-ial
uni-cam-er-al
uni-cam-er-al-ism
uni-cam-er-al-ist
uni-cel-lu-lar
uni-cel-lu-lar-ity
uni-col-our (*or* ·oured; *US* ·or *or* ·ored)
uni-corn
uni-cos-tate having one rib
uni-cy-cle
uni-cy-clist
un-iden-ti-fi-able
un-iden-ti-fied
uni-di-rec-tion-al
uni-fi-able
uni-fi-ca-tion
uni-fied
uni-fi-er
uni-fo-li-ate botany term
uni-fo-lio-late botany term
uni-form
uni-formi-tar-ian
uni-formi-tari-an-ism geological theory
uni-form-ity (*plural* ·ities)
uni-form-ly
uni-form-ness
uni-fy (·fies, ·fy·ing, ·fied)
uni-ju-gate botany term
uni-lat-er-al
uni-lat-er-al-ism (*or* ·ity)
uni-lat-er-al-ly
un-il-lus-trat-ed
uni-locu-lar botany term
un-im-agi-nable
un-im-agi-nably

un-im-agi-na-tive
un-im-ag-ined
un-im-paired
un-im-peach-abil-ity (*or* ·able·ness)
un-im-peach-able
un-im-ped-ed
un-im-por-tant
un-im-pos-ing
un-im-pressed
un-im-pres-sive
un-im-proved
un-in-cor-po-ra-ted
un-in-flu-enced
un-in-formed
un-in-hab-it-able
un-in-hab-it-ed
un-in-hib-it-ed
un-in-jured
un-in-spired
un-in-spir-ing
un-in-sur-able
un-in-sured
un-in-tel-li-gence
un-in-tel-li-gent
un-in-tel-li-gibie
un-in-tel-li-gibly
un-in-tend-ed
un-in-ten-tion-al
un-in-ten-tion-ally
un-in-ter-est-ed not interested; *compare* disinterested
un-in-ter-est-ed-ly
un-in-ter-est-ed-ness
un-in-ter-est-ing
un-in-ter-rupt-ed
uni-nu-cleate
un-in-vit-ed
un-in-vit-ing
un-ion
un-ion-ism
un-ion-ist
un-ion-is-tic
un-ioni-za-tion (*or* ·sa·tion)
un-ion-ize (*or* ·ise) join trade union
un-ionized not ionized
uni-para *variant of* primipara
unip-ar-ous biology term
uni-per-son-al
uni-per-son-al-ity
uni-pla-nar
uni-pod one-legged support

uni·po·lar
uni·po·lar·ity
unique
unique·ly
unique·ness
uni·ra·mous undivided
uni·sep·tate biology term
uni·sex
uni·sexu·al
uni·sexu·al·ity
uni·son
uniso·nous (or ·nal, ·nant)
unit
Uni·tar·ian
uni·tar·ian
Uni·tari·an·ism Christian belief
uni·tari·an·ism centralized government
uni·tary
unite
unit·ed
unit·ed·ly
unit·ed·ness
unit·er
uni·tive
unity (plural unities)
uni·va·len·cy
uni·va·lent
uni·valve zoology term
uni·ver·sal
uni·ver·sal·ism
uni·ver·sal·ist
uni·ver·sal·is·tic
uni·ver·sal·ity (plural ·ities)
uni·ver·sali·za·tion (or ·sa·tion)
uni·ver·sal·ize (or ·ise)
uni·ver·sal·ly
uni·ver·sal·ness
uni·verse
uni·ver·sity (plural ·sities)
uni·vo·cal unambiguous
un·just
un·jus·ti·fi·able
un·jus·ti·fied
un·just·ness
un·kempt
un·kempt·ness
un·kenned Dialect unknown
un·ken·nel (·nel·ling, ·nelled; US ·nel·ing, ·neled)

un·kind
un·kind·li·ness
un·kind·ness
un·knit (·knit·ting, ·knit·ted or ·knit)
un·know·able
un·know·able·ness (or ·abil·ity)
un·know·ing
un·know·ing·ly
un·known
un·known·ness
un·la·belled (US ·beled)
un·lace
un·lade unload
un·la·den
un·lady·like
un·laid
un·lam·ent·ed
un·lash
un·latch
un·law·ful
un·law·ful·ly
un·law·ful·ness
un·lay (·lay·ing, ·laid) untwist
un·lead printing term
un·lead·ed
un·learn (·learn·ing, ·learnt or ·learned)
un·learn·ed ignorant
un·leash
un·leav·ened
un·less
un·let·tered
un·li·censed
un·like
un·like·li·ness (or ·li·hood)
un·like·ly
un·lim·ber prepare for use
un·lim·it·ed
un·lined
un·list·ed
un·lit
un·live
un·lived-in
un·load
un·load·er
un·lock
un·lock·able
unlooked-for
un·loose (or ·loos·en)
un·lov·able
un·loved

un·love·ly
un·lov·ing
un·lucki·ly
un·lucki·ness
un·lucky (·lucki·er, ·lucki·est)
un·made
un·make (·mak·ing, ·made)
un·mak·er
un·man (·man·ning, ·manned)
un·man·age·able
un·man·li·ness
un·man·ly
un·manned
un·man·nered
un·man·ner·li·ness
un·man·ner·ly
un·marked
un·mar·riage·able
un·mar·ried
un·mask
un·mask·er
un·matched
un·mean·ing
un·meant
un·meas·ur·able unable to be measured; compare immeasurable
un·meas·ured
un·meet unsuitable
un·men·tion·able
un·men·tion·ables
un·mer·ci·ful
un·mer·ci·ful·ly
un·mer·it·ed
un·mind·ful
un·mis·tak·able (or ·take·)
un·mis·tak·ably (or ·take·)
un·miti·gat·ed
un·mixed
un·mo·lest·ed
un·moor
un·mor·al amoral
un·mo·ral·ity
un·mount·ed
un·mourned
un·moved
un·mu·si·cal
un·mu·si·cal·ly
un·mu·si·cal·ness
un·muz·zle

unnameable

un·name·able
un·named
un·natu·ral
un·natu·ral·ly
un·natu·ral·ness
un·navi·gable
un·nec·es·sari·ly
un·nec·es·sary
un·neigh·bour·ly (*US* ·bor·)
un·nerve
un·nerv·ing
un·no·ticed
un·num·bered
un·ob·jec·tion·able
un·ob·scured
un·ob·ser·vant
un·ob·served
un·ob·struct·ed
un·ob·tain·able
un·ob·tru·sive
un·ob·tru·sive·ly
un·ob·tru·sive·ness
un·oc·cu·pied
un·of·fend·ing
un·of·fi·cial
un·of·fi·cial·ly
un·opened
un·op·posed
un·or·gan·ized (*or* ·ised)
un·origi·nal
un·ortho·dox
un·owned
un·pack
un·pack·er
un·paged
un·paid
un·paint·ed
un·pained
un·pal·at·able
un·par·al·leled
un·par·don·able
un·par·lia·men·ta·ry
un·pat·ent·ed
un·pat·ri·ot·ic
un·paved
un·peeled
un·peg (·peg·ging, ·pegged)
un·peo·ple (*verb*)
un·per·ceived
un·per·fo·rat·ed
un·per·son
un·per·turbed
un·pick

un·pin (·pin·ning, ·pinned)
un·pity·ing
un·place·able
un·placed
un·planned
un·play·able
un·pleas·ant
un·pleas·ant·ness
un·pleas·ing
un·plug (·plug·ging, ·plugged)
un·plumbed
un·poli·tic
un·po·liti·cal
un·polled
un·pol·lut·ed
un·popu·lar
un·popu·lar·ity
un·posed
un·prac·ti·cal impractical
un·prac·ti·cal·ity (*or* ·ness)
un·prac·tised (*US* ·ticed)
un·prec·edent·ed
un·pre·dict·abil·ity (*or* ·able·ness)
un·pre·dict·able
un·pre·dict·ably
un·preju·diced
un·pre·medi·tat·ed
un·pre·medi·ta·tion
un·pre·pared
un·pre·par·ed·ness
un·pre·pos·sess·ing
un·pre·sent·able
un·pre·ten·tious
un·pre·ten·tious·ness
un·pre·vent·able
un·priced
un·prin·ci·pled
un·print·able
un·pro·duc·tive
un·pro·fessed
un·pro·fes·sion·al
un·pro·fes·sion·al·ly
un·prof·it·abil·ity (*or* ·able·ness)
un·prof·it·able
un·prof·it·ably
un·prom·is·ing
un·prompt·ed
un·pro·nounce·able
un·pro·tect·ed
un·prov·able

un·proved
un·prov·en
un·pro·vid·ed
un·pub·lished
un·punc·tual
un·pun·ished
un·put·down·able
un·quali·fi·able
un·quali·fied
un·quench·able
un·ques·tion·abil·ity (*or* ·able·ness)
un·ques·tion·able
un·ques·tion·ably
un·ques·tioned
un·ques·tion·ing
un·qui·et
un·quote
un·rav·el (·el·ling, ·elled; *US* ·el·ing, ·eled)
un·rav·el·ler (*US* ·el·er)
un·rav·el·ment
un·reach·able
un·read
un·read·abil·ity (*or* ·able·ness)
un·read·able
un·readi·ness
un·ready
un·real
un·re·al·is·tic
un·re·al·isti·cal·ly
un·re·al·ity
un·re·al·ized (*or* ·ised)
un·rea·son
un·rea·son·able
un·rea·son·able·ness
un·rea·son·ably
un·rea·son·ing
un·reck·on·able
un·rec·og·niz·able (*or* ·nis·able)
un·rec·og·nized (*or* ·nised)
un·rec·on·ciled
un·re·con·struct·ed
un·re·cord·ed
un·reeve (·reev·ing, ·rove *or* ·reeved) nautical term
un·re·fined
un·re·flect·ed
un·re·flec·tive
un·re·gard·ed
un·re·gen·era·cy

un·re·gen·er·ate
   unrepentant
un·reg·is·tered
un·re·hearsed
un·re·lat·ed
un·re·lent·ing
un·re·li·abil·ity (or
   ·able·ness)
un·re·li·able
un·re·li·ably
un·re·mit·ting
un·re·paired
un·re·peat·able
un·re·pent·ant
un·re·port·ed
un·rep·re·senta·tive
un·rep·re·sent·ed
un·re·quit·ed
un·re·served
un·re·serv·ed·ly
un·re·serv·ed·ness
un·re·sist·ing
un·re·solved
un·re·spon·sive
un·rest
un·re·strained
un·re·strict·ed
un·re·ward·ed
un·re·ward·ing
un·rhymed
un·rid·able
un·rid·dle solve
un·rid·dler
un·ri·fled
un·rig (·rig·ging, ·rigged)
un·right·eous
un·rip (·rip·ping, ·ripped)
un·ripe (or ·rip·ened)
un·ri·valled (US ·valed)
un·roll
un·root
un·round·ed
un·rove nautical term
un·ruf·fled
un·ruf·fled·ness
un·ruled
un·ru·li·ness
un·ru·ly (·li·er, ·li·est)
un·sad·dle
un·safe
un·said
un·sale·able (US
   ·sal·able)
un·salt·ed
un·sanc·tioned

un·sani·tary
un·sat·is·fac·tori·ly
un·sat·is·fac·tory
un·sat·is·fied
un·sat·is·fy·ing
un·satu·rat·ed
un·satu·ra·tion
un·saved
un·sa·vouri·ly (US ·vori·)
un·sa·vouri·ness (US
   ·vori·)
un·sa·voury (US ·vory)
un·say (·say·ing, ·said)
un·scal·able
un·scarred
un·scathed
un·scent·ed
un·sched·uled
un·schooled
un·sci·en·tif·ic
un·sci·en·tifi·cal·ly
un·scram·ble
un·scram·bler
un·scratched
un·screened
un·screw
un·script·ed
un·scru·pu·lous
un·scru·pu·lous·ness (or
   ·los·ity)
un·seal
un·seal·able
un·seam
un·search·able
un·sea·son·able
un·sea·son·ably
un·sea·soned
un·seat
un·sea·worthy
un·secured
un·seed·ed
un·seem·li·ness
un·seem·ly
un·seen
un·seg·re·gat·ed
un·self·con·scious
un·self·ish
un·self·ish·ness
un·sepa·rat·ed
un·ser·vice·able
un·set
un·set·tle
un·set·tled
un·set·tle·ment
un·sex

un·shack·le
un·shad·ed
un·shak·able (or ·shake·)
un·shak·en
un·shap·en
un·shav·en
un·sheathe
un·shed
un·ship (·ship·ping,
   ·shipped)
un·shock·able
un·sight·ed
un·sight·li·ness
un·sight·ly
un·signed
un·sink·able
un·skil·ful (US ·skill·ful)
un·skilled
un·slaked
un·sling (·sling·ing,
   ·slung)
un·smil·ing
un·smoked
un·snap (·snap·ping,
   ·snapped)
un·snarl
un·so·ciabil·ity (or
   ·ciable·ness)
un·so·ciable
un·so·ciably
un·so·cial
un·sold
un·so·lic·it·ed
un·solv·able
un·solved
un·so·phis·ti·cat·ed
un·so·phis·ti·cat·ed·ness
   (or ·ca·tion)
un·sort·ed
un·sought
un·sound
un·spar·ing
un·speak·able
un·speak·ably
un·spe·cif·ic
un·speci·fied
un·spent
un·spoiled (or ·spoilt)
un·spo·ken
un·sport·ing
un·spot·ted
un·sta·ble
un·stamped
un·steadi·ly
un·steadi·ness

unsteady

un·steady (*adj* ·steadi·er,
    ·steadi·est; *verb*
    ·steadies, ·steady·ing,
    ·stead·ied)
un·step (·step·ping,
    ·stepped) nautical term
un·stick (·stick·ing,
    ·stuck)
un·stint·ing
un·stop (·stop·ping,
    ·stopped)
un·stop·pable
un·stopped
un·strained
un·strap (·strap·ping,
    ·strapped)
un·strati·fied
un·stressed
un·stri·at·ed
un·string (·string·ing,
    ·strung)
un·striped
un·struc·tured
un·strung
un·stuck
un·stud·ied
un·sub·stan·tial
un·sub·stan·ti·al·ity
un·sub·stan·ti·at·ed
un·suc·cess·ful
un·suc·cess·ful·ly
un·sug·ared
un·suit·abil·ity (*or*
    ·able·ness)
un·suit·able
un·suit·ably
un·suit·ed
un·sul·ied
un·sung
un·sure
un·sur·passed
un·sus·pect·ed
un·sus·pect·ing
un·swathe
un·swear (·swear·ing,
    ·swore, ·sworn) retract
un·sweet·ened
un·swept
un·swerv·ing
un·sym·pa·thet·ic
un·sym·pa·theti·cal·ly
un·sys·tem·at·ic
un·taint·ed
un·tame·able
un·tamed

un·tan·gle
un·tapped
un·tast·ed
un·taught
un·teach (·teach·ing,
    ·taught)
un·teach·able
un·tear·able
un·ten·abil·ity (*or*
    ·able·ness)
un·ten·able
un·ten·ant·ed
Un·ter·wal·den Swiss
    canton
un·test·ed
un·thanked
un·thank·ful
un·thank·ful·ness
un·think (·think·ing,
    ·thought)
un·think·abil·ity (*or*
    ·able·ness)
un·think·able
un·think·ably
un·think·ing
un·thought-of
un·thread
un·ti·di·ly
un·ti·di·ness
un·ti·dy (*adj* ·di·er,
    ·di·est; *verb* ·dies,
    ·dy·ing, ·died)
un·tie (·ty·ing, ·tied)
un·til
un·time·ly
un·tinged
un·tir·ing
un·tit·led
unto
un·told
un·touch·abil·ity
un·touch·able
un·touched
un·to·ward
un·trace·able
un·trained
un·tram·melled (*US*
    ·meled)
un·trans·lat·able
un·trav·elled (*US* ·eled)
un·treat·able
un·treat·ed
un·tried
un·trod·den
un·true

un·truss
un·trust·worthy
un·truth
un·truth·ful
un·truth·ful·ly
un·truth·ful·ness
un·tuck
un·turned
un·tu·tored
un·typi·cal
un·us·able
un·used
un·usual
un·usu·al·ly
un·ut·ter·able
un·ut·tered
un·val·ued
un·var·ied
un·var·nished
un·vary·ing
un·veil
un·veil·ing
un·versed
un·voice phonetics term
un·voiced
un·want·ed
un·war·rant·able
un·war·rant·ed
un·wari·ly
un·wari·ness
un·wary
un·washed
un·watched
un·wat·ered
un·wa·ver·ing
un·wear·able
un·wea·ried
un·weary·ing
un·wed
un·weighed
un·wel·come
un·well
un·wept
un·whole·some
un·whole·some·ly
un·whole·some·ness
un·wieldi·ly (*or*
    ·wield·li·ly)
un·wieldi·ness (*or*
    ·wield·li·ness)
un·wieldy (*or* ·wield·ly)
un·willed
un·will·ing
un·will·ing·ness

un·wind (·wind·ing, ·wound)
un·wind·able
un·wind·er
un·wink·ing
un·wise
un·wise·ly
un·wish
un·wished
un·wit·nessed
un·wit·ting
un·wont·ed
un·work·able
un·world·li·ness
un·world·ly
un·worn
un·worthi·ly
un·worthi·ness
un·wor·thy (·thi·er, thi·est)
un·wound
un·wrap (·wrap·ping, ·wrapped)
un·writ·ten
un·yield·ing
un·yoke
un·zip (·zip·ping, ·zipped)
up (up·ping, upped)
up-anchor
up-and-coming
up-and-under
Upani·shad Hindu treatise
upas tree
up·beat
up-bow musical term
up·braid
up·braid·er
up·bring·ing
up·build (·build·ing, ·built)
up·build·er
up·cast (·cast·ing, ·cast)
up·country
up·date
up·dat·er
up·draught (US ·draft)
up·end
up·grade
up·grad·er
up·growth
up·heav·al
up·heave (·heav·ing, ·heaved or ·hove)
up·held
up·hill

up·hold (·hold·ing, ·held)
up·hold·er
up·hol·ster
up·hol·ster·er
up·hol·stery (plural ·steries)
up·hove variant of upheaved
uphroe variant spelling of euphroe
up·keep
up·land
up·lift
up·lift·er
up·lift·ing
up·most variant of uppermost
upon
up·per
upper-case (adj, verb)
upper-class (adj)
upper·cut (·cut·ting, ·cut)
upper·most (or up·most)
up·pish
up·pish·ness
up·pi·ty
Upp·sa·la (or Up·sa·la) Swedish city
up·raise
up·rais·er
up·rear
up·right
up·right·ness
up·rise (·ris·ing, ·rose, ·ris·en)
up·ris·er
up·ris·ing
up·river
up·roar
up·roari·ous
up·root
up·root·er
up·rose
up·rush
Up·sa·la variant spelling of Uppsala
up·set (·set·ting, ·set)
up·set·table
up·set·ter
up·set·ting
up·shot
up·side
upside-down
upside-downness
up·si·lon Greek letter
up·stage

uranographic

up·stairs
up·stand·ing
up·stand·ing·ness
up·start
up·state
up·stream
up·stretched
up·stroke
up·surge
up·sweep (·sweep·ing, ·swept)
up·swing (·swing·ing, ·swung)
upsy-daisy
up·take
up·throw
up·thrust
up·tight
up·tilt
up-to-date
up-to-dateness
up·town
up·turn
up·ward (adj)
up·ward·ly
up·ward·ness
up·wards (adv)
up·wind
Ur Sumerian city
ura·cil biochemical compound
urae·mia (US ure·)
urae·mic (US ure·)
urae·us (plural ·uses) sacred serpent
Ural Soviet river
Ural-Altaic language group
Ural·ic (or Ura·lian)
ural·ite mineral
ural·it·ic
Urals Soviet mountains
ura·naly·sis variant of urinalysis
Ura·nian of Uranus; celestial
uran·ic chemistry term
ura·nide chemical element
urani·nite mineral
ura·nite mineral
ura·nit·ic
ura·nium
ura·nog·ra·pher (or ·phist)
ura·no·graph·ic (or ·graphi·cal)

ura·nog·ra·phy star mapping
ura·nous chemistry term
Ura·nus planet
Uranus Greek god
ura·nyl chemical group
ura·nyl·ic
urate
urat·ic
ur·ban
ur·banc
ur·bane·ly
ur·bane·ness
ur·ban·ite
ur·ban·ity (*plural* ·**ities**)
ur·bani·za·tion (*or* ·**sa·tion**)
ur·ban·ize (*or* ·**ise**)
urbi et orbi papal blessing
ur·ceo·late pitcher-shaped
ur·chin
urd bean plant
urdé heraldic term
Urdu
urea
ureal (*or* **ureic**)
urease enzyme
ure·dial
uredium (*or* **uredin·ium**; *plural* **uredia** *or* **uredinia**) fungal structure
uredo (*plural* **uredi·nes**) urticaria
uredo·so·rus (*plural* ·**so·ri**) uredium
uredo·spore
ureic *variant of* **ureal**
ureide chemical compound
ure·mia *US spelling of* **uraemia**
ureter
ureter·al (*or* ·**ic**)
urethane (*or* **urethan**) chemistry term
urethra (*plural* **urethrae** *or* **urethras**)
urethral
urethrit·ic
urethri·tis
urethro·scope
urethro·scop·ic
urethros·co·py
uret·ic of urine
urge
ur·gen·cy
ur·gent
urg·er
urg·ing·ly
uric
uri·dine biochemical compound
uri·nal
uri·naly·sis (*or* **ura·**; *plural* ·**ses**)
uri·nant heraldic term
uri·nary (*plural* ·**naries**)
uri·nate
uri·na·tion
uri·na·tive
urine
uri·nif·er·ous transporting urine
uri·no·geni·tal *variant of* urogenital
uri·nous (*or* ·**nose**)
Ur·mia Iranian lake
urn
urn·field cemetery
urn·like
uro·chord zoology term
uro·chor·dal
uro·chor·date marine animal
uro·chrome pigment
uro·dele type of amphibian
uro·geni·tal (*or* **uri·no·**)
urog·enous producing urine
uro·lith stone in urinary tract
uro·lith·ic
uro·log·ic (*or* ·**logi·cal**)
urolo·gist
urol·ogy branch of medicine
uro·pod crustacean appendage
uropo·dal (*or* ·**dous**)
uro·pyg·ial
uro·pyg·ium base of bird's tail
uro·scop·ic
uros·co·pist
uros·co·py examination of urine
uro·style zoology term
ur·sine of bears
Ur·su·line nun
Ur·text *German* original text
ur·ti·ca·ceous botany term
ur·ti·caria nettle rash
ur·ti·car·ial (*or* ·**cari·ous**)
ur·ti·cate medical term
ur·ti·ca·tion
Urua·pan Mexican city
Uru·guay
Uru·guay·an
Urum·chi (*or* **Wu·lu·mu·ch'i**) Chinese city
uru·shi·ol poisonous liquid
us
us·abil·ity (*or* ·**able·ness, use·**)
us·able (*or* **use·**)
us·age
us·ance commerce term
use
use·abil·ity (*or* ·**able·ness**) *variants of* **usability**
use·able *variant spelling of* **usable**
used
use·ful
use·ful·ly
use·ful·ness
use·less
use·less·ness
user
Ush·ant French island
ush·er
ush·er·ette
Usk Welsh river
Üs·kü·dar Turkish town
us·que·baugh Irish liqueur
Usta·shi terrorist organization
Ust-Kameno·gorsk Soviet city
us·tu·la·tion burning
usu·al
usu·al·ly
usu·al·ness
usu·fruct legal term
usu·fruc·tu·ary (*plural* ·**aries**)
usu·rer
usu·ri·ous
usu·ri·ous·ness
usurp
usur·pa·tion
usur·pa·tive (*or* ·**tory**)
usurp·er
usurp·ing·ly
usu·ry (*plural* ·**ries**)
Utah
Utah·an

Ute (*plural* Utes *or* Ute) American Indian
uten·sil
uter·ine
uter·us (*plural* uteri)
Ut·gard Norse mythological place
Uti·ca ancient African city
utili·tar·ian
utili·tari·an·ism
util·ity (*plural* ·ities)
uti·liz·able (*or* ·lis·able)
uti·li·za·tion (*or* ·sa·tion)
uti·lize (*or* ·lise)
uti·liz·er (*or* ·lis·er)
ut in·fra *Latin* as below
uti pos·si·detis legal term
ut·most (*or* utter·)
Uto-Aztecan language
Uto·pia
Uto·pian (*or* uto·)
Uto·pi·an·ism (*or* uto·)
Utrecht Dutch province
utri·cle (*or* utricu·lus; *plural* utri·cles *or* utricu·li) part of ear
utricu·lar (*or* ·late)
utricu·li·tis
ut su·pra *Latin* as above
Ut·tar Pra·desh Indian state
ut·ter
ut·ter·able
ut·ter·able·ness
ut·ter·ance
ut·ter·er
ut·ter·ly
utter·most *variant of* utmost
U-turn
uva·rov·ite green garnet
uvea part of eye
uveal (*or* uveous)
uveit·ic
uveitis
uvu·la (*plural* ·las *or* ·lae)
uvu·lar
uvu·li·tis
Ux·bridge
uxo·rial wifely
uxo·ri·cid·al
uxo·ri·cide
uxo·ri·ous wife-loving
uxo·ri·ous·ness
Uz·bek (*plural* ·beks *or* ·bek)
Uz·beki·stan Soviet republic

V

Vaal South African river
vac *Slang* vacation
va·can·cy (*plural* ·cies)
va·cant
va·cant·ness
va·cat·able
va·cate
va·ca·tion
va·ca·tion·ist (*or* ·er)
vac·ci·nal
vac·ci·nate
vac·ci·na·tion
vac·ci·na·tor
vac·cine
vac·cinia cowpox
vac·cin·ial
vac·il·lant
vac·il·late
vac·il·lat·ing
vac·il·lat·ing·ly
vac·il·la·tion
vac·il·la·tor
vacua *plural of* vacuum
va·cu·ity (*plural* ·ities)
vacuo·lar
vacuo·late
vacuo·la·tion
vacu·ole cell cavity
vacu·ous
vacu·ous·ness
vacuum (*plural* vacuums *or* vacua)
vacuum-packed
vade me·cum handbook
Va·do·da·ra Indian city
va·dose geology term
Va·duz Liechtenstein capital
vag *Austral* vagrant
vaga·bond
vaga·bond·age
vaga·bond·ism
va·gal of the vagus
va·gary (*plural* ·garies)
va·gi·na (*plural* ·nas *or* ·nae)
vagi·nal
vagi·nate botany term
vagi·nec·tomy (*plural* ·tomies)
vagi·nis·mus vaginal spasm
vagi·ni·tis
va·goto·my (*plural* ·mies) surgery of the vagus
va·go·to·nia overactivity of the vagus
va·go·trop·ic affecting the vagus
va·gran·cy (*plural* ·cies)
va·grant
va·grant·ness
vague
vague·ly
vague·ness
va·gus (*plural* ·gi) nerve
va·hana mythological vehicle
vain conceited; *compare* vane
vain·glo·ri·ous
vain·glo·ry
vain·ly
vain·ness
vair fur trimming
Va·lais Swiss canton
val·ance drapery; *compare* valence
val·anced
Val-de-Marne French department
Val-d'Oise French department
vale *Latin* farewell
vale valley; *compare* veil
val·edic·tion
val·edic·tory (*plural* ·tories)
va·lence (*or* ·len·cy; *plural* ·lences *or* ·cies) chemistry term; *compare* valance
Va·len·cia Spanish port

Valenciennes

Va·len·ci·ennes French town; lace
va·len·cy *variant of* valence
val·en·tine
va·lerian plant
va·leri·a·na·ceous
va·ler·ic
val·et
va·leta *variant spelling of* veleta
Va·let·ta *variant spelling of* Valletta
val·etu·di·nar·ian (*or* ·nary; *plural* ·ians *or* ·naries)
val·etu·di·nar·ian·ism
val·gus medical term
Val·hal·la
val·iance (*or* ·ian·cy, ·iant·ness)
val·iant
val·id
vali·date
vali·da·tion
vali·da·tory
va·lid·ity
val·id·ness
va·line amino acid
va·lise
Valium (*Trademark*)
Val·kyrie (*or* **Wal·kyrie**, **Val·kyr**)
Va·lla·do·lid Spanish city
val·la·tion building fortifications
val·lecu·la (*plural* ·lae) biology term
val·lecu·lar (*or* ·late)
Val·le d'Ao·sta Italian region
Val·let·ta (*or* **Va·let·ta**) Maltese capital
val·ley
va·lo·nia acorns used in tanning
val·ori·za·tion (*or* ·sa·tion)
val·or·ize (*or* ·ise) fix price for
val·or·ous
val·our (*US* ·or)
Val·pa·rai·so Chilean port
valse French waltz
valu·able
valu·able·ness
valu·ably
valu·ate
valua·tion
valua·tion·al
valua·tor
value (**valu·ing**, **valued**)
value·less
value·less·ness
valu·er
valu·ta currency exchange rate
val·vate
valve
valve·less
val·vu·lar
val·vule (*or* **valve·let**)
val·vu·li·tis heart-valve inflammation
vam·brace armour
va·moose
vamp
vam·pire
vam·pir·ic (*or* ·ish)
vam·pir·ism
Van Turkish city
van
vana·date chemical compound
va·nad·ic
va·nadi·nite mineral
va·na·dium chemical element
vana·dous
va·na·spa·ti vegetable fat
Van·cou·ver
van·da orchid
Van·dal Germanic invader
van·dal destroyer
van·dal·ism
van·dal·is·tic (*or* ·dal·ish)
van·dal·ize (*or* ·ise)
Van·dyke beard; collar
vane flat blade; *compare* vain
vang nautical term
van·guard
va·nil·la
va·nil·lic
van·il·lin
van·ish
van·ish·er
van·ish·ing·ly
van·ish·ment
van·ity (*plural* ·ities)
van·quish
van·quish·able
van·quish·er
van·quish·ment
van·tage
Vanu·atu island republic
van·ward
vap·id
va·pid·ity
vap·id·ness
va·por·es·cence
va·por·es·cent
va·po·ret·to (*plural* ·ti *or* ·tos) steamboat
va·por·if·ic
va·por·im·eter
va·por·iz·able (*or* ·is·able)
va·pori·za·tion (*or* ·sa·tion)
va·por·ize (*or* ·ise)
va·por·iz·er (*or* ·is·er)
va·por·ous
va·por·ous·ness (*or* ·os·ity)
va·pour (*US* ·por)
va·pour·abil·ity (*US* ·por·)
va·pour·able (*US* ·por·)
va·pour·er (*US* ·por·)
va·pour·ish (*US* ·por·)
va·pour·ish·ness (*US* ·por·)
var unit of power
vara unit of length
va·rac·tor electronic device
Va·ra·na·si Indian city
Va·ran·gian medieval Scandinavian
var·ec seaweed
varia literary miscellany
vari·abil·ity (*or* ·able·ness)
vari·able
vari·ably
vari·ance
vari·ant
vari·ate a random variable
vari·ation
vari·ation·al (*or* ·ative)
vari·cel·la chickenpox
vari·cel·lar
vari·cel·late ridged
vari·cel·loid
vari·ces *plural of* varix
vari·co·cele medical term
vari·col·oured (*US* ·ored)
vari·cose

vari·co·sis
vari·cos·ity (plural ·ities)
vari·coto·my (plural
    ·mies) varicose-vein
    surgery
var·ied
var·ied·ness
varie·gate
varie·gat·ed
varie·ga·tion
va·ri·etal
va·ri·ety (plural ·eties)
vari·form
va·rio·la smallpox
va·rio·lar
va·rio·late inoculate
va·rio·la·tion
vari·ole geology term
vari·olite rock
vario·lit·ic
vario·loid mild smallpox
va·rio·lous of smallpox
vari·om·eter
vario·rum annotated text
vari·ous
vari·ous·ly
vari·ous·ness
var·is·cite mineral
var·is·tor electronic
    component
vari·type
Vari·typ·er (Trademark)
    justifying typewriter
vari·typ·ist
var·ix (plural vari·ces)
    varicose vein
var·let
var·mint
Var·na Bulgarian port
var·na Hindu caste
var·nish
var·nish·er
var·sity (plural ·sities)
    Slang university
var·us medical term
varve geology term
vary (varies, vary·ing,
    var·ied)
vary·ing·ly
vas·al of vas deferens;
    compare vassal
vas·cu·lar conducting fluids
vas·cu·lar·ity
vas·cu·lari·za·tion (or
    ·sa·tion) medical term

vas·cu·lum (plural ·la or
    ·lums) plant-specimen
    container
vas de·fe·rens (plural
    vasa de·fe·ren·tia)
    anatomy term
vase
vas·ec·to·mize (or ·mise)
vas·ec·to·my (plural
    ·mies)
Vas·eline (Trademark)
vaso·active affecting blood
    vessels
vaso·con·stric·tion
vaso·con·stric·tive
vaso·con·stric·tor
vaso·di·la·tion
vaso·di·la·tor
vaso·in·hibi·tor
vaso·in·hibi·tory
vaso·mo·tor
vaso·pres·sin hormone
vas·sal feudal tenant;
    compare vasal
vas·sal·age
vas·sal·ize (or ·ise)
vast
Väs·ter·ås Swedish city
vas·tity
vast·ness
vasty (vasti·er, vasti·est)
    Archaic vast
vat (vat·ting, vat·ted)
vat·ic of a prophet
Vati·can
Vati·can·ism
Vau·cluse French
    department
Vaud Swiss canton
vau·de·ville
vau·de·vil·lian
vau·de·vil·list
Vau·dois (plural ·dois) of
    Vaud; Waldenses
vault
vault·ed
vault·er
vault·ing
vaunt
vaunt·er
vaunt·ing·ly
vava·sor (or ·sour) vassal
veal
veal·er veal calf
vec·tor

vec·to·rial
Veda Hindu scriptures
ve·da·lia ladybird
Ve·dan·ta Hindu school of
    philosophy
Ve·dan·tic
Ved·da (or ·dah; plural
    ·da, ·das or ·dah, ·dahs)
    Sri Lankan people
Ved·doid
ve·dette
Ve·dic of the Veda
veer
veer·ing·ly
veery (plural veeries) bird
veg Slang vegetables
Vega star
ve·gan
veg·eta·ble
veg·etal of plants;
    nonsexual
veg·etar·ian
veg·etari·an·ism
veg·etate
veg·eta·tion
veg·eta·tion·al
veg·eta·tive
veg·eta·tive·ness
ve·he·mence
ve·he·ment
ve·hi·cle
ve·hicu·lar
Veii Etruscan city
veil head covering; compare
    vale
veiled
veil·ed·ly
veil·er
veil·ing
vein
vein·ing
vein·let
vein·stone ore material
veiny (veini·er, veini·est)
ve·la·men (plural
    ·lami·na) biology term
ve·lar biology or phonetics
    term
ve·lar·ium (plural ·laria)
    awning in Roman theatre
ve·lari·za·tion (or
    ·sa·tion)
ve·lar·ize (or ·ise)
    phonetics term
ve·late biology term

Velcro

Vel·cro (*Trademark*)
veld (*or* **veldt**)
ve·leta (*or* **va·**) dance
veli·ger mollusc larva
ve·li·tes Roman troops
vel·le·ity (*plural* **·ities**) a wish
Vel·lore Indian town
vel·lum parchment; *compare* velum
ve·lo·ce musical term
ve·loci·pede early bicycle
ve·loc·ity (*plural* **·ities**)
ve·lo·drome cycle-racing arena
ve·lours (*or* **·lour**) fabric
ve·lou·té sauce
ve·lum (*plural* **·la**) biology term; *compare* vellum
ve·lure velvet
ve·lu·ti·nous covered with hairs
vel·vet
vel·vet·een
vel·vety
vena (*plural* **venae**) vein
vena cava (*plural* **venae cavae**)
ve·nal open to bribery; *compare* venial
ve·nal·ity
ve·nal·ly
ve·nat·ic (*or* **·nati·cal**) of hunting
ve·na·tion arrangement of veins; *compare* vernation
ve·na·tion·al
vend
Ven·da (*plural* **·da** *or* **·das**) African people
ven·dace (*plural* **·daces** *or* **·dace**) fish
Ven·dée French department
ven·dee buyer
vend·er variant spelling of vendor
ven·det·ta
ven·det·tist
vend·ibil·ity (*or* **·ible·ness**)
vend·ible
vend·ing
ven·di·tion
ven·dor (*or* **vend·er**)
ven·due US public sale
ve·neer

ve·neer·er
ve·neer·ing
ven·epunc·ture variant spelling of **venipuncture**
ven·er·abil·ity (*or* **·able·ness**)
ven·er·able
ven·er·ably
ven·er·ate
ven·era·tion
ven·era·tion·al (*or* **·era·tive**)
ven·era·tor
ve·nereal
ve·nere·olo·gist
ve·nere·ol·ogy
ven·ery hunting; sexual gratification
ven·esec·tion incision into vein
Ve·netia ancient Italian region
Ve·netian
Ve·net·ic language
Ve·neto Italian region
Ven·ezue·la
Ven·ezue·lan
venge·ance
venge·ful
venge·ful·ly
venge·ful·ness
ve·nial easily forgiven; *compare* venal
ve·ni·al·ity (*or* **·al·ness**)
ve·nial·ly
Ven·ice
ven·in poison
veni·punc·ture (*or* **ven·epunc·ture**)
ve·ni·re fa·ci·as legal term
veni·son
Ve·ni·te 95th psalm
Venn dia·gram
ven·om
ven·om·ous
ve·nose
ve·nos·ity
ve·nous
ve·nous·ness
vent
vent·age small hole
ven·tail armour
ven·ter biology or legal term
ven·ti·lable
ven·ti·late

ven·ti·la·tion
ven·ti·la·tive
ven·ti·la·tor
ven·ti·la·tory
ven·tral
ven·tral·ly
ven·tri·cle
ven·tri·cose biology term
ven·tri·cos·ity
ven·tricu·lar
ven·tricu·lus (*plural* **·li**) zoology term
ven·tri·lo·quial (*or* **·qual**)
ven·trilo·quism (*or* **·quy**)
ven·trilo·quist
ven·trilo·quis·tic
ven·trilo·quize (*or* **·quise**)
ven·trilo·quy variant of ventriloquism
ven·ture
ven·tur·er
ven·ture·some (*or* **·tu·rous**)
ven·ture·some·ness
Venturi tube
venue
venu·lar
ven·ule small vein
Ve·nus planet
Venus Roman goddess
Ve·nu·sian
ve·ra·cious truthful; *compare* voracious
ve·ra·cious·ness
ve·rac·ity (*plural* **·ities**)
Vera·cruz Mexican state
ve·ran·da (*or* **·dah**)
ve·ran·daed (*or* **·dahed**)
ve·ra·tri·dine chemical compound
vera·trine (*or* **·trin**) former medicine
verb
ver·bal
ver·bal·ism
ver·bal·ist
ver·bali·za·tion (*or* **·sa·tion**)
ver·bal·ize (*or* **·ise**)
ver·bal·iz·er (*or* **·is·er**)
ver·bal·ly
ver·ba·tim
ver·be·na
ver·be·na·ceous botany term

ver·bi·age
ver·bid *linguistics term*
ver·bi·fi·ca·tion
ver·bi·fy (·fies, ·fy·ing, ·fied)
ver·bose
ver·bose·ly
ver·bos·ity (*or* ·bose·ness)
ver·bo·ten *German* forbidden
ver·dan·cy
ver·dant
ver·der·er
ver·dict
ver·di·gris
ver·din *bird*
ver·dure
ver·dur·ous
Ve·ree·ni·ging *South African city*
verge
ver·ger
ver·glas (*plural* ·glases) *thin ice*
ve·ridi·cal *truthful*
ve·ridi·cal·ity
veri·fi·able
veri·fi·ca·tion
veri·fi·ca·tive (*or* ·tory)
veri·fi·er
veri·fy (·fies, ·fy·ing, ·fied)
veri·ly
veri·simi·lar *likely*
veri·si·mili·tude
ver·ism *extreme realism*
ve·ris·mo *type of opera*
ver·ist
ve·ris·tic
veri·table
veri·table·ness
veri·tably
ver·ity (*plural* ·ities)
ver·juice
ver·kramp·te *Afrikaner nationalist*
ver·lig·te *South African liberal*
ver·meil *gilded metal*
ver·mi·cel·li
ver·mi·cid·al
ver·mi·cide
ver·micu·lar *wormlike*
ver·micu·late
ver·micu·la·tion

ver·micu·lite *mineral*
ver·mi·form
ver·mi·fuge *worm-expelling drug*
ver·mil·ion (*or* ·mil·lion)
ver·min
ver·mi·na·tion *infestation with vermin*
ver·mi·nous
ver·min·ous·ness
ver·mis (*plural* ·mes) *part of brain*
ver·mivo·rous *worm-eating*
Ver·mont
Ver·mont·er
ver·mouth
ver·nacu·lar
ver·nacu·lar·ism
ver·nal
ver·nali·za·tion (*or* ·sa·tion)
ver·nal·ize (*or* ·ise) *botany term*
ver·nal·ly
ver·na·tion *leaf arrangement in bud; compare* venation
ver·ni·er *measuring scale*
ver·nis·sage *opening of art exhibition*
Ve·ro·na *Italian city*
Vero·nal (*Trademark*) *drug*
ve·roni·ca *shrub*
ver·ru·ca (*plural* ·cae *or* ·cas)
ver·ru·cose (*or* ·cous)
ver·ru·cos·ity
Ver·sailles
ver·sant *mountain side*
ver·sa·tile
ver·sa·til·ity (*or* ·tile·ness)
verse
versed
ver·si·cle
ver·si·col·our (*US* ·or)
ver·si·fi·ca·tion
ver·si·fi·er
ver·si·fy (·fies, ·fy·ing, ·fied)
ver·sion
ver·sion·al
vers li·bre *French* free verse
ver·so (*plural* ·sos) *left-hand page*

ver·sus *against*
vert *heraldry term*
ver·te·bra (*plural* ·brae *or* ·bras)
ver·te·bral
ver·te·brate
ver·te·bra·tion
ver·tex (*plural* ·texes *or* ·tices) *apex; compare* vortex
ver·ti·cal
ver·ti·cal·ity (*or* ·ness)
ver·ti·cal·ly
ver·ti·ces *plural of* vertex
ver·ti·cil *biology term*
ver·ti·cil·las·ter *botany term*
ver·ti·cil·las·trate
ver·tic·il·late
ver·tic·il·la·tion
ver·tigi·nous *of vertigo*
ver·tigi·nous·ness
ver·ti·go (*plural* ·ti·goes *or* ·tigi·nes)
ver·tu *variant spelling of* virtu
Vertumnus *Roman god*
(verucca) *incorrect spelling of* verruca
Veru·la·mium *Latin* St Albans
ver·vain *plant*
verve
ver·vet *monkey*
very
Very light
vesi·ca (*plural* ·cae) *bladder*
vesi·cal *of the bladder; compare* vesicle
vesi·cant (*or* ·ca·tory; *plural* ·cants *or* ·ca·tories) *blistering substance*
vesi·cate
vesi·ca·tion
vesi·cle *small cavity; compare* vesical
ve·sicu·lar
ve·sicu·late
ve·sicu·la·tion
ves·per *evening prayer*
ves·per·al *prayer book*
ves·pers *canonical hour*
ves·per·tilio·nid *zoology term*
ves·per·tilio·nine

vespertine

ves·per·tine occurring in the evening
ves·pi·ary (*plural* ·aries) wasps' nest
ves·pid entomology term
ves·pine of wasps
ves·sel
vest
Ves·ta asteroid
Vesta Roman goddess
ves·ta wooden match
ves·tal virgin
vest·ed
ves·ti·ary (*plural* ·aries) room for clothes
ves·tibu·lar
ves·ti·bule
ves·tige
ves·tig·ial
vest·ment
vest·ment·al
vest·ment·ed
ves·tral
ves·try (*plural* ·tries)
vestry·man (*plural* ·men)
ves·tur·al
ves·ture garment
ve·su·vi·an·ite mineral
Ve·su·vi·us
vet (vet·ting, vet·ted)
vetch
vetch·ling
vet·er·an
vet·eri·nar·ian
vet·eri·nary
veti·ver a grass
veto (*noun, plural* vetoes; *verb* vetoes, ve·to·ing, ve·toed)
ve·to·er
vet·ted
vet·ting
vex
vexa·tion
vexa·tious
vexa·tious·ness
vex·ed·ly
vex·ed·ness
vex·er
vex·il·lary (*or* ·lar)
vex·il·late
vex·il·lolo·gist
vex·il·lol·ogy study of flags
vex·il·lum (*plural* ·la) biology term

vex·ing·ly
via
vi·abil·ity
vi·able
Via Dolo·ro·sa road to Calvary
via·duct
vial *less common spelling of* phial
via me·dia *Latin* compromise
vi·and a food
vi·ands provisions
vi·ati·cum (*plural* ·ca *or* ·cums)
vibes *Slang* vibrations; vibraphone
vib·ist vibraphone player
vi·bracu·lar
vi·bracu·loid
vi·bracu·lum (*plural* ·la) zoology term
vi·bra·harp musical instrument
vi·bran·cy
vi·brant
vi·bra·phone
vi·bra·phon·ist
vi·brate
vi·bra·tile
vi·bra·til·ity
vi·brat·ing·ly
vi·bra·tion
vi·bra·tion·al
vi·bra·tive
vi·bra·to (*plural* ·tos)
vi·bra·tor
vi·bra·tory
vib·rio (*plural* ·rios) bacterium
vib·ri·oid
vi·bris·sa (*plural* ·sae) whisker
vi·bris·sal
vi·bron·ic physics term
vi·bur·num
vic·ar
vic·ar·age
vi·car·ial
vi·cari·ate (*or* vic·ar·ship)
vi·cari·ous
vi·cari·ous·ness
vice sin; deputy; in place of
vice (*US* vise) tool
vice ad·mi·ral

498

vice-admiral·ty
vice-chairman (*plural* -chairmen)
vice-chairman·ship
vice chan·cel·lor
vice-chancellor·ship
vice·ge·ral
vice·ge·ren·cy (*plural* ·cies)
vice·ge·rent deputy
vice·like (*US* vise·)
vic·enary of 20
vi·cen·nial 20 years
Vi·cen·za Italian city
vice-presiden·cy (*plural* ·cies)
vice presi·dent
vice-presiden·tial
vice·re·gal of viceroy
vice·reine viceroy's wife
vice·roy
vice·roy·al·ty (*plural* ·ties)
vice·roy·ship
vice ver·sa
Vi·chy French town
vi·chy·ssoise soup
vici·nal
vi·cin·ity (*plural* ·ities)
vi·cious
vi·cious·ness
vi·cis·si·tude
vi·cis·si·tu·di·nary (*or* ·di·nous)
Vicks·burg US city
vi·comte (*fem* ·com·tesse) French noble
vic·tim
vic·timi·za·tion (*or* ·sa·tion)
vic·tim·ize (*or* ·ise)
vic·tim·iz·er (*or* ·is·er)
vic·tor
Vic·to·ria place name
vic·to·ria carriage; plum; water lily
Vic·to·rian
Vic·to·ri·ana
Vic·to·ri·an·ism
vic·to·ri·ous
vic·to·ri·ous·ness
vic·to·ry (*plural* ·ries)
vict·ual (·ual·ling, ·ualled; *US* ·ual·ing, ·ualed)
vict·ual·ler (*US also* ·ual·er)

vict·uals
vi·cu·ña
vide *Latin* see
vi·deli·cet *Latin* namely
video (*noun, plural* videos; *verb* videos, video·ing, videoed)
vid·eo·phone
vid·eo·phon·ic
video-tape (*verb*)
vidi·con small television camera tube
vie (vying, vied)
Vi·en·na Austrian capital
Vienne French river; department
Vi·en·nese (*plural* ·nese)
Vien·ti·ane Laotian capital
Vi·et·cong (*or* Viet Cong)
Vi·et·minh (*or* Viet Minh)
Vi·et·nam
Vi·et·nam·ese (*plural* ·ese)
view
view·able
view·er
view·finder
view·ing
view·less
view·point
vi·gesi·mal of 20
vig·il
vigi·lance
vigi·lant
vigi·lan·te
vi·gnette
vi·gnet·ting photography term
vi·gnet·tist
Vigo Spanish port
vi·go·ro·so musical term
vig·or·ous
vig·or·ous·ness
vig·our (*US* ·or)
Vi·jaya·wa·da Indian town
Vi·king
vi·la·yet Turkish administrative division
vile
vile·ly
vile·ness
vili·fi·ca·tion
vili·fi·er
vili·fy (·fies, ·fy·ing, ·fied)

vili·pend treat with contempt
vil·la
vil·lage
vil·lag·er
Vil·la·her·mo·sa Mexican town
vil·lain (*fem* ·lain·ess) wicked person; *compare* villein
vil·lain·ous
vil·lain·ous·ness
vil·lainy (*plural* ·lainies)
vil·la·nel·la (*plural* ·las) song
vil·la·nelle verse form
Vil·la·no·van archaeology term
vil·lat·ic rustic
vil·lein serf; *compare* villain
Ville·ur·banne French town
vil·li *plural of* villus
vil·li·form
vil·los·ity (*plural* ·ities)
vil·lous
vil·lus (*plural* ·li)
Vil·ni·us (*or* ·ny·) Soviet city
vim *Slang* vigour
vi·men (*plural* vimi·na) plant shoot
Vimi·nal Roman hill
vi·min·eous
vina musical instrument
vi·na·ceous
Viña del Mar Chilean city
vinai·grette
vi·nasse residue in a still
vin·cible
vin·cu·lum (*plural* ·la) maths symbol; anatomy term
vin·di·cabil·ity
vin·di·cable
vin·di·cate
vin·di·ca·tion
vin·di·ca·tor
vin·di·ca·tory
vin·dic·tive
vin·dic·tive·ly
vin·dic·tive·ness
vine
vine·dresser
vin·egar

vin·egar·roon arachnid
vin·egary
vin·ery (*plural* ·eries) place for growing grapes
vine·yard
vine·yard·ist
vingt-et-un card game
vi·nic of wine
vini·cul·tur·al
vini·cul·ture
vini·cul·tur·ist
vi·nif·er·ous
vi·nifi·ca·tion
vi·nifi·ca·tor wine-making apparatus
Vin·land *Viking name for* NE America
Vin·ni·tsa Soviet city
vino (*plural* vinos) *Slang* wine
vin or·di·naire (*plural* vins or·di·naires)
vi·nos·ity
vi·nous
vin·tage
vin·tag·er grape harvester
vint·ner
viny
(vinyard) *incorrect spelling of* vineyard
vi·nyl
vi·nyli·dene chemistry term
viol
vio·la
vio·labil·ity (*or* ·lable·ness)
vio·lable
vio·la·ceous botany term
vio·la da gam·ba
vio·la d'amore
vio·late
vio·la·tion
vio·la·tive
vio·la·tor (*or* ·lat·er)
vio·lence
vio·lent
vio·let
vio·lin
vio·lin·ist
vi·ol·ist
vio·lon·cel·list
vio·lon·cel·lo (*plural* ·los) cello
vio·lone musical instrument
vi·per

viperine

vi·per·ine
vi·per·ous (or ·ish)
vi·ragi·nous
vi·ra·go (plural ·goes or ·gos)
vi·ral
vir·elay poem
vireo (plural vireos) bird
vi·res·cence
vi·res·cent becoming green
vir·ga meteorology term
vir·gate rod-shaped; obsolete land measure
vir·gin
vir·gin·al
vir·gin·al·ly
Vir·ginia
Vir·gin·ian
vir·gin·ity
virgin's-bower plant
Vir·go constellation; sign of zodiac
Vir·goan
vir·go in·tac·ta virgin
vir·gu·late rod-shaped
vir·gule printing term
viri·des·cence
viri·des·cent becoming green
vi·rid·ian green pigment
vi·rid·ity greenness
vir·ile
viri·lism medical term
vi·ril·ity
vi·ro·logi·cal
vi·rolo·gist
vi·rol·ogy
vir·tu (or ver·) connoisseurship
vir·tual
vir·tu·al·ity
vir·tu·al·ly
vir·tue
vir·tu·os·ic
vir·tu·os·ity
vir·tuo·so (plural ·sos or ·si)
vir·tu·ous
vir·tu·ous·ness
viru·lence
viru·lent
vi·rus (plural ·ruses)
visa (vi·sa·ing, vi·saed)
vis·age

Vi·sa·kha·pat·nam variant of Vishakhapatnam
vis-à-vis
Vi·sa·yan (plural ·yans or ·yan) Philippine people
vis·ca·cha (or viz·) animal
vis·cera (sing. ·cus) internal organs
vis·cer·al
vis·ce·ro·mo·tor physiology term
vis·cid
vis·cid·ity (or ·ness)
vis·coid (or ·coi·dal)
vis·com·eter (or ·co·sim·eter)
vis·co·met·ric (or ·ri·cal)
vis·com·etry
vis·cose
vis·cos·ity (plural ·ities)
vis·count
vis·count·cy (or ·county; plural ·cies or ·counties)
vis·count·ess
vis·cous thick; compare viscus
vis·cous·ness
vis·cus sing. of viscera; compare viscous
vise US spelling of vice
Vi·sha·kha·pat·nam (or Vi·sa·kha·pat·nam, Vi·za·ga·pa·tam) Indian port
Vishnu Hindu god
vis·ibil·ity
vis·ible
vis·ible·ness
vis·ibly
Visi·goth
vi·sion
vi·sion·al
vi·sion·ari·ness
vi·sion·ary (plural ·aries)
vis·it
vis·it·able
visi·tant
vis·ita·tion
vis·ita·tion·al
vis·ita·to·rial of official visitation
visi·tor
visi·to·rial
vi·sor (or ·zor)
vi·sored (or ·zored)

500

vis·ta
vis·taed
Vis·tu·la Polish river
vis·ual
visu·ali·za·tion (or ·sa·tion)
visu·al·ize (or ·ise)
visu·al·iz·er (or ·is·er)
visu·al·ly
vi·ta·ceous botany term
vi·tal
vi·tal·ism philosophical doctrine
vi·tal·ist
vi·tal·is·tic
vi·tal·ity (plural ·ities)
vi·tali·za·tion (or ·sa·tion)
vi·tal·ize (or ·ise)
vi·tal·iz·er (or ·is·er)
vi·tal·ly
vi·tals
vita·min
vita·min·ic
Vi·tebsk Soviet city
vi·tel·lin protein
vi·tel·line of egg yolk
vi·ti·able
vi·ti·ate
vi·tia·tion
vi·tia·tor
viti·cul·tur·al
viti·cul·ture grape cultivation
viti·cul·tur·er (or ·ist)
viti·li·go unpigmented skin
Vi·to·ria Spanish city
Vi·tó·ria Brazilian port
vit·rain coal
vit·re·ous
vit·re·ous·ness (or ·os·ity)
vi·tres·cence
vi·tres·cent
vit·ric of glass
vit·ri·fi·abil·ity
vit·ri·fi·able
vit·ri·fi·ca·tion
vit·ri·form
vit·ri·fy (·fies, ·fy·ing, ·fied)
vit·rine glass display case
vit·ri·ol (·ol·ing, ·oled or ·ol·ling, ·olled)
vit·ri·ol·ic
vit·ri·oli·za·tion (or ·sa·tion)

vit·ri·ol·ize (or ·ise)
vit·ta (plural ·tae) biology term
vit·tate
vi·tu·line of calves
vi·tu·per·ate
vi·tu·per·a·tion
vi·tu·pera·tive
vi·tu·pera·tor
viva (vi·va·ing, vi·vaed) short for viva voce
vi·va·ce musical term
vi·va·cious
vi·va·vious·ly
vi·va·cious·ness
vi·vac·ity (plural ·ities)
vi·var·ium (plural ·iums or ·ia)
viva voce oral exam
vi·ver·rine zoology term
viv·id
viv·id·ness
vivi·fi·ca·tion
vivi·fi·er
vivi·fy (·fies, ·fy·ing, ·fied)
vivi·par·ity (or vi·vipa·rism, vi·vipa·rous·ness)
vi·vip·ar·ous
vivi·sect
vivi·sec·tion
vivi·sec·tion·al
vivi·sec·tion·ist
vivi·sec·tor
vix·en
vix·en·ish
vix·en·ish·ness
Vi·yel·la (Trademark)
Vi·za·ga·pa·tam variant spelling of Vishakhapatnam
viz·ard mask
viz·ca·cha variant spelling of viscacha
vi·zier
vi·zier·ate
vi·zor variant spelling of visor
Vlach (or Wa·lach) medieval European people
Vla·di·mir Soviet port
Vla·di·vos·tok Soviet port
vo·cab short for vocabulary
vo·cable vocal sound
vo·cabu·lary (plural ·laries)
vo·cal

vo·cal·ic
vo·cal·ise vocal exercise; variant spelling of vocalize
vo·cal·ism
vo·cal·ist
vo·cal·ity (or ·ness)
vo·cali·za·tion (or ·sa·tion)
vo·cal·ize (or ·ise)
vo·cal·iz·er (or ·is·er)
vo·cal·ly
vo·ca·tion
vo·ca·tion·al
voca·tive
vo·cif·er·ance
vo·cif·er·ant
vo·cif·er·ate
vo·cif·era·tion
vo·cif·era·tor
vo·cif·er·ous
vo·cif·er·ous·ness
vod·ka
vogue
voguish
Vo·gul (plural ·gul or ·guls) Siberian people
voice
voiced
voice·ful
voice·less
voice·less·ness
voice-over
voice·print
voic·er
void
void·able
void·able·ness
void·ance annulment
void·ed
void·er
voile fabric
Voio·tia Greek department
voir dire legal term
Voj·vo·di·na (or Voi·) Yugoslav region
Vo·lans constellation
vo·lant
Vola·puk artificial language
Vola·puk·ist
vo·lar anatomy term
vola·tile
vola·til·ity
vo·lati·liz·able (or ·lis·able)

vo·lati·liza·tion (or ·lisa·tion)
vo·lati·lize (or ·lise)
vol-au-vent
vol·can·ic
vol·cani·cal·ly
vol·can·ic·ity
vol·can·ism (or vul·)
vol·cani·za·tion (or ·sa·tion)
vol·can·ize (or ·ise)
vol·ca·no (plural ·noes or ·nos)
vol·cano·logi·cal (or vul·)
vol·can·olo·gist (or vul·)
vol·can·ol·ogy (or vul·)
vole
Vol·ga Soviet river
Vol·go·grad Soviet port
voli·tant moving rapidly
vo·li·tion
vo·li·tion·al (or ·ary)
voli·tive of the will
vol·ley
volley·ball
vol·ley·er
Vo·log·da Soviet city
vo·lost peasant community
vol·plane glide without power
Vol·sci Latin people
volt
Vol·ta African river or lake
vol·ta (plural ·te) dance
volt·age
vol·ta·ic
vol·ta·ism
vol·tam·eter instrument measuring electric charge; compare voltmeter
volt·am·meter instrument measuring volts or amperes; compare voltmeter
volt-ampere unit
Vol·ta Re·don·da Brazilian city
volte-face (plural volte-face) reversal of opinion
volt·me·ter instrument measuring volts; compare voltameter; voltammeter
vol·ubil·ity (or ·uble·ness)
vol·uble
vol·ubly
vol·ume

volumed

vol·umed
vo·lu·meter
volu·met·ric
volu·met·ri·cal·ly
vo·lu·metry
vo·lu·mi·nos·ity (or ·nous·ness)
vo·lu·mi·nous
vol·un·tar·ily
vol·un·tari·ness
vol·un·ta·rism (or ·tary·)
vol·un·ta·rist (or ·tary·)
vol·un·ta·ris·tic
vol·un·tary (plural ·aries)
vol·un·teer
vo·lup·tu·ary (plural ·aries)
vo·lup·tu·ous
vo·lup·tu·ous·ness (or ·os·ity)
vol·ute
vo·lu·tion
vol·va (plural ·vae or ·vas) mushroom sheath; compare vulva
vol·vate
Volvo (Trademark)
vol·vox microscopic animal
vol·vu·lus (plural ·luses) intestinal disorder
vo·mer bone
vo·mer·ine
vom·it
vom·it·er
vomi·tive
vomi·tory (plural ·tories)
vomi·tu·ri·tion retching
vomi·tus (plural ·tuses) vomited matter
voo·doo (noun, plural ·doos; verb ·doos, ·doo·ing, ·dooed)
voo·doo·ism
voo·doo·ist
voo·doo·is·tic
Voor·trek·ker Afrikaner settler
vo·ra·cious greedy; compare veracious
vo·rac·ity (or ·ra·cious·ness)
Vor·arl·berg Austrian province
vor·la·ge skiing position

Vo·ro·nezh Soviet city
Vo·ro·shi·lov·grad Soviet city
vor·tex (plural ·texes or ·ti·ces) whirling mass; compare vertex
vor·ti·cal
vor·ti·cel·la (plural ·lae) protozoan
vor·ti·ces plural of vortex
vor·ti·cism art movement
vor·ti·cist
vor·tigi·nous
Vosges French mountain range
Vos·tok Soviet spacecraft
vot·able (or vote·)
vo·tar·ess (or vo·tress)
vo·ta·rist
vo·ta·ry (plural ·ries)
vote
vote·able variant spelling of votable
vot·er
vo·tive
vo·tive·ness
vo·tress variant of votaress
Vo·ty·ak (plural ·aks or ·ak) Finnish people
vouch
vouch·er
vouch·safe
vouch·safe·ment
vouge weapon
vous·soir wedge-shaped stone
Vou·vray wine
vow
vow·el
vow·eli·za·tion (or ·sa·tion)
vow·el·ize (or ·ise)
vowel·less
vow·er
vox (plural vo·ces) voice
vox hu·ma·na organ stop
vox po·pu·li public opinion
voy·age
voy·ag·er
vo·ya·geur Canadian woodsman
vo·yeur

vo·yeur·ism
vo·yeur·is·tic
vo·yeur·is·ti·cal·ly
vrai·sem·blance verisimilitude
vroom exclamation
vug mining term
Vulcan Roman god
vul·ca·nian volcanic
vul·can·ism variant spelling of volcanism
vul·can·ite hard rubber
vul·can·iz·able (or ·is·able)
vul·cani·za·tion (or ·sa·tion)
vul·can·ize (or ·ise)
vul·can·iz·er (or ·is·er)
vul·can·ol·ogy variant spelling of volcanology
vul·gar
vul·gar·ian
vul·gar·ism
vul·gar·ity (plural ·ities)
vul·gari·za·tion (or ·sa·tion)
vul·gar·ize (or ·ise)
vul·gar·iz·er (or ·is·er)
vul·gar·ness
Vul·gate Latin Bible
vul·gate commonly accepted text
vul·ner·abil·ity (or ·able·ness)
vul·ner·able
vul·ner·ably
vul·ner·ary (plural ·aries) wound-healing drug
Vul·pecu·la constellation
vul·pine (or ·pecu·lar) of foxes
vul·ture
vul·tur·ine
vul·tur·ous
vul·va (plural ·vae or ·vas) female external genitals; compare volva
vul·val (or ·var, ·vate)
vul·vi·form
vul·vi·tis
vul·vo·vagi·ni·tis
vy·ing

W

Wa·bash US river
wacky (**wacki·er,** **wacki·est**)
wad (**wad·ding, wad·ded**)
wad·able (*or* **wade·**)
wad·ding
wad·dle
wad·dler
wad·dling·ly
wad·dy (*noun, plural* **·dies;** *verb* **·dies, ·dy·ing, ·died**) Aboriginal club; *compare* **wadi**
wade
wade·able *variant spelling of* **wadable**
wad·er
wad·ers
wadi (*or* **wady;** *plural* **wadis** *or* **wa·dies**) watercourse; *compare* **waddy**
Wadi Hal·fa Sudanese town
Wad Me·da·ni Sudanese town
wad·sct (**·set·ting, ·set·ted**) *Scot* mortgage
wady *variant spelling of* **wadi**
wae *Dialect* woe
wa·fer
wa·fery
waff *Dialect* gust
waf·fle
waft
waft·age
waft·er
wag (**wag·ging, wagged**)
wage
wa·ger
wa·ger·er
wages
wag·ga *Austral* blanket
Wag·ga Wag·ga Australian city
wagged
wag·gery
wag·ging
wag·gish
wag·gish·ness
wag·gle
wag·gling·ly
wag·gly
Wag·ne·rian
wag·on (*or* **wag·gon**)
wag·on·er (*or* **wag·gon·**)
wag·on·ette (*or* **wag·gon·**)
wagon-lit (*plural* **wagons-lits**) sleeping car
wagon·load (*or* **waggon·**)
wag·tail
Wah·ha·bi (*or* **Wa·ha·bi;** *plural* **·bis**) conservative Muslim
wa·hi·ne Polynesian woman
wa·hoo (*plural* **·hoos**) tree; fish
waif
Wai·ka·to New Zealand river
Wai·ki·ki Hawaiian resort
wail
wail·er
wail·ful
wail·ing·ly
wain farm wagon; *compare* **wane**
wain·scot
wain·scot·ed
wain·scot·ing (*or* **·scot·ting**)
wain·wright
waist
waist·band
waist·coat
waist·ed
waist·less
waist·line
wait
wait·er
wait·ress
waive relinquish; *compare* **wave**
waiv·er relinquishment; *compare* **waver**
Wa·kash·an American Indian language
Wa·ka·ya·ma Japanese city
wake (**wak·ing,** **woke, wok·en**)
Wake·field
wake·ful
wake·ful·ly
wake·ful·ness
wake·less
wak·en
wak·en·er
wak·er
wake·rife *Dialect* wakeful
wake-robin plant
wak·ing
Wa·lach *variant of* **Vlach**
Wa·la·chia (*or* **Wal·la·chia**) former European principality
Wał·brzych Polish city
Wal·che·ren Dutch island
Wal·den·ses Catholic sect
wald·grave medieval German forest officer
Wal·dorf sal·ad
wale weal; ridge
Wa·ler horse; *compare* **whaler**
Wales
walk
walk·able
walk·about
walk·er
walkie-talkie (*or* **walky-talky;** *plural* **-talkies**)
walk-in (*adj*)
walk·ing
walk-on (*noun, adj*)
walk·out (*noun*)
walk·over (*noun*)
walk·way
Wal·kyrie *variant spelling of* **Valkyrie**
walky-talky *variant spelling of* **walkie-talkie**
wall
wal·la·by (*plural* **·bies** *or* **·by**)
Wal·la·chia *variant spelling of* **Walachia**
wal·lah (*or* **wal·la**) *Slang* person in charge

wallaroo

wal·la·roo (*plural* ·**roos** *or* ·**roo**) large kangaroo
Wal·la·sey Merseyside town
wall·board
walled
wal·let
wall·eye (*plural* ·**eyes** *or* ·**eye**)
wall·eyed
wall·flower
wall-like
Wal·loon French-speaking Belgian
wal·lop
wal·lop·er
wal·lop·ing
wal·low
wal·low·er
wall·paper
Walls·end English town
wall-to-wall
wal·ly *Slang* idiot; *Scot* made of china
wal·nut
Wal·pur·gis Night
wal·rus (*plural* ·**ruses** *or* ·**rus**)
Wal·sall
waltz
waltz·er
wame *Dialect* belly; womb
wam·pum shell money
wan (*adj* **wan·ner**, **wan·nest**; *verb* **wan·ning**, **wanned**)
wand
wan·der
wan·der·er
wan·der·ing
wan·der·ing·ly
wan·der·lust
wan·deroo (*plural* ·**deroos**) monkey
wan·doo (*plural* ·**doos**) tree
Wands·worth
wane decrease; *compare* **wain**
waney (*or* **wany**; **wani·er**, **wani·est**)
Wan·ga·nui New Zealand port
wan·gle
wan·gler
wank
wan·na *Slang* want to
wanned
wan·ner
wan·nest
wan·ning
want
want·er
want·ing
wan·ton
wan·ton·ness
wap·en·take former county division
wapi·ti (*plural* ·**tis**) deer
wap·pen·shaw gathering of clans
war (**war·ring**, **warred**)
Wa·ran·gal Indian city
wa·ra·tah shrub
warb *Austral* dirty person
war·ble
war·bler
ward
ward·ed
war·den
war·den·ry
war·der (*fem* ·**dress**)
ward·robe
ward·room
ward·ship
ware *Archaic* beware
ware·house
ware·house·man (*plural* ·**men**)
wares goods
war·fare
war·fa·rin
war·head
war·horse
wari·ly
wari·ness
wari·son bugle note
War·ley English town
war·like
war·lock
war·lord
warm
warm-blooded
warm-blooded·ness
warm·er
warm-hearted
warm-hearted·ness
warm·ish
warm·ness
war·monger
warmth
warm-up (*noun*)
warn
warn·er
warn·ing
warp
warp·age
war·path
warp·er
war·plane
war·rant
war·rant·abil·ity
war·rant·able
war·rant·ably
war·rant·ee
war·rant·er one who warrants
war·ran·tor warranty giver
war·ran·ty (*plural* ·**ties**)
warred
war·ren
war·rig·al *Austral* dingo
war·ring
War·ring·ton Cheshire town
war·ri·or
War·saw
war·ship
war·sle *Dialect* wrestle
wart
wart·ed
war·time
warty (**warti·er**, **warti·est**)
War·wick
War·wick·shire
wary (**wari·er**, **wari·est**)
was
wash
wash·abil·ity
wash·able
wash·basin
wash·board
wash·bowl
wash·day
wash·er
washer·man (*plural* ·**men**)
washer·woman (*or* **wash·woman**; *plural* ·**women**)
wash·ery (*plural* ·**eries**)
wash·house
washi·ly
wash·in aeronautics term
washi·ness
wash·ing
Wash·ing·ton

Wash·ing·to·nian
washing-up
wash·out (*noun*)
wash·rag *US* face cloth
wash·room
wash·stand
wash·tub
wash·woman *variant of* washerwoman
washy (washi·er, washi·est)
wasn't
wasp
waspi·ly
waspi·ness
wasp·ish
wasp·ish·ness
waspy
was·sail
was·sail·er
wast·able
wast·age
waste
waste·ful
waste·ful·ly
waste·ful·ness
waste·land
waste·paper
wast·er
waste·weir water channel
wast·rel
wat Thai monastery
wa·tap American Indian thread
watch
watch·case
watch·dog
watch·er
watch·ful
watch·ful·ly
watch·ful·ness
watch-glass
watch·maker
watch·making
watch·man (*plural* ·men)
watch·strap
watch·tower
watch·word
wa·ter
wa·ter·age transportation by ship
water·bed
water·borne
water·buck antelope
water·colour (*US* ·color)

water·colour·ist (*US* ·color·)
water-cool
water-cooled
water·course
water·craft
water·cress
wa·ter·er
water·fall
Wa·ter·ford
water·fowl
water·front
Water·gate
wa·teri·ness
wa·ter·less
water·logged
Wa·ter·loo
water·man (*plural* ·men)
water·man·ship
water·mark
water·melon
water·proof
water·proof·ness
water-repellent
water-resistant
water·scape
water·shed
water-sick excessively irrigated
water·side
water-ski (*noun, plural* -skis; *verb* -skis, -skiing, -skied *or* ski'd)
water-skier
water·spout
water·tight
water·tightness
water·way
water·weed
water·works
water·worn
wa·tery
Wat·ford
watt unit
watt·age
watt-hour
wat·tle
wattle·bird
watt·meter
Wa·tu·si (*or* ·tut·; *plural* ·sis *or* ·si) African people
waul (*or* wawl) wail
wave undulation, etc.; move to and fro; *compare* waive
wave·band

wave·form physics term
wave·guide electronics term
wave·length
wave·let
wave·like
wa·vell·ite mineral
wave·meter
wave·off signal to aircraft
wa·ver hesitate; one who waves; *compare* waiver
wa·ver·er
wa·ver·ing·ly
wavi·ly
wavi·ness
wavy (wavi·er, wavi·est)
wawl *variant spelling of* waul
wax
wax·berry (*plural* ·berries)
wax·bill bird
wax·en
wax·er
waxi·ly
waxi·ness
wax·like
wax·plant
wax·wing bird
wax·work object
wax·work·er
wax·works exhibition
waxy (waxi·er, waxi·est)
way
way·bill document
way·farer
way·faring
Way·land legendary smith
way·lay (·lay·ing, ·laid)
way·lay·er
way-out
way·side
way·ward
way·ward·ness
wayz·goose printers' annual outing
Wa·ziri·stan Asian region
we
weak
weak·en
weak·en·er
weak·fish (*plural* ·fish *or* ·fishes)
weak-kneed
weak·li·ness
weak·ling
weak·ly (·li·er, ·li·est)

weak-minded

weak-minded
weak-minded·ness
weak·ness
weak-willed
weal prosperity
weal (*or* wheal) mark on skin
Weald English region
weald open country; *compare* wield
wealth
wealthi·ly
wealthi·ness
wealthy (wealthi·er, wealthi·est)
wean
wean·er
wean·ling
weap·on
weap·oned
weap·on·eer
wea·pon·ry
Wear English river
wear (wear·ing, wore, worn)
wear·abil·ity
wear·able
wear·er
wea·ri·ful *variant of* wearisome
wea·ri·less
wea·ri·ly
wea·ri·ness
wear·ing
wear·ing·ly
wea·ri·some (*or* ·ful)
wea·ri·some·ness (*or* ·ful·ness)
wear·proof
wea·ry (*adj* ·ri·er, ·ri·est; *verb* ·ries, ry·ing, ·ried)
wea·ry·ing·ly
wea·sand *Dialect* windpipe
wea·sel (*plural* ·sel *or* ·sels)
wea·sel·ly
weath·er climatic conditions; *compare* wether; whether
weath·er·abil·ity
weather-beaten
weather-board
weather-boarding
weather-bound
weather-cock
weath·er·er
weather·glass
weath·er·ing
weath·er·ly nautical term
weather·man (*plural* ·men)
weather-proof
weather-wise
weather-worn
weave (weav·ing, wove *or* weaved, wo·ven *or* weaved)
weav·er one who weaves; *compare* weever
weaver-bird
weav·ing
web (web·bing, webbed)
web·bing
web·by (·bi·er, ·bi·est)
we·ber unit
web·foot
web-footed
web-toed
wed (wed·ding, wed·ded *or* wed)
we'd we had; we would
wed·ding
wed·el·ing skiing turn
wedge
Wedg·wood (*Trademark*) pottery
wedgy
wed·lock
Wednes·day
wee (wee·ing, wee'd) *Slang* tiny; to urinate
weed
weed·er
weedi·ly
weedi·ness
weed·killer
weedy (weedi·er, weedi·est)
week
week·day
week·end
week·end·er
week·ly (*plural* ·lies)
week·night
wee·ny (*or* ween·sy; ·ni·er, ·ni·est *or* ·si·er, ·si·est)
weep (weep·ing, wept)
weep·er
weepi·ness
weep·ing
weep·ing·ly
weepy (*adj* weepi·er, weepi·est; *noun, plural* weepies)
wee·ver fish; *compare* weaver
wee·vil
wee·vily
weft
Wehr·macht German armed service
wei·ge·la shrub
weigh
weigh·able
weigh·bridge
weigh·er
weight
weight·er
weighti·ly
weighti·ness
weight·ing
weight·less
weight·less·ness
weight·lifter
weight·lifting
weighty (weighti·er, weighti·est)
Wei·hai Chinese port
Wei·mar East German city
Wei·mar·an·er dog
(Weir) *incorrect spelling of* Wear
weir
weird
weir·die (*or* ·do; *plural* ·dies *or* ·dos)
weird·ness
Weis·mann·ism biological theory
weka bird
Welch *variant spelling of* Welsh, now obsolete except in regimental names, esp. Royal Welch Fusiliers
welch *variant spelling of* welsh
wel·come
wel·come·ly
wel·come·ness
wel·com·er
weld
weld·abil·ity
weld·able
weld·er (*or* wel·dor)

wel·fare
(welk) *incorrect spelling of* whelk
Wel·kom South African town
well
we'll we will; we shall
well-accustomed
well-acquaint·ed
well-acted
well-adapted
well-advised
well-appoint·ed
well-argued
well-assort·ed
well-attend·ed
well-aware
well-balanced
well-behaved
well·being
well-bred
well-built
well-connect·ed
well-construct·ed
well-defined
well-deserved
well-developed
well-disposed
well-document·ed
well-done
well-dressed
well-educat·ed
well-endowed
well-equipped
well-established
well-favoured (*US* ·favored)
well-fed
well-found
well-founded
well-groomed
well-grounded
well·head
well-heeled
well-hung
wel·lies *Slang* Wellington boots
well-informed
Wel·ling·ton New Zealand capital; boot
well-intentioned
well-judged
well-knit
well-known
well-mannered

well-matched
well-meaning
well-nigh
well-off
well-oiled
well-organized (*or* -organised)
well-paid
well-pleased
well-preserved
well-propor·tioned
well-provid·ed
well-qualified
well-read
well-received
well-rounded
Wells Somerset city
well-situat·ed
well-spent
well-spoken
well·spring
well-support·ed
well-tempered
well-thought-of
well-timed
well-to-do
well-tried
well-turned
well-wisher
well-wishing
well-worded
well-worn
Welsh
welsh (*or* welch) fail in obligation
Welsh·man (*plural* ·men)
Welsh·woman (*plural* ·women)
welt
wel·ter
wel·ter·weight
wel·witschia plant
Wel·wyn Gar·den City
Wem·bley
wen cyst
wench
wench·er
Wend Slavonic people
wend
Wend·ish
Wen·dy house
Wens·ley·dale Yorkshire town; cheese
went
wen·tle·trap mollusc

wept
were
we're we are
weren't were not
were·wolf (*plural* ·wolves)
wer·gild (*or* were·gild, wer·geld) price on life
wer·ner·ite mineral
Wes·ley·an
Wes·ley·an·ism
Wes·sex
west
west·bound
West Brom·wich
west·er to move towards west
west·er·ing
west·er·li·ness
west·er·ly (*plural* ·lies)
west·ern
west·ern·er
west·ern·ism
west·erni·za·tion (*or* ·sa·tion)
west·ern·ize (*or* ·ise)
west·ern·most
West Ger·man
West Ger·many
West In·dian
West In·dies
west·ing westerly movement
West·meath Irish county
West·min·ster
West·mor·land former English county
west-northwest
Weston-super-Mare
West·pha·lia
West·pha·lian
west-southwest
west·ward (*adj*)
west·wards (*adv*)
wet (*adj* wet·ter, wet·test; *verb* wet·ting, wet *or* wet·ted) not dry; make wet; *compare* whet
weth·er male sheep; *compare* weather; whether
wet·lands
wet·ness
wet-nurse (*verb*)
wet·tabil·ity
wet·table
wet·ted
wet·ter

wettest

wet·test
wet·ting
wet·tish
we've we have
Wex·ford Irish county
Wey·mouth
whack
whack·er
whack·ing
whacko exclamation
whale (*plural* whales *or* whale)
whale·boat
whale·bone
whal·er whale catcher; whaleboat; *compare* **Waler**
whal·ing
wham (wham·ming, whammed)
whang
Whan·ga·rei New Zealand port
whangee bamboo grass
whare Maori hut
wharf (*plural* wharves *or* wharfs)
wharf·age
wharf·in·ger
wharve flywheel; pulley
what
what·ev·er
what·not
what·sit
what·so·ev·er
whaup *Scot* curlew
wheal *variant spelling of* weal
wheat
wheat·ear bird
wheat·en
wheat·worm
whee·dle
whee·dler
whee·dling·ly
wheel
wheel·bar·row
wheel·base
wheel·chair
wheel·er
wheeler-dealer
wheel·house
wheelie skateboarding manoeuvre
wheel·less
wheel·work
wheel·wright

wheen *Dialect* few
wheeze
wheez·er
wheezi·ly
wheezi·ness
wheez·ing·ly
wheezy (wheezi·er, wheezi·est)
whelk
whelp
when
whence
whene'er
when·ever
when·so·ever
where
where·abouts
where·as
where·at
where·by
where'er
where·fore
where·from
where·in
where·into
where·of
where·on
where·so·ever
where·to
where·upon
wher·ever
where·with
where·with·al
wher·rit worry
wher·ry (*plural* ·ries) boat
wherry·man (*plural* ·men)
whet (whet·ting, whet·ted) sharpen; stimulate; *compare* wet
wheth·er (*conj*) *compare* weather; wether
whet·stone
whet·ter
whey watery liquid
whey·ey (*or* ·ish, ·like)
whey·face
whey·faced
which
which·ever
whick·er whinny; *compare* wicker
whid·ah *variant spelling of* whydah
whiff
whiff·er

508

whif·fle
whif·fler
whif·fle·tree crossbar in harness
Whig political party
Whig·gery (*or* ·gism)
Whig·gish
Whig·gish·ness
while during the time that; *note* while away; *compare* wile
whilst
whim
whim·brel bird
whim·per
whim·per·er
whim·per·ing·ly
whim·si·cal
whim·si·cal·ity (*plural* ·ities)
whim·si·cal·ly
whim·si·cal·ness
whim·sy (*or* ·sey; *noun*, *plural* ·sies *or* ·seys; *adj* ·si·er, ·si·est)
whin gorse
whin·chat bird
whine
whin·er
whinge
whin·ing·ly
whin·ny (*verb* ·nies, ·ny·ing, ·nied; *noun*, *plural* ·nies)
whin·stone
whiny (whini·er, whini·est) peevish; *compare* winy
whip (whip·ping, whipped)
whip·cord
whip·lash
whip·like
whip·per
whipper-in (*plural* whippers-in)
whip·per·snap·per
whip·pet
whip·ping
whip·poor·will
whippy (whip·pier, whip·piest)
whip-round (*noun*)
whip·saw
whip·stall aeronautics term
whip·stitch

whip·stock whip handle
whip·worm
whir (or whirr; whir·ring, whirred)
whirl spin; confusion; compare whorl
whirl·about
whirl·er
whirli·gig
whirl·ing·ly
whirl·pool
whirl·wind
whirly·bird
whirr variant spelling of whir
whish swish
whisk
whisk·er
whisk·ered
whisk·ers
whisk·ery
whis·key Irish or US whisky
whis·ky (plural ·kies)
whis·per
whis·per·er
whist
whis·tle
whis·tler
whis·tling
Whit Christian festival
whit iota
white
white·bait
white·beam tree
white·cap white-crested wave
White·chapel
white-collar (adj)
white·damp mine gas
whit·ed sep·ul·chre
white-eye bird
white·fish (plural ·fish or ·fishes)
white·fly (plural ·flies)
White·hall
white-hot
white-livered
whit·en
whit·en·er
white·ness
whit·en·ing
white-out
whites
white-slaver
white·smith metal polisher
white·throat bird

white·wall tyre
white·wash
white·wash·er
white·wood
whit·ey (or wity; plural ·eys or wities)
whith·er
whit·ing (plural ·ing or ·ings) fish
whit·ing (or ·en·ing) ground chalk
whit·ish
whit·low
Whit·sun
Whit·sun·tide
whit·tle
whit·tler
whit·tlings wood shavings
whity whitish; variant spelling of whitey
whiz (or whizz; whiz·zing, whizzed)
whiz-bang (or whizz-)
whiz·zer
who
whoa
who'd who had; who would
who·dun·it (or ·dun·nit)
who·ever
whole
whole·food
whole·hearted
whole·hearted·ness
whole·meal
whole·ness
whole·sale
whole·sal·er
whole·some
whole·some·ly
whole·some·ness
who'll who will; who shall
whol·ly
whom
whom·ever
whom·so·ever
whoop
whoo·pee
whoop·er swan
whoop·ing cough
whoops exclamation
whoosh (or woosh)
whop (or wop; whop·ping, whopped or wop·ping, wopped) hit
whop·per

whop·ping
whore
whore·dom
whore·house
whore·monger
whore·son
whor·ish
whorl spiral pattern or arrangement; compare whirl
whorled
whortle·berry (plural ·berries)
who's who is
whose of who
who·so·ever (or who·so)
why (plural whys)
Why·al·la Australian port
whyd·ah (or whid·) bird
Wichi·ta US city
Wick Scottish town
wick
wick·ed
wick·ed·ness
wick·er flexible twig; compare whicker
wicker·work
wick·et
wicket·keeper
wick·ing
wicki·up American Indian hut
Wick·low Irish county
wico·py plant
wid·der·shins variant spelling of withershins
wide
wide-awake
wide-awakeness
wide-eyed
wide·ly
wid·en
wid·en·er
wide·ness
wide-open
wide-ranging
wide-screen (adj)
wide·spread
widg·eon variant spelling of wigeon
widg·et
widgie Austral unruly woman
wid·ish
Wid·nes Cheshire town

widow

wid·ow
wid·ow·er
wid·ow·hood
width
width·wise (or ·ways)
wield manipulate; compare
　weald
wield·able
wield·er
wieldy (wieldi·er,
　wieldi·est)
Wie·ner schnit·zel
(wier) incorrect spelling of
　weir
(wierd) incorrect spelling of
　weird
Wies·ba·den West German
　city
wife (plural wives)
wife·li·ness
wife·ly
wig (wig·ging, wigged)
Wig·an
wig·eon (or widg·) duck
wigged
wig·ging
wig·gle
wig·gler
wig·gly
Wight (Isle of)
wig·wag (·wag·ging,
　·wagged)
wig·wag·ger
wig·wam
wil·co signalling expression
wild
wild·cat (·cat·ting,
　·cat·ted)
wild·cat·ter
wil·de·beest (plural
　·beests or ·beest)
wil·der·ness
wild-eyed
wild·fire
wild·fowl
wild·fowl·er
wild·fowl·ing
wild-goose chase
wild·ing (or ·ling)
wild·life
wild·ness
wile craftiness; trick;
　compare while
wil·ful (US will·)
wil·ful·ly (US will·)

wil·ful·ness (US will·)
Wil·helms·ha·ven West
　German port
wili·ly
wili·ness
will
will·able
wil·lem·ite mineral
will·er
wil·let bird
will·ful US spelling of wilful
Wil·liams·burg US city
wil·lies Slang fright
will·ing
will·ing·ness
wil·li·waw US turmoil
will-o'-the-wisp
wil·low
wil·low·herb
wil·lowy
will·power
willy-nilly
wilt
Wil·ton carpet
Wilt·shire
wily (wili·er, wili·est)
wim·ble tool
Wim·ble·don
wimp
wimp·ish
wim·ple
Wim·py (Trademark)
　hamburger
win (win·ning, won)
wince
winc·er
win·cey fabric
win·cey·ette
winch
winch·er
Win·ches·ter English city;
　rifle
win·ches·ter large bottle
winc·ing·ly
wind (wind·ing, wound)
　coil
wind (wind·ing, wind·ed)
　air current, etc.
wind·able
wind·age
wind·bag
wind·blown
wind·borne
wind·bound
wind·break

wind-broken asthmatic
wind·burn
wind·burnt (or ·burned)
wind·cheater
wind·ed
wind·er
Win·der·mere
wind·fall
wind·flower
wind·gall fetlock swelling
wind·galled
Wind·hoek Namibian
　capital
wind·hover Dialect kestrel
windi·ly
windi·ness
wind·ing
wind·ing·ly
wind·jam·mer
wind·lass
win·dle·straw Dialect dried
　grass
wind·mill
win·dow
window-dresser
window-dressing
window·pane
window-shop (-shopping,
　-shopped)
window-shopper
window·sill
wind·pipe
wind-pollinat·ed
wind-pollina·tion
wind·row line of hay
wind·row·er
wind·sail
wind·screen
wind·shield
wind·sock
Wind·sor
wind·storm
wind·sucker
wind-sucking
wind·swept
wind-up (noun)
wind·ward
windy (windi·er,
　windi·est)
wine
wine-bibber
wine-bibbing
wine-glass
wine-glass·ful
wine·press

win·ery (*plural* ·eries)
wine·skin
wing
wing·ding *US* party
winged
wing·er
wing·less
wing·less·ness
wing·let
wing·like
wing·over aircraft
    manoeuvre
wing·span (*or* ·spread)
wink
wink·er
win·kle
win·nable
Win·ne·ba·go (*plural* ·gos
    or ·go) *US* lake;
    American Indian
win·ner
win·ning
win·ning·ness
win·nings
Win·ni·peg
Win·ni·peg·ger
Win·ni·pego·sis Canadian
    lake
win·now
win·now·er
wino (*plural* winos) *Slang*
    wine drinker
win·some
win·some·ly
win·some·ness
Winston-Salem *US* city
win·ter
winter·bourne stream
win·ter·er
winter·feed (·feeding,
    ·fed)
winter·green shrub
winter·kill
winter·time
win·tri·er
win·tri·est
win·tri·ly
win·tri·ness (*or* ·teri·ness)
win·try (*or* ·tery; ·tri·er,
    ·tri·est)
winy (wini·er, wini·est)
    like wine; *compare* whiny
winze mining shaft
wipe
wipe-out (*noun*)

wip·er
wire
wire·draw (·draw·ing,
    ·drew, ·drawn)
wire-gauge
wire-haired
wire·less
wire·man (*plural* ·men)
    US electrician
wir·er
wire·work
wire·worker
wire·works
wire·worm
wire-wove
wiri·ly
wiri·ness
wir·ing
wir·ra Irish exclamation
Wir·ral English peninsula
wiry (wiri·er, wiri·est)
Wis·con·sin
Wis·con·sin·ite
wis·dom
wise
wisea·cre
wise·crack
wise·crack·er
wise·ly
wise·ness
wi·sent European bison
wish
wish·bone
wish·er
wish·ful
wish·ful·ly
wish·ful·ness
wishy-washy
wisp
wispi·ly
wispi·ness
wispy (wispi·er, wispi·est)
wis·te·ria
wist·ful
wist·ful·ly
wist·ful·ness
wit
wit·an Anglo-Saxon council
witch
witch·craft
witch elm *variant spelling of*
    wych elm
witch·ery (*plural* ·eries)
witch·et·ty edible grub

witch ha·zel (*or* wych
    hazel)
witch-hunt
witch-hunter
witch-hunting
witch·ing
witch·like
wite *Scot* blame
wit·ena·gamot witan
with
with·al
with·draw (·draw·ing,
    ·drew, ·drawn)
with·draw·able
with·draw·al
with·draw·er
with·drawn
with·drawn·ness
with·drew
withe (*or* withy; *plural*
    withes *or* withies)
    flexible twig
with·er
with·ered·ness
with·er·er
with·er·ing·ly
with·er·ite mineral
with·ers
with·er·shins (*or* wid·der·)
with·hold (·hold·ing,
    ·held)
with·hold·er
with·in
with·out
with·stand (·stand·ing,
    ·stood)
with·stand·er
with·stood
withy (*plural* withies)
    willow tree; *variant
    spelling of* withe
wit·less
wit·less·ness
wit·loof Belgian chicory
wit·ness
wit·ness·able
wit·ness·er
wits
wit·ter
wit·ti·cism
wit·ti·ly
wit·ti·ness
wit·ting·ly intentional
wit·ty (·ti·er, ·ti·est)

Witwatersrand

Wit·wa·ters·rand South African region
wive *Archaic* to marry
wi·vern *variant spelling of* wyvern
wives *plural of* wife
wiz·ard
wiz·ard·ry
wiz·en
wiz·ened
woad
woad·ed
wob·be·gong shark
wob·ble
wob·bler
wob·bli·ness
wob·bly (·bli·er, ·bli·est)
Woden (*or* **Wodan**) Anglo-Saxon god
wodge
woe
woe·be·gone
woe·ful
woe·ful·ly
woe·ful·ness
wog·gle
wok
woke
wok·en
Wo·king
wold upland
wolf (*plural* **wolves**)
wolf·bane (*or* **wolfs·bane**, **wolf's-bane**) plant
wolf·er *variant of* wolver
wolf·fish (*plural* ·fish *or* ·fishes)
wolf·hound
wolf·ish
wolf·ish·ness
wolf·like
wolf·ram tungsten
wolf·ram·ite mineral
wolfs·bane (*or* **wolf's-bane**) *variants of* wolfbane
wolf·whistle (*verb*)
wol·las·ton·ite mineral
Wol·lon·gong Australian city
wol·ly (*plural* ·lies) *Dialect* pickled cucumber; *compare* wally
Wol·of (*plural* ·of *or* ·ofs) African people

wolv·er (*or* **wolf·**) wolf hunter
Wol·ver·hamp·ton
wol·ver·ine animal
wolves *plural of* wolf
wom·an (*plural* ·en)
wom·an·hood
wom·an·ish
wom·an·ish·ness
wom·an·ize (*or* ·ise)
wom·an·iz·er (*or* ·is·er)
wom·an·kind
woman-like
wom·an·li·ness
wom·an·ly
womb
wom·bat
womb-like
wom·en
women-folk
wom·era *variant spelling of* woomera
won *past tense of* win
won (*or* **hwan**; *plural* **won** *or* **hwan**) North Korean currency
won·der
won·der·er
won·der·ful
won·der·ful·ly
won·der·ful·ness
wonder·land
won·der·ment
wonder·work miracle
wonder-worker
wonder-working
won·drous
won·drous·ness
won·ky (·ki·er, ·ki·est)
Won·san North Korean port
wont accustomed; custom
won't will not
wont·ed
won ton Chinese food
woo (**woos**, **woo·ing**, **wooed**)
wood
wood·bine
wood·borer beetle larva
wood·carver
wood·carving
wood·chat bird
wood·chuck
wood·cock

wood·craft
wood·crafts·man (*plural* ·men)
wood·cut
wood·cut·ter
wood·cutting
wood·ed
wood·en
wooden·head
wood·en·ness
wood·grouse
woodi·ness
wood·land
wood·lander
wood·lark
wood·louse (*plural* ·lice)
wood·man (*plural* ·men)
wood·note natural song
wood·pecker
wood·pile
wood·print
wood·ruff plant
wood·rush
wood·screw
wood·shed
wood·sia fern
woods·man (*plural* ·men)
wood·wind
wood·work
wood·worker
wood·working
wood·worm
woody (**woodi·er**, **woodi·est**)
wooed
woo·er
woof weft; bark of dog
woof·er loudspeaker
woo·ing
wool
wool·gather·er
wool·gather·ing
wool·grower
wool·growing
wool·len (*US* **wool·en**)
wool·li·ly
wool·li·ness
wool·ly (*US also* **wooly**; *adj* ·li·er, ·li·est; *noun*, *plural* ·lies)
wool·pack
wool·sack
Woom·era Australian town
woom·era (*or* **wom·era**) Aboriginal spear thrower

wrecker

Woop Woop *Austral* remote town
woosh *variant spelling of* whoosh
woozi·ly
woozi·ness
woozy (woozi·er, woozi·est)
wop *variant spelling of* whop; *Slang* Italian
Worces·ter
Worces·ter·shire *former county; note* Worcestershire sauce
word
word·age
word-blind
word·book
word·break
word-deaf
wordi·ly
wordi·ness
word·ing
word·less
word·less·ness
word-perfect
word·play
word·smith
wordy (wordi·er, wordi·est)
wore
work
work·abil·ity (*or* ·able·ness)
work·able
worka·day
worka·hol·ic
work·bag
work·bench
work·book
work·box
work·day
work·er
worker-priest
work·folk
work-harden
work-harden·ing
work·horse
work·house
work-in (*noun*)
work·ing
work·load
work·man (*plural* ·men)
work·man·like
work·man·ly
work·man·ship
work-out (*noun*)
work·people
work·piece
work·room
works
work·shop
work·shy
Work·sop English town
work·table
work-to-rule (*noun*)
world
world-beater
world-beating
world·li·ness
world·ling
world·ly (·li·er, ·li·est)
worldly-wise
world-shaking
world-weariness
world-weary
world·wide
worm
worm·cast
worm-eaten
worm·er
worm·hole
worm·like (*or* ·ish)
worm·seed
worm·wood
wormy (wormi·er, wormi·est)
worn
worn-out
wor·ri·er
wor·ri·ment
wor·ri·some
wor·rit *Dialect* tease
wor·ry (*verb* ·ries, ·ry·ing, ·ried; *noun, plural* ·ries)
wor·ry·wart worrier
worse
wors·en
wor·ship (·ship·ping, ·shipped; *US* ·ship·ing, ·shiped)
wor·ship·able
wor·ship·ful
wor·ship·ful·ly
wor·ship·ful·ness
wor·ship·per
wor·ship·ping·ly
worst
wor·sted fabric
worst·ed defeated
wort soaked malt
worth
wor·thi·ly
wor·thi·ness
Wor·thing
worth·less
worth·less·ly
worth·less·ness
worth·while
worth·while·ness
wor·thy (*adj* ·thi·er, ·thi·est; *noun, plural* ·thies)
Wotan Germanic god
would
would-be
wouldn't
wouldst
wound
wound·able
wound·ed
wound·er
wound·ing·ly
wound·wort
wove
wo·ven
wow
wow·ser *Austral* puritanical person
wrack seaweed; *variant spelling of* rack
wraith
wraith·like
wran·gle
wran·gler
wrap (wrap·ping, wrapped)
wrap·over (*or* ·around, ·round)
wrap·per
wrap·ping
wrasse fish; *compare* rasse
wrath anger; *compare* wroth
wrath·ful
wrath·ful·ly
wrath·ful·ness
wreak
wreak·er
wreath (*noun, plural* wreaths)
wreathe (*verb*)
wreck
wreck·age
wreck·er

wreckfish

wreck·fish (*plural* ·fish *or* ·fishes)
Wre·kin English hill
Wren member of WRNS
wren bird
wrench
wrest
wrest·er
wres·tle
wres·tler
wres·tling
wretch miserable person; *compare* **retch**
wretch·ed
wretch·ed·ness
Wrex·ham
wried contorted
wri·er variant spelling of **wryer**
wri·est variant spelling of **wryest**
wrig·gle
wrig·gler
wrig·gling·ly
wrig·gly (·gli·er, ·gli·est)
wright maker or repairer
wring (wring·ing, wrung)
wring·er
wrin·kle
wrin·kly
wrist
wrist·band
wrist·let bracelet
wrist·lock
wrist·watch
writ
writ·able
write (writ·ing, wrote, writ·ten)
write-off (*noun*)
writ·er
writhe
writh·er
writh·ing·ly
writ·ing
writ·ten
Wro·cław Polish city
wrong
wrong·doer
wrong·doing
wrong·er
wrong-foot (*verb*)
wrong·ful
wrong·ful·ly
wrong·ful·ness
wrong-headed
wrong-headed·ness
wrong·ly
wrong·ness
wrote
wroth *Archaic* angry; *compare* **wrath**
wrought
wrought-up
wrung
wry (*adj* wry·er, wry·est *or* wri·er, wri·est; *verb* wries, wry·ing, wried)
wry·bill bird
wry·ing
wry·ly
wry·neck
wry·ness

Wu Chinese dialect
Wu·han Chinese city
Wu-hsi variant spelling of **Wusih**
Wuhu Chinese port
wul·fen·ite mineral
Wu-lu-mu-ch'i variant of **Urumchi**
wun·der·kind (*plural* ·kinds *or* ·kind·er) child prodigy
Wup·per·tal West German city
wurley (*or* **wurlie**) Aboriginal hut
wurst German sausage
Würt·tem·berg former German state
Würz·burg West German city
wus Welsh term of address
Wu·sih (*or* **Wu-hsi**) Chinese city
Wy·an·dotte domestic fowl
wych elm (*or* **witch elm**)
wych hazel variant spelling of **witch hazel**
Wyc·lif·fite (*or* **Wyc·lif·ite**)
Wye British river
Wyke·ham·ist member of Winchester College
wynd *Scot* lane
Wyo·ming
wy·vern (*or* **wi·**) heraldic beast

X

xan·thate chemical compound
xan·tha·tion
xan·the·in plant pigment
xan·thene chemical compound
xan·thic chemistry or botany term
xan·thin plant pigment
xan·thine chemical compound
xan·thoch·ro·ism animal skin condition
xan·tho·ma (*plural* ·mas *or* ·ma·ta) skin nodule
xan·tho·phyll plant pigment
xan·tho·phyll·ous
xan·thous having yellowish hair
Xan·thus ancient Asian city
x-axis
X-chromosome
xe·bec (*or* **ze·bec**, **ze·beck**) ship
xe·nia botany term
xe·nial
xeno·cryst
xe·noga·mous
xe·noga·my cross-fertilization
xeno·gen·esis botany term
xeno·genet·ic (*or* ·**gen·ic**)
xeno·glos·sia language ability
xeno·lith geology term
xeno·lith·ic
xeno·mor·phic geology term

yearning

xeno·mor·phi·cal·ly
xen·on chemical element
xeno·phile
xeno·phobe
xeno·pho·bia
xeno·pho·bic
xer·arch ecology term
xe·ric of dry conditions
xe·ri·cal·ly
xe·ro·der·ma (or ·mia) dry skin
xe·ro·der·mat·ic (or ·ma·tous)
xe·rog·ra·pher
xe·ro·graph·ic
xe·ro·graphi·cal·ly
xe·rog·ra·phy photocopying
xe·ro·mor·phic botany term
xe·ro·phile
xe·rophi·lous living in dry conditions
xe·rophi·ly
xe·roph·thal·mia (or xe·ro·ma) eye disease
xe·roph·thal·mic
xe·ro·phyte
xe·ro·phyt·ic
xe·ro·phyti·cal·ly
xe·ro·phyt·ism
xe·ro·sere ecology term
xe·ro·sis dryness of tissues
xe·rot·ic
Xer·ox (Trademark)
Xho·sa (plural ·sa or ·sas) African people
Xho·san
xi (plural xis) Greek letter
xiphi·ster·num (plural ·na) part of breastbone
xiph·oid anatomy or biology term
xipho·su·ran zoology term
Xmas
X-radiation
X-ray (or x-ray)
xy·lan biochemistry term
xy·lem plant tissue
xy·lene chemical compound
xy·li·dine chemical compound
xy·lo·carp botany term
xy·lo·car·pous
xy·lo·graph wood engraving
xy·log·ra·pher
xy·lo·graph·ic (or ·graphi·cal)
xy·log·ra·phy
xy·loid woody
xy·lol chemical compound
xy·lopha·gous wood-eating
xy·lo·phone
xy·lo·phon·ic
xy·lopho·nist
xy·lose sugar
xy·loto·mist
xy·loto·mous wood-boring
xy·loto·my preparing wood for microscopy
xy·lyl chemistry term
xyst (or xys·tus, xys·tos) portico
xys·ter surgical file

Y

yacht
yacht·ing
yachts·man (plural ·men)
yachts·man·ship (or yacht·)
yachts·woman (plural ·women)
ya·hoo (plural ·hoos) coarse person
ya·hoo·ism
yak (yak·king, yakked)
Ya·kut (plural ·kuts or ·kut) Soviet people
Ya·kutsk Soviet port
Yale US university; (Trademark) lock
Yal·ta Soviet port
yam
yam·mer
yam·mer·er
yang Chinese masculine principle; compare yin
Yang·tze
yank tug
Yank (or Yan·kee) Slang American
Yan·kee·ism
Ya·oun·dé (or Ya·un·de) Cameroon capital
yap (yap·ping, yapped)
ya·pok animal
ya·pon variant spelling of yaupon
yapped
yap·per
yap·ping
yap·py
yar·bor·ough bridge or whist term
yard·age
yard·arm
yard·stick
Yar·mouth
yar·mul·ke skullcap
yarn
yarn-dyed
Ya·ro·slavl Soviet city
yar·row
yash·mak (or ·mac)
yata·ghan sword
Ya·un·de variant spelling of Yaoundé
yau·pon (or ya·pon) shrub
yau·tia plant
yaw
yawl
yawn
yawn·er
yawn·ing·ly
yaws disease
y-axis
Y-chromosome
ye
yea
yean·ling goat's or sheep's young
year
year·book
year·ling
year·long
year·ly (plural ·lies)
yearn
yearn·er
yearn·ing

yeast

yeast
yeasti·ly
yeasti·ness
yeasty (yeasti·er, yeasti·est)
yell
yell·er
yel·low
yellow·bark
yellow-belly (plural -bellies)
yellow·bird
yellow·hammer
yel·low·ish
yellow·legs bird
yel·lows disease
Yellow·stone
yellow·tail (plural ·tails or ·tail) fish
yellow·weed
yellow·wood
yel·lowy
yelp
yelp·er
Yem·en
Yem·eni
yen (yen·ning, yenned)
yen (plural yen) Japanese currency
Ye·ni·sei Soviet river
Yen·tai (or Yen-t'ai) Chinese port
yeo·man (plural ·men)
yeo·man·ry (plural ·ries)
Yeo·vil
yer·ba beverage
Ye·re·van Armenian capital
yes
yes-man (plural -men)
yes·ter·day
yes·ter·year
yeti
yew
Ygg·dra·sil mythological tree
Yid·dish
yield
yield·able
yield·er
yield·ing·ly
yield·ing·ness
yin Chinese feminine principle; compare yang
Ying·kow (or Ying-k'ou) Chinese port

yip·pee
ylang-ylang (or ilang-ilang) tree
ylem original matter of universe
yob (or yob·bo; plural yobs or yob·bos)
yo·del (·del·ling, ·delled; US ·del·ing, ·deled)
yo·del·ler (US ·del·er)
yoga
yo·ghurt (or ·gurt)
yogi (plural yo·gis or yo·gin) yoga master
yo·gic
yo·gism
yo·gurt variant spelling of yoghurt
yo·him·bine medicinal substance
yoicks huntsman's exclamation
yoke frame; burden; link; part of garment; compare yolk
yo·kel
yo·kel·ish
Yo·ko·ha·ma Japanese city
Yok·ya·kar·ta (or Jog·ja·) Indonesian city
yolk part of egg; compare yoke
yolky
Yom Kip·pur
yon (or yond)
yon·der
yoni female genitalia
Yon·kers US city
Yonne French department and river
yon·nie Austral stone
yoo-hoo
yore
York
york·er cricket term
York·ist
York·shire
Yorkshire·man (plural ·men)
Yo·ru·ba (plural ·bas or ·ba) African people
Yo·ru·ban
Yo·semi·te US national park
Yoshkar-Ola Soviet city

516

you
you'd you would; you had
you'll you will; you shall
young
young·berry (plural ·berries)
young·ish
young·ster
Youngs·town US city
your of you
you're you are
yours
your·self (plural ·selves)
youth
youth·ful
youth·ful·ly
youth·ful·ness
you've you have
yowl
yowl·er
yo-yo (plural -yos)
Ypres
Yquem French vineyard
yt·ter·bia chemical compound
yt·ter·bite mineral
yt·ter·bium chemical element
yt·tria chemical compound
yt·tric
yt·trif·er·ous
yt·trium chemical element
yuan (plural yuan) Chinese currency
Yu·ca·tán Mexican state
yuc·ca
Yuga Hindu age
Yu·go·slav (or Ju·)
Yu·go·sla·via (or Ju·)
Yu·go·sla·vian (or Ju·)
yuk
yuk·ky
Yu·kon
Yu·kon·er
yu·lan tree
yule
yule·tide
Yu·man language group
yum·my (·mi·er, ·mi·est)
Yün·nan Chinese province
yup Slang yes
yup·pie
Yve·lines French department

Z

za·ba·glio·ne
Za·brze Polish city
Za·ca·te·cas Mexican state
zaf·fer (or zaf·fre) pigment
Zaga·zig (or Zaqa·ziq) Egyptian city
Za·greb
zai·bat·su Japanese wealthy families
Za·ire African republic
za·ire (plural ·ïre) African currency
Za·ir·ese
Za·ir·ian
Zama ancient African city
Zam·be·zi (or ·se)
Zam·be·zian
Zam·bia
Zam·bian
Zam·bo·an·ga Philippine port
za·mia plant
za·min·dar (or ze·) Indian landowner
za·min·dari (or ze·; plural ·daris) estate
za·ni·ly
za·ni·ness
Zan·te Greek island
zan·thoxy·lum tree
zany (adj zani·er, zani·est; noun, plural zanies)
Zan·zi·bar
Zan·zi·ba·ri
zap (zap·ping, zapped)
za·pa·dea·do (plural ·dos) dance
Za·po·rozh·ye Soviet city
Za·po·tec (plural ·tecs or ·tec) American Indian
Zapo·tec·an
Zaqa·ziq variant of Zagazig
Za·ra·go·za Spanish city
zara·tite mineral
za·reba (or ·ree·ba) African enclosure
zarf coffee-cup holder
Zar·ga (or Sar·ka) Jordanian town

Za·ria Nigerian city
zar·zue·la Spanish opera
z-axis
zeal
Zea·land Danish island; compare Zeeland
zeal·ot
zeal·ot·ry
zeal·ous
zeal·ous·ness
ze·bec (or ·beck) variant spellings of xebec
Zebedee biblical character
zeb·ra (plural ·ras or ·ra)
zebra-like (or ze·bra·ic)
zebra·wood
ze·brine (or ·broid)
zebu ox
zec·chi·no (plural ·ni) coin
zed
zedo·ary condiment
zee US zed
Zee·brug·ge
Zee·land Dutch province; compare Zealand
Zee·land·er
zein protein
Zeist Dutch city
Zeit·geist German outlook
ze·min·dar variant spelling of zamindar
ze·min·dari variant spelling of zamindari
Zen
ze·na·na women's part of house
Zen·ic
Zen·ist
zen·ith
zen·ith·al
zeo·lite mineral
zeo·lit·ic
zeph·yr breeze; fabric
Zephyrus Greek god
zep·pe·lin
zero (noun, plural zeros or zeroes; verb zeroes, ze·ro·ing, ze·roed)
zero-rated
zeroth

zest
zest·ful
zest·ful·ly
zest·ful·ness
zesty
zeta Greek letter
zeug·ma figure of speech
zeug·mat·ic
zeug·mati·cal·ly
Zeus
Zhda·nov Soviet port
Zhi·to·mir Soviet city
zho variant spelling of zo
zib·el·ine fur
zib·et animal
ziff Austral beard
zig·gu·rat (or zik·ku·rat, ziku·rat) temple tower
zig·zag (·zag·ging, ·zagged)
zig·zag·ged·ness
zig·zag·ger
zila (or zil·la, zil·lah) Indian administrative district
zilch
zil·lion (plural ·lions or ·lion)
Zim·ba·bwe
Zim·ba·bwe·an
zinc
zin·cate
zinc·ic (or ·ous, ·oid)
zinc·if·er·ous
zinck·en·ite variant spelling of zinkenite
zincky (or zincy, zinky)
zin·co (plural ·cos) short for zincograph
zin·co·graph zinc printing-plate
zin·cog·ra·pher
zin·co·graph·ic (or ·graphi·cal)
zin·cog·ra·phy
zincy variant spelling of zincky
Zin·fan·del wine grape
zing

zingaro

zin·ga·ro (*fem* ·ra; *plural* ·ri *or* ·re) gipsy
zin·gi·bera·ceous botany term
zingy
zin·jan·thro·pus fossil hominid
zin·ken·ite (*or* zinck·en·ite) mineral
zinky *variant spelling of* zincky
zin·nia plant
Zion (*or* Sion)
Zi·on·ism
Zi·on·ist
Zi·on·is·tic
zip (zip·ping, zipped)
zip·per
zip·py (·pi·er, ·pi·est)
zirc·al·loy
zir·con
zir·co·nia chemical compound
zir·con·ic
zir·co·nium chemical element
zith·er
zith·er·ist
Zla·to·ust Soviet town
zlo·ty (*plural* ·tys *or* ·ty) Polish currency
zo (*or* zho, dzo; *plural* zos, zhos, dzos *or* zo, zho, dzo) cattle
zo·di·ac
zo·dia·cal
Zo·har Jewish text
zois·ite mineral
Zom·ba Malawian city
zom·bie (*or* ·bi; *plural* ·bies *or* ·bis)
zom·bi·ism
zon·al (*or* zona·ry)
zon·ate (*or* zo·nat·ed)
zo·na·tion
Zond Soviet spacecraft
zone
zone·time
zonu·lar
zon·ule
zoo (*plural* zoos)
zoo·chemi·cal
zoo·chem·is·try
zoo·chore botany term
zoo·geo·gra·pher

zoo·geo·graph·ic (*or* ·graphi·cal)
zoo·geo·graphi·cal·ly
zoo·geog·ra·phy
zoo·gloea (*US* ·glea; *plural* ·gloeas *or* ·gloeae, *US* ·gleas *or* ·gleae) bacterial mass
zoo·gloeal (*US* ·gleal)
zo·og·ra·pher
zoo·graph·ic (*or* ·graphi·cal)
zo·og·ra·phy
zo·oid
zo·ol·at·er
zo·ola·trous
zo·ola·try worship of animals
zoo·logi·cal
zo·olo·gist
zo·ol·ogy (*plural* ·ogies)
zoom
zoo·met·ric (*or* ·ri·cal)
zo·om·etry
zoo·mor·phic
zoo·mor·phism
zo·ono·sis (*plural* ·ses) pathology term
zo·opha·gous feeding on animals
zoo·phile
zoo·philia fondness for animals
zoo·phil·ic
zo·ophi·lism sexual attraction to animals
zo·ophi·lous pollinated by animals
zoo·pho·bia
zo·opho·bous
zoo·phyte
zoo·phyt·ic (*or* ·phyti·cal)
zoo·plank·ton
zoo·plas·tic
zoo·plas·ty surgical transplantation
zoo·sperm
zoo·sper·mat·ic
zoo·spo·ran·gial
zoo·spo·ran·gium (*plural* ·gia)
zoo·spore
zoo·spor·ic (*or* zo·os·por·ous)
zo·os·ter·ol biochemical compound

518

zoo·tech·nics
zoo·tom·ic (*or* ·tomi·cal)
zoo·tomi·cal·ly
zo·oto·mist
zo·oto·my animal dissection
zoo·tox·ic
zoo·tox·in
zo·ril·la (*or* zo·rille) animal
Zo·ro·as·trian
Zo·ro·as·tri·an·ism
zos·ter shingles
Zou·ave French infantryman
zounds archaic exclamation
zoy·sia grass
zuc·chet·to (*plural* ·tos) skullcap
zuc·chi·ni (*plural* ·ni *or* ·nis)
zug·zwang chess position
Zui·der Zee (*or* Zuy·)
Zulu (*plural* Zulus *or* Zulu)
Zu·lu·land
Zü·rich
Zwickau East German city
zwie·back toasted rusk
Zwing·lian denoting religious movement
zwit·teri·on
zwit·teri·on·ic
zyg·apo·phys·eal (*or* ·ial)
zyga·pophy·sis (*plural* ·ses) part of vertebra
zy·go·dac·tyl ornithology term
zy·go·dac·tyl·ism
zy·go·dac·ty·lous
zy·go·ma (*plural* ·ma·ta) bone
zy·go·mat·ic
zy·go·mor·phic (*or* ·phous) botany term
zy·go·mor·phy (*or* ·phism)
zy·go·phyl·la·ceous botany term
zy·go·phyte
zy·gose
zy·go·sis (*plural* ·ses) biology term
zy·go·spore
zy·go·spor·ic
zy·gote fertilized egg cell

zy·go·tene stage of cell division
zy·got·ic
zy·goti·cal·ly
zy·mase enzyme
zy·mo·gen enzyme precursor
zy·mo·gen·esis
zy·mo·gen·ic
zy·mo·log·ic (*or* **·logi·cal**)
zy·molo·gist
zy·mol·ogy
zy·moly·sis fermentation
zy·mo·lyt·ic
zy·mom·eter
zy·mo·sis (*plural* **·ses**) disease
zy·mot·ic
zy·moti·cal·ly
zy·mur·gy branch of chemistry
Zyr·ian language

First Names

Aaron
Abbey (*or* Abbie, Abby)
Abe
Abel
Abigail
Abner
Abraham
Abram
Absalom
Ada
Adah
Adair
Adam
Adamina
Adamnan
Addie (*or* Addy)
Adela
Adelaide
Adele
Adelheid
Adelina
Adeline
Adlai
Adolf (*or* Adolph, Adolphe)
Adolphus
Adrian
Adriana
Adrianne (*or* Adrienne)
Aeneas
Afra
Agacia
Agatha
Aggie
Agnes
Agneta
Aidan
Aileen
Ailie
Ailis
Ailith
Ailsa
Aimee
Aine
Ainslie (*or* Ainsley)
Aisling
Aislinn
Aithne
Al
Alain

Alan (*or* Allan, Allen, Alun)
Alana (*or* Alanna)
Alaric
Alasdair (*or* Alastair) *variant spellings of* Alistair
Alban
Albany
Alberic
Albert
Alberta
Albertina
Albertine
Albin
Albina
Albinia
Albreda
Alda
Alden
Aldhelm
Aldis
Aldith
Aldo
Aldous (*or* Aldus)
Aldred
Aldreda
Aldwyn (*or* Aldwin)
Alec
Aled
Aledwen
Alethea
Alex
Alexa
Alexander
Alexandra
Alexandria
Alexandrina
Alexia
Alexis
Alf
Alfie
Alfonso *variant spelling of* Alphonso
Alfred
Alfreda
Algar
Alger
Algernon
Algie (*or* Algy)
Alice (*or* Alys)

Alicia
Alick
Alina
Aline
Alison (*or* Allison)
Alistair (*or* Alasdair, Alastair)
Alix
Allan *variant spelling of* Alan
Allegra
Allen *variant spelling of* Alan
Ally (*or* Allie)
Alma
Alonso (*or* Alonzo)
Aloysia (*or* Aloisia)
Aloysius
Alphonse
Alphonsine
Alphonso (*or* Alfonso)
Alphonsus
Althea
Alun *variant spelling of* Alan
Alured
Alva (*or* Alvah)
Alvar
Alvie
Alvin
Alvina
Alvis
Alwyn
Alys *variant spelling of* Alice
Amabel
Amalia
Amalie
Amanda
Amaryllis
Amata
Amber
Ambrose
Ambrosina
Ambrosine
Ambrosius
Amelia
Amias *variant spelling of* Amyas
Amice
Amicia
Aminta
Amos

Amy

Amy
Amyas (*or* Amias)
Anastasia
Ancel
André
Andrea
Andreas
Andrée
Andrew
Andy
Aneira
Aneurin (*or* Aneirin)
Angel
Angela
Angelica
Angelina
Angeline
Angelique
Angelo
Angharad
Angie
Angus
Anis (*or* Annis, Annice)
Anita
Ann *variant spelling of* Anne
Anna
Annabel (*or* Annabelle)
Annabella
Annalisa
Annaple
Anne (*or* Ann)
Anneliese
Annette
Annice *variant spelling of* Anis
Annie
Annika
Annis
Annora
Anona
Anouska
Ansel (*or* Ansell)
Anselm
Anselma
Anstey
Anstice
Anthea
Anthony (*or* Antony)
Antoine
Antoinette
Anton
Antonia
Antonina
Antonio
Antony *variant spelling of* Anthony
Anwen
Anya
Aphra
Apollonia
Appolina
Appoline
April
Aquila
Arabella
Araminta
Archelaus
Archer
Archibald
Archie (*or* Archy)
Ariadne
Ariane
Arianna
Arlene (*or* Arleen) *variant spellings of* Arline
Arletta
Arlette
Arline (*or* Arlene, Arleen)
Armand
Armin
Armina
Armine
Arnaud
Arnold
Art
Artemas (*or* Artemus)
Artemisia
Arthur
Arthuretta
Arthurina
Arthurine
Artie (*or* Arty)
Asa
Asher
Ashley
Aspasia
Astra
Astrid
Athelstan
Athene
Athol
Auberon
Aubert
Aubrey
Aud
Audra
Audrey
August
Augusta
Augustina
Augustine (*or* Augustin)
Augustus
Aulay
Aurea
Aurelia
Aurelian
Aureola
Aureole
Auriel
Auriol
Aurora
Aurore
Austen
Austin
Ava
Aveline
Averil
Avery
Avis (*or* Avice)
Avril
Axel
Aylmer
Aylwin
Azariah
Bab
Babette
Babs
Baldie
Baldwin
Balthasar (*or* Balthazar)
Barbara (*or* Barbra)
Barbary
Barbie
Barclay *variant spelling of* Berkeley
Bardolph
Barnabas
Barnaby
Barnard
Barnet
Barney
Baron (*or* Barron)
Barrett
Barrington
Barry (*or* Barrie)
Bart
Bartholomew
Bartle
Bartlett (*or* Bartlet)
Basie
Basil
Basilia
Basilie
Basilla

Bastian
Bathsheba
Baubie
Bea (or Bee)
Beata
Beatrice
Beatrix
Beattie (or Beatty)
Beau
Becky
Bedelia
Bedford
Bee variant spelling of Bea
Belinda
Bella
Belle (or Bell, Bel)
Ben
Benedict (or Benedick)
Benedicta
Benet variant spelling of Bennet
Benita
Benito
Benjamin
Benjy
Bennet (or Bennett, Benet)
Benny
Bentley
Berengaria
Berenger
Berenice
Berkeley (or Barclay)
Bernadette
Bernadina
Bernadine
Bernard
Bernardina
Bernardine
Bernhard
Bernice
Bernie (or Berny)
Berry
Bert
Berta
Bertha
Berthold
Bertie
Bertram
Bertrand
Beryl
Bess
Bessie (or Bessy)
Beta
Beth
Bethan

Bethany
Bethel (or Bethell)
Bethia
Betsy
Bette
Bettina
Bettrys
Betty
Beulah
Beverley (or Beverly)
Bevis
Bianca
Biddy
Bill
Billy (or Billie)
Bina
Bing
Birdie
Birgit
Birgitta
Bjorn
Blaine (or Blane)
Blair
Blaise (or Blase)
Blake
Blanche (or Blanch)
Blane variant spelling of Blaine
Blodwen
Blodyn
Blossom
Blythe
Boaz
Bob
Bobby (or Bobbie)
Bonamy
Bonar
Boniface
Bonita
Bonnie (or Bonny)
Boris
Botolph (or Botolf, Botulf)
Boyce
Boyd
Brad
Bradley
Bram
Brandon (or Brandan)
Branwen
Brenda
Brendan
Brent
Brett (or Bret)
Brian (or Bryan)

Brice variant spelling of Bryce
Bride
Bridget (or Brigit, Brigitte)
Bridie
Brighid (or Brigid)
Brigitta
Briony variant spelling of Bryony
Brita
Britannia
Britt
Brock
Broderick
Bronwen (or Bronwyn)
Bruce
Brunetta
Bruno
Bryan variant spelling of Brian
Bryce (or Brice)
Bryn
Bryony (or Briony)
Bud
Burt
Buster
Byron
Cadel (or Cadell)
Caesar
Cai
Caitlin
Caius
Caleb
Calum (or Callum)
Calvin
Cameron
Camilla
Camille
Camillus
Campbell
Candace
Candice
Candida
Candy
Canice
Cara (or Kara)
Caradoc (or Caradog)
Carey variant spelling of Cary
Carina (or Karina)
Carita
Carl (or Karl)
Carla
Carleen (or Carlene)
Carlo

Carlos
Carlotta
Carlton (or Carleton)
Carly
Carmel
Carmela
Carmelita
Carmen
Carol (or Carole)
Carola
Carolina
Caroline
Carolus
Carolyn
Carrie
Carter
Carthach
Carthage
Cary (or Carey)
Caryl
Carys
Casey
Casimir
Caspar
Cass
Cassandra
Cassie
Cath (or Kath)
Catherine (or Katherine, Katharine, Catharine)
Cathleen variant spelling of Kathleen
Cathy (or Kathy)
Catrin
Catriona
Cecil
Cecile
Cecilia
Cecily (or Cecilie)
Cedric (or Cedrych)
Ceinwen
Celeste
Celestina
Celestine
Celia
Celina variant spelling of Selina
Celine
Cerdic
Ceri
Ceridwen
Cerys
Chad
Charis
Charissa

Charity
Charlene
Charles
Charlie (or Charley)
Charlotte
Charlton
Charmaine
Charmian
Chas
Chattie
Chauncey (or Chauncy)
Chay
Cherie (or Sherry, Sherri)
Cherry
Cheryl
Chester
Chloe
Chris
Chrissie (or Chrissy)
Christabel
Christian
Christiana
Christiania
Christie (or Christy)
Christina (or Kristina)
Christine (or Kristine)
Christmas
Christopher
Christy variant spelling of Christie
Chrystal variant spelling of Crystal
Chuck
Cicely
Cilla
Cinderella
Cindy
Cis (or Ciss)
Cissy (or Cissie, Sissy, Sissie)
Claire (or Clare)
Clara
Clarence
Claribel
Clarice
Clarinda
Clarissa
Clark
Clarrie
Claud (or Claude)
Claudette
Claudia
Claudine
Claudius
Clayton

Cledwyn
Clem
Clemence
Clemency
Clement
Clementia
Clementina
Clementine
Cleo
Cleopatra
Cliff
Clifford
Clifton
Clint
Clinton
Clive
Clodagh
Clotilda
Clyde
Colette
Colin
Colina
Colleen
Colley
Colm
Colum
Columba
Columbina
Columbine
Conan
Concepta
Concetta
Conn
Connie
Connor (or Conor)
Conrad
Constance
Constancy
Constant
Constantia
Constantine
Cora
Coral
Coralie
Cordelia
Corinna
Corinne
Cormac
Cornelia
Cornelius
Corney
Cosimo
Cosmo
Courtney (or Courtenay)
Craig

Cressida
Crispian
Crispin
Crystal (*or* Chrystal)
Cuddy (*or* Cuddie)
Curt *variant spelling of* Kurt
Curtis
Cuthbert
Cy
Cynthia
Cyprian
Cyril
Cyrus
Cytherea
Daff *variant spelling of* Daph
Dafydd
Dagmar
Dai
Daisy
Dale
Damaris
Damian (*or* Damien)
Damon
Dan
Dana
Dane
Danette
Daniel
Daniella
Danielle
Danita
Danny
Dante
Danuta
Daph (*or* Daff)
Daphne
Darby (*or* Derby)
Darcy (*or* D'Arcy)
Darlene
Darren
Darryl (*or* Darrell, Daryl, Darrel)
Dave
David
Davida
Davina
Davinia
Davy
Dawn
Dean
Deanna
Deanne
Deb
Debbie
Deborah

Debra
Decima
Decimus
Declan
Dee
Deirdre
Del
Delia
Delilah
Della
Delphine
Delwyn (*or* Delwen)
Delyth
Demelza
Denholm
Denise
Dennie (*or* Denny)
Dennis (*or* Denis, Denys)
Denzil
Derby *variant spelling of* Darby
Derek (*or* Derrick, Deryck, Deryk)
Dermot
Derry
Deryn
Des
Desdemona
Desiree
Desmond
Dewi
Dexter
Diamond
Diana
Diane (*or* Dianne)
Diarmuid (*or* Diarmait)
Dick
Dickie (*or* Dicky)
Dickon
Digby
Diggory
Dillon
Dilys
Dinah
Dion
Dione (*or* Dionne)
Dionysia
Dionysius
Dirk
Dodie
Doll
Dolly
Dolores
Dominic (*or* Dominick)
Dominica

Dominique
Don
Donal
Donald
Donalda
Donaldina
Donna
Donny
Donovan
Dora
Doran
Dorcas
Doreen
Dorette
Doria
Dorian
Dorinda
Doris (*or* Dorice)
Dorita
Dorothea
Dorothy
Dorrie
Dot
Dottie
Doug
Dougal
Dougie (*or* Duggie)
Douglas
Dowsabel
Dreda
Drew
Drogo
Drusilla
Duane (*or* Dwayne)
Dudley
Dugald
Duggie *variant spelling of* Dougie
Duke
Dulce
Dulcibella
Dulcie
Duncan
Dunstan
Durand
Dustin
Dwayne *variant spelling of* Duane
Dwight
Dylan
Dymphna
Dympna
Eamon (*or* Eamonn)
Earl (*or* Erle)

Earnest

Earnest *variant spelling of* Ernest
Eartha
Easter
Eben
Ebenezer
Ed
Eda
Eddie (*or* Eddy)
Eden
Edgar
Edie
Edith
Edmund (*or* Edmond)
Edna
Edom
Edward
Edwin (*or* Edwyn)
Edwina
Effie
Egbert
Egidia
Egidius
Eileen
Eiluned *variant spelling of* Eluned
Eilwen
Eily
Eira
Eirian
Eithne
Elain
Elaine
Eldon
Eldred
Eldreda
Eleanor (*or* Elinor)
Eleanora
Eleazar
Elena
Eleonora
Elfreda (*or* Elfrida)
Eli
Elias
Elihu
Elijah
Elined *variant spelling of* Eluned
Elinor *variant spelling of* Eleanor
Eliot *variant spelling of* Elliott
Elisabeth *variant spelling of* Elizabeth
Elise
Elisha
Elissa
Eliza
Elizabeth (*or* Elisabeth)
Elkanah
Ella
Ellen
Ellery
Ellie
Elliott (*or* Elliot, Eliot)
Ellis
Elma
Elmer
Eloisa
Eloise
Elroy
Elsa
Elsie
Elspeth
Elspie
Elton
Eluned (*or* Elined, Eiluned)
Elvie
Elvin
Elvina
Elvira
Elvis
Elwyn
Emanuel (*or* Emmanuel)
Emanuela (*or* Emmanuela)
Emblem
Emblyn
Emeline *variant spelling of* Emmeline
Emelyn
Emerald
Emery
Emil (*or* Emile)
Emilia
Emily
Emlyn
Emma
Emmanuel *variant spelling of* Emanuel
Emmanuela *variant spelling of* Emanuela
Emmeline (*or* Emeline)
Emmie
Emrys
Ena
Enid
Enoch
Enos
Eoghan
Ephraim
Eppie
Erasmus
Eric (*or* Erik)
Erica (*or* Erika)
Erin
Erle *variant spelling of* Earl
Ermintrude (*or* Ermyntrude)
Ernest (*or* Earnest)
Ernestine
Ernie
Errol
Erwin *variant spelling of* Irwin
Esau
Esme (*or* Esmee)
Esmeralda
Esmond
Essie
Estella
Estelle
Esther
Ethan
Ethel
Ethelbert
Etheldreda
Ethelinda
Ethelred
Ethne
Etta
Ettie (*or* Etty)
Eugene
Eugenia
Eugenie
Eulalia
Eulalie
Eunice
Euphemia
Eustace
Eustacia
Eva
Evadne
Evan
Evangelina
Evangeline
Eve
Eveleen
Evelina
Eveline
Evelyn
Everard
Everild
Evie
Evita

Evonne *variant spelling of* Yvonne
Ewan (*or* Ewen)
Ezekiel
Ezra
Fabian
Fabiana
Faith
Fanny
Farquhar
Farran (*or* Farren, Faron)
Faustina
Fay (*or* Faye)
Feargus *variant spelling of* Fergus
Fedora
Felice
Felicia
Felicity
Felix
Fenella
Feodora
Ferdinand
Fergie
Fergus (*or* Feargus)
Fern
Fernando
Fidel
Fidelia
Fifi
Finlay
Finola
Fiona
Fionnuala (*or* Fionnghuala)
Fitzroy
Flavia
Fletcher
Fleur
Flora
Florence
Floretta
Florette
Florian
Florinda
Florrie
Floss
Flossie
Flower
Floy
Floyd
Fluellen
Flurry
Fortunatus
Fortune
Foster

Franca
Frances (*fem*)
Francesca
Francesco
Francie
Francine
Francis (*masc*)
Francisca
Francisco
Franco
Frank
Frankie
Franklin
Frannie (*or* Franny)
Fraser (*or* Frazer)
Fred
Freda
Freddie (*or* Freddy)
Frederica (*or* Frederika, Fredrica, Fredrika)
Frederick (*or* Frederic, Fredrick, Fredric)
Freya
Frieda
Fulbert
Gabby (*or* Gabbie, Gabi, Gaby)
Gabriel
Gabriella
Gabrielle
Gaenor *variant spelling of* Gaynor
Gail (*or* Gayle, Gale)
Gaius
Gamaliel
Gareth
Garfield
Garnet
Garret (*or* Garrett)
Garrick
Garth
Gary (*or* Garry)
Gaspar
Gavin
Gawain
Gay (*or* Gaye)
Gayle *variant spelling of* Gail
Gaylord
Gaynor (*or* Gaenor)
Gemma (*or* Jemma)
Gene
Genevieve
Genevra *variant spelling of* Ginevra
Geoff (*or* Jeff)

Geoffrey (*or* Jeffrey, Jeffery)
Geordie
George
Georgette
Georgia
Georgiana
Georgie
Georgina
Geraint
Gerald
Geraldine
Gerard (*or* Gerrard)
Gerda
Germaine (*or* Germain)
Gerontius
Gerry (*or* Jerry)
Gershom
Gert
Gertie
Gertrude
Gervase (*or* Gervais)
Gerwyn
Gethin
Ghislaine
Gideon
Gil
Gilbert
Gilberta
Gilbertine
Gilda
Giles (*or* Gyles)
Gill (*or* Jill)
Gillian (*or* Jillian, Gillean)
Gilroy
Gina
Ginette
Ginevra (*or* Genevra)
Ginger
Ginny
Gisela
Giselle
Glad
Gladys
Glen (*or* Glenn)
Glenda
Glenna
Glenys (*or* Glenis)
Gloria
Glyn
Glynis (*or* Glinys)
Godfrey
Godwin
Goldie
Goldwin (*or* Goldwyn)

Gordon

Gordon	Hamlyn	Hester
Grace	Hammond	Hetty
Gracie	Hamnet	Heulwen
Graham (*or* Graeme, Grahame)	Hamo	Hew *variant spelling of* Hugh
	Hamon	Hezekiah
Grainne	Hank	Hieronymus
Grania	Hannah	Hilary (*or* Hillary)
Grant	Hannibal	Hilda (*or* Hylda)
Granville	Hans	Hildebrand
Greg (*or* Gregg)	Hardy	Hildegard (*or* Hildegarde)
Gregor	Harley	Hillary *variant spelling of* Hilary
Gregory	Harold	
Grenville	Harriet (*or* Harriette)	Hippolyta
Greta	Harriot	Hippolytus
Gretchen	Harrison	Hiram
Gretel	Harry	Hob
Griffith	Hartley	Hobart
Griselda	Harvey	Holden
Grizel (*or* Grizzel)	Hattie (*or* Hatty)	Holly
Grover	Haydn (*or* Haydon, Hayden)	Homer
Guendolen *variant spelling of* Gwendoline	Hayley	Honor (*or* Honour)
	Hazel	Honora
Guido	Heath	Honoria
Guinevere	Heather	Hope
Gulielma	Hebe	Horace
Gunter (*or* Gunther)	Heber	Horatia
Gus	Hector	Horatio
Gussie	Hedda	Horry
Gusta	Hedley	Hortense
Gustave (*or* Gustav, Gustaf)	Hedwig	Hortensia
Gustavus	Hedy	Howard
Guy	Heidi	Howell (*or* Howel) *variant spellings of* Hywel
Gwen	Helen	
Gwenda	Helena	Hubert
Gwendoline (*or* Gwendolyn, Gwendolen, Guendolen)	Helene	Hugh (*or* Huw, Hew)
	Helewise	Hughie (*or* Huey)
Gwenllian	Helga	Hugo
Gwilym (*or* Gwylim)	Héloïse	Huldah, Hulda
Gwladys	Hennie (*or* Henny)	Humbert
Gwyn	Henri	Humph
Gwyneth (*or* Gwynneth, Gwynedd)	Henrietta	Humphrey
	Henriette	Huw *variant spelling of* Hugh
Gwynfor	Henry	Hyacinth
Gyles *variant spelling of* Giles	Hephzibah	Hyacintha
	Hepsie (*or* Hepsey, Hepsy)	Hylda *variant spelling of* Hilda
Hadassah	Hepzibah	
Hadrian	Herb	Hyman
Hagar	Herbert	Hymie
Haidee	Herbie	Hypatia
Hal	Hereward	Hywel (*or* Howell, Howel)
Halcyon	Herman (*or* Hermann)	Iago
Ham	Hermia	Ian (*or* Iain)
Hamilton	Hermione	Ianthe
Hamish	Hervé	Ibbie (*or* Ibby)
Hamlet	Hervey	Ichabod

Ida
Idonea
Idris
Ifor
Ignatius
Igor
Ike
Ilma
Ilona
Ilse
Immy
Imogen
Ina
Inez
Inga
Inge
Ingeborg
Ingram
Ingrid
Ingvar
Inigo
Iola
Iolanthe
Iolo
Iona
Iorwerth
Ira
Irene
Iris
Irma
Irvin (*or* Irvine)
Irving
Irwin (*or* Erwin)
Isa
Isaac (*or* Izaak)
Isabel (*or* Isabelle)
Isabella
Isadora
Isaiah
Iseult
Ishbel
Isidora
Isidore
Isla
Ismay
Isobel
Isolda
Isolde
Israel
Issy (*or* Izzy)
Ita
Ithel
Ivah
Ivan
Ives

Ivo
Ivor
Ivy
Izaak *variant spelling of* Isaac
Izzy *variant spelling of* Issy
Jabez
Jacinta
Jacinth
Jack
Jackie (*or* Jacky, Jacqui)
Jacob
Jacoba
Jacobina
Jacqueline (*or* Jacquelyn)
Jacques
Jacquetta
Jacqui *variant spelling of* Jackie
Jade
Jael
Jago
Jake
James
Jamesina
Jamie
Jan
Jane (*or* Jayne)
Janet
Janetta
Janette
Janice (*or* Janis)
Janie (*or* Janey)
Janine
Japheth
Jarrod (*or* Jarred, Jared)
Jarvis
Jasmine
Jason
Jasper
Jay
Jayne *variant spelling of* Jane
Jean
Jeanette (*or* Jeannette)
Jeanne
Jeannie (*or* Jeanie)
Jeannine
Jed
Jedidiah
Jeff *variant spelling of* Geoff
Jefferson
Jeffrey (*or* Jeffery) *variant spellings of* Geoffrey
Jehane

Jem
Jemima
Jemma *variant spelling of* Gemma
Jemmy
Jenna
Jennifer (*or* Jenifer)
Jenny (*or* Jennie)
Jephthah
Jeremiah
Jeremias
Jeremy
Jermaine
Jerome
Jerry *variant spelling of* Gerry
Jess
Jessamine (*or* Jessamyn)
Jesse
Jessica
Jessie
Jesus
Jethro
Jewel
Jill *variant spelling of* Gill
Jillian *variant spelling of* Gillian
Jim
Jimmy
Jinny
Jo
Joachim
Joan
Joanna
Joanne
Job
Jocasta
Jocelyn (*or* Joscelin)
Jock
Jodie (*or* Jodi, Jody)
Joe
Joel
Joey
Johanna
Johannes
John (*or* Jon)
Johnny (*or* Johnnie)
Jolene (*or* Joleen)
Jolyon
Jonah
Jonas
Jonathan
Jonquil
Jordan

Joscelin

Joscelin *variant spelling of* Jocelyn
José
Joseph
Josepha
Josephine
Josette
Josh
Joshua
Josiah
Josias
Josie
Joss
Jotham
Joy
Joyce
Juan
Juanita
Judah
Judas
Judd
Jude
Judith
Judoc
Judy (*or* Judi)
Jules
Julia
Julian
Juliana
Julianne
Julie
Julienne
Juliet (*or* Juliette)
Julitta
Julius
June
Junior
Juno
Justin
Justina
Justine
Kane
Kara *variant spelling of* Cara
Karel
Karen
Karin
Karina *variant spelling of* Carina
Karl *variant spelling of* Carl
Karol
Kate
Kath *variant spelling of* Cath
Katherine (*or* Katharine) *variant spellings of* Catherine
Kathleen (*or* Cathleen)
Kathryn
Kathy *variant spelling of* Cathy
Katie (*or* Katy)
Katrina
Katrine
Kay
Keeley
Keir
Keith
Kelda
Kelly (*or* Kellie)
Kelvin
Ken
Kendal (*or* Kendall)
Kendra
Kenelm
Kenneth
Kenny
Kenrick
Kent
Kentigern
Kenton
Keren
Kerenhappuch
Kerry (*or* Kerrie, Kerri, Keri)
Kester
Keturah
Kevin
Keziah (*or* Kezia)
Kieran
Kim
Kimball
Kimberly (*or* Kimberley)
Kinborough
King
Kingsley
Kirby
Kirk
Kirsten
Kirsty
Kit
Kitty
Kris
Kristen (*or* Kristin)
Kristina *variant spelling of* Christina
Kristine *variant spelling of* Christine
Kurt (*or* Curt)
Kyle
Kylie
Laban
Lachlan
Laetitia (*or* Letitia)
Lalage
Lambert
Lana
Lance
Lancelot
Lanty
Laraine (*or* Larraine)
Larissa
Larry
Lars
Launce
Launcelot
Laura (*or* Lora)
Lauraine
Laureen (*or* Loreen)
Laurel
Lauren
Laurence (*or* Lawrence)
Laurencia (*or* Laurentia)
Lauretta *variant spelling of* Loretta
Laurette (*or* Lorette)
Laurie (*or* Lauri, Lori)
Laurina
Laurinda *variant spelling of* Lorinda
Laverne
Lavina (*or* Lavena)
Lavinia
Lawrence *variant spelling of* Laurence
Lawrie
Layton *variant spelling of* Leighton
Lazarus
Leah
Leander
Leanne (*or* Lianne)
Lee (*or* Leigh)
Leighton (*or* Layton)
Leila (*or* Leilah, Lela)
Lelia
Lemmy
Lemuel
Lena
Lennox
Lenny (*or* Lennie)
Lenore
Leo
Leofric
Leoline
Leon
Leona

Leonard
Leonie
Leonora
Leopold
Leroy
Lesley (*fem*)
Leslie (*masc or fem*)
Lester
Leta
Letitia (*or* **Laetitia**)
Lettice
Letty (*or* **Lettie**)
Levi
Lew
Lewis
Liam
Liana
Lianne *variant spelling of* **Leanne**
Libby
Liddy
Liesl (*or* **Liesel**)
Lila
Lilac
Lili
Lilian (*or* **Lillian**)
Lilias (*or* **Lillias**)
Lilith
Lilla (*or* **Lillah**)
Lily (*or* **Lillie**)
Lina
Lincoln
Linda (*or* **Lynda**)
Lindsay (*masc or fem*)
Lindsey (*fem*)
Lindy
Linette *variant spelling of* **Lynette**
Linnet
Lionel
Lisa
Lisbeth *variant spelling of* **Lizbeth**
Lise
Lisette
Lita
Liz
Liza
Lizanne
Lizbeth (*or* **Lisbeth**)
Lizzie (*or* **Lizzy**)
Llewellyn (*or* **Llewelyn**)
Llinos
Lloyd
Lois

Lola
Lolita
Lolly
Lonnie
Lora *variant spelling of* **Laura**
Loraine *variant spelling of* **Lorraine**
Loreen *variant spelling of* **Laureen**
Loren (*or* **Lorin**)
Lorenzo
Loretta (*or* **Lauretta**)
Lorette *variant spelling of* **Laurette**
Lori *variant spelling of* **Laurie**
Lorin
Lorinda (*or* **Laurinda**)
Lorna
Lorne (*or* **Lorn**)
Lorraine (*or* **Loraine**)
Lottie (*or* **Lotty**)
Lou
Louella (*or* **Luella**)
Louie
Louis
Louisa
Louise
Loveday
Lovell
Lowell
Lucas
Lucasta
Luce
Lucetta
Lucette
Lucia
Lucian (*or* **Lucien**)
Luciana
Lucie
Lucienne
Lucilla
Lucille
Lucina
Lucinda
Lucius
Lucky
Lucrece
Lucretia
Lucrezia
Lucy
Ludo
Ludovic

Luella *variant spelling of* **Louella**
Luke
Lulu
Luther
Lydia
Lyle
Lyn *variant spelling of* **Lynn**
Lynda *variant spelling of* **Linda**
Lyndon
Lynette (*or* **Lynnette**, **Linette**)
Lynn (*or* **Lynne**, **Lyn**)
Lynsey
Lyra
Lyulf (*or* **Lyulph**)
Mabel (*or* **Mable**)
Mabella
Mabelle
Maddie (*or* **Maddy**)
Madeleine (*or* **Madeline**)
Madelina
Madge
Madoc
Mae
Maeve (*or* **Meave**)
Magda
Magdalena
Magdalene (*or* **Magdalen**)
Maggie
Magnolia
Magnus
Mahala (*or* **Mahalah**)
Mahalia
Maidie
Mair
Maire
Mairin
Maisie
Malachi (*or* **Malachy**)
Malcolm
Malise
Mallory (*or* **Malory**)
Malvin
Malvina
Mamie
Manasseh
Manasses
Mandy
Manfred
Manley
Manny
Mansel (*or* **Mansell**)
Manuel

Manuela

Manuela
Manus
Mara (or Marah)
Marc
Marcel
Marcella
Marcelle
Marcellus
Marcia
Marcie (or Marcy)
Marco
Marcus
Margaret
Margareta (or Margaretta)
Margarita (or Marguerita)
Marge
Margery variant spelling of
 Marjorie
Margie
Margot (or Margo)
Marguerite
Maria
Mariabella
Mariam (or Mariamne)
Marian variant spelling of
 Marion
Marianne
Marie
Mariel
Marietta (or Mariette)
Marigold
Marilyn
Marina
Mario
Marion (or Marian)
Marisa (or Marissa)
Marita
Marius
Marjorie (or Margery)
Mark
Marla
Marlene
Marlin (or Marlyn)
Marmaduke
Marnie (or Marni)
Marsha
Marshall (or Marshal)
Marta
Martha
Marti (or Martie)
Martin (or Martyn)
Martina
Martine
Marty
Marvin (or Marvyn)

Mary
Matilda
Matt (or Mat)
Matthew
Matthias
Mattie (or Matty)
Maud (or Maude)
Maudie
Maura variant spelling of
 Moira
Maureen
Maurice (or Morris)
Mavis
Max
Maximilian
Maxine
Maxwell
May
Maynard
Meave variant spelling of
 Maeve
Meg
Megan (or Meghan)
Meggie (or Meggy)
Mehala (or Mehalah,
 Mehalia)
Mehetabel (or Mehitabel)
Meirion (or Merrion)
Mel
Melania
Melanie (or Melloney)
Melba
Melicent (or Melisent)
Melinda
Meliora
Mélisande
Melissa
Melody (or Melodie)
Melva
Melville
Melvin (or Melvyn)
Melvina
Mercedes
Mercia
Mercy
Meredith
Meriel
Merilyn (or Merrilyn)
Merle
Merlin
Merrion variant spelling of
 Meirion
Merry
Merton
Merv

Mervyn (or Mervin)
Meryl
Meta
Mia
Micah
Michael
Michaela
Michelle (or Michele)
Mick
Mickey (or Micky)
Mignon
Mike
Milborough
Milburn
Mildred
Miles (or Myles)
Millicent
Millie (or Milly)
Milo
Milton
Mima
Mimi
Mina
Minerva
Minna
Minnie
Minty
Mira variant spelling of
 Myra
Mirabel (or Mirabelle)
Mirabella
Miranda
Miriam
Mitch
Mitchell
Mitzi
Modesty
Moira (or Moyra, Maura)
Moll
Molly
Mona
Monica
Monique
Montague (or Montagu)
Montgomery
Monty (or Monte)
Morag
Moray
Mordecai
Morgan
Morna
Morris variant spelling of
 Maurice
Mort
Mortimer

Morty
Morwenna
Moses
Moshe
Moss
Moyna
Moyra *variant spelling of* Moira
Muir
Mungo
Murdoch
Muriel
Murray
Murtagh
Myfanwy
Myles *variant spelling of* Miles
Myra (*or* Mira)
Myrna
Myron
Myrtilla
Myrtle
Mysie
Nada
Nadia
Nadine
Nahum
Nan
Nance
Nancy
Nanette
Nanny
Naomi
Napoleon
Narcissus
Nat
Natalia
Natalie
Natasha
Nathan
Nathaniel (*or* Nathanael)
Neal *variant spelling of* Neil
Ned
Neddie (*or* Neddy)
Nehemiah
Neil (*or* Neill, Neal, Niall)
Nell
Nellie (*or* Nelly)
Nelson
Nerina
Nerissa
Nerys
Nessa
Nessie
Nest

Nesta
Netta
Nettie
Neva
Neville (*or* Nevil)
Newton
Niall *variant spelling of* Neil
Nichola *variant spelling of* Nicola
Nicholas (*or* Nicolas)
Nick
Nicky (*or* Nikki)
Nicodemus
Nicol
Nicola (*or* Nichola)
Nicolas *variant spelling of* Nicholas
Nicole
Nicolette
Nigel
Nikki *variant spelling of* Nicky
Nina
Ninette
Ninian
Nita
Noah
Noel (*or* Nowell)
Noeleen (*or* Noeline)
Noelle (*or* Noele)
Nola
Nolan
Nona
Nora (*or* Norah)
Norbert
Noreen
Norm
Norma
Norman
Norris
Norton
Nova
Nowell *variant spelling of* Noel
Nuala
Nye
Nyree
Obadiah
Oberon
Octavia
Octavian
Octavius
Odette
Odile
Odilia

Odo
Ogden
Olaf
Olave (*or* Olav)
Olga
Oliff
Oliva
Olive
Oliver
Olivet
Olivia
Olivier
Ollie
Olwen (*or* Olwyn)
Olympia
Omar
Ona
Onuphrius
Oonagh (*or* Oona)
Opal
Ophelia
Oriana
Oriel
Orlando
Orrell
Orson
Orval
Orville
Osbert
Osborn (*or* Osborne)
Oscar
Osmond (*or* Osmund)
Ossy (*or* Ossie)
Oswald
Oswin
Otho
Otis
Ottilia
Ottilie
Otto
Owen (*or* Owain)
Owena
Ozzy (*or* Ozzie)
Pablo
Paddy
Padraig
Palmer
Pam
Pamela
Pamelia
Pandora
Pansy
Paolo
Parker
Parnel (*or* Parnell)

Parry

Parry
Parthenia
Pascal
Pascale
Pascoe
Pat
Patience
Patricia
Patrick
Patsy
Patti (*or* Patty, Pattie)
Paul
Paula
Paulette
Pauline
Peace
Pearl
Pearlie
Pedro
Peg
Peggy
Pelham
Penelope
Penny
Pepin
Pepita
Perce
Percival (*or* Perceval)
Percy
Perdita
Peregrine
Peronel
Perpetua
Perry
Peta
Pete
Peter
Petra
Petrina
Petronella
Petronilla
Petula
Phebe *variant spelling of* Phoebe
Phemie
Phil
Philadelphia
Philemon
Philibert
Philip (*or* Phillip)
Philippa (*or* Phillipa, Phillippa)
Phillida *variant spelling of* Phyllida

Phillis *variant spelling of* Phyllis
Philomena
Phineas (*or* Phinehas)
Phoebe (*or* Phebe)
Phyllida (*or* Phillida)
Phyllis (*or* Phillis)
Pia
Pierre
Piers
Pip
Pippa
Piran
Pleasance
Poldie
Poll
Polly
Pollyanna
Poppy
Portia
Preston
Primrose
Prince
Prisca
Priscilla
Prissy
Pru (*or* Prue)
Prudence
Prunella
Queena
Queenie (*or* Queeny)
Quentin (*or* Quintin)
Quincy
Quinn
Quintin *variant spelling of* Quentin
Rab
Rabbie
Rachel (*or* Rachael)
Radcliff (*or* Radcliffe)
Rae
Raelene
Rafael *variant spelling of* Raphael
Rafaela *variant spelling of* Raphaela
Rafe
Raina
Raine
Rainer *variant spelling of* Rayner
Ralph
Ramon
Ramona
Ramsay (*or* Ramsey)

Ranald
Randall (*or* Randal)
Randolph
Randy
Raoul
Raphael (*or* Rafael)
Raphaela (*or* Rafaela)
Ray
Raymond (*or* Raymund)
Raymonde
Rayner (*or* Raynor, Rainer)
Rebecca (*or* Rebekah)
Redvers
Reg
Reggie
Regina
Reginald
Reine
Rena (*or* Rina)
Renata
René (*masc*)
Renée (*fem*)
Renie (*or* Rene)
Reuben
Rex
Reynard
Reynold
Rhea (*or* Ria)
Rhiannon
Rhoda
Rhona
Rhonda
Rhonwen
Rhys
Ria *variant spelling of* Rhea
Rica (*or* Rika)
Ricarda
Ricardo
Rich
Richard
Richenda
Richie
Richmal
Rick
Ricky (*or* Ricki, Rikki)
Rika *variant spelling of* Rica
Rina *variant spelling of* Rena
Rita
Roald
Rob
Robbie
Robert
Roberta
Robin
Robina

Robyn
Rochelle
Rod
Roddy
Roderick
Rodge
Rodger *variant spelling of* Roger
Rodney
Rodolph
Rodrigo
Roger (*or* Rodger)
Roisin
Roland (*or* Rowland)
Rolf (*or* Rolph)
Rollo
Rolly
Rolph *variant spelling of* Rolf
Roly
Roma
Romaine
Ron
Rona
Ronald
Ronalda
Ronna
Ronnette
Ronnie
Rory
Ros
Rosa
Rosabel (*or* Rosabelle)
Rosabella
Rosaleen
Rosalia
Rosalie
Rosalind
Rosalinda
Rosaline (*or* Rosalyn)
Rosamund (*or* Rosamond)
Rosanna (*or* Roseanna)
Rosanne (*or* Roseann, Roseanne)
Rose
Roseline (*or* Roselyn)
Rosemary (*or* Rosemarie)
Rosetta
Rosie
Rosina
Rosita
Roslyn (*or* Rosslyn)
Ross
Rowan
Rowena

Rowland *variant spelling of* Roland
Roxana
Roxane (*or* Roxanne)
Roxanna
Roxy
Roy
Royal
Royston
Rubina
Ruby
Rudolph (*or* Rudolf)
Rudy (*or* Rudi)
Rufus
Rupert
Ruperta
Russ
Russell (*or* Russel)
Ruth
Ruthie
Ryan
Sabina
Sabrina
Sacha
Sacheverell
Sadie
Saffron
Sal
Salamon
Salena (*or* Salina)
Sally
Salome
Salvador
Salvatore
Sam
Samantha
Sammy
Samson (*or* Sampson)
Samuel
Sanchia
Sandra
Sandy (*or* Sandie)
Sapphira
Sapphire
Sarah (*or* Sara, Sarra)
Sarai
Saranna
Sarina
Sarita
Sarra *variant spelling of* Sarah
Saul
Saxon
Scarlett (*or* Scarlet)
Scott

Seamus (*or* Shamus)
Sean (*or* Shaun, Shawn)
Seb
Sebastian
Sefton
Selby
Selina (*or* Selena, Celina)
Selma
Selwyn
Senga
Septima
Septimus
Seraphina
Serena
Serge
Sergei
Sergio
Sergius
Seth
Seumas
Seward
Sextus
Seymour
Shamus *variant spelling of* Seamus
Shane
Shani
Shannon
Shari
Sharon (*or* Sharron)
Shaun *variant spelling of* Sean
Shauna
Shaw
Shawn *variant spelling of* Sean
Sheba
Sheena (*or* Shena)
Sheila (*or* Shelagh, Sheelagh, Sheilah)
Sheldon
Shelley (*or* Shelly)
Shem
Shena *variant spelling of* Sheena
Sheridan
Sherry (*or* Sherri) *variant spellings of* Cherie
Sheryl
Shirl
Shirley
Sholto
Shona
Shushana (*or* Shushanna)
Sian

Sibbie

Sibbie (*or* Sibby)
Sibella
Sibilla
Sibyl
Sibylla
Sid (*or* Syd)
Sidney (*or* Sydney)
Sidonia
Sidony (*or* Sidonie)
Siegfried
Sigismund
Sigmund
Silas
Síle
Silvana
Silvanus (*or* Sylvanus)
Silvester
Silvia
Sim
Simeon
Simon
Simona
Simone
Sinclair
Sìne
Sinead
Siobhan
Sisley
Sissy (*or* Sissie) *variant spellings of* Cissy
Solly
Solomon
Sonia (*or* Sonya, Sonja)
Sophia
Sophie (*or* Sophy)
Sophronia
Sorcha
Spencer
Stacey (*or* Stacy)
Stafford
Stan
Stanford
Stanislas (*or* Stanislaus)
Stanley
Steenie
Stella
Stephanie (*or* Stefanie)
Stephen (*or* Steven)
Steve
Stevie
Stewart *variant spelling of* Stuart
Stirling
St John
Stuart (*or* Stewart)

Sue
Sukey
Susan
Susannah (*or* Susanna, Suzanna)
Susie (*or* Suzy)
Suzanne (*or* Susanne)
Suzette
Suzy
Swithin
Sybella
Sybil (*or* Sibyl)
Sybilla
Syd *variant spelling of* Sid
Sydney *variant spelling of* Sidney
Sylvanus *variant spelling of* Silvanus
Sylvester (*or* Silvester)
Sylvia (*or* Silvia)
Sylvie
Tabitha
Tacey (*or* Tacy)
Taffy
Talbot
Taliesin
Talitha
Tallulah
Tam
Tamar
Tamara
Tamasine
Tammy
Tamsin
Tancred
Tania *variant spelling of* Tanya
Tanith
Tansy
Tanya (*or* Tania)
Tara
Tarquin
Tatiana
Taylor
Ted
Teddy (*or* Teddie)
Tegan
Tegwen
Temperance
Terence (*or* Terrence)
Teresa (*or* Theresa)
Terry (*or* Terri)
Tertius
Tess
Tessa

Tessie
Tetty
Tex
Thaddeus
Thea
Thekla (*or* Thecla)
Thelma
Theo
Theobald
Theodora
Theodore
Theodoric
Theodosia
Theophania
Theophila
Theophilus
Theresa *variant spelling of* Teresa
Thérèse
Theresia
Thirza (*or* Thirsa)
Thom
Thomas
Thomasin
Thomasina
Thomasine
Thora
Thorley
Thornton
Thurstan (*or* Thurston)
Thyra
Tibby
Tiffany
Tilda
Tilly
Tim
Timmy
Timothea
Timothy
Tina
Tirzah
Tisha
Titus
Tobias
Toby
Todd
Tolly
Tom
Tommy
Toni
Tonia (*or* Tonya)
Tony
Topsy
Torquil
Totty

Tracy (*or* Tracey)
Travers
Travis
Trevor (*or* Trefor)
Tricia (*or* Trisha)
Trina
Trissie
Tristan
Tristram
Trix
Trixie
Troy
Trudy (*or* Trudie, Trudi)
Tryphena
Tudor
Turlough
Tybalt
Tyra
Tyrone
Ulric
Ulrica
Ulysses
Una
Unity
Upton
Urban
Uriah
Ursula
Val
Valda
Valentina
Valentine
Valeria
Valerie
Vanda
Vanessa
Vashti
Vaughan (*or* Vaughn)
Velda
Velma
Venetia
Venus
Vera
Vere
Verena
Verity
Verna
Vernon
Verona
Veronica
Véronique
Vic (*or* Vick)
Vicky (*or* Vicki, Vickie, Vikki)
Victor

Victoria
Victorine
Vida
Vilma
Vin
Vina
Vince
Vincent
Vincentia
Vinnie (*or* Vinny)
Vinny
Viola
Violet
Violetta
Violette
Virgil
Virginia
Vita
Vitus
Viv
Viva
Vivia
Vivian (*or* Vivien, Vyvyan)
Viviana
Vivienne
Wade
Wal
Walburga
Waldo
Wallace (*or* Wallis)
Wally
Walt
Walter
Wanda
Ward
Warner
Warren
Warwick
Washington
Wat
Wayne
Wenda
Wendell
Wendy
Wesley
Wilbert
Wilbur
Wilf
Wilfred (*or* Wilfrid)
Wilfrida (*or* Wilfreda)
Wilhelmina
Will
Willa
Willard
William

Williamina
Willie (*or* Willy)
Willis
Willoughby
Wilma
Wilmer
Wilmot
Win
Windsor
Winfred (*or* Winfrid)
Winifred (*or* Winnifred, Winefred)
Winnie
Winston
Winthrop
Woodrow
Wyatt
Wybert
Wyndham
Wynford
Wynn (*or* Wynne)
Wystan
Xanthe
Xavier
Xenia
Yasmin
Yehudi
Yolanda
Yolande
Yves
Yvette
Yvonne (*or* Evonne)
Zacchaeus
Zachariah
Zacharias
Zachary
Zak (*or* Zack)
Zana
Zandra
Zane
Zara
Zechariah
Zedekiah
Zelda
Zelma
Zena
Zenobia
Zephaniah
Zillah
Zinnia
Zita
Zoë (*or* Zoe)
Zola
Zora (*or* Zorah)
Zuleika

Biographical Names

Aalto, Alvar
Aaltonen, Wäinö
Abbas
Abbas, Ferhat
Abd Allah (*known as* the Khalifa)
'Abd al-Malik ibn Marwan
'Abd ar-Rahman III an-Nasir
Abdelkader
Abdulhamid
Abdullah
Abdul Rahman, Tunku
Abel, Sir Frederick Augustus
Abel, Niels Henrik
Abelard, Peter
Abercrombie, Sir (Leslie) Patrick
Abercromby, Sir Ralph
Aberdeen, George Hamilton-Gordon, 4th Earl of
Absalom son of King David
Absalon 12th-century Danish statesman
Abu al-Wafa
Abu Bakar sultan of Johore
Abu Bakr first caliph
Abu Hanifah
Abu Nuwas
Accius, Lucius
Accoramboni, Vittoria
Achard, Franz Karl
Achebe, Chinua
Acheson, Dean (Gooderham)
Acton, John Emerich Edward Dalberg-Acton, 1st Baron
Adalbert
Adam, Adolphe-Charles
Adam, James
Adam, Robert
Adam, William
Adamnan, St
Adamov, Arthur
Adams, Charles Francis
Adams, Henry

Adams, John
Adams, John Couch
Adams, John Quincy
Adams, Richard
Adams, Samuel
Adamson, Robert
Addington, Henry, 1st Viscount Sidmouth
Addinsell, Richard
Addison, Joseph
Addison, Thomas
Adenauer, Konrad
Ader, Clément
Adler, Alfred
Adler, Felix
Adler, Larry
Adrian, Edgar Douglas, 1st Baron
Aelfric
Aeneas Silvius
Aeschines
Aeschylus
Aesop
Aetius, Flavius
Afghani, Jamal ad-Din al-
Aga Khan
Agassiz, Alexander
Agassiz, Jean Louis Rodolphe
Agathocles
Agee, James
Agesilaus
Agha Mohammad Khan
Agnesi, Maria Gaetana
Agnew, Spiro T(heodore)
Agnon, Shmuel Yosef
Agostini, Giacomo
Agricola, Georgius
Agricola, Gnaeus Julius
Agricola, Johann
Agrippa, Marcus Vipsanius
Agrippina
Ahad Ha'am
Ahmad Khan, Sir Sayyid
Ahmad Shah Durrani
Ahmed

Ahmose
Aiken, Howard Hathaway
Ailred of Rievaulx, St
Ainsworth, W(illiam) Harrison
Airy, Sir George Biddell
Aistulf
Akbar
Akhenaton (*or* Ikhnaton)
Akhmatova
Akiba ben Joseph
Alain-Fournier
Alanbrooke, Alan Francis Brooke, 1st Viscount
Alarcón, Pedro Antonio de
Alarcón y Mendoza, Juan Ruiz de
Alba, Fernando Alvarez de Toledo, Duke of
Albee, Edward
Albéniz, Isaac Manuel Francisco
Alberoni, Giulio
Albers, Josef
Alberti, Leon Battista
Alberti, Raphael
Albertus Magnus, St
Albinoni, Tomaso
Alboin
Albuquerque, Alfonso de
Alcaeus
Alcibiades
Alcmacon
Alcock, Sir John (William)
Alcoforado, Marianna
Alcott, Louisa May
Alcuin
Aldanov, Mark
Aldhelm, St
Aldington, Richard
Aldiss, Brian W(ilson)
Aldrich, Thomas Bailey
Aldridge, Ira Frederick
Alegría, Ciro
Alekhine, Alexander
Alemán, Mateo

Alexander

Alexander, Sir William, 1st Earl of Stirling
Alexander of Tunis, Harold, 1st Earl
Alexius Comnenus
al-Farabi, Mohammed ibn Tarkhan
Alfieri, Vittorio, Count
Alfonso Spanish king
Alfvén, Hannes Olof Gösta
Algirdas
Algren, Nelson
Ali
Ali, Muhammad
Ali Pasa, Mehmed Emin
Alkan, Charles Henri Valentin
al-Khwarizmi, Muhammed ibn Musa
Al-Kindi, Abu Yusuf Ya'qub ibn Ishaq
Allbutt, Sir Thomas Clifford
Allegri, Gregorio
Allen, Ethan
Allen, William, Cardinal
Allen, Woody
Allenby, Edmund Henry Hynman, 1st Viscount
Allende (Gossens), Salvador
Alleyn, Edward
Allingham, Margery
Allston, Washington
Alma-Tadema, Sir Lawrence
Almeida, Francisco de
Alp Arslan
Alphege, St
Altdorfer, Albrecht
Althusius, Johannes
Altichiero
Alvarado, Pedro de
Alvarez, Luis Walter
Álvarez Quintero, Joaquin
Álvarez Quintero, Serafin
Alyattes
Alypius
Amadeus the Peaceful
Amalasuntha
Amalia, Anna
Amanollah Khan
Amati, Andrea
Amati, Antonio
Amati, Girolamo
Amati, Nicolò
Ambartsumian, Viktor A(mazaspovich)
Ambler, Eric
Amenemhet
Amenhotep
Amherst, Jeffrey, Baron
Amici, Giovanni Battista
Amiel, Henri Frédéric
Amin Dada, Idi
Amis, Kingsley
Amis, Martin
Ammanati, Bartolommeo
Ampère, André Marie
Amr ibn al-As
Amundsen, Roald
Amyot, Jacques
Anacreon
Ananda
Anastasius
Anaxagoras
Anaximander
Anaximenes
Anchieta, José de
Andersen, Hans Christian
Anderson, Carl David
Anderson, Elizabeth Garrett
Anderson, John, 1st Viscount Waverley
Anderson, Sherwood
Andrássy, Gyula, Count
André, John
Andrea del Sarto
Andrewes, Lancelot
Andrić, Ivo
Andropov, Yuri Vladimirovich
Aneirin
Angelico, Fra
Angell, Sir Norman
Anglesey, Henry William Paget, 1st Marquess of
Angoulême, Charles de Valois, Duc d'
Angoulême, Margaret of
Ångström, Anders Jonas
Ankhesenamen
An Lu Shan
Annigoni, Pietro
Anouilh, Jean

540

Ansbach, Caroline of
Anselm of Canterbury, St
Ansermet, Ernest
Ansgar, St
Anson, George Anson, Baron
Antelami, Benedetto
Antenor
Antheil, George
Antigonus
Antiochus
Antipas, Herod
Antipater
Antiphon
Antisthenes
Antonello da Messina
Antonescu, Ion
Antoninus Pius
Antonioni, Michelangelo
Anville, Jean-Baptiste Bourguignon d'
Anzengruber, Ludwig
Apelles
Aphraates
Apollinaire, Guillaume
Apollonius
Appert, Nicolas
Apuleius, Lucius
Aquaviva, Claudio
Aquinas, St Thomas
Arafat, Yassir
Arago, (Dominique) François (Jean)
Aragon, Louis
Arakcheev, Aleksei Andreevich, Count
Aram, Eugene
Arany, János
Arbuthnot, John
Arc, St Joan of
Archer, Frederick Scott
Archer, Thomas
Archer, William
Archilochus
Archimedes
Archipenko, Alexander
Archytas
Arcimboldo, Giuseppe
Ardashir
Arduin
Aretino, Pietro
Argyll, Archibald Campbell, 1st Marquess of

Arimathea, St Joseph of
Ariosto, Ludovico
Aristagoras
Aristarchus
Aristides
Aristippus
Aristophanes
Aristotle
Arius
Arkwright, Sir Richard
Arlington, Henry
  Bennet, 1st Earl of
Arminius
Arminius, Jacobus
Armstrong, Edwin
  Howard
Armstrong, Louis
Armstrong, William
  George, Baron
Arnauld, Antoine
Arne, Thomas Augustine
Arnold, Benedict
Arnold, Malcolm
Arnold, Matthew
Arnold, Thomas
Arp, Jean (Hans)
Árpád
Arrabal, Fernando
Arrau, Claudio
Arrhenius, Svante
  August
Arrian
Arrowsmith, Aaron
Arrowsmith, John
Arsinoe
Artaud, Antonin
Artaxerxes
Artevelde, Jacob van
Arthur, Chester A(lan)
Artigas, José Gervasio
Arundel, Thomas
Asch, Sholem
Ascham, Roger
Ashcroft, Dame Peggy
Ashe, Arthur (Robert)
Ashkenazy, Vladimir
Ashley Cooper, Anthony
Ashton, Sir Frederick
  (William Mallandaine)
Ashurbanipal
Ashurnasirpal
Asimov, Isaac
Aske, Robert
Asoka
Asquith, Anthony

Asquith, Herbert Henry,
  1st Earl of Oxford
Asquith, Margot
Assad, Hafiz al-
Asser
Assisi, St Francis of
Astaire, Fred
Astbury, John
Aston, Francis William
Astor, John Jacob
Astor, Nancy Witcher,
  Viscountess
Astor, Waldorf, 2nd
  Viscount
Asturias, Miguel Ángel
Atahuallpa
Atatürk, Kemal
Atget, (Jean) Eugène
  (Auguste)
Athanasius, St
Athelstan
Athenagoras
Athlone, Alexander
  Cambridge, 1st Earl of
Attalus Soter
Attenborough, Sir David
Attenborough, Sir
  Richard
Atterdag, Valdemar
Attila
Attlee, Clement
  (Richard), 1st Earl
Auber, Daniel François
  Esprit
Aubrey, John
Aubusson, Pierre d'
Auchinleck, Sir Claude
Auckland, George Eden,
  Earl of
Auden, W(ystan) H(ugh)
Audubon, John James
Augereau, Pierre
  François Charles, Duc
  de Castiglione
Aung San
Aurangzeb
Aurelian(us), Lucius
  Domitius
Auric, Georges
Ausonius, Decimus
  Magnus
Austen, Jane
Austin, Herbert, 1st
  Baron
Austin, John
Austin, John Langshaw

Averroes
Avery, Oswald Theodore
Avicenna
Ávila, St Teresa of
Avogadro, Amedeo,
  Conte di Quaregna e
  Ceretto
Avon, (Robert) Anthony
  Eden, 1st Earl of
Awolowo, Obafemi
Ayatollah Ruholla
  Khomeini
Ayckbourn, Alan
Ayer, Sir Alfred (Jules)
Ayesha
Aylward, Gladys
Ayub Khan, Mohammad
Azaña, Manuel
Azikiwe, (Benjamin)
  Nnamdi
Aznavour, Charles
Azorín
Azuela, Mariano
Ba'al Shem Tov
Babbage, Charles
Babbitt, Irving
Babbitt, Milton
Babel, Isaac
  Emmanuilovich
Babeuf, François-Noël
Babington, Anthony
Babur
Bacchylides
Bach, Johann Christian
Bach, Johann Sebastian
Bach, Karl Philipp
  Emanuel
Bach, Wilhelm
  Friedemann
Bacon, Francis
Bacon, Francis, 1st
  Baron Verulam,
  Viscount St Albans
Bacon, John
Bacon, Roger
Baden-Powell, Robert
  Stephenson Smyth,
  1st Baron
Badoglio, Pietro
Baeck, Leo
Baedeker, Karl
Baekeland, Leo Hendrik
Baer, Karl Ernest von
Baeyer, (Johann
  Friedrich Wilhelm)
  Adolf von

Baez

Baez, Joan
Baffin, William
Bagehot, Walter
Baily, Francis
Bain, Alexander
Baird, John Logie
Bairnsfather, (Charles) Bruce
Baker, Sir Benjamin
Baker, Dame Janet (Abbott)
Baker, Sir Samuel White
Bakewell, Robert
Bakst, Léon
Bakunin, Mikhail Aleksandrovich
Balakirev, Mili Alekseevich
Balanchine, George
Balboa, Vasco Núñez de
Balchin, Nigel
Balcon, Sir Michael
Baldwin, James Arthur
Baldwin of Bewdley, Stanley, 1st Earl
Balenciaga, Cristóbal
Balfour, Arthur James, 1st Earl of
Ball, John
Balla, Giacomo
Balliol, Edward de
Balliol, John de
Balzac, Honoré de
Bana
Banda, Hastings Kamuzu
Bandaranaike, Sirimavo Ratwatte Dias
Bandaranaike, S(olomon) W(est) R(idgeway) D(ias)
Bandeira, Manuel Carneiró de Sousa
Bankhead, Tallulah
Banks, Sir Joseph
Bannister, Sir Roger (Gilbert)
Banting, Sir Frederick Grant
Banville, Théodore Faullain de
Barbarossa
Barber, Samuel
Barbirolli, Sir John
Barbour, John
Barbusse, Henri
Barclay de Tolly, Mikhail Bogdanovich, Prince
Bardeen, John
Bardot, Brigitte
Barents, Willem
Barère, Bertrand
Barham, Richard Harris
Bar Hebraeus
Baring, Evelyn
Barker, George
Barker, Harley Granville
Barkhausen, Heinrich
Bar Kokhba
Barlach, Ernst
Barnard, Christiaan Neethling
Barnard, Edward Emerson
Barnardo, Thomas John
Barnave, Antoine Pierre
Barnes, William
Barnum, Phineas Taylor
Baroja, Pío
Barras, Paul François Jean Nicolas, Vicomte de
Barrault, Jean-Louis
Barrès, Maurice
Barrie, Sir James (Matthew)
Barry, Sir Charles
Barrymore, Ethel
Barrymore, John
Barrymore, Lionel
Bart, Jean
Bart, Lionel
Barth, Heinrich
Barth, John
Barth, Karl
Bartholdi, Frédéric August
Bartók, Béla
Bartolommeo, Fra
Barton, Clara
Barton, Sir Edmund
Barton, Elizabeth
Baruch, Bernard
Basie, Count
Baskerville, John
Bassano, Jacopo
Bates, H(erbert) E(rnest)
Bates, Henry Walter
Bateson, William
Báthory, Stephen
Batista y Zaldívar, Fulgencio
Battani, al-
Batten, Jean
Battenberg, Prince Louis of
Baudelaire, Charles
Baudouin
Baum, L(yman) Frank
Baumgarten, Alexander Gottlieb
Baur, Ferdinand Christian
Bax, Sir Arnold Edward Trevor
Baxter, Richard
Bayar, Mahmud Celal
Bayard, Pierre Terrail, Seigneur de
Baybars
Bayezid
Bayle, Pierre
Baylis, Lilian
Bayliss, Sir William Maddock
Bazaine, Achille François
Beadle, George Wells
Beale, Dorothea
Beardsley, Aubrey Vincent
Beaton, Sir Cecil (Walter Hardy)
Beaton, David
Beatty, David, 1st Earl
Beaufort, Henry
Beaufort, Margaret
Beauharnais, Alexandre, Vicomte de
Beauharnais, Eugène de
Beauharnais, Hortense de
Beaumarchais, Pierre-Augustin Caron de
Beaumont, Francis
Beaumont, William
Beauvais, Vincent of
Beauvoir, Simone de
Beaverbrook, Max(well) Aitken, 1st Baron
Bebel, August
Beccaria, Cesare Bonesana, Marchese de
Bechet, Sidney

Becket, St Thomas
Beckett, Samuel
Beckford, William
Beckmann, Max
Bequerel, Antoine César
Becquerel, (Antoine) Henri
Beddoes, Thomas Lovell
Bede, St
Bedford, John, Duke of
Beebe, Charles William
Beecham, Sir Thomas
Beecher, Henry Ward
Beerbohm, Sir Max
Beethoven, Ludwig van
Beeton, Isabella Mary
Begin, Menachem
Behan, Brendan
Behn, Aphra
Behrens, Peter
Behring, Emil Adolf von
Behzad
Beiderbecke, Bix
Béjart, Maurice
Belinsky, Vissarion
Belisarius
Bell, Alexander Graham
Bell, Gertrude
Bellay, Joachim de
Bellingshausen, Fabian Gottlieb, Baron von
Bellini, Gentile
Bellini, Giovanni
Bellini, Jacopo
Bellini, Vincenzo
Bello, Andrés
Belloc, (Joseph-Pierre) Hilaire
Bellow, Saul
Belmonte y Garcia, Juan
Belyl, Andrel
Bembo, Pietro
Ben Bella, Ahmed
Benbow, John
Benchley, Robert Charles
Benda, Julien
Beneš, Edvard
Benét, Stephen Vincent
Ben-Gurion, David
Benn, Anthony (Neil) Wedgwood
Benn, Gottfried
Bennett, (Enoch) Arnold
Bennett, James Gordon

Bennett, Richard
Bedford, Viscount
Bennett, Richard Rodney
Bennett, Sir William Sterndale
Benoit de Sainte-Maure
Benson, Sir Frank
Bentham, Jeremy
Bentinck, Lord William (Henry Cavendish)
Bentley, Edmund Clerihew
Bentley, Richard
Benton, Thomas Hart
Benz, Karl (Friedrich)
Ben-Zvi, Itzhak
Bérain the Elder, Jean
Beranger, Pierre Jean de
Berdyaev, Nikolai
Berenson, Bernard
Berg, Alban
Bergius, Friedrich
Bergman, Hjalmar (Fredrik Elgérus)
Bergman, Ingmar
Bergman, Ingrid
Bergson, Henri
Beria, Lavrenti Pavlovich
Bering, Vitus Jonassen
Berio, Luciano
Beriosova, Svetlana
Berkeley, Busby
Berkeley, George
Berkeley, Sir Lennox Randal Francis
Berkeley, Sir William
Berlichingen, Götz von
Berlin, Irving
Berlin, Sir Isaiah
Berlinguer, Enrico
Berlioz, (Louis) Hector
Bernadotte, Folke, Count
Bernadotte, Jean Baptiste Jules
Bernanos, Georges
Bernard, Claude
Bernardin de Saint-Pierre, Jacques Henri
Bernhard of Saxe-Weimar, Duke
Bernhardt, Sarah
Bernini, Gian Lorenzo
Bernoulli, Daniel
Bernoulli, Jaques

Biddle

Bernoulli, Jean
Bernoulli, Nicolas
Bernstein, Eduard
Bernstein, Leonard
Berruguete, Alonso
Berruguete, Pedro
Berry, Chuck
Berry, Jean de France, Duc de
Berry, Marie-Caroline de Bourbon-Sicile, Duchesse de
Berthelot, (Pierre Eugène) Marcelin
Berthollet, Claude Louis, Comte
Bertillon, Alphonse
Bertillon, Jacques
Bertolucci, Bernardo
Bertrand, Henri Gratien, Comte
Bertran de Born
Berwick, James Fitzjames, Duke of
Berzelius, Jöns Jakob, Baron
Besant, Annie
Besant, Sir Walter
Bessarion, John
Bessemer, Sir Henry
Best, Charles Herbert
Bestuzhev-Riumin, Aleksei Petrovich, Count
Bethe, Hans Albrecht
Bethlen, Gábor
Bethmann-Hollweg, Theobald von
Betjeman, Sir John
Betterton, Thomas
Betti, Ugo
Beust, Friedrich Ferdinand, Count von
Bevan, Aneurin
Beveridge, William Henry Beveridge, 1st Baron
Bevin, Ernest
Bewick, Thomas
Beza, Theodore
Bhoskhara
Bhutto, Benazir
Bhutto, Zulfikar Ali
Bialik, Chaim Nachman
Bidault, Georges
Biddle, John

Bierce, Ambrose
  Gwinnett
Bilderdijk, Willem
Billroth, Christian Albert
  Theodor
Binet, Alfred
Bing, Sir Rudolf
Binyon, Laurence
Birendra Bir Bikram
  Shah Dev
Birkbeck, George
Birkenhead, F(rederick)
  E(dwin) Smith, 1st
  Earl of
Birkhoff, George David
Biró, Laszlo
Birtwistle, Harrison
Bishop, Sir Henry
  Rowley
Bismarck, Otto Eduard
  Leopold, Prince von
Bizet, Georges
Bjerknes, Jakob
Bjerknes, Vilhelm
  Friman Koren
Bjørnson, Bjørnstjerne
  (Martinius)
Black, Joseph
Blackett, Patrick
  Maynard Stuart,
  Baron
Blackmore, R(ichard)
  D(oddridge)
Blackstone, Sir William
Blackwood, Algernon
  Henry
Blake, Peter
Blake, Robert
Blake, William
Blanc, Louis
Blanchard, Jean Pierre
  François
Blanqui, Louis Auguste
Blasco Ibáñez, Vicente
Blasis, Carlo
Blavatsky, Helen
  Petrovna
Blenkinsop, John
Blériot, Louis
Blessington, Marguerite,
  Countess of
Bligh, William
Bliss, Sir Arthur Edward
  Drummond

Blixen, Karen, Baroness
Blixen-Finecke (pen
  name Isak Dinesen)
Bloch, Ernest
Bloch, Felix
Blok, Aleksandr
  Aleksandrovich
Blondel, Maurice
Blondin, Charles
Blood, Colonel Thomas
Bloomfield, Leonard
Blow, John
Blücher, Gebhard
  Leberecht von, Prince
  of Wahlstatt
Blum, Léon
Blunden, Edmund
  Charles
Blunt, Anthony
Blyton, Enid
Boadicea (or Boudicca)
Boas, Franz
Boccaccio, Giovanni
Boccherini, Luigi
Boccioni, Umberto
Bodawpaya
Bodhidharma
Bodin, Jean
Bodoni, Giambattista
Boehm, Theobald
Boehme, Jakob variant
  spelling of Böhme, Jakob
Boethius, Anicius
  Manlius Severinus
Bogarde, Dirk
Bogart, Humphrey
Bohemond
Böhm, Karl
Böhme (or Boehme), Jakob
Bohr, Aage
Bohr, Niels Henrik
  David
Boiardo, Matteo Maria,
  Conte di Scandiano
Boileau(-Despréaux),
  Nicolas
Boito, Arrigo
Bokassa
Bolden, Buddy
Bolesław
Boleyn, Anne
Bolingbroke, Henry St
  John, 1st Viscount
Bolívar, Simón
Böll, Heinrich

Bologna, Giovanni da
Bolt, Robert Oxton
Boltzmann, Ludwig
  Eduard
Bolyai, János
Bonaparte, Carlo
Bonaparte, Jérôme
Bonaparte, Joseph
Bonaparte, Louis
Bonaparte, Lucien
Bonaparte, Napoleon
Bonaventure, St
Bond, Edward
Bondi, Sir Hermann
Bonham-Carter, Lady
  Violet, Baroness
  Asquith
Bonhoeffer, Dietrich
Boniface, St
Bonington, Chris
Bonington, Richard
  Parkes
Bonnard, Pierre
Bonnet, Charles
Boole, George
Boone, Daniel
Booth, Charles
Booth, Edwin
Booth, Evangeline
Booth, John Wilkes
Booth, William
Booth, William Bramwell
Borden, Sir Robert Laird
Bordet, Jules Jean
  Baptiste Vincent
Borelli, Giovanni
  Alfonso
Borg, Bjorn
Borges, Jorge Luis
Borgia, Cesare
Borgia, Lucrezia
Borglum, Gutzon
Borlaug, Norman
Bormann, Martin
Born, Max
Borodin, Aleksandr
  Porfirevich
Borromeo, St Charles
Borromini, Francesco
Borrow, George Henry
Boru, Brian
Bosanquet, Bernard
Bosch, Carl
Bosch, Hieronymus

Bose, Sir Jagadis Chandra
Bose, Subhas Chandra
Bossuet, Jacques Bénigne
Boswell, James
Botha, Louis
Botha, Pieter Willem
Bothe, Walther Wilhelm Georg Franz
Bothwell, James Hepburn, 4th Earl of
Botticelli, Sandro
Botvinnik, Mikhail Moiseivich
Boucher, François
Boucher de Perthes, Jacques
Boudicca *variant spelling of* Boadicea
Boudin, Eugène
Bougainville, Louis Antoine de
Bouillon, Godfrey of
Boulanger, Nadia (Juliette)
Boulez, Pierre
Boulle, André Charles
Boult, Sir Adrian (Cedric)
Boulter, Hugh
Boulton, Matthew
Boumédienne, Houari
Bourbaki, Nicolas
Bourdelle, Émile
Bourgeois, Léon
Bourmont, Louis Auguste Victor de Ghaisnes, Comte de
Bouts, Dierick
Boveri, Theodor Heinrich
Bovet, Daniel
Bow, Clara
Bowdler, Thomas
Bowen, Elizabeth
Bowen, Norman Levi
Bower, Frederick Orpen
Bowie, David
Boyce, William
Boycott, Charles Cunningham
Boyd-Orr of Brechin Mearns, John, 1st Baron
Boyer, Charles

Boyle, Robert
Bo Zhu Yi (*or* Po Chü-i)
Brabham, Jack
Bracegirdle, Anne
Bracton, Henry de
Bradbury, Ray
Bradford, William
Bradlaugh, Charles
Bradley, Andrew Cecil
Bradley, Francis Herbert
Bradley, Omar Nelson
Bradman, Sir Donald George
Braganza, Catherine of
Bragg, Sir (William) Lawrence
Bragg, Sir William Henry
Brahe, Tycho
Brahms, Johannes
Braille, Louis
Bramah, Joseph
Bramante, Donato
Brancusi, Constantin
Brandes, Georg Morris Cohen
Brando, Marlon
Brandt, Bill British photographer
Brandt, Willy German statesman
Brant, Joseph
Brant, Sebastian
Branting, Karl Hjalmar
Brantôme, Pierre, Abbé and Seigneur de Bourdeille
Braque, Georges
Bratby, John
Brattain, Walter Houser
Brauchitsch, Walther von
Braun, Eva
Brazza, Pierre Paul François Camille Savorgnan de
Bream, Julian Alexander
Brébeuf, St Jean de
Brecht, Bertolt
Brendel, Alfred
Brentano, Clemens
Brentano, Franz
Bresson, Robert
Breton, André
Breuer, Josef

Breuer, Marcel Lajos
Breuil, Henri
Brewster, Sir David
Brezhnev, Leonid Ilich
Brian, Havergal
Briand, Aristide
Bridge, Frank
Bridges, Robert Seymour
Bridgman, Percy Williams
Bridie, James
Briggs, Henry
Bright, John
Bright, Richard
Brillat-Savarin, Anthelme
Brindley, James
Brissot, Jacques-Pierre
Britten, (Edward) Benjamin, Baron
Broadwood, John
Broch, Hermann
Broglie, Louis Victor, 7th Duc de
Bronowski, Jacob
Brontë, Anne
Brontë, Charlotte
Brontë, Emily
Brontë, Patrick Branwell
Bronzino
Brook, Peter
Brooke, Sir James
Brooke, Rupert (Chawner)
Brookeborough, Basil Stanlake Brooke, 1st Viscount
Broome, David
Brough, Louise
Brouwer, Adriaen
Brouwer, L(uitzen) E(gbertus) J(an)
Brown, Sir Arthur
Brown, Capability
Brown, Ford Madox
Brown, George (Alfred), Baron George-Brown
Brown, John
Brown, Robert botanist
Browne, Hablot Knight (*known as* Phiz)
Browne, Robert Puritan
Browne, Sir Thomas

Browning

Browning, Elizabeth
  Barrett
Browning, Robert
Brubeck, Dave
Bruce, James
Bruce, Robert the
Bruce of Melbourne,
  Stanley Melbourne,
  1st Viscount
Bruch, Max
Bruckner, Anton
Brueghel, Jan
Brueghel, Pieter
Brummel, George Bryan
Brunel, Isambard
  Kingdom
Brunel, Sir Marc
  Isambard
Brunelleschi, Filippo
Brüning, Heinrich
Brunner, Emil
Bruno, Giordano
Brunswick, Caroline of
Brutus, Marcus Junius
Bryant, William Cullen
Bryce, James, 1st
  Viscount
Buber, Martin
Bucer, Martin
Buchan, John, 1st Baron
  Tweedsmuir
Buchanan, George
Buchanan, James
Büchner, Georg
Buck, Pearl
  S(ydenstricker)
Buckingham, George
  Villiers, Duke of
Buddha
Buddhaghosa
Budé, Guillaume
Budge, (James) Don(ald)
Bueno, Maria (Esther)
Buffalo Bill *see* Cody,
  William F(rederick)
Buffet, Bernard
Buffon, Georges Louis
  Leclerc, Comte de
Bugatti, Ettore (Arco
  Isidoro)
Bukhari, al-
Bukharin, Nikolai
  Ivanovich
Bulganin, Nikolai
  Aleksandrovich
Bull, John

Bülow, Bernhard
  Heinrich, Fürst von
Bülow, Hans Guido,
  Freiherr von
Bultmann, Rudolf (Karl)
Bulwer-Lytton, Edward
  George Earle, 1st
  Baron Lytton
Bunche, Ralph
Bunin, Ivan Alekseevich
Bunsen, Robert Wilhelm
Buñuel, Luis
Bunyan, John
Burbage, Richard
Burbank, Luther
Burckhardt, Jacob
  Christoph
Bürge, Joost
Bürger, Gottfried
Burgess, Anthony
Burgess, Guy
Burgh, Hubert de
Burghley, Robert Cecil,
  1st Earl of Salisbury
Burghley, William Cecil,
  Lord
Burgoyne, John
Buridan, Jean
Burke, Edmund
Burke, Robert O'Hara
Burke, William
Burlington, Richard
  Boyle, 3rd Earl of
Burne-Jones, Sir Edward
  Coley
Burnet, Sir Frank
  Macfarlane
Burnet, Gilbert
Burnett, Frances Eliza
  Hodgson
Burney, Charles
Burney, Fanny
Burns, John Elliot
Burns, Robert
Burr, Aaron
Burra, Edward
Burroughs, Edgar Rice
Burroughs, William
Burton, Sir Richard
Burton, Richard
Burton, Robert
Busby, Matt
Bush, Alan Dudley
Bushnell, David
Busoni, Ferruccio

Buss, Frances Mary
Bustamante y Sirvén,
  Antonio Sánchez de
Bute, John Stuart, 3rd
  Earl of
Butler, Benjamin
  Franklin
Butler, Joseph
Butler, R(ichard)
  A(usten), Baron
Butler, Reg(inald)
  Cotterell
Butler, Samuel
Butler, Samuel
Butor, Michel
Butt, Dame Clara
Butterfield, William
Buxtehude, Dietrich
Bylot, Robert
Byng, George, Viscount
  Torrington
Byng, John
Byng of Vimy, Julian,
  1st Viscount
Byrd, Richard E(velyn)
Byrd, William
Byron, George Gordon,
  Lord
Caballé, Montserrat
Cabot, John
Cabot, Sebastian
Cabral, Pedro Álvares
Cabrini, St Frances
  Xavier
Caccini, Giulio
Cadbury, George
Cadbury, Richard
Cade, Jack
Cadwallader (*or* Cadwaladr)
Caedmon
Caesar, (Gaius) Julius
Cage, John
Cagliostro, Alessandro,
  Conte di
Cagney, James
Caillaux, Joseph
Cain
Calas, Jean
Calder, Alexander
Calderón de la Barca,
  Pedro
Calhoun, John
  C(aldwell)
Caligula
Callaghan, (Leonard)
  James, Baron

Callas, Maria
Calles, Plutarco Elías
Callias
Callicrates
Callimachus
Callot, Jacques
Calmette, Albert Léon Charles
Calvin, John
Calvin, Melvin
Cambacérès, Jean Jacques Régis, Duc de
Cambyses II
Camden, William
Cameron, Julia Margaret
Camões, Luís de
Campanella, Tommaso
Campbell, Colin, Baron Clyde
Campbell, Donald Malcolm
Campbell, Gina
Campbell, Sir Malcolm
Campbell, Mrs Patrick
Campbell, Roy (Dunnachie)
Campbell, Thomas
Campbell-Bannerman, Sir Henry
Campi, Antonio
Campi, Giulio
Campi, Vincenzo
Campion, Edmund
Campion, Thomas
Camus, Albert
Canaletto
Candela, Felix
Canning, Charles John, Earl
Canning, George
Cannizzaro, Stanislao
Cannon, Walter Bradford
Cano, Juan Sebastián del
Canova, Antonio
Cánovas del Castillo, Antonio
Cantor, Georg
Canute
Cao Chan (*or* Ts'ao Chan, Zao Zhan)
Capablanca y Graupera, José Raúl
Capone, Al

Capote, Truman
Capp, Al
Capra, Frank
Caracalla
Caratacus (*or* Caractacus)
Caravaggio
Cardano, Girolamo
Cárdenas, Lázaro
Cardigan, James Thomas Brudenell, 7th Earl of
Cardin, Pierre
Carducci, Giosuè
Cardwell, Edward, Viscount
Carew, Thomas
Carey, William
Carl Gustaf Swedish king
Carlos, Don
Carlyle, Thomas
Carnap, Rudolf
Carné, Marcel
Carnegie, Andrew
Carnera, Primo
Carnot, Lazare Nicolas Marguerite
Carnot, (Nicolas Léonard) Sadi
Caro, Joseph
Carossa, Hans
Carpaccio, Vittore
Carpentier, Georges
Carpini, Giovanni da Pian del
Carr, Robert
Carracci, Agostino
Carracci, Annibale
Carracci, Ludovico
Carranza, Venustiano
Carrel, Alexis
Carrington, Peter Alexander Rupert Carrington, 6th Baron
Carroll, Lewis *pen name of* Charles Lutwidge Dodgson
Carson, Edward Henry, Baron
Carson, Kit
Carson, Rachel Louise
Carte, Richard D'Oyly
Carter, Elliott (Cook)
Carter, Howard
Carter, Jimmy
Cartier, Jacques
Cartier-Bresson, Henri

Cartwright, Edmund
Caruso, Enrico
Carver, George Washington
Cary, (Arthur) Joyce (Lunel)
Casals, Pablo
Casanova, Giovanni Giacomo, Chevalier de Seingalt
Casement, Sir Roger (David)
Cassander
Cassatt, Mary
Cassiodorus, Flavius Magnus Aurelius
Cassirer, Ernst
Cassius Longinus, Gaius
Cassivelaunus
Casson, Sir Hugh (Maxwell)
Casson, Sir Lewis
Castagno, Andrea del
Castelo Branco, Camilo
Castiglione, Baldassare
Castilho, Antonio Feliciano de
Castlereagh, Robert Stewart, Viscount
Castro (Ruz), Fidel
Catesby, Robert
Catiline
Catlin, George
Cato
Catullus, Valerius
Cauchy, Augustin Louis, Baron
Cavafy, Constantine
Cavalcanti, Guido
Cavalli, Francesco
Cavallini, Pietro
Cavell, Edith
Cavendish, Henry
Cavour, Camillo Benso di, Count
Cawley, Evonne (*maiden name* Goolagong)
Caxton, William
Cayley, Arthur
Cayley, Sir George
Ceauşescu, Nicolae
Cecil, Lord David
Cecil, Robert Gascoyne-Cecil, 1st Viscount
Céline, Louis Ferdinand
Cellini, Benvenuto

Celsus, Aulus Cornelius
Cennini, Cennino (di
  Drea)
Cervantes, Miguel de
Cetshwayo
Cézanne, Paul
Chabrier, Emmanuel
Chabrol, Claude
Chadwick, Sir Edwin
Chadwick, Sir James
Chadwick, Lynn
Chagall, Marc
Chain, Sir Ernst Boris
Chaliapin, Feodor
  Ivanovich
Challoner, Richard
Chalmers, Thomas
Chamberlain, Sir
  (Joseph) Austen
Chamberlain, Joseph
Chamberlain, (Arthur)
  Neville
Chamberlain, Owen
Chambers, Sir William
Champaigne, Philippe de
Champlain, Samuel de
Champollion, Jean-
  François
Chandler, Raymond
Chandra Gupta
Chandragupta Maurya
Chandrasekhar,
  Subrahmanyan
Chanel, Coco
Chaplin, Charlie
Chapman, George
Charcot, Jean-Martin
Chardin, Jean-Baptiste-
  Siméon
Charlemagne
Charles, Ray
Charlton, Bobby
Charlton, Jackie
Charpentier, Gustave
Charron, Pierre
Charteris, Leslie
Chartier, Alain
Chateaubriand, Vicomte
  de
Chatham, William Pitt,
  1st Earl of
Chatterjee, Bankim
  Chandra
Chatterton, Thomas
Chaucer, Geoffrey
Chausson, Ernest
Chebishev, Pafnuti
  Lvovich
Chekhov, Anton
  Pavlovich
Cheng Ch'eng-kung *variant spelling of* Zheng
  Cheng Gong
Cheng Ho *variant spelling of* Zheng He
Chénier, André de
Cheops *Greek name of* Khufu
Chephren *Greek name of* Khafre
Cherenkov, Pavel
  Alekseievich
Cherubini, Maria Luigi
Cheshire, (Geoffrey)
  Leonard
Chesterfield, Philip
  Dormer Stanhope, 4th
  Earl of
Chesterton, G(ilbert)
  K(eith)
Chevalier, Maurice
Chiang Ch'ing *variant spelling of* Jiang Qing
Chiang Ching-kuo *variant spelling of* Jiang Jing Guo
Chiang Kai-shek (*or* Jiang Jie Shi)
Chicherin, Georgi
  Vasilievich
Chichester, Sir Francis
  (Charles)
Ch'ien-lung *variant spelling of* Qian Long
Chifley, Joseph Benedict
Chikamatsu Monzaemon
Childers, Erskine
Childers, Robert Erskine
Chippendale, Thomas
Chirac, Jacques
Chirico, Giorgio de
Chodowiecki, Daniel
  Nikolaus
Choiseul, Étienne
  François, Duc de
Chomsky, Noam
Chopin, Frédéric
  (François)
Chou En-lai (*or* Zhou En Lai)
Chrétien de Troyes
Christie, Dame Agatha
Christoff, Boris
Christophe, Henri
Chrysoloras, Manuel
Chrysostom, St John
Chuang-tzu *variant spelling of* Zhuangzi
Ch'ü Ch'iu-pai *variant spelling of* Qu Qiu Bai
Chulalongkorn
Churchill, Charles
Churchill, Lord
  Randolph Henry
  Spencer
Churchill, Sir Winston
  (Leonard Spencer)
Churriguera
Chu Teh *variant spelling of* Zhu De
Chu Xi (*or* Chu Hsi)
Chu Yuan
Ciano, Galeazzo
Cibber, Colley
Cicero, Marcus Tullius
Cimabue, Giovanni
Cimarosa, Domenico
Cimon
Cincinnatus, Lucius
  Quinctius
Cinna, Lucius Cornelius
Clair, René
Clare, John
Clarendon, Edward
  Hyde, 1st Earl of
Clare of Assisi, St
Clark, Jim
Clark, (Charles) Joseph
Clark, Kenneth
  (Mackenzie), Baron
Clarke, Jeremiah
Clarke, Marcus (Andrew Hislop)
Clarkson, Thomas
Claudel, Paul
Claude Lorraine
Claudian *Roman poet*
Claudius *Roman emperor*
Clausewitz, Karl von
Clausius, Rudolf Julius
  Emanuel
Clay, Cassius *original name of* Muhammad Ali
Clay, Henry
Cleanthes
Cleisthenes

Cleland, John
Clemenceau, Georges
Clementi, Muzio
Cleon
Cleopatra
Cleveland, Stephen Grover
Cleves, Anne of
Clinton, De Witt
Clive of Plassey, Robert, Baron
Clodion
Clouet, François
Clouet, Jean
Clovis
Coates, Joseph Gordon
Cobbett, William
Cobden, Richard
Cochise
Cochrane, Thomas, 10th Earl of Dundonald
Cockcroft, Sir John Douglas
Cockerell, Charles Robert
Cocteau, Jean
Cody, William F(rederick) (known as Buffalo Bill)
Coen, Jan Pieterszoon
Coeur, Jacques
Cohn, Ferdinand Julius
Coke, Sir Edward
Coke, Thomas William, Earl of Leicester of Holkham
Colbert, Claudette
Colbert, Jean-Baptiste
Coleridge, Samuel Taylor
Coleridge-Taylor, Samuel
Colet, John
Colette, Sidonie Gabrielle Claudine
Coligny, Gaspard de, Seigneur de Châtillon
Collier, Jeremy
Collingwood, Cuthbert, 1st Baron
Collingwood, Robin George
Collins, Michael
Collins, William
Collins, William Wilkie
Colman, George

Colman, Ronald
Colombo, Matteo Realdo
Colum, Padraic
Columba, St founder of Ionian monastery
Columban, St founder of monasteries in Gaul and Italy
Columbus, Christopher
Comaneci, Nadia
Comenius, John Amos
Commodus, Lucius Aelius Aurelius
Commynes, Philippe de
Comnena, Anna
Compton, Arthur Holly
Compton, Denis (Charles Scott)
Compton-Burnett, Dame Ivy
Comte, Auguste
Condillac, Étienne Bonnot de
Condorcet, Marie Jean Antoine de Caritat, Marquis de
Confucius
Congreve, William
Connors, Jimmy
Conrad, Joseph
Conscience, Hendrik
Constable, John
Constant, Benjamin
Constantine, Learie Nicholas, Baron
Cook, Captain James
Cook, Sir Joseph
Cook, Thomas
Coolidge, John Calvin
Cooper, Gary
Cooper, James Fenimore
Cooper, Samuel
Copernicus, Nicolaus
Copland, Aaron
Coralli, Jean
Corbusier, Le
Corday, Charlotte
Corelli, Arcangelo
Corelli, Marie
Corneille, Pierre
Cornelius, Peter von
Cornforth, Sir John Warcup
Cornwallis, Charles, 1st Marquess

Crichton

Corot, Jean Baptiste Camille
Correggio
Correns, Carl Erich
Cort, Henry
Cortés, Hernán
Cortot, Alfred
Corvo, Baron pseudonym of Frederick William Rolfe
Cosgrave, Liam
Cosgrave, William Thomas
Cosmas, St
Cosway, Richard
Cotman, John Sell
Coulomb, Charles Augustin de
Couperin, François
Courbet, Gustave
Courrèges, André
Court, Margaret
Cousin, Jean
Cousin, Victor
Cousteau, Jacques Yves
Coverdale, Miles
Covilhã, Pêro da
Coward, Sir Noel
Cowdrey, (Michael) Colin
Cowell, Henry
Cowley, Abraham
Cowper, William
Crabbe, George
Craig, Edward Henry Gordon
Craik, Dinah Maria Mulock
Cram, Steve
Cranach the Elder, Lucas
Crane, Hart
Crane, Stephen
Crane, Walter
Cranko, John
Cranmer, Thomas
Crashaw, Richard
Crassus, Marcus Licinius
Crawford, Joan
Creed, Frederick
Creeley, Robert
Cressent, Charles
Crèvecoeur, Michel-Guillaume-Jean de
Crichton, James

Crick

Crick, Francis Harry Compton
Crippen, Hawley Harvey
Cripps, Sir (Richard) Stafford
Cristofori, Bartolommeo
Crivelli, Carlo
Croce, Benedetto
Crockett, Davy
Crockford, William
Croesus
Crome, John
Crome, John Bernay
Cromer, Evelyn Baring, 1st Earl of
Crompton, Richmal
Crompton, Samuel
Cromwell, Oliver
Cromwell, Richard
Cromwell, Thomas, Earl of Essex
Cronin, A(rchibald) J(oseph)
Cronje, Piet Arnoldus
Crookes, Sir William
Crosby, Bing
Crossman, Richard (Howard Stafford)
Cruden, Alexander
Cruft, Charles
Cruikshank, George
Cruyff, Johann
Cruz, Sor Juana Inéz de la
Csokonai Vitéz, Mihaly
Cudworth, Ralph
Culbertson, Ely
Culpeper, Nicholas
Cumberland, Richard
Cumberland, William Augustus, Duke of
cummings, e(dward) e(stlin)
Cunningham, Merce
Cunobelinus
Curie, Marie
Curie, Pierre
Curry, John (Anthony)
Curtin, John Joseph
Curtiss, Glenn (Hammond)
Curwen, John
Curzon, Sir Clifford

Curzon, George Nathaniel, 1st Marquess
Cusa, Nicholas of
Cushing, Harvey Williams
Custer, George A(rmstrong)
Cuvier, Georges, Baron
Cuyp, Aelbert Jacobsz
Cuyp, Jacob Gerritsz
Cymbeline
Cynewulf
Cyrano de Bergerac, Savinien
Czerny, Karl
Dadd, Richard
Dafydd ap Gwilym
Dagly, Gerhard
Daguerre, Louis-Jacques-Mandé
Dahl, Roald
Daigo
Daimler, Gottlieb (Wilhelm)
Daladier, Édouard
Dale, Sir Henry Hallett
d'Alembert, Jean le Rond
Dalhousie, James Ramsay, 1st Marquess of
Dali, Salvador
Dallapiccola, Luigi
Dalton, John
Dam, Carl Peter Henrik
Damian, St 4th-century martyr
Damien, Father 19th-century missionary
Dampier, William
Danby, Francis
Danby, Thomas Osborne, 1st Earl of
Dance, George
Dandolo, Enrico
Dangerfield, Thomas
Daniel, Samuel
Daniell, John Frederic
D'Annunzio, Gabriele
Dante Alighieri
Danton, Georges Jacques
Da Ponte, Lorenzo
Darío, Rubén
Darius

Darlan, Jean (Louis Xavier) François
Darling, Grace
Darnley, Henry Stuart, Lord
Darrow, Clarence
Darwin, Charles Robert
Darwin, Erasmus
Datini, Francesco
Daubenton, Louis Jean Marie
Daubigny, Charles-François
Daudet, Alphonse
Daudet, Léon
Daumier, Honoré
Davenant, Sir William
Davenport, Charles Benedict
David, Gerard
David, Jacques Louis
David ap Gruffudd
Davies, Sir Peter Maxwell
Davies, W(illiam) H(enry)
da Vinci, Leonardo
Davis, Bette
Davis, Sir Colin
Davis, Jefferson
Davis, John
Davis, Miles
Davitt, Michael
Davy, Sir Humphry
Dawes, Charles G(ates)
Dayan, Moshe
Day Lewis, C(ecil)
Dazai Osamu
Deák, Ferenc
Deakin, Alfred
Dean, James
Deane, Silas
de Bary, Heinrich Anton
Debray, (Jules) Régis
Debré, Michel
Debrett, John
de Broglie, Louis Victor, 7th Duc
Debs, Eugene V(ictor)
Deburau, Jean-Gaspard
Debussy, Claude (Achille)
Debye, Peter Joseph Wilhelm
Decatur, Stephen

Decius, Gaius Messius Quintus Trajanus
Dedekind, (Julius Wilhelm) Richard
de Duve, Christian
Dee, John
Defoe, Daniel
De Forest, Lee
Degas, (Hilaire Germain) Edgar
De Gasperi, Alcide
de Gaulle, Charles André Joseph Marie
De Havilland, Sir Geoffrey
Dekker, Thomas
de Kooning, Willem
Delacroix, Eugène
De la Mare, Walter
De la Roche, Mazo
Delaroche, (Hippolyte) Paul
De La Rue, Warren
Delaunay, Robert
Delcassé, Théophile
Deledda, Grazia
Delescluze, Louis Charles
Delibes, Leo
Delius, Frederick
della Robbia, Andrea
della Robbia, Giovanni
della Robbia, Girolamo
della Robbia, Luca
Delorme, Philibert
Delvaux, Paul
de Mille, Agnes
de Mille, Cecil B(lount)
Democritus
De Morgan, Augustus
Demosthenes
Dempsey, Jack
Deng Xiao Ping *variant spelling of* Teng Hsiao-p'ing
Denham, Sir John
Denikin, Anton Ivanovich
Denis, Maurice
Denis, St
Denning, Alfred Thompson, Baron
d'Éon, Charles de Beaumont, Chevalier
Depretis, Agostino

De Quincey, Thomas
Derain, André
Derby, Edward (George Geoffrey Smith) Stanley, 4th Earl of
Desai, (Shri) Morarji (Ranchhodji)
Descartes, René
De Sica, Vittorio
Desiderio da Settignano
Desmond, Gerald Fitzgerald, 15th Earl of
Desmoulins, Camille
des Prez, Josquin
Dessalines, Jean Jacques
Destutt, Antoine Louis Claude, Comte de Tracy
Deus, João de
De Valera, Eamon
de Valois, Dame Ninette
Devine, George
Devonshire, Spencer Compton Cavendish, 8th Duke of
de Vries, Hugo Marie
de Wet, Christian Rudolf
Dewey, George
Dewey, John
De Wint, Peter
Diaghilev, Sergei (Pavlovich)
Dias, Bartolomeu
Díaz, Porfirio
Dibdin, Charles
Dickens, Charles
Dickinson, Emily
Diderot, Denis
Diefenbaker, John G(eorge)
Diels, Otto Paul Hermann
Dieman, Anthony van
Dietrich, Marlene
Digby, Sir Kenelm
Dilthey, Wilhelm
Dimitrii Donskoi
Dimitrov, Georgi
D'Indy, Vincent
Dinesen, Isak *pen name of* Karen Blixen
D'Inzeo, Piero
D'Inzeo, Raimondo
Dio Cassius
Dio Chrysostom

Diocletian(us), Gaius Aurelius Valerius
Diodorus Siculus
Diogenes
Dionysius
Diophantus
Dior, Christian
Dioscorides Pedanius
Dirac, Paul Adrien Maurice
Disney, Walt
Disraeli, Benjamin, 1st Earl of Beaconsfield
Djilas, Milovan
Djoser (*or* Zoser)
Dobzhansky, Theodosius
Dodgson, Charles Lutwidge (*pen name* Lewis Carroll)
Dodsley, Robert
Dogen
Dohnányi, Ernö
Dolci, Danilo
D'Oliviera, Basil Lewis
Dollfuss, Engelbert
Dolmetsch, Arnold
Dolmetsch, Carl
Domagk, Gerhard
Domenichino
Domenico Veneziano
Domingo, Placido
Domino, Fats
Domitian(us), Titus Flavius
Donatello
Donatus, Aelius
Dönitz, Karl
Donizetti, Gaetano
Donleavy, J(ames) P(atrick)
Donne, John
Doolittle, Hilda
Doppler, Christian Johann
Doré, (Paul) Gustave (Louis Christophe)
Dorgon
Dornier, Claudius
Dos Passos, John
Dostoievski, Fedor Mikhailovich
Dou, Gerrit
Doughty, Charles Montagu
Douglas, Gavin

Douglas

Douglas, (George) Norman
Douglas-Home, Alec, Baron Home of the Hirsel
Dowding, Hugh Caswall Tremenheere, 1st Baron
Dowland, John
Dowson, Ernest (Christopher)
Doyle, Sir Arthur Conan
D'Oyly Carte, Richard
Drabble, Margaret
Draco
Drake, Sir Francis
Drayton, Michael
Dreiser, Theodore
Dreyer, Carl Theodor
Dreyer, Johan Ludvig Emil
Dreyfus, Alfred
Driesch, Hans Adolf Eduard
Drinkwater, John
Droste-Hülshoff, Annette von
Drummond of Hawthornden, William
Dryden, John
Drysdale, Sir (George) Russell
Du Barry, Marie Jeanne Bécu, Comtesse
Dubček, Alexander
Dubuffet, Jean (Phillipe Arthur)
Du Cange, Charles du Fresne, Sieur
Duccio di Buoninsegna
Duchamp, Marcel
Dufay, Guillaume
Du Fu (*or* Tu Fu)
Dufy, Raoul
Duhamel, Georges
Dukas, Paul
Duke, Geoffrey E.
Dulles, John Foster
Dumas, Alexandre
Du Maurier, Dame Daphne
Du Maurier, George (Louis Palmella Busson)
Du Mont, Allen Balcom
Dumont d'Urville, Jules Sébastien César
Dumouriez, Charles François du Périer
Dunant, (Jean-)Henri
Dunbar, William
Duncan, Isadora
Dundee, John Graham of Claverhouse, 1st Viscount
Dunlop, John Boyd
Dunois, Jean d'Orléans, Comte de
Dunsany, Edward John Moreton Drax Plunkett, 18th Baron
Duns Scotus, John
Dunstable, John
Duparc, Henri
du Pré, Jacqueline
Dupré, Marcel
Duras, Marguerite
Dürer, Albrecht
Durham, John George Lambton, 1st Earl of
Durkheim, Emile
Durrell, Gerald Malcolm
Durrell, Lawrence George
Dürrenmatt, Friedrich
Duse, Eleonora
Duval, Claude
Duvalier, François
Duvalier, Jean-Claude
Dvořák, Antonín
Dylan, Bob
Eadred
Eads, John Buchanan
Eadwig (*or* Edwy)
Eakins, Thomas
Eanes, António dos Santos Ramalho
Earhart, Amelia
Eastman, George
Ebert, Friedrich
Eccles, Sir John Carew
Ecevit, Bülent
Echegaray y Eizaguirre, José
Eck, Johann Maier von
Eckermann, Johann Peter
Eckert, John Presper
Eckhart, Meister
Eddington, Sir Arthur Stanley
Eddy, Mary Baker
Eden, (Robert) Anthony, 1st Earl of Avon
Edgar the Aetheling
Edgeworth, Maria
Edison, Thomas Alva
Edwards, Jonathan
Edwy *variant of* Eadwig
Egmont, Lamoraal, Graaf van
Ehrenberg, Iliya Grigorievich
Ehrlich, Paul
Eichendorff, Josef, Freiherr von
Eichler, August Wilhelm
Eichmann, Adolf
Eijkman, Christiaan
Einhard
Einstein, Albert
Einthoven, Willem
Eisenhower, Dwight D(avid)
Eisenstein, Sergei
El Cid (*or* Rodrigo Diáz de Vivar)
Elgar, Sir Edward
El Greco
Eliot, George
Eliot, Sir John
Eliot, T(homas) S(tearns)
Ellenborough, Edward Law, Earl of
Ellington, Duke
Ellis, (Henry) Havelock
Elton, Charles
Éluard, Paul
Elyot, Sir Thomas
Emerson, Ralph Waldo
Emin Paşa, Mehmed
Emmet, Robert
Empedocles
Empson, Sir William
Enders, John Franklin
Endlicher, Stephan Ladislaus
Enesco, Georges
Engels, Friedrich
Engler, Gustav Heinrich Adolf
Ennius, Quintus
Ensor, James Sydney, Baron
Enver Pasha

Epaminondas
Epictetus
Epicurus
Epstein, Sir Jacob
Erasistratus of Ceos
Erasmus, Desiderius
Eratosthenes of Cyrene
Erceldoune, Thomas of
Ercilla, Alonso de
Erhard, Ludwig
Ericsson, John
Erigena, John Scotus
Erik Swedish king
Erlanger, Joseph
Ernst, Max
Erskine, Thomas
Erskine, 1st Baron
Erté
Esarhaddon
Eschenbach, Wolfram von
Escoffier, Auguste
Essex, Robert Devereux, Earl of
Estienne, Henri
Estienne, Robert
Ethelwulf
Etherege, Sir George
Etty, William
Eucken, Rudolf Christoph
Euclid
Eudoxus of Cnidus
Eugène of Savoy, Prince
Eugénie empress of France
Euler, Leonhard
Euphronios
Eupolis
Euripides
Eusebius of Caesarea
Eustachio, Bartolommeo
Evans, Sir Arthur John
Evans, Dame Edith
Evans, Sir Geraint
Evans, Oliver
Evelyn, John
Evert, Chris(tine)
Ewald, Johannes
Exekias
Eyre, Edward John
Eysenck, Hans Jürgen
Fabergé, Peter Carl
Fabius Maximus, Quintus
Fabre, Jean Henri

Fabricius ab Aquapendente, Hieronymus
Fabritius, Carel
Fabry, Charles
Fadden, Sir Arthur William
Fa-hsien *variant spelling of* Fa Xian
Faidherbe, Louis (Léon César)
Fairbanks, Douglas
Fairfax, Thomas, 3rd Baron
Faisal
Faisal Ibn Abdul Aziz
Fakhr ad-Din II
Falla, Manuel de
Fallopius, Gabriel
Fangio, Juan Manuel
Fa Ngum
Fantin-Latour, (Ignace) Henri (Joseph Théodore)
Faraday, Michael
Farel, Guillaume
Fargo, William
Farnaby, Giles
Farnese, Alessandro, Duke of Parma
Farouk
Farquhar, George
Fassbinder, Rainer Werner
Fateh Singh, Sant
Fatimah
Faulkner, William
Fauré, Gabriel (Urbain)
Fawcett, Henry
Fawcett, Dame Millicent Garrett
Fawkes, Guy
Fa Xian (*or* Fa-hsien)
Fechner, Gustav Theodor
Feininger, Lyonel (Charles Adrian)
Fellini, Federico
Fénelon, François de Salignac de la Mothe
Ferlinghetti, Lawrence
Fermat, Pierre de
Fermi, Enrico
Fernandel
Ferrar, Nicholas
Ferrier, Kathleen

Ferrier, Susan Edmonstone
Feuchtwanger, Lion
Feuerbach, Ludwig Andreas
Feuillère, Edwige
Feydeau, Georges
Feynman, Richard Phillips
Fibonacci, Leonardo
Fichte, Johann Gottlieb
Ficino, Marsilio
Field, Cyrus West
Field, John
Fielding, Henry
Fields, Gracie
Fields, W. C.
Fife, Duncan *variant spelling of* Phyfe, Duncan
Filarete
Fillmore, Millard
Finlay, Carlos Juan
Finney, Albert
Finsen, Niels Ryberg
Firbank, (Arthur Annesley) Ronald
Firdausi
Firth, J(ohn) R(upert)
Fischer, Bobby
Fischer, Emil Hermann
Fischer-Dieskau, Dietrich
Fischer von Erlach, Johann Bernhard
Fisher, Andrew
Fisher, John Arbuthnot, 1st Baron
Fisher, St John
Fitzgerald, Edward
Fitzgerald, Ella
Fitzgerald, F(rancis) Scott (Key)
Fitzgerald, George Francis
Fitzsimmons, Bob
Flagstad, Kirsten Malfrid
Flaherty, Robert (Joseph)
Flamininus, Titus Quinctius
Flaminius, Gaius
Flamsteed, John
Flaubert, Gustave
Flaxman, John Henry
Flecker, (Herman) James Elroy

Flémalle

Flémalle, Master of
Fleming, Sir Alexander
Fleming, Ian (Lancaster)
Fleming, Sir John Ambrose
Fleming, Paul
Fletcher, John
Fleury, André Hercule de, Cardinal
Flinders, Matthew
Flood, Henry
Florey, Howard Walter, Baron
Florio, John
Floris, Cornelis
Floris, Frans
Flotow, Friedrich von
Fludd, Robert
Flynn, Errol
Foch, Ferdinand
Fokine, Michel
Fokker, Anthony Hermann Gerard
Foley, John Henry
Fonda, Henry
Fonda, Jane
Fonda, Peter
Fontana, Domenico
Fontane, Theodor
Fontanne, Lyn
Fontenelle, Bernard le Bovier de
Fonteyn, Dame Margot
Foot, Michael (Mackintosh)
Forbes, George William
Ford, Ford Madox
Ford, Gerald R(udolph)
Ford, Henry
Ford, John
Forester, C(ecil) S(cott)
Forman, Miloš
Forster, E(dward) M(organ)
Fortescue, Sir John
Foscolo, Ugo
Foster, Stephen Collins
Fothergill, John
Foucault, Jean Bernard Léon
Fouché, Joseph, Duc d'Otrante
Fouqué, Friedrich Heinrich Karl, Baron de la Motte
Fouquet, Jean
Fouquet, Nicolas
Fourier, (François Marie) Charles
Fourier, Jean Baptiste Joseph, Baron
Fourneyron, Benoît
Fowler, Francis
Fowler, H(enry) W(atson)
Fowles, John
Fox, Charles James
Fox, George
Foxe, John
Fragonard, Jean Honoré
Frampton, Sir George James
France, Anatole
Francis, Sir Philip
Franck, César Auguste
Franck, James
Franco, Francisco
Frank, Anne
Frankfurter, Felix
Franklin, Benjamin
Franklin, Sir John
Fraser, (John) Malcolm
Fraser, Peter
Fraunhofer, Joseph von
Frazer, Sir James George
Frazier, Joe
Frederick Barbarossa
Frege, Gottlob
Frei (Montalva), Eduardo
Frémont, John C(harles)
French, John, Earl of Ypres
Freneau, Philip
Fresnel, Augustin Jean
Freud, Anna
Freud, Clement
Freud, Lucian
Freud, Sigmund
Friedman, Milton
Friedman, Rose
Friedrich, Caspar David
Friml, Rudolph
Frisch, Karl von
Frisch, Max
Frisch, Otto Robert
Frisch, Ragnar
Frobisher, Sir Martin
Fröding, Gustaf
Froebel, Friedrich Wilhelm August
Froissart, Jean
Fromm, Erich
Frontenac, Louis de Buade, Comte de Palluau et de
Frost, Robert Lee
Froude, James Anthony
Fry, Christopher
Fry, Elizabeth
Fry, Roger (Eliot)
Fu'ad
Fuchs, (Emil Julius) Klaus
Fuchs, Sir Vivian (Ernest)
Fugard, Athol
Fuller, J(ohn) F(rederick) C(harles)
Fuller, Richard Buckminster
Fuller, Roy (Broadbent)
Fuller, Thomas
Fulton, Robert
Furtwängler, Wilhelm
Fuseli, Henry
Fust, Johann
Gabin, Jean
Gable, Clark
Gabo, Naum
Gabor, Dennis
Gabrieli, Andrea
Gabrieli, Giovanni
Gaddafi, Moammar al-
Gaddi, Agnolo
Gaddi, Taddeo
Gagarin, Yuri Alekseevich
Gage, Thomas
Gainsborough, Thomas
Gaitskell, Hugh (Todd Naylor)
Galbraith, John Kenneth
Galen
Galerius
Galileo Galilei
Gall, Franz Joseph
Galle, Johann Gottfried
Galli-Curci, Amelita
Gallup, George Horace
Galois, Évariste
Galsworthy, John
Galt, John
Galton, Sir Francis

Galuppi, Baldassare
Galvani, Luigi
Galway, James
Gama, Vasco da
Gambetta, Léon
Gamliel
Gandhi, Indira
Gandhi, Mohandas Karamchand
Gandhi, Rajiv
Gandhi, Sanjay
Garbo, Greta
García Lorca, Federico
Gardiner, Stephen
Garibaldi, Giuseppe
Garland, Judy
Garrick, David
Gaskell, Elizabeth Cleghorn
Gassendi, Pierre
Gasser, Herbert Spencer
Gates, Horatio
Gaudier-Brzeska, Henri
Gaudí y Cornet, Antonio
Gauguin, Paul
Gaunt, John of, Duke of Lancaster
Gauss, Karl Friedrich
Gautama Siddhartha *original name of* Buddha
Gautier, Théophile
Gay, John
Gay-Lussac, Joseph Louis
Geber
Gediminas
Geiger, Hans
Gell-Mann, Murray
Genet, Jean
Genghis Khan
Genseric
Gentile, Giovanni
Gentile da Fabriano
Geoffroy Saint-Hilaire, Étienne
George, Stefan
Gérard, François (Pascal Simon), Baron
Géricault, (Jean Louis André) Théodore
Germanicus Julius Caesar
Geronimo
Gershwin, George
Gershwin, Ira

Gerson, Jean de
Gesner, Conrad
Gesualdo, Carlo, Prince of Venosa
Getty, J(ean) Paul
Geulincx, Arnold
Ghazna, Mahmud of
Ghiberti, Lorenzo
Ghirlandaio, Domenico
Giacometti, Alberto
Giambologna
Gibbon, Edward
Gibbons, Grinling
Gibbons, Orlando
Gibbs, James
Gibbs, Josiah Willard
Gibran, Khalil
Gide, André
Gielgud, Sir (Arthur) John
Gierek, Edward
Gigli, Beniamino
Gilbert, Sir Humphrey
Gilbert, William
Gilbert, Sir William Schwenk
Giles, Carl Ronald
Gill, (Arthur) Eric (Rowton)
Gillespie, Dizzy
Gillray, James
Ginkel, Godert de, 1st Earl of Athlone
Ginsberg, Allen
Giordano, Luca
Giorgione
Giotto
Giraldus Cambrensis
Giraudoux, Jean
Girtin, Thomas
Giscard d'Estaing, Valéry
Gish, Dorothy
Gish, Lillian
Gislebertus
Gissing, George Robert
Giulini, Carlo Maria
Giulio Romano
Gladstone, W(illiam) E(wart)
Glanville, Ranulf de
Glaser, Donald Arthur
Glazunov, Aleksandr Konstantinovich
Glendower, Owen

González de Mendoza

Glinka, Mikhail Ivanovich
Gluck, Christoph Willibald
Gneisenau, August (Wilhelm Anton), Graf Neithardt von
Gobbi, Tito
Gobind Singh (*or* Govind Singh)
Gobineau, Joseph Arthur, Comte de
Godard, Jean-Luc
Goddard, Robert Hutchings
Gödel, Kurt
Goderich, George Frederick Samuel Robinson, Viscount
Godiva, Lady
Godolphin, Sidney, Earl of
Godoy, Manuel de
Godunov, Boris (Fedorovich)
Godwin, William
Goebbels, (Paul) Joseph
Goes, Hugo van der
Goethe, Johann Wolfgang von
Gogol, Nikolai Vasilievich
Gold, Thomas
Golding, William
Goldoni, Carlo
Goldschmidt, Richard Benedict
Goldsmith, Oliver
Goldwyn, Samuel
Golgi, Camillo
Gollancz, Victor
Golovkin, Gavrīl Ivanovich, Count
Gómez, Juan Vicente
Gomułka, Władysław
Goncharov, Ivan Aleksandrovich
Goncourt, Edmond de
Goncourt, Jules de
Gondomar, Diego Sarmiento de Acuña, Conde de
Góngora y Argote, Luis de
González de Mendoza, Pedro

Goodman

Goodman, Benny
Goodyear, Charles
Goolagong, Evonne *maiden name of* Evonne Cawley
Goossens, Sir Eugene
Goossens, Leon
Gordon, Charles George
Göring, Hermann Wilhelm
Gorki, Maksim
Gorky, Arshile
Gorton, John Grey
Gossaert, Jan *(known as* Mabuse)
Gosse, Sir Edmund
Gottfried von Strassburg
Gottsched, Johann Christoph
Goujon, Jean
Gounod, Charles François
Govind Singh *variant spelling of* Gobind Singh
Gower, John
Gowon, Yakubu
Goya (y Lucientes), Francesco (Jose) de
Goyen, Jan Josephszoon van
Gozzi, Carlo
Gozzoli, Benozzo
Gracchus, Gaius Sempronius
Gracchus, Tiberius Sempronius
Grace, W(illiam) G(ilbert)
Graham, Billy
Graham, Martha
Graham, Thomas
Grahame, Kenneth
Grainger, Percy Aldridge
Gramsci, Antonio
Granados, Enrique
Granby, John Manners, Marquess of
Grant, Cary
Grant, Duncan James Corrowr
Grant, Ulysses S(impson)
Granville, Granville George Leveson-Gower, 2nd Earl

Granville, John Carteret, 1st Earl
Granville-Barker, Harley
Grappelli, Stephane
Grass, Günter
Gratian(us), Flavius
Grattan, Henry
Graves, Robert (Ranke)
Gray, Asa
Gray, Thomas
Greeley, Horace
Green, Henry
Greenaway, Kate
Greene, (Henry) Graham
Greene, Nathaneal
Greene, Robert
Greenough, Horatio
Greenwood, Walter
Gregory, Lady Augusta
Gregory, James
Greig, Tony
Grenville, George
Grenville, Sir Richard
Grenville, William (Wyndham), Baron
Gresham, Sir Thomas
Grétry, André Ernest Modeste
Greuze, Jean-Baptiste
Greville, Fulke, 1st Baron Brooke
Grey, Charles, 2nd Earl
Grey, Sir George
Grey, Henry George, 3rd Earl Grey
Grey, Lady Jane
Grey of Fallodon, Edward, 1st Viscount
Grieg, Edvard Hagerup
Grierson, John
Griffith, Arthur
Griffith, D(avid) W(ark)
Grillparzer, Franz
Grimaldi, Joseph
Grimm, Jakob
Grimm, Wilhelm
Grimmelshausen, Hans Jacob Christoph von
Grimond, Jo(seph), Baron
Gris, Juan
Grivas, Georgios
Gromyko, Andrei
Gropius, Walter

556

Gros, Antoine Jean, Baron
Grosseteste, Robert
Grossmith, George
Grossmith, Weedon
Grosz, George
Grotefend, Georg Friedrich
Grotius, Hugo
Grove, Sir George
Groves, Sir Charles
Grünewald, Matthias
Guang Xu (*or* Kuang-hsü)
Guardi, Francesco
Guardi, Giovanni Antonio
Guarini, Giovanni Battista
Guarini, Guarino Italian architect
Guarneri, Andrea Italian violin maker
Guarneri, Giuseppe
Guercino
Guericke, Otto von
Guesclin, Bertrand du
Guevara, Che
Guicciardini, Francesco
Guido d'Arezzo
Guillaume de Lorris
Guinness, Sir Alec
Guiscard, Robert
Guitry, Sacha
Guizot, François (Pierre Guillaume)
Gunn, Thom(son William)
Gurdjieff, George Ivanovitch
Gustavus II Adolphus
Gustavus I Vasa
Gutenberg, Johann
Guthrie, Arlo
Guthrie, (William) Tyrone
Guthrie, Woody
Guzmán Blanco, Antonio
Gwyn, Nell
Haakon
Haber, Fritz
Hadrian
Haeckel, Ernst Heinrich
Hafiz, Shams al-Din Muhammad
Hagen, Walter Charles

Haggard, Sir H(enry) Rider
Hahn, Kurt
Hahn, Otto
Hahnemann, Samuel Christian Friedrich
Haig, Douglas, 1st Earl
Haile Selassie
Hailsham, Douglas McGarel Hogg, 1st Viscount
Hailsham of St Marylebone, Quintin McGarel Hogg, Baron
Hailwood, Mike
Haitink, Bernard
Hakluyt, Richard
Haldane, John Burdon Sanderson
Haldane, John Scott
Haldane, Richard Burdon, 1st Viscount
Hale, Sir Matthew
Halévy, Jacques François
Halifax, Charles Montagu, 1st Earl of
Halifax, Edward Frederick Lindley Wood, 1st Earl of
Halifax, George Savile, 1st Marquess of
Hall, Sir Peter
Halle, Adam de la
Hallé, Sir Charles
Haller, Albrecht von
Halley, Edmund
Hals, Frans
Halsey, William F(rederick)
Hamilcar Barca
Hamilton, Alexander
Hamilton, Emma, Lady
Hamilton, James, 1st Duke of
Hamilton, Sir William Rowan
Hammarskjöld, Dag (Hjalmar Agne Carl)
Hammerstein, Oscar
Hammett, Dashiell
Hammond, Dame Joan
Hammond, Wally
Hammurabi
Hampden, John
Hampton, Lionel

Hamsun, Knut
Hancock, Tony
Handel, George Frederick
Handley Page, Sir Frederick
Handy, William Christopher
Han fei zi
Hardecanute (*or* Harthacnute)
Hardenberg, Karl (August), Fürst von
Hardie, J(ames) Keir
Hardinge of Lahore, Henry, 1st Viscount
Hardinge of Penshurst, Charles, 1st Baron
Hardouin-Mansart, Jules
Hardy, G(odfrey) H(arold)
Hardy, Oliver
Hardy, Thomas
Hare, William
Hargreaves, James
Harishchandra
Harlan, John Marshall
Harley, Robert, 1st Earl of Oxford
Harlow, Jean
Harmsworth, Alfred, 1st Viscount Northcliffe
Harmsworth, Harold, 1st Viscount Rothermere
Harnack, Adolf von
Harriman, W(illiam) Averell
Harrington, James
Harris, Joel Chandler
Harris, Roy
Harrison, Benjamin
Harrison, George
Harrison, William Henry
Harsa (*or* Harsha)
Hart, Moss
Harte, (Francis) Bret(t)
Hartley, L(esley) P(oles)
Hartmann, (Karl Robert) Eduard von
Hartmann, Nicolai
Hartnell, Sir Norman
Harun ar-Rashid
Harvey, William
Hasan al-Basri, al-
Hasdrubal (Barca)
Hašek, Jaroslav

Helmholtz

Haselrig, Sir Arthur *variant spelling of* Hesilrig, Sir Arthur
Hassall, John
Hassan
Hastings, Francis Rawdon-Hastings, 1st Marquess of
Hastings, Warren
Hathaway, Anne
Hatshepsut
Hauptmann, Gerhart
Haussmann, Georges-Eugène, Baron
Haw-Haw, Lord *see* Joyce, William
Hawke, Edward, 1st Baron
Hawkins, Sir John
Hawkins, Sir Richard
Hawks, Howard
Hawksmoor, Nicholas
Haworth, Sir Walter Norman
Hawthorn, Mike
Hawthorne, Nathaniel
Hay, Will
Haya de la Torre, Victor Raúl
Haydn, Franz Joseph
Hayes, Rutherford B(irchard)
Hazlitt, William
Healey, Denis (Winston)
Hearst, William Randolph
Heath, Edward (Richard George)
Heaviside, Oliver
Hebbel, (Christian) Friedrich
Hébert, Jacques-René
Heenan, John Carmel, Cardinal
Hegel, Georg Wilhelm Friedrich
Heidegger, Martin
Heifetz, Jascha
Heine, Heinrich
Heisenberg, Werner Karl
Heller, Joseph
Hellman, Lillian
Helmholtz, Hermann Ludwig Ferdinand von

Helmont

Helmont, Jan Baptist van
Helpmann, Sir Robert
Helvétius, Claude Adrien
Hemingway, Ernest
Henderson, Arthur
Hendrix, Jimi
Henry, Joseph
Henry, O.
Henry, Patrick
Henryson, Robert
Henze, Hans Werner
Hepburn, Katharine
Hepplewhite, George
Hepworth, Dame Barbara
Heraclitus Greek philosopher
Heraclius Byzantine emperor
Herbart, Johann Friedrich
Herbert, George
Herder, Johann Gottfried
Hereward the Wake
Hermann von Reichenau
Hermite, Charles
Herod
Herodotus
Hero of Alexandria
Herophilus
Herrera, Francisco de
Herrera, Juan de
Herrick, Robert
Herriot, Édouard
Herschel, Caroline
Herschel, Sir John
Herschel, Sir William
Hertz, Heinrich Rudolf
Hertzog, James Barry Munnik
Herzen, Aleksandr (Ivanovich)
Herzl, Theodor
Herzog, Werner
Hesilrige (or Haselrig), Sir Arthur
Hesiod
Hess, Dame Myra
Hess, Rudolf
Hess, Victor Francis
Hesse, Hermann
Hevesy, George Charles von

Heyerdahl, Thor
Heywood, Thomas
Hezekiah
Hickok, James Butler
Hideyoshi
Highsmith, Patricia
Hilbert, David
Hill, Archibald Vivian
Hill, David Octavius
Hill, Graham
Hill, Octavia
Hill, Sir Rowland
Hillary, Sir Edmund (Percival)
Hillel
Hillery, Patrick (John)
Hilliard, Nicholas
Hilton, James
Himmler, Heinrich
Hincmar of Reims
Hindemith, Paul
Hindenburg, Paul von Beneckendorff und von
Hines, Earl (Fatha)
Hinkler, Herbert John Lewis
Hinshelwood, Sir Cyril Norman
Hipparchus
Hippocrates
Hirohito
Hiroshige
Hitchcock, Sir Alfred
Hitler, Adolf
Hoad, Lew(is Alan)
Hobbema, Meindert
Hobbes, Thomas
Hobbs, Jack
Hochhuth, Rolf
Ho Chi Minh
Hockney, David
Hoddinott, Alun
Hodgkin, Alan Lloyd
Hodgkin, Dorothy Mary Crowfoot
Hodgkin, Thomas
Hoffman, Dustin
Hofmann, Joseph Casimir
Hofmannsthal, Hugo von
Hofmeister, Wilhelm Friedrich Benedict
Hogan, Ben
Hogarth, William

Hogg, James
Hohenlohe-Schillingsfürst, Chlodwig Karl Viktor, Fürst zu
Hokusai
Holbein, Hans
Holberg, Ludvig, Baron
Hölderlin, (Johann Christian) Friedrich
Holiday, Billie
Holinshed, Raphael
Holland, Henry
Holland, Sir Sidney (George)
Hollar, Wenceslaus
Holles, Denzil, Baron
Holliger, Heinz
Holmes, Oliver Wendell
Holst, Gustav (Theodore)
Holt, Harold (Edward)
Holyoake, Sir Keith Jacka
Home, Daniel Douglas
Home of the Hirsel, Alec Douglas-Home, Baron
Homer
Homer, Winslow
Honecker, Erich
Honegger, Arthur
Hong-wu (or Hung-wu)
Hong Xiu Quan (or Hung Hsiu-ch'uan)
Honorius
Honthorst, Gerrit von
Hooch, Pieter de
Hood, Samuel, 1st Viscount
Hood, Thomas
Hooft, Pieter Corneliszoon
Hooke, Robert
Hooker, Sir Joseph Dalton
Hooker, Richard
Hooker, Sir William Jackson
Hoover, Herbert (Clark)
Hoover, J(ohn) Edgar
Hope, Anthony
Hope, Bob
Hopkins, Sir Frederick Gowland
Hopkins, Gerard Manley
Hopkins, Harry (Lloyd)

Hopkinson, John
Hoppner, John
Hore-Belisha, (Isaac) Leslie, 1st Baron
Horn, Filips van Montmorency, Graaf van
Horowitz, Vladimir
Horta, Victor
Horthy de Nagybánya, Miklós
Hotspur *see* Percy, Sir Henry
Hotter, Hans
Houdini, Harry
Houdon, Jean Antoine
Houphouët-Boigny, Félix
Housman, A(lfred) E(dward)
Hovell, William Hilton
Howard, Catherine
Howard, Sir Ebenezer
Howard, Henry, Earl of Surrey
Howard, John
Howard, Leslie
Howard, Trevor
Howard of Effingham, Charles, 2nd Baron
Howe, Elias
Howe, Sir (Richard Edward) Geoffrey
Howe, Richard, Earl
Howe, William, 5th Viscount
Hoxha, Enver
Hoyle, Edmond
Hoyle, Sir Fred
Hsia Kuci *variant spelling of* Xia Gui
Hsuan-tsang *variant spelling of* Xuan Cang
Hua Guo Feng (*or* Hua Kuo-feng)
Huascar
Hubble, Edwin Powell
Huddleston, Trevor
Hudson, Henry
Hudson, W(illiam) H(enry)
Huggins, Sir William
Hughes, Howard (Robard)
Hughes, Richard
Hughes, Ted
Hughes, Thomas
Hughes, William M(orris)
Hugo, Victor (Marie)
Huizinga, Johan
Hull, Cordell
Humbolt, (Friedrich Wilhelm Karl Heinrich) Alexander von
Humboldt, (Karl) Wilhelm von
Hume, Basil George, Cardinal
Hume, David
Hume, Hamilton
Hume, Joseph
Hummel, Johann Nepomuk
Humperdinck, Engelbert
Humphrey, Hubert Horatio
Hung Hsiu-ch'uan *variant spelling of* Hong Xiu Quan
Hung-wu *variant spelling of* Hong-wu
Hunt, Henry
Hunt, James
Hunt, (Henry Cecil) John, Baron
Hunt, (James Henry) Leigh
Hunt, William Holman
Hunter, John
Hunter, William
Huntingdon, Selina Hastings, Countess of
Hunyadi, János
Hus, Jan
Husák, Gustáv
Hussein (ibn Talal)
Husserl, Edmund
Huston, John
Hutcheson, Francis
Hutten, Ulrich von
Hutton, James
Hutton, Len
Huxley, Aldous
Huxley, Sir Andrew Fielding
Huxley, Sir Julian
Huxley, Thomas Henry
Huygens, Christiaan
Huysmans, Joris Karl
Hyde, Douglas
Hyder Ali
Ibarruri, Dolores (*known as* La Pasionaria)
Ibert, Jacques
Iberville, Pierre le Moyne, Sieur d'
Ibn al-'Arabi, Muhyi-l-din
Ibn Battutah
Ibn Ezra, Abraham Ben Meir
Ibn Gabirol, Solomon
Ibn Khaldun
Ibn Saud
Ibrahim Pasha
Ibsen, Henrik
Ictinus
Ignatiev, Nikolai Pavlovich, Count
Ignatius Loyola, St
Ikhnaton *variant spelling of* Akhenaton
Illich, Ivan
Ilyushin, Sergei Vladimirovich
Imhotep
Ine
Inge, William Ralph
Ingenhousz, Jan
Ingres, Jean-Auguste-Dominique
Innocent pope
Inönü, Ismet
Ionesco, Eugène
Ipatieff, Vladimir Nikolaievich
Iqbal, Mohammed
Ireland, John Nicholson
Ireton, Henry
Ironside, William Edmund, 1st Baron
Irving, Sir Henry
Irving, Washington
Isaacs, Jorge
Isabey, Eugène
Isabey, Jean Baptiste
Isherwood, Christopher
Isma'il Pasha
Isocrates
Ito Hirobumi
Itúrbide, Agustín
Ivanovna, Anna
Ives, Charles (Edward)
Jabir ibn Hayyan
Jackson, Andrew

Jackson

Jackson, Glenda
Jackson, Stonewall
Jacobsen, Arne
Jacopo della Quercia
Jacopone da Todi
Jacquard, Joseph-Marie
Jagan, Cheddi Berrat
Jagan, Janet
Jagger, Mick
Jahangir
James, Henry
James, William
Jameson, Sir Leander Starr
Janáček, Leoš
Jansen, Cornelius Otto
Jansky, Karl Guthe
Januarius, St
Jaques-Dalcroze, Émile
Jarry, Alfred
Jaspers, Karl (Theodor)
Jaurès, Jean
Jawara, Sir Dawda
Jawlensky, Alexey von
Jay, John
Jayawardene, J(unius) R(ichard)
Jean de Meun
Jeans, Sir James Hopwood
Jeeps, Dickie
Jefferies, Richard
Jeffers, Robinson
Jefferson, Thomas
Jeffrey, Francis, Lord
Jeffreys of Wem, George, 1st Baron
Jeffries, John
Jellicoe, John Rushworth, 1st Earl
Jenkins, Roy (Harris)
Jenner, Edward
Jensen, Johannes (Vilhelm)
Jenson, Nicolas
Jespersen, Otto
Jevons, William Stanley
Jewel, John
Jiang Jing Guo (or Chiang Ching-kuo)
Jiang Qing (or Chiang Ch'ing)
Jiménez, Juan Ramón
Jimmu
Jinnah, Mohammed Ali

Joachim, Joseph
Jochho
Jochum, Eugen
Jodl, Alfred
Joffre, Joseph Jacques Césaire
Johannsen, Wilhelm Ludvig
John, Augustus (Edwin)
John, Barry
John, Elton
John, Gwen
Johns, Jasper
Johnson, Amy
Johnson, Andrew
Johnson, Cornelius
Johnson, Lyndon Baines
Johnson, Samuel
Johnson, Virginia Eshelman
Joinville, Jean de
Joliot, Frédéric
Joliot-Curie, Irène
Jolliet, Louis
Jolson, Al
Jones, (Alfred) Ernest
Jones, Bobby
Jones, Daniel
Jones, David
Jones, Inigo
Jones, Jack
Jones, John Paul
Jones, LeRoi
Jones, Sir William
Jongkind, Johan Barthold
Jonson, Ben
Joplin, Scott
Jordaens, Jakob
Jordan, Dorothy
Joselito
Joseph, Sir Keith (Sinjohn)
Josephson, Brian David
Josephus, Flavius
Josquin des Prez
Joubert, Piet
Joule, James Prescott
Jouvet, Louis
Jovian, Flavius
Jowett, Benjamin
Joyce, James
Joyce, William (known as Lord Haw-Haw)
Juantorena, Alberto

Juárez, Benito (Pablo)
Judah ha-Levi
Jugurtha
Jung, Carl Gustav
Jussieu, Antoine de
Jussieu, Antoine-Laurent de
Jussieu, Bernard de
Jussieu, Joseph de
Justinian
Juvenal
Kádár, János
Kafka, Franz
Kahn, Louis I(sadore)
Kaiser, Georg
Kakinomoto Hitomaro
Kalidasa
Kalinin, Mikhail Ivanovich
Kamehameha
Kamenev, Lev Borisovich
Kandinsky, Wassily
Kang Xi (or K'ang-hsi)
Kang You Wei
Kant, Immanuel
Kapitza, Peter Leonidovich
Karageorge
Karajan, Herbert von
Karamanlis, Constantine
Karloff, Boris
Károlyi, Mihály, Count
Karpov, Anatoly
Kasavubu, Joseph
Kassem, Abdul Karim
Kästner, Erich
Katsura Taro
Kauffmann, Angelica
Kaufman, George S(imon)
Kaunda, Kenneth (David)
Kaunitz, Wenzel Anton, Count von
Kawabata Yasunari
Kay, John
Kazan, Elia
Kazantzakis, Nikos
Kean, Edmund
Keaton, Buster
Keats, John
Keble, John
Keegan, Kevin
Keene, Charles Samuel

Keitel, Wilhelm
Kekulé von Stradonitz, (Friedrich) August
Keller, Gottfried
Keller, Helen Adams
Kelly, Grace
Kelly, Ned
Kelvin, William Thomson, 1st Baron
Kemal, (Mehmed) Namik
Kemble, Charles
Kemble, Frances Ann
Kemble, John Philip
Kemble, Roger
Kempe, Margery
Kempe, Rudolf
Kempis, Thomas à
Kendall, Edward Calvin
Kendall, Henry
Kendrew, Sir John Cowdery
Kennedy, Edward Moore
Kennedy, John Fitzgerald
Kennedy, Joseph Patrick
Kennedy, Robert Francis
Kennelly, Arthur Edwin
Kent, William
Kenyatta, Jomo
Kenyon, Dame Kathleen
Kepler, Johannes
Kerenski, Aleksandr Feodorovich
Kern, Jerome (David)
Kerouac, Jack
Kertanagara
Kesey, Ken
Kesselring, Albert
Ketch, Jack
Kettering, Charles Franklin
Keynes, John Maynard, 1st Baron
Khachaturian, Aram Ilich
Khafre
Khalid Ibn Abdul Aziz
Khalifa *see* Abd Allah
Khama, Sir Seretse
Khlebnikov, Velimir
Khomeini, Ayatollah Ruholla
Khorana, Har Gobind
Khosrow
Khrushchev, Nikita S(ergeevich)
Khufu
Kidd, William
Kidinnu
Kierkegaard, Søren
Kilvert, Francis
Kim Il Sung
King, Billie Jean
King, Martin Luther
King, William Lyon Mackenzie
Kingsley, Charles
Kingsley, Mary Henriette
Kinsey, Alfred
Kipling, (Joseph) Rudyard
Kirchhoff, Gustav Robert
Kirchner, Ernst Ludwig
Kirk, Norman (Eric)
Kirov, Sergei Mironovich
Kissinger, Henry (Alfred)
Kitagawa Utamaro
Kitasato, Shibasaburo
Kitchener of Khartoum, Horatio Herbert, 1st Earl
Kivi, Alexis
Klaproth, Martin Heinrich
Kléber, Jean Baptiste
Klebs, Edwin
Klee, Paul
Klein, Melanie
Kleist, Heinrich von
Klemperer, Otto
Klimt, Gustav
Klinger, Friedrich Maximilian von
Klint, Kaare
Klopstock, Friedrich Gottlieb
Kneller, Sir Godfrey
Knight, Harold
Knight, Dame Laura
Knox, John
Knox, Ronald (Arbuthnott)
Kobayashi Masaki
Koch, Robert
Köchel, Ludwig von
Kodály, Zoltan
Koestler, Arthur
Koffka, Kurt
Köhler, Wolfgang
Kokoschka, Oskar
Kolbe, (Adolf Wilhelm) Hermann
Kolchak, Alexander Vasilievich
Koldewey, Robert
Kolmogorov, Andrei Nikolaevich
Koniecpolski, Stanisław
Koniev, Ivan Stepanovich
Konoe Fumimaro, Prince
Korchnoi, Victor
Korda, Sir Alexander
Kornberg, Arthur
Kornilov, Lavrentia Georgievich
Koroliov, Sergei Pavlovich
Kosciuszko, Tadeusz Andrezei Bonawentura
Kossuth, Lajos
Kosygin, Aleksei Nikolaevich
Kotzebue, August von
Koussevitsky, Sergei
Koxinga *see* Zheng Cheng Gong
Kozirev, Nikolai Aleksandrovich
Krafft-Ebing, Richard von
Krebs, Sir Hans Adolf
Kreisky, Bruno
Kreisler, Fritz
Křenek, Ernst
Kreutzer, Rodolphe
Krishna Menon
Krochmal, Nachman
Kropotkin, Peter, Prince
Kruger, (Stephanus Johannes) Paul(us)
Krum
Krupp, Alfred
Krupp, Alfried
Krupp, Arndt
Krupp, Bertha
Krupp, Friedrich
Krupp, Gustav von Bohlen und Halbach
Kuang-hsü *variant spelling of* Guang Xu
Kubelik, Jan

Kubelik

Kubelik, Rafael
Kublai Khan
Kubrick, Stanley
Kukai
Kun, Béla
Kuo Mo-jo
Kurchatov, Igor Vasilievich
Kurosawa, Akira
Kusunoki Masashige
Kutuzov, Mikhail Ilarionovich, Prince of Smolensk
Kuznets, Simon
Kyd, Thomas
Kyprianou, Spyros
Labiche, Eugène
La Bruyère, Jean de
Laclos, Pierre Choderlos de
La Condamine, Charles Marie de
Laënnec, René Théophile Hyacinth
Lafayette, Marie Joseph Gilbert Motier, Marquis de
La Fayette, Mme de
Lafontaine, Henri-Marie
La Fontaine, Jean de
Laforgue, Jules
Lagerkvist, Pär (Fabian)
Lagerlöf, Selma Ottiliana Lovisa
Lagrange, Joseph Louis, Comte de
La Guardia, Fiorello Henry
Laing, R(onald) D(avid)
Laird, Macgregor
Lalande, Joseph-Jérôme Le Français de
Lalique, René
Lally, Thomas, Comte de
Lalo, (Victor Antoine) Édouard
Lalor, Peter
Lamarck, Jean-Baptiste de Monet, Chevalier de
Lamartine, Alphonse de
Lamb, Lady Caroline
Lamb, Charles
Lamb, Henry
Lamb, Sir Horace
Lambert, Constant
Lambert, Johann Heinrich
Lambert, John
Lamerie, Paul de
Lampedusa, Giuseppe Tomasi di
Lancaster, Sir Osbert
Lanchester, Frederick William
Land, Edwin Herbert
Landau, Lev Davidovich
Landor, Walter Savage
Landowska, Wanda
Landseer, Sir Edwin Henry
Landsteiner, Karl
Lane, Sir Allen
Lanfranc
Lang, Andrew
Lang, Fritz
Langland, William
Langley, Samuel Pierpont
Langmuir, Irving
Langton, Stephen
Langtry, Lillie
Lanier, Sidney
Lankester, Sir Edwin Ray
Lansbury, George
Lansdowne, Henry Charles Keith Petty-Fitzmaurice, 5th Marquess of
Lao Zi (*or* Lao Tzu)
Laplace, Pierre Simon, Marquis de
Lardner, Ring
Larkin, Philip
La Rochefoucauld, François, Duc de
Larousse, Pierre
Lars Porsena
Lartet, Édouard Armand Isidore Hippolyte
La Salle, Robert Cavelier, Sieur de
Lascaris, Theodore
Las Casas, Bartolomé de
Las Cases, Emmanuel, Comte de
Lasdun, Sir Denys
Lasker, Emanuel
Laski, Harold Joseph
Laski, Marghanita
Lassalle, Ferdinand
Lassus, Roland de
László
Latimer, Hugh
Latini, Brunetto
La Tour, Georges de
La Tour, Maurice-Quentin de
Laud, William
Lauda, Niki
Lauder, Sir Harry
Lauderdale, John Maitland, Duke of
Laue, Max Theodor Felix von
Laughton, Charles
Laurel, Stan
Laurier, Sir Wilfrid
Lautréamont, Comte de
Laval, Pierre
La Vallière, Louise de Françoise de la Baume le Blanc, Duchesse de
Laver, Rod(ney George)
Laveran, Charles Louis Alphonse
Lavoisier, Antoine Laurent
Law, (Andrew) Bonar
Law, William
Lawes, Sir John Bennet
Lawler, Ray
Lawrence, St
Lawrence, D(avid) H(erbert)
Lawrence, Ernest Orlando
Lawrence, Gertrude
Lawrence, John Laird Mair, 1st Baron
Lawrence, T(homas) E(dward)
Lawrence, Sir Thomas
Laxness, Halldór (Kiljan)
Layamon
Layard, Sir Austen Henry
Leach, Bernard (Howell)
Leacock, Stephen (Butler)
Leadbelly
Leakey, Louis Seymour Bazett
Leakey, Mary
Leakey, Richard
Lean, Sir David

Lear, Edward
Leavis, F(rank) R(aymond)
Le Brun, Charles
Le Carré, John
Le Châtelier, Henri-Louis
Leconte de Lisle, Charles Marie René
Lecoq de Boisbaudran, Paul-Émile
Le Corbusier
Lederberg, Joshua
Le Duc Tho
Lee, Bruce
Lee, Gypsy Rose
Lee, Jenny, Baroness
Lee, Robert E(dward)
Lee, Tsung-Dao
Leech, John
Lee Kuan Yew
Leeuwenhoek, Antonie van
Le Fanu, (Joseph) Sheridan
Legendre, Adrien Marie
Léger, Fernand
Lehár, Franz
Lehmann, Lilli
Lehmann, Lotte
Leibniz, Gottfried Wilhelm
Leicester, Robert Dudley, Earl of
Leichardt, (Friedrich Wilhelm) Ludwig
Leif Eriksson
Leigh, Vivien
Leighton of Stretton, Frederic, Baron
Leland, John
Lely, Sir Peter
Lemaître, Georges Édouard, Abbé
Le Nain, Antoine
Le Nain, Louis
Le Nain, Mathieu
Lenclos, Ninon de
L'Enfant, Pierre-Charles
Lenglen, Suzanne
Lenin, Vladimir Ilich
Lennon, John
Le Nôtre, André
Lenya, Lotte
Leonardo da Vinci

Leoncavallo, Ruggiero
Leonidas
Leonov, Leonid
Leopardi, Giacomo
Leopold
Lepidus, Marcus Aemilius
Lermontov, Mikhail
Lerner, Alan Jay
Lesage, Alain-René
Leschetizky, Theodor
Lescot, Pierre
Lesseps, Ferdinand de
Lessing, Doris
Lessing, Gotthold Ephraim
Leszczyński, Stanisław
Le Tellier, Michel
Leucippus
Leuckart, Karl Georg Friedrich Rudolph
Le Vau, Louis
Leven, Alexander Leslie, 1st Earl of
Leverhulme, William Hesketh Lever, 1st Viscount
Leverrier, Urbain Jean Joseph
Lévesque, René
Lévi-Strauss, Claude
Lewes, George Henry
Lewis, C. Day
Lewis, C(live) S(taples)
Lewis, Matthew Gregory
Lewis, (Harry) Sinclair
Lewis, (Percy) Wyndham
Libby, Willard Frank
Lichtenstein, Roy
Liddell Hart, Sir Basil Henry
Lie, Trygve (Halvdan)
Liebig, Justus, Baron von
Liebknecht, Karl
Liebknecht, Wilhelm
Lifar, Serge
Ligeti, György
Li Hong Zhang (or Li Hung-chang)
Lilburne, John
Lilienthal, Otto
Liliuokalani
Lillie, Beatrice

Limburg, de
Limosin, Léonard
Linacre, Thomas
Lin Biao (or Lin Piao)
Lincoln, Abraham
Lind, Jenny
Lindbergh, Charles A(ugustus)
Lindsay, (Nicholas) Vachel
Lindwall, Raymond Russell
Linklater, Eric
Linnaeus, Carolus
Lin Ze Xu (or Lin Tse-hsü)
Liouville, Joseph
Lipchitz, Jacques
Li Bo (or Li Po)
Lippershey, Hans
Lippi, Filippino
Lippi, Fra Filippo
Lipscomb, William Nunn
Lissitzky, El
List, Friedrich
Lister, Joseph, 1st Baron
Liszt, Franz
Littlewood, Joan
Litvinov, Maksim Maksimovich
Liu Shao Qi (or Liu Shao-sh'i)
Liverpool, Robert Banks Jenkinson, 2nd Earl of
Livia Drusilla
Livingstone, David
Livy
Llewellyn, Harry
Llewellyn, Richard
Lloyd, Harold
Lloyd, Marie
Lloyd George, David, 1st Earl
Lloyd George, Dame Margaret
Lloyd Webber, Andrew
Lloyd Webber, Julian
Llywelyn ap Gruffudd
Llywelyn ap Iorwerth
Lobachevski, Nikolai Ivanovich
Lobengula
Lochner, Stefan
Locke, John
Locke, Matthew

Lockhart

Lockhart, Sir (Robert Hamilton) Bruce
Lockhart, John Gibson
Lockyer, Sir Joseph Norman
Lodge, Henry Cabot
Lodge, Sir Oliver Joseph
Lodge, Thomas
Loeb, Jacques
Loeffler, Friedrich August Johannes
Loewe, Frederick
Loewi, Otto
Lomax, Alan
Lomax, John Avery
Lombard, Peter
Lombardo, Antonio
Lombardo, Pietro
Lombardo, Tullio
Lombroso, Cesare
Lomonosov, Mikhail Vasilievich
London, Jack
Longfellow, Henry Wadsworth
Longhi, Alessandro
Longhi, Pietro
Longinus
Lonsdale, Gordon Arnold
Lonsdale, Dame Kathleen
Loos, Adolph
Lope de Vega
López, Carlos Antonio
López, Francisco Solano
López de Ayala, Pero
Lorca, Federico Garcia
Loren, Sophia
Lorentz, Hendrick Antoon
Lorenz, Konrad
Lorenzetti, Ambrogio
Lorenzetti, Pietro
Lorenzo Monaco
Lorrain, Claude
Lorraine, Charles, Cardinal de
Los Angeles, Victoria de
Losey, Joseph
Lothair
Loti, Pierre
Lotto, Lorenzo
Louis, Joe
Louis Philippe

Louvois, Michel Le Tellier, Marquis de
Lovecraft, H(oward) P(hilips)
Lovelace, Richard
Lovell, Sir Bernard
Lovett, William
Low, Sir David (Alexander Cecil)
Lowell, Amy
Lowell, James Russell
Lowell, Percival
Lowell, Robert
Lowry, L(awrence) S(tephen)
Lowry, (Clarence) Malcolm
Lubitsch, Ernst
Lucan
Lucas van Leyden
Luce, Clare Booth
Luce, Henry R(obinson)
Lucretius
Lucullus, Lucius Licinius
Ludendorff, Erich
Lugard, Frederick Dealtry, 1st Baron
Lu Hsün
Lukacs, Giorgi
Lull, Ramón
Lully, Jean Baptiste
Lumière, Auguste
Lumière, Louis
Lumumba, Patrice (Hemery)
Lunt, Alfred
Lynne Fontanne
Lurçat, Jean
Luria, Isaac
Luther, Martin
Lutoslawski, Witold
Lutuli, Albert (John Mvumbi)
Lutyens, Sir Edwin Landseer
Lutyens, Elisabeth
Luxemburg, Rosa
Lvov, Georgi Yevgenievich, Prince
Lyautey, Louis Hubert Gonzalve
Lydgate, John
Lyell, Sir Charles
Lyly, John
Lynch, Jack

Lynd, Helen
Lynd, Robert Staughton
Lyons, Joseph Aloysius
Lysander
Lysenko, Trofim Denisovich
Lysias
Lysippus
Lyttelton, Humphrey
Lytton, Edward George Earle Bulwer-Lytton, 1st Baron
Maazel, Lorin
Mabuse see Gossaert, Jan
McAdam, John Loudon
MacAlpine, Kenneth
MacArthur, Douglas
Macarthur, John
Macaulay, Dame Rose
Macaulay, Thomas Babington, 1st Baron
Macbeth
MacBride, Seán
McBride, Willie John
McCarthy, Joseph R(aymond)
McCarthy, Mary
McCartney, Linda
McCartney, Paul
McClellan, George B(rinton)
McClure, Sir Robert John Le Mesurier
McCullers, Carson
MacDiarmid, Hugh
MacDonald, Flora
Macdonald, Sir John (Alexander)
MacDonald, (James) Ramsay
McEnroe, John (Patrick)
McGonagall, William
Mach, Ernst
Machaut, Guillaume de
Machel, Samora Moïses
Machen, Arthur (Llewellyn)
Machiavelli, Niccolò
McIndoe, Sir Archibald Hector
Macintosh, Charles
Macke, August
McKenna, Siobhán
Mackenzie, Sir (Edward Montague) Compton

Mackerras, Sir Charles
Mackinder, Sir Halford John
McKinley, William
Mackintosh, Charles Rennie
Maclean, Donald
Macleish, Archibald
Macleod, Iain (Norman)
Macleod, John James Rickard
Mac Liammóir, Micheál
Maclise, Daniel
McLuhan, (Herbert) Marshall
MacMahon, Marie Edme Patrice Maurice, Comte de
McMahon, William
Macmillan, Alexander
Macmillan, Daniel
McMillan, Edwin Mattison
Macmillan, (Maurice) Harold, 1st Earl of Stockton
MacMillan, Sir Kenneth
Macmillan, Kirkpatrick
MacMurrough, Dermot
MacNeice, Louis
Maconchy, Elizabeth
Macquarie, Lachlan
McQueen, Steve
Macready, William Charles
Madariaga y Rojo, Salvador de
Maderna, Carlo
Madison, James
Maecenas, Gaius
Maes, Nicolas
Maeterlinck, Maurice
Magellan, Ferdinand
Magendie, François
Magnani, Anna
Magritte, René
Mahavira *title of* Vardhamana
Mahdi, al-
Mahler, Gustav
Mahmud
Mailer, Norman
Maillol, Aristide
Maimonides, Moses
Maintenon, Mme de
Maistre, Joseph de
Makarios
Malachy, St
Malamud, Bernard
Malan, Daniel F(rançois)
Malaparte, Curzio
Malcolm, George (John)
Malebranche, Nicolas
Malenkov, Georgi Maksimilianovich
Malesherbes, Chrétien Guillaume de Lamoignon de
Malevich, Kazimir
Malherbe, François de
Malik-Shah
Malinowski, Bronisław
Malipiero, Gian Francesco
Mallarmé, Stéphane
Malmesbury, William of
Malory, Sir Thomas
Malpighi, Marcello
Malraux, André
Malthus, Thomas Robert
Ma'mun, al-
Manasseh ben Israel
Mandela, Nelson (Rolihlahla)
Mandela, Winnie
Mandelstam, Osip
Mandeville, Sir John
Manet, Edouard
Manin, Daniele
Manley, Michael
Mann, Heinrich
Mann, Thomas
Mannerheim, Carl Gustaf Emil, Baron von
Manning, Henry Edward, Cardinal
Mansart, François
Mansfield, Katherine
Mansfield, William Murray, 1st Earl of
Mansholt, Sicco
Mansholt Plan
Mansur, Abu Ja'far al-
Mantegna, Andrea
Manutius, Aldus
Manutius, Paulus
Manzoni, Alessandro

Martin

Mao Tse-tung (*or* Mao Ze Dong)
Marat, Jean Paul
Marc, Franz
Marceau, Marcel
Marcellus, Marcus Claudius
Marchand, Jean Baptiste
Marconi, Guglielmo
Marcos, Ferdinand E(dralin)
Marcus Aurelius
Marcuse, Herbert
Marenzio, Luca
Margrethe Danish queen
Mariette, Auguste Ferdinand François
Marinetti, Filippo Tommaso
Marini, Marino
Maritain, Jacques
Marius, Gaius
Marivaux, Pierre Carlet de Chamblain de
Mark Antony
Markiewicz, Constance, Countess of
Markov, Andrei Andreevich
Markova, Dame Alicia
Marks, Michael
Marks, Simon, 1st Baron
Marlborough, John Churchill, 1st Duke of
Marlborough, Sarah Churchill, Duchess of
Marlowe, Christopher
Marot, Clément
Marquand, J(ohn) P(hillips)
Marquette, Jacques
Marryat, Captain Frederick
Marsh, Dame Ngaio
Marshall, George C(atlett)
Marshall, John
Marsilius of Padua
Marston, John
Martel, Charles
Martel, Geoffrey
Martí, José Julián
Martial
Martin, Archer John Porter

Martin

Martin, John
Martin, Pierre-Émile
Martin, Richard
Martin du Gard, Roger
Martineau, Harriet
Martini, Simone
Martinu, Bohuslav
Marvell, Andrew
Marx, Chico
Marx, Groucho
Marx, Gummo
Marx, Harpo
Marx, Karl (Heinrich)
Marx, Zeppo
Masaccio
Masaryk, Jan (Garrigue)
Masaryk, Tomáš (Garrigue)
Mascagni, Pietro
Masefield, John
Masinissa
Masolino
Mason, A(lfred) E(dward) W(oodley)
Masséna, André
Massenet, Jules
Massey, Anna
Massey, Daniel
Massey, Raymond
Massey, William Ferguson
Massine, Léonide
Massinger, Philip
Massys, Quentin
Masters, Edgar Lee
Masters, William Howell
Mastroianni, Marcello
Mata Hari
Matisse, Henri
Matsuo Basho
Matteotti, Giacomo
Matthews, Sir Stanley
Mauchly, John W.
Maudslay, Henry
Maugham, Robin
Maugham, W(illiam) Somerset
Maupassant, Guy de
Maupertuis, Pierre Louis Moreau de
Mauriac, François
Maurois, André
Maurras, Charles
Maxim, Sir Hiram Stevens

Maxwell, James Clerk
Mayakovskii, Vladimir
Mayer, Julius Robert von
Mayer, Louis B.
Mayer, Sir Robert
Mayhew, Henry
Mayo, Charles Horace
Mayo, Charles William
Mayo, William James
Mayo, William Worrall
Mazarin, Jules, Cardinal
Mazzini, Giuseppe
Mboya, Tom
Mead, Margaret
Meade, Richard
Meads, Colin Earl
Mechnikov, Ilya *variant spelling of* Metchnikov, Ilya
Medawar, Sir Peter Brian
Medici, Catherine de'
Medici, Cosimo de'
Medici, Lorenzo de'
Medici, Piero de'
Médicis, Marie de
Meegeren, Hans van
Mehemet Ali
Meiji *title of* Mutsuhito
Meir, Golda
Meissonier, Jean-Louis-Ernest
Meitner, Lise
Melanchthon, Philip
Melba, Dame Nellie
Melbourne, William Lamb, 2nd Viscount
Melchett, Alfred Mond, 1st Baron
Melchior, Lauritz
Mellon, Andrew William
Melville, Herman
Memling, Hans
Menander
Mencius
Mencken, H(enry) L(ouis)
Mendel, Gregor Johann
Mendeleyev, Dimitrii Ivanovich
Mendelssohn, Felix
Mendelssohn, Moses
Menderes, Adnan
Mendès-France, Pierre

Mendoza, Antonio de
Menelik
Menes
Mengelberg, William
Mengs, Anton Raphael
Menno Simons
Menon, Krishna
Menotti, Gian Carlo
Menuhin, Hephzibah
Menuhin, Jeremy
Menuhin, Yaltah
Menuhin, Sir Yehudi
Menzies, Sir Robert Gordon
Mercator, Gerardus
Mercer, David
Mercouri, Melina
Meredith, George
Meredith, Owen *pen name of* Robert Bulmer-Lytton, 1st Earl of Lytton
Mérimée, Prosper
Merleau-Ponty, Maurice
Merneptah
Mesmer, Franz Anton
Messager, André (Charles Prosper)
Messalina, Valeria
Messerschmitt, Willy
Messiaen, Olivier
Messier, Charles
Meštrović, Ivan
Metastasio, Pietro
Metaxas, Ioannis
Metchnikov (*or* Mechnikov), Ilya Ilich
Methodius, St
Metsu, Gabriel
Metternich, Klemens Wenzel Nepomuk Lothar, Fürst von
Meyerbeer, Giacomo
Meyerhof, Otto Fritz
Meyerhold, Vsevolod Emilievich
Michelangelo Buonarroti
Michelet, Jules
Michelin, André
Michelin, Édouard
Michelozzo di Bartolommeo
Michelson, Albert Abraham
Mickiewicz, Adam
Middleton, Thomas

Mies van der Rohe, Ludwig
Mihajlović, Draža
Miles, Bernard, Baron
Milhaud, Darius
Mill, James
Mill, John Stuart
Millais, Sir John Everett
Millay, Edna St Vincent
Miller, Arthur
Miller, Glenn
Miller, Henry
Millet, Jean François
Millikan, Robert Andrews
Mills, Hayley
Mills, Sir John
Mills, Juliet
Milne, A(lan) A(lexander)
Milner, Alfred, Viscount
Miloš
Milstein, Nathan
Miltiades
Milton, John
Minamoto Yoritomo
Minamoto Yoshitsune
Mindszenty, József, Cardinal
Mingus, Charlie
Minnelli, Liza
Mintoff, Dom(inic)
Mirabeau, Honoré Gabriel Riquetti, Comte de
Miró, Joan
Mishima, Yukio
Mistinguett
Mistral, Frédéric
Mistral, Gabriela
Mitchell, Margaret
Mitchell, R(eginald) J(oseph)
Mithridates
Mitterrand, François (Maurice)
Mizoguchi Kenji
Mobutu, Sese Seko
Mocenigo, Andrea
Mocenigo, Giovanni
Mocenigo, Pietro
Mocenigo, Tommaso
Modigliani, Amedeo
Mohammed (or Muhammad)

Mohammed Askia
Moholy-Nagy, László
Molière
Molina, Luis de
Molinos, Miguel de
Molnár, Ferenc
Molotov, Vyacheslav Mikhailovich
Moltke, Helmuth, Graf von
Moltke, Helmuth Johannes Ludwig von
Mommsen, Theodor
Mond, Alfred, 1st Baron Melchett
Mond, Ludwig
Mondrian, Piet
Monet, Claude
Monge, Gaspard
Moniz, Antonio Egas
Monk, Thelonius (Sphere)
Monmouth, James Scott, Duke of
Monnet, Jean
Monod, Jacques-Lucien
Monroe, James
Monroe, Marilyn
Monsarrat, Nicholas
Montagu, Lady Mary Wortley
Montaigne, Michel de
Montale, Eugenio
Montcalm, Louis Joseph de Montcalm-Grozon, Marquis de
Montefeltro, Federigo, Duke of Urbino
Montefiore, Sir Moses
Montespan, Françoise Athénaïs de Rochechouart, Marquise de
Montesquieu, Charles Louis de Secondat, Baron de
Monteux, Pierre
Monteverdi, Claudio
Montez, Lola
Montezuma
Montfort, Simon de, Earl of Leicester
Montgolfier, Jacques-Étienne
Montgolfier, Joseph-Michel

Montgomery of Alamein, Bernard Law, 1st Viscount
Montherlant, Henry de
Montrose, James Graham, 1st Marquess of
Moody, Dwight Lyman
Moore, Bobby
Moore, G(eorge) E(dward)
Moore, Gerald
Moore, Henry
Moore, Sir John
Moore, Marianne
Moore, Thomas
Morandi, Giorgio
Moravia, Alberto
Moray, James Stuart, Earl of
More, Henry
More, Sir Thomas
Moreau, Gustave
Moreau, Jean Victor
Morgagni, Giovanni Battista
Morgan, Charles
Morgan, Sir Henry
Morgan, John Pierpont
Morgan, Thomas Hunt
Mörike, Eduard Friedrich
Morison, Stanley
Morisot, Berthe
Morland, George
Morley, Edward Williams
Morley, Robert
Morley, Thomas
Mornay, Philippe de, Seigneur du Plessis Marly
Moro, Aldo
Moroni, Giovanni Battista
Morphy, Paul Charles
Morris, Desmond John
Morris, William
Morrison, Herbert Stanley, Baron
Morse, Samuel Finley Breese
Mortier, Édouard Adolphe Casimir Joseph, Duc de Trévise

Mortimer, Roger de, 1st
  Earl of March
Morton, James Douglas,
  4th Earl of
Morton, Jelly Roll
Morton, John
Moseley, Henry Gwyn
  Jeffries
Mosley, Sir Oswald
  Ernald
Moss, Stirling
Motherwell, Robert
Mo-tzu *variant spelling of*
  Mo-Zi
Mountbatten of Burma,
  Louis, 1st Earl
Mozart, Wolfgang
  Amadeus
Mo-Zi (*or* Mo-tzu)
Muʻawiyah
Mugabe, Robert
  (Gabriel)
Muhammad *variant spelling of* Mohammed
Muhammad Ahmad *original name of* al-Mahdi
Muir, Edwin
Mujibur Rahman, Sheik
Muller, Hermann Joseph
Müller, Paul Hermann
Mulliken, Robert
  Sanderson
Mulready, William
Mumford, Lewis
Munch, Charles
Munch, Edvard
Münchhausen, Karl
  Friedrich, Freiherr von
Munnings, Sir Alfred
Munro, H(ector) H(ugh)
  (*pen name* Saki)
Munthe, Axel
Müntzer, Thomas
Murasaki Shikibu
Murat, Joachim
Murdoch, Dame Iris
Murdock, William
Murillo, Bartolomé
  Esteban
Murray, Gilbert
Murray, Sir James
  (Augustus Henry)
Murray, Len
Murrow, Edward
  R(oscoe)
Murry, John Middleton

Musgrave, Thea
Musil, Robert
Musset, Alfred de
Mussolini, Benito
  (Amilcare Andrea)
Mussorgski, Modest
  Petrovich
Mutanabbi, Abu At-
  Tayyib Ahmad Ibn
  Husayn al-
Mutesa
Mutsuhito
Muybridge, Eadweard
Muzorewa, Bishop Abel
  (Tendekayi)
Myers, F(rederic)
  W(illiam) H(enry)
Myrdal, Alva
Myrdal, Gunnar
Mzilikazi
Nabokov, Vladimir
Nadar
Nader, Ralph
Nader Shah
Naevius, Gnaeus
Nagarjuna
Nagy, Imre
Naipaul, V(idiadhur)
  S(urajprasad)
Namier, Sir Lewis
  Bernstein
Nanak
Nana Sahib
Nansen, Fridtjof
Napier, Sir Charles
  James
Napier, John
Napier of Magdala,
  Robert Cornelis, 1st
  Baron
Narses
Nash, John
Nash, Ogden
Nash, Paul
Nash, Richard
Nash, Sir Walter
Nashe, Thomas
Nasser, Gamal Abdel
Nazianus, St Gregory of
Nebuchadnezzar
Necker, Jacques
Neer, Aert van der
Nefertiti
Negrín, Juan
Nehru, Jawaharlal

Neill, A(lexander)
  S(utherland)
Nekrasov, Nikolai
  Alekseevich
Nelson, Horatio,
  Viscount
Nemery, Jaafar
  Mohammed al
Nennius
Neri, St Philip
Nernst, Walther
  Hermann
Nero (Claudius Caesar)
Neruda, Pablo
Nerva, Marcus Cocceius
Nerval, Gérard de
Nervi, Pier Luigi
Nesbit, Edith
Nesselrode, Karl Robert,
  Count
Neto, Agostinho
Neumann, (Johann)
  Balthasar
Neumann, John von
Nevsky, Alexander
Newcastle, Thomas
  Pelham-Holles, 1st
  Duke of
Newcastle, William
  Cavendish, Duke of
Newcombe, John
Newcomen, Thomas
Ne Win
Newman, John Henry,
  Cardinal
Newman, Paul
Newton, Sir Isaac
Nexø, Martin Andersen
Ney, Michel, Prince of
  Moscow
Ngo Dinh Diem
Niarchos, Stavros
  Spyros
Nicholson, Ben
Nicholson, Jack
Nicholson, William
Nicias
Nicklaus, Jack William
Nicolai, Otto Ehrenfried
Nicolson, Sir Harold
  (George)
Niebuhr, Barthold Georg
Nielsen, Carl (August)
Niemeyer, Oscar
Niemöller, Martin
Nietzsche, Friedrich

Nightingale, Florence
Nijinsky, Vaslav
Nikisch, Arthur
Nilsson, Birgit Marta
Nimitz, Chester W(illiam)
Nirenberg, Marshall Warren
Nithsdale, William Maxwell, 5th Earl of
Niven, David
Nixon, Richard Milhous
Nizam al-Mulk
Nkomo, Joshua
Nkrumah, Kwame
Nobel, Alfred Bernhard
Nobile, Umberto
Noble, Sir Andrew
Nobunaga Oda
Noel-Baker, Philip John
Noguchi, Hideyo
Nolan, Sir Sidney
Nolde, Emil
Nollekens, Joseph
Nono, Luigi
Nordenskjöld, Nils Adolf Erik, Baron
Norfolk, Thomas Howard, Duke of
North, Frederick, Lord
North, Sir Thomas
Northcliffe, Alfred Charles William Harmsworth, 1st Viscount
Northrop, John Howard
Northumberland, John Dudley, Duke of
Nostradamus
Novalis
Novello, Ivor
Novotný, Antonín
Noyes, Alfred
Nu, U
Nuffield, William Richard Morris, 1st Viscount
Nureyev, Rudolf
Nurhachi
Nurmi, Paavo Johannes
Nyerere, Julius (Kambarage)
Nyssa, St Gregory of
Oakley, Annie
Oastler, Richard

Oates, Lawrence Edward Grace
Oates, Titus
Obote, (Apollo) Milton
O'Brien, Conor Cruise
O'Brien, Flann
O'Brien, William
O'Brien, William Smith
O'Casey, Sean
Ockham, William of
O'Connell, Daniel
O'Connor, Feargus
O'Connor, Frank
Oda Nobunaga
Odets, Clifford
Odoacer
Oehlenschläger, Adam (Gottlob)
Oersted, Hans Christian
Offa
Offenbach, Jacques
O'Flaherty, Liam
Ogden, C(harles) K(ay)
Ogdon, John
Oglethorpe, James Edward
O'Hara, John (Henry)
O'Higgins, Bernardo
Ohm, Georg Simon
Oistrakh, David
Oistrakh, Igor
O'Keeffe, Georgia
Okeghem, Jean d'
Olbers, Heinrich Wilhelm Matthäus
Oldcastle, Sir John
Oldenbarneveldt, Johan van
Oldenburg, Claes (Thure)
Oliphant, Sir Mark Laurence Elwin
Olivares, Gaspar de Guzmán, Conde-Duque de
Oliver, Isaac
Olivier, Laurence (Kerr), Baron
Omar Khayyam
Onassis, Aristotle Socrates
Oñate, Juan de
O'Neill, Eugene
O'Neill, Terence, Baron
Onsager, Lars

Ophüls, Max
Opie, John
Opitz (von Boberfeld), Martin
Oppenheimer, J. Robert
Orcagna, Andrea
Orczy, Baroness Emmusca
Oresme, Nicole d'
Orff, Carl
Origen
Orlando, Vittorio Emanuele
Orléans, Charles, Duc d'
Orléans, Louis Philippe Joseph, Duc d'
Orlov, Aleksei Grigorievich
Orlov, Grigori Grigorievich, Count
Ormandy, Eugene
Ormonde, James Butler, 1st Duke of
Orozco, José
Ortega y Gasset, José
Ortelius, Abraham
Ortoli, François Xavier
Orwell, George
Osborne, Dorothy
Osborne, John
O'Shea, Katherine Page
Osler, Sir William
Osman
Ossian
Ossietsky, Carl von
Ostade, Adrian van
Ostrovskii, Aleksandr Nikolaevich
Ostwald, (Friedrich) Wilhelm
Oswald, Lee Harvey
Oswiu
Otis, Elisha Graves
Otto, Nikolaus August
Otway, Thomas
Oudry, Jean-Baptiste
Ouida
Ouspensky, Peter
Outram, Sir James
Ovid
Owen, Alun Davies
Owen, Dr David (Anthony Llewellyn)
Owen, Robert
Owen, Wilfred

Owens

Owens, Jesse
Oxenstierna, Axel, Count
Pabst, G(eorge) W(ilhelm)
Pachomius, St
Pachymeres, Georgius
Paderewski, Ignacy (Jan)
Páez, José Antonio
Paganini, Niccolò
Page, Sir Earle (Christmas Grafton)
Page, Sir Frederick Handley
Pahlavi, Mohammed Reza
Pahlavi, Reza Shah
Paine, Thomas
Paisley, Ian
Palaeologus, Michael
Palestrina, Giovanni Pierluigi da
Paley, William
Palgrave, Francis Turner
Palissy, Bernard
Palladio, Andrea
Palma Vecchio, Jacopo
Palmer, Arnold
Palmer, Samuel
Palmerston, Henry John Temple, 3rd Viscount
Pandit, Vijaya Lakshmi
Pan Gu (or P'an Ku)
Panini
Pankhurst, Dame Christabel
Pankhurst, Emmeline
Pankhurst, Sylvia
Papadopoulos, George
Papen, Franz von
Pappus of Alexandria
Paracelsus
Paré, Ambroise
Pareto, Vilfredo
Paris, Matthew
Park, Mungo
Park Chung Hee
Parker, Charlie (Christopher)
Parker, Dorothy Rothschild
Parker, Matthew
Parkes, Sir Henry
Parkinson, (Cyril) Northcote
Parkman, Francis
Parmenides
Parmigianino
Parnell, Charles Stewart
Parr, Catherine
Parry, Sir Hubert
Parry, Sir William Edward
Parsons, Sir Charles Algernon
Partridge, Eric Honeywood
Pascal, Blaise
Pašić, Nicola
Pasionaria, La see Ibarruri, Dolores
Pasmore, Victor
Pasolini, Pier Paolo
Passy, Frédéric
Pasternak, Boris
Pasteur, Louis
Pater, Walter (Horatio)
Paterson, William
Patinir, Joachim
Patmore, Coventry
Paton, Alan
Patti, Adelina
Patton, George S(mith)
Pauli, Wolfgang
Pauling, Linus Carl
Paulinus of Nola, St
Paulus, Friedrich
Pausanias
Pavarotti, Luciano
Pavese, Cesare
Pavlov, Ivan Petrovich
Pavlova, Anna
Paxinou, Katina
Paxton, Sir Joseph
Paz, Octavio
Peacock, Thomas Love
Peake, Mervyn
Pears, Sir Peter
Pearse, Patrick Henry
Pearson, Lester B(owles)
Peary, Robert Edwin
Peckinpah, Sam
Peel, Sir Robert
Peele, George
Péguy, Charles
Peirce, Charles Sanders
Pelagius
Pelé
Pelham, Henry
Pelletier, Pierre Joseph
Penda
Penderecki, Krzysztof
Pendlebury, John Devitt Stringfellow
Penn, William
Penney, William George, Baron
Pepys, Samuel
Perceval, Spencer
Percy, Sir Henry (known as Harry Hotspur)
Percy, Bishop Thomas
Perelman, S(idney) J(oseph)
Pérez Galdós, Benito
Pergolesi, Giovanni (Battista)
Pericles
Perkin, Sir William Henry
Perón, Evita
Perón, Isabel
Perón, Juan (Domingo)
Pérotin
Perrault, Charles
Perrin, Jean-Baptiste
Perry, Fred(erick John)
Perry, Matthew C(albraith)
Perse, Saint-John
Pershing, John J(oseph)
Perugino
Perutz, Max Ferdinand
Pestalozzi, Johann Heinrich
Pétain, (Henri) Philippe
Peterson, Oscar Emmanuel
Petipa, Marius
Petit, Roland
Petőfi, Sándor
Petrarch
Petrie, Sir (William Matthew) Flinders
Petronius Arbiter
Petrosian, Tigran Vartanovich
Pevsner, Antoine
Pevsner, Sir Nikolaus (Bernhard Leon)
Phaedrus
Phalaris
Phidias
Phidippides
Philadelphus, Ptolomy

Philby, Harold Adrian Russell
Philby, H(arry) St John (Bridge)
Philemon
Philidor, André Danican
Philidor, François André Danican
Phillip, Arthur
Philo Judaeus
Phiz see Browne, Hablot Knight
Phryne
Phyfe (or Fife), Duncan
Piaf, Edith
Piaget, Jean
Picabia, Francis
Picasso, Pablo
Piccard, Auguste
Piccard, Jacques
Piccard, Jean-Félix
Pickford, Mary
Pico della Mirandola, Giovanni, Conte
Pieck, Wilhelm
Piero della Francesca
Piero di Cosimo
Piggott, Lester Keith
Pilate, Pontius
Piłsudski, Józef Klemens
Pinckney, Charles
Pinckney, Charles Cotesworth
Pinckney, Thomas
Pindar
Pinero, Sir Arthur Wing
Pinkerton, Allan
Pinochet, Augusto
Pinter, Harold
Pinturicchio
Piozzi, Hester Lynch (married name Thrale)
Piper, John
Pirandello, Luigi
Piranesi, Giambattista
Pisanello
Pisano, Andrea
Pisano, Giovanni
Pisano, Nicola
Pisistratus
Pissarro, Camille
Pissarro, Lucien
Pitman, Sir Isaac
Pitt, William
Pitt-Rivers, Augustus Henry Lane Fox
Pius pope
Pizarro, Francisco
Place, Francis
Planck, Erwin
Planck, Max Karl Ernst Ludwig
Plantagenet surname of English kings 1154–1485
Plath, Sylvia
Plato
Plautus, Titus Maccius
Pleasence, Donald
Plekhanov, Georgi Valentinovich
Pliny
Plomer, William
Plotinus
Plowright, Joan
Plunket, St Oliver
Plutarch
Pocahontas
Po Chü-i variant spelling of Bo Zhu Yi
Podgorny, N(ikolai) V(iktorovich)
Poe, Edgar Allan
Poggio Bracciolini, Giovanni Francesco
Poincaré, Jules Henri
Poincaré, Raymond
Poisson, Siméon Dénis
Poitiers, Diane de, Duchesse de Valentinois
Polanski, Roman
Pole, Reginald, Cardinal
Polignac, Auguste Jules Armand Marie, Prince de
Poliziano
Polk, James K(nox)
Pollaiuolo, Antonio
Pollaiuolo, Piero
Pollock, Jackson
Polo, Marco
Polybius
Polycarp, St
Polyclitus
Polycrates
Pombal, Sebastião José de Carvalho e Mello, Marquês de
Pompadour, Mme de
Pompey
Pompidou, Georges (Jean Raymond)
Ponce de Leon, Juan
Poniatowski, Józef
Poniatowski, Stanisław
Pontiac
Pontormo, Jacopo da
Pope, Alexander
Popov, Aleksandr Stepanovich
Popov, Oleg Konstantinovich
Popper, Sir Karl Raimund
Porphyriogenitus, Constantine
Porphyry
Porter, Cole (Albert)
Porter, Katherine Anne
Porter, Peter
Portland, William Henry Cavendish Bentinck, 3rd Duke of
Potemkin, Grigori Aleksandrovich
Potter, Beatrix
Potter, Paul
Potter, Stephen
Poulenc, Francis
Pound, Ezra
Poussin, Nicolas
Powell, Anthony
Powell, Cecil Frank
Powell, (John) Enoch
Powys, John Cowper
Powys, Theodore Francis
Praetorius, Michael
Prandtl, Ludwig
Prasad, Rajendra
Praxiteles
Preminger, Otto (Ludwig)
Prescott, William Hickling
Presley, Elvis (Aaron)
Prester John
Pretorius, Andries (Wilhelmus Jacobus)
Pretorius, Marthinus Wessel
Prévert, Jacques
Previn, André
Prévost d'Exiles, Antoine François, Abbé

Pride

Pride, Thomas
Priestley, J(ohn) B(oynton)
Priestley, Joseph
Primo de Rivera, José Antonio
Primo de Rivera, Miguel
Prior, Matthew
Priscian
Pritchett, V(ictor) S(awden)
Proclus
Procopius
Prokofiev, Sergei
Prokop
Propertius, Sextus
Protagoras
Proudhon, Pierre Joseph
Proust, Joseph-Louis
Proust, Marcel
Prout, William
Prud'hon, Pierre Paul
Prynne, William
Psamtik
Pseudo-Dionysius the Areopagite
Ptolemy
Puccini, Giacomo
Pucelle, Jean
Pudovkin, Vsevolod
Pufendorf, Samuel von
Pugachov, Yemelyan Ivanovich
Pugin, Augustus Welby Northmore
Pulci, Luigi
Pullman, George Mortimer
Purcell, Edward Mills
Purcell, Henry
Purchas, Samuel
Pusey, Edward Bouverie
Pushkin, Aleksandr
Puvis de Chavannes, Pierre (Cécile)
Pu Yi, Henry
Pym, John
Pynchon, Thomas
Pyrrhon
Pyrrhus
Pythagoras
Pytheas
Qaboos ibn Sa'id
Qaddafi, Moammar al-
Qian Long (or Ch'ien-lung)

Quant, Mary
Quasimodo, Salvatore
Queneau, Raymond
Quercia, Jacopo della
Quesnay, François
Quesnel, Pasquier
Quiller-Couch, Sir Arthur Thomas
Quine, Willard van Orman
Quintilian
Quisling, Vidkun (Abraham Lauritz Jonsson)
Qu Qiu Bai (or Ch'ü Ch'iu-pai)
Rabelais, François
Rabi, Isidor Isaac
Rachmaninov, Sergei
Racine, Jean
Rackham, Arthur
Radcliffe, Ann (Ward)
Radcliffe-Brown, Alfred Reginald
Radek, Karl
Radić, Stjepan
Radiguet, Raymond
Raeburn, Sir Henry
Raeder, Erich
Raffles, Sir Thomas Stamford
Raglan, FitzRoy James Henry Somerset, 1st Baron
Raikes, Robert
Raine, Kathleen
Rainier, Prince
Rais, Gilles de
Rákóczy, Ferenc
Raleigh, Sir Walter
Ramakrishna
Raman, Sir Chandrasekhara Venkata
Ramanuja
Rambert, Dame Marie
Rameau, Jean Philippe
Ramón y Cajal, Santiago
Ramsay, Allan
Ramsay, Sir William
Ramses
Ramsey, Alf
Ram Singh
Ramus, Petrus
Ranjit Singh, Maharaja

Ranjitsinhji Vibhaji, Kumar Shri, Maharajah Jam Sahib of Nawanagar
Rank, J(oseph) Arthur, 1st Baron
Rank, Otto
Ranke, Leopold von
Ransom, John Crowe
Ransome, Arthur Mitchell
Raphael
Rashi
Rasmussen, Knud Johan Victor
Rasputin, Grigori Yefimovich
Rathenau, Walther
Rattigan, Sir Terence
Rauschenberg, Robert
Ravel, Maurice
Rawlinson, Sir Henry Creswicke
Rawsthorne, Alan
Ray, John
Ray, Man
Ray, Satyajit
Rayleigh, John William Strutt, 3rd Baron
Rayleigh, Robert John Strutt, 4th Baron
Razi, ar-
Razin, Stenka
Read, Sir Herbert
Reade, Charles
Reading, Rufus Daniel Isaacs, 1st Marquess of
Réaumur, René-Antoine Ferchault de
Reber, Grote
Recamier, Jeanne Françoise Julie Adelaide
Redford, Robert
Redgrave, Corin
Redgrave, Lynn
Redgrave, Sir Michael
Redgrave, Vanessa
Redmond, John Edward
Redon, Odilon
Redouté, Pierre Joseph
Reed, Sir Carol
Reed, John
Reed, Walter
Reeves, William Pember

Reger, Max
Regiomontanus
Regnier, Henri François Joseph de
Regulus, Marcus Attilus
Rehoboam
Reich, Wilhelm
Reid, Sir George Houston
Reid, Thomas
Reinhardt, Django
Reinhardt, Max
Reith, John Charles Walsham, 1st Baron
Remarque, Erich Maria
Rembrandt (Harmenszoon) van Rijn
Remington, Eliphalet
Renan, (Joseph) Ernest
Reni, Guido
Rennie, John
Renoir, Jean
Renoir, Pierre Auguste
Resnais, Alain
Respighi, Ottorino
Retz, Jean François Paul de Gondi, Cardinal de
Reuter, Paul Julius, Baron von
Revere, Paul
Reynaud, Paul
Reynolds, Sir Joshua
Rhee, Syngman
Rheticus
Rhine, Joseph Banks
Rhodes, Cecil (John)
Rhodes, Wilfred
Rhys, Jean
Ribbentrop, Joachim von
Ribera, José de
Ricardo, David
Ricci, Marco
Ricci, Matteo
Ricci, Sebastiano
Riccio, David
Rich, Richard, 1st Baron
Richards, Frank
Richards, Sir Gordon
Richards, I(vor) A(rmstrong)
Richardson, Henry Handel
Richardson, Henry Hobson

Richardson, Sir Ralph
Richardson, Samuel
Richelieu, Armand Jean du Plessis, Cardinal de
Richler, Mordecai
Richter, Hans
Richter, Johann Paul Friedrich.
Richter, Sviatoslav (Teofilovitch)
Richthofen, Manfred, Freiherr von
Ridley, Nicholas
Ridolfi, Roberto
Riebeeck, Jan van
Riefensthal, Leni
Riel, Louis
Riemann, Georg Friedrich Bernhard
Rienzo, Cola di
Riesman, David
Riley, Bridget Louise
Rilke, Rainer Maria
Rimbaud, Arthur
Rimsky-Korsakov, Nikolai
Rivera, Diego
Rizzio, David
Roach, Hal
Robbe-Grillet, Alain
Robbins, Frederick Chapman
Robbins, Jerome
Roberts, Frederick Sleigh, 1st Earl
Roberts, Tom
Robeson, Paul
Robespierre, Maximilien François Marie Isidore de
Robey, Sir George
Robinson, Edward G.
Robinson, Edwin Arlington
Robinson, John (Arthur Thomas)
Robinson, Sir Robert
Robinson, Sugar Ray
Robinson, William Heath
Robson, Dame Flora
Rochester, John Wilmot, 2nd Earl of
Rockefeller, John D(avison)

Rossetti

Rockefeller, Nelson A(ldrich)
Rockingham, Charles Watson-Wentworth, 2nd Marquess of
Roderic Irish king
Rodgers, Richard Charles
Rodin, Auguste
Rodney, George Brydges, 1st Baron
Rodrigo, Joaquín
Roebling, John Augustus
Roebling, Washington Augustus
Roentgen, Wilhelm Konrad
Rogers, Ginger
Rogers, John
Roget, Peter Mark
Röhm, Ernst
Rokitansky, Karl, Freiherr von
Rolfe, Frederick William
Rolland, Romain
Rolls, Charles Stewart
Romains, Jules
Rommel, Erwin
Romney, George
Romulus Augustulus
Ronsard, Pierre de
Roon, Albrecht, Graf von
Roosevelt, Eleanor
Roosevelt, Franklin D(elano)
Roosevelt, Theodore
Root, Elihu
Rory O'Connor
Rosa, Salvator
Roscelin
Roscius, Quintus
Rosebery, Archibald Philip Primrose, 5th Earl of
Rosenberg, Ethel
Rosenberg, Julius
Rosewall, Ken(neth Ronald)
Ross, Sir James Clark
Ross, Sir Ronald
Rosse, William Parsons, 3rd Earl of
Rossellini, Roberto
Rossetti, Christina Georgina
Rossetti, Dante Gabriel

Rossini

Rossini, Gioacchino Antonio
Rostand, Edmond
Rostropovich, Mstislav
Roth, Philip
Rothermere, Harold Sydney Harmsworth, 1st Viscount
Rothko, Mark
Rothschild, James
Rothschild, Karl Mayer
Rothschild, Lionel Nathan
Rothschild, Mayer Amschel
Rothschild, Nathan Mayer
Rothschild, Nathaniel Mayer Victor, 3rd Baron
Rothschild, Salomon Mayer
Rouault, Georges (Henri)
Roubillac, Louis François
Rouget de l'Isle, Claude Joseph
Rousseau, Henri
Rousseau, Jean Jacques
Rousseau, (Pierre Étienne) Théodore
Roussel, Albert
Roussel, Raymond
Roux, Pierre Paul Emile
Rowe, Nicholas
Rowlandson, Thomas
Rowley, Thomas
Rowse, A(lfred) L(eslie)
Royce, Sir (Frederick) Henry
Royce, Josiah
Rubbra, Edmund
Rubens, Peter Paul
Rubinstein, Anton
Rubinstein, Artur
Rublyov, Andrey
Ruggles, Carl
Ruisdael, Jacob van
Ruysdael, Salomon van
Ruiz, Juan
Rumford, Benjamin Thompson, Count
Rundstedt, (Karl Rudolf) Gerd von
Runeberg, Johan Ludwig
Runyon, Damon
Rurik
Rushdie, Salman
Rusk, (David) Dean
Ruskin, John
Russell, Bertrand Arthur William, 3rd Earl
Russell, John, 1st Earl
Russell, Ken
Russell, Lord William
Russell, Sir William Howard
Rutherford, Ernest, 1st Baron
Rutherford, Dame Margaret
Rutherford, Mark
Ruyter, Michiel Adriaanszoon de
Ryder, Sue, Baroness
Rykov, Aleksei Ivanovich
Ryle, Gilbert
Ryle, Sir Martin
Saarinen, Eero
Sabatier, Paul
Sachs, Hans
Sachs, Nelly (Leonie)
Sackville, Thomas, 1st Earl of Dorset
Sadat, Anwar
Sade, Donatien Alphonse François, Marquis de
Sa'di
Sagan, Françoise
Saigo Takamori
Sainte-Beuve, Charles-Augustin
Saint-Exupéry, Antoine de
Saint-Just, Louis (Antoine Léon) de
Saint-Laurent, Yves
Saint-Saëns, Camille
Saint-Simon, Claude Henri de Rouvroy, Comte de
Saint-Simon, Louis de Rouvroy, Duc de
Sakharov, Andrei Dimitrievich
Saki *pen name of* H(ector) H(ugh) Munro
Saladin
Salam, Abdus
Salazar, António de Oliveira
Sales, St Francis of
Salieri, Antonio
Salinger, J(erome) D(avid)
Salisbury, Robert Arthur Talbot Gascoyne-Cecil, 3rd Marquess of
Salisbury, Robert Cecil, 1st Earl of
Sallust
Samudra Gupta
Samuel, Herbert Louis, 1st Viscount
Sand, George
Sandage, Allan Rex
Sandburg, Carl
Sandwich, John Montagu, 4th Earl of
Sanger, Frederick
Sankara
San Martin, José de
Santa Anna, Antonio López de
Santayana, George
Sapir, Edward
Sapper *pen name of* H(erman) C(yril) McNeile
Sappho
Sardou, Victorien
Sargent, John Singer
Sargent, Sir Malcolm
Sargon
Saroyan, William
Sarraute, Nathalie
Sarto, Andrea del
Sartre, Jean-Paul
Sassetta
Sassoon, Siegfried
Satie, Erik
Sato Eisaku
Saud
Saussure, Ferdinand de
Savage, Michael Joseph
Savage, Richard
Savery, Thomas
Savonarola, Girolamo
Saxe, Maurice, Comte de
Saxe-Weimar, Duke Bernhard of
Saxo Grammaticus
Sayers, Dorothy L(eigh)

Scaliger, Joseph Justus
Scaliger, Julius Caesar
Scarfe, Gerald
Scarlatti, Alessandro
Scarlatti, Domenico
Scarron, Paul
Schacht, Hjalmar
Scheel, Walter
Scheele, Carl Wilhelm
Schelling, Friedrich
Schiaparelli, Elsa
Schiele, Egon
Schiller, (Johann Christoph) Friedrich (von)
Schlegel, August Wilhelm von
Schegel, (Carl Wilhelm) Friedrich von
Schleiden, Matthias Jakob
Schlesinger, John
Schlick, Moritz
Schlieffen, Alfred, Graf von
Schliemann, Heinrich
Schmeling, Max
Schmidt, Helmut
Schnabel, Artur
Schnitzler, Arthur
Schoenberg, Arnold
Schopenhauer, Arthur
Schreiner, Olive
Schrödinger, Erwin
Schubert, Franz (Peter)
Schuman, Robert French statesman; compare Schumann, Robert
Schuman, William (Howard)
Schumann, Clara
Schumann, Elisabeth
Schumann, Robert (Alexander) German composer; compare Schuman, Robert
Schuschnigg, Kurt von
Schütz, Heinrich
Schwann, Theodor
Schwarzenberg, Felix, Fürst zu
Schwarzkopf, Elisabeth
Schweitzer, Albert
Schwitters, Kurt

Scipio Aemilianus Africanus grandson of Scipio Africanus
Scipio Africanus
Scofield, (David) Paul
Scott, Sir George Gilbert
Scott, Sir Giles Gilbert
Scott, Sir Peter Markham
Scott, Robert Falcon
Scott, Ronnie
Scott, Sir Walter
Scriabin, Alexander
Scullin, James Henry
Seaborg, Glenn Theodore
Searle, Ronald William Fordham
Seddon, Richard John
Seeger, Pete
Seferis, George
Seghers, Hercules Pieterzoon
Segovia, Andrés
Segrè, Emilio
Selden, John
Seleucus I Nicator
Selkirk, Alexander
Sellers, Peter
Selwyn Lloyd, John, Baron
Selznick, David O(liver)
Semiramis
Sempringham, St Gilbert of
Senanayake, D(on) S(tephen)
Senanayake, Dudley
Seneca
Senefelder, Aloys
Senghor, Léopold Sédar
Sennacherib
Sennett, Mack
Sergius of Radonezh, St
Servetus, Michael
Sesostris
Sesshu
Sessions, Roger
Seton, Ernest Thompson
Seurat, Georges
Severini, Gino
Severus, Lucius Septimius
Severus Alexander

Sévigné, Marie de Rabutin-Chantal, Marquise de
Seymour, Jane
Shackleton, Sir Ernest Henry
Shadwell, Thomas
Shaffer, Anthony
Shaffer, Peter
Shaftesbury, Anthony Ashley Cooper, Earl of
Shah Jahan
Shahn, Ben
Shaka
Shakespeare, William
Shankar, Ravi
Shapur
Sharp, Cecil (James)
Shastri, Shri Lal Bahadur
Shaw, Artie
Shaw, George Bernard
Shaw, (Richard) Norman
Sheene, Barry
Shelburne, William Petty Fitzmaurice, 2nd Earl of
Shelley, Mary Wollstonecraft
Shelley, Percy Bysshe
Shenstone, William
Shepard, Ernest Howard
Shepard, Allan Bartlett
Sheppard, Jack
Sheraton, Thomas
Sheridan, Philip H(enry)
Sheridan, Richard Brinsley
Sherman, John
Sherman, William Tecumseh
Sherrington, Sir Charles Scott
Shockley, William Bradfield
Sholes, Christopher Latham
Sholokhov, Mikhail
Shostakovich, Dmitri
Shostakovich, Maxim
Shovell, Sir Cloudesley
Shrapnel, Henry
Shute, Nevil
Sibelius, Jean
Sica, Vittoria De
Sickert, Walter Richard

Siddons, Sarah
Sidgwick, Henry
Sidmouth, Henry Addington, 1st Viscount
Sidney, Algernon
Sidney, Sir Philip
Siemens, Ernst Werner von
Siemens, Friedrich
Siemens, Karl
Siemens, Sir William
Sienkiewicz, Henryk
Sieyès, Emmanuel Joseph
Siger of Brabant
Signac, Paul
Signorelli, Luca
Sigurdsson *variant spelling of* Sverrir
Sihanouk, Norodim, Prince
Sikorski, Władysław Polish statesman
Sikorsky, Igor Ivan US engineer
Sillitoe, Alan
Silone, Ignazio
Si-ma Qian (*or* Ssu-ma Ch'ien)
Simenon, Georges
Simeon Stylites, St
Simms, William Gilmore
Simnel, Lambert
Simon, John Allsebrook, 1st Viscount
Simonov, Konstantin
Simpson, George Gaylord
Simpson, N(orman) F(rederick)
Sinatra, Frank
Sinclair, Upton
Singer, Isaac Bashevis
Singer, Isaac Merrit
Siqueiros, David Alfaro
Sisley, Alfred
Sitwell, Edith
Sitwell, Sir Osbert
Sitwell, Sacheverell
Sivaji
Sixtus pope
Skalkottas, Nikos
Skanderbeg
Skelton, John

Skinner, Burrhus Frederic
Slade, Felix
Slánský, Rudolf
Slim, William Joseph, 1st Viscount
Sloane, Sir Hans
Sluter, Claus
Smart, Christopher
Smetana, Bedřich
Smiles, Samuel
Smith, Adam
Smith, Bessie
Smith, Harvey
Smith, Ian (Douglas)
Smith, John
Smith, Joseph
Smith, Sir Keith Macpherson
Smith, Maggie
Smith, Sir Ross Macpherson
Smith, Stevie
Smithson, Alison
Smithson, Peter
Smollett, Tobias (George)
Smuts, Jan (Christiaan)
Smythe, Pat
Snefru
Snow, C(harles) P(ercy), Baron
Snowdon, Antony Armstrong-Jones, Earl of
Snyders, Frans
Soames, (Arthur) Christopher (John), Baron
Soane, Sir John
Soares, Mario
Sobers, Gary
Sobieski, John
Socinus, Faustus
Socinus, Laelius
Socrates
Soddy, Frederick
Söderblom, Nathan
Solon
Soloviov, Vladimir Sergevich
Solti, Sir Georg
Solzhenitsyn, Aleksandr
Somers, John, Baron

Somerset, Edward Seymour, 1st Duke of
Somerset, Robert Carr, Earl of
Sommerfeld, Arnold Johannes Wilhelm
Sondheim, Stephen (Joshua)
Song (*or* Sung), T. V.
Song Qing-ling (*or* Sung Ch'ing-ling)
Song Mei-ling (*or* Sung Mei-ling)
Sophocles
Sopwith, Sir Thomas Octave Murdoch
Soranus of Ephesus
Sorel, Georges
Sosigenes of Alexandria
Soter, Ptolomy
Soto, Hernando de
Soufflot, Jacques Germain
Soult, Nicolas Jean de Dieu, Duc de Dalmatie
Souphanouvong, Prince
Sousa, John Philip
Soustelle, Jacques (Émile)
Southampton, Henry Wriothesley, 3rd Earl of
Southcott, Joanna
Southey, Robert
Soutine, Chaim
Soyinka, Wole
Spaak, Paul Henri
Spallanzani, Lazzaro
Spark, Muriel
Spartacus
Spassky, Boris
Spearman, Charles Edward
Speke, John Hanning
Spence, Sir Basil
Spencer, Herbert
Spencer, Sir Stanley
Spencer, Thomas
Spender, Stephen
Spengler, Oswald
Spenser, Edmund
Speranski, Mikhail Mikhailovich
Spillane, Mickey
Spinoza, Benedict

Spitz, Mark (Andrew)
Spock, Benjamin McLane
Spohr, Louis
Spooner, William Archibald
Ssu-ma Ch'ien *variant spelling of* Si-ma Qian
Staël, Anne Louise Germaine Necker, Madame de
Stahl, Georg Ernst
Stainer, Sir John
Stalin, Joseph
Stamitz, Johann
Standish, Myles
Stanford, Sir Charles (Villiers)
Stanhope, Charles, 3rd Earl
Stanhope, James, 1st Earl
Stanislavsky, Konstantin
Stanisław, St
Stanley, Sir Henry Morton
Stark, Dame Freya (Madeline)
Starr, Ringo
Staudinger, Hermann
Stauffenberg, Claus, Graf von
Steel, David (Martin Scott)
Steele, Sir Richard
Steen, Jan
Stefan Dušan
Stein, Sir (Marc) Aurel
Stein, Gertrude
Stein, Karl, Freiherr vom
Steinbeck, John
Steiner, Rudolf
Steinmetz, Charles Proteus
Steinway, Henry (Engelhard)
Stendhal
Steno, Nicolaus
Stephen, Sir Leslie
Stephenson, George
Stephenson, Robert British civil engineer; *compare* Stevenson, Robert Louis
Stern, Isaac
Sternberg, Josef von
Sterne, Laurence
Stevens, Wallace
Stevenson, Adlai E(wing)
Stevenson, Frances
Stevenson, Robert Louis Scottish novelist; *compare* Stephenson, Robert
Stewart, Jackie
Stewart, James (Maitland)
Stewart, Rod
Stieglitz, Alfred
Stiernhielm, Georg Olofson
Stilicho, Flavius
Stilwell, Joseph W(arren)
Stirling, James
Stockhausen, Karlheinz
Stoker, Bram
Stokes, Sir George Gabriel
Stokowski, Leopold
Stolypin, Petr Arkadievich
Stopes, Marie Charlotte Carmichael
Stoppard, Miriam
Stoppard, Tom
Storey, David
Storm, (Hans) Theodor Woldsen
Stoss, Veit
Stowe, Harriet Beecher
Strabo
Strachey, (Giles) Lytton
Stradivari, Antonio
Strafford, Thomas Wentworth, 1st Earl of
Stratton, Charles (*known as* Tom Thumb)
Strauss, Johann
Strauss, Richard
Stravinsky, Igor
Strawson, Peter Frederick
Streicher, Julius
Streisand, Barbra
Stresemann, Gustav
Strindberg, August
Stroheim, Erich von
Strong, Sir Roy (Colin)
Struve, Otto
Stuart surname of Scottish and English monarchs
Stuart, John McDouall
Stubbs, George
Stubbs, William
Sturluson, Snorri
Sturt, Charles
Stuyvesant, Peter
Suárez (Gonzalez), Adolfo, Duke of
Suarez, Francisco de
Suckling, Sir John
Sucre, Antonio José de
Su Dong Po (*or* Su Tung-p'o)
Sue, Eugène
Suetonius
Suger of Saint-Denis
Suharto
Sukarno
Suleiman
Sulla, Lucius Cornelius
Sullivan, Sir Arthur
Sullivan, John Lawrence
Sullivan, Louis Henry
Sully, Maximilien de Béthune, Duc de
Sully-Prudhomme, René François Armand
Sunderland, Robert Spencer, 2nd Earl of
Sun Yat-sen (*or* Sun Zhong Shan)
Suppiluliumas
Surrey, Henry Howard, Earl of
Surtees, John
Surtees, Robert Smith
Suslov, Mikhail
Sutcliffe, Herbert
Sutherland, Graham Vivian
Sutherland, Dame Joan
Sutton, Walter Stanborough
Suvorov, Aleksandr Vasilievich, Count
Sverrir (*or* Sigurdsson)
Svevo, Italo
Swammerdam, Jan
Swan, Sir Joseph Wilson
Swedenborg, Emanuel
Sweyn Forkbeard
Swift, Jonathan
Swinburne, Algernon Charles
Swithin, St
Symonds, John Addington

Symons, Arthur (William)
Synge, John Millington
Szell, George
Szent-Györgyi, Albert (von Nagyrapolt)
Szewinska, Irena
Szilard, Leo
Szymanowski, Karol
Tabari, Muhammad ibn Jarir al-
Tacitus, Cornelius
Taft, Robert Alphonso
Taft, William Howard
Tagore, Debendranath
Tagore, Rabindranath
Taine, Hippolyte Adolphe
Talbot, William Henry Fox
Taliesin
Talleyrand
Tallien, Jean Lambert
Tallis, Thomas
Tamerlane *variant of* Timur
Tancred
Tange Kenzo
Tanguy, Yves
Tanizaki Jun-ichiro
Tannhäuser
Tasman, Abel Janszoon
Tasso, Torquato
Tate, Allen
Tate, Harry
Tate, Nahum
Tati, Jacques
Tattersall, Richard
Tatum, Art(hur)
Tatum, Edward Lawrie
Tavener, John 20th-century British composer
Taverner, John 16th-century English composer
Tawney, R(ichard) H(enry)
Taylor, A(lan) J(ohn) P(ercivale)
Taylor, Brook
Taylor, Elizabeth
Taylor, Frederick Winslow
Taylor, Jeremy
Taylor, Zachary
Tchaikovsky, Peter Ilich
Teach, Edward

Teck, Mary of
Tecumseh
Tedder, Arthur William, 1st Baron
Teilhard de Chardin, Pierre
Te Kanawa, Dame Kiri
Telemann, Georg Philipp
Telesio, Bernardino
Telford, Thomas
Teller, Edward
Temple, Frederick
Temple, Shirley
Temple, William
Teng Hsiao-p'ing *variant spelling of* Deng Xiao Ping
Teniers, David
Tenniel, Sir John
Tennyson, Alfred, Lord
Tenzing Norgay
Terborch, Gerard
Terbrugghen, Hendrik
Terman, Lewis Madison
Terry, Dame Ellen (Alice)
Tertullian(us), Quintus Septimius Florens
Tesla, Nikola
Tetrazzini, Luisa
Tetzel, Johann
Teyte, Dame Maggie
Thackeray, William Makepeace
Thais
Thales
Thatcher, Margaret (Hilda)
Themistocles
Thenard, Louis-Jacques
Theocritus
Theodorakis, Mikis
Theodoric
Theodosius
Theophrastus
Thespis
Thibaud, Jacques
Thiers, Louis Adolphe
Thistlewood, Arthur
Thomas, Dylan
Thomas, Edward
Thompson, Francis
Thomson, Sir George Paget
Thomson, James

Thomson, Sir Joseph John
Thomson, Kenneth Roy, 2nd Baron
Thomson, Virgil
Thomson, William, 1st Baron Kelvin
Thomson of Fleet, Roy Herbert, 1st Baron
Thoreau, Henry David
Thorndike, Dame Sybil
Thornhill, Sir James
Thorpe, (John) Jeremy
Thorvaldsen, Bertel
Thrale, Hester Lynch (*maiden name* Piozzi)
Throckmorton, Francis
Throckmorton, Sir Nicholas
Thucydides
Thurber, James
Thutmose
Tibaldi, Pellegrino
Tiberius
Tibullus, Albius
Tieck, (Johann) Ludwig
Tiepolo, Giovanni Battista
Tiepolo, Giovanni Domenico
Tiglath-pileser
Tilak, Bal Gangadhar
Tillett, Benjamin
Tilley, Vesta
Tillich, Paul (Johannes)
Tilly, Johan Tserclaes, Graf von
Timoshenko, Semyon Konstantinovich
Timur (*or* Tamerlane)
Tinbergen, Jan
Tinbergen, Niko(laas)
Tintoretto
Tippett, Sir Michael
Tipu Sahib
Tirpitz, Alfred von
Tirso de Molina
Tissot, James Joseph Jacques
Titian
Tito
Titus (Flavius Vespasianus)
Tobey, Mark
Tocqueville, Alexis de

Todd, Alexander
  Robertus, Baron
Toghril Beg
Togliatti, Palmiro
Togo Heihachiro
Tojo Hideki
Tokugawa Ieyasu
Tolkien, J(ohn) R(onald)
  R(euel)
Toller, Ernst
Tolstoy, Leo
  (Nikolaevich), Count
Tom Thumb see Stratton,
  Charles
Tone, (Theobald) Wolfe
Tong Zhi (or T'ung-chih)
Tooke, John Horne
Torquemada, Tomás de
Torricelli, Evangelista
Tortelier, Paul
Toscanini, Arturo
Tostig
Totila
Toulouse-Lautrec, Henri
  (Marie Raymond) de
Touré, (Ahmed) Sékou
Tournefort, Joseph
  Pitton de
Tourneur, Cyril
Tours, St Gregory of
Toussaint-L'Ouverture,
  François Dominique
Townes, Charles Hard
Townshend, Charles, 2nd
  Viscount
Townshend, Pete
Toynbee, Arnold
  (Joseph)
Toynbee, (Theodore)
  Philip
Tracy, Spencer
Traherne, Thomas
Trajan(us), Marcus
  Ulpius
Traven, B(en) US novelist
Travers, Ben(jamin) British dramatist
Tree, Sir Herbert
  (Draper) Beerbohm
Trenchard, Hugh
  Montague, 1st
  Viscount
Trevelyan, George
  Macaulay
Trevelyan, Sir George
  Otto

Trevino, Lee
Trevithick, Richard
Trevor-Roper, Hugh
  Redwald, Baron Dacre
Trilling, Lionel
Trollope, Anthony
Tromp, Cornelis
  (Martenszoon)
Tromp, Maarten
  (Harpertszoon)
Trotsky, Leon
Trudeau, Pierre Elliott
Trueman, Freddy
Truffaut, François
Trujillo (Molina), Rafael
  (Leónidas)
Truman, Harry S.
Tryggvason, Olaf
Ts'ao Chan *variant spelling
  of* Cao Chan
Tshombe, Moise
  (Kapenda)
Tsiolkovski, Konstantin
  Eduardovich
Tsvetaeva, Marina
Tubman, William
  V(acanarat)
  S(hadrach)
Tu Fu *variant spelling of* Du
  Fu
Tull, Jethro
Tulsidas
T'ung-chih *variant spelling
  of* Tong Zhi
Tunney, Gene
Tupac Amarú
Tupolev, Andrei
  Niklaievich
Turenne, Henri de la
  Tour d'Auvergne,
  Vicomte de
Turgenev, Ivan
Turgot, Anne Robert
  Jacques, Baron de
  l'Aulne
Turishcheva, Ludmilla
Turner, Joseph Mallord
  William
Turner, Nat
Turpin, Dick
Tussaud, Marie
Tutankhamen
Tutuola, Amos
Twain, Mark
Tyler, John
Tyler, Wat

Tylor, Sir Edward
  Burnett
Tyndale, William
Tyndall, John
Tzimisces, John
Tz'u-hsi *variant spelling of*
  Zi Xi
Uccello, Paolo
Udall, Nicholas
Uhland, (Johann)
  Ludwig
Ulanova, Galina
Ulbricht, Walter
Umberto
Unamuno y Jugo,
  Miguel de
Undset, Sigrid
Ungaretti, Giuseppe
Updike, John (Hoyer)
Urban pope
Urey, Harold Clayton
Urfé, Honoré d'
Ussher, James
Ustinov, Peter
  (Alexander)
Utagawa Kuniyoshi
Utamaro, Kitagawa
Utrillo, Maurice
Valdemar (or Waldemar)
Valens
Valentinian
Valentino, Rudolf
Valera, Eamon De
Valéry, Paul
Valla, Lorenzo
Valois, Dame Ninette de
Valois, Margaret of
Van Allen, James Alfred
Vanbrugh, Sir John
Van Buren, Martin
Vance, Cyrus
Vancouver, George
Vanderbilt, Cornelius
Van der Post, Sir
  Laurens
Van der Waals,
  Johannes Diderik
van de Velde, Adriaen
van de Velde, Esaias
van de Velde, Henry
van de Velde, Willem
van Dieman, Anthony
Van Dyck, Sir Anthony
Vane, Sir Henry
van Eyck, Hubert

van Eyck

van Eyck, Jan
Van Gogh, Vincent
Vansittart, Robert Gilbert, 1st Baron
Van't Hoff, Jacobus Henricus
Vardhamana *see* Mahavira
Varèse, Edgard
Vargas, Getúlio
Varro, Marcus Terentius
Vasarely, Victor
Vasari, Giorgio
Vauban, Sébastian Le Prestre de
Vaughan, Henry
Vaughan Williams, Ralph
Vavilov, Nikolai Ivanovich
Vega (Carpio), Lope Félix de
Velázquez, Diego Rodriguez de Silva
Vendôme, Louis Joseph, Duc de
Venizélos, Eleuthérios
Ventris, Michael
Vercingetorix
Verdi, Giuseppe
Verhaeren, Émile
Verlaine, Paul
Vermeer, Jan
Verne, Jules
Vernon, Edward
Veronese, Paolo
Verrocchio, Andrea del
Verwoerd, Hendrik Frensch
Vesalius, Andreas
Vespasian
Vespucci, Amerigo
Vicente, Gil
Vicky *pen name of* Victor Weisz
Vico, Giambattista
Victor Emmanuel Italian king
Victoria, Tomás Luis de
Vidal, Gore
Vidal de la Blache, Paul
Vignola, Giacomo da
Vigny, Alfred de
Villa, Pancho
Villa-Lobos, Heitor
Villars, Claude Louis Hector, Duc de
Villehardouin, Geoffroi de
Villeneuve, Pierre
Villiers de l'Isle-Adam, Philippe Auguste, Comte de
Villon, François
Vincent de Paul, St
Viollet-le-Duc, Eugène Emmanuel
Virchow, Rudolf
Viren, Lasse Artturi
Visconti, Luchino
Vitruvius
Vittorini, Elio
Vittorino da Feltre
Vivaldi, Antonio
Vivekananda, Swami
Vivés, Juan Luis
Vladimir, St
Vlaminck, Maurice de
Volta, Alessandro Giuseppe Antonio Anastasio, Count
Voltaire
Vondel, Joost van den
Vonnegut, Kurt
Voroshilov, Kliment Yefremovich
Vorster, Balthazar Johannes
Voysey, Charles Francis Annesley
Voznesenskii, Andrei
Vuillard, (Jean) Édouard
Vyshinskii, Andrei Yanuareevich
Wace
Wade, Virginia
Wagner, (Wilhelm) Richard
Wagner, Siegfried
Wagner, Wieland
Wagner von Jauregg, Julius
Wain, John British novelist; *compare* Wayne, John
Wajda, Andrzej
Wakefield, Edward Gibbon
Waksman, Selman Abraham
Walafrid Strabo
Walburga, St
Waldemar *variant spelling of* Valdemar
Waldheim, Kurt
Waley, Arthur
Wallace, Alfred Russel
Wallace, Edgar
Wallace, Lew(is)
Wallace, Sir William
Wallenstein, Albrecht Wenzel von
Waller, Edmund
Waller, (Thomas) Fats
Wallis, Sir Barnes (Neville)
Walpole, Horace 4th Earl of Orford
Walpole, Sir Hugh (Seymour)
Walpole, Sir Robert, 1st Earl of Orford
Walsingham, Sir Francis
Walter, Bruno
Walter, Hubert
Walter, John
Walther von der Vogelweide
Walton, Ernest Thomas Sinton
Walton, Izaak
Walton, Sir William (Turner)
Wang An Shi (*or* Wang An-shih)
Wang Jing Wei (*or* Wang Ching-wei)
Warbeck, Perkin
Ward, Artemus
Ward, Barbara, Baroness Jackson
Ward, Mrs Humphry
Ward, Sir Joseph George
Ward, Sir Leslie
Warhol, Andy
Warlock, Peter
Warren, Earl
Warton, Joseph
Warton, Thomas
Warwick, Richard Neville, Earl of
Washington, Booker T(aliaferro)
Washington, George
Wasserman, August von
Waterhouse, Alfred
Watson, James Dewey

Watson, John Broadus
Watson, John Christian
Watson-Watt, Sir Robert Alexander
Watt, James
Watteau, (Jean) Antoine
Watts, George Frederick
Waugh, Alec (Raban)
Waugh, Auberon
Waugh, Evelyn (Arthur St John)
Wavell, Archibald Percival, 1st Earl
Wayne, John US actor; *compare* Wain, John
Webb, Beatrice (Potter)
Webb, Mary
Webb, Sidney (James), Baron Passfield
Weber, Carl Maria von
Weber, Ernst Heinrich
Weber, Max
Weber, Wilhelm Eduard
Webern, Anton von
Webster, John
Webster, Noah
Wedekind, Frank
Wedgwood, Dame Cicely Veronica
Wedgwood, Josiah
Weelkes, Thomas
Wegener, Alfred Lothar
Weil, Simone
Weill, Kurt
Weismann, August Friedrich Leopold
Weiss, Peter
Weissmuller, Johnny
Weisz, Victor (*pen name* Vicky)
Weizmann, Chaim (Azriel)
Welensky, Sir Roy
Welles, (George) Orson
Wellesley, Richard Colley, Marquess
Wellesz, Egon
Wellington, Arthur Wellesley, 1st Duke of
Wells, Henry
Wells, H(erbert) G(eorge)
Wenceslas
Wentworth, Thomas, 1st Earl of Strafford

Wentworth, William Charles
Werfel, Franz
Wergeland, Henrik Arnold
Wesker, Arnold
Wesley, Charles
Wesley, John
Wesley, Samuel
Wesley, Samuel Sebastian
West, Benjamin
West, Mae
West, Nathanael
West, Dame Rebecca
Weyden, Rogier van der
Wharton, Edith (Newbold)
Wheatstone, Sir Charles
Wheeler, Sir (Robert Eric) Mortimer
Whistler, James (Abbott) McNeill
Whistler, Laurence
Whistler, Rex
White, Gilbert
White, Patrick
White, T(erence) H(anbury)
Whitefield, George
Whitehead, A(lfred) N(orth)
Whitelaw, William (Stephen Ian), 1st Viscount
Whitgift, John
Whitlam, (Edward) Gough
Whitman, Walt
Whitney, Eli
Whittier, John Greenleaf
Whittington, Dick
Whittle, Sir Frank
Whorf, Benjamin Lee
Whymper, Edward
Widor, Charles Marie
Wieland, Christoph Martin
Wiener, Norbert
Wigner, Eugene Paul
Wilberforce, William
Wilde, Oscar
Wilder, Billy
Wilder, Thornton
Wilkes, John

Wilkie, Sir David
Wilkins, Sir George Hubert
Wilkins, Maurice Hugh Frederick
Williams, John
Williams, J(ohn) P(eter) R(hys)
Williams, Roger
Williams, Shirley (Vivien Teresa Brittain)
Williams, Tennessee
Williams, William Carlos
Williams-Ellis, Sir Clough
Williamson, Henry
Williamson, Malcolm
Willis, Ted
Wills (Moody), Helen
Wilson, Sir Angus
Wilson, Charles Thomson Rees
Wilson, Colin
Wilson, Edmund
Wilson, Edmund Beecher
Wilson, (James) Harold, Baron
Wilson, Sir Henry Hughes
Wilson, Henry Maitland, 1st Baron
Wilson, Richard
Wilson, (Thomas) Woodrow
Winckelmann, Johann Joachim
Wingate, Orde Charles
Winkler, Hans Günter
Winstanley, Gerrard
Winterhalter, Franz Xavier
Winthrop, John
Wise, Thomas James
Wiseman, Nicholas Patrick Stephen
Wishart, George
Wissler, Clark
Witt, Johan de
Witte, Sergei Yulievich
Wittgenstein, Ludwig
Wodehouse, Sir P(elham) G(renville)
Woffington, Peg
Wöhler, Friedrich
Wolf, Hugo

Wolfe

Wolfe, Charles
Wolfe, James
Wolfe, Thomas
Wolfenden, John
 Frederick, Baron
Wolf-Ferrari, Ermanno
Wölfflin, Heinrich
Wolfit, Sir Donald
Wolfram von
 Eschenbach
Wolfson, Sir Isaac
Wollstonecraft, Mary
Wolseley, Garnet
 Joseph, 1st Viscount
Wolsey, Thomas,
 Cardinal
Wood, Aaron
Wood, Enoch
Wood, Sir Henry
 (Joseph)
Wood, John
Wood, Ralph
Woodville, Elizabeth
Woodward, Robert
 Burns
Woolf, Leonard (Sidney)
Woolf, (Adeline)
 Virginia
Woollett, William
Woolley, Sir Leonard
Woolworth, F(rank)
 W(infield)
Wootton, Barbara,
 Baroness
Wordsworth, William
Wotton, Sir Henry
Wouwerman, Jan
Wouwerman, Philips
Wouwerman, Pieter
Wrangel, Ferdinand
 Petrovich, Baron von
Wrangel, Peter
 Nikolaievich, Baron
Wren, Sir Christopher
Wren, P(ercival)
 C(hristopher)
Wright, Frank Lloyd
Wright, Judith
Wright, Orville
Wright, Richard
Wright, Wilbur

Wu Hou
Wundt, Wilhelm
Wyatt, James
Wyatt, Sir Thomas
Wycherley, William
Wycliffe, John
Wykeham, William of
Wyss, Johann Rudolph
Wyszyński, Stefan,
 Cardinal
Xanthippe
Xenakis, Yannis
Xenophanes
Xenophon
Xerxes
Xia Gui (or Hsia Kuei)
Xuan Cang (or Hsuan-
 tsang)
Yamagata Aritomo
Yang, Chen Ning
Yeats, Jack Butler
Yeats, William Butler
Yesenin, Sergei
 Aleksandrovich
Yevtushenko, Yevgenii
Yoko Ono
Yonge, Charlotte
Yong Le (or Yung-lo)
Young, Andrew
Young, Arthur
Young, Brigham
Young, Thomas
Younghusband, Sir
 Francis Edward
Yuan Shi Kai (or Yüan
 Shih-k'ai)
Yukawa, Hideki
Zabaleta, Nicanor
Zadkine, Ossip
Zaghlul, Saad
Zaharoff, Sir Basil
Zamyatin, Yevgenii
 Ivanovich
Zao Zhan variant spelling of
 Cao Chan
Zapata, Emiliano
Zarathustra variant spelling
 of Zoroaster
Zátopek, Emil
Zeami Motokiyo

Zedekiah
Zeeman, Pieter
Zeffirelli, G. Franco
Zeiss, Carl
Zenobia
Zeno of Citium
Zeno of Elea
Zernicke, Frits
Zetkin, Clara
Zeuxis
Zheng Cheng Gong (or
 Cheng Ch'eng-kung;
 known as Koxinga)
Zheng He (or Cheng Ho)
Zhivkov, Todor
Zhuangzi (or Chuang-tzu)
Zhu De (or Chu Teh)
Zhukov, Georgi
 Konstantinovich
Zia ul-Haq, Gen
 Mohammad
Ziaur Rahman
Ziegfeld, Florenz
Ziegler, Karl
Zinoviev, Grigori
 Yevseevich
Zinzendorf, Nikolaus
 Ludwig, Graf von
Zi Xi (or Tz'u-hsi)
Žižka, Jan, Count
Zoffany, Johann
Zog
Zola, Émile
Zorn, Anders (Leonard)
Zoroaster (or Zarathustra)
Zorrilla y Moral, José
Zoser variant spelling of
 Djoser
Zsigmondy, Richard
 Adolph
Zuccarelli, Francesco
Zuccari, Federico
Zuccari, Taddeo
Zuckerman, Solly, Baron
Zurbarán, Francisco de
Zweig, Arnold
Zweig, Stefan
Zwingli, Ulrich
Zworykin, Vladimir
 Kosma